INTERNATIONAL BIBLIOGRAPHY OF HISTORICAL SCIENCES

INTERNATIONALE BIBLIOGRAPHIE DER GESCHICHTSWISSENSCHAFTEN
BIBLIOGRAFIA INTERNACIONAL DE CIENCIAS HISTORICAS
BIBLIOGRAPHIE INTERNATIONALE DES SCIENCES HISTORIQUES
BIBLIOGRAFIA INTERNAZIONALE DELLE SCIENZE STORICHE

VOLUME LXIV
1995

Edited by Massimo Mastrogregori

with the contribution of a number of scholars,
under the auspices of the
International Committee of Historical Sciences

K·G·SAUR MÜNCHEN 2000

The IBOHS for the years 1978 to 1992 (Vol. 47 – 61) was edited by
Michel François and Michael Keul for Vol. 47/48 (1978/1979) and
Jean Glénisson and Michael Keul for Vol. 49 – 61 (1980 – 1992)
on behalf of the International Committee of Historical Sciences
and was published by K. G. Saur Munich.

Die Deutsche Bibliothek - CIP-Einheitsaufnahme
International bibliography of historical sciences
= Internationale Bibliographie der Geschichtswissenschaften
= Bibliografia internacional de ciencias historicas /
Ed. by Massimo Mastrogregori - München : Saur
ISSN 0074-2015
Erscheint jährl.

Vol. 45/46. 1976/77 ff.–1980 ff.
Auf der Haupttitels. auch: Comité International
des Sciences Historiques.– Bis Vol. 43/44.
1974/75 im Verl. Colin, Paris.

Printed on acid-free paper / Gedruckt auf säurefreiem Papier

©2000 by K. G. Saur Verlag GmbH & Co. KG, München
Part of Reed Elsevier
Printed in the Federal Republic of Germany

All Rights Strictly Reserved / Alle Rechte vorbehalten
No part of this publication may be reproduced, stored in a retrieval system,
or transmitted in any form or by any means, electronic, mechanical, photocopying,
recording, or otherwise, without permission in writing from the publisher /
Jede Art der Vervielfältigung ohne Erlaubnis des Verlags ist unzulässig

Technical partner: Dr. Rainer Ostermann, München
Managing partner and technical support: Ellediemme libri dal mondo, Roma
Printed and Bound by Strauss Offsetdruck GmbH, Mörlenbach

ISSN 0074-2015
ISBN 3-598-20419-1

General editor

Massimo MASTROGREGORI, Roma

Assistant editor

Carlo COLELLA, Roma

Advisory board

Maria Teresa AMADO, Instituto superior de novas profissoes, Lisboa
Girolamo ARNALDI, Istituto storico italiano per il Medioevo, Roma
Yuri BESSMERTNY, Institute of General History, Russian Academy of Sciences, Moscow
Wieslaw BIENKOWSKI, Polska Akademia Nauk
Làszlò BIRÒ, Hungarian Academy of sciences, Budapest
Th. S. H. BOS, Gouda, The Netherlands
Luciano CANFORA, Università di Bari
Alejandro CATTARUZZA, University of Buenos Aires, Argentina
Anne EIDSFELDT, Universitetsbiblioteket I Oslo, Norway
Jean GLENISSON, Comité International des Sciences Historiques, Paris
Alexander KAN, Uppsala Universitet, Sweden
Kazuhiko KONDO, University of Tokyo
Mario MAZZA, Università di Roma "La Sapienza"
Matjaz REBOLJ, Ljubljana
Jacques REVEL, Ecole des Hautes Etudes en Sciences Sociales, Paris
Ruggiero ROMANO, Ecole des Hautes Etudes en Sciences Sociales, Paris
Gabrielle M. SPIEGEL, Johns Hopkins University, Baltimore
Martina STERCKEN, Universität Zurich
Natasa STERGAR, Ljubljana
Serban TURCUS, Università di Cluj Napoca, Romania
Ilse VAHAKYRO, Turku University Library, Finland
Romain VAN EENOO, Universiteit Gent, Belgium
Nenad VEKARIC, Dubrovnik
Bahaeddin YEDIYLDIZ, Hacettepe Universitesi, Ankara

Contributing editors

Maria Teresa AMADO, Instituto superior de novas profissoes, Lisboa (*Portuguese historiography*)
Vassili N. BABENKO, Russian Academy of Sciences, Moscow (*Russian historiography*)
Wieslaw BIENKOWSKI, Polska Akademia Nauk (*Polish historiography*)
Wolfdieter BIHL, Institut für Geschichte, Universität Wien (*Austrian historiography*)
Làszlò BIRÒ, Hungarian Academy of sciences, Budapest (*Hungarian historiography*)
Rosa CAROLI, Università di Venezia (*Japanese historiography*)
Vera BRENOVA, Institute of Contemporary History, Prague (*Czech historiography*)
Alejandro CATTARUZZA, University of Buenos Aires, Argentina (*Latin American historiography*)
Gaetana COVIELLO, Università di Roma "La Sapienza" (*Ancient history*)

Emanuele CUTINELLI-RENDINA, Université de Lausanne (*Modern religious history, History of modern culture*)
Laura DE GIORGI, Università di Venezia (*Chinese historiography*)
Anne EIDSFELDT, Universitetsbiblioteket I Oslo, Norway (*Norwegian historiography*)
Timophey GUIMON, Institute of General History, Russian Academy of Sciences, Moscow (*Russian historiography*)
Dario IPPOLITO, Roma (*History of international relations*)
Libby KAHANE, The Jewish National and University Library, Jerusalem (*Historiography of Israel*)
Alexander KAN, Uppsala Universitet, Sweden (*Slavonic historiography*)
Kazuhiko KONDO, University of Tokyo (*Japanese historiography*)
Mauro LENZI, Istituto italiano per gli studi storici B. Croce, Napoli (*Palaeography, Diplomatics, History of the book*)
Massimo MASTROGREGORI, Roma (*Auxiliary sciences, General works, Modern history, Modern economic and social history, Modern legal and constitutional history*)
Matjaz REBOLJ, Ljubljana (*Slovenian historiography*)
Evgeni SAVIZKI, Russian State University of Humanities, Moscow (*Russian Historiography*)
Natale SPINETO, Università di Milano (*History of religions*)
Martina STERCKEN, Universität Zurich (*Swiss historiography*)
Natasa STERGAR, Ljubliana (*Slovenian historiography*)
Kristine STREUBÜR, Istituto storico germanico, Roma (*History of the middle ages: history of music*)
Serban TURCUS, Università di Cluj Napoca, Romania (*Romanian historiography*)
Ilse VAHAKYRO, Turku University Library, Finland (*Finnish historiography*)
Romain VAN EENOO, Universiteit Gent, Belgium (*Belgian historiography*)
Nenad VEKARIC, Institute of historical sciences, Dubrovnik (*Croatian historiography*)
Amedeo VISCONTI, Roma (*Ancient history*)
Bahaeddin YEDIYLDIZ, Hacettepe Universitesi, Ankara (*Historiography of Turkey*)

Consulting editors

Maurice AYMARD, Maison des sciences de l'homme, Paris
Eric BRIAN, Centre Alexandre Koyré, Paris
Louis CHATELLIER, Université de Nancy II
Sten EBBESEN, University of Copenhagen
Carlo FRANCO, Venezia
Olivier GUYOTJEANNIN, Ecole nationale des Chartes, Paris
Daniele MENOZZI, Istituto per le scienze religiose, Bologna
Michel MORINEAU, Paris
Brian TIERNEY, Cornell University, Ithaca
Giusto TRAINA, Università di Lecce
Pietro VANNICELLI, Istituto per gli studi micenei ed egeo-anatolici, CNR, Roma
André VAUCHEZ, Ecole Française de Rome

Special Assistant editor

Dario IPPOLITO (*Index of names, Geographical index*)

INHALTSVERZEICHNIS

	Seite
VORBEMERKUNG	IX
INHALT	XIII
ALLGEMEINE HISTORISCHE BIBLIOGRAPHIEN	XVII
BIBLIOGRAPHIE	1
AUTOREN- UND PERSONENREGISTER	363
GEOGRAPHISCHES REGISTER	431

VORBEMERKUNG

Die *Internationale Bibliographie der Geschichtswissenschaften* ist eine Auswahl- und Hinweisbibliographie. Die in ihr aufgeführten Arbeiten – Monographien und Zeitschriftenartikel – sind nach einem systematischen und chronologischen Schlüssel geordnet. Dieser Schlüssel wurde von der Bibliographischen Kommission des Internationalen Komitees für Geschichtswissenschaft seinerzeit erarbeitet und in der Folge geringfügig verbessert.

Im folgenden sind die Grundsätze für die Auswahl der einzelnen Arbeiten sowie die Regeln für die Gliederung zusammengefaßt.

A. Richtlinien für die Auswahl

Das Redaktionsbüro ist bestrebt, der I.B.O.H.S. den Charakter einer allgemeinen Bibliographie zu geben, die das Ganze der Geschichtswissenschaft zu erfassen sucht. Gleichzeitig soll sie Historikern und Bibliothekaren in jährlich erscheinenden Bänden die wichtigsten Neuerscheinungen der Welt auf dem Gebiet der historischen Wissenschaften anzeigen.

In der Tat schien es angesichts der wachsenden Anzahl von Spezialbibliographien erforderlich zu sein, sowohl Einzelwissenschaftlern als auch wissenschaftlichen Organisationen, die sich diese Spezialbibliographien nicht vollzählig beschaffen können, ein Hilfsmittel in die Hand zu geben, das sie über den jährlichen Fortschritt der historischen Wissenschaften orientiert. Natürlich müssen diese Spezialbibliographien gleichwohl erwähnt werden. Dies geschieht auf zweifache Weise: Unter der Rubrik „Allgemeine Historische Bibliographien" werden alle großen internationalen oder nationalen Bibliographien aufgenommen, die sich auf einzelne Länder beziehen und in denen grundsätzlich die gesamten Neuerscheinungen aus diesem Land enthalten sind. Diese allgemeinen Bibliographien sind nicht in die systematischen Abteilungen eingegliedert, sondern werden ihnen vorangestellt. Im Gegensatz dazu haben innerhalb der systematischen Abteilungen – und zwar jeweils am Beginn der entsprechenden Abschnitte oder Unterabschnitte – alle jene Bibliographien ihren Platz gefunden, die einzelne Gegenstände, Autoren oder Landschaften betreffen; die Titel dieser Bibliographien sind mit einem Sternchen (*) versehen.

Die I.B.O.H.S. will ein Arbeitsinstrument von hohem wissenschaftlichem Rang und internationaler Bedeutung sein. Sie kann daher in ihre Spalten keine Titel aufnehmen, die nur von lokalem Interesse sind. Aus dem gleichen Grunde muß sie Kurzbesprechungen oder Gefälligkeitsanzeigen zurückweisen. Bewußt wurde auch auf die Aufnahme von Neuauflagen, Übersetzungen, Grabungsberichten ohne neue Ergebnisse, nicht wissenschaftlich kommentierten Ausstellungskatalogen, vulgarisierender oder Propagandaliteratur verzichtet.

Hingegen wird angestrebt, alle diejenigen Arbeiten anzuzeigen, die trotz ihres geringen Umfanges oder ihrer zunächst nur lokalen Thematik einen echten Beitrag zur allgemeinen Geschichte oder zur Lösung aktueller Fragestellungen bieten; das ist z. B. der Fall bei bestimmten Grabungsberichten oder bei Aufsätzen, die kontroverse Fragen der Verfassungs- oder Kulturgeschichte betreffen. In diesen Fällen wurde der Titel, wenn möglich noch ergänzt durch eine kurze, in eckige Klammern gesetzte Erläuterung oder Datumsangabe, wie das auch bei ungenauen Titeln zur besseren Orientierung des Lesers gehandhabt wird. Dieses Verfahren wurde in den letzten Bänden in wachsendem Maße angewendet und erhöht zweifellos den Nutzwert der Bibliographie. Sie soll deshalb aber keine analytische oder kritische Bibliographie werden – dieser Charakter ist der Spezialbibliographie vorbehalten –, sondern bleibt eine Auswahl- und Hinweisbibliographie.

Im Gegensatz zu den meisten historischen Nationalbibliographien, die eine oft sehr willkürliche zeitliche Begrenzung aufweisen, enthält die I.B.O.H.S. auch Arbeiten zur jüngsten Geschichte, insbesondere zu den internationalen Beziehungen (P § 8). Sie muß allerdings hierbei in ihrer Auswahl um so strenger sein, je näher der behandelte Stoff zur Gegenwart liegt.

Diese Grundsätze geben der I.B.O.H.S. ihr eigenes Gepräge. Sie möchte keine bereits bestehende Bibliographie ersetzen. Sie will auch anderwärts geleistete Arbeit nicht wiederholen. Wenn dennoch Überschneidungen vorkommen, weil sie sich nie vermeiden lassen, so wird die Wissenschaft auch aus ihnen sicherlich Gewinn ziehen.

B. Grundregeln für die Gliederung

Der Band LXIV, 1995, enthält diejenigen Werke, die im Jahr 1995 veröffentlicht wurden. Innerhalb eines jeden Abschnitts oder Unterabschnitts werden die Titel in der alphabetischen Reihenfolge der Autorennamen aufgeführt. Slawische Namen werden in lateinische Buchstaben umgeschrieben und sind ebenfalls entsprechend dem lateinischen Alphabet eingeordnet. Die diakritischen Zeichen ć, č, ś, š usw. finden keine Berücksichtigung. Bei germanischen und skandinavischen Eigennamen werden die Umlaute ä, ö, ø, ü aufgelöst in a, o und u. Die Zusammenziehungen Mc und M' werden wie das ausgeschriebene Mac behandelt.

Anonyme oder kollektive Werke werden alphabetisch nach dem charakteristischen Hauptwort (Stichwort) ihres Titels eingeordnet.

Fettgedruckt werden die Namen jener Gelehrten, denen eine ausführliche biographische Notiz gewidmet ist (B § 2 b), sowie die Namen von Heiligen (G § 4, I § 13 d). In dem ersten Fall erfolgt die Einordnung entsprechend den betreffenden Personennamen.

Nicht nur Spezialbibliographien, sondern auch Quellenveröffentlichungen sind aus der alphabetischen Einordnung der einzelnen Abschnitte oder Unterabschnitte herausgezogen und jeweils an deren Anfang, unmittelbar hinter die Bibliographien gesetzt worden. Sie sind durch zwei Sternchen (**) gekennzeichnet. Auf diese Weise übersieht der Leser sofort die neuesten Bibliographien und Quellenausgaben, die zu einer bestimmten Frage oder zu einem Zeitabschnitt erschienen sind. Lediglich bei den Kapiteln E, F, G, H und I wurde dieses Verfahren nicht angewendet, weil hier ja jeweils ein eigener Abschnitt für Quellen vorgesehen ist.

Soweit das laufende Jahr Gedenkjahr eines bestimmten historischen Ereignisses war, werden die in diesem Zusammenhang erschienenen Arbeiten gesondert und unter einer eigenen Überschrift am Ende jenes Unterabschnitts gruppiert, in den dieses Ereignis normalerweise eingeordnet worden wäre. Gelegentlich sind auch sonst mehrere Bücher oder Artikel der gleichen Frage oder Persönlichkeit gewidmet. In diesem Fall sind die entsprechenden Titel in der alphabetischen Reihenfolge der Autorennamen eingeordnet und dabei mit der gleichen laufenden Nummer versehen, wie die innerhalb der Unterabschnitte alphabetisch eingeordneten Stichwörter oder Personennamen.

Wenn ein bereits früher erschienenes Werk in der Folgezeit Gegenstand einer Besprechung ist, so wird auf eine ausführliche bibliographische Beschreibung verzichtet und lediglich unter dem Autorennamen mit einem Kurztitel auf die Nummer desjenigen Bandes der I.B.O.H.S. verwiesen, in dem dieses Werk ausführlich angezeigt wurde.

Zur besseren Übersichtlichkeit wurde versucht, die Bezeichnungen für Seiten, Tafeln, Illustrationen usw. möglichst zu vereinheitlichen, indem auf die französische oder englische Sprache zurückgegriffen wurde, da diese beiden Sprachen die meisten gleichen Wörter oder Wortabkürzungen dieser Art besitzen. Querverweise für Titel, die außer dem Abschnitt, in den sie gehören, auch andere Sachgebiete berühren, erfolgen durch *Cf. n°...* und sind jeweils am Schluß der betreffenden anderen Abschnitte zusammengefaßt.

Im Autoren- und Personenregister wurden die Namen der Heiligen, Päpste und römischen Kaiser in ihrer lateinischen Form aufgeführt.

INHALT

A

HILFSWISSENSCHAFTEN
(p. 1–18)

§ 1. Paläographie. 1-44. – § 2. Urkundenlehre. 45-76. – § 3. Buchwesen und Buchgeschichte (*a*. Volumen, Kodex, Handgeschriebenes Buch; *b*. Buchgeschichte). 77-258. – § 4. Chronologie. 259-269. – § 5. Genealogie. 270-273. – § 6. Siegel- und Wappenkunde. 274-291. – § 7. Münz-, Maß- und Gewichtskunde. 292-328. – § 8. Sprachliche Hilfsmittel. 329-367. – § 9. Historische Geographie und Geschichte der Geographie. 368-402. – § 10. Ikonographie. 403-417.

B

HANDBÜCHER, ALLGEMEINE ÜBERSICHTSWERKE
(p. 19–61)

§ 1. Archive, Bibliotheken und Museen (*a*. Archive; *b*. Bibliotheken; *c*. Museen). 418-506. – § 2. Geschichte der Geschichtswissenschaft (*a*. Allgemeines; *b*. Spezialarbeiten). 507-847. – § 3. Methodenlehre, Geschichtsphilosophie und Geschichtsunterricht. 848-983. – § 4. Völker und Volkskunde. 984-1059. – § 5. Allgemeine Geschichte. 1060-1173. – § 6. Staats- und Gesellschaftslehre. 1174-1231. – § 7. Rechts- und Verfassungsgeschichte. 1232-1249. – § 8. Wirtschafts- und Sozialgeschichte. 1250-1320. – § 9. Kultur-, Wissenschafts- und Unterrichtsgeschichte. 1321-1365. – § 10. Kunst- und Kunstgewerbegeschichte. 1366-1375. – § 11. Religions- und Kirchengeschichte (*a*. Allgemeines; *b*. Spezialarbeiten). 1376-1505. – § 12. Geschichte der Philosophie. 1506-1523. – § 13. Literaturgeschichte. 1524-1568.

C

VOR- UND FRÜHGESCHICHTE
(p. 63–69)

§ 1. Allgemeines. 1569-1595. – § 2. Paläolithikum und Mesolithikum. 1596-1625. – § 3. Neolithikum. 1626-1652. – § 4. Bronzezeit. 1653-1676. – § 5. Eisenzeit. 1677-1691. – § 6. Frühgeschichtliche Völker Europas mit Ausnahme Griechenlands und Italiens. 1692-1718.

D

DIE VÖLKER DES ALTEN ORIENTS
(die hellenistischen Staaten inbegriffen)
(p. 71–79)

§ 1. Allgemeines. 1719-1737. – § 2. Vorderasien (Allgemeines). 1738-1758. – § 3. Ägypten. 1759-1804. – § 4. Mesopotamien. 1805-1857. – § 5. Hethiter. 1858-1884. – § 6. Juden und semitische Stämme bis zum Ausgang des Altertums. 1885-1939. – § 7. Iran. 1940-1964.

E

GRIECHISCHE GESCHICHTE
(p. 81–96)

§ 1. Klassisches Altertum im Allgemeinen. 1965-1993. – § 2. Vorhellenische Zeit. 1994-2025. – § 3. Quellen und Quellenkunde (*a*. Epigraphische Quellen; *b*. Literarische Quellen). 2026-2112. – § 4. Allgemeine und politische Geschichte. 2113-2153. – § 5. Rechts- und Verfassungsgeschichte. 2154-2181. – § 6. Wirtschafts- und Sozialgeschichte. 2182-2232. – § 7. Literatur-, Philosophie- und Wissenschaftsgeschichte. 2233-2344. – § 8. Religion und Mythologie. 2345-2384. – § 9. Archäologie und Kunstgeschichte. 2385-2438.

F

GESCHICHTE ROMS, DES ALTEN ITALIENS UND DES RÖMISCHEN KAISERREICHS
(p. 97–114)

§ 1. Die Völkerschaften Italiens. 2439-2487. – § 2. Etruskologie. 2488-2507. – § 3. Quellen und Quellenkunde (*a*. Epigrafische Quellen; *b*. Literarische Quellen). 2508-2604. – § 4. Allgemeine und politische Geschichte. 2605-2676. – § 5. Rechts- und Verfassungsgeschichte. 2677-2709. – § 6. Wirtschafts- und Sozialgeschichte. 2710-2748. – § 7. Literatur-, Philosophie- und Wissenschaftsgeschichte. 2749-2825. – § 8. Religion und Mythologie. 2826-2858. – § 9. Archäologie und Kunstgeschichte. 2859-2921.

G

GESCHICHTE DER ALTEN KIRCHE BIS AUF GREGOR DEN GROSSEN
(p. 115–119)

§ 1. Quellen. 2922-2945. – § 2. Allgemeines. 2946-2959. – § 3. Spezialarbeiten. 2960-3031. – § 4. Hagiographie. 3032-3044.

H

BYZANTINISCHE GESCHICHTE
(Seit Justinian)
(p. 121–126)

§ 1. Quellen. 3045-3091. – § 2. Allgemeines. 3092-3105. – § 3. Spezialarbeiten. 3106-3177.

I

GESCHICHTE DES MITTELALTERS
(p. 127–180)

§ 1. Quellen. Quellenkritik (*a*. Urkunden; *b*. Literarische Quellen). 3178-3336. – § 2. Allgemeine Darstellungen. 3337-3396. – § 3. Politische Geschichte (*a*. Allgemeines; *b*. 476–900; *c*. 900–1300; *d*. 1300–1500). 3397-3517. – § 4. Juden. 3518-3542. – § 5. Islam. 3543-3574. – § 6. Wikinger. 3575-3590. – § 7. Rechts- und Verfassungsgeschichte. 3591-3689. – § 8. Wirtschafts- und Sozialgeschichte. 3690-3893. – § 9. Kultur-, Literatur- und Unterrichtsgeschichte. 3894-4175. – § 10. Kunstgeschichte (*a*. Allgemeines; *b*. Spezialarbeiten). 4175 a)-4239. – § 11. Musikgeschichte. 4240-4266. – § 12. Geschichte der Philosophie. 4267-4395. – § 13. Kirchengeschichte (*a*. Allgemeines; *b*. Geschichte des Papsttums; *c*. Ordensgeschichte; *d*. Hagiographie; *e*. Spezialarbeiten). 4396-4539. – § 14. Siedlungsgeschichte, Ortsnamenforschung und Städtebaukunst. 4540-4579.

K

NEUZEIT, ALLGEMEINE WERKE
(p. 181–224)

§ 1. Allgemeines. 4580-4665. – § 2. Einzelne Staaten. 4666-5620. – § 3. Erdentdeckung. 5621-5632.

L

RELIGIONSGESCHICHTE DER NEUZEIT
(p. 225–238)

§ 1. Allgemeines. 5633-5678. – § 2. Katholizismus (*a.* Allgemeines; *b.* Geschichte des Papsttums; *c.* Spezialarbeiten; *d.* Ordensgeschichte; *e.* Missionsgeschichte). 5679-5818. – § 3. Orthodoxie. 5819-5840. – § 4. Protestantismus. 5841-5897 – § 5. Nichtchristliche Religionen und Sekten. 5898-5964.

M

BILDUNGSGESCHICHTE DER NEUZEIT
(p. 239–275)

§ 1. Allgemeines. 5965-6056. – § 2. Akademien und wissenschaftliche Organisationen. 6057-6082. – § 3. Unterrichtsgeschichte. 6083-6153. – 4. Pressewesen. 6154-6215. – § 5. Philosophie und Weltanschauung. 6216-6375. – § 6. Exakte Wissenschaften. Technik, Naturwissenschaften und Medizin. 6376-6512. – § 7. Literatur (*a.* Allgemeines; *b.* Renaissance; *c.* Klassizismus; *d.* Romantik und Gegenwart). 6513-6713. – § 8. Bildende Kunst (*a.* Allgemeines; *b.* Architektur; *c.* Bildhauerei, Malerei, Graphik und Zeichenkunst; *d.* Kunstgewerbe und Volkskunst). 6714-6878.– § 9. Musik, Theater und Film. 6879-6986.

N

WIRTSCHAFTS- UND SOZIALGESCHICHTE DER NEUZEIT
(p. 277–298)

§ 1. Volkswirtschaftslehre. 6987-7042. – § 2. Allgemeine Wirtschaftsgeschichte. 7043-7145. – § 3. Industrie, Bergbau und Verkehr. 7146-7199. – § 4. Handel. 7200-7232. – § 5. Landwirtschaft und Agrarprobleme. 7233-7268. – § 6. Geld- und Finanzwesen. 7269-7301. – § 7. Bevölkerungsbewegung und Städtebaukunst. 7302-7346. – § 8. Sozial- und Sittengeschichte. 7347-7489– § 9. Arbeiterbewegung und Sozialismus. 7490-7533.

O

RECHTS- UND VERFASSUNGSGESCHICHTE DER NEUZEIT
(p. 299–304)

§ 1. Allgemeine Rechtsgeschichte. 7534-7551. – § 2. Geschichte des Verfassungsrechts. 7552-7574. – § 3. Staatsrecht und öffentliche Einrichtungen. 7575-7616. – § 4. Zivil- und Strafrecht. 7616-7660. – § 5. Völkerrecht. 7661-7669.

P

GESCHICHTE DER BEZIEHUNGEN ZWISCHEN DEN MODERNEN STAATEN
(p. 305–344)

§ 1. Allgemeines. 7670-7795. – § 2. Kolonialgeschichte und Dekolonisation (*a.* Allgemeines; *b.* Asien; *c.* Afrika; *d.* Amerika; *e.* Ozeanien). 7796-7910. – § 3. Geschichte von 1500–1789 (*a.* Allgemeines; *b.* 1500–1648; *c.* 1648–1789). 7911-7973. – § 4. Geschichte von 1789–1815. 7974-8011. – § 5. Geschichte von 1815–1910. 8012-8071. – § 6. Geschichte von 1910–1935. Der Erste Weltkrieg. 8072-8199. – § 7. Geschichte von 1935–1945. Der Zweite Weltkrieg (*a.* Allgemeines; *b.* Diplomatie. Wirtschaft; *c.* Kriegshandlungen; *d.* Widerstand). 8200-8419. – § 8. Geschichte seit 1945. 8420-8802.

R

ASIEN
(p. 345–355)

§ 1. Allgemeines. 8803-8809. – § 2. West- und Zentralasien. 8810-8814. – § 3. Südasien. 8815-8819. – § 4. Südostasien. 8820-8824. – § 5. China. 8825-9017. – § 6. Japan (vor 1868). 9018-9068. – § 7. Korea. 9069-9075.

S

AFRIKA
(*von der Urzeit bis zur Kolonisation*)
(p. 357–358)

N°s 9076-9106

T

AMERIKA
(*von der Urzeit bis zur Kolonisation*)
(p. 359)

N°s 9107-9118

U

OZEANIEN
(*von der Urzeit bis zur Kolonisation*)
(p. 361)

N°s 9119-9122

ALLGEMEINE HISTORISCHE BIBLIOGRAPHIEN

I. [Afrika] Histoire africaine en Afrique (L'): recensement analytique des travaux universitaires inédits soutenus dans les universités francophones d'Afrique noire. Ed. par Chantal CHANSON-JABEUR et Catherine COQUERY-VIDROVITCH. Paris, L'Harmattan, 95, 245 p. (Cahier Afrique noire. Laboratoires „Tiers-Mondes, Afrique" Dynamique des sociétés en développement, ERS CNRS 91-Université Paris VII-Denis Diderot, 16).

II. [Belgien] Bibliographie de l'histoire de Belgique. Bibliografie van de geschiedenis van België 1993. [1992. Cf. Bibl. 94, n° II.] Ed. par Romain VAN EENOO, Jean BOVESSE [et alii]. *Revue Belge de Philologie et d'Histoire – Belgisch Tijdschrift voor Filologie en Geschiedenis*, 95, 73, 2, p. 10*-351*. –De vele gezichten van de nieuwste geschiedenis = Les multiples visages de l'histoire contemporaine: Bibliografie van licentiaats- en doctoraatsverhandelingen betreffende de Belgische nieuwste geschiedenis, tot stand gebracht aan de Belgische universiteiten, buiten de seminaries voor nieuwste geschiedenis, 1991–1994. Vol. 2. Door L. FRANÇOIS; met medewerking van V. AELBRECHT [et al.]. Gent, Academia Press, Belgische Vereniging voor Nieuwste Geschiedenis, 95, [s. p.].

III. [Brasilien] Produção historica no Brasil 1985–1994: catalogo de dissertações e teses dos programas e cursos de pos-graduação em historia. Coordenação de Maria Helena ROLIM CAPELATO. Sao Paulo, Xama, 95, 3 vol., [s. p.].

IV. [El Salvador] Bibliografía historiogràfica de El Salvador. Coordinación, Mario R. VASQUES. San Salvador, Universidad de El Salvador, Instituto de Estudios Históricos, Antropológicos y Arqueológicos, 95, 50 p. (Colección Antropologia e historia, 2).

V. [Finnland] ANTIN (Kirsti). Finländsk historisk litteratur 1993. Bibliografiskt urval. [1992. Cf. Bibl. 94, n° IV.] (Bibliographie choisie d'ouvrages d'histoire publiés en Finlande en 1992). *Historisk tidskrift (Finland)*, 95, 80, p. 164-177. – Suomen historiallinen bibliografia 1981–1985. Ed. Raija MANKKI, Tuula RANIANEN. Helsinki, SHS 95, XVIII-699 p. (Finnish Historical Society Käsikirjoja, 16).

VI. [Frankreich] Bibliographie annuelle de l'histoire de France, du Ve siècle à 1958. Année 1994. [1993. Cf. Bibl. 94, n° V.] Réd. par Colette ALBERT-SAMUEL et Brigitte KERIVEN. Paris, Ed. du C.N.R.S., 95, LXXXVI-1045 p.

VII. [Deutschland] Historische Bibliographie. Berichtsjahr 1994 [1993. Cf. Bibl. 94, n° VI.] Hrsg. von der Arbeitsgemeinschaft ausseruniversitärer Forschungseinrichtungen in der Bundesrepublik Deutschland. München, Oldenbourg, 95, 761 p. – Jahresberichte für Deutsche Geschichte. Neue Folge. 45. Jahrgang 1993. Mit Nachträgen. [44. Jahrgang 1992. Cf. Bibl. 94, n° VI.] Hrsg. von der Berlin-Brandenburgischen Akademie der Wissenschaften. Berlin, Akademie Verlag, 95, VI-784 p.

VIII. [Großbritannien] Annual bibliography of British and Irish history. Publications of 1994. [1993. Cf. Bibl. 94, n° VII.] General editors: Barbara ENGLISH and John Joseph N. PALMER, for the Royal Historical Society and in association with the Institute of Historical Research. London, Oxford U. P., 95, XI-293 p. – Historical research for higher degrees in the United Kingdom. List n° 56. Part 1. Theses completed 1994. Part 2. Theses in progress 1995. London, Institute of historical research, 95, 2 vol., 37 p., 138 p.

IX. [Indien] CHATURVEDI (D. D.). Research in history. New Delhi, Anmol Publications, 95, VIII-421 p.

X. International Committee of Historical Sciences. Comité International des Sciences Historiques, Lausanne-Paris. International bibliography of historical sciences. Internationale Bibliographie der Geschichtswissenschaften. Bibliografía internacional de ciencias históricas. Bibliographie internationale des sciences historiques. Bibliografia internazionale delle scienze storiche. Vol. LX, 1991. [Vol. LIX, 1990. Cf. Bibl. 94, n° VIII.] Ed. with the contribution of the national committees by Jean GLENISSON a. Michael KEUL. Published with the assistance of Unesco and under the patronage of the International Council for Philosophy and Humanistic Studies. München, New Providence, London a. Paris, K. G. Saur, 95, XXII-477 p.

XI. [Irland] Major Accessions to Repositories [in Great Britain and Ireland] Relating to Irish History, 1993. [1992. Cf. Bibl. 94, n° IX.] *Irish Historical Studies*, 95, 115, p. 385-386.

XII. [Italien] Bibliografia storica nazionale. Anni LIII–LIV, 1991–1992. [Anni LI–LII, 1989–1990. Cf. Bibl. 93, n° *VIII.*] Ed. dalla Giunta centrale per gli studi storici. Roma e Bari, Laterza, 95, XXXVIII-599 p.

XIII. [Japan] Historical studies in Japan (VIII), 1988–1992. Ed. by The National Committee of Japanese Historians. Tokyo, Yamakawa, 95, 246 p.

XIV. [Mexiko] BELTRAN BERNAL (Trinidad), MONTES DE OCA NAVAS (Elvia). Bibliografía histórica del Estado de Mexico. Toluca, Colegio Mexiquense, 95, 4 vol., VI-556 p.

XV. [Niederlande] Repertorium van boeken en tijdschriftartikelen betreffende de geschiedenis van Nederland. (Repertoire de livres et articles concernant l'histoire des Pays-Bas). 1991. [1990. Cf. Bibl. 94, n° *XIII.*] Samengest. door Th. S. H. BOS en M. E. J. VAN WEERT-GAALMAN m. m. v. M. T. A. SCHOUTEN en A. H. SLINGS. Den Haag, Instituut voor Nederlandse Geschiedenis, 95, LXXXVII-559 p. (R. G. P.).

XVI. [Österreich] Österreichische historische Bibliographie. Austrian historical bibliography. 1993. [1992. Cf. Bibl. 94, n° *I.*] Hrsg. v. Günther HÖDL u. Wolfdieter BIHL. Bearb. v. Ulrike WINKLER, Elfriede SIEDLER, Uta HÖDL u. Bettina KUTTIN. Graz, Neugebauer u. Santa Barbara, Clio, 95, 671 p.

XVII. [Polen] Bibliografia historii polskiej za rok 1993. [1990–1992. Cf. Bibl. 94, n° *XIV.*] (Bibliographie de l'histoire polonaise pour l'année 1993). Aut.: Wojciech FRAZIK, Stefan GĄSIOROWSKI, Anna GRUCA, Zbigniew SOLAK. Réd. Wiesław BIEŃKOWSKI. Kraków, Wydawn. Profesjonalnej Szkoły Biznesu, 95, IX-487 p. (Pol. Akad. Nauk, Inst. Hist. Zakł. Bibliografii Bieżącej).

XVIII. [Portugal] Repertório bibliográfico da historiografia portuguesa: 1974–1994. Instituto Camoes, Faculdade de Letras da Universidade de Coimbra. Ed. Maria Helena da Cruz COELHO, Maria Manuela Tavares RIBEIRO, Joaqui RAMOS DE CARVALHO. Coimbra, Universidade de Coimbra, Fac. Letras, 95, 753 p. – ALMEIDA (M. M.). Indices da Revista Portuguesa de História (1941–1993). Coimbre, Instituto de História económica e social, Faculdade de Letras, 95, 45 p.

XIX. [Schweiz] Bibliographie der Schweizergeschichte. Bibliographie de l'histoire de Suisse. 1992. [1991. Cf. Bibl. 94, n° *XVIII.*] Bearb. v./ établie par Pierre Louis SURCHAT. Hrsg. v. Schweizerischen Landesbibliothek./ publ. par la Bibliothèque Nationale Suisse. Bern, Eidgenössische Drucksachen- und Materialzentrale, 95, XXVII-236 p.

XX. [Slowakei] Historiografia na Slovensku 1990–1994. (Historiography in Slovakia 1990–1994). Ed by Alžbeta SEDLIAKOVÁ. Bratislava, Historický ústav Slovenskej akadémie vied, 95, 188 p.

XXI. [Slowenien] JANŠA-ZORN (Olga), HOLZ (Eva), KANDUS (Nataša). Slovenian historiography in foreign languages, published from 1918–1993: on the occasion of the 18th International Congress of Historical Sciences, Montréal 1995. Ed. by Sergij VILFAN, translation by Cvetka VODE. Ljubljana, Research Center of the Slovenian Academy, Institute of Contemporary History, 95, VIII-118 p.

XXII. [Spanien] Indice histórico español. Publicación semestral del centro de estudios históricos internacionales. Ed. por Rosa ORTEGA CANADELL, Pere MOLAS RIBALTA. Vol. 33, n. 103-104, 1995. [1994. Cf. Bibl. 94, n° *XVI.*] Barcelona, Publicacions de la Universitat de Barcelona, 95, 2 vol., 292 p., 390 p.

XXIII. [Ungarn] Történeti bibliográfia 1993. [1991–1992. Cf. Bibl. 94, n° *XIX.*] (Bibliographie historique 1993.). Réd. par János POTO. Budapest, História-MTA Történettud. Int., 95, 192 p. (História könyvtár, bibliográfiák, 4).

A

HILFSWISSENSCHAFTEN

§ 1. Paläographie. 1-44. – § 2. Urkundenlehre. 45-76. – § 3. Buchwesen und Buchgeschichte (*a.* Volumen, Kodex, Handgeschriebenes Buch; *b.* Buchgeschichte). 77-258. – § 4. Chronologie. 259-269. – § 5. Genealogie. 270-273. – § 6. Siegel- und Wappenkunde. 274-291. – § 7. Münz-, Maß- und Gewichtskunde. 292-328. – § 8. Sprachliche Hilfsmittel. 329-367. – § 9. Historische Geographie und Geschichte der Geographie. 368-402. – § 10. Ikonographie. 403-417.

§ 1. Paläographie.

* 1. BMB. Bibliografia dei manoscritti in scrittura beneventana. Dati relativi a pubblicazioni apparse a partire dal 1990. Vol. 3. [Vol. 2. Cf. Bibl. 94, n° 1.]. Raccolti da Cristina ARESTI [et al.] ed elaborati da Francesco BIANCHI e Antonio MAGI SPINETTI. Roma, Viella, 95, 404 p.

* 2. COCKSHAW (Pierre), MANNING (Eugène). Bulletin codicologique. 1995. [1994. Cf. Bibl. 94, n° 3.]. *Scriptorium*, 95, 49, 1, p. 1*-82*; 2, p. 83*-233*.

3. AKTAN (Ali). Osmanlı Paleografyası ve Siyasi Yazışmaları. (Paléographie ottomane et ses correspondances politiques). İstanbul, Osmanlılar İlim ve İrfan Vakfı, 95, 189 p.

4. Aproximación a la cultura escrita: material de apoyo. Madrid, Playor, 95, 238 p. (Textos y recuperación).

5. BANTI (O.). Epigrafia medioevale e paleografia. Specificità dell'analisi epigrafica. *Scrittura e civiltà*, 95, 19, p. 31-52.

6. BARTOLONI (F.). Scritti. A cura di Vittorio DE DONATO e Alessandro PRATESI. Spoleto, Centro italiano di studi sull'alto medioevo, 95, XV-582 p. (Collectanea, 6).

7. BURGERS (J. W. J.). De paleografie van de documentaire bronnen in Holland en Zeeland in de dertiende eeuw. 1: Onderzoek. 2: Bijlagen. 3: Afbeeldingen. Leuven, Peeters, 95, 3 vol. (Schrift en Schriftdragers in de Nederlanden in de Middeleeuwen, 1).

8. CARLETTI (Carlo). «Viatores ad martyres». Testimonianze scritte alto-medievali nelle catacombe romane. *In*: Epigrafia medievale greca e latina [Cf. n° 15], p. 197-225.

9. Cavallo (GUGLIELMO), Magistrale (FRANCESCO). Mezzogiorno normanno e scritture esposte. *In*: Epigrafia medievale greca e latina [Cf. n° 15], p. 293-329.

10. Codices Sangallenses: Festschrift für Johannes Duft zum 80. Geburtstag. Hrsg. v. P. OCHSENBEIN u. E. ZIEGLER. Sigmaringen, J. Thorbecke, 95, XVI-216 p. (taf.).

11. CONDELLO (E.). Tra littera textualis e littera bastarda: scritture e codici di Guillaume de Breuil. *Scrittura e civiltà*, 95, 19, p. 235-250.

12. CRISTIN (A.-M.). L'image écrite ou la déraison graphique. Paris, Flammarion, 95, 248 p. (pl., ill.) (Idées et recherches).

13. DURLIAT (Jean). Epigraphie chrétienne de langue latine. *In*: Epigrafia medievale greca e latina [Cf. n° 15], p. 227-266. – IDEM. Epigraphie et société. Problèmes de méthode. *In*: Epigrafia medievale greca e latina [Cf. n° 15], p. 169-196.

14. EDROIU (Nicolae). Paleografia româno-chirilică (sec. XVI–XIX). (Romanian-Cyrillic paleography, XVIth–XIXth centuries). Oradea, Fundaţia Culturală "Cele Trei Crişuri", 95, 148 p.

15. Epigrafia medievale greca e latina. Ideologia e funzione. Atti del seminario di Erice, 12–18 settembre 1991. A cura di Guglielmo CAVALLO e Cyril MANGO. Spoleto, Centro Italiano di Studi sull'Alto Medioevo, 95, XIV-329 p. (tav., ill.) (Biblioteca del «Centro per il collegamento degli studi medievali e umanistici in Umbria», 11). [Cf. n[os] <scelta> 8, 9, 13.]

16. Escribir y leer en Occidente. Ed. a cargo de Armando PETRUCCI i Francisco M. GIMENO BLAY. València, Departament de història de la Antigüedat i de la cultura escrita, Universitat de València, 95, 254 p. (Seminario internacional de estudios sobre la cultura escrita «José Tenchs y Odena»). [Cf. n° <selección> 212.]

17. EVANGELISTI (C.). Accepto calamo, manu propria scripsi. Prove e perizie grafiche nella Bologna di fine Cinquecento. *Scrittura e civiltà*, 95, 19, p. 251-276.

18. FAVREAU (R.). Etudes d'épigraphie médiévale. Recueil d'articles rassemblés à l'occasion de son départ à la retraite. T. 1. Texte. T. 2. Index et planches. Limoges, PULIM, 95. 2 vol., XLII-622, 108 p. (ill.).

19. FRIOLI (D.). La 'grammatica della leggibilità' nel manoscritto cistercense. L'esempio di Aldersbach. *Studi Medievali*, 95, 36, 2, p. 743-776.

20. GANZ (David). Book production in the Carolingian empire and the spread of Caroline minuscule. *In:* New Cambridge medieval history [Cf. n° 3378], p. 786-808.

21. GIMENO BLAY (F. M.). Sobre la enseñanza de las escrituras antiguas. *Scrittura e civiltà*, 95, 19, p. 353-366.

22. GÖBEL (Robert), RÓNA-TAS (András). Die Inschriften des Schatzes von Nagy-Szentmiklós: eine paläographische Dokumentation. Wien, Verlag der Österreichischen Akademie der Wissenschaften, 95, 78-XXIV p. (ill.) (Österreichische Akademie der Wissenschaften, Phil.-hist. Klasse. Denkschriften, 240. Veröffentlichungen der Numismatischen Kommission. Österreichische Akademie der Wissenschaften, 31. Mitteilungen der Prähistorischen Kommission der Österreichischen Akademie der Wissenschaften, 29).

23. GULLICK (M.). Calligraphy. London, Studio Editions, 95, 62 p. (ill.) (The Treasury of decorative art).

24. Inschriften bis 1300. Probleme und Aufgaben ihrer Erforschung. Referate der Fachtagung für mittelalterliche und frühneuzeitliche Epigraphik, Bonn 1993. Hrsg. v. Helga GIERSIEPEN u. Raymund KOTTJE. Opladen, Westdeutscher Verlag, 95, 218 p.

25. KHATIBI (A.), SIJELMASSI (M.). L'arte calligrafica dell'Islam. A c. di P. ALBONICO e M. DE GIOVANNI BUZZONI. Milano, Garzanti, 95, 240 p. (ill.) (Gli Illustrati Vallardi). – IDEM. Splendour of Islamic calligraphy. London, Thames and Hudson, 95, 240 p. (ill.).

26. KRAUSE (W.). Les runes. Paris, Porte-Glaive, 95, 180 p. (ill.) (Patrimoine de l'Europe).

27. *Vacat.*

28. MASTRUZZO (A.). Ductus, corsività, storia della scrittura: alcune considerazioni. *Scrittura e civiltà*, 95, 19, p. 403-464.

29. Methoden der Schriftbeschreibung. I. Paläographische Methoden. Akten des 4. Internationalen Kolloquiums für historische Hilfswissenschaften, Marburg 1990. Marburg an der Lahn, Institut für Historische Hilfswissenschaften, 95, 250 p. (ill., pl.) (Elementa diplomatica, 4).

30. OVERGAAUW (Eef). Fast or slow, professional or monastic. The writing speed of some latin medieval scribes. *Scriptorium*, 95, 49, 2, p. 211-227.

31. PACI (G.). Epitafio urbano con fraintendimenti della minuta. *Scrittura e civiltà*, 95, 19, p. 53-66.

32. Pages of Perception. Islamic Calligraphy and Miniatures from the Oriental Institute of the Russian Academy of Sciences. New York, Abbeville Press, 95, 304 p. (ill.).

33. Palaeobyzantine Notations. A Reconsideration of the Source Material. Ed. by J. RAASTED a. C. TROELSGARD. Hernen, A. A. Bredius stichting, 95, VIII-172 p.

34. PEREZ MARTIN (Immaculada). Irene Cumno y el 'Taller de la Paleologuina'. *Scrittura e civiltà*, 95, 19, p. 223-234. – EADEM. El Vaticanus gr. 112 y la evolucion de la grafia de Jorge Galesiotos. *Scriptorium*, 95, 49, 1, p. 42-59.

35. PETRUCCI (Armando). Writers and Readers in Medieval Italy. Studies in the History of Written Culture. Ed. by M. C. RADDING. New Haven, Yale U. P., 95, 272 p. (ill.).

36. ROMERO TALLAFIGO (M.), RODRÍGUEZ LIAÑEZ (L.), SÁNCHEZ GONZÁLEZ (A.). Arte de leer escrituras antiguas: paleografía de lectura. Huelva, Universidad de Huelva, 95, 340 p. (ill.) (Instrumenta studiorum, 2).

37. SAFWAT (N. F.). The Art of the Pen. Calligraphy of the 14th to the 19th centuries. Oxford, Oxford U. P. and The Nour Foundation and Azimuth Ed., 95, 320 p. (pl.) (Nasser D. Khalili collection of Islamic art, 5).

38. Scribi e colofoni: le sottoscrizioni di copisti dalle origini all'avvento della stampa. Atti del seminario di Erice, X Colloquio del Comité international de paléographie latine, 23–28 ottobre 1993. A cura di Emma CONDELLO e Giuseppe DE GREGORIO. Spoleto, Centro italiano di studi sull'alto Medioevo, 95, X-565 p. (tav., ill.) (Biblioteca del Centro per il collegamento degli studi medievali e umanistici in Umbria, 14).

39. SIGNORINI (M.). Il copista di testi volgari (secoli X–XIII). Un primo sondaggio delle fonti. *Scrittura e civiltà*, 95, 19, p. 123-198.

40. STIENNON (J.). L'écriture. Turnhout, Brepols, 95, 132 p. (Typologie des sources du Moyen Age occidental, 72) (pl.).

41. STONE (Michael E.). The Album of Armenian paleography. With some picking from Armenian colophon. Gazette du livre médiéval, 26, 1, 95, p. 8-17.

42. SUPINO MARTINI (P.). Sul metodo paleografico: formulazione di problemi per una discussione. *Scrittura e civiltà*, 95, 19, p. 5-30.

43. TEDESCHI (C.). Osservazioni sulla paleografia delle iscrizioni britanniche paleocristiane (V–VII secolo). *Scrittura e civiltà*, 95, 19, p. 67-122.

44. VALSECCHI (B.). La scrittura carolina nei documenti notarili milanesi: proposta e ricezione di un modello (secc. XI–X). *Aevum*, 95, 69, p. 311-345.

Cf. n°s 45-76, 1354, 1588, 3178-3336

§ 2. Urkundenlehre.

45. AKYILDIZ (Ali). Tanzimat Döneminde Belgelerin Şekil, Dil ve Muhteva Yönünden Geçirdiği Bazı Değişiklikler, 1839–1856. (Quelques changements des documents du point de vue de la forme, de la langue et du contexte à l'époque de Tanzimat, 1839–1856). *Osmanlı Araştırmaları*, 95, 15, p. 221-237.

46. BANTI (Ottavio). Scritti di storia, diplomatica ed epigrafia. A cura di Silio P. P. SCALFATI. Ospedaletto e Pisa, Pacini, 95, XII-582 p. (ill.) (Biblioteca del Bollettino storico pisano. Collana storica, 43).

47. BARROW (Geoffrey W. S.). The English Royal Chancery in the earlier 13th century. *Archiv für Diplomatik, Schriftgeschichte Siegel- und Wappenkunde*, 95, 41, p. 241-248.

48. BATTELLI (Giulio). José Trenchs Òdena e i nuovi orientamenti della diplomatica pontificia. *In*: Misc.lània d'estudis dedicats a la memòria de Professor Josep Trenchs i Òdena [Cf. n° 67], p. 9-15.

49. BORRERO FERNANDEZ (Mercedes), FERNÁNDEZ GÓMEZ (Marcos), IGLESIA FERREIRÓS (Aquilino), OSTOS SALCEDO (Pilar), PARDO RODRÍGUEZ (María Luisa). Sevilla, ciudad de privilegios. Sevilla, Ayuntamiento de Sevilla, Universidad de Sevilla, Fundación el Monte, 585 p.

50. BROMM (G.). Die Entwicklung der Großbuchstaben im Kontext hochmittelalterlicher Papsturkunden. Marburg an der Lahn, Institut für Historische Hilfswissenschaften, 95, 272 p. (ill., taf.) (Elementa diplomatica, 3).

51. BTANDTL (Markus). Kanzlei und Verwaltung unter König Manfred – das Mandat. Mit einem Anhang ungedruckter Mandate. *Archiv für Diplomatik, Schriftgeschichte Siegel- und Wappenkunde*, 95, 41, p. 339-363.

52. Diplomatik der Bischofsurkunden vor 1250 (Die). La diplomatique épiscopale avant 1250. Referate zum VIII. Internationalen Kongress für Diplomatik. Innsbruck, 27. September bis 3. Oktober 1993. Hrsg. v. Christoph HAIDACHER u. Werner KÖFLER. Innsbruck, [s. n.], 564 p.

53. DUFOUR (Jean). Peut-on parler d'une organisation de la chancellerie de Philippe Auguste? *Archiv für Diplomatik, Schriftgeschichte Siegel- und Wappenkunde*, 95, 41, p. 249-261 (tab.).

54. FRENZ (Thomas). Zur Herkunft des päpstlichen Breve. Beobachtungen zur reduzierten Urkundenform mit «en vedette» gesetzter Intitulatio im späten Mittelalter. *In*: Misc.lània d'estudis dedicats a la memòria de Professor Josep Trenchs i Òdena [Cf. n° 67], p. 571-576.

55. FÜGEDI (Erik). Ai confini tra l'uso orale e l'uso scritto. La pratica della cancelleria in Ungheria. *In*: Spiritualità e lettere nella cultura italiana e ungherese del basso medioevo [Cf. n° 4128], p. 377-387.

56. GRABOWSKI (Janusz). Dokumenty i kancelaria Kazimierza I Trojdenowica księcia warszawskiego (1349–1355). (Chancellerie et documents de Casimir I duc de Varsovie 1349–1355). *Archeion*, 95, 95, p. 7-29. [Eng. Summary, Rés. franç.].

57. GROTEN (Manfred). Die Arengen der Urkunden Kaiser Heinrichs IV. und König Philipps I. von Frankreich im Vergleich. *Archiv für Diplomatik, Schriftgeschichte Siegel- und Wappenkunde*, 95, 41, p. 49-72.

58. HIESTAND (Rudolf). Das feierliche Privileg Hadrians IV. für das Kanonissenstift Fishbeck vom 11. Mai 1158. Zugleich ein Beitrag zur Fälschungsproblematik von Papsturkunden aus der Mitte des 12. Jahrhunderts. *Archiv für Diplomatik, Schriftgeschichte Siegel- und Wappenkunde*, 95, 41, p. 73-103.

59. HÖFLINGER (Klaus). Zu den Datierungen der Urkunden Kaiser Friedrichs II. *Archiv für Diplomatik, Schriftgeschichte Siegel- und Wappenkunde*, 95, 41, p. 325-337.

60. KOCH (Walter). Sizilisches im deutschen Umfeld. Auf dem Wege zur Urkunde der Kaiserzeit Friedrichs II. (1212–1220). *Archiv für Diplomatik, Schriftgeschichte Siegel- und Wappenkunde*, 95, 41, p. 290-309 (taf.).

61. KÖLZER (Theo). Die normannisch-staufische Kanzlei (1130–1198). *Archiv für Diplomatik, Schriftgeschichte Siegel- und Wappenkunde*, 95, 41, p. 273-289.

62. Kommunales Schriftgut in Oberitalien. Formen, Funktionen, Überlieferung. Hrsg. v. Hagen KELLER u. Thomas BEHRMANN. München, Wilhelm Fink, 95, XIV-380 p. (Münstersche Mittelalterschriften, 68) (taf.).

63. KORTÜM (Hans-Henning). Zur päpstlichen Urkundensprache im frühen Mittelalter. Die päpstlichen Privilegien, 896–1046. Sigmaringen, J. Thorbecke, 95, 464 p. (Beiträge zur Geschichte und Quellenkunde des Mittelalters, 17).

64. LUNARI (Marco). «De mandato domini archiepiscopi in hanc publicam formam redici, tradidi et scripsi». Notai di curia e organizzazione notarile nella diocesi di Milano (sec. XV). *Rivista di storia della Chiesa in Italia*, 49, 2, 95, p. 486-508.

65. LÜTKE WESTHUES (P.). Die Kommunalstatuten von Verona im 13. Jahrhundert. Formen und Funktionen von Recht und Schrift in einer oberitalienischen Kommune. Frankfurt am Main, Berlin u. Bern, Lang, 95, 324 p. (Gesellschaft, Kultur und Schrift. Mediëvistische Beiträge, 2).

66. Memoria (La) delle chiese. Cancellerie vescovili e culture notarili nell'Italia centro-settentrionale (secoli X-XIII). A cura di Patrizia CANCIAN. Torino, *Scriptorium*, 95, 208 p. (I Florilegi, 4).

67. Misc.lània d'estudis dedicats a la memòria de Professor Josep Trenchs i Òdena. Ed. por Francisco M. GIMENO BLAY y María Luz MANDIGORRA LLAVATA. Castelló, Diputació de Castelló, 95, 2 vol., 1536 p. [Cf. n[os] <selecíon> 48, 54, 284, 821, 3216, 3676.]

68. MOSIICI (Luciana). Osservazioni diplomatiche e paleografiche su alcune imbreviature di un notaio pratese (1235). *In*: Studi in onore di Arnaldo D'Addario [Cf. n° 452], p. 773-988.

69. MURRAY (James), PREVENIER (Walter), OOSTERBOSCH (Michel). Notarial instruments in Flanders between 1280 and 1452. Bruxelles, Commission Royale d'Histoire, Koninklijke Commissie vor Geschiedenis, 95, XXVII-349 p.

70. Ordinamenti di giustizia fiorentini. Studi in occasione del VII centenario. A cura di Vanna ARRIGHI. Firenze, Archivio di Stato, 95, 182 p. (Archivio di Stato di Firenze, Scuola di archivistica, paleografia e diplomatica, 4) (tav.).

71. ÖZ (Baki). Alevilikle İlgili Osmanlı Belgeleri: Fermanlar, Beratlar. (Les Documents ottomans relatifs aux Alévites: Firmans et Brevets impériaux). İstanbul, Can yayınları, 95, [s. p.].

72. PETERSEN (E. Ladewig). A note on Danish royal diplomas, 12th and 13th centuries. *Scandinavian Journal of History*, 95, 20, p. 141-146.

73. PETERSOHN (Jürgen). Kaiserliche Skriniare in Rom bis zum Jahre 1200. *Quellen und Forschungen aus italienischen Archiven und Bibliotheken*, 95, 75, p. 1-31 (taf.).

74. RABIKAUSKAS (Paulius). Die Arbeitsweise der päpstlichen Kanzlei (Ende 12.–Anfang 13. Jahrhundert). *Archiv für Diplomatik, Schriftgeschichte Siegel- und Wappenkunde*, 95, 41, p. 263-271.

75. RUBIO VELA (Agustín). L'escrivania municipal de València als segles XIV i XV: burocràcia, política i cultura. València, Generalitat Valenciana, 95, 141 p. (ill.).

76. SPIEGEL (Joachim). Zur Besiegelungstechnik der Urkunden Kaiser Friedrichs II. *Archiv für Diplomatik, Schriftgeschichte Siegel- und Wappenkunde*, 95, 41, p. 311-324 (taf.).

Cf. n°s 3178-3336

§ 3. Buchwesen und Buchgeschichte.

a. Volumen, Kodex, Handgeschriebenes Buch.

77. Aelfwine's Prayerbook: London, British Library, Cotton Titus D. XXVI–XXVII. Ed. by B. GÜNZEL. Woodbridge, Boydell and Brewer, 95, 244 p. (Henry Bradshaw Society).

78. ALVAREZ MARQUEZ (Carmen). Catalogo de los colofones de la Biblioteca Capitular y Colombina de Sevilla. *Scriptorium*, 95, 49, 2, p. 283-311.

79. AUTENRIETH (Johane). Bücher im Übergang von der Spätantike zum Mittelalter. *Scriptorium*, 95, 49, 2, p. 169-179.

80. AVELLINI (Luisa). Il supporto della memoria: fenomenologia libraria delle scritture storiche bolognesi. *In*: Memoria (La) e la città. Scritture storiche tra medioevo e età moderna [Cf. n° 3303], p. 579-599.

81. Bible moralisée (Wien, Österrreichische Nationalbibliothek, Cod. Vind. 2554). Ed. by G. GUEST. London, Harvey Miller, 95, 320 p., 136 pl. (Manuscripts in miniature, 2).

82. Biblia pauperum. Die Bilderhandschrift des Codex Palatinus Latinus 871 im Besitz der Biblioteca Apostolica Vaticana. Hrsg. von C. WETZEL und H. DRECHSLER. Stuttgart, Belser, 95, 112 p. (ill.).

83. Biblioteca Apostolica Vaticana. Archivio San Pietro B 79. Antifonario della Basilica di San Pietro (sec. XII). A c. di B. G. BAROFFIO, Soo Jung KIM. Roma, Torre d'Orfeo, 95, 2 vol., 324 p., (ill., tav.). (Musica Italiae liturgica, 1).

84. Biblioteca comunale, Treviso. Catalogo dei manoscritti nn. 1700–2150. A cura di E. LIPPI. Treviso, Comune, 95, 344 p.

85. Bibliothèque (La) du prince. Château de Chantilly: les manuscrits. Paris, Editerra, 95, 350 p., (ill.).

86. Bibliothèque nationale de France, Département des manuscrits. Catalogue des manuscrits arabes. 2e partie. Manuscrits musulmans. T. 5. Nos 1465–1685. Réd. par Y. SAUVAN et M.-G. BALTY-GUESDON. Paris, Bibliothèque nationale de France, 95, 334 p.

87. BISCHOFF (F. M.), MANIACI (M.). Pergamentgrösse – Handschriftenformate – Lagenkonstruktion. *Scrittura e civiltà*, 95, 19, p. 277-320.

88. BLACKMAN (S. A.). The Manuscripts and Patronage of Jacques d'Armagnac, Duke of Nemours (1433–1477). Ann Arbor, U.M.I., 95, 2 vol., XIV-790 p., (ill.).

89. BOFFEY (J.), EDWARDS (A.). Chaucer: works (Oxford, Bodleian Library, ms Arch. Selden B. 24). Facsimile edition. Woodbridge, Boydell and Brewer, 95.

90. Book in the Islamic world (The): the written word and communication in the Middle East. Ed. by George N. ATIYEH. Albany, State University of New York Press a. Washington, Library of Congress, 95, XVIII-305 p. (ill.).

91. British (The) Library Catalogue of Additions to the Manuscripts. New series, 1976–1980. Additional manuscripts 59652–61100, 61711–61890. Egerton manuscripts 3796–3802. Additional charters and rolls 75845–75881. Detached seals and casts CCIV. 1–8. Pt. 1. Descriptions. Pt. 2. Index. London, British Library, 1995. 2 vol., XIV-316 p., 370 p.

92. CAPASSO (Mario). Volumen: aspetti della tipologia del rotolo librario antico. Napoli, Procaccini, 95, 162 p. (Cultura, 3).

93. CARDON (B.), LIEVENS (R.), SMEYERS (M.). Typologische taferelen uit het leven van Jesus. A manu-

3. BUCHWESEN UND BUCHGESCHICHTE

script from the Gold scrolls group (Bruges, ca. 1440) in the Pierpont Morgan Library, New York, ms Morgan 649. An edition of the text, a reproduction of the manuscript and a study of the miniatures. Leuven, Peeters, 95, 208 p., (facsim., ill.) (Corpus van verluchte handschriften = Corpus of illuminated manuscripts, 1).

94. CATALDI PALAU (Annaclara). La biblioteca del cardinale Giovanni Salviati: alcuni nuovi manoscritti greci in biblioteche diverse dalla Vaticana. *Scriptorium*, 95, 49, 1, p. 60-94.

95. Catalogue of Arabic Manuscripts in SS. Cyril and Methodius National Library, Sofia, Bulgaria. T. 1. Hadith Sciences. Ed. by S. Kenderova and M. I. Walley. London, Al-Furqan Islamic heritage foundation, 95, XXX-460 p., (facs.) (Al-Furqan Islamic heritage foundation. Publications, 7).

96. Catalogus codicum Graecorum Bibliothecae nationalis neapolitanae. T. II. Rec. M. R. FORMENTIN. Roma, Istituto poligrafico e Zecca dello Stato, 95, XXX-232 p. (ill.) (Ministero per i beni culturali e ambientali. Indici e cataloghi. N.S., 8).

97. Codices miniati Medii Aevi. Microfiches. Vol. 37. Antiphonarium, Karlsruhe, Badische Landesbibliothek, Aug. perg. 60 (Zwiefalten, 3. Viertel 12. Jh., mit Ergänzungen). Hrsg. von H. MÖLLER. 10 microf., 42-IV-87 p. – Vol. 38. John LYGDATE, The Siege of Troye, Manchester, John Rylands University Library, English MS 1 (England, beginning of 15th c.). Ed. by W. G. BUSSE. 6 microf., 30 p. – Vol. 39. Apokalypse, Ars moriendi, Medizinische Traktate, Tugend- und Lasterlehren, London, Wellcome Institute for the history of Medicine, Western MS 49 (South-Eastern Germany, ca. 1420). Ed. by A. SEEBOHM. 3 microf., 80 p. – Vol. 40. Sacramentarium, Berlin, Staatsbibliothek Preussischer Kulturbesitz, Ms. theol. lat. fol. 2 (St. Gallen, 1022/1036) Hrsg. von M. KLÖCKENER und A. VON EUW. 11 microf., 60 p. – Vol. 41. Heinrich LAUFENBERG, Regimen, Zürich Zentralbibliothek, Ms. C 1026 (Oberrhein/Bodensee, um 1450). Hrsg. von B. SCHNELL. 5 microf., 30 p. – Vol. 42. Orationale des St. Galler Abtes Ulrich Rösch, Einsiedeln, Stifstsbibliothek, Cod. 285 (Wiblingen, 1472). Hrsg. von P. OCHSENBEIN und B. KONRAD. 4 microf., 40 p. München, Edition Helga Lengenfelder, 95.

98. Codicology (The) of Islamic Manuscripts. Proceedings of the 2nd Conference of Al-Furqan Islamic Heritage Foundation. Ed. by Y. DUTTON. London, Al-Furqan Islamic Heritage Foundation, 95, 160 p. (ill.) (Al-Furqan Islamic heritage foundation. Publications).

99. COLL I ROSELL (G.). Manuscrits jurídics i il·luminació: estudi d'alguns còdexs dels Usatges i constitucions de Catalunya i del Decret de Gracià, 1300–1350. Barcelona, Curial i Montserrat, Abadia, 95, 376 p. (ill.) (Textos i estudis de cultura catalana, 38).

100. Corali (I) del monastero di Santa Maria degli Angeli e le loro miniature asportate. Firenze, Centro Di, 95, 206 p. (ill.).

101. CROSS (F. M.). The Ancient Library of Qumran. Sheffield, Sheffield Academic Press, 1995, 204-16 p. (ill., facsim.) (The Biblical seminar, 30).

102. DE HAMEL (C.). Une histoire des manuscrits enluminés. London, Phaidon Press, 95, 272 p. (ill.).

103. De sphaera. Ed. facsimile del manoscritto membranaceo lat. 209 (a. X. 2. 14, Spherae coelestis et planetarum descriptio). A cura di E. MILANO, L. VENTURA e G. MALACARNE. Modena, Il Bulino, 95, 2 vol.

104. DESHMAN (R.). The Benedictional of Aethelwold (Cambridge, University Library, ms L. 1. 1. 10). Lawrenceville, Princeton U. P., 95, 432 p. (ill.) (Studies in manuscript illumination).

105. DIAZ Y DIAZ (Manuel C.). Manuscritos visigóticos del sur de la península: ensayo de distribución regional. Sevilla, Universidad de Sevilla, Secretariado de publicaciones, 95, 200 p. (pl.) (Historia y geografía, 11).

106. DOLBEAU (F.), PETITMENGIN (P.). Indices librorum. T. II. Catalogues anciens et modernes des manuscrits médiévaux en écriture latine (1984–1990) et compléments d'années antérieures (1977–1983). Paris, Presses de l'Ecole normale supérieure, 95, XVI-296 p. (Bibliothèque de l'Ecole normale supérieure. Guides et inventaires bibliographiques, 5).

107. DOMÍNGUEZ RODRÍGUEZ (A.), F. J. DOCAMPO CAPILLA (F. J.). Diminuto devocionario del Museo arqueológico nacional: estudio del códice y sus miniaturas. Madrid, Ediciones Grial, 95, 130 p. (ill.).

108. English Manuscripts Studies 1100–1700. Ed. by Peter BEAL and Jeremy GRIFFITH. Vol. 5. Oxford, Basil Blackwell, 95, VI-246 p.

109. EVANS (M. J.). Rereading Middle English Romance: manuscript layout, decoration and the lay-out of composite structure. Montréal, McGill-Queen's U. P., 95, 208 p.

110. Fabula in tabula. Una storia degli indici dal manoscritto al testo elettronico. Atti del convegno di studio della Fondazione Ezio Franceschini e della Fondazione IBM Italia, Certosa del Galluzzo (Firenze), 1994. A cura di Claudio LEONARDI, Marcello MORELLI e Francesco SANTI. Spoleto, centro di studi sull'Alto medioevo, 95, X-482 p. (Quaderni di cultura mediolatina, 13). [contiene: GARFAGNINI (Gian Carlo), Fare indici e storiografia, p. 301-14. TOSCHI (Luca), L'ipertesto d'autore. Per una teoria del testo d'autore, p. 439-73].

111. Facsimile (A) edition of Sefer Pitron Torah: a collection of Midrashim and interpretation, Jewish National and University Library, Jerusalem, ms Heb. 4° 5767. Jerusalem, Magnes Press, 95, [s. p.].

112. FEDERICO II. De arte venandi cum avibus. Facsimile ed edizione critica del manoscritto fr. 12400 della Bibliothèque nationale de France. Napoli, Electa, 95, 606 p. (Fridericiana ars).

113. Fihris makhtutat markaz Ahmad Baba lil-Watha'iq wa-'l-Buthuth al-Tarikhiyyah bi Tumbuktu (= Inventaire des manuscrits du Centre de Documentation et de recherches historiques Ahmed Baba, Tombouctou). T. 1. Ed. by Sidi Amar Ould ELY and J. JOHANSEN. London, Al-Furqan Islamic Heritage Foundation, 95, 592 p. (Handlist of Islamic manuscript series, 5. African collections, Mali).

114. FOHLEN (Jeannine). Comment «fabriquer» un exemplaire complet des Epistolae ad Lucilium. *Scriptorium*, 95, 49, 1, p. 95-105.

115. FRYDE (E. B.). Greek manuscripts in the private library of the Medici, 1469–1510. Aberystwyth, National Library of Wales, 95, 2 vol., 870 p.

116. GAMESON (Richard). Alfred the Great and the destruction and production of Christian books. *Scriptorium*, 95, 49, 2, p. 180-210.

117. GOLOB (N.). Twelfth century Cistercian manuscripts from Sitticum. London, Harvey Miller, 95, 340 p. (ill.).

118. Grandes (Les) Heures de Charles VIII, roi de France (Madrid, Biblioteca nacional, Vitr. 24-1). Facsímil con estudio crítico de A. DOMINGUEZ RODRIGUEZ, transcripción y traducción. Barcelona, M. Moleiro, 95, 2 vol., 232 p.

119. Greek papyri from Dublin (P. Dub.). Ed. by B. C. MAC GING. Bonn, Habelt, 95, XXVIII-230 p. (ill.) (Papyrologische Texte und Abhandlungen, 42).

120. GÜNTHER (J.). Mittelalterliche Handschriften und Miniaturen. Holm, Ed. Herms, 95, [s. p.].

121. HACO (M.). El horóscopo de Felipe II. A c. di D. SANTOS SANTOS. Madrid, Patrimonio nacional y Valencia, Grial, 95, 132 p. (fac-sim).

122. Handschriften (Die) der Universitätsbibliothek München. 1. Die Deutschen mittelalterlichen Handschriften. 2. Die Lateinischen mittelalterlichen Handschriften. 3. Die Musikhandschriften. Erlangen, H. Fischer, 95, 2871 microf.

123. Handschriften (Die) des 12. Jahrhunderts der Staatsbibliothek Bamberg. Hrsg. von Gude SUCKALE-REDLEFSEN. Wiesbaden, O. Harrassowitz, 95, XLVI-206 p. (Katalog der illuminierten Handschriften der Staatsbibliothek Bamberg, 2).

124. HANGARTNER (B.). Missalia Einsidlensia. Studien zu drei neumierten Handschriften des 11.–12. Jahrhunderts. St. Ottilien, EOS Verlag Erzabtei St. Ottilien, 95, 278 p. (ill.) (Bayerische Benediktinerakademie. Studien und Mitteilungen zur Geschichte des Benediktinerordens und seiner Zweige, 36. Ergänzungsband).

125. HÄRTEL (Helmar). Anmerkungen zu einem Katalogprojekt der mittelalterlichen Liturgica aus der Stiftskirche St. Blasius in Braunschweig. *In*: Welfen und ihr Braunschweiger Hof im hohen Mittelalter (Die) [Cf. n° 3486], p. 227-236.

126. HAUCAP-NASS (Anette). Der Braunschweiger Stadtschreiber Gerwin von Hameln und seine Bibliothek. Wiesbaden, O. Harrassowitz, 95, VI-376 p. (Wolfenbütteler Mittelalter-Studien. Bd. 8). – EADEM. Die Stiftsbibliothek von St. Blasius in Braunschweig. Ein Überblick mit einer Handliste der nachweisbaren Handschriften und Drucke aus dem Blasiusstift. *In*: Welfen und ihr Braunschweiger Hof im hohen Mittelalter (Die) [Cf. n° 3486], p. 205-225.

127. HEINZER (Felix). Die neuen Standorte der ehemals Donaueschinger Handschriftensammlung. *Scriptorium*, 95, 49, 2, p. 312-319.

128. HERNANDO (Joseph). Llibres i lectors a la Barcelona del s. XIV. Barcelona, Pagès, 95, 2 vol., 802 p. (Textos i documents, 30–31).

129. HOFFMANN (Hartmut). Bamberger Handschriften des 10. und des 11. Jahrhunderts. Hannover, Hahn, 95., XIV-210 p. (Monumenta Germaniae historica. Schriften, 39) (taf.).

130. Hours of Mary of Burgundy (The). Codex Vindobonensis 1857, Vienna, Österreichische Nationalbibliothek. Comm. by Eric INGLIS. London, Harvey Miller, 95, VII-80 p. (Manuscripts in Miniature).

131. HUNGER (H.). Katalog der griechischen Handschriften der Österreichischen Nationalbibliothek [Wien]. Band 4. Supplementum graecum. Wien, In Kommission bei Verlag Brüder Hollinek, 95, XIV-422 p. (Museion. Veröffentlichungen der Österreichischen Nationalbibliothek. N. F., 4. Reihe: Veröffentlichungen der Handschriftensammlung, 1, 4).

132. Jagdbuch (Das) des Mittelalters (Paris, Bibliothèque nationale, Ms. fr. 616). Hrsg. von M. THOMAS und W. SCHLAG. Graz Graz, Akademische Druck- und Verlagsanstalt, 95, 82 p., 276 taf. (Glanzlichter der Buchkunst, 4).

133. JOUANNA (Jacques). L'Hippocrate de Modène: Mut. Est. gr. 233, 220 et 227. *Scriptorium*, 95, 49, 2, p. 273-282.

134. KALATZI (Maria). Corpus Christi College 224: the missing link. *Scriptorium*, 95, 49, 2, p. 262-263.

135. Katalog der lateinischen Handschriften der Bayerischen Staatsbibliothek München. Die Handschriften aus St. Emmeram in Regensburg. T. 1. Clm. 14000–14130. Hrsg. von E. WUNDERLE. Wiesbaden, O. Harrassowitz, 95, XXVIII-450 p. (Catalogus codicum manu scriptorum Bibliothecae Monacensis, t. 4. Ser. nova, pars 2, 1).

136. KOCH (Petra). Die Statutengesetzgebung der Kommune Vercelli im 13. und 14. Jahrhundert. Untersuchungen zur Kodikologie, Genese und Benützung der überlieferten Handschriften, Gesellschaft, Kultur und Schrift. Frankfurt am Main u. Bern, Peter Lang, 95, 369 p. (Mediävistische Beiträge, 1).

137. LENZUNI (Anna). Note su alcuni codici patristici della Biblioteca Medicea Laurenziana. *In*: Tradi-

zione patristica (La). Alle fonti della cultura medievale [Cf. n° 4151], p. 115-125.

138. Liber testamentorum ecclesiae Ovetensis. Barcelona, M. Moleiro, 95, 824 p. (fac-sim.).

139. Libraria Domini. I manoscritti della Biblioteca Malatestiana: testi e decorazioni. Catalogo. A cura di F. LOLLINI e P. LUCCHI. Casalecchio di Reno, Grafis, 95, 432 p. (ill.).

140. Libri (I) di San Marco: manoscritti liturgici della basilica Marciana. Catalogo della mostra, Libreria Sansoviniana, Venezia, 1995. A c. di S. MARCON. Venezia, Il Cardo, 95, 198 p. (ill.).

141. Libro de horas de Carlos VIII, rey de Francia (Madrid, Bibl. nac., ms Vitr. 24. 1). Fac símil y estudio introductorio por A. DOMÍNGUEZ RODRÍGUEZ. Madrid, Biblioteca nacional y Barcelona, M. Moleiro, 95, 432 p. (Texte).

142. LIGHT (L.). Catalogue of Medieval and Renaissance Manuscripts in the Houghton Library, Harvard University. Vol. 1. Mss. lat. 3–179. Binghampton, State University of New York, Center for medieval and early Renaissance studies, 95, XXX-348 p., 67 pl. (Medieval and Renaissance texts and studies, 145).

143. Liturgia in figura: codici liturgici rinascimentali della Biblioteca Apostolica Vaticana. A cura di G. MORELLO e S. MADDALO. Città del Vaticano, Biblioteca Apostolica Vaticana e Roma, De Luca, 95, 36 p. (ill.).

144. Liturgical books af Anglo-Saxon England (The). Ed. by Richard W. PFAFF. Kalamazoo, Western Michigan University, Medieval Institute Publications, VI-128 p.

145. Livres parcours: manuscrits et merveilles de la Bibliothèque de Valenciennes. Catalogue de l'exposition, Valenciennes, Bibliothèque, 1995. Valenciennes, Ville de Valenciennes, 95, 140 p. (ill.) (Trésors de la bibliothèque de Valenciennes, 1).

146. MAC KITTERICK (Rosamond). Essai sur le représentations de l'écrit dans les manuscrits carolingiens. In: Symbolique du livre (La) dans l'art occidental [Cf. n° 183], p. 37-63.

147. Making the medieval book: techniques of production: proceedings of the Fourth Conference of the Seminar in the History of the Book to 1500, Oxford, July 1992. Ed. by Linda L. BROWNRIGG. Los Altos Hills, Anderson-Lovelace a. London, Red Gull Press, 95, XIV-246 p. (ill.).

148. MALAGUZZI (F.). De libris compactis. Legature di pregio in Piemonte. Vol. 1. Il Canavese. Torino, Centro studi piemontesi e Regione Piemonte, Assessorato alla cultura, 95, 170 p. (tav., ill.).

149. MANIACI (Marilena), ORNATO (Ezio). Intorno al testo: il ruolo dei margini nell'impaginazione dei manoscritti greci e latini. *Nuovi annali della Scuola speciale per archivisti e bibliotecari*, 9, 95, p. 175-194.

150. MANIACI (Marilena). Considerazioni intorno all'elaborazione di un glossario codicologico in lingua italiana. *Gazette du livre médiéval*, 26, 1, 95, p. 1-7. – EADEM. Ricette di costruzione della pagina nei manoscritti greci e latini. *Scriptorium*, 95, 49, 1, p. 16-41.

151. Manuscrits enluminés d'origine germanique. T. 1. X^e–XIVe siècle. Ed. par François. AVRIL et Claudia RABEL. Paris, Bibliothèque nationale de France, Département des manuscrits, Centre de recherche sur les manuscrits enluminés, 95, XXVI-220 p. (pl.).

152. MARCO POLO. Le Livre des Merveilles (Paris, Bibliothèque nationale, ms. fr. 2810): édition en facsimilé. Luzern, Faksimile Verlag, 95, 2 vol., [s. p.].

153. MARIANI CANOVA (G.). Guglielmo Giraldi: miniatore estense. Modena, F. C. Panini, 95, 208 p. (ill.).

154. MARROW (J. H.). As horas de Margarida de Cleves (Lisboa, Museu Calouste Gulbenkian, ms LA 148). Lisboa, Museu Calouste Gulbenkian, 95, 186 p. (ill.).

155. MASSING (J. M.). Erasmian wit and proverbial wisdom. Illustrated moral compendium for François I: facsimile of a dismembered manuscript with introduction and description. London, Warburg Institute, 95, 136 p., 48 p. fac-sim (ill.) (Studies of the Warburg Institute, 43).

156. MEEHAN (B.). The Book of Kells: an illustrated introduction to the manuscript in Trinity College Dublin [ms 58 (A. 1. 6)]. London, Thames and Hudson, 95, 96 p. (ill.).

157. MEYER (Christian). Le diagramme lamboïde du ms. Oxford Bodleian Library Auct. F.3.15. *Scriptorium*, 95, 49, 2, p. 228-237.

158. Mittelalterliche (Die) Musik-Handschrift. W1. Vollständige Reproduktion des Manuskripts der Herzog August Bibliothek Wolfenbüttel, Cod. Guelf. 628 Helmst. Hrsg. von M. STÄHLI. Wiesbaden, O. Harrassowitz, 95, 50 p., 394 p. (fac-sim.) (Wolfenbütteler Mittelalter-Studien, 9).

159. Mittelalterliche Handschriften der Universitätsbibliothek Uppsala. Katalog. Hrsg. v. M. ANDERSSON-SCHMITT, H. HALLBERG u. M. HEDLUND. Bd. 7. Supplement und Hauptregister. Bd. 8. Spezialregister. Stockholm, Almqvist & Wiksell Int., 95, XX-430 p., 514 p. (ill.) (Acta Bibliothecae R. Universitatis Upsaliensis, 26).

160. NARKISS (B.). Golden Haggadah (London, Br. Libr., Add. ms 27210). London, British Library, 95, 64 p. (ill.).

161. NEMIROVSKIJ (E. L.). Gesamtkatalog der Frühdrucke in kyrillischer Schrift. Bd. 1. Inkunabeln. Baden-Baden, V. Koerner, 95, 318 p. (Bibliotheca bibliographica Aureliana, 140).

162. Neri da Rimini: il Trecento riminese tra pittura e scrittura. Catalogo della mostra, Rimini, Museo della Città, 1995. Milano, Electa, 95, 224 p. (ill.).

163. New (The) Ellesmere Chaucer (San Marino, Huntington Library, ms El 26 C 9). Facsimile. Ed. by D. WOODWARD and M. STEVENS. San Marino, Huntington Library a. Yushodo, 95, 2 vol., [s.p.].

164. NOEL (W.). The Harley Psalter (London, Br. Libr., Harley ms 603). Cambridge, Cambridge U. P., 95, XVIII-232 p. (ill.) (Cambridge studies in palaeography and codicology, 4).

165. OLIVER (Judith). The Mount St Mary' Missel leaf and Parisan gothic manuscripts. *Scriptorium*, 95, 49, 2, p. 243-249.

166. Oliveriano 1 (Pesaro, Biblioteca oliveriana, ms 1). Facsimile del codice e commento. A c. di C. EGGENBERGER e L. MIGLIO. Roma, Istituto poligrafico e Zecca dello Stato, 95, 2 vol., [s. p.].

167. PAGE (R. I.), BUDNY (Mildred), HADGRAFT (Nicholas). Two fragments of an old English manuscript in the library of Corpus Christi College, Cambridge. *Speculum*, 95, 70, 3, p. 502-529.

168. PASTOUREAU (Michel). La symbolique médiévale du livre. *In*: Symbolique du livre (La) dans l'art occidental [Cf. n° 183], p. 17-36.

169. PELLEGRINI (Letizia). I predicatori e i loro manoscritti. *In*: Predicazione dei frati (La) [Cf. n° 4451], p. 114-139.

170. PERANI (Mauro). La «Ghenizah» italiana. Migliaia di frammenti ebraici rinvenuti negli archivi italiani. *Gazette du livre médiéval*, 26, 1, p. 18-26.

171. PETRUS DE EBULO, Liber ad honorem Augusti, sive de rebus Siculis (Codex 120 II der Burgerbibliothek Bern). Eine Bilderchronik der Stauferzeit. Hrsg. von T. KÖLZER und M. STÄHLI. Sigmaringen, J. Thorbecke, 95, 304 p., (taf.).

172. PLANAS BADENAS (Josefina). Una Biblia manuscrita de la Cartuja de Portaceli en la Hispanic-Society of America. *Anuario de estudios medievales*, 95, 25, 1, p. 287-295.

173. Pratiques de la culture écrite en France au XVe siècle. Actes du colloque international du C.N.R.S., Paris, 16–18mai 1992, organisé en l'honneur de Gilbert Ouy par l'unité de recherche CEMAT (Culture écrite du Moyen Age tardif). Ed. par Monique ORNATO et Nicole PONS. Louvain-la-Neuve, Fédération internationale des Instituts d'études médiévales, 95, XV-592 p. (pl.). (Fédération internationale des Instituts d'études médiévales. Textes et études du Moyen Age, 2).

174. Répertoire de réglures dans les manuscrits grecs sur parchemin. Base de données établie par J.-H. SAUTEL à l'aide du fichier Leroy et des catalogues récents à l'IRHT (C.N.R.S.). Turnhout et Paris, Brepols, 95, 410 p. (Bibliologia. Elementa ad librorum studia pertinentia, 13).

175. RIOU (Yves-François). Alfarabi, Aristotele, Platon, Plutarque et Ptolémée à Reims ver 1479. *Scriptorium*, 95, 49, 1, p. 106-133.

176. Rotolo (Il) librario. Fabbricazione, restauro, organizzazione interna. A cura di M. CAPASSO. Galatina, Congedo, 95, 264 p. (ill.) (Università di Lecce. Dipartimento di filologia classica e medievale. Papirologia, 3).

177. RUDLOFF STANTON (Anne). Notes on the codicology of the Queen Mary Psalter. *Scriptorium*, 95, 49, 2, p. 250-261.

178. SÁNCHEZ MARIANA (Manuel). Catálogo de manuscritos de la Real Biblioteca (Madrid). Madrid, Patrimonio nacional, 95, 3 vol., [s. p.]. – IDEM. Introducción al libro manuscrito. Madrid, Arco Libros, 95, 166 p. (Instrumenta bibliologica).

179. SERRAI (Alfredo). Storia della bibliografia. Vol. 6. La maturità disciplinare. A cura di Gabriella MIGGIANO; con contributi di Maria COCHETTI. Roma, Bulzoni, 95, 431 p. (Il bibliotecario, 4. Nuova serie, Manuali).

180. Shadow of Montecassino (In the). Nuove ricerche dai frammenti di codice dell'Archivio di Stato di Frosinone: catalogo della mostra organizzata dall'Archivio di Stato di Frosinone. A c. di R. SANTORO, V. FONTANA, G. BIANCHINI. Frosinone, Archivio di Stato di Frosinone e Ente provinciale per il turismo di Frosinone, 95, 102 p. (tav.) (Quaderni dell'Archivio di Stato di Frosinone, 3).

181. SPATHARAKIS (I.). Studies in Byzantine manuscript illumination and iconography. London, Pindar Press, 95, 390 p. (ill.) (Selected studies in the history of art).

182. STOLTE (A.). Frühe Miniaturen zu Dantes "Divina Commedia": der Codex Egerton 943 der British Library Reihe. Münster und Hamburg, Lit, 95, 350 p. (Kunstgeschichte, 47).

183. Symbolique du livre (La) dans l'art occidental du haut Moyen Age à Rembrandt. *Revue française d'histoire du livre*, 95, 64, 86-87, 217 p. [Cf. n^{os} <sélection> 146, 168, 213.]

184. TELESKO (W.). Göttweiger Buchmalerei des 12. Jahrhunderts: Studien zur Handschriftenproduktion eines Reformklosters. St. Ottilien, EOS Verlag Erzabtei St. Ottilien, 95, 196-22 p. (ill.) (Studien und Mitteilungen zur Geschichte des Benediktinerordens und seiner Zweige. Ergzbd., 37).

185. Treasures from the National Library of Ireland. Ed. by N. KISSANE. London, Alpine, 95, 244 p. (ill.) (Fine arts collection).

186. VAN BREE (C.). Lotgevallen van de codex Argenteus (Uppsala, Universitetsbiblioteket, DG 1): de wisselende waarde van een handschrift. Amsterdam, De Buitenkant, 95, 40 p., (ill.) (Bert van Selm-lezing, 4).

187. Verzeichnis der orientalischen Handschriften in Deutschland. Bd. 21. Koptische Handschriften. 2. Die Handschriften der Staats- und Universitätsbibliothek

Hamburg. Teil 2. Die Handschriften aus Dair Anb Maqr. Hrsg. von L. STÖRK. Stuttgart, F. Steiner, 95, 696 p.

188. Vie (La) de sainte Radegonde par Fortunat [Poitiers, Bibl. mun. ms. 250 (136)]. Ed. par R. FAVREAU. Paris, Le Seuil, 95, 270 p. (ill.), 47 pl. (fac-sim. intégral en couleur de la partie enluminée.).

189. VILLA (Claudia). Die Horazüberlieferung und die «Bibliothek Karls des Großen». Zum Werkverzeichnis der Handschrift Berlin Diez B. 66. *Deutsches Archiv für Erforschung des Mittelalters*, 95, 51, p. 29-52.

190. WENZEL (Horst). Hören und Sehen. Schrift und Bild. Kultur und Gedächtnis im Mittelalter. München, C. H. Beck, 95, 626 p. (ill.).

191. WIERDA (L.). De Sarijs-handschriften. Studie naar een groep laat-middeleeuwse handschriften uit de IJsselstreek (voorheen toegeschreven aan de Agnietenberg bij Zwolle). Zwolle, Waanders, 95, 212 p., (ill., taf., floppy).

192. Winchcombe sacramentary (The) (Orléans, Bibliothèque municipale, 127 [105]). Ed. by Anselme DAVRIL. Woodbridg a. Rochester, Boydell and Brewer, 95, VII-453 p. (Henry Bradshaw Society, 109).

b. Buchgeschichte.

* 193. ABHB. Annual bibliography of the history of the printed book and libraries. Ed. by the Department of Special Collections of the Koninklijke Bibliotheek, The Hague. Vol. 24. [Vol. 23. Cf. Bibl. 94, n° 63.]. Dordrecht, Kluwer Academic Publishers, 520 p.

* 194. Bibliographie der Buch- und Bibliotheksgeschichte (BBB). Vol. 13. 1993 (mit Nachträgen aus den Jahren 1980 bis 1992) [Vol. 12. 1992. Cf. Bibl. 94, n° 64.]. Hrsg. v. Horst MEYER. Bad Iburg, Bibliographischer Verlag Dr. Horst Meyer, 94, 638 p.

* 195. CHARON (Annie), GUILLEMINOT (Geneviève). L'histoire du livre en France au XVIe siècle: bilan bibliographique (1980–1993) – seconde partie. *Nouvelle revue du XVIe siècle*, 95, 13, 1, p. 105-123.

* 196. ROSENBLUM (Joseph). A bibliographic history of the book: an annotated guide to the literature. Metuchen, Scarecrow Press a. Pasadena, Salem Press, 95, XIII-425 p. (Magill bibliographies).

197. ANGERHOFER (Paul J.), ADDY MAXWELL (May Ann), MAXWELL (Robert L.). In Aedibus Aldi: the legacy of Aldus Manutius and his press. Provo, Friends of the Harold B. Lee Library a. Brigham Young University, 95, IX-172 p.

198. Antiquario (L') Felice Feliciano veronese tra epigrafia antica, letteratura e arti del libro. Atti del convegno di studi, Verona 1993. A cura di A. CONTÒ e L. QUAQUARELLI. Padova, Antenore, 95, XVI-430 p. (ill.) (Medioevo e umanesimo, 89).

199. Arbeitsgemeinschaft Sammlung Deutscher Drucke 1450–1912. Das deutsche Buch: die Sammlung deutscher Drucke 1450–1912. Bilanz der Förderung durch die Volkswagen-Stiftung. Hrsg. v. B. FABIAN u. E. MITTLER. Wiesbaden, L. Reichert, 95, 164 p. (ill.).

200. AVRIL (F.), REYNAUD (N.). Les manuscrits à peintures en France, 1440–1520. Publ. à l'occasion de l'exposition "Quand la peinture était dans les livres: les manuscrits enluminés en France, 1440–1520", Paris, Bibliothèque nationale, 1993–1994. Paris, Flammarion et Bibliothèque nationale, 95, 440 p. (ill.).

201. BACKHOUSE (J.). Lindisfarne Gospels (London, British Library, ms Cotton Nero D. IV): masterpiece of book painting. London, British Library, 95, 64 p. (Manuscripts in colour).

202. BARBIER (Frederic). L'empire du livre: le livre imprimé et la construction de l'Allemagne contemporaine, 1815–1914. Préface par Henri-Jean MARTIN. Paris, Ed. du Cerf, 95, XI-612 p. (ill.). (Bibliotheque franco-allemande).

203. BECHTEL (G.). Gutenberg. Torino, S.E.I., 95, VI-474 p.

204. BRAIDA (Ludovica). Il commercio delle idee. Editoria e circolazione del libro nella Torino del Settecento. Firenze, Olschki, 95, 403 p. (Fondazione Luigi Firpo. Centro di Studi sul pensiero Politico. Studi e testi, 2).

205. BROWN (Cynthia J.). Poets, patron, and printers. Crisis of authority in late medieval France. Ithaca a. London, Cornel U. P., 95, 293 p. (ill., bibl.).

206. BRUGNOLI (Giorgio), SANTINI (Carlo). L'Additamentum Aldinum di Silio Italico. Roma, Accademia Nazionale dei Lincei, 95, 111 p. (Bollettino dei Classici, Supplemento, 14).

207. Buchkultur im 15. und 16. Jahrhundert (Die). Hamburg, Maximilian-Gesellschaft, 95, 325 p. (ill.).

208. BURGOS RINCON (Javier). La edición española en el siglo XVIII. Un belance historiografico. *Hispania*, 95, 55, 190, p. 589-627.

209. CAMPOS (A.). Breve historia do livro. Porto Alegre, Mercado Alberto, 95, 240 p.

210. Catàleg dels incunables de la Biblioteca de la Universitat de Barcelona. Ed per J. TORRA I M. LAMARCA. Barcelona, Universitat de Barcelona, Publicacions, 95, 322 p. (pl.).

211. Catalogues régionaux des incunables des bibliothèques publiques de France. T. 12. Ed. par Y. FERNILLOT. Paris, Ministère de la Culture et de la francophonie. Direction du Livre et de la lecture et Paris, Klincksieck, 95, 360 p. (ill.).

212. CHARTIER (Roger). Lecteurs dans la longue durée: du codex à l'écran. *In:* Histoires de la lecture [Cf.

n° 231], p. 271-283. – IDEM. Lectures, lecteurs et littératures 'populaires' en Europe à la Renaissance. *In*: Escribir y leer en Occidente [Cf. n° 16], p. 145-162.

213. CHATELAIN (Jean-Marc). Livres d'emblèmes et livres du monde. *In*: Symbolique du livre (La) dans l'art occidental [Cf. n° 183], p. 87-104.

214. CISAŘOVSKA (Blanka). Libri prohibiti – nezávislá knihovna a studovna. (Libri prohibiti. The Independent Library and Reading Room). *Soudobé dějiny*, 95, 2, 1, p. 108-115.

215. COSTA (S.), NICOLINI (S.). Manuale di storia della grafica e della stampa dal XV al XX secolo. Roma, Memini, 95, 228 p. (ill.).

216. DAVIES (M.). Aldus Manutius, printer and publisher of Renaissance Venice. London, British Library, 95, 64 p.

217. DEVAUCHELLE (R.). La reliure: recherches historiques, techniques et biographiques sur la reliure française. Paris, Filigranes, 95, 318 p.

218. DIONISOTTI (Carlo). Aldo Manuzio umanista e editore. Milano, Il Polifilo, 95, 144 p. (Documenti sulle arti del libro, 18).

219. Early Printed books 1478–1840: Catalogue of the British Architectural Library early imprints collection. Ed. by British Architectural Library, Royal Institute of British Architects. Part. 2. E–L. London, Bowker-Saur, 95, XXII-500 p. (tab.).

220. Edizioni (Le) aldine della Biblioteca nazionale Braidense di Milano. A cura di G. MONTECCHI. Milano, Rovello, 95, 322 p. (ill.) (Almanacco del bibliofilo, 1994).

221. FRIEDMAN (J. B.). Northern English books: owners and makers in the late Middle Ages. Syracuse, Syracuse U. P., 95, 352 p.

222. GARCÍA ORO (José). Los reyes y los libros: la política libraria de la Corona en el siglo de oro (1475–1598). Madrid, Cisneros, 95, 142 p.

223. GASKELL (Philip). A new introduction to bibliography. Winchester, St. Paul's Bibliographies a. New Castle, Oak Knoll Press, 95, 438 p. (ill.).

224. GAUDRIAULT (R.). Filigranes et autres caractéristiques des papiers fabriqués en France aux XVIIe et XVIIIe siècles. Paris, CNRS-Editions et J. Telford, 95, 322 p., 150 pl.

225. GERHARD (H.). Schicksal der alten Hamburger Bibliotheken vom 16. Jahrhundert bis zur Gegenwart: Untersuchungen an Hand der Inkunabeln und Frühdruckbestände der Hessischen Landesbibliothek Fulda und der Bibliothek des Franziskanerklosters Altstadt. Würzburg, Freunde Mainfränkischer Kunst und Geschichte, Schweinfurt, Historischer Verein, 95, 220 p. (ill.) (Mainfränkische Studien, 57).

226. German (The) book, 1450–1750. Mélanges offerts à David L. Paisey. Ed. by J. L. FLOOD and W. A. KELLY. London, British Library and Toronto, University of Toronto Press, 95, 480 p. (ill.) (The British Library studies in the history of the book).

227. GILIBERTI (F.). Notamento delle tipografie messe in Italia nel XV secolo (L'arte della stampa in Italia). A cura di G. MASTRULLO. Milano, La Vita felice, 95, 128 p. (Liberilibri, 1).

228. Graphische Porträts in Büchern des 15. bis 19. Jahrhunderts. Hrsg. von P. BERGHAUS. Wiesbaden, O. Harrassowitz, 95, 218 p. (ill.) (Wolfenbütteler Forschungen, 63).

229. GRENDLER (P. F.). Books and schools in the Italian Renaissance. Aldershot, Variorum, 95, 288 p. (ill.) (Collected studies series, 473).

230. Handbuch der historischen Buchbestände in Österreich, unter Ltg. von H. W. LANG. Band 2. Wien. T. 2. Hrsg. von der Österreichischen Nationalbibliothek. Hildesheim, Olms-Weidmann, 95, 350 p.

231. Histoires de la lecture: un bilan des recherches: actes du colloque des 29 et 30 janvier 1993, Paris. Sous la direction de Roger CHARTIER. Paris, IMEC et Maison des sciences de l'homme, 95, 316 p. (In octavo, 2). [Cf. n° <sélection> 212.]

232. Histoires du livre: nouvelles orientations. Actes du colloque, Göttingen 1990. Ed. par H.-E. BÖDEKER. Paris, IMEC, 95, 450 p. (In Octavo).

233. I läslampens sken. Bokhistoriska uppsatser. (At the light of a reading lamp. Articles on the history of the book [in a Swedish province]). Ed. by Rolf KARLBOM. Göteborg, Karlstads högskola, Historiska institutionen, 95, 94 p.

234. Imprimeurs et libraires parisiens du XVIe siècle. Ouvrage publié d'apres les manuscrits de Philippe RENOUARD par le service des Travaux historiques de la ville de Paris avec le concours de la Bibliothèque nationale, Jean Loys. Ed. par Marie-Josèphe BREAUD-GAMBIER et Sylvie POSTEL-LECOCQ. Paris, Paris-Musées, 95, XXXIX-349 p. (pl.).

235. Incunabula: printing revolution in Europe, 1455–1500. Ed. by L. HELLINGA. Units 7–10. Printing in Italy before 1472 (parts I–IV and guide). Units 11–15. Medical incunabula (part I–V). Reading, Primary Source Media Ltd., 95, 1456 fiches-221 p., 1662 fiches.

236. KIND (H.), ROHLFING (H.). Gutenberg und der europäische Frühdruck: zur Erwerbungsgeschichte der Göttinger Inkunabelsammlung. Göttingen, Wallstein-Verl., 95, 112 p. (ill.).

237. KIND (H.). Incunabula Gottingensia. Inkunabelkatalog der Niedersächsischen Staats- und Universitätsbibliothek Göttingen. Bd. 1. Abteilung Adagia bis Biblia. Hrsg. von E. MITTLER. Wiesbaden, O. Harrassowitz, 95, X-322 p.

238. LANKHORST (Otto Stephanus), HOFTIJZER (P. G.). Drukkers, boekverkopers en lezers in Nederland tijdens de Republiek: een historiografische en biblio-

grafische handleiding. Den Haag, Sdu Uitgevers, 95, IX-227 p. (ill.). (Nederlandse cultuur in Europese context, 1).

239. LE ROY LADURIE (Emmanuel). Une histoire sérielle du livre (XVe–XXe siècle). *Histoire et société*, 95, 4, p. 1-24.

240. Lexikon der Buchkunst und Bibliophilie. Hrsg. von K. K. WALTHER. Augsburg, Weltbild-Verl., 95, 386 p. (ill.).

241. Literature in the marketplace: nineteenth-century British publishing and reading practices. Ed. by John O. JORDAN a. Robert L. PATTEN. Cambridge, Cambridge U. P., 95, XIV-338 p. (ill.). (Cambridge studies in nineteenth-century literature and culture, 5).

242. Livres en broderie. Reliures françaises du Moyen Age à nos jours. Catalogue de l'exposition, Paris, Bibliothèque de l'Arsenal, 1995–1996. Ed. par S. CORON et M. LEFEVRE. Paris, Bibliothèque nationale de France et D.M.C., 95, 192 p. (ill.).

243. MEIRELES (Maria Adelaide). Os livreiros no Porto no seculo XVIII: produção e comercio. Porto, Associacao Portuguesa de Livreiros Alfarrabistas, 95, 62 p.

244. MEYER-NOIREL (G.). Répertoire général des ex-libris français des origines à l'époque moderne, 1496–1920. Suppl. au t. III. Bi–BU. T. IV. Ca–Ce–Cha. Tomblaine, G. Meyer-Noirel, 95, 2 vol., 14 p., 246 p., XV f. de pl.

245. MONDRAIN (Brigitte). Un nouveau manuscrit d'Hérodote: le modèle de l'édition aldine. *Scriptorium*, 95, 49, 2, p. 263-272.

246. New Science out of Old Books. Studies in manuscripts and early printed books in honour of A. I. Doyle. Ed. by R. BEADLE and A. J. PIPER. Aldershot, Scholar Press, 95, 600 p., 60 pl.

247. PASTENA (C.). Libri, editori e tipografi a Palermo nei secoli XV e XVI. Saggio bibliografico. Palermo, Biblioteca centrale della Regione siciliana, 95, 184 p.

248. PETRUS BERTIUS. Nomenclator. The First Printed Catalogue of Leiden University Library (1595). A facsimile edition. Ed. by R. BREUGELMANS and J. J. WITKAM. Leiden, Leiden University Library, 95, XIV p., 108 p. of facs., XXII p.

249. PETTAS (William). A sixteenth-century Spanish bookstore: the inventory of Juan de Junta. Philadelphia, American Philosophical Society, 95, 247 p. (Transactions of the American Philosophical Society, 85, 1).

250. Praise of Aldus Manutius (In). A Quincentenary Exhibition, New York and Los Angeles 1995. Ed. by H. G. FLETCHER. New York, Pierpont Morgan Library, 95, XII-130 p.

251. Private libraries in Renaissance England. A collection and catalogue of Tudor and early Stuart book-lists. Vol. 4: PLRE 87–112. Ed. by R. J. FEHRENBACH and E. S. LEEDHAM-GREEN. Albany, State University of New York Press e Binghampton, Medieval and Renaissance Texts and Studies, 95, XXX-350 p.

252. RHODES (Dennis Everard). Silent printers: anonymous printing at Venice in the sixteenth century. London, British Library, 95, XIX-286 p. (ill.). (The British Library studies in the history of the book).

253. SCARSELLA (A.). Sul libro antico. Viterbo, BetaGamma, 95, 194 p.

254. Sociétés et cabinets de lecture entre lumières et romantisme. Actes du colloque organisé à Genève par la Société de lecture, le 20 novembre 1993. Genève, Société de lecture, 95, 155 p. (ill.).

255. Storia della lettura nel mondo occidentale. A cura di G. CAVALLO e R. CHARTIER. Roma e Bari, Laterza, 95, 516 p. (Storia e società).

256. Türkiye Yazma Eser Kütüphaneleri ve Bu Kütüphanelerde Bulunan Yazmalarla İlgili Yayınlar Bibliyografyası. (Bibliography on manuscript libraries in Turkey). Ed. by Ekmeleddin İHSANOGLU, Nimet BAYRAKTAR a. Mihin LUGAL. İstanbul, [s. n.], 95, [s. p.].

257. VERNUS (M.). Histoire du livre et de la lecture. De l'invention de l'imprimerie à nos jours. Dijon, Bibliest, Université de Bourgogne, Bibliothèque de l'Université, Section Droit-Lettres, 95, 118 p. (ill.).

258. ZAPPELLA (Giuseppina). Archeologia del libro. L'ispezione dei filoni nell'analisi bibliologica. *Nuovi annali della Scuola speciale per archivisti e bibliotecari*, 9, 95, p. 147-165.

Cf. n°s 6154-6215

§ 4. Chronologie.

259. BARDIS (Panos D.). Cronus in the Eternal City: scientific, social, and philosophical aspects of time in ancient Rome. Essen, [s.n.], 95, [s. p.]

260. GACK-SCHEIDING (Chr.). Johannes de Muris, Epistola super reformatione antiqui kalendarii. Ein Beitrag zur Kalenderreform im XIV. Jht. (Diss.). Hannover, Hahnsche Buchhandlung, 95, XXVI-164 p.

261. GRANT (George Parkin). Time as history. Edited with an introduction by William Christian. Toronto a. London, University of Toronto Press, 95, XLI-81 p.

262. Handbuch der Orientalistik. Abteilung 3. Südostasien. Band 9. EADE (John Christopher). The calendrical system of mainland south-east Asia. Leiden, New York a. Köln, E. J. Brill, 95, XVI-182 p. (ill.).

263. KAVYRCHINE (M.). Le traité de Kirik sur la chronologie. Novgorod, XIIe s. *Revue des études slaves*, 95, 47, p. 265-286.

264. MORETON (Jennifer). Before Grosseteste: Roger of Hereford and calendar reform in eleventh- and twelfth-century England. *Isis*, 95, 86, 4, p. 562-586.

265. POOLE (Robert). "Give us our eleven days!" Calendar reform in eighteenth-century England. *Past and Present*, 95, 149, p. 95-139.

266. RAUTY (Natale). Un raro esempio di datazione con l'era della Passione in un testo agiografico del secolo XI. *In*: Studi in onore di Arnaldo D'Addario [Cf. n° 452], p. 415-419.

267. ROSEN (Kl.). Jesu Geburtsdatum, der Census des Quirinius und eine jüdische Steuererklärung aus dem Jahr 127 n. C. *Jahrbuch für Antike und Christentum*, 95, 38, p. 5-15.

268. RÜPKE (Jörg). Kalender und Öffentlichkeit. Die Geschichte der Repräsentation und religiösen Qualifikation der Zeit in Rom. Berlin u. New York, de Gruyter, 95, 740 p. (Religionsgeschichtliche Versuche und Vorarbeiten, 40).

269. SULZGRUBER (W.). Zeiterfahrung und Zeitordnung vom frühen Mittelalter bis ins XVI. Jht. Hamburg, Kovač, 95, 200 p.

Cf. n°s 580, 641, 729, 1797

§ 5. Genealogie.

* 270. Bibliografia heraldico-genealogico-nobiliaria de la Biblioteca Nacional: (impresos, 1959–1994). Ed. por Luis GARCIA CUBERO; prologo de Manuel CARRION GUTIEZ. Madrid, Biblioteca Nacional, 95, 300 p.

271. Diccionario hispanoamericano de heraldica, onomastica y genealogia. Vol. 9. Ed. por Endika DE MOGROBEJO, con la colaboracion de Aitziber IRANTZU y Garikoitz DE MOGROBEJO-ZABALA. Bilbao, Editorial Mogrobejo-Zabala, 95, [s. p.].

272. SARZI AMADE (Luca). Come svolgere ricerche sui propri antenati, Milano,Mursia, 1995, 173 p.

273. ŻYCHLIŃSKI (Teodor). Złota księga szlachty polskiej. (Le livre d'or de la noblesse polonaise). Annuaire 5. Poznań, Heroldium, 95, 490 p.

Cf. n°s 1349, 3816, 8824

§ 6. Siegel- und Wappenkunde.

* 274. HENNING (Eckart), JOCHUMS (Gabriele). Bibliographie zur Sphragistik: Schrifttum Deutschlands, Österreichs und der Schweiz bis 1990. Mit einem Geleitwort von Toni DIEDERICH. Wien, Köln u. Weimar, Böhlau, 95, XX-228 p. (Bibliographie der historischen Hilfswissenschaften, 2).

275. BAKALOV (Georgi). Srednovekovniiat bulgarski vladetel: titulatura i insignii. (Titles of honor and nobility and heraldry in Byzantine Empire and Bulgaria). Sofiia, Anubis, 95, 272 p. (Istoricheski etiudi).

276. CSÁKY (Imre). A magyar királyság vármegyéinek címerei a XVIII–XIX. században. (Les armoiries des comitats du Royaume de Hongrie aux XVIIIe–XIXe siècles). Budapest, Corvina, 95, 162 p.

277. CSAPODI (Csaba). A heraldika és kodikológia kapcsolata. (Les relations de l'héraldique et de la codicologie). *Turul*, 95, 68, 3-4, p. 71-78.

278. DHENIN (Michel). L'apparition des armoiries sur les monnaies. *Histoire et sociétés*, 95, 56, p. 33-46.

279. DIEM (Peter). Die Symbole Österreichs: Zeit und Geschichte in Zeichen. Wien, Kremayr u. Scheriau, 95, 446 p.

280. FOURNIOUX (B.). Les sceaux des nobles périgourdins aux XIIIe–XIVe s. *Annales du Midi*, 95, 107, p. 333-343.

281. GARCÍA-MERCADAL Y GARCÍA-LOYGORRI (Fernando). Estudios de derecho dinástico. Los titulos y la heráldica de los Reyes de España. Barcelona, Editorial Bosch, 95, 447 p.

282. HARVEY (Paul Dean Adshead), MAC GUINNESS (Andrew). Guide to British medieval seals. London, British Library, 95, 133 p.

283. HYE (Franz-Heinz). Das österreichische Staatswappen und seine Geschichte. Innsbruck u. Wien, Studienverlag, 95, 143 p. (ill.). – IDEM. Erzherzog Ferdinand II. von Österreich-Tirol (1529–1595) im Spiegel seiner heraldischen Denkmäler. *Haller Münzblätter*, 95, 6,5-6, p. 79-120 (ill.).

284. JAKOBS (Hermann). Le sceau de la ville de Trèves. Datation et iconographie. *In*: Misc.lània d'estudis dedicats a la memòria de Professor Josep Trenchs i Òdena [Cf. n° 67], p. 673-685.

285. Liber sigillorum: de zegels in het archief van de Ridderlijke Duitsche Orde, Balije van Utrecht, 1200–1811. Beschreven door J.H. DE VEY MESTADGH, met medewerking van J. A. DE BOO. Utrecht, Ridderlijke Duitsche Orde Balije van Utrecht, 95, 2 vol., (ill).

286. MAC DONALD (R. A.). Images of hebridean lordship in the late XIIth and early XIIIth cent. The seal of Raonall Mac Sorley. *Scottish historical review*, 9574, p. 129-143.

287. MENENDEZ PIDAL DE NAVASCUÉS (Faustino), RAMOS AGUIRRE (Mikel), OCHOA DE OLZA EGUIRAN (Esperanza). Sellos medievales de Navarra. Estudios y corpus descriptivo. Pamplona, Gobierno de Navarra, Departamento de Educacion y Cultura, 95, 1014 p.

288. MONTANER FRUTOS (Alberto). El señal del rey de Aragon: historia y significado. Zaragoza, Institucion Fernando el Catolico, 95, 186 p. (Anejo no. 1 de Emblemata: revista aragonesa de emblematica. Emblemata [Zaragoza, Spain]. Anejo, 1).

289. RÁCZ (György). Az ákos nemzetség címere. (Les armoiries du clan Ákos). *Turul*, 95, 68, 1-2, p. 11-34.

290. VAHL (W.). Ein Geschäftssiegel der Stadt Wetter aus dem XIV. Jht. *Hessisches Jahrbuch für Landesgeschichte*, 95, 45, p. 255-268.

291. VANDORPE (K.). Breaking the seal of secrecy: sealing-practices in Greco-Roman and Byzantine Egypt based on Greek, Demotic and Latin papyrological evidence. Leiden, Papyrologisch Instituut, 95, XII-73 p. (Uitgaven vanwege de stichting "Het Leids Papyrologisch Instituut", 18).

Cf. n° 3086

§ 7. Münz-, Maß- und Gewichtskunde.

* 292. Bibliography of weighing instruments. Ed. by Eric SOSLAU and Judy SOSLAU. Chicago, International Society of Antique Scale Collectors, 95, VIII-53 p.

* 293. HEIT (Alfred), PETRY (Klaus). Bibliographie zur historischen Metrologie. Teil 2. Trier, Auenthal, 95, XX-134 p. (Wissenschaftliche Arbeitshilfen zur Geschichte des Mittelalters und der Neuzeit, 7, 2).

* 294. SMITH (Thurman L.). Coins and medals of the Reformation: a select bibliography. St. Louis, Center for Reformation Research, 95, 122 p. (Sixteenth century bibliography, 32).

* 295. TALIBI (Faramarz), QA'INI (Farzanah). Kitabshinasi-i sikkah. (Bibliography of numismatics in Iran). Tihran, Sazman-i miras-i farhang-i kishvar, 95, 247 p. (Vizarat-i farhang va irshad-i islami, 27).

296. ARBEZ (Fernand), CHARLET (Christian). La réforme monétaire de 1726 et la stabilisation du cours des monnaies jusqu'à la Révolution. *Cahiers numismatiques*, 95, 32, 125, p. 39-46.

297. ARSLAN (Ermanno A.). LA moneta a Pavia. La monetazione dei Goti e dei Longobardi. *Bollettino della Società pavese di storia patria*, 95, 47, p. 53-70.

298. CUNIETTI-FERRANDO (Arnaldo J.). Historia de la Real Casa de Moneda de Potosí durante la dominacion hispanica, 1573–1825. Pt. 1. 1573–1652. Buenos Aires, [s.n.], 95, 267 p. (ill.).

299. DEKESEL (C. E.). Bibliotheca Numismatica Siliciana. Gandavum Flandrorum, Bibliotheca Numismatica Siliciana, 95, IX-1189p.

300. DEMBSKI (Günther). Vorrömische und keltische Funde aus dem nordöstlichen Niederösterreich. *Mittelungen der Österr. Numismatischen Ges.*, 95, 35, p. 65-72 (ill.).

301. FAVA (Anna Serena). Genesi e vicende della Storia Metallica della Real Casa di Savoia. *Bollettino di Numismatica*, 95, 13, 24, p. 45-51.

302. FORZONI (Angiolo). La moneta nella storia. Vol. 2. Dalla rivoluzione cesariana alla riforma di Caracalla. Vol. 3. Dai Severi a Costantino il Grande. Roma, Istituto poligrafico e Zecca dello Stato, 95, 2 vol., XVIII-411 p., XIX-448 p.

303. GEMMILL (Elizabeth), MAYHEW (Nicholas). Changing values in medieval Scotland: a study of prices, money, and weights and measures. Cambridge, Cambridge U. P., 95, XXI-419 p. (ill).

304. HENRICHS (Laurent). L'étrange circulation d'un manuscrit. L'œuvre inédite de Pierre-Eugène de Sürbeck (1678–1741). *Revue numismatique*, 95, 150, p. 240-250.

305. HOCQUET (Jean-Claude). La metrologie historique. Paris, PUF, 95, 128 p. (Que sais-je? 2972).

306. HUSZAR (Lajos). Az erdelyi fejedelemseg penzverese. (A catalogue of Hungarian and Romanian numismatics). Budapest, Akademiai Kiado, 95, 231 p. (ill.).

307. JAIN (Rekha). Ancient Indian coinage: a systematic study of money economy from Janapada period to early medieval period (600 BC to AD 1200). New Delhi, D.K. Printworld, 95, XII-247 p. (Reconstructing Indian history & culture, 8).

308. JENSEN (Jorgen Steen). Tusindtallets Danske Mönter fra Den kongelige Mont-og-Medaillesamling. (Danish coins from the 11th century in the Royal Collection of Coins and Medals, National Museet). København, [s. n.], 95, 172 p.

309. KOS (Peter), SEMROV (Andrej). Rimski novci in kontramarke iz 1. stoletja = Roman imperial coins and countermarks of the 1st century: Augustus-Traianus. Ljubljana, Narodni muzej, 95, 206 p. (Zbirka Numizmaticnega kabineta Narodnega muzeja = The collection of the Numismatic Cabinet of the National Museum, 2. Situla: razprave Narodnega muzeja v Ljubljani, 33).

310. KRUMME (Michael). Römische Sagen in der antiken Münzprägung. Marburg, Hitzeroth, 95, 477 p.

311. LENTINI (Maria Costanza), GARRAFFO (Salvatore). Il tesoretto di Naxos (1985): dall'isolato urbano C4, casa 1–2. Premessa di Paola PELAGATTI. Roma, Istituto italiano di numismatica, 95, XII-49 p. (ill.).

312. Memoria: VIII Congreso Nacional de Numismatica, Aviles, 1–4 Abril 1992. Ed. por Cesar RAMIREZ FERNANDEZ. Madrid, Fabrica Nacional de la Moneda y Timbre, 95, 655 p.

313. Moneda hispanica (La): ciudad y territorio: Actas del I Encuentro Peninsular de Numismatica Antigua. Ed. por Ma. Paz GARCIA-BELLIDO y Rui Manuel SOBRAL CENTENO. Madrid, C.S.I.C. y Sociedade Portuguesa de Numismatica, 95, XIII-428 p. (ill., maps). (Anejos de Archivo Espanol de Arqueologia, 14).

314. Numismatische Literatur 1500–1864: die Entwicklung der Methoden einer Wissenschaft. Hrsg. v. Peter BERGHAUS. Wiesbaden, Harrassowitz, 95, 247 p. (Wolfenbütteler Forschungen, 64).

315. OULMONT (Philippe). «Le mal de changer»: les Français et la révolution métrique. *Histoire et société*, 95, 59, p. 31-55.

316. PENNESTRI (S.). Storia, memoria, collezionismo e il concetto di Storia metallica tra XVI e XIX secolo. *Bollettino di numismatica*, 95, p. 15-21.

317. RETAMERO (Felix). Moneda i monedes arabs a l'Illa d'Eivissa. Eivissa, Museu Arqueologic d'Eivissa i Formentera, 95, 66 p. (ill.). (Trabajos del Museo Arqueologico de Ibiza).

318. SCHMIDT-DICK (Franziska). Die römischen Münzen des Medagliere im Castelvecchio zu Verona. Wien, Vlg der Österrr. Akad. der Wiss., 95, 2 vol., 704 p., 102 p. (ill.). (Thesaurus nummorum Romanorum et Byzantinorum, 9. Veröffentlichungen der Numismatischen Kommission der Österr. Akad. der Wiss., phil.-hist. Kl., 30. Denkschriften der Österr. Akad. der Wiss., phil.-hist. Kl., 239).

319. SHAMMA (Samir). Ahdath 'asr al-Ma'mun kama tarwiha al-nuqud. (The time of al-Ma'mun in the light of numismatic evidence). Irbid, Jami`at Yarmuk, 95, 907 p. (ill.).

320. SKAARE (Kolbjörn). Norges mynthistorie. Mynter og utmyntning i 1000 år. Pengesedler i 300 år. Numismatikkk i Norge. Vol. 1. Vol. 2. Katalog- og registerbind. Oslo, Universitetsforlaget, 95, 2 vol., 349 p., 276 p.

321. SOTNIKOVA (M. P.). Drevnejšie russkie monety X–XI vekov: Katalog- issledovanie. (The Russian ancient coins of the Xth–XIth centuries: Catalogue-research). Moskva: Banki i birži, 95, 318 p.

322. Svet merenja = The world of measurements. Odgovorni urednik Dragoslav SREJOVIC; autori izlozbe Srdan SPIRIDONOVIC, Jelenka PETKOVIC; prevod na engleski Bratislav PANTELIC, Slobodan RIBNIKAR, Srdan SPIRIDONOVIC. Beograd, Srpska akademija nauka i umetnosti, Muzej nauke i tehnike, 95, 368 p. (ill.). (Galerija Srpske akademije nauka i umetnosti, 80).

323. TRAVAINI (Lucia). La monetazione dell'Italia normanna. Roma, Istituto storico italiano per il Medio Evo, 95, VIII-487 p. (ill.). (Nuovi studi storici, 28).

324. Trouvailles monétaires d'églises: actes du premier colloque international du Groupe suisse pour l'étude des trouvailles monétaires (Lucerne, 19. November 1993) = Fundmünzen aus Kirchengrabungen: Sitzungsbericht des ersten internationalen Kolloquiums der Schweizerischen Arbeitsgemeinschaft für Fundmünzen (Luzern, 19. November 1993). Ed. par Olivier F. DUBUIS et Suzanne FREY-KUPPER. Lausanne, Editions du zebre, 95, 182 p. (ill.). (Etudes de numismatique et d'histoire monétaire, 1).

325. Tusindtallets danske mönter fra Den Kongelige Mönt- og Medaille-samling. Ed. by Jörgen STEEN JENSEN. København, Nationalmuseet i samarbejde med Forlaget Munksgaard, 95, 172 p. [Danish coins from the 11th century in the Royal Collection of Coins and Medals].

326. Vocabulary of metrology. Part 3. Guide to the expression of uncertainty in measurement. London, BSI, 95, VIII-101 p. (British Standard, PD 6461, part 3).

327. Wissenschaftsgeschichte der Numismatik. Beiträge zum 17. deutschen Numismatikertag 3.–5. März 1995 in Hannover. Hrsg.v. Rainer ALBERT u. Reiner CUNZ. Speyer, 95, 247 p. (Schriftenreihe der Numismatischen Gesellschaft Speyer, 36).

328. WITHERS (Paul), ROMLUND WITHERS (Bente). Lions, ships and angels: identifying coin-weights found in Britain. Llanfyllin, Galata, 95, 80 p. (ill.).

Cf. n[os] *1958, 2186, 2479, 2482, 2606, 3704*

§ 8. Sprachliche Hilfsmittel.

* 329. GAMKRELIDZE (T. V.), IVANOV (Vjaceslav V.). Indo-European and the Indo-Europeans: a reconstruction and historical analysis of a Proto-language and a Proto-culture. Part 2. Bibliography, indexes. With a preface by Roman JAKOBSON; English version by Johanna NICHOLS; edited by Werner WINTER. (Trends in linguistics. Studies and monographs, 80) Berlin a. New York, Mouton de Gruyter, 95, [s. p.].

---

330. BANNIARD (M.). La cité de la parole. S. Augustin entre la théorie et la pratique de la communication latinophone. *Journal des savants*, 95, p. 283-306.

331. BARRERA-GONZALEZ (Andres). Language, collective identities and nationalism in Catalonia, and Spain in general. Florence, European University Institute, 95, 92 p. (EUI working paper. EUF, 95/6).

332. BECCARIA (Gian Luigi). I nomi del mondo: santi, demoni, folletti e le parole perdute. Torino, Giulio Einaudi Editore, 95, XXXII-308 p. (Saggi, 799).

333. BELARDI (Walter). "Periferia" e "centro": un'antitesi nella "questione della lingua" di alcune storicità linguistiche. Roma, Dipartimento di studi glottologici, Universita "La sapienza", 95, 428 p. (Biblioteca di ricerche linguistiche e filologiche, 37).

334. BILLY (Pierre-Henri). Atlas linguae Gallicae. Hildesheim, Olms, 95, X-254 p. (Alpha-Omega. Reihe A, Lexika, Indizes, Konkordanzen zur klassischen Philologie, 161).

335. BOLTANSKI (Jean-Elie). La Linguistique diachronique. Paris, PUF, 95, 127 p. (ill.). (Que sais-je? 2965).

336. CZOPEK-KOPCIUCH (Barbara). Adaptacje niemieckich nazw miejscowych w języku polskim. (Adaptations en polonais des noms de lieux allemands). Kraków, 95, 247 p. (Prace Inst. Języka Polskiego Pol. Akad. Nauk, 98). [Deutsche Zsfassung].

337. DANGEL (Jacqueline). Histoire de la langue latine. Paris, PUF, 95, 126 p. (Que sais-je?).

8. SPRACHLICHE HILFSMITTEL

338. DELMAIRE (R.). «Invasor, invasio». Réflexions sur quelques textes de l'antiquité tardive. *In*: Sources de la gestion publique (Aux). Tome 2 [Cf. n° 4574], p. 77-88.

339. FOX (Anthony). Linguistic reconstruction: an introduction to theory and method. Oxford a. New York, Oxford U. P., 95, XVII, 372 p. (Oxford textbooks in linguistics).

340. GASPARI (Gianmarco). Lingua e rivoluzione. *Rivista storica italiana*, 95, 107, 2, p. 495-526.

341. GIMENO MENENDEZ (Francisco). Sociolinguistica histórica: siglos X–XII. Madrid, Visor Libros, Universidad de Alicante, 95, 251 p. (Biblioteca filologica hispana, 25).

342. HADROVICS (László). Magyar frazeológia. Történeti áttekintés. (Phraséologie hongroise. Aspect historique). Budapest, Akad. Kiadó, 95, 409 p.

343. Histoire de la langue française 1914–1945. Ed. par l'Institut National de la langue française; sous la direction de Gerald ANTOINE et Robert MARTIN. Paris, CNRS-Editions, 95, 1049 p. (ill.).

344. Historical linguistics, 1993: selected papers from the 11th International Conference on Historical Linguistics, Los Angeles, 16–20 August 1993. Ed. by Henning ANDERSEN. Amsterdam a. Philadelphia, John Benjamins Pub. Co, 95, IX-460 p. (ill.). (Amsterdam studies in the theory and history of linguistic science. Series IV: Current issues in linguistic theory, 124).

345. Historical roots of linguistic theories. Ed. by Lia FORMIGARI a. Daniele GAMBARARA. Amsterdam a. Philadelphia, J. Benjamins, 95, VIII-309 p. (Amsterdam studies in the theory and history of linguistic science. Series 3. Studies in the history of the language sciences, 74).

346. HOLZER (Georg). Die Einheitlichkeit des Slavischen um 600 n. Chr. und ihr Zerfall. *Wien. Slavistisches Jb.*, 95, 41, p. 55-89.

347. JONES (Charles). A language suppressed: the pronunciation of the Scots language in the 18th century. Edinburgh, John Donald, 95, IX-278 p.

348. KISS (Lajos). Földrajzi neveink nyelvi fejlődése. (Evolution linguistique des noms géographiques hongrois). Budapest, Akad. Kiadó, 95, 62 p. (Nyelvtudományi értekezések, 139).

349. KRASUSKI (Jerzy). Językowe podłoże podziału Europy [XI–XX w.]. (Bases linguistiques du partage de l'Europe.). *Przegląd Zachodni*, 95, 51, 1, p. 53-68.

350. Languages and jargons: contributions to a social history of language. Ed. by Peter BURKE a. Roy PORTER. Cambridge [England] a. Cambridge [USA], Polity Press, 95, VII-216 p. (ill.).

351. LEHMANN (Wilfred P.). Person marking in Indo-european. *Historische Sprachforschung*, 95, 107, p. 1-19.

352. LINDE (Samuel Bogumił). Słownik języka polskiego. (Dictionnaire de la langue polonaise). T. 4. P. T. 5. R–T. T. 6. p. 1. U–W. T. 6. p. 2. X–Ż. Warszawa, Gutenberg-Print, 95, 4 vol., 735 p., 758 p., 684 p., 685 p.

353. Magyar (A) nyelv történeti nyelvtana. (Grammaire historique de la langue hongroise). Red.-en-chef Loránd BENKŐ. 2/2. A kései magyar kor. Mondattan, szöveggrammatika. (La période hongroise tardive. Syntaxe, grammaire des textes). Réd. par Endre RACZ. Budapest, Akad. Kiadó, 95, 850 p.

354. MAIDEN (Martin). A linguistic history of Italian. London, Longman, 95, 352 p. (Longman linguistics library).

355. Medieval dialectology. Ed. by Jacek FISIAK. Berlin a. New York, Mouton de Gruyter, 95, VIII-331 p. (Trends in linguistics. Studies and monographs, 79).

356. MEILLET (Antoine). Pour un manuel de linguistique générale. Edizione di manoscritti inediti conservati al Collège de France raccolti e pubblicati a cura di Fiorenza GRANUCCI. Roma, Accademia Nazionale dei Lincei, 95, 243 p. (ill.). (Atti della Accademia nazionale dei Lincei. Memorie, Classe di scienze morali, storiche e filologiche).

357. MIDGETTE (Sally). The Navajo progressive in discourse: a study in temporal semantics. New York, P. Lang, 95, XIV-252 p. (History and language, 6).

358. MOGUS (Milan). A history of the Croatian language: toward a common standard. Zagreb, Nakladni Zavod Globus, 95, 255 p. (Series "Special editions").

359. MUGGLESTONE (Lynda). Talking proper: the rise of accent as social symbol. Oxford a. New York, Clarendon Press, 95, 353 p.

360. Problemes i metodes de la historia de la llengua. A cura de Sadurni MARTI i Francesc FELIU. Barcelona, Quaderns Crema, 95, 245 p. (Assaig Minor, 10).

361. ROCHETTE (Bruno). Grecs et latins face aux langues etrangeres. Contribution a l'étude de la diversité linguistique dans l'antiquité classique. *Revue Belge de Philologie et d'Histoire*, 95, 73, 1, p. 5-17.

362. SCHUSTER (Elisabeth). Niederösterreichische Ortsnamen magyarischer Herkunft. *Unsere Heimat*, 95, 66, 4, p. 291-300.

363. Siglo (Del) de Oro al Siglo de las Luces: lenguaje y sociedad en los Andes del siglo XVIII Ed. por Cesar ITIER. Cuzco, Centro de Estudios Regionales Andinos "Bartolome de Las Casas", 95, 119 p. (Estudios y debates regionales andinos, 89).

364. Sintassi dell'italiano letterario (La). A cura di Maurizio DARDANO e Pietro TRIFONE. Roma, Bulzoni, 95, 450 p. (Biblioteca di cultura, 500).

365. Sprache der Diktaturen und Diktatoren (Die). Hrsg. v. Klaus STEINKE. Heidelberg, Winter, 95, 370 p.

366. STRASSNER (Erich). Deutsche Sprachkultur: von der Barbarensprache zur Weltsprache. Tübingen, Niemeyer, 95, VIII-468 p.

367. Towards a history of the Basque language. Ed. by Jose Ignacio HUALDE, Joseba A. LAKARRA a. R.L. TRASK. Amsterdam, J. Benjamins, 95, 365 p. (Amsterdam studies in the theory and history of linguistic science. Series IV. Current issues in linguistic theory,. 131).

Cf. n°s 676, 920, 1560, 2320

§ 9. Historische Geographie und Geschichte der Geographie.

368. AHMAD (Sayyid Maqbul). A history of Arab-Islamic geography: (9th–16th century A.D.). Foreword by Muhammad ADNAN AL-BAKHIT. Amman, Al-al Bayt, 95, 454 p.

369. Atti dell'Incontro di studio Colonie africane e cultura italiana fra Ottocento e Novecento: le esplorazioni e la geografia: Istituto italo-africano, Roma, 20 maggio 1994. A cura di Claudio CERRETI. Roma, CISU, 95, IV-287 p.

370. BERNECKER (Walther L.). Großer historischer Weltatlas. T. 4. Neueste Zeit. München, Bayerischer Schulbuch-Verl., 95, VIII-28-12 p.

371. BORSDORF (Axel). 150 Jahre Russische Geographische Gesellschaft in St. Petersburg. *Mitteilungen der Österr. Geographischen Ges.*, 95, 137, p. 429-430.

372. BRAUER (Ralph W). Boundaries and frontiers in medieval Muslim geography. Philadelphia, American Philosophical Society, 95, 73 p. (Transactions of the American Philosophical Society, 85, 6).

373. BRUNET (Pierre), BERTRAND (Georges), RENARD (Jean). Géographie et histoire rurale. *In*: Histoire rurale en France (L') [Cf. n° 601], p. 65-77.

374. BRUNET (Pierre). La contribution des géographes à l'histoire rurale française. *In*: Histoire rurale en France (L') [Cf. n° 601], p. 25-30.

375. CHANNON (John), HUDSON (Robert). The Penguin historical atlas of Russia. London, Penguin, 95, 144 p.

376. CLANCY (Robert). The mapping of Terra Australis. Macquarie Park, Universal Press Pty Ltd, 95, VII-192 p.

377. CLAVAL (Paul). Histoire de la géographie. Paris, PUF, 95, 127 p. (Que sais-je? 65).

378. Counting and recounting: measuring inner and outer space in the Renaissance: proceedings of the conference held at the Faculty of Magistero, on October 14, 1991. Ed. by Paola BOTTALLA a. Michela CALDERARO. Trieste, Edizioni la Mongolfiera, 95, 231 p.

379. COUZINET (Marie-Domonique). Fonction de la géographie dans la connaissance historique: le modèle cosmographique de l'histoire chez F. Bauduin et J. Bodin. *Corpus*, 95, 28, p. 113-145.

380. CUNILL GRAU (Pedro). Las transformaciones del espacio geohistorico latinoamericano, 1930–1990. Mexico, Colegio de Mexico, Fideicomiso Historia de las Americas, Fondo de Cultura Economica, 95, 198 p. (Serie Ensayos. Fideicomiso Historia de las Americas; Seccion de obras de historia).

381. DESMARAIS (Gaetan). La morphogenèse de Paris: des origines à la Révolution. Préfaces de Jean PETITOT et Gilles RITCHOT. Paris, L'Harmattan et Sainte-Foy, CELAT, 95, 285 p. (Collection Géographies en liberté).

382. DÖRFLINGER (Johannes), [et al.]. Atlantes austriaci. Kommentierter Katalog der österreichischen Atlanten von 1561 bis 1994. Band 1. Österreichische Atlanten 1561–1918. Band 2. Österreichische Atlanten 1919–1994. Wien, Köln u. Weimar, Böhlau, 95, 2 vol., XXXII-852 p., XLV-405 p.

383. GAUTIER DALCHE (P.). Carte marine et portulan au XIIe s. Le Liber de existencia riveriarum et forma maris nostri Mediterranei (Pise, circa 1200). Roma, Ecole française de Rome, 95, XI-308 p. (Collection de l'Ecole française de Rome, 203).

384. Katalog dawnych map Rzeczypospolitej Polskiej w kolekcji Emeryka Hutten Czapskiego i w innych zbiorach. (Catalogue des anciennes cartes de la République de Pologne dans la collection d'Emeryk Hutten Czapski et dans d'autres collections). T. 2. Mapy XVII wieku. (Cartes du XVIIe s.). [cf. T. 1. Bibl. 78–79, n° 200]. Ed. Teresa PAĆKO, Danuta STACHNAL-TALANDA, Ewa GOŁĄB-JANKOWSKA. Wrocław, Zakł. Narod. im. Ossolińskich, 95, 250 p. (Pol. Akad. Nauk, Inst. Geografii i Przestrzennego Zagospodarowania).

385. KLEINPENNING (J. M. G.). Peopling the purple land: a historical geography of rural Uruguay, 1500–1915. Amsterdam, CEDLA, 95, XV-355 p. (Latin America studies, 73).

386. KONIAS (Andrzej). Kartograficzny obraz Śląska na podstawie map Księstw śląskich Jana Wolfganga Wielanda i Mateusza Schubartha z połowy XVIII w. (z oceną kartometryczna). (Illustration carthographique de la Silésie d'après les cartes des principautées de Silésie de Jan Wolfgang Wieland et Mateusz Schubarth de la moitié du XVIIIe s. avec évaluation carthométrique). Katowice, [s. n.], 95, 155 p. (English summary, Deutsche Zsfassung, cartes). (Prace Nauk. Uniw. Śląskiego w Katowicach, 1462).

387. Lexicon topographicum urbis Romae. Vol. 2. D–G. A cura di Eva Margareta STEINBY. Roma, Quasar, 95, 500 p. (ill.).

388. MACKOWSKI (R. M.). Cities of Jesus. A study of the «three degrees of importance» in the Holy Land. Roma, Pontifical Oriental Institute, 95, 114 p.

389. MAEDER (Ernesto J. A.), GUTIERREZ (Ramon). Atlas historico del nordeste argentino. Resistencia, Instituto de Investigaciones Geohistoricas, Conicet-Fundanord [y] Universidad Nacional del Nordeste, 95, 197 p.

390. MAGOCSI (Paul Robert.). Historical atlas of East Central Europe. Seattle a. London, University of Washington Press, 95, XIII-218 p. (A History of East Central Europe, 1).

391. Magyarország története térképeken elbeszélve. (Histoire de Hongrie racontée par des tableaux). Réd. par Ferenc GLATZ. 1. Virágkor és a pusztulás: a kezdetektő 1606-ig. (Epanouissement et catastrophe: des origines jusqu'à 1606). Textes par Pál ENGEL et Ferenc SZAKALY. Budapest, História-MTA Történettud. Int., 95, 67 p. (História könyvtár, Atlaszok Magyarország történetéhez, 1).

392. Neo-Assyrian geography. Ed. by Mario LIVERANI. Roma, Università di Roma, Dipartimento di scienze storiche, archeologiche e antropologiche dell'Antichita, 95, 282 p. (Quaderni di geografia storica, 5).

393. PELLETIER (Monique), OZANNE (Henriette). Portraits de la France: les cartes, témoins de l'histoire. Paris, Hachette et Bibliothèque nationale de France, 95, 239 p.

394. REISZ (T. Csaba). Lipszky János levelei gróf Festetics Györgyhöz. Adalékok a Mappa Generalis Regni Hungariae c. térkép születéséhez. (Les lettres de János Lipszky [1766–1828] au comte György Festetics [1755–1818]. Donnés concernant la naissance de la carte Mappa Generalis Regni Hungariae). Fons, 95, 2, 3, p. 317-348.

395. RIBEIRO (Orlando), LAUTENSACH (Hermann). Geografia de Portugal. Ed. Suzanne DAVEAU. Lisboa, Joao Sá da Costa, 95, XXIII-334 p. (ill., bibl.).

396. SEMOTANOVA (Eva). Historicka geografie ceskych zemi. (Historical geography of Czech republic). Praha, Historicky ustav, 95, 293 p. (Prace Historickeho ustavu AV CR. Rada A, Monografia, 16 = Opera Instituti Historici Pragae).

397. SMITH (C. D.). Map ownership in XVIth-cent. Cambridge. The evidence of probate inventories. Imago mundi, 95, 47, p. 67-93.

398. TYSZKA (Przemysław). O metodzie badań nad średniowiecznymi granicami lokalnymi. (Sur la méthode de recherche relative aux frontières locales médiévales). Kwartalnik Historii Materialnej Polskiej Akademii Nauk, 95, 43, 4, p. 423-431. [Deutsche Zsfassung].

399. WARDENGA (Ute). Geographie als Chorologie: zur Genese und Struktur von Alfred Hettners Konstrukt der Geographie. Stuttgart, Franz Steiner Verlag, 95, 255 p. (Erdkundliches Wissen, 100).

400. WITHERS (Charles W. J.). Geography, natural history and the eighteenth-century enlightenment. History Workshop, 95, 39, p. 137-164.

401. WOOD (Eric Stuart). Historical Britain: a comprehensive account of the development of rural and urban life and landscape from prehistory to the present day. London, Harvill Press, 95, XXII-624 p.

402. ZUBAREV (V. G.). Kharakter iskaženij i obščaja kartina severopričernomorskogo regiona v "Geografičeskom rukovodstve" Klavdija Ptolemeja. (Distorsions and the whole picture of the Northern Pontic area in "Guide to geography" by Ptolemy). Ros. arkheol., 95, 3, p. 47-59.

Cf. n°s 1340, 2088, 2602, 2615, 8881, 8995

§ 10. Ikonographie.

403. ALBERTAN-COPPOLA (Sylviane). Les images dans l'Histoire générale des voyages de l'abbé Prévost. Etudes de lettres, 95, 1-2, p. 81-98.

404. ALBERTSON (F. C.). An Isiac model for the Raising of Lazarus in early Christian art. Jahrbuch für Antike und Christentum, 95, 38, p. 123-132.

405. BLANC (Odile). Images du monde et portraits d'habits: les recueils de costumes à la Renaissance. Bulletin du bibliophile, 95, 2, p. 221-261.

406. BORGES (María Elizia). Arte funeraria: representação da crianca despida. História, 95, 14, p. 173-187.

407. CAHN (Walter). [Henri] Focillon's Jongleur. Art History, 95, 18, 3, p. 345-362.

408. CARAION (Marta). Un objet photogénique entre science et rêverie: la ruine. Etudes de lettres, 95, 1-2, p. 135-148.

409. Corse (La) [d'Emeric Feher, 1935, 1939, 1965, numéro spécial]. Cahier d'Anthropologie (Corte), 95, 2, p. 1-74.

410. FINNEY (P. C.). Abraham and Isaac iconography on late-antique amulets and seals: the Western evidence. Jahrbuch f Antike und Christentum, 95, 38, p. 140-166.

411. KALININA (I. V.), USTINOVA (E. A.). Ispol'zovanie čeljustej životnykh dlja ornamentacii drevnej keramiki. (The use of the animals jaws in the ornamentation of the ancient ceramics). Ros. arkheol., 95, 2, p. 69-83.

412. LAHARIE (Muriel). Les infirmes au Moyen Age (XIe–XVe siècles). Approche iconographique. In: Actes du 118e Congrès national des Sociétés savantes [Cf. n° 4540], p. 313-333.

413. LIMA (Robert). La «gueule de l'enfer»: iconographie de la damnation dans le théâtre à l'époque médiévale. In: Enfer et paradis [Cf. n° 1370], p. 205-218.

414. MILLIOT (Vincent). Le peuple travesti. Les représentations de petits métiers parisiens du XVIe au

XVIIIe siècles. Paris, Publications de la Sorbonne, 95, 480 p.

415. SANSTERRE (Jean-Marie). Vénération et utilisation apotropaique de l'image à Reichenau vers la fin du Xe siècle: un temoignage des gesta de l'abbe Witigowo. *Revue Belge de Philologie et d'Histoire*, 95, 73, 2, p. 281-287.

416. SIGNORI (Gabriela). Maria zwischen Kathedrale, Kloster und Welt. Hagiographische und historiographische Annäherungen an eine hochmittelalterliche Wunderpredigt. Sigmaringen, Thorbecke, 95, 336 p. (ill.).

417. VAYER (Lajos). I problemi iconologici del capolavoro aretino di Piero della Francesca. Il ciclo di affreschi della Leggenda della Santa Croce della Chiesa di San Francesco. *Acta hist. art. Acad. Sci. Hungaricae*, 94-95, 37, 1-4, p. 1-76.

Cf. n°s 625, 2453, 2488, 2896, 2972, 4020, 4189, 6837, 6838

B

HANDBÜCHER, ALLGEMEINE ÜBERSICHTSWERKE

§ 1. Archive, Bibliotheken und Museen (*a*. Archive; *b*. Bibliotheken; *c*. Museen). 418-506. – § 2. Geschichte der Geschichtswissenschaft (*a*. Allgemeines; *b*. Spezialarbeiten). 507-847. – § 3. Methodenlehre, Geschichtsphilosophie und Geschichtsunterricht. 848-983. – § 4. Völker und Volkskunde. 984-1059. – § 5. Allgemeine Geschichte. 1060-1173. – § 6. Staats- und Gesellschaftslehre. 1174-1231. – § 7. Rechts- und Verfassungsgeschichte. 1232-1249. – § 8. Wirtschafts- und Sozialgeschichte. 1250-1320. – § 9. Kultur-, Wissenschafts- und Unterrichtsgeschichte. 1321-1365. – § 10. Kunst- und Kunstgewerbegeschichte. 1366-1375. – § 11. Religions- und Kirchengeschichte (*a*. Allgemeines; *b*. Spezialarbeiten). 1376-1505. – § 12. Geschichte der Philosophie. 1506-1523. – § 13. Literaturgeschichte. 1524-1568.

§ 1. Archive, Bibliotheken und Museen.

a. Archive.

** 418. Archivi (Gli) degli istituti e delle aziende di credito e le fonti d'archivio per la storia delle banche: tutela, gestione, valorizzazione. Roma, Ministero per i Beni Culturali e Ambientali, Ufficio Centrale per i beni archivistici, 95, 701 p. (Pubblicazioni degli archivi di Stato. Saggi, 35).

419. Actas de las V Jornadas de Archivos Aragoneses: situación y perspectiva de los archivos de la administración local, los archivos policiales. Zaragoza, Gobierno de Aragón, Departamento de Educación y Cultura, 95, 427 p. (Colección Actas, 27). [Cf. n[os] <selección> 420, 425, 426, 431, 433, 441, 444, 447.]

420. ALLEGRIA DE RIOJA (Jesús). Los archivos militares en Zaragoza. *In*: Actas de las V Jornadas de Archivos Aragoneses [Cf. n° 419], p. 339-365.

421. Altı Numaralı Muhimme Defteri: 972/1564–1565 [Le Registre de Muhimme (affaires importantes): 972/1564–1565]. Ed. par Haci Osman YILDIRIM. Ankara, Osmanlı Arşivi Daire Başkanlığı, 95, [s. p.].

422. Archives contemporaines et histoire: journées d'étude de la Direction des archives de France, Vincennes, 28–29 novembre 1994. Paris, Archives nationales, 95, 126 p.

423. Archivio di Stato di Bologna (L'). A cura di Isabella ZANNI ROSIELLO. Firenze, Nardini, 95, 236 p. (ill.). (Tesori degli archivi).

424. Archivio di Stato di Firenze (L'). A cura di Rosalia Manno TOLU e Anna BELLINAZZI. Fiesole, Nardini, 95, 276 p. (I tesori degli archivi).

425. BARBADILLO ALONSO (Javier). Archivos municipales: cuestiones relacionadas con la administración de documentos. *In*: Actas de las V Jornadas de Archivos Aragoneses [Cf. n° 419], p. 147-166.

426. BORREGUERO (Epifanio). Los archivos militares. *In*: Actas de las V Jornadas de Archivos Aragoneses [Cf. n° 419], p. 329-338.

427. ÇETİN (Atilla). "Divan-ı Hümayun Beğlikçi Kaleminin Görevleri ve İşleyişi Hakkında Önemli Bir Belge" (Un Document important relatif au devoir et au fonctionnement du bureau de Beylikçi dans la Chancellerie de L'Empire Ottoman). *Vakıflar Dergisi*, 95, 26, p. 231-257.

428. CHARMASSON (Thérèse), DEMUELENAERE-DOUYERE (Christiane), GAZIELLO (Catherine), OGILVIE (Denise). Les archives personnelles des scientifiques. Classement et conservation. Paris, Archives nationales, 95, 98 p.

429. CHAULEUR (Andrée). Les archives notariales. Le Minutier central des notaires de Paris. *Histoire de la justice*, 95-96, 8-9, p. 69-111.

430. EMECEN (Feridun). "Mufassaldan İcmale" (Des Registres détaillés aux Résumés). *Osmanlı Araştırmaları*, 95, 15, p. 27-44.

431. ESTEBAN CASALDO (M. Eloísa). Los archivos policiales de Aragón. *In*: Actas de las V Jornadas de Archivos Aragoneses [Cf. n° 419], p. 409-420.

432. Fondo documental Secretaria Tecnica, 10 y 20 presidencia del teniente general Juan Domingo Perón (1946–1955). Ed. por l'Archivo General de la Nación. Buenos Aires, AGN, 95, 241 p. (Colección Referencia. Serie Descriptores, 3).

433. GARCÍA MERCADAL (F.). Los archivos judiciales militares. *In*: Actas de las V Jornadas de Archivos Aragoneses [Cf. n° 419], p. 367-375.

434. GRAF (Christoph). Die Archivierung audiovisueller Quellen. *Revue suisse d'histoire*, 95, 45, 4, p. 514-520.

435. HORWITZ (Henry). Chancery equity records and proceedings, 1600–1800: a guide to documents in the Public Record Office. London, HMSO, 95, XI-110 p. (Public Record Office handbooks, 27).

436. KERKKONEN (Martti). Finlands riksarkiv 1809–1917: det finska arkivvasendets historia fran Fredrikshamnsfreden till sjalvstandigheten. (History of Finnish archives). Stockholm, Svenska riksarkivet, 95, 216 p. (Skrifter utgivna av Svenska riksarkivet, 12).

437. KRAJEWSKA (Hanna). Polen-Österreich vom 16. bis zum 20. Jahrhundert. Ein Dokumentenführer. Warszawa, Educatio, 95, 217 p. (phot., dessins, cartes). (Naczelna Dyr. Archiwów Państw. w Warszawie, Bundesministerium für Wissenschaft und Forschung in Wien).

438. LUNDIN (A. G.). Arkhivy drevnego Jemena. (The archives of ancient Yemen). *Vestn. drev. Ist.*, 95, 3, p. 3-13.

439. MERLOTTI (Andrea). Negli archivi del re. La lettura negata delle opere di Giannone nel Piemonte sabaudo (1748–1848). *Rivista storica italiana*, 95, 107, 2, p. 332-386.

440. MOORE (Keith). A guide to the archives and manuscripts of the Royal Society. With additions by Mary SAMPSON. London, Royal Society, 95, VIII-73 p. (ill.).

441. PÉREZ LÓPEZ (Roberto), CAÑO SÁNCHEZ (Domingo), CORONA LORENZO (Mercedes), DE FRÍAS CONDE (Fernando), HUETE CABALLO (Ana Isabel), VICENTE SERRADILLA (Ana Isabel). La justicia militar republicana durante la Guerra Civil: tratamiento archivístico de los fondos de los Tribunales Militares de justicia militar. *In*: Actas de las V Jornadas de Archivos Aragoneses [Cf. n° 419], p. 377-382.

442. PITHON (Remy). Archive cinematographiques et recherche historique: un accord à trouver. *Revue suisse d'histoire*, 95, 45, 4, p. 528-532.

443. PROVIDENTI (Elio). Gli archivi del ministero della Real Casa e il «Fondo Cimeli». *Quaderni di storia*, 95, 21, 42, p. 131-180.

444. RODRIGUEZ CLAVEL (J. R.). Archivos de Diputaciones Provinciales. *In*: Actas de las V Jornadas de Archivos Aragoneses [Cf. n° 419], p. 21-106.

445. ROSELLI (Lucia). Gli strumenti della ricerca: esperienze e prospettive negli Archivi di Stato. *Archivio storico italiano*, 95, 153, 563, p. 145-150.

446. Salamanca letters (The): a catalogue of correspondence (1619–1871) from the Archives of the Irish colleges in Spain in the library of St. Patrick's College, Maynooth, Ireland = Las cartas salmantinas: un catalogo de correspondencia (1619–1871) de los colegios irlandeses en España en la biblioteca del Colegio de San Patricio, Maynooth, Irlanda. Ed. by Regina WHELAN RICHARDSON; listed and conserved by Paul HOARY; typescript prepared by Susan DURACK; foreword by Patrick J. CORISH. Maynooth, St Patrick's College, 95, X-603 p. (Library Archives, 9).

447. SALANOVA ALCALDE (Ramón). Los archivos de la administración local. *In*: Actas de las V Jornadas de Archivos Aragoneses [Cf. n° 419], p. 7-19.

448. SALOMONI (Antonella). Un savoir historique d'Etat: les archives soviétiques. *Annales*, 95, 50, 1, p. 3-28.

449. SCHIOPPA (Simonetta), FELICIANI (Angela). Per una critica dell'archivistica: il contributo dei periodici archivistici italiani dal 1857 al 1975. *Nuovi annali della Scuola speciale per archivisti e bibliotecari dell'Università degli studi di Roma «La Sapienza»*, 95, 9, p. 7-43.

450. SKOWRONEK (Jerzy). Misja archiwisty i problemy rewindykacji archiwów – specyfika Europy Środkowo-Wschodniej XIX i XX w. (La mission de l'archiviste et les problèmes de la revendication des archives – spécificité de l'Europe Centrale et Orientale aux XIXe et XXe siècles). *Archeion*, 95, 94, p. 7-21. [Rés. franç., Eng. Summary]. – IDEM. Odzyskane zbiory archiwum Poselstwa Polskiego w Meksyku (1918–1945) – charakterystyka zasobu. (Archives recouvrés de la Légation de Pologne au Méxique 1918–1945 – caractéristique des fonds). *Archeion*, 95, 95, p. 76-102. [Eng. Summary, Rés. franç.].

451. Slovenija in Dunaj: razstava Zgodovinskega arhiva Ljubljana in Dunajskega mestnega in deželnega arhiva, Ljubljana, Cankarjev dom, 6. februar–5. marec 1995, Dunaj, Avstrijska akademija znanosti, 5. april–12. maj 1995. (Exhibition of the Historical Archives of Ljubljana and the Vienna Municipal and Provincial Archives, Ljubljana, Cankarjev Dom, 6th February–5th March, 1995). Ljubljana, Zgodovinski arhiv, 95, 234 p.

452. Studi in onore di Arnaldo D'Addario. A cura di Luigi BORGIA, Francesco DE LUCA, Raffaella Maria ZACCARIA e Paolo VITI. Lecce, Conte Editore, 95, 5 vol., XXVII-1759 p. (Attraverso la storia, 1). [Cf. n^{os} <scelta> 68, 266, 691, 760, 3306, 3492, 3495, 3508, 3606, 3677, 3700, 3720, 3922, 3994, 4044, 4154, 4162, 4311.]

453. UNFRIED (Berthold). Vom Nutzen und Nachteil der Archive für die Historie. Stalinismusforschung und

1. ARCHIVE, BIBLIOTHEKEN UND MUSEEN

Komintern – Historiographie nach Öffnung der russischen Archive. *Zeitgeschichte*, 95, 22, 7-8, p. 265-284.

454. VIDAL (Nathalie). Les archives contemporaines de la justice: quelle conservation? Eléments de réflexion fondés sur le cas du Pas-de-Calais. *Histoire de la justice*, 95-96, 8-9, p. 253-266.

b. Bibliotheken.

455. BHATT (Rakesh Kumar). History and development of libraries in India. New Delhi, Mittal Publications, 95, XX-367 p.

456. CHARTIER (Roger). Libraries without walls. *In*: Future libraries [Cf. n° 462], p. 38-52.

457. CUGUERO I CONCHELLO (Maria C.), BOADA I VILALLONGA (Maria Teresa), ALLUE I BLANCH (Vicenc). El Servei de Biblioteques del Front, 1936–1939. Barcelona, Diputacio de Barcelona, 95, 308 p. (ill.). (Quaderns de treball. Escola Universitaria Jordi Rubio i Balaguer de Biblioteconomia i Documentacio, 14).

458. DAMIEN (Robert). Bibliothèque et Etat. Naissance d'une raison politique dans la France du XVIIe siècle. Paris, PUF, 95, 317 p.

459. DEBAE (Marguerite). La bibliothèque de Marguerite d'Autriche: essai de reconstitution d'après l'inventaire de 1523–1524. Leuven, Peeters, 95, XXIII-689 p.

460. DICKINSON (Donald C.). Henry E. Huntington's library of libraries. San Marino, Huntington Library, 95, XVII-286 p.

461. DOMINGOS (Manuela D.). Subsidios para a historia da Biblioteca Nacional. Lisboa, Presidencia do Conselho de Ministros, Secretaria de Estado da Cultura, Instituto da Biblioteca Nacional e do Livro, 95, 158 p. (Estudos, 1).

462. Future libraries. Ed. by R. Howard BLOCH a. Carla HESSE. Berkeley a. London, University of California Press, 95, VI-159 p. (ill). (Representations books, 7). [Cf. n° <choice> 456.]

463. KARKOWSKI (Bogumił). Dzieje bibliotek Joachima Lelewela. Studium bibliologiczne. (Histoire des bibliothèques de Joachim Lelewel. Etudes bibliologique). Łódź, Wydawn. Uniw. Łódzkiego, 95, 166 p.

464. Making of the Wren Library (The), Trinity College, Cambridge. Ed. by David MAC KITTERICK. Cambridge, Cambridge U. P., 95, XVII-153 p.

465. MARTANI (M.). Librerie a Parma nella seconda metà del XV secolo. *La Bibliofilia*, 95, 97, p. 211-244.

466. OLDEN (Anthony). Libraries in Africa: pioneers, policies, problems. Lanham a. London, Scarecrow Press, 95, XX-170 p.

467. PETRUCCI NARDELLI (Franca). La Biblioteca Visconteo-Sforzesca. Ubicazione e disposizione del materiale librario. *Bibliofilia*, 95, 97, p. 21-34.

468. REIFENBERG (Bernd). Lessing und die Bibliothek. Wiesbaden, Harrassowitz, 95, 144 p. (Wolfenbütteler Schriften für Geschichte des Buchwesens, 23).

469. SCALON (Cesare). Produzione e fruizione del libro nel basso Medioevo: il caso Friuli. Padova, Antenore, 95, XXI-734 p. (Medioevo e umanesimo, 88).

470. SNAPE (Robert John). Leisure and the rise of the public library. London, Library Association, 95, VII-148 p.

471. TROMBETTA (Vincenzo). Storia della Biblioteca universitaria di Napoli: dal Viceregno spagnolo all'Unita d'Italia. Prefazione di Maurizio TORRINI. Napoli, Vivarium, 95, 293 p. (Crisopoli. Istituto italiano per gli studi filosofici, 1).

472. VAN SLYCK (Abigail Ayres). Free to all: Carnegie libraries & American culture, 1890–1920. Chicago a. London, University of Chicago Press, 95, XXVII-276 p.

473. VENEZIANI (Paolo). La Biblioteca Vittorio Emanuele al Collegio Romano. *Roma moderna e contemporanea*, 95, 3, p. 693-725.

Cf. n°s 77-258, 1774, 3084, 5749

c. Museen.

474. ALARY (Luc). L'art vivant avant l'art moderne: la musée du Luxembourg [Paris], premier essai de muséographie pour l'«art vivant» en France. *Revue d'histoire moderne et contemporaine*, 95, 42, p. 219-239.

475. ANDERSON (R. G. W.). Connoisseurship, pedagogy or antiquarianism? What were instruments doing in the nineteenth-century national collections in Great Britain? Oxford, Oxford U. P., 95, p. 14 (ill.).

476. AUER (Alfred), IRBLICH (Eva). Natur und Kunst. Handschriften und Alben aus der Ambraser Sammlung Erzherzog Ferdinands II. (1529–1595). Ausstellung der Kunsthistorischen Nationalbibliothek im Schloß Ambras, Innsbruck vom 23. Juni bis 24. September 1995. Hrsg. Kunsthistorisches Museum Wien. Wien, Kunsthist. Museum, 95, 125 p. (ill., Karten).

477. BENNETT (Tony). The birth of the museum: history, theory, politics. London a. New York, Routledge, 95, X-278 p. (Culture).

478. Beschlagnahmt. Die Sammlung des Wiener Jüdischen Museum nach 1938. Eine Ausstellung des Jüdischen Museums der Stadt Wien an fünf Schauplätzen vom 12. Oktober bis 26. November 1995. Hrsg. v. Bernhard PURIN. Wien, Jüdisches Museum der Stadt Wien, 95, 80 p. (ill., Zusammenfassung).

479. BREDEKAMP (Horst). The lure of antiquity and the cult of the machine: the Kunstkammer and the evolution of nature, art and technology. Princeton, Markus Wiener Publishers, 95, 140 p.

480. BROWN (Jonathan). Kings and connoisseurs: collecting art in seventeenth-century Europe. Prince-

ton, Princeton U. P., 95, 264 p. (The A.W. Mellon lectures in the fine arts, 1994. Bollingen series, 35, 43).

481. BUTTLAR (Gertrud). Stadtmuseum Wiener Neustadt. Katalog. Hrsg. Kulturamt der Statutarstadt Wiener Neustadt. Wiener Neustadt, Merbod, 95, 382 p. (ill.).

482. COLE (Douglas). Captured heritage: the scramble for Northwest Coast artifacts. Norman, University of Oklahama Press, 95, XIII-373 p. (ill.).

483. GERMAIN (Marie-Odile). Barrès: le musée ou l'art déraciné? *In*: Littérature et musée [Cf. n° 491], p. 36-44.

484. GIORGIO (Arcangela Gabriela), PANELLA (Maria Antonietta). Per la storia del collezionismo cartografico: la raccolta di Onofrio Bonghi. Bari, Cacucci, 95, 193 p. (ill.). (Saggi e ricerche. Università degli studi di Bari, Dipartimento di scienze storiche e geografiche, 9).

485. HAUPT (Herbert). Der Versuchung erlegen. Das Kunsthistorische Museum unter nationalsozialistischer Herrschaft 1938 bis 1945. *Jb. d. Vereins f. Gesch. d. Stadt Wien*, 95, 51, p. 93-142 (ill.).

486. HEINZL (Brigitte). Das Museum Francisco Carolinum in Linz und seine Sammlungen bei Eröffnung im Jahre 1895. *Jb.d. Oberösterr. Musealvereines I*, 95, 140, p. 303-334 (ill.).

487. Historical consciousness in the early republic: the origins of state historical societies, museums, and collections, 1791-1861. Ed. by H.G. JONES. Chapel Hill, North Caroliniana Society and North Carolina Collection, 95, 262 p. (North Caroliniana Society imprints, 25).

488. JACOMY (Bruno). Du cabinet au Conservatoire: les instruments scientifiques du Conservatoire des Arts et Métiers à Paris. *In*: Origins and evolution of collecting scientific instruments [Cf. n° 497], p. 227-233.

489. KOWALSKI (Wojcľech). Straty wojenne muzeów w Polsce. Czy to już historia? (Pertes des musées en Pologne dues à la guerre. Est-ce déjà de l'histoire?). *Archiwa, Biblioteki i Muzea Kościelne*, 95, 63, p. 43-53 (phot.).

490. Krieg in Österreich '45 (Der). Katalog zur Sonderausstellung im Heeresgeschichtlichen Museum, Wien. Objektbeschreibung von Günter Dirrheimer. Hrsg. v. Heeresgeschichtliches Museum. Militärhist. Institut. Red. von Erwin A. SCHMIDL. Wien, Heeresgeschichtl. Museum, 95, 123 p. (ill.).

491. Littérature et musée. Actes du Colloque organisé à l'occasion du deuxième centenaire du musée du Louvre par la Société d'histoire littéraire de la France et le musée d'Orsay, 11 mars 1994. *Revue d'histoire littéraire de la France*, 95, 95, 1, p. 1-68. [Cf. n°s <sélection> 483, 495, 500, 504.]

492. LOLLIO BARBERI (Olga), PAROLA (G.), TOTI (M. P.). Le antichità egiziane di Roma imperiale. Roma, Istituto poligrafico e Zecca dello Stato, Libreria dello Stato, 95, 329 p.

493. MACCIONI RUJU (P. Alessandra), MOSTERT (Marco). The life and times of Guglielmo Libri (1802-1869): scientist, patriot, scholar, journalist, and thief: a nineteenth-century story. Hilversum, Verloren Publishers, 95, 448 p.

494. MANCINI (Vincenzo). Antiquari, "vertuosi" e artisti: saggi sul collezionismo tra Padova e Venezia alla meta del Cinquecento. Padova, Ars patavina, 95, 149 p.

495. MEYER-PETIT (Judith). La maison de Balzac [à Paris] et les paradoxes du musée littéraire. *In*: Littérature et musée [Cf. n° 491], p. 59-68.

496. MUYLLE (Marianne). Paradoxe artistique: quand le vandalisme révolutionnaire mène au musée. *Pensée et Hommes*, 95, 38, 30, p. 81-93.

497. Origins and evolution of collecting scientific instruments. Papers from the Conference held in Museum Boerhaave, Leiden, September 1994. *Journal of the history collections*, 95, 7, 2, p. 133-269. [Cf. n° <choice> 488.]

498. PARENTI (Adonella Barbara). «I segreti in vetrina». Utilità e danno per la storia delle mostre di documenti, libri e cimeli. *Archivio storico italiano*, 95, 153, 563, p. 151-158.

499. PEARCE (Susan Mary). On collecting: an investigation into collecting in the European tradition. London, Routledge, 95, XIV-440 p. (The Collecting cultures series).

500. PIERROT (Roger). Le département des Manuscrits de la Bibliothèque nationale: bibliothèque et/ou musée littéraire? *In*: Littérature et musée [Cf. n° 491], p. 45-53.

501. POMMIER (Edouard). Les Musées en Europe à la veille de l'ouverture du Louvre: actes du colloque organisé par le service culturel du musée du Louvre à l'occasion de la commémoration du bicentenaire de l'ouverture du Louvre les 3, 4, 5 juin 1993. Paris, Louvre, Klincksieck, 95, 649 p. (ill.). (Louvre conferences et colloques).

502. RASSE (Paul). Les musées d'entreprise: quelle médiation de l'histoire? *Communication & Organisation*, 95, 3, p. 71-83.

503. SALLOIS (Jacques). Les musées de France. Paris, PUF, 95, 127 p. (Que sais-je? 447).

504. SAVY (Nicole). Victor Hugo et le musée des Monuments français, les effets d'une enfance au musée. *In*: Littérature et musée [Cf. n° 491], p. 13-26.

505. TROCHET (Jean-René). Sciences humaines et musées: du musée d'ethnographie du Trocadéro [à Paris] au musée national des Arts et Traditions populaires. *Géographies Cultures*, 95, 16, p. 3-30.

506. Zgodovinski parki in vrtovi v Sloveniji. (Historical parks and gardens in Slovenia). Ed. by Jerneja BATIĆ. Ljubljana, Ministrstvo za kulturo, Uprava Republike Slovenije za kulturno dediščino, 95, 155 p.

§ 2. Geschichte der Geschichtswissenschaft.

a. Allgemeines.

* 507. Bibliographies [d'histoire rurale]. *In*: Histoire rurale en France (L') [Cf. n° 601], p. 37-48, p. 77, p. 109-111, p. 143-149, p. 198-201, p. 254-260.

* 508. Bollettino corrente di storia della storiografia e della tradizione storica dei ricordi. Vol. 5. 1991–1994. A cura di Massimo MASTROGREGORI. Pisa e Roma, Gruppo editoriale internazionale, 95, 106 p. (Supplemento bibliografico annuale della "Rivista di storia della storiografia moderna", 5).

* 509. MAGOON (Joseph). Biography: bibliography and historical survey. Bournemouth, J. Magoon, 95, 42 p.

* 510. MIRONOV (Konstantin Sergeevich). Istoriia Rossii v poezii i proze: bibliograficheskii ukazatel' istoriko-khudozhestvennoi literatury XX veka. (A bibliography of Russian historiography, literature and historical fiction, 20th century). Moskva, Rusland-Krik, 95, 141 p.

511. AKENSON (Donald Harman). The historiography of English-speaking Canada and the concept of diaspora: a sceptical appreciation. *Canadian Historical Review*, 95, 76, 1, p. 377-409.

512. ALIBERTI (Giovanni). L'Italia politica dal Risorgimento al fascismo: un'interpretazione a confronto. *Storia contemporanea*, 95, 26, 5, p. 789-816.

513. ALPERÓVICH (M. S.). La revolución mexicana en la interpretación soviética del periodo de la "guerra fría". *Historia Mexicana*, 94-95, 44, p. 675-688.

514. ALTEKAMP (Stefan). L'azione archeologica fra indirizzo scientifico e intervento politico: il caso dell'archeologia libica (1911–1943). *Quaderni di storia*, 95, 21, 41, p. 101-114.

515. AMELANG (James S.). Microhistory and its discontents: the view from Spain. *In*: Historia a Debate. Tomo 2 [Cf. n° 602], p. 307-314.

516. American retrospectives: historians on historians. Ed. by Stanley I. KUTLER. Baltimore a. London, Johns Hopkins U. P., 95, X-341p.

517. ANATRA (Bruno). Storia locale in veste regionale: il caso italiano. *In*: Historia a Debate. Tomo 3 [Cf. n° 602], p. 51-58.

518. ANAYA MERCHANT (Luis). La construcción de la memoria en la revisión de la Revolución. *Historia Mexicana*, 94-95, 44, p. 523-534.

519. AYMARD (Maurice), TATE (Georges), BOIS (Guy), GAVIGNAUD (Geneviève). Histoire économique et histoire rurale. *In*: Histoire rurale en France (L') [Cf. n° 601], p. 79-111.

520. BARRIERA (Darío). Notas sobre la Nouvelle Histoire. *Anuario de la Escuela de Historia-Universidad Nacional de Rosario*, 95-96, 17, segunda época, p. 481-495.

521. BASTIAN (Jean-Pierre). Una ausencia notoria: la francmasonería en la historiografía mexicanista. *Historia Mexicana*, 94-95, 44, p. 439-460.

522. *Vacat.*

523. BENEŠ (Zdeněk). Pojmy jako předmět historiografického studia. Příklad: Gollova historická škola a její zakladatel. (Die Begriffe als der Gegenstand des historischen Studiums. Eine Beispiel: [Jaroslav] Goll's historische Schule und ihr Gründer). *Český časopis historický*, 95, 93, 3, p. 359-397.

524. BENIGNO (Francesco). Specchi della rivoluzione: revisionismi storiografici a confronto. *Storica*, 95, 4, 2, p. 7-54.

525. BERGER (Stefan). Viewpoint: historians and nation-building in Germany after reunification. *Past and Present*, 95, 148, p. 187-222.

526. BERLIN (Gail Ivy). Memorization in Anglo-Saxon England. *In*: Oral tradition in the Middle Ages [Cf. n° 3381], [s. p.].

527. BERMEJO BARRERA (José C.). Histoire universelle: la crise d'une idée. *Rivista di storia della storiografia moderna*, 95, 16, 1-3, p. 193-238.

528. BERNARD (Jean-Paul). L'historiographie canadienne récente (1964–1994) et l'histoire des peuples du Canada. *Canadian Historical Review*, 95, 76, 3, p. 321-353.

529. BESSMERTNY (Youri L.), LEPETIT (Bernard), GRENIER (Jean-Yves). A proposito delle nuove «Annales». *Rivista di storia della storiografia moderna*, 95, 16, 1-3, p. 127-136.

530. BESSMERTNY (Yuri L.). L'histoire démographique anthropologiquement orientée et son devenir en Russie. *In*: Historia a Debate. Tomo 3 [Cf. n° 602], p. 121-126.

531. BIZZOCCHI (Roberto). Genealogie incredibili: scritti di storia dell'Europa moderna. Bologna, Il Mulino, 95, 228 p. (Annali dell'Istituto storico italo-germanico, 22). – IDEM. Rec. di A. GRANDAZZI, La fondazione di Roma (1993). *Storica*, 95, 1, p. 165-168.

532. BLOCH (Maurice). Mémoire autobiographique et mémoire historique du passé éloigné. *In*: Usages de la tradition [Cf. n° 718], p. 59-78.

533. BLUMENAU (Semen F.). Ot social'no-économičeskoj istorii k problematike massovogo soznanija. Francuzskaja istoriografija revolucii konca XVIII veka (1945–1993 gody). (From the social and economic history to the problems of the mass consciousness. The end of the XVIIIth century revolution in the French historiography. 1945–1993). Brjansk, In-t vseobščej istorii RAN, Brjanskij gosudarstvennyj pedagogičeskij universitet imeni I. G. Petrovskogo, 95, 336 p.

534. BODOR (András). Erdély ókori történetének kutatása a XIX. század közepéig. (L'étude de l'histoire antique de Transylvanie jusqu'à la moitié du XIXe siècle). Erdélyi múzeum, 95, 57, 3-4, p. 56-81.

535. BOGDANOV (Andrej P.). Ot letopisanija k issledovaniju: Russkie istoriki poslednej četverti XVII veka. (From the chronicles to the researches: The Russian historians of the late quarter of the XVIIth century). Moskva, RISC, 95, 556 p.

536. BOJOVIC (Bosko I.). L'idéologie monarchique dans les hagio-biographies dynastiques du Moyen Age serbe. Roma, Pontificio Istituto Orientale, 95, LII-727 p. (Orientalia Christiana analecta, 248).

537. BONK (Magdalena). Deutsche Philologie in München: zur Geschichte des Faches und seiner Vertreter an der Ludwig-Maximilians-Universität vom Anfang des 19. Jahrhunderts bis zum Ende des zweiten Weltkrieges. Berlin, Duncker & Humblot, 95, XIII-463 p. (Ludovico Maximilianea, forschungen, 16).

538. BOUJU (Jacky). Tradition et identité. La tradition Dogon entre traditionalisme rural et néo-traditionalisme urbain. In: Usages de la tradition [Cf. n° 718], p. 95-120.

539. BOUTRY (Philippe). Tradition et écriture. In: Usages de la tradition [Cf. n° 718], p. 39-58.

540. BRETTLER (Marc Zvi). The creation of history in ancient Israel. London, Routledge, XV-254 p.

541. BREUER (Tilmann). Metropole als Denkmaltypus. In: Hauptstadt: Historische Perspektiven eines deutschen Themas [Cf. n° 1271], p. 137-160.

542. BRUNEL (Ghislain), MORICEAU (Jean-Marc). L'histoire rurale en question. In: Histoire rurale en France (L') [Cf. n° 601], p. 11-18.

543. BUBNOV (Nikolaj Ju.). Staroobrjadčeskaja kniga v Rossii vo vtoroj polovine XVII veka: Istočniki, tipy i évolucija. (The old-believers writings in Russia in the second half of the XVIIth century: origins, types and evolution). Sankt-Peterburg, Biblioteka RAN, 95, 435 p.

544. BUGNARD (Pierre-Philippe). Les retrouvailles de la biographie et de la nouvelle histoire. Revue suisse d'histoire, 95, 45, 2, p. 236-254.

545. BURGUIERE (André). L'anthropologie historique et l'Ecole des Annales. In: Historia a Debate. Tomo 3 [Cf. n° 602], p. 127-138.

546. CANAL (Jordi). La storiografia della sociabilità in Spagna. Passato e presente, 95, 13, 34, p. 151-164.

547. CANCIAN (P.). LA memoria delle chiese: cancellerie vescovili e culture notarili nell'Italia centro-settentrionale (secoli X–XIII). Torino, Scriptorium, 95, 204 p.

548. CANFORA (Luciano). Politische Philologie. Altertumswissenschaften und moderne Staatsideologien. Stuttgart, Klett-Cotta, 95, 220 p.

549. CARRERA DAMAS (German). La disputa de la independencia y otras peripecias del metodo critico en historia de ayer y de hoy. Caracas, Ediciones Ge, 95, 260 p.

550. CASSINA (Cristina). L'obsession interminable. La révolution française dans la littérature ultra-royaliste au début de la Restauration. Storia della Storiografia, 95, 27, p. 17-38.

551. CATTARUZZA (Alejandro). Entre el análisis de la producción académica y la "historia de la historia". Una discusión sobre los objetos de estudio de la historia de la historiografía. Anuario de la Escuela de Historia-Universidad Nacional de Rosario, 95–96, 17, segunda época, p. 47-68. – IDEM. La situación actual de la historia de la historiografía. Rivista di storia della storiografia moderna, 95, 16, 1-3, p. 163-192.

552. COLLINS (Randal). Les traditions sociologiques. In: Usages de la tradition [Cf. n° 718], p. 11-38.

553. Concepts of national identity in the Middle Ages. Ed. by Simon FORDE, Lesley JOHNSON a. Alan V. MURRAY. Leeds, School of English, University of Leeds, 95, VIII-213 p. (ill.). (Leeds texts and monographs, 14). [Contents: JOHNSON (Lesley). Imagining communities: medieval and modern. – SMITH (Anthony D.). National identities: modern and medieval? – WOOD (Ian). Defining the Franks: Frankish origins in early medieval historiography. – MURRAY (Alan V.). Ethnic identity in the Crusader states. – GILLINGHAM (John). Henry of Huntingdon and the twelfth-century revival of the English nation. – LYDON (James F.). Nation and race in medieval Ireland. – JOHNSON (Lesley). Etymologies, genealogies, and nationalities (again). – BYRN (Richard F.M.). National stereotypes reflected in German literature. – GONZALEZ-CASANOVAS (Roberto J.). Alfonso X's concept of Hispania. – BLACK (Iris). Accidental tourist in the Hundred Years War: images of the foreign world in Eustache Deschamps. – BRUSH (Kathryn L.). Gothic sculpture as a locus for the polemics of national identity.]

554. CROSBY (Alfred W.). The past and present of environmental history. American Historical Review, 95, 100, 4, p. 1177-1189.

555. CROSSLEY (Ceri). L'histoire romantique comme support du sens: l'exemple des libéraux. In: Histoire au XIXe siècle (L') [Cf. n° 599], p. 177-192.

556. CURCHIN (Leonard A.). History effaced: the disappearance of ancient monuments in Central Spain. Quaderni di storia, 95, 21, 42, p. 101-110.

557. DANYEL (Jürgen). Die Historiker und die Moral. Anmerkungen zur Debatte über die Autorenrechte an der DDR-Geschichte. *Geschichte und Gesellschaft*, 95, 21, 2, p. 290-304.

558. DARBO-PESCHANSKI (Catherine). Fabriquer du continu (L'historiographie grecque face au temps). *Storia della Storiografia*, 95, 28, p. 17-34.

559. DARTON (Robert). Diffusion vs. discourse: conceptual shifts in intellectual history and the historiography of the French Revolution. *In*: Historia a Debate. Tomo 2 [Cf. n° 602], p. 179-192.

560. DE CONINCK-SMITH (Nina). Barndommens historikere i midten af 1990erne. (Childhood's historians in the midst of the 1990s). *Historisk Tidskrift* (Denmark), 95, 95, 1, p. 143-154.

561. DE ROSA (Gabriele). Verso quale storiografia di fine millennio? Bilancio e prospettive del nostro lavoro. *Ricerche di storia sociale e religiosa*, 95, 47, p. 7-22.

562. DECLICH (Francesca). "Gendered Narratives", history, and identity: two centuries along the Juba River among the Zigula and Shanbara. *History in Africa*, 95, 22, p. 93-122.

563. DEN BOER (Pim). Deux aspects de l'historiographie aux Pays Bas et en France vers 1900: le rôle des facultés de théologie et la non intervention de l'Etat. *Rivista di storia della storiografia moderna*, 95, 16, 1-3, p. 117-126.

564. DERWICH (Marek). Die Forschungsstelle zur Geschichte der Orden und Ordenskongregationen an der Breslauer Universität. *Inter finitimos*, 95, 8, p. 7-12.

565. Deutsche Rechtsgeschichte in der NS-Zeit (Die): ihre Vorgeschichte und ihre Nachwirkungen. Hrsg. v. Joachim RUCKERT u. Dietmar WILLOWEIT. Tübingen, J.C.B. Mohr, 95, VI-355 p. (Beiträge zur Rechtsgeschichte des 20. Jahrhunderts, 12).

566. DI CAMILLO (Ottavio). Interpretations of the Renaissance in Spanish historical thought. *Renaissance quarterly*, 95, 48, 2, p. 352-365.

567. Discovery of Australian history (The), 1890–1939. Ed. by Stuart MACINTYRE a. Julian THOMAS. Melbourne, Melbourne U. P., 95, IX-219 p.

568. DOSTÁLOVÁ (R.). Der Einfluss der Rhetorik auf die Objektivität der historischen Information in den Werken byzantinischer Historiker. *Byzantino-slavica*, 95, 56, p. 291-303.

569. DUCHET (Michele). Anthropologie et histoire au siècle des lumières. Postface de Claude BLANCKAERT. Paris, Albin Michel, 95, 611 p.

570. DUMOULIN (Olivier). La tribu des médiévistes. *Genèses*, 95, 21, p. 120-133.

571. EMMONS (Terence). Russia then and now in the pages of the American Historical Review and elsewhere: a few centennial notes. *American Historical Review*, 95, 100, 4, p. 1136-1149.

572. ERGENC (Ozer). XVI. Yüzyılda Ankara ve Konya: Osmanlı Klasik Donemi Kent Tarihciligi. 1. (Ankara et Konya au XVIe siècle: Historiographie urbaine de l'époque classique ottomane). Ankara, Ankara Enstitüsü Vakfı, 1995, 217 p.

573. ESCH (Arnold). Mittelalterforschung heute aus der Sicht eines historischen Auslandsinstituts. *In*: Mittelalterforschung nach der Wende 1989 [Cf. n° 660], p. 75-88.

574. Etnias, educación y archivos en la historia de Colombia. Ed. por Javier GUERRERO. Tunja, Universidad Pedagogica y Tecnologica de Colombia y Bogota, Archivo General de la Nación: Asociación Colombiana de Historiadores, 95, 262 p. (Colección Memorias de historia, 3).

575. FABRE (Pierre-Antoine). L'institution du texte fondateur. La tradition orale des «écrits» d'Ignace de Loyola dans l'histoire et dans l'historiographie de la Compagnie de Jésus au XVIe siècle. *In*: Usages de la tradition [Cf. n° 718], p. 79-94.

576. FEINER (Shmuel). Haskalah ve-historyah: toldoteha shel hakarat-`avar Yehudit modernit. (Haskalah and history). Yerushalayim, Merkaz Zalman Shazar le-toldot Yisra'el, 95, 523 p. (Monografyot be-toldot `am Yisra'el. Mi-pirsume Merkaz Zalman Shazar).

577. FERRETTI (Maria). La mémoire refoulée. La Russie devant le passé stalinien. *Annales*, 95, 50, 6, p. 1237-1258.

578. FLAMMARION (Edith), VOLPILHAC-AUGER (Catherine). L'Antiquité au XVIIIe siècle: état des recherches et tendances actuelles. *XVIIIe siècle*, 95, 27, p. 5-23.

579. FLEMING (Robin). Picturesque history and the Medieval in nineteenth-century America. *American Historical Review*, 95, 100, 4, p. 1061-1094.

580. FREITAG (Ulrike). Notions of time in Arab-Islamic historiography. *Storia della Storiografia*, 95, 28, p. 55-68.

581. GABBA (Emilio). Cultura classica e storiografia moderna. Bologna, Il mulino, 95, 451 p. (Collezione di testi e di studi. Storiografia).

582. GAILLARD (Michele). D'Hincmar à Michel Sot: jeu de miroirs autour de l'histoire de l'église de Reims. *Revue Belge de Philologie et d'Histoire*, 95, 73, 2, p. 401-409.

583. GARCÍA-CÁRCEL (Ricardo). La manipulación de la memoria histórica. *In*: Historia a Debate. Tomo 1 [Cf. n° 602], p. 291-298.

584. GARDIN (J. C.), BORGHETTI (M. N.). L'architettura dei testi storiografici. Bologna, Clueb, 95, 215 p. («Heuresis» IX, Scienze storiche, 1).

585. GAVIGNAUD (Geneviève). L'apport de l'Ecole des Annales à l'histoire rurale de l'époque contemporaine. *In*: Histoire rurale en France (L') [Cf. n° 601], p. 94-102.

586. GELLRICH (Jesse M.). Discourse and dominion in the fourteenth century: oral contexts of writing in philosophy, politics, and poetry. Princeton, Princeton U. P., 95, XIV, 304 p.

587. Genre des mémoires (Le), essai de definition: colloque international des 4–7 mai 1994. Organisé à l'Université des sciences humaines de Strasbourg par le Groupe de recherche "Littérature et politique sous l'Ancien Regime". Actes publiés par Madeleine BERTAUD et Francois-Xavier CUCHE. Paris, Klincksieck, 95, 371 p. (Actes et colloques, 44).

588. Geteilte Vergangenheit (Die): zum Umgang mit Nationalsozialismus und Widerstand in beiden deutschen Staaten. Hrsg. v. Jurgen DANYEL. Berlin, Akademie Verlag, 95, 266 p. (Zeithistorische Studien, 4).

589. GIARRIZZO (Giuseppe). Per una storia della storiografia europea. Gli storici, la storia. Acireale, Bonanno Editore, 95, 255 p. [Cf. n^{os} <scelta> 741, 768, 807, 813, 819, 845.]

590. GIUA (Maria). La storiografia antica fra ricerca e didattica. A proposito di un contributo recente. *Storia della Storiografia*, 95, 27, p. 85-89.

591. GLENCROSS (Michael J.). La représentation de la littérature française du Moyen Age dans l'historiographie romantique. *In*: Histoire au XIXe siècle (L') [Cf. n° 599], p. 193-213.

592. GOTTLOB (Michael). Writing the history of modern Indian historiography. *Storia della Storiografia*, 95, 27, p. 125-146.

593. GRANT (Michael). Greek and Roman historians. Information and misinformation. London a. New York, Routledge, 95, 172 p.

594. GRELL (Chantal). Le XVIIIe siècle et l'antiquité en France, 1680–1789. T. 1–2. Oxford, Voltaire Foundation, 95, XXIV-1336 p.

595. Guide to historiography in Slovakia (A). Ed. by Elena MANNOVÁ, David Paul DANIEL. Bratislava, Historický ústav SAV, 95, 209 p.

596. GUNST (Péter). A magyar történetírás története. (Histoire de l'historiographie hongroise). Debrecen, Csokonai, 5, 214 p.

597. HENDRIX (G.). Saint Bernard et son historiographie. *Revue d'Histoire Ecclésiastique*, 95, 90, 1-2, p. 80-103.

598. Histoire au temps de la Renaissance (L'). Directeur de la publication, M.T. JONES-DAVIES. Paris, Klincksieck, 95, 214 p.

599. Histoire au XIXe siècle (L'). 2e Journée du 46e Congrès de l'Association internationale des études françaises. *Cahiers de l'Association internationale des études françaises*, 95, 47, p. 173-343. [Cf. n^{os} <sélection> 555, 591, 756, 811, 838, 858.]

600. Histoire et le métier d'historien en France 1945–1995 (L'). Sous la dir. de François BEDARIDA, avec la coll. de Maurice AYMARD, Yves-Marie BERCE et Jean-François SIRINELLI; préf. de Jacques LE GOFF et Nicolas ROUSSELLIER. Paris, Editions de la Maison des sciences de l'homme, 95, X-437 p. [Cf. n° <sélection> 871.]

601. Histoire rurale en France (L'). Actes du Colloque de Rennes, 6–8 octobre 1994. Réun. Et prés. Par Ghislain BRUNEL et Jean-Marc MORICEAU. *Histoire et sociétés rurales*, 95, 3, p. 11-260. [Cf. n^{os} <sélection> 373, 374, 507, 519, 542, 585, 617, 875, 4871, 4886, 4888, 4914, 7234, 7235, 7252.]

602. Historia a Debate. Tomo 1. Pasado y futuro. Tomo 2. Retorno del sujeto. Tomo 3. Otros enfoques. Actas del congreso internacional "A Historia a Debate" celebrado el 7–11 de julio 1993 en Santiago de Compostela. Ed. por Carlos BARROS GUIMERANS. Santiago de Compostela, HAD, 95, 3 vol., 353 p., 365 p., 306 p. [Cf. n^{os} <selección> 512, 517, 530, 545, 559, 583, 633, 648, 863, 881, 915, 961, 963, 1280.]

603. Historische Forschung und sozialistische Diktatur. Beiträge zur Geschichtswissenschaft der DDR. Hrsg. v. Martin SABROW u. Peter T. WALTHER. Leipzig, Leipziger Universitätsverl., 95, 270 p. (Beiträge zur Universalgeschichte und vergleichenden Gesellschaftsforschung, 13). [Cf. n° <Auswahl> 696.]

604. HOBSBAWM (Eric). Inventing traditions. *In*: Usages de la tradition [Cf. n° 718], p. 171-192.

605. HOESLER (Joachim). Die sowjetische Geschichtswissenschaft 1953 bis 1991: Studien zur Methodologie- und Organisationsgeschichte. München, Sagner, 95, 359 p. (Marburger Abhandlungen zur Geschichte und Kultur Osteuropas, 34).

606. HOLT (Thomas C.). Marking: race, race-marking, and the writing of history. *American Historical Review*, 95, 100, 1, p. 1-20.

607. HOLZBACHOVÁ (Ivana). Škola Annales a současné pojetí dějin. (The Annales school and the contemporary conception of history). Brno, Masarykova univerzita, 95, 59 p.

608. *Vacat*.

609. HOURCADE (Eduardo). Un panorama de la Nouvelle Histoire. *Estudios*, 5, 95, p. 93-106.

610. HÜBINGER (Gangolf). Neue Aspekte der Kulturgeschichte. *Storia della Storiografia*, 95, 27, p. 121-124.

611. HUNT (Lynn). Forgetting and remembering: the French Revolution then and now. *American Historical Review*, 95, 100, 4, p. 1119-1135.

612. HUTTUNEN (Mika). Modernin musiikkinhistoriankirjoituksen synty Suomessa. (The beginnigs of modern music history writing in Finland). Helsinki, Suomen musiikkitieteellinen seura, 95, 305 p. (Acta musicologica Fennica, 18).

613. I arbeid for lokalhistorie og kulturvern: Landslaget for lokalhistorie 75 år 1920–1995. (National Federation of Local History Association, 1920–1995).

Ed. by Egil NYSÆTER, Dagfinn SLETTAN a. Harald WINGE. Trondheim, Landslaget for lokalhistorie, 95, 169 p. (Skrifter frå Landslaget for lokalhistorie, 8).

614. ISLAMOV (Tofik M.). Problemy nacii i nacionalizma v sovremennoj avstrijskoj istoriografii. (Today's Austrian historiography on ethno-national processes). *Nov. novejš. Ist.* , 95, 4, p. 28-43.

615. Istoriki Rossii XVIII–XX vekov. (Russian historians, XVIII–XX century). Sost. i otv. red. A. A. CHERNOBAEV. Moskva, Arkhivno-informatsionnoe agentstvo, Istoriko-arkhivnoe otd-nie Mezhdunar. akademii informatizatsii, 95, 3 vol., [s. p.] (Arkhivno-informatsionnyi biulleten', 9, 10, 14. "'Prilozhenie k zhurnalu 'Istoricheskii arkhiv'"').

616. Italia contemporanea (L') e la storiografia internazionale. A cura di Filippo MAZZONIS. Venezia, Marsilio, 95, 315 p.

617. JACQUART (Jean). Les grandes étapes historiographiques [de l'histoire rurale]. *In*: Histoire rurale en France (L') [Cf. n° 601], p. 19-24.

618. JARAUSCH (Konrad H.). Normalisierung oder Re-Nationalisierung? Zur Umdeutung der deutschen Vergangenheit. *Geschichte und Gesellschaft*, 95, 21, 4, p. 571-584.

619. JONSSON (Ulf). Fran internationalisering till globalisering – ett paradigmskifte? (From internationalization to globalization – a paradigm shift?). *Historisk Tidskrift* (Sweden), 95, 2, p. 194-209.

620. Junta de Historia y Numismatica Americana (La) y el movimiento historiografico en la Argentina, 1893–1938. Buenos Aires, Academia Nacional de la Historia, 95, [s. p.] (ill.).

621. KAUFMANN (D.). Die "Wilden" in der Geschichtsschreibung und Anthropologie der "Zivilisierten". Historische und aktuelle Kontroversen um Cooks Südseereisen und seinen Tod auf Hawaii 1779. *Historische Zeitschrift*, 95, 260, 1, p. 49-74.

622. KERSKEN (Norbert). Geschichtsschreibung im Europa der "nationes": Nationalgeschichte Gesamtdarstellungen im Mittelalter. Wien, Köln u. Weimar, Böhlau, 95, X-963 p. (Münstersche historische Forschungen, 8).

623. KHAĆTURJAN (Valerija M.). Theorija civilizacij v russkoj istoričeskoj mysli. (Theory of civilization in the Russian historical thought). *Nov. novejš. Ist.*, 95, 5, p. 8-18.

624. KHALIL (Elias L.). Has economics progressed? Rectilinear, historicist, essentialist, universalist, and evolutionary historiographies. *Hist. Polit. Ec.*, 95, 27, 1, p. 43-88.

625. KINTZINGER (Marion). Chronos und Historia: Studien zur Titelblattikonographie historiographischer Werke vom 16. bis zum 18. Jahrhundert. Wiesbaden, Harrassowitz, 95, IX-369 p. (Wolfenbütteler Forschungen, 60.).

626. KLEINERT (Claudia). Die Revision der Historiographie des Osmanischen Reiches am Beispiel von Abdulhamid II.: das späte Osmanische Reich im Urteil türkischer Autoren der Gegenwart (1930–1990). Berlin, K. Schwarz, 95, 262 p. (Islamkundliche Untersuchungen, 188).

627. KLOCZOWSKI (Jerzy). East Central Europe in the historiography of the countries of the region. Lublin, Institute of East Central Europe, 95, 53 p.

628. KOPIEC (Jan). Pięćdziesięciolecie Polskiego Instytutu Historycznego w Rzymie [1945–1995]. (Le 50e anniversaire de l'Institut Historique Polonais à Rome [1945–1995]). *Nasza Przeszłość*, 95, 84, p. 381-389 (phot.)

629. LAMBERT (Peter). Generations of German historians: patronage, censorship and the containment of generation conflict 1918–1945. *In*: Generations in conflict [Cf. n° 7388], p. 164-183.

630. LANGHANS (Erika). Die "Krise der Geschichtswissenschaft" in der Volksrepublik China (1986–1989). Bochum, N. Brockmeyer, 95, XXXVI-286 p. (Chinathemen. Serie Europäisches Projekt zur Modernisierung in China, 12).

631. LARSON (Pier M.). Multiple narratives, gendered voices: remembering the past in Highland Central Madagascar. *International Journal of African Historical Studies*, 95, 28, 2, p. 295-326.

632. LATVAKANGAS (Arto). Riksgrundarna. Varjagproblemet i Sverige från runinskrifter till enhetlig historisk tolkning. Turku, University of Turku, 95, 527 p. (Turun yliopiston julkaisua. Sarja B, Humaniora, 211). [The founders of the Russian realm. The early Swedish historiography on the Varangian problem].

633. LE GOFF (Jacques). Les retours dans l'historiographie français actuelle. *In*: Historia a Debate. Tomo 3 [Cf. n° 602], p. 157-166.

634. LEMANN (Nicholas). History solo: non-academic historians. *American Historical Review*, 95, 100, 3, p. 788-798.

635. LEWIS (Earl). To turn as on a pivot: writing African Americans into a history of overlapping diasporas. *American Historical Review*, 95, 100, 3, p. 765-787.

636. LEWIS (Jan). The double-consciousness of the academic historian. *Journal of social history*, 95, 29, p. 51-57.

637. Liberation of France (The): image and event. Ed. by H. R. KEDWARD and Nancy WOOD. Oxford, Berg, 95, XVI-369 p. (Berg French studies).

638. LIFSHITZ (Felice). The Norman conquest of pious Neustria: historiographic discourse and saintly relics, 684–1090. Toronto, Pontifical Institute of Mediaeval Studies, 95, XII-324 p. (Studies and texts. Pontifical Institute of Mediaeval Studies, 122).

639. LUND (Allan A.). Germanenideologie im Nationalsozialismus: zur Rezeption der Germania des Tacitus im "Dritten Reich". Heidelberg, Universitätsverlag C. Winter, 95, 182 p.

640. LUR'E (Jakov S.). Mikhail Dmitrievič Priselkov i voprosy izučenija russkogo letopisanija. (Mikhail Priselkov and the problems of studying Russian chronicles). *Oteč. Ist.*, 95, 1,p. 146-159.

641. LURAGHI (Nino), MÖLLER (Astrid). Time in the writing of history: perceptions and structures. *Storia della Storiografia*, 95, 28, p. 3-15.

642. Magyar (A) honfoglalás a külföldi történetírásban. (La conquête du pays par les Hongrois dans l'historiographie étrangère). *Magyar tudomány*, 95, 40, 12, p. 1401-1511.

643. Making a historical culture. Historiography in Norway. Ed. William H. HUBBARD, Jon E. MYHRE, Trond NORBY a. Sölvi SOGNER. Oslo, Scandinavian U. P., 95, 438 p.

644. Making alternative histories: the practice of archaeology and history in non-Western settings. Ed. by Peter R. SCHMIDT a. Thomas C. PATTERSON. Santa Fe, School of American Research Press, 95, XIII-312 p. (School of American Research advanced seminar series).

645. MARINO (Luigi). Praeceptores germaniae. Göttingen 1770–1820. Göttingen, Vandenhoeck & Ruprecht, 95, VII-475 p. (Göttingen Universitätsschriften, 10).

646. MARY (André). Religion de la tradition et religieux post-traditionel. *In*: Usages de la tradition [Cf. n° 718], p. 121-142.

647. MASSEY (Doreen). Places and their pasts. *History Workshop*, 95, 39, p. 182-192.

648. MASTROGREGORI (Massimo). Historiographie et tradition historique des souvenirs. Histoire «scientifique» des études historiques et histoire «global» du rapport avec le passé. *In*: Historia a Debate. Tomo 1 [Cf. n° 602], p. 269-278. – IDEM. El problema histórico de los primeros Annales (1929–1945). *Iztapalapa*, 95, 15, 1, p. 9-22.

649. MATOS (Sérgio Carneiro de Campos). Memória e nação: historiografia portuguesa de divulgação e nacionalismo (1846–1898). Lisboa, [s. n.], 95, V-791 p. (bibl.).

650. MATSUMOTO (Akira). Sengo-Rekishigaku to Ōtsuka-Shigaku. (Post-war historiography and the Otsuka School). *Rekishi Hyoron*, 95, 542, p. 52-59.

651. MEDICK (Hans). The so-called 'Laichingen Hunger Chronicle'. *History Workshop*, 95, 40, p. 207-219.

652. Medieval scholarship. Biographical studies on the formation of a discipline. Vol. 1. History. New York a. London, Garland, 95, XXXII-147 p. [Cf. n[os] <choice> 749, 765, 802.]

653. MEL'NIKOVA (Elena A.), PETRUKHIN (Vladimir Ja.). Legenda o "prizvanii varjagov" i stanovlenie drevnerusskoj istoriografii. (The legend about "the call for varjags" and the beginning of an ancient Russian historiography). *Vopr. Ist.*, 95, 2, p. 44-57.

654. Mémoire et histoire: la Résistance. Sous la dir. de Jean-Marie GUILLON et Pierre LABORIE; préf. de Philippe JOUTARD. Toulouse, Editions Privat, 95, 352 p. (Bibliotheque historique privat).

655. Memoria als Kultur. Hrsg. v. Otto Gerhard OEXLE. Göttingen, Vandenhoeck & Ruprecht, 95. 428 p. (Veröffentlichungen des Max-Planck-Instituts für Geschichte, 121).

656. MIEGGE (Mario). Il sogno del re di Babilonia: profezia e storia da Thomas Müntzer a Isaac Newton. Milano, Feltrinelli, 95, 219 p. (Campi del sapere. Filosofia).

657. MINERBI (Alessandra). Orientamenti e temi dell'Exilforschung. *Passato e presente*, 95, 13, 36, p. 117-128.

658. MINUTI (Rolando). Storia nazionale e cultura illuministica nella Scozia del '700. *Storia della Storiografia*, 95, 28, p. 87-97.

659. MITTAL (Satish Chandra). India distorted: a study of British historians on India. New Delhi, M.D. Publications, 95, [s. p.]

660. Mittelalterforschung nach der Wende 1989. Hrsg. v. Michael BORGOLTE. München, Oldenbourg, 95, 520 p. (Historische Zs. Beih., 20). [Cf. n[os] <Auswahl> 573, 668.]

661. MORSEY (R.). Gründung und Gründer der Kommission für Zeitgeschichte 1960–1962. *Historisches Jahrbuch*, 95, 115, p. 453-485.

662. MUCCHIELLI (Laurent). Aux origines de la nouvelle histoire en France: l'évolution intellectuelle et la formation du champ des sciences sociales (1880–1930). *Revue de synthèse*, 95, 116, 1, p. 55-98.

663. MYERS (David N.). Re-inventing the Jewish past: European Jewish intellectuals and the Zionist return to history. New York a. Oxford, Oxford U. P., 95, VIII-278 p. (Studies in Jewish history).

664. Narrativa cristiana antica (La): codici narrativi, strutture formali, schemi retorici: XXIII incontro di studiosi della antichità cristiana, 5–7 maggio 1994. Roma, Institutum Patristicum "Augustinianum", 95, 666 p. (Studia ephemeridis "Augustinianum", 50).

665. NELSON Limerick (Patricia). Turnerians all: the dream of a helpful history in an intelligible world. *American Historical Review*, 95, 100, 3, p. 697-716.

666. NGALAMULUME (Kalala). Mythe, politique et histoire: le mythe de Mande Katawa chez les "Luluwa" du Kasayi. *History in Africa*, 95, 22, p. 329-347.

667. NIEDERHAUSER (Emil). A történetírás története Kelet-Európában. (Histoire de l'historiographie en Eu-

2. GESCHICHTE DER GESCHICHTSWISSENSCHAFT

rope Orientale). Budapest, História-MTA Történettud. Int., 95, 696 p. (História könyvtár, monográfiák, 6).

668. OEXLE (Otto G.). Was deutsche Mediävisten an der französischen Mittelalterforschung interessieren muß. *In*: Mittelalterforschung nach der Wende 1989 [Cf. n° 660], p. 89-128.

669. OLDRINI (Guido). Le noyau humaniste de l'historiographie au XVIe siècle. *Corpus*, 95, 28, p. 27-41.

670. Oliveira Martins: e os criticos da historia de Portugal. Lisboa, Ministerio da Cultura, Instituto da Biblioteca Nacional e do Livro, 95, 87 p.

671. OMOSINI (Olufemi). Evolution of African historiography: an overview. Ile-Ife, Obafemi Awolowo U. P., 95, 21 p. (Inaugural lecture series, 97).

672. OTÁHAL (Milan). K některým otázkám dějin »normalizace«. (Some questions concerning the history of 'Normalization'). *Soudobé dějiny*, 95, 2, 1, p. 5-16.

673. PARADISO (Annalisa). Perrot d'Ablancourt, Marivaux, Mably, Lévesque e le traduzioni tucididee tra Sei e Settecento. *Quaderni di storia*, 95, 21, 41, p. 115-128. – IDEM. Tempo della tradizione, tempo dello storico: Thuc. I. 18 e la storia arcaica spartana. *Storia della Storiografia*, 95, 28, p. 35-46.

674. PARRY (Graham). The trophies of time: English antiquarians of the seventeenth century. Oxford, Oxford U. P., 95, VIII-382 p. (ill., ports.).

675. PASTOR (Rodolfo F.). De moros en la costa a negros de Castilla: representación y realidad en las crónicas del siglo XVII centroamericano. *Historia Mexicana*, 94-95, 44, p. 195-235.

676. PENALVER CASTILLO (Manuel). La escuela de Menendez Pidal y la historiografía linguistica hispánica: aproximación a su estudio. Almeria, Universidad de Almeria, 95, 152 p. (Coleccion Humanidades. Monografias, 9).

677. PETER (Jürgen). Der Historikerstreit und die Suche nach einer nationalen Identität der achtziger Jahre. Frankfurt am Main, Peter Lang, 95, 260 p. (Europäische Hochschulschriften. R. 31, 288).

678. PETERS (Edward). Jewish history and gentile memory: the expulsion of 1492. *Jewish History*, 95, 9, 1, p. 9-34.

679. PETRALIA (Giuseppe). A proposito dell'immortalità di «Maometto e Carlomagno» (o di Costantino). *Storica*, 95, 1, 1, p. 37-88.

680. PEZZINO (Paolo). L'oggetto misterioso: Mezzogiorno d'Italia e revisionismo storiografico. *Società e storia*, 95, 18, p. 373-384.

681. PICCIRILLI (Luigi). Questioni tucididee II. *Quaderni di storia*, 95, 21, 42, p. 65-80.

682. PICK (Daniel). Freud's group psychology and the history of the crowd. *History Workshop*, 95, 40, p. 39-62.

683. PIZARRO (Joaquin Martinez). Writing Ravenna: the Liber pontificalis of Andreas Agnellus. Ann Arbor, University of Michigan Press, 95, X-213 p. (Recentiores: later Latin texts and contexts).

684. REMENSNYDER (Amy Goodrich). Remembering kings past: monastic foundation legends in medieval southern France. Ithaca, Cornell U. P., 95, XIII-355 p.

685. Rethinking the African cultural script: an overview of African historiography. Ed. by Bassey W. ANDAH. Ibadan, West African Journal of Archaeology, 95, VI-188 p. (African peoples and their cultural resources series, 3).

686. REUSSE (F.). Das Denkmal an der Grenze seiner Sprachfähigkeit. Stuttgart, Klett-Cotta, 95, 389 p.

687. RITTER (Gerhard Albert). Der Umbruch von 1989/91 und die Geschichtswissenschaft. München, Verlag der Bayerischen Akademie der Wissenschaften, in Kommission bei der C. H. Beck'schen Verlagsbuchhandlung, 95, 46 p. (Bayerische Akademie der Wissenschaften. Philosophisch-Historische Klasse, Jg. 1995, Heft 5).

688. ROFFE (David). The Historya Croylandensis: a plea for reassessment. *English Historical Review*, 95, 110, 435, p. 93-108.

689. ROMANO (Andrea). Tra «società» e «patria»: la storia dell'Armata Rossa nei recenti studi russo-sovietici. *Società e storia*, 95, 18, p. 853-868.

690. ROMERO (Federico). L'Europa come strumento di nation building: storia e storici dell'Italia contemporanea. *Passato e presente*, 95, 13, 36, p. 19-32.

691. ROSELLI (Lucia). Origini e vicende dell'archivio del monastero di Santa Maria di Vallombrosa. *In*: Studi in onore di Arnaldo D'Addario [Cf. n° 452], p. 219-235.

692. ROSS (Dorothy). Grand narrative in American historical writing: from romance to uncertainty. *American Historical Review*, 95, 100, 3, p. 651-677.

693. ROSSIAUD (Jacques). Du récit judiciaire à l'histoire. Essai sur le 'Tractatus de bellis et induciis ...' et la préhistoire municipale de Lyon. *In*: Comprendre le XIIIe siècle [Cf. n° 3965], p. 73-83.

694. ROWSE (Alfred Leslie). Historians I have known. London, Duckworth, 95, IX-208 p.

695. RUIZ GOMEZ (Francisco). La historia reclama el "habeas corpus". a proposito de varias publicaciones recientes sobre la historia del cuerpo. *Hispania*, 95, 55, 190, p. 711-725.

696. SABROW (Martin). Schwierigkeiten mit der Historisierung. Die DDR-Geschichtswissenschaft als Forschungsgegenstand. *In*: Historische Forschung und sozialistische Diktatur [Cf. n° 603], p. 9-28.

697. SAHLINS (Marshall David). How "natives" think: about Captain Cook, for example. Chicago, University of Chicago Press, 95, X-318 p.

698. SALOMONI (Antonella). Ideologia e congiuntura. Modelli storiografici sovietici del «comunismo di guerra». *Società e storia*, 95, 18, p. 869-895.

699. SANTOMASSIMO (Gianpasquale). Gli storici italiani tra fascismo e repubblica. *Italia contemporanea*, 95, 198, p. 77-89.

700. SCHLICH (Thomas). How gods and saints became transplant surgeons: the scientific article as a model for the writing of history. *History of science*, 95, 33, p. 311-331.

701. SCHÖTTLER (Peter). Rec. di B. and M. LYON (eds), The Birth of Annales History (1991). *Revue Belge de Philologie et d'Histoire*, 95, 73, p. 1040-1044. – IDEM. The Rhine in Franco-German historiography, 1918–1939. *History Workshop*, 95, 39, p. 1-22.

702. SCHULTZ (Helga). Das Fiasko der historischen Gerechtigkeit. Ostdeutsche Geisteswissenschaften im Umbruch. *Geschichte und Gesellschaft*, 95, 21, 3, p. 430-439.

703. SHORE (Marlene). "Remember the future": the Canadian Historical Review and the discipline of history, 1920–1995. *Canadian Historical Review*, 95, 76, 1, p. 410-463.

704. SŁOCZYŃSKI (Henryk). Z dziejów czarnej legendy krakowskiej historiografii konserwatywnej. Józef Szujski w opiniach współczesnych i potomnych. (De l'histoire de la légende noire relative à l'historiographie conservatrice cracovienne. Józef Szujski dans les opinions des ses contemporains et de leurs descendants). *Kwartalnik Historyczny*, 95, 102, 3-4, p. 209-244. [Eng. Summary].

705. SMITH (Bonnie G.). Gender and the practices of scientific history: the seminar and archival research in the nineteenth century. *American Historical Review*, 95, 100, 4, p. 1150-1176.

706. SPARR (Martin). Tysk historieforskning 1980–1994. en kortfattad översikt. (The German historical studies 1980–1994. A short review). *Historisk Tidskrift* (Sweden), 95, 1, p. 54-66.

707. ŠPĚT (Jiří). Po stu letech. K výročí Českého časopisu historického. (Nach 100 Jahren: Zum Jahrestag der Tschechischen historischen Zeitschrift). *Český časopis historický*, 95, 93, 1, p. 3-24.

708. STADLER (Peter). Memoiren der Neuzeit. Betrachtungen zur erinnerten Geschichte. Zürich, Neue Zürcher Zeitung, 95, 347 p.

709. STAPLETON (Timothy J.). Oral evidence in a pseudo-ethnicity: the Fingo debate. *History in Africa*, 95, 22, p. 359-368.

710. STERN (Fritz). Les historiens et la Grande Guerre. Vécu personnel, écrits publics. *Cahiers Marc Bloch*, 95, 3, p. 29-45.

711. STURM (Peter). Literaturwissenschaft im Dritten Reich: germanistische Wissensformationen und politisches System. Wien, Edition Praesens, 95, 298 p.

712. TEMIMI (Abdeljelil). Travaux en langue arabe d'histoire morisque: un premier bilan. *Revue d'Histoire Maghrebine*, 95, 77-78, p. 157-162.

713. THAPAR (Romila). L'histoire de Rama. L'élaboration continue d'une tradition écrite. *In*: Usages de la tradition [Cf. n° 718], p. 143-170.

714. THOROCZKAY (Gábor). Az Anonymus-kérdés ktatásának történeti áttekintése. (Vue historique des recherches concernant la question d'Anonymus [chroniqueur]). *Fons*, 94, 1, 2, p. 93-149 et 95, 2, 2, p. 117-173.

715. TRAMPUS (Antonio). Il cammino della democrazia e la società tedesca di fine Settecento: orientamenti storiografici recenti. *Storia della Storiografia*, 95, 27, p. 91-119.

716. TURTOLA (Martti), RAUNIO (Ari). Katsaus poliittiseen ja sotahistoriaan liittyviin tutkimuksiin ja kirjoituksiin. (A survey of Finnish political and military historical writings). *Sotahist. aik.* 95, 14, p. 260-272.

717. Uniting the Kingdom? The making of British history. Ed. by Alexander GRANT and Keith J. STRINGER. London a. New York, Routledge, 95, VI-310 p.

718. Usages de la tradition. *Enquête*, 95, 2, 233 p. [Cf. n°ˢ <sélection> 532, 538, 539, 552, 575, 604, 646, 713, 864.]

719. Uso pubblico della storia (L'). Relazioni presentate al Convegno dell'Istituto romano per la storia d'Italia dal fascismo alla Resistenza, Roma, 1–3 marzo 1993. A cura di N. GALLERANO. Milano, Angeli, 95, 239 p.

720. VALENSI (Lucette). Histoire nationale, histoire monumentale. 'Les Lieux de mémoire' (note critique). *Annales*, 95, 50, 6, p. 1271-1278.

721. VAN ARK (Bart). Towards European historical national accounts. *Scandinavian Economic History Review*, 95, 43, 1, p. 3-16.

722. VERA (Domenico). «Storia di Roma»: note conclusive. *Rivista storica italiana*, 95, 107, 2, p. 478-494.

723. VICIANO (P.). La temptaciò de la memòria. Valencia, E. Climent, 95, 221 p. («la unitat», 162).

724. VILANOVA (Mercedes). International oral history. *History Workshop*, 95, 39, p. 67-70.

725. VISCEGLIA (Maria Antonietta). Burocrazia, mobilità sociale e patronage alla corte di Roma tra Cinque e Seicento. Alcuni aspetti del recente dibattito storiografico e prospettive di ricerca. *Roma moderna e contemporanea*, 95, 3, p. 11-55.

726. Vision and textuality. Ed. by Stephen MELVILLE and Bill READINGS. Basingstoke, Macmillan, 95, XVIII-391p.

727. WALDENBERG (Marek), ŚLIWA (Michał). I conti con il passato: la storiografia polacca contemporanea. *Passato e presente*, 95, 13, 34, p. 101-112.

728. WALLIS (Faith). The ambiguities of medieval "Memoria". *Canadian Journal of History*, 95, 30, 1, p. 77-84.

729. WANG (Qinjia E.). Time in history and tide of history: an ancient Chinese view. *Storia della Storiografia*, 95, 28, p. 69-86.

730. WEGELER (Cornelia). "... wir sagen ab der internationalen Gelehrtenrepublik". Altertumswissenschaft und Nationalsozialismus. Das Göttinger Institut für Altertumskunde 1921–1962. Wien, Köln u. Weimar, Böhlau, 95, 442 p.

731. WERNER (Karl Ferdinand). Marc Bloch und die Anfänge einer europäischen Geschichtsforschung. Praef. Kurt-Ulrich JÄSCHKE. Saarbrücken, Universität des Saarlandes, 95, 47 p. (Saarbrücker Universitätsreden, 38).

732. WHITELAM (Keith W.). The invention of ancient Israel: the silencing of Palestinian history. New York, Routledge, 95, VIII-281 p.

733. WOLF (K. B.). Making history. The Normans and their historians in XIth-cent. Italy. Philadelphia, University of Pennsylvania Press, 95, XIII-192 p.

734. WOOD (Gordon S.). A century of writing early American hstory: then and now compared; or how Henry Adams got it wrong. *American Historical Review*, 95, 100, 3, p. 678-696.

735. WREGLESWORTH (John). The Chronicle of Alfonso III and its significance for the historiography of the Asturian kingdom, 718–910 AD: a critical study of the content, purpose and themes of a late 9th-century historical text. Leeds, [s. n.], 95, VII-520 leaves

736. Zeitgeschehen und seine Darstellung im Mittelalter = L'actualité et sa représentation au Moyen Age. Hrsg. v. Christoph CORMEAU. Bonn, Bouvier, 95, 259 p. (Studium universale, 20).

737. ZHANG (Yisbeng). Les réunions du samedi à Strasbourg et la genèse des Annales. *Raison présente*, 95, 113, p. 93-112.

738. ZINGEL (Michael). Frankreich, das Reich und Burgund im Urteil der burgundischen Historiographie des 15. Jahrhunderts. (Vorträge und Forschungen. Sonderband, 40). Sigmaringen, Thorbecke, 95, 258 p.

Cf. n°s 171, 190, 259-269, 487, 1277, 2781, 2803, 2815, 2888, 3121, 3159, 3271, 3272, 3279, 3298, 3303, 3304, 3318, 3330, 3587, 4174, 4374, 8992

b. Spezialarbeiten.

739. LANDES (Richard). Relics, apocalypse and the deceits of history **Adémar of [de] Chabanne**s, 989–1034. Cambridge, Harvard U. P., 95, XII-404 p. (ill.). (Harvard Historical studies, 117).

740. AGRIPPA D'AUBIGNE. Histoire universelle. T. 9. 1594–1602. Ed. par André THIERRY. Genève, Droz, 95, 434 p. (TLF, 458). – BANDERIER (Gilles). L'image de l'Espagne dans l'Histoire universelle d'**Agrippa d'Aubigné**. *Estudios de Investigación franco-española*, 95, 12, p. 143-156.

741. GIARRIZZO (Giuseppe). La Sicilia di Michele **Amari** (1806–1889). *In*: Per una storia della storiografia europea [Cf. n° 589], p. 77-90.

742. VALENSI (Lucette). Eloge de l'Orient, éloge de l'Orientalisme. Le jeu d'echecs d'**Anquetil-Duperron**. *Revue de l'histoire des religions*, 95, 212, 4, p. 419-452.

743. BISCIONE (Michele). Note in margine. I. **Antoni**, Chabod e Momigliano. II. Il carteggio Croce-**Antoni**. *Rivista di storia della storiografia moderna*, 95, 16, 1-3, p. 7-38.

744. FLOTO (Inga). Venskab. Korrespondancen mellem Erik Arup og Lauritz Weibull. (Friendship. The Correspondence between Erik Arup and Lauritz Weibull). *Historisk Tidskrift* (Denmark), 95, 95, 2, p. 241-296. – SVENSTRUP (Thyge). Erik **Arup** og Brooks Adams. Et bidrag til Arups historie- og metodesyn. (Erik Arup and Brooks Adams. Towards an understanding of Arup's concept of history and methodology). *Historisk Tidskrift* (Denmark), 95, 95, 1, p. 1-21. – IDEM. Erik **Arup**s syn på Danmarks forsvar. (Erik Arups view of Denmark's defence). *Historisk Tidskrift* (Denmark), 95, 95, 2, p. 298-325.

745. FALOLA (Toyin). T. O. **Avoseh** on the history of Epe and its environs. *History in Africa*, 95, 22, p. 165-195.

746. **Bakhtin**ologiia: issledovaniia, perevody, publikatsii. Redaktsionaia kollegiia, A. P. VALITSKAIA [et al.]. Sankt-Peterburg, "Aleteiia", 95, 370 p. (Problemy bakhtinologii). – BOOKER (M. Keith), JURAGA (Dubravka). **Bakhtin**, Stalin, and modern Russian fiction: carnival, dialogism, and history. Westport, Greenwood Press, 95, XIV-181 p. (Contributions to the study of world literature, 58). – DENTITH (Simon). **Bakhtin**ian thought: an introductory reader. London a. New York, Routledge, 95, XV-265 p. (Critical readers in theory and practice). – FARRELL (Thomas J.). **Bakhtin** and medieval voices. Gainesville, University Press of Florida, 95, 240 p. – HAYNES (Deborah J). **Bakhtin** (Mikhail Mikhailovich), and the visual arts. Cambridge a. New York, Cambridge U. P., 95, XVI-217 p. (ill.). (Cambridge studies in new art history and criticism). – M. M. **Bakhtin** v zerkale kritiki: sbornik. (Bibliography and chronology of M. M. Bakhtin). Otvetstvennyi redaktor i sostavitel' T. G. IURCHENKO. Moskva, Rossiiskaia akademiia nauk, In-t nauchnoi informatsii po obshchestvennym naukam, 95, 191 p.

747. DEMENT'EV (Igor'P.). Čarl'z Ostin Bird (1874–1948) (Charles Ostin Beard. 1874–1948). *Nov. novejš. Ist.* , 95, 3, p. 180-197.

748. RUDOLPH (Kurt). In memoriam Ugo **Bianchi**. *Numen*, 95, 42, 3, p. 225-227.

749. Bibliographie des travaux sur Marc **Bloch**, 1944–1994. *Cahiers Marc Bloch*, 95, 2, p. 25-37; 3,

p. 109. – BLOCH (Marc). Histoire et historiens. Textes réunis par Etienne BLOCH. Paris, Armand Colin, 95, 278 p. – IDEM. Version française de The rise of dependent cultivation and seignorial institutions [de Marc **Bloch**]. Etablie par Etienne BLOCH et présentée par Emmanuel LE ROY LADURIE. *Cahiers Marc Bloch*, 95, 3, p. 47-106. – FINK (Carole). Marc Bloch (1886–1944). *In*: Medieval scholarship. Vol. 1 [Cf. n° 652], p. 205-217. – MASTROGREGORI (Massimo). Il manoscritto interrotto di Marc **Bloch**. Apologia della storia o Mestiere di storico. Pisa e Roma, Istituti editoriali poligrafici internazionali, 95, 139 p. (Piste, 1). – Propos (A) de La Société féodale [de Marc **Bloch**]. *Cahiers Marc Bloch*, 95, 2, p. 15-23. – RAULFF (Ulrich). Ein Historiker im 20. Jahrhundert: Marc **Bloch**. Frankfurt am Main, S. Fischer, 95, 510 p. – SCHÖTTLER (Peter). Marc **Bloch** et Lucien Febvre face à l'Allemagne nazie. *Genèses*, 95, 21, p. 75-95.

750. DAIX (Pierre). **Braudel**. Paris, Flammarion, 95, 567 p. (ill.). (Grandes biographies). – LAI (Cheng-Chung). Second thoughts on Fernand **Braudel**'s civilization and capitalism. *Journal of European economic history*, 95, 24, 1, p. 177-193. – ROMANO (Ruggiero). Un protagoniste de notre siècle: Fernand **Braudel**. *Cahiers Vilfredo Pareto*, 95, 33, 100, p. 127-147.

751. FLORKOWSKA-FRANČIĆ (Halina). Profesor Andrzej **Brożek** (1933–1994) jako badacz problematyki polonijnej. (Le Professeur Andrzej Brożek en tant que chercheur dans le domaine de la problématique de la diaspora polonaise.). *Historyka*, 95, 25, p. 99-107.

752. FIEL (A.). Un manoscritto di lettere del primo cancellierato di Leonardo **Bruni**. *Archivio Storico Italiano*, 95, 3, p. p. 573-575.

753. BRENNAN (Brian). **Burckhardt** and Ranke on the age of Constantine the Great. *Quaderni di storia*, 95, 21, 41, p. 53-66. – COHN (Samuel K.). **Burckhardt** revisited from social history. *In*: Language and images of Renaissance Italy [Cf. n° 6023], 217-234. – SAMMER (Marianne). Intuitive Geschichtsschreibung. Ein Versuch zum Verhältnis von Geschichtsdenken und kulturhistorischer Methode bei Jacob **Burckhardt**. München, Tuduv Verlagsges, 95, 144 p. (Kulturgeschichtliche Forschungen, 19).

754. SIMONCELLI (Paolo). Note **cantimoriane**. *Storia contemporanea*, 95, 26, 1, p. 57-74.

755. FUMAROLI (Marc). Le comte de **Caylus** et l'Académie des Inscriptions. *Académie des Inscriptions et Belles-Lettres. Comptes rendus*, 95, 1, p. 225-250.

756. BERGER (Guy). **Chateaubriand** face à l'histoire. *In*: Histoire au XIXe siècle (L') [Cf. n° 599], p. 283-303.

757. CAPPI (D.). Del Lungo editore di Dino **Compagni**: il problema del testo della «Cronica». Roma, Istituto storico italiano per il Medio Evo, 95, XIX-97 p.

758. DE ROSA (Gabriele). **Cornelio Fabro** fra S. Tommaso, Kirkegaard e la morte di Pompei. *Ricerche di storia sociale e religiosa*, 95, 48, p. 165-170.

759. CUTINELLI-RÈNDINA (Emanuele). Benedetto **Croce** e l'edizione del proprio carteggio con Karl Vossler. *La cultura*, 95, 33, 2, p. 307-321. – GARIN (E.). Conversando con B. **Croce**. *Belfagor*, 95, 6, p. 649-656. – IMBRUGLIA (G.). Filosofia e storiografia nell'Illuminismo da **Croce** a Venturi. *Belfagor*, 95, 4, p. 397-410. – LUPO (S.). **Croce**, Volpe e l'Italia liberale. *Storica*, 95, 1, p. 11-37.

760. INGROSSO (Lorella). Bibliografia di Arnaldo **D'Addario**. *In*: Studi in onore di Arnaldo D'Addario [Cf. n° 452], p. XIX-XXVII.

761. VISSER (R.). Pietro **de Francisci**'s idee van de «romanità» als cryptofascistische filosofie van de geschiedenis. *Theoretische geschiedenis*, 95, 22, p. 472-497.

762. GOICHOT (Emile). Don Giuseppe **De Luca** et l'histoire de la piété. *Ricerche di storia sociale e religiosa*, 95, 24, 48, p. 91-111.

763. SAINT-ROCH (Patrick). Correspondence de Giovanni Battista **De Rossi** et de Louis Duchesne (1873–1894). Roma, Ecole française de Rome, 95, 731 p. (Collection de l'Ecole française de Rome, 205).

764. Diario segreto (Il) di Gaetano **De Sanctis** (1917–1933). A cura di Silvio ACCAME. *Nuova Antologia*, 95, 130, 2193-2194, p. 263-296, p. 319-347.

765. BATES (David). Léopold **Delisle** (1826–1910). *In*: Medieval scholarship. Vol. 1 [Cf. n° 652], p. 101-113.

766. TRAINA (Giusto). Un testimone armeno sulla fortuna di **Diodoro**. *Quaderni di storia*, 95, 21, 42, p. 81-88.

767. KUČKIN (Vladimir A.). Dmitry **Donskoj**. *Vopr. Ist.*, 95, 5/6, p. 62-83.

768. GIARRIZZO (Giuseppe). Rileggere J. G. **Droysen** (1808–1884). *In*: Per una storia della storiografia europea [Cf. n° 589], p. 91-114. – SOUTHARD (Robert). **Droysen** and the Prussian school of history. Lexington, University Press of Kentucky, 95. VIII-247 p.

769. BOYER (Régis). Relire **Dumézil**. *Mediaevistik*, 95, 8, p. 13-25.

770. BOLGANI (Franco). Alcune osservazioni su «il presente cattolico» di Alphonse **Dupront**. *Rivista di storia e letteratura religiosa*, 95, 31, 2, p. 271-291.

771. SERRA (Enrico). Jean-Baptiste **Duroselle**. *Rivista storica italiana*, 95, 107, 1, p. 110-118.

772. JÄGER (Wolfgang). "Menschenwissenschaft" und historische Sozialwissenschaft. Zur Rezeption von Norbert **Elias**. *Archiv für Kulturgeschichte*, 95, 77, p. 85-116. – KOCKA (Jürgen). "Über den Prozeß der Zivilisation". Norbert **Elias** als Historiker. *In*: Konflikt und Reform. Festschrift Berding [Cf. n° 4624], p. 329-337.

773. TORTORELLI (Gianfranco). Lettere di Giorgio **Falco** ad Angelo Fortunato Formiggini e la sua collaborazione a «L'Italia che scrive». *Archivio storico italiano*, 95, 153, 563, p. 83-138.

2. GESCHICHTE DER GESCHICHTSWISSENSCHAFT

774. PELOSI (Hebe Carmen). La conyuntura enciclopedica del periodo entreguerras. El modelo de Lucien **Febvre**. *Rivista di storia della storiografia moderna*, 95, 16, 1-3, p. 97-116. – WESSEL (Marleen). Geschiedenis en sociale verantwoordelijkheid: de controverse rond Lucien **Febvre**. *Theoretische geschiedenis*, 95, 22, p. 241-253. – EADEM. Les «combats pour l'histoire» de Lucien **Febvre**: une relecture. *Rivista di storia della storiografia moderna*, 95, 16, 1-3, p. 75-96.

775. ANDREAU (Jean). Présentation: Vingt ans après 'L'Economie antique' de Moses I. **Finley**. *Annales*, 95, 50, 5, p. 947-960. – DESCAT (Raymond). 'L'Economie antique' [de Moses I. **Finley**] et la cité grecque. Un modèle en question. *Annales*, 95, 50, 5, p. 961-990.

776. SEMENČENKO (L. V.). Predstavlenie o vmešatel'stve božestva v khod voennykh dejstvij v "Iudejskikh drevnostjakh" iosifa Flavija. (The concept of divine interference in the course of hostilities in "The Jewish antiquities" by **Flavius Josephus**). *Vestn. drev. Ist.* , 95, 3, p. 173-180.

777. KELLEY (Donald). Robert **Flint** historian of ideas. *Storia della Storiografia*, 95, 27, p. 39-62.

778. Nicolas **Fréret**. Textes et documents réunis par Catherine VOLPILHAC-AUGER. *Corpus*, 95, 29, p. 7-163.

779. DIESENER (Gerald). Die schwierige Nachfolge. Hans **Freyer** als Direktor des Instituts für Universal- und Kulturgeschichte. *Archiv für Kulturgeschichte*, 77, p. 117-134.

780. NEEDELL (Jeffrey D.). Identity, race, gender, and modernity in the origins of Gilberto **Freyre**'s oeuvre. *American Historical Review*, 95, 100, 1, p. 51-77.

781. COLLARD (F.). Formes du récit et langue historique dans le Compendium de origine et gestis Francorum de R. **Gaguin**. *Bibliothèque d'Humanisme et Renaissance*, 95, 57, 1, p. 67-82. – COLLARD (Franck). Dates et datations dans le Compendium de origine et gestis Francorum de Robert **Gaguin** (1493). *Studi francesi*, 95, 39, 117, p. 443-455.

782. BIANCHI (Paola). Peter **Gay** e l'Illuminismo. Philosophes e modernità nel laboratorio di uno «storico sociale delle idee». *Rivista storica italiana*, 95, 107, 3, p. 727-830.

783. MORO (Renato). Religione e politica nell'età della secolarizzazione: riflessioni su di un recente volume di Emilio **Gentile**. *Storia contemporanea*, 95, 26, 2, p. 255-328.

784. CLAUSI (B.). Storia sacra e strategia retorica. Osservazioni sull'uso dell'"exemplum" biblico nell'Adversus Iovinianum di **Gerolamo**. *Cristianesimo nella storia*, 95, 16, 3, p. 457-484.

785. WAGNER (Jonathan F.). Germany's 19th century Cassandra. The liberal federalist Georg Gottfried **Gervinus**. Frankfurt am Main, Peter Lang, 95, 180 p. (American University studies, 9, 175).

786. PORTER (Roy). **Gibbon**: making history. London, Phoenix Giants, 95, X-187 p.

787. W kręgu badań Profesora Stanisława Gierszewskiego [1929–1993] Sesja naukowa poświęcona pamięci Profesora Stanisława Gierszewskiego. (Dans le cercle des recherches au Professeur Stanisław **Gierszewski** [1929–1993]. Session scientifique en hommage au Professeur Stanisław **Gierszewski**). Réd. Andrzej GROTH. Gdańsk, Marpress, 95, 199 p.

788. ZIMMERMANN (T. C. Price). Paolo **Giovio**: the historian and the crisis of sixteenth-century Italy. Princeton a. Chichester, Princeton U. P., 95, XII-391 p.

789. VEENSTRA (Jan R.). The new historicism of Stephen **Greenblatt**: on poetics of culture and the interpretation of Shakespeare. *History and Theory*, 95, 34, 3, p. 174-198.

790. DE NIE (Giselle). Die Sprache im Wunder – das Wunder in der Sprache. Menschenwort und Logos bei **Gregor von Tours**. *Mitteilungen des Instituts für Österreichische Geschichtsforschung*, 95, 103, 1-2, p. 1-25. – HEN (Y.). **Gregory of Tours** and the Holy Land. *Orientalia christiana periodica*, 95, 61 p. 47-64.

791. CHEDOZEAU (B.). Le P. **Hardouin** et le refus du rationalisme en religion. Une reconstruction ultramontaine de l'histoire? *Revue des sciences philosophiques et théologiques*, 95, 79, p. 249-281.

792. WEILL (Claudie). L'eredità scientifica di Georges **Haupt**. *Passato e presente*, 95, 13, 36, p. 85-92.

793. JORDAN (Stefan). G. W. F. **Hegels** Einfluß auf das philologische und altertumswissenschaftliche Schaffen J. G. Droysens. *Jb. für Hegelforschung*, 95, 1, p. 141-155.

794. PEARCE (Mark), GABBA (Emilio). Dalle terremare a Roma: Wolfgang **Helbig** e la teoria delle origini degli italici. *Rivista storica italiana*, 95, 107, 1, p. 119-132.

795. HEUSS (Alfred). Gesammelte Schriften in drei Bänden. 1. Griechische Geschichte, griechische und römische Geschichte, Weltgeschichte. 2. Römische Geschichte. 3. Wissenschaftsgeschichte und Theorie, Völkerrecht, Universitäts- und Schulreform. Stuttgart, Steiner, 95, IX-2720 p.

796. HUIZINGA (Johan). De taak der cultuurgeschiedenis. Samengesteld, verzorgd en van een nawoord voorzien door W. E. KRUL. Groningen, Historische Uitgeverij, 95, 348 p. – NAUTA (L.). **Huizinga**'s Lente der Middeleeuwen. De plaats van de XII[de]-eeuwse geschiedenis in Nederland. *Tijdschrift voor geschiedenis*, 95, 108, p. 3-23.

797. EFIMOV (Nikolaj A.). Sergej Mironovich **Kirov**. *Vopr. Ist.* , 95, 11/12, p. 49-67.

798. BYRNES (Robert Francis). V.O. **Kliuchevskii**, historian of Russia. Bloomington, Indiana U. P., 95, XXI-301 p.

799. DUSIŃSKA (Halina). Stanisław **Konopka** 1896–1982. Zarys monograficzny. (Stanisław Konopka 1896–1982. Esquisse monographique). Warszawa, Gł. Bibl. Lekarska, 95, 363 p.

800. PATRUŠEV (Aleksandr I.). Vzlet o nizverženie Karla Lamprekhta (1865–1915). (The flight and overthrow of Karl **Lamprecht**. 1865–1915). *Nov. novejš. Ist.*, 95, 4, p. 179-193. – STEINLE (Jürgen). Geschichtsmethode und -politik bei Karl **Lamprecht**. *Archiv für Kulturgeschichte*, 95, 77, p. 405-428.

801. COMPAGNON (Antoine). Deux absences remarquables en 1894: Brunetière, **Lanson** et la fondation de la 'Revue d'histoire littéraire de la France'. *In*: Histoire littéraire hier (L'), aujourd'hui et demain, ici et ailleurs [Cf. n° 1544], p. 29-53.

802. ARIS (Rutherford). Jean **Mabillon**, 1632–1707. *In*: Medieval scholarship. Vol. 1 [Cf. n° 652], p. 15-32.

803. RIEKS (Rudolf). Livius und **Machiavelli**. Prinzipien historischen Denkens und politischen Handelns. *Gymnasium*, 95, 102, p. 305-333.

804. KÜMIN (Beat). "How good Gierke is!" Frederic William **Maitland** in seinem europäischen Kontext. Ausschnitte aus einer akademischen Korrespondenz der Jahrhundertwende. *Zeitschrift für Neuere Rechtsgeschichte*, 95, 17, 3-4, p. 268-282. – MAITLAND (Frederic William). The letters of Frederic William **Maitland**. Vol. 2. Ed. for the Selden Society by P. N. R. ZUTSHI. London, Selden Society, 95, XXII-306 p. (Supplementary series, 11).

805. CIZEK (E.). La poétique de l'histoire chez Ammien **Marcellin**. *Bollettino di Studi Latini*, 95, 25, p. 550-564.

806. MARROU (Henri-Irenée). Tristesse de l'historien [article d'H.-I. **Marrou** dans l'Esprit, 1er avril 1939]. *XXe siècle*, 95, 45, p. 109-131.

807. GIARRIZZO (Giuseppe). Santo **Mazzarino**. Un maestro. *In*: Per una storia della storiografia europea [Cf. n° 589], p. 191-250.

808. MEINEKE (Stefan). Friedrich **Meinecke**. Persönlichkeit und politisches Denken bis zum Ende des ersten Weltkrieges. Berlin u. New York, de Gruyter, 95, XII-386 p. (Veröffentlichungen der historischen Kommission zu Berlin, 90).

809. BREUER (Edward). On miracles and events past: **Mendelssohn** on history. *Jewish History*, 95, 9, 2, p. 27-52.

810. LEHMANN (Gustav Adolf). Eduard **Meyer**, Oswald Spengler und die Epoche des Hellenismus. *Archiv für Kulturgeschichte*, 95, 77, p. 165-196.

811. MICHELET (Jules). Correspondance générale. Tome 3. 1839–1842. Tome 4. 1843–1845. Ed. par Louis LE GUILLOU. Paris, Champion, 95, 2 vol., 862 p., 982 p. – IDEM. Cours au Collège de France: 1838–1851. Tome 1. 1838–1844. Tome 2. 1845–1851. Publiés par Paul VIALLANEIX, avec la collaboration d'Oscar A. HAAC et d'Irene TIEDER. Paris, Gallimard, 95, 2 vol., [s. p.] (Bibliothèque des histoires). – TIEDER (Irène). **Michelet**, la tradition révolutionnaire et les Juifs. *Nouveaux cahiers*, 95, 120, p. 57-61. – VIALLANEIX (Paul). **Michelet**: le magistère de l'historien. *In*: Histoire au XIXe siècle (L') [Cf. n° 599], p. 247-264.

812. BOHN (Thomas). Russische Geschichtswissenschaft von 1880–1905. Pavel N. **Miljukov** und die "Moskauer Schule". Hamburg, Diss, 95, X-570 p.

813. CECCONI (Giovanni Alberto), LURAGHI (Nino), MARCONE (Arnaldo). Le «Sather Lectures» di Arnaldo **Momigliano**. Appunti per una discussione. *Storia della Storiografia*, 95, 27, p. 73-84. – FABRE (Giorgio). Arnaldo **Momigliano**: autobiografia scientifica (1936). *Quaderni di storia*, 95, 21, 41, p. 85-96. – GIARRIZZO (Giuseppe). Storia sacra, storia profana: per Arnaldo **Momigliano**. *In*: Per una storia della storiografia europea [Cf. n° 589], p. 155-174. – GRAFTON (Anthony). Arnaldo **Momigliano** e la storia degli studi classici. *Rivista storica italiana*, 95, 107, 1, p. 91-109.

814. BAJONI (M. G.). Due lettere inedite di Theodor **Mommsen**. *Italia medievale e umanistica*, 95, 38, p. 381-386. – DEMANDT (Alexander). **Mommsen** zum Niedergang Roms. *Historische Zeitschrift*, 95, 261, 1, p. 23-50. – IDEM. Theodor **Mommsen**. I Cesari e la decadenza di Roma. Prefazione di Carl NYLANDER; introduzione di Karl CHRIST. Roma, Unione internazionale degli istituti di archeologia storia e storia dell'arte di Roma, 95, 99 p. (ill.). (Conferenze, 12).

815. BIANCHI (Lorenzo). **Montesquieu** et Fréret: quelques notes. *Corpus*, 95, 29, p. 105-128. – BINOCHE (Bertrand). **Montesquieu** et la crise de la rationalité historique. *Revue germanique internationale*, 95, 3, p. 31-53. – MYERS (Richard). **Montesquieu** on the causes of Roman greatness. *History of political thought*, 95, 16, 1, p. 37-47.

816. POULOUIN (Claude). L'Antiquité expliquée et représentée en figures (1719–1724) par Bernard **de Montfaucon**. *XVIIIe siècle*, 95, 27, p. 43-60.

817. COTTIGNOLI (A.). Alla luce del vero. Studi sul **Muratori** storico. Bologna, Clueb, 95, 119 p.

818. COSTA (Milton Carlos). O historiador Joaquim **Nabuco** e a Guerra do Paraguai. *História*, 95, 14, p. 13-33.

819. GIARRIZZO (Giuseppe). Un caso: L. B. **Namier**. *In*: Per una storia della storiografia europea [Cf. n° 589], p. 175-190.

820. ALONSO-NUÑEZ (J. M.). Die Weltgeschichte des **Nikolaos von Damaskos**. *Storia della Storiografia*, 95, 27, p. 3-16.

821. BOSCA CODINA (José Vicente), [et al.]. José Trenchs **Òdena**: su contribución cientifica. *In*: Misc.lània d'estudis dedicats a la memòria de Professor Josep Trenchs i Òdena [Cf. n° 67], p. 37-50.

822. DURST (Margarete). Adolfo **Omodeo**, collaboratore della Enciclopedia Italiana di Scienze, Lettere e Arti. *Veltro*, 95, 39, 1-2, p. 147-156.

823. POLICHETTI (Antonio). Rassegna di studi **orosiani**. 2. *Koinonia*, 95, 19, p. 33-61.

824. LA ROCCA (Cristina). **Pacifico di Verona**: il passato carolingio nella costruzione della memoria urbana. Con una nota di Stefano ZAMPONI. Roma, Istituto storico italiano per il Medio Evo, 95, IX-263 p. (Nuovi studi storici. Istituto storico italiano per il Medio Evo, 31).

825. SUPPLE (James J.). Etienne **Pasquier** et les «mystères de Dieu». *Corpus*, 95, 28, p. 147-166.

826. CHANTRE (Benoît). **Péguy**, Révolution et histoire. *Amitié Charles Péguy*, 95, 18, 71, p. 144-167.

827. LEROY (B.). Un modèle de souverain au début du XVe siècle. Ferdinand d'Antequera, d'après les Chroniques de Castille de Fernan **Perez de Guzman**. *Revue Historique*, 95, 119, 596, p. 201-218.

828. ECKSTEIN (Arthur M.). Moral vision in the histories of **Polybius**. Berkeley, Los Angeles a. London, University of California Press, 95, 331 p.

829. TODD (Robert B.). [John] Enoch **Powell**'s classical scholarship: a bibliography. *Quaderni di storia*, 95, 21, 42, p. 9-96.

830. GARGALLO DI CASTEL LENTINI (Gioacchino). Letture di storici: dai Duchi di Borgogna di **Prosper de Barante** al moderno «narrativismo». *Rivista di storia della storiografia moderna*, 95, 16, 1-3, p. 39-52.

831. QUINET (Edgard). Lettres à sa mère. Tome 1. 1808-1820. Ed. par Simone BERNARD-GRIFFITHS et Gerard PEYLET. Paris, Champion, 95, 246 p. (ill.).

832. RENAN (Ernest). Correspondance générale. Tome 1. Enfance et jeunesse, 1836-1845. Ed. par Jean BALCOU. Paris, Champion, 95, 683 p. (ill.). – SALMERI (Giovanni). Del Marc Aurèle et la fin du monde antique de Ernest **Renan**. *Rivista di storia della storiografia moderna*, 95, 16, 1-3, p. 53-74.

833. SCARROCCHIA (S.). Alois **Riegl**: teoria e prassi della conservazione dei monumenti. Antologia di scritti, discorsi, rapporti 1898-1905. Bologna Accademia Clementina e Clueb, 95, 611 p.

834. BUSINO (Giovanni). Rosario **Romeo** tra storiografia ed impegno politico. *Rivista storica italiana*, 95, 107, 2, p. 387-477. – Rinnovamento della storiografia politica (II), studi in onore di R. **Romeo**. A cura di G. PESCOSOLIDO. Roma, Istituto della Enciclopedia italiana, 95, 210 p. [Con la bibliografia di R. Romeo, a cura di I. ROMEO]

835. BONGARD-LEVIN (G. M.). M. I. Rostovcev i I. I. Bikerman. (Novye arkhivnye materialy). (M. I. **Rostovtzeff** and E. Bickerman. New archival documents). *Vestn. Drev. Ist.*, 95, 4, p. 180-203. – SAPRYKIN (S. Ju.). Akademik M. I. Rostocev o Pontijskom i Bosporkom carstvakh v svete dostiženij sovremennogo antikovedenija. (Academician M. I. **Rostovtzeff** on the Pontus and Bosporus in the light of the achievements of contemporary classical studies). *Vestn. drev. Ist.*, 95, 1, p. 200-210.

836. POZZI (Regina). Armando **Saitta** storico della cultura francese dell'Ottocento. *In ricordo di Armando Saitta. Annuario dell'Istituto storico itaiano per l'Età moderna e contemporanea*, 95, 41-42, p. 139-171.

837. DE VIVO (A.). Piano narrativo e ideologia negli Annales di **Tacito**. *Bollettino di Studi Latini*, 95, 25, p. 576-584. – HIRSTEIN (James S.). **Tacitus'** Germania and Beatus Rhenanus, 1485-1547: a study of the editorial and exegetical contribution of a sixteenth century scholar. Frankfurt am Main a. New York, P. Lang, 95, 324 p. (Studien zur klassischen philologie, 91). – **Tacitus**: the classical heritage. Ed. by Ronald MELLOR. New York a. London, Garland Publishing, 95, 249 p. (Classical heritage series, 6. Garland reference library of the humanities, 1633).

838. TOMBS (Robert). **Thiers** historien. *In*: Histoire au XIXe siècle (L') [Cf. n° 599], p. 265-281.

839. BUTLER (Marilyn). Samples of the History Workshop conference of July 1994 **Thompson**'s second front. *History Workshop*, 95, 39, p. 71-78. – EASTWOOD (David). E. P. **Thompson**, Britain and Frech Revolution. *History Workshop*, 95, 39, p. 79-88. – PHILP (Mark). **Thompson**, Godwin and the French Revolution. *History Workshop*, 95, 39, p. 88-101.

840. MARVIN (Perry). Arnold **Toynbee** and the western tradition. Frankfurt am Main, Peter Lang, 95, 150 p. (American University studies, 5, 169).

841. LURAGHI (Nino). La tirannide siceliota nell'Archaiologia di **Tucidide**. *Quaderni di storia*, 95, 21, 42, p. 35-64. – SHRIMPTON (Gordon). Time, memory, and narrative in **Thucydides**. *Storia della Storiografia*, 95, 28, p. 47-54.

842. Franco **Venturi**: lettere da Mosca (1947-1948). A cura di Aldo AGOSTI e Giovanni DE LUNA. *Passato e presente*, 95, 13, 35, p. 97-110. – MANCA (Sergio). A proposito dell'Antichità svelata e l'idea del progresso in N.-A. Boulanger di Franco **Venturi**. *Studi storici*, 95, 36, 4, p. 1011-1021.

843. NEEDELL (Jeffrey D.). History, race, and the state in the thought of Oliveira **Viana**. *Hispanic American Historical Review*, 95, 75, 1, p. 1-30.

844. Inventaire **Voltaire**. Dir. par Jean GOULEMOT, André MAGNAN et Didier MASSEAU. Rév. gén. par André MAGNAN. Paris, Gallimard, 95, 1479 p.

845. GIARRIZZO (Giuseppe). Michel **Vovelle**: un saluto. *In*: Per una storia della storiografia europea [Cf. n° 589], p. 251-254.

846. BREUER (Stefan). Herrschaftsstruktur und städtischer Raum. Überlegungen im Anschluß an Max **Weber**. *Archiv für Kulturgeschichte*, 95, 77, p. 135-164. –

SCHRÖDER (Hans-Christoph). Max **Weber** und der Puritanismus. *Geschichte und Gesellschaft*, 95, 21, 4, p. 459-478.

847. LE VOT (Gérard). Paul **Zumthor** 1915–1995. *Heresis*, 95, 24, p. 1-8.

Cf. n^{os} *1984, 2055, 2272, 2310, 2338, 2475, 2536, 2538, 2548, 2549, 2553, 2559, 2568, 2618, 2750, 2789, 2800, 2805, 2929, 3288, 3302, 3333, 3382, 3558, 3931, 3934, 4362, 4409, 4518*

§ 3. Methodenlehre, Geschichtsphilosophie und Geschichtsunterricht.

848. ABU-LUGHOD (Janet). The world-system perspective in the construction of economic history. *History and Theory*, 95, 34, 2, p. 86-98.

849. Alfons Huber, Briefe (1859–1898). Ein Beitrag zur Geschichte der Innsbrucker Historischen Schule um Julius Ficker und Alfons Huber. Hrsg. v. Gerhard OBERKOFLER [u. a.]. Innsbruck u. Wien, Studien Vlg., 95, 578 p. (ill.).

850. ANGLET (Kurt). Messianität und Geschichte: Walter Benjamins Konstruktion der historischen Dialektik und deren Aufhebung ins Eschatologische durch Erik Peterson. Berlin, Akademie Verlag, 95, 322 p.

851. Ästhetik der Geschichte. Hrsg. v. Johann HOLZNER u. Wolfgang WIESMÜLLER. Innsbruck, Institut für Germanistik an der Universität Innsbruck, 95, 259 p. (Innsbrucker Beiträge zur Kulturwissenschaft. Germanistische Reihe, 54).

852. BAILYN (Bernard). Context in history. (North American studies Bernard Bailyn lecture, 1). Melbourne, La Trobe University, 95, 32 p.

853. BANN (Stephen). Romanticism and the rise of history. New York, Twayne Publishers a. Maxwell Macmillan International a. Toronto, Maxwell Macmillan Canada, 95, XIV-187 p. (Twayne's studies in intellectual and cultural history).

854. BARTOV (Omer). An idiot's tale: memories and histories of the Holocaust. *Journal of modern history*, 95, 67, 1, p. 55-82.

855. BATTISTINI (Andrea). La sapienza retorica di Giambattista Vico. Milano, Guerini, 95, 138 p. (Saggi. Istituto italiano per gli studi filosofici, 21).

856. BERGE (Anders). Att begripa det förflutna. Förklaring, klassificering, kolligation inom historievetenskapen. (To understand the past. Explanation, classification, in the historical science). Lund, Studentlitteratur, 95, 122 p.

857. BERMEJO BARRERA (José Carlos). El historiador, el silencio y el problema del mal: la historiographia como teodicea. *Quaderni di storia*, 95, 21, 42, p. 111-130.

858. BERNARD-GRIFFITHS (Simone). Histoire naturelle et histoire dans la philosophie d'Edgard Quinet. *In*: Histoire au XIXe siècle (L') [Cf. n° 599], p. 215-246.

859. BEVIR (Mark). Objectivity in history. *History and theory*, 95, 33, 3, p. 329-344.

860. BIDUSSA (David). Mito e storia in Furio Jesi. *Humanitas*, 95, 4, p. 585-602.

861. Bilder erzählen Geschichte. Hrsg. v. Helmut ALTRICHTER. Freiburg, Rombach, 95, 354 p. (Rombach Wisssenschaft. Reihe Historiae, 6).

862. BOURDIEU (Pierre). Sur les rapports entre la sociologie et l'histoire en Allemagne et en France. Entretiens avec Lutz Raphaël. *Actes de la recherche en sciences sociales*, 95, 106-107, p. 108-122.

863. BOUREAU (Alain). Histoire et psychologie. *In*: Historia a Debate. Tomo 3 [Cf. n° 602], p. 139-150.

864. BRIAN (Eric). Calepin. Repérage en vue d'une histoire réflexive de l'objectivation. *In*: Usages de la tradition [Cf. n° 718], p. 193-222.

865. BRINKS (J. H.). Einige Überlegungen zur politischen Instrumentalisierung Martin Luthers durch die deutsche Historiographie im 19. und 20. Jahrhundert. *Zeitgeschichte*, 95, 22, 7-8, p. 233-248.

866. CALLINICOS (Alex). Theories and narratives: reflections on the philosophy of history. Cambridge, Polity Press a. Durham, Duke U. P., 95, X-252 p. (Post-contemporary interventions).

867. CASTELLANI (Cecilia). Dalla cronologia alla metafisica della mente: saggio su Vico. Napoli, Societa Editrice il Mulino, 95, XVI-174 p. (Istituto italiano per gli studi storici, 38).

868. ČERNJAK (Efim. B.). Istorija i logika (Struktura istoričeskikh kategorij). (History and logic: the structure of historical categories). *Vopr. Ist.*, 95, 10, p. 29-43.

869. CETLIN (Ju. B.). Problemy naučnogo éksperimenta v izučenii drevnego gončarstva. (Problems of scientific experiments in the ancient pottery studies). *Ros. arkheol.*, 95, 2, p. 59-68.

870. Chaos theory and history revisited. [Contents: ROTH (Paul), RYCKMAN (Thomas). Chaos, Clio, and scientific illusions of understanding. – REISCH (George). Scientism without tears: a reply to Roth and Ryckmann. – SHERMER (Michael). Exorcising Laplace's demon: chaos and antichaos, history and metahistory]. *History and Theory*, 95, 34, 1, p. 30-83.

871. CHARTIER (Roger). History between narrative and knowledge. *Western Humanities Review*, 95, 49, 4, p. 367-381. – IDEM. L'histoire culturelle entre 'Linguistic Turn' et retour au sujet. *In*: Wege zu einer neuen Kulturgeschichte [Cf. n° 1364], p. 29-58. – IDEM. L'histoire culturelle. Positions et prepositions. *In*: Culture et politique [Cf. n° 1331], p. 7-21. – IDEM. Philosophie et histoire: un dialogue. *In*: Histoire et le métier d'historien en France 1945–1995 (L') [Cf. n° 600], p. 149-169.

872. CHAUDHURI (Kirti N). From the Atlantic to the Arabian sea: a polyphonic essay on history. Firenze, Schifanoia, 95, 84 p.

873. COHEN (Yves). Une histoire aussi technique. *Annales*, 95, 50, 3, p. 537-540.

874. COLLART (Yves). De l'audio-visuel comme source de l'histoire. *Revue suisse d'histoire*, 95, 45, 4, p. 521-527.

875. CONTE (Patrice). L'archéologie des silos médiévaux: apports, limites et perspectives. *In*: Histoire rurale en France (L') [Cf. n° 601], p. 190-197.

876. CORNELL (Saul). Splitting the difference: textualism, contextualism, and post-modern history. *American Studies*, 95, 36, p. 57-80.

877. CRIPPS (Thomas). Historical truth: an interview with Ken Burns. *American Historical Review*, 95, 100, 3, p. 741-764.

878. DI RIENZO (Eugenio). Illuminismo politico. Alcuni problemi di metodo sulla storiografia politica del Settecento. *Studi storici*, 95, 36, 4, p. 977-1010.

879. DRAY (William H.). History as re-enactment: R. G. Collingwood's idea of history. Oxford, Clarendon Press, 95, XII-347 p.

880. DUARA (Prasenjit). Rescuing history from the nation: questioning narratives of modern China. Chicago a. London, University of Chicago Press, 95, 275 p.

881. ELLIOTT (John H.). Comparative history. *In*: Historia a Debate. Tomo 3 [Cf. n° 602], p. 9-20.

882. ERASOV (Boris S.). Problemy teorii civilizacij. (The problems of the theory of civilizations). *Nov-novejš. Ist.* , 95, 6, 181-187.

883. FARGE (Arlette). Paroles sans histoire; histoire sans paroles. *L'Inactuel. Psychanalyse et culture*, 95, 4, p. 27-35.

884. FEDOSOVA (V. N.). O vozmožnostjakh ispol'zovanija antropologiceskikh dannikh dlja paleosocial'nykh rekonstrukcij. (The possibilities of the phisical anthropology in the paleosocial reconstructions). *Ros. arkheol.* , 95,2, p. 104-111.

885. FILIPPOV (Szergej). Történelembölcseleti elképzelések a 15–17. századi Oroszországban. (Considérations de philosophie de l'histoire dans la Russie des XVe–XVIIe siècles). *Aetas*, 95, 3, p. 5-31.

886. FOLKERS (Karl H.). Die kulturelle Evolution. Vom Sinn und Ziel der Geschichte. Frankfurt am Main, Haag u. Herchen, 95, 600 p.

887. FRANGEUR (Renée). Utanför systemet? Om genussystemteorins förklaringsvärde för (stats) feminismen pa 1930-talet. (Beyond the system? About the explanative value of gender system theory as regards the French state feminism during the 1930s). *Historisk Tidskrift* (Sweden), 95, 2, p. 209-216.

888. FUKUYAMA (Francis). The end of history, five years later. *History and Theory*, 95, 34, 2, p. 27-43.

889. GADDIS (John Lewis). On contemporary history: an inaugural lecture delivered before the University of Oxford on 18 May 1993. Oxford, Clarendon Press, 95, 25 p. (Inaugural lectures, University of Oxford).

890. GALUZZI (Massimo). Considerazioni sulla storia della matematica. *Rivista di storia della storiografia moderna*, 95, 16, 1-3, p. 149-152. [Cf. PANZA (Marco). Che cosa è la storiografia della matematica. Riflessioni di ispirazione crociana, in risposta all'intervento di Massimo Galuzzi]

891. GIARRIZZO (Giuseppe). Storia locale, storia regionale. *Miscellanea storica della Valdesa*, 95, 101, p. 123-138.

892. GINSBORG (Paul). Family, civil society and the state in contemporary European history: some methodological considerations. *Contemporary European History*, 95, 4, 3, p. 249-273.

893. GINZBURG (Carlo). Microhistoria: dos o tres cosa que sé de ella. *Entrepasados*, 95, 4, 8, p. 87-103.

894. GOERTZ (Hans-Jürgen). Umgang mit Geschichte. Eine Einführung in die Geschichtstheorie. Reinbek, Rowohlt, 95, 195 p.

895. GREEN (S. J. D.). The Tawney-Strauss connection: on historicism and values in the history of political ideas. *Journal of modern history*, 95, 67, 2, p. 255-277.

896. GREEN (William). Periodizing world history. *History and Theory*, 95, 34, 2, p. 99-111.

897. GROETHUYSEN (Bernhard). Philosophie et histoire. Ed. par Bernard DANDOIS. Paris, Albin Michel, 95, 359 p. (Bibliotheque Albin Michel des idees).

898. HACKING (Ian). Rewriting the soul: multiple personality and the sciences of memory. Princeton, Princeton U. P., 95, IX-336 p.

899. HAFNER (Ralph). Johann Gottfried Herders Kulturentstehungslehre: Studien zu den Quellen und zur Methode seines Geschichtsdenkens. Hamburg, Meiner, 95, XIII-355 p. (ill.). (Studien zum achtzehnten Jahrhundert, 19).

900. HARTOG (François). Temps et histoire. «Comment écrire l'histoire de France». *Annales*, 95, 50, 6, p. 1219-1236.

901. *Vacat.*

902. História ao documento (Da), do documento à historia. Org. Arquivos Nacionais Torre do Tombo. Lisboa, AN/TT, 95, XLV-45 p.

903. Histories: French constructions of the past. Ed. by Jacques REVEL a. Lynn HUNT. New York, The New Press, 95, XX-654 p. (Postwar French thought series).

904. History and the idea of progress. Ed. by Arthur M. MELZER, Jerry WEINBERGER a. M. Richard ZINMAN. Ithaca, Cornell U. P., 95, VIII-271 p.

905. HOMANN (Arne). Dilthey's Bruch mit der Metaphysik: die Aufhebung der Hegelschen Philosophie im

geschichtlichen Bewusstsein. Freiburg, K. Alber, 95, 367 p. (Symposion, 102).

906. HOURCADE (Eduardo), GODOY (Cristina), BOTALLA (Horacio). Luz y contraluz de una historia antropológica. Buenos Aires, Biblos, 95, 208 p.

907. HUPPERT (George). La rencontre de la philosophie avec l'histoire. *Corpus*, 95, 28, p. 11-26.

908. IGGERS (Georg G.). Zur "Linguistischen Wende" im Geschichtsdenken und in der Geschichtsschreibung. *Geschichte und Gesellschaft*, 95, 21, 4, p. 557-570.

909. JAEGER (Michael). Autobiographie und Geschichte: Wilhelm Dilthey, Georg Misch, Karl Löwith, Gottfried Benn, Alfred Döblin. Stuttgart, Metzler, 95, 376 p.

910. JELAVICH (Peter). Poststrukturalismus und Sozialgeschichte – aus amerikanischer Perspektive. *Geschichte und Gesellschaft*, 95, 21, 2, p. 259-289.

911. JENKINS (Keith). On "What is History?" From Carr and Elton to Rorty and White. London a New York, Routledge, 95, VII-200 p.

912. JOYCE (Patrick). The end of social history? *Social History*, 95, 20, 1, p. 73-91.

913. KIESEWETTER (Hubert). Geschichtswissenschaft und Erkenntnistheorie. *Zeitschrift für Geschichtswissenschaft*, 95, 43, 7, p. 581-614.

914. KISLYJ (A. E.). Paleodemografija i vozmožnosti modelirovanija struktury drevnego naselenija. (Palaeodemography and the possibilities of the ancient population modelling). *Ros. arkheol.*, 95, 2, p. 112-122.

915. KOPOSSOV (Nikolaï). Vers l'anthropologie de la raison historique. *In*: Historia a Debate. Tomo 1 [Cf. n° 602], p. 263-268.

916. KOTTMAN (Paul). The writing of an event. *Rivista di storia della storiografia moderna*, 95, 16, 1-3, p. 239-255.

917. KOVAL'ČENKO (Ivan D.). Teoretiko-metodologičeskie problemy istoričeskikh issledovanij. Zametki i razmyšlenija o novykh podkhodakh. (Theoretical and methodological problems of the studies in history. Contemplations on new approaches). *Nov. novejš. Ist.*, 95, 1, p. 3-33.

918. KOVALEVSKAJA (V. B.). Arkheologičeskaja kul'tura: praktika, teorija, komp'juter. (The archaeological culture: practice, theory, computers). Moskva, Fond arkheologii, In-t arkheologii RAN, Rossijskij fond fundamental'nykh issledovanij, 95, 193p.

919. LA CAPRA (Dominick). History, language, and reading: waiting for crillon. *American Historical Review*, 95, 100, 3, p. 799-828.

920. Language and the history of thought. Ed. by Nancy STRUEVER. Rochester a. Suffolk, University of Rochester Press, 95, XII-257 p. (Library of the history of ideas, 13).

921. LEMON (Michael C.). The discipline of history and the history of thought. London a. New York, Routledge, 95, VI-280 p.

922. LEPETIT (Bernard). Les formes de l'expérience: une autre histoire sociale. Paris, Michel, 95, 337 p. (L'Evolution de l'humanité).

923. LIVERANI (Mario). La rivoluzione neolitica e la fine delle ideologie. *Studi storici*, 95, 36, p. 901-922.

924. LOEWENBERG (Peter). Fantasy and reality in history. New York, Oxford U. P., 95, VIII-235 p.

925. LÖWY (Ilana). Le genre dans l'histoire sociale et culturelle des sciences. *Annales*, 95, 50, 3, p. 523-530.

926. MAC NEILL (William H.). The changing shape of world history. *History and Theory*, 95, 34, 2, p. 8-26.

927. MACEDO (Jorge Borges) A experiência histórica contemporânea. Lisboa, [s. n.], 95, 124 p.

928. MANCHEL (Frank). A real witness: Steven Spielberg's representation of the Holocaust in «Schindler's List». *Journal of modern history*, 95, 67, 1, p. 83-100.

929. MARWICK (Arthur). Two approaches to historical study: the metaphysical (including 'Postmodernism') and the historical. *Journal of Contemporary History*, 95, 30, 1, p. 5-36.

930. Meaning of historicism (The) and its relevance for contemporary history. [Contents: ANKERSMIT (F. R.). Historicism: an attempt at synthesis. – IGGERS (Georg G.). Comments on F. R. Ankersmit's paper, "Historicism: an attempt at synthesis". – ANKERSMIT (F. R.). Reply to professor Iggers]. *History and Theory*, 95, 34, 3, p. 143-173.

931. MELBERG (Arne). Theories of mimesis. Cambridge a. New York, Cambridge U. P., 95, VII-192 p. (Literature, culture, theory, 12).

932. MIYAKE (Masaki). The problem of narrativity and objectivity in historical writings, with particular reference to the case of Japan. Tokyo, Institute of Social Sciences, Meiji University, 95, 23 p. (Bulletin of the Institute of Social Sciences, Meiji University, 18, 3).

933. NEAL (Aubrey). The promise and practice of deconstruction. *Canadian Journal of History*, 95, 30, 1, p. 49-76.

934. New philosophy of history (A). Ed. by F. R. ANKERSMIT and Hans KELLNER. London, Reaktion, 95, 304 p. (Critical views series).

935. OLÁBARRI (Ignacio). "New" new history: a Longue Durée structure. *History and Theory*, 95, 34, 1, p. 1-29.

936. OPLL (Ferdinand). Nachrichten aus dem mittelalterlichen Wien. Zeitgenossen berichten. Wien, Köln u. Weimar, Böhlau, 95, 290 p. (ill.).

937. OTTO (A. C.). De kwade wil als motor van de geschiedenis. Verschillen en overeenkomsten in de cul-

3. METHODENLEHRE, GESCHICHTSPHILOSOPHIE UND GESCHICHTSUNTERRICHT

tuurkritiek van Da Costa, Huizinga en Van Deursen. *Theoretische geschiedenis*, 95, 22, p. 112-126.

938. PANZA (Marco). Che cosa è la storiografia della matematica. Riflessioni di ispirazione crociana, in risposta all'intervento di Massimo Galuzzi. *Rivista di storia della storiografia moderna*, 95, 16, 1-3, p. 153-162.

939. PARR (Joy). Gender history and historical practice. *Canadian Historical Review*, 95, 76, 1, p. 354-376.

940. Passés recomposés: champs et chantiers de l'histoire. Dir. par Jean BOUTIER et Dominique JULIA. *Autrement. Série Mutations*, 95, 150-151, p. 349 p.

941. PERROT (Jean-Claude). Les premières statistique au regard de l'histoire intellctuelle. *Revue suisse d'histoire*, 95, 45, 1, p. 51-62.

942. PESTRE (Dominique). Pour une histoire sociale et culturelle des sciences. Nouvelles définitions, nouveaux objets, nouvelles pratiques. *Annales*, 95, 50, 3, p. 487-522.

943. Philosophy, history and civilization: interdisciplinary perspectives on R.G. Collingwood. Ed. by David BOUCHER, James CONNELLY a. Tariq MODOOD. Cardiff, University of Wales Press, 95, XVIII-388 p.

944. PICON (Antoine). Construction sociale et histoire des techniques. *Annales*, 95, 50, 3, p. 531-536.

945. POMIAN (Krzysztof). Jak uprawiać historię kultury. (Comment pratiquer l'histoire de la culture). *Przegląd Historyczny*, 95, 86, 1, p. 1-13. [Eng. Summary].

946. POMPER (Philip). World history and its critics. *History and Theory*, 95, 34, 2, p. 1-7.

947. POSTER (Mark). The second media age. London, Polity Press a. New York, Basil Blackwell, 95, 186 p.

948. PULIT (Marcin). Poznanie historyczne według Johanna Gustawa Droysena. (La cognition historique selon Johann Gustav Droysen.). *Historyka*, 95, 25, p. 13-30.

949. Reflexiones sobre el oficio del Historiador. México, Universidad Nacional Autonoma de Mexico, 95, 247 p. (Serie divulgacion, 2). [Cf. n° <selección> 952.]

950. REVEL (Jacques). Ressources narratives et connaissance historique. *Enquête*, 95, 1, p. 43-70.

951. ROBERTS (David D.). Nothing but history: reconstruction and extremity after metaphysics. Berkeley, University of California Press, 95, XIII-324 p.

952. ROMANO (Ruggiero). Braudel e noi. Riflessioni sulla cultura storica del nostro tempo. Roma, Donzelli, 95, 103 p. – IDEM. Historia cuantitativa, historia económica e historia: algunas consideraciones sobre la historiografia francesa de hoy. *Anales de Historia Antigua y Medieval*, 95, 28, [s. p.]. – IDEM. La historia y la fotografia. *In*: Reflexiones sobre el oficio del Historiador [Cf. n° 949], p. 55-63.

953. ROTH (Michael S.). The ironist's cage. Memory, trauma, and the construction of history. New York, Columbia U. P., 95, VIII-240 p.

954. SANDERSON (Stephen K). Social transformations: a general theory of historical development. Cambridge, Blackwell, 95, XII-452 p.

955. SCHMIDT (Thomas C.). Die Entdeckung des Ostens und der Humanismus. Niccolò de' Conti und Poggio Bracciolinis Historia de Varietate Fortunae. *Mitt. d. Inst. f. Österr. Gesch.-Forsch.*, 95, 103, 3-4, p. 392-418.

956. SCHMITT (Carl). Carl Schmitt. Briefwechsel mit einem seiner Schüler. Hrsg. v. Armin MOHLER; in Zusammenarbeit mit Irmgard HUHN und Piet TOMMISSEN. Berlin, Akademie Verlag, 95, 473 p.

957. SCHWARCZ (Iskra I.). Der wissenschaftliche Nachlaß von Henryk Paszkiewicz. *Österr. Osthefte*, 95, 37, 3, p. 783-788.

958. SEIDENSTICKER (Mike). Werbung mit Geschichte. Ästhetik und Rhetorik des Historischen. Wien, Köln u. Weimar, Böhlau, 95, VI-198 p. (Beiträge zur Geschichtskultur, 10).

959. SELLIN (Volker). Einführung in die Geschichtswissenschaft. Göttingen, Vandenhoeck u. Ruprecht, 95, 223 p. (Sammlung Vandenhoeck).

960. SIEBERER (Wido). Das Bild Europas in den Historien. Studien zu Herodotus Geographie und Ethnographie Europas und seine Schilderung der persischen Feldzüge. Innsbruck, Vlg des Inst. für Sprachwissenschaft der Univ. Innsbruck, 95, 336 p. (Karten). (Innsbrucker Beiträge zur Kulturwissenschaft. Sonderheft 96).

961. SPIEGEL (Gabrielle M.). Towards a theory of the Middle Ground: historical writing in the age of postmodernism. *In*: Historia a Debate. Tomo 1 [Cf. n° 602], p. 169-176.

962. STELZER (Winfried). Die verschollene Trauttmansdorffer Handschrift des Anonymus Leobiensis: cvp. 3445, 8221 und ihre Kontamination in den "Commentarii" Anton Steyerers (1725). *Unsere Heimat*, 95, 66, 3, p. 189-199 (ill.). – IDEM. Studien zur österreichischen historiographie im 14. Jahrhundert. Die Chronik des "Anonymus Leobiensis" und die Leobener Martins-Chronik. *Mitt. d. Inst. f. Österr. Gesch.-Forsch.*, 95, 103, 3-4, p. 369-391.

963. STONE (Lawrence). The future of history. *In*: Historia a Debate. Tomo 1 [Cf. n° 602], p. 177-190.

964. ŠUBRT (Jiří). Sociální paměť a sociologický výzkum. (Social memory and sociological research). *Soudobé dějiny*, 95, 2, 2-3, p. 269-280.

965. TESSITORE (Fulvio). Contributi alla storia e alla teoria dello storicismo. Roma, Edizioni di storia e letteratura, 95, 2 vol., 886 p. (Storia e letteratura, 190–191).

966. THURNER (Eugen). Jahre der Vorbereitung. Jakob Fallmerayers Tätigkeiten nach der Rückker von der zweiten Orientreise: 1842–1845. Wien, Vlg. der Österr. Akad. der Wiss., 95, 49 p. (Sitzungsberichte der Österr. Akad. der Wiss., phil.-hist. Kl., 621).

967. TILLEY (Allen). Plots of time: an inquiry into history, myth, and meaning. Gainesville, University Press of Florida, 95, XI-128 p.

968. Time: histories and ethnologies. Ed. by Diane OWEN HUGHES and Thomas R. TRAUTMANN. Ann Arbor, University of Michigan Press, 95, XIII-306 p. (Comparative studies in society and history book series).

969. TODOROV (Tzvetan). La mémoire devant l'histoire. *Terrain*, 95, 25, p. 101-112.

970. Ut med historien: historieundervisningens upgifter idag. (Off with history. The tasks of history teaching today). Ed. by Lars EDGREN a. Eva ÖSTERBERG. Lund, Studentlitteratur, 95, 139 p.

971. VANSINA (Jan). Historians, are archaeologists your siblings? *History in Africa*, 95, 22, p. 369-408.

972. Veritas filia temporis?: Philosophiehistorie zwischen Wahrheit und Geschichte. Hrsg. v. Rolf W. PUSTER. Berlin, Walter de Gruyter, 95, 311 p. [Festschrift fur Rainer Specht zum 65. Geburtstag]

973. VESTER (Heinz-Günther). Geschichte und Gesellschaft. Ansätze historisch-komparativer Soziologie. Berlin u. München, Quintessenz, 95, VII-207 p.

974. VIDAL-NACQUET (Pierre). Les assassins de la mémoire, «un Eichmann de papier» et autres essais sur le révisionisme [de Faurisson]. Paris, Ed. du Seuil, 95, 231 p.

975. VOLK (Peter). Anton Ritter von Spauns Muthmassungen über Heinrich von Ofterdingen und sein Geschlecht 1839. Neue Aspekte zur Historizität Heinrichs von Ofterdingen und des Kürenbergers. *Jb. d. Oberösterr. Musealkundevereines I*, 95, 140, p. 83-138 (ill.).

976. WEHLER (Hans-Ulrich). Die Gegenwart als Geschichte: Essays. München, Beck, 95, 304 p.

977. WERNER (Michael). Présentation: Proto-industrialisation et 'Alltagsgeschichte'. *Annales*, 95, 50, 4, p. 719-724.

978. WESSELING (H. L.). Onder historici: opstellen over geschiedenis en geschiedschrijving. Amsterdam, Bert Bakker, 95, 357 p.

979. WHITE (Hayden). Response to Arthur Marwick. *Journal of Contemporary History*, 95, 30, 2, p. 233-246.

980. WILSON (Andrew). The Donbas between Ukraine and Russia: the use of history in political disputes. *Journal of Contemporary History*, 95, 30, 2, p. 265-290.

981. WURGAFT (Lewis). Identity in world history: a post-modern perspective. *History and Theory*, 95, 34, 2, p. 67-85.

982. YOO (Heon-Sik). Das Problem des Neuen im Geschichtsdenken Hegels. Frankfurt am Main, P. Lang, 95, 246 p. (Europäische Hochschulschriften. Reihe 20, Philosophie, 470).

983. ZUKIER (Henri). Historical reality and psychological truth. *Jewish History*, 95, 9, 2, p. 21-26.

Cf. n°s 1442, 1453, 1457, 1461, 4130

§ 4. Völker und Volkskunde.

* 984. APRILE (Renato). Indice delle fiabe popolari italiane di magia. Vol 1. AT 300–451. Berlin: Edimetheos, 95, 761 p. (ill.).

* 985. Bibliographien zu "Slawisch-folkloristisches Schrifgut" aus dem Vorlesungsrepertoire von Vladimir Propp und zu "Slawische Folklore und Folklore vom Balkan" von Nikita I. Tolstoi (ed.). Bearb. u. hrsg. v. Wulfhild ZIEL. Frankfurt am Main, Peter Lang, 95, XVI-176 p.

* 986. CAMARENA LAUCIRICA (Julio), CHEVALIER (Maxime). Catalogo tipologico del cuento folklorico español. Cuentos maravillosos. Madrid, Gredos, 95, 794 p. (Biblioteca romanica hispanica. IV. Textos, 24).

* 987. HULTS (David S.). A bibliography of Australian folklore, 1790 to 1990. Perth, Black Swan Press, 95, II-139 p.

* 988. Typenverzeichnis der bulgarischen Volksmärchen. Bearb. u. hrsg. v. Klaus ROTH. Übersetzung von Klaus ROTH, Juliana ROTH u. Gabi TIEMANN. Helsinki, Suomalainen Tiedeakatemia, 95, 424 p. (FF communications, 257).

---

989. Abdülaziz Bey. Osmanlı Adet-Merasim ve Tabirleri. Vol. 1–2. (Coutumes et usages ottomans et leurs significations). Ed. par Kazim ARISAN et Duygu ARISAN GÜNAY. İstanbul, Türkiye Ekonomik Ve Toplumsal Tarih Vakfı, 95, 2 vol., 315 p., 298 p.

990. After empire: towards an ethnology of Europe's barbarians. Ed. by G. AUSENDA. Woodbridge, Boydell Press, 95, 317 p (il., maps). (Studies in historical archaeoethnology, 1).

991. AHLSTRÖM (Christian). Spår av hav, yxa och penna: historiska sjöolyckor i Östersjön avspeglade i marinarkeologiskt källmaterial. (Historical shipwrecks in the Baltic reflected in marine archaeological source material). Helsingfors, Finska Vetenskaps-societeten, 95, 214 p. (Bidr. t. Känn. av Finl. natur folk, 148) (Ill., maps).

992. Antropologia do parentesco: estudos amerindios. Ed. por Eduardo VIVEIROS DE CASTRO. Rio de Janeiro, UFRJ, 95, 382 p.

993. Antropologia storica. Materiali per un dibattito. A cura di Gilberto MAZZOLENI, Adriano SANTIEMMA e Vito LATTANZI. Roma, Euroma, 95, 397 p. (Collana di contributi di antropologia storica).

994. Atlas der schweizerischen Volkskunde = Atlas de folklore suisse. Begründet v. Paul GEIGER u. Richard WEISS; fortgeführt v. Walter ESCHER, Elsbeth LIEBL u. Arnold NIEDERER. Basel, Schweizerische Gesellschaft fur Volkskunde, 95, [s. p.].

995. BABIČ (Irina L.). Narodnye tradicii v obščestevennom bytu kabardincev. (Folk traditions in the public life of the Kabardinians). Moskva, RAN. In-t étnologii i antropologii im. N. N. Miklukho-Maklaja, 95. 128 p.

996. BALUŠKO (V. G.). Indiciacii drevnerussikikh družinnikov. (The ancient Russian "druzhinniks" initiations). Étnogr. obozrenie, 95, 1, p. 35-44.

997. BELCEV (Tasko D.). Makedonija: cetiri iljadi godini istorija, civilizacija i pismenost, ili etnogenezata na makedonskiot narod. (Ethnology of Macedonia). Skopje, STRK, 95, 171 p. (Biblioteka Nauka. Skopje, Macedonia).

998. BINDER (Frederick M.), REIMERS (David M.). All the nations under heaven: an ethnic and racial history of New York City. New York, Columbia U. P., 95, XII-353 p. (Columbia history of urban life).

999. BUDINA (O. P.). Tradicii domostroitel'stva u Kompaktnykh étničeskikh grupp v inoétničeskom okruženii. (Housebuilding traditions of ethnic enclaves in foreign surroundings). Étnogr. obozrenie, 95, 5, p. 59-76.

1000. BUTANAEV (Viktor Iakovlevich). Khakasy: etnograficheskii ocherk. (Khakassians: ethnographical essays). Moskva, "INSAN", 95, 37 p. (ill., maps).

1001. CHAN (Selina Ching). Tradition inherited, tradition reinterpreted: a Chinese lineage in the 1990s. [S. l.], [s. n.], 95, VIII-302 leaves (ill).

1002. DELAMONT (Sara). Appetites and identities: an introduction to the social anthropology of Western Europe. London a. New York, Routledge, 95, X-254 p.

1003. DENING (Greg). "P 905 .A512 X 100": an ethnographic essay. American Historical Review, 95, 100, 3, p. 854-864.

1004. DIOP (Samba). The oral history and literature of the Wolof people of Waalo, northern Senegal: the master of the word (griot) in the Wolof tradition. Lewiston a. Lampeter, Edwin Mellen Press, 95, 389 p. (African studies, 36).

1005. Écologija étničeskikh kul'tur Sibiri nakanune XXI veka: Sbornik. (Ecology of the Siberian etnic cultures on the eve of the XXIth century. Collected studies). Sankt-Peterburg: Nauka, RAN. Muzei antroplogii i étnografii im. Petra Velikogo (Kunstamera), 95, 222 p.

1006. Encountering ethnicities. Ethnological aspects in ethnicity, identity and migration. Ed. by Teppo KORHONEN. Helsinki, Suomalaisen Kirjallisuuden Seura, 95, 261 p. (Studia Fennica Ethnologica, 3).

1007. Ethno-archéologie méditerranéenne: finalités, démarches et résultats: table ronde organisée par la Casa de Velazquez, avec le concours de l'U.R.A. 1225 du C.N.R.S. Actes préséntes par André BAZZANA et Marie-Christine DELAIGUE. Madrid, Casa de Velazquez, 95, 218 p. (ill., maps, plans). (Collection de la Casa de Velazquez, 54).

1008. Étničeskoe samosoznanie slavjan v XV stoletii. (The ethnic consciousness of the Slavs in the XVth century). O. A. AKIMOVA, G. G. LITAVRIN, I. F. MAKAROVA i drugie; RAN. In-t slavjanovedenija i balkanistiki; Redkol.: G. G. LITAVRIN (otv. red.) i drugie. Moskva, Nauka, 95, 240 p.

1009. FABIETTI (Ugo). L'identità etnica: storia e critica di un concetto equivoco. Roma, NIS, 95, 172 p. (Studi superiori NIS, 257).

1010. FAMICIN (A. S.). Božestva drevnikh slavjan. (The ancient Slavs' deities). Sankt-Peterburg, Aleteja, Posleslovie N. S. Dobronravin, 95, 346 p.

1011. Fieldwork and footnotes: studies in the history of European anthropology. Ed. by Hans F. VERMEULEN and Arturo ALVAREZ ROLDAN. London a. New York, Routledge, 95, XI-261 p.

1012. FROLOVA (A. V.). Ural'skoe kazačestvo. (Kratkij istoriko-étnografičeskij očerk). (The Urals Cossacks. A short outline of their history and ethnography). Étnogr. obozrenie, 95, 5, p. 37-48.

1013. GEORGES (Robert A.), JONES (Michael Owen). Folkloristics: an introduction. Bloomington, Indiana U. P., 95, [s. p.].

1014. Gesto (Il): nel rito e nel cerimoniale dal mondo antico ad oggi. A cura di Sergio BERTELLI e Monica CENTANNI. Firenze, Ponte delle Grazie, 95, 357 p. (ill.). (Laboratorio di storia, 9).

1015. GÖYÜNÇ (Nejat). Die Begriffe "Türke, Kurde" und "Araber" in einigen Osmanischen Geschichtswerken und Urkunden. Osmanlı Araştırmaları, 95, 15, p. 199-207.

1016. GRIBANOV (P. V.). Kreolizacia i mežétničeskaja integracija v poliétničnykh strankakh Karibsogo regiona. (Creolization and interethnic integration in Poly-ethnic countries of the CARIBBEAN). Étnogr. obzrenie, 95, 6, p. 102-110.

1017. GRINEV (A. V.). Totemizm u indejcev khajda, tlinkitov i cimsian. (Totemism among the Haida, Tlingit, and Ziimshian). Étnogr. obzrenie, 95, 4, p. 115-125.

1018. GROMYKO (M. M.). Étnografičeskoe izučenie religioznosti naroda: zamekti o predmete, podkhodakh i osobennostjakh sovremennogo étapa issledovanij. (Ethnographic study of a people's religiousness: notes of the subject, methods and distinctive features of the current stage of the research). *Étnogr. obzrenie*, 95, 5, p. 77-83.

1019. GRUEL-APERT (Lise). La tradition orale russe. Paris, PUF, 95, 300 p. (ill.). (Collection "Ethnologies").

1020. GRUSKO (Elena A.), MEDVEDEV (Jurij M.). Slovar' slavjanskoj mifologii. (The Slavonic mythological dictionary). Nižnij Novgorod: Russkij kupec: Brat'ja slavjane, 95, 367 p.

1021. GÜNAY (Selçuk). II. Abdülhamit Dönemi'nin Son Yıllarında Güneydoğu Anadolu İle Kuzey Irak'ta Aşiret Mücadeleleri Ve Milli Aşiret Reisi İbrahim Paşa" (Les querelles tribales au sud-est de l'Anatolie et au nord de l'Iraq aux dernières années du règne d'Abdülhamid II). *Atatürk Üniversitesi Türkiyat Araştırmaları Enstitüsü Dergisi*, 95, 2, p. 103-132.

1022. HAMLIN (William M.). The image of America in Montaigne, Spenser (Edmund) and Shakespeare: Renaissance ethnography and literary reflection. Basingstoke, Macmillan, 95, XX-234 p.

1023. Istorija i kul'tura khantov. (The Khanty history and culture). V. I. MOLODIN, N. V. LUKINA, V. M. KULEMZIN i drugie; Pod. red. N. V. LUKINOJ; Administracija Jamalo-Neneckogo avtonomnogo okruga, Okružnaja laboratorija étnografii i étnografii i étnolingvistiki Jamala. Tomsk, Izdatel'stvo Tomskogo universiteta, 95, 162 p.

1024. Itämerensuomalaiset: heimokansien historiaa ja kohtaloita. (The Baltic Finnish tribes. History and destinies of the kindred peoples). Ed. by Mauno JOKIPII. Jyväskylä, Atena, 95, 445 p.

1025. JDEY (Ahmed). La société des fractions tribales faibles dans la Tunisie au XIXe siècle: l'exemple des Gsarniya (1858–1868). *Revue d'Histoire Maghrebine* (Partie arabe), 95, 77-78, p. 105-137.

1026. Karaimskaja narodnaja énciklopedija. (Karaite folk encyclopaedia). Tom. 1. Vvodnyj (Introduction). Redkol.: M. S. SARAĆ (glavnyj redaktor) i drugie. Moskva, Centr kul'tury i razvitija karaimov "Koroilar", 95, 248 p.

1027. KHOMIČ (L. V.). Nency: Očerki tradicionnoj kul'tury. (The Nenets: essays in the traditional culture). Upravlenie kul'tury administracii jamalo-Neneckogo avtonomnogo okruga, Associacijja "Jamal-potomkam". Moskva, Russkij Dvor, 95, 334 p.

1028. KOLPAKOV (E. M.). Étnos i étničnost'. (Ethnos and ethnicity). *Étnogr. obzrenie*, 95, 5, p. 13-23.

1029. KORPELA (Jukka). Beiträge zur Bevölkerungsgeschichte und Prosographie der Kiever Rus' bis zum Tode von Wladimir Monomach. Jyväskylä, University of Jyväskylä, 95, 296 p. (Abstract in Eng.). (Studia historica Jyväskyläensia, 54).

1030. KOZLOV (V. I.). Problematika "étničnosti". (The problem of ethnicity). *Étnogr. obzrenie*, 95, 4, p. 39-54.

1031. KRASNOVSKAJA (N. A.). K istorii étnografičeskoj nauki v Italii. (A contribution to the history of ethnography in Italy). *Étnogr. obozrenie*, 95, 3, p. 133-149.

1032. Kulturen, Identitäten, Diskurse. Perspektiven Europäischer Ethnologie. Hrsg. v. Wolfgang KASHUBA. Berlin, Akademie, 95, 250 p. (Zeithorizonte, 1).

1033. KURPERSHOEK (P. M.). The story of a desert knight: the legend of Slewih al-Atawi and other Utaybah heroes: an edition with translation and introduction. Leiden, Brill, 95, XIV-512 p. (plates, ill., map). (Oral poetry and narratives from Central Arabia, 2. Studies in Arabic literature, 17, 2).

1034. LEPPIN (Volker). Der Lateinische Totentanz aus Cpg 314 als Ursprungstext der europäischen Totentanztradition. Eine alte These neu bedacht. *Archiv für Kulturgeschichte*, 95, 77, p. 323-344.

1035. LIPINSKAJA (V. A.). Konfessional'nye gruppy pravoslavnogo naselenija Zapadnoj Sibiri. (Vtoraja polovina XIX–načalo XX veka). (The Orthodox denomination of West Siberia population. Later half of the XIXth–early XXth centuries). *Étnogr. obozrenie*, 95, 2, p. 113-127.

1036. LOBAČEVA (N. P.). Čto takoe svadebnyj obrjad? (Opyt izučenija soderžanija bračno-svadebnoj obrjadnosti). (What is a wedding ceremony? A casestudy of wedding ceremonialism). *Étnogr. obozrenie*, 95, 4, p. 55-64.

1037. LORCIN (Patricia M. E.). Imperial identities: stereotyping, prejudice and race in colonial Algeria. London, I. B. Tauris, 95, X-323 p. (Society and culture in the modern Middle East).

1038. MAHN-LOT (M.). Un évangélisateur-ethnographe en Haiti. *Revue Historique*, 95, 119, 594, p. 251-262.

1039. MARKOV (G. E.). Ot upadka k vozroždeniju. (Nemeckoe narodovedenie posle vtoroj mirovoj vojny: problema teorii). (From decline to renaissance. The German Volkskunde after World War II: problems of theory). *Étnogr. obozrenie*, 95, 6, p. 31-49.

1040. Mify i magia indoevropejcev: Sbornik. (Myths and magic of the Indoeuropeans. Collected studies). Moskva, Menedžer, Pod red. A. PLATOVA, 95, Vyp. 1. (Pt. 1), 255p.

1041. Nga iwi o Tainui: the traditional history of the Tainui people (New Zealand): nga koorero tuku iho a nga tupuna. Compiled by Pei Te HURINUI JONES; edited and annotated by Bruce BIGGS. Auckland, Auckland U. P., 95, XIV-402 p.

1042. PANOURGIA (Eleni Neni K.). Fragments of death, fables of identity: an Athenian anthropography. Madison, University of Wisconsin Press, 95, XXIII-242 p. (New directions in anthropological writing).

1043. Primer Encuentro de Investigadores de la Costa Ecuatoriana en Europa: arqueologia, etnohistoria, antropologia sociocultural. Por Alvarez, AURELIO. Quito, Ediciones Abya-Yala, 95, 568 p.

1044. Representation in ethnography. Ed. by John VAN MAANEN. Thousand Oaks a. London, Sage Publications, 95, 276 p.

1045. REYNOLDS (Dwight Fletcher). Heroic poets, poetic heroes: the ethnography of performance in an Arabic oral epic tradition. Ithaca a. London, Cornell U. P., 95, XVIII-246 p. (Myth and poetics).

1046. Russkie narodnye tradicii i sovremennost'. (The Russian folk traditions and the present). Redkol. : T. A. LISTOVA (otv. red.) i drugie. Moskva, Nauka, RAN. In-t étnologii i antropologii im. N. N. Miklukho-Maklaja, 95, 304 p.

1047. SAVČUV (Valerij V.). Krov' i kul'tura. (The blood and the culture). Sankt-Peterburg, Sankt-Peterburgskij gosudarstvennyj universitet, 95, 178 p.

1048. SCARZANELLA (Eugenia). Indiani e «cacciatori d'ombre» in Tierra del Fuego: note su fotografia, etnografia e storia. *Storia contemporanea*, 95, 26, 4, p. 619-638.

1049. SMIRNOVA-SESLAVINSKAJA (M. V.). Magija ženskogo tela v istokakh cyganskogo tabornogo tanca. (Female body magic as a source of the gipsy band dance). *Étnogr. obozrenie*, 95, 3, p. 70-83.

1050. SOLOV'EVA (L. T.). Gruzuìja. Étnografija detstva. (Georgia. Ethnography of childhood). Moskva, RAN. In-t étnologii i antropologii im. N. N. Miklukho-Maklaja, 95, 129 p.

1051. SPOTTEL (Michael). Die ungeliebte "Zivilisation": Zivilisationskritik und Ethnologie in Deutschland im 20. Jahrhundert. Frankfurt am Main, P. Lang, 95, 275 p. (Europäische Hochschulschriften. Reihe 19, Volkskunde, Ethnologie. Abt. B, Ethnologie, 40. Europäische Hochschulschriften. Reihe 19, Ethnologie, Kulturanthropologie. Abteilung B, 40).

1052. STAVIG (Ward). "Living in offense of our lord": indigenous sexual values and marital life in the colonial crucible. *Hispanic American Historical Review*, 95, 75, 4, p. 597-622.

1053. SZABÓ (János). Vázlat egy ellenségkép történetéről. A tatárok emlékezete Erdélyben, 1241–1621. (Esquisse d'histoire d'une image de l'ennemi. La mémoire des Tartares en Transylvanie, 1241–1621). *Aetas*, 95, 1-2, p. 5-23.

1054. TADINA (Nadežda A.). Altajskaja svadebnaja obrjadnos'(XIX–XX veka). (The Altai wedding rite, the XIXth–20th centuries). Gorno-Altajsk: Respublikanskoe knižnoe izdatel'stvo: Juč-Sjumer, Gorno-Altajskij gosudarstvennyj universitet, 95, 215 p.

1055. TOUMARKINE (Alexandre). Les Lazes en Turquie (XIXe–XXe siècles). İstanbul, Isis, 95, X-163 p. (Les Cahiers du Bosphore, 11).

1056. TRIAUD (Jean-Louis). La légende noire de la Sanûsiyya. Une confrérie musulmane saharienne sous le regard français (1840–1930). Paris, Editions de la MSH, 95, 2 vol., 1151 p.

1057. VOSAHLIKOVA (Pavla). Češi na Slovensku – Slováci v Čechách a na Moravě. Tvůrci legend a mýtů na přelomu 19. a 20. století. (Czechs in Slovakia – Slovaks in the Czech Lands and Moravia. Creators of legends and myths). *Moderní dějiny*, 95, 3, p. 7-22.

1058. WARNER (Marina). From the beast to the blonde: on fairy tales and their tellers. London, Vintage, 95, XXI-458 p.

1059. WILSON (Lynn B.). Speaking to power: gender and politics in the western Pacific. New York a. London, Routledge, 95, XII-218 p.

§ 5. Allgemeine Geschichte.

* 1060. Cambridge history of Latin America (The). Ed. by Leslie BETHELL. Vol. 11. Bibliographical essays. Cambridge, Cambridge U. P., 95, XXVIII-1043 p.

* 1061. FRAME (Murray). The Russian Revolution, 1905–1921: a bibliographic guide to works in English. Westport a. London, Greenwood Press, 95, XVI-308 p. (Bibliographies and indexes in world history, 40).

* 1062. JETSON (Tim), ELY (Richard). History of West and South-West Tasmania: a guide to printed sources. Hobart, University of Tasmania, Centre for Tasmanian History, 95, XVI-198 p. (Historical bibliographies of Tasmania, 3).

* 1063. LATHAM (Anthony John Heaton). Africa, Asia, and South America since 1800: a bibliographical guide. Manchester, Manchester U. P., 95, XXXIII-259 p. (History and related disciplines select bibliographies).

* 1064. ORIS (Michel). Bibliographie de l'histoire des populations belges: bilan des travaux des origines a nos jours. Liege, Editions Derouaux Ordina, 95, 475 p.

* 1065. TEMIMI (Abdeljelil). al-Bibliyughrafiya al-'amma li al-dirasat al-Murisklyah al-Andalusiyah. (Bibliographie générale d'études morisques). Zaghouan, Fondation Temimi pour la Recherche Scientifique et l'Information, 95, 330-51 p.

** 1066. HILTON (Sylvia L.), GONZALEZ CASASNOVAS (Ignacio). Fuentes manuscritas para la historia de Iberoamerica: guia de instrumentos de investigación. Madrid, Fundacion Mapfre America, Instituto Historico Tavera, 95, XLIII-617 p.

** 1067. OLNEY (Richard John). Manuscript sources for British history: their nature, location and use. (IHR guides, 3). London, University of London, Institute of Historical Research, 95, X-72 p.

1068. AMINO (Yoshihiko). Les Japonais et la mer. *Annales*, 95, 50, 2, p. 235-258.

1069. ANDERSON (Sean), SLOAN (Stephen). Historical dictionary of terrorism. Metuchen a. London,

Scarecrow Press, 95, XLI-452 p. (Historical dictionaries of religions, philosophies, and movements, 4).

1070. Atlas historico y geografico del Peru. Ed. por Carlos MILLA BATRES. Lima, Editorial Milla Batres, 95, 4 vol., 290 p., 440 p., 414 p., 362 p. (ill., plates, maps, some col.).

1071. BECKA (Jan). Historical dictionary of Myanmar. Metuchen a. London, Scarecrow Press, 95, XXII-328 p. (Asian historical dictionaries, 15).

1072. BENNETT (Alvin LeRoy). Historical dictionary of the United Nations. Lanham a. London, Scarecrow Press, 95, XXXII-244 p. (International organizations series, 8).

1073. BÉRENGER (Jean). Die Geschichte des Habsburgerreiches 1273 bis 1918. Wien, Köln u. Weimar, Böhlau, 95, 885 p. (ill., Graph. Darstellungen).

1074. BERG (Warren G.). Historical dictionary of Malta. Lanham a. London, Scarecrow Press, 95, XXI-163 p. (European historical dictionaries, 10).

1075. BETHENCOURT (Francisco). L'Inquisition à l'époque moderne. Espagne, Portugal, Italie XVe–XIXe siècle. Paris, Fayard, 95, 539 p.

1076. BORGOLTE (Michael). Eine Anthropologie der Anfänge Deutschlands. *Göttingische Gelehrte Anzeigen*, 95, 247, p. 88-102.

1077. BURROWES (Robert D.). Historical dictionary of Yemen. (Asian historical dictionaries, 17). Lanham a. London, Scarecrow Press, 95, XV-507 p.

1078. ČESKOV (Marat A.). Mirocelostnost i ee istorija. (The world integrity and its history). *Vopr. Ist.*, 95, 2, p. 27-43.

1079. CHRISTIANSEN (Erik). A history of Rome. From town to empire and from empire to town. Aarhus, Aarhus University Press, 95, 221 p.

1080. Concise history of the language sciences: from the Sumerians to the cognitivists. Ed. by E. F. K. KOERNER a. R. E. ASHER. Oxford, Pergamon, 95, XII-497 p.

1081. CONSTANTIN (Ion). România, Marile Puteri şi problema Basarabiei. (Romania and the Bessarabian question). Bucureşti, Editura Enciclopedică, 95, 310 p.

1082. COOPER (Frederick). L'Africa e il mondo. *Passato e presente*, 95, 13, 35, p. 111-140.

1083. COUTO (J.). A construçao do Brasil: ameríndios, portugueses e africanos, do início do povoamento a finais de quinhentos. Lisboa, Cosmos, 95, 408 p. (ill.). (Cosmos História, 11).

1084. COVELL (Maureen). Historical dictionary of Madagascar. Lanham a. London, Scarecrow Press, XLVI-356 p. (African historical dictionaries, 50).

1085. DE MADDALENA (Aldo). Spazi, tempi e diversità socioculturali. *Rivista storica italiana*, 95, 107, 2, p. 269-288.

1086. Dizionario biografico degli italiani. Vol. 45. Farinacci–Fedrigo. Roma, Istituto della Enciclopedia Italiana, 95, XIX-815 p.

1087. Documenti e realtà nel Mezzogiorno italiano in età medievale e moderna. Atti delle giornate di studio in memoria di Jole Mazzoleni (Amalfi, 10–12 dicembre 1993). Amalfi, Centro di Cultura e Storia Amalfitana, 95, 339 p. (Atti, 6).

1088. Drevnejšie gosudartva Vostočnoj Evropy: Materialy i issledovanija, 1992–1993 gody. (The ancient states of the Eastern Europe: The materials and researches, 1992–1993). RAN. In-t rossijskoj istorii; Otv. red. A. P. NOVOSEL'CEV. Moskva: Nauka, 95,219 p.

1089. Dziejów integracji europejskiej (Z). Od średniowiecza po współczesność. (De l'histoire de l'intégration européenne. De Moyen Age jusqu'à nos jours.). Réd. par Michał PUŁASKI. *Zeszyty Naukowe Uniwersytetu Jagiellońskiego*, 95, 1177, *Prace Historyczne*, 118, *Studia Pol.-Danubiana et Balcanica*, 7, p. 1-213. [Deutsche Zsfassung].

1090. EDROIU (Nicolae), PUŞCAŞ (Vasile). Maghiarii din România. (Hungarians in Romania). Cluj-Napoca, Fundaţia Culturală Română, Centrul de Studii Transilvane, 95, 111 p. (Interferenţe, 1).

1091. Elites e potere in Sicilia: dal medioevo a oggi. A cura di Francesco BENIGNO e Claudio TORRISI. Catanzaro, Meridiana Libri, 95, XI-175 p. (Saggi, 9).

1092. EL-MARZOUKI (Fethi). Le Makhzen et les tribus makhzen en Tunisie à l'époque hafside et au début de l'époque moderne (1230–1686). *Revue d'Histoire Maghrébine* (Partie arabe), 95, 79-80, p. 617-631.

1093. En del kilder og litteratur til lokalhistorie. (Some sources and literature on local history). Ed. by Liv MARTHINSEN. Oslo, Norsk lokalhistorisk institutt, 95, 38 p. (Hjelperåder i lokalhistorisk arbeid, 1).

1094. Frauen. Ein historisches Lesebuch. Hrsg. v. Andrea VAN DÜLMEN. München, Beck, 95, 396 p. (Beck'sche Reihe, 4002).

1095. Furansu Shi. (History of France). Ed. by Kōichi KABAYAMA, Norihiko FUKUI a. Michio SHIBATA. Tokyo, Yamakawa Shuppansha, 95, 3 vol., 600 p., 600 p., 584 p.

1096. GERNER (Kristian), HEDLUND (Stefan), SUNDSTRÖM (Niclas). Hjärnridån: det europeiska projektet och det gåtfulla Ryssland. (The brain curtain. The European project and the enigmatic Russia). Stockholm, Fischer, 95, 311 p.

1097. GUGUEV (V. K.), TREJSTER (M. Ju). Khan'skie zerkala i podražanija im na territorii Juga Vostočnoj Evropy. (Han dynasty mirrors and the local imitation in the South of the Eastern Europe). *Ros. arkheol.*, 95, 3, p. 143-156.

1098. GUST (Wolfgang). Imperium der Sultane. Eine Geschichte des osmanischen Reichs. München u. Wien, Hanser, 95, 414 p. (Karten).

5. ALLGEMEINE GESCHICHTE

1099. HAHN (István). A zsidó nép története. A babiloni fogságtól napjainkig. (Histoire du peuple juif. De la captivité de Babylone jusq'à nos jours). Budapest, Makkabi, 95, 200 p.

1100. Handbook of European history 1400–1600. Late Middle Ages, Renaissance and Reformation. Vol. 2. Vision, programs and outcomes. Ed. by Thomas A. BRADY Jr. Leiden, New York a. Köln, 95, XXIII-722 p.

1101. Handbuch der Orientalistik. Abteilung 1. Der Nahe und der Mittlere Osten. Band 20. La Civilisation phénicienne et punique: manuel de recherche. Ed. par Veronique KRINGS. Leiden, New York a. Köln, E. J. Brill, 95, XX-923 p. (ill., maps).

1102. Historia dyplomacji polskiej (połowa X–XX w.). (Histoire de la diplomatie polonaise, moitié du Xe–XXe s.). Ouvrage collectif réd. par Gérard LABUDA. T. 4. 1918–1939. [T 3. cf. Bibl. 82, n° 734]. Réd. par Piotr ŁOSSOWSKI. Auteurs: Marian LECZYK [et al.]. Warszawa, Państw. Wydawn. PWN, 95, 718 p.

1103. History today companion to British history (The). Ed. by Juliet GARDINER a. Neil WENBORN. London, Collins a. Brown, 95, III-840 p.

1104. JENSEN (Bernard Eric). Dansk identitetshistorie. (The history of the Danish identity [national self consciouness]). *Historisk Tidskrift* (Denmark), 95, 95, 1, p. 75-98.

1105. Juden in Deutschland. Hrsg. v. Michael MATHEUS. Stuttgart, Steiner, 95, 144 p.

1106. Vacat.

1107. KAMM (Antony). The Romans. An introduction. London a. New York, Routledge, 95, XII-224 p. (ill.).

1108. KHAPAEVA (Dina). L'Occident sera demain. *Annales*, 95, 50, 6, p. 1259-1270.

1109. KIRK (Tim). The Longman companion to Nazi Germany. London a. New York, Longman, 95, VIII-277 p. (maps). (Longman companions to history).

1110. KLINGE (Matti). The Baltic world. Helsinki, Otava, 95, 176 p.

1111. KOMMISRUD (Arne). Stat nasjon imperium. Habsburgmonarkiet, Tsar-Russland og Sovjetunionen. Et historisk-sosiologiskt perspektiv. Oslo, Spartacus, 95, 384 p. [The national issue and nationality politics in Habsburg empire, tsarist Russia and the Soviet Union].

1112. Kōza Sekaishi. (World history). Vol. 1–6. Ed. by Rekishigaku Kenkyukai. Tokyo, University of Tokyo Press, 95, 6 vol., 360 p., 384 p., 392 p., 468 p., 400 p., 400 p.

1113. Kōza Surabu no Sekai. (The Slavic world). Ed. by Teruyuki HARA [et al.]. Vol. 1–3. Vol. 6–8. Tokyo, Kōbundo, 95, 6 vol., 352 p., 392 p., 408 p., 416 p., 376 p., 400 p.

1114. KRUHEK (Milan). Krajiške utvrde Hrvatskog kraljevstva. (Frontier fortifications of the Croatian Kingdom). Zagreb, Institut za suvremenu povijest, 95, 404 p.

1115. KURUCZ (Görgy). Érdekek és előítéletek. A brit diplomácia és Magyarország a 18. század végéig. (Intérêts et préjugés. La diplomatie britannique et la Hongrie jusq'à la fin du XVIIIe siècle). *Századok*, 95, 129, 2, p. 253-284.

1116. LANDA (Robert G.). Vostok: civilizacija, formacija, socium. (The East: civilization, structure). *Vopr. Ist.*, 95, 4, p. 47-56.

1117. LERSKI (Jerzy Jan). Historical dictionary of Poland, 966–1945. With special editing and emendations by Piotr WROBEL a. Richard J. KOZICKI. Foreword by Aleksander GIEYSZTOR. Westport a. London, Greenwood Press, 95, XXV-750 p.

1118. Lexikon des Mittelalters. T. 7. Fasc. 6. Russkaja Pravda – Samson. Fasc. 7. Samsun – Schriftsinne. Fasc. 8. Schriftstellerkataloge – Servatius. Fasc. 9. Servicios – Snorri Sturluson. Fasc. 10. Soares – Stadt (Rus'). München, Artemis u. LexMA, 95, col. 1121-1344, 1345-1568, 1569-1792, 1793-2016, VIII-2017-2221.

1119. LIBAEK (Ivar), SÖRENSEN (Öivind). A history of Norway: from the ice age to the age of petroleum. Oslo, Gröndal & Dreyer, 95, 181 p.

1120. LINDE-LAURSEN (Anders). Det nationales natur. Studier i dansk-svenske relationer. (The nature of the national. Studies in Danish-Swedish relations). København, Nordisk Ministerråd, 95, 254 p.

1121. LORENTZ (John Henry). Historical dictionary of Iran. (Asian historical dictionaries, 16). Lanham a. London, Scarecrow Press, 95, XXIV-325 p.

1122. LOTZE (Detlef). Griechische Geschichte. Von den Anfängen bis zum Hellenismus. München, Beck, 95, 113 p.

1123. MACAN (Trpimir). Hrvatska povijest: pregled. (Croatian history: a survey). Zagreb, Matica hrvatska, 95, 239 p.

1124. Magyarok (A) krónikája. (La Chronique des Hongrois). Réd. par Ferenc GLATZ. Budapest, Officina Nova, 95, 816 p.

1125. MANTINI (Silvia). Un recinto di identificazione: le mura sacre della città. Riflessioni su Firenze dall'età classica al Medioevo. *Archivio storico italiano*, 95, 153, 564, p. 211-262.

1126. Mare Balticum – Baltics 2000 Years. Ed. by Ulla EHRENSVÄRD [et al.]. Helsinki, Otava & John Nurminen Foundation, 95, 287 p. (ill., maps).

1127. MATEI (Horia C.). Enciclopedia antichității. București, Editura Meronia, 95, 494 p. (ill.).

1128. MATERNA (Ingo). Brandenburgische Geschichte. Berlin, Akademie Verlag, 95, 891 p.

1129. MATOSO (José). Identificação de um País. Lisboa, Estampa, 95, 2 vol., 467 p., 408 p.

1130. MAUDE (George). Historical dictionary of Finland. Lanham a. London, Scarecrow Press, 95, XXIII-356 p. (European historical dictionaries, 8).

1131. MEDINA (Joao). História de Portugal dos tempos pré-históricos ãs nossos dias. Lisboa, Clube Internacional do Livro, 95, 15 vol., 364 p., 459 p., 403 p., 379 p., 378 p., 388 p., 457 p., 347 p., 403 p., 372 p., 355 p., 409 p., 411 p., 380 p., 492 p. (ill., bibl.).

1132. MENDEZ SALCEDO (Ildefonso). Seis temas de historia venezolana. Caracas, [s. n.], 95, 123 p.

1133. Monta tietä menneisyteen. (Several ways heading to the past). Ed. by Leena ROSSI a. Hanne KOIVISTO. Turku, Turun yliopisto, Kulttuurihistoria, 95, 348 p. (ill.). [Cf. nos <choice> 3356, 5598, 6933.]

1134. MORILLO (Stephen). Guns and government: a comparative study of Europe and Japan. *Journal of World History*, 95, 6, p. 75-106.

1135. MUNDT (Robert J.). Historical dictionary of Cote d'Ivoire (the Ivory Coast). Lanham a. London, Scarecrow Press, 95, XXXIV-367 p. (African historical dictionaries, 41).

1136. NIEDERHAUSER (Emil). Viharzóna a Balkánon. Bosznia-Hercegovina története. (Zone de tempête dans les Balkans. Histoire de la Bosnie-Herzégovine). *Magyar tudomány*, 95, 40, 6, p. 697-707.

1137. Nihon-Keiei-shi. (Japanese management history). Vol. 1–5. Ed. by Shigeaki YASOUKA, Matao MIYAMOTO, Tsunehiko YUI, Hiroaki YAMAZAKI, Hidemasa MORIKAWA, Masatoshi AMANO, Takeshi ABE, Eisuke DAITO, Takeo KIKKAWA a. Seiichirō YONEKURA. Tokyo, Iwanami Shoten, 95, 5 vol., 360 p., 360 p., 328 p., 338 p., 382 p.

1138. NIRENBERG (David). Les juifs, la violence et le sacré. *Annales*, 95, 50, 1, p. 109-132.

1139. Novgorod, Örebro, Lübeck after 700 years (1295–1995): lectures. Ed. by Pär HANSSON. Örebro, Bildningsförvaltningen, 95, 112 p.

1140. Oxford companion to the Second World War (The). General editor I.C.B. DEAR, consultant editor M.R.D. FOOT. Oxford, Oxford U. P., 95, XXII-1343 p. (ill.).

1141. PANTELI (Stavros). Historical dictionary of Cyprus. Lanham a. London, Scarecrow Press, 95, XXXI-223 p. (European historical dictionaries, 6).

1142. Penguin dictionary of ancient history (The). Ed. by Graham SPEAKE. London, Penguin, 95, X-758 p. (Penguin reference books).

1143. PETKOV (Kiril). A Korona elleni lázadóktól a fideli-nostri [!] Bulgariig. Az ortodox balkáni népekről alkotott kép Kelet-Közép-Európában. (Des émeutes contre la couronne jusq'aux fideles nostri Bulgari. L'image des peuples Balkaniques orthodoxes en Europe Centrale-Orientale). *Aetas*, 95, 3, p. 32-52.

1144. PIROUET (M. Louise). Historical dictionary of Uganda. Metuchen, Scarecrow Press, 95, XLV-533 p. (African historical dictionaries, 64).

1145. Polska na przestrzeni wieków. (Pologne à travers les siècles). Ouvr. collectif. réd. par Janusz TAZBIR. Auteurs: Tomasz KIZWALTER [et al.]. Warszawa, Wydawn. Nauk. PWN, 95, 763 p. (cartes).

1146. Polski słownik biograficzny. (Dictionnaire biographique polonais). T. 36. Fasc. 1–3. Warszawa et Kraków, Fundusz Nauki Pol., 95, 480 p. (Pol. Akad. Nauk, Inst. Hist.).

1147. Polskie tradycje wojskowe. (Les traditions militaires polonaises). T. 3. Tradycje walk wyzwoleńczych „Za naszą i waszą wolność". (Traditions des luttes indépendantistes "pour votre et notre liberté"). [T. 1 cf. Bibl.90, n° 708.] Réd. Józef Wiesław DYSKANT. Warszawa, Bellona, 95, 421 p. (phot., fig., cartes).

1148. PURVIS (Thomas L.). A dictionary of American history. Cambridge, Blackwell, 95, VIII-454 p. (Blackwell reference).

1149. RAFFESTIN (Claude). Géopolitique et histoire. Avec la coll. de Dario LOPRENO et Yvan PASTEUR. Lausanne et Paris, Payot, 95, 330 p.

1150. Rannie formy političeskoj organizacii: Ot pervobytnosti k gosugarstvennosti. (The early forms of political organization: from primitive society to statehood). Otv. red., sost., predislovie V. A. POPOVA. Moskva, Izdatel'skaja firma "Vostočnaja literatura" RAN, RAN. Muzej antropologii i étnografii im. Petra Velikogo (Kunstkamera), 95, 350p.

1151. RAO (A. M.). La Rivoluzione Francese e la scoperta della politica. *Studi Storici*, 95, 1, p. 163-214.

1152. RENSHAW (Patrick). Longman companion to America in the era of the two World Wars, 1910–45. New York, Longman, 95, 256 p. (maps). (Longman companions to history).

1153. Roldán Hervás (José Manuel). Historia de Roma. Salamanca, Ediciones Universidad de Salamanca, 95, 509 p. (Historia Salamanca de la Antigüedad).

1154. ROMANO (Ruggiero). L'idea dell'impero: da Roma a Carlo V. *In*: L'incidenza dell'antico [Cf. n° 6014], p. 69-79.

1155. ROVAN (Joseph). Geschichte der Deutschen. Von ihren Ursprüngen bis Heute. München u. Wien, Hanser, 95, 848 p.

1156. RUNBLOM (Harald). Majoritet och minoritet i Östersjöområdet: ett historiskt perspektiv. (National majorities and minorities in the Baltic: a historical perspective). Stockholm, Natur och Kultur. 95, 166 p. (Vittterhetsakademiens skriftserie om Europa).

1157. SCOBBIE (Irene). Historical dictionary of Sweden. Metuchen, Scarecrow Press, 95, XXII-314 p. (European historical dictionaries, 7).

1158. SKRYNNIKOV (Ruslan G.). Vojny Drevnej Rusi. (Wars of the Ancient Russ). *Vopr. Ist.*, 95, 11/12, p. 24-38.

1159. Society and culture. Poland in Europe. Studies in social and cultural history. Poland at the 18th International Congress of Historical Sciences in Montréal. Ed. by Maria BOGUCKA. Warszawa, Advancement of Sciences-Education „UN-O", 95, 146 p. (Pol. Acad. of Sciences, Commitee of Hist. Sciences. Inst. of History).

1160. STALLAERTS (Robert), LAURENS (Jeannine). Historical dictionary of the Republic of Croatia. Metuchen a. London, Scarecrow Press, 95, XLII-341 p. (European historical dictionaries, 9).

1161. STEINHÜBEL (Jan). Vel'komoravské územie v severovýchodnom Zadunajsku. (The area of Great Moravian Empire to the north-east of Transdanubianen). Bratislava, Veda, 95, 98 p.

1162. Studien zur Geschichte des Ostseeraumes. Vol. 1. Hrsg. v. Thomas RIIS. Odense, Odense U. P., 95, 148 p. (Dansk komité for Byhistorie. Byhistoriske skrifter, VII= Odense university studies in history and social sciences, 186).

1163. TAKAHASHI (Yoshito). Majo to Yōroppa. (Witches and Europe). Tokyo, Iwanami Shoten, 95, 312 p.

1164. TIMOŠČUK (Boris A.). Vostočnye slavjane: ot obščiny k gorodam. (The Eastern Slavs: from communities to towns). Otv. red. S. A. PLETNEVA. Moskva, Izdatel'stvo Moskovskogo universiteta, 95, 261 p.

1165. TOWNSON (Duncan). The new Penguin dictionary of modern history, 1789–1945. London, Penguin, 95, 941 p. (Penguin reference books).

1166. Treaties of the War of the Spanish Succession (The): an historical and critical dictionary. Ed. by Linda FREY a. Marsha FREY. Westport a. London, Greenwood Press, 95, XXVI-576p.

1167. TRUHART (Peter). Lexikon der historischen Staatennamen. München, New Providence, London u. Paris, K. G. Saur, 95, XXXIV-872 p.

1168. Türkische Wirtschafts- und Sozialgeschichte von 1071–1920. Hrsg. v. Raoul MOTIKA u. Hans G. MAJER. Wiesbaden, Harrassowitz, 95, VIII-373 p.

1169. VEREMES (Thanos M.), DRAGOUMIS (Mark). Historical dictionary of Greece. Metuchen a. London, Scarecrow Press, 95, XVII-258 p. (European historical dictionaries, 5).

1170. Vostočnyj Turkestan v drevnosti i rannem srednevekov'e: Khozjajstvo, material'naja kul'tura. (Eastern Turkestan in antiquity and early Medieval times: The economy, material culture). B. A. LITVINSKIJ, E. I. LUBO-LESNIČENKO, E. V. ANTONOVA i drugie. Pod. red. B. A. LITVINSKOGO. Moskva, Vostočnaja literatura, RAN, In-t vostokovedenija, 523 p.

1171. WEITHMANN (Michael W.). Balkanchronik. 2000 Jahre zwischen Orient und Okzident. Regensburg, Graz, Wien u. Köln, Pustet/Styria, 95, 542 p.

1172. WIN (May Kyi), SMITH (Harold E.). Historical dictionary of Thailand. Lanham, Scarecrow Press, 95, 296 p. (Asian historical dictionaries 18).

1173. ZABIB (Najib). 'al-Mawsu'ah 'al-`ammah lita'rikh 'al-Maghrib wa-'al-'Andalus. (General encyclopedia for history of Morocco and Al-Andalus). Bayrut, Dar 'al-Amir, 95, 5 vol., [s. p.] (ill., maps).

Cf. n°s 3353, 4580-4665

§ 6. Staats- und Gesellschaftslehre.

* 1174. Bibliographie [sur l'histoire des idées politiques]. *Revue française d'histoire des idées politiques*, 95, 2, p. 421-446.

* 1175. ECCLESHALL (Robert), KENNY (Michael). Western political thought: a bibliographical guide to post-war research. With the assistance of Michael DROLET, Gerard FITZPATRICK a. Gerard MAC CANN. Manchester, Manchester U. P., 95, XIV-342 p. (History and related disciplines select bibliographies).

** 1176. CUTINELLI-RÈNDINA (Emanuele). Rec. di N. Machiavelli, De principatibus. Testo critico a cura di G. INGLESE. *Studi e problemi di critica testuale*, 95, p. 192-206.

** 1177. MORELLET (André). Manoscritti storico-politici: testi inediti. A cura di Eugenio DI RIENZO. Firenze, Centro Editoriale Toscano, 95, VI-244 p. (Politica e storia, 46).

———

1178. ABROMAIT (Heidran). Volkssouveränität, Parlamentssouveränität, Verfassungssouveränität: Drei Realmodelle der Legitimation staatlichen Handelns. *Politische Vierteljahresschrift*, 95, 36, 1, p. 49-66.

1179. AGUET (Jean-Pierre). Tocqueville: democratie, armée et guerre. *Revue suisse d'histoire*, 95, 45, 3, p. 371-397.

1180. ANTER (Andreas). Max Webers Theorie des modernen Staates. Herkunft, Struktur und Bedeutung. Berlin, Duncker & Humblot, 95, 256 p. (Beiträge zur politischen Wissenschaft, 82).

1181. Aristotelismo politico e ragion di Stato: atti del convegno internazionale di Torino, 11–13 febbraio 1993. A cura di A. Enzo BALDINI. Firenze, Olschki, 95, 421 p. (Studi e testi. Fondazione Luigi Firpo, Centro di studi sul pensiero politico, 4). [Cf. n° <scelta> 1229.]

1182. ARMOGATHE (Jean-Robert). Contrat social et régicide [apport des théoriciens jésuites, XVIe–XVIIIe s.]. *Revue de sciences morales et politiques*, 95, 150, 1, p. 69-80.

1183. BARTELSON (Jens). A genealogy of sovereignty. Cambridge, Cambridge U. P., 95, X-317 p. (Cambridge studies in international relations, 39).

1184. BEHME (Thomas). Samuel von Pufendorf: Naturrecht und Staat. Eine Analyse und Interpretation seiner Theorie, ihrer Grundlagen und Probleme. Göttingen, Vandenhoeck & Ruprecht, 95, 195 p. (Veröffentlichungen des Max-Planck-Instituts für Geschichte, 112).

1185. BUCHHEIM (Hans). Das Prinzip "Nation" und der neuzeitliche Verfassungsstaat. *Zeitschrift für Politik*, 95, 42, 1, p. 60-67.

1186. CHANDHOKE (Neera). State and civil society: explorations in political theory. New Delhi a. London, Sage, 95, 266 p.

1187. CHENEVAL (Francis). Die Rezeption der Monarchia Dantes bis zur Editio Princeps im Jahre 1559: Metamorphosen eines philosophischen Werkes. Mit einer kritischen Edition von Guido Vernanis Tractatus de potestate summi pontificis. München, W. Fink, 95, XIII-490 p. (Humanistische Bibliothek. Reihe 1, Abhandlungen, 47).

1188. CLARK (Samuel). State and status: the rise of the state and aristocratic power in Western Europe. Cardiff, University of Wales Press, 95, XIII-502 p.

1189. Companion to contemporary political philosophy (A). Ed. by Robert E. GOODIN a. Philip PETTIT. Oxford, Blackwell, 95, XIII-679 p. (ill.). (Blackwell companions to philosophy).

1190. COUZINET (Marie-Dominique). Jean Bodin: état des lieux et perspectives de recherche. *Réforme, Humanisme, Renaissance*, 95, 21, 40, p. 11-22.

1191. CRUZ (Manuel B.). Instituiçoes políticas e processos sociais. Lisboa, Bertrand, 95, 503 p. (Ensaios e documentos, 21).

1192. DAVIDSON (Alastair). Dilemma of liberal socialism: the case of Norberto Bobbio. *Australian Journal of Politics and History*, 95, 41, 1, p. 47-54.

1193. DESBROUSSES (Hélène), PELOILLE (Bernard). De l'économie à la politique. Le thème des classes sociales [Turgot, Necker, Rousseau, Sieyès]. *Cahiers pour l'analyse concrète*, 95, 35, 78 p.

1194. EVZEROV (Robert Ja.). Leninskaja teorija imperializma: mify i realii. (The Leninist theory of imperialism: myths and reality). *Nov. novejš. Ist.*, 95, 3, p. 43-63.

1195. FERRARI (Jean). De la religion civile dans la pensée politique de Jean-Jacques Rousseau. *Etudes Jean-Jacques Rousseau*, 95, 7, p. 79-99.

1196. FREZZA (Daria). «Hitleristica abracadabra». Le scienze sociali americane e la crisi della democrazia (1920–1941). *Passato e presente*, 95, 13, 35, p. 37-64.

1197. GADŽIEV (kamaludin S.). Liberalizm: istorija i sovremennost'. (Liberalism. History and contemporaneity). *Nov. novejš. Ist.*, 95, 6, p. 15-31.

1198. GAUCHET (M.). La révolution des pouvoirs: la souveraineté, le peuple et la représentation. Paris, Gallimard, 95, 288 p.

1199. GLEASON (Abbot). Totalitarianism. New York, Oxford U. P., 307 p.

1200. GUBOGLO (Mikhail N.). Opyt i uroki suverenizacii (na materialakh Baškortostana I Tatarsana). (The experience and lessons of sovereignty. Case study of Bashkortostan and Tartastan, 1990s). *Oteč. Ist.*, 95, 2, p. 17-53.

1201. Hannah Arendt and Leo Strauss: German emigrés and American political thought after World War II. Ed. by Peter Graf KIELMANSEGG, Horst MEWES a. Elisabeth GLASER-SCHMIDT. Washington, German Historical Institute, a. Cambridge, Cambridge U. P., 95, X-208 p. (Publications of the German Historical Institute, Washington, D.C).

1202. HELLER (Leonid), Niqueux (Michel). Histoire de l'utopie en Russie. Paris, PUF, 95, 304 p.

1203. HINDESS (B.). Discourses of power: from Hobbes to Foucault. Oxford a. Cambridge, Blackwell, 95, VIII-183 p.

1204. HUTCHINGS (Kimberly). Kant, critique, and politics. London a. New York, Routledge, 95, XI-219 p.

1205. LARRERE (Catherine). Propriété et souveraineté chez Rousseau. *Droits*, 95, 22, p. 39-45.

1206. LIVORSI (Franco). Introduzione alla storia del pensiero politico. Torino, Tirrenia Stampatori, 95, 112 p.

1207. MOGIL'NICKIJ (Boris G.). N. A. Berdjaev o russkoj revolucii. (N. A. Berdyaev on the Russian revolution). *Nov. novejš. Ist.*, 95, 6, p. 54-67.

1208. MOHRS (Thomas). Vom Weltstaat: Hobbes' Sozialphilosophie, Soziobiologie, Realpolitik. Berlin, Akademie Verlag, 95, XXXVI-464 p. (Politische Ideen, 2).

1209. MOUREAUX (José-Michel). La politique de Voltaire dans le Portatif: de la première édition à l'article «Maître». *Revue d'histoire littéraire de la France*, 95, 2, p. 165-176.

1210. MÜLLER (Christian). Von der Gerechtigkeitstheorie zum Politischen Liberalismus. Rawls, Libertarians, Communitarians, und wieder Rawls. *Zeitschrift für Politik*, 95, 42, 3, p. 268-296.

1211. Naturrecht, Spätaufklärung, Revolution. Hrsg. v. Otto DANN u. Diethelm KLIPPEL. Hamburg, Meiner, 95, VI-303 p. (Studien zum achtzehnten Jahrhundert, 16).

1212. NAVET (Georges). Les échanges entre Proudhon et Michelet: fédération ou fédéralisme? Suivi de la correspondance de Michelet et de Proudhon [1851–1860]. *Archives proudhoniennes*, 95, p. 23-43.

1213. NEAUD (Pierrette M.). Montesquieu: biographie, étude de l'œuvre. Paris, A. Michel, 95, 191 p. (ill.).

1214. NITSCHKE (Peter). Staatsräson kontra Utopie?: von Thomas Müntzer bis zu Friedrich II. von Preussen. Stuttgart, J.B. Metzler, 95, XI-320 p.

1215. PAPPAS (Nickolas). Plato and the Republic. London a. New York, Routledge, 95, XIV-230 p. (Routledge philosophy guidebooks).

1216. PELTONEN (Markku). Classical humanism and republicanism in English political thought 1570–1640. Cambridge, Cambridge U. P., 95, XII-356 p. (Ideas in context, 36).

1217. Pluralisme et équité. La justice sociale dans la démocratie. Sous la dir. de Joëlle AFFICHARD et Jean-Baptiste DE FOUCAULD. Paris, Edition Esprit, Commissariat général du Plan, 95, 262 p.

1218. PROCACCI (Giuliano). Machiavelli nella cultura europea dell'età moderna. Roma e Bari, Laterza, 95, 494 p. (Collezione storica).

1219. RAPHAEL (L.). Freiheit und Wohlstand der Nationen. Alexander von Humboldts Analysen der politischen Zustände Amerikas und das politische Denken seiner Zeit. *Historische Zeitschrift*, 95, 260, 3, p. 749-776.

1220. REEDY (W. Jay). The traditionalist critique of individualism in post-revolutionary France: the case of Louis de Bonald. *History of political thought*, 95, 16, 1, p. 49-75.

1221. RENGGER (Nicholas J). Political theory, modernity, and postmodernity: beyond enlightenment and critique. Oxford, Blackwell, 95, XVII-253 p.

1222. Repubblica e virtù: pensiero politico e monarchia cattolica fra XVI e XVII secolo. A cura di Chiara CONTINISIO e Cesare MOZZARELLI. Roma, Bulzoni, 95, 611 p. (Biblioteca del Cinquecento, 67).

1223. RICHTER (Melvin). The history of political and social concepts. A critical introduction. New York a. Oxford, Oxford U. P., 95, 204 p.

1224. ROSEN (Stanley). Plato's Statesman: the web of politics. New Haven, Yale U. P., 95, X-197 p.

1225. SENELLART (Michel). Les arts de gouverner: du regimen médiéval au concept de gouvernement. Paris, Ed. du Seuil, 95, 311 p.

1226. SPRINGBORG (Patricia). Hobbes's biblical beasts: Leviathan and Behemoth. *Polit. Theory*, 95, 23, 2, p. 353-375.

1227. SYLOS LABINI (Paolo). La crisi italiana. Roma e Bari, Laterza, 95, XII-96 p. (Nocciolo, 11).

1228. TERNI (Massimo). La pianta della sovranità: teologia e politica tra Medioevo ed età moderna. Roma e Bari, Laterza, 95, 206 p. (Biblioteca di cultura moderna, 1083).

1229. VASOLI (Cesare). Il carattere "naturale" dello Stato e la sua "patologia" nella tradizione politica aristotelica. *In*: Aristotelismo politico e ragion di stato [Cf. n° 1181], p. 53-65.

1230. VORLÄNDER (Hans). Der ambivalente Liberalismus. Oder: Was hält die liberale Demokratie zusammen? *Zeitschrift für Politik*, 95, 42, 3, p. 250-267.

1231. ZARKA (Yves Charles). Hobbes et la pensée politique moderne. Paris, PUF, 95, 308 p. (Fondements de la politique. Serie Essais).

Cf. n°s 1973, 2643

§ 7. Rechts- und Verfassungsgeschichte.

1232. ANIL (Yaşar Şahin). Osmanlı Döneminde İki Dava. (Deux procès à l'époque ottomane). Ankara, Yapı Kredi Yayınları, 95, 208 p.

1233. ASCHERI (Mario). Tribunali, giuristi e istituzioni: dal Medioevo all'età moderna. Bologna, Il Mulino, 95, 282 p. (Ricerca).

1234. BÉLI (Gábor). Magyar jogtörténet az államalapítástól 1848-ig. (Histoire juridique hongroise de la constittion de l'Etat jusqu'à 1848). Pécs, JPTE ÁJK, 95, 170 p.

1235. BENACCHIO (Giannantonio). La circolazione dei modelli giuridici tra gli slavi del sud (sloveni, croati, serbi). Padova, Casa edit. dott. A. Milani C.E.D.A.M, 95, IX-305 p.

1236. GAUDEMET (Jean). Membrum, persona, status. *Studia et documenta historiae et iuris*, 95, 61, p. 1-16.

1237. Handbook of humanitarian law in armed conflicts (The). Ed. by Dieter FLECK, in collaboration with Michael BOTHE [et al.]. Oxford, Oxford U. P., 95, XVI-589 p. (ill.).

1238. Juristen: ein biographisches Lexicon von der Antike bis zum 20. Jahrhundert. Hrsg. v. Michael STOLLEIS. München, Beck, 95, 703 p.

1239. KNAFLA (Louis A.), BINNIE (Susan W.S.). Law, society and the state: essays in modern legal history. Toronto, University of Toronto Press, 95, XII-558 p.

1240. MOHNHAUPT (Heinz), GRIMM (Dieter). Verfassung. Zur Geschichte des Begriffs von der Antike bis zur Gegenwart. Zwei Studien. Berlin, Duncker & Humblot, 95, IX-144 p. (Schriften zur Verfassungsgeschichte, 47).

1241. PADOA-SCHIOPPA (Antonio). Il diritto nella storia d'Europa. Parte 1. Il Medioevo. Padova, Casa edit. dott. A. Milani C.E.D.A.M., 95, 290 p.

1242. PECORELLA (Corrado). Studi e ricerche di storia del diritto. Torino, G. Giappichelli, 95, LVI-630 p.

1243. ROULAND (Norbert). L'Etat français et le pluralisme. Histoire politique des institutions publiques de 476–1792. Paris, Ed. Odile Jacob, 95, 377 p.

1244. SAASTAMOINEN (Kari). The morality of the fallen man: Samuel Pufendorff on the natural law. Helsinki, SHS, 94, 190 p. (Studia historia, 52.).

1245. SANCHEZ BELLA (Ismael). Nuevos estudios de Derecho Indiano. Pamplona, EUNSA, 95, 404 p.

(Coleccion juridica. Universidad de Navarra. Facultad de Derecho, 112).

1246. STEPPAN (Markus). Das bäuerliche Recht an der Liegenschaft: vom Ende des 14. bis zum ausgehenden 18. Jahrhundert. Graz, Leykam-Verlag, 95, 144 p. (Grazer rechts- und staatswissenschaftliche Studien, 53).

1247. Thinking about law: perspectives on the history, philosophy and sociology of law. Ed. by Rosemary HUNTER, Richard INGLEBY a. Richard JOHNSTONE. St. Leonards, Allen & Unwin, 95, XIV-254 p.

1248. VAN CAENEGEM (Raoul C.). An historical introduction to Western constitutional law. Cambridge, Cambridge U. P., 95, X-338 p.

1249. WELCHMAN (Jennifer). Locke on slavery and inalienable rights. *Can. J. Phil.*, 95, 25, 1, p. 67-82.

Cf. n°s 7534-7551

§ 8. Wirtschafts- und Sozialgeschichte.

* 1250. MILLER (Joseph), GIBBS (Janis M.). Slavery: annual bibliographical supplement (1994). *Slavery and Abolition*, 95, 16, 3, p. 398-460.

1251. Alltagskulturen zwischen Erinnerung und Geschichte. Beiträge zur Volkskunde der Deutschen im und aus dem östlichen Europa. Hrsg. V. Kurt DRÖGE. München, Oldenbourg, 95, 278 p. (Schriften des Bundesinstituts für ostdeutsche Kultur und Geschichte, 6). [Cf. n° <Auswahl> 1270.]

1252. BAECHLER (Jean). Le capitalisme. Vol. 1. Les origines. Vol. 2. L'économie capitaliste. Paris, Gallimard, 442 p., 449 p.

1253. BAILLY (Antoine). Ville pratiquée, ville imaginée. *In*: Pour une histoire économique et sociale internationale [Cf. n° 1297], p. 611-616.

1254. BERGIER (Jean-François). Régions et histoire économique: quelques interrogations. *In*: Pour une histoire économique et sociale internationale [Cf. n° 1297], p. 101-110.

1255. BIAGIANTI (Ivo). La terra e gli uomini a San Marino. Agricoltura e rapporti di produzione dal Medioevo al Novecento. San Marino, Università degli Studi della Repubblica di San Marino, 95, 241 p. (Quaderni del Centro di Studi Storici, 11).

1256. BOLENS (Lucie). La notion de «développement» en al-Andalus. *In*: Pour une histoire économique et sociale internationale [Cf. n° 1297], p. 449-460.

1257. BUFFET (Jacky). Pour une approche «indisciplinée» des études du développement éléments du débat latino-américain et aspects de renouvellement. *In*: Pour une histoire économique et sociale internationale [Cf. n° 1297], p. 427-448.

1258. BUSINO (Giovanni). Les sciences sociales et l'histoire. *In*: Pour une histoire économique et sociale internationale [Cf. n° 1297], p. 85-100.

1259. CARLEVARO (Fabrizio), LOZA (Hugo). Analyse du développement économique d'une colonie agricole de l'Amazonie bolivienne. Un essai d'histoire économique mathématique. *In*: Pour une histoire économique et sociale internationale [Cf. n° 1297], p. 353-370.

1260. CASPRINI (Flavio). L'economia delle relazioni monetarie internazionali: teoria, storia e istituzioni. Roma, NIS, 95, 407 p. (Studi superiori Nis, 260).

1261. COQUERY-VIDROVITCH (Catherine). L'Afrique noire francophone au tournant de l'indépendence: les héritages. *In*: Pour une histoire économique et sociale internationale [Cf. n° 1297], p. 371-378.

1262. DEROUET (Bernard). Territoire et parenté. Pour une mise en perspective de la communauté rurale et des formes de reproduction familiale. *Annales*, 95, 50, 3, p. 645-686.

1263. DOCKES (Pierre). La logique du mercantilisme. *In*: Pour une histoire économique et sociale internationale [Cf. n° 1297], p. 483-498.

1264. ETEMAND (Bouda). Superficies et populations coloniales (XVIIIe–XXe siècles): questions de méthode. *In*: Pour une histoire économique et sociale internationale [Cf. n° 1297], p. 397-418.

1265. ETIENNE (Gilbert). Et si l'économie du développement élargissait son cadre? *In*: Pour une histoire économique et sociale internationale [Cf. n° 1297], p. 419-426.

1266. FOGEL (Robert W.). History with numbers. The American experience. *In*: Pour une histoire économique et sociale internationale [Cf. n° 1297], p. 47-56.

1267. GARRIER (Gilbert). Histoire sociale et culturelle du vin. Paris, Bordas, 95, 366 p.

1268. GINZBURG (Andrea). Nazionalismi ed economia: un rapporto complicato. *Passato e presente*, 95, 13, 34, p. 113-122.

1269. GLEJSER (Herbert). National X-Efficiency. *In*: Pour une histoire économique et sociale internationale [Cf. n° 1297], p. 301-312.

1270. GÖRNER (Karen). Familiale Traditionen in der Betrachtung über mehrere Generationen: ein Vergleich zwischen Einheimischen und Vertriebenen. *In*: Alltagskulturen zwischen Erinnerung und Geschichte [Cf. n° 1251], p. 67-81.

1271. Hauptstadt: Historische Perspektiven eines deutschen Themas. Hrsg. v. Hans M. KÖRNER u. Katharina WEIGAND. München, Deutscher Taschenbuch Verlag, 95, 280 p. [Cf. n^{os} <Auswahl> 541, 6111.]

1272. HOHENBERG (Paul M.), HOLLEN LEES (Lynn). The making of urban Europe, 1000–1994. Cambridge a. London, Harvard U. P., 95, IX-436 p.

8. WIRTSCHAFTS- UND SOZIALGESCHICHTE

1273. In vino veritas. Ed. by O. MURRAY a. M. TECUSAN. Roma, The British School at Rome, 95, 317 p. [Cf. n^{os} <choice> 2471, 2474, 2715, 2717, 2740, 2779, 2831, 2892.]

1274. ISSAWI (Charles). The Balkan and the Middle East: economic and social development in the Ottoman successor states. *In*: Pour une histoire économique et sociale internationale [Cf. n° 1297], p. 193-204.

1275. JAKIČ (Ivan). Gradovi, graščine in dvorci na Slovenskem. (Castles, mansion houses, and manor houses in Slovenia). Radovljica, Didakta, 95, 179 p.

1276. JONSSON (Ulf). Kommentar till Lena Sommestad: jordbrukets kvinnor i den svenska modellen. (Commentary to Lena Sommestad: women in agriculture according to the Swedish model). *Historisk Tidskrift* (Sweden), 95, 4, p. 528-536.

1277. KINDLEBERGER (Charles P.). Types of international economic history. *In*: Pour une histoire économique et sociale internationale [Cf. n° 1297], p. 33-46.

1278. KÜSTER (Hansjörg). Geschichte der Landschaft in Mitteleuropa von der Eiszeit bis zur Gegenwart. München, Beck, 95, 424 p.

1279. LANDERS (David S.). Convergence and divergence: what do numbers tell? *In*: Pour une histoire économique et sociale internationale [Cf. n° 1297], p. 111-120.

1280. LEPETIT (Bernard). La societé comme un tout. *In*: Historia a Debate. Tomo 1 [Cf. n° 602], p. 147-158.

1281. LITWIN (Jerzy). Polskie szkutnictwo ludowe XX wieku. (Construction navale populaire en Pologne en XX s.) Gdańsk, Marpress, 95, 375 p. (English summary, phot., dessins cartes). (Gdańsk Maritime Proceedings, 10).

1282. LOHRMANN (Dietrich). Von der östlichen zur westlichen Windmühle. *Archiv für Kulturgeschichte*, 95, 77, p. 1-32.

1283. LØKKE (Anne). No difference without a cause: infant mortality rates as a world view generator. *Scandinavian Journal of History*, 95, 20, p. 75-96.

1284. MALANIMA (Paolo). Economia preindustriale. Mille anni: dal IX al XVIII secolo. Milano, B. Mondadori, 95, X-630 p. (ill.).

1285. MAURO (Frédéric). La préindustrialisation du Brésil et la théorie de Hirschman: exposé d'un projet. *In*: Pour une histoire économique et sociale internationale [Cf. n° 1297], p. 341-352.

1286. MAYER (Jean). Esclavage et travail forcé en Afrique portugaise (1415–1975). *In*: Pour une histoire économique et sociale internationale [Cf. n° 1297], p. 379-396.

1287. Metamorfosi della città. A cura di Leonardo BENEVOLO. Milano, Scheiwiller, 95, XVI-492 p. (ill., tavole). (Civitas Europaea). [Cf. n° <scelta> 2875.]

1288. MITCHELL (Brian R.). International historical statistics. Africa, Asia and Oceania, 1750–1988. New York, Stockton a. Basingstoke, Macmillan, 95, XXIII-1089 p.

1289. NOLTE (Hans-Heinrich). Comparing internal peripheries. A plea for non-linear research. *In*: Pour une histoire économique et sociale internationale [Cf. n° 1297], p. 75-84.

1290. ORGANSKI (A. F. Kenneth), Kugler (Jacek), Abdollahian (M. Andrew). The mosaic of international power: reflections on general trends. *In*: Pour une histoire économique et sociale internationale [Cf. n° 1297], p. 169-192.

1291. ORTAYLI (İlber). İstanbul'dan Sayfalar. (Les pages de l'histoire d'İstanbul). İstanbul, İletişim Yayınları, 95, 250 p.

1292. OZTÜRK (Yücel). XIII ve XVII. Yüzyıllarda Karadeniz Ticareti. (Le commerce dans la Mer Noire aux XIIIe et XVIIe siècles). *Türk Dünyası Araştırmaları Dergisi*, 95, 97, p. 113-137.

1293. Panoramas urbains. Situation de l'histoire des villes. Ed. par Jean-Louis BIGET et Jean Claude HERVE. [S. l.], Editions Fontenay/Saint-Cloud, 95, 348 p.

1294. PERRENOND (Alfred). Le rôle de la migration dans la régulation démographique et son influence sur les comportements. *In*: Pour une histoire économique et sociale internationale [Cf. n° 1297], p. 571-594.

1295. PLACANICA (Augusto). Le conseguenze socio-economiche dei forti terremoti. Miti di capovolgimento e consolidamenti reali. *Rivista storica italiana*, 95, 107, 3, p. 831-839.

1296. POLLARD (Sidney). Marginal areas. Do they have a common history? *In*: Pour une histoire économique et sociale internationale [Cf. n° 1297], p. 121-136.

1297. Pour une histoire économique et sociale internationale. Mélanges offerts à Paul Bairoch. Ed. par Bouda ETEMAND, Jean BATOU et Thomas DAVID. Genève, Edition Passé Présent, 95, 619 p. [Cf. n^{os} <sélection> 1253, 1254, 1256, 1257, 1258, 1259, 1261, 1263, 1264, 1265, 1266, 1269, 1274, 1277, 1279, 1285, 1286, 1289, 1290, 1294, 1296, 1301, 1304, 1307, 1314, 1315, 1316, 1318, 4618, 7051, 7053, 7066, 7078, 7120, 7134, 7227, 7231, 7296, 7396.]

1298. RAEPSAET (Georges). Les prémices de la mécanisation agricole entre Seine et Rhin de l'Antiquité au XIIIe siècle. *Annales*, 95, 50, 4, p. 911-942.

1299. RICHTER (William Lee). The ABC-CLIO companion to transportation in America. Santa Barbara, ABC-CLIO, 95, XXXVI-653 p. (ABC-CLIO companions to key issues in American history and life).

1300. ROSAS (Fernando). Portugal entre a paz e a guerra: estudo do impacte da II Guerra Mundial na economia e na sociedade portuguesa 1939–1945. Lisboa, Estampa, 95, 484 p. (ill., bibl.).

1301. SACHS (Ignacy). L'historien et le développeur. *In*: Pour une histoire économique et sociale internationale [Cf. n° 1297], p. 57-62.

1302. SAFTIEN (Volker). Rhetorische Mimik und Gestik. Konturen epochenspezifischen Verhaltens. *Archiv für Kulturgeschichte*, 95, 77, p. 197-226.

1303. SANDGRUBER (Roman). Ökonomie und Politik. Österreichische Wirtschaftsgeschichte vom Mittelalter bis zur Gegenwart. Hrsg. v. Herwig Wolfram. Wien, Ueberreuter, 95, 669 p. (ill., Anhang, Personen- und Ortsreg.). (Österreichische Geschichte, 10).

1304. SARDET (Frédéric). Les frontières du commerce vertueux. Réflexions libres sur les échanges internationaux de médicaments (XVIIIe–XXe siècles). *In*: Pour une histoire économique et sociale internationale [Cf. n° 1297], p. 529-540.

1305. Siedler-Identität. Neun Fallstudien von der Antike bis zur Gegenwart. Hrsg. v. Christof DIPPER u. Rudolf HIESTAND. Frankfurt am Main, Berlin u. Bern, Lang, 95, 199 p.

1306. ŞIMŞIRGIL (Ahmet). XIII–XVI. Asırlarda Tokat Şehrinde İktisadi Hayat. (La vie économique dans la ville de Tokat aux XIIIe et XVIe siècles). *Tarih İncelemeleri Dergisi*, 95, 10, p. 187-211.

1307. SINGER (Hans W.). Historical background to the Bretton Woods system and its relation to the United Nations system. *In*: Pour une histoire économique et sociale internationale [Cf. n° 1297], p. 461-470.

1308. SOMMESTAD (Lena). Jordbrukets kvinno den svenska modellen. (Women in agriculture: the Swedish model). *Historisk Tidskrift* (Sweden), 95, 4, p. 508-528.

1309. Stadt und Kirche. Hrsg. v. Franz-Heinz HYE. Linz, Österreichischer Arbeitskreis für Stadtgeschichtsforschung, 95, 330 p. (Beiträge zur Geschichte der Städte Mitteleuropas, 13). [Cf. n^{os} <Auswahl> 3752, 4408, 4446, 4455, 5780.]

1310. TANDECKI (Janusz). Pozazawodowe funkcji i powinności korporacji rzemieślniczych w miastach Prus Krzyżackich i Królewskich w XIV–XVII wieku. (Fonctions et devoirs extraprofessionnels des corps des métiers dans les villes de Prusse Teutonique et Royale au XIVe–XVIIIe siècles). *Zapiski historyczne poświęcone historii Pomorza i Krajów Bałtyckich*, 95, 60, 1, p. 7-23. [Deutsche Zsfassung].

1311. THIVEAUD (Jean-Marie). Histoire de la finance en France. T. 1. Des origines jusqu'en 1775. [S. l.], Ed. P. A. U., 95, 418 p. (ill.).

1312. THOMES (Paul). Kommunale Wirtschaft und Verwaltung zwischen Mittelalter und Moderne. Bestandsaufnahme, Strukturen, Konjunkturen. Die Städte Saarbrücken und St. Johann im Rahmen der allgemeinen Entwicklung (1321–1768). Stuttgart, Steiner, 95, 446 p. (Karten). (Vierteljahrschrift für Sozial- und Wirtschaftsgeschichte, 118).

1313. TISSOT (Laurent). Histoire d'horlogers. *Revue suisse d'histoire*, 95, 45, 4, p. 502-506.

1314. TOBLER (Hans Werner). Facteurs externes et déroulement interne de deux révolutions: quelques remarques comparatives concernant le Mexique et la Chine. *In*: Pour une histoire économique et sociale internationale [Cf. n° 1297], p. 325-332.

1315. TOPOLSKI (Jerzy). Comparer c'est expliquer: un exemple de l'histoire économique européenne. *In*: Pour une histoire économique et sociale internationale [Cf. n° 1297], p. 63-74.

1316. VAN DER WEE (Herman). Small countries and foreign investment: the Belgian case from the Middle Ages to the present. *In*: Pour une histoire économique et sociale internationale [Cf. n° 1297], p. 471-482.

1317. VEKARIĆ (Nenad). Pelješki rodovi (A–K). (Family Names of the Pelješac Peninsula). Dubrovnik, Zavod za povijesne znanosti HAZU, 95, 387 p.

1318. WAELBROECK (Jean). China's growth in the light of the Western past. *In*: Pour une histoire économique et sociale internationale [Cf. n° 1297], p. 547-570.

1319. WEEBER (Karl-Wilhelm). Alltag im alten Rom. Ein Lexikon. Zürich, Artemis, 95, 447 p.

1320. WIESEMANN (Jörg). Steinkohlenbergbau in den Territorien um Aachen 1334–1794. Aix-la-Chapelle, Alano Verlag, 95, 335 p. (Aachener Studien zur älteren Energiegeschichte, 3).

§ 9. Kultur-, Wissenschafts- und Unterrichtsgeschichte.

* 1321. Bibliografia italiana di storia della scienza. 11. 1992. Addenda (1982–1991). [Vol. 9–10. Cf. Bibl. 94, n° 1043.] Direzione scientifica di Massimo BUCCIANTINI e Anna Corinna CITERNESI. Firenze, Olschki, 95, IX-258 p. (Biblioteca di bibliografia italiana, 139).

* 1322. HIGBY (Gregory J.), STROUD (Elaine C.). The history of pharmacy: a selected annotated bibliography. Associate editors David COWEN [et al.]. New York a. London, Garland, 95, XI-321 p. (Bibliographies on the history of science and technology, 25. Garland reference library of the humanities, 1366).

* 1323. Vacat.

1324. BEN-DOV (Yoav). Invitation à la physique. Edition établie par Christian JEANMOUGIN. Paris, Ed. du Seuil, 95, 208 p. (Points. Sciences, 107).

1325. BUICAN (Denis). Evolution de la pensée biologique. Paris, Hachette, 95, 155 p. (ill.). (Les Fondamentaux, 52).

1326. Bunmei-Gaku Gairon. (An introduction to history of civilization). [S. l.], Yamakawa Shuppansha, 95, 442 p. [Cf. n° <choice> 8864.]

9. KULTUR-, WISSENSCHAFTS- UND UNTERRICHTSGESCHICHTE

1327. CAHILL (Thomas). How the Irish saved civilization: the untold story of Ireland's heroic role from the fall of Rome to the rise of medieval Europe. London, Hodder & Stoughton, 95, X-246 p.

1328. Constructing knowledge in the history of science. Ed. by Arnold THACKRAY. Chicago, University of Chicago Press, 95, VIII-253 p. (Osiris. Second series, 10).

1329. Consuming Habits. Drugs in history and anthropology. Ed. by Jordan GOODMAN, Paul E. LOVEJOY, Andrew SHERRATT. London a New York, Routledge, 95, 244 p.

1330. COSMACINI (Giorgio). Storia della medicina e della sanità in Italia: dalla peste europea alla guerra mondiale, 1348–1918. Roma e Bari, Laterza, 95, XIV-448 p.

1331. Culture et politique. Textes réunis par Alexandru DUTU et Norbert DODILLE, Institut français de Bucarest. Paris, L'Harmattan, 95, [s. p.]. [Cf. n° <sélection> 871.]

1332. DRYGAS (Aleksander). Kształtowanie się postaw prawnych aptekarstwa w przekroju dziejowym. Studia nad podstawowymi źródłami do dziejów farmacji europejskiej i polskiej. Vol. 1. (wiek XII–XVIII). (Formation des attitudes juridiques des pharmaciens à travers les siècles. Etudes sur les sources de base relatives à l'histoire de la pharmacie européenne et polonaise). Gdańsk, Akad. Medyczna, 95, 161 p. (fig., carte).

1333. Essays in the history of the physiological sciences: proceedings of a network symposium of the European Association for the History of Medicine and Health held at the University Louis Pasteur, Strasbourg, on March 26th–27th, 1993. Ed. by Claude DEBRU. Amsterdam a. Atlanta, Rodopi, 95, 239 p. (The Wellcome Institute series in the history of medicine; Clio medica, 33).

1334. European integration and the European mind. Part 3–4. 3th international Conference of the international Society for the study of European ideas, Aalborg, 24–29 August 1992. History of European ideas, 95, 20, 1-3, 666 p.; 4-6, p. 663-972. [Cf. n^{os} <choice> 5929, 6006, 6024, 6025, 6028.]

1335. GLOSIKOVA (Viera). Handbuch der deutschsprachigen Schriftsteller aus dem Gebiet der Slowakei (17.–20. Jahrhundert). (Veröffentlichungen der Kommission für Literaturwissenschaft, 15; Sitzungsberichte/Österreichische Akademie der Wissenschaften. Philosophisch-historische Klasse, 625). Wien, Verlag der Österreichischen Akademie der Wissenschaften, 95, 169 p.

1336. Gobelin Europa: søkelys på europeisk kultur. (Focus on European culture). Ed. by Lars Martin FOSSE. Oslo, Sypress, 95, 303 p. (ill.).

1337. GURŠTEJN (A. A.). Zodiak i istoki evropejskoj kul'tury. (Zodiac and the sources of the European culture). Vestn. drev. Ist. , 95, 1, p. 153-160.

1338. Historia nauki polskiej. Wiek XX. Nauki ścisłe. (Histoire de la science polonaise. XXe siècle. Sciences exactes). Réd. Andrzej ŚRODKA. Z. 1. Matematyka, fizyka, chemia, astronomia [Cahier 1: mathématiques, physique, chimie, astronomie]. Warszawa, Wydawn. Inst. Hist. Nauki, 95, 377 p.

1339. KERESZTÉNY (Balázs). Magyar művelődési hagyományok kárpátaljai lexiona. (Encyclopédie de Ruthénie Subcarpatique des traditions culturelles hongroises). Ungvár et Budapest, Intermix, 95, 376 p. (Kárpátaljai magyar könyvek, 46).

1340. KLINGHAMMER (István), PAPAY (Gyula), TÖRÖK (Zsolt). Kartográfiatörténet. (Histoire de la cartographie). Budapest, Eötvös, 95, 189 p.

1341. LEERSSEN (josep). Wildness, wilderness, and Ireland: medieval and early-modern patterns in the demarcation of civility. Journal of the history of ideas, 95, 56, 1, p. 25-40.

1342. LUNDEN (Kåre). Bröd, roser og blod: kvinnehistoriske essayer. (Bread, roses and blood. Essays on the Norwegian women [from the Middle ages until our times]). Oslo, Universitetsforlaget, 95, 219 p.

1343. MAIOCCHI (Roberto). Storia della scienza in Occidente: dalle origini alla bomba atomica. Scandicci, La nuova Italia, 95, XII-598 p. (ill.). (Biblioteca di cultura, 200).

1344. MARDEŠIĆ (Ivo). Hrvatska – Velika Britanija: povijest kulturnih i književnih odnosa. (Croatia – Great Britain: the history of cultural and literary relations). Zagreb, Društvo hrvatskih književnika, 95, 243 p.

1345. Mexican studies in the history and philosophy of science. Ed. by Santiago RAMIREZ and Robert S. COHEN. Dordrecht a. London, Kluwer Academic, 95, XII-280 p. (Boston studies in the philosophy of science, 172).

1346. MICHELI (Gianni). Le origini del concetto di macchina. Firenze, Olschki, 95, 181 p. (ill.). (Biblioteca di Physis, 4).

1347. Mit Fremden Leben. Eine Kulturgeschichte von der Antike bis zur Gegenwart. Hrsg. v. Alexander DEMANDT [et al.]. München, Beck, 95, 313 p.

1348. MONGILI (Alessandro). La science russe: un système archaïque mais productif. Annales, 95, 50, 3, p. 541-562.

1349. NASSIET (Michel). Parenté et successions dynastiques aux XIVe et XVe siècles. Annales, 95, 50, 3, p. 621-644.

1350. NOWAK (Tadeusz Marian). Rozwój techniki rakietowej w świetle europejskich traktatów XIII–XVII wieku. (Développement de la technique de fusées à la lumière des traités européens du XIIIe–XVIIIe s). Warszawa, Retro-Art, 95, 264 p. (Rés. franç., Deutsche Zsfassung, dessins). (Kom. Hist. Nauki i Techn. Pol. Akad. Nauk, Rozpr. z Dziejów Nauki i Techn., 4).

1351. ÖDMAN (Per-Johan). Kontrasternas spel: en svensk mentalitets- och pedagogikhistoria. Part 1. Part 2. Stockhom, Norstedt, 95, 2 vol., XV-298 p., XI-333 p. (appendix). [A history of the Swedish mentality and indoctrination: pedagogics in a special hermeneutic sense].

1352. Osmanlı Bilimi Araştırmaları. (Recherches sur la science ottomane). Ed. par Feza GÜNERGUN. İstanbul, [s. n.], 95, 378 p. (İstanbul Üniversitesi Yayınları, 3911; Edebiyat Fakültesi Yayınları, 3401).

1353. PADEL (Ruth). Whom gods destroy. Elements of Greek and tragic madness. Princeton, Princeton U. P., 95, 276 p.

1354. PETRUCCI (Armando). Le scritture ultime: ideologia della morte e strategie dello scrivere nella tradizione occidentale. Torino, Einaudi, 95, XIX-186 p. (Saggi, 798).

1355. Physics, philosophy, and the scientific community: essays in the philosophy and history of the natural sciences and mathematics in honor of Robert S. Cohen. Ed. by Kostas GAVROGLU, John STACHEL a. Marx W. WARTOFSKY. Dordrecht a. London, Kluwer Academic, 95, XXVII-383 p. (Boston studies in the philosophy of science, 163).

1356. RYDSTRÖM (Jens). Homosexualitetens historia: ett försummat forskningsfält. (The history of homosexuality: a neglected investigation area). *Historisk Tidskrift* (Sweden), 95, 3, p. 338-354.

1357. SACKS (D.). Encyclopedia of the ancient Greek world. New York, Facts On File, 95, 320 p.

1358. SCHAMA (Simon). Landscape and memory. London, Harper Collins, 95, XI-652 p. (ill.).

1359. Science, reason, and rhetoric. Ed. by Henry KRIPS, J. E. MAC GUIRE a. Trevor MELIA. Pittsburgh, University of Pittsburgh Press a. Konstanz, Universitätsverlag Konstanz, 95, XIX-322 p. (Pittsburgh-Konstanz series in the philosophy and history of science).

1360. SKŁADANKOWA (Maria). Kultura perska. (Culture persane). Wrocław, Zakł. Narod. im. Ossolińskich, 95, 272 p. (phot., dessins).

1361. THEODORIDES (Jean). Histoire de la biologie. Paris, PUF, 95, 127 p. (ill.). (Que sais-je?, 1).

1362. Università in Europa. Le istituzioni universitarie dal Medio Evo ai nostri giorni, strutture, organizzazione, funzionamento. Atti del Convegno internazionale. Milazzo, 1993. A cura di Andrea ROMANO. Soveria Mannelli, Rubettino, 95, 748 p. (Materiali per una storia delle istituzioni giuridiche e politiche medievali, moderne e contemporanee. Atti, 2).

1363. VIROLI (Maurizio). Per amore della patria. Patriottismo e nazionalismo nella storia. Roma e Bari, Laterza, XII-223 p. (Storia e società).

1364. Wege zu einer neuen Kulturgeschichte. Mit Beiträgen von Rudolf VIERHAUS und Roger CHARTIER.

Göttingen, Wallstein Verlag, 95, [s. p.]. (Göttinger Gespräche zur Geschichtswissenschaft). [Cf. n° <Auswahl> 871.]

1365. WILSON (Alistair Macintosh). The infinite in the finite. Oxford, Oxford U. P., 95, XIII-524 p.

§ 10. Kunst- und Kunstgewerbegeschichte.

* 1366. BECKER (Jochen). Boekenwijsheid: inleiding in de kunsthistorische bibliografie. Leiden, Primavera Pers, 95, 112 p.

* 1367. BHA. Bibliography of the History of Art. Bibliographie de l'Histoire de l'Art. Vol. 5, 1-4, 1995. [Vol. 4, 1-4, 1994. Cf. Bibl. 94, n° 1089.]. Ed. by Michael RINEHART and Marise BIDEAULT. Paris, Centre National de la Recherche Scientifique a. Santa Monica, The J. Paul Getty Trust, 95, 4 vol., XXV-403 p., XXV-421 p., XXV-437 p., XXV-501 p.

* 1368. VICTORIA (José Guadalupe). Una bibliografía de arte novohispano. Con la colaboración de Pedro Angeles JIMENEZ, Norma FERNANDEZ QUINTERO y Maria Teresa VELASCO DE ESPINOSA. Mexico, Universidad Nacional Autonoma de Mexico, Instituto de Investigaciones Esteticas, 95, 364 p. (Apoyo a la docencia, 2).

1369. BLOOM (Ken). Hollywood song: the complete film and musical companion. New York, Facts on File, 95, 3 vol., XII-1504p.

1370. Enfer et paradis. L'au-delà dans l'art et la littérature en Europe. Actes du Colloque de Conques [Aveyron], 22–23 avril 1994. *Cahiers de Conques*, 95, 1, 427 p. [Cf. n^{os} <sélection> 413, 3947, 4046, 4136, 4201, 4202, 4203, 4205, 4209, 4215, 4223, 4228, 4229, 4232, 4233, 4234, 5902.]

1371. Katalog portretów osobistości polskich i obcych w Polsce działających. (Catalogue de portraits des personnalités polonaises et étrangères actives en Pologne). T. 5. T–Ż, suppléments. Réd. Hanna WIDACKA. Aut.: H. WIDACKA, Alicja ŻENDARA. Warszawa, [s. n.], 95, 385 p. (Katalogi Zakł. Zbiorów Ikonograficznych Bibl. Narod., Grafika, 1).

1372. KIVIKÄS (Pekka). Kalliomaalaukset. Muinainen kuva-arkisto. Paintings on the rock, an ancient picture archive. Jyväskylä, Atena, 95, 336 p. (ill., maps).

1373. KRASSOWSKI (Witold). Dzieje budownictwa i architektury na ziemiach Polski. (Histoire de génie civil et de l'architecture sur les terres de Pologne). T. 4. Budownictwo i architektura w warunkach rozkwitu folwarku pańszczyźnianego (XVI w.–pierwsza połowa XVII w.). (Le génie civil et l'architecture pendant la floraison des domaines de corvée XVIe s.–première moitié XVIIe s.). Warszawa, Arkady, 95, 434 p. (dessins., phot., cartes).

1374. Western medical tradition (The). 800 BC to AD 1800. Cambridge, Cambridge U. P., 95, XIV-556 p.

1375. ZOPPI (Mariella). Storia del giardino europeo. Roma e Bari, Laterza, 95, VIII-175 p. (ill.). (Grandi opere).

Cf. n° 183

§ 11. Religions- und Kirchengeschichte.

a. Allgemeines.

* 1376. Dictionnaire d'histoire et de géographie ecclésiastiques. Tome 25. Fasc. 146–147. Hyacinthe de Saint-Vincent–Inde. Fasc. 148–149. Inde–Iriarte Estañán et Supplément au tome 25. Dir. R. AUBERT, ass. de J.-P. HENDRICKX. Paris, Letouzey et Ané, 95, 2 vol., 511 p., 485 p.

* 1377. Ephemerides theologicae lovanienses. Elenchus bibliographicus. Tomus LXXI. [Tomus LXX. Cf. Bibl. 94, n° 1115.] Editae cura E. BRITO, L. DE FLEURQUIN, A. DE HALLEUX, J. ÉTIENNE, A. HAQUIN, J. LUST, F. NEIRYNCK, R. WIELOCKX, B. WILLAERT. Leuven, Peeters, 95, 680 p.

* 1378. Revue d'histoire ecclésiastique. Bibliographie. Tome 90. 1995. [Tome 89, 1994. Cf. Bibl. 94, n° 1117.] Ed. par M. HAVERALS. Louvain-la-Neuve, Bureaux de la R. H. E., Bibliothèque de l'université, 95, 511 p.

1379. Annuaire des sciences religieuses de l'École Pratique des Hautes Études. Résumé des conférences et travaux. T. 102. 1993–94. Paris, EPHE, 95, 489 p.

1380. Atlante delle religioni. Ideazione e realizzazione di Charles BALADIER. Ed. italiana a cura di Giovanni FILORAMO. Torino, UTET, 95, VIII-610 p. (ill.). [Cf. n° <scelta> 1391.]

1381. BARKER (E.). The scientific study of religion? You must be joking! *Journal for the Scientific Study of Religion*, 95, 34, p. 287-310.

1382. BIEDERMAN (S.). Scripture and knowledge. An essay on religious epistemology. Leiden, New York, Köln, Brill, 95, 256 p. (Studies in the History of Religions, Numen Bookseries, 69).

1383. BRINK (T.L.). Quantitative and / or qualitative methods in the scientific study of religion. *Zygon*, 95, 30, p. 179-184.

1384. CHARES (Mark), DEMERATH (N.J.), ELLISON (Christopher G.), IANNACCONE (Lawrence R.). Symposium on the rational choice approach to religion. *Journal for the Scientific Study of Religion*, 95, 34, p. 76-120.

1385. DUPUIS (J.). Communion universelle. Eglises chrétiennes et religions mondiales. *Cristianesimo nella storia*, 95, 16, 2, p. 361-381.

1386. Enciclopedia delle religioni. Vol. 5. Lo studio delle religioni. Discipline e autori. Diretta da Mircea ELIADE. Edizione tematica europea a cura di Dario M. COSI, Luigi SAIBENE, Roberto SCAGNO, da un primo progetto di tematizzazione di Ioan P. COULIANO. Settimo Milanese, Marzorati e Milano, Jaca Book, 95, 444 p.

1387. Female stereotypes in religious traditions. Ed. by Ria KLOPPENBORG a. Wouter J. HANEGRAAFF. Leiden, New York, Köln, Brill, 95, 263 p. (Studies in the History of Religions, Numen Bookseries, 66).

1388. Gestions religieuses de la santé (Les). Ed. par Françoise LAUTMAN et Jacques MAITRE. Paris, L'Harmattan, 95, 330 p.

1389. GIRAULT (René). Les religions orientales: hindouisme, bouddhisme, taoïsme. Paris, Plon et Mame, 95, 353 p.

1390. Gjør døren høy: kirken i Norge 1000 år. (The church in Norway through a thousand years). Ed. by Torstein JØRGENSEN, Ingun MONTGOMERY a. Jan SCHUMACHER. Oslo, Aschehoug, 95, XV-510 p. (ill.).

1391. GROTTANELLI (Cristiano). La storia delle religioni in Italia. *In*: Atlante delle religioni [Cf. n° 1380], p. 561-562.

1392. HAUSCHILD (Wolf-Dieter). Lehrbuch der Kirchen- und Dogmengeschichte. Band 1. Alte Kirche und Mittelalter. Gütersloh, Gütersloher Verlagshaus, 95, XVII-693 p.

1393. Herder-Lexikon der griechischen und römischen Mythologie: Götter, Helden, Ereignisse, Schauplätze. Freiburg, Herder Verlag, 95, 234 p.

1394. História religiosa. Propr. e ed. Centro de Estudos de História Religiosa, Universidade Católica Portuguesa. Lisboa, U.C.P., 95, [s. p.].

1395. JACOBSEN Buckley (Jorunn), BUCKLEY (Thomas). Anthropology, history of religions, and cognitive approach to religious phenomena. *Journal of the American Academy of Religion*, 95, 63, 2, p. 343-352.

1396. LAWSON (E. Thomas), MAC CAULEY (Robert N.). Carring for details: a humane reply to Buckley and Buckley. *Journal of the American Academy of Religion*, 95, 63, 2, p. 353-357.

1397. LE COZ (Raymond). Histoire de l'Eglise d'Orient. Chrétiens d'Irak, d'Iran et de Turquie. Paris, Editions du Cerf, 95, 441 p.

1398. Lexikon für Theologie und Kirche. Vol. 3. Dämon bis Fragmentenstreit. Vol. 4. Franca bis Hermenegild. Hrsg. v. W. KASPER. Freiburg, Herder, 95, 2 vol., 14*-1378 p., 14*-1450 p.

1399. MAC CHCHEON (R.T.). "Religion" in recent publications: a critical survey. *Numen*, 95, 42, p. 284-309.

1400. MARKSCHIES (Christoph). Arbeitsbuch zur Kirchengeschichte. Tübingen, Mohr, 95, XV-201 p. (UTB., 1857).

1401. MILLER (Alan S.), HOFFMAN (John P.). Risk and religion: an explanation of gender differences in religiosity. *Journal for the Scientific Study of Religion*, 95, 34, p. 63-75.

1402. MONROE (C. R.). World religions: an introduction. Amherst New York, Prometheus, 95, 439 p.

1403. MORGAN (Peggy). The study of religions and interfaith encounter. *Numen*, 95, 42, 2, p. 156-172.

1404. Off with her head! The denial of women's identity in myth, religion and culture. Berkeley, Los Angeles a. London, University of California Press, 95, IX-226 p.

1405. Ortodoxia (Az) története Magyarországon a XVIII. századig. (Histoire de l'orthodoxie en Hongrie jusqu'au XVIIIe siècle). Réd. par Imre TOTH. Szeged, JATE, 95, 120 p.

1406. Parlers de la foi (Les). Religion et langues régionales. Ed. par Michel LAGREE. Rennes, Presses Universitaires de de Rennes, 95, 162 p.

1407. Pluralism and Identity. Studies in Ritual Behaviour. Ed. by Jean PLATVOET a. Karel VAN DER TOORN. Leiden, New York, Köln, Brill, 95, 376 p. (Studies in the History of Religions, Numen Bookseries, 67).

1408. POLLAK (Detlef). Was ist Religion? Probleme der Definition. *Zeitschrift für Religionswissenschaft*, 95, 3, 2, p. 163-190.

1409. Regards nord-américains sur la religion: Contributions au colloque annuel de la Région internationale de l'Est. American Academy of Religion, Montréal, Université du Québec à Montréal, 22–24 avril 1994. North American Insights into Religion: Papers Presented in the Annual Meeting of the Eastern International Region, American Academy of Religion. Ed. by M. BOISVERT. Montréal, Département des Sciences Religieuses, 95, 375 p. (Religiologiques, 11).

1410. Religies en (on)gelijkheid in een plurale samenleving. Ed. R. KRANENBORG, W. STOKER. Leuven, Apeldoorn, Garant, 95, 256 p.

1411. Religion and secular humanism. *Journal of Dharma*, 95, 20, p. 317-400.

1412. SCOTT (David). Buddhism and Islam. Past to present encounters and interfaith lessons. *Numen*, 95, 42, 2, p. 141-156.

1413. SPEYER (Wolfgang). Religionsgeschichtliche Studien. Hildesheim, Zürich u. New York, Georg Olms, 95, XX-221 p. (Collectanea, 15).

1414. STEPHENSON (Gunther). Wege zur religiösen Wirklichkeit. Phänomene, Symbole, Werte. Darmstadt, Wissenschaftliche Buchgesellschaft, 95, 227 p.

1415. Storia della teologia. Vol. 1. Dalle origini a Bernardo di Chiaravalle. A cura di Enrico DAL COVOLO. Bologna, Edizioni Dehoniane, 95, 384 p.

1416. Storia delle religioni. Vol. 2. Ebraismo e cristianesimo. Vol. 3. Religioni dualiste. Islam. A cura di Giovanni FILORAMO. Roma e Bari, Laterza, 95, 2 vol., 704 p., 440 p.

1417. Symposium on Anthropology. *Religion*, 95, 25, p. 1-40.

1418. Theory and method in religious studies: contemporary approaches to the study of religion. Ed. by F. WHALING. Berlin a. New York, Mouton de Gruyter, 95, 427 p.

1419. TILLARD (J.-M. R.). Eglise catholique ou eglise universelle? *Cristianesimo nella storia*, 95, 16, 2, p. 341-361.

1420. Trattato di antropologia del sacro. Vol. 4. Crisi, rotture e cambiamenti. Diretto da Julien RIES. Milano, Jaca Book e Massimo, 95, 415 p.

Cf. n°s 5633-5678

b. Spezialarbeiten.

* 1421. Bibliographia Internationalis Spiritualitatis. T. 27. 1992. [T. 26, 1991. Cf. Bibl. 94, n° 1156.] Dir. by Juan Luis ASTIGARRAGA. Roma, Edizioni del Teresianum, 95, XXXI-541 p.

* 1422. Biographisch-Bibliographisches Kirchenlexicon. Band. 9. Scharling, Carl Henrik – Sheldon, Charles Monroe. Band. 10. Shelkow, Vladimir Anderyevich – Stoss, Andreas. [Bd. 7–8. Cf. Bibl. 94, n° 1158.] Begründet und herausgegeben von F.W. BAUTZ. Fortgeführt von T. BAUTZ. Herzberg, Traugott Bautz, 95, 2 vol., XXXIX p.-1600 col.; XXXIX p.-1600 col.

* 1423. Bulletin de bibliographie biblique. N. 13. Avril 95, XXIV-101 p. N. 14. Juillet 95, XXIV-79 p. N. 15. Déc. 95, IV-114 p. [N°s 10-12. Cf. Bibl. 94, n° 1159.]

* 1424. Index Islamicus 1993. Ed. by G.J. ROPPER, C.H. BLEANGY. Cambridge, Bowker a. Saur, 95, XXXVI-536 p.

* 1425. Internationale Zeitschriftenschau für Bibelwissenschaft und Grenzgebiete. International Review of Biblical Studies. Revue internationale des études bibliques. Band. XL 1993–1994. [Bd. XXXIX. Cf. Bibl. 94, n° 1161.] Düsseldorf, Patmon Verlag, 95, XIV-405 p.

* 1426. New Testament Abstracts. Vol. 39. [Vol. 38. Cf. Bibl. 94, n° 1163.] Cambridge, College School of theology, 95, 595 p.

* 1427. NORTH (Robert). Elenchus of Biblical Bibliography. Vol. 8. 1992. [Vol. 7, 1991. Cf. Bibl. 94, n° 1164.] Roma, Ed. Istituto Pontificio Biblico, 95, 1262 p.

* 1428. Old Testament Abstracts. Vol. 18. [Vol. 17. Cf. Bibl. 94, n° 1165.] Washington, Catholic University of America, 95, 722 p.

1429. AL-ASSIOUTY (Sawat Anis). Civilisations de répression et forgeurs de livres sacrés. Paris, Letouzey & Ané, 95, 415 p.

1430. ALBERT-LLORCA (Marlène), ALBERT (Jean-Pierre). Mahomet, la Vierge et la frontière. *Annales*, 95, 50, 4, p. 855-886.

1431. ALVAR (Jaime), [et al.]. Cristianismo primitivo y religiones mistéricas. Madrid, Cátedra, 95, 546 p.

1432. America's alternative religions. Ed. by Timothy MILLER. Albany, State University of New York Press, 95, 475 p.

1433. Americana. Ispanizzazione del cattolicesimo statunitense e altre ricerche sulle Americhe religiose. *Religioni e società*, 95, 10, 21, p. 3-129.

1434. Aspects of religious contact and conflict in the ancient world. Ed. by Pieter VAN DER HORST. Utrecht, Faculteit der Godgeleerdheid, 95, 166 p. (Utrechtse Theologische Reeks, 31).

1435. BAUMANN (Martin). "Merkwürdige Bundesgenossen" und "naive Sympathisanten". Die Ausgrenzung der Religionswissenschaft aus der bundesdeutschen Kontroverse um neue Religionen. *Zeitschrift für Religionswissenschaft*, 95, 2, 3, p. 111-136.

1436. BROWN (Peter). Authority and the Sacred. Aspects of the Christianisation of the Roman World. Cambridge, University of Cambridge Press, 95, XIII-91 p.

1437. Catholicisme hier aujourd'hui demain. Vol. 14. Fasc. 66. Structure – Tapper. Encyclopédie publiée sous le patronage de l'Institut Catholique de Lille par G. MATHON et G.H. BAUDRY. Paris, Letouzey & Ané, 95, 513-768 col.

1438. Chamanismo en Latinoamérica. Una revisión conceptual. Ed. por I. LAGARRIGA, J. GALINIER y M. PERRIN. Mexico, Plaza y Valdés, Universidad Iberoamericana, CEMCA, 95, 244 p.

1439. Chinese religion. An anthology of sources. Ed. by D. SOMMER. New York, Oxford U. P., 95, XXIII-375 p.

1440. CLADIS (M.S.). The French connection: Crea, Mauss, and the academic study of religion in the U.S.A. *Religion*, 95, 25, p. 179-184.

1441. Controverse religieuse (La) et ses formes. Ed. par Alain LE BOULLUEC. Paris, Ed. du Cerf, 95, 424 p.

1442. CULIANU (Ioan Petru). Mircea Eliade. Bucureşti, Nemira, 95, 320 p.

1443. DE LUCA (Giuseppe). La piété. Approche historique. Paris, Letouzey et Ané, 95, 172 p.

1444. DELUMEAU (Jean). Mille ans de bonheur. Paris, Fayard, 95, 496 p. (Une histoire du Paradis, 2).

1445. DENTIN (P.). Les Privilèges des papes devant l'Ecriture et l'histoire. Paris, Ed. du Cerf, 95, 291 p. (Parole présente).

1446. DIAKONOFF (Igor M.). Archaic myths of the Orient and the Occident. Göteborg, Acta Orientalia Gothuburgensis, 95, 216 p. (Orientalia Gothuburgensis 10).

1447. Dictionary of deities and demons in the Bible. Ed. by Karel VAN DER TOORN, Bob BECKING a. W. VAN DER PIETER. Leiden, New York, Köln, Brill, 95, 1774 col.

1448. Dictionnaire de spiritualité ascétique et mystique doctrine et histoire. Vol. 17. Tables générales. Fondé par M. VILLER, F. CAVALLERA, J. DE GUIBERT et A. RAYEZ. Continué par A. DERVILLE, P. LAMARCHE et A. SOLIGNAC. Paris, Beauchesne, 95, 732 p.

1449. DIEZ DE VELASCO (Francisco). Los caminos de la muerte. Religión, rito e imágines del paso al más allá en la Grecia antigua. Madrid, Trotta, 95, 198 p.

1450. DUMEZIL (Georges). Le roman des jumeaux et autres essais. Vingt-cinq esquisses de mythologie (76–100). Publiés par Joël H. GRISWARD. Paris, Gallimard, 95, 338 p.

1451. Encyclopaedia of Islam. New Edition. Volume VIII. Ned–Sam. Ed. by P. J. BEARMAN, T. BIANQUIS, C. E. BOSWORTH, E. VAN DONZEL a. W. P. HEINRICHS. Leiden, Brill, 95, 1056 p.

1452. Encyclopédie du protestantisme. Sou la direction de Pierre GISEL. Paris, Ed. du Cerf et Genève, Labor et fides, 95, 1712 p.

1453. Ernesto de Martino e il senso della storia. *Storia, antropologia e scienze del linguaggio*, 95, 10, 3, p. 9-185.

1454. Eugène Goblet d'Alviella, historien et francmaçon. Ed. par Alain DIERKENS. Bruxelles, Éditions de l'Université de Bruxelles, 95, 216 p.

1455. FAIVRE (Antoine), VOSS (K. C.). Western esotericism and the science of religions. *Numen*, 95, 42, 1, p. 48-77.

1456. FAJFAR (Britta). Die Verwaltungsnormen der Hirsauer Reform und ihre praktische Umsetzung in Admont bis ins 16. Jahrhundert. *Z. d. Hist. Vereines f. Steiermark*, 95, 86, p. 63-92.

1457. GIARRIZZO (Giuseppe). Note su Ernesto de Martino. *Archivio di storia della cultura*, 95, 8, p. 141-181.

1458. Histoire du christianisme des origines à nos jours. Dir. par Jean-Marie MAJEUR, Charles PIETRI, André VAUCHEZ et Marc VENARD. Vol. 11. Libéralisme, industrialisation, expansion européenne (1830–1914). Dir. par Jacques GADILLE et Jean-Marie MAJEUR. Paris, Desclée, 95, 1172 p.

1459. Image and ritual in Buddhism. *History of Religions*, 95, 34, 3, p. 201-280.

1460. JUNGINGER (Horst). Ein Kapitel Religionswissenschaft während der NS-Zeit: Hans-Alexander

Winkler (1900–1945). *Zeitschrift für Religionswissenschaft*, 95, 3, 2, p. 137-161.

1461. Károly Kerényi. La storia delle religioni nella cultura del Novecento. *Mythos. Rivista di storia delle religioni*, 95, 7, p. 3-115.

1462. KATZ (Nathan). The judaism of Kaifeng and Cochin. Parallel and divergent styles of religious acculturation. *Numen*, 95, 42, 2, p. 118-141.

1463. KERČMAR (Vili). Evangeličanska cerkev na Slovenskem. (Evangelical church in Slovenia). Murska Sobota, Evangeličanska cerkev v Sloveniji, 95, 331 p.

1464. KIPPENBERG (H. G.). Max Weber und die vergleichende Religionswissenschaft. *Revue internationale de philosophie*, 95, 49, p. 127-153.

1465. KIPPENBERG (Hans), STROUMSA (Guy G.). Secrecy and concealment. Studies in the history of Mediterranean and Near Eastern religions. Leiden, New York, Köln, Brill, 95, 406 p. (Studies in the History of Religions, Numen Bookseries, 65).

1466. KOMONCHAK (J. A.). Concepts of communion. Past and present. *Cristianesimo nella storia*, 95, 16, 2, p. 321-341.

1467. KUTTIANIMATTATHIL (J.). Elements of the emerging trends in the Christian understanding of others religions. *Vidyajyoti*, 95, 59, p. 281-289.

1468. LAMBERT (Jean). Le Dieu distribué. Une anthropologie comparée des monothéismes. Paris, Ed.du Cerf, 95, 405 p.

1469. LAUDE (P.). Une tentative de réduction du phénomène religieux: la pensée de René Girard. *Connaissance des religions*, 95, 43-44, p. 81-92.

1470. LIPINSKI (Edouard). Dieux et déesses de l'univers phénicien et punique. Leuven, Peeters, 95, 536 p. (Orientalia Lovaniensia Analecta, 64; Studia Phoeniciа, 14).

1471. Manichaean Nous (The). Proceedings of the International Symposion Louvain 1991. Ed. by A. VAN TONGERLOO, J. VAN OORT. Leuven, 95, 321 p. (Manichaean Studies, 2).

1472. MASSENZIO (Marcello). Dioniso e il teatro di Atene. Interpretazioni e prospettive critiche. Roma, La Nuova Italia Scientifica, 95, 142 p.

1473. MAZZOLENI (Gilberto). Atena e le altre: considerazioni in margine a una lettura. *Studi e materiali di storia delle religioni*, 95, 61, 2, p. 427-431.

1474. MERRAS (Merja). The origins of the celebration of the Christian feast of Epiphany: an ideological, cultural and historical study. Joensuu, University of Joensuu, 95, 218-10 p. (Joensuun yliopiston humanistisia julk, 16.).

1475. Mesoamerican religions. A special issue on the occasion of the seventeenth International Congress of the History of Religions, Mexico City, August 5–12. *History of Religions*, 95, 35, 1, p. 1-82.

1476. MONACO (Manuela). A proposito di fonti missionarie, di dèi aztechi e di sacrifici umani. *Studi e materiali di storia delle religioni*, 95, 61, 2, p. 209-218.

1477. MONTANARI (Enrico). Eliade e Guénon. *Studi e materiali di storia delle religioni*, 95, 61, 2, p. 131-149. – IDEM. Falsi e veri miti (antichi e moderni). *Studi e materiali di storia delle religioni*, 95, 61, 2, p. 441-452. – IDEM. Ugo Bianchi e gli studi sulla religione romano-italica. *Studi e materiali di storia delle religioni*, 95, 61, 1, p. 5-9.

1478. MORA (Fabio). Il pensiero storico-religioso antico. Autori greci a Roma. I. Dionigi d'Alicarnasso. Roma, L'Erma di Bretschneider, 95, 484 p. (Storia delle religioni, 12).

1479. MOSSAKOWSKI (Stanisław). Sztuka sakralna a tożsamość narodowa. (Art sacré et l'identité nationale). *Archiwa, Biblioteki i Muzea Kościelne*, 95, 63, p. 19-25.

1480. Møtet mellom hedendom og kristendom i Norge. (Paganism and christianity in Norway). Ed. by Hans-Emil LIDÉN. Oslo, Universitetsforlaget, 95, 300 p. (ill.).

1481. OLMEADOWS (Harry). Mircea Eliade and Carl Jung: Priests without Supplices? Reflections on the place of myth, religion and science in their work. Bendigo, Department of Humanities, La Trobe University, 95, 43 p.

1482. OVERBECK (Franz). Werke und Nachlass. Band. 4. Kirkenlexicon. Texte. Ausgewählte Artikel A–I; Band. 5. Kirkenlexicon. Texte. Ausgewählte Artikel J–Z. In Zusammenarbeit mit Marianne STAUFFACHER-SCHAUB herausgegeben von Barbara von REIBNITZ. Stuttgart u. Weimar, J.B. Metzler, 95, 2 vol., XLIV-692 p.; X-762 p.

1483. PIERARD (Richard). Civil religion critically revisited. *Kirchliche Zeitgeschichte*, 95, 8, 1, p. 203-219.

1484. POPKO (Maciej). Religions of Asia Minor. Warszawa, Academic Publications Dialog, 95, 230 p.

1485. PUŠKAREVA (N. L.). Sem'ja, ženščina, seksual'naja étika v pravoslavii i katolicizme: perspektivy svranitel'nogo pokhoda. (The family, woman, and sex ethnics in the Orthodox and Catholic churches: comparative perspective). *Étnogr. obozrenie*, 95, 3, p. 55-69.

1486. RENNIE (Brian S.). The religious creativity of modern humanity: some observations on Eliade's unfinished thought. *Religious Studies*, 95, 31, p. 221-235.

1487. REPSTAD (Pål). Civil religion in modern society. Some general and some nordic perspectives. *Kirchliche Zeitgeschichte*, 95, 8, 1, p. 159-175.

1488. RIES (Julien). L'homo religiosus, il sacro e il santuario. *In*: Terra sacra: Chiesa e teritorio (La). Seminario di studio, Università di Trento, 29–30 novembre 1994. A cura di F. DEMARCHI e S. ABRUZZESE. Rimini, Guaraldi, 95, [s. p.], p. 24-38.

1489. RIZZACASA (A.). Tempo e storia secondo una concezione di fenomenologia delle religioni: Riflessioni in merito ad alcuni sviluppi del pensiero di Mircea Eliade. *Convivium Assisiense*, 95, 3, p. 145-166.

1490. ROBERTS (R.H.). Globalised Religion? The "Parliament of the World's Religion" (Chicago 1993) in theoretical perspective. *Journal of Contemporary Religion*, 95, 20, p. 121-137.

1491. RUTHERFORD (Ian). Theoric crisis: the dangers of pilgrimage in Greek religion and society. *Studi e materiali di storia delle religioni*, 61, 95, 2, p. 274-292.

1492. SEIWERT (Hubert). Religion in der Geschichte der Moderne. *Zeitschrift für Religionswissenschaft*, 95, 3, 1, p. 91-101.

1493. ŠKVORČEVIĆ (Antun). Katolička crkva u Hrvatskoj i ekumenizam. *Bogoslovska smotra (Ephemerides theologicae Zagrabienses)*, 95, 65, p. 513-540.

1494. Studi sul cristianesimo antico e moderno in onore di Maria Grazia Mara. A cura di Manlio SIMONETTI e Paolo SINISCALCO. *Augustinianum*, 35, 95, 1-2, p. 1-941 p.

1495. SUNDERMEYER (T.). The meaning of tribal religions for the history of religion. *Studies in Interreligious Dialogue*, 95, 5, p. 169-177.

1496. SWEARER (Donald K.). The Buddhist world of Southeast Asia. Albany, State University of New York Press, 95, 258 p.

1497. TAVIANI (Paolo). Nazionalismo e integralismo religioso come attrazioni esotiche: Edith e Victor Turner al Purgatorio di San Patrizio. *Studi e materiali di storia delle religioni*, 95, 61, 2, p. 433-440.

1498. Thematic issue on "Religion and Food". *Journal of the American Academy of Religion*, 95, 63, 3, p. 429-482.

1499. Theologische Realenzyklopädie. Band. 25. Ochino – Parapsychologie. Hrsg. v. G. MÜLLER. Berlin u. New York, De Gruyter, 95, IV-787 p.

1500. Töten im Krieg. Hrsg. v. Heinrich von STIETENCRON u. Jörg RÜPKE. Freiburg u. München, [s. n.], 95, 494 p. (Veröffentlichungen des "Instituts für Historische Anthropologie e. V.", 6).

1501. TURNER (Victor), TURNER (Edith). Image and pilgrimage in Christian culture. Anthropological perspectives. New York, Columbia U. P., 95, 281 p. (Lectures on the History of Religions, 11).

1502. VERNETTE (Jean), MONCELON (Claire), Dictionnaire des groupes religieux aujourd'hui. Religions, églises, sectes, nouveaux mouvements religieux, mouvements spiritualistes, Paris, PUF, 95, 291 p.

1503. VISCA (Danila). Dei profeti dell'Occidente. Tre variazioni sul tema del profetismo. Roma, Euroma, 95, [s. p.].

1504. VISOTZKY (Burton L.). Fathers of the world. Essays in rabbinic and patristic literatures. Tübingen, J. C. B. Mohr, 95, VII-205 p. (Wissenschaftliche Untersuchungen zum N. T., 80).

1505. WIEBE (D.). Benson Saler, "Conceptualizing Religion". *Numen*, 95, 42, p. 78-88.

Cf. n°s 2363, 2988

§ 12. Geschichte der Philosophie.

* 1506. Bibliografia filosofica italiana, 1993. [1992. Cf. Bibl. 94, n° 1216.] A cura di Carlo SCALABRIN. Firenze, Olschki, 95, 217 p. (Biblioteca di bibliografia italiana, 138).

* 1507. Bibliography of philosophy = Bibliographie de la philosophie: a quarterly bulletin. Vol. 42, 1995. Fasc. 1–4. [Vol. 41, 1994. Cf. Bibl. 94, n° 1214.]. Paris, Vrin, 539 p.

* 1508. International philosophical bibliography = Répertoire bibliographique de la philosophie. Vol. 47, 1995. [Vol. 46, 1994. Cf. Bibl. 94, n° 1215.] Louvain, Ed. de l'Institut Supérieur de Philosophie, [s. p.].

1509. ARIEW (Roger). Ideas, in and before Descartes. *Journal of the history of ideas*, 95, 56, 1, p. 87-106.

1510. Aristotelian political philosophy. Ed. by K.J. BOUDOURIS. Athens, International Center for Greek Philosophy and Culture, 95, 2 vol., 252 p., 263 p. (Meletes sten Hellenike philosophia, 16–17. Meletes Hellenikes philosophias, 16–17).

1511. Cambridge companion to Aristotle (The). Ed. by Jonathan BARNES. (Cambridge companions). Cambridge, Cambridge U. P., 95, XXV-404 p.

1512. Cambridge companion to Husserl (The). Ed. by Barry SMITH and David WOODRUFF Smith. Cambridge, Cambridge U. P., 95, VIII-518 p.

1513. Cambridge companion to Leibniz (The). Ed. by Nicholas JOLLEY. Cambridge a. New York, Cambridge U. P., 95, XI-500 p. (Cambridge companions).

1514. CHAPPELL (Timothy D. J.). Aristotle and Augustine on freedom: two theories of freedom, voluntary action and akrasia. Basingstoke, Macmillan, 95, XII-212 p.

1515. Enzyklopädie Philosophie und Wissenschaftstheorie. Vol. 3. P–So. Hrsg. v. J. MITTELSTRASS. Stuttgart u. Weimar, J. B. Metzler, 95, 866 p.

1516. FLORIDI (Luciano). The diffusion of Sextus Empiricus's works in the Renaissance. *Journal of the history of ideas*, 95, 56, 1, p. 63-86.

1517. GUY (Alain). La philosophie espagnole. Paris, PUF, 95, 128 p. (Que sais-je? 3008).

1518. LANG (Helen s.). Aristotle's physics IV, 8. A vexed argument in the history of ideas. *Journal of the history of ideas* 95, 56, 3, p. 353-376.

1519. MARTINICH (Aloysius P.). A Hobbes dictionary. Oxford, Blackwell Publishers a. Cambridge, B. Blackwell, 95, XI-336 p. (The Blackwell philosopher dictionaries).

1520. Oxford companion to philosophy (The). Ed. by Ted HONDERICH. Oxford a. New York, Oxford U. P., 95, XX-1009 p. (ill.).

1521. Philosophical dialogues: Plato, Hume, Wittgenstein. Ed. by T.J. SMILEY. Oxford, Published for the British Academy by Oxford U. P., 95, X-83 p. (Proceedings of the British Academy, 85).

1522. SCOTT (Dominic). Recollection and experience: Plato's theory of learning and its successors. Cambridge, Cambridge U. P., 95, X-289 p.

1523. Storia della filosofia, storia della scienza: saggi in onore di Paolo Rossi. A cura di Antonello LA VERGATA e Alessandro PAGNINI. Scandicci, La nuova Italia, 95, X-432 p. (Biblioteca di cultura, 204).

Cf. n°s 6216-6375

§ 13. Literaturgeschichte.

* 1524. Bibliografia alla storiografia (Dalla): la critica dantesca nel mondo dal 1965 al 1990. A cura di Enzo ESPOSITO. Ravenna, Longo, 95, 269 p. (Bibliografia e storia della critica, 12).

* 1525. BIGLI. Bibliografia generale della lingua e della letteratura italiana. Vol. 3, 1993. Tomi 1-2. [Vol. 2, 1992. Tomi 1-2. Cf. Bibl. 94, n° 1241.] Diretta da Enrico MALATO. Roma, Salerno, 95, 2 vol., 753 p., 257 p. (Pubblicazioni del "Centro Pio Rajna").

* 1526. GRENVILLE (Anthony). Cockpit of ideologies: the literature and political history of the Weimar Republic. Bern a. New York, P. Lang, 95, 394 p. (Britische und irische Studien zur deutschen Sprache und Literatur = Etudes parues en Grande-Bretagne et en Irlande concernant la philologie et la littérature allemandes = British and Irish studies in German language and literature, 11. Britische und irische Studien zur deutschen Sprache und Literatur, 11).

1527. Alternative identities: the self in literature, history, theory. Ed. by Linda Marie BROOKS. New York a. London, Garland, 95, XV-327 p. (Wellesley studies in critical theory, literary history, and culture, 7. Garland reference library of the humanities, 1848).

1528. Authorship: from Plato to the postmodern: a reader. Ed. by Sean BURKE. Edinburgh, Edinburgh U. P., 95, XXX-349 p.

1529. BERCÉ (Yves-Marie). Histoire littéraire et histoire. In: Histoire littéraire hier (L'), aujourd'hui et demain, ici et ailleurs [Cf. n° 1544], p. 131-138.

1530. BOOKER (M. Keith). Joyce, Bakhtin, and the literary tradition: toward a comparative cultural poetics. Ann Arbor, University of Michigan Press, 95, 273 p.

1531. Cambridge companion to American realism and naturalism (The): from Howells to London. Ed. by Donald PIZER. Cambridge, Cambridge U. P., 95, XVI-287 p. (Cambridge companions to literature series).

1532. Cambridge history of American literature (The). Vol. 2. 1820–1865. Ed. by Sacvan BERCOVITCH a. Cyrus R. K. PATELL. Cambridge, Cambridge U. P., 95, XVIII-887 p.

1533. DE SOUSA (Celeste Ribeiro). O indio brasileiro na literatura alemá. Revista do Instituto de Estudos Brasileiros, 95, 38, p. 69-85.

1534. Dramat obcy w Polsce, Premiery, druki, egzemplarze 1765-1965. (Drame étranger en Pologne, premières, impréssions, exemplaires 1765-1965). Ouvrage collectif. Réd. en chef Jan MICHALIK. T. 1. Litera A. Réd. Stanisław HAŁUBA. Kraków, Księgarnia Akademicka, 95, 142 p.

1535. EDMUNDSON (Mark). Literature against philosophy, Plato to Derrida: a defence of poetry. Cambridge a. New York, Cambridge U. P., 95, XII-243 p.

1536. ERCİLASUN (Ahmet B.). İkinci Meşrutiyet Devrinde Edebi Tenkit (La Critique littéraire à l'époque de la Révolution de 1908). Ankara, Türk Kültürunu Araştırma Enstitusu, 95, 336 p. (Türk Kültürunu Araştırma Enstitusu yayınları, 146).

1537. Ernst Robert Curtius et l'idée d'Europe: actes du Colloque de Mulhouse et Thann des 29, 30 et 31 janvier 1992. Organise par Jeanne BEM et Andre GUYAUX. Paris, H. Champion, 95, 396 p. (Travaux et recherches des universites rhenanes, 10).

1538. FORSTER (Heinz) RIEGEL (Paul). Die Nachkriegszeit, 1945–1968. München, Deutscher Taschenbuch Verlag, 95, 489 p. (Deutsche Literaturgeschichte, 11).

1539. Garland companion to Vladimir Nabokov (The). Ed. by Vladimir E. ALEXANDROV. New York a. London, Garland, 95, XLIX-798 p. (Garland reference library of the humanities, 1474).

1540. Handbuch der Orientalistik. Abteilung 1. Der Nahe und Mittlere Osten. Band 13. Arabic literature of Africa. General editors J. O. HUNWICK and R. S. O'FAHEY. Vol. 2. The writings of Central Sudanic Africa. Compiled by John O. HUNWICK with the assistance of Razaq ABUBAKRE [et al]. Leiden, New York a. Köln, E. J. Brill, 95, 732 p.

1541. Handbuch der Orientalistik. Abteilung 2. Indien. Hrsg. v. J. BRONKHORST. Band 9. ZVELEBIL (Kamil). Lexicon of Tamil literature. Leiden, New York a. Köln, E. J. Brill, 95, XXIV-782p.

1542. HARRISON (Nicholas). Circles of censorship: censorship and its metaphors in French history, literature, and theory. Oxford, Clarendon Press, 95, 246 p.

1543. HAYRAPETEAN (Srbuhi Poghosi). A history of Armenian literature: from ancient times to the nineteenth century. Delmar, Caravan Books, 95, 650 p.

1544. Histoire littéraire hier (L'), aujourd'hui et demain, ici et ailleurs. Actes du Colloque des 17 et 18 novembre 1994. *Revue d'histoire littéraire de la France*, 95, 95, 6 (supplément), 190 p. [Cf. n^{os} <sélection> 801, 1529, 1567.]

1545. Historia de la literatura española. Tomo 6. El siglo XX. Obra dir. por Jean CANAVAGGIO con la colaboracion de Bernard DARBORD [et al.]. Barcelona, Editorial Ariel, 95, 401 p.

1546. Historia y critica de la literatura española. Al cuidado de Francisco RICO. 7. SANCHEZ VIDAL (Agustin). Epoca contemporanea: 1914–1939. Por. 1. Primer suplemento. Barcelona, Critica, 95, XII-636 p.

1547. History of Nordic neo-Latin literature (A). Ed. by Minna SKAFTE JENSEN. Odense, Odense U. P., 95, 380 p. (Odense University studies in Scandinavian languages and literatures, 32).

1548. HORSFALL (Nicholas). A companion to the study of Vergil. Leiden, New York a. Köln, E. J. Brill, 95, XIV-326 p. (Mnemosyne, bibliotheca classica Batava. Supplementum, 151).

1549. Letteratura italiana del Risorgimento. A cura di Gianfranco CONTINI. Firenze, Sansoni, 95, 504 p.

1550. Letteratura italiana: le opere. Dir. da Alberto ASOR ROSA. Vol. 3. Dall'Ottocento al Novecento. Vol. 4. Il Novecento. Parte 1. L'età della crisi. Parte 2. La ricerca letteraria. Torino, Einaudi, 95, 3 vol., 1141 p., 780 p., 1017 p., (ill.). (Letteratura italiana. Le opere, 3–4).

1551. Lexikon literaturtheoretischer Werke. Hrsg. v. Rolf Günther RENNER u. Engelbert HABEKOST. Stuttgart, Kröner, 95, XV-520 p. (Kröners Taschenausgabe, 425).

1552. MÜLLER (Ulrich). Künstlerische Fiktion zu Beginn des Ästhetischen Zeitalters. *Archiv für Kulturgeschichte*, 95, 77, p. 345-370.

1553. New Oxford companion to literature in French (The). Ed. by Peter FRANCE. Oxford, Oxford U. P., 95, LI-865 p. (maps).

1554. NISTICÒ (R.). Il soggetto desueto nella letteratura. *Belfagor*, 95, 6, p. 729-733.

1555. OVIEDO (Jose Miguel). Historia de la literatura hispanoamericana. Vol. 1. De los origenes a la emancipacion. Madrid, Alianza Editorial, 95, [s. p.]. (Alianza universidad textos, 151).

1556. Oxford book of letters (The). Ed. by Frank KERMODE a. Anita KERMODE. Oxford, Oxford U. P., 95, XXIV-559 p.

1557. PETRO (Peter). A history of Slovak literature. Liverpool, Liverpool U. P., 95, X-164 p.

1558. Reader's companion to twentieth-century writers (The). Ed. by Peter PARKER; consultant editor, Frank KERMODE. London, Fourth Estate/Helicon, 95, 900 p. (ill.).

1559. Secret texts: the literature of secret societies. Ed. by Marie MULVEY ROBERTS a. Hugh ORMSBY-LENNON. New York, AMS Press, 95, 349 p. (ill.). (AMS studies in cultural history, 1).

1560. SIHLER (A. L.). New comparative grammar of Greek and Latin. New York a. Oxford, Oxford U. P., 95, 686 p.

1561. SIRERA (Josep Lluis). Historia de la literatura valenciana. Valencia, Edicions Alfons el Magnanim, Institucio Valenciana d'Estudis i Investigacio, 95, 607 p.

1562. Slavjanskaja mifologija: Énciklopedičeskij slovar'. (The Slavonic mythology: Encyclopaedic dictionary). Naučnyj redaktor V. Ja. PETRUKHIN. Moskva, Ellis Lak, 95, 414 p.

1563. Słownik pseudonimów pisarzy polskich XV w.–1970 r. (Dictionnaire des pseudonymes des écrivains polonais, XVe s.–1970). Elab. par. l'équipe de Joanna KROL et autres sous la réd. d'Edmund JANKOWSKI. T. 2. J–Q. Wrocław, Zakł. Narod. im. Ossolińskich, 95, 862 p.

1564. SNODGRASS (Mary Ellen). Encyclopedia of utopian literature. Santa Barbara a. Oxford, ABC-CLIO, 95, XVI-644 p. (ill.). (ABC-CLIO literary companion).

1565. STEINER (George). What is comparative literature? An inaugural lecture delivered before the University of Oxford on 11 October, 1994. Oxford, Clarendon Press a. Oxford a. New York, Oxford U. P., 95, 19 p. (Inaugural lectures).

1566. THOMAS (Alfred). The labyrinth of the word. Truth and representation in Czech literature. München, Oldenbourg, 95, 174 p. (Veröffentlichungen des Collegium Carolinum, 78).

1567. THUILLIER (Jacques). Histoire littéraire et histoire de l'art. *In*: Histoire littéraire hier (L'), aujourd'hui et demain, ici et ailleurs [Cf. n° 1544], p. 150-156.

1568. Wielka literatura powszechna. (Grande littérature universelle). Réd. par Stanisław LAM. T. 1. BROMSKI (Józef) [et al.]. Wschód – literatury klasyczne. (Est – littératures classiques). Warszawa, Gutenberg-Print, 95, X-831 p. (phot., fig.).

Cf. n°s 1335, 6527

C

VOR- UND FRÜHGESCHICHTE

§ 1. Allgemeines. 1569-1595. – § 2. Paläolithikum und Mesolithikum. 1596-1625. – § 3. Neolithikum. 1626-1652. – § 4. Bronzezeit. 1653-1676. – § 5. Eisenzeit. 1677-1691. – § 6. Frühgeschichtliche Völker Europas mit Ausnahme Griechenlands und Italiens. 1692-1718.

§ 1. Allgemeines.

1569. ACKERLY (Neal W.). 'This does not compute': the All-American Pipeline Project revisited. *Antiquity*, 95, 69, 264, p. 596-601.

1570. ALLEN (Jim), HOLDXAY (Simon). The contamination of Pleistocene radiocarbon determinations in Australia. *Antiquity*, 95, 69, 262, p. 101-112.

1571. ANTHONY (David W.). Horse, wagon and chariot: Indo-European languages and archaeology. *Antiquity*, 95, 69, 264, p. 554-565.

1572. ANYON (Roger), FERGUSON (T. J.). Cultural resources management at the Pueblo of Zuni, New Mexico, USA. *Antiquity*, 95, 69, 266, p. 913-930.

1573. Arkheologičeeskoe nasledie Tjumenskoj oblasti: Pamjatniki lesostepi i podtaežnoj polosy. (The archaeological sites of the Tjumen region: monuments of the forest-steppes and taiga area). A. V. MATVEEV, N. P. MATVEEV, A. N. PANFILOV i drugie; Otv. red. V. I. MOLODIN; RAN. Sibirskoe otdelenie. Institut problem osvoenija Severa. Novosibirsk: Nauka. Sibirskaja izdatel'skaja firma, 95, 239 p.

1574. BADER (Tibor). Prähistorische Rekonstruktionen und experimentelle Archäologie im Keltenmuseum Hochdorf/Enz – Bundesrepublik Deutschland. *Acta archaeol. Acad. Sci. Hungaricae*, 95, 47, 1-4, p. 149-213.

1575. DÍAZ-ANDREU, MORA (Gloria). Arqueología y política: el desarollo de la arqueologia española en su contexto histórico. *Trabajos de Prehistoria*, 95, 52, 1, p. 25-38.

1576. EISELE (J. A.), FOWLER (D. D.), HAYNES (G.), LEWIS (R. A.). Survival and detection of blood residues on stone tools. *Antiquity*, 95, 69, 262, p. 36-46.

1577. FEATHERSTONE (Roger), HORNE (Peter), MAC LEOLD (David), BEWLEY (Robert). Aerial reconnaissance in England, summer 1995. *Antiquity*, 95, 69, 266, p. 981-988.

1578. HERNANDO GONZALO (Almudena). La etnoarqueología, hoy: una vía eficaz de aproximación al pasado. *Trabajos de Prehistoria*, 95, 52, 2, p. 15-30.

1579. HUBBARD (R.L.N.B.). Fallow deer in prehistoric Greece, and the analogy between faunal spectra and pollen analyses. *Antiquity*, 95, 69, 264, p. 527-538.

1580. HURCOMBE (Linda). Our own engendered species. *Antiquity*, 95, 69, 262, p. 87-100.

1581. MAC GLADE (James). Archaeology and ecodynamics of human-modified landscapes. *Antiquity*, 95, 69, 262, p. 113-132.

1582. MATJUKHIN (A. E.). Osobennosti analiza dvustoronne-obrabotannykh izdelij kamennogo veka. (Peculiarities of the analysis of the Stone Age bifacial treatment). *Ros. arkheol.*, 95, 3, p. 13-27.

1583. MATTHEWS (Keith J.). Archaeological data, subcultures and social dynamics. *Antiquity*, 95, 69, 264, p. 586-594.

1584. MEDEROS MARTÍN (Alfredo). ¿Retorno al pasado? Comercio o difusión en los análisis de los sistemas mundiales antiguos. *Trabajos de Prehistoria*, 95, 52, 2, p. 131-141.

1585. MESKELL (Lynn). Goddesses, Gimbutas and 'New Age' archaeology. *Antiquity*, 95, 69, 262, p. 74-86.

1586. NIEWĘGŁOWSKI (Andrzej). Archeologie – prahistoria – historie. Relacje przedmiotu i teorii badań. (Wstęp do dyskusji). [Archéologie, préhistoire, histoire. Relations entre l'objet et la théorie des recherches. (Introduction au débat)]. *Kwartalnik Historii Materialnej Polskiej Akademii Nauk*, 95, 43, 2, p. 229-254. [Deutsche Zsfassung].

1587. PEÑA (José Antonio), ESQUIVEL (José Antonio). El bricolage geoeléctrico: un recurso de bajo coste en la prospección arqueológica de subsuelo. *Trabajos de Prehistoria*, 95, 52, 1, p. 147-156.

1588. POSTGATE (Nicholas), WANG (Tao), WILKINSON (Toby). The evidence for early writing: utilitarian or ceremonial? *Antiquity*, 96, 69, 264, p. 459-480.

1589. RAO (Nandini). Politics and the World Archaeological Congress. *Trabajos de Prehistoria*, 95, 52, 1, p. 5-11.

1590. RODRIGUEZ ALCALDE (Angel), ALONSO JIMENEZ (Carmelo), VELAZQUEZ CANO (Julián). Fractales para la arqueología: un nuevo lenguaje. *Trabajos de Prehistoria*, 95, 52, 1, p. 13-34.

1591. SEALY (Judith), ARMSTRONG (Richard), SCHRIRE (Carmel). Beyond lifetime averages: tracing life histories through isotopic analysis of different calcified tissues from archaeological human skeletons. *Antiquity*, 95, 69, 263, p. 290-300.

1592. TRIGGER (Bruce G.). Expanding middle-range theory. *Antiquity*, 95, 69, 264, p. 449-458.

1593. VAN ANDEL (Tjeerd H.), RUNNELS (Curtis N.), The earliest farmers in Europe. *Antiquity*, 95, 69, 264, p. 481-500.

1594. VAZQUEZ VARELA (J. M.). Etnoarqueología de la extracción del oro de los ríos en el Noroeste de la Península Ibérica. *Trabajos de Prehistoria*, 95, 52, 2, p. 157-161.

1595. VILLOCH VAZQUEZ (Victoria). Monumentos y petroglifos: la construcción del espacio en las sociedades constructoras de túmulos del Noroeste peninsular. *Trabajos de Prehistoria*, 95, 52, 1, p. 39-55.

Cf. n° 2415

§ 2. Paläolithikum und Mesolithikum.

1596. AGUIRRE (Emiliano). Registro faunístico Pleistocenico Antiguo de Atapuerca (Burgos). *Trabajos de Prehistoria*, 95, 52, 2, p. 47-60.

1597. BAHN (Paul G.). Cave art without the caves. *Antiquity*, 95, 69, 263, p. 231-237.

1598. BEATON (J. M.). The transition on the coastal fringe of Greater Australia. *Antiquity*, 95, 69, 265, p. 798-806.

1599. BEDNARIK (Robert G.). The Côa petroglyphs: an obituary to the stylistic dating of Paleolithic rockart. *Antiquity*, 95, 69, 266, p. 877-883.

1600. BRADLEY (Bruce A.), ANIKOVICH (Michael), GIRIA (Engenii). Early Upper Palaeolithic in the Russian Plain: Streletskayan flaked stone artefacts and technology. *Antiquity*, 95, 69, 266, p. 989-998.

1601. CULLEN (Tracey). Mesolithic mortuary ritual at Franchthi Cave, Greece. *Antiquity*, 95, 69, 263, p. 270-289.

1602. EDWARDS (Douglas A.), O'CONNELL (James). Broad spectrum diets in arid Australia. *Antiquity*, 95, 69, 265, p. 769-783.

1603. FRANKEL (David). The Australian transition: real and perceived boundaries. *Antiquity*, 95, 69, 265, p. 649-655.

1604. GIRJA (E. Ju.), PITUL'KO (V. V.). Vkladyševye orudija i industrija obrabotki kamnja mezolitičeskoj stojanki na ostrove Žokhova. (Tools and stone industry from the Mesolithic site on Zhokhov island). *Ros. arkheol.*, 95, 1, p. 91-109.

1605. GOEBEL (Ted), AKSENOV (Mikhail). Accelerator radiocarbon dating of the initial Upper Paleolithic in southeast Siberia. *Antiquity*, 95, 69, 263, p. 349-357.

1606. HOLDAWAY (Simon). Stone artefacts and the transition. *Antiquity*, 95, 69, 265, p. 784-797.

1607. HOPE (Geoff), GOLSON (Jack). Late Quaternary change in the mountains of New Guinea. *Antiquity*, 95, 69, 265, p. 818-830.

1608. HOYOS (Manuel), AGUIRRE (Emiliano). El registro paleoclimático pleistoceno en la evolución del Karst de Atapuerca (Burgos): el corte de Gran Dolina. *Trabajos de Prehistoria*, 95, 52, 2, p. 31-45.

1609. KERSHAW (A. Peter). Environmental change in Greater Australia. *Antiquity*, 95, 69, 265, p. 656-675.

1610. KOHL (Philip L.). Prehistoric investigations in the Caucasus: international research in an Arena of national conflicts. *Altorientalische Forschungen*, 95, 22, 1, p. 87-102.

1611. LAUKHIN (S. A.). Zaselenie Severnoj Azii paleolitičeskim čelovekom i vozmožnosti Beringijskogo mosta. (The settlement of the Northern Asia by the Palaeolithic man and the Bering bridge possibilities). *Ros. arkheol.*, 95, 4, p. 7-19.

1612. LISICYN (N. F.). K voprosu o načal'nom ètape pozdnego paleolita Sibiri. (Concerning the beginning of the late Palaeolithic in Siberia. *Ros. arkheol.*, 95, 1, p. 5-13.

1613. LOZANO (Joan Miquel), SIMÓ (Rafel), GRIMALT (Joan O.), ESTÉVEZ (Jordi). Indicadores químicos de combustión en un hogar del Paleolítico Medio del yacimiento de Mediona I (Alt Penedès, Barcelona). *Trabajos de Prehistoria*, 95, 52, 2, p. 145-155.

1614. MAS CORNELLA (Martí), RIPOLL LOPEZ (SERGIO), MARTOS ROMERO (Juan Antonio), PANIAGUA PEREZ (José Pablo), LOPEZ MORENO DE REDROJO (José Ramón), BERGMANN (Lothar). Estudio preliminar de los grabados rupestres de la Cueva del Moro (Tarifa, Cádiz) y el arte paleolítico del Campo de Gibraltar. *Trabajos de Prehistoria*, 95, 52, 2, p. 61-81.

1615. MINZONI-DÉROCHE (Angela), MENU (Michel), WALTER (Philippe). The working of pigment during the Aurignacian period: evidence from Üçagizli cave (Turkey). *Antiquity*, 95, 69, 262, p. 153-158.

1616. O'CONNELL (James), ALLEN (JIM). Human reactions to the Pleistocene-Holocene transiction in Greater Australia: a summary. *Antiquity*, 95, 69, 265, p. 855-862.

1617. OTTE (Marcel), YALCINKAYA (Isin), LEOTARD (Jean-Marc), KARTAL (Metin), BAR-YOSEF (Ofer), KOZLOWSKI (Janusz), LÓPEZ BAYÓN (IGNACIO), MARSHACK (Alexander). The Epi-Palaeolithic of Öküzini cave (SW Anatolia) and its mobiliary art. *Antiquity*, 95, 69, 266, p. 931-944.

1618. PARDOE (Colin). Riverine, biological and cultural evolution in southeastern Australia. *Antiquity*, 95, 69, 265, p. 696-713.

1619. PORCH (Nick), ALLEN (Jim). Tasmania: archaeological and paleo-ecological perspectives. *Antiquity*, 95, 69, 265, p. 714-732.

1620. RIGAUD (Jean-Philippe), SIMEK (Jan F.), GE (Thierry). Mousterian fires from Grotte XVI (Dordogne, France). *Antiquity*, 95, 69, 266, p. 902, 912.

1621. TAÇON (Paul S. C.). Arnhem Land prehistory in landscape, stone and paint. *Antiquity*, 95, 69, 265, p. 676-695.

1622. TOMÁŠKOVÁ (Silvia). A site in history: archaeology at Dolnĕstonice/Unterwisternitz. *Antiquity*, 95, 69, 263, p. 301-316.

1623. VETH (Peter). Aridity and settlement in northwest Australia. *Antiquity*, 95, 69, 265, p. 733-746.

1624. YEN (D. E.). The development of Sahul agriculture with Australia as bystander. *Antiquity*, 95, 69, 265, p. 831-847.

1625. ZILHÃO (João). The age of the Côa valley (Portugal) rock-art: validation of archaeological dating to the Palaeolithic and refutation of 'scientific' dating to historic or proto-historic times. *Antiquity*, 95, 69, 266, p. 833-901.

§ 3. Neolithikum.

1626. AGRAWAL (D.P.), KHARAKWAL (Jeewan), KUSUMGAR (Sheela), YADAVA (M.G.). Cits burials of the Kumaun Himalayas. *Antiquity*, 95, 69, 264, p. 550-554.

1627. AKKEMANS (Peter M. M. G.), VERHOEVEN (Marc). An image of complexity: the burnt village at Late Neolithic Sabi Abyad, Syria. *American Journal of Archaeology*, 95, 99, 1, p. 5-32.

1628. ANZIDEI (Anna Paola), CARBONI (Giovanni). L'insediamento preistorico di Quadrato di Torre Spaccata (Roma) e osservazioni su alcuni aspetti tardo neolitici ed eneolitici dell'Italia centrale. *Origini. Preistoria e Protostoria delle Civiltà Antiche*, 95, 19, p. 55-225.

1629. AURISICCHIO (Carlo). Analisi chimico-mineralogica di una perlina in "steatite" proveniente dal sito del Neolitico Finale di Quadrato di Torre Spaccata (Roma). *Origini. Preistoria e Protostoria delle Civiltà Antiche*, 95, 19, p. 305-325.

1630. BAILO MODESTI (Gianni), SALERNO (Antonio). Il Gaudo di Eboli. *Origini. Preistoria e Protostoria delle Civiltà Antiche*, 95, 19, p. 327-393.

1631. BARCLAY (Gordon J.), MAXWELL (Gordon S.), SIMPSON (Ian A.), DAVIDSON (Donald A.). The Cleaven Dyke: a Neolithic cursus monument/bank barrow in Tayside Region, Scotland. *Antiquity*, 95, 69, 263, p. 317-326.

1632. BOWDLER (Sandra). Offshore islands and maritime explorations in Australian prehistory. *Antiquity*, 95, 69, 266, p. 945-958.

1633. CELANT (Alessandra). Macroresti vegetali del livello neolitico nell'insediamento di Quadrato di Torre Spaccata. *Origini. Preistoria e Protostoria delle Civiltà Antiche*, 95, 19, p. 277-286.

1634. COONEY (Gabriel), MANDAL (Stephen). Getting to the core of the problem: petrological results from the Irish Stone Axe Project. *Antiquity*, 95, 69, 266, p. 969-980.

1635. DE GROSSI MAZZORIN (Jacopo), MINNITI (Claudia). I resti faunistici dell'insediamento di Quadrato di Torre Spaccata nel contesto delle economie di allevamento del Neolitico finale ed Eneolitico in Italia centrale. *Origini. Preistoria e Protostoria delle Civiltà Antiche*, 95, 19, p. 287-295.

1636. DI LERNIA (Savino), FIORENTINO (Girolamo). Decoding an open-air archaeological deposit: the prehistoric settlement of Terragne (Manduria-Taranto, South Eastern Italy). Formation processes and spatial analysis. *Origini. Preistoria e Protostoria delle Civiltà Antiche*, 95, 19, p. 7-53.

1637. DRONFIELD (Jeremy). Subjective vision and the source of Irish megalithic art. *Antiquity*, 95, 69, 264, p. 539-459.

1638. GOSDEN (Chris). Arboriculture and agriculture in coastal Papua New Guinea. *Antiquity*, 95, 69, 265, p. 807-817.

1639. HARRIS (David). Early agriculture in New Guinea and the Torres Strait divide. *Antiquity*, 95, 69, 265, p. 848-854.

1640. KRIŽEVSKAJA (L. Ja.). Nekotorye novye dannye o khronologii neolita ural'skogo regiona i metodakh ee ustanovlenija. (The new data concerning the neolithic chronology of the Urals region and the methods of its determination). *Ros. arkheol.*, 95, 2, p. 5-10.

1641. LEMORINI (Cristina), ROSSETTI (Patrizia), CUONO (Giovanni), IOVINO (Maria Rosa). I materiali lavorati e le azioni effettuate: la ricostruzione funzionale dell'industria litica del giacimento neo-eneolitico di

Quadrato di Torre Spaccata (Roma) mediante l'analisi delle tracce d'uso. *Origini. Preistoria e Protostoria delle Civiltà Antiche*, 95, 19, p. 253-276.

1642. LENNEIS (Eva), NEUGEBAUER-MARESCH (Christine), RUTTKAY (Elisabeth). Jungsteinzeit im Osten Österreichs. St. Pölten u. Wien, Vlg. Niederösterr. Pressehaus, 95, 224 p. (ill., Karten, Graph. Darstellungen). (Schriftenreihe Niederösterreich, 102; Forschungsberichte zur Ur- und Frühgeschichte, 17).

1643. Mann im Eis (Der). 2. Neue Funde und Ergebnisse. Hrsg. v. Konrad SPINDLER [u. a.]. Wien u. New York, Springer, 95, X-320 p. (ill., Karten, Graph. Darstellungen). (Veröffentlichungen des Forschungsinstituts für Alpine Vorzeit der Universität Innsbruck, 2).

1644. MORWOOD (M. J.), HOBBS (D. R.). Themes in the prehistory of tropical Australia. *Antiquity*, 95, 69, 265, p. 747-768.

1645. MUSACCHIO (Alberto). L'industria litica dell'area 3 del sito neolitico di Quadrato di Torre Spaccata (Roma): analisi tecnologica della catena operativa delle punte di freccia ritoccate a pressione. *Origini. Preistoria e Protostoria delle Civiltà Antiche*, 95, 19, p. 227-251.

1646. PALLECCHI (Pasquino). Osservazioni sulla composizione e la tecnologia delle ceramiche dell'insediamento neolitico di Quadrato di Torre Spaccata (Roma). *Origini. Preistoria e Protostoria delle Civiltà Antiche*, 95, 19, p. 297-303.

1647. RYBICKA (Małgorzata). Przemiany kulturowe i osadnicze w III tysiącleciu przed Chrystusem na Kujawach. Kultura pucharów lejkowatych i amfor kulistych na Pagórach Radziejowskich. (Changements culturels et coloniaux au IIIe millénaire av. J. C. à Kujawy. Culture de coupes en forme d'entonnoir et d'amphores sphériques à Pagóry Radziejowskie). Łódź, 95, 275 p. (Eng. Summary, dessins, cartes). Bibl. Muzeum Archeolog. i Etnograf. w Łodzi, 28).

1648. SALERNO (Antonio). Revisione della tomba Brinson: i materiali. *Origini. Preistoria e Protostoria delle Civiltà Antiche*, 95, 19, p. 395-414.

1649. SCHUHMACHER (Thomas X.), WENIGER (G.-C.). Continuitad y cambio. Problemas de la neolitización en el Este de la Península Ibérica. *Trabajos de Prehistoria*, 95, 52, 2, p. 83-97.

1650. SIDOROV (V. V.). Neolit Desny i Volgo-Oskogo bassejna. (The Neolithic in the Desna and Volga-Oka rivers basins). *Ros. arkheol.*, 95, 1, p. 71-80.

1651. TELEGIN (D. Ja.). Neolitičeskaja keramika romankovskogo tipa v Kievskom Podneprov'e. (The Neolithic Romankovo type pottery in the Dnieper river region near Kiev). *Ros. arkheol.*, 95, 1, p. 110-120.

1652. YIOUNI (Paraskevi). Thechnological analysis of the Neolithic pottery from Makri. *Bulletin de Correspondance Hellénique*, 95, 119, 2, p. 607-620.

§ 4. Bronzezeit.

1653. ARMBRUSTER (Barbara R.). Sur la technologie et la typologie du collier de Sintra (Lisbonne, Portugal): un oeuvre d'orfèvrerie du Bronze Final Atlantique composé des types Sagrajas-Berzocana et Villena-Estremoz. *Trabajos de Prehistoria*, 95, 52, 1, p. 157-162.

1654. BARRIL VICENTE (Magdalena), MARTINEZ QUIRCE (Francisco J.). El disco de bronce y damasquinado en planta de Aguillar de Anguita (Guadalajara). *Trabajos de Prehistoria*, 95, 52, 1, p. 175-187.

1655. COMENDADOR REY (Beatriz). Caraterización de la metalurgia inicial gallega: una revisión. *Trabajos de Prehistoria*, 95, 52, 2, p. 11-129.

1656. CONTRERAS CORTES (Francisco), CAMARA SERRANO (Juan Antonio), LIZCANO PRESTEL (Rafael), PEREZ BAREAS (Cristóbal), ROBLEDO SANZ (Beatriz), TRANCHO GALLO (Gonzalo). Enterramientos y diferenciacion social I. El registro funerario del yacimiento de la Edad del Bronce de Peñalosa (Baños de la Encina, Jaén). *Trabajos de Prehistoria*, 95, 52, 1, p. 87-108.

1657. DELLA CASA (Philippe). The Cetina group and the transition from Copper to Bronze Age in Dalmatia. *Antiquity*, 95, 69, 264, p. 566-576.

1658. DI FRAIA (Tomaso). L'abitato dell'età del Bronzo Finale di Fonte Tasca (Comune di Archi, Chieti). Studio preliminare su alcune classi di manufatti. *Origini. Preistoria e Protostoria delle Civiltà Antiche*, 95, 19, p. 447-477.

1659. DÍAZ-DEL-RÍO ESPAÑOL (Pedro). Campesinado y gestión pluriactiva del ecosistema: un marco teórico para el análisis del III y II milenios A. C. en la Meseta peninsular. *Trabajos de Prehistoria*, 95, 52, 2, p. 99-109.

1660. FERNANDEZ-MIRANDA (Manuel), MONTERO RUIZ (Ignacio), ROVIRA LLORENS (Salvador). Los primeros objetos de Bronce en el Occidente de Europa. *Trabajos de Prehistoria*, 95, 52, 1, p. 57-69.

1661. FLEMING (Andrew). St Kilda: stone tools, dolerite querries and long-term survival. *Antiquity*, 95, 69, 262, p. 25-35.

1662. GOOD (Irene). On the question of silk in pre-Han Eurasia. *Antiquity*, 95, 69, 266, p. 959-968.

1663. GÖTZELT (Thomas). Complex simplicities: of periods and functions in Bronze Age Southern Turkmenistan. *Altorientalische Forschungen*, 95, 22, 1, p. 56-69.

1664. JOVER MAESTRE (Francisco Javier), LÓPEZ PADILLA (Juan Antonio). El Argar y el Bronce Valenciano. Reflexiones en torno al mundo funerario. *Trabajos de Prehistoria*, 95, 52, 1, p. 71-86.

1665. KADROW (Sławomir). Gospodarka i społeczeństwo. Wczesny okres epoki brązu w Małopolsce.

(Economie et société. L'âge précoce du bronze en Małopolska). Kraków, Inst. Archeologii i Etnografii Pol. Akad. Nauk, 95, 167 p. (Eng. summary).

1666. KUZ'MIN (Ja. V.), ORLOVA (L. A.), SULERŽICKIJ (L. D.), DŽALL(E. Dz.). Radiouglerodnaja khronologija drevnikh kul'tur épokh kamnja i bronzy Primor'ja. (Dal'nij Vostok Rossii). (Radiocarbon chronology of the Stone and Bronze Age cultures in Primorye. The Russian Far East). *Ros. arkheol.*, 95, 3, p. 5-12.

1667. LOCHNER (Michaela). Siedlungsgruben der älteren Urnenfelderzeit aus Oberbergern und Bronzefunde aus Unterbergern, Gem. Bergern im Dunkelsteinerwald, Niederösterreich. *Archaeologia Austriaca*, 95, 78, p. 69-98 (ill.).

1668. MERPERT (N. Ja.). O planirovke poselkov rannego bronzovogo veka v Verkhnefrakijskoj doline. (Južnaja Bolgarija). (Concerning the planning of the early Bronze Age settlements of the Upper Thracian valley. The Southern Bulgaria). *Ros. arkheol.*, 95, 3, p. 28-46.

1669. MONTERO (J. L.). Estudio provisional del ajuar metálico del conjunto funerario de los loci 12 E y 12 W. Tell Qara Q˝zýq (Siria). Campaña 1992. *Aula Orientalis*, 95, 13, 1, p. 25-30.

1670. OLÁVARRI (E.). Dos tumbas del Bronce Antiguo de Qara Qūzāq. *Aula Orientalis*, 95, 13, 1, p. 15-23. – IDEM. Excavaciones en Tell Qara Qūzāq. Informe provisional: campañas tercera y cuarta (1991–92). Misión arqueológica de la Universidad de Barcelona en Siria. *Aula Orientalis*, 95, 13, 1, p. 5-14.

1671. POTEMKINA (T. M.). Problema svjazej i smeny kul'tur naselenija Zaural'ja v épokhu bronzy (rannij i srednij étapy). (Problems of the cultures contacts and changes in region beyond the Urals in the Bronze Age. The early and the middle periods). *Ros. arkheol.*, 95, 1, p. 14-27. – IDEM. Problema svlazej i smeny kul'tur naselenija Zaural'ja v epokhu bronzy (pozdnij i final'nyj étapy). (Problems of the contacts and the cultures changing of the Bronze Age population lived beyond the Urals. The late and the final stages). *Ros. arkheol.*, 95, 2, p. 11-20.

1672. RADI (Giovanna). Le coste: stazioni dell'Eneolitico e della media età del Bronzo nel Fucino (Pescina, L'Aquila). *Origini. Preistoria e Protostoria delle Civiltà Antiche*, 95, 19, p. 415-445.

1673. RAUSCH (Andreas). Keltische Siedlungsfunde aus der Katastralgemeinde Schauboden im Erlauftal. *Unsere Heimat*, 95, 66, 3, p. 154-188 (ill., Karten, Tafeln).

1674. VALDES (C.). La cerámica de las tumbas del locus 12 (Tell Qara Qūzāq, Siria, campaña de 1992). *Aula Orientalis*, 95, 13, 1, p. 31-66.

1675. VIRÁG (Zsuzsanna). Die Hochkupferzeit in der Umgebung von Budapest und in NO-Transdanubien. Das Ludanice-Problem. *Acta archaeol. Acad. Sci. Hungaricae*, 95, 47, 1-4, p. p. 61-94.

1676. VRDOLJAK (Snježana), FORENBAHER (Stašo). Bronze-casting and organization of production at Kalnik-Igrišče (Croatia). *Antiquity*, 95, 69, 264, p. 577-582.

Cf. n° 1898

§ 5. Eisenzeit.

1677. AYALON (Etan). The Iron Age II pottery assemblage from Ḥorvat Teiman (Kuntillet 'Ajrud). *Tel Aviv*, 95, 22, 2, p. 141-212.

1678. BRAND (Cordula). Zur eisenzeitlichen Besiedlung des Durrnberges bei Hallei. Espelkamp, M. L. Leidorf, 95, 433 p. (Internationale Archäologie, 19).

1679. CUNLIFFE (Barry). Iron Age Britain. London, B. T. Batsford/English Heritage, 95, 128 p. (English Heritage).

1680. Different Iron Age. Studies on the Iron Age in temperate Europe. Edd. by J. D. HILL, C. G. CUMBERPATCH. Oxford, Tempus Reparatum, 95, 217 p. (BAR International series, 602).

1681. EGG (Markus). Die Metallzeit in Europa und im Vorderen Orient. Die Abteilung Vorgeschichte im Römisch-Germanischen Zentralmuseum. Mainz, Verlag der Römisch-Germanischen Zentralmuseums, 95, 236 p.

1682. FINKELSTEIN (Israel). Living on the fringe: the archaeology and history of the Negev, Sinai and neighbouring regions in the Bronze and Iron Ages. Sheffield, Sheffield Academic Press, 95, 197 p. (Monographs in Mediterranean Archaeology, 6).

1683. FORSBERG (Stig). Near Eastern destruction dating as sources for Greek and Near Eastern Iron Age chronology: archaeological and historical studies: the cases of Samaria (722 B. C.) and Tarsus (696 B.C.). Uppsala, Acta Universitatis Upsaliensis, 95, 106 p. (Boreas: Uppsala studies in ancient Mediterranean and Near Eastern civilizations, 19).

1684. KRENKE (N. A.). "Čertov gorodok" – selišče železnogo veka v okrestnostjakh sela Kolomenskogo. ("Tchertov gorodok", an iron Age site near Kolomenskoe). *Ros. arkheol.*, 95, 3, p. 165-178.

1685. MAKKAY (János). Decebál kincsei. (Les trésors de Décébale). *Századok*, 95, 129, 5, p. 967-1032.

1686. Nomads of the Eurasian steppes in the early Iron Age. Edd. by Jeannine DAVID-KIMBALL, Vladimir A. BASHILOV, Leonid T. YABLONSKY. Berkeley, Zinat Press, 95, 403 p.

1687. Nordiske jernalder – symposium (2:1992: Granavolden). Ed. by Heid GJÖSTEIN RESI. Oslo, Universitets oldsaksamling, 95, 225 p. [The iron age in the North].

1688. PARCERO OUBIÑA (César). Elementos para el estudio de los paisajes castreños del Noroeste peninsular. *Trabajos de Prehistoria*, 95, 52, 1, p. 127-144.

1689. PASTOR BORGOÑÓN (H.). La ocupación del Tell Kabri durante la edad del Hierro. *Aula Orientalis*, 95, 13, 2, p. 211-216.

1690. Sites and sights of the Iron Age. Essays on fieldwork and museum research presented to Ian Mathieson Stead. Edd. by Barry RAFTERY, Vincent MEGAW, Val RIGBY. Oxford, Oxbow, 95, 179 p. (Oxbow monograph, 56).

1691. Trans Europam: Beiträge zur Bronze- und Eisenzeit zwischen Atlantik und Altai. Festschrift für Margarita Primas. Hrsg. v. Biljana SCHMID-SIKIMIC, Philippe DELLA CASA. Bonn, R. Habelt, 95, 288 p. (Antiquitas, 34).

§ 6. Frühgeschichtliche Völker Europas mit Ausnahme Griechenlands und Italiens.

1692. Altes Germanien: Auszüge aus den antiken Quellen über die Germanen und ihre Beziehungen zum römischen Reich. Quellen der alten Geschichte bis zum Jahre 298 n. Chr. Hrsg. v. Hans-Werner GOETZ, Karl-Willhelm WELWEI. Darmstadt, Wissenschaftliche Buchgesellschaft, 95, 2 vol., 361 p., 422 p. (Ausgewählte Quellen zur deutschen Geschichte des Mittelalters, 1).

1693. BARCLAY (Alistair). Excavations at the Devil's Quits, Stanton Harcourt, Oxfordshire, 1972–73 and 1988. Oxford, Published for the Oxford Archaeological Unit by Oxford University Committee for Archaeology, 95, 138 p. (Thames Valley Landscapes. The Windrush Valley, 3).

1694. CAMPBELL (John Francis). The Celtic dragon myth. Felinfach, Lampeter, Llanerch Publishers, 95, 172 p.

1695. Celts (The). London, Thames and Hudson, 95, 78 p. (Sacred Symbols).

1696. CERDEÑO (Maria Luisa), PEREZ DE INESTROSA (José Luis), CABANES (Emilio). Cerámicas de importación mediterránea en un castro celtibérico. *Trabajos de Prehistoria*, 95, 52, 1, p. 163-173.

1697. CUNLIFFE (Barry). Danebury: an Iron Age hillfort in Hampshire. Vol. 6. A hillfort community in perspective. London, Council for British Archaeology, 95, 296 p. (CBA research report, 102).

1698. ELLIS (Peter Berresford). Celtic women. Women in Celtic society and literature. London, Constable, 95, 288 p. – IDEM. The Druids. London, Constable, 95, 304 p.

1699. Funzione dell'eroe germanico (La): storicità, metafora, paradigma. Atti del Convegno Internazionale di Studio, Roma, 6–8 maggio 1993. A cura di Teresa PAROLI. Roma, Calamo, 95, 376 p.

1700. GERLACH (Stefan). Der Eiersberg. Eine Höhensiedlung der vorrömischen Eisenzeit und ihre Stellung in der Siedlungslandschaft zwischen Rhön und Thüringer Wald. Kallmünz, Lassleben, 95, 178 p.

1701. GREEN (Miranda J.). Celtic goddesses. Warriors, virgins and mothers. London, British Museum Press, 95, 224 p.

1702. Heiligtümer und Opferkulte der Kelten. Hrsg. v. Alfred HAFFNER. Stuttgart, Theiss, 95, 121 p. (Archäologie in Deutschland).

1703. HILL (Jeremy David). Ritual and rubbish in the Iron Age of Wessex. A study on the formation of a specific archaeological record. Oxford, Tempus Reparatum, 95, 149 p. (BAR British Series, 242). – IDEM. The cultural world in Beowulf. Toronto a. Buffalo, University of Toronto Press, 95, 224 p. (Anthropological Horizons).

1704. JOACHIM (Hans-Eckart). Waldalgesheim: das Grab einer keltischen Fürstin. Köln, Rheinland-Verlag in Kommission bei R. Habelt, 95, 248 p. (Kataloge des Rheinischen Landesmuseums Bonn, 3).

1705. Kelten, Germanen, Römer im Mitteldonaugebiet. Vom Ausklang der Latene-Zivilisation bis zum 2. Jahrhundert. Hrsg. v. Jaroslav TEJRAL, Karol PIETA, Jan RAJTAR. Brno, Archäologisches Institut der Akademie der Wissenschaften der Tschechischen Republik Brno u. Nitra, Archäologisches Institut der Slowakischen Akademie der Wissenschaften Nitra, 95, 280 p.

1706. KURZ (Gabriele). Keltische Hort- und Gewässerfunde in Mitteleuropa. Deponierungen der Latenezeit. Stuttgart, Theiss, 95, 254 p. (Materialhefte zur Archäologie in Baden-Wurttemberg, 33).

1707. LAMBOT (Bernard). Une tombe à char de la Tene ancienne a Semide (Ardennes). Reims, Societé Archeologique Champenoise, 95, 106 p. (Memoire de la Société Archéologique Champenoise, 10).

1708. MATTHEWS (Caitlin). The Celtic book of days: a celebration of Celtic wisdom. New Alsresford, Godsfield, 95, 128 p. – IDEM. The Celtic tradition. Shaftesbury, Element, 95, 112 p. (The Element Library).

1709. PARFITT (Keith). Iron Age burials from Mill Hill, Deal. London, Published for the Trustees of the British Museum by British Museum Press, 95, 215 p.

1710. PRESCOTT (Christopher). From Stone Age to Iron Age. A study from Sogn, western Norway. Oxford, Tempus Reparatum, 95, 150 (BAR International Series, 603).

1711. RIECKHOFF-PAULI (Sabine). Süddeutschland im Spannungsfeld von Kelten, Germanen und Römern. Studien zur Chronologie der Spätlatenezeit im südlichen Mitteleuropa. Trier, Selbstverlag des Rheinischen Landesmuseums Trier, 95, 317 p. (Trierer Zeitschrift für Geschichte und Kunst des Landes Trier und seiner Nachbargebiete, 19).

1712. RODER (Brigitte). Frühlatenekeramik aus dem Breisgau. Ethnoarchäologisch und naturwissenschaftlich analysiert. Stuttgart, Theiss, 95, 257 p. (Materialhefte zur Archäologie in Baden-Württemberg, 30).

6. FRÜHGESCHICHTLICHE VÖLKER EUROPAS

1713. RUANO RUIZ (Encarnación), HOFFMAN (P.), RINCÓN (J. M.). Aproximación al estudio del vidrio preromano: los materiales procedentes de la necrópolis ibérica de El Cigarralejo (Mula, Murcia). Composición química de varias cuentas de collar. *Trabajos de Prehistoria*, 95, 52, 1, p. 189-206.

1714. SALISBURY (Chris). An 8th-century Mercian bridge over the Trent at Cromwell, Nottinghamshire, England. *Antiquity*, 95, 69, 266, p. 1015-1018.

1715. VOLLING (Thomas). Frühgermanische Gräber von Aubstadt im Grabfeldgau (Unterfranken). Kallmünz, M. Lassleben, 95, 123 p.

1716. WEBER-JENISCH (Gabriele). Der Limberg bei Sasbach und die spätlatenezeitliche Besiedlung des Oberrheingebietes. Stuttgart, Theiss, 95, 158 p; (Material zur Archäologie in Baden-Württemberg, 29).

1717. WILLIAMS (Robert John). Wavendon Gate. A late Iron Age and Roman settlement in Milton Keynes. Aylesbury, Buckinghamshire Archaeological Society, 95, 292 p. (Buchinghamshire Archaeological Society Monograph, 10).

1718. WOLFRAM (Herwig). Die Germanen. München, Beck, 95, 126 p.

D

DIE VÖLKER DES ALTEN ORIENTS
(die hellenistischen Staaten inbegriffen)

§ 1. Allgemeines. 1719-1737. – § 2. Vorderasien (Allgemeines). 1738-1758. – § 3. Ägypten. 1759-1804. – § 4. Mesopotamien. 1805-1857. – § 5. Hethiter. 1858-1884. – § 6. Juden und semitische Stämme bis zum Ausgang des Altertums. 1885-1939. – § 7. Iran. 1940-1964.

§ 1. Allgemeines.

1719. Archaeozoology of the Near East II. Proceedings of the second International Symposium on the Archaeozoology of Southwestern Asia and adjacent Areas. Ed. by H. BUITENHUIS, H.-P. UERPMANN. Leiden, Backhuys, 95, 155 p.

1720. AVALOS (Hector). Illness and health care in the ancient Near East. The role of the temple in Greece, Mesopotamia and Israel. Atlanta, Scholars Press, 95, 463 p. (Harvard Semitic Museum Publications, Harvard Semitic Monographs, 54).

1721. Civilizations of the ancient Near East. Ed. by M. SASSON. New York, Scribner a. London, Simon & Schuster and Prentice-Hall International, 95, 4 vol., 2966 p.

1722. COHEN (Raymond). On diplomacy in the ancient Near East. The Amarna Letters. Leicester, Centre for the Study of Diplomacy, University of Leicester, 95, 26 p. (Diplomatic Studies Programme, 2).

1723. COLLON (Dominique). Ancient Near Eastern art. London, British Museum Press, 95, 247 p.

1724. DELLER (K.), KLENGEL (H.). Keilschriftbibliographie. 54. *Orientalia*, 95, 64, p. 1*-100*.

1725. DEMANDT (Alexander). Antike Staatsformen. Eine vergleichende Verfassungsgeschichte der alten Welt. Berlin, Akademie, 95, 672 p.

1726. Egypt, the Aegean and the Levant: interconnections in the second millennium B. C. Ed. by W. V. DAVIES, L. SCHOFIELD. London, British Museum Press, 95, 156 p.

1727. GERGEN (Thomas). Die Ehe in der Antike: eine historische Rechtsvergleichung zu Ehe- und Ehegüterrecht bei den Ägyptern, Griechen und Römern. Marburg, Tectum Verlag, 95, 75 p.

1728. Immigration and emigration within the ancient Near East. Festschrift E. Lipinski. Ed. by K. VAN LERBERGHE, A. SCHOORS. Leuven, Uitgeverij Peeters en Departement Orientalistiek, 95, 458 p. (Orientalia Lovaniensia Analecta, 65).

1729. KUHRT (Amelie). The ancient Near East, c. 3000–330 B.C. London, Routledge, 95, 2. vol., [s. p.] (Routledge History of the Ancient World).

1730. LIM (R.). Public disputation, power and social order in late antiquity. Berkeley, Los Angeles a. London, University of California Press, 95, 278 p. (The Transformation of the Classical Heritage, 237).

1731. Od Nilu do Eufratu. Polska archeologia śródziemnomorska 1981–1994. (Du Nil à l'Euphrate. Archéologie méditerrannéenne polonaise 1981–1994). Réd. Maria Ludwika BERNHARD. Warszawa, Uniw. Warszawski, 95, 133 p. (phot., fig., dessins, carte 1).

1732. Religii drevnego Vostoka. (Religions of the Ancient East). Otv. red. G. M. BONGARD-LEVIN, A. N. MEŠČERJAKOV. Moskva, Vostočnaja literatura, RAN In-t vostokovedenija, 95, 344 p.

1733. State Archives of Assyria published by the Neo-Assyrian Text Corpus Project of the Academy of Finland in cooperation with Deutsche Orient-Gesellschaft. Vol. 11. Imperial administrative records. Part 2. Provincial and military administration. Ed. in chief Simo PARPOLA. Helsinki, Helsinki U. P., 95, XLII, 211 p.

1734. SUMMERS (G.D.), SUMMERS (M. E. F.), AHMET (K.). The regional survey at Kerkenes Dağ: an interim report on the seasons of 1993 and 1994. *Anatolian Studies*, 95, 45, p. 43-68.

1735. Trade, contact and the movement of peoples in the Eastern Mediterranean. Studies in honour of

J. Basil Hennessy. Edd. by Stephen BOURKE, Jean-Paul DESCOEUDRES. Sydney, MEDITARCH, 95, 339 p. [Cf. n[os] <choice> 1773, 1801, 1865, 1904, 1921, 1946.]

1736. WINKELMANN (Sylvia). Nordwestindische Bezüge auf baktrischen Siegeln. *Altorientalische Forschungen*, 95, 22, 1, p. 165-182.

1737. Year's work (The). *Anatolian Studies*, 95, 45, p. 3-22.

§ 2. Vorderasien (Allgemeines).

1738. ABRAMENKO (Andrik). Polykrates' Außenpolitik und Ende. Eine Revision. *Klio*, 95, 77, p. 35-54.

1739. BAKER (H. D.), COLLON (D.), HAWKINS (J. D.), POLLARD (T.), POSTGATE (J. N.), SYMINGTON (D.), THOMAS (D.). Kilise Tepe. *Anatolian Studies*, 95, 45, p. 139-191.

1740. BARATTOLO (Andrea). The temple of Hadrian-Zeus at Cyzicus. *Istanbuler Mitteilungen*, 95, 45, p. 57-108.

1741. CROW (James), HILL (Stephen). The Byzantine fortifications of Amastris in Paphlagonia. *Anatolian Studies*, 95, 45, p. 251-265.

1742. DEUBNER (Otfried). Lösung eines Stützenproblems in den Atlantenhöfen der Kizil Avlu in Pergamon. *Istanbuler Mitteilungen*, 95, 45, p. 175-177.

1743. DOUKELLIS (Panagiotis), DUFAURE (Jean-Jacques), FOUACHE (Eric). Le contexte géomorphologique et historique de l'aqueduc de Nicopolis. *Bulletin de Correspondance Hellénique*, 95, 119, 1, p. 209-233.

1744. ERDOĞU (Burçin). The mat white-painted pottery from Eastern Thrace. *Anatolian Studies*, 95, 45, p. 267-262.

1745. GATES (Marie-Henriette). Archaeology in Turkey. *American Journal of Archaeology*, 95, 99, 2, p. 207-255.

1746. HELD (Winfried). Wo stand die Hera von Samos? *Istanbuler Mitteilungen*, 95, 45, p. 13-23.

1747. HEUCK ALLEN (Susan). "Finding the walls of Troy": Frank Calvert, excavator. *American Journal of Archaeology*, 95, 99, 3, p. 379-407.

1748. HILL (Stephen). The first season of rescue excavation at Çiftlik (Sinop). *Anatolian Studies*, 95, 45, p. 219-231.

1749. Lexicography of the Ancient Near Eastern languages. Verona, Essedue, 95, 252 p. (Studi Epigrafici e Linguistici sul Vicino Oriente Antico, 12).

1750. LIPKA (Michael). Anmerkungen zu geographischen, wirtschaftlichen und sozialen Verhältnissen an der südöstlichen Schwarzmeerküste Ende des fünften/ Anfang des vierten Jhs. v. Chr. *Klio*, 95, 77, p. 65-74.

1751. MODE (Markus). Baktrisches Metall zwischen altvorderasiatischer Kunst und dem skytho-Tierstil. *Altorientalische Forschungen*, 95, 22, 1, p. 137-150.

1752. PARKER (Victor). Bemerkungen zu den Zügen der Kimmerier und der Skythen durch Vorderasien. *Klio*, 95, 77, p. 7-34.

1753. RUMSCHEID (Frank). Die Ornamentik des Apollon-Smintheus-Tempels in der Troas. *Istanbuler Mitteilungen*, 95, 45, p. 25-55.

1754. SAGONA (Antonio), SAGONA (Claudia), ÖZKORUCUKLU (Hilmi). Excavations at Sos Höyük. First preliminary report. *Anatolian Studies*, 95, 45, p. 193-218

1755. SCHWARTZ (Seth). Language, power and dientity in ancient Palestine. *Past and Present*, 95, 148, p. 3-47.

1756. Seals and sealing in the ancient Near East: proceedings of the symposium held on September 2, 1993, Jerusalem, Israel. Ed. by Joan GOODNICK WESTENHOLZ. Jerusalem, Bible Lands Museum, 95, 145 p. (Bible Lands Museum Jerusalem publications, 1).

1757. SMITH (R. R. R.), RATTÉ (Christopher). Archaeological research at Aphrodisias in Caria, 1993. *American Journal of Archaeoloy*, 95, 99, 1, p. 33-58.

1758. WEBER (Martha). Ein spätantikes Privatporträt aus Kleinasien. *Istanbuler Litteilungen*, 95, 45, p. 123-129.

§ 3. Ägypten.

1759. ABITZ (Friedrich). Pharao als Gott in den Unterweltsbüchern des Neuen Reiches. Freiburg, Universitätsverlag u. Göttingen, Vandenhoeck u. Ruprecht, 95, 219 p. (Orbis Biblicus et Orientalis, 146).

1760. ADAMS (Barbara). Ancient Nekhen. Garstgang in the city of Hirakonpolis. New Malden, Sia Publishing, 95, 206 p. (Egyptian Studies Association Publication, 3).

1761. ALSTON (R.). Soldier and society in Roman Egypt: a social history. London a. New York, Routledge, 95, 263, p.

1762. ANDORLINI (I.). Trattato di medicina su papiro. Edizione e commento. Firenze, Istituto Papirologico 'G. Vitelli', 95, 197 p.

1763. Archaeology of death in the Ancient Near East. Ed. by Stuart CAMPBELL, Anthony GREEN. Oxford, Oxbow Books, 95, 297 p. (Oxbow Monographs in Archaeology, 51).

1764. ASSMANN (Ian). Egyptian solar religion in the New Kingdom. Re, Amun and the crisis of polytheism. London a. New York, Kegan Paul International, 95, 233 p.

1765. BROWNE (Gerald M.). Miscellanea Nubiana II. *Orientalia*, 95, 64, 3, p. 450-459.

1766. CERVELLÓ AUTUORI (J.). ¿Un precedente del serej faraónico en la paleta predinástica de la caza? *Aula Orientalis*, 95, 13, 2, p. 169-175.

1767. CLAGETT (Marshall). Ancient Egyptian science. Vol. 2. Calendars, cloks, and astronomy. Philadelphia, American Philosophical Society, 95, 575 p.

1768. CLARYSSE (W.). Ptolemaic wills. *In*: Legal documents in the Hellenistic world [Cf. n° 2167], p. 88-105.

1769. DEPUYDT (Leo). Regnal years and civil calendar in Achaemenid Egypt. *The Journal of Egyptian Archaeology*, 95, 81, p. 151-173.

1770. DODSON (Aidan). Amenmesse in Kent, Liverpool, and Thebes. *The Journal of Egyptian Archaeology*, 95, 81, p. 115-128.

1771. Egyptian historical records of the Later Eighteenth Dynasty. Vol. 6. Ed. by Benedict G. DAVIES. Warminster, Arris a. Phillips, 95, 129 p.

1772. EIDE (T.), HÄGG (T.), HOLTON PIERCE (R.), TÖRÖK (L.). Fontes Historiae Nubiorum: textual sources for the history of the Middle Nile region between the eighth century B. C. and the sixth century A. D. Vol. I. From the eighth to the mid-fifth century B. C. Bergen, University of Bergen, 95, 343 p.

1773. ERIKSON (K. O.). Egyptian amphorae from late Cypriot contexts in Cyprus. *In*: Studies Hennessy [Cf. n° 1735], p. 199-205.

1774. ERSKINE (Andrew). Culture and power in Ptolemaic Egypt: the Museum and Library of Alexandria. *Greece and Rome*, 95, 42,1, p. 38-48.

1775. GOLOVINA (V. A.). Kdb: zemel'naja arenda v Egipte épochi rannego Srednego carstva. (Kdb: a special type of the lease of land in Egypt of the early Middle kingdom). *Vestn. drev. Ist.*, 95, 2, p. 4-27.

1776. GRATIEN (Brigitte). La Basse Nubie à l'Ancien Empire: Egyptiens et autochtones. *The Journal of Egyptian Archaeology*, 95, 81, p. 43-56.

1777. HENDRICKX (Stan). Analytical bibliography of the Prehistory and the Early Dynastic Period of Egypt and Northern Sudan. Leuven, Leuven U. P., 95, 328 p. (Egyptian Prehistory Monographs, 1).

1778. Hymns, prayers, and songs. An anthology of ancient Egyptian lyric poetry. Ed. by John L. FOSTER, Susan TOWER HOLLIS. Atlanta, Scholars Press, 95, 228 p.

1779. JACKSON (Howard M.). "The shadow of Pharaon, your lord, falls upon you": once again Wenamun 2.46. *Journal of Near Eastern Studies*, 95, 54, 4, p. 273-286.

1780. JANSEN-WINKELN (Karl von). Historische Probleme der 3. Zwischenzeit. *The Journal of Egyptian Archaeology*, 95, 81, p. 129-149.

1781. Juristische Literaturübersicht: 1990–1992 (mit Nachträgen). Hrsg. v. Joachim HENGSTL. *Archiv für Papyrusforschung*, 95, 41, 1, p. 232-262.

1782. KAPER (Olaf E.). The astronomical ceiling of Deir El-Haggar in the Dakhleh Oasis. *The Journal of Egyptian Archaeology*, 95, 81, p. 175-195.

1783. KEHOE (Dennis P.). Legal institutions and the bargaining power of the tenant in Roman Egypt. *Archiv für Papyrusforschung*, 95, 41, 2, p. 232-262.

1784. LACKENBACHER (S.). Les relations entre Ugarit et l'Égypte, à propos d'un text inédit. *In*: Relations internationales [Cf. n° 1985], p. 107-118.

1785. LECLANT (Jean), CLERC (Gisèle). Fouilles et travaux en Égypte et au Soudan, 1993–1994. *Orientalia*, 95, 64, 2, p. 225-355.

1786. MARTIN (Lutz). Ein elamisches Rollsiegel aus Bubastis. *Altorientalische Forschungen*, 95, 22, 1, p. 103-109.

1787. MATHIESON (Ian), BETTLES (Elizabeth), DAVIES (Sue), SMITH (H. S.). A stela of the Persian period from Saqqara. *The Journal of Egyptian Archaeology*, 95, 81, p. 23-41.

1788. MAXWELL-HYSLOP (K. R.). A note on the Anatolian connections of the Tôd treasure. *Anatolian Studies*, 95, 45, p. 243-250.

1789. MÉLÈZE-MODRZEJEWSKI (J.). Law and justice in Ptolemaic Egypt. *In*: Legal documents of the Hellenistic world [Cf. n° 2167], p. 1-19.

1790. MERKELBACH (R.). Isis Regina-Zeus Serapis: die griechischägyptische Religion nach den Quellen dargestellt. Stuttgart u. Leipzig, Teubner, 95, 722 p.

1791. PARKINSON (R. B.). Homosexual desire and Middle Kingdom literature. *The Journal of Egyptian Archaeology*, 95, 81, p. 57-76.

1792. PERPILLOU-THOMAS (F.). Sur les emplois de thallos, thallion à l'époque romaine et byzantine. *Revue des Etudes Grecques*, 95, 108, 1, p. 1-6.

1793. PESTMAN (P. W.). Appearance and reality in written contracts: evidence from bilingual family archives. *In*: Legal documents of the Hellenistic world [Cf. n° 2167], p. 79-87.

1794. REDMOUNT (Carol A.). The Wadi Tumilat and the "Canal of the Pharaons". *Journal of Near Eastern Studies*, 95, 54, 2, p. 127-135.

1795. RUSSMANN (Edna R.). Kushite headdresses and 'Kushite' style. *The Journal of Egyptian Archaeology*, 95, 81, p. 227-232.

1796. SCHOLL (R.). Zum ptolemäischen Sklavenrecht. *In*: Legal documents of the Hellenistic world [Cf. n° 2167], p. 149-172.

1797. SPALINGER (Anthony). Notes on the ancient Egyptian calendars. *Orientalia*, 95, 64, 1, p. 17-32. – IDEM. Some remarks on the epagomenal days in ancient Egypt. *Journal of Near Eastern Studies*, 95, 54, 1, p. 33-47.

1798. STEWART (Harry M.). Egyptian Shabtis. Princes Risborough, Shire Publications, 95, 64 p. (Shire Egyptology, 23).

1799. STOOF (Magdalena). Kauroide und Skaraboide in Kindergräbern des Neuen Reiches im Alten Ägypten. *Altorientalische Forschungen*, 95, 22, 1, p. 160-164.

1800. TAKÁCS (Sarolta A.). Isis and Sarapis in the Roman world. Leiden, New York a. Cologne, Brill, 95, 235 p. (Religions in the Graeco-Roman world, 124).

1801. WATSON (P. M.). Ceramic evidence for Egyptian links with Northern Jordan in the 6th–8th century AD. In: Studies Hennessy [Cf. n° 1735], p. 303-320.

1802. WEATHERHEAD (Frank). Wall-paintings from the King's House at Amarna. *The Journal of Egyptian Archaeology*, 95, 81, p. 95-113.

1803. WESTERN (A. C.), MAC LEOD (W.). Woods used in Egyptian bows and arrows. *The Journal of Egyptian Archaeology*, 95, 81, p. 77-94.

1804. WILKINSON (A. H.). A new king in the Western Desert. *The Journal of Egyptian Archaeology*, 95, 81, p. 205-210.

§ 4. Mesopotamien.

1805. ANTONOVA (E. V.). Simvoly kosmičeskikh sil i social'naja real'nost' Mesopotamii konca IV–III tysjačeletij do novoj éry. (Symbols of cosmic forces and social reality of Mesopotamia at the end of the IVth–IIIth millennium B. C.). *Vestn. drev. Is.*, 95, 4, p. 3-13.

1806. BASTERT (Katrin), DITTMAN (Reinhard). Anmerkung zu einigen Schmuckelementen eines mittelassyrischen Tempels in Kar-Tukulti-Ninurta (Iraq). *Altorientalische Forschungen*, 95, 22, 1, p. 8-29.

1807. BEAULIEU (Paul-Alain). Theological and philological speculations on the names of the goddess Antu. *Orientalia*, 95, 64, 2, p. 187-213.

1808. BELLOTTO (Nicoletta). I Lú.MEŠ.aḫ-ḫi-a a Emar. *Altorientalische Forschungen*, 95, 22, 2, p. 210-228.

1809. BÖCK (B.). Sumerisch a.rá und Divination in Mesopotamien. *Aula Orientalis*, 95, 13, 2, p. 151-159.

1810. BURGGRAAFF (W.). Belijatum: an agricultural entrepreneur in the Old Babylonian period. *Aula Orientalis*, 95, 13, 2, p. 161-167.

1811. CANCIK-KIRSCHBAUM (Eva). Konzeption und Legitimation von Herrschaft in neuassyrischer Zeit. *Die Welt des Orients*, 95, 26, p. 15-20.

1812. CASTEL (Corinne). Contexte archéologique et statut des documents. Les textes retrouvés dans les maisons mésopotamiennes du Ier millénaire av. J.-C. *Revue d'Assyriologie*, 95, 89, 2, p. 109-137.

1813. CAVIGNEAUX (Antoine), AL-RAWI (Farouk N. H.). Textes magiques de Tell Haddad. Deuxième partie. *Die Zeitschrift für Assyriologie*, 95, 85, 1, p. 19-46.
– IDEM. Textes magiques de Tell Haddad. Troisième partie. *Die Zeitschrift für Assyriologie*, 95, 85, 2, p. 169-220.

1814. CHARPIN (Dominique). La fin des archives dans le palais de Mari. *Revue d'Assyriologie*, 95, 89, 1, p. 29-40.

1815. CHARVÁT (Peter). Early texts and sealings: "divine journeys" in the Uruk IV Period? *Altorientalische Forschungen*, 95, 22, 1, p. 30-33.

1816. COLBOW (Gudrun). Die spätaltbabylonische Glyptik Südbabyloniens. München, Profil Verlag, 95, 220 p. (ill.). (Münchener vorderasiatische Studien, 17).
– EADEM. Samsu'iluna-zeitliche Abrollungen aus nordbabylonischen Archiven ausserhalb Sippars. *Revue d'Assyriologie*, 95, 89, 2, p. 149-189.

1817. CZICHON (Rainer Maria). Die Psychologie des künstlerischen Schaffensprozesses am Beispiel der Kilamuwastelen. *Altorientalische Forschungen*, 95, 22, 2, p. 352-373.

1818. D'AGOSTINO (F.). Umorismo e utilizzo del testo: a proposito de "Il medico di Isin". *Aula Orientalis*, 95, 13, 1 p. 67-74.

1819. DAVILA (James R.). The Flood hero as king and priest. *Journal of Near Eastern Studies*, 95, 54, 3, p. 199-214.

1820. ENGLUND (Robert K.). Regulating dairy productivity in the Ur III Period. *Orientalia*, 95, 64, 3, p. 377-429. – IDEM. There's a rat in my soup! *Altorientalische Forschungen*, 95, 22, 1,p. 37-55.

1821. FAIVRE (Xavier). Le recyclage des tablettes cunéiformes. *Revue d'Assyriologie*, 95, 89, 1, p. 57-66.

1822. FARBER (Gertrud). "Inanna and Enki" in Geneva: a Sumerian myth revisited. *Journal of Near Eastern Studies*, 95, 54, 4, p. 287-292.

1823. FERRARA (A. J.). Topoi and stock-strophes in Sumerian literary tradition: some observations, Part I. *Journal of Near Eastern Studies*, 95, 54, 2, p. 81-117.

1824. FINKEL (Irving L.). In black and white: remarks on the Assur psephomancy ritual. *Die Zeitschrift für Assyriologie*, 95, 85, 2, p. 271-276.

1825. FOXVOG (Daniel A.). Sumerian brands and branding-irons. *Die Zeitschrift für Assyriologie*, 95, 85, 2, p. 1-7.

1826. FRAME (Grant). Rulers of Babylonia. From the Second Dynasty of Isin to the end of Assyrian domination (1157–612 BC). Toronto, Buffalo a. London, University of Toronto Press, 95, 2 vol. 350 p. (The Royal Inscriptions of Mesopotamia. Babylonian Periods).

1827. HILLARD (Kent). Niga sá-du₁₁ as a fattening grade in Ur III texts. *Die Zeitschrift für Assyriologie*, 95, 85, 1, p. 8-18.

1828. HØYRUP (Jens). A note on an anomalous area measurement from Ur III (With a remark about confidence in experts). *Altorientalische Forschungen*, 95, 22, 1, p. 84-86.

1829. HRUXKA (Blahoslav). Herden für Götter und Könige. Schafe und Ziegen in der altsumerischen Zeit. *Altorientalische Forschungen*, 95, 22, 1, p. 73-83.

1830. INVERNIZZI (Antonio). The Jupiter statuette from Veh-Ardashir and the iconographical repertoire of 3th century Mesopotamia. *Iranica Antiqua*, 95, 30, p. 23-53.

1831. JONKER (Gerdien). The topography of remembrance: the dead, tradition and collective memory in Mesopotamia. Leiden a. New York, Brill, 95, XIV-284 p. (ill., maps). (Studies in the history of religions, 68).

1832. KATZ (Dina). Inanna's descent and undressing the dead as a divine law. *Die Zeitschrift für Assyriologie*, 95, 85, 2, p. 221-233.

1833. KOCH (Johannes). Der Dalbanna-Sternenkatalog. *Die Welt des Orients*, 95, 26, p. 43-85.

1834. KÜHNE (Hartmut). Der mittelassyrische "Cut Style". *Die Zeitschrift für Assyriologie*, 95, 85, 2, p. 277-301.

1835. LAFONT (Bertrand). La chute des Rois d'Ur et la fin des archives dans les grands centres administratifs de leur Empire. *Revue d'Assyriologie*, 95, 89, 1, p. 3-13.

1836. LION (Brigitte). La fin du site de Nuzi et la distribution chronologique des archives. *Revue d'Assyriologie*, 95, 89, 1, p. 77-88.

1837. MAC EWAN (G. J. P.). Family law in Hellenistic Babylonia. *In*: Legal documents of the Hellenistic world [Cf. n° 2167], p. 20-36.

1838. MAC GINNIS (John). The Šatammu of Sippar. *Die Welt des Orients*, 95, 26, p. 21-26.

1839. MARZAHN (Joachim), NEUMANN (Hans). Eine altsumerische Urkunde aus Girsu über Silberzählungen. *Altorientalische Forschungen*, 95, 22, 1, p. 110-116.

1840. MAUL (Stefan M.). Eine Rationenliste aus dem Königreich Arraphe. *Altorientalische Forschungen*, 95, 22, 1, p. 117-124.

1841. MAYER (Werner R.). Zum Terminativ-Adverbialis im Akkadischen: die Modalverbien auf -iš. *Orientalia*, 95, 64, 2, p. 161-186.

1842. MICHEL (Cécile). Validité et durée de vie des contrats et reconnaissances de dettes paléo-assyriens. *Revue d'Assyriologie*, 95, 89, 1, p. 15-27.

1843. MÜLLER (Manfred). Die "Großen Götter" Tiglatpilesars I. *Altorientalische Forschungen*, 95, 22, 1, p. 151-156.

1844. NEMET-NEJAT (Karen R.). Systems for learning mathematics in Mesopotamian scribal schools. *Journal of Near Eastern Studies*, 95, 54, 4, p. 241-260.

1845. OELSNER (Joachim). Recht im hellenistischen Babylonien: Tempel, Sklaven, Schuldrecht; allgemeine Charakterisierung. *In*: Legal documents of the Hellenistic world [Cf. n° 2167], p. 149-172. – IDEM. Spätbabylonische Texte aus Dēr. *Altorientalische Forschungen*, 95, 22, 2, p. 265-268.

1846. RENGER (Johannes). Zu den Besitzverhältnissen am Ackerland im altbabylonischen Uruk. *Altorientalische Forschungen*, 95, 22, 1, p. 157-159.

1847. SAUVAGE (Martin). Le contexte archéologique et la fin des archives a Khirbert ed-Diniyé – Harâdum. *Revue d'Assyriologie*, 95, 89, 1, p. 41-55.

1848. SCHAUDIG (Hanspeter). Ein Zylinder Nabonids im Vorderasiatischen Museum zu Berlin. *Altorientalische Forschungen*, 95, 22, 2, p. 247-264.

1849. SCHMIDT (Gérard). Die babylonische Renaissance. *Altorientalische Forschungen*, 95, 22, 2, p. 187-196.

1850. SELZ (Gebhard J.). Den Fährmann bezahlen! *Altorientalische Forschungen*, 95, 22, 2, p. 197-209.

1851. STRECK (Michael P.). Ittašab ibakki "weinend setzte er sich": iparras für die Vergangenheit in der akkadischen Epik. *Orientalia*, 95, 64, 1, p. 33-91.

1852. TROPPER (Josef). Akkadish nuḫḫutu und die Repräsentation des Phonems /ḫ/ im Akkadischen. *Die Zeitschrift für Assyriologie*, 95, 85, 1, p. 58-66.

1853. VILLARD (Pierre). Les derniers rapports des devins néo-assyriens. *Revue d'Assyriologie*, 95, 89, 2, p. 97-107.

1854. VINCENTE (Claudine-Adrienne). The Tall Leilān recension of the Sumerian King List. *Die Zeitschrift für Assyriologie*, 95, 85, 2, p. 234-270.

1855. WALKER (Christopher B. F.). The Dalbanna text: a Mesopotamian lstar-list. *Die Welt des Orients*, 95, 26, p. 27-42.

1856. ZACCAGNINI (Carlo). War and famine at Emar. *Orientalia*, 95, 64, 1, p. 92-109.

1857. ZAWADZKI (Stefan). A contribution to the chronology of the last days of the Assyrian Empire. *Die Zeitschrift für Assyriologie*, 95, 85, 1, p. 67-73. – IDEM. NER 18 and NER 70 as a source for the topography of Babylonia. *Altorientalische Forschungen*, 95, 22, 2, p. 240-246.

§ 5. Hethiter.

1858. Atti del II Congresso Internazionale di Hittitologia. A cura di Onofrio CARRUBA, Mauro GIORGIERI, Clelia MORA. Pavia, Gianni Iuculano Editore, 95, 400 p. (Studia Mediterranea, 9).

1859. BÖRKER-KLÄHN (Jutta). «Malnigal». *Istanbuler Mitteilungen*, 95, 45, p. 169-173.

1860. BRENTJES (Burchard). Der hethitische Königsfetisch ᴷᵁˣkurša auf ägyptischen Reliefs der Ramessidenzeit. *Altorientalische Forschungen*, 95, 22, 2, p. 334-347.

1861. CZICHON (Rainer Maria). Zur Komposition der Taprammi-Schale. *Istanbuler Mitteilungen*, 95, 45, p. 5-12.

1862. DE MARTINO (Stefano). Die Unternehmungen des Muršili. I. im südöstlichen Anatolien nach KUB XXXI 64 (CTH 12). *Altorientalische Forschungen*, 95, 22, 2, p. 282-296.

1863. EL-FAÏZ (Mohammed). L'agronomie de la Mésopotamie antique. Analyse du Livre de l'Agriculture Nabatéenne de Qûtâma. Leiden, New York et Köln, E. J. Brill, 95, [s. p.].

1864. Essays on ancient Anatolia and its surrounding civilizations. Ed. by Prince Takahito MIKASA. Wiesbaden, Harrassowitz Verlag, 95, 243 p. (Bulletin of the Middle Eastern Culture Center in Japan, 8).

1865. GILES (F. J.). The relative chronology of the Hittite conquest of Syria and Aitakama of Qadesh. *In*: Studies Hennessy [Cf. n° 1735], p. 137-148.

1866. GONG (Yushu). Die mittelbabylonischen Namen der Keilschriftzeichen aus Ḫattuša und Emar. *Die Zeitschrift für Assyriologie*, 95, 85, 1, p. 47-57.

1867. GRODDEK (Detlev). Fragmenta Hethitica dispersa II. *Altorientalische Forschungen*, 95, 22, 2, p. 323-333.

1868. GURNEY (O.R.). The hittite names of Kerkenes Daǧ and Kušakli Höyük. *Anatolian Studies*, 95, 45, p. 69-71.

1869. HAASE (Richard). Beobachtungen zur hethitischen Rechtsatzung nebst einem bibliographischen Anhang. Leonberg, R. Haase, 95, 51 p. – IDEM. Dienstleistungsverträge in der hethitischen Rechtssammlung. *Die Zeitschrift für Assyriologie*, 95, 85, 1, p. 109-115. – IDEM. Zur Stellung der Frau im Spiegel der hethitischen Rechtssammlung. *Altorientalische Forschungen*, 95, 22, 2, p. 277-281.

1870. HAWKINS (John David). The hieroglyphic inscription of the sacred pool complex at Hattusa (Sudburg). Wiesbaden, Harrassowitz, 95, 139 p. (Studien zur den Bogazkoy-Texten, 3).

1871. JASINK (Anna Margherita). Gli stati neo-ittiti. Analisi delle fonti scritte e sintesi storica. Pavia, Gianni Iuculano Editore, 95, 246 p. (Studia Mediterranea).

1872. KLINGER (J.). Das Corpus der Maşat-Briefe und seine Beziehungen zu den Texten aus Ḫattuša. *Die Zeitschrift für Assyriologie*, 95, 85, 1, p. 74-105.

1873. MEYER (Jan-Waalke). Ergänzende Bemerkungen zur Topographie von Ḫattuša. *Altorientalische Forschungen*, 95, 22, 1, p. 125-136.

1874. MILITAREV (A. Ju.). Šumery i afrazijcy? (Sumerians and Afrasians?). *Vestn. drev. Ist.*, 95, 2, p. 113-126.

1875. NAKAMURA (Mitsuo). Weitere Fragmente zum Orakeltext CTH 568. *Altorientalische Forschungen*, 95, 22, 2, p. 317-322.

1876. OSHIRO (Terumasa). Notes on the present tense in hieroglyphic Luwian. *Altorientalische Forschungen*, 95, 22, 2, p. 348-351.

1877. OTTEN (Heinrich). Die hethitischen Königssiegel der frühen Grossreichszeit. Mainz, Akademie der Wissenschaften und der Literatur u. Stuttgart, Franz Steiner Verlag, 95, 42 p. (Abhandlungen der Geistes- und Sozialwissenschaftlichen Klasse. Akademie der Wissenschaften und der Literatur; Jahrg. 1995, 7).

1878. STARKE (Frank). Ausbildung und Training von Streitwagenpferden: eine hippologisch orientierte Interpretation des Kikkuli-Textes. Wiesbaden, Harrassowitz, 95, 172 p. (Studien zu den Bogazkoy-Texten, 41).

1879. Studio historiae ardens. Ancient Near Eastern studies presented to Philo H. J. Houwink ten Cate on the occasion of his 65th birthday. Edd. by Theo P. J. VAN DEN HOUT, Johan DE ROOS. Istanbul, Nederlands Historisch-Archaeologisch Instituut te Istanbul, 95, 344 p. (Uitgaven van het Nederlands Historisch-Archaeologisch Instituut te Istanbul, 74).

1880. ÜNAL (Ahmet). Reminiszenzen an die Zeit der altassyrischen Handelskolonien in hethitischen Texten. *Altorientalische Forschungen*, 95, 22, 2, p. 269-276.

1881. VAN DEN HOUT (Theo P. J.). Der Ulmitesub-Vertrag: eine prosopographische Untersuchung. Wiesbaden, Harrassowitz, 95, 326 p. (Studien zu den Bogazkoy-Texten, 58).

1882. WEGNER (Ilse). Hurritische Opferlisten aus hethitischen Festbeschreibungen. Roma, Bonsignori Editore, 95, 231 p.

1883. WEGNER (Stefan). Die hurritischen Körperteilbezeichnungen. *Die Zeitschrift für Assyriologie*, 95, 85, 1, p. 116-126.

1884. YAMADA (Masamichi). The Hittite social concept of 'free' in the light of the Emar texts. *Altorientalische Forschungen*, 95, 22, 2, p. 297-316.

§ 6. Juden und semitische Stämme bis zum Ausgang des Altertums.

1885. ALEXANDRE (Yardenna). The 'Hippo' jar and other storage jars at Hurvat Rosh Zayit. *Tel Aviv*, 95, 22, 1, p. 77-88.

1886. BAALBAKI (Ramzi). Reclassification in Arab grammatical theory. *Journal of Near Eastern Studies*, 95, 54, 1, p. 1-13.

1887. BIKAI (Patricia M.), KOORING (Deborah). Archaeology in Jordan. *American Journal of Archaeology*, 95, 99, 3, p. 507-533.

1888. BONNET (Corinne). Phénicien Šrn= accadien šurinnu? À propos de l'inscription de Bodashtart CIS I 4*. *Orientalia*, 95, 64, 2, p. 214-222.

1889. BROWN (J. P.). Israel and Hellas. Berlin a. New York, De Gruyter, 95, 407 p. (Beihefte zur Zeitschrift für die alttestamentliche Wissenschaft, 231).

1890. BURNS (Ross). Monuments of Syria. An historical guide. London, I. B. Tauris, 95, 297 p.

1891. CORS I MEYA (Jordi). A concordance of the Phoenician history of Philo of Byblos. Barcelona, Editorial Ausa, 95, 119 p. (Aula Orientalis, 10).

1892. Dead Sea scrolls (The). Hebrew, Aramaic and Greek texts with English translations. Vol. 2. Damascus document, war scroll and related documents. Ed. by H. CHARLESWORTH. Tübingen, Mohr Siebeck a. Louisville, Westminster John Knox Press, 95, 229 p.

1893. DIJKSTRA (Klaas). Life and loyalty. A study in the socio-religious culture of Syria and Mesopotamia in Graeco-Roman period based on epigraphical evidence. Leiden, E. J. Brill, 95, 375 p. (Religions in the Graeco-Roman World, 128).

1894. Discourse analysis of biblical literature. What it is and what it offers. Ed. by Walter R. BODINE. Atlanta, Scholars Press, 95, 264 p. (The Society of Biblical Literature Semeia Studies).

1895. DOWNING (F. Gerald). Cosmic eschatology in the first century: «pagan», Jewish and Christian. *L'Antiquité Classique*, 95, 64, p. 99-109.

1896. ELAYI (J.). Algunos nuevos pequeños objectos fenicios inscritos. *Aula Orientalis*, 95, 13, 2, p. 197-201.

1897. Fenici (I): ieri, oggi, domani. Ricerche, scoperte, progetti (Roma, 3–5 marzo 1994). Promosso dall'Accademia Nazionale dei Lincei, Commissione per gli Studi Fenici e Punici, Consiglio Nazionale delle ricerche, Istituto per la Civiltà Fenicia e Punica. Roma, Istituto per la Civiltà Fenicia e Punica del Consiglio Nazionale delle Ricerche, 95, 552 p.

1898. FINKELSTEIN (Israel). The date of the settlement of the Philistines in Canaan. *Tel Aviv*, 95, 22, 2, p. 213-239. – IDEM. Two notes on early Bronze Age urbanization and urbanism. *Tel Aviv*, 95, 22, 1, p. 47-69.

1899. FROLOV (S.). Merneptah's Israel and Horite genealogy in Gen 36: 20-30. *Aula Orientalis*, 95, 13, 2, p. 203-209.

1900. GAL (Zvi). The diffusion of Phoenician cultural influence in light of the excavations at Hurvat Rosh Zayit. *Tel Aviv*, 95, 22, 1, p. 89-93.

1901. GOGRAFE (Rudiger). Syrien. München, Hirmer, 95, 247 p.

1902. GONZÁLEZ ECHEGARAY (J.). Investigaciones arqueológicas en Levante, V. *Aula Orientalis*, 95, 13, 2, p. 177-196.

1903. GREENHUT (Zvi). Early Bronze IV tombs and burials in Palestine. *Tel Aviv*, 95, 22, 1, p. 3-46.

1904. HADIDI (A.). Hyksos influence in Jordan and Palestine. *In*: Studies Hennessy [Cf. n° 1735], p. 133-136.

1905. HARRAK (Amir). Notes on Syriac inscriptions, I. The inscription of Ma'ar-zaytā (Syria). *Orientalia*, 95, 64, 1, p. 110-119.

1906. KUAN (Jeffrey K.). Neo-Assyrian historical inscriptions and Syria-Palestine. Israelite/Judean-Tyrian-Damascene political and commercial relations in the ninth-eighth centuries B. C. Sheffield, Sheffield Academic Press, 95, 281 p. (Jian Dao Dissertation Series, 1; Bible and Literature, 1).

1907. LACKENBACHER (Sylvie). Le correspondance internationale dans les archives d'Ugarit. *Revue d'Assyriologie*, 95, 89, 1, p. 67-76.

1908. LANCEL (Serge). Carthage. A history. Oxford a. Cambridge, Blackwell, 95, 474 p.

1909. LECKER (Michael). The conversion of Ḥimyar to Judaism and the Jewish Ban" Hadl of Medina. *Die Welt des Orients*, 95, 26, p. 129-136. – IDEM. Wāqidī's account on the status of the Jews of Medina: a study of combined report. *Journal of Near Eastern Studies*, 95, 54, 1, p. 15-32.

1910. LEV-YADUN (Simcha), HERZOG (Ze'ev), TSUK (Tsvika). Conifer beams of Juniperus phoenica found in the well of Tel Beer-sheba. *Tel Aviv*, 95, 22, 1, p. 128-136.

1911. LIPHSCHITZ (Nili), BIGER (Gideon). The timber trade in ancient Palestine. *Tel Aviv*, 95, 22, 1, p. 121-127.

1912. LOPEZ CASTRO (Jose Luis). Hispania poena: los fenicios en la Hispania romana (206 a. C.–96 d. C.). Barcelona, Grijalbo Mondadori, 1995, 373 p.

1913. MAEIR (Aren M.), STRAUSS (Yael). A pilgrim flask of Anatolian origin from late Byzantine/early Ummayad Jerusalem. *Anatolian Studies*, 95, 45, p. 237-241.

1914. MÜLLER (Hans-Peter). Ergative constructions in early Semitic languages. *Journal of Near Eastern Studies*, 95, 54, 4, p. 261-271.

1915. NA'AMAN (Nadav). Tiglath-Pileser III's campaigns against Tyre and Israel (734–732 B.C.E.). *Tel Aviv*, 95, 22, 2, p. 268-278.

1916. NIDITCH (Susan). War in the Hebrew Bible. A study in the ethics of violence. New York a. Oxford, Oxford University Press, 95, 180 p.

1917. Palmyrene Aramaic texts. Ed. by Delbert R. HILLERS, Eleonora CUSSINI. Baltimore, Johns Hopkins

University Press, 95, 458 p. (Publications of the Comprehensive Aramaic Lexicon Project).

1918. Pays d'Ougarit autour de 1200 av. J.-C., histoire et archéologie (Le). Actes du Colloque International, Paris, 28 juin–1er juillet 1993. Ed. par Marguerite YON, Maurice SZNYCER, Pierre BORDREUIL. Paris, Editions Recherche sur les civilisations, 95, 268 p. (Ras Shamra-Ougarit, 11).

1919. PETTINATO (G.). "Napoleone" ad Ebla: un generale o un verbo? Aula Orientalis, 95, 13, 1, p. 75-106.

1920. Pitcher is broken (The). Memorial essays for Gosta W. Ahlstrom. Ed. by Steven W. HOLLOWAY, Lowell K. HANDY. Sheffield, Sheffield Academic Press, 95, 474 p. (Journal for the Study of the Old Testament Supplement Series, 190).

1921. PRAG (K.). The 'built tomb' of the intermediate early-middle bronze age at Beitrawi, Jordan. In: Studies Hennessy [Cf. n° 1735], p. 103-113.

1922. Problematica del infanticidio en las sociedades fenicio-punicas (La). IX jornadas de arqueologia fenicio-punica (Eivissa, 1994). Elvissa, Museu Arqueologic d'Eivissa i Formentera, 95, 89 p. (Treballs del Museu Arqueologic d'Eivissa i Formentera, 35).

1923. Recent excavations in Israel: a view to the West. Reports on Kabri, Nami, Miqne-Ekron, Dor, and Ashkelon. Ed. by Seymour GITIN. Dubuque (Iowa), Kendall/ Hunt Publishing Company, 95, 122 p. (Archaeological Institute of America. Colloquia and Conference Papers, 1).

1924. ROSEN (Haiim Baruch). A note on the Middle Bronze Age cemetery at Jericho. Tel Aviv, 95, 22, 1, p. 70-76. – IDEM. Hebrew at the crossroads of cultures. From outgoing Antiquity to the Middle Ages. Leuven a. Paris, 95, 86 p. (Orbis, 3).

1925. RUTGERS (L. V.). The Jews in late ancient Rome: evidence of cultural interaction in the Roman diaspora. Leiden, New York a. Cologne, Brill, 95, 283 p. (Religions in the Graeco-Roman World, 126).

1926. SCHULTZ (J. P.), SPATZ (L.). Sinai and Olympus: a comparative study. Lanham, New York a. London, University Press of America, 95, 790 p.

1927. SODEN (Wolfram von). Die Nominalform uf'ūla/ uf'ūl im Schriftarabischen. Die Welt des Orients, 95, 26, p. 137-144.

1928. TORRES (Joan Ramon). Las anforas fenicio-punicas del Mediterraneo central y occidental. Barcelona, Universitat de Barcelona, 95, 661 p. (Collleccio Instrumenta, 2).

1929. TROPPER (J.). Epigraphische Anmerkungen zur Neuauflage von KTU. Aula Orientalis, 95, 13, 2, p. 231-239.

1930. ULLMANN (Manfred). Was bedeutet arabisch du'mūṣ? Die Welt des Orients, 95, 26, p. 145-160.

1931. URCIUOLI (G. M.). Šeš-II-ib Priests at Ebla. Aula Orientalis, 95, 13, 1, p. 107-126.

1932. USSISHKIN (David). The destruction of Megiddo at the end of the Late Bronze Age and its historical significance. Tel Aviv, 95, 22, 2, p. 240-267.

1933. VIGANÒ (Lorenzo). Rituals at Ebla. Journal of Near Eastern Studies, 95, 54, 3, p. 215-222.

1934. WAGNER (Carlos G.). Fenicios y autóctonos en Tartessos. Consideraciones sobre las relaciones coloniales y la dinámica de cambio en el Suroeste de la Península Ibérica. Trabajos de Prehistoria, 95, 52, 1, p. 109-126.

1935. WATSON (W. G. E.). Ugaritic onomastics (4). Aula Orientalis, 95, 13, 2, p. 217-229.

1936. WILKINSON (Tony J.). Settlement development in the North Jazira, Iraq. A study of the archaeological landscape. Warminster, Published for the British School of Archaeology in Iraq and the Departement of Antiquities & Heritage, Baghdad, Aris a. Phillips, 95, 228 p. (Iraq Archaeological Reports, 3).

1937. Wisdom in ancient Israel. Essays in honour of J. A. Emerton. Ed. by John DAY, Robert P. GORDON, H. G. M. WILLIAMSON. Cambridge, Cambridge U. P., 95, 311 p.

1938. ZIADEH (Ghada). Ethno-history and 'reverse chronology' at Ti'innik, a Palestinian village. Antiquity, 95, 69, 266, p. 999-1008.

1939. ZORN (Jeffrey R.). Three cross-shaped "tet" stamp impressions from Tell en-Nasbeh. Tel Aviv, 95, 22, 1, p. 98-106.

Cf. n°s 1101, 1470

§ 7. Iran.

1940. BILLOWS (R. A.). Kings and colonists: aspects of Macedonian imperialism. Leiden, New York a. Cologne, Brill, 95, 240 p. (Columbia Studies in the Classical Tradition).

1941. BIVAR (A.D.H.). The miller of Manjanīq. Iranica Antiqua, 95, 30, p. 217-227.

1942. Vacat.

1943. DANDAMAYEV (Muhammad A.). The Ebabbar temple and Iranian Magi. Altorientalische Forschungen, 95, 22, 1, p. 34-36.

1944. DE BRUIJN (Erik), DUDLEY (Dennine). The Humeima hoard: Byzantine and Sasanian coins and jewelry from southern Jordan. American Journal of Archaeology, 95, 99, 4, p. 683-697.

1945. DEPUYDT (Leo). Murder in Memphis: the story of Cambyses's mortal wounding of the Apis bull (ca. 523 B.C.E.). Journal of Near Eastern Studies, 95, 54, 2, p. 119-126.

1946. EDWARDS (P. C.), MACUMBER (P. G.). The last half milion years at Pella. *In*: Studies Hennessy [Cf. n° 1735], p. 1-14.

1947. GREGORY (Andrew Pearce). A Macedonian dynastes: evidence for the life and career of Pleistarchos Antipatrou. *Historia*, 95, 44, 1, p. 11-28.

1948. HELTZER (Michael). Zu einem Verwaltungsproblem in den Provinzen der V. Satrapie des Achämenidenreiches. *Altorientalische Forschungen*, 95, 22, 1, p. 70-72.

1949. HUFF (Dietrich). Beobachtungen zum Čahartaq und zur Topographie von Girre. *Iranica Antiqua*, 95, 30, p. 71-92.

1950. JAMZADEH (Parivash). Darius' thrones: temporal and eternal. *Iranica Antiqua*, 95, 30, p. 1-21.

1951. KETTENHOFEN (Erich). Die Eroberung von Nisibis und Karrahi durch die Sāsāniden in der Zeit Kaiser Maximins (235/236 n. Chr.). *Iranica Antiqua*, 95, 30, p. 159-177.

1952. KOSHELENKO (G.), BADER (A.), GAIBOV (V.). The Beginnings of Christianity in Merv. *Iranica Antiqua*, 95, 30, p. 55-70.

1953. LERNER (Judith). Central Asians in the sixth-century China: a Zoroastrian funerary rite. *Iranica Antiqua*, 95, 30, p. 179-190.

1954. MAC QUEEN (E. I.). Diodorus Siculus: the reign of Philip II. The Greek and the Macedonian narrative from Book XVI. A companion. London, Bristol Classical Press, 95, 202 p. (Classical Studies Series).

1955. MARCH (Duane A.). The kings of Makedon: 399–369 B.C. *Historia*, 95, 44, 3, p. 257-282.

1956. NICHOLSON (Oliver). The end of Mithraism, *Antiquity*, 95, 69, 263, p. 358-362.

1957. OVERLAET (Bruno). A chieftain's folding stool and the Cheragh Ali Tepe problem. *Iranica Antiqua*, 95, 30, p. 93-122.

1958. POTTS (D.T.), CRIBB (J.). Sasanian and Arab-Sasanian coins from Eastern Arabia. *Iranica Antiqua*, 95, 30, p. 123-139.

1959. REITER (Karin). Drei "kassitische" Rollsiegel. *Altorientalische Forschungen*, 95, 22, 2, p. 229-239.

1960. SIMPSON (John), HERRMANN (Georgina). 'Through the glass darkly'. Reflections on some ladies from Merv. *Iranica Antiqua*, 95, 30, p. 141-158.

1961. *Vacat*.

1962. TUBACH (Jürgen). Seleukos' Sieg über den medischen Satrapen Nikanor. *Die Welt des Orients*, 95, 26, p. 97-128.

1963. VELIGIANNI (Chrissoula). Gazoros und sein Umland. Polis und Komai. *Klio*, 95, 7, p. 139-148.

1964. WHITCOMB (Donald). Two glass medallions: Sasanian influence in early Islamic Aqaba. *Iranica Antiqua*, 95, 30, p. 191-206.

E

GRIECHISCHE GESCHICHTE

§ 1. Klassisches Altertum im Allgemeinen. 1965-1993. – § 2. Vorhellenische Zeit. 1994-2025. – § 3. Quellen und Quellenkunde (*a*. Epigraphische Quellen; *b*. Literarische Quellen). 2026-2112. – § 4. Allgemeine und politische Geschichte. 2113-2153. – § 5. Rechts- und Verfassungsgeschichte. 2154-2181. – § 6. Wirtschafts- und Sozialgeschichte. 2182-2232. – § 7. Literatur-, Philosophie- und Wissenschaftsgeschichte. 2233-2344. – § 8. Religion und Mythologie. 2345-2384. – § 9. Archäologie und Kunstgeschichte. 2385-2438.

§ 1. Klassisches Altertum im Allgemeinen.

* 1965. Bibliografia di Carlo Gallavotti. A cura di Silvio Mario MEDAGLIA e Camillo NERI. *Eikasmos*, 95, 6, p. 315-336.

* 1966. HOPWOOD (Keith). Ancient Greece and Rome: a bibliographical guide. Manchester a. New York, Manchester U. P., 95, XIV-450 p. (History and related disciplines select bibliographies).

* 1967. ROSENBERGER (Veit). Zeitschriftenreferat für den Jahrgang 1994. *Laverna*, 95, 6, p. 163-170.

1968. BAGNALL (R. S.). Reading papyri, writing ancient history. London a. New York, Routledge, 95, 145 p. (Approaching the Ancient World).

1969. Bałkany antyczne. (Balkans antiques). Réd. par Włodzimierz PAJĄKOWSKI et Leszek MROZEWICZ. Poznań, Wydawn. Nauk. A. Mickiewicza, 95, 415 p. (phot. dessins, cartes). (Balcanica Posn., Acta et Studia, 7). [Eng. summary].

1970. BLEICKEN (Jochen). Wann begann die athenische Demokratie? *Historische Zeitschrift*, 95, 260, 2, p. 337-364.

1971. CAWKWELL (George L.). Early Greek tyranny and the people. *Classical Quarterly*, 95, 45, 1, p. 73-86.

1972. Clisthène et la démocratie athénienne. Actes du colloque de la Sorbonne tenu le 15 janvier 1994 sous la présidence de Jean-Pierre Vernant. Éd. par Pierre LEVEQUE, Spyros SPATHIS. Paris, Les Belles Lettres, 95, 47 p.

1973. Demokratia. Der Weg zur Demokratie bei den Griechen. Hrsg. v. Konrad H. KINZL. Darmstadt, Wissenschaftliche Buchgesellschaft, 95, 452 p.

1974. DEMONT (Paul). À propos de la démocratie athénienne et de la cité grecque. *Revue des Etudes Grecques*, 95, 108, 1, p. 198-210.

1975. DOBESCH (G.). Das europäische 'Barbaricum' und die Zone der Mediterrankultur: ihre historische Wechselwirkung und das Geschichtsbild des Poseidonios. Wien, Holzhausen, 95, 118 p. (Tyche, 2).

1976. GERCMAN (E. V.). Muzyka Drevnej Grecii i Rima. (Music in the Ancient Greece and Rome). Sankt-Peterburg, Aleteja, 95, 336 p.

1977. GILL (C.). Greek thought. Oxford, Oxford U. P., 95, 103 p. (Greece and Rome: New Surveys in the Classics, 25).

1978. Görög történelem a kezdetektől Kr. e. 30-ig. (Histoire grecque des origines jusqu'à 30 avant J-Chr.). Szerk NÉMETH György. Budapest, Osiris, 95, 393 p.

1979. Handbuch der Orientalistik. Abteilung 1. Der Nahe und Mittlere Osten. Hrsg.v. H. ALTENMULLER, [et al.]. Band. 16–17. Judaism in late antiquity Pt. 1. The literary and archaeological sources. Pt. 2. Historical syntheses. Ed. by Jacob NEUSNER. Leiden, New York a. Köln, E. J. Brill, 95, 2 vol., XIV-276 p., XIV-318 p.

1980. Hellenika symmikta: histoire, linguistique, épigraphie. Vol. 2. Ed. par Claude BRIXHE. Nancy, ADRA at Paris, de Boccard, 95, 134 p. (Etudes d'archéologie classique, 8). [Cf. n° <sélection> 2155.]

1981. KATIČIĆ (Radoslav). Illyricum mythologicum. Zagreb, Izdanja Antibarbarus, 95, 482 p.

1982. KOLB (Frank). Rom. Die Geschichte der Stadt in der Antike. München, Beck, 95, 783 p.

1983. LEFEVRE (François). L'amphictionie de Delphes: mythe et réalité. *Cahiers du Centre George-Radet*, 95, 6, p. 13-31.

1984. PAYEN (Pascal). Comment résister à la conquête? Temps, espace et récit chez Hérodote. *Revue des Etudes Grecques*, 95, 108, 2, p. 308-338.

1985. Relations internationales (Les). Actes du Colloque de Strasbourg 15–17 juin 1993. Ed. par E. FREZOULS, A. JACQUEMIN. Paris, de Boccard, 95, 542 p. (Université des sciences humaines de Strasbourg. Travaux du Centre de recherches sur le Proche-Orient e la Grèce antiques, 13). [Cf. n^{os} <sélection> 1784, 2135, 2142, 2145, 2153, 2173, 2177, 2181, 2677, 2689, 2697.]

1986. Sources for the ancient Greek city-state. Symposium August, 24–27 1994. Acts of the Copenhagen Polis Centre. Ed. by M. H. HANSEN. Copenhagen, Det Kongelige Danske Videnskabernes Selskab, 95, 376 p., 2 voll. (Historisk-filosofiske Meddelelsar, 72).

1987. Stadtbild und Bürgerbild im Hellenismus: Kolloquium, München, 24. bis 26. Juni 1993 veranstaltet von der Kommission zur Erforschung des antiken Städtewesens der Bayerischen Akademie der Wissenschaften und der Kommission für alte Geschichte und Epigraphik des Deutschen Archäologischen Instituts. Ed. by M. WÖRRLE, P. ZANKER. München, Beck, 95, 263 p. (Vestigia, 47).

1988. Studies in the ancient Greek polis. Edd. by M. H. HANSEN, K. RAAFLAUB. Stuttgart, Franz Steiner, 95, 219 p. Stuttgart, Franz Steiner, 95, 219 p. (Historia Einzelschriften, 95. Papers from the Copenhagen Polis Centre, 2).

1989. TRACY (S. V.). Athenian democracy in transition: Attic Letter-Cutters of 340 to 290 B. C. Berkeley, Los Angeles a. London, University of California P., 95, 206 p. (Hellenistic Culture and Society, 20).

1990. VERNANT (Jean Pierre). Passé et présent: contributions à une psychologie historique réunies par Riccardo DI DONATO. Roma, Edizioni di storia e letteratura, 95, 2 vol., XII-786 p. (Storia e letteratura, 188–189).

1991. VIVIERS (Didier). Démocratie athénienne et symbolisme théséen. *Revue de Philosphie Ancienne*, 95, 13, 1, p. 67-80.

1992. WOLPERT (Andrew). Rebuilding the walls of Athens. Democratic ideology, civic discourse, and the reconciliation of 403. B. C. Chicago, The University of Chicago Press, 95, 192 p.

1993. ZAK (W. F.). The polis and the divine order. The Oresteia, Sophocles and the defense of democracy. Lewisburg, Bucknell U. P., 95, 320 p. (London: Associated University Presses).

Cf. n^{os} *593, 1142, 2215, 2787*

§ 2. Vorhellenische Zeit.

1994. Ages of Homer (The). A tribute to Emily Townsend Vermeule. Ed. by J. B. CARTER, S. P. MORRIS. Austin, University of Texas Press, 95, 210 p.

1995. ANDREEV (Ju. V) Meždu Euraziej i Evropoj. (K voprosu ob istoričeskoj specifike minojskoj civilizacii). (Between Eurasia and Europe. On historical specificity of the Minoan civilization). *Vestn. drev. Ist.*, 95, 2, p. 94-112.

1996. ANDREEV (Ju. V). Égejskij mir v preddverii civilizacii. (The Aegean world on the threshold of civilization). *Vestn. drev. Ist.*, 95, 2, p. 94-112.

1997. CARRUBA (Onofrio). L'arrivo dei Greci, le migrazioni indoeuropee e il «ritorno» degli Eraclidi. *Athenaeum*, 95, 83, 1, p. 5-44.

1998. GINDIN (L. A.), CYMBURSKIJ (V. L.). Troja i "Pra-Akhkhijava". (Troy and Proto-Ahijawa). *Vestn. drev. Ist.*, 95, 3, p. 14-37.

1999. GODART (Louis), TZEDAKIS (Yannis). La chute de Cnossos, le royaume de Kydonia et le scribe 115. *Bulletin de Correspondance Héllenique*, 95, 119, 1, p. 27-33.

2000. GULJAEV (V. I.), SAVČENKO (E. I.). Ternovoe I, novyj skhifskyj mogil'nik na Srednem Donu. (Ternovoe I, the new Scytian burial ground in the Middle Don region). *Ros. arkheol.*, 95, 4, p. 87-102.

2001. HAJNAL (Ivo). Studien zum mykenischen Kasussystem. Berlin u. New York, W. de Gruyter, 95, 377 p. (Untersuchungen zur indogermanischen Sprach- und Kulturwissenschaften, 7).

2002. Homeric questions. Essays in philology, ancient history, and archaeology, including the papers of a conference organized by the Netherlands Institute at Athens (15 May 1993). Ed. by Jan Paul CRIELAARD. Amsterdam, J. C. Gieben, 95, 316 p. (Publications of the Netherlands Institute at Athens, 2).

2003. IVANČIK (A. I.) K voprosu ob étničeskoj prinadležnosti i arkheologičeskoj kul'ture kimmerijcev. II. "Ranneskifskie" nakhodki v Maloj Azii. (On the question of the ethnic origin and archaeological culture of the Cimmerians. II. Early Scytian finds in Asia Minor). *Vestn. drev. Ist.*, 95, 1, p. 3-22.

2004. KANTOROVIČ (A. R.). Odin iz obrazov kopytnogo životnogo v iskusstve skifskogo zverinogo stilja. (One of the hoofed animal images in the Scythian animal style). *Ros. arkheol.*, 95, 4, p. 45-55.

2005. Klados. Essays in honour of J. N. Coldstream. Ed. by Christine MORRIS. London, University of London, Institute of Classical Studies, 95, 310 p. (Bulletin, 63).

2006. Kommos. An excavation on the South coast of Crete. Vol. I. The Kommos region and houses of the Minoan town. Part I. The Kommos region, ecology and Minoan industries. Edd. by J. W. SHAW, M. C. SHAW. Princeton, Princeton U. P., 95, 215 p.

2007. LEJEUNE (Michel), GODART (Louis). Le syllabogramme *56 dans linéaire B Thébain. *Rivista di Filologia e di Istruzione Classica*, 95, 123, 3, p. 272-277.

2008. MARČENKO (K. K.). Ékologičeskaja situacija i kul'turogenez v Severo-Vostocnom Priazov'e – Nižnen Podon'e skifskoj épokhi. (The ecological situation and the cultural genesis in the North-Eastern Sea of Azov – the Lower Don areas of Scythian epoch). *Vestn. drev. Ist.*, 95, 4, p. 96-105.

2009. MELJUKOVA (A. I.). Novye dannye o skifofrakijskikh vzaimootnošenijakh v IV–III vekakh do novoj éry. (The new data about the Scythians and Thracians relations in the IVth–IIIth centuries B. C.). *Ros. arkheol.*, 95, 1, p. 28-36.

2010. MOUNTJOY (Penelope A.). Mycenaean Athens. Jonsered, Åstroms Forlag, 95, 77 p. (Studies in Mediterranean Archaeology and Literature, 127).

2011. PELON (Olivier). Empreintes de sceaux et signe incisé sur deux tesson de Malia. *Bulletin de Correspondance Hellénique*, 95, 119, 2, p. 575-589.

2012. POLINGER FOSTER (Karen). A flight of swallows. *American Journal of Archaeology*, 95, 99, 3, p. 409-425.

2013. POPHAM (Mervyn R.), GILL (Margaret A. V.). The latest sealings from the palace and houses at Knossos. London, British School at Athens, 95, X-65 p. (British School at Athens studies, 1).

2014. RAEVSKIJ (D. S.) Rannie skify: sreda obitanija i khozjastvenno-kul'turnyj tip. (The early Scythians: enviroment and economic-cultural type). *Vestn. drev. Ist.*, 95, 4, p. 87-95.

2015. Role of the ruler in the prehistory of the Aegean (The). Proceedings of a panel discussion at the annual meeting of the Archaeological Institute of America, New Orleans, Lousiana, 28 December 1992. With additions. Ed. by P. REHAK. Liège et Austin, Université de Liège et University of Texas at Austin, 95, 211 p. (Aegaeum, 11).

2016. RUNNELS (Curtis). Review of Aegean Prehistory IV: the Stone Age of Greece from the Palaeolithic to the advent of the Neolithic. *American Journal of Archaeology*, 95, 99, 4, p. 699-728.

2017. RUUSKANEN (J.-P.), IKÄHEIMO (J.) Style and chronology of the Late Aegean seals-bulls with circular horns. *Faravid*, 93 (pr. 95), 17, p. 25-64 (ill.).

2018. SACCONI (Anna). Riflessioni sull'economia micenea. Economia di baratto o economia monetaria? *Rivista di Filologia e di Istruzione Classica*, 95, 123, 3, p. 257-271.

2019. Sceaux minoens et myceniens: 4[e] symposium international, 10–12 septembre 1992, Clermont-Ferrand. Redaktion Walter MULLER. Berlin, Mann, 95, XII-348 p. (Corpus der minoischen und mykenischen Siegel. Beiheft, 5).

2020. TOURNAVITOU (Iphigenia). The ivory houses at Mycenae. London, The British School at Athens, 95, 341 p. (British School at Athens, 24).

2021. TOURNAVITOU (Iphigenia). The Mycenaean ivories from the Artemision at Delos. *Bulletin de Correspondance Hellénique*, 95, 119, 2, p. 479-527.

2022. TSIPOPOULOU (Metaxia). Achladia. Scavi e ricerche della Missione Greco-Italiana in Creta Orientale (1991–1993). Roma, Gruppo Editoriale Internazionale, 95, 218 p. (Incunabula Graeca, 97).

2023. VINOGRADOV (Ju. A.)., MARĆENKO (K. K.). Greki i skify v Severo-Zapadnom Pričernomor'e v V veke do novoj éry. (Greeks and Scythians in the North-Western Black Sea region in the 5th century B. C.). *Vestn. drev. Ist.*, 95, 1, p. 80-84.

2024. WERNHER (Gretel). Micanas y Homero. A proposito de Iliada XV 187-193. Santafe de Bogota, Istituto Caro y Cuervo, 95, 216 p.

2025. WINGERATH (Halina). Studien zur Darstellung des Menschen in der minoischen Kunst der älteren und jungeren Palaszeit. Marburg, Tectum Verlag, 95, 276 p.

§ 3. Quellen und Quellenkunde.

a. Epigraphische Quellen.

2026. AVRAM (Alexandre). Un règlement sacré de Callatis. *Bulletin de Correspondance Hellénique*, 95, 119, 1, p. 235-252.

2027. BOFFO (Laura). Ancora una volta sugli «archivi» nel mondo greco: conservazione e «pubblicazione» epigrafica. *Athenaeum*, 95, 83, 1, p. 91-130.

2028. CHAMPION (Craige). The Soteria at Delphi: Aetolian propaganda in the epigraphical record. *American Journal of Philology*, 95, 116, 2, p. 213-220.

2029. *Vacat*.

2030. CURTY (O.). Les parentés légendaires entre cités grecques: catalogue raisonnée des inscriptions contenant le terme SYGGENEIA et analyse critique. Geneva, Droz, 95, 284 p. (Hautes études du monde gréco-romain, 20).

2031. DUBOIS (Laurent). Une tablette de malédiction de Pella: s'agit-il du premier texte macédonien? *Revue des Etudes Grecques*, 95, 108, 1, p. 190-197.

2032. FEISSEL (Denis). Notes d'épigraphie chrétienne (X). *Bulletin de Correspondance Hellénique*, 95, 119, 1, p. 375-389.

2033. GAUTHIER (Philippe). Du nouveau sur les courses aux flambeaux d'après deux inscriptions de Kos. *Revue des Etudes Grecques*, 95, 108, 2, p. 576-585.

2034. GUERRA (M.F.), BARRANDON (J.-N.). Les comptes de Pompidas (IG VII 2426). Drachmes d'argent symmachique et drachmes de bronze. *Bulletin de Correspondance Hellénique*, 95, 119, 1, p. 1-26.

2035. HALLOF (Klaus). Pleistias von Kos. *Klio*, 95, 77, p. 132-138.

2036. KAYA (Durmu). Zwei neugefundene Grabstelen aus Atabey (Isparta). *Istanbuler Mitteilungen*, 95, 45, p. 179-180.

2037. KONTORINI (Vassa), MIGEOTTE (Léopold). Logheia tas didrachmias à Rhodes. *Bulletin de Correspondance Hellénique*, 95, 119, 2, p. 621-628.

2038. MOURGUES (Jean-Louis). Le préambule de l'édit de Tiberius Julius Alexander, témoin des étapes de son élaboration. *Bulletin de Correspondance Hellénique*, 95, 119, 1, p. 415-435.

2039. NIGDELIS (Pantelis M.). Oberpriester und Gymnasiarchen im Provinziallandtag Makedoniens: eine neue Ehreninschrift aus Beroia. *Klio*, 95, 77, p. 170-183.

2040. PIERART (Marcel). Chios entre Athènes et Sparte. La contribution des exilés de Chios à l'effort de guerre lacédémonien pendant la guerre du Péloponnèse. IG V 1, 1 (SEG XXXIX 370). *Bulletin de Correspondance Hellénique*, 95, 119, 1, p. 253-282. – IDEM. Une dédicace partiellement inédite d'un temple d'Héra (SEG XI 340). *Bulletin de Correspondance Hellénique*, 95, 119, 2, p. 473-477.

2041. PUCCI BEN ZEEV (Miriam). Josephus, bronze tablets and Greek inscriptions. *L'Antiquité Classique*, 95, 64, p. 211-215.

2042. SALVIAT (François), LEFEVRE (François). Document amphictionique CID IV 2: restitution. Note additionnelle. *Bulletin de Correspondance Hellénique*, 95, 119, 2, p. 565-573.

2043. TORTORELLI GHIDINI (Marisa). Lettere d'oro per l'Ade. *La Parola del Passato*, 95, 50, 3-6, p. 468-482.

Cf. n° 2389

b. Literarische Quellen.

2044. [Aelius Promotus] IHM (S.). Der Traktat perì tôn hiobólon theríon kaì deleteríon pharmákon des sog. Aelius Promotus. Erstedition mit textkritischem Kommentar. Wiesbaden, Dr. Ludwig Reichert, 95, 164 p. (Serta Graeca. Beiträge zur Erforschung griechischer Texte, 4).

2045. Ancient Greek novels. Ed. by S. A. STEPHENS, J. J. WINKLER. Princeton, Princeton U. P., 95, 541 p.

2046. [Andocides] Andocide: Contro Alcibiade. Ed. da P. C. GHIGGIA. Pisa, Edizione Ets, 95, 309 p. (Studi e testi di storia antica, 4).

2047. [Andocides] Greek orators: Andocides. Ed. by M. J. EDWARDS. Warminster, Aris a. Phillips Ltd, 95, vol. 5, 216 p. (Classical Texts).

2048. [Aristophanes] Aristophanes: Birds. Ed. by N. DUNBAR. Oxford, Clarendon Press, 95, 782 p.

2049. [Aristoteles] Aristotle: On the Heavens I and II. Ed. by S. LEGGATT. Warminster, Aris a. Phillips, 95, 273 p. (Classical Texts).

2050. [Aristoteles] Aristotle: Politics, Books I and II. Ed. by T. J. SAUNDERS. Oxford, Clarendon Press, 95, 194 p. (Clarendon Aristotle Series).

2051. [Aristoteles, Demetrius, Longinus] Aristotle: On Poetics. Longinus: On the Sublime. Demetrius: On Style. Edd. by S. HALLIWELL, D. RUSSEL, W. H. FYFE, D. C. INNES, W. RHYS ROBERTS. Cambridge a. London: Harvard U. P., 95, 533 p. (Loeb Classical Library, 199).

2052. [Arrianus] Arrien: Périple du Pont-Euxin. Ed. par A. SILBERMAN. Paris, Les Belles Lettres, 95, 75 p. (Collection des Universités de France publiée sous le patronage de l'Association Guillaume Budé).

2053. BARKER (E.). Aristotle, Politics. Revisited with an introduction and notes by R. F. Stalley. Oxford, Oxford U. P., 95, 423 p. (The World's Classic).

2054. BLAISE (Fabienne). Solon. Fragment 36 W. Pratique et fondation des normes politiques. *Revue des Etudes Grecques*, 95, 108, 1, p. 24-37.

2055. BONELLI (Guido). La concezione tucididea dell'esercizio del potere. *L'Antiquité Classique*, 95, 64, p. 27-56.

2056. BRENNAN (Tad). The text of Anaxagoras fragment DK 59 B22. *American Journal of Philology*, 95, 116, 4, p. 533-537.

2057. [Charito] Chariton: Callirhoe. Ed. by G. P. GOOLD. Cambridge a. London, Harvard U. P., 95, 425 p. (Loeb Classical Library, 81).

2058. COLESANTI (Giulio). La disposizione delle armi in Alc. 140 V. *Rivista di Filologia e di Istruzione Classica*, 95, 123, 4, p. 385-408.

2059. COLLAS-HEDDELAND (Emmanuelle). Le culte impérial dans la compétition des titres sous le haut-empire. Une lettre d'Antonin aux Éphésiens. *Revue des Etudes Grecques*, 95, 108, 2, p. 410-429.

2060. Corpus dei Papiri Filosofici Greci e Latini (CPF). Testi e lessico nei papiri di cultura greca e latina. Parte III. Commentari. Unione Academica Nazionale. Accademia Toscana di Scienze e Lettere 'La Colombaria'. Firenze, Olschki, 95, 655 p.

2061. DAVID (Ephraim). Theramenes' speech at Colonus. *L'Antiquité Classique*, 95, 64, p. 15-25.

2062. DI BENEDETTO (Vincenzo). Callimaco, fr. 2, 4 PF. *Rivista di Filologia e di Istuzione Classica*, 95, 123, 2, p. 169-171.

2063. [Eratosthenes] ROSOKOKI (A.). Die Erigone des Eratosthenes. Eine kommentierte Ausgabe der Fragmente. Heidelberg, Universitätsverlag C. Winter, 95, 140 p. (Bibliothek der klassischen Altertumswissenschaften, 94).

2064. [Euripides] Eurípedes. Tragedias III. Medea; Hipólito. Ed. por F. R. ADRADOS, L. A. DE CUENCA. Madrid, Consejo Superior de Investigaciones Científicas, 95, 147 p. (Alma Mater, Colección de Autores Griegos y Latinos).

2065. [Euripides] Euripides: Bakkhai. Ed. by R. M. MEAGHER. Wauconda, Bolchazy-Carducci Publishers, 95, 97 p.

2066. [Euripides] Euripides: Children of Heracles, Hippolytus, Andromache, Hecuba. Ed. by D. KOVACS. Cambridge a. London, Harvard U. P., 95, 519 p. (Loeb Classical Library, 484, Euripides II).

2067. [Euripides] Euripides. Hippolytus. Warminster, Aris a. Phillips, 95, 275 p. (Classical Texts).

2068. [Euripides] Euripides: Selected fragmentary plays. Edd. by C. COLLARD, M. J. CROPP, K. H. LEE. Warminster, Aris a. Phillips, 95, 280 p. (Classical Texts).

2069. [Euripides] Euripides. Suppliant Women. Ed. by R. WARREN, S. SCULLY. New York, Oxford U. P., 95, 82 p. (Greek Tragedy in New Traslations).

2070. [Euripides] GÜNTHER (H.-C.). The manuscripts and the transmission of the Paleologan Scholia on the Euripidean triad. Stuttgart, Steiner, 95, 329 p. (Hermes-Einzelschriften, 68).

2071. [Galenus] BARRAS (V.), BIRCHLER (T.), MORAND (A.-F.), STAROBINSKI (J.). Galien: l'âme et ses passion. Paris, Les Belles Lettres, 95, 156 p. (La roue à livres).

2072. GAMBERALE (Leopoldo). Un probabile errore di latino in Plutarco, Tib. Gracch. 13, 6. *Rivista di Filologia e di Istuzione Classica*, 95, 123, 4, p. 433-440.

2073. GILULA (Dwora). Food. An effective tool of amatory persuasion. A commentary on Mnesimachus, fr. 4 K-A. *Athenaeum*, 95, 83, 1, p. 143-156.

2074. GORMAN (Vanessa B.). Aristotle's Hippodamos (Politics 2. 1267b22–30). *Historia*, 95, 44, 4, p. 385-395.

2075. Greek papyri from Kellis. (P. Kell. G.). Ed. by K. A. WORP. Oxford, Oxbow Books, 95, Vol. 1. 281 p. (Oxbow Monograph, 54).

2076. [Hermogenes] HEATH (M.). Hermogenes, On Issues. Strategies of argument in later Greek rhetoric. Oxford, Clarendon Press, 95, 274 p.

2077. [Hippocrates] Hippocrates. Vol. 8. Ed. by P. POTTER. Cambridge a. London, Harvard U. P., 95, 418 p. (Loeb Classical U. P.).

2078. HOFFER (Stanley E.). Telemachus' "laugh" (Odyssey 21.105): deceit, authority, and communication in the bow contest. *American Journal of Archaeology*, 95, 116, 4, p. 515-531.

2079. [Homerus] Homer: Iliad book nine. Ed. by J. GRIFFIN. Oxford, Clarendon Press, 95, 152 p.

2080. [Homerus] Homer. The Odyssey. Ed. by A. T. MURRAY a. G. E. DIMOCK. London, Harvard U. P., 95, 481 p. (Loeb Classical Library, 104 and 105).

2081. KEANEY (John J.). Androtion F6 and methodology. *Klio*, 95, 77, p. 126-131.

2082. LABARBE (Jules). Une allocation pour les filles d'Aristide. *L'Antiquité Classique*, 95, 64, p. 1-14.

2083. LOPEZ FEREZ (J. A.). De Homero a Libanio: estudios actuales sobre textos griegos II. Madrid, Ediciones Clásicas, 95, 402 p. (Estudios de Filología Griega, 2).

2084. [Lucianus] Luciano: Racconti fantastici. Ed. da M. MATTEUZZI. Milano, Garzanti, 95, 385 p.

2085. [Maximus Tyrius] Maximus Tyrius Philosophumena – *Dialexeis*. Ed by G. L. KONIARIS. Berlin u. New York, Walter de Gruyter, 95, 527 p. (Texte und Kommentare, 17).

2086. MEDDA (E.). Lisia, Orazioni XVI–XXXIV, Frammenti. Introduzione, traduzione e note. Milano, Biblioteca Universale Rizzoli, 95, 584 p. (I Classici della Bur).

2087. MONTANA (Fausto). Variae lectiones dell'Athenaion Politeia aristotelica in uno scolio al Pluto di Aristofane. *Athenaeum*, 95, 83, 2, p. 391-400.

2088. MUND-DOPCHIE (M.). La fortune du 'Périple d'Hannon' à la Renaissance et au XVIIe siècle: continuité et rupture dans la transmission d'un savoir géographique. Namur, Société des Etudes Classiques, 95, 178 p. (Collection d'Etudes Classiques, 8).

2089. MURPHY (David J.). Contribution to the history of some manuscripts of Plato. *Rivista di Filologia e di Istruzione Classica*, 95, 123, 2, p. 155-168.

2090. [Myrsilus] S. JACKSON. Myrsilus of Methymna: hellenistic paradoxographer. Amsterdam, Hakkert, 95, 124 p.

2091. NEHAMAS (A.), WOODRUFF (P.). Plato: Phaedrus. Translated, with introduction and notes. Indianapolis, Hackett Publishing Co., 95, 94 p.

2092. [Nonnus] Nonnos de Panopolis: Les Dionysiaques, Chants XI–XIII. Tome V. Ed. par F. VIAN. Paris, Les Belles Lettres, 95, 280 p. (Collection des Universités de France, Budé).

2093. Oxyrhynchus Papyri (The). Ed. by T. GAGOS, M. H. HASLAM, N. LEWIS. London, Egypt Exploration Society (for the British Academy), 95, vol. 61, 163 p. (Graeco-Roman Memoirs, 81).

2094. Oxyrhynchus Papyri (The). Ed. by J. C. SHELTON, J. E. G. WHITEHORNE. London, Egypt Exploration Society (for the British Academy), 95, vol. 62, 182 p. (Graeco-Roman Memoirs, 82).

2095. PAZDERNIK (Charles F.). Odysseus and his audience: Odyssey 9.39–40 and its formulaic resonances. *American Journal of Philology*, 95, 116, 3, p. 347-369.

2096. [Philodemus] On choices and avoidances. Ed. by G. INDELLI, V. TSOUNA-MAC KIRAHAN. Napoli, Bibliopolis, 95, 248 p. (Istituto Italiano per gli Studi Filosofici. La Scuola di Epicuro, Collezione di testi ercolanesi diretta da Marcello Gigante, 15).

2097. [Pindarus] Pindaro: Le Pitiche. Ed. da B. GENTILI, P. A. BERNARDINI, E. CINGANO, P. GIANNINI. Verona, Fondazione Lorenzo Valla, 95, 714 p. (Scrittori Greci e Latini).

2098. [Plato] Platonis opera: Euthyphro, Apologia Socratis, Crito, Phaedo, Cratylus, Theaetetus, Sophista, Politicus. Vol. 1. Ed. by E. A. DUKE, W. F. HICKEN, W. S. M. NICOLL, D. B. ROBINSON, J. C. G. STRACHAN. Oxford, Clarendon Press, 95, 572 p. (Oxford Classical Texts).

2099. [Plato] Plato: Statesman. Ed. by C. J. ROWE. Warminster, Aris a. Phillips, 95, 245 p. (Classical Texts).

2100. [Plato] Plato: Statesman. Ed. by J. ANNAS, R. WATERFIELD. Cambridge, Cambridge U. P., 95, 89 p. (Cambridge Texts in the History of Political Thought).

2101. [Plotinus] Plotino. Sul Bello. Enneade I, 6. Ed. da D. SUSANETTI. Padova, Imprimitur, 95, 164 p. (Studi Testi Documenti, 6).

2102. [Plotinus] Plotinus Ennead III 6, On the impassivity of the Bodiless. Translation and commentary. Oxford, Clarendon Press, 95, 314 p.

2103. [Plutarchus] Essays on Plutarch's Lives. Ed. by B. SCARDIGLI. Oxford, Clarendon Press, 95, 403 p.

2104. [Porphyrius Tyrius] Porphyre: De l'abstinence. Vol. 3. Parte IV. Ed. par M. PATILLON, A. P. SEGONDS. Paris, Les Belles Lettres, 95, 176 p. (Collection des Universités de France publiée sous le patronage de l'association Guillaume Budé).

2105. RADICKE (J.). Die Rede des Demosthenes für die Freiheit der Rhodier (or. 15). Stuttgart u. Leipzig, B. G. Teubner, 95, 214 p. (Beiträge zur Altertumskunde, 65).

2106. REQUES (Denis). La famille d'Hypatie (Synésios, epp. 5 et 16 G.). Revues des Etudes Grecques, 95, 108, 1, p. 128-149.

2107. SEGAL (Charles). Perseus and the Gorgon: Pindar Pythian 12.9–12 reconsidered. American Journal of Philology, 95, 116, 1, p. 7-17.

2108. [Sextus Empiricus] Sesto Empirico: Contro gli Etici. Ed. da E. SPINELLI. Napoli, Bibliopolis, 95, 450 p. (Elenchos: collana di testi e studi sul pensiero antico, 24).

2109. WILLCOCK (M. M.). Pindar, victory odes: Olympians 2, 7 and 11. Nemean 4. Isthmians 3, 4 and 7. Cambridge, Cambridge U. P., 95, 181 p. (Cambridge Greek and Latin Classics).

2110. [Xenophon] KRENTZ (P.). Xenophon: Hellenika II.3.11–IV.2.8. Warminster, Aris a. Phillips, 95, 220 p. (Classical Texts).

2111. [Xenophon] LENDLE (O.). Kommentar zu Xenophons Anabasis: Bücher 1–7. Darmstadt, Wissenschaftliche Buchgesellschaft, 95, 527 p.

2112. [Xenophon] STRONK (J. P.). The ten thousand in Trace: an archaeological and historical commentary on Xenophon's Anabasis, Books VI iii-vi – VIII. Amsterdam, J. C. Gieben, 95, 356 p. (Amsterdam Classical Monographs, 2).

§ 4. Allgemeine und politische Geschichte.

2113. Alexander the Great. Reality and myth. Ed. by Joseph ROISMAN. Lexington, D. C. Heath, 95, 241 p.

2114. BALCER (Jack Martin). The Persian conquest of the Greeks 545–450 B. C.. Konstanz, Universitäts-Verlag Konstanz, 95, 344 p.

2115. BLACKWELL (Christopher William). A questionable hegemony. Harpalus and the failure of Macedonian authority. Durham, Duke U. P., 95, 350 p.

2116. BLOEDOX (Edmund F.). Diplomatic negotiations between Darius and Alexander. Historical implications of the first phase at Marathus in Phoenicia in 333/332 B. C. The Ancient History Bulletin, 95, 9, 1, p. 93-110.

2117. BRIANT (P.), LEVEQUE (P.), BRULE (P.), DESCAT (R.), MACTOUX (M.-M.). Le monde grec aux temps classiques. Vol. 1. Le Ve siècle. Paris, Presses universitaires de France, 95, 456 p. (Nouvelle Clio: L'histoire et ses problèmes).

2118. BRUGNONE (Antonietta). In margine alle tradizioni ecistiche di Massalia. La Parola del Passato, 95, 50, 1, p. 46-66.

2119. BUCK (Robert J.). The character of Theramenes. The Ancient History Bulletin, 95, 9, 1, p. 14-24.

2120. BYLKOVA (V. P.). Greki i varvary v Nižnem Podneprov'e v konce V – pervoj treti III veka do novoj éry. (Po materialam raskopok poselenij). (The Greeks and Barbarians in the Lower Dnieper basin in the late Vth–first third of the IIIrd c. B. C. Based on the results of excavations of the settlements). Vestn. drev. Ist., 95, 4, p. 111-116.

2121. CARGILL (J.). Athenian settlements of the fourth century B. C. Leiden, New York a. Cologne, Brill, 95, 487 p. (Mnemosyne, 45).

2122. DE ROMILLY (Jacqueline). Alcibiade ou les dangers de l'ambition. Paris, de Fallois, 95, 282 p.

2123. DEPUYDT (Leo). The date of death of Artaxerxes I. Die Welt des Orients, 95, 26, p. 86-96.

2124. DORATI (Marco). Ctesia falsario? Quaderni di storia, 95, 21, 41, p. 33-52.

2125. DREHER (Martin). Hegemon und Symmachoi. Untersuchungen zum Zweiten Athenischen Seebund. Berlin, de Gruyter, 95, 316 p.

2126. FALKNER (Caroline). The battle of Syme, 411 B. C. (Thuc. 8. 42). The Ancient History Bulletin, 95, 9, 1, p. 117-124.

2127. GABELKO (O. L.). Nekotorye osobennosti carkoj vlasti v Vifinii. (K probleme vzaimodejstvija frakijskikh i obsceellinisticeskikh tradicii). (Some peculiarities of the king's power in Bithynia. To the problems of interrelations of Thracian and Hellenistic traditions). Vestn. drev. Ist., 95, 3, p. 161-172.

2128. GRAINGER (John D.). The expansion of the Aitolian league. *Mnemosyne*, 95, 48, 3, p. 313-343.

2129. HABICHT (Christian). Athen. Die Geschichte der Stadt in hellenistischer Zeit. München, Beck, 95, 406 p.

2130. HAMEL (Debra). Strategoi on the bema. The separation of political and military authority in fourth-century Athens. *The Ancient History Bulletin*, 95, 9, 1, p. 25-39.

2131. HARDING (Phillip). Athenian foreign policy in the fourth century. *Klio*, 95, 77, p. 105-125.

2132. HEFTNER (Herbert). Ps.-Andokides' Rede gegen Alkibiades ([And.] 4] und die politische Diskussion nach dem Sturz der 'Dreißig' in Athen. *Klio*, 95, 77, p. 75-104.

2133. HENRY (Madeleine Mary). Prisoner of history. Aspasia of Miletus and her biographical tradition. New York, Oxford U. P., 95, 201 p.

2134. KEEN (Antony G.). A "confused" passage of Philochoros (F 149 A) and the peace of 392/1 B.C. *Historia*, 95, 44, 1, p. 1-10.

2135. KNOEPFLER (Denis). Les relations des cités eubéennes avec Antigone Gonatas et la chronologie delphique au début de l'époque étolienne. *Bulletine de Correspondance Hellénique*, 95, 119, 1, p. 137-159. – IDEM. Une paix de cent ans et un conflit en permanence: étude sur les relations diplomatiques d'Athènes avec Érétrie et les autres cités de l'Eubée au IVe siècle av. J.-C.. *In*: Relations internationales [Cf. n° 1985], p. 309-364.

2136. LEFEVRE (François). La chronologie du IIIe siècle à Delphes, d'après les actes amphictioniques (280–200). *Bulletin de Correspondance Hellénique*, 95, 119, 1, p. 161-208.

2137. MAKAROV (I. A.). Tiranija i Del'fy v ramkakh političeskoj istorii Grecii vtoroj poloviny VII–VI veka do novoj éry. (Tyranny and Delphi within the framework of the political history of Greece of the second half of the VIIth–VIth century B. C.). *Vestn. drev. Ist.*, 95, 4, p. 117-131.

2138. MAROTI (Egon). Delphoi és Pythia sportversenyei. (Concours sportifs de Delphoi et Pythia). Budapest, Akad. Kiadó, 95, 128 p.

2139. MARR (John). The death of Themistocles. *Greece and Rome*, 95, 42, 2, p. 159-167.

2140. MASLENNIKOV (A. A.). Drevnie greki v Krymskom Priazov'e. (The ancient Greeks in the Crimean Azov sea region). *Vestn. drev. Ist.*, 95, 2, p. 78-93.

2141. MASTROCINQUE (Attilio). Iaso e i Seleucidi. *Athenaeum*, 95, 83, 1, p. 131-141.

2142. NIETO (F. J. Fernandez). Tregua sagrada, diplomacia y politica durante la guerra del Peloponneso. *In*: Relations internationales [Cf. n° 1985], p. 161-187.

2143. O'SULLIVAN (Neil). Pericles and Protagoras. *Greece and Rome*, 95, 42, 1, p. 15-23.

2144. PARKER (Victor). Zur Datierung der Dorischen Wanderung. *Museum Helveticum*, 95, 52, 2, p. 130-154.

2145. PIERART (M.). "Hyp'Argheion epeblethe zemie" (Hérodote, VI 92). Aspects des relations extérieures d'Argos au Ve siècle. *In*: Relations internationales [Cf. n° 1985], p. 297-308.

2146. PIMOUGUET (Isabelle). Défense et territoire. L'exemple milésien. *Dialogue d'Histoire Ancienne*, 95, 21, 1, p. 89-109.

2147. Schenkungen hellenistischer Herrscher an griechische Städte und Heiligtümer. T. 1. Zeugnisse und Kommentare. Hrsg. v. Klaus BRINGMANN. Berlin, Akademie, 95, XI-592 p.

2148. TAUDEND (Klaus). Pheidon von Argos und das argolische Aigina. *Grazer Beiträge*, 95, 21, p. 1-5.

2149. UIBOPUU (Kaja). Ein Vergleich zwischen Epidauros und Hermione: zur friedlichen Lösung zwischenstaatlicher Konflikte durch Schiedsgerichte. *Grazer Beiträge*, 95, 21, p. 61-70.

2150. VINOGRADOV (Ju. A.). Nekotorye diskussionye problemy grečeskoj kolonizacii Bospora Kimmerijskogo. (Some debatable problems of Greek colonization of the Cimmerian Bosporus). *Vestn. drev. Ist.*, 95, 3, p. 152-160.

2151. VIVIERS (Didier). Hérodote et la neutralité des Crétois en 480 avant notre ère: la trace d'un débat athénien? *Hermes*, 95, 123, 3, p. 257-269.

2152. WHEATLET (Pat). Ptolemy Soter's annexation of Syria 320 B. C. *Classical Quarterly*, 95, 45, 2, p. 433-440.

2153. WHITEHEAD (D.). The ten-day truce (Thucydides 5.26.2, etc.). *In*: Relations internationales [Cf. n° 1985], p. 189-210.

Cf. n°s 1122, 1357

§ 5. Rechts- und Verfassungsgeschichte.

2154. ALFIERI TONINI (Teresa). L'euergesia delle poleis nei decreti onorari ateniesi del V sec. a. C. *Dialogues d'histoire ancienne*, 95, 21, 2, p. 71-83.

2155. BILE (Monique). Le lois de Gortyne: nécessité d'une approche multidisciplinaire. *In*: Hellenika symmikta [Cf. n° 1980], p. 7-22.

2156. BILLOWS (Richard A.). The succession of the Epigonoi. *Syllecta Classica*, 95, 6, p. 1-11.

2157. CAREY (Christopher). Rape and adultery in Athenian law. *Classical Quarterly*, 95, 45, 2, p. 407-417. – IDEM. The witness's exomosia in the Athenian courts. *Classical Quarterly*, 95, 45, 1, p. 114-119.

2158. CHICHOVA (I. A.). Législation ancienne et formation de l'esclavage en Grèce. *In*: Esclavage et dépendance [Cf n° 2192], p. 59-72.

2159. COHEN (D.). Law, violence and community in classical Athens. Cambridge, Cambridge U. P., 95, 214 p. (Key Themes in Ancient History).

2160. DE BRUYN (O.). La compétence de l'Aréopage en matière de procès publics: des origin de la polis athénienne à la conquête romaine de la Grèce (vers 700–146 avant J.-C.). Stuttgart, Franz Steiner, 95, 226 p. (Historia Einzelschriften, 90).

2161. DIHLE (A.). Der Begriff des Nomos in der griechischen Philosophie. *In*: Nomos und Gesetz [Cf. n° 2174], p. 117-134.

2162. GARDIES (Jean-Louis). Ce que la raison doit au procès. *Archives de Philosophie du Droit*, 95, 39, p. 39-45.

2163. GEHRKE (H.-J.). Der Nomosbegriff der Polis. *In*: Nomos und Gesetz [Cf. n° 2174], p. 13-35.

2164. GUERBER (E.). Cité libre ou stipendiaire? A propos du statut juridique d'Éphèse a l'époque du haut empire romain. *Revue des Etudes Grecques*, 95, 108, 2, p. 388-409.

2165. JONES (Nicholas). The Athenian phylai as associations: disposition, function, and purpose. *Hesperia*, 95, 64, 4, p. 503-542.

2166. KATZOFF (R.). Hellenistic marriage contracts. *In*: Legal documents of the Hellenistic world [Cf. n° 2167], p. 37-45.

2167. Legal documents of the Hellenistic world. Papers from a seminar arranged by the Institute of Classical Studies, the Institute of Jewish Studies and the Warburg Institute, University of London. February to May 1986. Ed. by Markham GELLER, Herwig MAEHLER. London, The Warburg Institute, University of London, 95, 254 p. [Cf. n°s <choice> 1768, 1789, 1793, 1796, 1837, 1845, 2166, 2172, 2178.]

2168. LHUILLIER (Virginie). Le procès de Socrate. *Archives de Philosophie du Droit*, 95, 39, p. 47-71.

2169. LORAUX (Nicole). Le procès athénien et la justice comme division. *Archives de Philosophie du Droit*, 95, 39, p. 25-39.

2170. MAFFI (Alberto). Legislazione e retorica della Grecia classica. *In*: Senectus I [Cf. n° 2225], p. 265-275.

2171. MANUWALD (Bernd). Zur rechtlichen Problematik von Antiphon, or. 5. *Rheinisches Museum*, 95, 138, 1, p. 41-59.

2172. MARTIN (C. J.). Marriages, wills and leases of land: some notes on the formulae of demotic contracts. *In*: Legal documents of the Hellenistic world [Cf. n° 2167], p. 58-78.

2173. MOGGI (Mauro). I proxenoi e la guerra nel V secolo a. C. *In*: Relations internationales [Cf. n° 1985], p. 143-159.

2174. Nomos und Gesetz. Ursprünge und Wirkungen des griechischen Gesetzesdenkens. 6. Symposion der Kommission 'Die Funktion des Gesetzes in Geschichte und Gegenwart'. Hrsg. von Okko BEHRENDS, Wolfgang SELLERT. Göttingen, Vandenhoeck u. Ruprecht, 95, 261 p. [Cf. n°s <Auswahl> 2161, 2163.]

2175. REDEN (Sitta von). The Piraeus. A world apart. *Greece and Rome*, 95, 42, 1, p. 24-37.

2176. RHODES (P. J.). The "acephalous" *polis*? *Historia*, 95, 44, 2, p. 153-167.

2177. SALMON (P.). Le rôle des béotarques dans la confédération béotienne. *In*: Relations internationales [Cf. n° 1985], p. 365-383.

2178. SMITH (H. S.). Marrige and family law. *In*: Legal documents of the Hellenistic world [Cf. n° 2167], p. 46-57.

2179. SURIKOV (I. E.) Afinskij areopag v pervoj polovine V veka do novoj éry. (The Athenian areopagos in the first half of the Vth century B. C.). *Vestn. drev. Ist.*, 95, 1, p. 23-40.

2180. THOMAS (Rosalind). Written in stone? Liberty, equality, orality and the codification of law. *Bulletin of the Institute of Classical Studies*, 95, 40, p. 59-74.

2181. TRONCOSO (V. Alonso). Ultimatum et déclaration de guerre dans la Grèce classique. *In*: Relations internationales [Cf. n° 1985], p. 211-295.

§ 6. Wirtschafts- und Sozialgeschichte.

2182. ANNAS (J.). Aristotelian political theory in the Hellenistic period. *In*: Justice and generosity [Cf. n° 2287], p. 74-94.

2183. BABA (Keiji). Kodai Girisha no Sembotsusha Kokuso to Shijimbo. (State burial of the war dead and private gravestones in Ancient Greece). *Sundai Shigaku*, 95, 93, p. 28-100 (English summary).

2184. BEARZOT (Cinzia). Motivi socio-demografici nella colonizzazione ateniese del V secolo: promozione o relegazione? *In*: Coercizione e mobilità [Cf. n° 2620], p. 61-88.

2185. BLUNDELL (S.). Women in ancient Greece. Cambridge, Harvard U. P., 95, 224 p.

2186. CARRADICE (I.). Greek Coins. Austin, University of Texas Press, 95, 112 p.

2187. DALBY (A.). Siren feasts: a history of food and gastronomy in Greece. London a. New York, Routledge, 95, 320 p.

2188. DESTROOPER-GEORGIADES (Anne). Note sur les monnaies trouvées en 1991 près d'Alyki à Larnaca. *Bulletin de Correspondance Hellénique*, 95, 119, 2, p. 629-638.

6. WIRTSCHAFTS- UND SOZIALGESCHICHTE

2189. Distaff side (The): representing the female in Homer's Odyssey. Ed. by B. COHEN. Oxford a. New York, Oxford U. P., 95, 229 p.

2190. DUCAT (Jean). Un rituel samien. *Bulletin de Correspondance Hellénique*, 95, 119, 1, p. 339-368.

2191. EDWARDS (Martha Lynn). Physical disability in the ancient Greek world. Minneapolis, University of Minnesota Press, 95, 202 p.

2192. Esclavage et dépendance dans l'historiographie soviétique récente. Ed. par Marie-Madeleine MACTOUX, Évelyne GENY. Paris, Les Belles Lettres, 95, 210 p. [Cf. n° <sélection> 2158.]

2193. FINKELBERG (Margalit). Odysseus and the genus 'hero'. *Greece and Rome*, 95, 42, 1, p. 1-14.

2194. FINNEGAN (Rachel J.). The professional careers. Women pioneers and the male image seduction. *Classics Ireland*, 95, 2, p. 67-81.

2195. Food in antiquity. Ed. by J. WILKINS, D. HARVEY, M. DOBSON. Exeter, University of Exeter Press, 95, 459, p.

2196. FOULON (Eric). Misthophoroi et xenoi hellénistiques. *Revue des Etudes Grecques*, 95, 108, 1, p. 211-218.

2197. GABBA (Emilio). La concezione antica di aristocrazia. *Rendiconti dell'Accademia dei Lincei*, 95, 6, p. 461-468.

2198. GARLAND (R.). The eye of the beholder. Deformity and disability in the Graeco-Roman world. London, Duckworth, 95, 222 p.

2199. GJONGECAJ (Shpresa), NICOLET-PIERRE (Hélène). Le monnayage d'argent d'Égine et le trésor de Hollm (Albanie) 1991. *Bulletin de Correspondance Hellénique*, 95, 119, 1, p. 283-348.

2200. GOLDHILL (S.). Foucault's virginity. Ancient erotic fiction and the history of sexuality. Cambridge, Cambridge U. P., 95, 194 p. (The Stanford Memorial Lectures).

2201. HALL (Jonathan M.). The role of language in Greek ethnicities. *Proceedings of the Cambridge Philological Society*, 95, 41, p. 83-100.

2202. HARRIS (D.). The treasures of the Parthenon and Erechtheion. Oxford, Clarendon Press, 95, 306 p. (Oxford Monographs on Classical Archaeology).

2203. HOLLARD (Dominique). La crise de la monnaie dans l'Empire romain au IIIe siècle après J.-C. Synthèse des recherches et résultat nouveaux. *Annales*, 95, 50, 5, p. 1045-1078.

2204. HOSE (M.). Drama und Gesellschaft: Studien zur dramatischen Produktion in Athen am Ende des 5. Jahrhunderts. Stuttgart, M a. P., 95, 214 p. (Drama: Beiträge zum antiken Drama und seiner Rezeption, 3).

2205. KENNEL (N. M.). The gymnasium of virtue: education and culture in ancient Sparta. Chapel Hill a. London, The University of North Carolina P., 95, 241 p.

2206. KONSTANT (D.). Greek comedy and ideology. New York a. London, Oxford U. P., 95, 244 p.

2207. LAMBINI (Gérard). À propos de chansons de banquet: fragment d'une anthropologie de la Grèce antique. *Kentron*, 95, 11,1, p. 43-50.

2208. LAWALL (Mark Lewis). Transport amphoras and trademarks. Imports to Athens and economic diversity in the fifth century B. C. Ann Arbor, University of Michigan Press, 95, 435 p.

2209. LE GUEN (B.). Théâtre et cités à l'époque hellénistique. *Revue des Etudes Grecques*, 95, 108, 1, p. 59-90.

2210. LE RIDER (Georges). La politique monétaire des Séleucides en Coelé Syrie et en Phénicie après 200. *Bulletin de Correspondance Hellénique*, 95, 119, 1, p. 391-404.

2211. LETOUBLON (Françoise). Said over the dead or tant de marbre sur tant d'ombres. *Arethusa*, 95, 28, 1, p. 1-19.

2212. LORAUX (Nicole). La guerre civile grecque et la représentation anthropologique du monde à l'envers. *Revue de l'histoire des religions*, 95, 212, 3, p. 299-326.

2213. ŁOŚ (Andrzej). La condition sociale des affranchis privés au I^e siècle après J.-C. *Annales*, 95, 50, 5, p. 1011-1044.

2214. MASSON (Olivier). Kypriaka, XIX. *Bulletin de Correspondance Hellénique*, 95, 119, 1, p. 405-413.

2215. MATZ (D.). Ancient world lists and numbers: numerical phrases and rosters in the Graeco-Roman civilizations. Jefferson a. London, McFarland, 95, 254 p.

2216. NATALI (C.). Oikonomia in Hellenistic political thought. *In*: Justice and generosity [Cf. n° 2287], p. 95-128.

2217. Pandora: women in classical Greece. Ed. by E. D. REEDER. Baltimore a. Princeton, The Walters Art Gallery, Princeton U. P., 95, 431 p.

2218. PAPARIZOS (Antonios). «Logos» et violence en tant que principes de la politique et la démocratie des Athéniens. *Minerva*, 95, 9, p. 97-116.

2219. PAVLOVSKAJA (A. I.). O zapustenii zemel'v Fajume v IV–V vekakh novoj éry. (Land degradation in Fayum in the IVth–Vth centuries A. D.). *Vestn. drev. Ist.*, 95, 2, p. 28-38.

2220. Recueil de timbres sur amphores romaines (1987–1988). Ed. par M.-B. CARRE [et al.]. Aix-en-Provence, Université de Provence, 95, 194 p. (Travaux du Centre Camille Jullian, 16).

2221. REDEN (Sitta von). Exchange in ancient Greece. London, Duckworth, 95, X-244 p.

2222. RODRIGUEZ ADRADOS (F.). Sociedad, amor y poësía en la Grecia antigua. Madrid, Alianza Universidad, 95, 328 p.

2223. SCHEIDEL (Walter). The most silent women of Greece and Rome: rural labour and women's life in the ancient world. *Greece and Rome*, 95, 42, 2, p. 202-217.

2224. SEKUNDA (N.). Seleucid and Ptolemaic reformed armies 168–145 B.C. Vol. 2. The Ptolemaic army under Ptolemy VI Philometor. Stockport, Montvert, 95, 84 p.

2225. Senectus: la vecchiaia nel mondo classico. Vol. 1. La Grecia. Ed. da U. MATTIOLI. Bologna, Pàtron Editore, 95, 487 p. (Edizioni e saggi universali di filologia classica). [Cf. n° <scelta> 2170.]

2226. SHIFFMAN (Gary Adam). The political uses of mortality. Citizenship and solidarity in classical Athens. Ann Arbor, The University of Michigan Press, 95, 271 p.

2227. SOURVINOU-INWOOD (C.). 'Reading' Greek death to the end of the classical period. Oxford, Clarendon Press, 95, 489 p.

2228. Spettacolo delle voci (Lo). A cura di Francesco DE MARTINO, Alan Herbert SOMMERSTEIN. Bari, Levante, 95, 221 p.

2229. TCHERNIA (André). Moussons et monnaies: les voies du commerce entre le monde gréco-romain et l'Inde. *Annales*, 95, 50, 5, p. 991-1010.

2230. WARTENBERG (U.). After Marathon: war, society and money in fifth-century Greece. London, British Museum Press, 95, 64 p.

2231. WATSON (P. A.). Ancient stepmothers. Myth, misogyny and reality. Leiden, Brill, 95, 288 p. (Mnemosyne, 143).

2232. WEBER (Gregor). Herrscher, Hof und Dichter. Aspekte der Legitimierung und Repräsentation hellenistischer Könige am Beispiel der ersten drei Antigoniden. *Historia*, 95, 44, 3, p. 283-316.

Cf. n° 2018

§ 7. Literatur-, Philosophie- und Wissenschaftsgeschichte.

2233. ALBERTI (A.). The Epicurean theory of law and justice. *In*: Justice and generosity [Cf. n° 2287], p. 161-190.

2234. ALEXIOU (E.). Ruhm und Ehre: Studien zu Begriffen, Werten und Motivierungen bei Isokrates. Heidelberg, Universitätsverlag C. Winter, 95, 272 p. (Bibliothek der Klassischen Altertumswissenschaft, 2, 93).

2235. Ancient medicine in its socio-cultural context. Papers read at the Congress held at Leiden University, 13–15 April 1992. Ed. by Ph. J. VAN DER EIJK, H. F. J. HORSTMANSHOFF, P. H. SCHRIJVERS. Amsterdam a. Atlanta, Rodopi, 95, 2 vol., 637 p. (The Wellcome Institute Series in the History of Medicine, 27, 28).

2236. Aristotle and moral realism. Ed. by R. HEINAMAN. London, UCL P., 95, 239 p. (The Keeling Colloquia, 1).

2237. ARRIGHETTI (G.). Poesia greca. Pisa, Giardini, 95, 279 p. (Ricerche di Filologia Classica, 4).

2238. AUBERGER (Janick). Ctésias romancier. *L'Antiquité Classique*, 95, 64, p. 57-73.

2239. BARRET (James). Narrative and the messenger in Aeschylus' Persians. *American Journal of Philology*, 95, 116, 4, p. 539-557.

2240. BATCHELDER (A. G.). The seal of Orestes. Self-reference and authority in Sophocles's Electra. Lanham, Rowman and Littlefield, 95, 163 p. (Greek Studies: Interdisciplinary Approaches).

2241. BECKER (A. S.). The Shield of Achilles and the poetics of Ekphrasis. Lanham, Rowman a. Littlefield, 95, 191 p.

2242. BEGUIN (Daniel). Le problème de la connaissance dans le De Optima Doctrina de Galien. *Revue des Etudes Grecques*, 95, 108, 1, p. 107-127.

2243. Beyond Aristophanes: transition and diversity in Greek comedy. Ed. by G. W. DOBROV. Atlanta, Scholars Press, 95, 209 p. (American Philological Association: American Classical Studies, 38).

2244. BOURRIOT (F.). Kalos kagathos – Kalokagathia: d'un terme de propagande de sophistes à une notion sociale et philosophique. Etude d'histoire athénienne. Hildesheim, Zürich et New York, Georg Olms, 95, 2 vol., 654 p., 626 p. (Spoudasmata, 58).

2245. Boxen. Texte, Übersetzungen, Kommentar. Hrsg. v. Georg DOBLHOFER, Peter MAURITSCH. Köln u. Wien, Böhlau, 95, 361 p. (Quellendokumentation zur Gymnastik und Agonistik im Altertum, 4).

2246. BUCHER (Gregory S.). Appian BC 2. 24 and the trial De ambitu of M. Aemilius Scaurus. *Historia*, 95, 44, 4, p. 396-421.

2247. BURRIDGE (R. A.). What are the Gospels? A comparison with Graeco-Roman biography. Cambridge, Cambridge U. P., 95, 292 p. (Society for New Testament Studies. Monograph Series, 70).

2248. BURTON (J. B.). Theocritus's urban mimes. Mobility, gender and patronage. Berkeley, Los Angeles a. London, University of California Press, 95, 298 p. (Hellenistic Culture and Society, 19).

2249. CAMERON (A.). Callimachus and his critics. Princeton, Princeton U. P., 95, 534 p.

2250. CANFORA (Luciano). Il Pericle di Plutarco: forme del potere personale. *In*: Teoria e prassi politica nelle opere di Plutarco [Cf. n° 2334], p. 83-90. – IDEM. Pathos e storiografia drammatica. *Elenchos*, 95, 16, 1, p. 179-192.

2251. CASSON (Lionel). The feeding of the trireme crews and an entry in IG II^2 1631. *Transactions of the American Philosophical Society*, 95, 125, p. 261-269.

7. LITERATUR-, PHILOSOPHIE- UND WISSENSCHAFTSGESCHICHTE

2252. COLLARD (Christopher). Two early collectors of Euripidean fragments: Dirk Canter and Joshua Barnes. *L'Antiquité Classique*, 95, 64, p. 243-256.

2253. CYRINO (M. S.). In Pandora's jar: lovesickness in early Greek poetry. Lanham, University Press of America, 95, 197 p.

2254. DAVIES (Malcom). Theocritus' Adoniazusae. *Greece and Rome*, 95, 42, 2, p. 152-158.

2255. DECKER (Wolfgang). Sport in der Griechischen Antike. Vom minoischen Wettkampf bis zu den Olympischen Spielen. München, Beck, 95, 255 p.

2256. DEVINE (Andrew Mackay). Polybius' lost Tactica: the ultimate source for the tactical manuals of Asclepiodotus, Aelian, and Arrian? *The Ancient History Bulletin*, 95, 9, 1, p. 40-44.

2257. DI BENEDETTO (Vincenzo). Tifone in Pindaro e in Eschilo. *Rivista di Filologia e di Istruzione Classica*, 95, 123, 2, p. 129-139.

2258. DIK (H.). Word order in ancient Greek: a pragmatic account of word order variation in Herodotus. Amsterdam, J. C. Gieben, 95, 294 p. (Amsterdam Studies in Classical Philology, 5).

2259. DILCHER (R.). Studies in Heraclitus. Hildesheim, Zürich u. New York, Georg Olms, 95, 207 p. (Spudasmata, 56).

2260. DILLON (Matthew). By gods, tongues, and dogs: the use of oaths in Aristophanic comedy. *Greece and Rome*, 95, 42, 2, p. 135-151.

2261. DOHERTY (L. E.). Siren songs: gender, audiences and narrators in the Odyssey. Ann Arbor, The University of Michigan Press, 95, 220 p.

2262. DRÄGER (P.). Stilistische Untersuchungen zu Pherekydes von Athen. Ein Beitrag zur ältesten ionischen Prosa. Stuttgart, Franz Steiner, 95, 98 p. (Palingenesia, 52).

2263. DREW GRIFFITH (R.). A Homeric metaphor cluster describing teeth, tongue, and words. *American Journal of Philology*, 95, 116, 1, p. 1-5.

2264. DZIELSKA (M.). Hypatia of Alexandria. Cambridge a. London, Harvard U. P., 95, 157 p. (Revealing Antiquity, 8).

2265. ELLIOT SORUM (Christina). Euripides' judgment: literary creation in Andromache. *American Journal of Philology*, 95, 116, 3, p. 371-388.

2266. Ethics and rhetoric. Classical essays for Donald Russel on his seventy-fifth birthday. Ed. by D. C. INNES, H. M. HINE, C. B. R. PELLING. Oxford, Clarendon Press, 95, 378 p.

2267. FATTAL (Michel). La composition des concepts dans le De Anima (III, 6) d'Aristote. Commentaires grecs et arabes. *Revue des Etudes Grecques*, 95, 108, 2, p. 371-387.

2268. FEDERSPIEL (Michel). Sur l'opposition défini/indéfini dans la langue des mathématiques grecques. *Les Etudes Classiques*, 95, 63, 3-4, p. (249-293.

2269. FORTASSIER (P.). Le spondaïque expressif dans l'Iliade et dans l'Odyssée. Louvain et Paris, Peeters, 95, 194 p. (Bibliotheque d'Etudes Classiques, 5).

2270. GALEOTTI PAPI (Donatella). La scena di Macaria negli Eraclidi e l'oratoria funebre. *Rivista di Filologia e di Istruzione Classica*, 95, 123, 2, p. 140-154.

2271. GARBRECHT (Günther). Meisterwerke antiker Hydrotechnik. Stuttgart, Teubner, 95, 154 p.

2272. GRAY (Vivienne). Herodotus and the rhetoric of otherness. *American Journal of Philology*, 95, 116, 2, p. 185-211.

2273. Greek literary theory after Aristotle: a collection papers in honour of D. M. Schenkeveld. Ed. by J. G. J. ABBENES, S. R. SLINGS, I. SLUITER. Amsterdam, VU U. P., 95, 329 p.

2274. GREGORY (Justina). Genealogy and intertextuality in Hecuba. *American Journal of Philology*, 95, 116, 3, p. 389-397.

2275. Groningen Colloquia on the novel. Ed. by H. HOFMANN. Groningen, Egbert Forsten, 95, 183 p.

2276. HABASH (Martha). Two complementary festivals in Aristophanes' Acharnanians. *American Journal of Philology*, 95, 116, 4, p. 559-577.

2277. HAHM (D. E.). Polybius' applied political theory. In: Justice and generosity [Cf. n° 2287], p. 7-47.

2278. HANKINSON (R. J.). The sceptics. London a. New York, Routledge, 95, 376 p. (The Arguments of the Philosophers).

2279. HANSEN (Mogens Herman). The trial of Sokrates, from the Athenian point of view. København, Munksgaard, 95, 36 p. (Historisk-filosofiske meddelelser, 71).

2280. HELD (G. F.). Aristotle's theleological theory of tragedy and epic. Heidelberg, Universitätsverlag C. Winter, 95, 162 p.

2281. HERSHKOWITZ (Debra). Pliny the poet. *Greece and Rome*, 95, 42, 2, p. 168-181.

2282. History, tragedy, theory: dialogues on Athenian drama. Ed. by B. GOFF. Austin, University of Texas Press, 95, 228 p.

2283. HOLMBERG (Ingrid E.). Euripides' Helen: most noble and most chaste. *American Journal of Philology*, 95, 116, 1, p. 19-42.

2284. *Vacat.*

2285. HUYS (M.). The tale of the hero who was exposed at birth in Euripidean tragedy: a study of motifs. Leuven, Leuven U. P., 95, 446 p; (Symbolae, A 20).

2286. JOUANNA (Jacques). Espaces sacrés, rites et oracles dans l'Œdipe à Colone de Sophocle. *Revue des Etudes Grecques*, 95, 108, 1, p. 38-58.

2287. Justice and generosity. Studies in Hellenistic social and political philosophy. Proceedings of the sixth symposium Hellenisticum. Edd. by André LAKS, Malcolm SCHOFIELD. Cambridge, Cambridge U. P., 95, 304 p. [Cf. n^os <choice> 2182, 2216, 2233, 2277, 2304, 2324.]

2288. KATSOURIS (A. G.). Menander Bibliography. Thessaloniki, University Studio Press, 95, 159 p.

2289. KENDRICK PRITCHETT (W.). Thucydides' Pentekontaetia and other essays. Amsterdam, Gieben, 95, 279 p. (Archaia Hellas: Monograph on Ancient Greek History and Archaeology, 1).

2290. KINGSLEY (P.). Ancient philosophy, mystery and magic: Empedocles and Pythagorean tradition. Oxford, Clarendon Press, 95, 422 p.

2291. KNIGHT (V.). The renewal of epic: responses to Homer in the Argonautica of Apollonius. Leiden, New York u. Cologne, Brill, 95, 335 p. (Mnemosyne, 152).

2292. KRISCHER (Tilman). Die Rolle der Magna Grecia in der Geschichte der Mechanik. *Antike und Abendland*, 95, 41, p. 60-71.

2293. KUTSCHERA (F. von). Platons Parmenides. Berlin u. New York, Walter de Gruyter, 95, 171 p. (De Gruyter Studienbuch).

2294. LAROCHE (Roland A.). Popular symbolic/ mystical numbers in antiquity. *Latomus*, 95, 54, 3, p. 568-576.

2295. LEONTIS (A.). Topographies of Hellenism. Mapping the homeland. Ithaca a. London, Cornell U. P., 95, 257 p. (Myth and Poetics).

2296. LOPEZ CRUCES (J. L.). Les méliambes de Cercidas de Mégalopolis: politique et tradition littéraire. Amsterdam, A. M. Hakkert, 95, 319 p. (Classical and Byzantine Monographs, 32).

2297. MARASCO (Gabriele). Cleopatra e gli esperimenti su cavie umane. *Historia*, 95, 44, 3, p. 317-325.

2298. MARGEL (Serge). Les nourritures de l'âme. Essai sur la fonction nutritive et séminale dans la biologie d'Aristote. *Revue des Etudes Grecques*, 95, 108, 1, p. 91-106.

2299. MARR (John). Themistocles and the supposed second message to Xerses: the anatomy of a legend. *Acta Classica*, 95, 38, p. 57-69.

2300. MASARACCHIA (Agostino). Isocrate: retorica e politica. Roma, Gruppo Editoriale Internazionale, 95, 165 p; (Filologia e Critica, 73).

2301. MAUDUIT (Christine). Les morts de Philoclète. *Revue des Etudes Grecques*, 95, 108, 2 p. 339-370.

2302. MAURER (K.). Interpolation in Thucydides. Leiden, New York a. Köln, Brill, 95, 243 p. (Mnemosyne, 150).

2303. MEIKLE (S.). Aristotle's economic thought. Oxford, Clarendon Press, 95, 216 p.

2304. MOLES (J. L.). The Cynics and politics. *In*: Justice and generosity [Cf. n° 2287], p. 129-158.

2305. MÖLLENDORF (P. von). Grundlagen einer Ästhetik der Alten Komödie: Untersuchungen zu Aristophanes und Michail Bachtin. Tübingen, Günter Narr, 95, 297 p. (Classica Monacensia: Münchener Studien zur Klassischen Philologie, 9).

2306. MONTANARI (F.). Studi di filologia omerica antica II. Pisa, Giardini, 95, 153 p. (Biblioteca di Studi Antichi, 50).

2307. MOSSMAN (J.). Wild justice: a study of Euripides' Hecuba. Oxford, Clarendon Press, 95, 283 p.

2308. MÜLLER (Stefan). Das Volk der Athleten. Untersuchungen zur Ideologie und Kritik des Sports in der griechisch-römischen Antike. Trier, Wissenschaftlicher Verlag Trier, 95, 379 p.

2309. NEUMANN (U.). Gegenwart und mythische Vergangenheit bei Euripides. Stuttgart, Franz Steiner, 95, 191 p. (Hermes Einzelschriften, 69).

2310. NICOLAI (Roberto). Ktema es aiei. Aspetti della fortuna di Tucidide nel mondo antico. *Rivista di Filologia e di Istruzione Classica*, 95, 123, 1, p. 5-26.

2311. NIGHTINGALE (A. W.). Genres in Dialogue: Plato and the construct of philosophy. Cambridge, Cambridge U. P., 95, 222 p.

2312. OLSON (S. D.). Blood and Iron. Stories and storytelling in Homer's Odyssey. Leiden, New York a. Cologne, E. J. Brill, 95, 260 p. (Mnemosyne Supplement, 148).

2313. Passionate intellect (The). Essays on the transformation of classical traditions, presented to Professor I. G. Kidd. Ed. by L. AYRES. New Brunswick a. London, Transaction Publishers, 95, 376 p. (Rutgers University Studies in Classical Humanities, 7).

2314. PELLICCIA (H.). Mind, body and speech in Homer and Pindar. Göttingen, Vandenhoeck a. Ruprecht, 95, 389 p. (Hypomnemata, 107).

2315. PESELY (George E.). Aristotles's source for the tyranny of Peisistratos. *Athenaeum*, 95, 83, 1, p. 45-66.

2316. PRATT (Louise). The seal of Theognis, writing, and oral poetry. *American Journal of Philology*, 95, 116, 2, p. 171-184.

2317. PRICE (A. W.). Mental conflict. London, Routledge, 95, 218 p. (Issues in Ancient Philosophy).

2318. PRITCHARD (P.). Plato's philosophy of mathematics. Sankt Augustin, Academia Verlag, 95, 191 p. (International Plato Studies, 5).

2319. Reading the Statesman. Proceedings of the III Symposium Platonicum. Ed. by C. J. ROWE. Sankt Augustin, Academia Verlag, 95, 424 p. (International Plato Studies, 4).

2320. ROCHETTE (Bruno). Du grec au latin et du latin au grec. Les problèmes de la traduction dans l'antiquité gréco-latine. *Latomus*, 95, 54, 2, p. 245-261.

2321. ROQUES (D.). Synésios a Costantinople: 399–402. *Byzantion*, 95, 65, 2, p. 405-439.

2322. RUTHERFORD (R. B.). The art of Plato: ten essays in Platonic interpretation. London, Duckworth, 95, 335 p.

2323. SCHAMP (Jacques). Le Plutarque de Photios. *L'Antiquité Classique*, 95, 64, p. 155-184.

2324. SCHOFIELD (Malcolm). Two Stoic approaches to justice. *In*: Justice and generosity [Cf. n° 2287], p. 191-212.

2325. SCOTT (D.). Recollection and experience: Plato's theory of learning and its successors. Cambridge, Cambridge U. P., 95, 289 p.

2326. SEAFORD (Richard). Reciprocity and ritual. Homer and tragedy in the developing city-state. Oxford, Clarendon Press, 95, XIX-455 p.

2327. SEGAL (C.). Sophocles' tragic world: divinity, nature, society. Cambridge, Harvard U. P., 95, 276 p.

2328. Singer resumes the tale (The). Ed. by A. B. LORD, M. L. LORD. Ithaca a. London, Cornell U. P., 95, 258 p. (Myth and Poetics).

2329. SMITH (Thea Katharine). Water management in the Late Bronze Age Argolid, Greece. Cincinnati, Cincinnati U. P., 95, 344 p.

2330. Stage directions: essays in ancient drama in honour of E. W. Handley. Ed. by A. GRIFFITHS. London, Institute of Classical Studies, 95, 160 p; (Bulletin of the Institute of Classical Studies, 66).

2331. STERN-GILLET (S.). Aristotle's philosphy of friendship. Albany, State University of New York Press, 95, 233 p. (SUNY Series in Ancient Greek Philosophy).

2332. SULLIVAN (S. D.). Psychological and ethical ideas: what early Greeks say. Leide, Brill, 95, 262 (Mnemosyne, 114).

2333. SYME (Ronald). Anatolica. Studies in Strabo. Ed. by A. BIRLEY. Oxford, Clarendon Press, 95, 396 p.

2334. Teoria e prassi politica nelle opere di Plutarco. Atti del V Convegno Plutarcheo (e III Congresso Internazionale della International Plutarch Society). Certosa di Pontignano, 7–9 giugno 1993. Napoli, d'Auria, 95, 504 p. [Cf. n° <scelta> 2250.]

2335. THOME (J.). Psychotherapeutische Aspekte in der Philosophie Platons. Hildesheim, Ohms-Weidmann, 95, 288 p. (Altertumswissenschaftliche Texte und Studien, 29).

2336. TOO (Y. L.). The rhetoric of identity in Isocrates: text, power, pedagogy. Cambridge, Cambridge U. P., 95, 274 p. (Cambridge Classical Studies).

2337. TSAKMAKIS (Antonis). Das historische Werk von Stesimbrotos von Thasos. *Historia*, 95, 44, 2, p. 129-152.

2338. TZIFOPOULOS (Yannis Z.). Thucydidean rhetoric and the propaganda of the Persian wars topos. *La Parola del Passato*, 95, 50, 2, p. 91-115.

2339. UGOLINI (Gherardo). Aspetti politici dell'Aiace sofocleo. *Quaderni di storia*, 95, 21, 42, p. 5-34.

2340. VANSEVEREN (S.). Echo, verbe à sens neutre (dans l'épopée homérique). *L'Antiquité Classique*, 95, 64, p. 199-203.

2341. VINCENT (J.). Aux origines de l'individualisation des images historiques dans la production grecque. *Revue Historique*, 95, 119, 593, p. 3-22.

2342. WÖHRLE (Georg). Wer entdeckte die Quelle des Mondlichts? *Hermes*, 95, 123, 2, p. 244-247.

2343. WRIGHT (M. R.). Cosmology in antiquity. London a. New York, Routledge, 95, 201 p. (Sciences of Antiquity).

2344. ZAGDOUN (Mary-Anne). Plutarque à Delphes. *Revue des Etudes Grecques*, 95, 108, 2, p. 586-592.

Cf. n°s 1511, 1522, 2044-2112, 2161, 3095, 3096, 3097, 3099, 3101, 3102, 3116, 3117, 6222, 6229, 6236, 6242, 6254, 6261, 6286, 6308, 6327, 6331

§ 8. Religion und Mythologie.

* 2345. CHIANOTIS (Angelos), STAVRIANOPOULOU (Efychia). Epigraphic bulletin for Greek religion. (EBGR7). 1991. *Kernos*, 95, 8, p. 205-266.

2346. ALISON (Nick). The origins and practice of animal sacrifice in ancient Greece. *Pegasus*, 95, 38, p. 28-32.

2347. ALVIS (J.). Divine purpose and heroic response in Homer and Virgil: the political plan of Zeus. Lanham, Rowman a. Littlefield Publishers, 95, 269 p.

2348. ANTONACCIO (Carla M.). An archaeology of ancestors: tomb cult and hero cult in early Greece. Lanham, Rowman & Littlefield, 95, 295 p.

2349. AVRAM (A.), LEFEVRE (F.). Les cultes de Callatis et l'oracle de Delphes. *Revue des Etudes Grecques*, 95, 108, 1, p. 7-23.

2350. BARRINGER (J. M.). Divine escorts. Nereids in archaic and classical Greek art. Ann Arbor, University of Michigan Press, 95, 276 p.

2351. BEEKES (Robert S. P.). Where Europa bathed. *Mnemosyne*, 95, 48, 5, p. 579-581.

2352. BOULOGNE (Jacques). La leçon de Protée. *Uranie*, 95, 5, p. 9-32.

2353. BURGESS (Jonathan Seth). Achilles' heel: the death of Achilles in ancient myth. *Classical Antiquity*, 95, 14, 2, p. 217-243.

2354. BYNUM (Mary Rebecca). Studies in the topography of the southern Corinthia. Berkeley, University of California Press, 95, 231 p.

2355. CAPDEVILLE (Gérard). Mythes et cultes de la cité d'Aptera (Crète occidentale). *Kernos*, 95, 8, p. 41-84.

2356. CERRI (Giovanni). Cosmologia dell'Ade in Omero, Esiodo e Parmenide. *La Parola del Passato*, 95, 50, 3-6, p. 437-467.

2357. D'AGOSTINO (Bruno). Eracle e Gerione: la struttura del mito e la storia. *AION (archeologia)*, 95, 2, p. 7-13.

2358. DANDAMAEVA (M. M.). Legenda o trekh assirijskikh vladykakh (Rannjaja grečeskaja tradicija o Nine, Semiramide i Sardanapale). (The legend about three Assyrian rulers. The early Greek tradition about Ninus, Semiramis, and Sardanapalus). *Vestn. drev. Ist.*, 95, 4, p. 14-34.

2359. DAVIDSON (John). Two substitutions in Greek myth. *L'Antiquité Classique*, 95, 64, p. 205-210. – IDEM. Zeus and the stone substitute. *Hermes*, 95, 123, 3, p. 363-369.

2360. DERKS (H.). De koe van Troje. De mythe van de Griekse oudheid. Hilversum, Verloren, 95, 330 p.

2361. DUCAT (Jean). Un rituel samien. *Bulletin de Correspondance Hellénique*, 95, 119, 1, p. 339-368.

2362. DUCHEMIN (J.). Mythes grecs et sources orientales. Paris, Les Belles Lettres, 95, 350 p. (Vérité des mythes).

2363. Early Amazons (The). Modern and ancient perspectives on a persistent myth. Leiden a. New York, Brill, 95, 473 p.

2364. FAUTH (Wolfgang). Helios Megistos: zur synkretistischen Theologie der Spätantike. Leiden, Brill, 95, 268 p. (Religions in the Greek and Roman World, 125).

2365. GIAMMARCO RAZZANO (Maria Carla). Sincretismi euripidei: Demeter Auletris. *La Parola del Passato*, 95, 50, 2, p. 116-135.

2366. HILLGRUBER (Michael). Der Phaetonmythos als Gegenstand kosmologischer Spekulationen. *Gymnasium*, 95, 102, 6, p. 481-496.

2367. JOUAN (François). Le mythe de Bellérophon chez Pindare. *Revue des Etudes Grecques*, 95, 108, 2, p. 271-287.

2368. JOUANNO (Corinne). Alexandre et Olympias: de l'histoire au mythe. *Bulletin de l'Association Guillaume Budé*, 95, p. 211-230.

2369. KARWIESE (Stefan). Groß ist die Artemis von Ephesos. Die Geschichte einer der großen Städte der Antike. Wien, Phoibos Verlag, 95, 184 p. (ill., Karten).

2370. KOKOLAKIS (Minos). Zeus' tomb. An object of pride and reproach. *Kernos*, 95, 8, p. 123-138.

2371. LARSON (J.). Greek heroine cults. London a. Madison, University of Wisconsin Press, 95, 236 p. (Wisconsin Studies in Classics).

2372. MARCACCINI (Carlo). Considerazioni sulla morte di Orfeo in Thracia. *Prometheus*, 95, 21, 3, p. 241-252.

2373. MILANEZI (Silvia). Le rire d'Hadès. *Dialogues d'histoire ancienne*, 95, 21, 2, p. 231-345.

2374. MOREAU (Alain). La Niobé d'Eschyle: quelques jalons. *Revue des Etudes Grecques*, 95, 108, 2, p. 288-307.

2375. NAFISSI (Massimo). Zeus Basileus di Lebadea. La politica religiosa del Koinon beotico durante la guerra cleomenica. *Klio*, 95, 77, p. 149-169.

2376. OTTONE (Gabriella). Un episodio della saga di Cadmo alla luce delle tradizioni mitiche di Cirene. *Quaderni di Archeologia della Libia*, 95, 17, p. 31-39.

2377. PORTULAS (Jaume). De Oriente alla Grecia: las siete Pléyades, *Minerva*, 95, 9, p. 25-41.

2378. SMADJA (Élisabeth). Héraclès, héros et dieu: mythe et histoire. *Dialogues d'histoire ancienne*, 95, 21, 1, p. 241-246.

2379. STEINER (Deborah Tarn). Stoning and sight: a structural equivalence in Greek mythology. *Classical Antiquity*, 95, 14, 1, p. 193-211.

2380. TORRACA (Luigi). Le più antiche testimonianze letterarie. *La Parola del Passato*, 95, 50, 3-6, p. 414-424. [Sulla figura di Caronte].

2381. VERNANT (Jean-Pierre). Mythos und Religion im alten Griechenland. Frankfurt, Campus, 95, 101 p.

2382. WEST (David R.). Some cults of Greek goddesses and famale daemons of Oriental origin. Kevelaer, Butzon & Bercker a. Neukirchen-Vluyn, Neukirchener Verlag, 95, 373 p. (Alter Orient und Altes Testament, 233).

2383. WILLIAMS (Michael A.). The harvest of Hellenism and the category «gnosticism». *Syllecta Classica*, 95, 6, p. 87-104.

2384. ZAJKO (Vanda). Speaking myth. *Arethusa*, 95, 28, 1, p. 21-38.

Cf. n[os] *1393, 1893*

§ 9. Archäologie und Kunstgeschichte.

* 2385. BERGEMANN (Johannes). Attische Grabreliefs. Besprechung ausgewählter Beiträge aus den Jahren 1982 bis 1991. *Göttingische Gelehrte Anzeigen*, 95, 247, 1-2, p. 10-52.

* 2386. KIENAST (Hermann J.). Athener Trilogie. Klassizistische Architektur und ihre Vorbilder in der Hauptstadt Griechenlands. *Antike Welt*, 95, 26, 3, p. 161-176.

* 2387. ZAGDOUN (Mary-Anne). Bulletin archéologique: la sculpture hellénistique. *Revue des Études grecques*, 95, 108, p. 150-189.

2388. BELIS (Annie). La cithare du relief des Théores. Essai de datation. *Bulletin de Correspondance Hellénique*, 95, 119, 1, p. 369-374.

2389. BREUER (Christine). Reliefs und Epigramme griechischer Privatgrabmäler. Zeugnisse bürgerlichen Selbstverständnisse vom 4. bis 2. Jahrhundert v. Chr. Köln u. Wien, Böhlau, 95, 151 p.

2390. BROWN (B. R.). Royal portraits in sculpture and coins: Pyrrhos and the successors of Alexander the Great. New York, Peter Lang, 95, 121 p. (Hermeneutics of Art, 5).

2391. BRUNEAU (Philippe). Deliaca (X). *Bulletin de Correspondance Hellénique*, 95, 119, 1, p. 35-62.

2392. BUITRON-OLIVER (Diana). Douris. A master painter of Athenian red-figure vases. Mainz, von Zabern, 95, 115 p.

2393. CANTILENA (Renata). Un obolo per Caronte? *La Parola del Passato*, 95, 50, 3-6, p. 177.

2394. CIAMPOLTRINI (Giulio). Il vecchio, il mare, la nave. Una proposta per il fregio con thiasos marino di Telamone. *La Parola del Passato*, 95, 50, 1, p. 67-77.

2395. COATES (John). Tilley's and Morrison's triremes: evidence and practicality. *Antiquity*, 95, 69, 262, p. 159-162.

2396. EAVERLY (Mary Ann). Archaic Greek equestrian sculpture. Ann Arbor, University of Michigan Press, 95, 141 p.

2397. EITELJORG (Harrison). The entrance to the Athenian Acropolis before Mnesicles. Dubuque, Kendall/Hunt Publications Collection, 95, 146 p.

2398. ÉTIENNE (Roland), BRAUN (Jean-Pierre). L'autel monumental du théatre à Delos. *Bulletin de Correspondance Hellénique*, 95, 119, 1, p. 63-87.

2399. FOTIADIS (Michael). Modernity and the past-still-present: politics of time in the birth of regional archaeological projects in Greece. *American Journal of Archaeology*, 95, 99, 1, p. 59-78.

2400. FRONTISI-DUCROUX (F.). Du masque au visage. Aspects de l'identité en Grèce ancienne. Paris, Flammarion, 95, 192 p. (Idées et Recherches).

2401. GROSSMAN (Janet Burnett). The sculptured funerary monuments of the classical period in the Athenian Agora. New York, New York U. P., 95, 594 p.

2402. GUIMIER-SORBETS (Anne-Marie), NENNA (Marie-Dominique). Réflexions sur la couleur dans les mosaïques hellénistiques: Délos et Alexandrie. *Bulletin de Correspondance Hellénique*, 95, 119, 2, p. 529-563.

2403. HALL (Jonathan M.). How Argive was the "Argive" Heraion? The political and cultic geography of the Argive Plain, 900–400 B.C. *American Journal of Archaeology*, 95, 99, 4, p. 577-613.

2404. HAVELOCK (Christine Mitchell). The Aphrodite of Knidos and her successors. A historical review of the female nude in Greek art. Ann Arbor, University of Michigan Press, 95, 158 p.

2405. HERSCHER (Ellen). Archaeology in Cyprus. *American Journal of Archaeology*, 95, 99, 2, p. 257-294.

2406. HURWIT (Jeffrey M.). Beautiful evil: Pandora and the Athena Parthenos. *American Journal of Archaeology*, 95, 99, 2, p. 171-186.

2407. JARVA (E.). Archaiologia on archaic Greek body armour. Rovaniemi, Pohjois-Suomen Historiallinen Yhdistys, Societas Historica Finlandiae Septentrionalis, 95, 176 p. (Studia Archaeologica Septentrionalia, 3).

2408. JENKINS (Ian). The south frieze of the Parthenon: problems in arrangement. *American Journal of Archaeology*, 95, 99, 3, p. 445-456.

2409. JONES ROCCOS (Linda). The kanephoros and her festival mantle in Greek art. *American Journal of Archaeology*, 95, 99, 4, p. 641-666.

2410. KARAGEORGHIS (V.). The coroplastic art of ancient Cyprus. Vol. 4. The Cypro-Archaic Period: small male figurines. Nicosia, University of Cyprus, 95, 174 p.

2411. KEESLING (Catherine Marie). Monumental private votive dedications on the Athenian Acropolis, ca. 600–400 B. C. Ann Arbor, University of Michigan Press, 95, 550 p.

2412. KNELL (Heiner). Die Nike von Samothrake. Typus, Form, Bedeutung und Wirkungsgeschichte eines rhodischen Sieges-Anathems im Kabirenheiligtum von Samothrake. Darmstadt, Wissenschaftliche Buchgesellschaft, 95, 130 p.

2413. LAWTON (C. L.). Attic document reliefs: art and politics in ancient Athens. Oxford, Clarendon Press, 95, 167 p. (Oxford Monographs on Classical Archaeology).

2414. LENZ (Dirk). Vogeldarstellungen in der agäischen und zyprischen Vasenmalerei des 12.–9. Jahrhunderts v. Chr. Untersuchungen zu Form und Inhalt. Espelkamp, M. Leidorf, 95, 308 p.

2415. MAC GOVERN (Patrick E). Science in archaeology: a review. *American Journal of Archaeology*, 95, 99, 1, p. 79-142.

2416. MAC GOWAN (Elizabeth P.). Tomb marker and turning post: funerary columns in the Archaic period. *American Journal of Archaeology*, 95, 99, 4, p. 615-632.

2417. MARCHETTI (Patrick), RIZAKIS (Yvonne). Recherches sur les mythes et la topographie d'Argos. IV. L'agora revisitée. *Bulletin de Correspondance Hellénique*, 95, 119, 2, p. 437-472.

2418. MERSCH (Andrea). Archäologischer Kommentar zu den "Gräbern der Athener und Plataier" in Marathonia. *Klio*, 95, 77, p. 55-64.

2419. MOORE (Mary B.). The central group in the Gigantomachy of the Old Athena Temple on the Acropolis. *American Journal of Archaeology*, 95, 99, 4, p. 633-639.

2420. MUGIONE (Eliana). La raffigurazione di Caronte in età greca. *La Parola del Passato*, 95, 50, 3-6, p. 357-375.

2421. NEILS (Jenifer). The Euthymides krater from Morgantina. *American Journal of Archaeology*, 95, 99, 3, p. 427-444.

2422. NICGORSKI Ann m.). The iconography of the Herakles knot and the Herklesknot hairstyle of Apollo and Aphrodite. Chapel Hill, The University of North Carolina, 95, 555 p.

2423. PAPADOPOULOS (Stratis). L'organisation de l'espace dans deux ateliers de potiers traditionnels de Thasos. *Bulletin de Corespondance Hellénique*, 95, 119, 2, p. 591-606.

2424. PARISE (Nicola F.). 'Segni premonetari' ed obolo di Caronte. *La Parola del Passato*, 95, 50, 3-6, p. 179-183.

2425. PIKOULAS (Y. A.). Road network and defence from Corinth to Argos and Arkadia. Athens, Horos, 95, 450 p.

2426. Polykleitos. The Doryphoros and tradition. Ed. by W. G. MOON. Madison a. London, Univesity of Wisconsin Press, 95, 364 p. (Wisconsin Studies in Classics).

2427. PONTRANDOLFO (Angela). Olinto e Corinto. Considerazioni sul rituale funerario. *La Parola del Passato*, 95, 50, 3-6, p. 483-508.

2428. RHODES (R. F.). Architecture and meaning on the Athenian Acropolis. Cambridge, Cambridge U. P., 95, 218 p.

2429. Studien zur Bühnendichtung und zum Theaterbau der Antike. Hrsg. v. E. PÖHLMANN. New York, Peter Lang, 95, 264 p. (Studien zur klassischen Philologie, 93).

2430. SVENSON (Dominique). Darstellungen hellenistischer Könige mit Götterattributen. Bern u. Frankfurt, Lang, 95, 425 p.

2431. Time, tradition and society in Greek archaeology: bringing the 'Great divide'. Ed. by N. SPENCER. London a. New York, Routledge, 95, 179 p. (Theoretical Archaeology Group).

2432. TOWNSEND (R. F.). The East side of the Agora. The remains beneath of the Stoa of Attalos. Princeton, The American School of Classical Studies at Athens, 95, 248 p. (The Athenian Agora, 27).

2433. TUNA-NÖRLING (Y.). Die attisch-schwarzfigure Keramik und der attische Keramikexport nach Kleinasien. Tübingen, Ernst Wasmuth, 95, 180 p. (Istambuler Forschungen, 41).

2434. WANNAGAT (Detlev). Säule und Kontext. Piedestale und Teilkannelierung in der griechischen Architektur. München, Biering u. Brinkmann, 95, 154p.

2435. WHITBREAD (I. K.). Greek transport amphorae. A petrological and archaeological study. Athens, The British School at Athens, 95, 453 p. (British School at Athens. Fitch Laboratory Occasional Papers, 4).

2436. ZANKER (Paul). The mask of Socrates: the image of the intellectual in antiquity. Berkeley, Los Angeles a. London, University of California Press, 95, 426 p. (Sather Classical Lectures, 59).

2437. ZEVI (Fausto). Gli Eubei a Cuma. Dedalo e L'Eneide. *Rivista di Filologia e di Istruzione Classica*, 95, 123, 2, p. 178-192.

2438. ZOLOTAREV (M. I.). Khersonesskaja arkhaika. (The archaic finds from Chersonesus). *Vestn. drev. Ist.*, 95, 3, p. 138-151.

Cf. n° 6840

F

GESCHICHTE ROMS, DES ALTEN ITALIENS UND DES RÖMISCHEN KAISERREICHS

§ 1. Die Völkerschaften Italiens. 2439-2487. – § 2. Etruskologie. 2488-2507. – § 3. Quellen und Quellenkunde (*a*. Epigrafische Quellen; *b*. Literarische Quellen). 2508-2604. – § 4. Allgemeine und politische Geschichte. 2605-2676. – § 5. Rechts- und Verfassungsgeschichte. 2677-2709. – § 6. Wirtschafts- und Sozialgeschichte. 2710-2748. – § 7. Literatur-, Philosophie- und Wissenschaftsgeschichte. 2749-2825. – § 8. Religion und Mythologie. 2826-2858. – § 9. Archäologie und Kunstgeschichte. 2859-2921.

§ 1. Die Völkerschaften Italiens.

2439. AIGNER FORESTI (Luciana). La tradizione antica sul ver sacrum. *In*: Coercizione e mobilità [Cf. n° 2620], p. 141-147.

2440. Ancient Sicily. Ed. by Tobias FISHER-HANSEN. Copenhagen, University of Copenhagen, 95, 316 p. (ill.). (Danish studies in classical archaeology. Acta Hyperborea, 6) [Cf. n°[os] <choice> 2472, 2480.]

2441. ANDREAU (Jean). Italy, Europe and the Mediterranean: relations in banking and business during the last centuries BC. *In*: Italy in Europe [Cf. n° 2463], p. 305-312.

2442. BAGNASCO (Gianni), ROCCA (Giovanna). Note su alcune iscrizioni dell'Italia centrale. *Aevum*, 95, 69, p. 31-68.

2443. BARBANERA (Marcello). Il guerriero di Agrigento. Una probabile scultura frontale del Museo di Agrigento e alcune questioni di archeologia siceliota. Roma, L'Erma di Bretschneider, 95, 101 p. (ill., tavole). (Studia archaeologica, 77).

2444. BARELLO (Federico). Architettura greca a Caulonia. Edilizia monumentale e decorazione architettonica in una città della Magna Grecia. Firenze, Le Lettere, 95, XIII-138 p. (tavole). (Università degli Studi di Torino. Fondo di studi Parini-Chirio. Studi e materiali di archeologia, 9).

2445. BELLI PASQUA (Ribaerta). Sculture di età romana in basalto. Roma, L'Erma di Bretschneider, 95, 163 p. (ill., tavole). (Xenia antiqua. Monografie, 2).

2446. Brettii (I). Vol. 1. Cultura, lingua e documentazione storico-archeologica. Atti del I corso seminariale (Rossano, 20–26 febbraio 1992). A cura di Giovanna DE SENSI SESTITO. Soveria Mannelli, Rubbettino, 95, XI-346 p. (ill.).

2447. Brettii (I). Vol. 2. Fonti letterarie ed epigrafiche. A cura di Maria INTIERI e Antonio ZUMBO. Soveria Mannelli, Rubbettino, 95, 390 p.

2448. CAMPANILE (Enrico). L'iscrizione Vetter 196 e una ipotesi sulla genesi del meddicato duplice a Messina. *Athenaeum*, 95, 83, 2, p. 463-467.

2449. CANTILENA (Renata). La Campania preromana. *In*: Caronte [Cf. n° 2452], p. 217-239.

2450. CAPOZZA (M.), BUCHREITER (N.), TONELOTTO (S.). Donne italiote e donne romane nel Bruzio antico (un'ipotesi di lavoro). *Hesperìa*, 95, 5, p. 191-199.

2451. CARLUCCI (Claudia). Il santuario falisco di Vignale. Nuove acquisizioni. *Archeologia Classica*, 95, 47, p. 69-101.

2452. Caronte. Un obolo per l'aldilà. Napoli, Macchiaroli, 95, 381 p. (ill.). (La Parola del Passato, 95, 3-4) [Cf. n°[os] <scelta> 2449, 2458, 2469, 2490, 2866.]

2453. CASSIMATIS (Hélène). Fenêtre de l'au-delà dans l'iconographie italiote. *Mélanges de l'Ecole française de Rome. Antiquité*, 95, 107, 2, p. 1061-1092.

2454. CERCHIAI (Luca). I Campani. Milano, Longanesi, 95, 264 p. (ill.). (Biblioteca di Archeologia, 23).

2455. Corinto e l'Occidente. Atti del trentaquattresimo Convegno di Studi sulla Magna Grecia (Taranto, 7–11 ottobre 1994). Napoli, Istituto per la storia e l'archeologia della Magna Grecia, 95, 2 vol., 870 p. (tavole).

2456. CORNELL (T.J.). The beginnings of Rome. Italy and Rome from the bronze age to the Punic wars (c. 1000–264 BC). London a. New York, Routledge, 95, XX-507 p. (ill.). (Routledge history of the ancient world).

2457. CULASSO GASTALDI (Enrica). IG³ 228: Atene, Siracusa e i Siculi. *Hesperìa*, 95, 5, p. 145-162.

2458. CUTRONI (Aldina). La Sicilia. *In*: Caronte [Cf. n° 2452], p. 189-216.

2459. DE LA GENIERE (Juliette). Les Grecs et les autres. Quelques aspects de leurs relations en Italie du Sud à l'époque archaïque. *In*: Grecs et l'Occident [Cf. n° 2462], p. 29-40.

2460. FRIELINGHAUS (Heide). Einheimische in der apulischen Vasenmalerei. Ikonographie im Spannungsfeld zwischen Produzenten und Rezipienten. Berlin, Verlag Köster, 95, XII-241 p. (Taf.). (Wissenschaftliche Schriftenreihe Archäologie, 2).

2461. GRAS (Michel). La Méditerranée archaïque. Paris, Colin, 95, 189 p. (ill.). (Cursus).

2462. Grecs et l'Occident (Les). Actes du colloque de la Villa Kérylos (1991). Rome, Ecole française de Rome, 95, 159 p. (ill.) [Cf. n°s <sélection> 2459, 2482, 2484.]

2463. Italy in Europe: economic relations 700 BC– AD 50. Ed. by Judith SWADDLING, Susan WALKER a. Paul ROBERTS. London, The Trustees of the British Museum, 95, VII-353 p. (ill.). (British Museum, Department of Greek and Roman antiquities. Occasional papers, 97) [Cf. n°s <choice> 2441, 2497, 2503, 2713.]

2464. LIPPOLIS (E.), GARRAFFO (S.), NAFISSI (M.). Culti greci in occidente. Fonti scritte e documentazione archeologica. Vol. 1. Taranto, Istituto per la storia e l'archeologia della Magna Grecia, 95, 374 p. (tavole).

2465. LUCCA (Rita). Il culto di Pan Aktios a Sibari e a Turi. *Hesperìa*, 95, 5, p. 233-237.

2466. MARCHESINI VELASCO (Simona). Le piramidette messapiche iscritte. *Annali della Scuola Normale Superiore di Pisa*, 95, 25, p. 1359-1385.

2467. MAZZEI (Marina). Arpi. L'ipogeo della Medusa e la necropoli. Bari, Edipuglia, 95, 351 p. (ill.). (Ministero per i beni culturali e ambientali. Soprintendenza archeologica della Puglia).

2468. MENICHETTI (Mauro). Quoius forma uirtutei parisuma fuit: ciste prenestine e cultura di Roma mediorepubblicana. Roma, L'Erma di Bretschneider, 95, 148 p. (ill.). (Archaeologia Perusina, 12. Archaeologica, 116).

2469. PARENTE (Anna Rita). La Lucania: necropoli e monete in tombe (V–II secolo a.C.). *In*: Caronte [Cf. n° 2452], p. 276-288.

2470. PERUZZI (Emilio). La sacerdotessa di Corfinio. *La Parola del Passato*, 95, 50, p. 5-15.

2471. PONTRANDOLFO (Angela). Simposio e élites sociali nel mondo etrusco e italico. *In*: In vino veritas [Cf. n° 1273], p. 176-195.

2472. PROCELLI (E.). Cultures and societies in Sicily between the neolithic and the middle bronze age. *In*: Ancient Sicily [Cf. n° 2440], p. 13-32.

2473. PROHÁSZKA (Marianne). Reflections from the dead. The metal finds from the Pantanello necropolis at Metaponto. A comprehensive study of grave goods from the 5th to the 3rd centuries BC. Jonsered, Aströms, 95, 256 p. (ill., tab.). (Studies in mediterranean archaeology, 110).

2474. RATHJE (A.). Il banchetto in Italia centrale: quale stile di vita? *In*: In vino veritas [Cf. n° 1273], p. 167-175.

2475. RAVIOLA (Flavio). Napoli origini. Roma, L'Erma di Bretschneider, 95, 272 p. (carte). (Hesperìa, 6). – IDEM. Tucidide e Segesta. *Hesperìa*, 95, 5, p. 75-119.

2476. RONCONI (Lucia). Il muro sull'istmo (Ecateo, Antioco, Filisto). *Hesperìa*, 95, 5, p. 37-47.

2477. RUBY (Pascal). Le crépuscule des marges. Le premier âge du fer à Sala Consilina. Rome et Naples, Ecole française de Rome et Centre Jean Bérard, 95, 371 p. (ill.). (Bibliothèque des écoles françaises d'Athènes et de Rome, 290. Collection du Centre Jean Bérard, 12).

2478. SANCHEZ JIMENEZ (Francisco). Helánico y Dionisio sobre el origen pelásgico de los Tirrenos (D. H. I, 28, 3, = FgrH 4 F 4). *Quaderni di storia*, 95, 21, 41, p. 129-140.

2479. Sicilia tra l'Egitto e Roma (La). La monetazione siracusana dell'età di Ierone II. Atti del seminario di studi (Messina, 2–4 dicembre 1993). A cura di Maria CACCAMO CALTABIANO. Palermo, Accademia Peloritana dei Pericolanti, 95, 521 p. (ill.). (Atti dell'Accademia Peloritana dei Pericolanti, Suppl. 1, vol. 69).

2480. SIRONEN (T.). La cultura epigrafica dei Peligni. *In*: Acta colloquii epigraphici Latini [Cf. n° 2509], p. 343-346. – IDEM. Position of minority languages in Sicily: oscan and elymian. *In*: Ancient Sicily [Cf. n° 2440], p. 185-194.

2481. SOMMELLA (Paolo). Il culto di Apollo a Peltuinum città dei Vestini. *Caesarodunum*, 95, 30, p. 279-291.

2482. STAZIO (Attilio). Monetazione dei Greci d'Occidente. *In*: Grecs et l'Occident [Cf. n° 2462], p. 141-150.

2483. Studi sulla Campania preromana. A cura di Alessandra CASTORINA. Roma, L'Erma di Bretschneider, 95, VIII-259 p. (tavole). (Pubblicazioni scientifiche del Centro di studi della Magna Grecia dell'Università degli Studi di Napoli Federico II).

2484. TUSA (Vincenzo). Greci e Punici. *In*: Grecs et l'Occident [Cf. n° 2462], p. 19-28.

2485. WAARSENBURG (Demetrius J.). The northwest necropolis of Satricum. An iron age cemetery in Latium vetus. Amsterdam, Thesis publishers, 95, XXV-559 p. (maps). (Scrinium, 8. Satricum, 3).

2486. WERNER (R.). Untersuchungen zur Geschichte und Struktur des Italiotenbundes. *In*: Rom und der Griechische Osten [Cf. n° 2659], p. 287-296.

2487. ZORAT (Marta). Città italiote tra Timoleonte e Archidamo. *Hesperìa*, 95, 5, p. 171-181.

§ 2. Etruskologie.

2488. ADAM (Anne-Marie). Aspects de l'iconographie des cavaliers en Etrurie du VIe au IVe siècle avant notre ère: représentation et idéologie. *Mélanges de l'Ecole française de Rome. Antiquité*, 95, 107, 1, p. 71-96.

2489. BIEG (Gebhard), PRAYON (Friedhelm). Zu orvietaner Grabkontexte Komposition und Wert. *Revue des Etudes Anciennes*, 95, 97, p. 141-151.

2490. CERCHIAI (Luca). Daimones e Caronte sulle stele felsinee. *In*: Caronte [Cf. n° 2452], p. 376-394. – IDEM. Il programma figurativo dell'hydria Ricci. *Antike Kunst*, 95, 38, 2, p. 81-91.

2491. CHERICI (Armando). Un arciere a Orvieto? In margine alla stele di guerriero della Cannicella. *Athenaeum*, 95, 83, 2, p. 487-495. – IDEM. Vasellame metallico e tombe con armi in Etruria. *Revue des Etudes Anciennes*, 95, 97, p. 115-139.

2492. COLONNA (Giovanni). Gli scavi del 1852 ad Ardea e l'identificazione dell'Aphrodisium. *Archeologia Classica*, 95, 47, p. 1-67.

2493. Corpus speculorum etruscorum. Bundesrepublik Deutschland. Vol. 4. Staatliche Museen zu Berlin, Antikensammlung. München, Hirner, 95, 173 p. (ill.) [mit einem Beitrag von Josef RIEDERER und Helmut RIX].

2494. Corpus speculorum etruscorum. Italia. Vol. 2. Perugia, Museo Archeologico Nazionale. A cura di Alba FRASCARELLI. Roma, L'Erma di Bretschneider, 95, 179 p. (tavole).

2495. Corpus speculorum etruscorum. Italia. Vol. 3. Volterra, Museo Guarnacci. A cura di Gabriele CATENI. Roma, L'Erma di Bretschneider, 95, 194 p. (tavole).

2496. Corpus speculorum etruscorum. Stato della Città del Vaticano. Vol. 1. Città del Vaticano, Museo Profano della Biblioteca Apostolica Vaticana. Roma, Collezione di antichità dell'Abbazia di San Paolo fuori le mura. A cura di Roger LAMBRECHTS. Roma, L'Erma di Bretschneider, 95, 162 p. (tavole).

2497. CRISTOFANI (Mauro). Novità sul commercio etrusco arcaico: dal relitto del Giglio al contratto di Pech Maho. *In*: Italy in Europe [Cf. n° 2463], p. 131-137. – IDEM. Tabula Capuana. Un calendario festivo di età arcaica. Firenze, Olschki, 95, 136 p. (tavole). (Istituto nazionale di studi etruschi e italici. Biblioteca di Studi etruschi, 29).

2498. GRAIN-AYMERICH (Jean). Le bucchero et les vases métalliques. *Revue des Etudes Anciennes*, 95, 97, p. 45-76.

2499. JANNOT (Jean-René). A propos des cavaliers de la tombe Querciola. Développement d'une nouvelle cavalerie à l'aube du IVe siècle? *Mélanges de l'Ecole française de Rome. Antiquité*, 95, 107, 1, p. 13-31. – IDEM. Les représentations d'animaux dans l'imagerie étrusque: imitation de modèles ou témoignages réels? *In*: Homme et animal [Cf. n° 2633], p. 217-233. – IDEM. Les vases métalliques dans les représentations picturales étrusques. *Revue des Etudes Anciennes*, 95, 97, p. 167-182.

2500. MORANDI (Alessandro). A proposito di due epigrafi etrusche ceretane. *Revue Belge de Philologie et d'Histoire*, 95, 73, 1, p. 105-127.

2501. MORANDI (Massimo). Novità sui Velcha di Tarquinia. *Archeologia Classica*, 95, 47, p. 267-288.

2502. PFIFFIG (Ambros J.). Mi zinaku amprusale. Gesammelte Schriften zu Sprache und Geschichte der Etrusker. Herausgegeben zur Vollendung seines 85. Lebenjahres vom Institut für Alte Geschichte, Altertumskunde und Epigraphik der Universität Wien unter der Leitung von Luciana AIGNER-FORESTI und Ekkehard WEBER. Wien, Österr. Ges. für Archäologie, 95, 532 p. (ill.). (Althistorisch-epigraphische Studien, 3).

2503. SHEFTON (B.B.). Leaven in the dough: Greek and Etruscan imports north of the Alps – the classical period. *In*: Italy in Europe [Cf. n° 2463], p. 9-44.

2504. SORDI (Marta). Prospettive di storia etrusca. Como, Edizioni New Press, 95, 224 p. (Biblioteca di Athenaeum, 26).

2505. THUILLIER (Jean-Paul). Pretium victoribus: l'exemple des vases étrusques. *Revue des Etudes Anciennes*, 95, 97, p. 153-166.

2506. VAN DER MEER (L.B.). Interpretatio Etrusca. Greek myths on Etruscan mirrors. Amsterdam, Gieben, 95, 285 p. (Abb.).

2507. ZIMMER (Gerhard). Etruskische Spiegel. Technik und Stil der Zeichnungen. Berlin, de Gruyter, 95, 43 p. (Abb.). (Winckelmannprogramm der Archäologischen Gesellschaft zu Berlin, 135).

§ 3. Quellen und Quellenkunde.

a. Epigraphische Quellen.

* 2508. Année épigraphique 1992 (L'). Ed. par Mireille CORBIER et Patrick LE ROUX. Paris, Presses universitaires de France, 95, 664 p.

2509. Acta colloquii epigraphici Latini. Helsingiae 3–6 sept. 1991 habiti. Ed. by Heikki SOLIN, Olli SALOMIES, Uta-Maria LIERTZ. Helsinki, Societas scientiarum fennica, 95, 425 p. (ill.). (Commentationes humanarum litterarum, 104) [Cf. n^{os} <choice> 2480, 2511, 2519, 2521, 2524, 2526, 2718, 2839, 2869.]

2510. ADAMS (J.N.). The language of the Vindolanda writing tablets: an interim report. *Journal of Roman Studies*, 95, 85, p. 86-134.

2511. CAMODECA (Giuseppe). Nuovi dati sulla struttura e funzione documentale delle tabuale ceratae nella prassi campana. *In*: Acta colloquii epigraphici Latini [Cf. n° 2509], p. 59-77.

2512. CLOPPET (Christian). Observations sur un milliaire de Claude. A propos de C.I.L., XVII 2, 144 et des voies romaines de Lyon aux Alpes. *Latomus*, 95, 54, 4, p. 842-855.

2513. COTTON (H.M.), COCKLE (W.E.H.), MILLAR (F.G.B.). The papyrology of the Roman Near East: a survey. *Journal of Roman Studies*, 95, 85, p. 214-235.

2514. DAL CASON PATRIARCA (Francesca). Considerazioni demografiche sulla lista decurionale della Tabula di Canusium. *Athenaeum*, 95, 83, 1, p. 245-264.

2515. ECK (Werner). Augustus und Claudius in Perusia. *Athenaeum*, 95, 83, 1, p. 83-90.

2516. FALLETTI (E.). La rappresentazione dei funerali e delle onoranze funebri nell'epigrafia romana. *In*: Mort au quotidien [Cf. n° 2728], p. 225-234.

2517. FRANCE (J.), HESNARD (A.). Une statio du quarantième des Gaules et les opérations commerciales dans le port romain de Marseille (place Jules-Verne). *Journal of Roman Archaeology*, 95, 8, p. 79-93.

2518. GREGORY (Andrew P.). A study in survival. The case of the freedman L. Domitius Phaon. *Athenaeum*, 95, 83, 2, p. 401-410.

2519. HARRIS (W.V.). Instrumentum domesticum and Roman literacy. *In*: Acta colloquii epigraphici Latini [Cf. n° 2509], p. 19-27.

2520. LETTA (Cesare). ILAfr, 265 e il proconsolato d'Africa di C. Cingio Severo. *Latomus*, 95, 54, 4, p. 864-874.

2521. LEVICK (B.). The latin inscriptions of Asia Minor. *In*: Acta colloquii epigraphici Latini [Cf. n° 2509], p. 393-402.

2522. MAURIN (Louis). Pagus mercurialis veteranorum medelitanorum. Implantations vétéranes dans la vallée de l'oued Miliane. Le dossier épigraphique. *Mélanges de l'Ecole française de Rome. Antiquité*, 107, 1, p. 97-135.

2523. MAVROJANNIS (Theodoros). L'aedicula dei Lares Compitales nel compitum degli Hermaistai a Delo. *Bulletin de Correspondance Hellénique*, 95, 119, 1, p. 89-123.

2524. MILLAR (Fergus). Latin epigraphy of the Roman Near East. *In*: Acta colloquii epigraphici Latini [Cf. n° 2509], p. 403-419.

2525. MODONESI (Denise). Museo Maffeiano. Iscrizioni e rilievi sacri latini. Roma, L'Erma di Bretschneider, 95, 127 p. (tavole). (Studia archaeologica, 75).

2526. PANCIERA (Silvio). Le iscrizioni repubblicane di Roma. *In*: Acta colloquii epigraphici Latini [Cf. n° 2509], p. 319-342.

2527. PEDRONI (Luigi). Tessere da una collezione privata. *Archeologia Classica*, 95, 47, p. 161-201 [con Appendice tecnica di Guido DEVOTO].

2528. RAEPSAET-CHARLIER (Marie-Thérèse). Municipium Tungrorum. *Latomus*, 95, 54, 2, p. 361-369.

2529. SCHEID (John). Le desmos de Gaionas. Observations sur une plaque inscrite du sanctuaire des dieux syriens à Rome (IGUR 109). *Mélanges de l'Ecole française de Rome. Antiquité*, 95, 107, 1, p. 301-314.

2530. SIMONELLI (Antonietta). La gens Herennia ad Abellinum: testimonianze epigrafiche e monumenti. *Archeologia Classica*, 95, 47, p. 139-159.

Cf. n° 3203

b. Literarische Quellen.

2531. ADKIN (Neil). Self-imitation in Jerome's Libellus de virginitate servanda (Epist. XXII). *Athenaeum*, 95, 83, 2, p. 469-485.

2532. [Apuleius] APULEIUS MADAURENSIS. Metamorphoses. Book IX. Ed. by B.L. HIJMANS Jr., R.T. VAN DER PARDT, V. SCHMIDT *et al.* Groningen, Forsten, 95, XXII-436 p. (Groningen commentaries on Apuleius).

2533. BLECKMANN (Bruno). Bemerkungen zu den Annales des Nicomachus Flavianus. *Historia*, 95, 44, 1, p. 83-99.

2534. BODEL (John). Minicia Marcella: taken before her time. *American Journal of Philology*, 95, 116, 3, p. 453-460.

2535. [Manlius Severinus Boethius (Anicius)] BOECE. Institution arithmétique. Ed. par Jean-Yves GUILLAUMIN. Paris, Belles Lettres, 95, XCVII-253 p. (Collection des universités de France).

2536. BRUGNOLI (Giorgio). Curiosissimus excerptator. Gli Additamenta di Girolamo ai Chronica di Eusebio. Pisa, Edizioni ETS, 95, LIX-245 p. (Testi e studi di cultura classica, 12).

2537. BRUUN (Christer). The thick neck of the emperor Constantine. Slimy snails and Quellenforschung. *Historia*, 95, 44, 4, p. 459-480.

2538. BURGESS (R.W.). Jerome and the Kaisergeschichte. *Historia*, 95, 44, 3, p. 349-369.

2539. CAMERON (Alan). Ancient epigrams. *American Journal of Philology*, 95, 116, 3, p. 477-484.

2540. CAPE (Robert W., Jr.). The rhetoric of politics in Cicero's fourth Catilinarian. *American Journal of Philology*, 95, 116, 2, p. 255-277.

2541. [Valerius Catullus (Gaius)] CATULLUS. Poems 61–68. Ed. by John GODWIN. Warminster, Aris & Phillips, 95, IV-235 p.

3. QUELLEN UND QUELLENKUNDE

2542. [Celsus] CELSE. De la médecine. Vol. 1. Ed. par Guy SERBAT. Paris, Belles Lettres, 95, LXXVI-179 p. (Collection des universités de France).

2543. [Tullius Cicero (Marcus)] M. TULLI CICERONIS. Scripta quae manserunt omnia. Vol. 23. Orationes In P. Vatinium testem, Pro M. Caelio. Hrsg. v. Tadeusz MASLOWSKI. Stuttgart u. Leipzig, Teubner, 95, CXXI-156 p. (Abb.). (Bibliotheca Scriptorum Graecorum et Romanorum Teubneriana).

2544. [Tullius Cicero (Marcus)] M. TULLIUS CICERO. The letters of january to april 43 BC. Ed. by M.M. WILLCOCK. Warminster, Aris & Phillips, 95, VI-154 p.

2545. CLAUSS (James J.). A delicate foot on the wellworn threshold: paradoxical imagery in Catullus 68b. *American Journal of Philology*, 95, 116, 2, p. 237-253.

2546. DE AROZENA (B.P.). Retórica y burocracia: hapax y prima dicta en el lenguaje de las cancillerías. *Latomus*, 95, 54, 2, p. 370-376.

2547. DE CALLATAŸ (Godefroid). Les quatre arts d'Apollon dans l'Enéide. *Latomus*, 95, 54, 4, p. 812-821.

2548. DEN BOEFT (J.), DRIJVERS (J.W.), DEN HENGST (D.), TEITLER (H.C.). Philological and historical commentary on Ammianus Marcellinus XXII. Groningen, Forsten, 95, XIV-392 p.

2549. DEVILLERS (Olivier). Tacite, les sources et les impératifs de la narration: le récit de la mort d'Agrippine (Annales XIV, 1–13). *Latomus*, 95, 54, 2, p. 323-345.

2550. DI BENEDETTO (Vincenzo). La consapevolezza di morte in Turno. *Rivista di Filologia e di Istruzione Classica*, 95, 123, 1, p. 45-72.

2551. [Blossius Aemilius Dracontius] DRACONTIUS. Oeuvres. Vol. 3. La tragédie d'Oreste. Poèmes profanes I–V. Ed. par Jean BOUQUET et Etienne WOLFF. Paris, Belles Lettres, 95, 278 p. (Collection des universités de France).

2552. DYER (R.R.). Cicero at Caieta in Vergil's Aeneid. *Latomus*, 95, 54, 2, p. 290-297.

2553. [Eutropius] EUTROPII. Breviarium ab urbe condita. Hrsg. v. Friedhelm L. MÜLLER. Stuttgart, Steiner, 95, 336 p. (Palingenesia, 56).

2554. FABER (Riemer). Vergil eclogue 3.37, Theocritus 1 and hellenistic ekphrasis. *American Journal of Philology*, 95, 116, 3, p. 411-417.

2555. FRASCHETTI (Augusto). Sulla datazione della Consolatio ad Liviam. *Rivista di Filologia e di Istruzione Classica*, 95, 123, 4, p. 409-427.

2556. GAIDE (François). Intuitions linguistiques de Pétrone dans la mise en scène des affranchis de la Cena. *Latomus*, 95, 54, 4, p. 856-863.

2557. GONZALEZ PONCE (F.J.). Avieno y el Periplo. Sevilla, Editorial Graficas Sol, 95, 217 p.

2558. GREENE (Ellen). Elegiac woman: fantasy, materia and male desire in Propertius 1.3 and 1.11. *American Journal of Philology*, 95, 116, 2, p. 303-318.

2559. HÄNDL-SAGAWE (Ursula). Der Beginn des 2. Punischen Krieges. Ein historisch-kritischer Kommentar zu Livius' Buch 21. München, Editio Maris, 95, 432 p. (Karten). (Münchener Universitätsschriften. Münchener Arbeiten zur Alten Geschichte, 9).

2560. HAIG GAISSER (Julia). Threads in the labyrinth: competing views and voices in Catullus 64. *American Journal of Philology*, 95, 116, 4, p. 579-616.

2561. [Horatius Flaccus (Quintus)] Q. HORATI FLACCI. Epodes. Ed. by David MANKIN. Cambridge, Cambridge University Press, 95, VII-321 p. (Cambridge Greek and Latin Classics).

2562. [Horatius Flaccus (Quintus)] HORACE. Odes I: Carpe Diem. Ed. by D. WEST. Oxford, Clarendon Press, 95, XIII-203 p.

2563. HÜBNER (Wolfgang). Grade und Gradbezirke der Tierkreiszeichen. Der anonyme Traktat De stellis fixis, in quibus gradibus oriuntur signorum. Stuttgart u. Leipzig, Teubner, 95, 2 vol., 265 p., 272 p. (Sammlung wissenschaftlicher Kommentare).

2564. [Iulius Severianus] IULII SEVERIANI. Praecepta artis rhetoricae summatim collecta de multis ac syntomata. A cura di Anna Luisa CASTELLI MONTANARI. Bologna, Patron, 95, 130 p. (Edizioni e saggi universitari di filologia classica, 53).

2565. KRAUTSCHICK (Stefan). Die unmögliche Tatsache. Argumente gegen Johannes Antiochenus. *Klio*, 95, 77, p. 332-338.

2566. LANDOLFI (Luciano). Metro e forma. Lettura di Hor. c. I, 11. *L'Antiquité Classique*, 95, 64, p. 217-235.

2567. LANIADO (Avshalom). Some addenda to the Prosopography of the Later Roman Empire. *Historia*, 95, 44, 1, p. 121-128.

2568. [Titus Livius] TITE-LIVE. Histoire romaine. Vol. 18. Livre XXVIII. Ed. par Paul JAL. Paris, Belles Lettres, 95, LXI-148 p. (Collection des universités de France).

2569. [Annaeus Lucanus (Marcus)] MARCO ANNEO LUCANO. La guerra civile. A cura di Giovanni VIANSINO. Milano, Mondadori, 95, 2 vol., CXLII-1024 p. (Classici greci e latini, 89–90).

2570. [Lucretius Carus (Titus)] LUCRETIUS. On the nature of things. Ed. by A. ESOLEN. Baltimore, The Johns Hopkins University Press, 95, IX-296 p.

2571. MAC GUIRE (Donald T., Jr.). History compressed: the Roman names of Silius' Cannae episode. *Latomus*, 95, 54, 1, p. 110-118.

2572. [Manilius] MANILIO. Astronomica. Libro I. A cura di Dora LIUZZI. Galatina, Congedo, 95, 275 p. (Università degli Studi di Lecce, Dipartimento di filologia classica e medievale. Testi e studi, 8).

2573. MANZONI (Gian Enrico). Foroiuliensis poeta. Vita e poesia di Cornelio Gallo. Milano, Vita e pensiero, 95, VII-108 p. (Pubblicazioni dell'Università Cattolica del Sacro Cuore. Scienze filologiche e storia; Brescia, 7).

2574. [Valerius Martialis (Marcus)] MARTIAL. Epigrams V. Ed. by Peter HOWELL. Warminster, Aris & Phillips, 95, IV-172 p.

2575. MAZZINI (Innocenzo). Didone abbandonata: innamorata o pazza? La psichiatria antica, una chiave di lettura per il IV libro dell'Eneide. *Latomus*, 95, 54, 1, p. 92-105.

2576. MOLYVIATI-TOPTSIS (Urania). Sed falsa ad caelum mittunt insomnia manes (Aeneid 6.896). *American Journal of Philology*, 95, 116, 4, p. 639-652.

2577. MORGAN (Llewelyn). Underhand tactics: Milanion, Acontius and Gallus P. Qaṣr Ibrîm. *Latomus*, 95, 54, 1, p. 79-85.

2578. NENCI (Giuseppe). Onasus Segestanus in Girolamo, Ep. 40. *Rivista di Filologia e di Istruzione Classica*, 95, 123, 1, p. 90-94.

2579. NOSARTI (Lorenzo). Scafa l'investigatrice. Plaut. Most. 213. *Rivista di Filologia e di Istruzione Classica*, 95, 123, 1, p. 27-44.

2580. [Ovidius Naso (Publius)] P. OVIDII NASONIS. Epistularum ex Ponto liber II. A cura di Luigi GALASSO. Firenze, Le Monnier, 95, 489 p. (Biblioteca nazionale. Serie dei classici greci e latini. Testi con commento filologico, 2).

2581. [Ovidius Naso (Publius)] P. OVIDII NASONIS. Heroidum epistula IX: Deianira Herculi. A cura di Sergio CASALI. Firenze, Le Monnier, 95, 262 p. (Biblioteca nazionale. Serie dei classici greci e latini. Testi con commento filologico, 3).

2582. [Ovidius Naso (Publius)] P. OVIDII NASONIS. Tristia. Hrsg. v. John BARRIE HALL. Stuttgart u. Leipzig, Teubner, 95, XXX-263 p. (Bibliotheca Scriptorum Graecorum et Romanorum Teubneriana).

2583. [Ovidius Naso (Publius)] P. OVIDIUS NASO. Select epistles. Ed. by Peter E. KNOX. Cambridge, Cambridge University Press, 95, IX-329 p. (Cambridge Greek and Latin classics).

2584. PASCHALIS (Michael). Virgil's sixth eclogue and the Lament for Bion. *American Journal of Philology*, 95, 116, 4, p. 617-621.

2585. PELLEGRINO (Carlo). Per l'interpretazione di Properzio I, 21. *Latomus*, 95, 54, 3, p. 613-624.

2586. [Petronius Arbiter] PETRONII ARBITRI. Satyricon. A cura di Giancarlo GIARDINA e Rita CUCCIOLI MELLONI. Torino, Paravia, 95, XXI-193 p. (Corpus Scriptorum Latinorum Paravianum).

2587. [Petronius Arbiter] PETRONIUS. Satyricon reliquiae. Hrsg. v. Konrad MÜLLER. Stuttgart u. Leipzig, Teubner, 95, XLVIII-195 p. (Bibliotheca Scriptorum Graecorum et Romanorum Teubneriana).

2588. [Plinius Secundus] C. PLINII SECUNDI. Naturalis historiae libri XXXVII. Liber XVIII. Hrsg. v. Roderich KÖNIG. Zürich, Artemis & Winkler, 95, 406 p. (Sammlung Tusculum).

2589. PUTNAM (Michael C.J.). Ganymede and Virgilian ekphrasis. *American Journal of Philology*, 95, 116, 3, p. 419-440.

2590. ROSELLINI (Michela). Vicende umanistiche dei Carmina Duodecim Sapientium. *Rivista di Filologia e di Istruzione Classica*, 95, 123, 3, p. 320-346.

2591. ROSIVACH (Vincent J.). Seneca on the fear of poverty in the Epistulae Morales. *L'Antiquité Classique*, 95, 64, p. 91-98.

2592. SANTINI (Carlo). I frammenti di L. Cassio Emina. Introduzione, testo, traduzione e commento. Pisa, Edizioni ETS, 95, 225 p. (Testi e studi di cultura classica, 13).

2593. SCONOCCHIA (Sergio). Nuovi testimoni scriboniani tra tardo antico e medioevo. *Rivista di Filologia e di Istruzione Classica*, 95, 123, 3, p. 278-319.

2594. [Annaeus Seneca (Lucius)] SENECA. The tragedies. Vol. 2. Ed. by D.R. SLAVITT. Baltimore a. London, The Johns Hopkins University Press, 95, XLIV-261 p. (Complete Roman Draama in Translation).

2595. SHACKLETON BAILEY (D.R.). Onomasticon to Cicero's Letters. Stuttgart u. Leipzig, Teubner, XII-161 p.

2596. SOUBIRAN (Jean). Prosodie et métrique du Miles gloriosus de Plaute. Louvain et Paris, Peeters, 95, XI-311 p. (Bibliothèque d'études classiques).

2597. SUTHERLAND (Elizabeth H.). Audience manipulation and emotional experience in Horace's Pyrrha Ode. *American Journal of Philology*, 95, 116, 3, p. 441-452.

2598. [Aurelius Symmachus (Quintus)] SYMMAQUE. Lettres. Vol. 3. Livres VI–VIII. Ed. par Jean-Pierre CALLU. Paris, Belles Lettres, 95, XI-199 p. (Collection des universités de France).

2599. [Valerius Maximus] VALERE MAXIME. Faits et dits mémorables. Vol. 1. Livres I–III. Ed. par Robert COMBES. Paris, Belles Lettres, 95, 341 p. (Collection des universités de France).

2600. [Flavius Renatus Vegetius] P. FLAVII VEGETI RENATI. Epitoma rei militaris. Hrsg. v. Alf ÖNNERFORS. Stuttgart u. Leipzig, Teubner, 95, LXI-268 p. (Bibliotheca Scriptorum Graecorum et Romanorum Teubneriana).

2601. [Vitruvius Pollio] VITRUVE. De l'architecture. Vol. 7. Ed. par Bernard LIOU, Michel ZUINGHEDAU, Marie-Thérèse CAM. Paris, Belles Lettres, 95, LIV-195 p. (Collection des universités de France).

2602. WALSER (Gerold). Zu Caesars Tendenz in der geographischen Beschreibung Galliens. *Klio*, 95, 77, p. 217-223.

2603. WILLIAMS (Margaret H.). Tiberius and the disobliging grammarian of Rhodes. Suetonius, Vita Tiberi XXXII, 2 re-considered. *Latomus*, 95, 54, 3, p. 625-633.

2604. ZECCHINI (Giuseppe). Sallustio, Lucullo e i tre schiavi di C. Giulio Cesare (due nuovi frammenti delle Historiae?). *Latomus*, 95, 54, 3, p. 592-607.

§ 4. Allgemeine und politische Geschichte.

* 2605. Bulletin analytique d'histoire romaine. Vol. 4. 1995. Dir. par Hélène JOUFFROY. Strasbourg, Université de sciences humaines, Group de recherche d'histoire romaine, 95, 591 p.

2606. ABRAMZON (Mikhail G.). Monety kak sredstvo propagandy oficial'noj politiki Rimskoj imperii. (Propaganda and Roman imperial coin types). Moskva, RAN. In-t arkologii, 95, 654 p.

2607. AMIOTTI (Gabriella). Primi casi di relegazione e di deportazione insulare nel mondo romano. *In*: Coercizione e mobilità [Cf. n° 2620], p. 245-258.

2608. ANTONOVA (I. A), JAJLENKO (V. P.). Khersones, Severnoe Pričernomor'e i Markomannskie voiny po dannym khersonesskogo dekreta 174 goda novoj ery v čest'Tita Avrelija Kal'purniana Apollonoda. (Chersonesus, the Northern Black Sea coast and the Marcomannic wars according to the data of the Chersonesian decree of 174 A. D. in honour of Titus Aurelius Calpurnianus Apollonides). *Vestn. drev. Ist.*, 95, 4, p. 58-87.

2609. AUSTIN (N.J.E.), RANKOV (N.B.). Exploratio. Military and political intelligence in the Roman world from the second Punic war to the battle of Adrianople. London a. New York, Routledge, 95, XIII-292 p.

2610. BARNES (T.D.). Statistics and the conversion of the Roman aristocracy. *Journal of Roman Studies*, 95, 85, p. 135-147.

2611. BARTON (Tamsyn). Augustus and Capricorn: astrological polyvalency and imperial rhetoric. *Journal of Roman Studies*, 95, 85, p. 33-51.

2612. BONNEFOND-COUDRY (Marianne). Princeps et Sénat sous les Julio-Claudiens: des relations à inventer. *Mélanges de l'Ecole française de Rome. Antiquité*, 95, 107, 1, p. 225-254.

2613. BRINGMANN (K.). Die konstantinische Wende. Zum Verhältnis von politischer und religiöser Motivation. *Historische Zeitschrift*, 95, 260, 1, p. 21-48.

2614. BRIQUEL (Dominique). Le règne d'Ancus Marcius: un problème de comparaison indo-européenne. *Mélanges de l'Ecole française de Rome. Antiquité*, 95, 107, 1, p. 183-195.

2615. BRODERSEN (Kai). Terra cognita. Studien zur römischen Raumerfassung. Hildesheim u. Zürich u. New York, Olms, 95, 354 p. (Abb.). (Spoudasmata, 59).

2616. BROWN (Peter). Macht und Rhetorik in der Spätantike. Der Weg zu einem "christlichen Imperium". München, Deutscher Taschenbuch Verlag, 95, 205 p.

2617. BURGARELLA (F.). Pagani e cristiani tra IV e V secolo a Costantinopoli. *In*: Pagani e cristiani [Cf. n° 2655], p. 181-191.

2618. CHRIST (Karl). Caesar und die Geschichte. *In*: Historische Interpretationen [Cf. n° 2632], p. 9-22.

2619. Cicero öröksége. Tanulmányok a szónok-politikus születésének 2100. évfordulója alkalmából. = Hereditas Ciceroniana. Studia memoriae Ciceronis MMC annis ante nati dicata. Red. Ladislaus HAVAS. Debrecen, KLTE, 95, 304 p.

2620. Coercizione e mobilità umana nel mondo antico. A cura di Marta SORDI. Milano, Vita e pensiero, 95, VIII-277 p. (Contributi dell'Istituto di storia antica, 21) [Cf. n[os] <scelta> 2184, 2439, 2607, 2699.]

2621. Concordia e la X regio. Giornate di studio in onore di Dario Bertolini nel centenario della morte. Atti del convegno (Portogruaro, 22–23 ottobre 1994). A cura di Pierangela CROCE DA VILLA e Attilio MASTROCINQUE. Padova, Zielo, VII-329 p. (ill.). (Comune di Portogruaro. Soprintendenza archeologica del Veneto) [Cf. n[os] <scelta> 2828, 2842, 2918.]

2622. CONRAD (C.F.). A new chronology of the Sertorian war. *Athenaeum*, 95, 83, 1, p. 157-187.

2623. CRACCO RUGGINI (Lellia). Etablissements militaires, martyrs Bagaudes et traditions romaines dans la Vita Baboleni. *Historia*, 95, 44, 1, p. 100-119.

2624. DAL COVOLO (Enrico). I Severi precursori di Costantino? Per una messa a punto delle ricerche sui Severi e il cristianesimo. *Augustinianum*, 95, 35, 2, p. 605-622.

2625. DESNIER (Jean-Luc). Tenet nunc Parthenope. *Latomus*, 95, 54, 2, p. 298-304.

2626. DRUMMOND (Andrew). Law, politics and power. Sallust and the execution of the Catilinarian conspirators. Stuttgart, Steiner, 95, 136 p. (maps). (Historia Einzelschriften, 93).

2627. Frontières terrestres, frontières célestes dans l'antiquité. Ed. par Aline ROUSSELLE. Paris, Presses universitaires de Perpignan et de Boccard, 95, 457 p. (ill.). (Collection Etudes) [Cf. n[os] <sélection> 2640, 2666, 2877, 2965.]

2628. GOWERS (Emily). The anatomy of Rome from Capitol to Cloaca. *Journal of Roman Studies*, 95, 85, p. 23-32.

2629. GURVAL (Robert Alan). Actium and Augustus. The politics and emotions of Civil war. Ann Arbor, Michigan University Press, 95, XIV-337 p.

2630. HEATHER (Peter). The Huns and the end of the Roman Empire in Western Europe. *English Historical Review*, 95, 110, 435, p. 4-41.

2631. HEIL (Matthäus). Baebius und das erste Konsulat des Germanicus. *Klio*, 95, 77, p. 224-231.

2632. Historische Interpretationen. Gerold Walser zum 75. Geburtstag dargebracht von Freunden, Kollegen und Schülern. Hrsg. v. Marlis WEINMANN-WALSER. Stuttgart, Steiner, 95, 212 p. (Karten, Taf.). (Historia Einzelschriften, 100) [Cf. n^{os} <Auswahl> 2618, 2674.]

2633. Homme et animal dans l'antiquité romaine. Actes du Colloque de Nantes 1991. Tours, Centre de Recherches A. Piganiol, 95, 470 p. (ill.). (Caesarodunum Hors Série) [Cf. n^{os} <sélection> 2499, 2656, 2712, 2720, 2847, 2850.]

2634. INGLEBERT (Hervé). Les causes de l'existence de l'Empire romain selon les auteurs chrétiens des IIIe–Ve siècles. *Latomus*, 95, 54, 1, p. 18-50.

2635. KEAVENEY (Arthur). Sulla's Cilician command: the evidence of Apollinaris Sidonius. *Historia*, 95, 44, 1, p. 29-36.

2636. KETTENHOFEN (Erich). Tirdad und die Inschrift von Paikuli. Kritik der Quellen zur Geschichte Armeniens im späten 3. und frühen 4. Jahrhundert n. Chr. Wiesbaden, Reichert, 95, XXVIII-203 p.

2637. KOSTIAL (Michaela). Kriegerisches Rom? Zur Frage von Unvermeidbarkeit und Normalität militärischer Konflikte in der römischen Politik. Stuttgart, Steiner, 95, 192 p. (Palingenesia, 55).

2638. KREUTER (S.). Die Beziehungen zwischen Rom und Kreta vom Beginn des zweiten Jahrhunderts v. Chr. bis zur Einrichtung der römischen Provinz. *In*: Rom und der Griechische Osten [Cf. n° 2659], p. 135-150.

2639. Leaders and masses in the Roman world. Studies in honor of Zvi Yavetz. Ed. by Irad MALKIN. Leiden, New York a. Köln, Brill, 95, XVII-243 p. (Mnemosyne, 139).

2640. LEVEAU (Ph.). Le limes d'Afrique à l'épreuve de nouveaux concepts (apport du point de vue systématique à la notion de limite et de frontière). *In*: Frontières terrestres [Cf. n° 2627], p. 57-65.

2641. LIM (Richard). Religious disputation and social disorder in late antiquity. *Historia*, 95, 44, 2, p. 204-231.

2642. LINDSAY (Hugh). A fertile marriage: Agrippina and the chronology of her children by Germanicus. *Latomus*, 95, 54, 1, p. 3-17.

2643. LINKE (Bernhard). Von der Verwandtschaft zum Staat. Die Entstehung politischer Organisationsformen in der frührömischen Geschichte. Stuttgart, Steiner, 95, IX-214 p.

2644. LIZZI (Rita). Discordia in urbe: pagani e cristiani in rivolta. *In*: Pagani e cristiani [Cf. n° 2655], p. 115-140.

2645. LORETO (Luigi). La grande insurrezione civica contro Cartagine del 241–237 a.C. Una storia politica e militare. Rome, Ecole française de Rome, 95, X-238 p. (Collection de l'Ecole française de Rome, 211).

2646. LUSNIA (Susann S.). Julia Domna's coinage and Severan dynastic propaganda. *Latomus*, 95, 54, 1, p. 119-139.

2647. MALYŠEV (A. A.), MEDNIKOVA (M. B.). Naselenie Cemesskoj doliny v rimskoe vremja po dannym arkheologii i paleodemografii. (Tsemes valley population in the Roman times according to the archaeological and palaeodemographic data). *Ros. arkheol.*, 95, 4, p. 125-135.

2648. MARTÍNEZ-PINNA (Jorge). Tarquinio Prisco. Ensayo histórico sobre Roma arcaica. Madrid, Ediciones clásicas, 95, X-440 p.

2649. MASON (Hugh J.). The end of Antissa. *American Journal of Philology*, 95, 116, 3, p. 399-410.

2650. MASTINO (Attilio), RUGGERI (Paola). Claudia Augusti liberta Acte, la liberta amata da Nerone ad Olbia. *Latomus*, 95, 54, 3, p. 513-544.

2651. MINAMIKAWA (Takashi). Rōma-Kotei to Sono-Jidai: Genshuseiki Roma Teikoku Seijishi no Kenkyū. (Roman emperors and their ages: studies on the political history of the Principate period in the Roman empire). Tokyo, Sōbunsha, 95, 485 p.

2652. MOLEV (Evgenij A.). Vlastitel'Ponta: O Mitridate VI Evpatore. Monografija. (The sovereign of Pontos: about the Pontian king Mithridatos VI Eupatoros. Monograph). Nižny Novgorod, Izdatel'stvo Nižegorodskogo universiteta, Nižegorodskij gosudarstvennyj universitet imeni N. I. Lobačevskogo, 95, 144 p.

2653. MOLTHAGEN (Joachim). Die Lage der Christen im römischen Reich nach dem 1. Petrusbrief. Zum Problem einer domitianischen Verfolgung. *Historia*, 95, 44, 4, p. 422-458.

2654. NIPPEL (Wilfried). Public order in ancient Rome. Cambridge, Cambridge University Press, 95, X-163 p. (Key themes in ancient history).

2655. Pagani e cristiani da Giuliano l'Apostata al sacco di Roma. Atti del convegno internazionale di studi (Rende, 12–13 novembre 1993). A cura di Franca Ela CONSOLINO. Messina, Rubbettino, 95, 331 p. (Università degli Studi della Calabria, Dipartimento di filologia. Studi di filologia antica e moderna, 1) [Cf. n^{os} <scelta> 2617, 2644, 2762, 2798, 2820, 2837, 3011, 3040.]

2656. PEREZ (Christine). La symbolique de l'animal comme lieu et moyen d'expression de l'idéologie gentilice, personnellet et impérialiste de la Rome républicaine. *In*: Homme et animal [Cf. n° 2633], p. 235-282.

2657. PIATKOWSKI (A.). Nouvelles directions dans la politique culturelle du Principat après Tibère (37–193). *In*: Prinzipat und Kultur [Cf. n° 2810], p. 25-38.

2658. PRICKARTZ (Cherles). Philippe l'Arabe (244–249), civilis princeps. *L'Antiquité Classique*, 95, 64, p. 129-153.

2659. Rom und der Griechische Osten. Festschrift für Hatto Schmitt zum 65. Geburtstag dargebracht von

Schülern, Freunden und Münchener Kollegen. Hrsg. v. C. SCHUBERT und K. BRODERSEN. Stuttgart, Steiner, 95, 375 p. (Taf.) [Cf. n^{os} <Auswahl> 2486, 2638.]

2660. SCHLANGE-SCHÖNINGEN (Heinrich). Kaisertum und Bildungswesen im spätantiken Konstantinopel. Stuttgart, Steiner, 95, 189 p. (Karten). (Historia Einzelschriften, 94).

2661. SCHNURBEIN (Siegmar von). Vom Einfluß Roms auf die Germanen. Opladen, Westdeutscher Verlag, 95. 28 p. (Nordrhein-westfälische Akademie der Wissenschaften, Geisteswissenschaften, 331).

2662. SHAW (Brent D.). Josephus: Roman power and responses to it. *Athenaeum*, 95, 83, 2, p. 357-390.

2663. SMITH (Rowland). Julian's gods. Religion and philosophy in the thought and action of Julian the Apostate. London a. New York, Routledge, 95, XVII-300 p.

2664. SORICELLI (Gianluca). La Gallia transalpina tra la conquista e l'età cesariana. Como, Edizioni New Press, 95, 144 p. (Biblioteca di Athenaeum, 29).

2665. STEWART (Roberta). Catiline and the crisis of 63–60 B.C.: the Italian perspective. *Latomus*, 95, 54, 1, p. 62-78.

2666. THEBERT (Y.). Nature des frontières de l'empire romain: le cas germain. *In*: Frontières terrestres [Cf. n° 2627], p. 221-235.

2667. TOKMAKOV (V. N.). Struktura i boeve postroenie rimskogo vojska Rannej respubliki. (The structure and battle formation of the Roman troops of the Early republic). *Vestn. drev. Ist.*, 95, 4, p. 138-160.

2668. ULRICH (Jens). Barbarische Gesellschaftsstruktur und römische Außenpolitik zu Beginn der Völkerwanderung. Ein Versuch zu den Westgoten 365–377. Bonn, Habelt, 95, 229 p. (Habelts Dissertationsdrucke, Reihe alte Geschichte, 40).

2669. WELCH (Kathryn E.). Antony, Fulvia, and the ghost of Clodius in 47 B.C. *Greece & Rome*, 95, 42, 2, p. 182-201.

2670. WIEBE (Franz Josef). Kaiser Valens und die heidnische Opposition. Bonn, Habelt, 95, XII-407 p. (Antiquitas, Reihe 1. Abhandlungen zur Alten Geschichte, 44).

2671. WIEMER (Hans-Ulrich). Libanios und Julian. Studien zum Verhältnis von Rhetorik und Politik im vierten Jahrhundert n. Chr. München, C.H. Beck'sche Verlagsbuchhandlung, 95, XII-408 p. (Vestigia. Beiträge zur alten Geschichte, 46).

2672. WILLIAMS (Stephen). Theodosius. The empire at bay. New Haven a. London, Yale U.P., 95, 238 p.

2673. WIRTH (Gerhard). Rückschritte. Zur verlangten Dedition von 190 und den Schwierigkeiten des römisch-aetolischen Verhältnisses. Wien, Verlag der Österreichischen Akademie der Wissenschaften, 95, 43 p. (Sitzungsberichte der Österreichische Akademie der Wissenschaften. Philosophisch-historische Klasse, 627).

2674. ZAWADZKI (Tadeusz). Princeps necessarius magis quam bonus (HA A 37, 1). Quelques remarques sur la morale politique dans l'antiquité tardive. *In*: Historische Interpretationen [Cf. n° 2632], p. 203-212.

2675. ZIELIŃSKI (Tadeusz). Cesarstwo rzymskie. (Empire Romain). Ed. Grzegorz ŻUREK. Warszawa, Państw. Inst. Wydawn., 95, 477 p. (phot., fig.).

2676. ZIMMERMANN (Martin). Die restitutio honorum Galbas. *Historia*, 95, 44, 1, p. 56-82.

Cf. n°s 722, 1079, 1107, 1153, 1319

§ 5. Rechts- und Verfassungsgeschichte.

2677. AULIARD (C.). La spécificité des premiers contacts diplomatiques de Rome avec les monarchies hellénistiques avant la fin du IIIe siècle av. J.-C. *In*: Relations internationales [Cf. n° 1985], p. 433-452.

2678. BLEICKEN (Jochen). Cicero und die Ritter. Göttingen, Vandenhoeck & Ruprecht, 95, 128 p.

2679. BRIZZI (G.). La gerarchia militare in età repubblicana. *In*: Hiérarchie (Rangordnung) [Cf. n° 2691], p. 15-21.

2680. Collatio iuris romani. Etudes dédiées à Hans Ankum à l'occasion de son 65e anniversaire. Ed. par R. FEENSTRA, A.S. HARTKAMP, J.E. SPRUIT [et al.]. Amsterdam, Gieben, 95, 2 vol., XXVIII-710 p. (Studia Amstelodamensia ad epigraphicam, ius antiquum et papyrologicam pertinentia, 35).

2681. CORBIER (Mireille). Male power and legitimacy through women: the domus Augusta under the Julio-Claudians. *In*: Women in antiquity [Cf. n° 2748], p. 178-193.

2682. DAMON (Cynthia), MACKAY (Christopher S.). On the prosecution of C. Antonius in 76 B.C. *Historia*, 95, 44, 1, p. 37-55.

2683. DAVID (Jean-Michel). Le tribunal du préteur: contraintes symboliques et politiques sous la République et le début de l'Empire. *Klio*, 95, 77, p. 371-385.

2684. DELMAIRE (Roland). Les institutions du Bas-Empire romain de Constantin à Justinien. Vol. 1. Les institutions civiles palatines. Paris, Editions du Cerf et Editions du CNRS, 95, 202 p. (Initiations au christianisme ancien).

2685. Demokratie in Rom? Die Rolle des Volkes in der Politik der römischen Republik. Hrsg. v. Martin JEHNE. Stuttgart, Steiner, 95, VII-141 p. (Historia Einzelschriften, 96) [Cf. n^{os} <Auswahl> 2690, 2692, 2694.]

2686. DESIDERI (Paolo). Il trattamento del corpo dei suicidi. *In*: Mort au quotidien [Cf. n° 2728], p. 189-204.

2687. DOLATA (Jens). Promotio militaris – die Beförderung eines ritterlichen Offiziers. *Klio*, 95, 77, p. 255-265.

2688. ESTIEZ (O.). La translatio cadaveris, le transport des corps dans l'antiquité romaine. *In*: Mort au quotidien [Cf. n° 2728], p. 101-108.

2689. FERRARY (J.-L.). Ius fetiale et diplomatie. *In*: Relations internationales [Cf. n° 1985], p. 411-432.

2690. FLAIG (E.). Entscheidung und Konsens. Zu den Feldern der politischen Kommunikation zwischen Aristokratie und Plebs. *In*: Demokratie in Rom [Cf. n° 2685], p. 77-127.

2691. Hiérarchie (Rangordnung) de l'armée romaine sous le Haut-empire (La). Actes du congrès de Lyon (15–18 septembre 1994). Ed. par Yann LE BOHEC. Paris, de Boccard, 95, 480 p. (ill.). (Université de Lyon III, Centre d'études romaines et gallo-romaines) [Cf. n[os] <sélection> 2679, 2693.]

2692. HÖLKESKAMP (K.-J.). Oratoris maxima scaena: Reden vor dem Volk in der politischen Kultur der Republik. *In*: Demokratie in Rom [Cf. n° 2685], p. 11-49.

2693. ISAAC (B.). Hierarchy and command-structure in the Roman army. *In*: Hiérarchie (Rangordnung) [Cf. n° 2691], p. 23-31.

2694. JEHNE (Martin). Die Beeinflussung von Entscheidungen durch Bestechung: zur Funktion des ambitus in der römischen Republik. *In*: Demokratie in Rom [Cf. n° 2685], p. 51-76.

2695. KUNKEL (Wolfgang), WITTMANN (Roland). Staatsordnung und Staatspraxis der römischen Republik. Zweiter Abschnitt: Die Magistratur. München, Beck, 95, XVII-806 p. (Handbuch der Altertumswissenschaft, 10, 3, 2, 2; Rechtsgeschichte des Altertums, 2, 2).

2696. LEVI (Mario Attilio). Gentes e centurie dopo le XII Tavole. *Rivista di Filologia e di Istruzione Classica*, 95, 123, 2, p. 172-177.

2697. LINDERSKI (J.). Ambassadors go to Rome. *In*: Relations internationales [Cf. n° 1985], p. 453-478.

2698. MAGDELAIN (André). De la royauté et du droit de Romulus à Sabinus. Roma, L'Erma di Bretschneider, 95, 217 p. (Saggi di storia antica, 8).

2699. NEGRI (Giovanni). Aspetti giuridici delle deduzioni coattive nella fondazione di colonie latine. *In*: Coercizione e mobilità [Cf. n° 2620], p. 149-159.

2700. NOÈ (Eralda). Cedat forum castris: esercito e ascesa politica nella riflessione ciceroniana. *Athenaeum*, 95, 83, 1, p. 67-82.

2701. PINA POLO (Francisco). Procedures and functions of civil and military contiones in Rome. *Klio*, 95, 77, p. 203-216.

2702. *Vacat*.

2703. ROBINSON (O.F.). The criminal law of ancient Rome. Baltimore, The Johns Hopkins University Press, 95, X-212 p.

2704. ROSENSTEIN (Nathan). Sorting out the lot in Republican Rome. *American Journal of Philology*, 95, 116, 1, p. 43-75.

2705. SAAVEDRA GUERRERO (M.D.). La cooptatio patroni o el elogio de la virtus en el patronato colegial. *Athenaeum*, 95, 83, 2, p. 497-507.

2706. SCHOLTEN (Helga). Der Eunuch in Kaisernähe. Zur politischen und sozialen Bedeutung des praepositus sacri cubiculi im 4. und 5. Jahrhundert n. Chr. Frankfurt am Main u. Berlin u. Bern, Lang, 95, VII-291 p. (Abb.). (Prismata. Beiträge zur Altertumswissenschaft, 5).

2707. STERNBERG (Th.). Wesenszüge der römischen Rechtskultur im Prinzipat. *In*: Prinzipat und Kultur [Cf. n° 2810], p. 69-78.

2708. WITSCHEL (Christian). Die Entwicklung der Gesellschaft von Timgad im 2. bis 4. Jh. n. Chr. *Klio*, 95, 77, p. 266-331.

2709. ZUBAR' (Vitalij M.). Zur römischen Militärorganisation auf der Taurike in der zweiten Hälfte des 2. und am Anfang des 3. Jahrhunderts. *Historia*, 95, 44, 2, p. 192-203.

§ 6. Wirtschafts- und Sozialgeschichte.

2710. ALPERS (Michael). Das nachrepublikanische Finanzsystem. Fiscus und Fisci in der früheren Kaiserzeit. Berlin u. New York, de Gruyter, 95, VIII-349 p. (Untersuchungen zur antiken Literatur und Geschichte, 45).

2711. BEARD (M.). Re-reading (Vestal) virginity. *In*: Women in antiquity [Cf. n° 2748], p. 166-177.

2712. BODSON (Liliane). Points de vue romains sur l'animal domestique et la domestication. *In*: Homme et animal [Cf. n° 2633], p. 7-49.

2713. BURNETT (A.). The unification of the monetary system of the Roman West: accident or design? *In*: Italy in Europe [Cf. n° 2463], p. 313-320.

2714. CARLSEN (Jesper). Villici and Roman estate managers until AD 284. Roma, L'Erma di Bretschneider, 95, 208 p. (Analecta Romana Instituti danici Supplementum, 24).

2715. COARELLI (Filippo). Vino e ideologia nella Roma arcaica. *In*: In vino veritas [Cf. n° 1273], p. 196-213.

2716. CRACCO RUGGINI (Lellia). Les morts qui voyagent: le rapatriement, l'exil, la glorification. *In*: Mort au quotidien [Cf. n° 2728], p. 117-134.

2717. D'ARMS (J.H.). Heavy drinking and drunkenness in the Roman world: four questions for historians. *In*: In vino veritas [Cf. n° 1273], p. 304-317.

2718. ECK (Werner). Tituli honorarii, curriculum vitae und Selbstdarstellung in der höhen Kaiserzeit. *In*: Acta colloquii epigraphici Latini [Cf. n° 2509], p. 211-237.

2719. ERDKAMP (Paul). The corn supply of the Roman armies during the third and second centuries B.C. *Historia*, 95, 44, 2, p. 168-191.

2720. GOGUEY (Dominique). Les Romains et les animaux: regards sur les grands fauves, liens affectifs entre l'homme et l'animal. *In*: Homme et animal [Cf. n° 2633], p. 51-66.

2721. JACOBSEN (Gurli). Primitiver Austausch oder freier Markt? Untersuchungen zum Handel in den gallisch-germanischen Provinzen während der römischen Kaiserzeit. St. Katharinen, Scripta Mercaturae Verlag, 95, 237 p. (Pharos. Studien zur griechisch-römischen Antike, 5).

2722. KAJAVA (Mika). Roman female praenomina. Studies in the nomenclature of Roman women. Rome a. Helsinki, Institutum Romanum Finlandiae a. Helsinki University Press, 95, 289 p. (Acta Instituti Romani Finlandiae, 14).

2723. KORPELA (J.). Aromatarii, pharmacopolae, thurarii et ceteri. Zur Sozialgeschichte Roms. *In*: Ancient medicine [Cf. n° 2751], p. 101-118.

2724. KRAUSE (Jens-Uwe). Witwen und Waisen im römischen Reich. Vol. 3. Rechtliche und soziale Stellung von Waisen. Stuttgart, Steiner, 95, VII-316 p. (Heidelberger Althistorische Beiträge und Epigraphische Studien, 18).

2725. LOPEZ BARJA DE QUIROGA (Pedro). Freedmen social mobility in Roman Italy. *Historia*, 95, 44, 3, p. 326-348.

2726. MARTEM'JANOV (A. P.). Iz istorii zemledelija Frakii i Nižnej Mezii v pervykh vekakh novoj éry. (The Thracian and the Low Mesia agriculture of the first centuries A. D.). *Ros. Arkheol.*, 95, 1, p. 47-56.

2727. MASSA-PAIRAULT (Françoise-Hélène). Eques romanus – eques latinus (V^e–IVe siècle). *Mélanges de l'Ecole française de Rome. Antiquité*, 95, 107, 1, p. 33-70.

2728. Mort au quotidien dans le monde romain (La). Actes du colloque organisé par l'université de Paris IV (Paris-Sorbonne, 7–9 octobre 1993). Ed. par François HINARD et Marie-Françoise LAMBERT. Paris, de Boccard, 95, 259 p. (De l'archéologie à l'histoire) [Cf. n[os] <sélection> 2516, 2686, 2688, 2716, 2733, 2833, 2835.]

2729. NÄF (Beat). Senatorisches Standesbewußtsein in spätrömischer Zeit. Freiburg, Universitätsverlag Freiburg, Schweiz, 95, IX-344 p. (Paradosis, 40).

2730. OTT (Joachim). Die Beneficiarier. Untersuchungen zu ihrer Stellung innerhalb der Rangordnung des römischen Heeres und zu ihrer Funktion. Stuttgart, Steiner, 95, 246 p. (Karten). (Historia Einzelschriften, 92).

2731. PEDRONI (Luigi). Censo, moneta e rivoluzione della plebe. *Mélanges de l'Ecole française de Rome. Antiquité*, 95, 107, 1, p. 197-223.

2732. PLASS (P.). The game of death in ancient Rome. Arena sport and political suicide. Madison, The University of Wisconsin Press, 95, XIII-283 p. (Wisconsin Studies in Classics).

2733. PRESCENDI (F.). Il lutto dei padri nella cultura romana. *In*: Mort au quotidien [Cf. n° 2728], p. 147-154.

2734. RUGGINI (Lellia). Economia e societa nell'"Italia annonaria": rapporti fra agricoltura e commercio dal IV al VI secolo d. C. Bari, Edipuglia, 95, XXIV-750 p. (Munera, 2).

2735. SCHEIDEL (Walter). The most silent women of Greece and Rome: rural labour and women's life in the ancient world. Part I. *Greece & Rome*, 95, 42, 2, p. 202-217.

2736. SCHWARZ (Irene). Diaita. Ernährung der Griechen und Römer im klassischen Altertum. Eine altsprachlich-ernährungswissenschaftliche Studie. Innsbruck, Verlag des Instituts für Sprachwissenschaft der Universität Innsbruck, 95, 234 p. (Abb.). (Innsbrucker Beiträge zur Kulturwissenschaft, 94).

2737. Senectus. La vecchiaia nel mondo classico. A cura di Umberto MATTIOLI. Vol. 2. Roma. Bologna, Patron, 95, 392 p. (Edizioni e saggi universitari di filologia classica) [Contiene: MINARINI (A.). La palliata, p. 1-30. – R. CUCCIOLI, G. GIARDINA. I vari tipi di satira, p. 31-52. – E. RIGANTI. Virgilio e l'epica postclassica, p. 53-84. – M. BONVICINI. La lirica latina: Catullo e Orazio, p. 85-111. – M. BONVICINI. L'epigramma latino: Marziale, p. 113-136. – P. PINOTTI. Gli elegiaci. L'epica ovidiana, p. 137-182. – O. FUÀ. Da Cicerone a Seneca, p. 183-238. – P. SOVERINI, Senectus e res publica: la storiografia romana, p. 239-285. – D. DALLA, Le fonti giuridiche, p. 287-321. – P. DONATI GIACOMINI. La documentazione epigrafica, p. 323-337. – I. MAZZINI. La geriatria di epoca romana, p. 339-363. – R. TOSI. La tradizione proverbiale, p. 366-378].

2738. SHERBERG (Barbara). Das Vater-Sohn-Verhältnis in der griechischen und römischen Komödie. Tübingen, Narr, 95, 223 p. (ScriptOralia, 80).

2739. SZIDAT (Joachim). Staatlichkeit und Einzelschicksal in der Spätantike. *Historia*, 95, 44, 4, p. 481-495.

2740. TCHERNIA (A.). Le vin et l'honneur. *In*: In vino veritas [Cf. n° 1273], p. 297-303.

2741. THOMMEN (Lukas). Les lieux de la plèbe et de ses tribuns dans la Rome républicaine. *Klio*, 95, 77, p. 358-370.

2742. TONER (J.P.). Leisure and ancient Rome. Cambridge, Polity Press, 95, X-198 p. (pls.).

2743. VERA (Domenico). Dalla villa perfecta alla villa di Palladio: sulle trasformazioni del sistema agrario in Italia fra principato e dominato. *Athenaeum*, 95, 83, 1, p. 189-211. – IDEM. Dalla villa perfecta alla villa di Palladio: sulle trasformazioni del sistema agrario in Italia fra principato e dominato. Parte II. *Athenaeum*, 95, 83, 2, p. 331-356.

2744. Vicende e figure femminili in Grecia e a Roma. Atti del convegno (Pesaro, 28–30 aprile 1994). A cura di Renato RAFFAELLI. Ancona, Commissione per le pari opportunità tra uomo e donna della Regione Marche, 95, 541 p. (ill., tavole).

2745. VIRLOUVET (Catherine). Tessera frumentaria. Les procédures de distribution du blé public à Rome à la fin de la République et au début de l'Empire. Rome, Ecole française de Rome, 95, 424 p. (ill.). (Bibliothèque des écoles françaises d'Athènes et de Rome, 286).

2746. WIERSCHOWSKI (Lothar). Die regionale Mobilität in Gallien nach den Inschriften des 1. bis 3. Jahrhunderts n. Chr. Quantitative Studien zur Sozial- und Wirtschaftsgeschichte der westlichen Provinzen des römischen Reiches. Stuttgart, Steiner, 95, 400 p. (Karten). (Historia Einzelschriften, 91).

2747. WILMANNS (Juliane C.). Der Sanitätsdienst im römischen Reich. Eine sozialgeschichtliche Studie zum römischen Militärsanitätswesen nebst einer Prosopographie des Sanitätspersonals. Hildesheim u. Zürich u. New York, Olms-Weidmann, 95, X-341 p. (Abb.).

2748. Women in antiquity. New assessments. Ed. by Richard HAWLEY a. Barbara LEVICK. London a. New York, Routledge, 95, XIX-271 p. (ill., tab.) [Cf. n[os] <choice> 2681, 2711, 3175.]

Cf. n°s 2441, 2463

§ 7. Literatur-, Philosophie- und Wissenschaftsgeschichte.

2749. ADAMS (J. N.). Pelagonius and latin veterinary terminology in the Roman empire. Leiden a. New York a. Köln, Brill, 95, VIII-695 p. (Studies in ancient medicine, 11).

2750. ALONSO-NÚÑEZ (J. M.). Drei Autoren von Geschichtsabrissen der römischen Kaiserzeit: Florus, Iustinus, Orosius. *Latomus*, 95, 54, 2, p. 346-360.

2751. Ancient medicine in its socio-cultural context. Papers read at the congress held at Leiden University 13–15 april 1992. Ed. by Ph. VAN DER EIJK, H.F.J. HORSTMANSHOFF, P.H. SCHRIJVERS. Amsterdam a. Atlanta, Rodopi, 95, 2 vol., XXIII-319 p., 314 p. (Clio medica. The Wellcome Institute series in the history of medicine) [Cf. n[os] <choice> 2723, 2777, 2797, 2819, 2823.]

2752. ARENA (Antonella). Ovidio e l'ideologia augustea. I motivi delle Heroides ed il loro significato. *Latomus*, 95, 54, 4, p. 822-841.

2753. ARMISEN-MARCHETTI (Mireille). Sénèque et l'appropriation du temps. *Latomus*, 95, 54, 3, p. 546-567.

2754. BELL (Brenda M.). The contribution of Julius Caesar to the vocabulary of ethnography. *Latomus*, 95, 54, 4, p. 753-767.

2755. BINDER (G.). Öffentliche Autorenlesungen. Zur Kommunikation zwischen römischen Autoren und ihrem Publikum. *In*: Kommunikation durch Zeichen [Cf. n° 2787], p. 265-332.

2756. Biografia e autobiografia degli antichi e dei moderni. A cura di Italo GALLO e Luciano NICASTRI. Napoli, Edizioni scientifiche italiane, 95, 323 p. (Pubblicazioni dell'Università degli Studi di Salerno. Sezione Atti, convegni, miscellanee, 45) [Cf. n[os] <scelta> 2758, 2759, 2817.]

2757. BLANC (Bernard). Les Métamorphoses d'Ovide. Un vivier de légendes et de mythes. Paris, L'Harmattan, 95, 288 p.

2758. BRUGNOLI (Giorgio). Nascita e sviluppo della biografia romana: aspetti e problemi. *In*: Biografia e autobiografia [Cf. n° 2756], p. 79-107.

2759. CERESA GASTALDO (Aldo). Gerolamo e la biografia letteraria cristiana. *In*: Biografia e autobiografia [Cf. n° 2756], p. 137-147.

2760. CITRONI (M.). Poesia e lettori in Roma antica. Forme della comunicazione letteraria. Roma e Bari, Laterza, 95, XV-507 p.

2761. COLTON (Robert E.). Studies of imitation in some Latin authors. Amsterdam, Hakkert, 95, XI-396 p.

2762. CONSOLINO (Franca Ela). Pagani, cristiani e produzione letteraria latina da Giuliano l'Apostata al sacco di Roma. *In*: Pagani e cristiani [Cf. n° 2655], p. 311-328.

2763. CURCHIN (Leonard A.). Literacy in the Roman provinces: qualitative and quantitative data from central Spain. *American Journal of Philology*, 95, 116, 3, p. 461-476.

2764. DEHON (Pierre-Jacques). La Libye et la Scythie virgiliennes ou l'exotisme au service d'une idéologie. *L'Antiquité Classique*, 95, 64, p. 74-90.

2765. DEREMETZ (Alain). Le miroir des Muses. Poétiques de la réflexivité à Rome. Villeneuve d'Ascq Cédex, Presses universitaires du Septentrion, 95, 497 p. (Racines et modèles).

2766. DÖPP (S.). Zeitverhältnisse und Kultur im taciteischen Dialogus. *In*: Prinzipat und Kultur [Cf. n° 2810], p. 210-228.

2767. EBERSBACH (V.). Die humanitas des Petronius oder Diagnose eines gesellschaftlichen Verfalls. *In*: Prinzipat und Kultur [Cf. n° 2810], p. 192-202.

2768. Esegesi, parafrasi e compilazione in età tardoantica. Atti del Terzo Convegno dell'Associazione di Studi Tardoantichi. A cura di Claudio MORESCHINI. Napoli, D'Auria, 95, 406 p. (Collectanea, 9).

2769. FABRE-SERRIS (Jacqueline). Mythe et poèsie dans les Métamorphoses d'Ovide. Fonctions et significations de la mythologie dans la Rome augustéenne. Paris, Klincksieck, 95, 425 p. (Etudes et commentaires, 104).

2770. FEAR (A.T.). A Latin master from Roman Spain. *Greece & Rome*, 95, 42, 1, p. 57-69.

2771. FITZGERALD (William). Catullan provocation. Lyric poetry and the drama of position. Berkeley a. Los Angeles a. London, California University Press, 95, IX-310 p.

2772. FONTANELLA (Francesca). L'interpretazione ciceroniana del culto degli eroi e delle virtù: un contributo delle 'leges de religione' alla formazione morale della élite repubblicana. *Rivista storica italiana*, 95, 107, 1, p. 5-19.

2773. GALVAGNO (Rosalba). Le sacrifice du corps. Frayages du fantasme dans les Métamorphoses d'Ovid. Paris, Panormitis, 95, 153 p.

2774. GAZICH (Roberto). Exemplum ed esemplarità in Properzio. Milano, Vita e pensiero, 95, XV-341 p. (Pubblicazioni dell'Università Cattolica del Sacro Cuore; Scienze filologiche e storia, Brescia, 6).

2775. GLEASON (Maud W.). Making man. Sophist and self-presentation in ancient Rome. Princeton, Princeton U. P., 95, XXXII-193 p.

2776. GOLDBERG (S.M.). Epic in republican Rome. New York a. Oxford, Oxford University Press, 95, XII-196 p.

2777. GORDON (R.). The healing event in Graeco-Roman folk-medicine. *In*: Ancient medicine [Cf. n° 2751], p. 363-376.

2778. GREENE (Ellen). The Catullan ego: fragmentation and the erotic self. *American Journal of Philology*, 95, 116, 1, p. 77-93.

2779. GRIFFIN (J.). Regalis inter mensas laticemque Lycaeum: wine in Vergil and others. *In*: In vino veritas [Cf. n° 1273], p. 283-296.

2780. HERSHKOWITZ (Debra). Patterns of madness in Statius' Thebaid. *Journal of Roman Studies*, 95, 85, p. 52-64.

2781. Historiae Augustae colloquium Maceratense. A cura di Giorgio BONAMENTE e Gianfranco PACI. Bari, Edipuglia, 95, XIII-338 p. (Centro interuniversitario per gli studi sulla Historia Augusta Macerata-Perugia. Munera, 4).

2782. Homage to Horace. A bimillenary celebration. Ed. by S.J. HARRISON. Oxford, Clarendon Press, 95, X-380 p.

2783. HORSFALL (Nicholas). Rome without spectacles. *Greece & Rome*, 95, 42, 1, p. 49-56.

2784. JAMES (Sharon L.). Establishing Rome with the sword: condere in the Aeneid. *American Journal of Philology*, 95, 116, 4, p. 623-637.

2785. JANTZ (Martina). Das Fremdenbild in der Literatur der römischen Republik und der augusteischen Zeit. Vorstellungen und Sichtweisen am Beispiel von Hispanien und Gallien. Frankfurt am Main u. Berlin u. Bern, Lang, 95, X-295 p. (Europäische Hochschulschriften. Geschichte und ihre Hilfswissenschaften, 656).

2786. KNORR (Ortwin). The character of Bacchis in Terence's Heautontimorumenos. *American Journal of Philology*, 95, 116, 2, p. 221-235.

2787. Kommunikation durch Zeichen und Wort. Stätten und Formen der Kommunikation im Altertum. Vol. 4. Trier, Wissenschaftlicher Verlag Trier, 95, 370 p. (Bochumer Altertumswissenschaftliches Colloquium, 23) [Cf. n^os <Auswahl> 2755, 2816, 2821, 2824, 2825.]

2788. KRASSER (Helmut). Entwicklungen der römischen Lesekultur in trajanischer Zeit. *In*: Prinzipat und Kultur [Cf. n° 2810], p. 79-89. – IDEM. Horazische Denkfiguren. Theophilie und Theophanie als Medium der poetischen Selbstdarstellung des Odendichters. Göttingen, Vandenhoeck & Ruprecht, 95, 164 p. (Hypomnemata, 106).

2789. LANA (Italo). Q. Giulio Ilariano e il problema della storiografia latina cristiana nel IV secolo. *Rivista di Filologia e di Istruzione Classica*, 95, 123, 1, p. 73-89.

2790. LEFÈVRE (Eckard). Plautus und Philemon. Tübingen, Narr, 95, 179 p. (ScriptOralia, 73).

2791. Letture oraziane. A cura di Marcello GIGANTE e Salvatore CERASUOLO. Napoli, 95, 357 p. (Pubblicazioni del Dipartimento di Filologia classica dell'Università degli Studi di Napoli Federico II, 10).

2792. LYNE (R.O.A.M.). Horace: behind the public poetry. New Haven a. London, Yale University Press, 95, VIII-230 p.

2793. MACKENDRICK (P.). The Speeches of Cicero: context, law, rhetoric. London, Duckworth, 95, VIII-627 p. (maps).

2794. MAGGIULLI (Gigliola). Incipiant silvae cum primum surgere. Mondo vegetale e nomenclatura della flora di Virgilio. Roma, Gruppo editoriale internazionale, 95, 524 p. (Bibliotheca Athena, 5).

2795. MALEUVRE (J.-Y.). Les odes romaines d'Horace, ou un chef-d'oeuvre ignoré de la cacozelie (presque) invisible. *Revue Belge de Philologie et d'Histoire*, 95, 73, 1, p. 53-73.

2796. MAMBWINI KIVUILA-KIAKU (Joseph). Destin, liberté, nécessité chez Tacite ou la philosophie tacitéenne de la dignitas humana. *L'Antiquité Classique*, 95, 64, p. 111-127.

2797. MARASCO (Gabriele). L'introduction de la médecine grecque à Rome. Une dissension politique et idéologique à Rome. *In*: Ancient medicine [Cf. n° 2751], p. 35-48.

2798. MARCONE (Arnaldo). Il De civitate Dei e il suo pubblico. *In*: Pagani e cristiani [Cf. n° 2655], p. 267-277.

2799. MEULDER (Marcel). Bons et mauvais généraux chez Tacite. *Revue Belge de Philologie et d'Histoire*, 95, 73, 1, p. 75-91.

2800. MILES (Gary B.). Livy. Reconstructing early Rome. Ithaca a. London, Cornell University Press, 95, XI-251 p.

2801. Mistero nel racconto classico (Il). Atti del convegno del XIII Mystfestival (Cattolica, 29 giugno 1992). A cura di Renato RAFFAELLI. Urbino, Quattro Venti, 95, 69 p. (Letteratura e antropologia, 5).

2802. MÜNSTERMANN (Hans). Apuleius. Metamorphosen literarischer Vorlagen. Untersuchung dreier Episoden des Romans unter Berücksichtigung der Philosophie und Theologie des Apuleius. Stuttgart u. Leipzig, Teubner, 95, 226 p. (Beiträge zur Altertumskunde, 69).

2803. NÄF (Beat). Genealogia jako jedna z podstawowych form świadomości historycznej w okresie późnoantycznym i jej stosunek do historii. (Généalogie en tant qu'une des formes de base de la conscience historique dans la période de l'antiquité tardive et son rapport à l'histoire). Poznań, [s. n.], 95, 23 p. (Uniw. im. Adama Mickiewicza w Poznaniu. Inst Hist. Xenia Posnaniensia, 8).

2804. NEWLANDS (Carole E.). Playing with time. Ovid and the Fasti. Ithaca a. London, Cornell University Press, 95, XII-254 p. (Cornell studies in classical philology, 55).

2805. ONIGA (Renato). Sallustio e l'etnografia. Pisa, Giardini, 95, 147 p. (Biblioteca di Materiali e discussioni per l'analisi dei testi classici, 12).

2806. [OVIDE]. P. Ouidii Nasonis Tristia. Ed. by John Barrie HALL. Stuttgart a. Leipzig, Teubner, 95, XXX-263 p. (Bibliotheca scriptorum graecorum et romanorum Teubneriana).

2807. PANAYOTAKIS (C.). Theatrum Arbitri. Theatrical elements in the Satyrica of Petronius. Leiden a. New York a. Köln, Brill, 95, XXV-225 p. (Mnemosyne Suppl., 146).

2808. PASCHOUD (François). Mendacii splendor: formes d'entrée en matière et protestations de véridicité dans la littérature de fiction. *Latomus*, 95, 54, 2, p. 262-278.

2809. Plautus und die Tradition des Stegreifspiels. Festgabe für Eckard Lefèvre zum 60. Geburtstag. Hrsg. v. Lore BENZ, Ekkehard STÄRK, Gregor VOGT-SPIRA. Tübingen, Narr, 95, XI-270 p. (ScriptOralia, 75).

2810. Prinzipat und Kultur im 1. und 2. Jahrhundert. Wissenschaftliche Tagung der Friedrich-Schiller-Universität Jena und der Iwane-Dshawachischwili-Universität Tbilissi (27–30 Oktober 1992 in Jena). Hrsg. v. Barbara KÜHNERT, Volker RIEDEL und Rismag GORDESIANI. Bonn, Habelt, 95, X-332 p. (Taf.) [Cf. n[os] <Auswahl> 2657, 2707, 2766, 2767, 2788, 2811, 2818, 2829, 2887.]

2811. RIEDEL (Volker). Von Phaedrus bis Juvenal. Grundzüge, historischer Stellenwert und aktuelle Bedeutung der römischen Literatur im nachaugusteischen Jahrhundert. *In*: Prinzipat und Kultur [Cf. n° 2810], p. 1-17.

2812. RIGGSBY (Andrew M.). Pliny on Cicero and oratory: self-fashioning in the public eye. *American Journal of Philology*, 95, 116, 1, p. 123-135.

2813. Roman comedy, augustan poetry, historiography. Papers of the Leeds international Latin seminar 8, 1995. Leeds, Cairns, 95, X-307 p. (Arca. Classical and medieval texts, papers and monographs, 33).

2814. RULLI (Gabriella). Significato ideologico del mito in Properzio: un approccio metodologico. *Latomus*, 95, 54, 2, p. 305-314.

2815. RÜPKE (Jörg). Fasti: Quellen oder Produkte römischer Geschichtsschreibung? *Klio*, 95, 77, p. 184-202.

2816. STABRYŁA (S.). Die Funktion literarischer Gattungen bei griechischen und römischen Autoren. *In*: Kommunikation durch Zeichen [Cf. n° 2787], p. 207-227.

2817. STOK (F.). Ritratti fisiognomici in Svetonio. *In*: Biografia e autobiografia [Cf. n° 2756], p. 109-135.

2818. SZELEST (H.). Martials Ansichten über frühere und zeitgenössische Dichtung. *In*: Prinzipat und Kultur [Cf. n° 2810], p. 203-209.

2819. VAN MINNEN (P.). Medical care in late antiquity. *In*: Ancient medicine [Cf. n° 2751], p. 153-169.

2820. VINCHESI (M.A.). Il rapporto tra cristianesimo e cultura pagana in Paolino di Nola (con un'analisi tematica del propemptikon per Niceta, carm. 17). *In*: Pagani e cristiani [Cf. n° 2655], p. 299-310.

2821. VÖSSING (K.). Non scholae sed vitae – der Streit um die Deklamationen und ihre Funktion als Kommunikationstraining. *In*: Kommunikation durch Zeichen [Cf. n° 2787], p. 91-136.

2822. WHEELER (Stephen M.). Imago mundi: another view of the creation in Ovid's Metamorphoses. *American Journal of Philology*, 95, 116, 1, p. 95-121.

2823. WILMANNS (Juliane C.). Der Arzt in der römischen Armee der frühen und hohen Kaiserzeit. *In*: Ancient medicine [Cf. n° 2751], p. 171-187.

2824. WOS (K.). Die Funktionen der römischen literarischen Kommunikation. *In*: Kommunikation durch Zeichen [Cf. n° 2787], p. 247-264.

2825. WÜLFING (P.). Antike und moderne Redegestik. Eine frühe Theorie der Körpersprache bei Quintilian. *In*: Kommunikation durch Zeichen [Cf. n° 2787], p. 71-90.

Cf. n[os] *1548, 2531-2604*

§ 8. Religion und Mythologie.

2826. Aufstieg und Niedergang der römischen Welt. Geschichte und Kultur Roms im Spiegel der neueren Forschung. II. Principat. Vol. 26. Religion. Hrsg. v. Wolfgang HAASE. Berlin u. New York, de Gruyter, 95,

XIV-1120 p. [Cf. n^{os} <Auswahl> 2951, 2956, 2957, 2970, 2992, 3012, 3023, 3024, 3030.]

2827. BLAIVE (Fréderic). Le rituel romain des Robigalia et le sacrifice du chien dans le monde indo-européen. *Latomus*, 95, 54, 2, p. 279-289.

2828. BRIQUEL (Dominique). Il mito degli Iperborei: dal caput Adriae a Roma. *In*: Concordia [Cf. n° 2621], p. 189-195.

2829. CANCIK (H.)., CANCIK-LINDEMEIER (H.). Universalistische Tendenzen in der römischen Religion des 1. und 2. Jahrhunderts. *In*: Prinzipat und Kultur [Cf. n° 2810], p. 100-102.

2830. CAPDEVILLE (Gérard). Volcanus. Recherches comparatistes sur les origines du culte de Vulcain. Rome, Ecole française de Rome, 521 p. (Bibliothèque des écoles françaises d'Athènes et de Rome, 288).

2831. DE CAZANOVE (Olivier). Rituels romains dans les vignobles. *In*: In vino veritas [Cf. n° 1273], p. 214-223.

2832. DEMARIS (Richard E.). Demeter in Roman Corinth. Local development in a Mediterranean religion. *Numen*, 95, 42, 2, p. 105-118.

2833. DESCHAMPS (L.). Rites funéraires de la Rome républicaine. *In*: Mort au quotidien [Cf. n° 2728], p. 171-180.

2834. Discours religieux dans l'antiquité. Actes du colloque (Besançon, 27–28 janvier 1995). Ed. par Marie-Madeleine MACTOUX et Evelyne GENY. Besançon, Presses de l'Université de Besançon, 95, 324 p. (ill.). (Annales littéraires de l'Université de Besançon. Centre d'Histoire Ancienne, 150) [Cf. n^{os} <sélection> 2855, 2979.]

2835. DUCOS (M.). Le tombeau, locus religiosus. *In*: Mort au quotidien [Cf. n° 2728], p. 135-144.

2836. Estudios de religión y mito en Grecia y Roma. X Jornadas de filología clásica de Castilla y León. Ed. por Jesús-María NIETO IBAÑEZ. León, Universidad de León, 95, 294 p. (ill.).

2837. FRASCHETTI (Augusto). Trent'anni dopo. Il conflitto fra paganesimo e cristianesimo nel secolo IV. *In*: Pagani e cristiani [Cf. n° 2655], p. 5-14.

2838. KAZAKOV (M. M.). Rim na puti ot jazyčestva k khristianstvu. Altar'pobedy. (Rome on the way from Paganism to Christianity: the altar of victory). *Vestn. drev. ist.*, 95,4, p. 161- 174.

2839. LE GLAY (Marcel). L'inscription latine comme document d'histoire religieuse. *In*: Acta colloquii epigraphici Latini [Cf. n° 2509], p. 263-267.

2840. LIOU-GILLE (Bernadette). Une loi de Numa: ne supra genua tollito. *Euphrosyne*, 95, 23, p. 27-42.

2841. MAIER (Harry O.). The topography of heresy and dissent in late-fourth-century Rome. *Historia*, 95, 44, 2, p. 232-249.

2842. MASTROCINQUE (Attilio). Aspetti della religione pagana a Concordia e nell'alto Adriatico. *In*: Concordia [Cf. n° 2621], p. 269-287.

2843. MONTERO (Santiago). La interpretación romana de las prácticas hepatoscópicas extranjeras. *Gerión*, 95, 13, p. 155-167.

2844. MORESCHINI (Claudio). Il demone nella cultura pagana dell'età imperiale. *In*: Demonio [Cf. n° 2976], p. 75-110.

2845. PAILLER (Jean-Marie). Bacchus: figures et pouvoirs. Paris, Belles Lettres, 95, 230 p. (ill., pl.).

2846. POPESCU (Emilian). Christianitas Daco-Romana. Florilegium studiorum. Bucureşti, Editura Academiei Române, 95, 496 p.

2847. POPLIN (François). La chasse au sanglier et la vertu virile. *In*: Homme et animal [Cf. n° 2633], p. 445-467.

2848. POSSENTI (Livia Dina). Le divinità comites. *Annali della Facoltà di Lettere e Filosofia, Università di Macerata*, 95, 28, p. 141-170.

2849. PURCELL (Nicholas). Literate games: Roman urban society and the game of Alea. *Past and Present*, 95, 147, p. 3-37.

2850. RENARD (Etienne). Bovidés et rites agraires à l'époque gallo-romaine. *In*: Homme et animal [Cf. n° 2633], p. 435-444.

2851. RIVES (J.). Human sacrifice among pagans and christians. *Journal of Roman Studies*, 95, 85, p. 65-85.

2852. RIVES (James R.). Religion and authority in Roman Carthage from Augustus to Constantine. Oxford, Clarendon Press, 95, XIII-334 p. (maps).

2853. SCHEID (John). Les espaces cultuels et leur interprétation. *Klio*, 95, 77, p. 424-432.

2854. SEGARRA CRESPO (Diana). Pietas y simulación en la ofrenda privada romana. *Espacio, tiempo y forma. Historia*, 95, 8, p. 127-158.

2855. SMADJA (Elisabeth). Statue, image et culte de l'empereur en Afrique. *In*: Discours religieux dans l'antiquité [Cf. n° 2834], p. 279-294.

2856. TENNANT (P.M.W.). Reflections on a mirror: possible evidence for the early origin of the canonical version of the Roman foundation legend. *Akroterion*, 95, 40, 2, p. 64-79.

2857. WISEMAN (T. P.). Remus. A Roman myth. Cambridge, Cambridge University Press, 95, XV-243 p. – IDEM. The god of the Lupercal. *Journal of Roman Studies*, 95, 85, p. 1-22.

2858. ZUBAR' (V. M.). Kul't rimskikh imperatov v Severnom Pričernomor'e. (The Roman emperors cult in the Northern Pontic area). *Ros. Arkheol.*, 95,1, p. 57-63.

Cf. n°s 1393, 1436, 1478, 1800, 1893

§ 9. Archäologie und Kunstgeschichte.

2859. Antiken Sarkophagreliefs (Die). Vol. 5. II. Die stadt-römischen Eroten-Sarkophage. Hrsg. v. Bernhard ANDREAE u. Guntram KOCH. Berlin, Mann, 95, 112 p. (Taf.). (Deutsches Archäologisches Institut).

2860. BAZANT (Jan). Roman portraiture. A history of its history. Praha, Koniasch Latin, 95, 209 p. (ill).

2861. BEZECZKY (Tamás). Amphorae and amphora stamps from the Laecanius workshop. *Journal of Roman Archaeology*, 95, 8, p. 41-64.

2862. BIERING (Ralf). Die Odysseefresken vom Esquilin. München, Biering & Brinkmann, 95, 208 p. (Abb., Taf.).

2863. BLÁZQUEZ (J.M.). Arte provincial de la Hispania romana. Estelas de Lara de los Infantes (Burgos). *Latomus*, 95, 54, 4, p. 768-783.

2864. BONIFAY (Michel), PIERI (Dominique). Amphores du Ve au VIIe s. à Marseille: nouvelles données sur la typologie et le contenu. *Journal of Roman Archaeology*, 95, 8, p. 94-120.

2865. BONNEFOND-COUDRY (Marianne). Pouvoir des mots, pouvoir des images: Octave et la curia Iulia. *Klio*, 95, 77, p. 386-404.

2866. BRAGANTINI (Irene). La raffigurazione di Caronte in età romana. *In*: Caronte [Cf. n° 2452], p. 395-413.

2867. CASTELLVI (Georges), NOLLA (Josep M.), RODÀ (Isabel). La identificación de los trofeos de Pompeyo en el Pirineo. *Journal of Roman Archaeology*, 95, 8, p. 5-18.

2868. CASTRIOTA (David). The Ara pacis augustae and the imagery of abundance in later Greek and early Roman imperial art. Princeton, Princeton University Press, 95, XVIII-253 p. (ill.).

2869. CORBIER (Mireille). L'écriture dans l'image. *In*: Acta colloquii epigraphici Latini [Cf. n° 2509], p. 113-161.

2870. D'AMBRA (Eve). Mourning and the making of ancestors in the Testamentum relief. *American Journal of Archaeology*, 95, 99, 4, p. 667-681.

2871. DONDERER (Michael). Zu den Häusern des Kaisers Augustus. *Mélanges de l'Ecole française de Rome. Antiquité*, 95, 107, 2, p. 621-660.

2872. DOWNEY (Susan B.). Architectural terracottas from the Regia. Ann Arbor, Michigan University Press, 95, XVI-109 p. (ill., maps). (Papers and monographs of the American Academy in Rome, 30).

2873. ELSNER (Jás). Art and the roman viewer. The transformation of art from the pagan world to christianity. Cambridge, Cambridge University Press, 95, XXVI-375 p. (ill., tab). (Cambridge studies in new art history and criticism).

2874. FARRINGTON (Andrew). The Roman baths of Lycia. An architectural study. Oxford, Oxbow books, 95, XXV-176 p. (ill., maps).

2875. FRANCHETTI PARDO (Vittorio). Costantinopoli. La trasformazione di Bisanzio nella capitale imperiale. *In*: Metamorfosi della città [Cf. n° 1287], p. 3-72.

2876. FREED (Joann). The late series of Tunisian cylindrical amphoras at Carthage. *Journal of Roman Archaeology*, 95, 8, p. 155-191.

2877. GALINIER (M.). La colonne trajane: images et imaginaire de la frontière. *In*: Frontières terrestres [Cf. n° 2627], p. 273-288.

2878. GALLISTL (Bernhard). Maske und Spiegel. Zur Maskenszene des Pompejaner Mysterienfrieses. Hildesheim u. Zürich u. New York, Olms, 95, VIII-73 p. (Abb.). (Studien zur Kunstgeschichte, 101).

2879. GERMÁN RODRÍGUEZ MARTÍN (Francisco). La villa romana de Torre Águila (Barbaño-Montijo, Badajoz). *Journal of Roman Archaeology*, 95, 8, p. 313-316.

2880. GONZENBACH (Victorine von). Die römischen Terracotten in der Schweiz. Untersuchungen zu Zeitstellung, Typologie und Ursprung der mittelgallischen Tonstatuetten. Vol. 1. Tübingen u. Basel, Francke, 95, VIII-492 p. (Abb., Taf.). (Handbuch der Schweiz zur Römer- und Merowingerzeit).

2881. GRANT (Michael). Art in the Roman empire. London a. New York, Routledge, 95, XXII-146 p. (ill.).

2882. GUILLAUME-COIRIER (Germaine). Images du coronarius dans la littérature et l'art de Rome. *Mélanges de l'Ecole française de Rome. Antiquité*, 95, 107, 2, p. 1093-1151.

2883. Hellenistic and Roman pottery in the eastern mediterranean. Advances in scientific studies. Acts of the II Nieborów pottery workshop. Ed. by Henryk MEYZA a. Jolanta MŁYNARCZYK. Warsaw, Polish Academy of sciences, 95, X-497 p. (ill.).

2884. HESNARD (A.). Les ports antiques de Marseille, Place Jules-Verne. *Journal of Roman Archaeology*, 95, 8, p. 65-78.

2885. JACOBELLI (Luciana). Le pitture erotiche delle Terme Suburbane di Pompei. Roma, L'Erma di Bretschneider, 95, 133 p. (ill., tavole). (Ministero per i beni culturali e ambientali. Soprintendenza archeologica di Pompei. Monografie, 10).

2886. JASHEMSKI (Wilhelmina F.). Roman gardens in Tunisia: preliminary excavations in the House of Bacchus and Ariadne and in the east temple at Thuburbo Maius. *American Journal of Archaeology*, 95, 99, 4, p. 559-576 [with an appendix by J.E. FOSS, R.J. LEWIS, M.E. TIMPSON, and S.Y. LEE].

2887. KLUWE (E.). Künstlerischer Werkstattbetrieb und Kunsthandel in der römischen Kaiserzeit. *In*: Prinzipat und Kultur [Cf. n° 2810], p. 293-305.

9. ARCHÄOLOGIE UND KUNSTGESCHICHTE

2888. KOORTBOJIAN (Michael). Myth, meaning, and memory on Roman sarcophagi. Berkeley a. Los Angeles a. London, California University Press, 95, XX-172 p. (ill.).

2889. KRIERE (Karl R.). Sieg und Niederlage. Untersuchungen physiognomischer und mimischer Phänomene in Kampfdarstellungen der römischen Plastik. Wien, Phoibos, 95, 274 p. (Taf.). (Wiener Forschungen zur Archäologie, 1).

2890. KUTTNER (Ann L.). Dynasty and empire in the age of Augustus. The case of the Boscoreale cups. Berkeley a. Los Angeles a. Oxford, California University Press, 95, XIV-387 p. (ill.).

2891. LAFON (Xavier). Dehors ou dedans? Le vestibulum dans les domus aristocratiques à la fin de la République et au début de l'Empire. *Klio*, 95, 77, p. 405-423.

2892. LING (R.). The decoration of Roman triclinia. *In*: In vino veritas [Cf. n° 1273], p. 239-251.

2893. LUND (John). A synagogue at Carthage? Menorah-lamps from the Danish excavations. *Journal of Roman Archaeology*, 95, 8, p. 245-262.

2894. MANNELL (Joanne). The monopteroi in the west precint of Diocletian's palace at Split. *Journal of Roman Archaeology*, 95, 8, p. 235-244.

2895. MATTINGLY (David J.), HITCHNER (R.B.). Roman Africa: an archaeological review. *Journal of Roman Studies*, 95, 85, p. 165-213.

2896. MIKOCKI (Tomasz). Sub specie deae. Les impératrices et princesses romaines assimilées à des déesses. Etude iconologique. Roma, L'Erma di Bretschneider, 95, 311 p. (tab.)

2897. MORAWIECKI (Lesław). Monety rzymskie a źródła pisane. (Pièces de monnaie romains et les sources écrites). *Przegląd Historyczny*, 95, 85, 3, p. 207-220. (phot.). [Eng. Summary].

2898. PICCOTTINI (Gernot), DOLENZ (Heimo). Die Ausgrabungen in Virunum 1993 und 1994 – ein Vorbericht. *Carinthia I*, 95, 185, p. 163-173 (ill., Pläne).

2899. PICCOTTINI (Gernot). Die Ausgrabungen auf dem Magdalensberg 1993 und 1994 – ein Vorbericht. *Carinthia I*, 95, 185, p. 145-161 p. (ill., Pläne).

2900. PLOUG (Gunhild). Catalogue of the Palmyrene sculptures. Ed. by Anne Marie NIELSEN. København, Ny Carlberg Glyptotek, 95, 269 p.

2901. Recent work on villas around Ampurias, Gerona, Iluro, and Barcelona (NE Spain). *Journal of Roman Archaeology*, 95, 8, p. 271-312.

2902. RIBERA I LACOMBA (Albert). La primera evidencia arqueológica de la destrucción de Valentia por Pompeyo. *Journal of Roman Archaeology*, 95, 8, p. 19-40 [con analisis antropológico por Matías CALVO GALVEZ].

2903. RITTER (Stefan). Hercules in der römischen Kunst von den Anfängen bis August. Heidelberg, Verlag Archäologie und Geschichte, 95, 248 p. (Taf.). (Archäologie und Geschichte, 5).

2904. Roman and Byzantine Near East (The): some recent archaeological research. Ann Arbor, Humphrey, 95, 346 p. (ill.). (Journal of Roman Archaeology, Supplement 14).

2905. SCATOZZA-HÖRICHT (Lucia A.). Frammenti di lastre Campana da Cuma. *Latomus*, 95, 54, 4, p. 793-811.

2906. SCHNEIDER (Katja). Villa und Natur. Eine Studie zur römischen Oberschichtkultur im letzten vor- und ersten nachchristlichen Jahrhundert. München, tuduv-Verlagsgesellschaft, 95, 167 p. (Taf.). (Quellen und Forschungen zur antiken Welt, 18).

2907. SCHÖRNER (Günther). Römische Rankenfriese. Untersuchungen zur Baudekoration der späten Republik und der frühen und mittleren Kaiserzeit im Westen des Imperium Romanum. Mainz, von Zabern, 95, XIII-198 p. (Taf.). (Beiträge zur Erschließung hellenistischer und kaiserzeitlichen Skulptur und Architektur, 15).

2908. SPEIDEL (Michael P.). Die Garde des Maximus auf der Theodosiussäule. *Istanbuler Mitteilungen*, 95, 45, p. 131-136.

2909. STERNINI (Mara). La Fenice di sabbia. Storia e tecnologia del vetro antico. Bari, Edipuglia, 95, 217 p. (ill.). (Bibliotheca archaeologica, 2).

2910. STEVENS (Susan T.). A late-Roman urban population in a cemetery of Vandalic date at Carthage. *Journal of Roman Archaeology*, 95, 8, p. 263-270.

2911. STURGEON (Mary C.). The Corinth Amazon: formation of a Roman classical sculpture. *American Journal of Archaeology*, 95, 99, 3, p. 483-505.

2912. TANSINI (Raffaella). I ritratti di Agrippina maggiore. Roma, L'Erma di Bretschneider, 95, 137 p. (ill.).

2913. THOMAS (Renate). Die Dekorationssysteme der römischen Wandmalerei von augusteischer bis in trajanische Zeit. Mainz, von Zabern, 95, 352 p. (Abb., Taf.).

2914. TOUCHETTE (Lori-Ann). The dancing Maenad relief. Continuity and change in Roman copies. London, University of London, 95, X-119 p. (tab.). (Bulletin of the Institute of classical studies, Suppl. 62).

2915. TUSA (Vincenzo). I sarcofagi romani in Sicilia, Roma, L'Erma di Bretschneider, 95, XVI-119 p. (tavole). (Bibliotheca archaeologica, 14).

2916. VAQUERIZO GIL (D.), CARRILLO DIAZ-PINES (J.R.). The Roman villa of El Ruedo (Almedinilla, Cordoba). *Journal of Roman Archaeology*, 95, 8, p. 121-154.

2917. VARNER (Eric R.). Domitia Longina and the politics of portraiture. *American Journal of Archaeology*, 95, 99, 2, p. 187-206.

2918. VERZÁR-BASS (M.). La cultura artistica della X regio. *In*: Concordia [Cf. n° 2621], p. 127-148.

2919. WATTEL-DE CROIZANT (Odile). Les mosaïques représentant le mythe d'Europe (Ier–V^{er} siècles). Evolution et interprétation des modèles grecs en milieu romain. Paris, de Boccard, 95, 313 p. (tab.). (De l'archéologie à l'histoire).

2920. WOOD (Susan). Diva Drusilla Panthea and the sisters of Caligula. *American Journal of Archaeology*, 95, 99, 3, p. 457-482.

2921. ZANKER (Paul). Pompeji. Stadtbild und Wohngeschmack. Mainz, von Zabern, 95, 238 p. (Abb.). (Kulturgeschichte der antiken Welt, 61).

G

GESCHICHTE DER ALTEN KIRCHE BIS AUF GREGOR DEN GROSSEN

§ 1. Quellen. 2922-2945. – § 2. Allgemeines. 2946-2959. – § 3. Spezialarbeiten. 2960-3031. – § 4. Hagiographie. 3032-3044.

§ 1. Quellen

* 2922. KADEL (Andrew). Matrology: a bibliography of writings by Christian women from the first to the fifteenth centuries. New York, Continuum, 95, 191 p.

2923. CAMPLANI (Alberto). Epifanio (Ancoratus) e Gregorio di Nazianzo (Epistulae) in copto: identificazioni e status quaestionis. *Augustinianum*, 95, 35, 1, p. 327-347.

2924. Corpus orationum. Vol. 5. I–O: Orationes 3029–3699. Vol. 6. O–P: Orationes 3700–4334. Ed. par Bertrand COPPIETERS'T WALLANT [et al.]. Turnhout, Brepols, 95, 2 vol., LXIV-317 p., LXIV-283 p. (Corpus Christianorum. Series Latina, 160D–160E).

2925. CUSCITO (Giuseppe). Il Coemeterium Romanum a S. Calimero. Prolegomena ad ICI-Mediolanum. *Augustinianum*, 95, 35, 2, p. 779-786.

2926. FELLE (Antonio Enrico). Loci scritturistici nella produzione epigrafica romana. *Vetera Christianorum*, 95, 32, 1, p. 61-89.

2927. FOLLIET (Georges). Un témoin latin d'un florilège ascétique De discretione virtutum. *Augustinianum*, 95, 35, 1, p. 371-390.

2928. GRÉGOIRE DE NAZIANZE. Discours 6–12. Ed. par Marie-Ange CALVET-SEBASTI. Paris, Editions du Cerf, 95, 418 p. (Sources Chrétiennes, 405).

2929. HANSEN (G.C.), SIRINJAN (Manja). Sokrates. Kirchengeschichte. Berlin, Akademie Verlag, 95, LXII-501 p. (Berlinbrandenburgische Akademie der Wissenschaften. Die griechischen christlichen Schriftsteller der ersten Jahrhunderte, 1).

2930. Inscriptiones christianae Italiae septimo saeculo antiquiores. Vol. 9. Regio IX: Liguria reliqua trans et cis Appeninum. A cura di Giovanni MENNELLA e Giovanni COCCOLUTO. Bari, Edipuglia, 95, XXIII-113 p. (ill.).

2931. Inscriptiones christianae Italiae septimo saeculo antiquiores. Vol. 10. Regio V: Picenum. A cura di Gianfranco BINAZZI. Bari, Edipuglia, 95, XXIV-113 p. (ill.).

2932. Laici e laicità nei primi secoli della Chiesa. A cura di Enrico DAL COVOLO, Fernandino BERGAMELLI, Elena ZOCCA, Maria Grazia BIANCO. Torino, Edizioni Paoline, 95, 435 p. (Letture cristiane del primo millennio, 21).

2933. MAZZOLENI (Danilo). Considerazioni in margine alle Inscriptiones Christianae Aquileiae. *Augustinianum*, 95, 35, 2, p. 787-796.

2934. Millenarismo (Il): testi dei secoli I–II. A cura di Carlo NARDI. Firenze, Nardini, 95, 271 p. (Biblioteca patristica, 27).

2935. MOSSAY (Justin). Repertorium Nazianzenum. Orationes. Textus Graecus. Vol. 4. Codices Cypri, Graeciae (pars altera), Hierosolymorum. Paderborn u. München u. Wien, Ferdinand Schöningh, 95, 246 p. (Studien zur Geschichte und Kultur des Altertums. Forschungen zu Gregor von Nazianz im Auftrag des Görres-Gesellschaft, 11).

2936. NALDINI (Mario). Nuove testimonianze cristiane nelle lettere dei papiri greco-egizi (sec. II–IV). *Augustinianum*, 95, 35, 2, p. 831-846.

2937. Notre Père dans l'église ancienne (Le): choix des textes des Pères de l'église. Ed. par Adalbert-Gautier HAMMAN. Paris, Editions Franciscaines, 95, 224 p.

2938. ORIGENE. Homélies sur les Psaumes 36 à 38. Ed. par Emanuela PRINZIVALLI, Henri CROUZEL, Luc BRESARD. Paris, Editions du Cerf, 95, 494 p. (Sources chrétiennes, 411).

2939. PANIMOLLE (Salvatore A.). La cristologia di Luca 1–2. *Augustinianum*, 95, 35, 1, p. 61-75.

2940. Regola di San Benedetto e le regole dei Padri (La). A cura di Salvatore PRICOCO. Milano, Mondadori, 95, LXIV-416 p. (Fondazione Lorenzo Valla. Scrittori greci e latini).

2941. RIES (Julien). Notes de lecture du Contra epistulam fundamenti d'Augustin, à la lumière de quelques documents manichéens. *Augustinianum*, 95, 35, 2, p. 537-548.

2942. SCHOLTEN (Clemens). Antike Naturphilosophie und christliche Kosmologie in der Schrift De opificio mundi des Johannes Philoponos. Berlin u. New York, de Gruyter, 95, XI-488 p. (Patristische Texte und Studien, 45).

2943. STUDER (Basil). Zur Pneumatologie des Augustinus von Hippo (De trinitate 15,17,27–27,50). *Augustinianum*, 95, 35, 2, p. 567-583.

2944. TATIANI. Oratio ad Graecos. Hrsg. v. Miroslav MARCOVICH. Berlin u. New York, de Gruyter, 95, XII-192 p. (Patristische Texte und Studien, 43).

2945. VINEL (Fr.). Une étape vers l'affirmation du salut universel: Prosper d'Aquitaine: Lettre à Rufin sur la grâce et le libre arbitre. Introduction et traduction. *Revue d'Histoire Ecclésiastique*, 95, 90, 3-4, p. 367-395.

Cf. n°s 2247, 4298

§ 2. Allgemeines.

2946. BROWN (Peter). Potere e cristianesimo nella tarda antichità. Roma e Bari, Laterza, 95, 261 p.

2947. CHAU (Wai-Shing). The letter and the spirit: a history of interpretation from Origen to Luther. Bern u. Frankfurt am Main, 95, 250 p. (American university studies. Series 7. Theology and Religion, 167).

2948. GÜNTHER (Matthias). Die Frühgeschichte des Christentums in Ephesus. Bern u. Frankfurt am Main, Lang, 95, X-249 p. (Arbeiten zur Religion und Geschichte des Urchristentums, 1).

2949. Histoire du christianisme des origines à nos jours. Vol. 2. Naissance d'une chrétienté (250–430). Ed. par Charles et Luce PIETRI. Paris, Desclée, 95, 1096 p. (ill.).

2950. JENAL (Georg). Italia ascetica atque monastica: von den Anfängen bis zur Zeit der Langobarden (ca. 150/250–604). Stuttgart, Hiersemann, 95, 2 vol., XX-471 p., XI-553 p. (Monographien zur Geschichte des Mittelalters, 39).

2951. KIRCHSCHLÄGER (Walter). Die Entwicklung von Kirche und Kirchenstruktur zur neutestamentlichen Zeit. *In*: Aufstieg und Niedergang der römischen Welt [Cf. n° 2826], p. 1277-1356.

2952. KLAUCK (Hanz-Josef). Die religiöse Umwelt des Urchristentums. Vol. 1. Stadt- und Hausreligion, Mysterienkulte, Volksglaube. Stuttgart, Kohlhammer, 95, 207 p. (Kohlhammer Studienbücher Theologie, 9).

2953. LAMOREAUX (John C.). Episcopal courts in late antiquity. *Journal of Early Christian Studies*, 95, 3, 2, p. 143-167.

2954. MINNERATH (Roland). De Jérusalem à Rome: Pierre et l'unité de l'église apostolique. Paris, Beauchesne, 95, 618 p. (Théologie historique, 101).

2955. Origenes, vir ecclesiasticus. Symposion zu Ehren von Hernn Prof. Dr. H.-J. Vogt. Hrsg. v. Wilhelm GEERLINGS u. Hildegard KÖNIG. Bonn, Borengässer, 95, 103 p. [Cf. n[os] <Auswahl> 3018, 3028.]

2956. RHOADS (David M.). Network for mission: the social system of the Jesus movement as depicted in the narrative of the Gospel of Mark. *In*: Aufstieg und Niedergang der römischen Welt [Cf. n° 2826], p. 1692-1729.

2957. SCHENK (Wolfgang). Die ältesten Selbstverständnisse christlicher Gruppen im ersten Jahrhundert. *In*: Aufstieg und Niedergang der römischen Welt [Cf. n° 2826], p. 1357-1467.

2958. STEGEMANN (Ekkehard), STEGEMANN (Wolfgang). Urchristliche Sozialgeschichte: die Anfänge im Judentum und die Christusgemeinden in der mediterranen Welt. Stuttgart, Kohlhammer, 95, 416 p.

2959. THIESSEN (Werner). Christen in Ephesus: die historische und theologische Situation in vorpaulinischer und paulinischer Zeit und zur Zeit der Apostelgeschichte und der Pastoralbriefe. Tübingen, Francke, 95, 410 p. (Texte und Arbeiten zum neutestamentlichen Zeitalter, 12).

Cf. n°s 1392, 1398, 1416, 1431, 1952, 4086, 4151

§ 3. Spezialarbeiten.

2960. Apocryphal Acts of John (The). Ed. by Jan N. BREMMER. Kampen, Kok Pharos, 95, VI-243 p. (pl.).

2961. ARNALDI (Girolamo). Gregorio Magno e la giustizia. *In*: Giustizia (La) nell'Alto Medioevo [Cf. n° 3630], p. 57-102.

2962. ARNOLD (Clinton E.). The Colossian syncretism: the interface between christianity and folk belief at Colossae. Tübingen, Mohr, 95, XII-378 p. (Wissenschaftliche Untersuchungen zum Neuen Testament. Reihe 2, 77).

2963. BAUMGART (Susanne). Die Bischofsherrschaft im Gallien des 5. Jahrhunderts. Eine Untersuchung zu den Gründen und Anfängen weltlicher Herrschaft der Kirche. München, Editio Maris, 95, 220 p. (Münchener Universitätsschriften. Münchener Arbeiten zur Alten Geschichte, 8).

2964. BEAGON (Philip M.). The Cappadocian Fathers, women and ecclesiastical politics. *Vetera Christianorum*, 95, 49, p. 165-179.

2965. BIARNE (J.). Cloître, clôture, peregrinatio. *In*: Frontières terrestres [Cf. n° 2627], p. 389-407.

2966. BOWERSOCK (Glenn W.). Martyrdom and Rome. Cambridge, Cambridge U. P., 95, XII-106 p.

(The Wiles lectures given at the Queen University of Belfast).

2967. BRENT (Allen). Hippolytus and the Roman church in the third century: communities in tension before the emergence of a monarch-bishop. Leiden a. New York, Brill, 95, XII-611 p. (ill.). (Supplements to Vigiliae Christianae, 31).

2968. BUTTERWECK (Christel). Martyriumssucht in der alten Kirche? Studien zur Darstellung und Deutung frühchristlicher Martyrien. Tübingen, Mohr, 95, 288 p. (Beiträge zur historischen Theologie, 87).

2969. BYNUM (Caroline W.). The resurrection of the body in western christianity. Columbia, University of South Carolina Press, 95, XX-368 p. (ill.). (Lectures on the history of religions. New series, 15).

2970. CAPPER (Brian J.). Community of goods in the early Jerusalem church. *In*: Aufstieg und Niedergang der römischen Welt [Cf. n° 2826], p. 1730-1774.

2971. CLOKE (Gillian). This female man of God: women and spiritual power in the patristic age, AD 350–450. London a. New York, Routledge, 95, XI-243 p.

2972. CONSOLINO (Franca Ela). Il diavolo e l'iconografia. *In*: Demonio [Cf. n° 2976], p. 285-317.

2973. DASSMANN (Ernst). Ämter und Dienste in den frühchristlichen Gemeinden. Alfter, Borengässer, 95, X-244 p. (Karten).

2974. DE VIRGILIO (G.). Heuaggelixein in the third gospel. *Cristianesimo nella storia*, 95, 16, 3, p. 587-598.

2975. DECRET (François). La christologie manichéenne dans la controverse d'Augustin avec Fortunatus. *Augustinianum*, 95, 35, 2, p. 443-455.

2976. Demonio e i suoi complici (Il). Dottrine e credenze demonologiche nella tarda antichità. A cura di Salvatore PRICOCO. Messina, Rubbettino, 95, 321 p. (ill.). (Armarium. Biblioteca di storia e cultura religiosa, 6) [Cf. n[os] <scelta> 2844, 2972, 3004, 3016.]

2977. DESTRO (Adriana), PESCE (Mauro). Dialettica di riti e costruzione del movimento di Gesù nel Vangelo di Giovanni. *Augustinianum*, 95, 35, 1, p. 77-109.

2978. DOVERE (Elio). Ius principale e catholica lex dal Teodosiano agli editti su Calcedonia. Napoli, Jovene, 95, X-324 p. (Pubblicazioni del Dipartimento di diritto romano e storia della scienza romanistica dell'Università degli Studi di Napoli Federico II, 8).

2979. DUBOIS (Jean-Daniel). Vie de Jésus et vie de Mani au cœur des débats entre chrétiens orthodoxes et manichéens. *In*: Discours religieux dans l'antiquité [Cf. n° 2834], p. 177-187.

2980. EVIEUX (Pierre). Isidore de Péluse. Paris, Beauchesne, 95, XXVII-444 p. (Théologie historique, 99).

2981. FELBECKER (Sabine). Die Prozession: historische und systematische Untersuchungen zu einer liturgischen Ausdruckshandlung. Würzburg-Altenberg,

Echter-Oros Verlag, 95, 743 p. (Münsteraner theologische Abhandlungen, 39).

2982. FORBES (Christopher). Prophecy and inspired speech in early christianity and its hellenistic environment. Tübingen, Mohr, 95, XI-380 p. (Wissenschaftliche Untersuchungen zum Neuen Testament. Reihe 2, 75).

2983. FOSSUM (Jarl E.). The image of the invisible God: essays on the influence of Jewish mysticism on early christology. Göttingen u. Freiburg, Vandenhoeck & Ruprecht u. Universitätsverlag, 95, 181 p. (Novum Testamentum et orbis antiquus, 30).

2984. FREDOUILLE (Jean-Claude). L'apologétique chrétienne antique: métamorphoses d'un genre polymorphe. *Revue des Etudes Augustiniennes*, 95, 41, 2, p. 201-216.

2985. FRENSCHKOWSKI (Marco). Offenbarung und Epiphanie. Vol. 1. Grundlagen des spätantiken und frühchristlichen Offenbarungsglaubens. Tübingen, Mohr, 95, IX-481 p. (Wissenschaftliche Untersuchungen zum Neuen Testament, 2).

2986. GALVAO-SOBRINHO (Carlos R.). Funerary epigraphy and the spread of Christianity in the West. *Athenaeum*, 95, 83, 2, p. 431-462.

2987. GAMBLE (Harry Y.). Books and readers in the early church: a history of early christian texts. New Haven, Yale U. P., 95, XII-337 p.

2988. GAUDEMET (Jean). Notes sur l'excommunication. *Cristianesimo nella storia*, 95, 16, 2, p. 285-306.

2989. GEORGI (Dieter). The early church: internal Jewish migration or new religion? *Harvard Theological Review*, 95, 88, 1, p. 35-68.

2990. GRAPPE (Christian). Images de Pierre aux deux premiers siècles. Paris, Presses Universitaires de France, 95, 349 p. (Etudes d'histoire et de philosophie religieuses, 75).

2991. GUINOT (Jean-Noë). L'exégèse de Théodoret de Cyr. Paris, Beauchesne, 95, 879 p.

2992. HAACKER (Klaus). Die Stellung des Stephanus in der Geschichte des Urchristentums. *In*: Aufstieg und Niedergang der römischen Welt [Cf. n° 2826], p. 1515-1533. – IDEM. Zum Werdegang des Apostels Paulus: biographische Daten und ihre theologische Relevanz. *In*: Aufstieg und Niedergang der römischen Welt [Cf. n° 2826], p. 815-838.

2993. HAMMAN (Adalbert G.). Essai de chronologie de la vie et des œuvres de Justin. *Augustinianum*, 95, 35, 1, p. 281-239.

2994. HARRILL (James Albert). The manumission of slaves in early christianity. Tübingen, Mohr, 95, XVII, 255 p. (Hermeneutische untersuchungen zur Theologie, 32).

2995. IOANNIDES (Phôtios S.). Epidraseis tou monachismou tes anatoles ston kanona tou hosiou Benediktou (Les influences du monachisme anatolien dans la Règle de Saint Benoît). Katerinè, Ekdoseis Epektase, 95, 252 p.

2996. *Vacat.*

2997. KEE (Howard C.). Who are the people of God? Early christian models of community. New Haven, Yale U. P., 95, VII-231 p.

2998. KENNEL (Gunter). Frühchristliche Hymnen? Gattungskritische Studien zur Frage nach den Liedern der frühen Christenheit. Neukirchen-Vluyn, Neukirchener Verlag, 95, XV-334 p. (Wissenschaftliche Monographien zum Alten und Neuen Testament, 71).

2999. KRAUSE (Jens-Uwe). Witwen und Waisen im römischen Reich. Vol. 4. Witwen und Waisen im frühen Christentum. Stuttgart, Steiner, 95, 154 p. (Heidelberger Althistorische Beiträge und Epigraphische Studien, 19).

3000. LEVELEUX (Corinne). Des prêtresses déchues: l'image des Vestales chez les Pères de l'Eglise latine (fin IIe–début Ve siècle). Préf. de Michel HUMBERT. Paris, Editions LGDJ, 95, 172 p. (Travaux de Recherches Panthéon-Assaa Paris II).

3001. LUISELLI (Bruno). Il linguaggio della «evangelizatio pauperum» nella chiesa latina antica. *In*: Tradizione patristica (La). Alle fonti della cultura medievale [Cf. n° 4151], p. 31-58.

3002. MANNS (Frédéric). Lire les écritures en église. *Revue des sciences religieuses*, 95, 69, p. 436-452.

3003. MARKSCHIES (Christoph). Ambrosius von Mailand und die Trinitätstheologie. Kirchen- und theologiegeschichtliche Studien zu Antiarianismus und Neunizänismus bei Ambrosius und im lateinischen Westen (364–381 n.Chr.). Tübingen, Mohr, 95, XII-288 p. (Beiträge zur historischen Theologie, 90).

3004. MONACI CASTAGNO (A.). La demonologia cristiana fra secondo e terzo secolo. *In*: Demonio [Cf. n° 2976], p. 111-150.

3005. NORELLI (Enrico). Note sulla soteriologia di Marcione. *Augustinianum*, 95, 35, 1, p. 281-305.

3006. OTRANTO (Giorgio). Note sull'Italia meridionale paleocristiana nei rapporti col mondo bizantino. *Augustinianum*, 95, 35, 2, p. 859-884.

3007. PATRICH (Joseph). Palestinian desert monasticism. The monastic systems of Chariton, Gerasimus and Sabas. *Cristianesimo nella storia*, 95, 16, 1, p. 1-9.

3008. PERETTO (Elio). Tracce di preghiera eucaristica negli scritti di Ireneo di Lione. *Augustinianum*, 95, 35, 1, p. 267-280.

3009. PICCALUGA (Giulia). Fondazione della realtà e uscita dalla storia nel sermo De urbis excidio. *Augustinianum*, 95, 35, 2, p. 497-510.

3010. PILHOFER (Peter). Philippi. Vol. 1. Die erste christliche Gemeinde Europas. Tübingen, Mohr, 95,

XXII-311 p. (Wissenschaftliche Untersuchungen zum Neuen Testament, 87).

3011. PRICOCO (Salvatore). Il monachesimo tra pagani e cristiani da Giuliano al sacco di Roma. *In*: Pagani e cristiani [Cf. n° 2655], p. 193-206.

3012. RÄISÄNEN (Heikki). Die Hellenisten der Urgemeinde. *In*: Aufstieg und Niedergang der römischen Welt [Cf. n° 2826], p. 1515-1514.

3013. RIDINGS (Daniel). The Attic Moses. The dependency theme in some early christian writers. Göteborg, Acta Universitatis Gothoburgensis, 95, 270 p. (Studia Graeca et Latina Gothoburgensia, 59).

3014. ROMERO-POSE (Eugenio). Los ángeles de las Iglesias (Exégesis de Ticonio al Apoc. 1, 20-3, 22). *Augustinianum*, 95, 35, 1, p. 119-136.

3015. RORDORF (Willy). Bedeutung und Grenze der altkirchlichen ökumenischen Glaubensbekenntnisse. *Theologische Zeitschrift*, 95, 51, 1, p. 50-64.

3016. SARDELLA (T.). Diabolus instrumentum regni. Il diavolo nella politica papale (484–518). *In*: Demonio [Cf. n° 2976], p. 207-236.

3017. SAUZEAU (Pierre). Les chevaux colorés de l'Apocalypse. Parte I. L'Apocalypse de Jean, Zacharie et les traditions de l'Iran. *Revue de l'Histoire des Religions*, 95, 212, 3, p. 259-298. – IDEM. Les chevaux colorés de l'Apocalypse. II. Commentaires, iconographie et légendes de l'Antiquité au Moyen Age. *Revue de l'Histoire des Religions*, 95, 212, 4, p. 379-396.

3018. SCHOCKENHOFF (E.). Kirchliche Autorität als Hilfe zum Christsein? Zwei Antworten der frühen Kirche. *In*: Origenes, vir ecclesiasticus [Cf. n° 2955], p. 83-93.

3019. SCOTT (T. Kermit). Augustine. His thought in context. New York a. Mahwah, Paulist Press, 95, V-253 p.

3020. SIAT (Jeannine). La persécution des chrétiens au début du IIe s. d'après la lettre de Pline le Jeune et la réponse de Trajan en 112. *Les Etudes Classiques*, 95, 63, 2, p. 161-170.

3021. SIMONETTI (Manlio). La Sacra Scrittura nella Chiesa delle origini (I–III secolo): significato e interpretazioni. *Salesianum*, 95, 57, 1, p. 63-74.

3022. SINISCALCO (Paolo). Lo stile biblico nella riflessione di scrittori cristiani del II–III secolo. *Augustinianum*, 95, 35, 1, p. 215-230.

3023. SUHL (Alfred). Paulinische Chronologie im Streit der Meinungen. *In*: Aufstieg und Niedergang der römischen Welt [Cf. n° 2826], p. 939-1188.

3024. TAYLOR (Justin). St Paul and the Roman Empire: Acts of Apostles 13–14. *In*: Aufstieg und Niedergang der römischen Welt [Cf. n° 2826], p. 1189-1231.

3025. TAYLOR (Miriam S.). Anti-Judaism and early christian identity: a critique of the scholarly consensus.

Leiden a. New York, Brill, 95, 207 p. (Studia postbiblica).

3026. TOPOROV (Vladimir N.). Svjatos' i svjatye v russkoj dukhovnoj kul'ture. (Sanctity and the saints in the Russian spiritual culture). T. 1. Pervyj vek khristianstva na Rusi. (The first century of the Christianity in Rus'). Moskva, "Gnozis"-Škola "Jazyk russkoj kul'tury", Rossijskij gosudarstvennyj gumanitarnyj universitet, Institut vysšykh gumanitarnykh issledovanij, 95, 874 p.

3027. VIAN (Giovanni Maria). Ortodossia ed eresia nel IV secolo: la cristologia dei testi ariani di Verona. *Augustinianum*, 95, 35, 2, p. 847-858.

3028. ZIEGLER (G.). Der iubilus. Seine Beschreibung und Deutung bei Origenes, Augustinus und im frühen Mittelater. *In*: Origenes, vir ecclesiasticus [Cf. n° 2955], p. 95-100.

3029. ZINCONE (Sergio). Valore e funzione della preghiera comunitaria secondo Giovanni Crisostomo. *Augustinianum*, 95, 35, 2, p. 705-713.

3030. ZMIJEWSKI (Josef). Die Aufnahme der ersten Heiden in die Kirche nach Apg 10,1-11,18. Eine Interpretationsstudie. *In*: Aufstieg und Niedergang der römischen Welt [Cf. n° 2826], p. 1554-1601.

3031. ZOCCA (Elena). La senectus mundi. Significato, fonti e fortuna di un tema ciprianeo. *Augustinianum*, 95, 35, 2, p. 641-677.

§ 4. Hagiographie.

3032. DEVOS (Paul). Du nouveau sur Chrysostome et Chalkèdôn. *Analecta Bollandiana*, 95, 113, 1, p. 107-114.

3033. DOLBEAU (François). Un sermon inédit d'origine africaine pour la fête des saintes **Perpétue** et **Félicité**. *Analecta Bollandiana*, 95, 113, 1, p. 89-106.

3034. DONNINI (Mauro). In margine alla doctrina e alla ratio imitandi dell'agiografo di san Marino. *Hagiographica*, 95, 2, p. 137-143.

3035. KOOPER (Kate). A saint in exile: the early medieval Thecla at Rome and Meriamlik. *Hagiographica*, 95, 2, p. 1-23.

3036. LUONGO (Gennaro). Acacio di Melitene ed Andrea di Samosata. Agiografia e trasfigurazione nell'Encomio di **S. Acacio**. *Augustinianum*, 95, 35, 2, p. 815-830.

3037. MARTÍN IGLESIAS (J. C.). Una posible datación de la Passio sancti **Desiderii** BHL 2149. *Euphrosyne*, 95, 23, p. 439-456.

3038. MASTANDREA (Paolo). Passioni di martiri donatisti (BHL 4473 e 5271). *Analecta Bollandiana*, 95, 113, 1, p. 39-88.

3039. MUSSO (Olimpio), SANTI (Francesco). Un nuovo documento del culto di San **Varo** e i Templari di Casale Monferrato. *Hagiographica*, 95, 2, p. 177-186.

3040. SCORZA BARCELLONA (Francesco). Martiri e confessori dell'età di Giuliano l'Apostata: dalla storia alla leggenda. *In*: Pagani e cristiani [Cf. n° 2655], p. 53-83. – IDEM. Per una lettura della Passio **Typasii** veterani. *Augustinianum*, 95, 35, 2, p. 798-814.

3041. SUSI (Eugenio). La Vita beati Mauri Syri abbatis et Felicis eius filii apud Vallem Narci prope Naris ripam del Codice Alessandrino 89. *Hagiographica*, 95, 2, p. 93-136.

3042. VAN MINNEN (Peter). The earliest account of a martyrdom in coptic. *Analecta Bollandiana*, 95, 113, 1, p. 13-38.

3043. VERRANDO (Giovanni Nino). Per una nuova Biblioteca Hagiographica Latina, compilata sui manoscritti di origine italiana. *Hagiographica*, 95, 2, p. 277-308.

3044. WOODS (David). Ammianus Marcellinus and the deaths of **Bonosus** and **Maximilianus**. *Hagiographica*, 95, 2, p. 25-55.

H

BYZANTINISCHE GESCHICHTE
(Seit Justinian)

§ 1. Quellen. 3045-3091. – § 2. Allgemeines. 3092-3105. – § 3. Spezialarbeiten. 3106-3177.

§ 1. Quellen.

3045. ACCONCIA LONGO (Augusta). La Vita e i Miracoli di S. Fantino di Tauriana e l'identificazione dell'imperatore Leone eretico. *Rivista di Studi Bizantini e Neoellenici*, 95, 32, p. 77-90.

3046. Actes d'Iviron. Vol. 4. De 1328 au début du XVIe siècle. Ed. par Jacques LEFORT, Nicolas OIKONOMIDES, Denise PAPACHRYSSANTHIOU, Vassiliki KRAVARI. Paris, CNRS Editions, 95, XII-260 p. (tab.). (Archives de l'Athos, 19).

3047. AGAPETOS DIAKONOS. Der Fürstenspiegel für Kaiser Iustinianos. Hrsg. v. Rudolf RIEDINGER. Athena, 95, 89 p. (Etaireia philon tou laou. Kentron ereunes Byzantiou, 4).

3048. ALLEN (Pauline), MAYER (Wendy). The thirty-four Homilies on Hebrews: the last series delivered by Chrysostom in Constantinople? *Byzantion*, 95, 65, 2, p. 309-348.

3049. ARRANZ (Miguel, S.J.). Preghiere parapenitenziali di purificazione e di liberazione nella tradizione bizantina. *Orientalia Christiana Periodica*, 95, 61, 2, p. 425-494.

3050. AUZEPY (Marie-France). L'Adversus Constantinum Caballinum et Jean de Jérusalem. *Byzantinoslavica*, 95, 56, 2, p. 323-338.

3051. BARKHUIZEN (J.H.). Romanos Melodos: on earthquakes and fires. *Jahrbuch der Österreichischen Byzantinistik*, 95, 45, p. 1-18.

3052. BERGER (Albrecht). Leontios Presbyteros von Rom. Das Leben des heiligen Gregorios von Agrigent. Berlin, Akademie Verlag, 95, 425 p. (Berliner Byzantinische Arbeiten, 60).

3053. BROOCK (Sebastian P.). A syriac Narratio attributed to Abba Daniel of Sketis. *Analecta Bollandiana*, 95, 113, 2, p. 269-280.

3054. Byzantiner und ihre Nachbarn (Die). Die De administrando imperio genannte Lehrschrift des Kaisers Konstantinos Porphyrogennetos für seinen Sohn Romanos. Hrsg. v. Klaus BELKE u. Peter SOUSTAL. Wien, Fassbaender, 95, 358 p. (Byzantinische Geschichtsschreiber, 19).

3055. Corpus Iuris Civilis. Text und Übersetzung. Vol. 2. Digesten 1–10. Hrsg. v. Okko BEHRENDS, Rolf KNÜTEL, Berthold KUPISCH [et al.]. Heidelberg, C.F. Müller Juristischer Verlag, 95, XXVII-862 p. (Taf.).

3056. CROKE (Brian). The Chronicle of Marcellinus. Sydney, Australian association for Byzantine studies, 95, XXVII-152 p. (Byzantina Australiensia, 7).

3057. CUPANE (Carolina), SCHIFFER (Elisabeth). Das Register des Patriarchats von Konstantinopel. Indices. Wien, Österreichische Akademie der Wissenschaften, 95, 352 p.

3058. DEROCHE (Vincent). Etudes sur Léontios de Néapolis. Uppsala et Stockholm, Almqvist & Wiksell, 95, 316 p. (Acta Universitatis Upsaliensis. Studia Byzantina Upsaliensia, 3).

3059. EFTHYMIADIS (Stephanos). Living in a city and living in ascetis: the Dream of Eustathios the Banker. *Byzantinische Forschungen*, 95, 21, p. 11-29. – IDEM. Notes on the correspondence of Theodore the Studite. *Revue des Etudes Byzantines*, 95, 53, p. 141-163.

3060. FLORISTAN (José M.). Correspondencia inédita de Macario de Heraclea-Pelagonia con Antonio Perrenot, Cardenal de Granvela (1551). *Byzantion* 95, 65, 2, p. 495-524.

3061. FUSCO (Roberto). Un pamphlet antiariano. La Vita premetafrastica di S. Anfilochio di Iconio (BHG 75–75a). *Rivista di Studi Bizantini e Neoellenici*, 95, 32, p. 17-76.

3062. GLEI (Reinhold), KHOURY (Adel Theodor). Johannes Damaskenos und Theodor Abu Qurra. Schriften zum Islam. Echter-Oros Verlag, Würzburg-Altenberg,

95, XXI-341 p. (Corpus islamo-christianum, series Graeca 3).

3063. GREGORII ACINDYNI. Refutationes duae operis Gregorii Palamae cui titulus Dialogus inter Orthodoxum et Barlaamitam. Ed. par Juan NADAL CAÑELLAS. Turnhout et Leuven, Brepols et Leuven University Press, 95, CXC-485 p. (Corpus Christianorum. Series Graeca, 31).

3064. GREGORIO DI CORINTO. Esegesi al canone giambico per la Pentecoste attribuito a Giovanni Damasceno. A cura di Franco MONTANA. Pisa, Giardini, 95, LXXIII-97 p. (tavole). (Biblioteca di studi antichi, 76).

3065. GUILLOU (André), MAVROMATIS (Lénos), BENOU (Lisa), ODORICO (Paolo). Le cartulaire B du monastère Saint-Jean-Prodrome au mont Ménécée (Serrès). *Byzantion*, 95, 65, 1, p. 196-239.

3066. HUNGER (Herbert), KRESTEN (Otto), KISLINGER (Ewald), CUPANE (Carolina). Das Register des Patriarchats von Konstantinopel. II. Edition und Übersetzung der Urkunden aus den Jahren 1337–1350. Wien, Österreichische Akademie der Wissenschaften, 95, 518 p. (Pl., Taf.). (Corpus Fontium Historiae Byzantinae, 19, 2).

3067. HUNGER (Herbert). Aus den letzten Lebensjahren des Johannes Chortasmenos. Das Synaxarion im Cod. Christ Church Gr. 56 und der Metropolit Ignatios von Selybria. *Jahrbuch der Österreichischen Byzantinistik*, 95, 45, p. 159-218. – IDEM. Elemente der byzantinischen Urkundenschrift in literarischen Handschriften des 12. und 13. Jahrhunderts. *Röm. Hist. Mitt.*, 95, 37, p. 27-40.

3068. KALAMAKIS (D.). Une scolie inédite au passage Dorm. II 6, 34–37 de S. Jean Damascène. *Byzantion*, 95, 65, 1, p. 240-246.

3069. KOLBABA (Tia M.). Barlaam the Calabrian. Three treatises on papal primacy: introduction, edition, and translation. *Revue des Etudes Byzantines*, 95, 53, p. 41-115.

3070. KOLOVOU (Foteini). Euthymios Tornikes als Briefschreiber. Vier unedierte Briefe des Euthymios Tornikes an Michael Choniates im Codex Buc. Gr. 508. *Jahrbuch der Österreichischen Byzantinistik*, 95, 45, p. 53-74.

3071. Kresten (Otto). Diplomatische und historische Beobachtungen zu den in den Kanzleiregistern Papst Innozenz' III. überlieferten Auslandsschreiben byzantinischer Kaiser. *Röm. Hist. Mitt.*, 95, 37, p. 41-79.

3072. MACEDONIUS CONSUL. The Epigrams. Ed. by J.A. MADDEN. Hildesheim u. Zürich u. New York, Olms, 95, XVIII-321 p. (Spoudasmata, 60).

3073. MALECI (Stefano). Il codice Barberinianus Graecus 70 dell'Etymologicum Gudianum. Roma, Accademia nazionale dei Lincei, 95, 91 p. (Bollettino dei classici, suppl. 15).

3074. MANUEL II PALAIOLOGUS. Dialog mit einem Muslim. Vol. 2. Hrsg. v. Karl FÖRSTEL. Echter-Oros Verlag, Würzburg-Altenberg, 95, XXI-341 p. (Corpus islamo-christianum, series Graeca 4/2).

3075. ORTOLEVA (Vincenzo). La parafrasi della traduzione planudea dei Disticha Catonis nel Cod. Barocc. 71. *Byzantion*, 95, 65, 1, p. 89-97.

3076. PAPATHOMOPOULOS (Manolis), TSAVARI (Isabella)., RIGOTTI (Gianpaolo). Augoustinou Peri Triados biblia pentekaideka haper ek tes latinon dialektou eis ten Hellada metenenke Maximos ho Planoudes. (Les quinze livres du De trinitate de S. Augustin traduits du latin en grec par Maxime Planude). Athena, Kentron Ekdoseos Ergon Hellenon Syngrapheon, 95, 2 vol., CLVIII-1056 p. (Akademia Athenon. Bibliotheke A. Manouse, 3).

3077. Prosopographisches Lexikon der Palaiologenzeit. Addenda zu Faszikel 1–12. Hrsg. v. E. TRAPP, H.-V. BEYER, I.G. LEONTIADES. Wien, Österreichische Akademie der Wissenschaften, 95, 140 p. (Österreichische Akademie der Wissenschaften. Veröffentlichungen der Kommission für Byzantinistik, I/1–12 Add.).

3078. Register des Patriarchats von Konstantinopel (Das). 2. Edition und Übersetzung der Urkunden aus den Jahren 1337–1350. Indices. Teil 2. Indices zu den Urkunden aus den Jahren 1315–1350. Teil 1 und 2 erstellt von Carolina CUPANE und Elisabeth SCHIFFER. Hrsg. v. Herbert HUNGER [et al.]. Wien, Verlag der: Österreichischen Akademie der Wissenschaften, 95, 2 vol., 518 p., 352 p. (ill.). (Corpus fontium historiae Byzantinae. Series Vindobonensis, 19).

3079. Repertorium der Handschriften des byzantinischen Rechts. Parte I. Die Handschriften des westlichen Rechts (Nr. 1–327). Hrsg. v. Ludwig BURGMANN, Marie Theres FÖGEN, Andreas SCHMINCK, Dieter SIMON. Frankfurt am Main, Löwenklau-Gesellschaft, 95, XXVIII-466 p. (Forschungen zur byzantinischen Rechtsgeschichte, 20).

3080. RIGO (Antonio). La Vita di Pietro l'Athonita scritta da Gregorio Palama. *Rivista di Studi Bizantini e Neoellenici*, 95, 32, p. 177-190.

3081. Romanzi cavallereschi bizantini (Callimaco e Crisorroe, Beltandros e Crisanza, Storia di Achille, Florio e Plaziaflore, Storia di Apollonio di Tiro, Favola consolatoria sulla Cattiva e la Buona Sorte). A cura di Carolina CUPANE. Torino, Utet, 95, 734 p. (tavole). (Classici greci. Autori della tarda antichità e dell'età bizantina).

3082. RYDÉN (Lennart). The Life of St Andrew the Fool. Uppsala, Acta Universitatis Upsaliensis, 95, 2 vol., 304 p., 437 p. (Studia Byzantina Upsaliensia, 4.1–2).

3083. SALIBA (George). Paulus Alexandrinus in syriac and arabic. *Byzantion*, 95, 65, 2, p. 440-454.

3084. SEMENOVKER (Boris A.). Bibliografičeskie pamjatniki Vizantii. (The byzantine bibliographical texts.

between the VIth–VIIth centuries). Moskva, Arkheografičeskij centr, 95, 225 p.

3085. SINKEWICZ (Robert E.). Theoleptos of Philadelpheia. The monastic discourses. Turnhout, Brepols, 95, 418 p. (Pontifical Institute of Mediaeval Studies. Studies and texts, 111).

3086. Studies in Byzantine sigillography. 4. Ed. by Nicolas OIKONOMIDES. Washington, Dumbarton Oaks Research Library and Collection, XI-216 p.

3087. Testimonia najdawniejszych dzielow Slowian (Témoignages relatifs aux origines de l'histoire des Slaves). Warszawa, Polska Akademia Nauk, 95, 572 p. (Serie Grecka).

3088. Three medieval greek romances: Velthandros and Chrysandza, Kallimachos and Chrysorroi, Livistros and Rodamni. Ed. by G. BETTS. New York a. London, Garland, 95, XLI-192 p. (The Garland Library of Medieval Literature, 98).

3089. TINNEFELD (Franz). Es wäre gut für jenen Menschen, wenn er nicht geboren wäre. Eine Disputation am Hof Kaiser Manuels II. über ein Jesuswort vom Verräter Judas. Einleitung, kritische Erstedition und Übersetzung. *Jahrbuch der Österreichischen Byzantinistik*, 95, 45, p. 115-158.

3090. TOMPKINS (Ian G.). Problems of dating and pertinence in some letters of Theodoret of Cyrrhus. *Byzantion*, 95, 65, 1, p. 176-195.

3091. VERHELST (Stéphane). Les Présanctifiés de saint Jacques. *Orientalia Christiana Periodica*, 95, 61, 2, p. 381-405.

Cf. n°s 33, 181, 568

§ 2. **Allgemeines.**

* 3092. Byzantinische Zeitschrift. Begründet von Karl KRUMBACHER. Hrsg. v. Peter SCHREINER. Stuttgart u. Leipzig, Teubner, 95, XXXII-610 p. (Taf.).

3093. ANGOLD (Michael). Church and society in Byzantium under the Comneni, 1081–1261. Cambridge, Cambridge University Press, 95, XVI-604 p.

3094. Costantinople and its hinterland. Papers from the twenty-seventh Spring Symposium of Byzantines Studies (Oxford, april 1993). Ed. by Cyril MANGO a. Gilbert DAGRON. Aldershot, Variorum, 95, XI-426 p. (Society for the promotion of byzantine studies publications, 3).

3095. DEGANI (Enzo). La lessicografia. *In*: Spazio letterario [Cf. n° 3103], p. 505-527.

3096. ELEUTERI (Paolo). La filosofia. *In*: Spazio letterario [Cf. n° 3103], p. 437-464.

3097. IRMSCHER (Johannes). Il pensiero politico a Bisanzio. *In*: Spazio letterario [Cf. n° 3103], p. 529-561.

3098. KAZHDAN (Alexander). The Italian and late Byzantine city. *Dumbarton Oaks Papers*, 95, 49, p. 1-22.

3099. MALTESE (Enrico V.). La storiografia. *In*: Spazio letterario [Cf. n° 3103], p. 355-388.

3100. Originality in Byzantine literature, art and music. A collection of essays edited by A.R. LITTLEWOOD. Oxford, Oxbow Books, 95, X-228 p. (Oxbow Monographs, 50) [Cf. n^{os} <choice> 3112, 3113, 3119, 3129, 3144, 3152, 3155, 3173.]

3101. PONTANI (Anna). La filologia. *In*: Spazio letterario [Cf. n° 3103], p. 307-351.

3102. ROTOLI (Vincenzo). La poesia. *In*: Spazio letterario [Cf. n° 3103], p. 465-504.

3103. Spazio letterario della Grecia antica (Lo). A cura di Giuseppe CAMBIANO, Luciano CANFORA, Diego LANZA. Vol. 2. La ricezione e l'attualizzazione del testo. Roma, Salerno, 95, 834 p. (tavole) [Cf. n^{os} <scelta> 3095, 3096, 3097, 3099, 3101, 3102, 3116, 3117.]

3104. Studien zur byzantinischen Kunstgeschichte. Festschrift für Horst Hallensleben zum 65. Geburtstag. Hrsg. v. Brigitt BORKOPP, Barbara SCHELLEWALD, Lioba THEIS. Amsterdam, Hakkert, 95, 293 p. (Abb.).

3105. TREADGOLD (W.). Byzantium and its army, 284-1081. Stanford, Stanford University Press, 95, XIII-250 p.

§ 3. **Spezialarbeiten.**

3106. AUZÉPY (Marie-France). Les Vies d'Auxence et le monachisme auxentien. *Revue des Etudes Byzantines*, 95, 53, p. 205-235.

3107. BARBU (D.). L'église et l'empereur au XIVe siècle selon le témoignage de la peinture murale de Valachie. *Revue roumaine d'histoire*, 95, 34, 2, p. 131-139.

3108. BARTUSIS (Mark C.). The functions of archaizing in Byzantium. *Byzantinoslavica*, 95, 56, 2, p. 271-278.

3109. BERGER (Albrecht). Zur Topographie der Ufergegend am Goldenen Horn in der byzantinischen Zeit. *Istanbuler Mitteilungen*, 95, 45, p. 149-165.

3110. BISSINGER (Manfred). Kreta. Byzantinische Wandmalerei. München, Editio Maris, 368 p. (Taf.). (Münchener Arbeiten zur Kunstgeschichte und Archäologie, 4).

3111. BROWN (T. S.). Byzantine Italy, c. 680–c. 876. *In*: New Cambridge medieval history [Cf. n° 3378], p. 320-348.

3112. BROWNING (Robert). Tradition and originality in literary criticism and scholarship. *In*: Originality in Byzantine literature [Cf. n° 3100], p. 17-28.

3113. BRUBAKER (L.). Originality in Byzantine manuscript illumination. *In*: Originality in Byzantine literature [Cf. n° 3100], p. 147-165.

3114. Byzantine and early islamic Near East. Vol. 3. States, ressources and armies. Papers of the third workshop on late antiquity and early Islam. Ed. by Averil CAMERON. Princeton, The Darwin Press, 95, XV-491 p. (maps). (Studies in Late Antiquity and Early Islam, 1).

3115. Byzantine magic. Ed. by Henry MAGUIRE. Washington, Dumbarton Oaks, 95, VII-187 p. (ill.). (Dumbarton Oaks Research Library and Collection) [Cf. n^{os} <choice> 3122, 3125, 3130, 3136, 3144, 3163.]

3116. CANFORA (Luciano). Le collezioni superstiti. *In*: Spazio letterario [Cf. n° 3103], p. 95-261. – IDEM. Libri e biblioteche. *In*: Spazio letterario [Cf. n° 3103], p. 11-93.

3117. CAVALLO (Guglielmo). I fondamenti culturali della trasmissione dei testi antichi a Bisanzio. *In*: Spazio letterario [Cf. n° 3103], p. 265-306. – IDEM. Qualche riflessione sulla continuità della cultura greca in Oriente tra i secoli VII e VIII. *Byzantinische Zeitschrift*, 95, 88, p. 13-22.

3118. CIGGAAR (Krijnie N.). Une description de Constantinople dans le Tarragonensis 55. *Revue des Etudes Byzantines*, 95, 53, p. 117-140.

3119. CUNNINGHAM (M.B.). Innovation or mimesis in Byzantine sermons? *In*: Originality in Byzantine literature [Cf. n° 3100], p. 67-80.

3120. DENNERT (Martin). Mittelbyzantinische Ambone in Kleinasien. *Istanbuler Mitteilungen*, 95, 45, p. 137-147.

3121. DOSTALOVÁ (Růžena). Der Einfluß der Rhetorik auf die Objektivität der historischen Information in den Werken byzantinischer Historiker. *Byzantinoslavica*, 95, 56, 2, p. 291-303.

3122. DUFFY (John). Reactions of two Byzantine intellectuals to the theory and practice of magic: Michael Psellos and Michael Italikos. *In*: Byzantine magic [Cf. n° 3115], p. 83-97.

3123. DURLIAT (J.). Les transferts fonciers après la reconquête byzantine en Afrique et en Italie. *In*: Sources de la gestion publique (Aux). Tome 2 [Cf. n° 4574], p. 89-121.

3124. Empress Theophano (The). Byzantium and the west at the turn of the first millennium. Ed. by Adelbert DAVIDS. Cambridge, Cambridge U. P., 95, XVI-344 p.

3125. FÖGEN (Marie Theres). Balsamon on magic: from Roman secular law to Byzantine canon law. *In*: Byzantine magic [Cf. n° 3115], p. 99-115.

3126. FRANCESCHINI BOLOGNESI RECCHI (Eugenia). Winter in the great palace: the persistence of pagan festivals in christian Byzantium. *Byzantinische Forschungen*, 95, 21, p. 117-132.

3127. GARLAND (Lynda). Conformity and licence at the Byzantine court in the eleventh and twelfth centuries: the case of imperial women. *Byzantinische Forschungen*, 95, 21, p. 101-115.

3128. GERO (Stephen). Jannes and Jambres in the Vita Stephani Iunioris (BHG 1666). *Analecta Bollandiana*, 95, 113, 2, p. 281-292.

3129. GOUMA-PETERSON (Th.). Originality in Byzantine religious paintings (mosaics and frescoes). *In*: Originality in Byzantine literature [Cf. n° 3100], p. 125-145.

3130. GREENFIELD (Richard P.H.). A contribution to the study of palaeologican magic. *In*: Byzantine magic [Cf. n° 3115], p. 117-153.

3131. HARRIS (J.). Greek emigrés in the West, 1400–1520. Camberley, Porphyrogenitus, 95, XI-272 p.

3132. HOWARD-JOHNSTON (James D.). Crown lands and the defence of imperial authority in the tenth and eleventh centuries. *Byzantinische Forschungen*, 95, 21, p. 75-100.

3133. HUNGER (Herbert). Der Mythos der Hellenen in byzantinischem Ambiente. *Byzantinische Zeitschrift*, 95, 88, p. 23-37.

3134. HUTTER (Irmgard). Die Geschichte des Lincoln College Typikons. *Jahrbuch der Österreichischen Byzantinistik*, 95, 45, p. 79-114.

3135. KARPOZILOS (Apostolos). Realia in byzantine epistolography XIII-XV c. *Byzantinische Zeitschrift*, 95, 88, p. 68-84.

3136. KAZHDAN (Alexander). Byzantine town and trade as seen by Niketas Choniates. *Byzantinoslavica*, 95, 56, 1, p. 209-218. – IDEM. Holy and unholy miracle workers. *In*: Byzantine magic [Cf. n° 3115], p. 73-82. – IDEM. Some problems in the biography of John Mauropous. II. *Byzantion*, 95, 65, 2, p. 362-387.

3137. KISLINGER (Ewald). Byzantinische Kupfermünzen aus Sizilien (7.–9. Jh.) im historischen Kontext. *Jahrbuch der Österreichischen Byzantinistik*, 95, 45, p. 25-36.

3138. KOUTRAKOU (Nike). La rumeur dans la vie politique byzantine. Continuité et mutations (VIIIe-Xe siècles). *Byzantinoslavica*, 95, 56, 1, p. 62-73.

3139. KRESTEN (Otto), MÜLLER (Andreas E.). Samtherrschaft, Legitimationsprinzip und kaiserlicher Urkundentitel in Byzanz in der ersten Hälfte des 10. Jahrhunderts. Wien, Verlag der Österreichischen Akademie der Wissenschaften, 95, 87 p. (Sitzungsberichte der Österreichische Akademie der Wissenschaften. Philosophisch-historische Klasse, 630).

3140. LAIOU (Angeliki E.). Italy and the Italians in the political geography of the Byzantines (14th century). *Dumbarton Oaks Papers*, 95, 49, p. 73-98.

3. SPEZIALARBEITEN

3141. LOUNGHIS (Telemachos C.). Die byzantinische Ideologie der begrenzten Ökumene und die römische Frage im ausgehenden 10. Jh. *Byzantinoslavica*, 95, 56, 1, p. 117-128.

3142. MAC CORMICK (Michael). Byzantium and the West, 700–900. *In*: New Cambridge medieval history [Cf. n° 3378], p. 349-382.

3143. MACGEER (Eric). Sowing the dragon's teeth: Byzantine warfare in the tenth century. Washington, Dumbarton Oaks Research Library and Collection, 95, XVIII-405 p. (Dumbarton Oaks Studies, 33).

3144. MAGUIRE (Henry). Magic and christian image. *In*: Byzantine magic [Cf. n° 3115], p. 51-71. – IDEM. Originality in Byzantine art criticism. *In*: Originality in Byzantine literature [Cf. n° 3100], p. 101-114.

3145. MAKRIS (Georgios). Zur Epilepsie in Byzanz. *Byzantinische Zeitschrift*, 95, 88, p. 363-404.

3146. MALAMUT (Elisabeth). L'image byzantine des Petchénègues. *Byzantinische Zeitschrift*, 95, 88, p. 105-147.

3147. MALTESE (Enrico V.). Dimensioni bizantine. Donne, angeli e demoni nel medioevo greco. Torino, Scriptorium, 95, 191 p.

3148. MALTEZOU (Chryssa A.). Byzantine "consuetudines" in Venetian Crete. *Dumbarton Oaks Papers*, 95, 49, p. 269-280.

3149. MIMOUNI (Simon Claude). Dormition et assomption de Marie. Histoire des traditions anciennes. Paris, Beauchesne, 95, XXII-716 p. (Théologie historique, 98).

3150. MORRIS (Rosemary). Monks and laymen in Byzantium, 843–1118. Cambridge, Cambridge University Press, 95, XXII-330 p.

3151. MOYSIDOU (Jasmine). To Byzantio kai hoi boreioi gheitones tou ton 10. aiona. (L'empire byzantin et ses voisins du Nord pendant le Xe siècle). Athena, Basilopoulos, 95, 438 p. (Istorikes Monographies, 15).

3152. MULLETT (M.E.). Originality in the Byzantine letter: the case of exile. *In*: Originality in Byzantine literature [Cf. n° 3100], p. 39-58.

3153. NELSON (Robert S.). The Italian appreciation and appropriation of illuminated Byzantine manuscripts, ca. 1200–1450. *Dumbarton Oaks Papers*, 95, 49, p. 209-235.

3154. OCCHIATO (Giuseppe). Il duomo di Gerace: persistenze bizantine in un edificio romanico calabrese. *Byzantion*, 95, 65, 1, p. 33-68.

3155. OUSTERHOUT (R.). Beyond Hagia Sophia: originality in byzantine architecture. *In*: Originality in Byzantine literature [Cf. n° 3100], p. 167-185.

3156. PATRICH (Joseph). Sabas, leader of Palestinian monasticism. A comparative study in eastern monasticism, fourth to seventh centuries. Washington, Dumbarton Oaks, 95, XI-420 p. (Dumbarton Oaks Studies, 32).

3157. Peace and war in Byzantium. Essays in honor of George T. Dennis. Ed. by Timothy S. MILLER a. John NESBITT. Washington, Catholic University of America Press, 95, XX-282 p.

3158. PERRONE (Lorenzo). I monaci e gli altri. Il monachesimo come fattore d'interazione religiosa nella Terra Santa di epoca bizantina. *Augustinianum*, 95, 35, 2, p. 729-761.

3159. RAPP (Claudia). Byzantine hagiographers as antiquarians, seventh to tenth centuries. *Byzantinische Forschungen*, 95, 21, p. 31-44.

3160. RIGO (Antonio). Il monte Galesion (Alaman Dağ) e i suoi monasteri: da S. Lazzaro (m. 1053) alla conquista turca (ottobre 1304). *Cristianesimo nella storia*, 95, 16, 1, p. 11-43. – IDEM. Il monte Ganos e i suoi monasteri. *Orientalia Christiana Periodica*, 95, 61, 1, p. 235-248.

3161. ROHMANN (Jens). Einige Bemerkungen zum Ursprung des feingezahnten Akanthus. *Istanbuler Mitteilungen*, 95, 45, p. 109-121.

3162. RUGGIERI (Vincenzo, S.J.). Appunti sulla continuità urbana di Side, in Panfilia. *Orientalia Christiana Periodica*, 95, 61, 1, p. 95-116. – IDEM. L'architettura religiosa nell'impero bizantino (sec. VI–IX secolo). Messina, Rubbettino, 95, 206 p. (ill.). (Accademia Angelica Costantiniana di Lettere Arti Scienze – Saggi, Studi, Testi, 2).

3163. RUSSELL (James). The archaeological context of magic in the early Byzantine period. *In*: Byzantine magic [Cf. n° 3115], p. 35-50.

3164. SANSTERRE (Jean-Marie). La caution de S. Euphebius. Une variante napolitaine de la légende byzantine du Christ garant. *Analecta Bollandiana*, 95, 113, 2, p. 293-296.

3165. SARADI (Helen). Evidence of barter economy in the documents of private transactions. *Byzantinische Zeitschrift*, 95, 88, p. 405-418. – EADEM. The Byzantine tribunals: problems in the application of justice and state policy (9th–12th c.). *Revue des Etudes Byzantines*, 95, 53, p. 165-204.

3166. SCHMITT (Oliver J.). Zur Geschichte der Stadt Glarentza im 15. Jahrhundert. *Byzantion*, 95, 65, 1, p. 98-135.

3167. SCHOULER (B.). La définition de la rhétorique dans l'enseignement byzantin. *Byzantion*, 95, 65, 1, p. 136-175.

3168. SHAHÎD (Irfan). Byzantium and the Arabs in the sixth century. Washington, Dumbarton Oaks, 95, 2 vol., XXX-1030 p. (Dumbarton Oaks Research Library and Collection).

3169. SIGNES (Juan). El período del segundo iconoclasmo en Theophanes Continuatus. Análisis y comentario de los tres primeros libros de la crónica. Amsterdam, Hakkert, 95, 773 p.

3170. SPIESER (Jean-Michel). Portes, limites et organisation de l'espace dans les églises paléochrétiennes. *Klio*, 95, 77, p. 433-445.

3171. THIERRY (Nicole). De la datation des églises de Cappadoce. *Byzantinische Zeitschrift*, 95, 88, p. 419-455.

3172. *Vacat.*

3173. VELIMIROVI (M.). Originality and innovation in Byzantine music. *In*: Originality in Byzantine literature [Cf. n° 3100], p. 189-199.

3174. WALTER (Christopher). The origins of the cult of Saint George. *Revue des Etudes Byzantines*, 95, 53, p. 295-326.

3175. WILSON (A.). Female sanctity in the Greek calendar: the Synaxarion of Costantinople. *In*: Women in antiquity [Cf. n° 2748], p. 233-247.

3176. YANNOPOULOS (Panayotis). La Grèce dans la Vie de S. Fantin. *Byzantion*, 95, 65, 2, p. 475-494.

3177. ZUCKERMAN (Constantine). On the date of the Khazars' conversion to judaism and the chronology of the kings of the Rus Oleg and Igor. *Revue des Etudes Byzantines*, 95, 53, p. 237-270.

I

GESCHICHTE DES MITTELALTERS

§ 1. Quellen. Quellenkritik (*a.* Urkunden; *b.* Literarische Quellen). 3178-3336. – § 2. Allgemeine Darstellungen. 3337-3396. – § 3. Politische Geschichte (*a.* Allgemeines; *b.* 476–900; *c.* 900–1300; *d.* 1300–1500). 3397-3517. – § 4. Juden. 3518-3542. – § 5. Islam. 3543-3574. – § 6. Wikinger. 3575-3590. – § 7. Rechts- und Verfassungsgeschichte. 3591-3689. – § 8. Wirtschafts- und Sozialgeschichte. 3690-3893. – § 9. Kultur-, Literatur- und Unterrichtsgeschichte. 3894-4175. – § 10. Kunstgeschichte (*a.* Allgemeines; *b.* Spezialarbeiten). 4175 a)-4239. – § 11. Musikgeschichte. 4240-4266. – § 12. Geschichte der Philosophie. 4267-4395. – § 13. Kirchengeschichte (*a.* Allgemeines; *b.* Geschichte des Papsttums; *c.* Ordensgeschichte; *d.* Hagiographie; *e.* Spezialarbeiten). 4396-4539. – § 14. Siedlungsgeschichte, Ortsnamenforschung und Städtebaukunst. 4540-4579.

§ 1. Quellen. Quellenkritik.

a. Urkunden.

3178. ABBE (Jean-Loup). L'aménagement de l'espace: le parcellaire rural de la bastide de Saint-Denis (Aude). *In*: Campagnes médiévales [Cf. n° 3713], p. 103-120.

3179. Albori del Comune di San Gimignano e lo statuto del 1314 (Gli). A cura di Mario BROGI. Siena, Cantagalli, 95, 309 p.

3180. ANDERNACH (Norbert). Die Regesten der Erzbischöfe von Köln im Mittelalter. Band 12/1. 1411–1414. (Friedrich von Saarwerden). Düsseldorf, Droste, 95, XXX-491 p. (Publikationen der Gesellschaft für rheinische Geschichtskunde, 21).

3181. AYERBE IRIBAR (M. R.). Documentación medieval del valle de Legazpia (1290-1495). Donostia, Eusko Ikaskuntza, 95, XXVII-161 p. (Fuentes documentales medievales del País Vasco).

3182. Bakkalarenregister (Das) der Artistenfakultät der Universität Erfurt 1392–1521 (= Registrum baccalariorum de facultate arcium universitatis studii Errfordensis existencium). Hrsg. von R. C. SCHWINGES und K. WRIEDT. Jena u. Stuttgart, G. Fischer, 95, LXVI-488 p. (ill.) (Veröffentlichungen der Historischen Kommission für Thüringen. Große Reihe, 3).

3183. BAUMGÄRTNER (Ingrid). Regesten aus dem Kapitelarchiv von S. Maria in Via Lata (1201–1258). Teil II. *Quellen und Forschungen aus italienischen Archiven und Bibliotheken*, 95, 75, p. 32-177.

3184. Boniface VIII en procès. Articles d'accusation et déposition des témoins (1303–1311). Ed. par Jean COSTE. Préf. par André VAUCHEZ. Roma, L'Erma di Bretschneider, 95, LXI-966 p. (Pubblicazioni della Fondazione Camillo Caetani, Studi e Documenti d'Archivio, 5).

3185. Breve Mercadantie mercatorum Papie: la più antica legislazione mercantile pavese, 1295. A cura di Renata CROTTI PASI e Carla Maria CANTU. Pavia, Camera di commercio industria artigianato e agricoltura, 95, 516 p. (tav.,. ill.).

3186. Briefwechsel (Der) Karls des Kühnen (1433–1477). Inventar. Hrsg. von Werner PARAVICINI. Frankfurt am Main, Peter Lang, 95, 2 vol., 594 p., 638 p. (Kieler Werkstücke. Reihe D, Beiträge zur europäischen Geschichte des späten Mittelalters, 14).

3187. BROOKE (Christopher N. L.). English episcopal «Acta» of twelfth and thirteenth centuries. *In*: Medieval ecclesiastical studies [Cf. n° 4410], p. 41-56.

3188. Capitula episcoporum. Teil 2. Hrsg. von Rudolf POKORNY und Martina STRATMANN. Teil 3. Hrsg. von Rudolf POKORNY. Hannover, Hahnsche Buchhandlung, 95, 2 vol., XVI-242 p., XVIII-378 p. (Monumenta Germaniae Historica. Leges.).

3189. Carte (Le) del secolo XI dell'Archivio Arcivescovile di Lucca. Vol. 4. Dal 1044 al 1055. A cura di Giuseppe GHILARDUCCI, Lucca, San Marco, 95, 254 p.

3190. Carte (Le) della chiesa di S. Maria degli Armeni in Forenza, 1146-1548. A cura di Teresa COLAMARCO. Napoli, Edizioni Scientifiche Italiane, 95, XXVIII-143 p. (Istituto internazionale di studi federiciani, CNR Napoli, Acta et documenta, 1),

3191. Cartulaire du chapitre cathedral de Langres. Ed. par Hubert FLAMMARION. Nancy, A.R.T.E.M., 95, 448 p. (Diplomatica, textes et études).

3192. Cartulaire du Chapitre Cathédral Saint-Etienne d'Agde (Le). Ed. par Raymonde FOREVILLE. Paris, C. N. R. S., Institut de Recherche et d'Histoire de Textes, 95, 583 p. (Documents, études et répertoires).

3193. Collección de documentos de la Santa Hermandas (1300–1500). A cura de J. M. SANCHEZ BENITO. Toledo, Diputación Provincial, 95, 222 p. (Temas toledanos, 14).

3194. Collección diplomática de los reyes de Navarra de la dinastía de Champaña. Vol. 3. Enrique I de Navarra (1270–1274). Donostia, Eusko Ikaskuntza, 95, XIX-72 p. (Fuentes documentales medievales del País Vasco).

3195. Collección documental del Archivo Municipal de Bergara (1181–1497). Tomo 1. Donostia, Eusko Ikaskuntza, 95, XVII-84 p. (Fuentes documentales medievales del País Vasco).

3196. COLLOMB (Pascal). Les statuts du chapitre cathédral de Lyon (XIIe–XVe siècle): première exploitation et inventaire. *Bibliothèque de l'École des chartes*, 95, 153, 1, p. 5-52.

3197. Comacchio nelle antiche carte. Vol. 1. Per un codice diplomatico comacchiese, 715–1399. A cura di Paola BOZZINI e Aurelio GHINATO. Coordinamento scientifico di Antoinio SAMARITANI. Bologna, Nuova Alfa, 95, 154 p. (Per un museo delle culture umane del delta del Po in Comacchio, 6).

3198. COMPANYS I FARRERONS (Isabel), MONTARDT I BOFARULL (Núria). El castell del rei en temps de Jaume II. Edició comentada dels llibres de comptes de l'obra (1313–1317). Diputació de Tarragona, Institut d'Estudis Tarraconenses Ramon Berenguer IV, 95, [s. p.] (Secció d'Arqueologia i Història, 97).

3199. Comptes de l'écurie du Roi Charles VI. Vol. 1. Le registre KK 34 des Archives Nationales (1381–1387). Ed. par Guy-Michel LEPROUX. Paris, Diffusion De Boccard, 95, 272 p. (Recueil des historiens de la France. Documents financiers, 9).

3200. Comunità (Una) della valdelsa nel Medioevo: Poggibonsi e il suo statuto del 1332. A cura di Silvio PUCCI. Poggibonsi, Lalli, 92, 244 p.

3201. Consigli della Republica fiorentina (I). Libri fabarum XVII (1338–1340). A cura di Francesca KLEIN. Prefazione di Riccardo FUBINI. Roma, Ministero per i Beni Culturali e Ambientali, 95, XXXVII-481 p.

3202. Corpus des inscriptions de la France médiévale. Sous la dir. de E.-R. LABANDE. 18. Allier, Cantal, Loire, Haute-Loire, Puy-de-Dôme. Paris, par textes R. FAVREAU, J. MICHAUD, B. LEPLANT-MORA. Paris, C. N. R. S.-Editions, 95, 440 p. (pl., ill).

3203. Corpus Inscriptionum Latinarum. Editio altera. Volumen 2. Inscriptiones Hispaniae Latinae. Pars 14, Conventus Terraconensis. Fasciculus 1. Conventus Terraconensis, pars meridionalis. Ed. G. ALFÖLDY, M. CLAUSS. M. MAYER OLIVÉ. Berolini, Novi Eboraci, 95, XXX-167 p. (tab., ill., microfiches).

3204. Date (The), provenance and authorship of the pseudo-patrician canonical materials. Ed. by Aidan BREEN. *Zeitschrift der Savigny-Stiftung für Rechtsgeschichte. Kanonistisch Abteilung*, 95, 81, p. 83-129.

3205. DIEGO SANTOS (F.). Inscripciones medievales de Asturias. Oviedo, Principado de Asturias, Servicio de publicaciones, 95, 284 p. (ill.).

3206. Diplomatari (El) del monestir de Santa Cecilia de Montserrat. 2. Anys 1000–1077. Ed. por Francesc Xavier ALTES I AGUILO. *Studia monastica*, 95, 37, p. 301-394.

3207. Diplomatari de Santa Maria d'Amer. A cura de Esteve PRUENCA I BAYTONA i Josep M. MARQUÈZ I PLANAGUMÀ. Barcelona, Fundació Noguera, 95, 338 p. (Diplomataris, 7).

3208. Diplomatario del Cardenal Gil de Albornoz. Vol. 3. Cancilleria Pontificia (1357–1358). Ed. por María Teresa FERRER y Regina SÁINZ DE LA MAZA. Barcelona, Consejo Superior de Investigaciones Científicas, Escuela Española de Historia et Arqueología en Roma, 95, XXII-343 p. (tab.) (Monumenta Albornotiana).

3209. Documenti (I) del processo di Oderzo del 1285. A cura di Dario CANZIAN. Padova, Antenore, 95, LIII-247 p. (tav.) (Fonti per la storia della terraferma veneta, 9).

3210. Due libri mastri degli Alberti. Una grande compagnia di Calimala, 1348–1358. A cura di Richard A. GOLDTHWAITE, Enzo SETTESOLDI, Marco SPALLANZANI. Vol. 1. 1348–1350. Vol. 2. 1352–1358. Firenze, Cassa di Risparmio, CXLI-690 p.

3211. DUFOUR (Jean). Un acte inédit de Louis VI pour l'abbaye cistercienne de Loroy (1129). *Bibliothèque de l'École des chartes*, 95, 153, 1, p. 157-160.

3212. FABREGA I GRAU (Angel). Diplomatari de la catedral de Barcelona. Documents dels anys 844–1260. T. 1. Documents dels anys 844–1000. Amb l'estudi Dataciò dels documents de la Catedral de Barcelona (segles IX–XIII). Barcelona, Arxiu capítular de la catedral de Barcelona, 95, XV-706 (Arxiu capítular de la catedral de Barcelona, Publicacions, sèrie IV, Fonts documentals, I–1) (pl.).

3213. Fascicoli (I) della Cancelleria Angioina ricostruiti dagli Archivisti napoletani. Vol. 1. Fascicolo 9, 'olim' 82. Il computo del capitano Guglielmo di Recuperanza (1299–1301). A cura di Biagio FERRANTE. Napoli, Accademia Pontaniana, 95, LXVI-127 p. (Testi e documenti di storia napoletana pubblicati dall'Accademia Pontaniana. Serie III, 1).

3214. FUMAGALLI (F. M.), RICHLER (B.). Manoscritti e frammenti ebraici nell'Archivio di Stato di Cremona. Roma, La Fenice, 95, XII-126 p. (ill.). (Centro di studi delle testimonianze del giudaismo italiano, 4).

3215. GAUTIER DALCHE (Patrick). Carte marine et portulan au XIIe siècle. Le Liber de existencia riveriarum et forma maris nostri mediterranei (Pise, circa 1200). Roma, Ecole française de Rome, 95, XI-308 p. (Collection de l'Ecole française de Rome, 203).

3216. GONZALEZ BALASCH (M. T.), FERNANDEZ VIANA Y VIEITES (J. I.). La documentación pontificia en el «tumbo B» de la catedral de Santiago. In: Misc.lània d'estudis dedicats a la memòria de Professor Josep Trenchs i Òdena [Cf. n° 67], p. 627-646.

3217. HOCHHOLZER (E.). Ein Lambacher Kalendar-Nekrologfragment (11. Jahrhundert) aus Münsterschwarzach? Untersuchung zur Datierung und Entstehung von Lambach Fr. 4. Frühmittelalterliche Studien, 95, 29, p. 226-272.

3218. Jewish Inscriptions of Western Europe. Vol. 2. The City of Rome. Ed. by David NOY. Cambridge, Cambridge University Press, 95, XI-573 (ill., pl.).

3219. KEYNES (Simon). An Atlas of attestations in Anglo-saxon charters, c.670–1066. Cambridge, Department of Anglo-Saxon, Norse and Celtic, Univ. of Cambridge, 95, 78 tables in [c.250]p.

3220. LAFFONT (Pierre-Yves). Les chartriers seigneuriaux du XIIIe siècle: quelques réflexions sur une source méconnue au travers d'exemples du Haut-Languedoc. In: Comprendre le XIIIe siècle [Cf. n° 3965], p. 41-58.

3221. LARRAÑAGA ZULUETA (M.), LEMA PUEYO (J. A.). Colección de documentos medievales del Convento de San Bartolomé (San Sebastián), 1250–1515. Donostia, Eusko Ikaskuntza, 95, XXXIII-180 p. (Fuentes documentales medievales del País Vasco, 58).

3222. LEMAITRE (Jean-Loup). Les Obituaires du chapitre cathédral de Rodez. Paris, [s. n.], 95, 390 p. (Recueil Historiens de la France, Obituaires, 3).

3223. Liber tabuli Vitaliani Bonromei: mastro contabile del tesoriere ducale Vitaliano Borromeo (1426–1430). A cura di Pier Giacomo PISONI. Verbania-Intra, Alberti, 95, 340 p. (Raccolta verbanese, 8).

3224. Libro de actos judiciales de la alcaldía (1419–1499) y Libro de acuerdos y decretos municipales (1463) de la villa de Bilbao. Donostia, Eusko Ikaskuntza, 95, XXXVI-235 p. (Fuentes documentales medievales del País Vasco).

3225. Libro de privilegios de la Orden de San Juan de Jerusalén en Castilla y León (siglos XII–XV). Ed. por Carlos DE AYALA MARTINEZ. Madrid, Istituto Complutense de la Orden de Malta, 95, 864 p.

3226. MAIRE VIGUEUR (Jean-Claude). Révolution documentaire et révolution scripturaire: le cas de l'Italie médiévale. Bibliothèque de l'École des chartes, 95, 153, 1, p. 177-185.

3227. MARQUES PLANAGUMA (Josep M.). Escriptures de Santa Maria de Villabertran (968–1300). Figueres, Institut d'Estudis Empordanesos, 95, 404 p.

3228. MICHAUD (Jean). Les inscriptions romanes des musées Ochier et du Farinier à Cluny. Cahiers de civilisation médiévale, 95, 38, p. 165-172.

3229. MODIGLIANI (Anna). I protocolli notarili per la storia di Roma del secondo Trecento. Roma nel Rinascimento, 95, p. 151-158.

3230. MORDEK (Hubert). Bibliotheca capitularium regum Francorum manuscripta. Überlieferung und Traditionszusammenhang der fränkischen Herrschererlasse. München, Monumenta Germaniae Historica, 95, XLV-1158 p. (Monumenta Germaniae Historica, Hilfsmittel, 15).

3231. Notariato (Il) a Parma. La Matricula Collegii notariorum Parmae (1406–1805). A cura di Antonio ALIANI. Milano, A. Giuffrè, 95, XX-658 p. (tav., ill.). (Fonti e strumenti per la storia del notariato italiano, 7).

3232. Patti con Imola (I), 1099–1422. A cura di Andrea PADOVANI. Venezia, Il Cardo, 95, 74 p. (Pacta veneta, 5).

3233. Pergamene degli archivi di Bergamo (Le), aa. 1002–1058. A cura di Mariarosa CORTESI e Alessandro PRATESI. Edizione critica di Cristina CARBONETTI VENDITTELLI, Rita COSMA e Marco VENDITTELLI. Bergamo, Provincia di Bergamo, Assessorato alla cultura, Centro Documentazione Beni Culturali, 95, XVIII-618 p. (Fonti per lo studio del territorio bergamasco, 12. Carte medievali bergamasche, 2/1).

3234. PIANA TONIOLO (Paola). Notai genovesi in Oltremare. Atti rogati a Chio da Gregorio Panissaro (1403–1405). Genova, Accademia Ligure di Scienze e Lettere, 95, 312 p. (Collana storica di fonti e studi italo-ellenica, serie fonti, 2).

3235. PODHRADSKY (Gerhard). Handschriften aus dem 8.–11. Jahrhundert in Vorarlberg. Jb. d. Vorarlberger Landesmuseumsvereins, 95, 139, p. 31-48 (ill.).

3236. PONTAL (Odette). Les conciles de la France capétienne jusqu'en 1215. Paris, Ed. du Cerf et I. R. H. T. (C. N. R. S.), 95, 539 p. (Histoire).

3237. PUIG I USTRELL (Pere). El monestir de Sant Llorenç del Munt sobre Terrassa. Diplomatari dels segles XI i XII. Barcelona, Fundació Noguera, 95, 3 vol., [s. p.] (Diplomatari, 8–10).

3238. Regesta chartarum pistoriensium. Canonica di San Zenone. Vol. 2. Secolo XII. A cura di Natale RAUTY. Pistoia, Società pistoiese di storia patria, 95, LXI-314 p. (ill.). (Regesta chartarum pistoriensium. Fonti storiche pistoiesi, 12).

3239. Register (Die) Innocenz' III. Band 6. 6. Pontifikatsjahr 1203–1204. Texte und Indices. Hrsg. Othmar HAGENEDER, John C. MOORE, Andreas SOMMERLECHNER. Wien, Verlag der Österreichische Akademie der Wissenschaften, 95, LXVIII-487 p. (Publikationen des Historischen Instituts beim Österreichischen Kulturinstitut in Rom, II. Abteilung, Quelle, 1. Reihe, Die Register Innocenz' III., 6) (taf.).

3240. Register (The) of John Kirkby, Bishop of Carlisle, 1332–1352, and the Register of John Ross, Bishop of Carlisle, 1325–1332. Vol. 2. Ed. by R. L. STOREY. Leeds, Canterbury and York Society a. Rochester, Boydell & Brewer, 95, VI-186 p. (Canterbury and York Society, 81).

3241. Register (The) of Walter Bronescombe, Bishop of Exeter, 1258–1280. Ed. by O. F. ROBINSON. Leeds, Canterbury and York Society a. Rochester, Boydell & Brewer, 95, 224 p. (Canterbury and York Society, 82).

3242. Registri (I) della Cancelleria Angioina ricostruiti da Riccardo Filangieri con la collaborazione degli Archivisti napoletani. Vol. 42. 1268–1292. A cura di Stefano PALMIERI. Napoli, Accademia Pontaniana, 95, CCLXXIII-96 p.

3243. Reino de León (El) en la alta Edad Media. Vol. 8. La documentación real Astur-Leonesa (718–1072). Ed. por Manue Lucas ÁLVAREZ. Léon, Centro de Estudios e Investigación «San Isidoro», 95, 709 p. (Fuentes y Estudios de historia leonesa, 57).

3244. RUBELLIN (Michel). Les statuts synodaux. In: Comprendre le XIIIe siècle [Cf. n° 3965], p. 121-132.

3245. RUIZ DE LOIZAGA (S.), DIAZ BODEGAS (P.), SAINZ RIPA (E.). Documentación vaticana sobre la diócesis de Calahorra y la Calzada-Logroño (463–1342). Logroño, Gubierno de la Rioja, Instituto de Estudios Riojanos, 95, 314 p. (Biblioeca de temas riojanos, 98).

3246. RUIZ DE LOIZAGA (Saturnino). Los Cartularios Gótico y Galicano de Santa María de Valpuesta (1090–1140). Vitoria, Diputación Foral de Álava, 95, [s. p.].

3247. SCHUCHARD (Christiane). Bemerkungen zu den päpstlichen Registerbänden des 15. und frühen 16. Jahrhunderts in Paris. Quellen und Forschungen aus italienischen Archiven und Bibliotheken, 95, 75, p. 553-573.

3248. SCHÜTZ (Walter). Catalogus Comitum. Versuch einer Territorialgliederung Kampaniens unter den Normannen von 1000 bis 1140 von Benevent bis Salerno. Frankfurt a. M., Peter Lang, 95, 694 p. (Europäische Hochschulschriften, III, 641).

3249. Statuti pistoiesi del secolo XII. Breve di Consoli (1140–1180). Statuto del Podestà (1162–1180). A cura di N. RAUTY. Pistoia, Società pistoiese di storia patria, 95, 384 p. (Fonti storiche pistoiesi).

3250. Statuts (Les) synodaux français du XIIIe siècle. Tome 4. Les statuts synodaux de l'ancienne province de Reims (Cambrai, Arras, Noyon, Soissonne et Tournai). Ed. par J. AVRIL. Paris, Comité des travaux historiques et scientifiques, 95, XX-396 p. (Documents inédits de l'histoire de la France. Série in 8°, 23).

3251. STOKER (David). «Innumerable Letters o Goor Consequence in History»: the Discovery and First Publication of the Paston Letters. Tre Library, 17, 95, 2, p. 107-155.

3252. Storie a confronto. Le riformanze dei Comuni della Tuscia alla metà del Quattrocento. Manziana, Vecchiarelli e Roma, Roma nel Rinascimento, 95, 296 p.

3253. Summarium Heinrici. Band 3. Wortschatz, Register der deutschen Glossen und ihrer lateinischen Bezugswörter auf der Grundlage der Gesamtüberlieferung. Hrsg. von R. HILDEBRANDT und K. RIDDER. Berlin, W. de Gruyter, 95, XXXV-327 p. (taf.).

3254. TREMOLANTI (Ezio). I catasti dei contadini del secolo XV. Aspetti storici, socio-economici e demografici di ciascuna comunità costituente l'attuale municipalità larigiana. Ospedaletto e Pisa, Pacini, 95, VIII-544 p.

3255. Urkunden (Die) des Kloster Dalheim. Hrsg. H. MÜLLER. Münster, Aschendorff, 95, 282 p. (ill.) (Veröffentlichungen der Historischen Kommission für Westfalen. Westfälische Urkunden, 7).

3256. VENDITTELLI (Marco). Testimonianze sui rapporti tra «mercatores» romani e i vescovati di Metz e Verdun nel secolo XIII. Archivio della Società romana di storia patria, 118, 95, p. 69-99.

3257. VERGER (Jacques). Les statuts universitaires du XIIIe siècle. In: Comprendre le XIIIe siècle [Cf. n° 3965], p. 261-272.

3258. Women in Medieval England, c. 1275–1525. Documentary sources. Trans. by P. J. P. GOLDBERG. Manchester a. New York, Manchester U. P., 95, 307 p. (Manchester medieval sources series).

3259. ZEBALZA ALDAVE (M. I.). Archivo General de Navarra (1274–1321): documentación real. Donostia, Eusko Ikaskuntza, 95, XIX-309 p. (Fuentes documentales medievales del País Vasco, 61).

3260. ZUTSHI (Patrick N. R.). Collective indulgences from Rome and Avignon in English collections. In: Medieval ecclesiastical studies [Cf. n° 4410], p. 281-297.

Cf. n°s 1-44, 45-76, 3071, 4417

b. Literarische Quellen.

3261. AMIET (Robert). La tradition manuscrite du manuel ambrosien. Scriptorium, 95, 49, 1, p. 134-142.

3262. Anglo-Saxon chronicle (The). A collaborative edition. 1. Facsimile of MS. F: The Domitian bilingual. Ed. by David DUMVILLE a. Simon KEYNES. Woodbridge a. Rochester, Boydell and Brewer, 95, 23 p.

3263. Bouvines nach Segni (Von). Zwei Texte zur Geschichte Philipps II. Augustus. Hrsg. v. Rudolf HIESTAND. Francia, 95, 22, 1, p. 59-78.

3264. BOVEN (Walter). Scotichronicon. 3. Books V and VI. Ed. a. trans. John MAC QUEEN, Winfred MAC QUEEN a. D. E. R. WATT. Edinburgh, Mercat, 95, XXXII-521 p.

3265. BUTURAC (Josip). Pisani spomenici Požege i okolice: 1210–1536. (The written monuments of Požega and its surroundings, 1210–1536). Jastrebarsko, Naklada Slap, 95, 417 p.

3266. CAPGRAVE (John). Ye Solace of Pilgrimes. Una guida di Roma per i pellegrini del Quattrocento. A cura di Daniela GIOSUÈ. Roma, Roma nel Rinascimento, 95, 231 p.

3267. Career of Philip the Cleric (The), younger brother of Louis VII. Apropos of an unpublished charter. Ed. by Andrew W. LEWIS. *Traditio*, 95, 50, p. 111-127.

3268. CHIESA (Paolo). Vita e morte di Giovanni Calibita e Giovanni l'Elemosiniere. Due testi 'amalfitani' inediti. Salerno, Avagliano Editore, 95, 126 p. (Società salernitana di storia patria, Quaderni salernitani, 1).

3269. Chronica Hispana saeculi XII. Pars II. Chronica Naierensis. Ed. par Juan A. ESTEVEZ SOLA. Turnholt, Brepols, 95, CIX-230 p. (Corpus Christianorum continuatio mediaevalis, 71a).

3270. *Vacat*.

3271. CIAPPELLI (Giovanni). La memoria degli eventi storici nelle ricordanze private fiorentine (secc. XIII–XV). *In*: Memoria (La) e la città. Scritture storiche tra medioevo e età moderna [Cf. n° 3303], p. 123-150.

3272. CINGOLANI (Stefano Maria). Le storie dei Longobardi. Dalle origini a Paolo Diacono. Roma, Viella, 95, 206 p. (I libri di Viella, 6).

3273. COLLOMB (Pascal). Le 'Liber ordinarius', un livre liturgique, une source historique. *In*: Comprendre le XIIIe siècle [Cf. n° 3965], p. 97-109.

3274. Cronaca (La) di S. Domenico di Perugia. A cura di A. MAIARELLI. Spoleto, Centro italiano di studi sull'alto Medioevo, 95, LXVI-156 p. (ill.) (Quaderni del Centro per i collegamenti degli studi medievali e umanistici in Umbria, 36).

3275. Cronachetta di Urbino (1405–1444). A cura di Giovanni SCATENA. Urbino, Quattroventi, 95, 64 p. (ill., facs.) (Biblioteca del Rinascimento. Documenti e ricerche).

3276. DALENA (Pietro). Basilicata cistercense. Il codice Barb. lat. 3247. Galatina, Concedo, 95, 171 p. (ill.) [in appendice il testo del manoscritto] (Itinerari di ricerca storica. Supplementi, 14).

3277. DE CRESCENTIIS (Petrus). Ruralia commodalia. Das Essen des vollkommenen Landwirts um 1300. Teil 1. Einleitung mit Buch I–III. Hrsg. von Will RICHTER. Heidelberg, Universitätsverlag C. Winter, 95, LXXXVI-194 p. (Editiones Heidelbergenses, 25).

3278. DE VRIES (Kelly R.). Contemporary views of Edward III's failure at the siege of Tournai, 1340. *Nottingham Medieval Studies*, 95, 39, p. 70-105.

3279. DEFILIPPIS (Domenico), NUOVO (Isabella). Tra cronaca e storia: le forme della memoria nel Mezzogiorno. *In*: Memoria (La) e la città. Scritture storiche tra medioevo e età moderna [Cf. n° 3303], p. 419-466.

3280. DOIG (James A.). A new source for the siege of Calais in 1436. *English Historical Review*, 95, 110, 436, p. 404-416.

3281. FASOLI (Gina). Cronache medievali di Sicilia. Note d'orientamento. Testo riveduto da O. CAPITANI e F. BOCCHI. Bologna, Patron, 95, IX-78 p. (Il mondo medievale. Sezione di storia delle istituzioni, della spiritialità e delle idee, 21).

3282. Formative stages of classical traditions. Latin texts from Antiquity to the Renaissance. Proceedings of a Conference held at Erice, 16–22 October 1993, as the 6th course of International School for the Study of written records. Ed. by Oronzo PECERE a. Michael D. REEVE. Spoleto, Centro Italiano di Studi sull'Alto Medioevo, 95, XI-511 p. (Biblioteca del «Centro per il collegamento degli studi medievali e umanistici in Umbria», 15) [Cf. n^{os} <choice> 3313, 3319, 3328, 3332, 3982, 3988, 4119, 4141.]

3283. GIOVANNA MARIA DELLA CROCE. Vita. A cura di Cristina ANDREOLLI, Claudio LEONARDI, Diego LEONI. Spoleto, Centro italiano di studi sull'alto Medioevo, 95, XCIV-488 p. (tav., ill.) (Biblioteca del «Centro per il collegamento degli studi medievali e umanistici in Umbria», 12).

3284. HILEY (David). What St. Dunstan heard the angels sing. Notes on a pre-conquest Historia. *In*: Laborare fratres in unum [Cf. n° 4252], p. 105-115.

3285. Hofonglalás (A) kórának írott forrásai. (Les sources écrites de l'époque de la conquête du pays). Szerk. KRISTÓ Gyula. Szeged, Szegedi Középkorász Mühely, 95, 429 p. (Szegedy Középkortört. könyvtár, 7).

3286. IRACE (Erminia). La memoria formalizzata: dai libri di famiglia alle prove di nobiltà per gli Ordini cavallereschi. *In*: Memoria (La) e la città. Scritture storiche tra medioevo e età moderna [Cf. n° 3303], p. 73-103.

3287. Izbrano gradivo za zgodovino gozdarstva na Slovenskem v srednjem veku. (Selected materials for the history of forestry in Slovenia in the Middle Ages). Ed. by Bostjan ANKO. Ljubljana, Narodna in univerzitetna knjiznica, 95, 46 p. (Viri za zgodovino gozda in gozdarstva na Slovenskem, 8).

3288. JAURANT (Danielle). Rudolfs «Weltchronik» als offene Form. Überlieferungsstruktur und Wirkungsgeschichte. Tübingen u. Bâle, Francke Verlag, 95, X-407 p. (Bibliotheca Germanica, 34).

3289. JOHN OF WORCESTER. The chronicle of John of Worcester. 2. The annals from 450 to 1066. Ed. by R. R. DARLINGTON a. P. MAC GURK. Oxford, Clarendon Press, 95, LXXXVI-717 p. (Oxford Medieval Studies).

3290. JONAS D'ORLEANS. Le métier de roi (De Institutione regia). Ed. par A. DUBREUCQ. Paris, Ed. du Cerf, 95, 304 p. (Sources chrétiennes, 407).

3291. Jüngere (Die) Hildesheimer Briefsammlung. Hrsg. von Rolf DE KEGEL. München, Monumenta Germaniae Historica, 95, 284 p. (MGH. Epistolae, 2. Die Briefe der deutschen Keiserzeit, 7).

3292. Karolellus atque Pseudo-Turpini Historia Karoli Magni et Rotholandi. Ed. by Paul Gerhard SCHMIDT. Stuttgardiae, G. B. Teubner, 96. (Bibliotheca Scriptorum Graecorum et Romanorum Teubneriana).

3293. KNIGHTON (Henry) Knighton's Chronicle, 1337–1396. Ed. a. trans. by G. H. MARTIN. Oxford, Clarendon Press a. New York, Oxford U. P., 95, LXXXIX-593 p. (Oxford medieval texts).

3294. LARRINGTON (Caroline). Women and writing in medieval Europe. A sourcebook. London, Routledge, 95, XIV-277 p.

3295. LEONARDI (Claudio). Le cronache latine e la città italiana nel medioevo. In: Memoria (La) e la città. Scritture storiche tra medioevo e età moderna [Cf. n° 3303], p. 41-43.

3296. LEWIS (Peter S.). Some provisional remarks upon the chronicles of Saint-Denis and upon the [Grandes] Chroniques de France in the fifteenth century. Nottingham Medieval Studies, 95, 39, p. 146-181.

3297. Life (The) of Saint Francis of Assisi. A Critical Edition of the Ms. Paris, Bibl. Nat. fonds français 2094. Ed. by Janice M. PINDER. Grottaferrata, Collegio di S. Bonaventura, 95, X-167 p. (Editiones Archivum Franciscanum Historicum).

3298. LIFSCHITZ (Felice). The Norman conquest of Pious Neustria. Historiographic discourse and saintly relics, 684–1090. Toronto, Pontifical Institute of Medieval Studies, 95, XII-324 p. (Studies and texts, 122).

3299. Livre au roi (Le). Ed. par Myriam GREILSAMMER, foreword by Jean RICHARD. Paris, Académie des Inscriptions et Belles-Lettres, 95, 308 p. (Documents relatifs à l'histoire des Croisades, 17).

3300. LOMBARDI (Giuseppe). Cronache e libri di famiglia: il caso di Viterbo. In: Memoria (La) e la città. Scritture storiche tra medioevo e età moderna [Cf. n° 3303], p. 407-417.

3301. MAKK (Ferenc). Külföldi források és a korai magyar történelem. X–XI. század. (Les sources étrangères et la première période de l'histoire hongroise. X^e–XIe siècles). Acta univ. Szegediensis, Acta hist., 95, 102, p. 25-41.

3302. MARTINEZ PIZARRO (Joaquin). Writing Ravenna. The Liber Pontificalis of Andrea Agnellus. Ann Arbor, University of Michigan Press, 95, X-213 p. (Later Latin Texts and Contexts, 4).

3303. Memoria (La) e la città. Scritture storiche tra medioevo e età moderna. A cura di Patrizia BASTIA, Maria BOLOGNANI e Fulvio PEZZAROSSA; prefazione di Ezio RAIMONDI. Bologna, Il Nove, 95, 655 p. (Emilia Romagna. Biblioteche Archivi, 30). [Cf. n^{os} <scelta> 80, 3271, 3279, 3286, 3295, 3300, 3304, 3314, 3315, 3317, 3318, 3322, 3816, 3940, 3985, 4103, 4142.]

3304. MIGLIO (Massimo). La memoria e la città. Introduzione. In: Memoria (La) e la città. Scritture storiche tra medioevo e età moderna [Cf. n° 3303], p. 17-28.

3305. Mongolengeschichte (Die) des Johannes von Piano Carpine. Einführung, Text, Übersetzung, Kommentar. Hrsg. von Johannes GHISSAUF. Graz, Selbstverlag, 95, 265 p. (Schriften des Instituts für Geschichte).

3306. MORANDI (Ubaldo). Una fonte di storia senese del 1215: l'«Ordo officiorum Ecclesiae Senensis». In: Studi in onore di Arnaldo D'Addario [Cf. n° 452], p. 1101-1117.

3307. MOULINIER (Jean-Claude). Saint Victor de Marseille. Les recits de sa passion. Città del Vaticano, Pontificio istituto di archeologia cristiana, 95, XXI 662 p. (ill.) (Studi di antichità cristiana, 49).

3308. MÜLLER (Wolfgang P.). Eine neue Handschrift von Hugguccios Agiographia. Quellen und Forschungen aus italienischen Archiven und Bibliotheken, 95, 75, p. 545-552.

3309. OLAI (Ericus). Chronica Regni Gothorum. Band I. Textkritische Ausgabe. Hrsg. von Ella HEUMAN und Jan ÖBERG. Band II. Prolegomena und Indizes. Hrsg. von J. ÖBERG. Stockholm, Almquist & Wiksell International, 95, 85 p., 85 p. (Acta Universitatis Stockholmiensis. Studia Latina Stockholmiensia, 39).

3310. OTOREPEC (Božo). Gradivo za slovensko zgodovino v arhivih in bibliotekah Vidma (Udine): 1270–1405. (Materials for Slovene history in the archives and libraries of Udine: 1270–1405). Ljubljana, Slovenska akademija znanosti in umetnosti, Znanstvenoraziskovalni center SAZU, Zgodovinski inštitut Milka Kosa, 95, 335 p. (Viri za zgodovino Slovencev, 14).

3311. PAGNOTTA (L.). Sulle tracce di un libro d'autore. Il manoscritto Marciano It. IX 175 e la tradizione delle opere di Tommaso di Giunta. Studi Medievali, 95, 36, 1, p. 169-198.

3312. PANELLA (Emilio). Libri di Ricordanze di Santa Maria Novella in Firenze (XIV–XV sec.). Memorie domenicane, 95, 26, p. 319-367.

3313. PECERE (Oronzo). Il codice Palatino dell'Historia Augusta come «edizione» continua. In: Formative stages of classical traditions [Cf. n° 3282], p. 323-369.

3314. PESAVENTO (Luisa). La «pulcherrima urbs Mediolani» di Pietro Lazzaroni e la storiografia milanese di età sforzesca. In: Memoria (La) e la città. Scritture storiche tra medioevo e età moderna [Cf. n° 3303], p. 361-377.

3315. PEZZAROSSA (Fulvio). Alcune osservazioni sulle scritture storiche e di memoria nella Bologna tra medioevo ed età moderna. In: Memoria (La) e la città. Scritture storiche tra medioevo e età moderna [Cf. n° 3303], p. 495-522.

3316. PLEZIA (Marian). Wincenty Kadłubek – kronikarz krakowski. (Wincenty Kadłubek – chroniqueur cracovien). *Roczniki Krakowski*, 95, 61, p. 5-10. [Eng. Summary].

3317. QUAQUARELLI (Leonardo). Ricordanze familiari e lodi alla città. In margine al censimento dei generi memoriali non cronachistici bolognesi. *In*: Memoria (La) e la città. Scritture storiche tra medioevo e età moderna [Cf. n° 3303], p. 523-557.

3318. RAGONE (Franca). Il cronista e le sue fonti. Elementi del rapporto con la tradizione cittadina. *In*: Memoria (La) e la città. Scritture storiche tra medioevo e età moderna [Cf. n° 3303], p. 373-389.

3319. RIZZO (Silvia). Per una tipologia delle tradizioni manoscritte di classici latini in età umanistica. *In*: Formative stages of classical traditions [Cf. n° 3282], p. 371-400.

3320. RODRÍGUEZ DÍAZ (Elena E.). El libro de la «Regla colorada» de la catedral de Oviedo. Estudio y edición. Oviedo, Real Instituto de estudios asturianos, 95, XXXVII-639 p. (pl.) (Fuentes y estudios de historia de Asturias, 6).

3321. SADA (Luigi), VALENTE (Vincenzo). Liber de coquina. Libro della cucina del XII secolo. Il capostipite meridionale della cucina italiana. Bari, Puglie grafica sud, 1995, 195 p. (ill.) [in appendice il testo originale con traduzione italiana a fronte].

3322. SASSE TATEO (Barbara). Scrittura prammatica e memoria cittadina nel Mezzogiorno tardo medievale: i «libri rossi» di Puglia. *In*: Memoria (La) e la città. Scritture storiche tra medioevo e età moderna [Cf. n° 3303], p. 467-475.

3323. SBRIZIOLO (Itala Pia). Tipologia, struttura e stile dei poslanija della Rus, XIV–XVI secolo. Roma, Il calamo, 95, 136 p. (Biblioteca di ricerche linguistiche e filologiche, 36).

3324. SIGAL (Pierre-André). Les récits de miracles. *In*: Comprendre le XIIIe siècle [Cf. n° 3965], p. 133-144.

3325. Skriftlege kjelder til kunnskap om nordisk mellomalder. (Written sources concerning medieval Scandinavia). Ed. by Magnus RINDAL. Oslo, Noregs forskingsråd, 95, 70 p. (ill.). (KULTs skriftserie, 38).

3326. Somnium viridarii. Vol. 2. Ed. par Marion SCHNERB-LIEVRE. Paris, C. N. R. S., 95, 548 p. (Sources d'Histoire Médiévale).

3327. SOSZYŃSKI (Jacek). Kronika Marcina Polaka i jej średniowieczna tradycja rękopiśmienna w Polsce. (Chronique de Marcin le Polonais et sa tradition manuscrite médiévale en Pologne). Warszawa, 95, 190 p. (Pol. Akad. Nauk, Inst. Hist. Nauki, Studia Copernicana, 24). [Eng. summary].

3328. SPALLONE (Maddalena). «Edizioni» tardoantiche e tradizione medievale dei testi: il caso delle Epistulae ad Lucilium di Seneca. *In*: Formative stages of classical traditions [Cf. n° 3282], p. 149-196.

3329. STEFANO DI LECCE. Vita del beatissimo confessore Pietro Angelerio. A cura di Vincenzo LICITRA e Franco Lucio SCHIAVETTO. Istituto Molisano di Studi e Ricerche, Marinelli Editore, 95, 85 p.

3330. VAN HOUTS (Elisabeth M. C.). Local and regional chronicles. Turnhout, Brepols, 95, 60 p. (Typologie des sources du moyen age occidental, 74).

3331. VESZPRÉMY (László). La tradizione unnomagiara nella «Cronaca Universale» di fra' Paolino da Venezia. *In*: Spiritualità e lettere nella cultura italiana e ungherese del basso medioevo [Cf. n° 4128], p. 355-371.

3332. VILLA (Claudia). La tradizione di Orazio e la «biblioteca di Carlo Magno»: per l'elenco di opere nel codice Berlin, Diez B Sant. 66. *In*: Formative stages of classical traditions [Cf. n° 3282], p. 299-322.

3333. VILLANI (Matteo), VILLANI (Filippo). Cronica. Vol. 1. Libri I–VI. Vol. 2. Libri VII–XI e continuazione. A cura di G. PORTA. Parma, Fondazione Pietro Bembo e Guanda, 95, CLXXIII-889 p., 841 p. (Biblioteca di scrittori italiani).

3334. WARD (John O.). Ciceronian rhetoric in treatise, scholion and commentary. Turnhout, Brepols, 95, 373 p. (Typologie des sources de Moyen Age occidental, 58).

3335. WILLIAM OF JUMIÈGES, ORDERIC VITALIS, ROBERT OF TORIGNI. The Gesta Normannorum Ducum. Ed. by E. M. C. VAN HOUTS. Vol. 2. Books V–VIII. Oxford, Clarendon Press, 95, 360 p. (Oxford Medieval Texts).

3336. WOLFRAM (Herwig). Salzburg, Bayern, Österreich. Die Conversio Bagoariorum et Carantanorum und die Quellen ihrer Zeit. Wien u. München, Oldenbourg Verlag, 95. 464 p. (Mitteilungen des Instituts für Österreichische Geschichtsforschung. Ergänzungsband, 31).

Cf. n°s 1-44, 45-76, 1692

§ 2. Allgemeine Darstellungen.

* 3337. Bibliographie annuelle du moyen âge tardif. Auteurs et textes latins. T. 5. [T. 4. Cf. Bibl. 94, n° 3122.] Rassemblée et compilée par Jean-Pierre ROTHSCHILD, avec la collaboration de Pascal BERMON et Patrice SICARD. Paris et Turnhout, Brepols, 95, VIII-584 p.

* 3338. International medieval bibliography (450–1500). T. 28. Part 1. January–June 1994. Part 2. July–December 1994. [T. 27, part 1 and 2. Cf. Bibl. 94, n° 3123.] Ed. by S. FORDE a. A. V. MURRAY. Leeds, University, 95, 2 vol., XLVIII-457 p., LIII-480 p.

* 3339. Medioevo latino. Bollettino bibliografico della cultura europea da Boezio a Erasmo (secc. VI–XV). Vol. 16. [Vol. 15. Cf. Bibl. 94, n° 3124.] A cura di Claudio LEONARDI, L. PINELLI [et al.]. Spoleto, Centro Italiano di Studi sull'Alto Medioevo, 95, XXXVI-1027 p.

3340. 14. Jahrhundert (Das). Krisenzeit. Hrsg. v. Walter BUCKL. Regensburg, Pustet, 95, 240 p. (Eichstätter Kolloquium, 1).

3341. ANDERSEN (Per Sveas). Samlingen av Norge og kristningen av landet: 800–1130. (The unification of Norway and its conversion to Christianity, 800–1300). Oslo, Universitetsforlaget, 95, 381 p.

3342. Aquitaine and Ireland in the Middle Ages. Ed. by Jean-Michel PICARD. Forew. by Pierre RICHÉ. Dublin, Four Courts Press, 95, 272 p. (Four Courts Press, 6).

3343. Aufbruch – Wandel – Erneuerung. Beiträge zur «Renaissance» des 12. Jahrhunderts. 9. Blaubeurer Symposion vom 9. bis 11. Oktober 1992. Hrsg. v. Georg WIELAND. Stuttgart, Frommann u. Bad Cannstatt, Holzboog, 95, 279 p.

3344. BAGGE (Sverre). Nationalism in Norway in the Middle Ages. *Scandinavian Journal of History*, 95, 20, p. 1-18.

3345. BÁLINT (Csanád). Kelet, a korai avarok és Bizánc kapcsolatai. Régészeti tanulmányok. (Les relations de l'Orient, des premiers Avares et de Byzance. Etudes archéologiques). Szeged, JATE, 95, 348 p. (Magyar őstörténeti könyvtár, 8).

3346. BEJAN (Adrian). Banatul în secolele IV–XII. (Banat in the IVth–XIIth centuries). Timişoara, Editura de Vest, 95, 224 p. (ill.).

3347. BEZLER (Francis). Pénitence chrétienne et or musulman dans l'Espagne du Cid. *Annales*, 95, 50, 1, p. 93-108.

3348. Bilan et perspectives des études médiévales en Europe. Actes du premier Congrès européen d'Etudes Médiévales (Spoleto, 27–29 mai 1993). Ed. par Jacqueline HAMESSE. Louvain-La-Neuve, Institut d'Etudes Médiévales et Turnhout, Brepols, 95, 522 p.

3349. BONA (István). Az Árpádok korai váraíról. 11–12. századi ispáni várak és határvárak. (Des premiers châteaux-forts de l'époque des Árpad. Châteauxforts des comtes et se frontière au XIe–XIIe siècles). Debrecen, Ethnica, 95, 136 p.

3350. BORGOLTE (M.). Der mißlungene Aufbruch. Über Sozialgeschichte des Mittelalters in der Zeit der deutschen Teilung. *Historische Zeitschrift*, 95, 260, 2, p. 365-394.

3351. BRANDT (Miroslav). Srednjovjekovno doba povijesnog razvitka. (Medieval historical development). Zagreb, Školska knjiga, 95, 559 p.

3352. BROWN (Peter). La formazione dell'Europa cristiana. Universalismo e diversità. 200–1000 D. C. Roma e Bari, Laterza, 95, XII-438 p. (Fare l'Europa).

3353. BUNSON (Matthew). Encyclopedia of the Middle Ages. New York, Facts on File, 95, p. XIV-498 p.

3354. CARR (A. D.). Medieval Wales. New York, St. Martin's Press, 95, XVIII-165 p. (British history in perspective).

3355. Chūsei ni-okeru Kodai no Dentō. (Traditions of antiquity in the Middle Ages). Ed. by Jōchi Daigaku Chūseishisō Kenkyūjo. Tokyo, Sōbunsha, 95, 338 p.

3356. DE ANNA (Luigi G.) Mare Unicum: contantti tra il Baltico e il Mediterraneo in età medievale. *In:* Monta tietä menneisyteen [Cf. n° 1133], p. 51-62.

3357. Europa en los umbrales de la crisis (1250–1350). XXI Semaña de Estudios Medievales de Estella. Pamplona, Gobierno de Navarra, Departamento de Educación y Cultura, 95, 539 p. [Cf. n^{os} <selección> 3447, 3462, 3672, 3676, 3716, 3728, 3754, 3771, 3841, 3864, 4352, 4359, 4567.]

3358. FOLEY (John Miles). The implication of oral tradition. *In:* Oral tradition in the Middle Ages [Cf. n° 3381], [s. p.].

3359. FUMAGALLI (Vito). Scrivere la storia. Riflessioni di un medievista. Roma e Bari, Laterza, 95, VIII-109 p.

3360. GERICS (József). Egyház, állam és gondolkodás Magyarországon a középkorban. (Eglise, Etat et pensée en Hongrie au moyen-âge). Budapest, Metem, 95, 318 p.

3361. GOLDSTEIN (Ivo). Hrvatski rani srednji vijek. (Early Middle Ages in Croatia). Zagreb, Novi Liber, Zavod za hrvatsku povijest Filozofskog fakulteta, 95, 511 p.

3362. GRODECKI (Roman), ZACHOROWSKI (Stanisław), DĄBROWSKI (Jan). Dzieje Polski średniowiecznej. (L'histoire de la Pologne médiévale). T. 1. Do roku 1333. T. 2. Od roku 1333 do 1506 oprac. Jerzy WYROZUMSKI. Kraków, Universitas, 95, 426 p., 526 p.

3363. Histoire et archéologie des terres catalanes au Moyen Age. Dir. par Philippe SENAC. Perpignan, Presses Universitaires de Perpignan, 95, 445 p (Collection Etudes, centre de recherche sur les problèmes de la frontière).

3364. Vacat.

3365. JANIN (Valentin L.). Iz istorii novgorodsko – moskovskikh otnošenij v XV veke. (On history of Novgorod – Moscow relations in the XVth century). *Oteč. Ist.* , 95, 3, p. 150-157.

3366. KABAYAMA (Kōichi). Ikyō no Haken. (Discovery of the foreign world). Tokyo, University of Tokyo Press, 95, 261 p.

3367. KIDO (T.). The study of the medieval history of Europe in Japan. *Journal of Medieval History*, 95, 21, 2, p. 79-86.

3368. KOLANOVIĆ (Josip). Šibenik u kasnome srednjem vijeku. (Šibenik in the late Middle Ages). Zagreb, Školska knjiga, 95, 347 p.

3369. KOSI (Miha). Templarji na Slovenskem: prispevek k reševanju nekaterih vprašanj srednjeveške zgodovine Prekmurja, Bele Krajine in Ljubljane. (The Templars in Slovenia: a contribution to solving some problems of mediaeval history of the Prekmurje region, Bela Krajina region and Ljubljana). Ljubljana, Zveza zgodovinskih društev Slovenije, 95, 47 p. (Zbirka Zgodovinskega časopisa, 13).

3370. KRISTÓ (Gyula). A honfoglaló magyarok életmódjáról. Írott források alapján. (Sur le mode de vie des Hongrois conquêrants. Sur la base des sources écrites). *Századok*, 95, 129, 1, p. 3-62. – IDEM. A magyar álam megszületése. (La naissance de l'Etat hongrois). Szeged, Szegedi Középkorász Műhely, 95, 382 p. (Szegedi középkortört. könyvtár 8).

3371. LORD (Albert B.). Oral composition and "oral residue" in the Middle Ages. *In*: Oral tradition in the Middle Ages [Cf. n° 3381], [s. p.].

3372. LUNDEN (Kåre). Was there a Norwegian national identity in the Middle Ages? *Scandinavian Journal of History*, 95, 20, p. 19-34.

3373. MAC KITTERICK (Rosamond). Eight-century foundations. *In*: New Cambridge medieval history [Cf. n° 3378], p. 682-694.

3374. Magyarország történeti demográfiája. 1. A honfoglalás és az Árpád-kor népessége. (La démographie de la Hongrie. 1. La population de l'époque de la conquête du pays et des Árpád). Szerk. KOVACSICS József. Budapest, KSH, 95, 132 p.

3375. MAŽEIKA (R.). The Grand Duchy rejoins Europe: Post-Soviet developments in the historiography of pagan Lithuania. *Journal of Medieval History*, 95, 21, 3, p. 289-303.

3376. Medieval England. Ed. by H.W.C. DAVIS. London, Bracken, 95, XXI-632 p. (ill).

3377. MESTERHÁZY (Károly). A magyar fejedelem és kísérete a 10. században. (Le duc hongrois et son accompagnement au Xe siècle). *Századok*, 95, 129, 5, p. 1033-1052.

3378. New Cambridge medieval history (The). Vol. 2. C. 700–c. 900. Ed. by Rosamond MAC KITTERICK. Cambridge, Cambridge U. P., 95, XXXI-1082. [Cf. n^os <choice> 20, 3111, 3142, 3373, 3390, 3408, 3411, 3413, 3414, 3418, 3419, 3420, 3421, 3423, 3556, 3578, 3585, 3631, 3692, 3704, 3870, 3885, 3892, 3930, 3966, 4188, 4328, 4424, 4433, 4529.]

3379. NORDBERG (Michael). Den dynamiska medeltiden. (The dynamic Middle Ages [in Western Europe]). Stockholm, Tiden, 95, 429 p. – IDEM. I kung Magnus tid. Norden under Magnus Eriksson 1317–1374. (Nordic countries in king Magnus Eriksson's times, 1317–1374). Stockholm, Norstedt, 95, 361 p.

3380. O'CROININ (Daibhi). Early medieval Ireland, 400–1200. London a. New York, Longman, 95, XVI-379 p. (Longman history of Ireland, 1).

3381. Oral tradition in the Middle Ages. Ed. by W. F. H. NICOLAISEN. Binghamton, Medieval & Renaissance Texts & Studies, 95, 231 p. (ill., Papers presented at the 22nd Annual Conference of the Center for Medieval and Early Renaissance Studies, which was held Oct. 21–22, 1988, at the State University of New York at Binghamton). (Medieval & Renaissance texts & studies, 112). [Cf. n^os <choice> 526, 3358, 3371, 3533.]

3382. PLACANICA (A.). L'opera storiografica di Caffaro. *Studi Medievali*, 95, 36, 1, p. 1-62.

3383. PLJUKHANOVA (Marija B.). Sjužety i simvoly Moskovskogo carstva. (Themes and symbols of the Moscovite kingdom). Sankt-Peterburg, Akropol', 95, 335 p.

3384. RICHTER (Michael). Medieval Ireland. The enduring tradition. Foreword by Próinséas Ní CHATHÁIN. New York, St. Martin's Press, 95, XII-214 p.

3385. RILL (Bernd). Sizilien im Mittelalter. Das Reich der Araber, Normannen und Staufer. Stuttgart u. Zürich, Belser, 95, 335 p.

3386. RÓNA-TAS (András). A magyarság korai története. Tanulmányok. (Histoire initiale du peuple hongrois. Etudes). Szeged, JATE, 95, 329 p.

3387. SARAIVA (António José). O crepúsculo da Idade Média em Portugal. Ed. Manuel Joaquim VIEIRA. Lisboa, Gradiva, 95, 302 p. (Obras de António José Saraiva, 1).

3388. Seiō chūseishi. (The Medieval history of Western Europe). Ed. by Keizō ASAJI, Atsushi EGAWA a. Yoshihisa HATTORI. Kyoto, Minerva Shobō, 95, 3 vol., 285 p., 302 p., 333 p.

3389. Seiyō-Chūsei-zō no Kakushin. (Innovation of the images about the medieval western Europe). Ed. by Kōichi KABAYAMA. Tokyo, Tōsui-Shobō, 95, 397 p.

3390. SHEPARD (Jonathan). Slavs and Bulgars. *In*: New Cambridge medieval history [Cf. n° 3378], p. 228-248.

3391. Skånes och Blekinges riksgräns: dokumentation av de två danske landskapens gräns mot svenska Småland. Ed. by Bertil KARLSJÖ i samverkan med Göran HALLBERG. Lund, Halmstad, 95, 169 p. (Skrifter utgivna genom Dialekt- och ortsnamnarkivet i Lund, 8). [The documentation on the national border of medieval Scania and Blekinge].

3392. ŠKUNAEV (S. V.). Ranneirlandskaja tradicija i jazyčeskoe prošloe: problemy i perspektivy izučenija. (The early Irish tradition and the Pagan past: problems and prospects for study). *Vestn. drev. Ist.*, 95, 3, p. 38-47.

3393. Srednie veka: Sbornik. (The Middle Ages: Collected studies). Redkol.: O. I. VAR'JAŠ i drugie. Moskva, Nauka, RAN. In-t vseobščej istorii, 95, 298 p. Vyp. 58 (N 58).

3394. TAKAYAMA (Hiroshi). Shimpi no Chūsei-Ōkoku: Yōroppa, Bizantsu Isuramu Bunka no Jūji-ro. (A mysterious medieval kingdom: the crossroads of European, Byzantine and Islamic cultures). Tokyo, University of Tokyo Press, 95, 352 p.

3395. VAN HOUTS (Elisabeth). The Norman conquest through European eyes. *English Historical Review*, 95, 110, 438, p. 832-853.

3396. Zakon Krzyżacki a społeczeństwo państwa w Prusach. (Der Deutsche Orden und die Gesellschaft seines preussischen Staates). Studiensammlung hrsg. v. Zenon Hubert NOWAK. Toruń, Tow. Nauk. w Toruniu, 95, 197 p. (carte 1). [Deutsche Zsfassung].

Cf. n^{os} *1118, 5439*

§ 3. Politische Geschichte.

a. Allgemeines.

3397. BINSKI (Paul). Westminster Abbey and the Plantagenets. Kingship and the representation of power, 1200–1400. New Haven a. London, Yale U.P., 95, 241 p.

3398. GOLDBERG (Eric J.). Popular revolt, dynastic politics, and aristocratic factionalism in the early Middle Ages: the Saxon Stellinga reconsidered. *Speculum*, 95, 70, 3, p. 467-501.

3399. HELLE (Knut). Aschehougs Norgeshistorie. Vol. 3. Under kirke og kongemakt: 1130–1350. (Aschehoug's history of Norway. Vol. 3. Church and royal power 1130–1350). Ed. by Knut HELLE. Oslo, Aschehoug, 95, 239 p.

3400. Property and power in the early Middle Ages. Ed. by Wendy DAVIES a. Paul FOURACRE. Cambridge, Cambridge U. P., 95, XIV-322 p.

3401. Reino de León (El) en la alta Edad Media. Vol. 3. La monarquía astur-leonesa. De Pelayo a Alfonso VI (718–1109). León, Centro de Estudios e Investigación «San Isidoro», 95, 712 p. (Fuentes y Estudios de historia leonesa, 50).

3402. SEGURA GRAÍÑO (Cristina). Participación de las mujeres en el podere político. *Anuario de estudios medievales*, 95, 25, 2, p. 449-462.

3403. SIERCK (Michael). Festtag und Politik: Studien zur Tagewahl karolingischer Herrscher. Wien, Köln u. Weimar, Böhlau, 95, XIV-496 p. (Beihefte zum Archiv fur Kulturgeschichte, 38).

3404. TYERMAN (C. J.). Were there any crusades in the twelfth century? *English Historical Review*, 95, 110, 437, p. 553-577.

3405. VAN KAN (F. J. W). Elite and government in medieval Leiden. *Journal of Medieval History*, 95, 21, 1, p. 51-75.

3406. WERNER (Karl Ferdinand). Karl der Grosse oder Charlemagne? Von der Aktualitat einer überholten Fragestellung. München, Verlag der Bayerischen Akademie der Wissenschaften, In Kommission der C.H. Beck'schen Verlagsbuchh., 95, 62 p. (Sitzungsberichte der Bayerischen Akademie der Wissenschaften. Philosophisch-Historische Klasse; Jahrg. 1995, 4. Sitzungsberichte/Bayerische Akademie der Wissenschaften. Philologisch-Historische Klasse; Jahrg. 1995, 4).

b. 476–900.

3407. BOWLUS (Charles R.). Franks, Moravians, and Magyars. The struggle for the Middle Danube, 788–907. Philadelphia, University of Pennsylvania Press, 95, XVIII-420 p. (Middle Ages Series).

3408. COLLINS (Roger). Spain: the northern kingdoms and the Basques, 711–910. *In*: New Cambridge medieval history [Cf. n° 3378], p. 272-289.

3409. CUOZZO (Errico), MARTIN (Jean-Marie). Il particolarismo napoletano altomedievale. *In*: Particularisme napolitain au haut Moyen Age (Le) [Cf. n° 3422], p. 7-16.

3410. CUOZZO (Errico). La «militia Neapolitanorum»: un modello per i «milites» normanni di Aversa. *In*: Particularisme napolitain au haut Moyen Age (Le) [Cf. n° 3422], p. 31-38.

3411. DELOGU (Paolo). Lombard and Carolingian Italy. *In*: New Cambridge medieval history [Cf. n° 3378], p. 290-319.

3412. DELTERNE (M.). L'action de Philippe le Bel dans les «terres de débat» (1294–1301). *Annales du Cercle royal d'histoire et d'archéologie d'Ath et de la région et musées athois*, 95, 54, p. 39-72.

3413. FOURACRE (Paul). Frankish Gaul to 814. *In*: New Cambridge medieval history [Cf. n° 3378], p. 85-109.

3414. FRIED (Johannes). The Frankish kingdoms, 817–911: the east and middle kingdoms. *In*: New Cambridge medieval history [Cf. n° 3378], p. 142-168.

3415. GALASSO (Giuseppe). L'eredità municipale del ducato di Napoli. *In*: Particularisme napolitain au haut Moyen Age (Le) [Cf. n° 3422], p. 77-97.

3416. GNOCCHI (Claudia). Ausilio e Vulgario. L'eco della «questione formosiana» in area napoletana. *In*: Particularisme napolitain au haut Moyen Age (Le) [Cf. n° 3422], p. 65-75.

3417. JUSSEN (B.). Über 'Bischofsherrschaften' und die Prozeduren politisch-sozialer Umordnung in Gallien zwischen 'Antike' und 'Mittelalter'. *Historische Zeitschrift*, 95, 260, 3, p. 673-718.

3418. KEYNES (Simon). The British isles. England, 700–900. *In*: New Cambridge medieval history [Cf. n° 3378], p. 18-42.

3419. KITTERICK (Rosamond). The British isles. England and the continent. *In*: New Cambridge medieval history [Cf. n° 3378], p. 64-84.

3420. NELSON (Janet L.). Kingship and royal government. *In*: New Cambridge medieval history [Cf.

n° 3378], p. 383-431. – EADEM. The Frankish kingdoms, 814–898: the West. *In*: New Cambridge medieval history [Cf. n° 3378], p. 110-141.

3421. Ó CORRÁIN (Donnchadh). The British isles. Ireland, Scotland and Wales, c. 700 to the early eleventh century. *In*: New Cambridge medieval history [Cf. n° 3378], p. 43-63.

3422. Particularisme napolitain au haut Moyen Age (Le). Roma, Ecole française de Rome, 95, 329 p. (MEFRM, 107). [Cf. n^{os} <sélection> 3409, 3410, 3415, 3416, 4515.]

3423. SMITH (Julia M. H.). Fines imperii: the marches. *In*: New Cambridge medieval history [Cf. n° 3378], p. 169-189.

3424. SMYTH (Alfred P.). King Alfred the Great. Oxford, Oxford U. P., 95, 744 p.

3425. Teodorico e i Goti tra Oriente e Occidente. A cura di Antonio CARILE. Ravenna, Longo, 95, 422 p.

3426. TÓTH (Sándor László). A honfoglalás időpomtja. (Le temps précis de la conquête du pays). *Acta univ. Szegediensis, Acta hist.*, 95, 102, p. 3-10.

3427. WOLFRAM (Herwig). Grenzen und Räume. Geschichte Österreichs vor seiner Entstehung 378–907. Wien, Ueberreuter, 95, 503 p. (Österreichische Geschichte).

c. 900–1300.

3428. ARTIFONI (Enrico). Gli uomini dell'assemblea. L'oratoria civile, i concionatori e i predicatori nella società comunale. *In*: Predicazione dei frati (La) [Cf. n° 4451], p. 143-188.

3429. ASAJI (K.). The Barons' War and the hundred jurors in Cambridgeshire. *Journal of Medieval History*, 95, 21, 2, p. 153-165.

3430. BALESTRACCI (Duccio). Signorie, comunità e città. Le autonomie nella Toscana medievale (XIII–XV secolo). *In*: Libertà di decidere (La) [Cf. n° 3648], p. 185-205.

3431. BENSCH (Stephen P.). Barcelona and its rulers, 1096–1291. Cambridge, Cambridge U. P., 95, XVIII-457 p.

3432. BIAŁUŃSKI (Grzegorz). Wyprawa Bolesława Kędzierzawego na Prusy 1166 roku. (Expédition de Boleslas le Crépu contre la Prusse en 1166). *Zapiski historyczne poświęcone historii Pomorza i Krajów Bałtyckich*, 95, 60, 2-3, p. 7-19. [Deutsche Zsfassung].

3433. BLACK-VELDTRUP (Mechthild). Kaiserin Agnes (1043–1077). Quellenkritische Studien. Wien, Köln u. Weimar, Böhlau, 95, VII-478 p. (Münstersche historische Forschungen, 7).

3434. BOGUCKI (Ambroży). The administrative structure in Poland in the eleventh and twelfth century. *Acta Poloniae historica*, 95, vol. 72, p. 5-32.

3435. BOJKO (Krzysztof). Początki stosunków dyplomatycznych Wielkiego Księstwa Moskiewskiego z Rzeszą Niemiecką (1486–1493). (Relations du Grand Duché de Moscou avec le Reich Allemand: 1486–1493). *Studia Historyczne*, 95, 38, 2, p. 147-161. [Eng. Summary].

3436. BOSCHOF (Egon). Welfische Herrschaft und staufisches Reich. *In*: Welfen und ihr Braunschweiger Hof im höhen Mittelalter (Die) [Cf. n° 3486], p. 17-42.

3437. BRATCHELL (M. E.). Lucca, 1430–1494. The reconstruction of an Italian city-republic. Oxford, Clarendon Press, a. New York, Oxford U. P., 95, XII-346 p.

3438. CANAL SANCHEZ-PAGIN (José M.). La Casa de Haro en León y Castilla durante el siglo XII. Nuevas conclusiones. *Anuario de estudios medievales*, 95, 25, 1, p. 3-38.

3439. CARDINI (Franco). Crociata e religione civica nell'Italia medievale. *In*: Religion civique à l'époque médiévale et moderne (La) [Cf. n° 4528], p. 155-164.

3440. CORIA COLINO (Jesús I.). Intervención regia en el ámbito municipal. El concejo de Murcia (1252–1369). Murcia, Real Academia Alfonso X e Sabio, 95, [s. p.].

3441. DE ROSA (Daniele). Alle origini della Repubblica fiorentina. Dai consoli al "Primo Popolo" (1172–1260). Firenze, Arnaud, 95, 287 p.

3442. DERVILLE (Alain). La seigneurie artésienne (850–1350). *In*: Campagnes médiévales [Cf. n° 3713], p. 487-500.

3443. DI CAVE (Carlo). L'arrivo degli Ungheresi in Europa e la conquista della patria. Spoleto, Centro Italiano di Studi sull'Alto Medioevo, 95, 433 p. (Testi, studi, strumenti, 10).

3444. EHLERS (Joachim). Der Hof Heinrichs des Löwen. *In*: Welfen und ihr Braunschweiger Hof im hohen Mittelalter (Die) [Cf. n° 3486], p. 43-59.

3445. FONT (Márta). Magyar-orosz politikai kapcsolatok a 12. században, 1118–1199. (Relations politiques hungaro-russes au XIIe siècle). *Aetas*, 95, 3, p. 53-75.

3446. GALOPPINI (Laura), TANGHERONI (Marco). Le città della Sardegna tra Due e Trecento. *In*: Libertà di decidere (La) [Cf. n° 3648], p. 207-222.

3447. GENET (Jean-Philippe). Le développement des monarchies d'Occident est-il une conséquence de la crise? *In*: Europa en los umbrales [Cf. n° 3357], p. 247-273.

3448. GOEZ (Elke). Beatrix von Canossa und Tuszien. Eine Untersuchung zur Geschichte des 11. Jahrhunderts. Sigmaringen, Thorbecke, 95, 285 p. (Vorträge und Forschungen, 41). – EADEM. Die Markgrafen von Canossa und die Klöster. *Deutsches Archiv für Erforschung des Mittelalters*, 95, 51, p. 83-114.

3449. GÖRICH (K.). Der Herrscher als parteiischer Richter. Barbarossa in der Lombardei. *Frühmittelalter-

liche Studien, 95, 29, p. 273-288. – IDEM. Otto III., Romanus Saxonicus et Italicus: kaiserliche Rompolitik und sächsische Historiographie. Sigmaringen, J. Thorbecke, 95, 319 p. (Historische Forschungen, 18).

3450. GOUTTEBROZE (J. G.). Le duc, le comte et le peuple. Remarques sur une sédition des paysans en Normandie autour de l'an mil. *Moyen Age*, 95, 101, 3, p. 407-424.

3451. HABERSTUMPF (Walter). Dinastie europee nel Mediterraneo orientale. I Monferrato e i Savoia nei secoli XII–XV. Torino, Scriptorium, 95, 299 p. (Gli Alambicchi, 5).

3452. HELLE (Knut). Under kirke og kongemakt 1130–1319. Oslo, Aschehoug, 95, 239 p. (Aschehougs Norges historie, 3).

3453. HOFFMANN (Hartmut). Ottonische Fragen. *Deutsches Archiv für Erforschung des Mittelalters*, 95, 51, p. 53-82.

3454. JENKS (Stuart). Die Welfen, Lübeck und die werdende Hanse. *In*: Welfen und ihr Braunschweiger Hof im hohen Mittelalter (Die) [Cf. n° 3486], p. 483-522.

3455. KELLER (H.). Widukinds Bericht über die Aachener Wahl und Krönung Ottos I.. *Frühmittelalterliche Studien*, 95, 29, p. 390-453.

3456. KERBRAT (Pierre). Corps des saints et contrôle civique à Bologne du XIIIe siècle au début du XVI siècle. *In*: Religion civique à l'époque médiévale et moderne (La) [Cf. n° 4528], p. 165-185.

3457. KESSLER (Ulrike). Richard I. Löwenherz. König, Kreuzritter, Abenteurer. Graz, Wien und Köln, Styria, 95, 367 p.

3458. KIM (K.). Être fidèle au roi: XIIe–XIVe siècle. *Revue Historique*, 95, 119, 594, p. 225-250.

3459. KIS (Péter). A "király hű bárója". Ákos nembeli Ernye pályafutása. (Le "baron fidèle du roi". La carrière de Ernye de la génération Ákos [? 1225–1274/75]). *Fons*, 95, 2, 3, p. 273-316.

3460. KRISTÓ (Gyula), MAKK (Ferenc). Az Árpádház uralkodói. (Les rois de la dynastie des Árpáds). Budapest, I. P. C., 95, 288 p.

3461. LABUDA (Gerard). Śmierć Leszka Białego (1227). (La mort de Leszek Biały). *Roczniki Historyczne*, 95, 61, p. 7-36. [Deutsche Zsfassung].

3462. LADERO QUESADA (Miguel Ángel). La Corona de Castilla: transformaciones y crisis políticas. 1250–1350. *In*: Europa en los umbrales [Cf. n° 3357], p. 275-322.

3463. LANCONELLI (Angela). Autonomie comunali e potere centrale nel Lazio dei secoli XIII–XIV. *In*: Libertà di decidere (La) [Cf. n° 3648], p. 82-101.

3464. LAUDADIO (Valter). Uomini e potere dal Tronto al Potenza tra XI e XVI secolo. *In*: Libertà di decidere (La) [Cf. n° 3648], p. 131-154.

3465. MAC DONALD (R. A.). Matrimonial politics and core-periphery interactions in twelfth- and early thirteenth-century Scotland. *Journal of Medieval History*, 95, 21, 3, p. 227-247.

3466. MELVILLE (Gert). Um Welfen und Höfe. Streiflichter am Schluß einer Tagung. *In*: Welfen und ihr Braunschweiger Hof im hohen Mittelalter (Die) [Cf. n° 3486], p. 544-557.

3467. MILLER (Maureen C.). From episcopal to communal palaces. Places and power in northern Italy (1000–1250). *Journal of the Society of Architectural Historians*, 95, 54, 175-185.

3468. MOEGLIN (Jean-Marie). Zur Entwicklung dynastischen Bewußtseins der Fürsten im Reich von 13. zum 15. Jahrhundert. *In*: Welfen und ihr Braunschweiger Hof im hohen Mittelalter (Die) [Cf. n° 3486], p. 523-540.

3469. NOGRADY (Árpád). "Magistratus et comitatus tenentibus". 2. András kormányzati rendszerének kérdéséhez. (Données concernant la question du régime gouvernemental du roi András II [1205–1235]). *Századok*, 95, 129, 1, p. 157-194.

3470. ORTEGA PEREZ (Pascual). Aragonesisme i conflicte Ordes/vassalls a les Comandes templeres i hospitaleres d'Ascó, Horta i Miravet. *Anuario de estudios medievales*, 95, 25, 1, p. 151-178.

3471. PANERO (Francesco). Autonomie urbane e rurali nel Piemonte comunale: aspetti e problemi. *In*: Libertà di decidere (La) [Cf. n° 3648], p. 290-319.

3472. PASCUA ECHEGARAY (Esther). Violencia, escatologia y cambio social: la polemica en torno al movimiento de "la paz de dios". *Hispania*, 95, 55, 190, p. 727-737.

3473. POPPE (Andrzej). Spuścizna po Włodzimierzu Wielkim. Walka o tron kijowski 1015–1019. (Succession de Vladimir le Grand. Lutte pour le trône de Kiev en 1015–1019). *Kwartalnik Historyczny*, 95, 102, 3-4, p. 3-22. [Eng. Summary].

3474. RODGER (N. A. M.). Cnut's geld and the size of Danish ships. *English Historical Review*, 95, 110, 436, p. 392-403.

3475. *Vacat.*

3476. SAMSOMOWICZ (Henryk). La diversité ethnique au Moyen Age: le cas polonais. *Acta Poloniae historica*, 95, 71, p. 5-16.

3477. SCHNEIDMÜLLER (Bernd). Die Welfen und ihr Braunschweiger Hof im hohen Mittelalter. Zur Einführung. *In*: Welfen und ihr Braunschweiger Hof im hohen Mittelalter (Die) [Cf. n° 3486], p. 1-15.

3478. SIBYLLE (Eva), RÖSCH (Gerhard). Kaiser Friedrich II. und sein Königreich Sizilien. Sigmaringen, Thorbecke, 95, 200 p.

3479. SIMONETTA (S.). Una singolare alleanza: Wyclif e Lancaster. *Studi Medievali*, 95, 36, 2, p. 797-838.

3480. STALLS (Clay). Possessing the land: Aragon's expansion into Islam's Ebro frontier under Alfonso the Battler, 1104–1134. Leiden, New York a. Köln, E. J. Brill, 95, 337 p. (The Medieval Mediterranean, 7).

3481. STIH (Peter). Carniola, patria Sclavorum. *Österr. Osthefte*, 95, 37, 4, p. 845-861.

3482. Świat chrześćijański i Turcy Osmańscy w dobie bitwy pod Varną. (Le monde chrétien et les Turcs d'Osman à l'époque de la bataille de Varna.). Réd. par Danuta QUIRINI-POPŁAWSKA. *Zeszyty Naukowe Uniwerstyetu Jagiellońskiego*, 95, 1178, *Prace Historyczne*, 119, *Studia Pol.-Danubiana et Balcanica*, 8, p. 1-160. [Eng. Summary].

3483. TSURUSHIMA (H.). Feodum in Kent c. 1066–1215. *Journal of Medieval History*, 95, 21, 2, p. 97-115.

3484. TURNER (Ralph V.). The problem of survival for the Angevine "Empire": Henry II's and his sons' vision versus late twelfth-century realities. *American Historical Review*, 95, 100, 1, p. 78-96.

3485. VIGUERA MOLINS (María Jesús). De las taifas al reino de Granada, Al-Andalus, siglos XI–XV. Madrid, Edition Historia 16, 95, 145 p. (Historia de España, 9).

3486. Welfen und ihr Braunschweiger Hof im hohen Mittelalter (Die). Hrsg. v. Bernd SCHNEIDMÜLLER. Wiesbaden, Harrassowitz, 95, 559 p. (Wolfenbütteler Mittelalter-Studien, 7). [Cf. n^{os} <Auswahl> 125, 126, 3436, 3444, 3454, 3466, 3468, 3477, 3488, 3637, 3926, 3992, 4018, 4033, 4040, 4070, 4079, 4083.]

3487. WILLIAMS (Ann). The English and the Norman conquest. Woodbridge a. Rochester, Boydell and Brewer, 95, XV-264 p.

3488. WOLF (Armin). Gervasius von Tilbury und die Welfen. Zugleich Bemerkungen zur Ebstorfer Weltkarte. *In*: Welfen und ihr Braunschweiger Hof im hohen Mittelalter (Die) [Cf. n° 3486], p. 407-438.

d. 1300–1500.

3489. BACKMAN (Clifford R.). The decline and fall of medieval Sicily. Politics, religion, and economy in the reign of Frederick III, 1296–1337. Cambridge, Cambridge U. P., 95, XXII-352 p.

3490. CARRASCO MANCHADO (Ana Isabel). Propaganda política en los panegíricos poéticos de los Reyes Católicos: una aproximación. *Anuario de estudios medievales*, 95, 25, 2, p. 517-544.

3491. Crown, government and the people in the fifteenth century. Ed. by Rowena E. ARCHER. New York, St. Martin's Press, 95, VIII-252 p.

3492. DE ANGELIS (Laura). La fine della libertà pistoiese. *In*: Studi in onore di Arnaldo D'Addario [Cf. n° 452], p. 1157-1165.

3493. ESTOW (Clara). Pedro the Cruel of Castile, 1350–1369. Leiden, New York a. Köln, E. J. Brill, 95, XXXVIII-288 p. (The medieval Mediterranean: peoples, economies and cultures, 400–1453, 6).

3494. French descent (The) into Renaissance Italy: antecedents and effects. Ed. by David ABULAFIA. Aldershot, Variorum, 95, 496 p.

3495. GORI PASTA (Orsola). La crisi del regime mediceo del 1466 in alcune lettere inedite di Piero dei Medici. *In*: Studi in onore di Arnaldo D'Addario [Cf. n° 452], p. 809-825.

3496. GORSKIJ (Anton A.). Moskva, Tver'i Orda v 1300–1339 godakh. (Moscow, Tver and Orda in 1300–1339). *Vopr. Ist.*, 95, 4, p. 34-46.

3497. GREEN (Louis). Lucca under many masters. A fourteenth-century Italia commune in crisis (1328–1342). Firenze, Olschki, 95, VII-361 p. (Quaderni di «Rinascimento»).

3498. HILTON (Rodney H.). Inherent and derived ideology in the English rising of 1381. *In*: Campagnes médiévales [Cf. n° 3713], p. 399-408.

3499. HOENSCH (Jörg), KEES (Thomas), NIESS (Ulrich), ROSCHECK (Petra). Itinerar König und Kaiser Sigismunds von Luxemburg 1368–1437. Warendorf, Fahlbusch Verlag, 95, 170 p.

3500. KOVÁCZ (Péter). Miksa magyarországi hadjárata. (La campagne de Maximilien en Hongrie [1490]). *Tört. szle.*, 95, 37, 1, p. 35-49.

3501. LOPEZ PEREZ (María Dolores). La Corona de Aragón y el Magreb en el siglo 1331–1410. Madrid, CSIC, 95, 968 p.

3502. NIEDERSTÄTTER (Alois). Der Alte Zürichkrieg. Studien zum österreichisch-eidgenössischen Konflikt sowie zur Politik König Friedrichs III. in den Jahren 1440 bis 1446. Wien, Köln u. Weimar, Böhlau, 95, 443 p. (Forschungen zur Kaiser- und Papstgeschichte des Mittelalters, 14).

3503. NIETO SORIA (José Manuel). Enrique III de Castilla y la promoción eclesiástica del clero: las iniciativas políticas y las súplicas beneficiales (1390–1406). *Archivum historiae pontificiae*, 95, 33, p. 41-89. – IDEM. Propaganda política y poder real en la Castilla Trastámara: una perspectiva de análisis. *Anuario de estudios medievales*, 95, 25, 2, p. 489-516.

3504. OŻÓG (Krzysztof). Intelektualiści w służbie Królestwa Polskiego w latach 1306–1382. (Les intellectuels au service du Royaume de Pologne dans les années 1306–1382). Kraków, [s. n.], 95, 149 p. (Rés. français). (Uniw. Jagiell. Rozpr. Habil., 307).

3505. PAVIOT (Jacques). La politique navale des ducs de Bourgogne, 1384–1482. Lille, Presses Universitaires de Lille, 95, 387 p. (Economies et Sociétés).

3506. PONS ALOS (Vicent). El señorío de Sumacàrcer en la Baja Edad Media. De mudéjares a moriscos. [S. l.], Associació d'Amics de l'Ermita de Sumacàrcer, 95, 117 p. (ill.).

3507. RAMIREZ VAQUERO (Eloísa). Los resortes del poder en la Navarra bajomedieval. *Anuario de estudios medievales*, 95, 25, 2, p. 429-448.

3508. RAO (Ida Giovanna). Il Gran siniscalco Nicola Acciaioli e la vendita di Prato ai fiorentini. *In*: Studi in onore di Arnaldo D'Addario [Cf. n° 452], p. 799-808.

3509. RIEDMANN (Josef). Österreich und Italien im späten Mittelalter. *Röm. Hist. Mitt.*, 95, 37, p. 289-312 (ill.).

3510. RÖMER (Claudia). Osmanische Festungsbesatzungen in Ungarn zur Zeit Murads III. dargestellt anhand von Petitionen zur Stellenvergabe. Wien, Vlg der Österr. Akad. der Wiss., 95, 236 p. (Karten). (Schriften der Balkan-Kommission der Österr. Akad. der Wiss., phil.-hist. Kl., 35).

3511. SABATÉ (Flocel). Discurs i estratègies del poder reial a Catalunya al segle XIV. *Anuario de estudios medievales*, 95, 25, 2, p. 617-647.

3512. SAUL (Nigel). Richard II and the vocabulary of kingship. *English Historical Review*, 95, 110, 438, p. 854-877.

3513. SMOŁUCHA (Janusz). Między Warną a Mohaczem. Zagrożenie tureckie w świetle wybranych traktatów [1444–1526]. (Entre Varna et Mohàcs. Le menace turc à la lumière des traités choisis). *Studia Historyczne*, 95, 38, 4, p. 459-4791. [Eng. Summary].

3514. Ticino ducale (Il). Il carteggio e gli atti ufficiali. Vol. 1. Francesco Sforza. Tomo 3. 1462–1466. A cura di L. MORONI STAMPA e G. CHIESI. [S. l.], Edizioni dello stato del Canton Ticino, 95, XVII-627 p.

3515. Veneto nel medioevo (Il): le signorie trecentesche. A cura di Andrea CASTAGNETTI e Gian Maria VARANINI. Verona, Banca Popolare di Verona, 95, 465 p.

3516. Wars of the Roses in fiction (The). An annotated bibliography. Ed. by Roxane C. MURPH. Westport a. London, Greenwood Press, 95, IX-209 p. (Bibliographies and indexes in world history, 41).

3517. WITTLIN (Curt). El rei Pirro de Roma en el "Dotzè del Cristià" de Francesc Eiximenis. Crítica encoberta de la política sarda del rei Pere de Catalunya. *Anuario de estudios medievales*, 95, 25, 2, p. 647-658.

Cf. n°s 7920, 7929

§ 4. Juden.

** 3518. BATTENBERG (Friedrich). Quellen zur Geschichte der Juden im Hessischen Staatsarchiv Darmstadt 1080–1650. Wiesbaden, Kommission für die Geschichte der Juden in Hessen, 95, XVIII-636 p. (Quellen zur Geschichte der Juden in hessischen Archiven, 2). – IDEM. Herrschaft und Verfahren: politische Prozesse im mittelalterlichen Römisch-Deutschen Reich. Darmstadt, Wissenschaftliche Buchgesellschaft, 95, X-251 p.

** 3519. Żydzi w średniowiecznym Krakowie. Wypisy Łródłowe z ksiąg miejskich. (The Jews in Medieval Cracow. Selected records from Cracow municipal books). Ed. Bożena WYROZUMSKA. Kraków, Pol. Akad. Umiej., Uniw. Jagiell. w Krakowie, Izraelska Akad. Nauk, Uniw. Hebrajski w Jerozolimie, 95, 286 p.

3520. ESPOSITO (Anna). Un'altra Roma. Minoranze nazionali e comunità ebraiche tra Medioevo e Rinascimento. Roma, Il Calamo, 95, 345 p. (Pagine della memoria, 1).

3521. GOW (Andrew Colin). The red jews. Antisemitism in an apocalyptic age, 1200–1600. Leiden, New York a. Köln, E. J. Brill, 95, IX-420 p. (Studies in medieval and reformation thought, 55).

3522. HILLGARTH (Jocelyn Nigel). Sources for the history of the Jews of Majorca. *Traditio*, 95, 50, p. 334-341.

3523. HINOJOSA MONTALVO (José). Las tierras alicantinas en la Edad Media. Alicante, Diputación de Alicante, Instituto de Cultura "Juan Gil-Albert", 271 p. (Divulgación, 17).

3524. HOOD (John Y. B.). Aquinas and the jews. Philadelphia, Univeristy of Pennsylvania Press, 95, XIV-145 p. (Middle ages series).

3525. Italia Judaica. Gli ebrei in Sicilia sino all'espulsione del 1492. Atti del V convegno internazionale, Palermo, 15–19 giugno 1992. Roma, Ministero per i Beni Culturali e Ambientali, Ufficio Centrale per i beni archivistici, 95, 500 p. (Pubblicazioni degli Archivi di Stato. Saggi, 32).

3526. Jews in Western Europe (The), 1400–1600. Ed. by John EDWARDS. Manchester a. New York, Manchester U. P., 95, XVI-159 p. (Manchester medieval sources series).

3527. Jews of medieval Islam (The): community, society, and identity: proceedings of an international conference held by the Institute of Jewish Studies, University of London. Ed. by Daniel FRANK. Leiden, New York a. Köln, E. J. Brill, 95, XIV-357 p. (Etudes sur le judaisme médiéval, 16).

3528. Judios de Murcia en la Baja Edad Media (Los), 1350–1500. Recopilación y transcripción de Luis RUBIO GARCIA. Murcia, Universidad de Murcia, 1995, [s.p.].

3529. Judios, sefarditas, conversos: la expulsion de 1492 y sus consecuencias. Ed. por Angel ALCALA. Valladolid, Ambito, 95, 654 p.

3530. KENIG (Evelyne). Historia de los judios espanoles hasta 1492. Barcelona, Ediciones Paidos, 95, 164 p. (Paidos Studio, 109).

3531. KUBINYI (András). A magyarországi zsidóság története a középkorban. (L'histoire des Juifs en Hongrie au moyen-âge). *Soproni szle.*, 95, 49, 1, p. 2-37.

3532. Lettura ebraica delle Scritture (La). A cura di Sergio J. SIERRA. Bologna, EDB, 95, 525 p.

3533. LEVIN (Saul). The medieval transformation of the Jews' oral heritage. In: Oral tradition in the Middle Ages [Cf. n° 3381], [s. p.].

3534. LEWIS (Bernard). Cultures in conflict: Christians, Muslims, and Jews in the age of discovery. New York a. Oxford, Oxford U. P., 95, 101 p.

3535. Medieval studies: in honour of Avrom Saltman. Ed. by Albert BAT-SHEVA, Yvonne FRIEDMAN, Simon SCHWARZFUCHS. Ramat-Gan, Bar-Ilan U. P., 95, 292 p. (Bar-Ilan studies in history, 4; Bar-Ilan departmental researches).

3536. MENTGEN (Gerd). Studien zur Geschichte der Juden im mittelalterlichen Elsaß. Hannover, Hahnsche Buchhandlung, 95, XII-719 p. (Forschungen zur Geschichte der Juden, A/2).

3537. OCHMAN (Jerzy). Historia filozofii żydowskiej. (Histoire de la philosophie juive). T. 2. Średniowieczna filozofia żydowska. (La philosophie juive du Moyen-Age). Kraków, Universitas, 95, 512 p.

3538. ROTH (Norman). Conversos, inquisition, and the expulsion of the Jews from Spain. Madison, University of Wisconsin Press, 95, XVI-429 p.

3539. SAITTA (Biagio). L'antisemitismo nella Spagna visigotica. Roma, l'Erma di Bretschneider, 95, 158 p. (Studia historica, 130).

3540. SUAREZ BILBAO (Fernando). Las ciudades castellanas y sus juderias en el siglo XV. Madrid, Caja de Madrid, 95, 287 p (Coleccion Marques de Pontejos, 9).

3541. "Und groß war bei der Tochter Jehudas Jammer und Klage ..." Die Ermordung der frankfurter Juden im Jahre 1241. Hrsg. v. Fritz BACKHAUS. Sigmaringen, Thorbecke, 95, 116 p. (Schriftenreihe des jüdischen Museums Frankfurt am Main, 1).

3542. ZIWES (Franz-Josef). Studien zur Geschichte der Juden im mittleren Rheingebiet während des hohen und späten Mittelalters. Hannover, Hahnsche Buchhandlung, 95, XIII-374 p. (Forschungen zur Geschichte der Juden. Abteilung A, Abhandlungen, 1).

Cf. n° 170

§ 5. Islam.

3543. AL-TABARI (Abu Ja`far Muhammad b. Jarir). 'Abbasid authority affirmed. Ed. by Jane Dammen MAC AULIFFE. Albany, State University of New York Press, 95, XXIII-326 p. (The history of al-Tabari = Tarikh al-rusul wa'l-muluk, 28; SUNY series in Near Eastern studies; Bibliotheca Persica).

3544. AMITAI-PREISS (Reuven). Mongols and Mamluks: the Mamluk-Ilkhanid War, 1260–1281. Cambridge, Cambridge U. P., 95, XV-272 p. (geneal. tables, maps). (Cambridge studies in Islamic civilization).

3545. AZUAR (Rafael). Las técnicas constructivas en al-Andalus. El origen de la sillería y el hormigón de tapial. In: Semaña de Estudios Medievales (V) [Cf. n° 3568], p. 125-142.

3546. BERKEY (Jonathan P.). Tradition, innovation and the social construction of knowledge in the Medieval Islamic Near East. Past and Present, 95, 146, p. 38-65.

3547. CHALMETA (Pedro). Presupuestos políticos y instrumentos institucionales y jurídicos en al-Andalus. In: Semaña de Estudios Medievales (V) [Cf. n° 3568], p. 51-64.

3548. Civilización árabo-islámica (La). Ed. por Francisco VIDAL CASTRO. Jaén, Universidad de Jaén, 95, 173 p.

3549. ELAD (Amikam). Medieval Jerusalem and Islamic worship: holy places, ceremonies, pilgrimage. Leiden, New York a. Köln, E. J. Brill, 95, VII-196 p. (Islamic history and civilization: studies and texts, 8).

3550. Estudios sobre cementerios islámicos andalusíes. Ed. por Manuel ACIÉN, M. Paz TORRES PALOMO. Málaga, Universidad de Málaga, 95, 159 p. (Estudios y ensayos, 3).

3551. FELDBAUER (Peter). Die islamische Welt 600–1250. Ein Frühfall von Unterentwicklung? Wien, Promedia Druck- und Vlgs-Ges., 95, 612 p. (Karten). (Edition Forschung).

3552. Handbuch der Orientalistik. Abteilung 1. Der Nahe und der Mittlere Osten. Band 11. A Greek and Arabic lexikon: materials for a dictionary of the medieval translations from Greek into Arabic. Fasc. 3. Aslila. Ed. by Gerhard ENDRESS a. Dimitri GUTAS. Leiden, New York a. Köln, E. J. Brill, 95, 95 p.

3553. HOLT (Peter Malcolm). Early Mamluk diplomacy, 1260–1290: treaties of Baybars and Qalawun with Christian rulers. Leiden, New York a. Köln, E. J. Brill, 95, VIII-161 p. (Islamic history and civilization. Studies and texts, 12).

3554. HOSSEINI (Hamid). Understanding the market mechanism before Adam Smith: economic thought in medieval Islam. Hist. Polit. Ec., 95, 27, 3, p. 539-562.

3555. KALLFELZ (Wolfgang). Nichtmuslimische Untertanen im Islam: Grundlage, Ideologie und Praxis der Politik frühislamischer Herrscher gegenüber ihren nichtmuslimischen Untertanen mit besonderem Blick auf die Dynastie der Abbasiden, 749–1248. Wiesbaden, Harrassowitz, 95, IX-180 p. (Studies in Oriental religions, 34).

3556. KENNEDY (Hugh). The Muslims in Europe. In: New Cambridge medieval history [Cf. n° 3378], p. 249-271.

3557. Khadramaut: Arkheologičeskie, étnografičeskie i istoriko-kul'turnye issledovanija. Trudy sovetsko-jemenskoj kompleksnoj ėkspedicii. (Hadramawt: Archaeological, ethnographical and historical-cultural studies. Preliminary report of the Soviet-Yemeni joint complex expedition). RAN. In-t vostokovedenija i drugie, Redkol.: B. B. PIOTROVSKIJ (predsedatel') i drugie. T. 1. Otv. red. P. A. GRJAZNEVIČ, A. V. SEDOV. Moskva, Izdatel'skaja firma "Vostočnaja literatura". RAN, 95, 551 p.

3558. LAGARDERE (Vincent). Histoire et societé en Occident musulman au moyen âge. Analyse du MiYar d'al-Wansarisi. Madrid, Casa de Velazquez, 95, 536 p. (bibl.) (Collection de la casa de Velazquez, 53).

3559. LEVANONI (Amalia). A turning point in Mamluk history: the third reign of al-Nasir Muhammad ibn Qalawun (1310–1341). Leiden, New York a. Köln, E. J. Brill, 95, VI-221 p. (Islamic history and civilization. Studies and texts, 10). [Nasir Muhammad ibn Qalawun, Sultan of Egypt and Syria, 1285–1341]

3560. LOMBA (Joaquín). El Islam en el valle del Ebro: la cultura filosófica y científica. *In*: Semaña de Estudios Medievales (V) [Cf. n° 3568], p. 175-190.

3561. LORCH (Richard P.). Arabic mathematical sciences: instruments, texts, transmission. Aldershot, Variorum, 95, [s. p.]. (Variorum reprints. Collected studies series, CS517).

3562. MAILLO (Felipe). Doctrina islámica: principios y prácticas. *In*: Semaña de Estudios Medievales (V) [Cf. n° 3568], p. 23-34.

3563. MALPICA (Antonio). El agua en al-Andalus. Un debate historiográfico y una propuesta de análisis. *In*: Semaña de Estudios Medievales (V) [Cf. n° 3568], p. 65-85.

3564. MANZANO MORENO (Eduardo). El surgimiento del Islam en la Historia. *In*: Semaña de Estudios Medievales (V) [Cf. n° 3568], p. 11-21.

3565. NECIPOĞLU (Gürlu). The Topkapı scroll. Geometry and ornament in Islamic architecture. Santa Monica, Getty Center for the history of art and the humanities, 95, XIII-398 p. (Sketchbooks and albums). [With an essay on the geometry of the muqarnas by Mohammad al-Assad].

3566. *Vacat.*

3567. SAUNDERS (John Joseph). A history of medieval Islam. London a New York, Routledge, 95, XV-219 p. (maps).

3568. Semaña de Estudios Medievales (V). Najera del 1 al 5 de agosto de 1994. Ed. por José Ignacio DE LA IGLESIA. Logroño, Instituto de Estudios Riojanos, 95, 261 p. [Cf. n^{os} <seleción> 3545, 3547, 3560, 3562, 3563, 3564, 3569, 3571, 3572.]

3569. SOUTO (Juan Antonio). Las ciudades andalusíes. Morfologías fisicas. *In*: Semaña de Estudios Medievales (V) [Cf. n° 3568], p. 143-166.

3570. SPAULDING (Jay). Medieval christian Nubia and the Islamic world: a reconsideration of the Baqt treaty. *International Journal of African Historical Studies*, 95, 28, 3, p. 577-594.

3571. VALDÉS (Fernando). Datos sobre el comercio peninsular durante las primeras taifas: el reino de Badajoz. *In*: Semaña de Estudios Medievales (V) [Cf. n° 3568], p. 167-174.

3572. VIGUERA MOLINS (Maria Jesús). El establecimiento de los musulmanes en Spania al-Andalus. *In*: Semaña de Estudios Medievales (V) [Cf. n° 3568], p. 35-50. – EADEM. El Islam en Aragón. Saragoza, Caja de Ahorros de la Inmaculada, 95, 173 p. (Mariano de Pano y Ruata, 9).

3573. WASSERSTROM (Steven M). Between Muslim and Jew. The problem of symbiosis under early Islam. Princeton, Princeton U. P., 95, VIII-300 p.

3574. ZAKERI (Mohsen). Sasanid soldiers in early Muslim society: the origins of 'ayyaran and the futuwwa. Wiesbaden, Harrassowitz, 95, 391 p.

Cf. n^{os} *319, 1045, 1416, 1924, 1925, 3062, 3114, 3168, 3534*

§ 6. Wikinger.

3575. Agrip af Noregskonungasogum: a twelfth-century synoptic history of the kings of Norway. Ed. by M. J. DRISCOLL. London, Viking Society for Northern Research, University College London, 95, XXV-126 p. (Text series. Viking Society for Northern Research, 10).

3576. BJARNI (F. Einarsson). The settlement of Iceland, a critical approach: Granastadir and the ecological heritage. Reykjavik, Islenska bokmenntafelag, 95, 206 p. (ill., maps).

3577. CLARKE (Helen), AMBROSIANI (Bjorn). Towns in the Viking age. Leicester, Leicester U. P., 95, IX-210 p. (ill., plans).

3578. COUPLAND (Simon). The Vikings in Francia and Anglo-Saxon England to 911. *In*: New Cambridge medieval history [Cf. n° 3378], p. 190-201.

3579. FELLOWS JENSEN (Gillian). The Vikings and their victims: the verdict of the names. London, published for the University College London by the Viking Society for Northern Research, 95, 34 p. (Dorothea Coke memorial lecture in northern studies, 1994).

3580. FOLDÖY (Oddveig). The Viking in the Norwegian soul. Stavanger, Museum of Archaeology, 95, 23 p.

3581. GRAHAM-CAMPBELL (James). The Viking-Age gold and silver of Scotland (AD 850–1100). With contributions by Donald BATESON [et al.]. Edinburgh, National Museums of Scotland, 95, VIII-260 p. (ill., maps).

3582. GRIFFITH (Paddy). The Viking art of war. London, Greenhill Books a. Mechanicsburg, Stackpole Books, 95, 224 p (ill., maps).

3583. HAYWOOD (John). The Penguin historical atlas of the Vikings. London, Penguin, 95, 144 p. (ill, maps).

3584. KRAG (Claus). Aschehougs Norgeshistorie. Vol. 2. Vikingtid og rikssamling: 800–1130. (Aschehoug's history of Norway. Vol. 2: Viking Age and the Norwegian unification 800–1130). Ed. by Knut HELLE. Oslo, Aschehoug 95, 236 p.

3585. LUND (Niels). Scandinavi, c. 700–1066. In: New Cambridge medieval history [Cf. n° 3378], p. 202-227.

3586. MASONEN (Jaakko). Tracks, paths and roads: infrastructure and transport in Finland and the Baltic sea area from the Viking age to medieval times (800–1500 AD). Helsinki, Finnish national road administration, 95, 36 p. (maps). (Vagmuseets rapporter = Road museum reports, 1, 1995).

3587. PAGE (Raymond Ian). Chronicles of the Vikings. Records, memorials and myths. Toronto a. Buffalo, University of Toronto Press, 95, 240 p. – IDEM. Runes and runic inscriptions: collected essays on Anglo-Saxon and Viking runes. Ed. by David PARSONS with a bibliography by Carl T. BERKHOUT. Woodbridge, Boydell Press, 95, XIII-346 p. (maps).

3588. Scandinavian settlement in northern Britain: thirteen studies of place-name in their historical context. Ed. by Barbara CRAWFORD. London a. New York, Leicester U. P., 95, XV-248 p. (ill., maps).

3589. THUNMARK-NYLEN (Lena). Die Wikingerzeit Gotlands. Vol. 1. Abbildungen der Grabfunde. Stockholm, Kungl. Vitterhets Historie och Antikvitets Akademien, 95, [s. p.]

3590. *Vacat.*

§ 7. Rechts- und Verfassungsgeschichte.

3591. ANDREOLLI (Bruno). Per una morfologia della statutaria medievale emiliana: il caso modenese. In: Libertà di decidere (La) [Cf. n° 3648], p. 271-289.

3592. ANGIOLINI (Enrico). «Laudabiles consuetudines que tamen non sint a iure prohibite»: gli stretti margini di libertà delle comunità romagnole. In: Libertà di decidere (La) [Cf. n° 3648], p. 155-183.

3593. ARRIANZA (A.). Le statut nobiliaire adapté à la bourgeoisie: mobilité des statuts en Castille à la fin du Moyen Age. *Moyen Age*, 95, 101, 1, p. 89-102.

3594. AZZARA (Claudio). Il processo come gara. Aspetti ludici nel diritto processuale longobardo. *Ludica*, 95, 1, p. 7-17.

3595. BAAKEN (Gerhard). Das sizilische Königtum Kaiser Heinrichs VI. *Zeitschrift der Savigny-Stiftung für Rechtsgeschichte. Germanistische Abteilung*, 95, 112, p. 202-244.

3596. BADER (Karl Siegfried). Zum Unrechtsausgleich und zur Strafe im Frühmittelalter. *Zeitschrift der Savigny-Stiftung für Rechtsgeschichte. Germanistische Abteilung*, 95, 112, p. 1-63.

3597. BALLETTO (Laura). Novità e conservazione degli statuti liguri del tardo medioevo. In: Libertà di decidere (La) [Cf. n° 3648], p. 223-243.

3598. BARRIO BARRIO (Juan Alfonso). Gobierno municipal en Orihuela durante el reinado de Alfonso V, 1416–1458. Alicante, Universidad de Alicante, 95, 258 p.

3599. BARTOLO DA SASSOFERRATO. A grammar of signs. Bartolo da Sassoferrato's "Tract on Insignia and Coats of Arms". Ed. a. trans. by Osvaldo CAVALLAR, Susanne DEGENRING a. Julius KIRSHNER. Berkeley, Robbins Collection Publications, University of California Berkeley, 95, XVII-200 p. (Studies in comparative legal history).

3600. BAUMGÄRTNER (Ingrid). «Quidam presbiter beneficialis». Der niedere Klerus in den Rechtsgutachten des späten Mittelalters. *Zeitschrift der Savigny-Stiftung für Rechtsgeschichte. Kanonistische Abteilung*, 95, 81, p. 189-224.

3601. BOUGARD (François). La justice dans le royaume d'Italie de la fin du VIIIe siècle au début du XIe siècle. Roma, Ecole française de Rome, 95, III-504 p. (Bibliothèque de l'Ecole française d'Athènes et de Rome, 291).

3602. BOUREAU (Alain). Le droit de cuissage: la fabrication d'un mythe (XIIIe–XXe siècle). Paris, Albin Michel, 95, 327 p. (L'Evolution de l'Humanité).

3603. BRECHON (Franck). Autour du notariat et des nouvelles pratiques de l'écrit dans les régions méridionales aux XIIe et XIIIe siècles. In: Comprendre le XIIIe siècle [Cf. n° 3965], p. 161-172.

3604. BRETT (Martin). Canon law and litigation. The century before Gratian. In: Medieval ecclesiastical studies [Cf. n° 4410], p. 21-40.

3605. BRUNDAGE (James A.). Medieval canon law. London a. New York, Longman, 95, XII-260 p. – IDEM. The rise of professional canonists and development of the «Ius commune». *Zeitschrift der Savigny-Stiftung für Rechtsgeschichte. Kanonistische Abteilung*, 95, 81, p. 26-63.

3606. BUCCI (Oddo). Osservazioni sulla legislazione statutaria in materia di gestione dei documenti (secc. XIII–XIV). In: Studi in onore di Arnaldo D'Addario [Cf. n° 452], p. 59-73.

3607. CABEZUELO PLIEGO (José Vicente). "Procuració versus governació". El reino de Valencia ante la reforma gubernativa de 1344. *Anuario de estudios medievales*, 95, 25, 2, p. 571-592.

3608. CACIORGNA (Maria Teresa). L'influenza angioina in Italia: gli ufficiali nominati a Roma e nel

Lazio. *Mélanges de l'Ecole française de Rome. Moyen Age-Temps modernes*, 95, 107, p. 173-206.

3609. CARMONA RUIZ (M. Antonia). Usurpaciones de tierras y derechos comunales en Sevilla y su "tierra" durante el siglo XV. Madrid, Ministerio de Agricultura, Pesca y Alimentación, 95, 254 p.

3610. CATALAN MARTINEZ (Elena). La pervivencia del derecho patrimonial en la iglesia vasca durante el feudalismo desarrollado. *Hispania*, 95, 55, 190, p. 567-587.

3611. CLEMENTI (Alessandro). Autonomie negli Abruzzi: alcuni esempi (secc. XIII–XIV). *In*: Libertà di decidere (La) [Cf. n° 3648], p. 61-81.

3612. Consilia im späten Mittelalter. Zum historischen Aussagewert einer Quellengattung. Hrsg. v. Ingrid BAUMGÄRTNER. Sigmaringen, Thorbecke, 95, 95, 256 p. (Studi. Schriftenreihe des Deutschen Studienzentrums in Venedig. Centro tedesco di studi veneziani, 13).

3613. CONTE (Emanuele). Cose, persone, obbligazioni, consuetudini. Piccole osservazioni su grandi temi. *In*: Sol et l'immeuble (Le) [Cf. n° 3682], p. 27-39.

3614. CORRAO (Pietro). Città e normativa cittadina nell'Italia meridionale e in Sicilia nel medioevo: un problema storiografico da riformulare. *In*: Libertà di decidere (La) [Cf. n° 3648], p. 35-60.

3615. CORTESE (Ennio). Diritto nella storia medievale (Il). Vol. 1. L'alto Medioevo. Roma, Il Cigno G. Galilei, 95, VI-465 p. – IDEM. Il processo longobardo tra romanità e germanesimo. *In*: Giustizia (La) nell'Alto Medioevo [Cf. n° 3630], p. 621-647.

3616. DE BORCHGRAVE (Christian). De technische aspecten van de Bourgondische diplomatie onder hertog Jan zonder Vrees (1404–1419). *Revue belge de philologie et d'histoire*, 95, 73, p. 287-318.

3617. Dedalo statutario (Dal). Atti dell'incontro di studio dedicato agli Statuti, Centro seminariale Monte Verità, 11–13 novembre 1993. *Archivio storico ticinese*, 95, 32, p. 127-288 [Interventi di Pio CARONI, Antonio PADOA SCHIOPPA, Giorgio CHITTOLINI, Claudia STORTI STORCHI, Alessandro PASTORE, Ettore DEZZA, Gian Savino PENE VIDARI].

3618. DONDARINI (Rolando). «... terra Centi et Plebis regitur legibus et suis propriis statutis et ordinamentis sibi datis ...». Gli statuti medievali centopievesi come manifesto di autonomia di una comunità contesa. *In*: Libertà di decidere (La) [Cf. n° 3648], p. 397-410.

3619. DONNINI (Mauro). Sul lessico giuridico nelle fonti altomedievali: polisemia ed esattezza di significato in un latino fra letteratura e diritto. *In*: Giustizia (La) nell'Alto Medioevo [Cf. n° 3630], p. 1209-1240.

3620. Dret Comú i Catalunya (El). Actes del IV Simposi Internacional Homenatge al professor Josep M. Gay Escoda. Barcelona, 27–28 de maig de 1994. Ed. por Aquilino IGLESIA FERREIRÓS. Barcelona, Fundació Noguera, 95, 376 p. (Estudis, 9).

3621. ERDÖ (Peter). Diritto civile veneziano in Ungheria. *In*: Spiritualità e lettere nella cultura italiana e ungherese del basso medioevo [Cf. n° 4128], p. 389-399. – IDEM. Tribunali ecclesiastici medievali in Polonia e in Ungheria. *Studi Medievali*, 95, 36, 1, p. 323-344.

3622. ERRERA (Andrea). "Arbor actionum". Genere letterario e forma di classificazione delle azioni nella dottrina dei glossatori. Bologna, Monduzzi, 95, XVII-406 p. (Archivio per la storia del diritto medioevale e moderno, 1).

3623. FAVINO (L.). Giovanni di Capestrano ed il diritto civile. *Studi Medievali*, 95, 36, 1, p. 255-284.

3624. FEBRER ROMAGUERA (Manuel Vicent). Las servidumbres prediales en el Derecho foral valenciano medieval. *Anuario de estudios medievales*, 95, 25, 1, p. 67-80.

3625. FOURACRE (Paul). Carolingian justice. The rhetoric of improvement and context of abuse. *In*: Giustizia (La) nell'Alto Medioevo [Cf. n° 3630], p. 771-803.

3626. FOWLER (Elizabeth). Civil death and the maiden: agency and the conditions of contract in Piers Plowman. *Speculum*, 95, 70, 4, p. 760-792.

3627. FUMAGALLI (Vito). Le vicende delle formule giudiziarie nella documentazione altomedievale sino all'età carolingia. *In*: Giustizia (La) nell'Alto Medioevo [Cf. n° 3630], p. 607-619.

3628. GAUTHIEZ (Bernard). Le formes des immeubles et le statut juridique des terrains: l'exemple de Rouen du XIIIe au XVIIIe siècle. *In*: Sol et l'immeuble (Le) [Cf. n° 3682], p. 267-299.

3629. GEARY (Patrick J.). Extra-judicial means of conflict resolution. *In*: Giustizia (La) nell'Alto Medioevo [Cf. n° 3630], p. 568-601.

3630. Giustizia (La) nell'Alto Medioevo (secoli V–VIII). Spoleto, Centro Italiano di Studi sull'Alto Medioevo, 95, 2 vol., XVI-652 p., 627 p. (Settimane di studio, 42). [Cf. n^{os} <scelta> 2961, 3615, 3619, 3630, 3627, 3629, 3633, 3636, 3642, 3643, 3667, 3669, 3678, 3679, 3688, 4052, 4226, 4332, 4362.]

3631. GOETZ (Hans-Werner). Social and military institutions. *In*: New Cambridge medieval history [Cf. n° 3378], p. 451-480.

3632. GROSSI (Paolo). L'ordine giuridico medievale. Roma e Bari, Laterza, 95, VII-265 p.

3633. GUILLOT (Olivier). La justice dans le royaume franc à l'époque mérovingienne. *In*: Giustizia (La) nell'Alto Medioevo [Cf. n° 3630], p. 653-731.

3634. GUINOT RODRÍGUEZ (Enric). Organització i estructuració del poder al sí d'un Ordre Militar: el cas de l'Ordre de Montesa (segles XIV–XV). *Anuario de estudios medievales*, 95, 25, 1, p. 179-214.

3635. GUYADER (Josseline). L'appel en droit canonique médiéval. *In*: Voies de recours judiciaires (Les) [Cf. n° 3687], p. 31-51.

3636. HARTMANN (Wilfried). Der Bischof als Richter nach den kirchenrechtlichen Quellen des 4. bis 7. Jahrhunderts. *In*: Giustizia (La) nell'Alto Medioevo [Cf. n° 3630], p. 805-837.

3637. HASSE (Klaus-Peter). Hofämter am welfischen Fürstenhof. *In*: Welfen und ihr Braunschweiger Hof im hohen Mittelalter (Die) [Cf. n° 3486], p. 95-122.

3638. HEUCLIN (Jean). Biens ecclésiastiques et 'invasiones' au VIe siècle. *In*: Sources de la gestion publique (Aux). Tome 2 [Cf. n° 4574], p. 135-147.

3639. JACKMAN (Donald C.). Das Eherecht und der frühdeutsche Adel. *Zeitschrift der Savigny-Stiftung für Rechtsgeschichte. Germanistische Abteilung*, 95, 112, p. 158-201.

3640. KANAO (T.). Les messagers du Duc de Bourgogne au début du XVe siècle. *Journal of Medieval History*, 95, 21, 2, p. 195-226

3641. KELLY (Robert L.). Malory and the common law: Hasty judgement in the "Tale of the Death of King Arthur". *Medievalia et Humanistica*, 95, 22, p. 111-140.

3642. KOTTJE (Raymund). «Buße oder Strafe?» Zur «Iustitia» in den «libri penitentiales». *In*: Giustizia (La) nell'Alto Medioevo [Cf. n° 3630], p. 443-468.

3643. KROESCHELL (Karl). Recht und Gericht in den merowingischen «Kapitularien». *In*: Giustizia (La) nell'Alto Medioevo [Cf. n° 3630], p. 737-765.

3644. KUEHN (Thomas). Vicissitudini di un patrimonio fiorentino del XV secolo. *Quaderni storici*, 95, 30, 88 (1), p. 43-62.

3645. LANDAU (Peter). Ehetrennung als Strafe. Zum Wandel des kanonischen Eherechts im 12. Jahrhundert. *Zeitschrift der Savigny-Stiftung für Rechtsgeschichte. Kanonistische Abteilung*, 95, 81, p. 148-188.

3646. LEMARIGNIER (Jean-François). Structures politiques et religieuses dans la France du haut Moyen Age. Recueil d'articles rassemblés par ses disciples. Rouen, Publications de l'université de Rouen, 95, 446 p. (Publications de l'université de Rouen, 206).

3647. LEYTE (Guillaume). «Imperium» et «dominium» chez les glossateurs. *Droits*, 95, 22, p. 19-26.

3648. Libertà di decidere (La). Realtà e parvenze di autonomia nella normativa locale del medioevo. Atti del Convegno nazionale di studi. Cento, 6–7 maggio 1993. A cura di Rolando DONDARINI. Cento, Comune di Cento, 95, 415 p. [Cf. n^{os} <scelta> 3430, 3446, 3463, 3464, 3471, 3591, 3592, 3597, 3611, 3614, 3618, 3660, 3661, 3670, 3686, 3689.]

3649. LINGER (Sandrine). Acquisition et transmission de propriétés d'après le testament de Bertrand du Mans (27 mars 616). *In*: Sources de la gestion publique (Aux). Tome 2 [Cf. n° 4574], p. 171-194.

3650. LIZISOWA (Maria Teresa). Podstawowe terminy prawne w statutach staropolskich na tle słowiańskim [XIV–XV w]. Studium semantyczne. (Termes juridiques de base dans les anciens statuts polonais sur le fond slave, XIVe–XVe s. Etudes sémantique). Kraków, Wydawn. Nauk. Wyższej Szkoły Pedagog., 95, 283 p. (Eng. summary).

3651. LOGAN (F. Donald). The Cambridge canon law faculty. Sermons and addresses. *In*: Medieval ecclesiastical studies [Cf. n° 4410], p. 151-164.

3652. LOHRMANN (Dietrich). Zwei Mühlenstatuten von 1188 und 1212 aus der Picardie. *In*: Campagnes médiévales [Cf. n° 3713], p. 217-230.

3653. MAC HARDY (A. K.). Church courts and criminous clerks in the later Middle Ages. *In*: Medieval ecclesiastical studies [Cf. n° 4410], p. 165-183.

3654. MAGNOU-NORTIER (Elisabeth). L'enjeu des biens ecclésiastiques dans la crise du IXe siècle. *In*: Sources de la gestion publique (Aux). Tome 2 [Cf. n° 4574], p. 227-259. – EADEM. La confiscation des biens d'Eglise: un droit royal (VIe–VIIIe siècles). *In*: Sources de la gestion publique (Aux). Tome 2 [Cf. n° 4574], p. 149-169.

3655. MANSFIELD (Mary C.). The humiliation of sinners: public penance in thirteenth-century France. Ithaca a. London, Cornell U. P., 95, XV-343 p.

3656. MARTÍNEZ MARTÍNEZ (María). La territorialización del poder: los Adelantados mayores de Murcia (siglos XIII–XV). *Anuario de estudios medievales*, 95, 25, 2, p. 545-570.

3657. MINEO (E. Igor). Formazione delle élites urbane nella Sicilia del tardo medioevo: matrimonio e sistemi di successione. *Quaderni storici*, 95, 30, 88 (1), p. 9-42.

3658. MOLENAT (Jea-Pierre). Les Francs de Tolède aux XIIe et XIIIe siècles à travers les documents de la pratique. *In*: Comprendre le XIIIe siècle [Cf. n° 3965], p. 59-72.

3659. MORELLE (Laurent). La notice des plaids généraux de Corbie: une révision. *In*: Campagnes médiévales [Cf. n° 3713], p. 573-586.

3660. NEQUIRITO (Mauro). Le carte di regola delle comunità trentine dal medioevo all'età moderna. *In*: Libertà di decidere (La) [Cf. n° 3648], p. 367-385.

3661. NICO OTTAVIANI (Maria Grazia), BIANCIADI (Patrizia). L'Umbria tra potere pontificio e autonomie locali: Perugia e Spoleto nella normativa due-trecentesca. *In*: Libertà di decidere (La) [Cf. n° 3648], p. 103-130.

3662. NÖRR (Knut Wolfgang). Von der Textrationalität zur Zweckrationalität. Das Beispiel des summarischen Prozesses. *Zeitschrift der Savigny-Stiftung für Rechtsgeschichte. Kanonistische Abteilung*, 95, 81, p. 1-25.

3663. Oldenburger Sachsenspiegel (Der). Codex picturatus Oldenburgensis, CIM 1410 Landesbibliothek Oldenburg. Vollständige Faksimile-Ausgabe (zusammen mit 2 Kommentarbänden, die nach ihrem Erscheinen nachgeliefert werden). Graz, Akad. Druck- und Vlgsanstalt, 95, 135 p. (ill.). (Codices selecti, 101).

3664. OLEART (Oriol). La terra davant del monarca. Una contribució per a una tipologia de l'assemblea estamental catalana. *Anuario de estudios medievales*, 95, 25, 2, p. 593-616.

3665. OLIVERA SERRANO (Cesar). Servicio al rey y diplomacia castellana: Don Juan Manuel de Villena († 1462). *Anuario de estudios medievales*, 95, 25, 2, p. 463-488.

3666. Ordnung und Aufruhr im Mittelalter. Historische und juristische Studien zur Rebellion. Hrsg. v. Marie Theres FÖGEN. Frankfurt am Main, Klostermann, 95, 365 p. (Ius Commune. Veröffentlichungen des Max-Planck-Instituts für Europäische Rechtsgeschichte, 70).

3667. PADOA SCHIOPPA (Antonio). Discorso conclusivo. *In*: Giustizia (La) nell'Alto Medioevo [Cf. n° 3630], p. 1241-1276.

3668. PALACIOS MARTIN (Bonifacio). Sobre la redacción y difusión de las "Ordinacions" de Pedro IV de Aragón y sus primeros códices. *Anuario de estudios medievales*, 95, 25, 2, p. 659-682.

3669. PETIT (Carlos). «Iustitia y iudicium» en el Reino de Toledo. Un estudio de teología jurídica visigoda. *In*: Giustizia (La) nell'Alto Medioevo [Cf. n° 3630], p. 843-932.

3670. PIRILLO (Paolo). «E séco porta lettere d'ubidientia e di comandamento agli uomini dell'alpe». Le comunità appenniniche tra signoria locale e giurisdizione cittadina (secc. XIV–XVI). *In*: Libertà di decidere (La) [Cf. n° 3648], p. 245-269.

3671. PUTALLAZ (François-Xavier). Insolente liberté: controverses et condamnations au XIIIe siècle. Fribourg, Editions Universitaires et Paris, Ed. du Cerf, 95, XVI-339 p. (Vestigia, 15).

3672. RIGAUDIERE (Albert). L'essor de la fiscalité royale du règne de Philippe le Bel (1285–1314) à celui de Philippe VI (1328–1350). *In*: Europa en los umbrales [Cf. n° 3357], p. 323-391.

3673. ROSONI (Isabella). «Quale singula non prosunt collecta iuvant». La teoria della prova indiziaria nell'età medievale e moderna. Milano, Giuffrè e Macerata, Università di Macerata, 95, 373 p. (Pubblicazioni della facoltà di Giurisprudenza, 84).

3674. ROUCHE (Michel). La notion d'invasion dans les conciles mérovingiens. *In*: Sources de la gestion publique (Aux). Tome 2 [Cf. n° 4574], p. 125-134.

3675. RUSSOCKI (Stanisław). La naissance du parlementarisme polonais vue dans une perspective comparative. *Acta Poloniae historica*, 95, 72, p. 33-47.

3676. SANCHEZ MARTINEZ (Manuel). Fiscalidad pontificia y finanzas reales en Cataluña a mediados del s. XIV. Las décimas de 1349, 1351 y 1354. *In*: Misc.

lània d'estudis dedicats a la memòria de Professor Josep Trenchs i Òdena [Cf. n° 67], p. 1277-1296. – IDEM. La evolución de la fiscalidad regia en los países de la Corona de Aragón (c. 1280–1356). *In*: Europa en los umbrales [Cf. n° 3357], p. 393-428.

3677. SANTARELLI (Umberto). Il divieto delle usure da canone morale a regola giuridica. Modalità ed esiti di un «trapianto». *In*: Studi in onore di Arnaldo D'Addario [Cf. n° 452], p. 367-384.

3678. SCHOTT (Klausdieter). Traditionelle Formen der Konfliktlösung in der Lex Burgundionum. *In*: Giustizia (La) nell'Alto Medioevo [Cf. n° 3630], p. 933-961.

3679. SIEMS (Harald). Bestechliche und ungerechte Richter in frühmittelalterlichen Rechtsquellen. *In*: Giustizia (La) nell'Alto Medioevo [Cf. n° 3630], p. 509-563.

3680. SIMON (Thomas). Grundherrschaft und Vogtei. Eine Strukturanalyse spätmittelalterlicher und frühneuzeitlicher Herrschaftsbildung. Frankfurt am Main, Klostermann, 95, 446 p. (Karten). (Ius commune. Veröffentlichungen des Max-Planck-Instituts für europäische Rechtsgeschichte, Frankfurt am Main. Sonderhefte: Studien zur europäischen Rechtsgeschichte, 77).

3681. SMITH (David M.). The «Officialis» of the bishop in twelfth and thirteenth-century England. Problems of terminology. *In*: Medieval ecclesiastical studies [Cf. n° 4410], p. 201-220.

3682. Sol et l'immeuble (Le). Les formes dissociées de proprieté immobilière dans les villes de France et d'Italie (XIIe–XIXe siècles). Roma, Ecole française de Rome, 95, 342 p. (Collection de l'Ecole française de Rome, 206). [Cf. n^{os} <sélection> 3613, 3628, 3705, 3763, 3786, 3807, 3850, 3853.]

3683. TAKAYAMA (H.). The local administrative system of France under Philip IV (1285–1314) – bailis and seneschals. *Journal of Medieval History*, 95, 21, 2, p. 167-193.

3684. TONNERRE (Noël-Yves). Les biens des évêques mérovingiens en Armorique. *In*: Sources de la gestion publique (Aux). Tome 2 [Cf. n° 4574], p. 195-206.

3685. TURULL RUBINAT (Max). La formació del poder polític als segles XII–XV i els orígens medievals de l'Estat. Història política i història del Dret i de les institucions: bibliografia recent en llengua francesa (1984–1994). *Anuario de estudios medievales*, 95, 25, 2, p. 761-812.

3686. VARANINI (Gian Maria). Gli statuti e l'evoluzione politico istituzionale nel Veneto tra governi cittadini e dominazione veneziana (secoli XIV–XV). *In*: Libertà di decidere (La) [Cf. n° 3648], p. 321-358.

3687. Voies de recours judiciaires (Les), instruments de liberté. Ed. par Jean-Louis THIREAU. Paris, PUF, 95, 143 p. [Cf. n° <sélection> 3635.]

3688. WORMALD (Patrick). «Inter cetera bona ... genti suae». Law-making and peace-keeping in the ear-

8. WIRTSCHAFTS- UND SOZIALGESCHICHTE

liest english kingdoms. *In*: Giustizia (La) nell'Alto Medioevo [Cf. n° 3630], p. 963-993.

3689. ZACCHIGNA (Michele). Note per un inquadramento storico della produzione statutaria friulana. *In*: Libertà di decidere (La) [Cf. n° 3648], p. 387-395.

Cf. n°s 62, 65, 99, 136, 1241

§ 8. Wirtschafts- und Sozialgeschichte.

3690. ABERTH (J.). The Black Death in the diocese of Ely: the evidence of the bishop's register. *Journal of Medieval History*, 95, 21, 3, p. 275-287.

3691. Agriculture in the Middle Ages. Technology, practice, and representation. Ed. by Del SWEENEY. Philadelphia, University of Pennsylvania Press, 95, 365 p.

3692. AIRLIE (Stuart). The aristocracy. *In*: New Cambridge medieval history [Cf. n° 3378], p. 431-450.

3693. ALCAMO (Jean-Claude). Aide à l'installation et intégration socio-économique de nouveaux venus à Romans [-sur-Isère, Drôme] au milieu du XVe siècle. *In*: Actes du 118e Congrès national des Sociétés savantes [Cf. n° 4540], p. 275-295.

3694. AURELL (Martin). Les noces du comte. Mariage et pouvoir en Catalogne (785–1213). Paris, Publications de la Sorbonne, 95, 623 p. (Histoire Ancienne et Médiévale, 32).

3695. AURELL I CARDONA (Jaume), PUIGARNAU I TORELLÓ (Alfons). Iconografia a les llars mercantils del segle XV. Mentalitat, estètica i religiositat dels mercaders a Barcelona. *Anuario de estudios medievales*, 95, 25, 1, p. 295-334.

3696. BAILEY (Mark). The prior and convent of Ely and their management of the Manor of Lakenheath in the fourteenth century. *In*: Medieval ecclesiastical studies [Cf. n° 4410], p. 1-19.

3697. BARTHELEMY (Dominique). Les comtes, les sires et les «nobles de châteaux» dans la Touraine deu XIe siècle. *In*: Campagnes médiévales [Cf. n° 3713], p. 439-454.

3698. BENOIT (Paul), GUILLOT (Ivan), PLOQUIN (Alain). Les forges minières au Moyen Age et à la Renaissance: approche archéologique et paléométallurgique. *In*: Campagnes médiévales [Cf. n° 3713], p. 639-652.

3699. BERTHE (Maurice). Marché de la terre et hiérarchie paysanne dans le Lauragais toulousain vers 1270–vers 1320. *In*: Campagnes médiévales [Cf. n° 3713], p. 297-312.

3700. BERTI (Luca). I capitoli «De vestibus mulierum» del 1460, ovvero «status» personale e distinzioni sociali nell'Arezzo di metà Quattrocento. *In*: Studi in onore di Arnaldo D'Addario [Cf. n° 452], p. 1171-1214.

3701. BESSMERTNY (Youri). Le paysan vu par le seigneur: la France des XIe–XIIe siècles. *In*: Campagnes médiévales [Cf. n° 3713], p. 601-612.

3702. BIROLINI (Alain). Etude d'anthroponymie génoise. *In*: Genèse médiévale de l'anthroponymie moderne. L'espace italien [Cf. n° 3764], p. 467-496.

3703. BISSON (Thomas N.). Medieval lordship. *Speculum*, 95, 70, 4, p. 743-759.

3704. BLACKBURN (Mark). Money and coinage. *In*: New Cambridge medieval history [Cf. n° 3378], p. 553-562.

3705. BOUCHERON (Patrick). Pouvoir princier et structures de la propriété immobilière à Milan au temps des Sforza (1450–1500): questions et perspectives. *In*: Sol et l'immeuble (Le) [Cf. n° 3682], p. 207-226.

3706. BOURIN (Monique). Délimitation des parcelles et perception de l'espace en Bas-Languedoc aux Xe et XIe siècles. *In*: Campagnes médiévales [Cf. n° 3713], p. 73-86.

3707. BRUNE (Ghislain). Bêtes sauvages et bêtes d'élevage: l'exemple de la forêt de Retz (XIIe–XIVe siècles). *In*: Campagnes médiévales [Cf. n° 3713], p. 157-162.

3708. BUC (P.). Italian Hussies and German matrons. Liutprand of Cremona on dynastic Legitimacy. *Frühmittelalterliche Studien*, 95, 29, p. 207-225.

3709. BUDAK (Neven). I fiorentini in Slavonia e nella Croazia nei secoli XIV e Xv. *Archivio storico italiano*, 95, 153, 566, p. 681-696.

3710. Burg, Burgstadt, Stadt. Zur Genese mittelalterlicher nichtagrarischer Zentren in Ostmitteleuropa. Hrsg. v. Hansjürgen BRACHMANN. Berlin, Akademie, 95, 351 p. (Forschungen zur Geschichte und Kultur des östlichen Mitteleuropa).

3711. BUSCH (J. W.). Die Lombarden und die Langobarden. Alteingesessene und Eroberer im Geschichtsbild einer Region. *Frühmittelalterliche Studien*, 95, 29, p. 289-311.

3712. BUTLER (John). The quest for Becket's bones. The mystery of the relics of St. Thomas Becket of Canterbury. New Haven a. London, Yale U. P., 95, XII-180 p.

3713. Campagnes médiévales: l'homme et son espace. Etudes offertes à Robert Fossier. Ed. par Elisabeth MORNET. Paris, Publications de la Sorbonne, 95, 736 p. (Histoire ancienne et médiévale, 31). [Cf. n^{os} <sélection> 3178, 3442, 3498, 3652, 3659, 3697, 3698, 3699, 3701, 3706, 3707, 3718, 3721, 3726, 3731, 3733, 3734, 3735, 3736, 3739, 3744, 3746, 3747, 3748, 3750, 3761, 3776, 3778, 3782, 3784, 3800, 3801, 3802, 3803, 3804, 3806, 3808, 3813, 3819, 3833, 3840, 3846, 3851, 3853, 3882, 3885, 4003, 4315, 4447, 4579.]

3714. CAPANNELLI (E.), INSABATO (E.). Censimento degli archivi di persone fisiche in area fiorentina. Primo bilancio. *Studi Medievali*, 95, 36, 1, p. 483-512.

3715. CARMI PARSONS (John). Eleanor of Castile. Queen and society in thirteenth-century England. New York, St. Martin's Press, 95, XIX-364 p.

3716. CARRASCO (Juan). Europa en los umbrales de la crisis (1250–1350). In: Europa en los umbrales [Cf. n° 3357], p. 17-35.

3717. CATEURA BENNASSER (Pau). Prejuicio religioso y conflicto social en una pequeña sociedad mediterranea: el caso de Mallorca (1286–1435). Anuario de estudios medievales, 95, 25, 1, p. 235-254.

3718. CHEDEVILLE (André). La guerre des bourgs. Concurrence châtelaine et patrimoine monastique (XIe–XIIe siècles). In: Campagnes médiévales [Cf. n° 3713], p. 501-512.

3719. CHENE (Catherine). Juger les vers. Exorcismes et procès d'animaux dans le diocèse de Lausanne (XVe–XVIe s.). Lausanne, Université de Lausanne, Section d'Histoire, 95, 194 p. (Cahiers Lausannois d'Histoire Médiévale, 14).

3720. CHERUBINI (Giovanni). Un rigattiere fiorentino del Duecento. In: Studi in onore di Arnaldo D'Addario [Cf. n° 452], p. 761-772.

3721. CHEVALIER (Bernard). Les bonnes villes, l'Etat et la société dans la France de la fin du XVe siècle. Orléans, Paradigme, 95, 394 p. (Coll. Varia, 20). – IDEM. Un grand domaine agricole de Marmoutier: la grange de Meslay (IXe–XVIIIe siècles). In: Campagnes médiévales [Cf. n° 3713], p. 587-600.

3722. CHIESA (Paolo). Ladri di reliquie a Costantinopoli durante la quarta crociata. Studi Medievali, 95, 36, 1, p. 431-460.

3723. CIAPPELLI (Giovanni). Una famiglia e le sue ricordanze: i Castellani di Firenze nel Tre-Quattrocento. Firenze, Olschki, 95, V-251 p. (Quaderni di Rinascimento, 27).

3724. CLEMENS (Jacques). Le fouage de l'évêque d'Agen dans quelques paroisses rurales de la baylie de Lauzerte [Tarn-et-Garonne] en 1283–1284. In: Actes du 118e Congrès national des Sociétés savantes [Cf. n° 4540], p. 145-158.

3725. Commercialising economy (A). England 1086 to c. 1330. Ed. by Richard H. BRITNEL a. Bruce M. S. CAMPBELL. Manchester a. New York, Manchester U. P., 95, 228 p.

3726. CONTAMINE (Philippe). Le cheval dans l'économie rurale d'après les archives de l'ordre de l'Hôpital (France du Nord, XIVe siècle). In: Campagnes médiévales [Cf. n° 3713], p. 163-176.

3727. CORRARATI (Patrizia). Percorsi dell'antroponimia familiare: Milano e il Milanese nel XII secolo. In: Genèse médiévale de l'anthroponymie moderne. L'espace italien [Cf. n° 3764], p. 497-512.

3728. CORTONESI (Alfio). Note sull'agricoltura italiana fra XIII e XIV secolo. In: Europa en los umbrales [Cf. n° 3357], p. 87-128. – IDEM. Ruralia. Economie e paesaggi del medioevo italiano. Roma, Il Calamo, 95, XVI-424 p.

3729. Cultures of power. Lordship, status, and process in twelfth-century Europe. Ed. by Thomas N. BISSON. Philadelphia, University of Pennsylvania Press, 95, 347 p.

3730. CUOZZO (Enrico). Qualche nota sull'antroponimia aristocratica di Gaeta tra IX e XI secolo. In: Genèse médiévale de l'anthroponymie moderne. L'espace italien [Cf. n° 3764], p. 343-344.

3731. CURSENTE (Benoît). Une «populatio» béarnaise en quête d'église: Geup (1274). In: Campagnes médiévales [Cf. n° 3713], p. 121-134.

3732. CZAJA (Roman). Udział wielkich miast pruskich w handlu hanzeatyckim do połowy XIV wieku. (Cz. 1–2). [La part des grandes villes prussiennes dans le commerce hanséatique jusqu'à la moitié du XIVe siècle. (Parties 1–2)]. Zapiski historyczne poświęcone historii Pomorza i Krajów Bałtyckich, 95, 60, 2-3, p. 21-38; 4, p. 43-55. [Deutsche Zsfassung].

3733. DE LA RONCIERE (Charles M.). Propriétaires et fermiers dans la plaine de Florence (1300–1370). In: Campagnes médiévales [Cf. n° 3713], p. 681-696.

3734. DEBORD (André). Terres et revenus de N. D. de Barbezieux à la fin du XIIe siècle. In: Campagnes médiévales [Cf. n° 3713], p. 533-548.

3735. DELMAIRE (Bernard). Note sur la dîme des jardins, «mes» et courtils dans la France du Nord au Moyen Age. In: Campagnes médiévales [Cf. n° 3713], p. 231-246.

3736. DELORT (Robert). Percevoir la nature au Moyen Age: quelques réflexions. In: Campagnes médiévales [Cf. n° 3713], p. 31-44.

3737. DEPREUX (Ph.). Tassilon III et le roi des Francs: examen d'une vassalité controversée. Revue Historique, 95, 119, 593, p. 23-74.

3738. DERVILLE (Alain). L'économie française au moyen âge. Paris, Ophrys, 95, 262 p. (Synthèse Σ Histoire).

3739. DESPY (Georges). A propos de «désert» dans les campagnes au XIIe siècle. In: Campagnes médiévales [Cf. n° 3713], p. 549-562.

3740. DI CARPEGNA FALCONIERI (Tommaso). L'antroponomastica del clero di Roma nei secoli X–XII. In: Genèse médiévale de l'anthroponymie moderne. L'espace italien [Cf. n° 3764], p. 513-534.

3741. DINI (Bruno). Saggi su una economia-mondo. Firenze e l'Italia fra Mediterraneo e Europa (secc. XIII–XVI). Pisa, Pacini, 95, 326 p. (Rinascimento, 35, 424).

3742. DOHAR (William J.). The black death and pastoral leadership. The Diocese of Hereford in the fourteenth century. Philadelphia, University of Pennsylvania Press, 95, XVI-198 p. (Middle Ages Series).

3743. DOUMERC (B.). Les Vénitiens dans la tourmente de la guerre civile en Catalogne (1462–1472). *Moyen Age*, 95, 101, 1, p. 41-64.

3744. DUBOIS (Henri). Riches et pauvres à la campagne (Normandie 1381). *In*: Campagnes médiévales [Cf. n° 3713], p. 327-340.

3745. DUBUIS (Pierre). Les vifs, les morts et le temps qui court. Familles valaisannes, 1400–1550. Lausanne, Université de Lausanne, Section d'Histoire, 95, 318 p. (Cahiers Lausannois d'Histoire Médiévale, 16).

3746. DURAND (Aline). Les systèmes de culture dans les garrigues et premiers contreforts montagneux languedociens aux XIe et XIIe siècles. *In*: Campagnes médiévales [Cf. n° 3713], p. 177-188.

3747. DURAND (Robert). La mémoire des campagnes portugaises (XIIIe siècle). *In*: Campagnes médiévales [Cf. n° 3713], p. 363-374.

3748. DYER (Christopher). Were peasants self-sufficient? English villagers and the market, 1050–1350. *In*: Campagnes médiévales [Cf. n° 3713], p. 653-666.

3749. DZIEDUSZYCKI (Wojciech). Kruszce w systemach wartości i wymiany społeczeństwa Polski wczesnośredniowiecznej [X–XIII w.]. (Les mineraux dans les systémes de valeurs et d'échanges de la société polonaise du haut Moyen Age [X^e–XIIIe s.]). Poznań, 95, 192 p. (English summary). (Inst. Archeologii i Etnologii Pol. Akad. Nauk).

3750. FELLER (Laurent). Achats de terres, politiques matrimoniales et liens de clientèles en Italie centro-meridionale dans la seconde moitié du IXe siècle. *In*: Campagnes médiévales [Cf. n° 3713], p. 425-438.

3751. FERNANDEZ TRABAL (Josep). Una família catalana medieval. Els Bell-lloc de Girona 1267–1533. Barcelona, Publicacions de l'Abadia de Monserrat, 95, [s. p.].

3752. FLACHENECKER (Helmut). Geistlicher Stadtherr und Bürgerschaft. Zur politischen Führungsschicht Brixens am Ausgang des Mittelalters. *In*: Stadt und Kirche [Cf. n° 1309], p. 83-120.

3753. FLORI (Jean). La chevalerie en France au Moyen Age. Paris, PUF, 95, 127 p. (Col. Que sais-je?).

3754. FORTUN PEREZ DE CIRIZA (Luis Javier). Espacio rural y estructuras señoriales en Navarra (1250–1350). *In*: Europa en los umbrales [Cf. n° 3357], p. 129-169.

3755. FRYE (David). Transformation and tradition in the Merovingian civitas. *Nottingham Medieval Studies*, 95, 39, p. 1-11.

3756. FUHRMANN (Rosi). Kirche und Dorf. Religiöse Bedürfnisse und kirchliche Stiftung auf dem Lande vor der Reformation. Stuttgart, Jena u. New York, Fischer, 95, XI-506 p. (Karten). (Quellen und Forschungen zur Agrargeschichte, 40).

3757. FUMAGALLI (Vito). Uomini contro la storia. Bologna, Clueb, 95, 128 p. (Lexis, Biblioteca di scienze umane, 4).

3758. FURIO (Antoni). El mercado de la tierra en el pais valenciano a finales de la edad media. *Hispania*, 95, 55, 191, p. 887-919.

3759. GAIER (Claude). Armes et combats dans l'univers médiéval. Préf. de André JORIS. Bruxelles, De Boeck-Université, 95, 418 p. (ill.). (Bibliothèque du Moyen Age, 5).

3760. GANGENI (Maria Luisa). L'evoluzione antroponimica a Catania e Paternò attraverso le pergamene di S. Niccolò l'Arena. *In*: Genèse médiévale de l'anthroponymie moderne. L'espace italien [Cf. n° 3764], p. 393-413.

3761. GARCIA DE CORTAZAR (José Angel). Sociedad rural y organización del espacio en Castilla del año mil. *In*: Campagnes médiévales [Cf. n° 3713], p. 613-628.

3762. GARCÍA MARSILLA (Juan Vicente). Crédito y banca en el Mediterráneo medieval: la quiebra del cambista valenciano Francesc de Pals. *Anuario de estudios medievales*, 95, 25, 1, p. 127-150.

3763. GARZELLA (Gabriella). La proprietà frazionata nella gestione immobiliare di un ente monastico pisano (secoli XII–XIII). *In*: Sol et l'immeuble (Le) [Cf. n° 3682], p. 169-184.

3764. Genèse médiévale de l'anthroponymie moderne. L'espace italien. 2. Actes de la table ronde de Milan, 21–22 avril 1994. Ed. par Jean-Marie MARTIN et François MENANT. Roma, Ecole française de Rome, 95, 302 p. (MEFRM, 107). [Cf. n^{os} <sélection> 3702, 3727, 3730, 3740, 3760, 3778, 3808, 3812, 3815, 3854, 3858, 3886, 3891.]

3765. Genèse médiévale de l'anthroponymie moderne. T. 3. Enquêtes généalogiques et données prosopographiques. Ed. par Monique BOURIN et Pascal CHAREILLE. Tours, Publications de l'Université, 95, 241 p.

3766. GENICOT (L.). L'économie rurale namuroise au bas moyen âge. 4. La communauté et la vie rurales. Louvain-la-Neuve, Bureau du Recueil, Collège Erasme et Bruxelles, Nauwelaerts, 95, XVIII-514 p.

3767. GERMAIN (René). Le feu, un comportement social (Bourbonnais, XIVe–début XVIe siècle). *In*: Actes du 118e Congrès national des Sociétés savantes [Cf. n° 4540], p. 27-49.

3768. Gioco, civilizzazione, transizioni. Spiel, Zivilisation, Gesellschaftlicher Umbruch. Convegno internazionale organizzato dalla Fondazione Benetton Studi e Ricerche e dall'Historisches Seminar dell'Università di Bonn nei giorni 3, 4 e 5 febbraio 1994. Treviso, Fondazione Benetton Studi e Ricerche e Roma, Viella, 95, 200 p. [Cf. n^{os} <scelta> 3823, 3825, 3828, 3852, 3861.].

3769. GOLINELLI (Paolo). Quando il santo non basta più: simboli cittadini non religiosi nell'Italia bassomedievale. In: Religion civique à l'époque médiévale et moderne (La) [Cf. n° 4528], p. 375-389.

3770. GOMEZ VOZMEDIANO (Miguel Fernando). Rentas pecuarias de las santas hermandades viejas de ciudad real, Toledo y Talavera De La Reina durante la edad moderna. Hispania, 95, 55, 190, p. 527-546.

3771. GONZALES I JIMENEZ (Manuel). Poblamiento de la Baja Andalucía: de la repoblación a la crisis (1250–1350). In: Europa en los umbrales [Cf. n° 3357], p. 63-86.

3772. GONZALEZ ARCE (José Damián). El artesanado en los fueros del reino de Murcia. Anuario de estudios medievales, 95, 25, 1, p. 81-126.

3773. GOODICH (Michael E.). Violence and miracle in the fourteenth century. Private grief and public salvation. Chicago a. London, University of Chicago Press, 95, XI-220 p.

3774. GORE (Terry L.). Neglected Heroes. Leadership and war in the early medieval period. Westport a. London, Praeger, 95, XIII-213 p.

3775. GREILSAMMER (Myriam). Autour de la maison: trois études sur l'univers de la famille au moyen age. Revue Belge de Philologie et d'Histoire, 95, 73, 2, p. 409-433.

3776. GUERREAU (Alain). Remarques sur l'arpentage selon Bertrand Boysset (Arles, vers 1400–1410). In: Campagnes médiévales [Cf. n° 3713], p. 87-102.

3777. GUILBERT (Sylvette). Migrations de tisserands flamands et picards et agitation sociale à Châlons-sur-Marne au début du XIVe siècle. In: Actes du 118e Congrès national des Sociétés savantes [Cf. n° 4540], p. 267-273.

3778. GUYOTJEANNIN (Olivier). Problèmes de la dévolution du nom et du surnom dans les élites d'Italie centro-septentrionale (fin XIIe–XIIIe siècle). In: Genèse médiévale de l'anthroponymie moderne. L'espace italien [Cf. n° 3764], p. 557-594. – IDEM. Vivre libre dans une seigneurie juste. Note sur les préambules des chartes de franchise. In: Campagnes médiévales [Cf. n° 3713], p. 375-386.

3779. Habitat rural (L') du haut Moyen Age (France, Pays-Bas, Danemark et Grande-Bretagne). Ed. par Claude LORREN et Patrick PERIN. Rouen, Association française d'archéologie mérovingienne, 1995, 237 p. (Mémoires publiés par l'Association française d'archéologie mérovingienne).

3780. HALSALL (Guy). Settlement and social organization. The Merovingian region of Metz. Cambridge, Cambridge U. P., 95, XX-307 p.

3781. HAMMER (C. I.). Servile names and seigneurial organization in early-medieval Bavaria. Studi Medievali, 95, 36, 2, p. 917-928.

3782. HELAS (Jean-Claude). Prénoms en Gévaudan au début du XIVe siècle d'après les «Feuda Gabalorum». In: Campagnes médiévales [Cf. n° 3713], p. 341-354.

3783. HICKS (Michael). Bastard feudalism. London a. New York, Longman, 95, XII-243 p.

3784. HOCQUET (Jean-Claude). Productivity gains and technological change. Venetian naval architecture at the end of the Middle Ages. Journal of European Economic History, 95, 24, 3, p. 537-556. – IDEM. Des paysans de la mer. L'exploitation du sel en Picardie au Moyen Age. In: Campagnes médiévales [Cf. n° 3713], p. 629-638.

3785. HOSHINO (Hidetoshi). Chūsei-koki Firentsue Keorimono-Kōgyō-shi. (L'arte della lana in Firenze nel basso medioevo). Nagoya, University of Nagoya Press, 95, 402 p.

3786. HUBERT (Etienne). Gestion immobilière, propriété dissociée et seigneuries foncières à Rome aux XIIIe et XIVe siècle. In: Sol et l'immeuble (Le) [Cf. n° 3682], p. 185-205. – IDEM. Urbanisation, propriété et emphitéose au Moyen Age: remarques introductives. In: Sol et l'immeuble (Le) [Cf. n° 3682], p. 1-8.

3787. IRADIEL (P.), IGUAL (D.), NAVARRO (G.), APARICI (J.). Oficios artesanales y comercio en Castelló de la Plana (1371–1527). Castellón, Fundación Davalos-Fletcher, 95, 330 p.

3788. IWAŃCZAK (Wojciech). Ludzie miecza, modlitwy, pracy. Trójpodział społeczeństwa w średniowiecznej myśli czeskiej. (Hommes de l'épée, de la prière, du travail. La tripartition de la société dans la pensée médiévale tchèque). Kielce, Wyższa Szkoła Pedagog. im. Jana Kochanowskiego w Kielcach, 95, 277 p. (Eng. summary).

3789. JACOBS (Nicolas). The later version of "Sir Degarre". A study in textual degeneration. Oxford, Society for the Study of Mediaeval Languages and Literature, 95, X-127 p. (Medium Ævum Monographs, 18).

3790. JANSEN (K. L.). Mary Magdalen and the mendicants. The preaching of penance in the late Middle Ages. Journal of Medieval History, 95, 21, 1, p. 1-25.

3791. JANTZEN (Grace M.). Power, gender and christian mysticism. Cambridge, Cambridge U. P., 95, XVII-384 p. (Cambridge studies in ideology and religion, 8).

3792. JOCHENS (Jenny). Women in old Norse society. Ithaca a. London, Cornell U. P., 95, XV-266 p.

3793. JONES (E. D.). Death by document. A reappraisal of Spalding priory's census evidence for the 1260s. Nottingham Medieval Studies, 95, 39, p. 54-69.

3794. KLEINSCHMIDT (H.). Beyond conventionality. Recent work on the Germanic migration to the British isles. Studi Medievali, 95, 36, 2, p. 975-1010.

3795. KNIGHTINGALE (Pamela). A medieval mercantile community. The Grocers' company and the politics and trade London, 1000–1485. New Haven a. London, Yale U. P., 95, XI-640 p.

3796. Kommunikation und Mobilität im Mittelalter. Begegnungen zwischen dem Süden und der Mitte Europas (XI.–XIV. Jh.). Hrsg. v. Siegfried DE RACHEWILTZ u. Josef REIDMANN. Sigmaringen, Thorbecke, 95, 336 p.

3797. KÖRMENDY (Adrienne). Melioratio terrae. Vergleichende Untersuchungen über die Siedlungsbewegung in östlichen Mitteleuropa im 13.–14. Jahrhundert. Poznań, 95, 237 p. (cartes). (Pozn. Tow. Przyj. Nauk, Wydz. Hist. i Nauk społ., Prace Kom. Hist., 48).

3798. KOWALESKI (Maryanne). Local markets and regional trade in medieval Exeter. Cambridge, Cambridge U. P., 95, XVI-442 p.

3799. LAGUNAS (Cecilia). Una familia de escuderos en el Monasterio de San Marcos, León. El priorazgo de Diego Alfons (1376–1409). *Anuario de la Escuela de Historia-Universidad Nacional de Rosario*, 95-96, 17, segunda época, p. 481-495.

3800. LAURIOUX (Bruno). Des lasagnes romaines aux vermicelles arabes. Quelques réflexions sur les pâtes alimentaires au Moyen Age. *In*: Campagnes médiévales [Cf. n° 3713], p. 199-216.

3801. LE JAN (Régine). Entre maîtres et dépendants: réflexions sur la famille paysanne en Lotharingie, aux IXe et Xe siècles. *In*: Campagnes médiévales [Cf. n° 3713], p. 277-296. – EADEM. Famille et pouvoir dans le monde franc (VIIe–Xe siècle). Essai d'anthropologie sociale. Paris, Publications de la Sorbonne, 95, 571 p. (maps, tables). (Histoire Ancienne et Médiévale, 33).

3802. LE MENE (Michel). Métayage et bail à cheptel dans l'Ouest de la France (1335–1342). *In*: Campagnes médiévales [Cf. n° 3713], p. 697-708.

3803. LINDKVIST (Thomas). The peasantry and peasant communities in medieval Sweden. *In*: Campagnes médiévales [Cf. n° 3713], p. 387-398.

3804. LORCIN (Marie-Thérèse). Pariages et testaments en Forez au XVe siècle. *In*: Campagnes médiévales [Cf. n° 3713], p. 355-362.

3805. MAC KEE (Sally). Households in fourteenth-century Venetian Crete. *Speculum*, 95, 70, 1, p. 27-67.

3806. MANE (Perrine) Le paysan dans ses meubles. *In*: Campagnes médiévales [Cf. n° 3713], p. 247- 264.

3807. MARAZZI (Federico). Le proprietà immobiliari urbane della Chiesa romana tra IV e VIII secolo: reddito, struttura e gestione. *In*: Sol et l'immeuble (Le) [Cf. n° 3682], p. 151-168.

3808. MARTIN (Jean-Marie). Anthroponymie de l'Italie méridionale lombarde (VIIIe–IXe siècles). *In*: Genèse médiévale de l'anthroponymie moderne. L'espace italien [Cf. n° 3764], p. 333-342. – IDEM. Deux listes de paysans sud-italiennes du VIIIe siècle. *In*: Campagnes médiévales [Cf. n° 3713], p. 265-276.

3809. MATTOSO (José). O poder e a morte. *Anuario de estudios medievales*, 95, 25, 2, p. 395-428.

3810. MAUSKOPF DELIYANNIS (D.). Church Burial in Anglo-Saxon England: the prerogative of kings. *Frühmittelalterliche Studien*, 95, 29, p. 96-119.

3811. Mediaeval antiquity. Ed. by Andries WELKENHUYSEN, Herman BRAET an Werner VERBEKE. Leuven, Leuven U. P., 95, VIII-381 p. (Mediaevalia Lovaniensa, 1, 24).

3812. MENANT (François). Les modes de dénomination de l'aristocratie italienne aux XIe et XIIe siècle: premières réflexions à partir d'exemples lombards. *In*: Genèse médiévale de l'anthroponymie moderne. L'espace italien [Cf. n° 3764], p. 535-555.

3813. MICHAUD-FREJAVILLE (François). Hommes et femmes dépendants de Déols au XIIIe siècle. L'apport de l'étude anthroponymique. *In*: Campagnes médiévales [Cf. n° 3713], p. 313-326.

3814. MILLER (Edward), HATCHER (John). Medieval England. Towns, commerce and crafts, 1086–1348. London, Longman, 95, XVII-469 p.

3815. MIRAZITA (Iris). L'antroponimia nelle imbreviature del notaio Adamo de Citella (I registro: 1286–87). *In*: Genèse médiévale de l'anthroponymie moderne. L'espace italien [Cf. n° 3764], p. 415-425.

3816. MOLHO (Anthony), BARDUCCI (Roberto), BATTISTA (Gabriella), DONNINI (Francesco). Genealogia, parentado e memoria storica a Firenze nel XV secolo. *In*: Memoria (La) e la città. Scritture storiche tra medioevo ed età moderna [Cf. n° 3303], p. 235-270.

3817. MOLLAY (Károly). Egy évtized soproni külkereskedelmének társadalomtörténeti háttere, 1483–1489. (L'arrière-fond du commerce extérieur de Sopron pendant une décennie, 1483–1489). *Soproni szle.*, 95, 49, 4, p. 289-316.

3818. MORENZONI (Franco). Contribution a l'histoire des prix des cereales et des fèves en Valais à la fin du moyen âge d'après les comptes de Chatellenie (vers 1270–1450). *Revue suisse d'histoire*, 95, 45, 2, p. 175-204.

3819. MORIMOTO (Yoshiki). Sur les manses surpeuplés ou fractionnaires dans le polyptyque de Prüm: phénomènes marginaux ou signes de décadence? *In*: Campagnes médiévales [Cf. n° 3713], p. 409-424.

3820. MORLET (Marie-Thérèse). Les noms de personne à Blois et dans sa banlieue en 1389. *In*: Actes du 118e Congrès national des Sociétés savantes [Cf. n° 4540], p. 159-199.

3821. MOSHER STUARD (Susan). Ancillary evidence for the decline of medieval slavery. *Past and Present*, 95, 149, p. 3-28.

3822. MÜLLER (E. Maria). Jungfräulichkeit in Versepen des 12. und 13. Jahrhunderts. München, Wilhelm Fink Verlag, 95, 395 p.

3823. MÜLLER (Rainer A.). Il gioco degli scacchi come metafora della società tardomedievale. *In*: Gioco, civilizzazione, transizioni [Cf. n° 3768], p. 114-125.

3824. NICHOLAS (David). Child and adolescent labour in the late medieval city: a Flemish model in regional perspective. *English Historical Review*, 95, 110, 439, p. 1103-1131.

3825. NITSCHKE (August). Spiele der Identifikation in Mittelalter und früher Neuzeit. *In*: Gioco, civilizzazione, transizioni [Cf. n° 3768], p. 89-97.

3826. NOZAKI (Naoji). Doitsu-Chūsei-Shakaishi no Kenkyū. (Studies of the social history in medieval Germany). Tokyo, Waseda U. P., 95, 241 p.

3827. ORME (Nicholas), WEBSTER (Margaret). The English hospital, 1070–1570. New Haven a. London, Yale U. P., 95, XII-308 p.

3828. ORTALLI (Gherardo). Uncertain thresholds of tolerance: games and crisis in the Middle Age. *In*: Gioco, civilizzazione, transizioni [Cf. n° 3768], p. 56-68.

3829. OSTORERO (Martine). "Folâtrer avec les démons". Sabbat et chasse aux sorciers à Vevey (1448). Lausanne, Université de Lausanne, Faculté des Lettres, Section d'histoire, 95, 323 p. (Cahiers Lausannois d'Histoire Médiévale, 15).

3830. PACH (Zsigmond Pál). A debreceni posztószövők legrégibb céhszabadalma. (La plus ancienne lettre de maîtrise des tisseurs de drap de Debrecen). *Századok*, 95, 129, 1, p. 63-100. – IDEM. Hogyan lett a harmincadvámból huszad? (1436–1457). (Comment la douane de trentième est devenue de vingtième?). *Tört. szle.*, 95, 37, 3, p. 257-276.

3831. PALENCIA HERREJON (Juan Ramón). Los Ayala de Toledo: Desarrollo e Instrumentos de poder de un linaje nobiliario en el siglo XV. Toledo, [s. n.], 95, 165 p.

3832. PARAVICINI (Werner). Die Preussenreisen des europäischen Adels, 2. Sigmaringen, Thorbecke, 95, 346 p. (Beihefte der Francia, 17, 2).

3833. PARISSE (Michel). La petite noblesse et les nouveaux ordres: les bienfaiteurs de Riéval en Lorraine (XIIe–XIIIe siècles). *In*: Campagnes médiévales [Cf. n° 3713], p. 455-472.

3834. PASTOR (Reyna), [et al.]. Compraventa de tierras en Galicia. Microanalisis de la documentación del monasterio de Oseira. siglo XIII. *Hispania*, 95, 55, 191, p. 953-1024.

3835. Peasants and townsmen in medieval Europe. Studia in honorem Adriaan Verhulst. Ed. by Jean-Marie DUVOSQUEL et Erik THOEN. Gand, Snoeck-Ducaju en Zoon, 95, 787 p.

3836. PELTERET (David A. E.). Slavery in early medieval England from the reign of Alfred until the twelfth century. Woodbridge a. Rochester, Boydell and Brewer, 95, XVI-375 p. (Studies in Anglo-Saxon history, 7).

3837. PEÑA BOCOS (Esther). La atribución social del espacio en la Castilla altomedieval. Una nueva aproximación al feudalismo peninsular. Santander, Universidad de Cantabria, Asamblea Regional de Cantabria, 95, 406 p.

3838. Pescia e la Valdinievole nell'età dei comuni. A cura di C. VIOLANTE e A. SPICCIANI. Pisa, Edizioni ETS, 95, IX-210 p. (Studi Medievali, 1).

3839. PICHOT (Daniel). Le Bas-Maine du Xe au XIIIe siècle: étude d'une société. Laval, Société d'Archéologie et d'Histoire de la Mayenne, 95, 455 p. (La Mayenne: Archéologie, Histoire – Supplément, 7).

3840. PICHOTTE (Daniel). Les Deux-Evailles: une famille de la petite aristocratie du Bas-Maine (1211–1358). *In*: Campagnes médiévales [Cf. n° 3713], p. 473-486.

3841. PINTO (Giuliano). Popolazione e comportamenti demografici in Italia (1250–1348). *In*: Europa en los umbrales [Cf. n° 3357], p. 37-61.

3842. Pohl-Resl (Brigitte). Vorsorge, Memoria und soziales Ereignis: Frauen als Schenkerinnen in den bayerischen und alemannischen Urkunden des 8. und 9. Jahrhunderts. *Mitt. d. Inst. f. Österr. Gesch.-Forsch.*, 95, 103, 3-4, p. 265-287.

3843. POSTLES (D.). Noms de personnes en langue française, dans l'Angleterre du Moyen Age. *Moyen Age*, 95, 101, 1, p. 7-22.

3844. Progetti e dinamiche nella società comunale italiana. A cura di Renato BORDONE e Giuseppe SERGI. Napoli, Liguori, 95, 424 p.

3845. RAUKAR (Tomislav). I fiorentini in Dalmazia nel secolo XIV. *Archivio storico italiano*, 95, 153, 566, p. 657-680.

3846. REDON (Odile). Le notaire au village. Enquête en pays siennois dans la deuxième moitié du XIIIe siècle et au début du XIVe siècle. *In*: Campagnes médiévales [Cf. n° 3713], p. 667-680.

3847. Représentation, pouvoir et royauté à la fin du Moyen Age. Ed. par Joël BLANCHARD. Postface de Philippe CONTAMINE. Paris, Picard, 95, 340 p.

3848. REYNOLDS (Susan). Ideas and solidarities of the medieval laity: England and Western Europe. Aldershot, Variorum, 95, VIII-253 p. (Collected Studies Series).

3849. RIGBY (S. H.). English society in the later Middle Ages. Class, status and gender. New York, St. Martin's Press, 95, XII-408 p.

3850. RINALDI (Rossella). Forme di gestione immobiliare a Bologna nei secoli centrali del Medioevo tra normativa e preassi. *In*: Sol et l'immeuble (Le) [Cf. n° 3682], p. 41-69.

3851. RIPPE (Gérard). «Il combattimento di pane et polenta». *In*: Campagnes médiévales [Cf. n° 3713], p. 189-198.

3852. RIZZI (Alessandra). Dal divieto alla moralizzazione: il gioco e la predicazione al tramonto del medio evo. *In*: Gioco, civilizzazione, transizioni [Cf. n° 3768], p. 157-170.

3853. ROUX (Simone). Etre propriétaire à Paris à la fin du Moyen Age. *In*: Sol et l'immeuble (Le) [Cf. n° 3682], p. 71-83. – IDEM. Les laboureurs de Paris à la fin du Moyen Age. *In*: Campagnes médiévales [Cf. n° 3713], p. 723-732.

3854. RUGOLO (Carmela Maria). L'antroponimia nelle carte latine di alcune abbazie calabresi nei secoli XI–XIII. *In*: Genèse médiévale de l'anthroponymie moderne. L'espace italien [Cf. n° 3764], p. 381-392.

3855. RUSSELL (P. E.). Portugal, Spain and the African Atlantic, 1343–1490. Chivalry and Crusade from John of Gaunt to Henry the Navigator. Aldershot, Variorum, 95, XIV-327 p.

3856. SALICRÚ I LLUCH (Roser). El tràfic de mercaderies a Barcelona segons els comptes de la Lleuda de Mediona (febrer de 1434). Barcelona, CSIC, Institució Milà i Fontanals, 95, XIV-431 p. (Anuario de Estudios Medievales, Annex 30).

3857. SALRACH (Josep M.). El mercado de la tierra en la economia campesina medieval. Datos de fuentes catalanas. *Hispania*, 95, 55, 191, p. 921-952.

3858. SALVATORI (Enrica). Il sistema antroponimico a Pisa nel Duecento: la città e il territorio. *In*: Genèse médiévale de l'anthroponymie moderne. L'espace italien [Cf. n° 3764], p. 427-466.

3859. SANCHEZ MARTINEZ (Manuel). El naixement de la fiscalitat d'estat a Catalunya (segles XII–XIV). Girona, EUMO, Universitat de Girona i Estudis Universitaris de Vic, 95, 147 p. (Biblioteca Universitària, Història, 4).

3860. SCHULTZ (James A.). The knowledge of childhood in the German Middle Ages, 1100–1350. Philadelphia, Univeristy of Pennsylvania Press, 95, XX-318 p. (Middle ages series).

3861. SCHWERHOFF (Gerd). Der blasphemische Spieler. Zur Deutung eines Verhaltenstypus im späten Mittelalter und in der frühen Neuzeit. *In*: Gioco, civilizzazione, transizioni [Cf. n° 3768], p. 98-113.

3862. SCULLY (D. Eleanor), SCULLY (Terence). Early French cookery. Sources, history, original recipes and modern adaptations. Ann Arbor, University of Michigan Press, 95, XI-377 p.

3863. SCULLY (Terence). The art of cookery in the Middle Ages. Woodbridge a. Rochester, Boydell and Brewer, 95, VIII-276 p.

3864. SESMA MUÑOZ (José Ángel). Producción para el mercado, comercio y desarrolo mercantil en espacios interiores (1250–1350): el modelo del sur de Aragón. *In*: Europa en los umbrales [Cf. n° 3357], p. 205-246.

3865. SHERMAN SEVERIN (Dorothy). Witchcraft in "Celestina". London, University of London, Queen Mary and Westfield College, Department of Hispanic Studies, 95 58 p. (Papers of the medieval Hispanic research seminar, 1).

3866. SIMON (Larry J.). Iberia and the Mediterranean world of the late Middle Ages. Studies in honor of Robert I. Burns S. I. Vol. 1. Leiden, New York a. Köln, E. J. Brill, 95, 373 p.

3867. SIMONITI (Vasko). Die Wüstungen im 14. und 15. Jahrhundert mit besonderer Berücksichtigung des slowenischen Gebietes. *Mitt. d. Inst. f. Österr. Gesch.-Forsch.*, 95, 103, 1-2, p. 44-55.

3868. SINGMAN (Jeffrey L.), MAC LEAN (Will). Daily life in Chaucer's England. Westport a. London, Greenwood Press, 95, XIII-253 p. (Daily life through history).

3869. SKINNER (Patricia). Family power in southern Italy. The Duchy of Gaeta and its neighbours, 850–1139. Cambridge, Cambridge U. P., 95, XII-322 p. (Cambridge studies in medieval life and thought. Fourth series, 29). – EADEM. Politics and piracy: the Duchy of Gaeta in the twelfth century. *Journal of Medieval History*, 95, 21, 4, p. 307-319.

3870. SMITH (Julia M. H.). Religion and lay society. *In*: New Cambridge medieval history [Cf. n° 3378], p. 654-680.

3871. Società fiorentina nel Basso Medioevo (La). Per Elio Conti (Dipartimento di storia dell'Università di Firenze. Istituto storico italiano per il Medio Evo. Roma-Firenze, 16–18 dicembre 1992). A cura di Renzo NINCI. Roma, Istituto storico italiano per il Medio Evo, 95, XVI-272 p.

3872. SOUSA (Bernardo Vasconcelos e). Os Pimentéis: percursos de uma linhagem da nobreza medieval portuguesa (séculos XIII–XIV). Lisboa, [s. n.], 95, 511 p. (Tese dout. Hist. Económica Social – Sécs. III–XIV, Univ. Nova Lisboa).

3873. SOWINA (Urszula). Średniowieczna działka miejska w świetle źródeł pisanych. (Parcelle municipale au Moyen Age à la lumière des sources écrites.). *Kwartalnik Historii Materialnej Polskiej Akademii Nauk*, 95, 43, 3, p. 323-331. [Deutsche Zsfassung].

3874. STÖKLY (Doris). Le système de l'Incanto des galées du marché à Venise (fin XIIIe–milieu XVe siècle). Leiden, New York a. Köln, E. J. Brill, 95, XVII-434 p. (The Medieval Mediterranean, 5).

3875. TEKE (Zsuzsa). Firenzei kereskedőtársaságok, kereskedők Magyarországon Zsigmond uralmának megszilárdulása után, 1404–1437. (Associations de commerçants, commerçants de Florence en Hongrie après la stabilisation du regne de Sigismond, 1404–1437). *Századok*, 95, 129, 1, p. 195-214. – EADEM. Firenzei üzletemberek Magyarországon 1373–1403. (Gens d'affaires florentins en Hongrie en 1373–1403). *Tört. szle.*, 95, 37, 2, p. 129-150. – EADEM. L'economia fiorentina e l'Europa centro-orientale nei secoli XIV e XV (Introduzione). *Archivio storico italiano*, 95, 153, 566, p. 631-632. – EADEM. Operatori economici in Ungheria nel tardo Trecento e nel primo Quattrocento. *Archivio storico italiano*, 95, 153, 566, p. 697-708.

3876. TERPSTRA (Nicholas). Lay confraternities and civic religio in Renaissance Bologna. Cambridge, Cambridge U. P., 95, XX-251 p. (Cambridge studies in Italian history and culture).

3877. THOMPSON (Michael). The medieval hall. The basis of secular domestic life, 600–1600 AD. Aldershot a. Brookfield, Scolar Press, 95, XII-212 p.

3878. THUMSER (Matthias). Rom und der römische Adel in der späten Stauferzeit. Tübingen, Max Niemeyer Verlag, 95, 425 p. (Bibliothek des Deutschen Historischen Instituts in Rom, 81).

3879. *Vacat.*

3880. TODESCHINI (Giacomo). Testualità francescana e linguaggi economici nelle città italiane del Quattrocento. *Quaderni medievali*, 95, 40, p. 21-49.

3881. TOUBERT (Pierre). Dalla terra ai castelli. Paesaggio, agricoltura e poteri nell'Italia medievale. A cura di Giuseppe SERGI. Torino, Einaudi, 95, XX-360 p. (Biblioteca studio, 7).

3882. TRICARD (Jean). Livres de raison et présence de la bourgeoise dans la campagnes limousines (XIVe–XVe siècles). *In*: Campagnes médiévales [Cf. n° 3713], p. 709-722.

3883. VALENTE (C.). Simon de Montfort, Earl of Leicester, and the utility of sanctity in thirteenth-century England. *Journal of Medieval History*, 95, 21, 1, p. 27-49.

3884. VAN VLECK (Amelia). Textiles as testimony in Marie de France and Philomena. *Medievalia et Humanistica*, 95, 22, p. 31-60.

3885. VERHULST (Adriaan). Economic organisation. *In*: New Cambridge medieval history [Cf. n° 3378], p. 481-509. – IDEM. Les biens et revenus du chapitre Saint-Donatien de Bruges en 1089. *In*: Campagnes médiévales [Cf. n° 3713], p. 513-532.

3886. VILLANI (Matteo). L'antroponimia nelle carte napoletane (secc. X–XII). *In*: Genèse médiévale de l'anthroponymie moderne. L'espace italien [Cf. n° 3764], p. 345-359.

3887. VIÑA BRITO (Ana). Deudas e indemnizaciones. Aspectos negativos de la herencia de los primeros condes de Ureña. *Anuario de estudios medievales*, 95, 25, 1, p. 255-266.

3888. VINCENT (Catherine). Lieux de piètè et lieux de pouvoir à Poitiers entre le XIIIe et le XVe siècle: la confrérie du Corps de ville dite aussi du Cent. *In*: Religion civique à l'époque médiévale et moderne (La) [Cf. n° 4528], p. 429-444.

3889. VIOLANTE (Cinzio). Prospettive storiografiche sulla società medioevale. Milano, Angeli, 95, 188 p.

3890. WAMERS (E.). Eine burgundische Pyxis 'vom Niederrhein'. Zu merowingerzeitlichen Amulettkapseln und Kosmetikbüchsen. *Frühmittelalterliche Studien*, 95, 29, p. 144-166.

3891. WANDRUSZKA (Nikolai). Die Entstehung des Familiennamens in Bologna (XII. und XIII. Jahrhundert). *In*: Genèse médiévale de l'anthroponymie moderne. L'espace italien [Cf. n° 3764], p. 595-625.

3892. WICKHAM (Chris). Rural society in Carolingian Europe. *In*: New Cambridge medieval history [Cf. n° 3378], p. 510-552.

3893. WINDEMUTH. (Marie-Luise). Das Hospital als Träger der Armenfürsorge im Mittelalter. Stuttgart, Steiner, 95. 164 p. (Sudhoffs Archiv, 36).

§ 9. Kultur-, Literatur- und Unterrichtsgeschichte.

** 3894. Altenglische (Die) Interlinearversion zu De vitiis et peccatis in der Hs. British Library, Royal 7 C IV. Textausgabe mit Kommentar und Glossar von R. CORNELIUS. Bern u. Frankfurt am M. u. New York u. Paris, P. Lang, 95, 238 p. (Europäische Hochschulschriften. Reihe 14, 296).

** 3895. Belle (La) Hélène de Constantinople. Chanson de geste du XIVe siècle. Ed. par Claude ROUSSEL. Genève, Droz, 95, 942 p. (Texte littéraires français, 454).

** 3896. CABALLINUS DE CERRONIBUS (Ioannes). Polistoria de virtutibus et dotibus Romanorum. Hrsg. von Marc LAUREYS. Stuttgart u. Lipsia, Teubner, 95, LXII-375 p. (Bibliotheca scriptorum Graecorum et Romanorum Teubneriana).

** 3897. CHASTELAIN (G.). Le miroir de mort. Ed. critique par T. VAN HEMELRYCK. Louvain-la-Neuve, Istitut d'études médiévales de l'Université catholique, 95, 187 p. (ill.) (Textes, études, congrès. Publications de l'Institut d'études médiévales de Louvain-la-Neuve, 17).

** 3898. Commentary (A) on the Penitentiam Psalms translated by Dame Eleanor Hull. Ed. by A. BARRATT. Oxford, Early English Texts Society, Oxford University Press, 95, 500 p. (Early English Text Society. Original Series, 307).

** 3899. Copie (La) de Guiot fol. 79v–105r du manuscrit f. fr. 794 de la Bibliothèque Nationale, "Li chevaliers au lyeon" de Chretien de Troyes. Ed. par K. MEYER. Amsterdam et Atlanta, Rodopi, 95, 342 p. (51 facs.) (Faux titre. Études de langue et littérature française, 104).

** 3900. DANTE ALIGHIERI. Convivio. A cura di F. BRAMBILLA AGENO. Vol. 1–2. Introduzione. Vol. 3. Testo. Firenze, Le lettere, 95, 3 vol., 1443 p. (Le opere di Dante Alighieri. Edizione nazionale a cura della Società Dantesca Italiana, 3).

** 3901. DANTE ALIGHIERI. Epistola a Cangrande. A cura di E. CECCHINI. Firenze, Giunti, 95, LII-52 p. (Biblioteca del Medioevo latino)

.** 3902. FRANCESCO DA BARBERINO. Reggimento e costumi di donna. Ed. crit. a cura di G. E. SANSONE. Roma, Zauli, 95, CII-322 p. (I topazi. Testi volgari antichi, 3).

** 3903. GIOVANNI DI GARLANDIA. Epithalamium beatae Virginis Mariae. Ed. crit. a cura di A. SAIANI. Firenze, L. S. Olschli, 95, 948 p. (Accademia toscana di scienze e lettere «La Colombaria», 139).

** 3904. GUILLELMUS DURANTUS. Rationale divinorum officiorum, I–IV. Ed. par Anselme DAVRIL et Thimothy M. THIBODEAU. Turnhout, Brepols, 95, XXIV-602 p. (Corpus christianorum, continuatio mediaevalis, 140).

** 3905. Index (The) of Middle English Prose. Handlist 11. Manuscripts in the Library of Trinity College, Cambridge. Ed. by L. R. MOONEY. Woodbridge, D. S. Brewer, 95, XXXVIII-252 p.

** 3906. Metaura (La) d'Aristotile. Volgarizzamento fiorentino anonimo del XIV secolo. Ed. crit. di R. LIBRANDI. Napoli, Liguori, 95, 2 vol., 616 p. (Romanica neapolitana, 29).

** 3907. Middle English Romances. Ed. by S. H. A. SHEPHERD. New York, W. W. Norton & C., 95, 488 p. (Norton Critical Editions).

** 3908. Novellino (The). Ed. by R. L. PAYNE and J. L. SMARR. Frankfurt am Main, Peter Lang, 95, XVII-154 p. (Studies in Italian Culture: Literature in History, 15).

** 3909. Perilous (The) Cemetery (L'atre périlleux). Ed. by N. B. BLACK. New York a. London, Garland Publishing, 95, 480 p. [original text and English transl.] (Garland Library of Medieval Literature. Series A, 104).

** 3910. PIERO DELLA FRANCESCA. Libellus de quinque corporibus regularibus. Testi e note, disegni, facsimile (Codex Vaticanus Urb. lat. 632). A cura di C. GRAYSON, M. DALAI EMILIANI, C. MACCAGNI. Firenze, Giunti, 95, 3 vol. (Edizione nazionale degli scritti di Piero della Francesca, 1).

** 3911. Poesia (La) carolingia, testo latino a fronte. A cura di Francesco STELLA. Firenze, Le Lettere, 95, 526 p. (Le Lettere. Università, 3. Antologie, 1).

** 3912. Repues (Les) franches de maistre François Villon et de ses compagnons. Ed. crit. de J. KOOPMANS et P. VERHUYCK. Genève, Droz, 95, 208 p. (Textes littéraires français, 455).

** 3913. RINUCCINI (C.). Rime. Ed. crit. a cura di G. BALBI. Torino, Casa Editrice Le Lettere, 95, 208 p. (Fondo di studi Parini-Chirio. Filologia. Testi e studi, 4).

** 3914. ROBERT DE BORON. Joseph d'Arimathie. Critical ed. by Richard O'GORMAN. Toronto, Pontifical Institute of Medieval Studies, 95, 587 p. (Studies and Texts, 120).

** 3915. Roman (Le) de Tristan en prose. Publié sous la dir. de P. MENARD. Tome 8. De la quête de Galaad à la destruction du château de la lépreuse. Ed. par B. GUIDOT et J. SUBRENAT. Genève, Droz, 95, 408 p. (Textes littéraires français, 462).

** 3916. SERCAMBI (G.). Novelle. Nuovo testo critico a cura di G. SINICROPI. Torino, Casa editrice Le Lettere, 95, 2 vol., 1467 p. (Fondo di studi Parini-Chirio. Filologia. Testi e studi, 5).

** 3917. Songs (The) of the Women Troubadours. Ed. by M. T. BRUCKNER, L. SHEPARD and S. WHITE, New York a. London, Garland Publishing, 95, 275 p. [original text and English transl.] (Garland Library of Medieval Literature. Series A, 97).

** 3918. Sticker (Der), Daniel von dem Blühenden Tal. Hrsg. von M. RESLER. Tübingen, M. Niemeyer, 95, XXVI-364 p. [2. neu bearb. Auflage] (Altdeutsche Textbibliothek, 92).

** 3919. VESPASIANO DA BISTICCI. Große Männer und Frauen der Renaissance. Achtunddreißig biographische Porträts. Hrsg. von Bernd ROECK. München, Beck, 95, 471 p. (taf.).

** 3920. VINCENTIUS BELVACENSIS. De morali principiis institutione. Ed. par Robert J. SCHNEIDER. Turnhout, Brepols, 95, LXXXVIII-184 p. (Corpus christianorum, continuatio mediaevalis, 137).

3921. Actas I Congreso nacional de latín medieval (Léon, 1–4 de diciembre de 1993). Ed. por Maurilio PÉREZ GONZÁLEZ. Léon, Universdad de Léon, Secretariado de Publicaciones, 95, 670 p.

3922. ADORNO (Francesco). La crisi dell'Umanesimo civile fiorentino da Alamanno Rinuccini al Machiavelli. In: Studi in onore di Arnaldo D'Addario [Cf. n° 452], p. 561-583.

3923. ÆLFRIC. Ælfric's prefaces. Ed. by Jonathan WILCOX. Durham, University of Durham, Department of English Studies, 95, VII-202 p. (Durham medieval texts, 9).

3924. Aetates ovidianae. Lettori di Ovidio dall'Antichità al Rinascimento. A cura di I. GALLO e L. NICASTRI. Napoli, Edizioni scientifiche italiane, 95, 384 p.

3925. ALPHANDERY (Paul), DUPRONT (Alphonse). La Chrétienté et l'idée de Croisade. Postface de Michel BALARD. Paris, Albin Michel, 95, 597 p. (Bibliothèque de "L'Evolution de l'Humanité Albin Michel").

3926. ALTHOFF (Gerd). Die Historiographie bewältigt. Der Sturz Heinrichs des Löwen in der Darstellung Arnolds von Lübeck. In: Welfen und ihr Braunschweiger Hof im hohen Mittelalter (Die) [Cf. n° 3486], p. 163-182.

3927. ALVIRA CABRER (Martin). La muerte del enemigo en el pleno medievo: cifras e ideologia (el modelo de las navas de Tolosa). Hispania, 95, 55, 190, p. 403-424.

3928. ARMSTRONG (A.). More manuscript copies of Jean Bouchet's verse: Mss. B. N. fr. 2206 and 2231. *Bibliothèque d'Humanisme et Renaissance*, 95, 57, 1, p. 89-100.

3929. ASPERTI (Stefano). Carlo I d'Angiò e i trovatori. Componenti "provenzali" e angioine nella tradizione manoscritta della lirica trobadorica. Ravenna, Longo, 95, 270 p. (Memoria del tempo, 3).

3930. BANNIARD (Michel). Language and communication in Carolingian Europe. *In*: New Cambridge medieval history [Cf. n° 3378], p. 695-708.

3931. BARLOW (J.). Gregory of Tours and the myth of the Trojan origins of the Franks. *Frühmittelalterliche Studien*, 95, 29, p. 86-95.

3932. BARTHELEMY (Dominique). Du nouveau sur le Conventum Hugonis? *Bibliothèque de l'École des chartes*, 95, 153, 2, p. 483-495.

3933. BARTLETT (Anne Clark). Male authors, female readers. Representation and subjectivity in middle English devotional literature. Ithaca a. London, Cornell U. P., 95, XII-212 p.

3934. BAXTER WOLF (Kenneth). Making history: the Normans and their historians in eleventh-century Italy. Philadelphia, University of Pennsylvania Press, 95, XIII-192 p. (Middle Ages Series).

3935. BEECH (George), CHAUVIN (Yves), PON (Georges). Le «Conventum» (vers 1030), un précurseur aquitain des premières épopées. Geneve, Droz, 95, 190 p. (Publications romanes et françaises, 212) (pl.).

3936. BELL (D. N.). What nuns read: books and libraries in medieval English nunneries. Kalamazoo, Cistercian publications, 95, 300 p. (Cistercian studies series, 158).

3937. BELTRAN (E.). L'Oratio funebris pro Alberto rege Romanorum de Jean Jouffroy (1412–1473). *Bibliothèque d'Humanisme et Renaissance*, 95, 57, 3, p. 599-614.

3938. BENHAMAMOUCHE (Fatima). Ramon Llull (1232–1315) y el mundo islamico: una relacion apasionada. *Revue d'Histoire Maghrébine*, 95, 77-78, p. 113-125.

3939. BERLIOZ (Jacques), POLO DE BEAULIEU (Marie-Anne). Les prologues des recueils d'exempla (XIIIe–XIVe siècles). Une grille d'analyse. *In*: Predicazione dei frati (La) [Cf. n° 4451], p. 269-299.

3940. BLASIO (Maria Grazia). Memoria filologica e memoria politica in Biondo Flavio. Il significato della «instauratio Urbis». *In*: Memoria (La) e la città. Scritture storiche tra medioevo e età moderna [Cf. n° 3303], p. 307-317.

3941. BOLAND (Margaret M.). Architectural structure in the "Lais" of Marie de France. New York, Lang, 95, X-226 p. (Currents in comparative romance languages and literatures, 21).

3942. BOND (Gerald A.). The loving subject. Desire, eloquence, and power in romanesque France. Philadelphia, Univeristy of Pennsylvania Press, 95, IX-276 p. (Middle ages series).

3943. BÖNINGER (Lorenz). Un illustre abate siciliano, l'«Audientia litterarum contradictarum» e una donazione di reliquie a Santa Maria del Fiore nel 1439. *Archivio storico italiano*, 95, 153, 565, p. 427-486.

3944. BONNET (Marie Rose). Livres de raison et de comptes e Provence, fin du XIVe siècle-début du XVIe siècle. Aix en Provence, Publications de l'Université de Provence, 95, 177 p.

3945. BONOCORE (Marco). Properzio nei codici della Biblioteca Apostolica Vaticana. Assisi, Accademia Properziana del Subasio, 95, 138 p.

3946. BORST (A.). Das Buch der Naturgeschichte: Plinius und seine Leser im Zeitalter des Pergaments. Heidelberg, Winter, 95, X-434 p.

3947. BOZOKY (Edina). Les démons et les morts: croyances et pratiques pour protéger les morts contre les démons au Moyen Age. *In*: Enfer et paradis [Cf. n° 1370], p. 311-331.

3948. BRAND (Paul). Learning English customary law: education in the London Law School, 1250–1500. *In*: Vocabulary of teaching [Cf. n° 4164], p. 199-213.

3949. BRETEL (Paul). Les ermites et les moines dans la littérature française du Moyen Age (1150–1250). Paris, Champion, 95, 810 p. (Nouvele Bibliothèque du Moyen Age, 32).

3950. BÜHLER (Pierre). Présence, sentiment et rhétorique de la nature dans la littérature latine de la France médiévale. Paris, Champion, 95, 2 vol., 722 p., 698 p.

3951. BURGESS (Glyn S.). The old French narrative lay. An analytical bibliography. Woodbridge a. Rochester, Boydell and Brewer, 95, VIII-140 p.

3952. BYRHTFERTH. Byrhtferth's Enchiridion. Ed. a. trans. by Peter S. BAKER a. Michael LAPIDGE. Oxford, Oxford U. P., 95, CXXXIII-480 p. (Early English text society, 15).

3953. Centers of learning. Learning and location in pre-modern Europe and the Near-East. Ed. by Jan Willem DRIJVERS a. Alasdair A. MAC DONALD. Leiden, New York a. London, E. J. Brill, 95, XIV-340 p. (Brill's studies in intellectual history, 61). [Cf. n° <choice> 3975, 4076, 4156, 4314, 4319, 4349, 4380, 4385, 4386, 4387.]

3954. CEPEDA (Isabel Vilares). Bibliografía da prosa medieval em língua portuguesa: subsídios. Lisboa, Inst. da Biblioteca Nacional e do Livro, 95, 265 p.

3955. Chansons des trovères. Chanter m'estuet. Ed. et trad. par Samuel N. ROSENBERG, Hans TISCHLER et Marie-Geneviève GROSSEL. Paris, La Livre de Poche, 95, 1089 p. (Lettres gothiques).

9. KULTUR-, LITERATUR- UND UNTERRICHTSGESCHICHTE

3956. CHAUCER (Geoffrey). A Variorum edition of the works of Geoffry Chaucer. 2. The Canterbury tales. 7. Summoner's tale. Ed. by John F. PLUMMER III. Norman a. London, Univerity of Oklahoma Press, 95, XXVIII-242 p.

3957. CHIESA (Paolo). «Autographa Medii Aevi»: nel laboratorio degli scrittori medievali. *Studi Medievali*, 95, 36, 1, p. 477-482.

3958. CHRETIEN DE TROYES. La copie de Guiot, fol. 79v–105r du manuscrit f. fr. 794 de la Bibliothèque Nationale, "Li chevaliers au lyeon" de Crestien de Troyes. Ed. par Kajsa MEYER. Amsterdam et Atlanta, Rodopi, 95, 342 p. (Faux titre, 104).

3959. Chūsei no Gakumon-kan. (Thought of learning in the Middle Ages). Ed. by Jōchi Daigaku Chūseishisō Kenkyūjo. Tokyo, Sōbunsha, 95, 400 p.

3960. CLASSEN (A.). Minnesang als Spiel. Sinnkonstitution auf dem «Schachbrett» der Liebe. *Studi Medievali*, 95, 36, 1, p. 211-240.

3961. Classical (The) tradition in the Middle Ages and the Renaissance. Proceedings of the first European science foundation workshop on "The reception of classical texts", Florence, Certosa del Galluzzo, 26–27 June 1992. Ed. by Claudio LEONARDI a. Birger MUNK OLSEN. Spoleto, Centro Italiano di Studi sull'Alto Medioevo, 95, X-283 p. (ill) (Biblioteca di Medioevo Latino, 15).

3962. CLEMOES (Peter). Interaction of thought and language in old English poetry. Cambridge, Cambridge U. P., 95, XVII-523 p. (Cambridge studies in Anglo-Saxon England, 12).

3963. COBBY (Anne Elizabeth). Ambivalent conventions. Formula and parody in old French. Amsterdam a. Atlanta, Rodopi, 95, IX-180 p. (Faux titre, 101).

3964. COLINET (A.). Le livre d'Hermès intitulé «Liber dabessi» ou «Liber rebis». *Studi Medievali*, 95, 36, 2, p. 1011-1052.

3965. Comprendre le XIIIe siècle. Etudes offertes à Marie-Thérèse Lorcin. Dir. par Pierre GUICHARD et Danièle ALEXANDRE-BIDON. Lyon, Presses Universitaires, 95, 313 p. [Cf. n^{os} <sélection> 693, 3220, 3244, 3257, 3273, 3324, 3603, 3658.]

3966. CONTRENI (John J.). The Carolingian renaissance: education and literary culture. *In*: New Cambridge medieval history [Cf. n° 3378], p. 709-757.

3967. *Vacat*.

3968. COULSON (F. T.). A newly discovered copy of the 'Vulgate' commentary on Ovid's «Metamorphoses» in an «Incunabulum» in the British Library. *Studi Medievali*, 95, 36, 1, p. 321-322.

3969. Creating French culture. Treasures from the Bibliothèque nationale de France. Ed. by Marie-Hélène TESNIÈRE and Prosser GIFFORD, introduction by Emmanuel LE ROY LADURIE. New Haven a. London, Yale U. P., 95, XL-480 p.

3970. CRISCIANI (Chiara). Aspetti della trasmissione del sapere nell'alchimia latina. Un'immagine di formazione, uno stile di commento. *In*: Crisi dell'alchimia (Le) [Cf. n° 4318], p. 149-184.

3971. Cross cultural convergences in the Crusade period. Essays presented to Aryeth Graboïs on his sixty-fifth birthday. Ed. by M. GOODICH, S. MENACHE a. S. SCHEIN. New York, Lang, 95, [s. p.].

3972. CSAPODI (Csaba). A magyar könyvkultúra Zsigmond korában. (La culture de livre hongroise à l'époque du roi Sigismond [1387–1437]). *Magyar könyvszle.*, 95, 111, 1, p. 1-14.

3973. Dante now. Current trends in Dante studies. Ed. by Theodore J. CACHEY Jr. Notre Dame a. London, University of Notre Dame Press, 95, XXI-283 p. (William and Katherine Devers series in Dante studies, 1).

3974. DANTE. Monarchia. Ed. a. trans. Prue SHAW. Cambridge, Cambridge U. P., 95, XLVI-186 p. (Cambridge medieval classics, 4).

3975. DE BOER (Dick E. H.). Ludwig the Bavarian and the scholars. *In*: Centers of learning [Cf. n° 3953], p. 229-244.

3976. DE MERINDOL (Christian). Iconographie de sceau de ville en France à l'èpoque médiévale et religion civique. *In*: Religion civique à l'époque médiévale et moderne (La) [Cf. n° 4528], p. 415-428.

3977. DELCORNO (Carlo). La lingua dei predicatori. Tra latino e volgare. *In*: Predicazione dei frati (La) [Cf. n° 4451], p. 21-46. – IDEM. Le «Vitae Patrum» nella letteratura religiosa medievale (secc. XIII–XV). *In*: Spiritualità e lettere nella cultura italiana e ungherese del basso medioevo [Cf. n° 4128], p. 179-201.

3978. DI FRANCESCO (Amedeo). La letteratura monastica e gli inizi della drammaturgia e della novellistica in lingua ungherese. *In*: Spiritualità e lettere nella cultura italiana e ungherese del basso medioevo [Cf. n° 4128], p. 211-230.

3979. DIJKSTRA (C. Th. J.). La chanson de croisade. Etude thématique d'un genre hybride. Amsterdam, Schiphouwer en Brinkman, 95, V-233 p.

3980. DRONKE (P.). Medieval sibyls: their character and their «Auctoritas». *Studi Medievali*, 95, 36, 2, p. 581-616.

3981. DUFOURNET (J.). Philippe de Remy et la réécriture. 1. Jehan et Blonde comme réécriture de Joufroi de Poitiers (XIIIe siècle). D'un roman anglais à l'autre. *Moyen Age*, 95, 101, 3, p. 425-446.

3982. DUMVILLE (David N.). The early medieval insular churches and the preservation of Roman literature. Towards a historical and plaeographical revaluation. *In*: Formative stages of classical traditions [Cf. n° 3282], p. 197-237.

3983. Ellesmere Chaucer (The). Essays in interpretation. Ed. by Martin STEVENS a. Daniel WOODWARD.

San Marino, Huntington Library a. Tokyo, Yushodo, 95, XVI-363 p.

3984. Europe des Humanistes (L') (XIVᵉ–XVIIᵉ siècles). Répertoire établi par J. F. MAILLARD, J. KECSKEMETI et M. PORTALIER. Paris, CNRS Editions et Turnhout, Brepols, 95, 544 p. (Documents, études et répertoires publiés pa l'Institut de Recherche et d'Histoire des Textes).

3985. FARENGA (Paola). La memoria di una minoranza: la città dei Romani. *In*: Memoria (La) e la città. Scritture storiche tra medioevo e età moderna [Cf. n° 3303], p. 319-329.

3986. FEISTNER (Edith). Historische Typologie der deutschen Heiligenlegende des Mittelalters von der Mitte des 12. Jahrhunderts bis zur Reformation. Wiesbaden, Dr. Ludwig Reichert, 95, IX-411 p. (Wissenliteratur im Mittelalter, 20).

3987. Femme (Une) de lettres au Moyen Age: études autour de Christine de Pizan. Articles inédits réunis par L. DULAC et B. RIBEMONT. Orléans, Paradigme, 95, 526 p. (ill.) (Etudes médiévales)

3988. FERA (Vincenzo). Un laboratorio filologico di fine Quattrocento: la «Naturalis Historia». *In*: Formative stages of classical traditions [Cf. n° 3282], p. 435-466.

3989. FOSS (Michael). The world of Camelot: King Arthur and the Knights of the Round Table. New York, Sterling, 95, 212 p.

3990. FREDELL (Joel). Reading the dream miniature in the Confessio Amantis. *Medievalia et Humanistica*, 95, 22, p. 61-94.

3991. FREIRE (José Geraldes). Oração de sapiência. O latin medieval em Portugal. Lingua e literatura. Coimbra, Universidade de Coimbra, 95, 56 p.

3992. FREISE (Eckhard). Die Welfen und der Sachsenspiegel. *In*: Welfen und ihr Braunschweiger Hof im hohen Mittelalter (Die) [Cf. n° 3486], p. 439-482.

3993. FREUND (Stephan). Studien zur literarischen Wirksamkeit des Petrus Damiani. Hannover, Hahnsche Buchhandlung, 95, XII-305 p. (Monumenta Germaniae Historica. Studien und Texte, 13).

3994. FUBINI (Riccardo). Cristoforo Landino, le «Disputationes Camaldulenses» e il volgarizzamento di Plinio: questioni di cronologia e di interpretazione. *In*: Studi in onore di Arnaldo D'Addario [Cf. n° 452], p. 535-560.

3995. FURNO (Martine). Le «Cornu copiae» de Niccolo Perotti. Culture et méthode d'un humaniste qui aimait les mots. Genève, Droz, 95, 251 p. (Travaille d'Humanisme et Renaissance, 194).

3996. GAFFURI (Laura). Nell'«Officina» del predicatore: gli strumenti per la composizione dei sermoni latini. *In*: Predicazione dei frati (La) [Cf. n° 4451], p. 82-111.

3997. GARCIA TERUEL (G.). Les opinions sur le femme dans quelques récits du XIIᵉ et du XIIIᵉ siècles. *Moyen Age*, 95, 101, 1, p. 23-40.

3998. GAUNT (Simon). Gender and genre in medieval French literature. Cambridge, Cambridge U. P., 95, X-372 p. (Cambridge studies in French, 53).

3999. Gentle voices of teachers (The). Aspects of learning in the Carolingian Age. Ed. by Richard E. SULLIVAN. Columbus, Ohio State U. P., 95, 361 p.

4000. GEORGIANNA (Linda). The Clerk's tale and the grammar of assent. *Speculum*, 95, 70, 4, p. 793-821.

4001. GREGORY (T.). I «thesauri» dei padri greci e latini. *Studi Medievali*, 95, 36, 1, p. 461-476.

4002. GUERIN (M. Victoria). The fall of kings and princes and destruction in Arthurian tragedy. Stanford, Stanford U. P., 95, XV-336. (Figurae. Reading Medieval Culture).

4003. GUERREAU-JALABERT (Anita). L'essart comme figure de subversion de l'ordre spatial dans les romans arthuriens. *In*: Campagnes médiévales [Cf. n° 3713], p. 59-72.

4004. GUNNELL (Terry). The origins of drama in Scandinavia. Woodbridge a. Rochester, Boydell and Brewer, 95, XXVI-414 p.

4005. Gyðinga saga (Rit, 42.). Ed. by Kirsten WOLF. Reykjavík, Stofnun Árna Magnússonar á Íslandi, 95, CLXVI-233 p.

4006. HAMESSE (Jacqueline). Approche terminologique de certaines méthodes d'enseignement et de recherche à la fin du moyen âge. «Declarare», «recitare», «conclusio». *In*: Vocabulary of teaching [Cf. n° 4164], p. 8-28. – EADEM. La prédication universitaire. *In*: Predicazione dei frati (La) [Cf. n° 4451], p. 49-79.

4007. Handbook of the Troubadours (A). Ed. by F. R. P. AKEHURST a. Judith M. DAVIS. Berkeley, Los Angeles a. London, University of California Press, 95, VII-502 p. (Publications of the UCLA Center for Medieval and Renaissance studies, 26).

4008. HARÐARSON (Gunnar). Littérature et spiritualité en Scandinavie médiévale. La traduction norroise du "De arrha animae" de Hugues de Saint-Victor. Paris et Turnhout, Brepols, 95, X-275 p. (Bibliotheca Victorina, 5).

4009. HASSIG (Debra). Medieval Bestiaries. Text, image, ideology. Cambridge, Cambridge U. P., 95, XX-300 p. (RES Monographs on Anthropology and Aesthetics).

4010. HAUG (Walter). Brechungen auf dem Weg zur Individualität. Kleine Schriften zur Literatur des Mittelalters. Tübingen, Max Niemeyer Verlag, 95, XIV-685 p.

4011. HAUSTEIN (Jens). Marner-Studien. Tübingen, Max Niemeyer Verlag, 95, IX-285 p. (Münchener Texte und Untersuchungen zur deutschen Literatur des Mittelalters, 109).

4012. HEN (Yitzhak). Culture and religion in merovingian Gaul, A. D. 481–751. Leiden, New York a. Köln, E. J. Brill, 95, XIV-308 p. (Cultures, beliefs and traditions. Medieval and early modern peoples, 1).

4013. HERMANN (John P.). Boniface and Dokkum: terror, repetition, allegory. *Medievalia et Humanistica*, 95, 22, p. 1-30.

4014. HILL (John M.). The cultural world in "Beowulf". Toronto, University of Toronto Press, 95, X-224.

4015. HOENEN (Maarten J. F. M.). Late medieval schools of thought in the mirror of University textbooks. The «Promptuarium argumentorum» (Cologne 1492). *In*: Philosophy and learning [Cf. n° 4363], p. 329-370.

4016. HOLL (Béla). Sulla poesia liturgica dei domenicani in Ungheria a cavallo fra il Duecento e il Trecento. *In*: Spiritualità e lettere nella cultura italiana e ungherese del basso medioevo [Cf. n° 4128], p. 39-52.

4017. HOLZNAGEL (Franz-Joseph). Wege in die Schriftlichkeit. Untersuchungen und Materialen zur Überlieferung der mittelhochdeutschen Lyrik. Tübingen u. Basel, Francke, 95, 664 p. (Bibliotheca Germanica, 32).

4018. HUCKER (Bernd Ulrich). Literatur im Umkreis Kaiser Ottos IV. *In*: Welfen und ihr Braunschweiger Hof im hohen Mittelalter (Die) [Cf. n° 3486], p. 377-406.

4019. HUTCHINSON (Ann M.). What the nuns read: literary evidence from the English Bridgettine House, Syon abbey. *Mediaeval Studies*, 95, 57, p. 205-222.

4020. Image (La): fonction et usage des images dans l'Occident médiéval. Actes du colloque d'Erice 1992. Ed. par J. BASCHET et J.-C. SCHMITT. Paris, Le Léopard d'or, 95, 240 p. (ill.) (Les Cahiers du Léopard d'or, 5).

4021. In supreme dignitatis. Per la storia dell'Università di Ferrara (1391–1991). A cura di Patrizia CASTELLI. Firenze, Olschki, 95, XXVIII-615 p. (Pubblicazioni dell'Università di Ferrara, 3).

4022. JOHANNES DE GARLANDIA. Compendium Gramatice. Hrsg. v. Thomas HAYE. Wien, Köln u. Weimar, Böhlau, 95, VIII-327 p. (Ordo, Studien zur Literatur und Gesellschaft des Mittelalters und der frühen Neuzeit, 5).

4023. JONES (Frederic J.). The structure of Petrarch's "Canzoniere". A chronological, Psychological and stylistic analysis. Woodbridge a. Rochester, Boydell and Brewer, 95, XII-328 p.

4024. JÓNSSON (Einar Már). Le miroir. Naissance d'un genre littéraire. Paris, Les Belles Lettres, 95, 238 p. (il.). (Histoire).

4025. JUDITH (George). Venantius Fortunatus: personal and political poems. Liverpool, Liverpool U. P., 95, 156 p. (Translated texts for historians, 23).

4026. KAHN (Didier). Littérature et alchimie au Moyen Age: de quelques textes alchimiques attribués à Arthur et Merlin. *In*: Crisi dell'alchimia (Le) [Cf. n° 4318], p. 227-262.

4027. KAY (Sarah). "Chanson de geste" in the age of romance. Political fictions. Oxford, Clarendon Press a. New York, Oxford U. P., 95, VII-273 p. – EADEM. The Romance of the Rose. London, Grant & Cutler, 95, 125 p. (Critical guide to French texts, 110).

4028. KELLY (Douglas). Internal difference and meanings in the "Roman of Rose". Madison, University of Wisconsin Press, 95, IX-228 p.

4029. KENNEDY (Thomas C.). The translator's voice in The Second Nun's Invocacio: gender, influence, and textuality. *Medievalia et Humanistica*, 95, 22, p. 95-110.

4030. KENT (Bonnie). Virtues of the will. The transformation of ethics in the late thirteenth century. Washington, Catholic University of America Press, 95, IX-270 p.

4031. KERN (Manfred). Agamemnon weint, oder arthurische Metamorphose und trojanische Destruktion im "Göttweiger Trojanerkrieg". Erlangen u. Jena, Palm & Enke, 95, IX-251 p. (Erlanger Studien, 104).

4032. KIENING (Christian). Le double décomposé. Rencontres des vivants et des morts à la fin du Moyen Age. *Annales*, 95, 50, 5, p. 1157-1190.

4033. KINTZINGER (Martin). Bildung und Wissenschaft im hochmittelalterlichen Braunschweig. *In*: Welfen und ihr Braunschweiger Hof im hohen Mittelalter (Die) [Cf. n° 3486], p. 183-203.

4034. KLASSEN (Thomas). Chaucer on love, knowledge and sight. Woodbridge a. Rochester, Boydell and Brewer, 95, XI-225 p. (Chaucer studies, 21).

4035. KLEIN (T. A.-P.). Der «Ernestus» des Odo von Magdeburg: Studien zur Textkritik und Interpretation. *Studi Medievali*, 95, 36, 2, p. 1053-1058.

4036. KOLLER (Heinrich). Zu Bedeutung des Vokalspiels AEIOU. *Österreich in Geschichte und Literatur mit Geographie*, 95, 39, 3, p. 162-170.

4037. Koninc Ermenríkes Dôt. Die niederdeutsche Flugschrift "Van Dirick van dem Berne" und "Van Juncker Baltzer". Hrsg. v. Hilkert WEDDIGE. Tübingen, Max Niemeyer Verlag, 95, VII-170 p. (Hermanea. Germanistische Forschungen, 76).

4038. KRISTENSSON (Gillis). A survey of middle English dialects, 1290–1350. The east midland counties. Lund, Lund U. P., 95, XIV-199 p. (Skrifter Utgivna av Vetenskapssocieteten i Lund, Publications of the New Society of Letters at Lund, 88).

4039. KRISTÓ (Gyula). Latini, Italiani e Veneziani nella cronaca ungherese. *In*: Spiritualità e lettere nella cultura italiana e ungherese del basso medioevo [Cf. n° 4128], p. 343-354.

4040. KROOS (Renate). Welfische Buchmalereiaufträge des 11. bis 15. Jahrhunderts. *In*: Welfen und ihr Braunschweiger Hof im hohen Mittelalter (Die) [Cf. n° 3486], p. 263-278.

4041. KUCZYNSKI (Michael P.). Prophetic song. The Psalms as moral discourse in late medieval England. Philadelphia, Univeristy of Pennsylvania Press, 95, XXX-292 p. (Middle Ages Series).

4042. Kul'tura srednevekovoj Moskvy, XIV–XVII veka. (Culture of the medieval Moscow, the XIVth– the XVIIth centuries). Redkol.: B. A. RYBAKOV (otv. red.) i drugie. Moskva, Nauka, RAN. Naučnyj sovet po istorii mirovoj kul'tury, Sekcija po kul'ture Drevnej Rusi, 95, 271 p.

4043. KULCSAR (Péter). Bonfini-kéziratok. (Manuscrits de Bonfini [Antonio, entre 1427–34–vers 1503]). *Magyarkönyvszle.*, 95, 111, 3, p. 213-237.

4044. LANZA (Loredana). Ideologia e politica nei «Commentarii» di Pio II: le descrizioni di città. *In*: Studi in onore di Arnaldo D'Addario [Cf. n° 452], p. 521-533.

4045. LASKAYA (Anne). Chaucer's approach to gender in the "Canterbury Tales". Woodbridge a. Rochester, Boydell and Brewer, 95, VIII-224 p. (Chaucer studies, 23).

4046. LAVÈNE (Béatrice). Enfer et paradis dans les sermons anonymes du manuscrit 50 de la B. M. de Rodez (fin XIVe–début XVe siècle). *In*: Enfer et paradis [Cf. n° 1370], p. 301-309.

4047. LAW (Vivien). Wisdom, authority and grammar in the seventh century. Decoding Virgilius Maro Grammaticus. Cambridge, Cambridge U. P., 95, X- 170 p.

4048. LE BLANC (Yvonne). Va lettre va. The French epistle (1400–1550). Birmingham, Summa Publications, 95, 264 p.

4049. LECLERCQ (Jean). Temi monastici nell'opera del Petrarca. *In*: Spiritualità e lettere nella cultura italiana e ungherese del basso medioevo [Cf. n° 4128], p. 149-162.

4050. LECOUTEUX (Claude). Au-delà du merveilleux. Des croyances du Moyen Age. Paris, Presses de l'Université de Paris-Sorbonne, 95, 255 p. (Cultures et civilisations médiévales, 13).

4051. LEHTONEN (Tuomas M. S.). Fortuna, money and the sublunar world. Twelfth-century ethical poetics and the satirical poery of the Carmina Burana. Helsinki, Finnish Historical Society, 95, 188 p. (Bibliotheca Historica, 9).

4052. LEONARDI (Claudio). Gustavo Vinay e la poesia mediolatina. *In*: Giustizia (La) nell'Alto Medioevo [Cf. n° 3630], p. 9-33.

4053. Lessico critico decameroniano. A cura di Renzo BRIGANTINI e Pier Massimo FORNI. Torino– Bollati Boringhieri, 95, 498 p.

4054. LETALDO DI MICY. Within piscator. Ed. a. trans. by Ferruccio BERTINI. Firenze, Giunti, 95, XXIII-77 p. (Biblioteca del medioevo latino).

4055. LEWIS (S.). Reading Images. Narrative Discourse and Reception in the thirteenth-century Illuminated Apocalypse. Cambridge, Cambridge U. P., 95, 448 p. (ill.).

4056. Lexikon der Romanischen Linguistik. Band 2. Die einzelnen romanischen Sprachen und Sprachgebiete vom Mittelalter bis zur Renaissance. Hrsg. v. G. HOLTUS, M. METZELTIN u. Ch. SCHMITT. Tübingen, Max Niemeyer Verlag, 95, [s. p.]. [Cf. n° <Auswahl> 4097.]

4057. LINDSAY (W. M.). Studies in Early Medieval Latin Glossaries. Ed. by M. LAPIDGE. Aldershot, Variorum, 95, 370 p. (ill.) (Collected studies series, 467).

4058. LULL (Ramon). Llibre d'Amic i Amat. Edició critica d'Albert SOLER I LLOPART. Barcelona, Editorial Barcino, 95, 310 p. (Els Nostres Clàssics, Col.lecció B, 13).

4059. LYNCH (Kathryn L.). East meets west in Chaucer's squire's and Franklin's tales. *Speculum*, 95, 70, 3, p. 530-551.

4060. MAC KITTERICK (R.). The Frankish Kings and Culture in the Early Middle Ages. Aldershot, Variorum, 95, 326 p. (ill.) (Collected studies series, 477).

4061. MADAS (Edit). «Légende dorée» – «Historia Lombardica» – en Hongrie. *In*: Spiritualità e lettere nella cultura italiana e ungherese del basso medioevo [Cf. n° 4128], p. 53-61.

4062. MAGGIONI (Giovanni Paolo). Appelli al lettore e definizioni di apocrifo nella «Legenda aurea». A margine della legenda di Giuda Iscariota. *Studi Medievali*, 95, 36, 1, p. 241-254. – IDEM. Ricerche sulla composizione e sulla trasmissione dell'«Legenda Aurea». Spoleto, Centro Italiano di Studi sull'Alto Medioevo, 95, XII-610 p. (Bibliioteca di Medioevo Latino, 8).

4063. MAIER (C. T.). Crusade and rhetoric against the Muslim colony of Lucera: Eudes of Chateauroux's Sermones de Rebellione Sarracenorum Lucherie in Apulia. *Journal of Medieval History*, 95, 21, 4, p. 343-385.

4064. MARTELLI (Mario). Angelo Poliziano. Storia e metastoria. Lecce, Conte, 95, 334 p. (Attraverso la storia).

4065. MARX (C. W.). The devil's rights and the redemption in the literature of Medieval England. Woodbridge a. Rochester, Boydell and Brewer, 95, X-184 p.

4066. MASON CLARK (Francelia). Theme in oral epic and in "Beowulf". New York a. London, Garland, 95, XXXVI-252 p. (Milman Parry studies in oral tradition).

4067. MENJOT (D.). Le castillan dialectal de Murcie au bas Moyen Age. *Moyen Age*, 95, 101, 3, p. 447-460.

9. KULTUR-, LITERATUR- UND UNTERRICHTSGESCHICHTE

4068. MICHAŁOWSKA (Teresa). Średniowiecze. (Moyen-Age). Warszawa, Wydawn. Nauk. PWN, 95, 905 p. (phot., fig., dessins, notes). (Wielka Hist. Literatury Pol.).

4069. MICHON (P.). L'épisode de la folie de Tristan dans le Tristano Panciatichiano. *Moyen Age*, 95, 101, 3, p. 461-474.

4070. MILDE (Wolfgang). Christus verheißt das Reich des Lebens. Krönungsdarstellungen von Schreibern und Stiftern. *In*: Welfen und ihr Braunschweiger Hof im hohen Mittelalter (Die) [Cf. n° 3486], p. 279-296.

4071. MINNIS (A. J.), SCATTERGOOD (V. J.), SMITH (J. J.). The shorter poems. Oxford, Clarendon Press a. Oxford U. P., 95, XIV-578 p. (Oxford guides to Chaucer).

4072. MONSON (Don A.). The Troubadour's lady reconsidered again. *Speculum*, 95, 70, 2, p. 255-274.

4073. MOONEY (Linne R.). The index of middle English prose. Handlist 11. Manuscripts in the library of Trinity College, Cambridge. Woodbridge a. Rochester, Boydell and Brewer, 95, XXXVIII-251 p.

4074. MOULINIER (Laurence). Le manuscrit perdu de Strasbourg. Enquête sur l'œuvre scientifique de Hildegarde. Paris, Publications de la Sorbonne et Saint-Denis, Presses Universitaires de Vincennes, 95, 288 p. (Série Histoire ancienne et médiévale, 35).

4075. MUIR (Lynette R.). The biblical drama of Medieval Europe. Cambridge, Cambridge U. P., 95, XXIII-320 p.

4076. MULDER-BAKKER (Anneke B.). The reclusorium as an informal centre of learning. *In*: Centers of learning [Cf. n° 3953], p. 245-254.

4077. MUNK OLSEN (Birger). Les classiques latins et la critique textuelle médiévale (IXe-XIIe siècles). *Académie des Inscriptions et Belles-Lettres, comptes rendu*, 95, 3, p. 817-827. – IDEM. La réception de la littérature classique au Moyen Age (IXe-XIIe siècle). Choix d'articles publié par des collègues à l'occasion de son soixantième anniversaire. København, Museum Tusculanum Press et Université de Copenhague, 95, 282 p.

4078. NALDINI (Mario). Nel solco dell'Umanesimo: la «biblioteca patristica». *In*: Tradizione patristica (La). Alle fonti della cultura medievale [Cf. n° 4151], p. 105-114.

4079. NASS (Klaus). Geschichtsschreibung am Hofe Heinrichs des Löwen. *In*: Welfen und ihr Braunschweiger Hof im hohen Mittelalter (Die) [Cf. n° 3486], p. 123-161.

4080. NEWMAN (Barbara). From virile woman to Woman Christ. Studies in medieval religion and literature. Philadelphia, University of Pennsylvania Press, 95, VI-335 p. (Middle Ages Series).

4081. Non recedent memoria eius. Beiträge zur lateinischen Philologie des Mittelalters im Gedenken an Jakob Werner (1861–1944). Hrsg. v. Peter STOTZ u. Michele C. FERRARI. Frankfurt am Main, Peter Lang, 95, 265 p. (Lateinische Sprache und Literatur des Mittelalters, 28).

4082. OBERMAIER (Sabine). Von Nachtigallen und Handwerkern: "Dichtung über Dichtung" in Minnesang und Sangspruchdichtung. Tübingen, Max Niemeyer Verlag, 95, XIV-401 p. (Hermaea, Germanistische Forschungen, Neue Folge, 75).

4083. OEXLE (Otto Gerhard). Welfische Memoria. Zugleich ein Beitrag über adlige Hausüberlieferung und die Kriterien ihrer Erforschung. *In*: Welfen und ihr Braunschweiger Hof im hohen Mittelalter (Die) [Cf. n° 3486], p. 61-94.

4084. OLEF-KRAFFT (F.). Œdipe au château du Graal. *Moyen Age*, 95, 101, 2, p. 227-258.

4085. *Vacat.*

4086. OLSON (Paul A.). The journey to Wisdom. Self-education in patristic and medieval literature. Lincoln a. London, University of Nebraska Press, 95, XXI-297 p.

4087. ORCHARD (Andy). Pride and prodigies. Studies in the monsters of the "Beowulf"-manuscript. Woodbridge a. Rochester, Boydell and Brewer, 95, VIII-352 p.

4088. Ordbog over det norrøne prosasprog. A dictionary of old Norse prose. 1. A–bam. Ed. by Helle DEGNBOL [et al.]. København, Arnamagnæanske Kommission, 95, VIII-906 p.

4089. ORME (Nicholas). The culture of children in Medieval England. *Past and Present*, 95, 148, p. 48-88.

4090. PALUDAN (Helge). Familia og familie. To europeiske kulturelementers möde i höjmiddelalderens Danmark. Aarhus, Aarhus Universitets Forlag, 95, 231 p. [A study on the interaction of different European culture elements in Denmark during the Higher Middle Ages].

4091. PÀROLI (Teresa). Il «Lamento di Maria» tra lauda e dramma. *In*: Spiritualità e lettere nella cultura italiana e ungherese del basso medioevo [Cf. n° 4128], p. 231-293.

4092. Patrimoine littéraire européen. Anthologie en langue française. Dir. Par Jean-Claude POLET. T. 5. Premières mutations: de Pétrarque à Chaucer (1304–1400). T. 6. Prémices de l'Humanisme (1400–1515). Bruxelles, De Boeck-Université, 95, 2 vol. XXXIX-827 p., XXXV-902 p.

4093. PENSOM (Roger). Reading Béroul's "Tristan". A poetic narrative and the anthropology of its receptio. Bern, Lang, 117 p.

4094. PERUGI (Maurizio). Saggi di linguistica trovadorica. Saggi su "Girart de Roussillon", Marcabruno, Bernart de Ventadorn, Raimbaut d'Aurenga, Arnaut

4095. Daniel e sull'uso letterario di oc e oil nel trecento italiano. Tübingen, Stauffenburg, 95, 197 p. (Romanica et Comparatistica, 21).

4096. PETRARCH. Petrachs "Songbook", "Rerum vulgarium fragmenta". A verse translation. Trans. by James Wyatt COOK, introduction by Germaine WARKENTIN, with an edition of the Italian text by Gianfranco CONTINI. Binghamton, State University of New York at Birmingham, Center for Medieval and Early Renaissance Studies, 95, XIII-447 p. (Medieval and Renaissance texts and studies, 151).

4097. PETRUKHIN (Vladimir Ja.). Načalo étnokul'turnoj istorii Rusi IX–XI vekov. (The original ethnocultural history of Rus'in the IXth–XIth centuries). Smolensk: Rusič; Moskva. Gnozis, RAN. In-t slavjanovedenija i balkanistiki, 95, 317p.

4098. PFISTER (Max), GLESSGEN (Martin-Dietrich). Okzitanische Koine; Okzitanische Skriptaformen I. Limousin/Périgord. LODGE (R. Anthony). Okzitanische Skriptaformen II. Auvergne. GLESSGEN (Martin-Dietrich). Okzitanische Skriptaformen III. a). Provence. WÜEST (Jakob). Okzitanische Skriptaformen III. b). Dauphinois. WÜEST (Jakob). Okzitanische Skriptaformen IV. Languedoc. ALLIERES (Jacques). Okzitanische Skriptaformen V. Gaskogne, Béarn. *In*: Lexikon der Romanischen Linguistik. Band 2 [Cf. n° 4056], p. 406-466.

4099. Premier (Le) mythographe du Vatican. Ed. par Nevio ZORZETTI, trad. par Jacques BERLIOZ. Paris, Les Belles Lettres, 95, LX-181 p. (Collection des Universités de France, Série latine, 328).

4100. PUTTER (Ad). "Sir Gawain and the Green Knight" and French Arthurian romance. Oxford, Clarendon Press, 95, XII-279 p.

4101. RABE (Susan A.). Faith, art, and politics at Saint Riquier. The symbolic vision of Angilbert. Philadelphia, Univeristy of Pennsylvania Press, 95, XVII-220 p. (Middle Ages Series).

4102. RAFTI (P.). Alle origini dei Rerum vulgarium fragmenta. *Scrittura e civiltà*, 95, 19, p. 199-222.

4103. RAYNAUD (C.). Le sacrifice d'Abraham dans quelques représentations de la fin du Moyen Age. *Journal of Medieval History*, 95, 21, 3, p. 249-274.

4104. REGOLIOSI (Mariangela). «Res gestae patriae» e «res gestae ex universa Italia»: la lettera di Lapo da Castiglionchio a Biondo Flavio. *In*: Memoria (La) e la città. Scritture storiche tra medioevo e età moderna [Cf. n° 3303], p. 273-305.

4105. Reino de León (El) en la alta Edad Media. Vol. 7. León, Centro de Estudios e Investigación «San Isidoro», 95, 597 p. (Fuentes y Estudios de historia leonesa, 58).

4106. RIZZO (Silvia). Sulla terminologia dell'insegnamento grammaticale nelle scuole umanistiche. *In*: Vocabulary of teaching [Cf. n° 4164], p. 29-44.

4107. ROCCARO (Cataldo). La «scrittura» dei sermoni latini: struttura e tecnica compositiva fra enunciazione teoriche ed applicazione pratica. *In*: Predicazione dei frati (La) [Cf. n° 4451], p. 231-265.

4108. ROCKWELL (Paul Vincent). Rewriting resemblance in medieval French romance. "Ceci n'est pas un Graal". New York a. London, Garland, 95, XVI-245 p. (Garland studies in medieval literature, 13. Garland reference library of the humanities, 1908).

4109. ROHR (Christoph). Der Theoderich-Panegyricus des Ennodius. Hannover, Hahnsche Buchhandlung, 95, XXXVII-309 p. (Monumenta Germaniae Historica. Studien und Texte, 12).

4110. RUHRBERG (Christine). Der literarische Körper der Heiligen. Leben und Viten der Christina von Stommeln (1242–1312). Tübingen u. Basel, Francke, 95, X-487 p. (Bibliotheca Germanica, 35).

4111. RUS (Martijn). Da la conception à l'au dela. Textes et documents français d'un siècle qui n'en est pas un (1450–1550). Amsterdam, [s. n.], 95, 339 p. (Etudes de langue françaises, 103).

4112. RUSCONI (Roberto). «Trasse la storia per farne la tavola»: immagini di predicatori degli ordini mendicanti nei secoli XIII e XIV. *In*: Predicazione dei frati (La) [Cf. n° 4451], p. 497-450.

4113. RYŚ (Jan). Szkolnictwo parafialne w miastach Małopolski w XV wieku. (Education paroissiale dans les villes de la Małopolska au XVe s.). Warszawa, Pol. Akad. Nauk, Inst. Hist. Nauki, 95, 150 p. (Eng. Summary). (Pol. Akad. Nauk, Inst. Hist. Nauki, Zakł. Dziejów Oświaty, Monogr. z Dziejów Oświaty, 37).

4114. SABBADINI (Remigio). Opere minori. Vol. 1. Classici e umanisti da codici latini inesplorati. Saggi riveduti e corretti dall'autore. A cura di Tino FOFFANO. Padova, Antenore, 95, LXXXIII-368 p. (tav.) (Medioevo e umanesimo, 87).

4115. SALICRÚ I LLUCH (Roser). La coronació de Ferran d'Antequera: l'organització i els preparatius de la festa. *Anuario de estudios medievales*, 95, 25, 2, p. 699-760.

4116. SALVINI-PLAWEN (Luitfried). Zur Datierung des Nibelungenliedes. Bezüge zum Haus Andechs-Meranien. *Mitt. d. Inst. f. Österr. Gesch.-Forsch.*, 95, 103, 1-2, p. 26-43.

4117. SCALIA (Giuseppe). Annalistica e poesia epicostorica pisana nel secolo XII. *In*: Senso della storia (Il) nella cultura medievale italiana [Cf. n° 4374], p. 105-124.

4118. SCHAFFNER (Paul). The errant Morsel in Solomon and Saturn II: liturgy, lore, and lexicon. *Mediaeval Studies*, 95, 57, p. 223-258.

4119. SCHALLER (Dieter). Studien zur lateinischen Dichtung des Frühmittelalters. Stuttgart, Anton Hiersemann, 95, XI-469 p. (Quellen und Untersuchungen zur lateinischen Philologie des Mittelalters, 11).

9. KULTUR-, LITERATUR- UND UNTERRICHTSGESCHICHTE

4120. SCHINDEL (Ulrich). Frühe Stufen der Quintilian-Überlieferung. In: Formative stages of classical traditions [Cf. n° 3282], p. 64-82.

4121. SCHMIDT (Paul Gerhard). Das Interesse am mittellateinischer Literatur. Freiburg, Universitätsverlag Freiburg Schweiz, 95, 43 p. (Wolfgang Stammler Gastprofessur für Germanische Philologie, Vorträge, 3).

4122. SCHULER (S.). Excerptoris morem gerere. Zur Kompilation und Rezeption klassisch-lateinischer Dichter im 'Speculum historiale' des Vinzenz von Beauvais. *Frühmittelalterliche Studien*, 95, 29, p. 312-348.

4123. SEYMOUR (M. C.). A catalogue of Chaucer manuscripts. 1. Works before the "Canterbury Tales". Aldershot a. Brookfield, Scholar Press, 95, X-171 p.

4124. SHANK (Michael H.). University and church in late medieval Vienna. Modi docendi et operandi, 1388–1421. In: Philosophy and learning [Cf. n° 4363], p. 43-62.

4125. SHERMAN (Claire Richter). Imaging Aristotle. Verbal and visual representation in XIVth century France. Berkeley, Los Angeles a. London, University of California Press, 95, XXIV-423 p. (ill.).

4126. Siena, Florence and Padua: art, society and religion, 1280–1400. Vol. 1. Interpretative essays. Volume 2. Case studies. Ed. by Diana NORMAN. New Haven a. London, Yale U. P. in ass. with The Open University, 95, 2 vol., X-260 p., XI-290 p. (plates).

4127. SIMS-WILLIAMS (P.). Britain and Early Christian Europe: Studies in History and Culture. Aldershot, Variorum, 95, 350 p. (Collected studies series, 515).

4128. SMITH (Susan L.). The power of women. A "Topos" in medieval art and literature. Philadelphia, Univeristy of Pennsylvania Press, 95, XVII-294 p.

4129. Spiritualità e lettere nella cultura italiana e ungherese del basso medioevo. Atti del convegno di studio promosso e organizzato dalla Fondazione Giorgio Cini in collaborazione con l'Accademia ungherese delle scienze. A cura di Cesare VASOLI, prefazione di Sante GRACIOTTI. Firenze, Olschki e Venezia, Fondazione Giorgio Cini, 95, XIV-414 p. (Civiltà veneziana. Studi, 46). [Cf. n^{os} <scelta> 55, 3331, 3621, 3977, 3978, 4016, 4039, 4049, 4061, 4091, 4150, 4163, 4437, 4466, 4467, 4468, 4479, 4488, 4510, 4535.]

4130. Sprachtheorien in Spätantike und Mittelalter. Hrsg. v. Sten EBBESEN. Tübingen, G. Narr, 95, XX-408 p. (Geschichte der Sprachtheorie, 3).

4131. STAUBACH (N.). Christiana tempora. Augustin und das Ende der alten Geschichte in der Weltchronik Frechulfs von Lisieux. *Frühmittelalterliche Studien*, 95, 29, p. 167-206.

4132. STEVENS (W. M.). Cycles of Time and Scientific Learning in Medieval Europe. Aldershot, Variorum, 95, 350 p. (ill.) (Collected studies series, 482).

4133. STEVENSON (Jane). The "Laterculus Malalianus" and the school of Archbischop Theodore. Cambridge, Cambridge U. P., 95, XIII-254 p. (Cambridge studies in Anglo-Saxon England, 14).

4134. Storia della fortuna postmedievale di Marziano Capella (Per una): i primi volgarizzamenti italiani delle "Nozze di Mercurio e Filologia". A c. di G. MORETTI. Trento, Università di Trento, 95, 328 p. (ill.) (Reperti, 1).

4135. Storia della letteratura italiana. Vol. 2. Il Trecento. Roma, Salerno, 95, XIII-1042 p.

4136. STRAUB (Richard E. F.). David Aubert, escripvain et clerc. Amsterdam et Atlanta, Rodopi, 95, V-378 p. (Faux titre, 96).

4137. SUBRENAT (Jean). Il est monté aux enfers. Il est monté aux cieux. Enfer et paradis d'après les 'Mystères de la Passion' au XVe siècle. In: Enfer et paradis [Cf. n° 1370], p. 195-203.

4138. SULLIVAN (Thomas). Benedectine Monks at the University of Paris, A. D. 1229–1500. A Biographical Register. Leiden, E. J. Brill, 95, 458 p. (Education and society in the Middle Age and Renaissance, 4).

4139. SURTZ (Ronald E.). Writing women in late medieval and early modern Spain. The mothers of Saint Theresa of Avila. Philadelphia, Univeristy of Pennsylvania Press, 95, XI-223 p. (Middle Ages Series).

4140. TANAKA (Mineo). Chi no Undō: Juni-Seiki Runessansu kara Daigaku e. (Dynamism of Knowledge: from Renaissance in the twelfth century to the universities). Kyōto, Minerva Shobō, 95, 597 p.

4141. TARGOSZ (Karolina). Korzenie i kształty teatu do 1500 roku w perspektywie Krakowa. (Les racines et les formes du théatre jusqu'à 1500 vues de la perspective de Cracovie). Kraków, Secesja, 95, 307 p. (dessins). Tow. Miłośników Hist. i Zabytków Krakowa. [Rés. franç.].

4142. TARRANT (Richard J.). The «Narrationes» of «Lactantius» and the transmission of classical tradition of Ovid's «Metamorphoses». In: Formative stages of classical traditions [Cf. n° 3282], p. 83-115.

4143. TATEO (Francesco). Epidittica e antiquaria nelle memorie cittadine del Mezzogiorno. In: Memoria (La) e la città. Scritture storiche tra medioevo e età moderna [Cf. n° 3303], p. 29-39.

4144. Textes d'étude (ancien et moyen français). Ed. par Robert-Léon WAGNER. Genève, Droz, 95, XIV-382 p. (Textes littéraires français).

4145. Thesaurus of old English (A). vol. 1. Introduction and Thesaurus. Vol. 2. Index. Ed. by Jane ROBERTS a. Christian KAY. London, Centre for late antique and medieval studies, King's College London, 95, 2 vol., XXXV-716 p., IV-838 p. (King's College London medieval studies, 11).

4146. THOMSON (R. W.). A bibliography of classical Armenian literature to 1500 AD. Turnhout, Brepols, 95, 324 p. (Corpus Christianorum).

4147. THOMSON (Rodney M.). Robert Amiclas: a twelfth-century Parisian master and his books. *Scriptorium*, 95, 49, 2, p. 238-242.

4148. TIEKEN-BOON VAN OSTADE (Ingrid). The two versions of Malory's "Morte Darthur". Multiple Negation and the editing of the text. Woodbridge a. Rochester, Boydell and Brewer, 95, IX-169 p.

4149. TILATTI (Andrea). Dall'agiografia alla cronaca. Le «inventiones» degli antichi patroni padovani fra interpretazione storiografica e sviluppo di una coscienza civile (sec. XI–XII). *In*: Religion civique à l'époque médiévale et moderne (La) [Cf. n° 4528], p. 47-64.

4150. TOBIN (Frank). Mechthild von Magdeburg. A medieval mystic in modern eyes. Columbia, Camden House, 95, XI-152 p. (Studies in German literature, linguistics, and culture: literacy criticism in perspective).

4151. TÖRÖK (József). Gherardus de Venetis auctor et monachus? (Un clerc médiéval et la Bible). *In*: Spiritualità e lettere nella cultura italiana e ungherese del basso medioevo [Cf. n° 4128], p. 203-209.

4152. Tradizione patristica (La). Alle fonti della cultura medievale. A cura di Mario NALDINI. Fiesole, Nardini, 95, 128 p. (Letture patristiche, 2). [Cf. n^os <scelta> 137, 3001, 4078, 4158.]

4153. TRANSMUNDUS. Introductiones dictandi. Ed. a. trans. by Ann DALZELL. Toronto, Pontifical Institute of Mediaeval Studies, 95, X-254 p. (Studies and texts, 123).

4154. TROTTA (S.). L'«Elegia di Madonna Fiammetta» di Giovanni Boccaccio e un volgarizzamento delle «Epistulae heroidum» di Ovidio attribuito a Filippo Ceffi. *Italia medievale e umanistica*, 95, 38, p. 217-262.

4155. TURRINI (Patrizia). Le disavventure senesi delle «Historiae» di Sigismondo Tizio. *In*: Studi in onore di Arnaldo D'Addario [Cf. n° 452], p. 645-656.

4156. VAN EMDEN (Wolfgang). La chanson de Roland. London, Grant & Cutler, 95, 135 p. (Critical guides to French texts, 113).

4157. VANDERJAGT (Ario J.). Classical learning and the building of power at the fifteenth-century Burgundian court. *In*: Centers of learning [Cf. n° 3953], p. 267-277.

4158. VARVARO (A.). Karel ende Elegast et la tradition folklorique. *Moyen Age*, 95, 101, 2, p. 259-276.

4159. VASOLI (Cesare). Umanesimo e patristica. *In*: Tradizione patristica (La). Alle fonti della cultura medievale [Cf. n° 4151], p. 9-19.

4160. VECCHIO (Silvana). Le Prediche e l'istruzione religiosa. *In*: Predicazione dei frati (La) [Cf. n° 4451], p. 303-335.

4161. VERGER (Jacques). Les universités françaises au Moyen Age. Leiden, New York a. Köln, E. J. Brill, 95, XIII-244 p. (Education and society in the Middle Ages and Renaissance, 7).

4162. VILLAR (Milagros). Códices petrarquescos en España. Padova, Editrice Antenore, 95, 451 p.

4163. VITI (Paolo). Un nuovo testimone dell'«Epistola de coronatione Sigismundi Imperatoris» di Poggio Bracciolini. *In*: Studi in onore di Arnaldo D'Addario [Cf. n° 452], p. 517-519.

4164. VIZKELETY (András). I «sermonaria» domenicani in Ungheria nei secoli XIII–XIV. *In*: Spiritualità e lettere nella cultura italiana e ungherese del basso medioevo [Cf. n° 4128], p. 29-38.

4165. Vocabulary of teaching and research between Middle Ages and Renaissance. Proceedings of the colloquium, London, Warburg Institute, 11–12 March 1994. Ed. by Olga WEIJERS. Turnhout, Brepols, 95, 256 p. (CIVICIMA. Etudes sur le vocabulaire intellectuel du Moyen Age, 8). [Cf. n^os <choice> 3948, 4006, 4105, 4308, 4321, 4326, 4341, 4346, 4356, 4357.]

4166. Wace à Lawamon (De). Le "Roman de Brut" de Wace. Texte original (extraits). Le "Brut" de Lawamon. Text original, traduction (extraits). Trad. par Marie-Françoise ALAMICHEL. Paris, Association des Médiévistes Anglicistes de l'Enseignement Supérieur, 95, 2 vol., XI-311 p., I-331 p. (Pubblications de l'Association des Médiévistes Anglicistes de l'Enseignement Supérieur, 20).

4167. WALTERS ROBERTSON (Anne). Remembering the annunciation in medieval polyphony. *Speculum*, 95, 70, 2, p. 275-304.

4168. WARNER OF ROUEN. Moriuht. A Norman Latin poem from the early eleventh century. Ed. a. trans. by Christopher MAC DONOUGH. Toronto, Pontifical Institute of medieval studies, 95, X-230 p. (Studies and texts, 121).

4169. WATSON (Nicholas). Censorship and cultural change in late-medieval England: vernacular theology, the Oxford translation debate, and Arundel's constitutions of 1409. *Speculum*, 95, 70, 4, p. 822-864.

4170. WEISL (Angela Jane). Conquering the reign of femeny. Gender and genre in Chaucer's romance. Woodbridge a. Rochester, Boydell and Brewer, 95, IX-133 p. (Chaucer studies, 22).

4171. WENZEL (Siegfried). Academic sermons at Oxford in the early fifteenth century. *Speculum*, 95, 70, 2, p. 305-329.

4172. WOLF (Aloise). Heldensage und Epos: Zur Konstituierung einer mittelalterlichen volkssprachlichen Gattung im Spannungsfeld von Mündlichkeit und Schriftlichkeit. Tübingen, Gunter Narr, 95, (ScriptOralia, 68).

4173. Women, the Book and the Godly. Vol. 1. Selected Proceedings of the St. Hilda's Conference, Women and the Book in the Middle Ages, Oxford 1993. Ed. by L. SMITH and J. H. M. TAYLOR. Cambridge, Brewer, 95, XIV-192 p.

4174. Women, the Book and the Wordly. Selected proceedings of the St. Hilda's Conference, 1993. Vol. 2. Ed. by Lesley SMITH a. Jane H. M. TAYLOR. Woodbridge a. Rochester, Boydell and Brewer, 95, XIV-193 p.

4175. WRIGHT (Neil). History and literature in late antiquity and the early medieval West. Studies in intertextuality. Aldershot, Variorum, 95, XIV-301 p. (Collected studies series, 495).

Cf. n° 6515

§ 10. Kunstgeschichte.

a. Allgemeines.

4175. a) ABAS (Syed Jan), SALMAN (Amer Shaker). Symmetries of Islamic geometrical patterns. Forewords by Ahmed MOUSTAFA and Sir Michael ATIYAH. Singapore a. London, World Scientific, 95, XXII-396 p. (ill.).

4176. Artistic integration in Gothic buildings. Ed. by Virginia CHIEFFO RAGUIN, Kathryn BRUSH a. Peter DRAPER. Toronto a. London, University of Toronto Press, 95, XIII-348 p. (ill.).

4177. Benedetto Antelami e il Battistero di Parma A cura di Chiara FRUGONI. Scritti di Albert DIETL [et al.]. Torino, Einaudi, 95, XXXII-294 p. (Saggi, 801).

4178. BERNARDI (Philippe). Métiers du bâtiment et techniques de construction à Aix-en-Provence à la fin de l'époque gothique (1400–1550). Aix-en-Provence, Publications de l'Université de Provence, 95, 501 p.

4179. BINDING (Günther). Beiträge zum Gotik-Verständnis. Köln, 95, 179 p. (Veröffentlichungen der Abteilung Architektur des kunsthistorischen Instituts der Universität Köln, 53).

4180. Corso (XLI) di cultura sull'arte ravennate e bizantina: seminario internazionale sul tema: "Ravenna, Costantinopoli, Vicino Oriente", Ravenna, 12–16 settembre 1994: in memoria di Friedrich Wilhelm Deichmann. Ravenna, Edizioni del girasole, 95, 700 p. (ill.).

4181. DUBY (Georges). Le Moyen Age. Avec la participation de Xavier BARRAL I ALTET [et al.]. Paris, Ed. du Seuil, 95, 395 p. (Librairie européenne des idées; Histoire artistique de l'Europe).

4182. Federico II: immagine e potere. A cura di Maria Stella CALO MARIANI e Raffaella CASSANO. Venezia, Marsilio, 95, XXXI-603 p. – Federico II e le nuove culture. Atti del 31° Convegno storico internazionale, Todi 1994. Spoleto, Centro di studi sull' Alto Medioevo, 95, 570 p. (ill.) (Atti del Centro italiano di studi sul Basso Medioevo-Accademia Tudertina e del Centro di studi sulla spiritualità medievale. N. S., 8). – Federico II e l'Italia: percorsi, luoghi, segni e strumenti. Roma, De Luca e Editalia, 95, XV-381 p.

4183. FOLDA (Jaroslav). The art of the Crusaders in the Holy Land, 1098–1187. Cambridge, Cambridge U. P., 95, XXX-672 p.

4184. From the isles of the North: early medieval art in Ireland and Britain: proceedings of the third International Conference on Insular Art, held in the Ulster Museum, Belfast, 7–11 April, 1994. Ed. by Cormac BOURKE. Belfast, HMSO, 95, XI-280 p. (ill.).

4185. KRAUTHEIMER (Richard). Idéologie de l'art antique du IVe au XVe siècle. Paris, Gerard Monfort, 95, 120 p.

4186. LAFONTAINE-DOSOGNE (Jacqueline). Histoire de l'art byzantin et chrétien d'Orient. Louvain, Institut Orientaliste, Université Catholique de Louvain, 95, XXVI-293 p. (Publications de l'Institut Orientaliste de Louvain, 45).

4187. Literatur, Musik und Kunst im Übergang vom Mittelalter zur Neuzeit. Bericht über Kolloquien der Kommission zur Erforschung der Kultur des Spätmittelalters 1989 bis 1992. Hrsg. v. Hartmut BOOCKMANN, Ludger GRENZMANN, Bernd MOELLER u. Martin STAEHELIN. Göttingen, Vandenhoeck & Ruprecht, 95, 470 p.

4188. NEES (Lawrence). Art and architecture. *In:* New Cambridge medieval history [Cf. n° 3378], p. 809-844.

4189. RAYNAUD (Christiane). Mythes, cultures et sociétés (XIIe–XVe siècles): images de l'Antiquité et iconographie politique à la fin du Moyen Age. Paris, Le Léopard d'or, 95, 362 p. (ill.).

4190. Sacred image East and West (The). Ed. by Robert OUSTERHOUT a. Leslie BRUBAKER. Urbana, University of Illinois Press, 95, XIII-312 p. (Illinois Byzantine studies, 4).

4191. SCHELLER (Robert Walter Hans Peter). Exemplum: model-book drawings and the practice of artistic transmission in the Middle Ages (ca. 900–ca. 1470). Amsterdam, Amsterdam U. P., 95, XI-434 p. (ill.).

4192. SCHMIDT (Victor Michael). A legend and its image: the aerial flight of Alexander the Great in Medieval art. Groningen, Egbert Forsten, 95, XIV-293 p. (Mediaevalia Groningana, 17).

4193. SCHUNK-HELLER (Sabine). Die Darstellung des ungläubigen Thomas in der italienischen Kunst bis um 1500 unter Berücksichtigung der lukanischen Ostentatio Vulnerum. München, Scaneg, 95, 202 p. (Beiträge zur Kunstwissenschaft, 59).

4194. TIGLER (Guido). Il portale maggiore di San Marco a Venezia. Aspetti iconografici e stilistici dei rilievi duecenteschi. Venezia, Istituto Veneto di Scienze, Lettere ed Arti, 95, 579 p. (Memorie. Classe di scienze morali, lettere ed arti, 59).

4195. WILSON (David M.). Vikingatidens konst. (Viking art). Lund, Bokforlaget Signum, 95, 238 p. (ill.). (Signums svenska konsthistoria).

4196. *Vacat.*

b. Spezialarbeiten.

4197. ALBRECHT (Uwe). Der Adelssitz im Mittelalter. Studien zum Verhältnis von Architektur und Lebensform in Nord- und Westeuropa. München u. Berlin, Deutscher Kunstverlag, 95, 279 p.

4198. Architektura gotycka w Polsce. (Architecture gothique en Pologne). T. 1. Réd. Teresa MROCZKO et Marian ARSZYŃSKI. T. 2. Katalog zabytków. (Catalogue de monuments). T. 3. Album ilustracji. (Album d'illustrations). Réd. par Andrzej WŁODAREK. Warszawa, Inst. Sztuki Pol. Akad. Nauk, 95, 3 vol., 172 p., 603 p., 801 p. (Dzieje Sztuki Pol., 2).

4199. Architettura cistercense. Fontenay e le abbazie in Italia dal 1120 al 1160. A cura di Goffredo VITI. Firenze, Ed. Casamari, 95, 349 p.

4200. AVRIL (F.). L'enluminure à l'époque gothique, 1200–1420. Paris, Bibliothèque de l'image, 95, 144 p. (ill.).

4201. BOUSQUET (Jacques). Enfer et paradis au tympan de Conques [Anveyron]. Réflexions complémentaires. *In*: Enfer et paradis [Cf. n° 1370], p. 53-65.

4202. CASSAGNES (Sophie). Géographie du paradis dans l'art bourguignon médiéval. *In*: Enfer et paradis [Cf. n° 1370], p. 111-124.

4203. CAUSSE (Louis). La question du déplacement du Tympan de Conques. *In*: Enfer et paradis [Cf. n° 1370], p. 79-92.

4204. COCKE (Thomas), BUTTRESS (Donald). 900 years. The restorations of Westminster Abbey. London, Harvey Miller, 95, 172 p.

4205. COURTILLE (Anne). Enfer et paradis dans la peinture murale d'Auvergne au Moyen Age. *In*: Enfer et paradis [Cf. n° 1370], p. 125-135.

4206. DE MERINDOL (Christian). Portrait et généalogie: la genèse du portrait réaliste et individualisé. *In*: Actes du 118ᵉ Congrès national des Sociétés savantes [Cf. n° 4540], p. 219-248.

4207. EBERLEIN (Johann Konrad). Miniatur und Arbeit. Frankfurt am Main, Suhrkamp, 95, 501 p.

4208. FALCON PEREZ (M. P.). Estudio artístico de los manuscritos iluminados de la catedral de Tarazona: análisis y catalogación. Zaragoza, Departamento de Educación y cultura, 95, 550 p. (ill.) (Colección Estudios y monografías, 22).

4209. FAU (Jean-Claude). L'ange à l'encensoir à Sainte-Foy de Conques [Aveyron] et à Saint-Jacques-de-Compostelle. *In*: Enfer et paradis [Cf. n° 1370], p. 71-77.

4210. FAVREAU (Robert). Les inscriptions des fonts baptismaux d'Hildesheim. Baptême et quaternité. *Cahiers de civilisation médiévale*, 95, 38, p. 115-140.

4211. Flanders in an European perspective. Manuscript illumination around 1400 in Flanders and abroad.

Proceedings of the International Colloquium. Leuven, 7–10 sept. 1993. Ed. by Maurits SMEYERS a. Bert CARDON. Leuven, Peeters, 95, XIII-799 p. (Corpus of illuminated manuscripts, 8).

4212. FORSYTH (William H.). The Pietà in French late gothic sculpture. Regional variations. New York, Metropolitan Museum of Art, 95, 219 p.

4213. FRENCH (Thomas). York Minster. The great east window. Oxford a. New York, Oxford U. P., 95, XIV-161 p. (Corpus Vitrearum Medii Aevi, Great Britain, Summary Catalogue, 2).

4214. GADOMSKI (Jerzy). Gotyckie malarstwo tablicowe Małopolski 1500–1540. (Peinture gothique sur bois en Małopolska 1500–1540). Warszawa, Wydawn. Nauk. PWN, 95, 131 p.

4215. GUERET-LAFERTE (Michèle). L'Orient: enfer ou paradis? Les représentations de l'au-delà dans quelques relations de voyage en Asie (XIIIᵉ–XIVᵉ siècles) [à travers les récits de Joinville]. *In*: Enfer et paradis [Cf. n° 1370], p. 233-244.

4216. HARF (L.). La Serpente et le Sanglier: les manuscrits enluminés des deux romans français de Mélusine. *Moyen Age*, 95, 101, 1, p. 65-88.

4217. HARRIS (J.). Two Byzantine craftsmen in fifteenth-century London. *Journal of Medieval History*, 95, 21, 4, p. 387-403.

4218. HOLL (Imre). Neutronenaktivierungsanalyse mittelalterlicher Ofenkacheln. 2. Beobachtungen zur Fertigungstechnik, Viervielfältigung, Ton- und Engobeauswahl. *Acta archaeol. Acad. Sci. Hungaricae*, 95, 47, 1-4, p. 257-294.

4219. KALICZ (Nándor). Die älteste transdanubische (mitteleuropäische) Linienbandkeramik. Aspekte zu Ursprung, Chronologie und Beziehungen. *Acta archaeol. Acad. Sci. Hungaricae*, 95, 47, 1-4, p. 23-59.

4220. KENAAN-KEDAR (Nurith). Marginal sculpture in medieval France. Towards the deciphering of an enigmatic pictorial language. Aldershot a. Brookfield, Scholar Press, 95, XVIII-210 p.

4221. KOLLER (Manfred). Studien zur gefaßten Skulptur des Mittelalters in Österreich. Der Flügelaltar aus Mechelin in der Deutschordenskirche zu Wien. *Österreichische Zeitschrift für Kunst und Denkmalpflege*, 95, 49, 1-2, p. 90-104.

4222. KORNBLUTH (Genevra). Engraved gems of the Carolingian empire. University Park, Pennsylvania State U. P., 95, XXV-139.

4223. LANÇON (Pierre). La «Maison des singularités» d'Hélyon Jouffroy ou l'enfer à domicile. *In*: Enfer et paradis [Cf. n° 1370], p. 335-345.

4224. MARCHAL (Guy P.). Jalons pour une histoire de l'iconoclasme au Moyen Age. *Annales*, 95, 50, 5, p. 1135-1156.

4225. MARSDEN (Richard). Job in his place: the Ezra miniature in the Codex Amiatinus. *Scriptorium*, 95, 49, 1, p. 3-15.

4226. MORDEK (Hubert). Frühmittelalterliche Gesetzgeber und Iustitia in Miniaturen weltlicher Rechtshandschriften. *In*: Giustizia (La) nell'Alto Medioevo [Cf. n° 3630], p. 997-1052.

4227. MUIR WRIGHT (Rosemary). Art and antichrist in Medieval Europe. Manchester a. New York, Manchester U. P., 95, XII-244 p.

4228. OURSEL (Raymond). Le portrait eschatologique du prieuré d'Anzy-le-Duc [Saône-et-Loire]. *In*: Enfer et paradis [Cf. n° 1370], p. 103-110.

4229. PICCAT (Marco). Sulla tradizione della salita al paradiso dell'imperatore Carlo Magno [représenté sur le tympan de Conques]. *In*: Enfer et paradis [Cf. n° 1370], p. 245-257.

4230. PRIAMI (E.). La miniatura gotica. Milano, Opportunity books, 95, 160 p. (ill.) (Elite. Arti e stili).

4231. RUBINSTEIN (Nicolai). The Palazzo Vecchio 1298–1532. Government, architecture, and imagery in the civic palace of the Florentine Republic. Oxford, Clarendon Press, 95, XVIII-154 p. (Oxford-Warburg Studies).

4232. SALSON (Jean-Marie). Entre la porte du paradis et la gueule de l'enfer: la fresque du Jugement dernier de Nicolï Greschny dans la chapelle Notre-Dame-de-Treize-Pierres à Villefranche-de-Rouergue. *In*: Enfer et paradis [Cf. n° 1370], p. 371-382.

4233. SEGURET (Pierre). Le dévoilement: enfer voilé, paradis dévoilé. Interprétation des messages iconographiques du tympan de Conques. *In*: Enfer et paradis [Cf. n° 1370], p. 93-102.

4234. SUAU (Jean-Pierre). Le thème du livre individuel de consciences sur les peintures murales méridionales du Jugement dernier, à la fin du Moyen Age. *In*: Enfer et paradis [Cf. n° 1370], p. 147-175.

4235. SUCKALE (Robert). Eine unbekannte Madonnenstatuette der Wiener Hofkunst um 1350. *Österr. Z. f. Kunst und Denkmalpflege*, 95, 49, 3, p. 147-159. (ill.).

4236. VENARD (Marc). La religion civique exprimée par l'image. Les saints tutèlaires et protecteurs de l'ancienne citè d'Avignon. *In*: Religion civique à l'époque médiévale et moderne (La) [Cf. n° 4528], p. 471-479.

4237. WILLIAMS (J.). The illustrated Beatus: a corpus of the illustrations of the Commentary on the Apocalypse. T. 2. The tenth and eleventh centuries. London, Harvey Miller, 95, 320 p. (ill.).

4238. ZEMAN (Georg). Studien zur Skulptur am Hof des Jean de Berry: Stilfragen. *Wien. Jb. f. Kunstgesch.*, 95, 48, p. 165-214 (ill.).

4239. ZIRLIN (Yael). Joel meets Johannes: a fifteenth century Jewish-Christian collaboration in manuscript illumination. *Viator. Medieval and Renaissance Studies*, 26, 95, p. 265-282 (ill.).

Cf. n° 417

§ 11. Musikgeschichte.

4240. ATKINSON (Charles). Johannes Afflighemensis as a historian of mode. *In*: Laborare fratres in unum [Cf. n° 4252], p. 1-10.

4241. BAILEY (Terence). Ambrosian double antiphons. *In*: Laborare fratres in unum [Cf. n° 4252], p. 11-24.

4242. BREWER (Charles). «Cantiones et moteti populi». Towards a definition of popular song and poliphony in central and east central Europe. *In*: Laborare fratres in unum [Cf. n° 4252], p. 25-36.

4243. COLETTE (Marie-Noël). Grégorien et vieux-romain: deux méthodes différentes de collectage de mélodies traditionelles? *In*: Laborare fratres in unum [Cf. n° 4252], p. 37-52.

4244. Essays on medieval music in honor of David G. Hughes. Ed. by Graeme BOONE. Cambridge, Cambridge U. P., 95, XIV-196 p. (Isham library papers, 4).

4245. GONCHAROVA (Victoria). The prose «Adest praecelsa cunctis» for St. Mary Magdalene in manuscript Lat.Q.v.I.51 of the Saltikov-Shchedrin Library, St. Petersburg. *In*: Laborare fratres in unum [Cf. n° 4252], p. 63-77.

4246. HAGGH (Barbara). The late-medieval liturgical books of Cambrai Cathedral. A brief survey of the evidence. *In*: Laborare fratres in unum [Cf. n° 4252], p. 79-85.

4247. HUGLO (Michel). Exercitia vocum. *In*: Laborare fratres in unum [Cf. n° 4252], p. 117-123.

4248. IVERSEN (Gunilla). «Cantans-orans-exultans». Interpretations of chants of the introit liturgy. *In*: Laborare fratres in unum [Cf. n° 4252], p. 125-150.

4249. KARP (Theodore). The offertory «In die solemnitatis». *In*: Laborare fratres in unum [Cf. n° 4252], p. 151-165.

4250. KELLY (Thomas Forrest). The liturgical Rotulus at Benevento. *In*: Laborare fratres in unum [Cf. n° 4252], p. 167-186.

4251. KISS (Gábor). Die Beziehung zwischen Ungebundenheit und Traditionalismus im Messordinarium. *In*: Laborare fratres in unum [Cf. n° 4252], p. 187-200.

4252. Laborare fratres in unum. Festschrift László Dobszay zum 60. Geburtstag. Hrsg. v. Janka SZENDEI u. David HILEY. Hildesheim, Weidmann, 95, XV-349 p. (Spolia Berolinensia, 7). [Cf. n°s <Auswahl> 3824, 4240, 4241, 4242, 4243, 4245, 4246, 4247, 4248, 4249, 4250,

4251, 4254, 4255, 4256, 4257, 4258, 4259, 4261, 4263, 4265, 4266.]

4253. Lexicon musicum Latinum medii aevi. Wörterbuch der lateinischen Musikterminologie des Mittelalters bis zum Ausgang des 15. Jahrhunderts. Dictionary of medieval latin musical terminology to the end of the 15th century. 2. A–authenticus. Ed. by Michael BERNHARD. München, Bayerische Akademie der Wissenschaften, 95, XIII-80 p.

4254. MAC KINNON (James W.). Lector chant versus Schola chant. A question of historical plausibility. *In*: Laborare fratres in unum [Cf. n° 4252], p. 201-211.

4255. MAITRE (Claire). Des sons et des couleurs: étude chromatique d'un manuscrit liturgique noté. *In*: Laborare fratres in unum [Cf. n° 4252], p. 213-228.

4256. MÖLLER (Hartmut). Christliches Kultdrama im Mittelalter. Neue Perspektiven. *In*: Laborare fratres in unum [Cf. n° 4252], p. 229-239.

4257. NILSSON (Ann-Marie). «Discubuit»: a service, a procession, or both? Some notes on the «Discubuit Jesus» in north European traditions. *In*: Laborare fratres in unum [Cf. n° 4252], p. 241-248.

4258. SCHLAGER (Karlheinz). Frigdola=Frigdora? Spekulationen um einen Sequenzentitel. *In*: Laborare fratres in unum [Cf. n° 4252], p. 279-284.

4259. SEVESTRE (Nicole). Fragments d'un prosaire aquitain inédit. *In*: Laborare fratres in unum [Cf. n° 4252], p. 285-295.

4260. SHEHADI (Fadlou). Philosophies of music in medieval Islam. (Brill's studies in intellectual history, 67). Leiden, New York a. Köln, E. J. Brill, 95, 175 p.

4261. STEINER (Ruth). Antiphons for lauds on the Octave of Christmas. *In*: Laborare fratres in unum [Cf. n° 4252], p. 307-315.

4262. SWITTE (Margaret L.). Music and poetry in the Middle Ages. A guide to research on French and Occitan songs, 1100–1400. New York a. London, Garland, 95, XXXI-452. (Garland Medieval Bibliographies, 19. Garland Reference Library of Humanities, 1102).

4263. SZENDREI (Janka). Quilisma und Diastematie. *In*: Laborare fratres in unum [Cf. n° 4252], p. 317-330.

4264. Two offices for St Elizabeth of Hungary. "Gaudeat Hungaria" and "Letare Germania". Ed. by Barbara HAGGH. Ottawa, Institute of Mediaeval Music, 95, XXV-48 p. (Wissenschaftliche Abhandlungen/Musicological Studies, 65; Historiae, 1).

4265. VAN DEUSEN (Nancy). Institutional context and musical construct. A paradigm in medieval France. *In*: Laborare fratres in unum [Cf. n° 4252], p. 53-61.

4266. WITKOWSKA-ZAREMBA (Elzbieta). «Mi contra fa» and «Divisio toni». *In*: Laborare fratres in unum [Cf. n° 4252], p. 331-340.

Cf. n° 158

§ 12. **Geschichte der Philosophie.**

** 4267. Aristote. Metaphysica (lib. I–XIV). Recensio et translatio Guillelmi de Moerbeka. Ed. by Gudrun VUILLEMIN-DIEM. Leiden, New York a. Köln, E. J. Brill, 95, 2 vol., XII-375 p., 479 p. (ill.). (Aristoteles latinus, XXV, 3.1, 2).

** 4268. BEDA IL VENERABILE. Esposizione e revisione degli Atti degli Apostoli. A cura di Giuseppina Abbolito SIMONETTI. Roma, Città Nuova, 95, 304 p. (Collana di testi patristici, 121).

** 4269. BERNARD OF CLAIRVAUX. On loving God. Comm. by Emero STIEGMAN. Kalamazoo, Cistercian Publications, 95, V-219 p. (Cistercian fathers series, 13B).

** 4270. Bibliotheca (Die) Amploniana. Ihre Bedeutung im Spannungsfeld von Aristotelismus, Nominalismus und Humanismus. Hrsg. von A. SPEER. Berlin u. New York, W. De Gruyter, 95, XVI-512 p. (Miscellanea medievalia, 23).

** 4271. BONAVENTURA DA BAGNOREGIO. Opera omnia di San Bonaventura. A cura di J. G. BOUGEROL, C. DEL ZOTTO e L. SILEO. Vol. 6. Sermoni teologici. A cura di B. DE ARMELLADA. Roma, Città Nuova, 95, 404 p. (ill.) (Sancti Bonaventurae Opera, 6).

** 4272. Clavis patrum latinorum. Ed. 3ª, aucta et emendata. Steenbrugis, in abbatia Sancti Petri et Turnholti, Brepols, 95, XXXII-934 p. (Corpus christianorum. Series latina).

** 4273. Codices Boethiani. A conspectus of manuscripts of the works of Boethius. 1. Great Britain and the Republic of Ireland. Ed. by M. T. GIBSON, Lesley SMITH a. Joseph ZIEGLER. London, University of London, Warburg Institute, 95, XV-288 p. (Warburg Institute surveys and texts, 25).

** 4274. Corpus orationum. Inchoante E. MOELLER, subsequente I. M. CLÉMENT, totum opus perfecit B. COPPIETERS 'T WALLANT. T. 7. P–Q. Orationes 4335–4954. Turnhout, Brepols, 95, LXIV-324-8 p. (Corpus christianorum. Series latina, 160E–F).

** 4275. *Vacat.*

** 4276. Espositiones Pauli epistularum ad Romanos, Galathas et Ephesios e codice Sancti Michaelis in periculo Maris. Ed. G. DE MARTEL. Turhnolti, Brepols, 95, 303 p. (tab.) (Corpus christianorum continuatio mediaevalis, 151).

** 4277. FEROTIN (M). Le «Liber mozarabicus sacramentorum» et les manuscrits mozarabes. A cura di A. WARD e C. JOHNSON. Roma, Centro liturgico vincenziano, 95, 728 p. (Bibliotheca Ephemerides liturgicae. Subsidia, 78).

** 4278. GIOACCHINO DA FIORE. Introduzione all'Apocalisse. A cura di Kurt-Victor SELGE e Gian Luca POTESTÀ. Roma, Viella, 95, 65 p. (Centro internazionale di Studi Gioachimiti S. Giovanni in Fiore. Opere di Gioacchino da Fiore, Testi e strumenti, 6). –

IDEM. Dialogi de prescientia Dei et predestinatione electorum. A cura di Gian Luca POTESTÀ. Roma, Istituto Storico Italiano per il Medio Evo, 95, XIV-158 p. (Fonti per la storia dell'Italia medievale. Antiquitates, 4).

** 4279. GUILLELMUS DE LA MARE. Scriptum in secundum librum Sententiarum. Hrsg. v. Hans KRAML. München, Beck u. Bayerische Akademie der Wissenschaften, 95, 579 p. (Bayerische Akademie der Wissenschaften, 18).

** 4280. GUILLELMUS DE MOERBEKA. Metaphysica. Lib. I–XIV. Ed. by Gudrun VUILLEMIN-DIEM. Leiden, New York a. Köln, E. J. Brill, 95, 2 vol., XII-375 p., VII-459 p. (Aristotels Latinus, 25, 3, 1–2).

** 4281. HILDEGARDIS BINGENSIS. Liber vitae meritorum. Ed. A. CARLEVARIS. Turnholti, Brepols, 95, 495 p. (Corpus christianorum continuatio mediaevalis, 90).

** 4282. HUGUES DE BALMA. Théologie mistique. Ed. par F. RUELLO et J. BARBET. Tome 1. Paris, Cerf, 95, 280 p. (Sources chrétiennes, 408).

** 4283. Index des citations et allusions bibliques dans la littérature patristique. Paris, C.N.R.S.-Editions, 95, 416 p. [et CD-ROM]. (Biblia patristica, 6).

** 4284. Vacat.

** 4285. IOHANNES SCOTTUS ERIUGENA. Periphyseon (De diuisione naturae). Liber quartus. Ed. by Edouard A. JEANEAU a. Mark A. ZIER, trans. by John J. O'MEARA a. I. P. SHELDON-WILLIAMS. Dublin, School od Celtic Studies, Dublin Institute for Advanced Studies, 95, XLIV-338 p. (Scriptores Latini Hiberniae, 13).

** 4286. JOHANNES BURIDANUS. Summulae de praedicabilibus. Ed. by L. M. DE RIJK. Nijmegen, Ingenium, 95, XLIV-82 p.

** 4287. Logica antiquioris mediae aetatis. Vol. 1. Excerpta isagogarum et categoriarum. Ed. I. D'ONOFRIO. Turnholti, Brepols, 95, 312 p. (tab.) (Corpus christianorum continuatio mediaevalis, 120).

** 4288. LOHR (C. H.). Aristotelica Helvetica. Catalogus codicum latinorum in bibliothecis Confederationis Helveticae asservatorum quibus versiones expositionesque operum Aristotelis continentur. Freiburg/Schweiz, Universitätsverlag, 95, XII-388 p. (ill.) (Scrinium Friburgense; Sonderbd, 6). – ** IDEM. Latin Aristotle commentaries. T. 3. Index initiorum, index finium. Firenze, L. S. Olschki, 95, XVI-290 p. (Corpus philosophorum Medii Aevi. Subsidia, 10).

** 4289. LULLUS (R.). Opera latina. Nn. 106–113. Ed. J. GAYÀ ESTELRICH. Turnholti, Brepols, 95, 575 p. (Corpus christianorum continuatio mediaevalis, 113).

** 4290. MICHAELIS DE MARBASIO. Summa de modis significandi. Critical edition with an introduction by Louis G. KELLY. Stuttgart, Fromann a. Bad Cannstatt, Holzboog, 95, LXI-199 p. (Grammatica speculativa. Sprachtheorie und Logik des Mittelalters. Theory of language and logic in the Middle Ages, 5).

** 4291. Myrour of recluses (The). A middle English translation of "Speculum inclusorum". Ed. by Marta POWELL HARLEY. Madison a. Teaneck, Fairleigh Dickinson U. P. a. London, Associated University Presses, 95, XXXIII-90 p.

** 4292. NICOLAUS ORESME. Expositio et Quaestiones in Aristotelis "De Anima". Ed. par Benoît PATAR et Claude GAGNON. Louvain-la-Neuve, Institut Supérieur de Philosophie et Louvain, Peeters, 95, 621 p. (Philosophes Médiévaux, 32).

** 4293. OCKHAM (William of). A Letter to the Friars Minor and Other Writings. Ed. by A. S. MAC GRADE and J. KILCULLEN. Cambridge, Cambridge University Press, 95, 288 p. (Cambridge Texts in the History of Political Thought).

** 4294. PETRUS DE CRESCENTIIS. Ruralia commoda: das Wissen des volkommenen Landwirts um 1300, Einleitung mit Buch I–III. T. 1. Hrsg. v. Will RICHTER u. Reinhilt RICHTER-BERGMEIER. Heidelberg, Universitätsverlag C. Winter, 95, LXXXIV-193 p. (Editiones Heidelbergenses, 25).

** 4295. RAIMUNDUS LULLUS. Opera Latina, 20. Ed. by Jordi GAYÀ ESTELRICH. Turnhout, Brepols, 95, LXXVIII-494 p. (Corpus Christianorum, Continuatio Mediaeualis, 113).

** 4296. Repertorium Nazianzenum. Orationes. Textus Graecus. 4. Codices Cypri, Graeciae (pars altera), Hierosolymorum. Rec. I. Mossay. Paderborn, F. Schöningh, 95, 246 p. (Studien zur Geschichte und Kultur des Altertums. N. F. 2. Reihe, 11).

** 4297. ROBERT GROSSETESTE. Opera. Vol. 1. Expositio in Epistolam sancti Pauli ad Galatas. Glossarium in sancti Petri fragmenta. Tabula. Ed. J. MAC EVOY, L. RIZZERIO, R. C. DALES, P. W. ROSEMANN. Turnholti, Brepols, 95, 351 p. (tab.) (Corpus christianorum continuatio mediaevalis, 130).

** 4298. SAINT JEROME. Saint Jerome's "Hebrew Questions on Genesis". Trans. by C. T. R. HAYWARD. Oxford, Clarendon Press, a. New York, Oxford U. P., 95, XIII-274 p. (Oxford early christian studies).

** 4299. STRABO (Walahfrid). Walahfrid Strabo's «Libellus de exordiis et incrementis». Ed. by A. HARTING-CORRÊA. Leiden u. New York, E. J. Brill, 95, 220 p. (Mittellateinische Studien und Texte, 19).

** 4300. THEODORE. The Laterculus Malalianus and the School of Archbishop Theodore. Ed. by J. STEVENSON. Cambridge, Cambridge University Press, 95, XIII-254 p. [Latin and English text] (Cambridge Studies in Anglo-Saxon England, 14).

4301. Albertus Magnus und der Albertismus. Deutsche philosophische Kultur des Mittelalters. Hrsg. v. Maarten J. F. M. HOENEN u. Alain DE LIBERA. Leiden, New York u. Köln, E. J. Brill, 95, 391 p. (Studien und Texte zur Geistesgeschichte des Mittelalters, 48).

4302. Aristotelica et Lulliana magistro doctissimo Charles H. Lohr septuagesimum annum feliciter agenti dedicata. Hrsg. v. Fernando DOMÍNGUEZ REBOIRAS, Ruedi IMBACH, Theodor PINDL-BÜCHEL u. Peter WALTER. Steenbrugge, The Hague u. Sint Pietresabdij, M. Nijhoff Internation, 95, IX-598 p. (Instrumenta patristica, 26). [Cf. n^{os} <Auswahl> 4303, 4305, 4321, 4322, 4325, 4329, 4334, 4335, 4339, 4340, 4364, 4367, 4368, 4372, 4384, 4388, 4391.]

4303. BERTELLONI (Francisco). Presupuestos de la recepción de la «Politica» de Aristóteles. In: Aristotelica et Lulliana [Cf. n° 4302], p. 35-54.

4304. BIANCHI (S.). La trasmissione della logica aristotelica nell'Occidente latino: il caso del «Periherrmeneais» di Apuleio. Studi Medievali, 95, 36, 1, p. 63-86.

4305. BONNER (Anthony). Syllogisms, fallacies and hypotheses. Llull's new weapons to combat the partisan Averroists. In: Aristotelica et Lulliana [Cf. n° 4302], p. 457-475.

4306. BOUREAU (Alain). Conclusion. In: Crisi dell'alchimia (Le) [Cf. n° 4318], p. 347-353.

4307. BOYLE (John F.). The ordering of Trinitarion teaching in Thomas Aquinas' second commentary on Lombard's sentences. In: Thomistica [Cf. n° 4381], p. 125-136.

4308. BURNETT (Charles Stuart F.). The institutional context of Arabic-Latin translations of the Middle Ages. A reassessment of the «School of Toledo». In: Vocabulary of teaching [Cf. n° 4164], p. 214-235.

4309. CADDEN (Joan). Science and rhetoric in the middle ages: the natural philosophy of William of Conches. Journal of the history of ideas, 95, 56, 1, p. 1-24.

4310. CALVET (Antoine). Mutations de l'alchimie médicale au XVe siècle. A propos des textes authentiques et apocryphes d'Arnaud de Villeneuve. In: Crisi dell'alchimia (Le) [Cf. n° 4318], p. 185-209.

4311. CAROTI (Stefano). L'oggetto della conoscenza secondo Nicole Oresme («Quaestiones super Physicam», I, 2). In: Studi in onore di Arnaldo D'Addario [Cf. n° 452], p. 455-469.

4312. CARUSI (Paola). Animalis Herbalis Naturalis. Considerazioni parallele sul «De anima in arte alchimiae» attribuito ad Avicenna e sul «Miftāḥ al-Ḥikma» (Opera di un allievo di Apollonio di Tiana). In: Crisi dell'alchimia (Le) [Cf. n° 4318], p. 45-74.

4313. CHASE (Steven). Angelic Wisdom. The cherubin and the grace of contemplation in Richard of St. Victor. Notre Dame a. London, University of Notre Dame Press, 95, XXVI-273 p. (Studies in spirituality and theology, 2).

4314. COLISH (Marcia L.). The development of Lombardian theology, 1160–1215. In: Centers of learning [Cf. n° 3953], p. 207-216.

4315. COMET (Georges). L'iconographie des «plantes nouvelles» en Europe, ou une approche des débuts de la botanique moderne. In: Campagnes médiévales [Cf. n° 3713], p. 45-58.

4316. CONSTABLE (Giles). Three studies in medieval religious and social thought. Cambridge, Cambridge U. P., 95, XIV-423 p.

4317. COURTENAY (William J.). Was there an Ockhamist School? In: Philosophy and learning [Cf. n° 4363], p. 263-292.

4318. Crisi dell'alchimia (Le). The crisis of alchemy. Pref. di Agostino PARAVICINI BAGLIANI. Turnhout, Brepols, 95, VIII-387 p. [Cf. n^{os} <scelta> 3970, 4026, 4306, 4310, 4312, 4351, 4358, 4361, 6463.]

4319. DE JONG (Mayke). Old law and new-found power. Hrabanus Maurus and the Old Testament. In: Centers of learning [Cf. n° 3953], p. 161-176.

4320. DE LIBERA (Alain). Albert le Grand et la mystique allemande. In: Philosophy and learning [Cf. n° 4363], p. 29-42.

4321. DE RIJK (Lambert Marie). Ockham as the commentator of «His» Aristotle: his treatment of «Posterior Analytic». In: Aristotelica et Lulliana [Cf. n° 4302], p. 77-127. – IDEM. Teaching and inquiry in 13th–14th century logic and metaphysics. In: Vocabulary of teaching [Cf. n° 4164], p. 83-95.

4322. DOMINGUEZ REBOIRAS (Fernando). Raimundo Lulio y el ideal mendicante. Afinidades y divergencias. In: Aristotelica et Lulliana [Cf. n° 4302], p. 377-413.

4323. DREYER (Mechthild). Die literarische Gattung der Theoremata als Residuum einer Wissenschaft «more geometrico». In: Philosophy and learning [Cf. n° 4363], p. 123-136.

4324. EMERY (Glles). La Trinité créatrice: Trinité et création dans les commentaires aux "Sentences" de Thomas d'Aquin et de ses précurseurs Albert le Grand et Bonaventure. Paris, J. Vrin, 95, 590 p. (Bibliothèque Thomiste, 47).

4325. EULER (Walter Andreas). «De adventu Messiae». Ramón Lulls Beitrag zur Christlich-Judischen Messiaskontroverse. In: Aristotelica et Lulliana [Cf. n° 4302], p. 429-441.

4326. EVANS (Gillian Rosemary). Theology. The vocabulary of teaching and research 1300–1600: words and concepts. In: Vocabulary of teaching [Cf. n° 4164], p. 118-133.

4327. GALLOWAY (Andrew). The rhetoric of riddling in late-medieval England: the "Oxford" riddles, the Secretum philosophorum, and the riddles in Pier Plowman. Speculum, 95, 70, 1, p. 68-105.

4328. GANZ (David). Theology and the organisation of thought. In: New Cambridge medieval history [Cf. n° 3378], p. 758-785.

4329. GAYA ESTELRICH (Jordi). Significación y demonstración en el «Libre de contemplació» de Ramon Llull. *In*: Aristotelica et Lulliana [Cf. n° 4302], p. 477-499.

4330. GIBSON (Craig A.), NEWTON (Francis). Pandulf of Capua's De calculatione: an illustrated abacus treatise and some evidence for the Hindu-Arabic numerals in eleventh-century South Italy. *Mediaeval Studies*, 95, 57, p. 293-336.

4331. GONTHIER (N.). Les médecins et la justice au XVe siècle à travers l'exemple dijonnais. *Moyen Age*, 95, 101, 2, p. 277-296.

4332. GREGOIRE (Réginald). Le interpretazioni altomedievali dei testi veterotestamentari sulla giustizia. *In*: Giustizia (La) nell'Alto Medioevo [Cf. n° 3630], p. 423-440.

4333. HALVERSON (James). Franciscan thelogy and predestinarian pluralism in late-medieval thought. *Speculum*, 95, 70, 1, p. 1-26.

4334. HAMESSE (Jacqueline). Le rôle joué par divers ordres religieux dans la composition des florilèges d'Aristote. *In*: Aristotelica et Lulliana [Cf. n° 4302], p. 289-310.

4335. HILLGARTH (Jocelyn Nigel). An unpublished Lullian sermon by Pere Deguí. *In*: Aristotelica et Lulliana [Cf. n° 4302], p. 561-569.

4336. HOLCOT (Robert). Seeing the future clearly. Questions on future contingents by Robert Holcot. Ed. by Paul STREVELER, Katherine H. TACHAU [et al.]. Toronto, Pontifical Institute of Mediaeval Studies, 95, IX-223 p. (Studies and texts, 119).

4337. HOLLYWOOD (Amy). The soul as virgin wife. Mechthild of Magdeburg, Marguerite Porete, and Meister Eckhart. Notre Dame a. London, University of Notre Dame Press, 95, X-331 p. (Studies in spirituality and theology, 1).

4338. HONNEFELDER (Ludger). Scotus und der Scotismus. Ein Beitrag zur Bedeutung der Schulbildung in der mittelalterlichen Philosophie. *In*: Philosophy and learning [Cf. n° 4363], p. 249-262.

4339. HÖSLE (Vittorio). Platonism and anti-platonism in Nicholas of Cusa's philosophy of mathematics. *In*: Aristotelica et Lulliana [Cf. n° 4302], p. 517-543.

4340. JACOBI (Klaus), STRAUB (Christian). Peter Abaelard als Kommentator. *In*: Aristotelica et Lulliana [Cf. n° 4302], p. 11-34.

4341. JACQUART (Danielle). Les «Concordances» de Pierre de Saint-Flour et l'enseignement de la médecine à Paris dans la second moitié du XIV siècle. *In*: Vocabulary of teaching [Cf. n° 4164], p. 172-183.

4342. JOHNSON (Mark F.). St. Thomas, obediential potency, and the infused virtues: De virtutibus in communi, a. 10. ad 13. *In*: Thomistica [Cf. n° 4381], p. 27-34.

4343. JOLIVET (Jean). Philosophie médiévale arabe et latine. Recueil d'articles. Paris, J. Vrin, 95, 319 p. (Etudes de philosophie médiévale, 73).

4344. JUSSILA (Päivi Hannele). Peter Abelard on imagery. Theory and practice with special reference to his Hymns. Helsinki, Suomalainen Tiedeakatemia, 95, XVIII-237 p. (Suomalainen Tiedeakatemiam Toimituksia, Annales Academiae Scientiarum Fennicae, B-280).

4345. KALUZA (Zénon). La crise des années 1474–1482. L'interdiction du nominalisme par Louis XI. *In*: Philosophy and learning [Cf. n° 4363], [s. p.].

4346. KNEEPKENS (Corneille). «Ordo naturalis» and «Ordo artificialis». A note on the terminology of thirteenth-century university grammar. *In*: Vocabulary of teaching [Cf. n° 4164], p. 59-82.

4347. KUKSEWICZ (Zdzisław). Der lateinische Averroismus im Mittelalter und in der Früh-Renaissance. *In*: Philosophy and learning [Cf. n° 4363], p. 371-386.

4348. MAAS (Pauline Henriëtte Joanna Theresia). The Liber sententiarum Magistri A. Its place amidsr the sentences collections of the first half of the XIIth century. Nijmegen, Katholieke Universiteit Nijmegen, Centrum Middeleeuwse Studies, 95, XI-365 p. (Middeleeuwse Studies, 11).

4349. MAKDISI (George). Baghdad, Bologna, and scolasticism in Centers of learning. *In*: Centers of learning [Cf. n° 3953], p. 141-157.

4350. MANSINI (Guy). Duplex Amor and the structure of love in Aquinas. *In*: Thomistica [Cf. n° 4381], p. 137-196. – IDEM. Similitudo, Communicatio, and the friendship of Charity in Aquinas. *In*: Thomistica [Cf. n° 4381], p. 1-26.

4351. MATTON (Sylvain). L'influence de l'humanisme sur la tradition alchimique. *In*: Crisi dell'alchimia (Le) [Cf. n° 4318], p. 279-345.

4352. MATTOSO (José). Da teoria à prática: o mundo das ideias no princípio do século XIV. *In*: Europa en los umbrales [Cf. n° 3357], p. 429-462.

4353. MAYESKI (Marie Anne). Dhuoda. Ninth century mother and theologian. Scranton, University of Scranton Press, 95, XII-177 p.

4354. MIETHKE (Jürgen). Señorio y libertad en la teoría política del siglo XIV. *Patristica et medievalia*, 95, 16, p. 3-32.

4355. NEDERMAN (Cary J.). Community and consent. The secular political theory of Marsiglio of Padua's "Defensor pacis". Lanham a. London, Rowman and Littlefield, 95, X-163 p.

4356. NORTH (John D.). Aspects of language of medieval mathematics. *In*: Vocabulary of teaching [Cf. n° 4164], p. 134-150.

4357. NUTTON (Vivian). The changing language of medicine, 1450–1550. *In*: Vocabulary of teaching [Cf. n° 4164], p. 184-198.

4358. OBRIST (Barbara). Vers une histoire de l'alchimie médiévale. In: Crisi dell'alchimia (Le) [Cf. n° 4318], p. 3-43.

4359. PALACIOS MARTIN (Bonifacio). El mundo de las ideas políticas en los tratados doctrinales españoles: los «espejos de príncipes» (1250–1350). In: Europa en los umbrales [Cf. n° 3357], p. 463-483.

4360. PARENS (Joshua). Metaphysics as rhetoric. Alfarabi's "Summary of Plato's 'Laws'". Albany, State University of New York Press, 95, XXXVIII-195 p. (SUNY Series in middle eastern studies).

4361. PEREIRA (Michela). Teorie dell'elixir nell'alchimia medievale. In: Crisi dell'alchimia (Le) [Cf. n° 4318], p. 103-148.

4362. PETRI (Luce). Grégoire de Tours et la justice dans le royaume des Francs. In: Giustizia (La) nell'Alto Medioevo [Cf. n° 3630], p. 475-506.

4363. Philosophy and learning. Universities in the Middle Ages. Ed. by Maarten J. F. M. HOENEN, Jakob Hans Josef SCHNEIDER a. Georg WIELAND. Leiden, New York a. Köln, E. J. Brill, 95, XIV-435 p. (Education and society in the Middle Ages and Renaissance, 6). [Cf. n°s <choice> 4015, 4123, 4317, 4320, 4323, 4338, 4345, 4347.]

4364. PINDL-BÜCHEL (Theodor). Ramon Lull, Thomas le Myésier und die Miniaturen des «Breviculum ex artibus Raimundi electum». In: Aristotelica et Lulliana [Cf. n° 4302], p. 501-516.

4365. QUINTO (Riccardo). Per la storia del trattato tomistico «de passionibus animae»: il «timor» nella letteratura teologica tra il 1200 ed il 1230 ca. In: Thomistica [Cf. n° 4381], p. 35-87.

4366. Reading and Wisdom. The «De Doctrina Christiana» of Augustine in the Middle Ages. Ed. by Edward D. ENGLISH. Notre Dame a. London, University of Notre Dame Press, 95, XI-188 p. (Notre Dame conferences in medieval studies, 6).

4367. REINHARDT (Klaus). Ramón Lull und die Bibel. In: Aristotelica et Lulliana [Cf. n° 4302], p. 311-331.

4368. RIEDLINGER (Helmut). Zu Ramon Lulls gegenwärtiger Bedeutung. In: Aristotelica et Lulliana [Cf. n° 4302], p. 571-580.

4369. ROJAS (José). St. Thomas' treatise on self-defense. In: Thomistica [Cf. n° 4381], p. 89-123.

4370. Saint Thomas et l'onto-théologie. Actes du colloque tenu à l'Institut Catholique de Toulouse 3–4 juin 1994. Préf. par Serge-Thomas BONINO. Toulouse et Bruxelles, Ecole de théologie, 95, 192 p.

4371. San Tommaso teologo. San Tommaso filosofo. Ricerche in occasione dei due centenari accademici. A cura di Antonio PIOLANTI. Città del Vaticano, Pontificia Accademia Romana di San Tommaso e Libreria Editrice Vaticana, 95, 2 vol., 337 p., 384 p. (Studi tomistici, 59, 60).

4372. SANTI (Francesco). «Utrum resurrectio sit naturalis». Preservazione della natura non razionale oltre la fine del mondo. Studi Medievali, 95, 36, 1, p. 199-210. – IDEM. Guglielmo di Saint Thierry (non) fonte di Raimondo Lullo. In: Aristotelica et Lulliana [Cf. n° 4302], p. 333-354.

4373. Scholing in de middeleeuwen. Ed. by René Ernst Victor STUIP a. Kees VELLEKOOP. Hilversum, Verloren, 95, 256 p. (Utrechtse bijdragen tot de mediëvistiek, 13).

4374. Senso della storia (Il) nella cultura medievale italiana (1100–1350). Atti del quattordicesimo Convegno Internazionale di studio tenuto a Pistoia nei giorni 14–17 maggio 1993. Bologna, Editografica, 95, [s. p.]. [Cf. n°s <scelta> 4116, 4465.]

4375. SHAW (Gregory). Theurgy and the soul. The neoplatonism of Iamblichus. University Park, Pennsylvania State U. P., 95, XI-268 p. (Hermeneutics. Studies in the history of religions).

4376. SOUTHERN (R. W.). Scholastic Humanism and the unification of Europe. Vol. 1. Foundations. Oxford a. Cambridge, Blackwell, 95, XXI-330 p.

4377. SPEER (Andreas). Die entdeckte Natur. Untersuchungen zu Begründungsversuchen einer "scientia naturalis" im 12. Jahrhundert. Leiden, New York u. Köln, E. J. Brill, 95, XI-365 p. (Studien und Texte zur Geistesgeschichte des Mittelalters, 45).

4378. STECHER (Gudrun Theresia). Magnetismus im Mittelalter. Von den Fähigkeit und der Verwendung des Magneten in Dichtung, Alltag und Wissenschaft. Göppingen, Kümmerle Verlag, 95, 162 p. (Göppinger Arbeiten zur Germanistik, 622).

4379. SYNAN (Edward A.), JEAUNEAU (Edouard). Some remarks on the Muckle translation of Abelard's adversities. Mediaeval Studies, 95, 57, p. 337-344.

4380. THIJSSEN (Johannes M. M. H.). Academic heresy and intellectual freedom at the University of Paris, 1200–1378. In: Centers of learning [Cf. n° 3953], p. 217-228.

4381. Thomistica. Ed. par Eugène MANNING. Leuven, Peeters, 95, 201 p. (Recherches de théologie ancienne et médiévale. Supplementa, 1). [Cf. n°s <sélection> 4307, 4342, 4350, 4365, 4369, 4307.]

4382. TROTTMANN (Christian). La vision béatifique. Des disputes scolastiques à sa définition par Benoît XII. Roma, Ecole française de Rome, 95, IV-899 p. (Bibliothèque des Ecoles françaises d'Athènes et de Rome, 289).

4383. TURNER (Denys). The darkness of God. Negativity in Christian mysticism. Cambridge, Cambridge U. P., 95, X-278 p.

4384. URVOY (Dominique). Nature et portée des liens de Ramon Llull avec l'univers arabe. In: Aristotelica et Lulliana [Cf. n° 4302], p. 415-427.

4385. VAN LIERE (Franciscus A.). Andrew of St Victor (d. 1175). Scholar between cloister and school. *In*: Centers of learning [Cf. n° 3953], p. 187-195.

4386. VAN ZWIETEN (Jan W. M.). Scientific and spiritual culture in Hugh of St Victor. *In*: Centers of learning [Cf. n° 3953], p. 177-186.

4387. VAN'T SPIJKER (Ienje). Learning by experience. Twelfth-century monastic ideas. *In*: Centers of learning [Cf. n° 3953], p. 197-206.

4388. VERBEKE (Gérard). La réception de la Physique d'Aristote. Philopon et Thomas d'Aquin. *In*: Aristotelica et Lulliana [Cf. n° 4302], p. 55-75.

4389. Via Scoti. Methodologica ad mentem Johannis Duns Scoti. Atti del congresso scotistico internazionale. Roma, 9–11 marzo 1993. A cura di Leonardo SILEO. Roma, Ed. Antonianum, 95, 2 vol., X-1220 p.

4390. WALKER BYNUM (Caroline). The resurrection of the body in Western Christianity, 200–1336. New York, Columbia U. P., 95, XXI-368 p. (Lectures on the history of religion, 15).

4391. WALTER (Peter). Jacobus Faber Stapulensis als Editor des Raimundus Lulles, dargestellt am Beispiel des «Liber Natalis pueri parvuli Christi Jesu». *In*: Aristotelica et Lulliana [Cf. n° 4302], p. 545-559.

4392. WAWRYKOW (Joseph P.). God's grace and human action. "Merit" in the theology of Thomas Aquinas. Notre Dame a. London, University of Notre Dame Press, 95, X-293 p.

4393. WEIJERS (Olga). La "disputatio" à la Faculté des arts de Paris (1200–1350 environ). Esquisse d'une typologie. Turnhout, Brepols, 95, 175 p. (Studia Artistarum. Etudes sur la Faculté des Arts dans les Universités Médiévales, 2).

4394. WILKS DOLNIKOWSKI (Edith). Thomas Bradwardine. A view of time and a vision of eternity in fourteenth-century thought. Leiden, New York a. Köln, E. J. Brill, 95, IX-250 p. (Studies in the History of ChristianThought, 65).

4395. ZUPKO (Jack). Freedom of choice in Buridan's moral psychology. *Mediaeval Studies*, 95, 57, p. 75-100.

§ 13. Kirchengeschichte.

a. Allgemeines

4396. BARRELL (Andrew D. M.). The Papacy, Scotland, and northern England, 1342–1378. Cambridge, Cambridge U. P., 95, XXV-291 p. (Cambridge Studies in medieval life and thought).

4397. *Vacat.*

4398. BROSSE (Jacques). Histoire de la chrétienté d'Orient et d'Occident: de la conversion des Barbares au sac de Constantinople, 406–1204. Paris, A. Michel, 95, 1110 p.

4399. Chiesa e mondo feudale nei secoli X–XII: atti della dodicesima settimana internazionale di studio della Mendola, 24–28 Agosto 1992. Milano, Vita e pensiero, 95, 640 p. (Miscellanea del Centro di studi medioevali, 14; Scienze storiche, 59).

4400. COWAN (Ian Borthwick). The medieval church in Scotland. Ed. by James KIRK. Edinburgh, Scottish Academic Press, 95, XV-254 p.

4401. English episcopal acta. 10. Bath and Wells 1061–1205. Ed. by Frances M. R. RAMSEY. Oxford, Published for The British Academy by Oxford U. P., XCIX-252 p.

4402. *Vacat.*

4403. *Vacat.*

4404. FRIEDRICH SILBER (Ilana). Virtuosity, charisma, and social order. A comparative sociological study of monasticism in Theravada buddhism and medieval catholicism. Cambridge, Cambridge U. P., 95, X-250 p. (Cambridge Cultural Social Studies).

4405. GANDINO (Germana). Il vocabolario politico e sociale di Liutprando di Cremona. Roma, Istituto Storico Italiano per il Medioevo, 95, 308 p. (Nuovi studi storici, 27).

4406. *Vacat.*

4407. HINSON (E. Glenn). The church triumphant: a history of Christianity up to 1300. Macon, Mercer U. P., 95, XXI-494 p.

4408. KUBINYI (András). Stadt und Kirche in Ungarn im Mittelalter. *In*: Stadt und Kirche [Cf. n° 1309], p. 179-198.

4409. MAC CREADY (William D.). Bede and the Isidorian legacy. *Mediaeval Studies*, 95, 57, p. 41-74.

4410. Medieval ecclesiastical studies in honour of Dorothy M. Owen. Ed. by Michael J. FRANKLIN a. Christopher HARPER-BILL. Woodbridge, Boydell Press, 95, XXI-310 p. (Studies in the history of medieval religion, 7). [Cf. n[os] <choice> 3187, 3260, 3604, 3651, 3653, 3681, 3696, 4412, 4503, 4506, 4507, 4533, 4534, 4575.]

4411. Quellen zur Kirchenreform im Zeitalter der Großen Konzilien des 15. Jahrhunderts. Acta ad ecclesiam in Generalibus saeculi XV Conciliis reformandam spectantia. T. 1. Die Konzilien von Pisa (1409) und Konstanz (1414–1418). Ausgewählt und übersetzt von Jürgen MIETHKE und Lorenz WEINRICH. Darmstadt, Wissenschaftliche Buchgesellschaft, 95, X-555 p. (Ausgewählte Quellen zur deutschen Geschichte des Mittelalters, 38a).

4412. RABAN (Sandra). The church in the 1279 Hundred Rolls. *In*: Medieval ecclesiastical studies [Cf. n° 4410], p. 185-200.

4413. *Vacat.*

4414. SMITH (Julia M. H.). The problem of female sanctity in Carolingian Europe c.780–920. *Past and Present*, 95, 146, p. 3-37.

4415. Soldiers of Christ: saints and saints lives from late antiquity and the early Middle ages. Ed. by Thomas F. X. NOBLE a. Thomas HEAD. University Park, Pennsylvania State U. P. a. London, Sheed & Ward, 95, XLIV-383 p.

4416. WERNER (Ernst). Religion und Gesellschaft im Mittelalter. Mit einem Vorwort von Cinzio VIOLANTE; hrsg. v. Silio P. P. SCALFATI. Spoleto, Centro italiano di studi sull'alto Medioevo, 95, XV-685 p. (Collectanea/Centro italiano di studi sull'alto Medioevo, 2).

4417. WOLL (Ingrid). Untersuchungen zu Überlieferung und Eigenart der merowingischen Kapitularien. Frankfurt am Main, Peter Lang, 95, XI-311 p. (Freiburger Beiträge zur mittelalterlichen Geschichte, 6).

Cf. n°s 1390, 1392, 1398, 1400, 1419, 1437, 1445

b. Geschichte des Papsttums.

4418. AZZARA (C.). «Pater vester, clementissimus imperator». Le relazioni tra i Franchi e Bisanzio nella prospettiva del papato del VI secolo. *Studi Medievali*, 95, 36, 1, p. 303-320.

4419. BEATTIE (Blake). Local reality and papal policy: papal provision and the church of Arezzo, 1248–1327. *Mediaeval Studies*, 95, 57, p. 131-154.

4420. COWDREY (H. E. J.). Pope Urban II and the idea of Crusade. *Studi Medievali*, 95, 36, 2, p. 721-742.

4421. DESWARTE (Th.). Rome et la spécificité catalane. La papauté et ses relations avec la Catalogne et Narbonne (850–1030). *Revue Historique*, 95, 119, 595, p. 3-43.

4422. EGGER (Christoph). Handschriften aus der päpstlichen Bibliothek von Avignon-Peniscola. Beobachtungen zur Überlieferungsgeschichte der theologischen Schriften Papst Innocenz' III. *Röm. Hist. Mitt.*, 95, 37, p. 81-96.

4423. MACCARRONE (Michele). Nuovi studi su Innocenzo III. prefazione di Ovidio CAPITANI. A cura di Roberto LAMBERTINI. Roma, Istituto storico italiano per il Medio Evo, 95, XXIV-437 p. (Nuovi studi storici, 25).

4424. NOBLE (Thomas F. X.). The papacy in the eight and ninth centuries. *In*: New Cambridge medieval history [Cf. n° 3378], p. 563-586.

4425. PARAVICINI BAGLIANI (Agostino). La cour des papes au XIIIe siecle. Paris, Hachette, 95, 314 p.

4426. VOCI (Anna Maria). Giovanna I d'Angiò e l'inizio del Grande Scisma d'Occedente. La doppia elezione del 1378 e la proposta conciliare. *Quellen und Forschungen aus italienischen Archiven und Bibliotheken*, 95, 75, p. 178-255.

4427. WEIß (Stefan). Die Urkunden der päpstlichen Legaten von Leo IX. bis Coelestin III. (1049–1198). Wien, Köln u. Weimar, Böhlau, 95, XVIII-461 p. (Forschungen zur Kaiser- und Papstgeschichte des Mittelalters, 13. Beihefte zu F. J. Böhmer, Regesta Imperii, 13).

c. Ordensgeschichte.

4428. ALBERZONI (Maria Pia). L'Ordine di San Damiano in Lombardia. RSCI, 95, 49, p. 1-42.

4429. ARSZYŃSKI (Marian). Budownictwo warowne zakonu krzyżackiego w Prusach, 1230–1454. (Ouvrages fortifiés des chevaliers teutoniques en Prusse, 1230–1454). Toruń, 95, 269 p. (Uniw. Mikołaja Kopernika).

4430. Badań nad dziejami klasztorów w Polsce (Z). ([Extraits] des recherches sur l'histoire des couvents en Pologne). Réd. Jerzy OLCZAK, Wojciech CHUDZIAK. Toruń, [s. n.], 95, 260 p., (phot., dessins). (Uniw. Mikołaja Kopernika. Uniw. Centrum Archeologii Średniowiecza i Nowożytności. Ser. Archeologia Hist. Pol., 2). [Deutsche Zsfassung, Eng. Summary].

4431. CABY (Cécile). Culte civique et «inurbamento» monastique en Italie à la fin du Moyen Age. Le culte du B. Parisio de Trévise. *In*: Religion civique à l'époque médiévale et moderne (La) [Cf. n° 4528], p. 219-234.

4432. COELHO DIAS (Geraldo J. A.). Perspectivas bíblicas da mulher e monaquismo feminino. *Revista da Faculdade de letras do Porto, Série de História*, 95, 12, p. 9-45.

4433. DE JONG (Mayke). Carolingian monasticism: the power of prayer. *In*: New Cambridge medieval history [Cf. n° 3378], p. 622-653.

4434. DILWORTH (Mark). Scottish monasteries in the late Middle Ages. Edinburgh, Edinburgh U. P., 95, VIII-102 p.

4435. DRACK (Walter), LÜTHI (Alfred). Zum kulturgeographischen Umfeld zur Zeit der Gründung des Zisterzienserklosters Maris Stella/Wettingen (1227). *Jb. d. Vorarlb. Landesmuseumsvereins*, 95, 139, p. 61-91 (ill., Reg.).

4436. Dziedzictwo kulturowe cystersów na Pomorzu. Materiały z seminarium, które odbyło się 18 września 1994 roku w Kołbaczu. (Patrimoine culturel des Cysterciens en Poméranie. Matériaux du séminaire tenu le 18 septembre 1994 à Kołbacz). Réd. Kazimiera KALITA-SKWIRZYŃSKA, Małgorzata LEWANDOWSKA. Szczecin, Regionalny Ośrodek Studiów i Ochrony Środowiska Kult., 95, 168 p. (Deutsche Zsfassung).

4437. ÉRSZEGI (Géza). Delle Beghine in Ungheria (ovvero l'insegnamento di un codice di Siena). *In*: Spiritualità e lettere nella cultura italiana e ungherese del basso medioevo [Cf. n° 4128], p. 63-73.

4438. FLACHENECKER (Helmut). Schottenklöster. Irische Benediktinerkonvente im hochmittelalterlichen

Deutschland. Paderborn, München u. Wien, Schöningh, 95, 401 p. (Quellen und Forschungen aus dem Gebiet der Geschichte, 18).

4439. Fontes Franciscani. A cura di Enrico MENESTÒ, Stefano BRUFANI, Giuseppe CREMASCOLI, Emore PAOLI, Luigi PELLEGRINI e Stanislao DA CAMPAGNOLA. S. Maria degli Angeli, Edizioni Porziuncola, 95, XVI-2582 p. (Medioevo Francescano. Testi, 2).

4440. GOLDING (Brian). Gilbert of Sempringham and the Gilbertine Order, c. 1130–c. 1300. Oxford, Clarendon Press a. New York, Oxford U. P., 95, XVI-508 p.

4441. HERRERA (Lorenzo). Historia de la Orden de Císter. Documentación. Burgos, Monasterio de las Huelgas, 95, 601 p. (Col. Epiritualidad Monástica, 30).

4442. HOUBEN (Hubert). Die Abtei Venosa und das Mönchtum im normannisch-staufischen Süditalien. Tübingen, Max Niemeyer Verlag, 95, IX-498 p. (Bibliothek des Deutschen Historschen Institut in Rom, 80).

4443. JOTISCHKY (Andrew). The perfection of solitude: hermits and monks in the Crusader states. University Park, Pennsylvania State U. P., 95, XVIII-198 p.

4444. KAISER (R.). Quêtes itinérantes avec des reliques pour financer la construction des églises (XIe–XIIe siècles). *Moyen Age*, 95, 101, 2, p. 205-226.

4445. Klasztor w kulturze średniowiecznej Polski. (Monastère dans la culture médiévale en Pologne). Matériaux de la conférence scientifique organisée à Dąbrowa Niemodlińska les 4–6, XI, 1993 par Instytut Historii Wyższej Szkoły Pedagogicznej d' Opole et Instytut Historyczny Uniwersytetu Wrocławskiego. Réd. Anna POBOG-LENARTOWICZ et Marek DERWICH. Opole, Wydawn. św. Krzyża, 95, 550 p. (English summary, phot., fig., dessins, carte). (Inst. Hist. Uniw. Opolskiego, Inst. Hist. Uniw. Wrocławskiego, Sympozja, 9).

4446. KLOS-BUZEK (Friederike). Kartause und mittelalterliche Stadt. *In*: Stadt und Kirche [Cf. n° 1309], p. 301-312.

4447. LEBECQ (Stéphane). Vaucelles et la terre aux XIIe–XIIIe siècles. Contribution à l'histoire foncière des Cisterciens en Picardie du Nord. *In*: Campagnes médiévales [Cf. n° 3713], p. 563-572.

4448. LUTTERBACH (Hubertus). Monachus factus est. Die Mönchwerdung im frühen Mittelalter. Zugleich ein Beitrag zur Frömmigkeits- und Liturgiegeschichte. Münster, Aschendorff, 95, LVI-347 p. (Beiträge zur Geschichte des alten Mönchtums und des Benediktinertums, 44).

4449. MAITRE (Claire). La réforme cistercienne du plain-chant. Etude d'un traité théorique. Préf. de Georges DUBY. Brecht, Abdij Nazareth, 95, 453 p. (ill.).

4450. O'CARROLL (Maura). The friars and the liturgy in the thirteenth century. *In*: Predicazione dei frati (La) [Cf. n° 4451], p. 191-227.

4451. Predicazione dei frati (La): dalla metà del '200 alla fine del '300. Atti del XII Convegno internazionale. Assisi, 13–15 ottobre, 1994. Spoleto, Centro Italiano di Studi sull'Alto Medioevo, 95, 496 p. [Cf. n^{os} <scelta> 169, 3428, 3939, 3977, 3996, 4006, 4106, 4111, 4159, 4450, 4464.]

4452. REITER (Eric H.). A treatise on confession from secular/mendicant dispute: The Casus abstracti a iure of Herman of Saxony, O. F. M. *Mediaeval Studies*, 95, 57, p. 1-40.

4453. Ritterorden und Region. Politische, soziale und wirtschaftliche Verbindungen im Mittelalter. Hrsg. v. Zenon Hubert NOWAK. Toruń, [s. n.], 95, 171 p. (carte). (Univ. Nicolai Copernici, Ordines Militares, 8. Colloquia Torunensia Hist.).

4454. ROGGEN (Héribert). De Clarissenorde in de Nederlanden. Sint-Truiden, Institut voor Franciscaanse Geschiedenis, 95, 289 p. (Instrumenta franciscana, 1).

4455. STÜDELI (Bernhard). Minoriten- und andere Mendikanten-Niederlassungen als Gemeinschaftszentren im öffentlichen Leben der mittelalterlichen Stadt. *In*: Stadt und Kirche [Cf. n° 1309], p. 239-256.

4456. ULPTS (Ingo). Die Bettelorden in Mecklenburg. Ein Beitrag zur Geschichte der Franziskaner, Klarissen, Dominikaner und Augustiner-Eremiten im Mittelalter. Werl, D. Coelde, 95, XIV-556 p. (Saxonia Franciscana, 6).

4457. WYRWA (Andrzej Marek). Procesy fundacyjne wielkopolskich klasztorów cysterskich linii altenberskiej. Łekno, Ląd, Obra. (Processus de fondation en Grande Pologne des couvents cisterciens du type "Altenberg". Łekno, Ląd, Obra). Poznań, [s. n.], 95, 293 p. (Publikacje Inst. Hist. Uniw. Adama Mickiewicza w Poznaniu, 3). [Eng. Summary].

d. Hagiographie.

4458. BEATO DE LIÉBANA. Obras completas. Ed. por Joaquín Gonzales ECHEGARAY, Alberto DEL CAMPO y Leslie G. FREEMAN. Toledo y Madrid, Estudio teológico de San Ildefonso, Biblioteca de Autores Cristianos, 95, LXII-953 p. (BAC Maior, 47).

4459. BONADONNA RUSSO (M. T.). L'amicizia spirituale tra s. **Caterina de'Ricci** e s. **Filippo Neri**. *Studi Medievali*, 95, 36, 2, p. 957-974.

4460. CANNON (Joanna). **Marguerite** et les Cortonais: iconographie d'un «culte civique» au XIVe siècle. *In*: Religion civique à l'époque médiévale et moderne (La) [Cf. n° 4528], p. 403-413.

4461. **Chiara d'Assisi** e la memoria di **Francesco**. Atti del convegno per l'VIII centenario della nascita di Santa Chiara. Fara Sabina, 19–20 maggio 1994. A cura di Alfonso MARINI e Maria Beatrice MISTRETTA, pref. di Renato BONELLI. Fara Sabina, Centro Francescano Santa Maria in Castello-Petruzzi, 95, 158 p.

4462. COULET (Noël). Dévotions communales: Marseille entre saint **Victor**, saint **Lazare** e saint **Louis** (XIIIᵉ–XVᵉ siècle). In: Religion civique à l'époque médiévale et moderne (La) [Cf. n° 4528], p. 119-133.

4463. Culte des saints (Le) au IXᵉ–XIIIᵉ siècles. Actes du colloque de Poitiers, 15–17 septembre 1993. Poitiers, Centre d'Etudes Supérieures de Civilisation Médiévale, 95, 167 p. (Civilisation médiévale, 1).

4464. DALARUN (Jacques). **Francesco** nei sermoni: agiografia e predicazione. In: Predicazione dei frati (La) [Cf. n° 4451], p. 339-404.

4465. GOLINELLI (Paolo). L'agiografia cittadina: dall'autocoscienza all'autorappresentazione (sec. IX–XII; Italia settentrionale). In: Senso della storia (Il) nella cultura medievale italiana [Cf. n° 4374], p. 253-274.

4466. GRACIOTTI (Sante). Per una rilettura della «Leggenda» su Elisabetta d'Ungheria, tra biografia e agiografia. In: Spiritualità e lettere nella cultura italiana e ungherese del basso medioevo [Cf. n° 4128], p. 111-131.

4467. KLANICZAY (Gábor). I modelli di santità femminile tra i secoli XIII e XIV in Europa centrale e in Italia. In: Spiritualità e lettere nella cultura italiana e ungherese del basso medioevo [Cf. n° 4128], p. 75-109.

4468. KLANICZAY (Tibor). La fortuna di Santa Margherita d'Ungheria in Italia. In: Spiritualità e lettere nella cultura italiana e ungherese del basso medioevo [Cf. n° 4128], p. 3-27.

4469. KRETZENBACHER (Leopold). St. **Ivo**, der bretonische Armenanwalt und Juristenpatron, in der Grazer Herrengasse. Z. d. Hist. Vereines f. Steiermark, 95, 86, p. 187-208 (ill.).

4470. LORENZO PINAR (Francisco Javier). Beatas y mancebas. Zamora, Editorial Semuret, 95, 159 p.

4471. LUTTERBACH (Hubertus). 'Pastor noster Anskarius'. Das Hirten-Ideal des Hl. **Ansgar** im Kontext der Entwicklungsgeschichte christlicher Frömmigkeit. Archiv für Kulturgeschichte, 95, 77, p. 279-300.

4472. MARBODO DI RENNES. Vita beati **Roberti**. Ed. and trans. by Antonella DEGL'INNOCENTI. Firenze, Giunti, LXXV-99 p. (Biblioteca del medioevo latino).

4473. REAL (I.). Vie et Vita de sainte **Ségolène**, abbesse du Troclar au VIIᵉ siècle. Moyen Age, 95, 101, 3, p. 385-406.

4474. RHEIN (Reglinde). Die Legenda Aurea des Jacobus de Voragine. Die Entfaltung von Heiligkeit in "Historia" und "Doctrina". Wien, Köln u. Weimar, Böhlau, 95, 308 p. (Beihefte zum Archiv für Kulturgeschichte, 40).

4475. RIGON (Antonio). S. Antonio da «pater Padue» a «patronus civitatis». In: Religion civique à l'époque médiévale et moderne (La) [Cf. n° 4528], p. 65-76.

4476. ROBERTSON (Duncan). The medieval saints' lives. Spiritual renewal and old French literature. Lexington, French Forum, 95, 290 p. (Edward C. Armstrong monographs on medieval literature, 8).

4477. Sainte Claire d'Assise et sa posterité. Actes du colloque international organisé à l'occasion du VIIIᵉ Centenaire de la naissance de sainte Claire. U. N. E. S. C. O. (29 septembre–1ᵉʳ octobre 1994). Ed. par Geneviève BRUNEL-LOBRICHON, Jacqueline GREAL, Dominique DINET et Damien VORREUX. Nantes et Paris, Association Claire Aujourd'hui et Ed. Franciscaines, 95, 540 p. (Publications du Comité du VIIIᵉ centenaire de Sainte Claire).

4478. SARADI (H.). Constantinople and its saints (IVᵗʰ–VIᵗʰ c.). The image of the city and social considerations. Studi Medievali, 95, 36, 1, p. 87-110.

4479. SZÖRÉNYI (László). La problematica del codice «Jókai» alla luce degli studi recenti sulle leggende di San **Francesco**. In: Spiritualità e lettere nella cultura italiana e ungherese del basso medioevo [Cf. n° 4128], p. 133-147.

Cf. n° 188

e. Spezialarbeiten.

4480. ANGENENDT (A.), BRAUCKS (T.), BUSCH (R.), LENTES (T.), LUTTERBACH (H.). Gezählte Frömmigkeit. Frühmittelalterliche Studien, 95, 29, p. 1-71.

4481. Archbishop Theodore. Commemorative studies on his life and influence. Ed. by Michael LAPIDGE. Cambridge, Cambridge U. P., 95, 95, XIII-343 p. (Cambridge studies in Anglo-Saxon England, 11).

4482. BEATTIE (Blake). A book of the schismatic pope Benedict XIII († 1423)? Clues to the ownership of a collection of coran papa sermons. Mediaeval Studies, 95, 57, p. 345-356.

4483. BELTJENS (Alain). Aux origines de l'Ordre de Malte. De la fondation de l'Hôpital de Jérusalem à sa transformation en ordre militaire. Bruxelles, Chez l'auteur, 95, 516 p.

4484. BENVENUTI (A.). Da San Salvatore a Santa Maria del Fiore. Itinerario di una cattedrale. Studi Medievali, 95, 36, 1, p. 111-151.

4485. BORK (B.), VON DER NAHMER (D.). Das Kloster des Honoratus von Fundi und das Praetorium Speculancae. Studi Medievali, 95, 36, 2, p. 617-656.

4486. BORNSTEIN (D.). Le donne di Giovanni Dominici: un caso nella recezione e trasmissione dei messaggi religiosi. Studi Medievali, 95, 36, 1, p. 355-362.

4487. BORNSTEIN (Daniel E.). Corporazioni spirituali: proprietà delle confraternite e pietà dei laici. Ricerche di storia sociale e religiosa, 95, 48, p. 77-90. – IDEM. Le Conseil de Dix et le controle de la vie religieuse à Venise à la fin du Moyen Age. In: Religion civique à l'époque médiévale et moderne (La) [Cf. n° 4528], p. 187-200.

13. KIRCHENGESCHICHTE

4488. BRANCA (Vittore). Ripiegamenti spirituali di mercanti fra Medioevo e Rinascimento. In: Spiritualità e lettere nella cultura italiana e ungherese del basso medioevo [Cf. n° 4128], p. 163-177.

4489. BRENON (Anne). Les hérésies de l'an Mil: nouvelles perspectives sur les origines du catharisme. Heresis, 95, 24, p. 21-36.

4490. BROWN (Andrew D.). Popular piety in late Medieval England. The Diocese of Salisbury, 1250–1550. Oxford, Clarendon Press, 95, X-297 p. (Oxford Historical Monographs).

4491. BYLINA (Stanisław). La religion civique et la religion populaire en Pologne au bas Moyen Age. In: Religion civique à l'époque médiévale et moderne (La) [Cf. n° 4528], p. 323-335.

4492. CASAGRANDE (Giovanna). Religiosità penitenziale e città al tempo dei Comuni. Roma, Istituto storico dei cappuccini, 95, 511 p. (Bibliotheca seraphicocapucina, 48).

4493. Clergé rural (Le) dans l'Europe médiévale et moderne. Ed. par Pierre BONNASSIE. Toulouse, Presses Universitaires du Mirail, 95, 291 p.

4494. CLUSE (Chr.). Stories of breaking and taking the cross. A possible context for the Oxford incident of 1268. Revue d'Histoire Ecclésiastique, 95, 90, 3-4, p. 396-442.

4495. COOPE (Jessica). The martyrs of Córdoba. Community and family conflict in an age of mass conversion. Lincoln a. London, University of Nebraska Press, 95, XIX-113.

4496. DE SANDRE GASPARINI (Giuseppina). L'amministrazione pubblica dell'evento religioso: qualche esempio della Terraferma veneta nel secolo XV. In: Religion civique à l'époque médiévale et moderne (La) [Cf. n° 4528], p. 201-217.

4497. DOBOSZ (Józef). Działalność fundacyjna Kazimierza Sprawiedliwego. (Activité de fondation de Casimir le Juste). Poznań, 95, 252 p. (Eng. Summary, cartes). (Publikacje Inst. Historii Uniw. im. A. Mickiewicza w Poznaniu, 2).

4498. DOMAŃSKI (Juliusz). La tolleranza religiosa e la guerre giusta negli scritti di Stanislas di Scarbimiria e di Paolo Vladimiri. Odrodzenie i Reformacja w Polsce, 95, 39, p. 19-30.

4499. EDDEN (Valerie). Marian devotion in a Carmelite sermon collection of the late Middle Ages. Mediaeval Studies, 95, 57, p. 101-130.

4500. ERLER (Mary C.). English vowed women at the end of the Midlle Ages. Mediaeval Studies, 95, 57, p. 155-204.

4501. FLORI (Jean). Faut-il réhabiliter Pierre L'Ermite? (Une réévalutation des sources de la première croisade). Cahiers de civilisation médiévale, 95, 38, p. 35-54.

4502. FORSTNER (Karl). Quellenkundliche Beobachtungen an den ältesten Salzburger Güterverzeichnissen und an der Vita s. Ruperti. Mitt. d. Ges. f. Salzburg. Landeskde., 95, 135, p. 465-488.

4503. FRANKLIN (Michael J.). Bodies in medieval Northampton. Legatine intervention in the twelfth century. In: Medieval ecclesiastical studies [Cf. n° 4410], p. 57-81.

4504. Geschichte der christlichen Spiritualität. 2. Hochmittelalter und Reformation. Hrsg. v. Jill RAITH. Würzburg, Echter, 95, 488 p.

4505. GRIBBIN (Joseph A.). Aspects of Carthusian liturgical practice in later medieval England. Salzburg, Universität Salzburg, Institut für Anglistik und Amerikanistik, 95, IX-86 p. (Analecta Cartusiana, 99, 33).

4506. HARPER-BILL (Christopher). John of Oxford, diplomat and bishop. In: Medieval ecclesiastical studies [Cf. n° 4410], p. 83-105.

4507. KEMP (Brian). Informing the Archdeacon on ecclesiastical matters in twelfth-century England. In: Medieval ecclesiastical studies [Cf. n° 4410], p. 131-149.

4508. KRZYŻANIAKOWA (Jadwiga). Henryk Totting z Oyty i jego prascy uczniowie. (Henryk Totting d'Oyta et ses disciples de Prague [IIe moitié du XIVe siècle]). Roczniki Historyczne, 95, 61, p. 87-109. [Deutsche Zsfassung].

4509. Księga Jadwiżańska, Międzynarodowe sympozjum naukowe. "Święta Jadwiga w dziejach i kulturze Śląska", Wrocław-Trzebnica, 21–23 września 1993 roku. (Livre d'Hédvige, Symposium scientifique internationale „Sainte Hédvige dans l'histoire et culture de la Silésie", Wrocław-Trzebnica, les 21–23 septembre 1993). Wrocław, 95, 494 p. (Deutsche Zsfassung). (Acta Univ. Wratislaviensis, 1720).

4510. KULCSAR (Péter). L'unione contro i Turchi e l'unità religiosa nell'Ungheria quattrocentesca. In: Spiritualità e lettere nella cultura italiana e ungherese del basso medioevo [Cf. n° 4128], p. 319-328.

4511. LEPINE (David). A brotherhood of canons serving god. English secular cathedrals in the later Middle Ages. Woodbridge a. Rochester, Boydell and Brewer, 95, XII-240 p. (Studies in history of medieval religion, 8).

4512. LEWIS (Andrew W.). Toward the identification of Fulcher (ob. 1171), Abbot of Pontlevoy and of Saint-Père at Chartres. Revue bénédictine, 95, 105, 415-432.

4513. LUTTERBACH (H.). Intentions- oder Tathaftung? Zum Bußverständnis in den frühmittelalterlichen Bußbüchern. Frühmittelalterliche Studien, 95, 29, p. 120-143.

4514. MARSDEN (Richard). The text of the Old Testament in Anglo-Saxon England. Cambridge, Cambridge U. P., 95, XIX-506 p. (Cambridge studies in Anglo-Saxon England, 15).

4515. MARTIN (Jean-Marie). Le rôle de l'Eglise de Naples dans le Midi. A propos de deux assemblées ecclésiastiques du IX siècle et de leurs actes. In: Particularisme napolitain au haut Moyen Age (Le) [Cf. n° 3422], p. 39-64.

4516. MESTRE GODES (Jesús). Los cátaros. Barcelona, Península Ediciones, 95, 268 p. (Historia, Ciencia, Sociedad, 241).

4517. MONTESANO (Marina). Aspetti e conseguenze della predicazione civica di Bernardino da Siena. In: Religion civique à l'époque médiévale et moderne (La) [Cf. n° 4528], p. 265-275.

4518. MOORHEAD (J.). Gregory of Tours on the Arian kingdoms. Studi Medievali, 95, 36, 2, p. 903-916.

4519. MOREROD (J.-D.). Influences extérieures et innovation dans l'Eglise de Lausanne. Le rôle d'un évêque «étranger», Roger de Vico Pisano (1178–1212), et de son entourage. Studi Medievali, 95, 36, 1, p. 151-168.

4520. MUÑOZ FERNÁNDEZ (Ángela). Acciones e intenciones de mujeres en la vida religiosa de los siglos XV y XVI. Madrid, horas y Horas, 95, 222 p. (ill.).

4521. MURDOCH (B.). Various Gospels. The «Sermone» of Pietro da Barsegapè, the middle high German «Erlösung» and the «Pascon agan Arluth». Studi Medievali, 95, 36, 2, p. 777-796.

4522. PACIOCCO (R.). The Franciscus and female saintliness, the case of Chiara of Montefalco between 1290 and 1331. Cristianesimo nella storia, 95, 16, 3, p. 485-520.

4523. PADBERG (Lutz E. von). Mission und Christianisierung. Formen und Folgen bei Angelsachsen und Franken im 7. und 8. Jahrhundert. Stuttgart, Steiner, 95, 419 p.

4524. Parrocchia nel medio evo (La). Economia, scambi, solidarietà. A cura di Agostino PARAVICINI BAGLIANI e Véronique PASCHE. Roma, Herder, 95, 325 p. (Italia sacra. Studi e documenti di storia ecclesiastica, 53).

4525. Peregrinationes. Pielgrzymki w kulturze dawnej Europy. (Pélerinages dans la culture de l'ancienne Europe). Réd. par Halina MANIKOWSKA et Hanna ZAREMSKA. Warszawa, 95, 349 p. (phot., fig., dessins carte). (Inst. Hist Pol. Akad. Nauk, Colloquia Medievalia Varsoviensia, 2).

4526. PIXTON (Paul B.). The German Episcopacy and the implementation of the decrees of the Fourth Lateran Council, 1216–1245: watchmen on the tower. Leiden, New York a. Köln, E. J. Brill, 95, XV-543 p. (Studies in the history of christian thought, 64).

4527. RADZIMIŃSKI (Andrzej). Duchowieństwo kapituł katedralnych w Polsce XIV i XV w. na tle porównawczym. Studium nad rekrutacją i drogami awansu. (Les ecclésiastiques des chapitres des cathédrales en Pologne aux XIV et XVème siècles du point de vue comparatif).Toruń, [s. n.], 95, 312 p. (Deutsche Zsfassung). (Uniw. Mikołaja Kopernika, Rozpr.).

4528. Religion civique à l'époque médiévale et moderne (La) (Chrétienté et Islam). Actes du colloque organisé par le Centre de recherche «Histoire sociale et culturelle de l'Occident. XIIe–XVIIIe siècles» de l'Université de Paris X-Nanterre et l'Institut Universitaire de France (Nanterre, 21–23 juin 1993). Ed. par André VAUCHEZ. Roma, Ecole française de Rome, 95, 571 p. (Collection de l'Ecole française de Rome, 213). [Cf. n^{os} <sélection> 3439, 3456, 3769, 3888, 3976, 4148, 4236, 4431, 4460, 4462, 4475, 4487, 4491, 4496, 4517, 5758, 6849.]

4529. REYNOLDS (Roger E.). The organisation, law and liturgy of the Western church, 700–900. In: New Cambridge medieval history [Cf. n° 3378], p. 587-621.

4530. SCHMUGGE (Ludwig). Kirche, Kinder, Karrieren. Päpstliche Dispense von der unehelichen Geburt im Spätmittelalter. Zürich, Artemis & Winkler, 95, 511 p.

4531. SIMONETTI (Adele). I Sermoni di Umiltà da Faenza. Studio e edizione. Spoleto, Centro Italiano di Studi sull'Alto Medioevo, 95, XCIV-194 p. (Biblioteca di Medioevo Latino, 14).

4532. STAITI (C.). Agli inizi della produzione catechetica in volgare tedesco. L'«ordo» per la confessione dei peccati del codice Pal. lat. 485. Studi Medievali, 95, 36, 2, p. 657-720.

4533. STOREY (Robin Linsday). Malicious indictments of Clergy in the fifteenth century. In: Medieval ecclesiastical studies [Cf. n° 4410], p. 221-240.

4534. SWANSON (R. N.). Parochialism and particularism. The dispute over the status of Dichford Frary, Warwickshire, in the early fifteenth century. In: Medieval ecclesiastical studies [Cf. n° 4410], p. 241-257. – IDEM. Religion and devotion in Europe, c. 1215–c. 1515. Cambridge, Cambridge U. P., 95, XV-377 p. (Cambridge medieval textbooks).

4535. SZÉKELY (György). Efforts vers une réforme religieuse en Hongrie et ses racines italiennes. In: Spiritualità e lettere nella cultura italiana e ungherese del basso medioevo [Cf. n° 4128], p. 329-341.

4536. SZYMAŃSKI (Józef). Kanonikat świecki w Małopolsce od końca XI do połowy XIII wieku. (Canonicat laïque en Małopolska de la fin du XIe s jusqu'à la moitié du XIIIe s.). Lublin, Agencja Wydawn. – Handlowa AD, 95, 143 p. [Rés. franç.]

4537. TELESKO (Werner). Zum antihäretischen Bildprogramm der Apsisreliefs von Schöngrabern. Unserer Heimat, 95, 66, 1, p. 15-22 (ill.).

4538. TREXLER (R. C.). Francis of Assisi, his mother's son ... Studi Medievali, 95, 36, 1, p. 363-374.

4539. VALERIO (A.). Domenica da paradiso e la mistica femminile dopo Savonarola. Studi Medievali, 95, 36, 1, p. 345-354.

§ 14. Siedlungsgeschichte, Ortsnamenforschung und Städtebaukunst.

4540. Actes du 118ᵉ Congrès national des Sociétés savantes, Pau, 25–29 octobre 1993. Section Histoire médiévale et philologie. Population et démographie au Moyen Age. Paris, Ed. du CTHS, 95, 350 p. [Cf. nᵒˢ <sélection> 412, 3693, 3724, 3767, 3777, 3820, 4206, 4550, 4553, 4554, 4557, 4558.]

4541. AILLOT (Michelle). L'habitat du haut Moyen Age en Picardie: état de la question. *In:* Sources de la gestion publique (Aux). Tome 2 [Cf. n° 4574], p. 269-293.

4542. ALCOCK (Leslie), STEVENSON (S. J.), MUSSON (C. R.). Cadbury Castle, Somerset. The early medieval archaeology. Cardiff, University of Wales Press, 95, X-188 p.

4543. ALEKSEEV (L. V.). Mstislavl'skij detinec v XII–XIV vekakh. (Mstislavl's fortress in the XIIᵗʰ–XIVᵗʰ centuries). *Ros. arkheol.*, 95, 3, p. 60-76.

4544. BOCCHI (Francesca). Bologna. 2. Il Duecento. Bologna, Grafis Edizioni, 95, 216 p. (ill.). (Atlante storico delle città italiane. Emilia-Romagna).

4545. BRUNTERC'H (Jean-Pierre). Le manse et la dîme en Limousin à la fin du IXᵉ siècle. *In:* Sources de la gestion publique (Aux). Tome 2 [Cf. n° 4574], p. 261-265.

4546. Burg und Schloß als Lebensorte in Mittelalter und Renaissance. Hrsg. v. Wilhelm G. BUSSE. Düsseldorf, Droste, 95, 262 p. (Studia humaniora, 26).

4547. CABERO DOMÍNGUEZ (C.). Astorga y su territorio en la Edad Media. León, Universidad de León, 95, 301 p.

4548. CASTRILLO LLAMAS (M. Concepción). Fortificaciones elementos defensivos y organización militar en los fueros castellanos y leoneses de la Edad Media. *Anuario de estudios medievales*, 95, 25, 1, p. 39-66.

4549. CASTRITIUS (H). Barbari – antiqui barbari. Zur Besiedlungsgeschichte Südostnorikums und Südpannoniens in der Spätantike (Ende des 4. bis Mitte des 6. Jahrhunderts n. Chr.). *Frühmittelalterliche Studien*, 95, 29, p. 72-85.

4550. CLAVAUD (Florence). Evolution et structures de la population à Cajarc [Lot], consulat du Haut-Quercy, au XIVᵉ siècle: un exemple du cas des petites villes. *In:* Actes du 118ᵉ Congrès national des Sociétés savantes [Cf. n° 4540], p. 51-83.

4551. CROUZET-PAVAN (Elisabeth). La mort lente de Torcello. Histoire d'une cité disparue. Paris, Fayard, 95 432 p. (maps).

4552. DARKEVIČ (V. P.), BORISEVIČ (G. V.). Drevnjaja stolica Rjazanskoj zemli, XI–XIII veka. (The ancient capital of the Ryazan'land, the XIᵗʰ–XIIIᵗʰ centuries). Moskva: Krug', 95, 448 p.

4553. DOUMERC (Bernard). L'emigration française à Raguse (Dubrovnik) au XVᵉ siècle. *In:* Actes du 118ᵉ Congrès national des Sociétés savantes [Cf. n° 4540], p. 297-304.

4554. FOSSIER (Robert). Aperçus sur la démographie médiévale. *In:* Actes du 118ᵉ Congrès national des Sociétés savantes [Cf. n° 4540], p. 9-23.

4555. Freiburg 1091–1120. Neue Forschungen zu den Anfängen der Stadt. Hrsg. v. Hans SCHADECK u. Thomas ZOTZ. Sigmaringen, Thorbecke, 95, 276 p. (ill., Karten, Bibl.). (Archäologie und Geschichte, 7).

4556. GARCIA BIOSCA (J. E.). Els orígens del terme de Lleida. La formació d'un territori urbà (segles XI–XII). Anjuntament d'Alguaire, Patronat Municipal "Josep Lladonosa i Pujol"-La Mañana, 95, 221 p.

4557. GERMAIN (René). Les migrations comme facteur d'équilibre démographique (Bourbonnais, XIVᵉ–XVᵉ siècles). *In:* Actes du 118ᵉ Congrès national des Sociétés savantes [Cf. n° 4540], p. 251-266.

4558. GOURDIN (Pierre). Le terrier de l'aumônerie de Saumur [Maine-et-Loire] 1452. *In:* Actes du 118ᵉ Congrès national des Sociétés savantes [Cf. n° 4540], p. 201-217.

4559. GUINOT RODRÍGUEZ (Enric). Els límits del regne. El procés de formació territorial del País Valencià medieval (1238–1500). València, Edicions Alfons el Magnànim, Institució Valenciana d'Estudis i Investigació, Generalitat Valenciana, Diputació Provincial de València, 95, 163 p. (Col·lecció Politècnica, 58).

4560. HILTON (R. H.). English and French towns in feudal society. A comparative study. Cambridge, Cambridge U. P., 95, XI-171 p. (Past and present publications).

4561. IOGNA-PRAT (Dominique). Cluny à la mort de Maïeul (994–998). *Bulletin de la Société des fouilles archéologiques et des monuments historiques de l'Yonne*, 95, 12, p. 13-23.

4562. JANIN (Valentin L.), BASSALYGO (Leonid A.). Velikolukskaja zemlja v XV veke: territorija i granicy. (The Velikie Luki land in the XVᵗʰ century: territory and borders). *Oteč. Ist.*, 95, 6, p. 45-58.

4563. LORANS (Elisabeth). La 'villa' de Courcay [Indre-et-Loire] en Touraine: approche historique et archéologique. *In:* Sources de la gestion publique (Aux). Tome 2 [Cf. n° 4574], p. 295-312.

4564. LOUIS (E.). Fouilles archéologiques sur le site du monastère mérovingien puis carolingien de Hamage (France, dép. Du Nord). *Handelingen der Maatschappij voor geschiedenis en oudheidkunde te Gent*, 95, 49, p. 45-70.

4565. MACHAČEK (Jiří). Das Brandgräberfeld von Břeclav-Pohansko. Bemerkungen zur slawischen Ethnogenese in Mitteleuropa. *Archaeologia Austriaca*. 95, 78, p. 219-231.

4566. MACIAS (Santiago A. F.). O Bairro de Alcácova de Mértola: imagens de um conjunto urbano nos finais do período islâmico. Lisboa, [s. n.], 95, 2 vol., 739 p. (ill., bibl.).

4567. MAIRE VIGUEUR (Jean-Claude). L'essor urbain dans l'Italie médiévale: aspects et modalités de la croissance. *In*: Europa en los umbrales [Cf. n° 3357], p. 171-204.

4568. MANTINI (Silvia). Lo spazio sacro della Firenze Medicea. Trasformazioni urbane e cerimoniali pubblici tra Quattrocento e Cinquecento. Prefazione di Guido CLEMENTE. Firenze, Loggia de' Lanzi, 95, 293 p.

4569. PERTICI (Petra). La città magnificata. Interventi edilizi a Siena nel Rinascimento. L'Ufficio dell'Ornato (1428–1480). Con fotografie di Gigi LUSINI. Siena, Il Leccio, 95, XIII-189 p. (Sena Vetus. Argomenti Senesi, 5).

4570. RACINET (Philippe). Une 'villa', un château, un prieuré: le site de Nottonville (Clustines, Eure-et-Loir). *In*: Sources de la gestion publique (Aux). Tome 2 [Cf. n° 4574], p. 313-343.

4571. REGLERO DE LA FUENTE (Carlos). El poblamiento del noreste de la cuenca del duero en el siglo XV. *Hispania*, 95, 55, 190, p. 425-493.

4572. ROMANINI (Angiola Maria). Una città in forma di palazzo. Potere signorile e forma urbana nella Mantova medievale e moderna. Mantova e Brescia, Centro di ricerche storiche e sociali F. Odorici, 95, XVII-211 p. (Quaderni di Cheiron, 1).

4573. RUBIO VELA (Agustin). La población de Valencia en la baja edad media. *Hispania*, 95, 55, 190, p. 495-525.

4574. Sources de la gestion publique (Aux). Tome 2. L'invasio des villae ou la villa comme enjeu de pouvoir. 2ᵉ journée d'étude, Lille. Textes réunis par Elisabeth MAGNOU-NORTIER. Lille, Presses Universitaires de Lille, 95, 350 p. (Publications du Centre de recherche sur l'Antiquité et le haut moyen âge, IVᵉ–XIIᵉ s. Coll. UL3. Travaux et recherches). [Cf. nᵒˢ <sélection> 338, 3123, 3638, 3649, 3654, 3674, 3684, 4541, 4545, 4563, 4570.]

4575. TAYLOR (Pamela). Boundaries and margins. Barnet, Finchley and Totteridge. *In*: Medieval ecclesiastical studies [Cf. n° 4410], p. 259-279.

4576. VERHULST (Adriaan). Landschap en Landbouw in Middeleeuws Vlaanderen. Bruxelles, Crédit communal, 95, 191 p. (ill.). – IDEM. Le paysage rural: les structures parcellaires de l'Europe du Nord-Ouest. Turnhout, Brepols, 95, 82 p. (ill.). (Typologie des sources du Moyen Age occidental, 73).

4577. WALLERSTRÖM (Thomas). Norrbotten, Sverige och medeltiden: problem kring makt och bosättning i en europeiskt perspektiv. Part 1. Part 2: supplement. (Norrbotten, Sweden and the middle ages: problems concerning power and settlement on a European periphery). Stockholm, Almqvist & Wiksell International, 95, 381 p., 4 microfiche. (Lund studies in mediaeval archaeology, 15).

4578. WHARTON (Annabel Jane). Refiguring the post classical city. Dura Europos, Jerash, Jerusalem and Ravenna. Cambridge, Cambridge U. P., 95, XVIII-238 p.

4579. ZADORA-RIO (Elisabeth). Le village des historiens et le village des archéologues. *In*: Campagnes médiévales [Cf. n° 3713], p. 145-156

K

NEUZEIT, ALLGEMEINE WERKE

§ 1. Allgemeines. 4580-4665. – § 2. Einzelne Staaten. 4666-5620. – § 3. Erdentdeckung. 5621-5632.

§ 1. Allgemeines.

* 4580. Bibliographie zur Zeitgeschichte. Zusammengestellt von Christoph WIESZ u. Ingeborg ÜNAL. Jahrgang 43, 1995 [42, 1994. Cf. Bibl. 94, n° 4071.]. München, Oldenbourg, 144 p.

* 4581. CONLON (Pierre M.). Le siècle des lumières: bibliographie chronologique. Tome 15. 1767–1769. Geneve, Droz, 95, XXXI-512 p. (Histoire des idées et critique littéraire, 346).

** 4582. Dreissigjähriger Krieg und Zeitalter Ludwigs XIV. (1618–1715). Bearbeitet von Winfried BECKER. Darmstadt, Wissenschaftliche Buchgesellschaft, 95, X-187 p. (Quellenkunde zur deutschen Geschichte der Neuzeit von 1500 bis zur Gegenwart, 2).

** 4583. Fonti diplomatiche in età moderna e contemporanea (Le). Roma, Ministero per i Beni Culturali e Ambientali, Ufficio Centrale per i beni archivistici, 95, 635 p. (Pubblicazioni degli Archivi di Stato, 33).

4584. 20. [Huszadik] századi egyetemes történet. I. 1890–1945. (Histoire générale du XXe siècle. I. 1890–1945). Szerk. DIÓSZEGI István. Budapest, Korona, 95, 588 p.

4585. AGOSTON (Gábor). Az európai hadügyi forradalom és az oszmánok. (La révolution militaire en Europe et les Ottomans). *Tört. szle.*, 95, 37, 4, p. 465-485.

4586. Vacat.

4587. Aufgabe der Freiheit (Von der). Politische Verantwortung und bürgerliche Gesellschaft im 19. und 20. Jahrhundert. Festschrift für Hans Mommsen zum 5. 11. 95. Hrsg. v. Christian JANSEN, Lutz NIETHAMMER u. B. WEISBROD. Berlin, Akademie Verlag, 95, 758 p. [Cf. n° <Auswahl> 4884.]

4588. Balkany: meždu prošlym i buduščim. (The Balkan countries: between the past and future, the XXth century). RAN. In-t meždunarodnykh ékonomičeskikh i političeskikh issledovanij; Redkol.: A. A. JAZ'KOVA i drugie. Moskva: Aprel'- 85, 95, 222 p.

4589. BANTI (Alberto Mario). Nazione e cittadinanza in Francia e Germania. *Storica*, 95, 1, 1, p. 141-164.

4590. BARDACH (Juliusz). De la nation politique à la nation ethnique dans le Centre-Est de l'Europe. *Acta Poloniae historica*, 95, 71, p. 17-35.

4591. BELCHEM (John). Nationalism, republicanism and exile: Irish emigrants and the revolutions of 1848. *Past and Present*, 95, 146, p. 103-135.

4592. BERG (Roald). Nation-building, state structure and ethnic groups: the Scandinavian Sámis 1905–1919. *Scandinavian Journal of History*, 95, 20, p. 61-70.

4593. BEVIR (Mark). British socialism and American romanticism. *English Historical Review*, 95, 110, 438, p. 878-901.

4594. BOLKHOVITINOV (Nikolaj N.). Otliki v SŠA na otmenu krepostnogo prava v Rossii. (The reaction of the USA to the abolition of the serfdom in Russia). *Vopr. Ist.*, 95, 8, p. 126-132.

4595. BORA (Siren). Birinci Dünya Savaşı ve Yahudiler (1914–1918). [La Première Guerre Mondiale et les Juifs (1914–1919)]. *Çağdaş Türkiye Tarihi Araştırmaları Dergisi*, 95, 2, 4-5, p. 19-27.

4596. CANNISTRARO (Philip V.). Per una storia dei Fasci negli Stati Uniti (1921–1929). *Storia contemporanea*, 95, 26, 6, p. 1061-1144.

4597. CARLEY (Michael Jabara). Generals, statesmen, and international politics in Europe, 1898–1945. *Canadian Journal of History*, 95, 30, 2, p. 289-322.

4598. CARMILLY-WEINBERGER (Moshe). A zsidóság története Erdélyben, 1623–1944. (Histoire des Juifs en Transylvanie, 1623–1944). Szerk. KOMOROCZY Géza. Budapest, MTA Judaisztikai Kutatócsoport, 95, 389 p.

4599. CHABOD (Federico). Idea di Europa e politica dell'equilibrio. A cura di Luisa AZZOLINI. Bologna, Il

Mulino, 95, LIX-292 p. (Istituto italiano per gli studi storici. Testi storici, filosofici e letterari, 4).

4600. CHAUNU (Pierre). Nous et les leçons de l'Histoire. *In*: Enjeux de la paix (Les) [Cf. n° 4605], p. 1-37.

4601. Citizenship identity and social history. Ed. by Ch. TILLY. *International review of social history*, 95, 40, Supplement 3, [s. p.].

4602. Crimini nazisti (I), la memoria, l'Europa di oggi. [Interventi di Gabriele RANZATO, Charles MAIER e Stuart WOOLF]. *Passato e presente*, 95, 13, 34, p. 15-38.

4603. CSAPODI (Zoltán). Thököly-felkelés visszhangja a Német-római Birodalom területén. (Les échos du soulèvement de Thököly [Imre, 1657–1705, prince de Haute-Hongrie] sur le territoire de l'empire germanique). *Aetas*, 95, 1-2, p. 140-170.

4604. EL MALKI (M'hamed). Les mouvements nationaux maghrébins et leur projet pour l'établissement de l'Etat moderne (1950–1962). *Revue d'Histoire Maghrébine* (Partie arabe), 95, 77-78, p. 229-256.

4605. Enjeux de la paix (Les). Nous et les autres XVIIIe–XXIe siècle. Ed. par Pierre CHAUNU. Paris, PUF, 95, 355 p. [Cf. n° <sélection> 4600.]

4606. Europa im Blick der Historiker. Europäische Integration im 20. Jh. Bewußtsein und Institutionen. Hrsg. v. Rainer HUDEMANN, Hartmut KAELBLE u. Klaus SCHWABE. München, Oldenbourg, 95, VIII-273 p. (Historische Zs. Beih, 21).

4607. Europa im Umbruch 1750–1850. Hrsg. v. Dieter ALBRECHT, Karl O. Frhr. von ARETIN u. Winfried SCHULZE. München, Oldenbourg, 95, X-422 p.

4608. European nobilities in the seventeenth and eighteenth centuries (The). Vol. 1. Western Europe. Vol. 2. Northern Central and Eastern Europe. Ed. by H. M. SCOTT. London a. New York, Longman, 95, 2 vol., VIII-286 p., 315 p. ·

4609. FIMIANI (Enzo). Per una storia delle teorie e pratiche plebiscitarie nell'Europa moderna e contemporanea. *Annali dell'Istituto storico italo-germanico di Trento*, 95, 21, p. 267-333.

4610. GENTILE (Emilio). Un'apocalisse nella modernità. La Grande Guerra e il mito della rigenerazione della politica. *Storia contemporanea*, 95, 26, 5, p. 733-788.

4611. GEYER (Michael), BRIGHT (Charles). World history in a global age. *American Historical Review*, 95, 100, 4, p. 1034-1060.

4612. GOSEWINKEL (Dieter). Staatsbürgerschaft und Staatsangehörigkeit. *Geschichte und Gesellschaft*, 95, 21, 4, p. 533-556.

4613. GUIOMAR (Jean-Yves). De l'Allemagne et de la France. Les faux-semblants d'une opposition. *Débat*, 95, 84, p. 70-88.

4614. HARDEN (David J.). Liberty caps and liberty trees. *Past and Present*, 95, 146, p. 66-102.

4615. HENNESSY (Peter). Searching for the 'Great Ghost': the palace, the premiership, the cabinet and the constitution in the Post-War period. *Journal of Contemporary History*, 95, 30, 2, p. 211-232.

4616. HESSE (Joachim Jens), JOHNSON (Nevil). Constitutional policy and change in Europe. Oxford, Oxford U. P., 95, 403 p.

4617. HIPPEL (Wolfgang von). Armut, Unterschichten, Randgruppen in der frühen Neuzeit. München, Oldenbourg, 95, 161 p. (Enzyklopädie deutscher Geschichte, 34).

4618. HOBSBAWM (Eric). Nationalism and nationality in Latin America. *In*: Pour une histoire économique et sociale internationale [Cf. n° 1297], p. 313-324.

4619. JARA (Álvaro). La nueva sociedad colonial americana: un panorama trisecular. *Revista Chilena de Historia y Geografía*, 94-95, 161, p. 73-98.

4620. JONES (Adrian). After empire: the contemporary modern-mediaeval revolutions of Europe's East. *Australian Journal of Politics and History*, 95, 41, 1, p. 70-89.

4621. KASCHUBA (Wolfgang). Kulturalismus: Kultur statt Gesellschaft? *Geschichte und Gesellschaft*, 95, 21, 1, p. 80-95.

4622. KAŠUBA (Margarita S.), MARTYNOVA (Marina Ju.). Novaja étnopolitičeskaja karta Balkan. (A new ethnopolitical map of the Balkan countries, 1990's). Moskva, RAN. In-t étnologii i antropologii im. N. N. Miklukho-Maklaja, 95, 163 p.

4623. KENDE (Tamás). Vérvád. Egy előítélet működése az újkori Közép- és Kelet-Európában. (Accusation du sang. Le mécanisme d'un préjugée en Europe Centrale et Orientale aux temps contemporains). Budapest, Századvég, 95, 183 p.

4624. Konflikt und Reform. Festschrift für Helmut Berding. Hrsg. u. W. STEITKAMP u. H.-P. ULMANN. Göttingen, Vandenhoeck u. Ruprecht, 95, 342 p. [Cf. n° <Auswahl> 772]

4625. LA FEBER (Walter). The world and the United States. *American Historical Review*, 95, 100, 4, p. 1015-1033.

4626. LANGEWIESCHE (Dieter). Nation, Nationalismus, Nationalstaat. Forschungsstand und Forschungsperspektiven. *Neue Politische Literatur*, 95, 40, 2, p. 190-236.

4627. LIEVEN (Dominic). The Russian empire and the Soviet Union as imperial polities. *Journal of Contemporary History*, 95, 30, 4, p. 607-636.

4628. MAC INTYRE (Arnold Meredith). Trade and economic development in small open economies: the case of the Caribbean countries. Westport, Praeger, 95, 185 p. (graph.).

4629. MAFRICI (Mirella). Mezzogiorno e pirateria nell'età moderna: secoli XVI–XVIII. Napoli, ESI, 95, 349 p. (Pubblicazioni dell'Università degli studi di Salerno. Sezione di studi storici, 7).

4630. MAIER (Charles S.). After communism: rethinking the histories of the postwar epoch. *Australian Journal of Politics and History*, 95, 41, 1, p. 1-13.

4631. MAIER (Hans). "Totalitarismus" und "politische Religionen". Konzepte des Diktaturvergleichs. *Vierteljahrshefte für Zeitgeschichte*, 95, 95, 43, 3, p. 387-406.

4632. MARRUS (Michael R.). Jewish resistance to the Holocaust. *Journal of Contemporary History*, 95, 30, 1, p. 83-110.

4633. MÜLLER (Rainer A.). Der Fürstenhof in der frühen Neuzeit. München, Oldenbourg, 95, 131 p. (Enzyklopädie deutscher Geschichte 33).

4634. MUSILOVÁ (Dana). Životní příběhy ročníku 1924. Lidský osud v dějinách 20. století. (The life stories of some people born in 1924. Human destiny in the history of the 20th century). Tomo 1. Historicko-biografický výzkum. Praha, Ústav pro soudobé dějiny AV ČR, 95, 95 p. (Studijní materiály výzkumného projektu Československo 1945–1967, 1).

4635. Nacional'nyj vopros v Vostočnoj Evrope: Prošloe i nastojaščee. (The national problem in the Eastern Europe: the background and contemporary state, XIXth–XXth century). Redkol : R. P. GRIŠINA, M. D. EREŠČENKO (otv. red.), Moskva, RAN. In-t slavjanovedenija i balkanistiki. Naučnyj centr obščeslavjanskikh issledovanij, 95, 298 p.

4636. Nation und Emotion. Deutschland und Frankreich im Vergleich. 19. und 20. Jahrhundert. Hrsg. v. Etienne FRANÇOIS. Göttingen, Vandenhoeck & Ruprecht, 95, 408 p. (Kritische Studien zur Geschichtswissenschaft, 110).

4637. NEDREBØ (Tore). Den tyske utfordringa. Tyskland, Noreg og det nye Europa. (The German challenge. Germany, Norway and the "new" Europe). Oslo, Samlaget, 95, 263 p. (ill.).

4638. NIKLÍČEK (Ladislav). Českoslovenští komunisté mezi Kominternou a středoevropskou demokracií. (Czechoslovak Communists between the Comintern and Central European Democracy). *Soudobé dějiny*, 95, 2, 2-3, p. 237-253.

4639. NOIRIEL (Gérard). Socio-histoire d'un concept. Les usages du mot «nationalité» au XIXe siècle. *Genèses*, 95, 20, p. 4-23.

4640. NOVOPAŠIN (Jurij S.). Vostočnaja Evropa posle 80-kh: Tendecii i problemy. (The Eastern Europe after 1980's. Tendency and problems). *Vopr. Ist.*, 95, 4, p. 129-136.

4641. OSTAPENKO (Galina S.). Britanskie konservatory i dekolonizacija. (The British conservatories and decolonization). Moskva, RAN. In-t vseobščej istorii, 95, 173 p.

4642. PAGEL (Jgen). Souveränität oder Bevormundung? Die Baltischen Staaten zwischen Deutschland, Polen und der Sowjetunion 1933–34. *Vierteljahrshefte für Zeitgeschichte*, 95, 95, 43, 1, p. 37-74.

4643. PÓCZIK (Szilveszter). Fasizmusértelmezések. (Interprétations du fascisme). Budapest, Biadrukt, 95, 262 p.

4644. Pride and prejudice. National stereotypes in XIXth and XXth century Europe East to West. Ed. by László KONTLER. Budapest, Central Europ. Univ., 95, 211 p.

4645. Problemy social'noj istorii Evropy: ot antičnosti do novogo vremeni: Sbornik statej. (The problems of the European social history: from the Antiquity to the modern time. Collected studies). Redkol. : A. M. DUBROVSKIJ i drugie. Brjansk, Brjanskij gosudarstvennyj pedagogičeskij universitet imeni akademika I. G. Petrovskogo, 95, 185 p.

4646. Revolusjon og resonnement: festskrift til Kåre Tönnesson på 70-årsdagen den 1. januari 1996. Ed. by Øystein RIAN [et al.]. Oslo, Universitetsforlaget, 95, 335 p.

4647. Ricerche di storia moderna. 1. In onore di Mario Mirri. A cura di Giuliana BIAGIOLI. Pisa, Pacini, 95, 415 p. (Pubblicazioni dell'Istituto di storia, Facoltà di lettere dell'Università di Pisa). [Cf. n° <scelta> 5036.]

4648. Rossija i Evropa: Diplomatija i kul'tura. Sbornik statej. (Russia and Europe: Diplomacy and culture). Redkol.: A. S. NAMAZOVA (otv. red.) i drugie. Moskva, Nauka, RAN, In-t vseobščej istorii, 95, 223 p.

4649. RYCROFT (Simon), COSGROVE (Denis). Mapping the modern nation. *History Workshop*, 95, 40, p. 91-105.

4650. SCHMIDT-NOWARA (Christopher Ebert). The problem of slavery in the Age of Capital: Abolitionism, Liberalism, and Counter-Hegemony in Spain, Cuba and Puerto Rico, 1833–1886. [s. l., s. e.], 95, VI-471 p.

4651. Severnaja Evropa: Problemy istorii. Sbornik naučnykh trudov. (The Northern Europe: Issues of history. Collection of research papers). In-t vseobščej istorii, centr istorii i kul'tury Severnoj Evropy; Meždunarodnyj redakcionnyj sovet: A. O. ČUBAR'JAN i drugie; Redkol. : O. V. ČERNYŠEVA (otv. red.) i drugie. Moskva, Progress-Akademija, RAN, 95, 381 p.

4652. ŠIRINJA (Kirill K.). Ideja mirivoj revoljucii v strategii Kominterna. (The idea of the world revolution in Comintern's strategy). *Nov. novejš. Ist.*, 95, 5, p. 46-61.

4653. Sōryoku-Sen to Gendaika. (Total war and modernization). Ed. by Yasushi YAMANOUCHI. Tokyo, Kashiwa-Shobō, 95, 344 p.

4654. Sovětizace východní Evropy. Země střední a jihovýchodní Evropy v letech 1944–1948. (The Sovietization of Eastern Europe. The countries of central and south-east Europe, 1944–1948). Praha, Historický ústav AV ČR, 95, 283 p. (Práce Historického ústavu AV ČR, C/12)

4655. Spain, Europe and the Atlantic world: essays in honour of John H. Elliott. Ed. by R. L. KAGAN a. G. PARKER. Cambridge, Cambridge U. P., 95, 330 p.

4656. Stato e società locale: una discussione. *Società e storia*, 95, 18, p. 11-140 [Interventi di Angelo TORRE, Alberto Mario BANTI, Daniele ANDREOZZI, Arturo PACINI, Maria MONTACUTELLI].

4657. STJERNØ (Steinar). Mellom kirke og kapital: tysk velferdspolitikk – med sideblikk til britisk, svensk og norsk. (Between church and capital: German welfare policy – "sideblikk" to British, Swedish and Norwegian). Oslo, Universitetsforlaget, 95, 283 p.

4658. Terms of survival: the Jewish world since 1945. Ed. by Robert S. WISTRICH. London a New York, Routledge, 95, [s. p.].

4659. Totalitarizm: Istoričeskij opyt Vostočnoj Evropy. (Totalitarianism: a historical experience of the Eastern Europe, 1945–1989's). Otv. red. V. V. MAR'INA. Moskva, RAN. In-t slavjanovedenija i balkanistiki. Naučnyj centr obščeslavjanskikh issledovanij, 95, 287 p.

4660. VERGA (Marcello). Tra Sei e Settecento: un'età delle preriforme? *Storica*, 95, 1, 1, p. 89-121.

4661. Visions allemandes de la France (1871–1914). Hrsg. v. Michel GRUNEWALD u. Helga ABRET. Frankfurt am Main, Berlin u. Bern, Lang, 95, 444 p. (Contacts, 2, 15).

4662. VORONKOV (Vladimir I.). Sobytija 1980–1981 godov v Pol'še. Vzgljad so Staroj ploščadi. (The events of 1980–1981 in Poland. A view from Moscow). *Vopr. Ist.*, 95, 10, p. 92-121.

4663. WINTER (Jay Murray). Sites of memory, sites of mourning: the Great War in European cultural history. Cambridge, Cambridge U. P., 95, X-310 p. (ill.).

4664. YELVINGTON (Kevin A.). Producing power: ethnicity, gender, and class in a Caribbean workplace. Philadelphia, Temple U. P., 95, 286 p. (map.).

4665. ZUBKOVA (Elena Ju.). Obščestvo, vyšedšee iz vojny: russkie i nemcy v 1945 godu. (The post-war society: the Russians and Germans in 1945). *Oteč. Ist.*, 95, 3, p. 90-100.

Cf. n°s 1060-1173, 1288, 7670-7795, 7953

§ 2. Einzelne Staaten.

Afghanistan

** 4666. Sowjetische Geheimdokumente zum Afghanistankrieg (1978–1991). Hrsg. v. Pierre ALLAN [et al.]. Zürich, Hochschulverlag, 95, 801 p. (Strategische Studien, 8).

4667. GALEOTTI (Mark). Afghanistan: the Soviet Union's last war. London, Frank Cass, 95, IX-242 p.

4668. GRASSELLI (Gabriella). British and American responses to the Soviet invasion of Afghanistan. Aldershot, Hants. a. Brookfield, Dartmouth, 95, VI-216 p.

4669. KAKAR (M. Hasan). Afghanistan: the Soviet invasion and the Afghan response, 1979–1982. Berkeley, University of California Press, 95, 380 p.

4670. MERIMSKIJ (Viktor A.). Vojna v Afganistane: Zapiski učastika. (The Afghan war. Memoirs of a person partecipated in it). *Nov. novejš. Ist.*, 95, 3, p. 74-117.

Cf. n° 8492

Ägypten

4671. SAGIV (David). Fundamentalism and intellectuals in Egypt, 1973–1993. London, F. Cass, 95, 188 p.

4672. State and its servants (The): administration in Egypt from Ottoman times to the present. Ed. by N. HANNA. Cairo, American University in Cairo Press, 95, 128 p.

Cf. n°s 7867, 7993, 7999, 8441, 8730

Albanien

4673. BARTL (Peter). Albanien: vom Mittelalter bis zur Gegenwart. Regensburg, F. Pustet, 95, 304 p.

4674. PLAVA (Elmaz B.). Plava e Gucia ne levizjen kombetare shqiptare: kujtime dhe dokumente historike. Tirane, Marin Barleti, 95, 259 p.

4675. VICKERS (Miranda). The Albanians: a modern history. London, I. B. Tauris, 95, 262 p.

Cf. n° 8503

Algerien

4676. COLONNA (Fanny). Les versets de l'invincibilité. Permanence et changements religieux dans l'Algérie contemporaine. Paris, Presses de la Fondation nationale de sciences politiques, 95, 397 p.

4677. HIDOUCI (Ghazi). Algerie: la liberation inachevée. Paris, La Decouverte, 95, 302 p.

4678. NOUSCHI (André). L'Algérie amère (1914–1994). Paris, Maison de Science de l'Homme, 95, 350 p.

Cf. n°s 7858, 7864, 7876, 8759

Argentinien

4679. BALZE (Felipe A. M. de la). Remaking in Argentina Economy. New York, Council on Foreign Relations Press, 95, VIII-196 p.

2. EINZELNE STAATEN

4680. BECKERMAN (Paul). Central-Bank 'Distress' and hyperinflation in Argentina, 1989–90. *Journal of Latin American Studies*, 95, 27, p. 663-682.

4681. BURDICK (Michael A.). For God and the Fatherland: religion and politics in Argentina. Albany, State University of New York Press, 95, 283 p. (bibl., ind.).

4682. CAIMARI (Lila M.). Perón y la iglesia católica: religión, estado y sociedad en la Argentina (1943–1955). Buenos Aires, Ariel Historia, 95, 390 p. (map., graph.).

4683. COLÁS (Santiago). Postmodernity in Latin America: the Argentine paradigm. Durham, Duke U. P., 95, 224 p. (bibl.).

4684. FOSTER (David William). Violence in Argentina Literature: cultural responses to tyranny. Columbia, University of Missouri Press, 95, [s. p.].

4685. GUTIÉRREZ (Leandro H.), ROMERO (Luis Alberto). Sectores populares, cultura y política: Buenos Aires en la entreguerra. Buenus Aires, Editorial Sudamericana, 95, 212 p.

4686. HOROWITZ (Joel). Argentina's failed General Strike of 1921: a critical moment in the Radicals' relations with Unions. *Hispanic American Historical Review*, 95, 75, p. 57-80.

4687. IVEREIGH (Austen). Catholicism and politics in Argentina, 1810–1960. Basingstoke, Macmillan Press, 95, XIII-275 p.

4688. MAYO (Carlos A.). Estancia y sociedad en la Pampa, 1740–1820. Buenos Aires, Editorial Biblos, 95, 202 p.

4689. MERCADO (Ruben Jose) Historia economica Argentina: desde 1900 hasta 1955. Buenos Aires, Ediciones Theoria, 95, [s. p.],

4690. MORENO (José Luis). Gauchos et peones du Rio de la Plata. Réflexion sur l'histoire rurale de l'Argentine coloniale. *Annales*, 95, 50, 6, p. 1351-1360.

4691. Nationalsozialismus und Argentinien. Beziehungen, Einflüsse und Nachwirkungen. Hrsg. v. Holger M. MEDING. Frankfurt am Main, Berlin u. Bern, Lang, 95, 250 p.

4692. NICOLAU (Juan Carlos). Proteccionismo y libre comercio en Buenos Aires (1810–1850). Cordoba, Centro de Estudios Historicos, 95, 128 p.

4693. Orden y virtud: el discurso republicano en el regimen rosista. Buenos Aires, Universidad Nacional de Quilmes, 95, 310 p. (Ideologia argentina)

4694. RANIS (Peter). Class, democracy, and labor in contemporary Argentina. New Brunswick, Transaction Publishers, 95, 313 p.

4695. ŠOKINA (Izabella E.). Khuan Domingo Peron. (Juan Domingo Peron). *Vopr. Ist.*, 95, 1, p. 59-77.

4696. ZIMMERMANN (Eduardo). Los liberales reformistas: la cuestion social en la Argentina, 1890–1916. Buenos Aires, Editorial Sudamericana, Universidad de San Andres, 95, 250 p.

Cf. n°s 432, 7768

Armenien

** 4697. Armenians in Ottoman documents, 1915–1920. Ankara, General Directorate of the State Archives, Directorate of Ottoman Archives, 95, XLIV-641 p. (Turkey. Osmanli Arsivi Daire Baskanligi. Yayin, 25).

4698. SOMAKIAN (Manoug Joseph). Empires in conflict: Armenia and the great powers, 1895–1920. London a. New York, Tauris Academic Studies, 95, XI-276 p. (International library of historical studies, 2).

Äthiopien

4699. DEL BOCA (Angelo). Il Negus. Vita e morte dell'ultimo Re dei Re. Bari, Laterza, 95, 394 p.

4700. O'KANE (Rosemary H. T.). Reigns of terror in the Ethiopian and Iranian revolutions. Keele, University of Keele, Department of Politics, 95, 27 p.

4701. TESHALE (Tibebu). The making of modern Ethiopia: 1896–1974. Lawrenceville, The Red Sea Press, 95, 246 p.

Cf. n° 7877

Australien

4702. ALSTON (Philip), CHIAM (Madelaine). Treaty-making and Australia: globalisation versus sovereignty? Australia, The Federation Press, 95, 309 p.

4703. BURGMAN (Verity). Revolutionary industrial unionism: the industrial workers of the world in Australia. Cambridge, Cambridge U. P., 95, 346 p.

4704. GALLIGAN (Brian). A federal republic: Australia's constitutional system of government. Cambridge, Cambridge U. P., 95, 283 p.

4705. Gender at war: Australians at war in the twentieth century. Ed by J. DAMOUSI and M. LAKE. Cambridge, Cambridge U. P., 95, VIII-351 p. (ill.).

4706. MARSH (Ian). Beyond the two party system: rapresentation, competitiveness and the structure of Australian politics. Cambridge, Cambridge U. P., 95, 409 p.

4707. OLIVER (Bobbie). War and peace in Western Australia: the social and political impact of the Great War, 1914–1926. Nedlands, University of Western Australia Press, 95, 314 p.

4708. RUBINSTEIN (W. D.). The Cold War, the Australian Jewish community, and the marginalisation of the Jewish left, 1942–1960. *Australian Journal of Politics and History*, 95, 41, 3, p. 373-390.

4709. TROY (Patrick). Australian cities: issues, stategies and policies for urban Australia in the 1990s. Cambridge, Cambridge U. P., 95, 310 p.

Cf. n°ˢ 8074, 8081, 8636, 8767

Belarus

4710. Belarus: the end of independence? Parliamentary elections and referendum, May 1995: report. By the British Helsinki Human Rights Group. Oxford, British Helsinki Human Rights Group, 95, 43 p.

4711. Occasional papers in Belarusian studies No.1. Ed. by James DINGLEY a. Arnold MAC MILLIN. London, School of Slavonic and East European Studies, University of London, 95, VIII-73 p. (SSEES occasional papers, 27).

Cf. n° 8402

Belgien

** 4712. Archives scabinales et communales du Brabant. Ed. par André VANRIE. Bruxelles, Archives generales du Royaume, 95, 607 p. (Archives generales du Royaume et Archives de l'Etat dans les provinces. Guides, 16. Guide des fonds et collections des Archives generales du Royaume, 16).

** 4713. D'HOOP (Alfred). Inventaire sommaire des archives des Etats de Brabant: Cartons. Bruxelles, Archives Generales du Royaume, 95, 27 p. (Inventaires/ Archives Generales du Royaume, 104/2).

4714. DE VILLERS (Gauthier). De Mobutu à Mobutu: trente ans de relations Belgique-Zaire. Bruxelles, De Boeck-Wesmael, 95, 256 p.

4715. DELAUNOIS (Jean-Marie). Un cas de collaboration "nationale" en Belgique francophone: José Streel, penseur du rexisme. *Guerres Mondiales et conflits contemporains*, 95, 45, 180, p. 89-104.

4716. DUJARDIN (Vincent). Belgique 1949–1950: entre regence et royauté. Préface de Pierre HARMEL. Bruxelles, Racine, 95, 207 p.

4717. HUYSE (Luc), HOFLACK (Kris). Life after prison: the purge and the reintegration of wartime collaborators in Belgium, Holland and France (1944–1994). *In*: 1945: consequences and sequels of the Second World War [Cf. n° 8422], p. 257-280.

4718. KIKKERT (J. G). Geld, macht & eer: Willem I, Koning der Nederlanders en Belgen, 1772-1843. Utrecht, Scheffers, 95, 254 p.

4719. ŁAPTOS (Józef). Historia Belgii. (Histoire de la Belgique). Wrocław, Zakł. Narod. im. Ossolińskich, 95, 328 p. (phot., fig, cartes).

4720. MOULAERT (Jan). Rood en zwart: de anarchistische beweging in Belgie 1880–1914. Leuven, Davidsfonds, 95, 462 p.

4721. VANSCHOENBEEK (Guy). Novecento in Gent: de wortels van de sociaal-democratie in Vlaanderen. Antwerpen, Hadewijch, 95, 269 p.

Cf. n°ˢ 8026, 8180, 8261

Bolivien

4722. CUETO (Marcos). Saberes andinos, ciencia y tecnología en Bolivia, Ecuador y Peru. Lima, Instituto de Estudios Peruanos, 95, 213 p.

4723. MORALES (Juan Antonio), LA TORRE (Gilka). Inflación, estabilización y crecimiento. La experiencia boliviana de 1982 a 1993. La Paz, Universidad Católica Boliviana de Investigaciones Socio-económicas, 95, 495 p.

Bosnien-Herzegowina

4724. CALIC (Marie-Janine). Der Krieg in Bosnien-Hercegovina: Ursachen, Konfliktstrukturen, internationale Lösungsversuche. Frankfurt am Main, Suhrkamp, 95, 256 p. (Edition Suhrkamp. Neue Folge, 943).

4725. KOSLOWSKI (Gerd). Die NATO und der Krieg in Bosnien-Herzegowina: Deutschland, Frankreich und die USA im internationalen Krisenmanagement. Vierow bei Greifswald, SH-Verlag, 95, 228 p. (Kölner Arbeiten zur internationalen Politik, 2).

4726. O'BALLANCE (Edgar). Civil war in Bosnia, 1992–94. Basingstoke, Macmillan, 95, XXIII-269 p.

4727. Sarajevska raskrsca: dnevnik i kazivanja izbeglica = The crossroads of Sarajevo: diary and testimonies of refugees. Organiser Momcilo MITROVIC. Beograd, Novinsko-izdavacka ustanova "Vojska", 95, 313 p.

Brasilien

* 4728. Bibliografia comentada: industrialização, urbanização e migrações: São Paulo, séculos XIX e XX. Orientadora, Zilda Marcia GRICOLI IOKOI. Sao Paulo, Departmento de Historia-USP, 95, IX-205 p. (ill.). (Serie Iniciacao, 2).

4729. BOONE (Christopher). Streetcar and Politics in Rio de Janeiro: private enterprise versus Municipal Government in the provision of Mass Transit, 1903–1920. *Journal of Latin American Studies*, 95, 27, p. 343-366.

4730. DANAHER (Kevin), SHELLENBERGER (Michael). Fighting for the soul of Brazil. New York, Monthly Review Press, 95, 271 p. (map.).

4731. DIACON (Todd). Bringing the countryside back in: a case study of military intervention as State building in Brazilian Old Republic. *Journal of Latin American Studies*, 95, 27, p. 569-592.

4732. LESSER (Jeff). Welcoming the undesirables: Brazil and the Jewish question. Berkeley, University of California Press, 95, XVIII-280 p. (ill.)

4733. MAC MILLAN (Gordon). At the end of the rainbow? Gold, land, and people in the Brazilian Amazon. New York, Columbia U. P., 95, 199 p. (phot., map.).

4734. MATTOS DE CASTRO (Hebe Maria). Das cores do silêncio: os significados de liberdade no sudeste ascravista, Brasil, século XIX. Rio de Janeiro, Arquivo nacional, 95, [s. p.].

4735. NAVA (Carmen). Patria and patriotism: nationalism and national identity in Brazilian public schools, 1937–1974. Ann Arbor, UMI, 95, XII-293 p. (ill.).

4736. SEGATTO (Jose Antonio). Reforma e revolução: as vicissitudes políticas do PCB (1954–1964). Rio de Janeiro, Civilização Brasileira, 95, 271 p.

4737. SUMM (Harvey). Brazilian mosaic: portraits of a diverse people and culture. Wilmington, SR Books, 95, 209 p.

4738. WELCH (Cliff). Rivalry and unification: mobilising rural workers in São Paulo on the eve of the Brazilian Golpe of 1964. *Journal of Latin American Studies*, 95, 27, p. 161-188.

4739. WILLIS (Eliza J.). Explaining bureaucratic independence in Brazil: the experience of the National Economic Development Bank. *Journal of Latin American Studies*, 95, 27, p. 625-662.

Cf. n°s 7768, 7937

Bulgarien

* 4740. MUTAFCHIEVA (Vera P.). Sudut nad istoritsite: bulgarskata istoricheska nauka. T. 1. Dokumenti i diskusii 1944–1950. Sofiia, Akademichno izd-vo "Marin Drinov", 95, [s. p.].

4741. Bulharsko a československá krize 1968. (Bulgaria and the Czechoslovak crisis of 1968). Praha, Ústav pro soudobé dějiny AV ČR, 95, 51 p. (Materiály, studie, dokumenty, 11).

4742. KOSTADINOVA (Tatiana). Bulgaria, 1879–1946: the challenge of choice. Boulder, East European Monographs, 95, 122 p. (East European monographs, 429).

4743. LAZAROV (Ivan), PAVLOV (Plamen), TIUTIUNDZHIEV (Ivan). Istoriia na Bulgariia ch. 2. XVIII vek – 1947 g. Bulgarsko vuzrazhdane. Bulgariia v novoto vreme, Veliko Turnovo, Slovo, 95, [s. p.].

Chile

4744. ETCHEPARE (Jaime Antonio), STEWART (Hamish I.). Nazism in Chile: a particular type of fascism in South America. *Journal of Contemporary History*, 95, 30, 4, p. 577-606.

4745. HOFMEISTER (Wilhelm). La opción por la democracía: democracía cristiana y desarrollo politico en Chile, 1964–1994. Santiago, Konrad Adenauer Stiftung, 95, 345 p.

4746. MURDOCK (Carl J.). Physician, the State and public health in Chile, 1881–1891. *Journal of Latin American Studies*, 95, 27, p. 551-568.

4747. OXHORN (Philiph D.). Organizing civil society: the popular sectors and the struggle for democracy in Chile. University Park, Penn State Press, 95, XVI-373 p.

4748. SCHNEIDER (Cathy Lisa). Shanytown protest in Pinochet's Chile. Philadelphia, Temple U. P., 95, XXIV-269 p.

4749. TOKMAN (Victor E.), KLEIN (Emilio). Regulation and informal economy: microenterprises in Chile, Ecuador, and Jamaica. Boulder a. London, Lynne Rienner Publshers, 95, VI-24 p.

4750. VALDÈS (Juan Gabriel). Pinochet's economists: the Chicago School in Chile. New York a. Cambridge, Cambridge U. P., 95, XIII-334 p.

China

Cf. n°s 7706, 7789, 8016, 8080, 8444, 8542, 8544, 8568, 8608, 8619, 8629, 8651, 8684, 8725, 8739, 8794, 8801, 8825-9017

Dänemark

4751. BARFOD (Jörgen H.). Christian 3.s flåde. København, Gyldendal, 95, 297 p. (Marinehistorisk Selskabs skrift, 25). [The Danish navy under Christian III, i.e. in 16th century].

4752. KIRCHHOFF (Hans). Denmark: a light in the darkness of the Holocaust? A reply to Gunnar S. Paulsson. *Journal of Contemporary History*, 95, 30, 3, p. 465-480. [Cf. n° 4755: PAULSSON (Gunnar S.). The 'Bridge over the Øresund']

4753. Kong Christian VIIIs dagböger og optegnelser 1839–1848. Vol. 4. Part 1–3. Ed. by Anders Monrad MÖLLER. København, Det Kongelige Danske selskab for Faedrelandets Historie, 95, 1207 p. [The diaries and notes of the Danish monarch Christian VIII].

4754. LAURIDSEN (John T.). Nazister i Danmark 1930–45. En forskningsoversigt. (Nazis in Denmark 1930–1945. A review of studies). *Historisk Tidskrift* (Denmark), 95, 95, 1, p. 99-142.

4755. PAULSSON (Gunnar S.). The 'Bridge over the Øresund': the historiography on the expulsion of the

Jews from Nazi-occupied Denmark. *Journal of Contemporary History*, 95, 30, 3, p. 431-464. [Cf. n° 4752: KIRCHHOFF (Hans). Denmark: a light in the darkness]

4756. ROSLYNG-JENSEN (Palle). Befrielsesjubilæet og den nyeste besættelseslitteratur. Idealister og "materialister" i besættelsesforskningen. (The liberation jubilee and the recent occupation studies. Idealists and "materialists" in the investigation of the German occupation period [1940–1945]). *Historisk Tidskrift* (Denmark), 95, 95, 2, p. 367-398.

Cf. n°s 7934, 8424, 8600, 8782

Deutschland

* 4757. RUCK (Michael). Bibliographie zum Nationalsozialismus. Köln, Bund-Verlag, 95, 1428 p.

4758. BARANOWSKI (Shelley). The sanctity of rural life: nobility, protestantism, and nazism in Weimar Prussia. New York, [s. n.], 95, X-267 p.

4759. BARCLAY (David E.). Frederick William IV and the Prussian Monarchy, 1840–1861. Oxford, Clarendon Press, 95, XIII-335 p.

4760. BARKIN (Kenneth). Bismarck in a postmodern world. *German Studies Review*, 95, 18, 2, p. 241-252.

4761. BEHREND (Hanna). German unification: the destruction of an economy. London, Pluto, 95, 232 p.

4762. BENZ (Wolfgang). Germans, Jews and antisemitism in Germany. *Australian Journal of Politics and History*, 95, 41, 1, p. 118-129.

4763. BERGER (Helge), RITSCHL (Albrecht). Die Rekonstruktion der Arbeitsteilung in Europa. Eine neue Sicht des Marshallplans in Deutschland 1947–1951. *Vierteljahrshefte für Zeitgeschichte*, 95, 43, 3, p. 473-519.

4764. BIEFANG (Andreas). Der deutsche Nationalverein 1859–1867. Vorstands- und Ausschußprotokolle. Düsseldorf, Droste, 95, LIII-528 p.

4765. BLASCHKE (O. R.). Der Altkatholizismus 1870 bis 1945. Nationalismus, Antisemitismus und Nationalsozialismus. *Historische Zeitschrift*, 95, 261, 1, p. 51-100.

4766. BÖMELBURG (Hans-Jürgen). Zwischen polnischer Ständegesellschaft und preußischem Obrigkeitsstaat. Vom königlichen Preußen zu Westpreußen (1756–1806). München, Oldenbourg, 95, XI-549 p. (Schriften des Bundesinstituts für ostdeutsche Kultur und Geschichte, 5).

4767. Bürokratie und Kult. Das Parteizentrum der NSDAP am Königsplatz in München. Geschichte und Rezeption. Hrsg. v. Piero STEINLE, Julian ROSEFELDT u. Iris LAUTERBACH. München, Deutscher Kunstverl., 95, 368 p. (Veröff. des Zentralinstituts für Kunstgeschichte, 10).

4768. CANNARELLA (Carmelo). Dal muro di Berlino al muro verde. L'impatto della riunificazione tedesca nel settore agricolo dei Länder orientali. Milano, F. Angeli, 95, 102 p.

4769. CLARK (Christopher). The limits of the confessional state: conversions to Judaism in Prussia 1814–1843. *Past and Present*, 95, 147, p. 159-179.

4770. COLLOTTI (Enzo). La storia infinita: i diari di Goebbels. *Passato e presente*, 95, 13, 34, p. 165-170.

4771. DAHM (Volker). Nationale Einheit und partikulare Vielfalt. Zur Frage der kulturpolitischen Gleichschaltung im Dritten Reich. *Vierteljahrshefte für Zeitgeschichte*, 95, 95, 43, 2, p. 221-266.

4772. DARTMANN (Christoph). The State and economic crisis in 20th Century Germany. *The Journal of the German History Society*, 95, 13, p. 80-83.

4773. Dritte Reich (Das). Ein Lesebuch zur deutschen Geschichte 1933–1945. Hrsg. v. Christoph STUDT. München, Beck, 95, 346 p. (Beck'sche Reihe, 1089).

4774. ENGELMANN (Roger), HENKE (Klaus-Dietmar). Aktenlage: die Bedeutung der Unterlagen des Staatssicherheitsdienstes für die Zeitgeschichtsforschung. Berlin, Ch. Links, 95, 244 p. (Analysen und Dokumente, 1).

4775. FABREGUET (Michel). Les historiens face aux témoignages des rescapés des camps de concentration nationaux-socialistes. *In*: Nouvelles recherches sur l'univers concentrationnaire et d'extermination nazi [Cf. n° 4805], p. 199-207.

4776. FARBMAN (Nikolaj V.). Gustav Štrezman: čelovek i gosudarstvenny dejatel'. (Gustav Stresemann: man and statesman). *Nov. novejš. Ist.*, 95, 5, p. 167-190.

4777. FERGUSON (Niall). Hamburg business and German politics in the era of Inflation, 1897–1927. Cambridge, Cambridge U. P., 95, XII-539 p.

4778. FEST (Joachim). Joseph Goebbels. Eine Porträtskizze. *Vierteljahrshefte für Zeitgeschichte*, 95, 43, 4, p. 565-580.

4779. FISCHER (Albert). Hjalmar Schacht und Deutschlands "Judenfrage". Der "Wirtschaftsdiktator" und die Vertreibung der Juden aus der deutschen Wirtschaft. Köln, Weimar u. Wien, Böhlau, 95, 252 p. (Wirtschafts- und sozialhistorische Studien, 2).

4780. FULBROOK (Mary). Anatomy of dictatorship: inside the GDR 1949–1989. Oxford, Oxford U. P., 95, 307 p.

4781. GABEL (Helmut). Widerstand und Kooperation. Studien zur politische Kultur rheinischer und maasländischer Kleinterritorien (1648–1794). Tübingen, Bibliotheca Academica, 95, 480 p. (Frühneuzeitforschungen, 2).

4782. GERBI (Sandro). Benjamin Franklin antisemita? Un falso della propaganda nazista. *Passato e presente*, 95, 13, 36, p. 129-140.

2. EINZELNE STAATEN

4783. HARRINGTON (Joel). Reorderind marriage and society in reformation Germany. Cambridge, Cambridge U. P., 95, XV-315 p.

4784. HENTSCHEL (Klaus), RENNEBERG (Monika). Eine akademische Karriere. Der Astronom Otto Heckmann im Dritten Reich. *Vierteljahrshefte für Zeitgeschichte*, 95, 95, 43, 4, p. 581-610.

4785. JAKUŠEVSKIJ (Anatolij S.). Vnutrennij krizis Germanii v 1944–1945 godakh. (Home crisis in Germany in 1944–1945). *Nov. novejš. Ist.*, 95, 2, p. 47-64.

4786. JESSEN (Ralph). Die Gesellschaft im Staatssozialismus. Probleme einer Sozialgeschichte der DDR. *Geschichte und Gesellschaft*, 95, 21, 1, p. 96-110.

4787. KARSTEN (Rudolph). Die sächsische Sozialdemokratie vom Kaiserreich zur Republik (1871–1923). Wien, Köln u. Weimar, Böhlau, 95, 455 p. (Demokratische Bewegung in Mitteldeutschland, 1).

4788. KERSHAW (Ian). L'opinion allemande sous le nazisme. Bavière 1933–1945. Paris, CNRS Editions, 95, 375 p.

4789. KESSLER (Ralf), HARTMUT (Rüdiger Peter). Antifaschisten in der SBZ. Zwischen elitärem Selbstverständnis und politischer Instrumentalisierung. *Vierteljahrshefte für Zeitgeschichte*, 95, 95, 43, 4, p. 611-634.

4790. KLENKE (D.). Nationalkriegerisches Gemeinschaftsideal als politische Religion. Zum Vereinsnationalismus der Sänger, Schützen und Turner am Vorabend der Einigungskriege. *Historische Zeitschrift*, 95, 260, 2, p. 395-448.

4791. KOZIEŁŁO-POKLEWSKI (Bohdan). Antyhitlerowska opozycja klasy robotniczej w Prusach Wschodnich [1932–1939]. (Opposition antihitlérienne de la classe ouvrière en Prusse Orientale [1932–1939]). *Komunikaty Mazursko-Warmińskie*, 95, 39, 1, p. 65-81. [Deutsche Zsfassung].

4792. KRAUS (Antje). Quellen zur Bevölkerungs-, Sozial- und Wirtschaftsstatistik Deutschlands 1815–1875. Band. 3. Quellen zur Berufs- und Gewerbestatistik Deutschlands 1816–1875: norddeutsche Staaten. Band. 4. Quellen zur Berufs- und Gewerbestatistik Deutschlands 1816–1875: mitteldeutsche Staaten. Band. 5. Quellen zur Berufs- und Gewerbestatistik Deutschlands 1816–1875: süddeutsche Staaten. Hrsg. v. Wolfgang KOLLMANN. Boppard, Boldt, 3 vol., 95, X-829 p., X-685 p., IX, 655 p. (Forschungen zur deutschen Sozialgeschichte, 2, 3, 5).

4793. KRETININ (Sergej V.). Karl Kautskij (1845–1938): opyt pereosmyslenija. (Karl Kautsky: an experience of recomprehension). *Nov. novejš. Ist.*, 95, 1, p. 141-160.

4794. LAMBERT (Peter). Germans historians and nazy ideology. The parameters of the Volksgemeinschaft and the problem of historical legitimation, 1930–45. *European History Quarterly*, 95, 25, p. 555-582.

4795. LAPP (Benjamin). A 'National' socialism: the old Socialist Party of Saxony, 1926–32. *Journal of Contemporary History*, 95, 30, 2, p. 291-310.

4796. LE TURDU (Anna). L'exploitation des témoignages oraux. *In*: Nouvelles recherches sur l'univers concentrationnaire et d'extermination nazi [Cf. n° 4805], p. 215-229.

4797. LEBIODA (Tadeusz). Nowopolityczne instytuty wychowawcz w II Rzeszy jako instrument kształtowania faszystowskiej elity. (Instituts éducatifs du nouveau type au IIIe Reich en tant qu'instrument de formation de l'élite nazi). *Śląski Kwartalnik Historyczny. Sobótka*, 95, 50, 1-2, p. 45-58. [Deutsche Zsfassung].

4798. LORENZ (Chris). Beyond good and evil? The German Empire of 1871 and modern German historiography. *Journal of Contemporary History*, 95, 30, 4, p. 729-765.

4799. MANCA (Anna Gianna). La sfida delle riforme. Costituzione e politica nel liberalismo prussiano (1850–1866). Bologna, Il Mulino, 95, 684 p. (Annali dell'Istituto storico italo-germanico, monografia, 21).

4800. MILTON (Sybil). Vorstufe zur Vernichtung. Die Zigeunerlager nach 1933. *Vierteljahrshefte für Zeitgeschichte*, 95, 95, 43, 1, p. 115-130.

4801. MITCHELL (Maria). Materialism and secularism: CDU politicians and national socialism, 1945–1949. *Journal of modern history*, 95, 67, 2, p. 278-308.

4802. MOMMSEN (Hans). Noch einmal: Nationalsozialismus und Modernisierung. *Geschichte und Gesellschaft*, 95, 21, 3, p. 391-402.

4803. MOMMSEN (Wolfgang J.). Bürgerstolz und Weltmachtstreben. Deutschland unter Wilhelm II. 1890 bis 1918. Berlin, Propyläen, 95, 946 p. (Propyläen Geschichte Deutschlands, 7/2).

4804. National Socialist cultural policy. Ed. by Glenn R. CUOMO. New York, [s. n.], 95, IV-252 p.

4805. Nouvelles recherches sur l'univers concentrationnaire et d'extermination nazi. Actes d'un Colloque tenu à Paris IV-Sorbonne, les 2 et 3 février 1995. *Revue d'Allemagne*, 95, 27, 2, p. 143-304. [Cf. n^{os} <sélection> 4775, 4796, 4824, 4894, 5860.]

4806. OVERESCH (Manfred). Buchenwald und die DDR, oder die Suche nach Selbstlegitimation. Göttingen, Vandenhoeck & Ruprecht, 95, 350 p.

4807. PAUL (Gerhard) [et al.]. Milieus und Widerstand. Eine Verhaltensgeschichte der Gesellschaft im Nationalsozialismus. Bonn, Dietz, 95, 663 p. (Widerstand und Verweigerung im Saarland 1935–1945, 3).

4808. POHL (Karl Heinrich). Adolf Müller, Geheimagent und Gesandter in Kaiserreich und Weimarer Republik. Köln, Bund, 95, 388 p.

4809. PULZER (Peter). German politics 1945–1995. Oxford, Oxford U. P., 95, 195 p.

4810. RADICE (Giles). The new Germans. London, Michael Joseph, 95, 255 p.

4811. ROBINSON (Philip). Die Fürstabtei St. Gallen und ihr Territorium 1463–1529. Eine Studie zur Entwicklung territorialer Staatlichkeit. St. Gallen, Selbstverlag des Staatsarchivs und Stiftsarchivs St. Gallen, 95, 361 p. (St. Galler Kultur und Geschichte, 24).

4812. ROSEMAN (Mark). Gender in German history. *The Journal of the German History Society*, 95, 13, p. 83-90.

4813. ROWLANDS (Alison). Women, gender and power in Rothenburg ob der Tauber and its rural environs, 1500–c.1618. *The Journal of the German History Society*, 95, 13, p. 95-96.

4814. RUBLACK (Ulinka). Women and crime in South-West Germany 1500–1700. *The Journal of the German History Society*, 95, 13, p. 372-373.

4815. Russische Emigration in Deutschland 1918 bis 1941: Leben im europäischen Bürgerkrieg. Hrsg. v. Karl SCHLÖGEL. Berlin, Akademie Verlag, 95, 550 p. (ill.).

4816. SCHMÄDEKE (Jürgen). Wählerbewegung im wilhelminischen Deutschland. Band. 1. Die Reichstagswahlen von 1890 bis 1912: eine historisch-statistische Untersuchung. Band. 2. Die Reichstagswählen von 1890 bis 1912: Wählergebnisse und Strukturen im Kartenbild. Berlin, Akademie, 95, 2 vol., XXXVI-1020 p.

4817. SCHRÖDER (Iris). Wohlfahrt, Frauenfrage und Geschlechterpolitik. Konzeptionen der Frauenbewegung zur kommunalen Sozialpolitik im Deutschen Kaiserreich 1871–1914. *Geschichte und Gesellschaft*, 95, 21, 3, p. 368-390.

4818. SCHWARZ (Hans-Peter). Konrad Adenauer: a German politician and statesman in a period of war, revolution, and reconstruction. Volume I. From empire to the Federal Republic, 1876–1952. Providence, Berghahn Books, 95, 759 p.

4819. SONDHAUS (Lawrence). 'The Spirit of the Army' at sea. The Prussian-German naval officer corps, 1847–1897. *International History Review*, 95, 17, p. 459-484.

4820. Tag X, 17. Juni 1953 (Der). Die "innere Staatsgründung" der DDR als Ergebnis der Krise 1952–54. Hrsg. v. Ilko-Sache KOWALCZUK [et al.]. Berlin, Links, 95, 359 p. (Forschungen zur DDR-Geschichte, 3).

4821. THEIBAULT (John C.). German villages in crisis. Rural life in Hesse-Kassel and the Thirty Years' War, 1580–1720. Atlantic Highlands, Humanities Press, 95, XI-237 p.

4822. TOKODY (Gyula). Pártok és pártrendszerek a második világháború utáni Németországban, 1945–1990. (Partis et systèmes de partis en Allemagne après la deuxième guerre mondiale, 1945–1990). *Múltunk*, 95, 40, 4, p. 3-32.

4823. TRIBE (Keith). Strategies of economic order. German economic discourse 1750–1950. Cambridge, Cambridge U. P., 95, IX-285 p.

4824. TROTIGNON (Yves). Le témoignage écrit. *In*: Nouvelles recherches sur l'univers concentrationnaire et d'extermination nazi [Cf. n° 4805], p. 209-213.

4825. VJATKIN (Kirill S.). Helmut Kohl. *Vopr. Ist.*, 95, 3, p. 46-66.

4826. VOTH (Hans-Joachim). Did high wages or high interest rates bring down the Weimar Republic? A cointegration model of investment in Germany, 1925–1930. *Journal of Economic History*, 95, 55, 4, p. 801-821.

4827. WEEKS (Gregory). Der nationalsozialistische Traum von einem Deutsch-Mittelafrikanischen Reich, 1933–1943. *Geschichte und Gegenwart*, 95, 14, 3, p. 148-160.

4828. WEHLER (Hans-Ulrich). Deutsche Gesellschaftsgeschichte. Band 3. Von der "deutschen Doppelrevolution" bis zum Beginn des ersten Weltkrieges 1849–1914. München, Beck, 95. XVIII-1515 p.

4829. WISTRICH (Robert S.), HOLLAND (Luke). Weekend in Munich: art, propaganda, and terror in the Third Reich. London, Pavilion, 95, 176 p. (ill.). (Channel Four Television Company).

Cf. n^{os} *603, 677, 1109, 7703, 7716, 7754, 7995, 8036, 8052, 8138, 8141, 8145, 8146, 8165, 8249, 8260, 8302, 8318, 8335, 8430, 8450, 8460, 8605, 8623, 8676, 8727, 8734, 8735, 8793, 8799*

Dominikanische Republik

4830. BETANCES (Emelio). State and society in the Dominican Republic. Boulder, Wetsview press, 95, 162 p. (map.).

4831. LEGRAND (Catherine C.). Informal resistance on a Dominican sugar plantation during the Trujillo dictatorship. *Hispanic American Historical Review*, 95, 75, p. 555-596.

4832. PONS (Frank Moya). The Dominican Republic: a national history. New Rochelle, Hispaniola Books, 95, 543 p. (map.).

Estland

4833. Éstonija: stoličnye žiteli. (Estonia: inhabitants of the capital, the end of the 80's–the beginning of the 90's). Moskva, RAN. In-t étnologii i antropologii im. N. N. Miklukho- Maklaja; Avtorskaja programa, rukoviditel' issledovanij Ju. V. Arutjunjan, 95, 269 p.

4834. GEISTLINGER (Michael). Estonia. A new framework for the Estonian majority and the Russian minority. Vienna, Braumuller, 95, 159 p.

4835. Viro: historia, kansa, kulttuuri. (Estonia: history, folk, culture). Ed. by Seppo ZETTERBERG. Hel-

2. EINZELNE STAATEN

sinki, SKS, 95, 402 p. (Dt. Zfassung, Eng. Summary). (Suomal. kirjallisuuden seuran toim., 610.).

Finnland

4836. ALENIUS (Kari). Ahkeruus, edistys, ylimielisyys. Virolaisten Suomi-kuva kansallisen heräämisen ajasta tsaarinvallan päättymiseen (n. 1850–1917). [Hardworking, progressive, arrogant: the image of Finland in the eyes of the Estonians from the period of national awekening to the end of the tsarist era (approx. 1850–1917)]. Oulu, Pohjoinen, 96, in-8, 259 p. (Studia historica septentrionalia, 27).

4837. ENGMAN (Max). Förvaltningen och utvandringen till Ryssland 1809–1917. Helsingfors, Förvalningshistoriekommitténs publikationer, 95, 275 p. (Hallintohistoriallisia tutkimuksia, 20). [Administration and the Finnish emigration to Russia].

4838. Vacat.

4839. Finland 1917–1920. Vol. 2. Ett folk i kamp. Vol. 3. Ett stat tar form. Ed. Ohto MANNINEN. Helsingfors, Tryckericentralen Riksarkivet, 95, 2 vol., 782 p., 550 p. [The early political history of independent Finland].

4840. HIETANIEMI (Tuija). Totuuden jäljillä. Suomalaisen rikospoliisin taival. (Criminal investigation in the history of the Finnish police). Vantaa, Keskusrikospoliisi, 95, 473 p. (Eng. summary, ill.).

4841. JUSSILA (Osmo), HENTILÄ (Seppo), NEVAKIVI (Jukko). Suomen poliittinen historia 1809–1955. (Political history of Finland). Porvoo, WSOY 95, 354 p.

4842. KRONLUND (Jarl). Vom Volksaufstand zur Institution: die Verteidigungskräfte Finnlands 1918–1993. Helsinki, Informationsstab des Oberkommandos, 95, 53 p. (ill., maps).

4843. LIIKANEN (Ilkka). Fennomania ja kansa: joukkojärjestäytymisen läpimurto ja Suomalaisen puolueen synty. (Fennomania and the people: the breaktrough of massa organization and the birth of the Finnish Party). Helsinki, SHS, 95, 363 p. (Eng. summary, ill., maps, tables). (Hist. tutkim., 191).

4844. LINDHOLM (Marcus). Lotsverkets förryskning – myt och verklighet. (Russification of the Finnish administration of pilotage, lighthouses and buoyes,1899–1914). Sjöhistorisk årsskrift för Åland 94-95. p. 105-123 (Eng. Summary, ill.).

4845. MICKWITZ (Joachim). Folkbildning, företag och propaganda, finsk icke-fiktiv film på det fält där nationellt symbolgods skapades under mellankrigtiden. (Film, Big business, Propaganda: The Finnish nonfiction film as an element in the national propaganda of the inter-war period). Helsingfors, SHS, 95, 301 p. (Eng. Summary, ill.). (Hist. tutkim., 190).

4846. SINERMA (Martti). Lauri Malmberg ja Suojeluskunnat. (Lauri Malmberg, artillery general and commandant of the Civil Guards in the Finnish political crisis of Mäntsälä uprising). Helsinki, Otava, 95, 395 p. (ill.).

4847. YLI-JOKIPII (Pentti), KOSKI (Arto). The changing pattern of Finnish regional politics. *Fennia* 95, 173 2, p. 53-67 (maps).

4848. ZILLIACUS (Kim O.K.). Finländsk kommunism i ljuset av väljarstöd 1945–1991. (Finnish communism in the light of electoral support, 1945–1991). Helsingfors, Finska Vetenskaps-Societen, 95, 294 p. (Eng. Summary). (Bidr. t. Känn. av Finl. natur folk, 149).

Cf. n°s 7789, 8057, 8271, 8552, 8576, 8800

Frankreich

* 4849. AUBIN (Paul), ROUILLARD (Jacques). Bibliographie d'histoire de l'Amérique française [1993–1994]. *Revue d'histoire de l'Amérique française*, 95, 48, 3, p. 453-458; 4, p. 595-603.

* 4850. DUCLERT (Vincent). Bibliographie internationale du centenaire de l'affaire Dreyfus en 1993–1995. *Cahiers Jean Jaurès*, 95, 138, p. 130-181.

4851. ACCAMPO (Elinor A.), FUCHS (Rachel G.), STEWART (Mary Lynn). Gender and the politics of social reform in France, 1870–1914. Baltimore, Johns Hopkins U. P., 95, 241 p.

4852. An II (L'). Communications présentées les 17 et 18 juin 1994, Institut d'Histoire de la Révolution française. *Annales historiques de la Révolution française*, 95, 300, p. 137-301. [Cf. n^{os} <sélection> 4865, 4876, 4881, 4891, 4896, 4900, 4902, 4918, 6159, 7506, 7592, 7624, 7802.]

4853. BARBAS (Jean-Claude). L'idée de Patrie et de Nation dans les discours de Philippe Pétain, chef de l'Etat français (juin 1940–août 1944). *Guerres Mondiales et Conflits Contemporains*, 95, 45, 177, p. 31-65.

4854. BARZMAN (John). "La gravité du fléchissement qui s'était produit au Havre..." Grèves et opposition à la guerre en 1917–1918. *Guerres Mondiales et Conflits Contemporains*, 95, 45, 179, p. 115-134.

4855. BAUREPAIRE (P.-Y.). Le rayonnement international et le recrutement étranger d'une loge maçonnique au service du négoce protestant: Saint-Jean d'Écosse à l'Orient de Marseille au XVIIIe siècle. *Revue Historique*, 95, 119, 594, p. 263-288.

4856. BELL (David). Lingua populi, lingua dei: language, religion, and the origins of French revolutionary nationalism. *American Historical Review*, 95, 100, 5, p. 1403-1437.

4857. BERSTEIN (Serge), MILZA (Pierre). Histoire de la France au XXe siècle. Paris, Editions Complexe, 95, 1406 p.

4858. BIARD (Michel). Collot d'Herbois, légendes noires et révolution. Lyon, Presses Universitaires de Lyon, 95, 225 p.

4859. BORELLA (Vincent), HARBULOT (Jean-Pierre), DIWO (Gérard), RICHEZ (Jean-Claude), WAHL (Alfred). Les pouvoirs locaux en France, 1935–1953 [enquête de l'Institut d'histoire du temps présent: la Lorraine et l'Alsace]. *Bulletin de l'Institut d'histoire du temps présent*, 95, 59, p. 15-25.

4860. BOURGEON (Jean-Louis). Charles IX devant la Saint-Barthélemy. Genève, Droz, 95, 207 p.

4861. BOVYKIN (Dmitrij Ju.). Ljudovik XVIII: žizn'i legenda. (Louis XVIII: Life and Legend). *Nov. novejš. Ist.*, 95, 4, p. 168-178.

4862. BUCHER (Bernadette). Descendants de chouans. Histoire et culture populaire dans la Vendée contemporaine. Paris, Editions de la MSH, 95, 338 p.

4863. COLLINS (James B.). The state in the early modern France. Cambridge, Cambridge U. P., 95, XXXIV-280 p.

4864. DARTNELL (Michael Y.). Action directe: ultra-left terrorism in France, 1979–1987. London, Frank Cass, 95, 209 p.

4865. DE COCK (Jacques). Marat, prophète de la Terreur? *In*: An II (L') [Cf. n° 4852], p. 261-269.

4866. DEHAY (Valérie). L'école et l'enfance dans la Somme pendant la Grande Guerre. *Guerres Mondiales et Conflits Contemporains*, 95, 45, 179, p. 99-114.

4867. Dictionnaire historique de la vie politique française au XXe siècle. Sous la dir. de J. F. SIRINELLI. Paris, PUF, 95, XX-1067 p.

4868. DILKS (David N.). Rights, wrongs and rivalries: Britain and France in 1945. *In*: 1945: consequences and sequels of the Second World War [Cf. n° 8422], p. 41-70.

4869. DOYLE (William). Officers, nobles, and revolutionaries: essays on eighteenth-century France. London a. Rio Grande, Hambledon Press, 95, [s. p.].

4870. DUCLERT (Vincent). L'affaire Dreyfus et le tournant critique (note critique). *Annales*, 95, 50, 3, p. 563-578.

4871. DUPUY (Roger). Le comportement politique de la paysannerie française du XVIe siècle à la fin des années 1950. *In*: Histoire rurale en France (L') [Cf. n° 601], p. 113-116.

4872. ÉDOUARD-LAURENT (S.). Problématique d'une monarchie au XVIe siècle: Philippe II, un roi absolu? *Revue Historique*, 95, 119, 596, p. 225-242.

4873. FAVI (Dolcino). Bernanos e Dreyfus. *Storia contemporanea*, 95, 26, 2-3, p. 227-254, p. 405-440.

4874. Fédéralismes (Les). Réalités et représentations, 1789–1874. Actes du colloque de Marseille, septembre 1993. Aix-en-Provence, Publications de l'Université de Provence, 95, 448 p.

4875. FISHMAN (Sarah). The power of myth: five recent works on Vichy France. *Journal of modern history*, 95, 67, 3, p. 666-673.

4876. FOURNIER (Georges). La vie politique au village en l'an II [en Languedoc]. *In*: An II (L') [Cf. n° 4852], p. 271-282.

4877. GAILLARD (Jean-Michel). L'E. N. A. miroir de l'Etat de 1945 à nos jours. Bruxelles, Ed. Complexe, 95, 238 p.

4878. GARRISSON (Janine). A history of sixteenth-century France, 1483–1598: Renaissance, Reformation and Rebellion. London, Macmillan Press, 95, 438 p.

4879. GILCHER-HOLTEY (Ingrid). Robespierre: Die Charismatisierung der Vernunft. *Geschichte und Gesellschaft*, 95, 21, 2, p. 248-258.

4880. GOBLOT (Jean-Jacques). La jeune France libérale: le Globe et son groupe littéraire, 1824–1830. Paris, Plon, 95, 710 p.

4881. GUILHAUMOU (Jacques), LAPIED (Martine). La mission Maignet [dans les Bouches-du-Rhône et le Vaucluse]. *In*: An II (L') [Cf. n° 4852], p. 283-294.

4882. HALLS (W. D.). Politics, society and christianity in Vichy France. Oxford, Berg, 95, 450 p.

4883. HARDMAN (John). French politics, 1774–1789: from the accession of Louis XVI to the fall of the Bastille. London, Longman, 95, X-283 p.

4884. HERBERT (Ulrich). Die deutsche Militärverwaltung in Paris und die Deportation der französischen Juden. *In*: Aufgabe der Freiheit (Von der) [Cf. n° 4587], p. 427-450.

4885. HERMAN (Arthur L. Jr.). The language of fidelity in early modern France. *Journal of modern history*, 95, 67, 1, p. 1-24.

4886. HUBSCHER (Ronald). Une histoire en quête d'auteurs: les paysans et la politique au XXe siècle. *In*: Histoire rurale en France (L') [Cf. n° 601], p. 137-142.

4887. Immortels du Sénat (Les), 1875–1918. Les cent seize inamovibles de la Troisième République. Sous la direction de Alain CORBIN et Arlette SCHWEITZ. Paris, Publications de la Sorbonne, 95, 512 p. (Histoire de la France aux XIXe et XXe siècles, 37).

4888. JESSENNE (Jean-Pierre). Du sujet au citoyen: la participation rurale aux affaires publiques de l'Ancien Régime au Consulat. *In*: Histoire rurale en France (L') [Cf. n° 601], p. 123-132.

4889. JONES (Peter M.). Reform and Revolution in France: the politics of transition, 1774–1791. Cambridge, Cambridge U. P., 95, XV-275 p.

4890. KAWANO (Kenji). Furansu Kakumei no Shisō to Kodo. (Thought and behaviour in the French Revolution). Tokyo, Iwanami Shoten, 95, 446 p.

2. EINZELNE STAATEN

4891. LEMARCHAND (Guy). Mouvements paysans en période révolutionnaire: Angleterre des années 1640, France de l'an II. *In*: An II (L') [Cf. n° 4852], p. 141-160.

4892. LERNER (Henri). Le nazisme et l'idéologie de Vichy dans la pensée du général de Gaulle. *Guerres Mondiales et conflits contemporains*, 95, 45, 180, p. 63-88.

4893. LEROY (Géraldi). Andler, Jaurès, Herr, Péguy en 1913: la polémique sur la social-démocratie. *Amitié Charles Péguy*, 95, 18, 70, p. 66-78.

4894. LESOURD (Céline). Etude démographique du groupe national français à Mauthausen. *In*: Nouvelles recherches sur l'univers concentrationnaire et d'extermination nazi [Cf. n° 4805], p. 291-294.

4895. LESPAGNOL (André). La course malouine au temps de Louis XIV, entre l'argent et la gloire. Rennes, Editions Apogée, 95, 189 p.

4896. LIRIS (Elisabeth). On rougit ici d'être riche [la politique sociale mise en œuvre par Fouché, dans l'Allier]. *In*: An II (L') [Cf. n° 4852], p. 295-301.

4897. MARCUS (Jonathan). The National Front and French politics: the resistible rise of Jean-Marie Le Pen. London, Macmillan, 95, 212 p.

4898. MARKOFF (John). Violence, emancipation, and democracy: the countryside and the French Revolution. *American Historical Review*, 95, 100, 2, p. 360-386.

4899. MERLE (Gabriel). Emile Combes. Paris, Fayard, 95, 664 p.

4900. MONNIER (Raymonde). Cordeliers, sans-culottes et Jacobins. *In*: An II (L') [Cf. n° 4852], p. 249-260.

4901. ODANAKA (Naoki). Furansu Kindai Shakai 1814–1852: Chitsujo to Tochi. (French modern society 1814–1852: order and government). Tokyo, Bokutakusya, 95, 478 p.

4902. PETITFRÈRE (Claude). La Vendée en l'an II: défaite et répression. *In*: An II (L') [Cf. n° 4852], p. 73-185.

4903. POTTER (David). A history of France, 1460–1560. The emergence of a nation state. New York, St. Martin's Press, 95, XVI-438 p. – IDEM. Kingship in the Wars of Religion: The reputation of Henry III of France. *European History Quarterly*, 95, 25, p. 485-528.

4904. Pouvoir local et Révolution. La frontière intérieure. Ed. par Roger DUPUY. Rennes, Presses Universitaires de Rennes, 95, 586 p.

4905. Pouvoirs locaux en France (Les), 1935–1953. Comment mesurer le renouvellement des élus au sein des conseils généraux. Réunion des correspondants de l'I. H. T. P., 15 mars 1995. *Bulletin de l'Institut d'histoire du temps présent*, 95, 60, p. 25-36.

4906. PRICE (Munro). Preserving the monarchy: the comte de Vergennes, 1774–1787. Cambridge, Cambridge U. P., 95, XI-256 p.

4907. PROCHASSON (Christophe). Sur le cas Maurras: biographie et histoire des idées politiques (note critique). *Annales*, 95, 50, 3, p. 579-588.

4908. PROUD (Judith K.). Children and propaganda: il était une fois – fiction and fairy tale in Vichy France. Forward by H. R. KEDWARD. London, Intellect, 95, VI-80 p. (European studies series).

4909. RODRÍGUEZ (Jesús Antonio). Mayo del 68: una razón histórica. Santafé de Bogotá, Oficina de Publicaciones Universidad Distrital Francisco José de Caldas, 95, 98 p.

4910. ROGISTER (John). Louis XV and the Parlement of Paris, 1737–1755. Cambridge, Cambridge U. P., 95, XXV-288 p. (ill.). (Studies presented to the International Commission for the History of Representative and Parliamentary Institutions).

4911. ROUSSO (Henry). La France inconsolable ou le deuil perpétuel des années noires. *In*: 1945: consequences and sequels of the Second World War [Cf. n° 8422], p. 325-338.

4912. ŚLIWA (Monika). Szkic biografii politycznej Léona Bluma [1872–1950]. (Esquisse de la biographie politique de Léon Blum [1872–1950]. *Dzieje najnowsze*, 95, 27, 1, p. 47-61.

4913. SOUCY (Robert). French fascism: the second wave, 1933–1939. New Haven, Yale U. P., 95, XII-352 p.

4914. SOURIAC (René). Les paysans et la politique au XVIe et XVIIe siècles. *In*: Histoire rurale en France (L') [Cf. n° 601], p. 117-122.

4915. SWANN (Julian). Politics and the Parlement of Paris under Louis XV, 1754–1774. New York, Cambridge U. P., 95, X-390 p.

4916. TATARINOV (Jurij B.). "Železnaja maska" – gosudarstvennaja tajna Burbonov XVII veka. (The "iron mask": the state secret of the Bourbons. The XVIIth century). *Nov. novejš. Ist.*, 95, 1, p. 176-205.

4917. TOUZERY (Mireille). Atlas de la Généralité de Paris au XVIIIe siècle. Un paysage retrouvé. Paris, Comité pour l'histoire économique et financière de la France, 95, 175 p.

4918. WAHNICH (Sophie), BELISSA (Marc). Les crimes des Anglais: trahir le droit. *In*: An II (L') [Cf. n° 4852], p. 233-248.

4919. WALKER (Anita M.), DICKERMAN (Edmund H.). Mind of an Assassin: Ravaillac and the Murder of Henry IV of France. *Canadian Journal of History*, 95, 30, 2, p. 201-230.

4920. WINOCK (Michel). La droite depuis 1789: les hommes, les idées, les reseaux. Paris, Editions du Seuil, 95, 414 p. (Collection points).

4921. ZIELINSKI (Bernd). Staatskollaboration: Vichy und der Arbeitskräfteeinsatz im Dritten Reich. Münster, Westfalisches Dampfboot, 95, 292 p. (Theorie und Geschichte der bürgerlichen Gesellschaft, 11).

Cf. n°s 7698, 7715, 7754, 7817, 7850, 7864, 7913, 7914, 7916, 7937, 7943, 7961, 7970, 7975, 7983, 7979, 8002, 8003, 8012, 8029, 8043, 8060, 8064, 8089, 8104, 8126, 8130, 8144, 8156, 8176, 8193, 8210, 8213, 8216, 8255, 8261, 8264, 8307, 8330, 8338, 8371, 8406, 8419, 8465, 8541, 8611, 8736, 8791, 8802

Ghana

4922. EDGERTON (Robert Breckenridge). The fall of the Asante Empire: the hundred-year war for Africa's Gold Coast. New York a. London, The Free Press, 95, X-293 p. (ill., maps).

4923. LI (Anshan). Asafo and destoolment in colonial Southern Ghana, 1900–1953. *International Journal of African Historical Studies*, 95, 28, 2, p. 327-358.

4924. MEYER (Birgit). Translating the devil: an African appropriation of Pietist Protestantism: The case of the Peki Ewe in Southeastern Ghana 1847–1992. Amsterdam, Universiteit van Amsterdam, 95, XIV-408 p.

Cf. n° 7886

Griechenland

4925. BASCH (Sophie). Le mirage grec: la Grèce moderne devant l'opinion française depuis la création de l'Ecole d'Athènes jusqu'à la guerre civile grecque (1846–1946). Préface de Robert JOUANNY. Paris et Athènes, Hatier, 95, 541 p. (Collection Confluences).

4926. BOUNIALES (Marinos Tzane). Ho Kretikos polemos: 1645–1669. Epimeleia, Stylianos ALEXIOU, Martha APOSKITE. Athena, Stigme, 95, 631 p

4927. CLOSE (David H). The origins of the Greek civil war. London a. New York, Longman, 95, XIV-248 p. (Origins of modern wars).

4928. Erträumte Nation (Die): Griechenlands Wiedergeburt im 19. Jahrhundert. Hrsg. v. Reinhard HEYDENREUTER, Jan MURKEN u. Raimund WUNSCHE. München, Biering & Brinkman, 95, 235 p.

4929. KIRIAKOPOULOS (G. C.). The Nazi occupation of Crete, 1941–1945. Westport a. London, Praeger, 95, XVI-248 p.

4930. MYLONAKI (Ioanna). Die Suche nach der "Nationalen Identität": eine griechische literarische Zeitschrift der Zwischenkriegszeit. Frankfurt am Main, Peter Lang, 95, 179 p. (Studien zur Geschichte Südosteuropas, 13).

4931. NIKITINA (Tat'jana N.). Élefterios Venizelos – ideolog i praktik grečeskogo liberalizma (1864–1936). (Eleftherios Venizelos, ideologist and practician of the Greek liberalism, 1864–1936). *Nov. novejš. Ist.*, 95, 2, p. 135-155.

4932. TODOROV (Vurban Nikolov). Greek federalism during the nineteenth century: ideas and projects. Boulder, East European Quarterly, 95, XIII-181 p. (East European monographs, 408).

4933. ULUNJAN (A. A.). Kommunističeskaja partija Grecii: Istorija-Ideologija-Politika, 1956–1974. (The communist party of Greece. History. Ideology. Politics, 1956–1974). Moskva: Firma "Grom", Fond Grečeskikh Issledovanij, 95, 283 p.

4934. VARPHES (Kostes A.). Venetotourkikoi kai Rosotourkikoi polemoi stis Hellenikes thalasses, 1453–1821. Athena, Iris, 95, 144 p. (Historia, laographia, taxidia, 3).

Cf. n°s 1169, 8059, 8181, 8754

Großbritannien

4935. ANDREWS (Goeff), FISHMAN (Nina), MORGAN (Kevin). Opening the books: essays on the social and cultural history of the British Communist Party. London, Pluto, 95, 275 p.

4936. BARNETT (Correlli). The lost victory: British dreams, British realities 1945–1950. London, Macmillan, 95, 514 p.

4937. Conquest and union. Fashioning a British state, 1485–1725. Ed. by Steven G. ELLIS a. Sarah BARBER. London a. New York, Logman, 95, XII- 336 p.

4938. CORR (Helen). Dominies and domination in nineteenth-century Scotland. *History Workshop*, 95, 40, p. 151-164.

4939. CRAGOE (Matthew). Conscience or coercion? Clerical influence at the general election of 1868 in Wales. *Past and Present*, 95, 149, p. 140-169.

4940. CUST (Richard). Honour and politics in Early Stuart England: the case of Beaumont v. Hastings. *Past and Present*, 95, 149, p. 57-94.

4941. DONAGAN (Barbara). Halcyon days and the literature of war: England's military education before 1642. *Past and Present*, 95, 147, p. 65-100.

4942. DONALDSON (Gordon). Scotland's history, approaches and reflections. Edinburgh, Scottish Academic Press, 95. XVI-165 p.

4943. ENGEHAUSEN (Frank). Von der Revolution zur Restauration. Die englischen Nonkonformisten 1653–1662. Heidelberg, Winter, 95, 500 p. (Heidelberger Forschungen, 30).

4944. Era of the reform league (The): English labour and radical politics 1857–1872. Ed. by John BREUILLY, Gottfried NIEDHART a. Antony TAYLOR. Mannheim, Palatium im J. & J. Verlag 1995. XI, 369 s., 98 dm. (Mannheimer historische Forschungen, 8).

4945. First World war in British history (The). Ed. by S. CONSTANTINE, M. W. KIRBY, M. B. ROSE, London a. New York, St. Martin's Press, 95, IX-286 p.

4946. HENDLEY (Matthew). "Help us to secure a strong, healthy, prosperous and peaceful Britain": the social arguments of the campaign for compulsory military service in Britain, 1899–1914. *Canadian Journal of History*, 95, 30, 2, p. 261-288.

4947. KNIF (Henrik). Gentlemen and spectators: studies in journals, opera and the social scene in late Stuart London. Helsinki, Finnish Historical Society, 95, 302 p. (Bibliotheca historica, 7).

4948. KURIEV (Murat M.). Artur Uéllesli, gercog Vellington (1769–1852). (Arthur Wellesly, duke Wellington. 1769–1852). *Nov. novejš. Ist.*, 95, 6, p. 144-180. – IDEM. Gercog Vellington. (The Duke of Wellington 1769–1852). Moskva, RADIKS, 95, 254 p.

4949. LAMBERT (Nicholas A.). British naval policy, 1913–1914: financial limitation and strategic revolution. *Journal of modern history*, 95, 67, 3, p. 595-626.

4950. LAMOINE (Georges). Histoire constitutionnelle anglaise. Paris, Presses universitaires de France, 95, 127 p. (Que sais-je?).

4951. LANG (Timothy). The Victorians and the Stuart heritage. Interpretations of a discordant past. Cambridge, Cambridge U. P., 95, XIV-233 p.

4952. LUCKETT (D. A.). Crown patronage and political morality in early Tudor English: the case of Giles, Lord Daubeney. *English Historical Review*, 95, 110, 437, p. 578-595.

4953. MAC KEAN (Charles). A Scottish modernism, 1933–1939. *History Workshop*, 95, 40, p. 165-172.

4954. MAC ROBBIE (Angela). Catholic Glasgow: a map of the city. *History Workshop*, 95, 40, p. 173-180.

4955. MILLER (John). Representatives and represented in England, 1660–89. *Parliements, Estates and Representation*, 95, 15, p. 125-132.

4956. NICHOLLS (Mark). Sir Walter Ralegh's treason: a prosecution document. *English Historical Review*, 95, 110, 438, p. 902-924.

4957. OLDFIELD (John R.). Popular politics and British anti-slavery. The mobilisation of public opinion against the slave trade, 1787–1807. Manchester a. New York, Manchester U. P., 95. X-197 p.

4958. PHILLIPS (John A.), WETHERELL (Charles). The Great Reform Act of 1832 and the political modernization of England. *American Historical Review*, 95, 100, 2, p. 411-436.

4959. POPE (Rex). British demobilization after the Second World War. *Journal of Contemporary History*, 95, 30, 1, p. 65-82.

4960. SCHRÖDER (Hans-Christoph). Englische Geschichte. München, Beck, 95, 136 p.

4961. SEARLE (Geoffrey R.). Country before party: coalition and the idea of "national government" in modern Britain, 1885–1987. London a. New York, Logman, 95, IX-309 p.

4962. Voting records of the British House of Commons, 1761–1820. Vol. 1–6. Ed. by Donald E. GINTER. London, Hambledon Press, 95, 6 vol., 130 p., 560 p., 560 p., 560 p., 645 p., 645 p.

4963. WAHRMAN (Dror). Imagining the middle class. The political representation of class in Britain, c. 1780–1840. Cambridge, Cambridge U. P., 95, XIV-428 p.

4964. WILLIAMSON (Arthur H.). Union with England traditional, union with England radical: Sir James Hope and the mid-seventeenth-century British state. *English Historical Review*, 95, 110, 436, p. 303-322

4965. Winston Churchill: studies in statesmanship. Ed. by R.A.C. PARKER, in association with Correlli BARNETT and Churchill College. London a. Washington, Brassey's, 95, XXI-259 p. (plates, ill.). [Cf. n° <choice> 5037.]

Cf. nos 717, 1067, 1103, 7692, 7714, 7753, 7755, 7804, 7812, 7817, 7819, 7851, 7877, 8030, 8044, 8052, 8062, 8074, 8089, 8104, 8112, 8126, 8135, 8156, 8175, 8209, 8246, 8253, 8294, 8307, 8321, 8339, 8348, 8378, 8382, 8439, 8460, 8611, 8639, 8697, 8766, 8767, 8794

Guatemala

4966. BROWN (Richmond F.). Profits, prestige, and persistence. Juan Fermin de Aycinena and the spirit of enterprise in the kingdom of Guatemala. *Hispanic American Historical Review*, 95, 75, 3, p. 405-440.

4967. CARMACK (Robert M.). Rebels of highland Guatemala: the Quiche-Mayas of Momostenango. Norman, University of Oklahoma Press, 95, XXXIV-525 p. (Civilization of the American Indian series)

4968. DOSAL (Paul Jaime). Power in transition: the rise of Guatemala's industrial oligarchy, 1871–1994. Westport, Praeger, 95, XII-223 p.

4969. LLOSA (Alvaro Vargas), AROCA (Santiago). Riding the tiger: Ramiro de León Carpio's battle for human rights in Guatemala. Miami, Brickell Communications Group, 95, 25 p. (phot.).

4970. LOVELL (George W.). A beauty that hurts: life and death in Guatemala. Toronto, Between the Lines, 95, 161 p. (map.).

4971. PIEL (Jean). El departamento del Quiche bajo la dictadura liberal, 1880–1920. [s. l.], Centro de Estudios Mexicanos y Centroamericanos, 95, 164 p. (ill., 1 map).

Haïti

4972. MARTINEZ (Samuel). Peripheral migrants: Haitians and Dominican Republic sugar plantation. Knoxville, University of Tennessee Press, 95, 228 p. (maps, graph.).

4973. PERUSSE (Roland I.). Haitian democracy restored 1991–1995. Lanham, University Press of America, 95, 170 p.

4974. SOUFFRANT (Claude). Sociologie prospective d'Haiti. Montréal, Ed. du CIDIHCA, 95, 347 p.

4975. VEGA (Bernardo). Trujillo y Haití, 1937–1938. Santo Domingo, Fundación Cultural Dominicana, 95, 427 p. (phot.).

Indien

4976. BAHL (Vinay). The making of the Indian working class: a case of the Tata Iron and Steel Company, 1880–1946. New Delhi a. London, Sage Publications, 95, 432 p.

4977. BOWYER (T. H.). India and the personal finances of Philip Francis. *English Historical Review*, 95, 110, 435, p. 122-131.

4978. GRIFFO (Maurizio). Politica e istituzioni nell'India tardo-coloniale. Un'introduzione al dibattito storiografico. *Rivista storica italiana*, 95, 107, 1, p. 68-90.

4979. GRIGG (John). Myths about the approach to Indian independence. Austin, College of Liberal Arts, Harry Ransom Humanities Research Center, University of Texas at Austin, 95, 25 p. (British studies distinguished lectures)

4980. KHAN (Ansar Hussain). The rediscovery of India: a new subcontinent. With a foreword by Sarvepalli GOPAL. New Delhi, Orient Longman, 95, 351 p. (ill.)

4981. PEERS (Douglas M.). Sepoys, soldiers and the lash: race, caste and army discipline in India. The *Journal of Imperial and Commonwealth History*, 95, 23, p. 211-247.

4982. SETH (Sanjay). Marxist theory and nationalist politics: the case of colonial India. New Delhi, Thousand Oaks, Sage Publications, 95, 256 p.

4983. SIMEON (Dilip). The politics of labour under late colonialism: workers, unions, and the state in Chota Nagpur, 1928–1939. New Delhi, Manohar, 95, XIX-398 p. (ill., 1 folded map)

4984. SINGH (R. G.). GADKAR (R. D.). Social development and justice in India. London, Sangam, 95, 274 p.

4985. THAKUR (Ramesh). The government and politics of India. London, Macmillan, 95, 395 p.

Cf. n°s 7815, 7823, 7824, 7830, 7833, 7834, 7839, 7881, 7882, 8038, 8471, 8731, 8753

Indonesien

4986. BARNES (Philip). Indonesia: the political economy of energy. Oxford, Oxford U. P., 95, 193 p.

4987. CRIBB (Robert). Modern Indonesia: a history since 1945. London a. New York, Longman, 95, XVI-192 p. (Postwar world).

4988. RAMAGE (Douglas E.). Politics in Indonesia: democracy and the ideology of tolerance. London, Routledge, 95, 272 p.

4989. TABALUJAN (Carlo Hein). Fifty years of business in Indonesia (1945–95). Cambridge, Pentland Press, 95, 182 p.

Iran

4990. Iran after the revolution: crisis of an Islamic state. Ed. by S. RAHNEMA and S. BEHDAD. London, Tauris, 95, XII-292 p. (ill.)

Cf. n°s 7975, 8425, 8613, 8656

Irak

4991. TAUBER (Eli'ezer). The formation of modern Syria and Iraq. Ilford a. Portland, Frank Cass, 95, X-417 p.

Cf. n°s 7744, 8760

Irland

4992. COOGAN (Tim Pat). The troubles: Ireland's ordeal 1966–1995 and the search for peace. London, Hutchinson, 95, 460 p.

4993. CRONIN (Mike). The Bleushirt Movement, 1932–35: Ireland's fascists? *Journal of Contemporary History*, 95, 30, 2, p. 311-332.

4994. DUNNINGAN (John P.). Deep-rooted conflict and the IRA case-fire. Lanham, University Press of America, 95, 112 p.

4995. HERLIHY (Kevin). The Irish dissenting tradition, 1650-1750. Dublin, Four Courts Press, 95, 130 p.

4996. Ireland: from independence to occupation, 1641–1660. Ed. by Jane OHLMEYER. Cambridge, Cambridge U. P., 95, 324 p.

4997. JACKSON (Alvin). Colonel Edward Saunderson: land and loyalty in Victorian Ireland. Oxford, Clarendon Press, 95, XII-276 p.

4998. NEWSINGER (John). The Catholic Church in the Nineteenth-Century Ireland. *European History Quarterly*, 95, 25, p. 247-268.

4999. O'DAY (Alan). Terrorism laboratory: the case of Northen Ireland. Aldershot a. Hants, Dartmouth, 95, 255 p.

5000. O'HAGAN (J. W.). The economy of Ireland. London, Macmillan, 95, 406 p.

5001. PROUDFOOT (Lindsay J.). Urban patronage and social authority. The management of the duke of

2. EINZELNE STAATEN

Devonshire's towns in Ireland, 1764–1891. Washington, Catholic University of America Press, 95, XIV-398 p.

5002. SCALLY (Robert James). The end of hidden Ireland: rebellion, famine, and emigration. New York a. Oxford, Oxford U. P., 95, X-266 p.

5003. SMITH (M. L. R.). Fighting for Ireland? The military stategy of the Irish republican movement. London, Routledge, 95, 265 p.

Cf. n°s 7731, 7971, 8125, 8206

Island

5004. SIGURDSSON (Jón Vidar). Forholdet mellom frender, hushold og venner på Island i fristatstiden. (The relationship between kinsmen, household and friends on Iceland in the free state period). *Historisk Tidsskrift* (Norway), 95, 74, p. 311-330.

Israel

5005. Shaping of Israeli identity (The): myth, memory, and trauma. Ed. by Robert S. WISTRICH a. David OHANA. London a. Portland, Frank Cass, 95, [s. p.].

Cf. n°s 8519, 8537, 8538, 8552, 8577, 8599, 8625, 8644

Italien

5006. BATKIN (Leonid M.). Ital'janskoe vozroždenie: Problemy i ljudi. (The Italian Renaissance: problems and persons). Moskva, Rossijskij gosudarstvennyj gumanitarnyj universitet, 95, 446 p.

5007. BATTISTELLI (Pier Paolo). Il «buco nero» della storia della RSI. Analisi storiografica dell'apparato militare della repubblica di Salò. *Storia contemporanea*, 95, 26, 1, p. 101-132.

5008. BÖNINGER (Lorenz). Die Ritterwürde in Mittelitalien zwischen Mittelalter und früher Neuzeit. Mit einem Quellenanhang: päpstliche Ritterernennungen 1417–1564. Berlin, Akademie, 95, VI-366 p.

5009. CAMMARANO (Fulvio). La costruzione dello stato e la classe dirigente italiana (1861–1887). *In*: Storia d'Italia. Vol. 2 [Cf. n° 5047], p. 3-112.

5010. CASELLA (Mario). Massoni e massoneria nel Vallo di Diano tra Ottocento e Novecento (Appunti per una ricerca). *Archivio storico italiano*, 95, 153, 563, p. 3-82.

5011. COFRANCESCO (Dino). Considerazioni sul gramsciazionismo. A proposito dell'ultimo scritto di Alessandro Galante Garrone. *Storia contemporanea*, 95, 26, 1, p. 75-100.

5012. COZZI (G.). Venezia barocca: conflitti di uomini e idee nella crisi del Seicento veneziano. Venezia, Il Cardo, 95, 422 p.

5013. CRAVERI (Piero). La Repubblica dal 1958 al 1992. Torino, UTET, 95, XV-1074 p.

5014. DE FELICE (Alessandro). La socialdemocrazia e la scelta occidentale dell'Italia (1946–1947). *Storia contemporanea*, 95, 26, 1, p. 5-46.

5015. DE FELICE (Franco). La crisi della nazione italiana. *Passato e presente*, 95, 13, 36, p. 5-18.

5016. DE LUNA (Giovanni), REVELLI (Marco). Fascismo, antifascismo: le idee, le identità. Scandicci, La Nuova Italia, 95, 167 p.

5017. DOLHAR (Rafko). Leva sredina in tržaški Slovenci. (The Centre-Left and the Slovenes of Trieste). Trst, Krožek za družbena vprašanja Virgil Šček, 95, 155 p.

5018. DUNNAGE (Jonathan). Law and order in Giolittian Italy: a case study of the province of Bologna. *European History Quarterly*, 95, 25, p. 381-408.

5019. FIOCCA (Giorgio). Il terzo partito: un aspetto della «milanesità» in età giolittiana. *Passato e presente*, 95, 13, 36, p. 33-54.

5020. GALLERANO (Nicola). Antifascismo, Resistenza, identità nazionale. *Passato e presente*, 95, 13, 36, p. 141-148.

5021. GENTILE (Emilio). La politica estera del partito fascista. Ideologia e organizzazione dei Fasci Italiani all'estero (1920–1930). *Storia contemporanea*, 95, 26, 6, p. 897-956.

5022. GHISALBERTI (Carlo). Aspetti istituzionali della crisi del 1943. *Clio*, 95, 31, p. 97-118.

5023. Governo Parri (Il). Atti del Convegno, Roma, 13 e 14 dicembre 1994, Archivio centrale dello Stato. Organizzato dalla FIAP, Federazione italiana associazioni partigiane. Roma, FIAP, 95, 194 p. (ill.).

5024. Innovazione e modernizzazione in Italia fra Otto e Novecento. A cura di Enrico DECLEVA, Carlo G. LACAITA e Angelo VENTURA. Milano, Franco Angeli, 95, 658 p. (La società moderna e contemporanea. Analisi e contributi, 43).

5025. Italy in the Cold War: politics, culture, and society, 1948–58. Ed. by C. DUGGAN and C. WAGSTAFF. Oxford, Berg, 95, [s. p.]

5026. KROGEL (Wolfgang). Dante und die italienische Nation. Untersuchung der 600-Jahr-Feiern zu Ehren Dantes in Florenz 1865 bis 1921. *Archiv für Kulturgeschichte*, 95, 77, p. 429-458.

5027. LEPRE (Aurelio). Mussolini l'italiano: il Duce nel mito e nella realtà. Milano, A. Mondadori, 95, 368 p. (Le scie).

5028. MERLIN (Pierpaolo). Emanuele Filiberto. Un principe tra il Piemonte e l'Europa. Torino, Società Editrice Internazionale, 95, X-370 p.

5029. Mito del Risorgimento nell'Italia unita (Il). Atti del Convegno, Milano, 9–12 novembre 1993. *Ri-*

sorgimento, 95, 47, p. 5-575 [Scritti di Giovanni SPADOLINI, Roberto VIVARELLI, Franco DELLA PERUTA, Fernando MAZZOCCA, Giovanna ROSA, Paolo ALATRI, Cosimo CECCUTI, Fabrizio DOLCI, Ilaria PORCIANI, Bruno TOBIA, Giovanni SABBATUCCI, Carlo GHISALBERTI, Giuseppe PARLATO, Maria Luisa CICALESE, Arturo COLOMBO, Zeffiro CIUFFOLETTI, Andrea RICCARDI, Gabriella CIAMPI, Paul GINSBORG, Aldo ALBONICO, Vittorio SPINAZZOLA, Jens PETERSEN, Fabrizio PANZERA, Matteo SANFILIPPO, Fusatoshi FUJISAVA, Giorgio RUMI, Angelo VARNI, Sergio ROMANO].

5030. MITTERMAIER (Karl). Mussolinis Ende. Die Republik von Salo 1943–1945. München, Langen Müller, 95, 256 p.

5031. MITTERMAIR (Veronika). Von der Illegalität zur Macht. Soziale Merkmale des Völkischen Kampfringes Südtirols und der Arbeitsgemeinschaft der Optanten. *Zeitgeschichte*, 95, 22, 5-6, p. 211-222.

5032. MORNATI (Lorenzo). Gli intellettuali, il partito e il fascismo italiano a Losanna. *Storia contemporanea*, 95, 26, 6, p. 1003-1061.

5033. NERI SERNERI (Simone). Classe, partito, nazione: alle origini della democrazia italiana 1919–1948. Manduria, P. Lacaita Editore, 95, 299 p. – IDEM. Resistenza e democrazia dei partiti. I socialisti nell'Italia del 1943–1945. Manduria, P. Lacaita, 95, XIX-534 p.

5034. NICCOLI (Ottavia). Il seme della violenza: putti, fanciulli e mammoli nell'Italia tra Cinque e Seicento. Roma, Laterza, 95, XXIII-210 p. (Quadrante).

5035. PACE (Enzo). L'unità dei cattolici in Italia. Origini e decadenza di un mito collettivo. Milano, Guerini e Associati, 95, 179 p.

5036. PEZZINO (Paolo). Appunti sul tema delle classi dirigenti nella storia dell'Italia contemporanea. *In*: Ricerche di storia moderna. 1 [Cf. n° 4647], p. 343-375. – IDEM. Mafia: industria della violenza. Scritti e documenti inediti sulla mafia dalle origini ai giorni nostri. Firenze, La Nuova Italia, 95, 400 p.

5037. POMBENI (Paolo). Churchill and Italy 1922–1940. *In*: Winston Churchill: studies in statesmanship [Cf. n° 4965], 65-82.

5038. REGELE (Ludwig W.). Bleiber, Optanten, Juden und Widerstand in Südtirol. Verfassungsrechtliche Lage in Italien nach dem Sturz Mussolinis. *Österr. i Gesch. u. Lit.*, 95, 39, 2, p. 77-88.

5039. ROMANELLI (Raffaele). Il comando impossibile. Stato e società nell'Italia liberale. Bologna, Il Mulino, 95, 360 p. (Saggi, 430). – IDEM. Individuo, famiglia e collettività nel codice civile della borghesia italiana. *In*: Saperi della borghesia [Cf. n° 6043], p. 351-399. – IDEM. La nobiltà nella costituzione dell'Italia contemporanea. *Storia Amministrazione Costituzione. Annale ISAP*, 95, 3, p. 247-267.

5040. ROMANO (Ruggiero). Quale "Risorgimento"? *RES*, 95, 5, 9, p. 39-41.

5041. SANTOMASSIMO (Gianpasquale). Fascismo e antifascismo nel paese delle "anomalie". *Passato e presente*, 95, 13, 34, p. 5-14.

5042. SAROGNI (Emilia). La Donna Italiana. Il lungo cammino verso i diritti, 1861–1994. Parma, Nuova Pratiche Editrice, 95, 226 p.

5043. SCOPPOLA (Pietro). 25 aprile: liberazione. Torino, Einaudi, 95, 101 p.

5044. SCRIBA (Friedemann). Il mito di Roma, l'estetica e gli intellettuali negli anni del consenso: la Mostra Augustea della Romanità 1937–38. *Quaderni di storia*, 95, 21, 41, p. 67-84.

5045. SOMOGYI (Stefano), SOMOGYI (Rosa Anna). Il suicidio in Italia dal 1864 ad oggi. Roma, Kappa, 95, 246 p.

5046. STILLE (Alexander). Exellent cadavers: the Mafia and the death of the first Italian Republic. London, Cape, 95, 467 p.

5047. Storia d'Italia. Vol. 2. Il nuovo stato e la società civile: 1861–1887. A cura di Giovanni SABBATUCCI e Vittorio VIDOTTO. Roma e Bari, Laterza, 95, XI-644 p. [Cf. n° <scelta> 5009.]

5048. Storia dello stato italiano. Dall'unità a oggi. A cura di Raffaele ROMANELLI. Roma, Donzelli, XVI-511 p. [Cf. n[os] <scelta> 7561, 7589, 7598, 7599, 7607, 7609, 7637, 7653.]

5049. SUZZI VALLI (Roberta). Il fascio italiano a Londra. L'attività politica di Camillo Pellizzi. *Storia contemporanea*, 95, 26, 6, p. 957-1002.

5050. TASCA (Angelo). Nascita e avvento del fascismo. A cura di Sergio SOAVE. Scandicci, La Nuova Italia, 95, XXVIII-583 p. (Biblioteca di storia).

5051. TRANFAGLIA (Nicola). La prima guerra mondiale e il fascismo. Torino, UTET, 95, XVI-690 p.

5052. VILLARI (P.). I mali d'Italia. Scritti su mafia, camorra e brigantaggio. Intr. di E. GARIN. Firenze, Vallecchi, 95, 339 p.

5053. VIVANTI (Corrado). The history of the Jews in Italy and the history of Italy. *Journal of modern history*, 95, 67, 2, p. 309-357.

Cf. n[os] *1086, 4629, 7703, 7712, 7724, 7920, 7991, 8005, 8010, 8210, 8094, 8398, 8410, 8477, 8569*

Japan

5054. IWAMI (Toru). Japan in the international financial system. London, Macmillan, 95, 186 p.

5055. MOSK (Carl). Competition and cooperation in Japanese labour markets. London, Macmillan, 95, 290 p.

5056. RAMSEYER (J. Mark), ROSENBLUTH (Frances M.). The politics of oligarchy: institutional choice in imperial Japan. Cambridge, Cambridge U. P., 95, 224 p.

2. EINZELNE STAATEN

5057. SENATOR (Aleksej I.). Političeskie partii Japonii: Sravnitel'nyj analiz programm, organizacionnoj i parlamentskoj dejatel'nosti (1945–1992). (The Japanese political parties: the comparative analysis of programmes, organization and parliamentary activities, 1945–1992). Moskva, Vostočnaja literatura, RAN. In-t sravnitel'noj politologii i problem rabočego dviženija, 95, [s. p.].

5058. SEVOST'JANOV (Grigorij N.). Japonija 1945 goda v ocenke sovetskikh diplomatov. Novye arkhivnye materialy. (Japan of 1945 in the assessment of the Soviet diplomats. New archival materials). *Nov. novejš. Ist.*, 95, 6, p. 32-53.

5059. SMITH (Dennis B.). Japan since 1945: the rise of economic superpower. London, Macmillan, 95, 180 p.

5060. TAKAHASHI (Mutsuko). Japanese welfare society: analysing the Japanese welfare discourses. Tampere, Tampereen yliopisto, 95, 288 p. (Acta Univ. Tamperensis, A 462).

5061. YOSHIMI (Shun'ya). Les rituels politiques du Japon moderne. Tournées impériales et stratégies du regard dans le Japon de Meiji. *Annales*, 95, 50, 2, p. 341-372.

5062. YUI (Daizaburō). Nichi-Bei-Sensō-kan no Sōkoku. (Conflicting views of war between Japan and United States). Tokyo, Iwanami Shoten, 95, 236 p.

Cf. n°s 7735, 8064, 8112, 8147, 8209, 8287, 8301, 8320, 8345, 8373, 8470, 8536, 8561, 8563, 8574, 8591, 8601, 8651, 8664, 8737, 8756, 8776, 8795

Jugoslawien

5063. BANAC (Ivo). Nacionalno pitanje u Jugoslaviji: porijeklo, povijest, politika. (The national issue in Yugoslavia: origin, history, politics). Zagreb, Durieux, 95, 374 p.

5064. CSUKA (János). A délvidéki magyarság története, 1918–1941. (Histoire des Hongrois du Sud). Budapest, Püki, 95, 499 p.

5065. DURIĆ (Rašid). Mißbrauch des Mythos in der serbischen Literatur und zeitgenössischen Politik. *Österr. Z. f. Volkskde.*, 95, 49 (98), 4, p. 397-422.

5066. KUDRJAVCEVA (Elena P.). Korolevskie dinastii Jugoslavii. (The Jugoslav king dynasties). *Nov. novejš. Ist.*, 95, 3, p. 145-157.

5067. MOSETTIG (Ivan). Obmane: splitska viđenja započeta 1941. (Misinterpretations: Split views beginning with 1941). Split, Književni krug, 95, 250 p.

5068. PIRJEVEC (Jože). Jugoslavija: nastanek, razvoj ter razpad Karadjordjevićeve in Titove Jugoslavije. (Yugoslavia 1918–1992. The formation, development and collapse of Karadjordevic's and Tito's Yugoslavia). Koper, Lipa, 95, 461 p. (ill.).

5069. ŠETIĆ (Nevio). Istra između tradicionalnog i modernog ili O procesu integracije suvremene hrvatske nacije u Istri. (Istria between the traditional and modern, or on the process of integration of modern Croat nation in Istria). Pazin, Naša sloga, 95, 160 p.

5070. TOLDI (Ferenc). A jugoszláv állam kialakulása és felbomlása. (La formation et la dissolution de l'État yougoslave). Budapest, MTA Állam-és Jogtud. Int., 95, 182 p.

Cf. n°s 7771, 8485, 8679, 8713, 8742

Kambodscha

5071. MARTELLI (Fabio). Crescita economica e autoritarismo in Cambogia. *Relazioni Internazionali*, 95, 59, 33, p. 50-62.

Cf. n° 8673

Kanada

* 5072. BELL (Sandra M.). Victory bonding: wartime messages from Canada's government, 1939–1945: a bibliography = Victoire oblige: les messages du gouvernement canadien pendant la guerre 1939–1945: une bibliographie. Ottawa, National Library of Canada, 95, 15 p.

5073. BOTHWELL (Robert). Canada and Quebec: one country, two histories. Vancouver, UBC Press, 95, xiv-269 p.

5074. DOUGLAS (William Alexander Binney), GREENHOUS (Brereton). Out of the shadows: Canada in the Second World War. Toronto a. Oxford, Dundurn Press, 95, 304 p.

5075. HANNANT (Larry). The infernal machine: investigating the loyalty of Canada's citizens. Toronto, University of Toronto Press, 95, IX-330 p.

5076. JOHNSTON (Wendy). Aux sources du développement inégal: le financement de l'enseignement public à Montreal de 1920 a 1945. *Canadian Historical Review*, 95, 76, 1, p. 43-80.

5077. MARTIN (Ged). Britain and the origins of Canadian confederation, 1837–67. Basingstoke, Macmillan, 95, XI-388 p.

5078. REID (Jennifer). Myth, symbol, and colonial encounter: British and Mi'kmaq in Acadia, 1700–1867. Ottawa, University of Ottawa Press, 95, 133 p. (Religions and beliefs series, 4).

5079. TRUDEL (Marcel). La population du Canada en 1666: recensement reconstitué. Sillery, Septentrion, 95, 379 p.

5080. WAITE (P. B.). Journeys through thirteen volumes: the dictionary of Canadian biography. *Canadian Historical Review*, 95, 76, 1, p. 464-481.

5081. WYNN (Graeme). Maps and dreams of nationhood: a (re)view of the historical atlas of Canada. *Canadian Historical Review*, 95, 76, 1, p. 482.

Cf. nº 7746

Kenia

5082. ASKWITH (Tom). From Mau Mau to Harambee: memoirs and memoranda of colonial Kenya. Cambridge, African Studies Centre, University of Cambridge, 95, VIII-221 p.

5083. HAUGERUD (Angelique). The culture of politics in modern Kenya. Cambridge. Cambridge U. P., 95, XVI-266 p. (ill., maps).

5084. SHAW (Carolyn Martin). Colonial inscriptions: race, sex, and class in Kenya. Minneapolis a. London, University of Minnesota Press, 95, IX-250 p. (ill., map).

Cf. nº 7880

Kolumbien

5085. ANRUP (Roland). Ordet och svärdet. Maktsymbolik och diskursiv kamp i columbiansk politik och historia. (Word and sword. Power symbols and argument struggle in Columbian politics and history). *Historisk Tidskrift* (Sweden), 95, 1, p. 34-53.

5086. CARMONA (Darío Acevedo). La mentalidad de las élites sobre la violencia en Colombia (1936–1949). Bogotá, Instituto de Estudios Políticos y Relaciones Internacionales y El Ancora Editores, 95, 224 p.

5087. ROBAYO (Juan Manuel). Iglesia, tierra y credito en la colonia: Tunja y su provincia en el siglo XVIII. Tunja, Universidad Pedagogica y Tecnologica de Colombia, 95, 92 p.

5088. RUEDA MENDEZ (David). Esclavitud y sociedad en la provincia de Tunja, siglo XVIII. Tunja, Universidad Pedagogica y Tecnologica de Colombia, 95, 169 p. (ill., maps).

5089. STOLLER (Richard). Alfonso López Pumerejo and Liberal Radicalism in 1930s Colombia. *Journal of Latin American Studies*, 95, 27, p. 367-398.

Korea

Cf. nᵒˢ 7734, 8025, 8568, 8638, 8660, 8705, 9069-9075

Kroatien

5090. BIĆANIĆ (Rudolf). Ekonomska podloga hrvatskog pitanja i drugi radovi. (Economic framework of the Croatian issue and other papers). Zagreb, Pravni fakultet, 95, 504 p.

5091. JAREB (Jere). Pola stoljeća hrvatske politike: povodom Mačekove autobiografije. (Fifty years of Croatian politics: occasioned by Maček's autobiography). Zagreb, Institut za suvremenu povijest, 95, 180 p.

5092. MATKOVIĆ (Hrvoje). Suvremena politièka povijest Hrvatske. (A modern political history of Croatia). Zagreb, Ministarstvo unutarnjih polova Republike Hrvatske, 95, 262 p. – IDEM. Svetozar Pribićević: ideolog, stranački vođa, emigrant. (Svetozar Pribićević: ideologist, party leader, emigrant). Zagreb, Hrvatska sveučilišna naklada, 95, 330 p.

Kuba

5093. DANIEL (Yvonne). Rumba: dance and social change in contemporary Cuba. Bloomington, Indiana U. P., 95, 196 p. (maps, graphs., fig., phot.).

5094. DE LA FUENTE (Alejandro). Race and inequality in Cuba, 1899–1981. *Journal of Contemporary History*, 95, 30, 1, p. 131-168.

5095. HELG (Aline). Our rightful share: the Afro-Cuban struggle for equality, 1886–1912. Chapel Hill a. London, University of North Carolina Press, 95, XII-361 p. (ill., map)

5096. HERNÁNDEZ GONZÁLES (Pablo J.). Cuba en la octava decada del siglo XVII: visita del obispo Diaz Vara Calderon. *Boletin de la Academia Nacional de la Historia*, 95, 78, 3, [s. p.].

5097. OPATRNÝ (Josef). Cuba: algunos problemas de su historia. Prague, Charles University, 95, 179 p.

5098. PARKER (Dick). La Revolución Cubana. Caracas, Biblioteca Nacional Facultad de ciencias Economicas y Sociales, UCV, 95, XXXIX-172 p.

5099. PEREZ (Louis A.). Essays on Cuban history: historiography and research. Gainesville, University Press of Florida, 95, XIV-306 p.

5100. SOTO (Lionel). La revolución precursora de 1933: un momento trascendental en la continuidad revolucionaria de Jose Marti: ensayo de indagación politico-social y economico en un periodo reciente de la historia de Cuba. Ciudad de La Habana, Editorial SI-MAR, S.A., 95, 765 p.

Cf. nᵒˢ 8049, 8709, 8723

Libanon

5101. SALEM (Elie A.). Violence and diplomacy in Lebanon: the troubled years, 1982–1988. London, Tauris, 95, VII-296 p.

Libyen

5102. VENDEWALLE (Dirk). Qadhafi's Libya 1969–1994. London, Macmillan, 95, 256 p.

Cf. nº 7852

2. EINZELNE STAATEN

Luxemburg

5103. SPANG (Paul). Etat general des Fonds conservés aux Archives nationales du Grand-Duché de Luxembourg et aux archives de la Section historique de l'Institut Grand-Ducal. Luxembourg, Section historique de l'Institut Grand-Ducal de Luxembourg, 95, [s. p.].

Malaysia

5104. LEARY (John). Violence and the dream people: the Orang Asli in the Malayan emergency, 1948–1960. Athens a. Ohio, Ohio University Center for International Studies, 95, XIII-238 p. (ill., maps). (Monographs in international studies. Southeast Asia series).

5105. LEE (Hoong Phun). Constitutional conflicts in contemporary Malaysia. Kuala Lumpur a. Oxford, Oxford U. P., 95, 184 p.

Cf. n°s 7820, 8744

Marokko

5106. FAROUK (Ahmed), De La Veronne (Chantal). Sources françaises de l'histoire du Maroc au XVIIIe siècle: année 1740. *Revue d'Histoire Maghrébine*, 95, 77-78, p. 191-221.

5107. SUKER (Dahir Mohamed). Political crisis in Morocco 1951: a study based on Iraqi documents. *Revue d'Histoire Maghrébine* (Partie arabe), 95, 77-78, p. 167-185.

Cf. n°s 7846, 7849, 7869

Mauritania

5108. TAYLOR (Raymond M.). Warriors, tributaries, blood money and political transformation in nineteenth-century Mauritania. *Journal of African History*, 95, 36, 3, p. 419-442.

Mazedonien

5109. MAMUROVSKI (Tasko). Makedoncite vo Egejska Makedonija, 1945–1946. Skopje, In-t za nacionalna istorija, 95, 224 p.

5110. PANOVSKA (Liljana). Terorot vo Egejskiot del na Makedonija pod germansko-italijanska okupacija, 1941–1944. (Terror in the Aegean part of Macedonia under German and Italian occupation, 1941–1944). Skopje, Institut za nacionalna istorija, 95, 159 p.

5111. TOKAY (A. Gül). Makedonya Sorunu: Jön Türk İhtilalinin Kökenleri (1903–1908). (Le Problème de Macédoine: les racines de la Révolution de Jeune Turc). İstanbul, Afa Yayınları, 95, [s. p.].

Cf. n°s 8045, 8268

Mexiko

5112. ALONSO (Ana María). Thread of blood: colonialism, revolution, and gender on Mexico's northern frontier. Tucson, University of Arizona Press, 95, 303 p. (map.).

5113. BECKER (Marjorie). Setting the Virgin of Fire: Lázaro Cárdenas, Michoacán Peasants, and the redemption of the Mexican Revolution. Berkeley, University of California Press, 95, 188 p. (map.).

5114. BOYER (Richard). Lives of the bigamists: marriage, family, and community in Colonial Mexico. Albequerque, University of New Mexico Press, 95, 340 p. (ill., map.).

5115. CARROLL (Patrick J.). Los mexicanos negros, el mestizaje y los fundamentos olvidados de la Raza Cósmica: una perspectiva regional. *Historia Mexicana*, 94-95, 44, p. 403-438.

5116. FICKER (Sandra Kuntz). Empresa extranjera y mercado interno: el ferrocarril central mexicano, 1880–1907. Mexico City, El Colegio de México, 95, 390 p. (map., graph.).

5117. GARAVAGLIA (Juan Carlos). Atlixco: l'eau, les hommes et la terre dans une vallée mexicaine (XVe–XVIIe s.). *Annales*, 95, 50, 6, p. 1309-1350.

5118. GLEDHILL (John). Neoliberism, transnationalization, and rural poverty: a case study of Michoacán, Mexico. Boulder, Westview Press, 95, 243 p. (map.).

5119. GUARDINO (Peter). Barbarism or republican law? Guerrero's peasants and national politics, 1820–1846. *Hispanic American Historical Review*, 95, 75, 2, p. 185-214.

5120. HALE (Charles A.). Frank Tannenbaum and the Mexican revolution. *Hispanic American Historical Review*, 95, 75, 2, p. 215-246.

5121. HODGES (Donald C.). Mexican anarchism after the revolution. Austin, University of Texas Press, 95, 251 p.

5122. JOSEPH (Gilbert M.), NUGENT (Deniel). Everyday forms of state formation: revolution and negotiation of rule in modern Mexico. Durham and London, Duke U. P., 95, XIX-432 p.

5123. LERNER SIGAL (Victoria). Espionaye y revolución mexicana. *Historia Mexicana*, 94-95, 44, p. 615-641.

5124. MALLON (Florencia E.). Peasant and nation: the making of postcolonian Mexico and Peru. Berkeley a. London, University of California Press, 95, XXII-472 p.

5125. MIDDLEBROOK (Kevin J.). The paradox of revolution: labor, the state, and authoritarianism in Mexico. Stanford, Stanford U. P., XIX-578 p.

5126. MILLER (Simon). Landlords and haciendas in modernizing Mexico: essays in radical rappraisal. Amsterdam, CEDLA, 95, 203 p.

5127. NEEDLER (Martin C.). Mexican politics: the containment of conflict. New York, Praeger, 95, 144 p.

5128. PONIATOWSKA (Elena). Nothing, nobody: the voice of the Mexico City earthquake. Philadelphia, Temple U. P., 95, 327 p. (phot., maps).

5129. SALMERÓN CASTRO (Alicia). El general agrarista en la lucha contra los cristeros. El movimiento en Aguascalientes y las razones de Genovevo de la O. *Historia Mexicana*, 94-95, 44, p. 535-577.

5130. SERRANO (Monica). The armed branch of the state: civil-military relations in Mexico. *Journal of Latin American Studies*, 95, 27, p. 423-448.

5131. TAYLOR HANSEN (Lawrence Douglas). ¿Charlatán o filibustero peligroso? El papel de Richard "Dick" Ferris en la revuelta magonista de 1911 en Baja California. *Historia Mexicana*, 94-95, 44, p. 579-614.

5132. TORO (María Celio). Mexico's "war" on drugs: causes and consequences. Boulder a. London, Lynne Rienner Publishers, 95, XI-109 p.

5133. YANKELEVICH (Pablo). Una mirada argentina de la revolución mexicana. La gesta de Manuel Ugarte (1910-1917). *Historia Mexicana*, 94-95, 44, p. 643-674.

Cf. n°s 7758, 7905, 8113, 8681

Mosambik

5134. ISHEMO (Shubi Lugemalila). The Lower Zambezi Basin: a study in economy and society, 1850-1920. Aldershot, Avebury, 95, XII-292 p. (maps).

5135. PENVENNE (Jeanne Marie). African workers and colonial racism: Mozambican strategies and struggles in Lourenco Marques, 1877-1962. Portsmouth, Heinemann a. Johannesburg, Witwatersrand U. P., 95, XVII- 229 p. (ill., maps).

5136. TEIXEIRA (Francisco Nuñes). A igreja em Mocambique na hora da independencia. Coimbra, Grafica de Coimbra, 95, 160 p.

Cf. n°s 7855, 7860

Namibia

5137. GROTH (Siegfried). Namibia, the wall of silence: the dark days of the liberation struggle. Wuppertal, Hammer, 95, 206 p.

5138. LEYS (Colin). Namibia's liberation struggle: the two-edged sword. London, James Currey, 95, X-212 p.

5139. PELTOLA (Pekka). The lost May Day: Namibian workers struggle for independence. Helsinki, Finnish Anthropological Society, in association with the Nordic Africa Institute, 95, 302 p.

Cf. n° 7882

Neuseeland

5140. CRAIG (Dick). The realms of King Tawhiao: with review of causes of 1860-64 Waori Wars. [S. l.], [s. n.], 95, 141 p.

5141. Te pukaki Maori: a guide to Maori sources at National Archives. Wellington, National Archives, 95, 100 p.

Niederlande

** 5142. GROTIUS (Hugo). Liber de antiquitate reipublicae Batavicae. Vertaald en ingeleid door het Collegium Classicum c.n. E.D.E.P.O.L. Arnhem, Gouda Quint, 95, XXIX-179 p.

5143. De staatsregeling van 1801: bronnen voor de totstandkoming. Bewerkt door L. DE GOU. Den Haag, Instituut voor Nederlandse Geschiedenis, 95, XLIII-721 p. (Rijks geschiedkundige publicatien. Kleine serie, 85).

5144. Gestalten van de Gouden Eeuw: een Hollands groepsportret. Onder redactie van H. M. BELIEN, A. Th. VAN DEURSEN en G.J. VAN SETTEN. Amsterdam, Bert Bakker, 95, 420 p.

5145. GORTER-VAN ROYEN (Laetitia V. G.). Maria van Hongarije, regentes der Nederlanden: een politieke analyse op basis van haar regentschaps-ordonnanties en haar correspondentie met Karel V. Hilversum, Verloren, 95, 383 p.

5146. GROENVELD (S.). Was de Nederlandse Republiek verzuild? Over segmentering van de samenleving binnen de Verenigde Nederlanden: rede. Leiden, Rijksuniversiteit Leiden, 95, 30 p.

5147. HELLEMA (Duco). The relevance and irrelevance of Dutch anti-communism: the Netherlands and the Hungarian revolution, 1956-1957. *Journal of Contemporary History*, 95, 30, 1, p. 169-186.

5148. ISRAEL (Jonathan). The Dutch Republic. Its rise, greatness, and fall, 1477-1806. Oxford, Clarendon Press, 95, XXX-1231 p.

5149. KAPLAN (Benjamin J.). Calvinists and Libertines: confession and community in Utrecht, 1578-1620. Oxford, Clarendon Press, 95, [s. p.]

5150. KLEIN (S. R. E.). Patriots republikanisme. Politieke cultuur in Nederland (1766-1787). Amsterdam, Amsterdam U. P., 95, 340 p.

5151. KOOLE (R. A.). Politieke partijen in Nederland: onstaan en ontwikkeling van partijen en partijstelsel. Utrecht, Het Spectrum, 95, 400 p.

5152. Miracle mirrored (A): the Dutch Republic in European perspective. Ed. by Karel DAVIDS a. Jan LUCASSEN. Cambridge a. New York, Cambridge U. P., 95, XX-539 p.

5153. Sporen en spiegels: beschouwingen over geschiedenis en identiteit. Onder redactie van J. C. DEKKER. Tilburg, Tilburg U. P., 95, 139 p.

Cf. n°s 7819, 7852, 7925, 8344, 8363

Niger

5154. COOPER (Barbara M.). Women's worth and wedding gift exchange in Maradi, Niger, 1907–1989. *Journal of African History*, 95, 36, 1, p. 121-140.

Nikaragua

5155. SPOOR (Max). The state and domestical agricultural markets in Nicaragua: from interventionism to neoliberalism. Basingstoke, Macmillan in association with the Institute of social Studies, 95, XXXIV-298 p.

Norwegen

5156. DE FIGUEIREDO (Ivo). Ideologiens primat. Nasjonal Samling 1937–1940. (The primacy of ideology. Norwegian fascism in the late 1930's). *Historisk Tidsskrift* (Norway), 95, 74, p. 370-390.

5157. EGGE (Åsmund). Komintern og krisen i det norske arbeiderparti. (Komintern and the crisis in the Norwegian Labour Party). Oslo, Universitetsforlaget, 95, 134 p.

5158. FELDBÆK (Ole). Frederik 6. og Norge i januar 1814. (Frederik VI and Norway in January 1814). *Historisk Tidsskrift* (Norway), 95, 74, p. 283-310.

5159. GUSTAFSSON (Harald). Om norsk och annan nationalism: slutreplik till Kåre Lunden. (About the Norwegian nationalism and other: reply to Kåre Lunden). *Historisk Tidskrift* (Sweden), 95, 3, p. 355-357.

5160. HAUG (Eldbjørg). Erik av Pommerns norske kroning. (The Norwegian coronation of Erik the Pomeranian). *Historisk Tidsskrift* (Norway), 95, 74, p. 1-21.

5161. HELLE (Egil). Kyrre Grepp. Oslo, Tiden, 95, 219 p.

5162. IMSEN (Steinar). Norsk bondekommunalisme: fra Magnus Lagabøte til Kristian Kvart. Vol. 2. Lydriketiden. (Norwegian communalism from King Magnus Lagabøte to King Kristian Kvart. Vol 2. 1537–1814). Trondheim, Historisk institutt, Universitetet i Trondheim, 95, 289 p. (Skriftserie fra Historisk institutt, 7).

5163. JACOBSEN (Roy). Trygve Bratteli. En fortelling. Oslo, Cappelen, 1995, 615 p.

5164. LIE (Einar). Ambisjon og tradisjon: Finansdepartementet 1945–1965. (Ambition and tradition. The history of the Norwegian Ministry of Finance 1945–1965). Oslo, Universitetsforlaget, 95, 493 p. (ill.).

5165. LUNDEN (Kåre). Norge i 1814. (Norway in 1814). *Historisk Tidskrift* (Sweden), 95, 1, p. 75-77.

5166. Norsk historisk leksikon. Naeringsliv, rettsvesen, administrasjon, mynt, mått og vekt, militaere forthold, byggeskikk m.m 1500–1850. 2. utg. Ed. Rolf FLADBY, Steinar IMSEN, Harald WINGE. Oslo, Cappelen, 95, 389 p.

5167. RIAN (Øystein). Aschehougs Norgeshistorie. Vol. 5. Den nye begynnelsen 1520–1660. (Aschehoug's history of Norway. Vol. 5. The new beginning: 1520–1660). Ed. by Knut HELLE. Oslo, Aschehoug, 95, 263 p.

5168. SEIP (Anne-Lise). Nation-building within the union: politics, class and culture in the Norwegian nation-state in the nineteenth century. *Scandinavian Journal of History*, 95, 20, p. 35-50.

Cf. n°s 7759, 7760, 7933, 8085, 8115, 8242, 8463

Österreich (Österreich-Ungarn)

5169. BEER (Siegfried). Wien in der frühen Besatzungszeit. Erkundigungen des US-Geheimdienstes OSS/SSU im Jahre 1945. Eine exemplarische Dokumentation. *Jb. d. Vereins f. Gesch. d. Stadt Wien*, 95, 51, p. 35-92 (Dok.).

5170. BOWMAN (William D.). Regional history and the Austrian nation. *Journal of modern history*, 95, 67, 4, p. 873-897.

5171. CZÖVEK (István). Der slawische Kongreß 1867 und die Nationalitäten des Habsburgerreiches. *Mitt. d. Inst. f. Österr. Gesch.-Forsch.*, 95, 103, 1-2, p. 101-108.

5172. DICKSON (P. G. M.). Monarchy and bureaucracy in late eighteenth-century Austria. *English Historical Review*, 95, 110, 436, p. 323-367.

5173. DIÓSZEGI (István). Közjogi kérdések a közös minisztertanács előtt 1883–1895. (Questions de droit public au conseil des ministres communs entre 1883–1895). *Levéltári szle.*, 95, 45, 2, p. 3-20.

5174. Dokumentationen. Der Bericht des US-Geheimagenten Jack H. Taylor über das Konzentrationslager Mauthausen. *Zeitgeschichte*, 95, 22, 9-10, p. 318-341 (ill., Faksimiles).

5175. ETZERDORFER (Irene). Arisiert. Eine Spurensuche im gesellschaftlichen Untergrund der Republik. Wien, Kremayr & Scheriau, 95, 204 p. (ill.).

5176. FALCH (Sabine). "Legaler Sturz des Systems von unten her auf dem Wege über die Länder und Gemeinden". Zu den NS-Erfolgen bei den Gemeinderatswahlen in Tirol 1932 und 1933. *Zeitgeschichte*, 95, 22, 5-6, p. 188-210 (Tab., Graph. Darstellungen).

5177. GÓRALSKI (Zbigniew). Maria Teresa [Cesarzowa Austrii]. (Marie Thérèse [impératrice d'Autriche]). Wrocław, Zakł. Narod. im. Ossolińskich, 95, 256 p.

5178. GRÜNBART (Michael). Jakob Philipp Fallmerayer und sein türkischer Orden. Briefe und Aktenstücke aus den Jahren 1847 bis 1849. *Biblos*, 95, 44, 2, p. 271-295 (ill.).

5179. HAGSPIEL (Hermann). Die Ostmark. Österreich im Großdeutschen Reich 1938 bis 1945. Wien, Braumüller, 95, VIII-466 p.

5180. HAUPTNER (Rudolf). Das "Luftschutz-Raumnetz Innere Stadt" in Wien 1944–45. *Wien. Gesch.-Bl.*, 95, 50, 2, p. 96-104 (Pläne).

5181. HEISZLER (Vilmos). Birodalmi és nemzeti szimbólumok Bécsben és Budapesten, 1867–1918. (Symboles impériaux et nationaux à Vienne et à Budapest, 1867–1918). *Budapesti negyed*, 95, 3, 3, p. 173-192.

5182. HINTERHUBER (Hartmann). Ermordet und vergessen. Nationalsozialistische Verbrechen an psychisch Kranken und Behinderten in Nord- und Südtirol. Innsbruck u. Wien, Vip-Vlg. Integrative Psychiatrie, 95, 133 p. (ill., Karten).

5183. MAKKAI (Béla). Magyar szórványgondozás Bosznia-Hercegovinában. (Le patronage des Hongrois en Bosnie-Herzégovine). *Regio*, 95, 6, 3, p. 65-88.

5184. MALINA (Peter). Die "vergessenen Opfer" des Nationalsozialismus in Wien. Ergebnisse einer fragmentarischen archivalischen Spurensuche. *Jb. d. Vereins f.Gesch. d. Stadt Wien*, 95, 51, p. 143-176.

5185. OGRIS (Alfred). Spittal an der Drau als zeitweiliger Sitz der Kärntner Landesregierung und der provisorischen Landesversammlung im Jahre 1919. Gedanken zum 75. Jahrestag im Jahre 1994. *Carinthia I*, 95, 185, p. 557-566 (ill.).

5186. PERZ (Bertrand). "Auf Wunsch des Führers ..." Der Bau von Luftschutzkellern in Linz durch Häftlinge des Konzentrationslagers Linz II. *Zeitgeschichte*, 95, 22, 9-10, p. 342-356.

5187. PETZNEK (Fridrich). Das kaiserlichkönigliche Flüchtlingslager in Bruck an der Leitha 1914–1918. Bruck an der Leitha, Kultur- und Museumsverein, 95, 44 p. (ill., Karten).

5188. POKORNÝ (Jiři). Die Tschechen für oder gegen Österreich. *Der Donauraum*, 95, 35, 3, p. 28-36.

5189. PORĘBSKI (Andrzej). Dylematy narodowe Austriaków. (Dilemmes nationaux des Autrichiens). *Przegląd Polonijny*, 95, 21, 1, p. 47-70. [Eng. Summary].

5190. RAINER (Johann). General De Bono und die italienische Besetzung Kärntens 1919–1920. *Carinthia I*, 95, 185, p. 537-548.

5191. REBHANN (Fritz M.). Die braunen Jahre. Wien 1938–1945. Wien, Wiener Journal, Zeitschriftenvlg, 95, 323 p. (Edition Atelier).

5192. Russen in Wien (Die): die Befreiung Österreichs, Wien 1945. Augenzeugenbericht und über 400 unpublizierte Fotos aus Rußland. Hrsg. v. Erich KLEIN. Wien, Falter Verlag, 95, 247 p. (ill.).

5193. SCHAUSBERGER (Franz). Ins Parlament, um es zu zerstören. Das "parlamentarische" Agi(ti)eren der Nationalsozialisten in den Landtagen von Wien, Niederösterreich, Salzburg und Vorarlberg nach den Landtagswählen 1932. Wien, Köln u. Weimar, Böhlau, 95, 424 p. (ill.). (Schriftenreihe des Forschungsinstitutes für Politisch-Historische Studien der Dr.-Wilfried-Hauslauer-Bibliothek, Salzburg, 1).

5194. SCHMIDL (Erwin A.). Die 40. südafrikanische Staffel in Mödendorf und Klagenfurt. Eine wenig bekannte Episode aus der frühen Nachkriegszeit. *Carinthia I*, 95, 185, p. 319-342. (ill., Anhang).

5195. SCHOBER (Richard). Auf dem Weg zum Anschluß. Tirols Nationalsozialisten 1927–1938. *Tiroler Heimat*, 95, 59, p. 131-161.

5196. SELIGER (Maren). Groß- und Klein-Wien? Politische Auseinandersetzungen um die Nachkriegsgrenzen und Stadtentwicklungsziele. *Jb. d. Vereins f. Gesch. d. Stadt Wien*, 95, 51, p. 209-241 p. (Karten).

5197. SENEKOWITSCH (Martin). Feldmarschallleutnant Johann Friedländer, 1882–1945. Ein vergessener Offizier des Bundesheeres. Wien, BMLV, Büro für Wehrpolitik, 95, 31 p. (ill.).

5198. SOMOGYI (Éva). A "közös ügyek", 1867–1914. Abszolutista és alkotmányos elemek a közösügyes politikában. (Les "affaires communes", 1867–1914. Eléments absolutistes et constitutionnels dans la politique des affaires communes). Budapest, História-MTA Történettud. Int., 95, 28 p. (Előadások a történettud. műhelyeiből, 7).

5199. TUMA (Renate). Die Probleme der territorialen Integrität Österreichs 1945–1947. Unter besonderer Berücksichtigung der Grenzziehung gegenüber Deutschland, der Tschechoslowakei und Ungarn. Wien, WUV-Univ.-Vlg, 95, 358 p. (Karten). (Dissertationen der Universität Wien. N. F., 6).

5200. TWERASER (Kurt). US-Militärregierung Oberösterreich. 1: Sicherheitspolitische Aspekte der amerikanischen Besatzung in Oberösterreich-Süd 1945–1950. Linz, Oberösterr. Landesarchiv, 95, 448 p. (ill., Graph. Darstellungen). (Beiträge zur Zeitgeschichte Oberösterreichs, 14).

5201. WEISZ (Franz). Das Hauptquartier der Wiener Gestapo: das Haus am Morzinplatz Nr. 4. *Jb. d. Vereins f. Gesch. d. Stadt Wien*, 95,51, p. 243-264.

5202. WEYSS (Norbert). Maria Theresia, Kaiserin. *Österreich in Geschichte und Literatur mit Geographie*, 95, 39, 5b/6, p. 313-326. (Stammtafeln).

5203. Zeit-Zeugen der Besatzungs-Zeit. 1945–1955 - Bezirk Horn. Für das Niederösterreichische Bildungs- und Heimatwerk hrsg. v. Erwin FRANK. Wien, Niederösterr. Bildungs- und Heimatwerk, Dorferneuerungskomitee, 95, 112 p.

Cf. n°s 1073, 1303, 7977, 8114, 8140, 8499, 8354

Pakistan

5204. MALUKA (Zulfikar Khalid). The myth of constitutionalism in Pakistan. Karachi a. Oxford, Oxford U. P., 95, XII-362 p.

5205. PAIDAR (Parvin). Women and the political process in twentieth-century Iran. Cambridge, Cambridge U. P., 95, XVI-401 p. (Cambridge Middle East studies).

5206. SAMAD (Yunas), A nation in turmoil: nationalism and ethnicity in Pakistan, 1937–1958. New Delhi a. Thousand Oaks a. London, Sage, 95, 232 p.

5207. SHIHAB (Rafi`ullah). The political history of Pakistan. Lahore, Dost Associates, 95 360 p.

Cf. n° 7830

Palästina

* 5208. GOLDSCHMIDT-LEHMANN (Ruth P.). Britain and the Holy Land, 1800–1914: a select bibliography. London, Jewish Historical Society of England, 95, XI-168 p.

5209. BARNAY (Y.). Historyografyah u-le'umiyut: megamot be-heker Erets-Yisra'el ve-yishuvah ha-Yehudi, 634-1881 (Historiography and nationalism). Yerushalayim, Hotsa'at sefarim `al shem Y.L. Magnes, ha-Universitah ha-`Ivrit, 755, 95, 249 p. (Mekorot u-mehkarim / ha-Universitah ha-`Ivrit bi-Yerushalayim, ha-Makhon le-heker toldot Yisra'el `a. sh. B. Ts. Dinur).

5210. DOUMANI (Beshara). Rediscovering Palestine: merchants and peasants in Jabal Nablus, 1700–1900. Berkeley, University of California Press, 95, XI-340 p.

5211. GALNOOR (Itzhak). The partition of Palestine: decision crossroads in the Zionist movement. Albany, State University of New York Press, 95, IX-379 p. (SUNY series in Israeli studies).

5212. SEIKALY (May). Haifa: transformation of a Palestinian Arab society, 1918–1939. Foreword by Walid Khalidi. London; New York, I.B. Tauris, 95, XV-284 p.

5213. ZADKA (Saul). Blood in Zion: how the Jewish guerrillas drove the British out of Palestine. London a. Washington, Brassey's, 95, XVIII-227 p.

Cf. n°s 8538, 8577

Paraguay

5214. ABOU (Selim). La "República" jesuítica de los Guaranies (1609–1768) y su herencia. Buenos Aires, M. Zago Ediciones, 95, 157 p.

5215. KIDD (Stephen W.). Land, politics and benevolent Shamanism: The Enxet Indians in a democratic Paraguay. *Journal of Latin American Studies*, 95, 27, p. 43-76.

Peru

5216. PARKER (David S.). Peruvian politics and the eight-hour day: rethinking the 1919 general strike *Canadian Journal of History*, 95, 30, 3, p. 417-438.

5217. PEÑA (Milagros). Thelogies and liberation in Peru: the role of ideas in social movements. Philadelphia, Temple U. P., 95, 222 p.

5218. SELINGMANN (Linda J.). Between reform and revolution: political struggles in the Peruvian Andes, 1969–91. Stanford, Stanford U. P., 95, X-268 p.

5219. STARN (Orin), DEGREGORI (Carlos Ivàn), KIRK (Robin). The Peru reader: history, culture, politics. Durham a. London, Duke U. P., 95, XI-530 p.

5220. STARN (Orin). Maoism in the Andes: The Communist Party of Peru Shining-Path and the refusal of history. Savage in Dominican Dystopia. *Journal of Latin American Studies*, 95, 27, p. 399-422.

5221. SUAREZ (Margarite). Comercio y fraude en el Perú colonial: les estrategias mercantiles de un banquero. Lima, Instituto de Estudios Peruanos, Banco Central de Reserva, 95, 137 p. (graph.).

5222. THURNER (Mark). 'Republicanos' and 'Communidad de Peruanos': unimagined political communities in postcolonial Andean Peru. *Journal of Latin American Studies*, 95, 27, p. 291-318.

Philippinen

5223. HIDALGO NUCHERA (Patricio). Encomienda, tributo y trabajo en Filipinas, 1570–1608. Madrid, Universidad Autonoma de Madrid, Ediciones Polifemo, 95, 352 p.

5224. KUNZ (Hildegard). Von Marcos zu Aquino: der Machtwechsel auf den Philippinen und die katholische Kirche. Hamburg, Institut fur Asienkunde, 95, 190 p. (Mitteilungen des Instituts fur Asienkunde Hamburg)

5225. Primeros de Filipinas (Los): cronicas de la conquista del archipielago de San Lazaro. Madrid, Miraguano Ediciones, Ediciones Polifemo, 95, 367 p. (maps) (Biblioteca de viajeros hispanicos).

5226. RIEDINGER (Jeffrey). Agrarian reform in the Philippines: democratic transitions and redistributive reform. Stanford, Stanford U. P., 95, 366 p.

Polen

* 5227. FEDEROWICZ (Grażyna), GROMADZIŃSKA (Krystyna), KACZYŃSKA (Maria). Bibliografia podziemnych druków zwartych z lat 1976–1989. (Bibliographie des livres clandestins 1976–1989). Warszawa, Bibl. Narod., 95, 498 p.

** 5228. Materiały źródłowe do dziejów Żydów w księgach grodzkich dawnego województwa krakowskiego z lat 1647-1696. (Matériaux - sources relatifs à l'histoire des Juifs dans les registres municipaux de l'ancienne voiévodie de Cracovie entre 1674 et 1696). Etablie par Adam KAŹMIERCZYK, Kraków, Universitas, 95, XXIV-263 p. (Studia Pol.-Judaica. Ser. Fontium, 4).

** 5229. Podstępne uwięzienie profesorów Uniwersytetu Jagiellońskiego i Akademii Górniczej (6 XI 1939). Dokumenty. [Emprisonnement artificieux des professeurs de l'Université Jagellonne et de l'Académie des Mines (6 XI 1939) Documents]. Choisi et élab. par Józef BUSZKO et Irena PACZYŃSKA. Kraków, 95, 947 p. (Uniw. Jagiell. Varia, 348).

** 5230. Protokoły posiedzeń Prezydium Krajowej Rady Narodowej 1944-1947. (Procès verbaux du Conseil National d'Etat 1944-1947). Ed. et avant propos: Jerzy KOCHANOWSKI. Warszawa, Wydawn. Sejmowe, 95, 347 p. (Arch. Sejmu PRL).

** 5231. Protokoły Rady Stanu Księstwa Warszawskiego. (Procès verbaux du Conseil d'Etat du Duché de Varsovie). T. 3. 1re partie. Ed.Tadeusz MENCEL et Mariusz KALLAS. Warszawa, Wydawn. Sejmowe, 95, 281 p. (Z prac Tow. Nauk. w Toruniu, Fontes 79).

** 5232. Protokoły z posiedzeń Rady Ministrów Rzeczypospolitej. (Procès verbaux des séances du Conseil des Ministres de la République Polonaise). Réd. Marian ZGORNIAK. T. 2. Czerwiec 1940-czerwiec 1941. (Juin 1940-juin 1941). Ed. Wojciech ROJEK avec la collab. d'Andrzej SUCHCITZ. Kraków, Secesja, 95, XXXIII-416 p. (Pol. Akad. Umiej. Wydz. Hist.-Filozof. Archiwum Komisji dla Badania Dziejów Władz Rzeczypospolitej na Uchodźstwie, 1939–1990. Cz. 1: Druga Wojna Światowa. Ser. A).

** 5233. Sejm Królestwa Polskiego o działalności rządu i stanie kraju 1816-1830. (Diète du Royaume Polonais sur l'activité et l'état du pays 1816-1830). Ed. et avant-propos Janina LESKIEWICZOWA et Franciszka RAMOTOWSKA. Warszawa, Wydawn. Sejmowe, 95, 453 p.

5234. ALEKSIUN-MĄDRZAK (Natalia). Materiały dotyczące historii Żydów w Polsce w latach 1945-1950 w archiwach wojewódzkich. (Matériaux relatifs à l'histoire des Juifs en Pologne dans les années 1945–1950 dans les archives des voïvodies.). *Biuletyn Żydowskiego Instytutu Historycznego w Polsce*, 95, 42, 1-3, p. 151-162.

5235.BERNHARD (Michael), SZLAJFER (Henryk). From the Polish underground: selections from Krytyka, 1978–1993. University Park, Penn State Press, 95, 458 p.

5236.CURRY (JaneLeftwich), FAJFER (Luba). Poland's permanent revolution: people vs. elites 1956–1990. Lanham, American U. P., 95, 450 p.

5237. DALEWSKI (Zbigniew) Ceremoniał koronacyjny królów polskich w XV i początkach XVI wieku. (Le cérémonial de couronnement des rois polonais au XVe et au début du XVIe siècle). *Kwartalnik Historyczny*, 95, 102, 3-4, p. 37-60. [Eng. Summary].

5238. DEJMEK (Jindřich). Coup d'état Józefa Piłsudského v květnu 1926 v pohledu československé diplomacie. (Czechoslovak Diplomacy's view of the Józef Piłsudski's Coup d'état in May 1926). *Moderní dějiny*, 95, 3, p. 101-128.

5239. Dom sapieżyński [XV-XX w.]. (La maison des Sapieha [XV–XX w.]). Ed. Eustachy SAPIEHA. Warszawa, Państw. Wydawn. Nauk. PWN, 95, 804 p. (phot., fig., carte).

5240. Dziedzictwo. Ziemianie polscy i udział ich w życiu narodu. Réd. Tadeusz CHRZANOWSKI. (Patrimoine. La noblesse polonaise et sa participation à la vie de la nation). Kraków, Znak, 95, 296 p. (Eng. summary, phot., fig., dessins., carte).

5241. Dziejów Polski i Skandynawii (Z): rozprawy i studia na X-lecie Instytutu Polsko-skandynawskiego. (From the history of Poland and Scandinavia. To the honour of the Polish-Scandinavian history in Copenhagen). Ed. by Eugeniusz S. KRUSZEWSKI. København, Instytut Polsko-Skandynawski, 95, 196 p.

5242. Elity mieszczańskie i szlacheckie Prus Królewskich i Kujaw w XIV–XVIII wieku. (Les élites bourgeoises et nobles de la Prusse Royale et de Kujawy en XIVe–XVIIIe s.). Ouvrage collectif. Réd. Jacek STASZEWSKI. Toruń, Uniw. Mikołaja Kopernika, 95, 137 p. (Deutsche Zsfassung).

5243. FURIER (Andrzej). Polskie Ślady w czeczeńskiej historii [I poł. XIX w.–1920]. (Traces polonaises dans l'histoire de la Tchetchénie [1e moitié du XIXe s.–1920]). *Przegląd Polonijny*, 95, 21, 3, p. 17-34. [Eng. Summary].

5244. Galicja i jej dziedzictwo. Materiały z międzynarodowej konferencji naukowej, Łańcut i Rzeszów w dn. 14–18 września 1992 r. (La Galicie et son patrimoine. Matériaux de la conférence scientifique internationale, Łańcut et Rzeszów les 14–18 septembre 1992). Com. de réd. Zbigniew SOWA [et al.]. T.2. Społeczeństwo i gospodarka. (Société et économie). Réd. Jerzy CHŁOPECKI, Helena MADUROWICZ-URBAŃSKA. T. 3. Nauka i oświata. (Science et éducation). Réd. Andrzej MEISSNER, Jerzy WYROZUMSKI. Rzeszów, Wydawn. Wyższej Szkoły Pedagog., 95, 2 vol., 284 p., 286 p. (Eng. summary, Deutsche Zsfassung).

5245. GŁEMBICKA (Halina). Ormianie w życiu kulturalnym i artystycznym Galicji. (Les Arméniens dans la vie culturelle et artistique de la Galicie). *Przegląd Wschodni*, 95, 3, 3, p. 507-524. [Eng. Summary].

5246. KALIŃSKI (Janusz). Gospodarka Polski w latach 1944–1989: przemiany strukturalne. (Economie polonaise dans les années 1944–1989: changements structuraux). Warszawa, Państw. Wydawn. Ekonom., 95, 251p.

5247. KRIEGSEISEN (Wojciech). Sejm Rzeczypospolitej szlacheckiej (do 1763 roku). Geneza i kryzys władzy ustawodawczej. [Diète de la République Polonaise des nobles (jusqu'à 1763): Genèse et crise du pouvoir législatif]. Warszawa, Wydawn. Sejmowe, 95, 222 p.

5248. KUPIECKI (Robert), SZCZEPANIK (Krzysztof). Polityka zagraniczna Polski 1918–1994. (Politique étrangère de la Pologne 1918–1994). Warszawa, Scholar, 95, 295 p. (Fundacja Studiów Międzynarod.).

5249. ŁODZIŃSKI (Sławomir). Polityka państwa polskiego wobec mniejszości narodowych w latach 1989–1993. (Politique de l'état polonais par rapport aux minorités nationales dans les années 1989–1993). *Przegląd Polonijny*, 95, 21, 1, p. 123-149. [Eng. Summary].

5250. Ludy i kultury Europy w relacjach Polaków [XIX–XX w]. (Peuples et cultures dans les relations des Polonais, XIXe–XXe s.). Etablie par Mieczysław TROJAN. Wrocław, Katedra Etnologii Uniw. Wrocł., 95, 238 p.

5251. Nad Odrą, Olzą i Bierawką podczas III Powstania Śląskiego [1921]. Materiały z V Ogólnopolskiego Seminarium Historyków Powstań Śląskich i Plebiscytu zorganizowanego w dniach 27–28 maja 1993 roku w Rybniku, Wodzisławiu Śląskim i Raciborzu. (Au bord de l'Oder, Olza et Bierawka lors de la troisième insurection silésienne de 1921. Matériaux du Ve séminaire polonais des historiens spécialistes d'insurrections silésiennes et du plebiscite, organisé les 27–28 mai 1993 à Rybnik, Wodzisław Śląski et Racibórz). Ouvrage collectif. Réd. Zbigniew KAPAŁA, Wacław RYŻEWSKI. Bytom-Zabrze, Muzeum Górnośląskie, 95, 4231 p.

5252. NICIEJA (Stanisław Sławomir). Lwów – fenomen miasta wielu kultur i narodów. (Vvov – le phénomène d'une ville multiculturelle et multiéthnique.). *Przegląd Wschodni*, 95, 3, 4, p. 717-732. [Eng. Summary].

5253. NOWIŃSKI (Franciszek). Polacy na Syberii Wschodniej. Zesłańcy polityczni w okresie międzypowstaniowym [1832–1863]. (Les Polonais en Syberie Orientale. Les déportés politiques dans la période de l'entre-deux-insurrections [1832–1863]). Gdańsk, Wydawn. Gdańskie, 95, 433 p. (Eng. summary). (Gdańskie Tow. Nauk. Wydz. 1 Nauk Społ. i Humanist., Ser. Monografii, 99).

5254. ODYNIEC (Wacław). Polskie dominium maris Baltici w XVI i XVII wieku. Koncepcje i realizacja. (Le dominium maris Baltici polonais au XVIe et XVIIe siècles. Conceptions et réalisation.). *Komunikaty Mazursko-Warmińskie*, 95, 39, 3, p. 223-232. [Deutsche Zsfassung].

5255. PACZKOWSKI (Andrzej). Pół wieku dziejów Polski 1939–1989. (Un demi siècle de l'histoire de la Pologne 1939–1989). Warszawa, Wydawn. Nauk. PWN, 95, 599 p. (phot., cartes).

5256. PAJEWSKI (Janusz). Budowa Drugiej Rzeczypospolitej 1918–1926. (Construction de la Deuxième République Polonaise 1918–1926). Kraków, 95, 266 p. (Pol. Akad. Umiej. Rozpr. Wydz. Hist.-Filozof., og. zb., 79).

5257. PIETKIEWICZ (Krzysztof). Wielkie Księstwo Litewskie pod rządami Aleksandra Jagiellończyka. Studia nad dziejami państwa i społeczeństwa na przełomie XV i XVI wieku. (Grand Duché Lithuanien sous le règne d'Alexandre le Jagellon. Etudes sur l'histoire de l'Etat et de la société entre XVe et XVIe siècles). Poznań, Uniw. im. Adama Mickiewicza w Poznaniu, 95, 256 p. (Eng. summary). (Uniw. im. Adama Mickiewicza w Poznaniu. Historia, 185).

5258. Powstanie styczniowe 1863–1864. Aspekty militarne i polityczne. Materiały z sympozjum. (Insurrection de Janvier 1863–1864. Aspects militaires et politiques. Matériaux du symposium). Réd. Janusz WOJTASIK. Warszawa, Bellona, 95, 215 p. (phot., fig., cartes)

5259. PRIZEL (Ilya), MICHTA (Andrew A.). Polish foreign policy reconsidered: challenges of independence. London, Macmillan, 95, 174 p.

5260. Programy partii i ugrupowań parlamentarnych 1989–1991. (Programmes des partis et des groupements parlementaires 1989–1991). Ed. Inka SŁODKOWSKA. Cz. 1–2. Warszawa, Inst. Studiów Polit. Pol. Akad. Nauk, 95, XX-289 p., 318 p. (Eng. summary).

5261. ROK (Bogdan). Hiszpania w opinii społeczeństwa Rzeczypospolitej Obojga Narodów w XVIII wieku. (L'Espagne dans l'opinion de la population de la République des Deux Nations au XVIIIe siècle). *Studia Historyczne*, 95, 38, 3, p. 335-352. [Eng. Summary].

5262. Rola i miejsce Górnego Śląska w Drugiej Rzeczypospolitej. Matriały sesji naukowej zorganizowanej w dniach 15–16 czerwca 1992 roku w 70 rocznicę przyłączenia części odzyskanego Górnego Śląska do Macierzy. (Rôle et place de la Haute Silésie dans la seconde République Polonaise. Matériaux de session scientifique, organisée les 15–16 juin 1992 pour le 70e anniversaire de l'adhésion à la Pologne de la partie récupérée de la Haute Silésie). Ouvrage collectif réd. par Maria WANATOWICZ. Bytom et Katowice, Muzeum Górnośląskie, Muzeum Śląskie, 95, 343 p. (phot., fig., cartes).

5263. SALMONOWICZ (Stanisław). Studia historyczno-prawne [XVI–XIX]. (Etudes historiques et juridiques XVIe–XIXe s). Toruń, Uniw. Mikołaja Kopernika, 95, 179 p. (Deutsche Zsfassung, Rés. Franç).

5264. Śląsk – etniczno – kulturowa wspólnota i różnorodność. (Silésie – communauté et diversité technique et culturelle). Réd. Barbara BAZIELICH. Aut. Wojciech WRZESIŃSKI [et al.]. Wrocław, Uniw. Wrocł., 95, 177 p. [Deutsche Zsfassung].

5265. Stulecie Młodej Polski. Studia. (Le centenaire de la "Jeune Pologne". Etudes). Réd. par Maria PODRAZA-KWIATKOWSKA. Kraków, Universitas, 95, 616 p.

5266. SZAROTA (Tomasz). National stereotypes as the theme of historical research in Poland. *Acta Poloniae historica*, 95, 71, p. 55-68.

5267. TARAS (Raymond). Consolidating democracy in Poland. Boulder a. Oxford, Westview, 95, 276 p.

5268. Toruń i Pomorze pod władzą pruską. (Toruń et Poméranie sous le règne prusssien). Matériaux de la conférence du 10–11 décembre 1993 à Toruń. Réd. Szczepan WIERZCHOSŁAWSKI. Toruń, 95, 128 p. (carte).

5269. WRONA (Janusz). System partyjny w Polsce 1944–1950. Miejsce, funkcje, relacje partii politycznych w warunkach budowy i utrwalania systemu totalitarnego. (Régime des partis en Pologne 1944–1950. Place, fonctions, relations des partis politiques pendant la mise en place et fixation du système totalitaire.). Lublin, Wydawn. Uniw. M. Curie-Skłodowskiej, 95, 345 p.

5270. ŻYGULSKI (Zdzisław jun.). Walka Polaków o skarby narodowe [1921–1977]. (Combat des Polonais pour leurs trésors nationaux [1921–1977]). *Archiwa, Biblioteki i Muzea Kościelne*, 95, 63, p. 27-40 (phot.).

Cf. n^{os} *1117, 7678, 7784, 7927, 7947, 8142, 8159, 8166, 8176, 8200, 8202, 8224, 8236, 8241, 8262, 8276, 8348, 8540, 8605*

Puerto Rico

5271. CLARK (Truman R.). Prohibition in Puerto Rico, 1917–1933. *Journal of Latin American Studies*, 95, 27, p. 77-98.

5272. MORRIS (Nancy). Puerto Rico: culture, politics and identity. Westport, Praeger, 95, 205 p. (map.).

Portugal

5273. CONFRARIA (Joao). Desenvolvimento econômico e política industrial: a economia portuguesa no processo de integração européia. Lisboa, Universidade Catolica Editora, 95, 145 p.

5274. DE OLIVEIRA MARQUES (A. H.). A maçonaria portuguesa e o estado novo. Lisboa, Dom Quixote, 95, 391 p. (bibl.). (Tradição, 8). – IDEM. Breve história de Portugal. Lisboa, Presença, 95, 763 p. (bibl.).

5275. FERREIRA (Jaime Alberto do Couto). A dessacralização do pão: políticas de abastecimento no Antigo Regime: do concelho ao Estado iluminista. Porto, Campo das Letras, 95, 270 p. (ill.).

5276. GOMES (Rita Costa). A corte dos reis de Portugal no final da idade media. Lisboa, Difel, 95, IV-386 p. (Memoria e Sociedade)

5277. GONÇALVES (Eduardo Candido Cordeiro). Ressonâncias em Portugal da implantação da República no Brasil, 1889–1895. Porto, Reitoria da Universidad do Porto, 95, XXXIII-186 p. (ill.).

5278. HESPANHA (António Manuel). História de Portugal moderno político e institucional. Lisboa, Universidade Aberta, 95, 302 p. (ill.). (Textos de base, 69).

5279. KENNETH (Maxwell). The making of Portuguese democracy. Cambridge, Cambridge U. P., 95, 250 p.

5280. LAINS (Pedro). A economia portuguesa no seculo XIX: crescimento econômico e comércio externo, 1851–1913. Lisbon, Imprensa Nacional Casa da Moeda, 95, 273 p.

5281. LOURENCO (Maria Paula Marcal). A Casa e o Estado do Infantado, 1654–1706: formas e praticas administrativas de um patrimônio senhorial. Lisboa, Centro de Historia da Universidade de Lisboa, 95, 268 p. (ill.).

5282. MENDONCA (Manuela). Cidades, vilas e aldeias de Portugal: estudos de historia regional portuguesa. Lisboa, Edições Colibri, 95, [s. p.]

5283. PATRIARCA (Fátima). A questao social no Salazarismo: 1930–1947. Lisboa, Imp. Nac.-Casa da Moeda, 95, 2 vol., 666 p. (Análise social).

5284. PINTO (Antonio Costa). Salazar's dictatorship and European fascism: problems of interpretation. Boulder, Social Science Monographs, 95, VIII-230 p.

5285. RIBEIRO (Maria da Conceição). A polícia política no Estado Novo, 1926–1945. Lisboa, Editorial Estampa, 95, 314 p. (ill., map). (Historias de Portugal).

5286. SANCHEZ CERVELLO (Josep). La Revolución Portuguésa y su influencia en la transición española, 1961–1976. Madrid, Nerea, 95, XIX-377 p. (maps).

5287. SARAIVA (António José). Para a história da cultura em Portugal. Lisboa, Gradiva, 95, 2 vol., 607 p. (Obras de António José Saraiva, 11, 12).

5288. VAQUINHAS (Irene Maria). Violência, justiça e sociedade rural: os campos de Coimbra, Montemor-o-Velho e Penacova de 1858 a 1918. Porto, Edições Afrontamento, 95, 542 p. (ill.)

Cf. n^{os} *1300, 7672, 7774, 7797, 7798, 7825, 7855, 8208, 8663, 8185*

Ruanda

5289. KANYAMACHUMBI (P.). Société, culture et pouvoir politique en Afrique interlacustre: Hutu et Tutsi de l'ancien Rwanda. Kinshasa, Editions Select, 95, 349 p. (ill., maps).

5290. MAC CULLUM (Hugh). The angels have left us: the Rwanda tragedy and the churches. Geneva, WCC Publications, 95, XXIV, 115 p.

5291. PRUNIER (Gerard). The Rwanda crisis: history of a genocide. New York, Columbia U. P., 95, XIV-389 p. (ill.)

Rumänien

5292. BÁRDI (Nándor). A Keleti Akció. A romániai magyar intézmények anyaországi támogatása az 1920-as években. (L'Action orientale. Le support des institutions hongroises de la Roumanie par la Hongrie dans les années vingt du XXᵉ siècle). *Regio*, 95, 6, 3, p. 89-134; 4, p. 3-28.

5293. BORSI-KÁLMÁN (Béla). Illúziókergetés vagy ismétléskényszer? Román-magyar nemzetpolitikai elgondolások és megegyezési kísérletek a XIX. században. (Poursuite des illusions ou répétition forcée? Considérations de politique nationale roumaine et hongroise au XIXᵉ siècle). Budapest, Balassi, 95, 232 p.

5294. BRĂTIANU (Gheorghe I.). Sfatul domnesc și Adunarea stărilor în Principatele române. (The Princely Council and the Estates' Assembly in the Romania principalities). București, Editura Enciclopedică, 95, 328 p.

5295. CIOBANU (Mircea). În fața neamului meu. Convorbiri cu Mihai I al României. (In front of my people. A dialog with Mihai I of Romania). Iași, Editura Princeps, 95, 384 p.

5296. COJOCARIU (Mihai). Partida nationala si constituirea statului roman, 1856–1859. Iasi, Editura Universitatii "Al. I. Cuza", 95, 428 p.

5297. GALLAGHER (Tom). Romania after Ceausescu: the politics of intolerance. Edinburgh, Edinburgh U. P., 95, VIII-267 p. (map)

5298. MOROZOV (Nikolaj N.). Gogencollerny v Rumynii. (The Hohenzollerns in Romania). *Nov. novejš. Ist.*, 95, 1, p. 161-175.

5299. ORNEA (Zigu). Anii treizeci. Extrema dreaptă românească. (The Thirties. The Romanian Far Right). București, Editura Fundației Culturale Române, 95, 474 p.

5300. RĂDUȚIU (Aurel), GYEMANT (Ladislau). Repertoriul izvoarelor statistice privind Transilvania 1690–1847. (The repertory of statistic sources concerning Transylvania, 1690–1847). București, Editura "Univers Enciclopedic", 95, CX-819 p.

Cf. n°s 8119, 8160, 8177, 8186, 8225, 8326, 8338, 8353, 8699

Rußland

* 5301. BEYER-THOMA (Hermann). International bibliography of pre-Petrine Russia 1993. München, Osteuropa-Institut, 95, 158 p. (Mitteilungen. Osteuropa-Institut München, 4).

5302. 1812 god v vospominanijakh sovremennikov. (1812. The memoirs of the contemporaries). RAN. In-t rossijskoj istorii; Redkol.: A. G. TARTAKOVSKIJ (otv. red.) i drugie. Moskva, Nauka, 95, 202 p.

5303. ALBATS (Yevgenia). KGB: state within a state. The secret police and its hold on Russia's past, present and future. London, Tauris, 95, 401 p.

5304. Aleksander Vtoroj. Vospomitanija, dnevniki. (Alexander the second. Memoirs, diaries. Russia, the 19th century). Vstupitel'naja stat'ja, sostavlenie, primečanja i podgotovka texta V. G. ČERNUKHA; A. S. PROKHVATILOVA. Sankt-Peterburg, Puškinskij fond, 95, 446 p.

5305. ASCHER (Abraham). Prime minister P. A. Stolypin and his 'Jewish' adviser. *Journal of Contemporary History*, 95, 30, 3, p. 513-532.

5306. Aviastroenie Rossii. (The Russian aircraft, the XIXth–XXth centuries). A. G. BRATUKHIN, A. M. BATKOV, A. F. VOJNOV i drugie; Pod. red. A. G. BRATUKHINA. Moskva, Mašinostroenie, 95, 390 p.

5307. BALUEV (Boris P.). Liberal'noe narodničestvo na rubeže XIX–XX vekov. (The Russian liberal narodnik movement in the late of the XIXth–the beginning of the XXthcenturies). Moskva, RAN. In-t rossijskoj istorii, Nauka, 95, 267 p.

5308. BELJAKOV (Aleksej A.). Vnutrennie vodnye puti Rossii v pravitel'stvennoj politike konca XIX–načala XX veka. (Russia's internal waterways in the government policies of the late XIXth–early XXth centuries). *Oteč. Ist.*, 95, 2, p. 154-165.

5309. BORTNEVSKIJ (Viktor G.). Belaja razvedka i kontrrazvedka na Juge Rossii vo vremja graždanskoj vojny. (The white intelligence and counter-intelligence during the civil war in the South of Russia). *Oteč. Ist.*, 95, 5, p. 88-100.

5310. BUTOV (S. E.). "Zasluga nevoznagradimaja ...": Očerki o morjakakh-dekabristakh. (Great services ..." : Essays about the Decembrist-seamen, the XIXth century). Rossijskij gosudarstvennyj morskoj istoriko-kul'turnyj centr pri Pravitel'stve Rossijskoj Federacii. Moskva, Meždunarodnyj gumanitarnyj fond "Znanie", 95, 255 p.

5311. CHWALBA (Andrzej). Imperium korupcji w Rosji i Królestwie Polskim w latach 1861–1917. Postface: Józef SMAGA. Korupcja w pierwszym państwie robotników i chłopów (1917–1995). (Empire de la corruption en Russie et dans le Royaume de Pologne dans les années 1861–1917. Postface: Józef SMAGA. La corruption dans le premier Etat d'ouvriers et de paysans [1917–1995]). Kraków, Universitas, 95, 359 p. [Eng. summary].

5312. CLARK (Katerina). Petersburg: crucible of the cultural revolution. Cambridge, Harvard U. P., 95, XII-377 p.

5313. CZERSKA (Danuta). Dymitr Samozwaniec. (Dimitre l'Imposteur). Wrocław, Zakł. Narod. im. Ossolińskich, 95, 255 p.

5314. DORONCHENKOV (Askol'd Ivanovich). Mežnatsional'nye otnosheniia i natsional'naia politika v

Rossii: aktual'nye problemy teorii, istorii i sovremennoi praktiki: etnopolitologicheskii ocherk. (Irredentism and national politics in Russian federation). Sankt-Peterburg, TSentr. in-t povysheniia kvalifikatsii rukovodiashchikh rabotnikov i spetsialistov professional'nogo obrazovaniia Ministerstva obrazovaniia Rossiiskoi Federatsii, 95, 199 p.

5315. DUZ' (Petr D.). Istorija vozdukhoplavanija i aviacii v Rossii: Period do 1914 goda. (A history of the aeronautics and aviation in Russia till 1914). RAN. Moskva: Nauka, 95, 495 p.

5316. Dvorjanskie rody Rossijskoj imperii: V 10 tomakh. (Families of the nobility of the Russia empire. In 10 volumes). Rukovoditel'avtorskogo kollektiva P. Kh. GREBEL'SKIJ. Tom 2. Knjaz'ja (Princes). Naučnyj redaktor S. V. DUMIN. Sankt-Peterburg, IPK. "Vesti", 95, 263 p.

5317. ÉDEL'MAN (Ol'ga V.). Vospominanija dekabristov o sledstvii kak istoričeskij istočnik. (The Decembrist's reminiscenses of their inquest as a historical source). Oteč. Ist., 95, 6, p. 34-44.

5318. Ékonomika russkoj civilizacii. (Economy of the Russian civilization). Moskva, Rodnik, Sost. O. A. Platonov, 95, 383 p.

5319. FROJANOV (Igor' Ja.). Drevnjaja Rus': Opyt issledovanija istorii social'noj i političeskoj bor'by. (Old Rus'. History of the social and political struggle. Experience of the researches). Sankt-Peterburg, Zlatoust, Pod red. A. Ja. DEGTJAREVA, 95, 704 p.

5320. GUBOGLO (M. N.). Tri nacional'noj politiki v postkommunističeskoj Rossii. (Trends in nationalities policy of the postcommunist Russia). Étnogr. obzrenie, 95, 5, p. 110-124.

5321. Vacat.

5322. IOFFE (Genrikh Z.). Semnadcatyj god: Lenin, Kerenskij, Kornilov. (The 1917: Lenin, Kerensky, Korniloff). Moskva, Nauka, RAN. In-t rossijskoj, 95, 238 p.

5323. IŠIN (Vjačeslav V.). Socialisty-revoljucionery v Rossii konca XIX načala XX veka. (The Russian Socialist-Revolutionaries at the end of the XIXth century–the beginning of XXth centuries). Astrakhanskij gosudarstvennyj pedagogičeskij institut imeni S. M. KIROVA. Astrakhan', Izdatel'stvo Astrakhanskogo pedagogičeskogo instituta, 95, 240 p.

5324. ISTOMINA (Énessa G.). Lesookhranitel'naja polotika Rossii v XVIII–načale XX vekov. (Forest preservation policy in Russia from the XVIIIth century to early XXth century). Oteč. Ist., 95, 4, p. 34-51.

5325. JAHN (Hubertus F.). Patriotic culture in Russia during world war I. Ithaca a. London, Cornell U. P., 95, XII-229 p.

5326. KAMENSKIJ (Aleksandr B.). Soslovnaja politika Ekateriny II. (The estate policy of Ekaterina the Second). Vopr. Ist., 95, 3, p. 29-45.

5327. KHAZANOV (Anatolii Mikhailovich). After the USSR: ethnicity, nationalism and politics in the Commonwealth of Independent States. Madison, University of Wisconsin Press, 95, XXI-311 p.

5328. KLIER (John Doyle). Imperial Russia's Jewish question 1855–1881. Cambridge, Cambridge U. P., 95, 534 p.

5329. Knjaz' Aleksandr Nevskij i ego épokha: Issledovanija i materialy. (Prince Alexander Nevsky and his epoch: the researches and materials). Pod. red. Ju. K. BEGUNOVA, A. N. KIRPIČNIKOVA. Sankt-Peterburg, Dmitrij Bulanin, Mérija Sankt-Peterburga, RAN. In-t istorii material'noj kul'tury, 95, 214 p.

5330. KONEV (Aleksej Ju.). Korennye narody Severo-Zapadnoj Sibiri v administrativnoj sisteme Rossijskoj imperii (XVIII–načalo XX veka). (Aboriginal population of the North-Western Siberia and the Russian administrative system, the XVIIIth– the beginning of the XXth centuries). Moskva, RAN. In-t étnologii i antropologii im. N. N. Miklukho-Maklaja, 95, 217 p.

5331. KOROLEVA (N. G.). Zemstvo na perelome (1905–1907 gody). (Zemstvo on the eve of the upheaval, 1905–1907). Moskva, RAN. In-t rossijskoj istorii, 95, 236 p.

5332. KORŽIKHINA(T. P.), SENIN (A. S.). Istorija rossojzskoj gosudarstvennosti. (The history of the Russian statesmanship). Moskva: Interpraks, 95, 348 p.

5333. KOZLOV (Aleksandr I.). Anton Ivanovich Denikin. Vopr. Ist., 95, 10, p. 54-73.

5334. KRSANOV (Nikolaj A.). Nacional'nye formirovanija Krasnoj Armii v Velikoj Otečestvennoj vojne 1941–1945. (National units of the red Army in the Great Patriotic War, 1941–1945). Oteč. Ist., 95, 4, p. 116-125.

5335. Kto byl kto v Velikoj Otečestvennoj vojne: Ljudi. Sobytija. Fakty. Kratkij spravočnik. (Who was who during the Great Patriotic War. People. Events. Facts. Reference-book). Pod. red. O. A. RŽEŠEVSKOGO; Sostavitel'hroniki E. K. ŽIGUNOV. Moskva, Respublika, 95, 416 p.

5336. KULAVIG (Erik). Russisk nationalisme 1986–1992. Odense, Odense University Press, 95, 96 p. (Odense university Slavic studies, 8).

5337. KUVŠINOV (Vladimir A.). Kadety v Rossii i émigracii. (The constitutional democrats in Russian and emigration). Nov. novejš. Ist., 95, 4, p. 44-63.

5338. LITVIN (Alter L.). Krasnyj i belyj terror v Rossii, 1918–1922 gody. (The red and white terror in Russia, 1918–1922). Kazan', Tatarskoe gazetno-žurnal'noe izdatel'stvo, 95, 328p.

5339. Ljudskie poteri SSSR v period vtoroj mirovoj vojny: Sbornik statej. (Human losses of the USSR during the War of 1941–1945. Collections of articles). Podgotovil N. A. ARALOVEC i drugie. Sankt-Peterburg, RAN. Otdelenie istorii i drugie, 95, 192 p.

2. EINZELNE STAATEN

5340. LÖWENHARDT (John). The reincarnation of Russia with the legacy of communism, 1990–1994. London, Longman, 95, 238 p.

5341. MARGOLIS (A. D.). Tjur'ma i ssylka v imperatorskoj Rossii:Issledovanija i arkhivyne nakhodki. (Prisons and exile in the imperial Russia: Researches and archival finds, the XVIIIth–XIXth centuries). Moskva, Lanterna-Vita, 95, 207 p.

5342. MASSIE (Robert K.). The Romanovs: the final chapter. New York, Random House, 95, 308 p.

5343. MAU (V. A.). Ékonomika i vlast': Političeskaja istorija ékonomičeskoj reformy v Rossii, 1985–1994. (Economy and state power: the political history of the Russian economic reform, 1985–1994). Moskva, Akademija narodnogo khozjajstva pri Pravitel'stve Rossijskoj Federacii, Delo, 95, 111 p.

5344. MICHAILENKO (Valerij). Centro e periferia nello stato russo. *Relazioni Internazionali*, 95, 59, 34, p. 38-45.

5345. PERRIE (Maureen). Pretenders and popular monarchism in Early Modern Russia: the false Tsars of the time of troubles. Cambridge, Cambridge U. P., 95, 269 p.

5346. RAKHMATULLIN (Morgan A.). Imperator Nikolaj I i sem'i dekabristov. (Emperor Nicholas I and the families of the Decembrists). *Oteč. Ist.*, 95, 6, p. 3-20.

5347. Rossija, 1913 god: Statistiko-dokumental'nyj spravočnik. (Russia in 1913. Statistic and dokumental reference book). Red. – sost.: A. M. ANFIMOV, A. P. KORELIN; Otv. red. A. P. KORELIN. Sankt-Peterburg, BLIC, RAN. In-t rossijskoj istorii, 95, 416p.

5348. Rossijskie reformatory, XIX–načalo XX veka. (The Russian reformers, the XIXth–the beginning of the XXth centuries). Sost. i otv. red. A. P. KORELIN; Vsupitel'naja stat'ja A. N. SAKHAROV. Moskva, Meždunarodyne otnošenija, 95, 318 p.

5349. Russischen Zaren 1547–1917 (Die). Hrsg. v. Hans-Joachim TORKE. München, Beck, 95, 406 p.

5350. SOGRIN (Vladimir V.). 1985–1995: realii i utopii novoj Rossii. (1985–1995: real life and utopianism in a new Russia). *Oteč. Ist.*, 95, 2, p. 3-16.

5351. STEINBERG (Mark), KHRUSTALEV (Vladimir). The fall of the Romanovs: political dreams and personal struggles in a time of revolution. New Haven a. London, Yale U. P., 95, XVIII-444 p.

5352. Vlast'i oppozicija: Rossijskij političeskij process XX stoletija. (State power and the opposition: The Russian political processes in the XXth century). Ju. V. AKSJUTIN, O. V. VOLOBUEV, A. A. DANILOV i drugie. Moskva, ROSSPEN, Associacija "Rossijskaja političeskaja énciklopedija", Rossijskij nezavisimyj institut social'nykh i nacional'nykh problem i drugoe, 95, 400 p.

5353. VOLKOV (Mikhail Ja.). O rynke nedvižimosti v Evropejskoj Rossii konca XVII – pervoj četverti XVIII veka. (Real estate market in European Russia in the late XVIIth–first quarter of the XVIIIth centuries). *Oteč. Ist.*, 95, 2, p. 105-120.

5354. VOLKOVA (Irina V.), KURUKIN (Igor V.). Fenomen dvorcovykh perevorotov v političeskoj istorii Rossii XVII–XX vekov. (The palace coup d'etat, phenomen in the political history of Russia in the XVIIth–XXth centuries). *Vopr. Ist.*, 95, 5/6, p. 40-61.

5355. WOJNA (Romuald). ZSRR jako zjawisko historyczne. (L'URSS en tant que phénomène historique.). *Kwartalnik Historyczny*, 95, 102, 1, p. 67-78. [Eng. Summary].

5356. WORTMAN (Richard S.). Scenarios of power: myth and ceremony in Russian monarchy. Vol. 1. From Peter the Great to the death of Nicholas I. Princeton, Princeton U.P., 95, XVII-469 p.

Cf. n°s 7673, 7755, 7757, 7763, 7778, 7975, 8015, 8037, 8054, 8063, 8134, 8157, 8173, 8188, 8205, 8506, 8528, 8651, 8618, 8684, 8764

Saudi-Arabien

5357. MAC LOUGHLIN (Leslie J.). Ibn Saud: founder of a kingdom. Basingstoke, Macmillan in association with St. Antony's College, 95, XVI-240 p.

Schweden

5358. ÅHSBERG (Bengt). Studenter och storpolitik: Sverige och det internationella studentsamarbetet 1919–1931. (Students and the international politics. Sweden and the international student colllaboration). Lund, Lund U. P., 95, 337 p. (Bibliotheca historica Lundensis, 83).

5359. BERGGREN (Henrik). Seklets ungdom: retorik, politik och modernitet 1900–1939. (Youth of the century: rhetoric, politics and modernity, 1900–1939). Stockholm, Tiden, 95, 302 p.

5360. GUNNARSSON (Lars). Kyrkan, nazismen och demokratin: åsiktsbildning kring svensk kyrklighet 1919–1945. (Church, nazism and democracy: opinions about the Swedish Church, 1919–1945). Stockholm, Almqvist & Wiksell International, 95, 256 p. (Stockholm studies in history, 52).

5361. HADENIUS (Sven). Svensk politik under 1900-talet: konflikt och samförstånd. (Swedish politics during the 20th century, conflict and consensus). Stockholm, Tiden, 95, 280 p.

5362. ISAKSSON (Christer). Revanschen: Ingvar Carlssons väg tillbaka. Stockholm, Ekelid, 95, 288 p. [The election victory of the social-democrats with Ingvar Carlsson in 1994].

5363. JOHANSSON (Alf W.). Herbert Tingsten och det kalla kriget: anticommunism och liberalism i tiden 1946–1952. Stockholm, Tiden, 95, 376 p. [The well-known liberal publicist's and editor's impact upon Swedish politics].

5364. KARLSSON (Michael). Partistrategi och utrikespolitik: interna motiveringar och dagspressens agerande i Catalina-affären 1952 och EEC-frågan 1961–62. (Stockholm studies in politics, 52). Party strategy and foreign policy: internal motives and the action of the daily press in the Catalina affair 1952 and the EEC question 1961–62). Stockholm, Stockholm U. P., 95, VI-177 p.

5365. VEGESACK (Thomas von). Smack för frihet: opinionsbildningen i Sverige 1755–1830. (The taste for freedom: the growth of public opinion in Sweden, 1755–1830). Stockholm, Natur och Kultur, 95, 378 p.

5366. VIRRANKOSKI (Pentti). Anders Chydenius: demokratisk politiker i upplysningens tid. (Anders Chydenius: a democratic politician in the times of Enlightment). Stockholm, Timbro, 95, 455 p.

Cf. n°s 8094, 8323, 8763

Schweiz

5367. BUSSET (Thomas). La mise en place du bureau fédéral de statistique. *Revue suisse d'histoire*, 95, 45, 1, p. 7-28.

5368. EBNÖTHER (Karl). Polizeigeschichte in der Schweiz. *Revue suisse d'histoire*, 95, 45, 4, p. 458-489.

5369. EVERS (Meindert). Gabriel de Convenant, avoué de la "glorieuse rentrée" des Vaudois: correspondence avec les Etats-Generaux des Provinces-Unies, 1688–1690. Geneve, Droz, 95, 236 p.

5370. FINK (Paul). Die "Komplimentswahl" von Amtierenden Bundesräten in den Nationalrat 1851–1896. *Revue suisse d'histoire*, 95, 45, 2, p. 214-235.

5371. GROSSE (Christian). L'excommunication de Philibert Berthelier: histoire d'un conflit d'identité aux premiers temps de la Réforme genèvoise (1547–1555). Genève, Société d'Histoire et d'Archeologie de Genève, 95, II-181 p.

5372. HEAD (Randolph C.). Early modern democracy in the Grisons: social order and political language in a Swiss mountain canton, 1470–1620. Cambridge, Cambridge U. P., 95, XVII-287 p. (ill., maps). – IDEM. William Tell and his comrades: association and fraternity in the propaganda of fifteenth-and sixteenth-century Switzerland. *Journal of modern history*, 95, 67, 3, p. 527-557.

5373. Vacat.

5374. KINGDON (Robert McCune). Adultery and divorce in Calvin's Geneva. Cambridge a. London, Harvard U. P., 95, IX-214 p.

5375. MANGO-TOMEI (Elsa). Materiali e documenti ticinesi 1975–1995. *Revue suisse d'histoire*, 95, 45, 4, p. 507-512.

5376. SURDEZ (Muriel). Quand les frontières se font statistiques. La constitution d'un espace national considerée à travers le prisme des recensements. *Revue suisse d'histoire*, 95, 45, 1, p. 63-79.

5377. SUTER (Andreas). Regionale politische Kulturen von Protest und Widerstand im Spätmittelalter und der Frühen Neuzeit. Die schweizerische Eidgenossenschaft als Beispiel. *Geschichte und Gesellschaft*, 95, 21, 2, p. 161-194. – IDEM. Verschwörungen in der schweizerischen Eidgenossenschaft der frühen Neuzeit. *Revue suisse d'histoire*, 95, 45, 3, p. 330-370.

5378. TANNER (Albert). Arbeitsame Patrioten, wohlanständige Damen: Bürgertum und Bürgerlichkeit in der Schweiz 1830–1914. Zürich, Orell Fussli, 95, IX-848 p.

5379. WALTER (François). La Suisse urbaine, 1750–1950. Préf. de André CORBOZ. Genève, Editions Zoé, 95, 454 p.

5380. WANDEL (Lee Palmer). Voracious idols and violent hands: iconoclasm in Reformation Zurich. Cambridge a. New York, Cambridge U. P., 95, XII-205 p. (ill.)

5381. WIEDMANN (Arnd). Imperialismus, Militarismus, Sozialismus: der deutschschweizerische Protestantismus in seinen Zeitschriften und die grossen Fragen der Zeit 1900–1930. Bern, Peter Lang, 95, 562 p.

5382. WÜRGLER (Andreas). Das Modernisierungspotential von Unruhen im 18. Jahrhundert. Ein Beitrag zur Entstehung der politischen Öffentlichkeit in Deutschland und der Schweiz. *Geschichte und Gesellschaft*, 95, 21, 2, p. 195-217.

Cf. n°s 7673, 7697, 7740, 8069

Simbabwe

5383. RANGER (Terence). Are we not also men? The Samkange family and African politics in Zimbabwe 1920–64. London, James Currey, 95, XII-211 p. (ill.).

5384. SKALNES (Tor). The politics of economic reform in Zimbabwe. London, Macmillan, 95, 217 p.

Cf. n°s 7845, 7847

Singapore

5385. HILL (Michael), FEE (Lian Kwen). The politics of nation building and citizenship in Singapore. London, Routledge, 95, 285 p.

Cf. n° 8168

Slowakei

5386. Diktatúry k diktatúre (Od). Slovensko v rokoch 1945–1953. (From dictatorship to dictatorship. Slovakia from 1945 to 1953). Ed. by Michal BARNOVSKÝ. Bratislava, Veda, 95, 196 p.

5387. HALLON (Ľudovít). Industrializácia Slovenska 1918–1938. (Die Industrialisation der Slowakei. 1918–1938). Bratislava, Veda, 211 p.

5388. KOCSIS (Károly). Közigazgatási változások Szlovákibián. (Echanges administratives en Slovaquie). *Regio*, 95, 6, 4, p. 29-59.

5389. Slovenská akadémia vied a umení. (Slovak Academy of Sciences on Culture). Zusammengestellt Ondrej POSS. Bratislava, Historický ústav Slovenskej akadémie vied, 95, 100 p.

Cf. n° 8304

Slowenien

5390. CEPIC (Zdenko). Agrarna reforma in kolonizacija v Sloveniji, 1945–1948. Maribor, Zalozba "Obzorja", 95, 282 p. (ill.)

5391. HRIBAR (Tine). Slovenci kot nacija: soočanja s sodobniki. (The Slovenes as a nation). Ljubljana, Narodna in univerzitetna knjiznica, 95, 270 p.

5392. MAVCIC (Arne). Slovenian constitutional review: its position in the world and its role in the transition to a new democratic system. Ljubljana. Nova revija, 95, 235 p.

5393. Slovenska kronika XX. Stoletja. Knj. 1. 1900–1941. (Slovene chronicle of the 20th century). Ljubljana, Nova revija, 95, 457 p.

Somalia

5394. GHALIB (Jama Mohamed). The cost of dictatorship: the Somali experience. New York, NY, Lilian Barber, 95, 289 p.

5395. KAPTEIJNS (Lidwien). Gender relations and the transformation of the Northern Somali pastoral tradition. *International Journal of African Historical Studies*, 95, 28, 2, p. 241-260.

Sowietunion (U. d. S. S. R.)

5396. ARALOVEC (Natal'ja A.). Poteri naselenija sovetskogo obščestva v 1930-e gody: problemy, istočniki, metody izučenija v otečestvennoj istoriografii. (Population losses of the Soviet society in the 1930's: problems, sources, methods of research). *Oteč. Ist.*, 95, 1, p. 135-145.

5397. BOFFA (Giuseppe). Dall'URSS alla Russia. Storia di una crisi non finita. Bari, Laterza, 95, XII-421 p.

5398. BREUER (Claudia). Die "russische Sektion" in Riga. Amerikanische diplomatische Berichterstattung über die Sowjetunion, 1922–1933. Stuttgart, Steiner, 95, 238 p. (Transatlantische historische Studien, 3).

5399. BUŠKOV (V. I.), MIKUĽ SKIJ (D. V.). "Tadžikskaja revolucija" i graždanskažja gojna (1989–1994 gody). ("The Tajic revolution" and the civil war, 1989–1994). Moskva, RAN. Centr po izučeniju mežnacional'nykh otnošenij Instituta étnologii i antropologii im. N. N. Miklukho-Maklaja, 95, 310 p.

5400. DOMNIN (Igor'V.). Russkoe voennoe zarubež'e: dela, ljudi i mysli (20–30-e gody). (The Russian war emigration: problems, people and ideas, the 20's–30's years). *Vopr. Ist.*, 95, 7, p. 109-120.

5401. DUNN (Walter Scott). The Soviet economy and the Red Army, 1930–1945. Westport a. London, Praeger, 95, IX-256 p.

5402. GAREEV (Makhmut A.). O voennoj nauke i voennom iskusstve v Velikoj Otečestvennoj vojne. (On the military art in the Great Patriotic War). *Nov. novejš. Ist.*, 95, 2, p. 3-17.

5403. GIMPEL'SON (Efim G.). Formirovanie sovetskoj političeskoj sistemy, 1917–1923 gody. (The formation of the Soviet political system, 1917–1923). Moskva, Nauka, RAN. In. t rossijkoj istorii, 95, 231 p.

5404. HOFFMANN (Joachim). Stalins Vernichtungskrieg 1941–1945. München, Verlag für Wehrwissenschaften, 95, 336 p.

5405. Intimacy and terror: Soviet diaries of the 1930s. Ed. by Veronique GARROS, Natalya KORENEV-SKAYA a. Thomas LAHUSEN. New York, New Press, 95, XX-394 p.

5406. IZMOZIK (V. S.). Glaza i ushi rezhima: Gosudarstvennyi politicheskii kontrol' za naseleniem Sovetskoi Rossii v 1918–1928 godakh. Sankt Peterburg, Sank Peterburg Universiteit Ekonomiki i Finansov, 95, 164 p.

5407. KEEP (John). Last off the Empires: a history of the Soviet Union 1945–1991. Oxford, Oxford U. P., 95, 477 p.

5408. KOTKIN (Stephen). Magnetic mountain: Stalinism as a civilization. Berkeley a. London, University of California Press, 95, XXV-639 p N8

5409. KRAUSZ (Tamás). Sztálin. Történelmi esszé. (Stalin. Essay historique). Budapest, Útmutató, 95, 128 p.

5410. MALIA (Martin). La tragédie soviétique: histoire du socialisme en Russie, 1917–1991. Paris, Ed. du Seuil, 95, 633 p.

5411. Moskva voennaja, 1941–1945: Memuary i arkhivnye dokumenty. (Moscow in the 1941–1945. Memoirs and archival documents). Red. sovet. : V. A. ZOLOTAREV i drugie; Sost. : K. I. BUKOV i drugie. Moskva, Izddatel'stvo ob "edineija "Mosgorarkhiv", 95, 743 p.

5412. MURIN (Jurij G.). Kak fal'sificirovalos' "delo Bukharina". (The forcing of N. I. Bukharin's case). *Nov. novejš. Ist.*, 95, 1, p. 61-76.

5413. ODINCOV (Mikhail I.). Religioznye organizacii v SSSR nakanune i v gody Velikoj Otečestvennoj vojny, 1941–1945. (The religious organizations in the

USSR on the eve and during the Great Patriotic War, 1941-1945). Moskva, Rossijskaja akademija gosudarstvennoj služby pri Prezidente RF., 95, 221p.

5414. OMEL'ČENKO (Nikolaj A.). Russkij opyt: revoljucija 1917 goda v Rossii i političeskaja praktika bol'ševizma v obščestvenno-političeskoj mysli rossiskogo zarubež'ja (1917–načalo 1930- kh godov). [The Russian experience. Revolution of the 1917 in Russia and political thought of the Russian emigration (1917–the beginning of the 1930's)]. Moskva, Gosudarstvennaja akademija upravlenija im. Ordžonikidze, 95, 160 p.

5415. Organy gosudarstvennoj bezopasnosti SSSR v Velikoj Otečestvennoj vojne: Sbornik dokumentov. (The Soviet state security bodies during the Great Patriotic War: Documental collected papers). Redkol.: S. V. STEPAŠIN (predsedatel') i drugie. Tom 1. Nakanune. (On the eve). Kniga 1. (Nojabr'1983 goda–dekabr'1940 goda). (The november 1938–December 1940). Kniga 2. (1 janvarja–21 ijunja 1941 goda). (The 1st January–21 June, 1941). Sostaviteli: V. P. JAMPOL'SKIJ i drugie. Federal'naja služba kontrrazvedki Rossijskoj Federacii, Akademija Federal'noj služby kontrrazvedki Rossijskoj Federacii. Moskva, Kniga i biznes, 95, 2 vol., 452 p., 398 p.

5416. OSOKINA (Elena A.). Ljudi i vlast'v uslovijakh krizisa snabženija. 1939–1941 gody. (People and power under supply crisis conditions in the USSR, 1939–1941). Oteč. Ist., 95, 3, p. 16-32.

5417. PIKHOJA (Rudol'f G.). O vnutripolitičeskoj bor'be v sovetskom rukovodstve. 1945–1958 gody. (On the inner political struggle in the soviet leadership. 1945–1958). Nov. novejš. Ist., 95, 6, p. 3-15.

5418. PIPES (Richard). A concise history of the Russian Revolution. New York, Knopf, 95, XVII-431 p.

5419. PRYCE-JONES (David). The war that never was: the fall of the Soviet empire 1958–1991. London, Weidenfeld & Nicolson, 95, 456 p.

5420. Stalin: v vospominanijakh sovremennikov i dokumentakh épokhi. (Stalin: memoires of the contemporaries and documents of his epoch). Moskva, Novaja kniga, Sostavitel'M. Lobanov, 95, 735 p.

5421. Stalinskoe Politbjuro v 30-e gody: Sbornik dokumentov. (The Stalinist Politburo in the 1930s: Collected documental materials). Moskva: AIRO-XX, Centr social'no-gumanitarnogo obrazovanija MGU im. M. V. LOMOSOVA i drugie; Sostavitel' O. V. KLEVNJUK i drugie; Redkol. : A. V. KVAŠONKIN i drugie, 95, 340 p.

5422. SUVENIROV (Oleg F.). Voennaja kollegija Verkhovnogo suda SSSR (1937–1939 gody). (The military board of the USSR Supreme court. 1937–1939). Vopr. Ist., 95, 4, p. 137-146.

5423. VETTER (Matthias). Lasar Moisejewitsch Kaganowitsch. 1893–1991. Biographische Skizze. Zeitgeschichte, 95, 22, 1-2, p. 46-61.

5424. VYLCAN (Mikhail A.). Deportacija narodov v gody Velikoj Otečestvennoj vojny. (Deportation of peoples during the Great Patriotic War). Étnogr. obozrenie, 95, 3, p. 26-44. – IDEM. Prikaz i propoved': sposoby mobilizacii resursov derevni v gody vojny. (The oder and the sermon: ways of mobilizing rural resources in the war years, 1941–1945). Oteč. Ist., 95, 3, p. 69-80.

5425. WAGNER (Armin). Das Bild Sowjetrußlands in den Memoiren deutscher Diplomaten der Weimarer Republik. Münster u. Hamburg, Lit, 95, V-165 p. (Studien zur Weimarer Geschichte, 2).

5426. ZASLAVSKY (Victor). Storia del sistema sovietico. L'ascesa, la stabilità, il crollo. Roma, La Nuova Italia Scientifica, 95, 290 p.

5427. ZEZINA (Marija R.). Šokovaja terapija ot 1953-go k 1956 godu. (Shock therapy: from 1953 to 1956. Stalins's death in the social consciousness). Oteč. Ist., 95, 2, p. 121-134.

5428. ZIMA (Veniamin F.). Poslevoennoe obščestvo: golod i prestupnost' (1946–1947 gody). (The post-war society: famine and criminality, the USSR, 1946–1947). Oteč. Ist., 95, 5, p. 45-59.

5429. ZUBKOVA (Elena Ju.). Malenkov i Khruščev: ličnyj faktor v politike poslestalinskogo rukovodstva. (Malenkov and Khruschev: a personal factor in the post-Stalin leadership policy). Oteč. Ist., 95,4, p. 103-115.

5430. ŽUKOV (Jurij N.). Bor'ba za vlast' v rukovdstve SSSR v 1945–1952 godakh. (The struggle for power in the USSR leadership in the 1945–1952). Vopr. Ist., 95, 1, p. 23-39.

Cf. n°s 448, 577, 1061, 4627, 5339, 5355, 7759, 7893, 8237, 8251, 8253, 8304, 8306, 8353, 8452, 8473, 8535, 8576, 8641, 8672, 8686, 8707, 8719, 8772

Spanien

* 5431. Historia contemporanea de Andalucia. Madrid, CSIC (Centro de Informacion y Documentacion Cientifica), 95, X-199 p (Bibliografías de historia de España, 5).

* 5432. Relaciones iglesia-estado (ss. XV–XX). Madrid, CINDOC, 95, XII-131 p (Bibliografías de historia de España, 6).

5433. ANDREW (Christopher). Introduction to 'The ISOS years: Madrid 1941–3'. Journal of Contemporary History, 95, 30, 3, p. 355-358. [Cf. n° 5434: BENTON (Kenneth). The ISOS years: Madrid 1941–3].

5434. BENTON (Kenneth). The ISOS years: Madrid 1941–3. Journal of Contemporary History, 95, 30, 3, p. 359-410. [Cf. n° 5433: ANDREW (Christopher). Introduction to 'The ISOS years: Madrid 1941–3'].

2. EINZELNE STAATEN

5435. BOLADO (Alvarez Alfonso). Para gagnar la guerra, para gagnar la paz. Iglesia y guerra civil: 1936–39. Madrid, Universidad Pontificia Comillas, 95, 716 p.

5436. CATALAN (Jordi). La economía española y la Segunda Guerra Mundial. Barcelona, Editorial Ariel, 95, 283 p. (ill.)

5437. DADSON (Trevor J.). The Duke of Lerma and the Count of Salinas: Politics and Friendship in Early Seventeenth-Century Spain. *European History Quarterly*, 95, 25, p. 5-38.

5438. ESENWEIN (George), SHUBERT (Adrian). Spain at war: the Spain Civil War and historical perspective. London, Longman, 95, 313 p. (map.).

5439. GLICK (Thomas F.). From Muslim fortress to Christian castle: social and cultural change in Medieval Spain. Manchester, Manchester U. P., 95, 201 p. (map.).

5440. LOPEZ (Roberto J.). Ceremonia y poder a finales del Antiguo Régimen. Galicia, 1700–1833. Santiago de Compostela, Universidade de Santiago de Compostela, 95, 296 p.

5441. PÉREZ SARRIÓN (G.). Hidraulic policy and irrigation works in Spain in the second half of eighteenth-century. *Journal of European Economic History*, 95, 24, 1, p. 131-144.

5442. Relations entre hommes et femmes en Espagne aux XVIe et XVIIe siècles: realités et fictions. Ed. par A. REDONDO. Paris, Publications de la Sorbonne, Presses de la Sorbonne Nouvelle, 95, 220 p. (ill.)

5443. REQUENA GALLERO (Manuel). El triunfo monarquico en las elecciones municipales de 1931 en Castilla-La Mancha. *Hispania*, 95, 55, 190, p. 673-691.

5444. RUIZ IBAÑEZ (José Javier). Las dos caras de Jano. Monarquia, ciudad e individuo. Murcia, 1588–1648. Murcia, Universidad de Murcia-Ayuntamiento de Murcia, 95, 387 p.

5445. SALVADÓ (Francisco J. Romero). Spain in the First World War: The structural crisis of the liberal monarchy. *European History Quarterly*, 95, 25, p. 529-554.

5446. SEIDEL (Carlos Collado). Zufluchtsstätte für Nationalsozialisten? Spanien, die Alliierten und die Behandlung deutscher Agenten 1944–1947. *Vierteljahrshefte für Zeitgeschichte*, 95, 95, 43, 1, p. 131158.

Cf. n°s 7774, 7809, 7817, 7829, 7889, 7894, 7921, 7944, 8019, 8049, 8149, 8185, 8307, 8313, 8472, 8551, 8666

Südafrika

5447. BEINHART (William), DUBOW (Saul). Segregation and apartheid in twentieth century South Africa. London, Routledge, 95, 288 p.

5448. BICKFORD-SMITH (Vivian). Black ethnicities, communities and political expression in late Victorian Cape Town. *Journal of African History*, 95, 36, 3, p. 443-466.

5449. BRECKENRIDGE (Keith). 'Money with dignity': migrants, minelords and the cultural politics of the South African gold standard crisis, 1920–33. *Journal of African History*, 95, 36, 2, p. 271-304.

5450. EPPRECHT (Marc). Democratizing the Southern African past. *Canadian Journal of History*, 95, 30, 2, p. 323-329.

5451. FEINBERG (H. M.). South Africa and land ownership: What's in a Deed? *History in Africa*, 95, 22, p. 439-443.

5452. HYSLOP (Jonathan). Incident at Ziman brothers: the politics of gender and race in a Pretoria factory, 1934. *International Journal of African Historical Studies*, 95, 28, 3, p. 509-526. – IDEM. White working-class women and invention of Apartheid: 'Purified' Afrikaner nationalist agitation for legislation against 'mixed' marriages. *Journal of African History*, 95, 36, 1, p. 57-82.

5453. JEANNOTAT (Claire-Marie). Histoire inavouée de l'apartheid: chronique d'une resistance populaire. Paris, L'Harmattan, 95, 253 p. (Memoires africaines)

5454. JOHNS (Sheridan). Raising the red flag: the International Socialist League and the Communist Party of South Africa 1914–1931. Cape Town, Mayibuye Books, 95, 309 p.

5455. JUCKES (Tim J.). Opposition in South Africa: the leadership of Z. K. Matthews, Nelson Mandela and Stephen Biko. Westport, Praeger, 95, 206 p.

5456. LE MAY (Godfrey Hugh Lancelot). The Afrikaners: an historical interpretation. Oxford, Blackwell, 95, 280 p. (ill., maps)

5457. NASSON (Bill). War opinion in South Africa. *The Journal of Imperial and Commonwealth History*, 95, 23, p. 248-276.

5458. SCULLY (Pamela). Rape, race, and colonial culture: the sexual politics of identity in the nineteenth-century cape colony, South Africa. *American Historical Review*, 95, 100, 2, p. 335-359.

5459. Segregation and apartheid in twentieth-century South Africa. Ed. by W. BEINART and S. DUBOW. London, Routledge, 95, XII-288 p. (Rewriting histories)

5460. SPARKS (Alister). Tomorrow is another country: the inside story of South Africa's negotiated revolution. London, Heinemann, 95, 254 p.

5461. WALSHE (Peter). Prophetic Christianity and the liberation movement in South Africa. Pietermaritzburg, Cluster Publications, 95, 180 p.

Cf. n° 8570

Sudan

5462. DENG (Francis M.). War of visions: conflict of identities in Sudan. Washington DC, The Brooking Institution, 95, 577 p.

5463. ELTIGANI (Eltigani E.). War and drought in Sudan: essays on population displacement. Gainesville, University of Florida Press, 95, 114 p.

5464. HAMAD (Bushra). Sudan notes and records and Sudanese nationalism, 1918–1956. *History in Africa*, 95, 22, p. 239-270.

5465. LOBEHE (Placido Alema). A history of the Catholic Church in the Sudan from 1846 to 1920. Khartoum, [s.n.], 95, [s. p.].

5466. RUGIIREHEH-RUNAKU (James B. N. M.). The chaotic Horn of Africa. Matsapha a. Swaziland, Green Shoots, 95, IV-180 p. (ill.).

Cf. n° 7885

Syrien

5467. PERTHES (Volker). The political economy of Syria under Asad. London, I. B. Tauris, 95, 298 p.

Cf. n°s 8027, 8425, 8644, 8714

Tanzania

5468. SHETLER (Jan). A gift for generations to come: a Kiroba popular history from Tanzania and identity as social capital in the 1980s. *International Journal of African Historical Studies*, 95, 28, 1, p. 69-112.

Cf. n° 7862

Thailand

5469. Regions and national integration in Thailand, 1892–1992. Ed. by V. GRABOWSKY. Wiesbaden, Harrassowitz, 95, VIII-296 p.

Tschechoslowakei

5470. BENEŠ (Edvard). Nezveřejněné projevy prezidenta Beneše. Rok 1946. (Unpublished addresses by President Beneš, 1946). Tomo 1–2. Ed. by Jiří KOCIAN a. Jana VÁCHOVÁ. Praha, Ústav pro soudobé dějiny AV ČR, 95, 2 vol., 213 p., 153 p. (Studijní materiály výzkumného projektu Československo 1945–1967, 3–4).

5471. BÍLEK (Jiří), PILÁT (Vladimír). Závodní, Dělnické a Lidové milice v Československu. (The factory militias, workers' militia, and People's Militia in Czechoslovakia). *Historie a vojenství*, 95, 44, 3, p. 78-106. – IDEM. Československá armáda a měnová reforma v roce 1953. (The Czechoslovak Army and the currency reform in 1953). *Historie a vojenství*, 95, 44, 1, p. 66-91.

5472. BLODIG (Vojtěch). Puč v Židenicích a Národní obec fašistická v roce 1933. (Der Putsch in Židenice und die Nationale faschistische Gemeinde im Jahre 1933). *Paginae historiae*, 95, 3, p. 146-160.

5473. BUBENÍK (Jaroslav), KŘESŤAN (Jiří). Zjišťování národnosti jako problém statistický a politický. Zkušenosti ze sčítání lidu za první republiky. (Die Nationalitätenfeststellung als statistisches Problem. Erfahrungen von den Volkszählungen in der Zeit der ersten Republik). *Paginae historiae*, 95, 3, p. 119-140.

5474. CIGÁNEK (František). Národní shromáždění 21.–28. srpna 1968. (The Czechoslovak National Assembly, August 1968). Brno, Doplněk, 95, 316 p. (bibl.). (Prameny k dějinám československé krize 1967–1970, 3).

5475. GALANDAUER (Jan). Zachvěl se, zakymácel rudý prapor náš. Vojensko-civilní pohřeb Klementa Gottwalda. (It trembled, it swayed, that red flag of ours. The military-civilian funeral of Klement Gottwald). *Historie a vojenství*, 95, 44, 1, p. 40-65.

5476. HAVRÁNEK (Jan). Sociální struktura pražských Němců a Čechů, křesťanů a židů ve světle statistik z let 1890–1930. (Die Sozialstruktur der Prager Deutschen und Tschechen, Christen und Juden im Lichte der Statistiken aus den Jahren 1890–1930). *Český časopis historický*, 95, 93, 3, p. 470-480.

5477. HRBEK (Jaroslav). Americký dokument o odsunu Němců z Československa. (American document on the transfer of the Germans from Czechoslovakia). *Historie a vojenství*, 95, 44, 5, p. 139-171.

5478. JANIŠOVÁ (Milena), KAPLAN (Karel). Katolická církev a pozemková reforma 1945–1948. Dokumentace. (Catholic Church and the Land Reform, 1945–1948). Brno, Doplněk, 95, 499 p.

5479. KAPLAN (Karel). Československo v RVHP 1949–1956. (Czechoslovakia's first seven years in the CMEA, 1949–1956). Praha, Ústav pro soudobé dějiny AV ČR, 95, 519 p. (Studie – materiály – dokumenty, 4).

5480. KÁRNÍK (Zdeněk). Fenomén první republiky v proudu dějin. (The phenomenon of the First Czechoslovak Republic, 1918–1938). *Soudobé dějiny*, 95, 2, 2-3, p. 147-156.

5481. KLIPA (Bohumír). Italská vojenská mise v Československu. (The Italian military mission in Czechoslovakia). *Historie a vojenství*, 95, 44, 3, p. 26-78.

5482. KOCIAN (Jiří). »Benešova strana« a »její« prezident za druhé světové války. ('Beneš's Party' and 'its' President during the Second World War). *Moderní dějiny*, 95, 3, p. 159-171.

5483. KREJČOVÁ (Helena), HYNDRÁKOVÁ (Anna). Postoj Čechů k židům. Z politického zpravodajství okupační správy a protektorátního tisku v letech 1939–1941. (The Czech attitude towards Jews. From the political reports of the occupation administration and from the protectorate press, 1939–1941). *Soudobé dějiny*, 95, 2, 4, p. 578-605.

5484. KUBŮ (Eduard). Zátěž dějinného dědictví, chybné kalkulace, osudová neschopnost, či neúprosná logika vývoje?. Zahraničněpolitické sekvence. (The

2. EINZELNE STAATEN

Burden of historical heritage, bad calculation, unavoidable incompetence or the relentless logic of development? A foreign policy progression). *Soudobé dějiny*, 95, 2, 2-3, p. 254-268.

5485. KUČERA (Martin). Pekař proti Masarykovi. Historik a politika. ([Josef] Pekař versus [Tomaš Garrigue] Masaryk. Historian and politician). Praha, Ústav T. G. Masaryka, 95, 87 p. (photogr.).

5486. MAŇÁK (Jiří). Komunisté na pochodu k moci. Vývoj početnosti a struktury KSČ v období 1945–1948. (Communists on the march to power. The evolution of the size and structure of the Czechoslovak Communist Party, 1945-1948). Praha, Ústav pro soudobé dějiny AV ČR, 95, 73 p. (tab.). (Studijní materiály výzkumného projektu Československo 1945–1967, 2). – IDEM. Proměny strany moci. Studie a dokumenty k vývoji Komunistické strany Československa v období 1948–1968. (Essays and documents on the evolution of the Czechoslovak Communist Party, 1948-1968). Tomo 1–2. Praha, Ústav pro soudobé dějiny AV ČR, 95, 2 vol., 199 p., 146 p. (Studijní materiály výzkumného projektu Československo 1945–1967, 8–9).

5487. MUDRA (Miroslav). České národní povstání v květnu 1945. (The Czech national uprising, May 1945). Praha, Ministerstvo obrany, 95, 105 p. (photogr.).

5488. MUSIL (Jiri). The end of Czechoslovakia. Budapest, Central European U. P., 95, 283 p.

5489. MUSIL (Michal). Příběh Háchova politického sekretáře. Josef Kliment před Národním soudem roku 1947. (The fate of Hácha's political secretary. Josef Kliment on trial in the National Court, 1947). *Soudobé dějiny*, 95, 2, 4, p. 530-544.

5490. NEČAS (Ctibor). Kolik vězňů prošlo internacemi v protektorátních cikánských táborech. (The number of prisoners interned in Gypsy camps during the Protectorate). *Časopis Matice moravské*, 95, 114, 2, p. 354-364.

5491. PECKA (Jindřich), BELDA (Josef), HOPPE (Jiří). Občanská společnost 1967–1970. Emancipační hnutí uvnitř Národní fronty. (Civil society in Czechoslovakia, 1967–1970. Attempts at emancipation within the National Front). Brno, Doplněk, 95, 586 p. (Prameny k dějinám československé krize 1967–1970, 2/1).

5492. POPÉLY (Gyula). Esterházy János gróf pályaképe. (Vue de la carrière du comte János Esterházy). *Valóság*, 95, 38, 12, p. 60-76.

5493. Prameny k dějinám 3. odboje. Přehledy a dokumenty k československé politice v letech 1948–1949 (1951). [Sources on the history of the Third Resistance. Surveys and documents on Czechoslovak policy, 1948–1949 (1951)]. Tomo 1–3/2. Olomouc, Vyd. Univerzity Palackého, 95, 5 vol., 987 p., 415 p., 357 p., 464 p., 531 p.

5494. PREČAN (Vilém). Dokumenty sovětské éry v ruských archivech – nový pramen k československým dějinám 1941–1945. Badatelské zkušenosti z let 1994 a 1995. (New Soviet documents on Czechoslovak history, 1941–45. A researcher's recent experiences in the Russian archives). *Soudobé dějiny*, 95, 2, 4, p. 609-628. – IDEM. Novoroční filipika 1995. Disent a Charta 77 v pojetí Milana Otáhala. (A new year's philippic for 1995. Dissent and Charter 77 according to Milan Otáhal). Praha, Ústav pro soudobé dějiny AV ČR, 95, 39 p.

5495. Přehled o zasedáních ÚV KSČ, o personálním složení ústředního výboru a jeho orgánů od XIV. do XV. sjezdu KSČ (1971–1976). (Survey of sessions of the Central Committee [CC] of the Czechoslovak Communist Party [CPCz], concerning personnel composition of the CC and its organs from the 14th to 15th CPCz Congress, 1971–1976). Praha, Ústav pro soudobé dějiny AV ČR, 95, 29 p. (Materiály, studie, dokumenty, 2/1995).

5496. Proměny politického systému v Československu na přelomu let 1989–1990. (Changes in the Czechoslovak political system, 1989–90). Praha, Nadace Heinricha Bölla, 95, 128 p. (photogr.).

5497. První světová válka, moderní demokracie a T. G. Masaryk. (The First World War, modern democracy, and T. G. Masaryk). Ed. by Jaroslav OPAT. Praha, Ústav T. G. Masaryka, 95, 352 p.

5498. R. W. Seton-Watson. His relations with the Czechs and Slovaks. Documents 1906–1951. Tomo 1. Ed. by Jan RYCHLÍK, Thomas D. MARZIK a. Miroslav BIELIK. Praha, Ústav T. G. Masaryka, 95, 648 p. (photogr.).

5499. RAFAJ (Pavel). Soupisy zahraničních pramenů k dějinám Československa 1938–1945. (Foreign Primary Sources on Czechoslovak History, 1938–1945). *Soudobé dějiny*, 95, 2, 4, p. 606-608.

5500. RATAJ (Jan). Komunistické Československo. (Communist Czechoslovakia). Tomo 1. 1948–1960. Plzeň: Pedagogická fakulta ZČU, 95, 170 p.

5501. Sborník dokumentů k vnitřnímu vývoji v českých zemích za 1. světové války 1914–1918. (Documents on internal developments in the Bohemian Lands during World War I, 1914–1918). Tomo 3. 1916. Praha, Státní ústřední archiv, 95, 313 p. (ill.).

5502. Spor o smysl českých dějin 1895–1938. (Debate on the meaning of Czech history, 1895–1938). Ed. by Miloš HAVELKA. Praha, Torst, 95, 867 p.

5503. STARZYCZNÁ (Halina), STEINER (Jan). Proměny obchodního podnikání v českých zemích v letech (1930–) (1945–1950). [Verwandlungen im Geschäftsunternehmen in den tschechischen Ländern (1930–) (1945–1950)]. *Slezský sborník*, 95, 93, 3, p. 218-231.

5504. SUK (Jiří). Vznik Občanského fóra a proměny jeho struktury. 19. listopad–10. prosinec 1989. (The creation of the Civic Forum. 19 November–10 December 1989). *Soudobé dějiny*, 95, 2, 1, p. 17-41.

5505. VADKERTY (Katalin). A telepítéspolitika a magyarkérdés megoldásában Csehszlovákiában, 1945–

1948. (La politique de colonisation dans la solution de la question hongroise en Tchécoslovaquie, 1945–1948). *Agrártört. szle.*, 95, 37, 1-4, p. 183-189.

5506. VANĚK (Miroslav). O některých problémech ekologického hnutí v českých zemích před rokem 1989. (The environmentalist movement in Bohemia and Moravia, before 1989). *Soudobé dějiny*, 95, 2, 1, p. 42-57.

5507. WAIC (Marek). Československá obec sokolská v politickém životě první republiky. (The Czechoslovak Sokol organization in the political life of the First Republik). *Moderní dějiny*, 95, 3, p. 83-100.

5508. Zpráva Dokumentační komise K 231. (Report of the K 231 documentation commission). Ed. by Otakar RAMBOUSEK a. Ladislav GRUBER. Praha, Dokumentační komise, 95, 97 p.

Cf. n[os] *8123, 8283, 8370, 8381, 8450, 8452, 8594, 8695, 8712*

Tunesien

5509. SRAIEB (Noureddine). Le college Sadiki de Tunis 1875–1956: enseignement et nationalisme. Paris, CNRS éditions, 95, 346 p.

Cf. n[os] *7843, 8566*

Türkei

5510. AKŞİN (Sina). Fransiz İhtilali'nin II. Meşrutiyet Öncesi Osmanlı Devleti Üzerindeki Etkileri Üzerine Bazı Görüşler. (Quelques observations sur les influences de la Révolution Francaise sur l'Etat Ottoman avant la Réforme de 1908). *Ankara Üniversitesi Siyasal Bilgiler Fakültesi Dergisi*, 95, 49, 3-4, p. 23-29.

5511. ÇAHA (Ömer). Osmanlı'da Sivil Toplum. (La Société civile dans l'Empire Ottoman). *Ankara Üniversitesi Siyasal Bilgiler Fakültesi Dergisi*, 95, 49, 3-4, p. 79-99.

5512. ÇAVDAR (Tevfik). Türkiye'nin Demokrasi Tarihi (1839–1950). (Histoire de la Démocratie turque). 1. Basim. Ankara, İmge Yayınları, 95, 512 p.

5513. Defterdar Sarı Mehmet Paşa. Zübde-i Vekayiat-Tahlili ve Metin (1066–1116/1656–1704*)* (L'Essence des évenements de Defterdar Sari Mehmet Paşa. Le Texte et son analyse). Ed. par Abdülkadir ÖZCAN. Ankara, [s. n.], 95, 907 p.

5514. DEMIR (Fevzi). İzmir Sancağı'nda 1908 Meclis-i Mebusan Seçimleri. (Les élections des députés de la Chambre au 1908 dans le Sandjak d'Izmir). *Çağdaş Türkiye Tarihi Araştırmaları Dergisi*, 95, 2, 4-5, p. 137-156.

5515. FAROQHI (Suraiya). Making a living in the Ottoman lands 1480–1820. Istanbul, Isis Press, 95, VI-330 p.

5516. FODOR (Pál). Török és oszmán. Az oszmán rabszolga-elit azonosságtudatáról. (Turc et Ottoman. De la notion d'identité de l'élite Ottomane des esclaves). *Tört. szle.*, 95, 37, 4, p. 367-383.

5517. INALCIK (Halil). From empire to republic: essays on Ottoman and Turkish social history. Istanbul, Isis Press, 95, 179 p.

5518. KAFADAR (Cemal). Between two worlds: the construction of the Ottoman state. Berkeley a. London, University of California Press, 95, XX-221 p.

5519. KANSU (Aykut). 1908 Devrimi (La Révolution de 1908). İstanbul, İletişim Yayınları, 1995, 482 p.

5520. KARAGÖZ (Mehmet). Osmanlı Devleti'nde Islahat Hareketleri. (Les mouvements de réforme dans l'Etat Ottoman). *Osmanlı Tarihi Araştırma Merkezi Dergisi*, 95, 6, p. 173-194.

5521. KÜÇÜKDAG (Yusuf). II. Bayezid, Yavuz ve Kanuni Devirlerinde Cemali Ailesi. (La famille de Cemalî aux époques de Bajazed II, de Yavuz et de Soliman le Magnifique). İstanbul, Aksarayi Vakfı, 95, 217 p.

5522. NAGATA (Yuzo). Studies on the social and economic history of the Ottoman Empire. Izmir, Akademi Kitabevi, 95, 139 p.

5523. ORTAYLI (İlber). Tarikatler ve Tanzimat Dönemi Osmanlı Yönetimi. (Les Ordres mistiques et l'administration ottoman à l'époque de Tanzimat). *Osmanlı Tarihi Araştırma Merkezi Dergisi*, 95, 6, p. 221-288.

5524. ÖZCAN (Abdulkadir). "Cülus ve Cülusla İlgili Meseleler" (L'avènement Impérial et ses problèmes). *Mimar Sinan Üniversitesi Fen/ Edebiyat Fakültesi Dergisi*, 95, 2, p. 163-184. – IDEM. II. Mahmud ve Reformları Hakkında Bazı Gözlemler" (Quelques observations sur Mahmud II et ses réformes). *Tarih İncelemeleri Dergisi*, 95, 10, p. 13-41.

5525. ÖZDEMIR (Rifat). Osmanlı Devletinin Tarikat, Tekke ve Zaviyelere Karşı Takip Ettiği Siyaset. (La politique de l'Etat Ottoman contres les ordres mistiques). *Osmanlı Tarihi Araştırma ve Uygulama Merkezi Dergisi*, 95, 5, p. 259-310.

5526. PANZAC (D.). Histoire économique et sociale de l'Empire Ottoman et de la Turquie (1326–1960). Paris, Peeters, 95, XXIII-882 p. (Collection Turcica).

5527. RAUF (Bulent). The last sultans. Ed. by Meral ARIM and Judy KEARNS. Roberton, Meral Arim, 95, 366 p. (ill.)

5528. ROZALIEV (Jurij N.). Mustafa Kemal Ataturk. *Vopr. Ist.*, 95, 8, p. 57-77.

5529. ŞENTÜRK (Hüdai). Tuna Vilayeti'nin Teşkiline, Karadağ Ve Hersek Vukuatina (1861) Dair Cevdet Paşa Tarafından Kaleme Alınan Layiha. (Le Projet écrit par Cevdet Paşa à propos de formation de la province de Tuna et des événements de Monténégro et Herzégovine). *Belleten*, 95, 59, 226, p. 715-737.

5530. SHAKER (Sallama). State, society, and privatization in Turkey, 1979–1990. Washington, Woodrow Wilson Center Press, 95, 101 p.

5531. Suleyman the Magnificent and his age: the Ottoman Empire in the early modern world. Ed. by M. KUNT and C. WOODHEAD Publisher. London a. New York, Longman, 95, III-218 p.

5532. TOPRAK (Zafer). İttihat Terakki ve Devletçilik: Türkiye'de Ekonomi ve Toplum: 1908–1950 (İttihat Terakki et étatisme: l'économie et la société dans la Turquie: 1908–1950). İstanbul, Tarih Vakfı Yurt Yayınları, 95, [s. p.].

5533. TUŞ (Muhittin). Osmanlı'da Baskı Gruplarının Rolü Üzerine Bir Deneme. (Un essai sur le role des groupes de pression dans l'Empire Ottoman). *Ankara Üniversitesi Osmanlı Tarihi Araştırma ve Uygulama Merkezi Dergisi*, 95, 6, p. 319-324.

5534. Workers and the working class in the Ottoman Empire and the Turkish Republic 1839–1950. Ed. by D. QUATAERT and E. J. ZURCHER. London, Tauris, 95, 208 p.

Cf. n°s 7713, 8109, 8173, 8175

Uganda

5535. KASOZI (Abdu Basajabaka Kawalya). The social origins of violence in Uganda, 1964–1985. With the assistance and collaboration of Nakanyike MUSISI and James MUKOOZA SEJJENGO. Montreal, McGill-Queen's U. P., 95, XV-347 p. (ill., maps)

5536. ODED (Arye). Religion and politics in Uganda: a study of Islam and Judaism. Nairobi, East African Educational Publishers, 95, XII-123 p. (ill., maps).

5537. WHITE (Louise). "They could make their victims dull": genders and genres, fantasies and cures in colonial Southern Uganda. *American Historical Review*, 95, 100, 5, p. 1379-1402.

Cf. n° 7884

Ukraine

5538. BAKHMATOVA (Marina). L'Ucraina di Kuchma. *Relazioni Internazionali*, 95, 59, 34, p. 35-39.

Cf. n°s 8063, 8176

Ungarn

** 5539. HARSANYI (Iván). 1943–1944 magyarországi eseményei spanyol diplomáciai iratok tükrében. (Des documents diplomatiques espagnols sur les événements des années 1943–1944 en Hongrie). *Századok*, 95, 129, 3, p. 629-694.

** 5540. Országgyűlési almanach. Történelmi sorozat 1. Az Ideiglenes Nemzetgyűlés almanachja, 1944–1945. (Almanach parlementaire. Série historique. 1 Almanach de l'Assemblée nationale transitoire, 1944–1945). Főszerk. VIDA István. Budapest, Magyar Országgyűlés, 94, 597 p.

5541. BARTA (János). Illúziók és realitás a magyar jakobinusok mozgalmában. (Illusion et réalité dans le mouvement des Jacobins hongrois). *Századok*, 95, 129, 4, p. 883-989.

5542. BENKŐ (Péter). A Hazafias Népfront és a népi mozgalom 1957-ben. (Le Front populaire patriotique et le mouvement populaire en 1957). *Múltunk*, 95, 40, 3, p. 73-98.

5543. BÉRI-LICHTNER (János). Együttélés. A zsidóság szerepe Magyarország legújabbkori történetében, 1790–1918. (Cohabitation. Le rôle des Juifs dans l'histoire contemporaine de Hongrie, 1790–1918). Budapest, Argumentum, 95, 409 p.

5544. BOTOS (János). A Belügyminisztérium története a Monarchia széthullásától a második világháborúvégéig. (Histoire du Ministère de l'Intérieur de la dissolution de la Monarchie [Austro-Hongroise] jusqu'à la fin de la deuxième guerre mondiale). Budapest, BM, 95 p.

5545. CSIZMADIA (Ervin). A magyar demokratikus ellenzék, 1968–1988. (L'opposition hongroise démocratique, 1968–1988). Budapest, T-Twins, 95, 3 vol., 550 p., 380 p., 551 p.

5546. CSOHÁNI (János). Die politischen Beziehungen von Gábor Bethlen zum reformierten Europa. *Jb. f. d. Gesch. d. Protestantismus i. Österr.*, 94-95, 110-111, p. 87-98.

5547. DEÁK (Ágnes). Társadalmi ellenállási stratégiák Magyarországon az abszolutista kormányzat ellen 1851–1852-ben. (Stratégies de résistance sociale contre le gouvernement absolutistique en Hongrie en 1851–1852). *Aetas*, 95, 4, p. 27-59.

5548. ETENYI (Nóra). A 17. századi közvéleményformálás és propaganda Érsekújvár 1663-as ostromának tükrében. (Formation de l'opinion publique et propagande au XVIIe siècle dans le miroir du siège de Érsekújvár [Nové Zámky] en 1663). *Aetas*, 95, 1-2, p. 95-139.

5549. FEITL (István). Viták az Ideiglenes Nemzeti Kormányban. (Discussions au sein du Gouvernement national provisoire). *Társad. Szle.*, 95, 50, 4, p. 85-95.

5550. FÖLDES (György). Az eladósodás politikatörténete, 1957–1986. (Histoire politique de l'endettement, 1957–1986). Budapest, Maecenas, 95, 269 p.

5551. FÖLDESI (Margit). A Szövetséges Elenőrző Bizottság Magyarországon: visszaemlékezések, diplomáciai jelentések tükrében, 1945–1947. (La Commission de contrôle Alliée en Hongrie dans le miroir des mémoires, des rapports diplomatiques en 1945–1947). Budapest, Ikva, 95, 203 p.

5552. GERÖ (András). Modern Hungarian society in the making. London, Central European Press, 95, 276 p.

5553. GYARMATI (György). A parlamentarizmus korlátai és annak következményei az Ideiglenes Nemzetgyűlés tevékenységére. (Les barrières du parlamentarisme et ses conséquences sur l'activité du parlement national provisoire). *Társad. szle.*, 95, 50, 4, p. 76-85.

5554. HEGYI (Klára). Török berendezkedés Magyarországon. (Etablissement turc en Hongrie). Budapest, História-MTA Történettud. Int., 95, 204 p. (História könyvtár, monográfiák, 7). – EADEM. Török katonaság a magyarországi hódoltságban. (Soldats ottomans sur le territoire de Hongrie, dominé par l'empire ottoman). *Keletkutatás*, 95, p. 45-59.

5555. IZSÁK (Lajos). Rákosi-rendszer, 1948 ősze–1956 nyara. (Régime Rákosi, automne 1948–été 1956). *Tört. szle.*, 95, 37, 1, p. 51-67.

5556. LUKÁCS (Lajos). Chapters on the Hungarian political emigration, 1849–1867. Budapest, Akad. Kiádó, 95, 188 p. (Studia hist. Acad. Sci. Hungaricae, 196).

5557. Magyarország története, 1918–1990. Egyetmi tankönyv. (Histoire de Hongrie, 1918–1990. Manuel universitaire). Szerk. PÖLÖSKEI Ferenc, GERGELY Jenő. Budapest, Korona, 95, 347 p.

5558. MELINZ (Gerhard), ZIMMERMANN (Susan). Armenfürsorge, Kinderschutz und Sozialreform in Budapest und Wien 1870–1914. *Geschichte und Gesellschaft*, 95, 21, 3, p. 338-367.

5559. MOLNÁR (András). "A kormányt hatalmának visszaélésével vádolom!" Batthyány Lajos gróf az 1839/40-es országgyűlésen. ("J'accuse le gouvernement de l'abus du pouvoir!" Le comte Lajos Batthyány à la diète de 1839/40). *Levéltári szle.*, 95, 45, 1, p. 3-22. – IDEM. Batthyány Lajos és a Széchenyi-Kossuth vita, 1841–1843. (Lajos Batthyány et la discussion entre Széchenyi etá Kossuth). *Soproni szle.*, 95, 49, 4, p. 316-326. – IDEM. Deák Ferenc és a rendszeres bizottsági munkálatokra tett zalai észrevételek. (Ferenc Deák et les remarques du comitat de Zala faits sur les opérations systhématiques). *Századok*, 95, 129, 2, p. 381-406.

5560. MOLNÁR (Judit). Zsidósors 1944-ben az V. (szegedi) csendőrkerületeben. [Les juifs dans le rayon No V. (Szeged) des gendarmes]. Budapest, Cserépfalvi, 95, 223 p.

5561. NAGY (Ferenc). Visszaemlékezések, tanulmányok, cikkek. Összeáll., bevez. CSICSERY-RONAY István. (Memoires, études, articles). Budapest, Occidental press, 95, 161 p.

5562. NAGY (József). IV. Károly. Az utolsó magyar király. (Charles IV. Le dermier roi de Hongrie). Budapest, Göncöl, 95, 199 p.

5563. NEMESKÜRTY (István). Búcsúpillantás. A Magyar Királyság és kormányzója, 1920–1944. (Regard d'adieu. Le Royaume de Hongrie et son gouverneur, 1920–1944). Budapest, Szabad Tér, 95, 310 p.

5564. ÓDOR (Imre). A "hivatali elit" Baranya vármegyében 1711–1813. (L'élite officielle au comitat Baranya entre 1711–1813). *Levéltári szle.*, 95, 45, 2, p. 21-34.

5565. OROSZ (István). Hagyományok és megújulás. Válogatott tanulmányok a magyar mezővárosok történetéből. (Traditions et renouvellement. Etudes choisies de l'histoire des bourgades de Hongrie). Debrecen, Csokonai, 95, 295 p.

5566. PALASIK (Mária). A jogállam csapdái Magyarországon 1947 első felében. A Magyar Közösség pere mint eszköz a kisgazdapárt hatalomból történő kiszorításához. (Les pièges de l'État constitutionnel dans la première moitié de l'année 1947 en Hongrie. Le procès contre la Communauté hongroise comme instrument d'exclure le Parti des petits propriétaires du pouvoir). *Századok*, 95, 129, 6, p. 1305-1330.

5567. PÁLFFY (Géza). A magyarországi és délvidéki végvárrendszer 1576. és 1852. Évi jegyzékei. (Les registres du système des châteaux-forts des confins hongrois et méridionaux de 1576 et de 1582). *Hadtört. közl*, 95, 108, 1, p. 114-185. – IDEM. A magyarországi török és királyi végvárrendszer fenntartásának kérdéséhez. (Données concernant la question du maintien du système des châteaux-fort aux confins ottomans et royaux en Hongrie). *Keletkutatás*, 95, p. 61-86. – IDEM. Katonai igazságszolgáltatás a királyi Magyarszágon a XVI–XVII. században. (Juridiction militaire en Hongrie royale aux XVI–XVII siècles). Győr, Győr-Moson-Sopron Megyei Levéltár, 95, 342 p.

5568. POPRADY (Judit). A Magyarországi Németek Szövetségének története. (Histoire de l'Union des Allemands de Hongrie). *Fons*, 95, 2, p. 221-258.

5569. RAINER (M. János). Nagy Imre szovjet emigrációban, 1930–1939. (Imre Nagy [1875–1958] en émigration soviétique, 1930–1939). *Tört.szle.*, 95, 37, 3, p. 317-343.

5570. RÉTI (György). Hungary and the Problems of National Minorities. *Rivista di studi politici internazionali*, 95, 62, p. 265-278.

5571. SIMON (Zsuzsanna). Erdély köz-és szakigazgatása a második bécsi döntés után. (Administration publique et profesionelle de Transylvanie [du Nord] après le deuxième arbitrage de Vienne [1940]). *Regio*, 95, 6, 4, p. 60-82.

5572. STARK (Tamás). Zsidóság a vészkorszakban és a felszabadulás után, 1939–1955. (Les juifs dans la période du danger et aprés la liberation, 1939–1955). Budapest, MTA Történettud. Int., 95, 109 p. (Társadalom-és művelődéstörténeti tanulmányok 15).

5573. STIPA (István). Törekvések a vármegyék polgári átalakítására. Tervezetek, javaslatok, törvények. (Efforts pour la réorganisation bourgeoise des comitats. Plans, propositions, lois). Budapest, Osiris, 95, 194 p.

5574. SZKÁLY (Ferenc). Mezőváros és reformáció. Tanulmányok a korai magyar polgárosodas kérdéséhez. (Bourgade et réformation. Etudes concernant la question de l'embourgeoisement hongrois au temps moderne). Budapest, Balassi, 95, 486 p.

5575. TÜDŐS (S. Kinga). Erdélyi védőrenszerek a VX–XVII. században. Háromszéki templomvárak. (Systèmes de fortification en Transylvanie aux XV–XVII siècles. Eglises fortifiées dans le comitat de Háromszék). Budapest, Püski, 95, 230 p.

5576. UDVARI (István). Ruszin (kárpátukrán) hivatalos írásbeliség a XVIII. századi Magyarországon. (Ecriture officielle ruthéne (carpato-ukrainienne) en Hongrie au XVIII siècle). Budapest, 95, 168 p.

5577. VARGA (János). Románok és magyarok 1848–1849-ben. (Roumains et hongrois en 1848–1849). Budapest, MOL, 72 p.

5578. VÖRÖS (Károly). Wahrmann Mór-egy zsidó politikus a dualizmus korában. (Mór Wahrmann un politicien juif à l'époque du dualisme). *Budapesti negyed*, 95, 3, 2, p. 22-40.

5579. ZACHAR (József). A magyarországi hadügy jogi keretei, 1648–1848. (Les cadres juridiques des affaires militaires de Hongrie, 1648–1848). *Hadtört. közl.*, 95, 108, 2, p. 3-24.

Cf. n°s 7710, 7747, 7930, 7942, 7997, 8024, 8087, 8098, 8257, 8315, 8440, 8727

Uruguay

5580. ROSENTHAL (Anton). The arrival of the electric streetcar and the conflict over progress in early 20th century Montevideo. *Journal of Latin American Studies*, 95, 27, p. 319-342.

Cf. n°s 8498, 8711, 8790

Venezuela

5581. ANGULO RIVAS (Alfredo). La union federal republicana: politica, autonomia y religion en Merida. *Boletin de la Academia Nacional de la Historia*, 95, 78, 2, [s. p.].

5582. GOODMAN (Louis W.), Lessons of the Venezuelan Experience. Baltimore and London, Johns Hopkins U. P., 95. XVI-420 p.

5583. MAC COY (Jennifer), SERBIN (Andrés), SMITH (William C.), STAMBOULI (Andrés). Venezuelan democracy under stress. New Brunswick a. London, Transaction Publisher, 95, VI-288 p.

5584. SOSA LLANOS (Pedro Vicente). La policia en la Venezuela colonial (siglo XVIII). *Boletin de la Academia Nacional de la Historia*, 95, 78, 4, [s. p.].

Vereinigten Staaten von Amerika

* 5585. KREWSON (Margrit Beran). New Netherland, 1609–1664: a selective bibliography. Washington, Library of Congress, 95, 92 p.

* 5586. MERRIAM (Louise Alice), OBERLY (James W.). United States history: a bibliography of the new writings on American history. Manchester, Manchester U. P., 95, XI-227 p. (History and related disciplines select bibliographies).

———

5587. Amerikanischen Präsidenten (Die). 41. Historische Portraits von George Washington bis Bill Clinton. Hrsg. v. Jürgen HEIDEKING. München, Beck, 95, 468 p.

5588. AYERS (Edward L.). Southern crossing: a history of the American South, 1877–1906. Oxford a. New York, Oxford U. P., 95, X-288 p

5589. BOGART (Leo). Cool wars, cold war: a new look at USA's premises for propaganda. Washington, The American Univerity Press, 95, 250 p.

5590. CARDOZIER (Virgus Ray). The mobilization of the United States in World War II: how the government, military and industry prepared for war. Jefferson, London, McFarland, 95, VII-269 p.

5591. DANBOM (David B.). Born in the country: a history of rural America. Baltimore, Johns Hopkins U. P., 95, XII-306 p. (Revisiting rural America).

5592. FONER (Eric). Free soil, free labor, free men: the ideology of the Republican Party before the Civil War. Oxford a. New York, Oxford U. P., 95, XLIV-353 p.

5593. France de la Révolution et les Etats-Unis d'Amérique (La). Colloque tenu à la Fondation Singer-Polignac de Paris, 5 novembre 1994. Paris, Masson et Fondation Singer-Polignac, 95, X-139 p. [Cf. n^{os} <sélection> 7569, 7982, 7983, 7996, 8003, 8009.]

5594. FRANZINA (Emilio). Gli italiani al Nuovo mondo: l'emigrazione italiana in America, 1492–1942. Milano, A. Mondadori, 95, 644 p. (La storia).

5595. HAMPTON (Henry), FAYER (Steve), FLYNN (Sarah). Voices of freedom: an oral history of the civil rights movement from the 1950's through the 1980's. London, Vintage, 95, XXVIII-692 p.

5596. HARRIS (J. William). Etiquette, lynching, and racial boundaries in Southern history. A Mississipi example. *American Historical Review*, 95, 100, 2, p. 387-410.

5597. Historia Stanów Zjednoczonych Ameryki. (Histoire des Etats Unis d'Amérique). Réd. Andrzej BARTNICKI, Donald T. CRITCHLOW, Krzysztof MICHAŁEK. T. 1. 1607–1763. Auteurs: Patricia U. BONOMI [et al.]. T. 2. 1763–1848. Auteurs: Lance BANNING [et al.]. T. 3. 1848–1917. Auteurs: Donna R. GABACCIA [et al.]. T. 4. 1917–1945. Auteurs A. BARTNICKI [et al.]. T. 5. 1945–1990. Auteurs: Paul BOYER [et al.]. Warszawa, Wydawn. Nauk. PWN, 95, 5 vol., 281 p., 357 p., 385 p., 388 p., 399 p. (phot., fig, cartes).

5598. HOLLI (Melvin G.). German American ethnic and cultural identity from 1890 onward. *In:* Monta tietä menneisyteen [Cf. n° 1133], p. 63-76.

5599. KAZIN (Michael). The populist persuasion: an American history. New York, BasicBooks, 95, X-381 p.

5600. KING (Desmond S.). Separate and unequal: Black Americans and the US federal government. Oxford, Clarendon Press a. New York, Oxford U. P., 95, XIV-352 p.

5601. KLEHR (Harvey), HAYNES (John Earl), FIRSOV (Fridrikh Igorevich). The secret world of American communism. New Haven, Yale U. P., 95, XXXII-348 p. (Annuals of communism).

5602. LÁNG (Imre). Az Egyesült Államok története 1945 után. A Truman-korszak. (Histoire des États-Unis après 1945. La période Truman). Budapest, Universitas, 95, 242 p.

5603. LEFF (Mark H.). Revisioning U. S. political history. *American Historical Review*, 95, 100, 3, p. 829-853.

5604. LIND (Michael). The next American nation: the new nationalism and the fourth American revolution. New York a. London, Free Press, 95, VII-436 p.

5605. MAMMARELLA (Giuseppe). L'America a destra. La fine dello Stato sociale e la crisi dello Stato nazione nel futuro dell'America. Politica e cultura negli Stati Uniti dalla Seconda guerra mondiale a oggi. Firenze, Ponte alle Grazie, 95, 173 p.

5606. MISA (Thomas J). A nation of steel: the making of modern America, 1865–1925. Baltimore a. London, Johns Hopkins U. P., 95, XXVI-367 p. (Studies in the history of technology).

5607. O'REILLY (Kenneth). Nixon's piano: presidents and racial politics from Washington to Clinton. New York a. London, Free Press, 95, X-525 p.

5608. PURSELL (Carroll W.). The machine in America: a social history of technology. Baltimore, Johns Hopkins U. P., 95, XVI-358 p.

5609. Republic of letters (The): the correspondence between Thomas Jefferson and James Madison, 1776–1826. Ed. by James Morton SMITH. New York a. London, Norton 95, 3 vol., XVII-2073 p.

5610. SHERRY (Michael S.). In the shadow of war: the United States since the 1930s. New Haven a. London, Yale U. P., 95, XII-595 p.

5611. ŠPOTOV (Boris M.). Henry Ford. *Vopr. Ist.*, 95, 4, p. 57-77.

5612. TESTI (Arnaldo). The gender of reform politics: Theodore Roosevelt and the culture of masculinity. *Journal of American History*, 95, 81, p. 1509-1533.

5613. WARD (Harry Merrill). The American Revolution: nationhood achieved, 1763–1788. New York, St. Martin's Press, 95, XIV-432 p. (ill., maps). (The St. Martin's series in U.S. history).

5614. WIEBE (Robert Huddleston). Self-rule. A cultural history of American democracy. Chicago a. London, University of Chicago Press, 95, X-321 p.

5615. WRIGHT (Esmond). A History of the United States of America. Vol. I. The search for liberty: from origins to independence. Cambridge, Blackwell, 95, XVI-582 p.

Cf. n°s 1148, 1152, 7729, 7750, 7758, 7819, 7824, 7851, 7865, 7877, 7893, 7974, 7983, 8003, 8009, 8015, 8107, 8113, 8151, 8152, 8246, 8253, 8256, 8297, 8320, 8429, 8336, 8339, 8439, 8464, 8470, 8509, 8517, 8519, 8526, 8561, 8529, 8621, 8622, 8625, 8629, 8643, 8651, 8657, 8688, 8694, 8697, 8700, 8705, 8725, 8728, 8794, 8796, 8776

Vietnam

5616. ENGELBERT (Thomas), GOSCHA (Christopher E.). Falling out of touch: a study on Vietnamese communist policy towards an emerging Cambodian communist movement, 1930–1975. Clayton, Centre of Southeast Asian Studies, Monash Asia Institute, Monash University, 95, XVI-165 p.

5617. MARR (David George). Vietnam 1945: the quest for power. Berkeley, University of California Press, 95, XXVIII-602 p.

5618. VAN KY (Nguyen). La société vietnamienne face à la modernité: le Tonkin de la fin du XIXe siècle à la seconde guerre mondiale. Paris, L'Harmattan, 95, 432 p. (ill.). (Recherches asiatiques).

5619. WEST (Richard). War and peace in Vietnam. London, Sinclair-Stevenson, 95, 365 p.

Cf. n°s 8486, 8504, 8548, 8550, 8638, 8680, 8704, 8726

Zypern

5620. Visitors, immigrants, and invaders in Cyprus. Ed. by P. W. WALLACE. Albany, Institute of Cypriot Studies, 95, VI-201 p. (ill., maps).

Cf. n° 8653

§ 3. Erdentdeckung.

* 5621. GARCIA-ROMERAL PEREZ (Carlos). Bio-bibliografía de viajeros españoles (siglo XIX). Madrid, Ollero & Ramos, 95, 307 p.

* 5622. GRIEP (Wolfgang) PELZ (Annegret). Frauen Reisen: ein bibliographisches Verzeichnis deutschsprachiger Frauenreisen 1700 bis 1810. Bremen, Temmen, 95, 438 p. (ill.). (Eutiner Kompendien, 1).

** 5623. BARTOLOME DE LAS CASAS). La Destruction des Indes (1552). Trad. de Jacques DE MIGGRODE (1579), gravures de Théodore DE BRY (1598). Introduction historique de Alain MILHOU, établ. du texte et analyse icon. de Jean-Paul DUVIOLS. Paris, Editions Chandeigne, 95, 219 p. (Collection Magellane).

5624. BOERLIN-BRODBECK (Yvonne). Le rôle de la France dans la découverte de la Suisse. *In*: Paysage en Europe du XVIe au XVIIIe siècle (Le) [Cf. n° 6759], p. 257-276.

5625. DOUGNAC RODRÍGUEZ (Antonio). Impresiones y vicisitudes de una viajera chilena del siglo XIX: Maipina de la Barra. *Revista Chilena de Historia y Geografía*, 94-95, 161, p. 117-146.

5626. Globe encircled and the world revealed (The). Ed. by Ursula LAMB. Aldershot, Variorum, 95, XXXI-315 p. (An expanding world: the European impact on world history 1450–1800, 3).

5627. HAFID-MARTIN (Nicole). Voyage et connaissance au tournant des Lumières (1780–1820). Oxford, Voltaire Foundation, 95, V-264 p. (Studies on Voltaire and the eighteenth century, 334).

5628. MOREIRA (Rafael). A arquitectura militar na Expansão Portuguesa. Ed. Comissão Nacional para as Comemoraçoes dos Descobrimentos Portugueses. Porto, C.N.C.D.P., 95, 160 p. (ill.).

5629. PINAULT SORENSEN (Madeleine). Le voyage de Houël en Sicile. *In*: Paysage en Europe du XVIe au XVIIIe siècle (Le) [Cf. n° 6759], p. 119-135.

5630. Portugal, the pathfinder: journeys from the medieval toward the modern world, 1300–ca. 1600. Ed. by George D. WINIUS. Madison, Hispanic Seminary of Medieval Studies, 95, XI-428 p. (Portuguese series, 2).

5631. Tratado de Tordesillas (El) y su Epoca. Congreso Internacional de Historia, [Setubal, 2 de junio, Salamanca 3, 4 de junio, Tordesillas 5, 6, 7 de junio de 1994]. Coordinador general Luis Antonio RIBOT GARCIA. Madrid, Sociedad 5. centenario del tratado de Tordesillas, 95, 3 vol., XVIII-629 p., 714 p., 572 p. [Cf. n° <selección> 7449.]

5632. Voyage de Gonneville (Le) (1503–1505) et la découverte de la Normandie par les Indiens du Brésil. Ed. et comm. de Lyla PERRONE-MOISES, trad. par Arianne WITKOWSKI. Paris, Editions Chandeigne, 95, 224 p. (ill.). (Collection Magellane) [En anexe la lettre de Perô Vaz de Caminha sur la découverte du Brésil, 1500].

Cf. n° 5225

L

RELIGIONSGESCHICHTE DER NEUZEIT

§ 1. Allgemeines. 5633-5678. – § 2. Katholizismus (a. Allgemeines; b. Geschichte des Papsttums; c. Spezialarbeiten; d. Ordensgeschichte; e. Missionsgeschichte). 5679-5818. – § 3. Orthodoxie. 5819-5840. – § 4. Protestantismus. 5841-5897 – § 5. Nichtchristliche Religionen und Sekten. 5898-5964.

§ 1. Allgemeines.

* 5633. Bibliotheca dissidentium: répertoire des nonconformistes religieux des seizième et dix-septième siècles. Ed. par André SEGUENNY, en collaboration avec Jean ROTT. Tome 17. 1. MULLER (Franck). Jacob Kautz. 2. BOYD (Stephen). Pilgram Marpeck, Hans Schlaffer, Leonhard Schiemer. Baden-Baden, [s. n.], 95, 122 p. (Bibliotheca bibliographica Aureliana, 146).

5634. ASANTE (Emmanuel). Toward an African Christian theology of the Kingdom of God: the kingship of Onyame. Lewiston, Mellen University Press, 95, VIII-197 p.

5635. BIAGIONI (Mario). Prospettive di ricerca su Francesco Pucci. *Rivista storica italiana*, 95, 107, 1, p. 133-152.

5636. BIDERMAN (S.). Scripture and knowledge: an essay on religious epistemology. Leiden a. New York, Brill, 95, 256 p. (Studies in the history of religion, 69).

5637. BRUCE (Steve). Religion in modern Britain. Oxford, Oxford U.P., 95, XII-143 p. (ill.). (Oxford modern Britain).

5638. CAPPS (Walter H.). Religious studies: the making of a discipline. Minneapolis, Fortress Press, 95, XXII-368 p.

5639. CESAREO (Vincenzo). La religiosità in Italia. Milano, Mondadori, 95, XII-369 p. (ill.).

5640. CORTES PENA (Antonio Luis). Entre la religiosidad popular y la institucional. Las rogativas en la España moderna. *Hispania*, 95, 55, 191, p. 1027-1042.

5641. CROCE (Paul Jerôme). Science and religion in the era of William James. Eclipse of certainty, 1820–1880. Chapel Hill a. London, University of North Carolina Press, 95, XX-350 p. (ill.).

5642. DAVIES (Jon). The Christian warrior in the twentieth century. Lewiston a. Lampeter, Edwin Mellen, 95, X-158 p. (ill.).

5643. DE GRUCHY (John W.). Christianity and democracy. A theology for a just world order. Cambridge a. New York, Cambridge U.P., 95, XVI-291 p. (Cambridge studies in ideology and religion).

5644. DE ROSA (Gabriele). I codici di lettura del vissuto religioso. Roma e Bari, Laterza, 95, 70 p.

5645. DORRIEN (Gary J.). Soul in society: the making and renewal of social Christianity. Minneapolis, Fortress Press, 95, X-389 p.

5646. ELLINGSEN (Mark). A common sense theology: the Bible, faith, and American society. Macôn, Mercer, 95, XII-251 p. (Studies in American biblical hermeneutics, 9).

5647. FODOR (James). Christian hermeneutics: Paul Ricoeur and the refiguring of theology. Oxford a. New York, Clarendon Press a. Oxford U.P., 95, XIV-370 p.

5648. GRANT (Jacquelyn). Perspectives on womanist theology. Atlanta, ITC Press, 95, 259 p. (Black church scholars series, 7).

5649. HANEGRAAFF (Wouter J.), KLOPPENBORG (Ria). Female stereotypes in religious traditions. Leiden a. New York, Brill, 95, XII-261 p. (Studies in the history of religions, 66).

5650. HAUGHT (John F.). Science and religion: from conflict to conversation. New York, Paulist Press, 95, 225 p.

5651. HEINRICH (Clark). Strange fruit. Alchemy, religion and magical foods: a speculative history. London, Bloomsbury, 95, XI-212 p. (ill.).

5652. KARWALE (W.R.). Divergents interpretations in the relationship between concept of God in the Old testament and in African traditional religions. *Old Testament Essays*, 95, 8, p. 7-30.

5653. KILANI (Mondher). De l'universel et du particulier en antropologie de la religion. *Studia religiosa helvetica*, 95, 1, p. 49-69.

5654. KROEKER (P. Travis). Christian ethics and political economy in North America: a critical analysis. Montreal a. London, McGill-Queen's U.P., 95, XVI-201 p. (McGill-Queen's studies in the history of religion, 17).

5655. KÜNG (Hans). Christentum und Weltreligionen. München, Piper, 95, 234 p.

5656. LAUSTEN (Martin Schwarz). Christian 2. mellem paven og Luther. Tro og politik omkring "den röde konge" i eksilet og i fangenskabet (1523–1559). København, Akademisk forlag, 95, 504 p. (Institut for Kirkehistorie, Köbenhavn universitet. Kirkehistoriske studier III, 3). [Danish king Christian II dethroned in 1523 between the Pope and Luther].

5657. LAZEROW (Jama). Religion and the working class in antebellum America. Washington a. London, Smithsonian Institution Press, 95, XXII-353 p.

5658. LOVIN (Robin W.). Reinhold Niebuhr and Christian realism. Cambridge, Cambridge U. P., 95, X-255 p.

5659. MARTIN (Philippe). Le chemin du sacré. Paroisses, processions, pélerinages en Lorraine du XVIe au XIXe siècle. Metz, Serpenoise, 95, 358 p.

5660. MAZHAR NOOR (Giovanni). Catholic attitudes to evolution in nineteenth-century Italian literature. Venezia, Istituto veneto di scienze, lettere ed arti, 95, 284 p. (Istituto veneto di scienze, lettere ed arti. Classe di scienze, morali, lettere ed arti, 60).

5661. NICHOLLS (David). God and government in an age of reason. London a. New York, Routledge, 95, X-278 p.

5662. NICHOLS (Francis W.). Christianity and the stranger: historical essays. Atlanta, Scholars Press, 95, 297 p. (South Florida-Rochester-Saint Louis studies on religion and the social order, 12).

5663. NITOBURG (Éduard L.). Cerkov' afroamerikancev v SŠA. (The Church of the African-Americans in the USA). Moskva, Nauka, RAN. In-t étnologii i antropologii, 95, 267 p.

5664. OSTERLIN (Lars). The churches of northern Europe in profile: a thousand years of Anglo-Nordic perspective. Norwich, Canterbury Press, 95, X-317 p. (ill.).

5665. Papers of the Seventeenth György Ránki Hungarian Chair Conference. "Religion and Churches in Modern Hungary"– Indiana University, Bloomington, April 23–25, 1993. *Hungarian studies*, 95, 10, 1, p. 3-147.

5666. ROEMER (Thomas). L'Ancien testament: une littérature de la crise. *Revue de théologie et philosophie*, 95, 127, p. 321-38.

5667. SEAGER (Richard Hughes). The World's Parliament of Religions: the East/West encounter, Chicago, 1893. Bloomington, Indiana U.P., 95, XXXII-208 p. (ill.).

5668. SILK (Mark). Unsecular media: making news of religion in America. Urbana, University of Illinois Press, 95, XIV-181 p.

5669. Storia dell'Italia religiosa. 3. L'Età contemporanea. A cura di Gabriele DE ROSA. Roma e Bari, Laterza, 95, XXXVI-620 p. (Storia e società). [contiene: DE ROSA (Gabriele). Introduzione. p. V-XXXVI. – AGOSTINI (Filiberto). la riforma statale della chiesa nell'Italia napoleonica, p. 3-24. – DE MARCO (Vittorio). I santi nella restaurazione: le nuove congregazioni missionarie e assistenziali, p. 25-38. – GIOVAGNOLI (Agostino). Il neoguelfismo, p. 39-60. – TRINCHESE (Stefano). Chiesa e stato nel magistero di Leone XIII, p. 61-86. – STELLA (Pietro). Il clero e la sua cultura nell'Ottocento, p. 87-114. – STELLA (Pietro). Prassi religiosa, spiritualità e mistica nell'Ottocento, p. 115-42. – ZAMBARBIERI (Annibale). Fede e religiosità fra tendenze laiche e modernismo cattolico, p. 143-88. – MALGERI (Francesco). La Chiesa, i cattolici e la prima guerra mondiale, p. 189-223. – DE ROSA (Gabriele), MALGERI (Francesco). L'impegno politico dei cattolici, p. 223-56. – TRANIELLO (Francesco). L'Italia cattolica nell'era fascista, p. 257-301. – MALGERI (Francesco). Chiesa, clero e laicato cattolico tra guerra e Resistenza, p. 303-334. – RICCARDI (Andrea). La Chiesa cattolica in Italia nel secondo dopoguerra, p. 335-360. – MELLONI (Alberto). Da Giovanni XXIII alle Chiese italiane del Vaticano II, p. 361-404. – RICCA (Paolo). Le Chiese evangeliche, p. 405-440. – CAVIGLIA (Stefano). Gli ebrei tra Ottocento e Novecento, p. 441-470. – LA TORRE (Giuseppe). Minoranze musulmane in Italia nel XX secolo, p. 471-500. – FILORAMO (Giovanni). Nuovi movimenti religiosi: l'influsso del misticismo orientale, p. 501-516. – TURCHINI (Angelo). Iconografia e vita religiosa. Committenza e commercio, p. 517-532. Cartografia, p. 533-542. – Bibliografia, p. 543-588. – Indici dei nomi]

5670. STROUMSA (Gedaliahu A. G.), KIPPENBERG (Hans G.). Secrecy and concealment: studies in the history of Mediterranean and Near Eastern religions. Leiden a. New York, Brill, 95, XXIV-406 p. (ill.). (Werner-Reimers-Stiftung; Studies in the history of religions, 65).

5671. TODD (Margo). Reformation to revolution: politics and religion in early modern England. London a. New York, Routledge, 95, XIV-269 p. (ill.). (Rewriting histories).

5672. VAN DER TOORN (K.), PLATVOET (Jan). Pluralism and identity: studies in ritual behaviour. Leiden a. New York, Brill, 95, VI-376 p. (Studies in the history of religions, 67).

5673. VISCHER (Lukas), SCHENKER (Lukas), DELLSPERGER (Rudolf), FATIO (Olivier). Histoire du christianisme en Suisse: une perspective oecumenique. Genève et Fribourg, Editions Labor et Fides, 95, 345 p. (ill.).

5674. WALZ (R.). Der vormoderne Antisemitismus: Religiöser Fanatismus oder Rassenwahn? *Historische Zeitschrift*, 95, 260, 3, p. 719-748.

5675. WESSELS (Anton). Arab and Christian? Christians in the Middle East. Kampen, Kok Pharos, 95, 320 p.

5676. WHALING (Frank). Theory and method in religious studies: contemporary approaches to the study of religion. Berlin u. New York, Mouton de Gruyter, 95, 427 p.

5677. YORK (Michael). The Church universal and triumphant. *Journal of contemporary religion*, 95, 10, p. 71-82.

5678. ZEILSTRA (Jurjen A.). European unity in ecumenical thinking, 1937-1948. Zoetermeer, Uitgeverij Boekencentrum, 95, XVII-454 p.

Cf. n°s 1376-1420

§ 2. Katholizismus.

a. Allgemeines.

* 5679. DEGLER-SPENGLER (Brigitte). Helvetia sacra. Arbeitsbericht 1994. *Revue suisse d'histoire*, 95, 45, 2, p. 255-259.

* 5680. LANGLOIS (Claude). Histoire du christianisme, XVIe–XXe siècles: les livres de 1994, bibliographie annotée de langue française. Paris, GDR 1095 Histoire du Christianisme et CNRS, 95, 35 p.

5681. BIZZOCCHI (Roberto), ROSA (Mario). Clero e società nell'Italia moderna. Roma e Bari, Laterza, 95, XL-394 p.

5682. BORZOMATI (Pietro). I cattolici e il Mezzogiorno. Roma, Studium, 95, 263 p. (Pensiero politico e sociale dei cattolici italiani, 23).

5683. BOUDON (J.-O.). Le Saint-Siège et le recrutement des évêques français au lendemain de la Séparation: une enquête de 1908 sur le candidats à l'épiscopat. *Revue d'Histoire Ecclésiastique*, 95, 90, 3-4, p. 443-470.

5684. CATTANEO (Massimo). Gli occhi di Maria sulla rivoluzione: "miracoli" a Roma e nello Stato della Chiesa (1796–1797). Roma, Istituto nazionale di studi romani, 95, XII-279 p. (ill.).

5685. CHÂTELLIER (Louis). Le catholicisme en France, 1500–1650. T. 1. Le XVIe siècle. T. 2. Le XVIIe siècle. 1600–1650. Paris, SEDES, 95, 2 vol., 499 p.

5686. DAL TOSO (Paola). L'associazionismo giovanile in Italia. Gli anni sessanta-ottanta. Torino, Società Editrice Internazionale, 95, XII-358 p.

5687. EIRE (Carlos M.N.). From Madrid to Purgatory. The art and craft of dying in sixteenth-century Spain. Cambridge, Cambridge U.P., 95, XIV-572 p.

5688. Ethique, économie et developpement: l'enseignement des évêques des cinq continents (1891–1991). Actes du Colloque organisé a Fribourg, du 1er au 3 avril 1993. Ed. par Roger BERTHOUZOZ et Roberto PAPINI. Fribourg, Editions Universitaires et Paris, Editions du Cerf, 95, 270 p. (Université de Fribourg Institut de theologie morale / Institut international Jacques Maritain / Studien zur theologischen Ethik, Etudes d'éthique chretienne, 62).

5689. FERRONE (Vincenzo). The intellectual roots of the Italian Enlightenment: Newtonian science, religion, and politics in the early eighteenth century. Atlantic Highlands, Humanities Press, 95, XIV-396 p.

5690. FIRPO (Massimo), MARCATTO (Dario). Il processo inquisitoriale del cardinal Giovanni Morone. Volume 6. Appendice 2. Summarium processus originalis. Documenti. Roma, Istituto storico italiano per l'età moderna e contemporanea, 95, 459 p.

5691. Foi, fidelité, amitié en Europe a la période moderne. Mélanges offerts à Robert Sauzet. Ed. par Brigitte MAILLARD. Tours, Publication de l'Université de Tours, 95, XII-558 p. (ill.).

5692. *Vacat.*

5693. Katholische Konfessionalisierung (Die). Wissenschaftliches Symposion der Gesellschaft zur Herausgabe des Corpus Catholicorum und des Vereins für Reformationsgeschichte 1993. Hrsg. v. Wolfgang REINHARD u. Heinz SCHILLING. Gütersloh, Gütersloher Verlagshaus, 95, XIII-472 p. (Gesellschaft zur Herausgabe des Corpus Catholicorum, Verein für Reformationsgeschichte, Schriften des Vereins für Reformationsgeschichte, 198).

5694. KIEFER (Thomas). Ehekatechese. Ein didaktisches Modell zur Ehevorbereitung und -begleitung. Freiburg im Breisgau, Herder, 95, 293 p. (Freiburger theologische Studien, 156).

5695. LEB (Ioan-Vasile). Orthodoxie und Altkatholizismus: eine hundert Jahre ökumenische Zusammenarbeit (1870–1970). Cluj-Napoca, Presa Universitara Clujeeana, 95, 262 p. ("Babes-Bolyai" Universität).

5696. MAC GINNESS (Frederick J.). Right thinking and sacred oratory in Counter-Reformation Rome. Princeton, Princeton U. P., 95, 368 p.

5697. MAUGENEST (Denis). Le discours social de l'Eglise catholique de France (1891–1992). Textes majeurs de l'Episcopat francais. Paris, Editions du Cerf, 95, 749 p. (Documents des Eglises).

5698. MENOZZI (Daniele). Regalità sociale di Cristo e secolarizzazione. Alle origini della quas primas. *Cristianesimo nella storia*, 95, 16, 1, p. 79-114.

5699. MILTON (Anthony). Catholic and Reformed: the Roman and Protestant churches in English Protestant thought, 1600–1640. Cambridge a. New York, Cambridge U.P., 95, XVI-599 p. (Cambridge studies in early modern British history).

5700. MOLETTE (Charles). La foi de Marie, mère du redempteur: 51ᵉ session de la Societé française d'études mariales, Rocamadour, 1994. Paris, Mediaspaul, 95, 132 p. (Société française d'études mariales).

5701. Mysterium Christi. Symbolgegenwart und theologische Bedeutung. Festschrift für Basil Studer. Hrsg. v. Magnus LOHRER u. Elmar SALMANN. Roma, Pontificio Ateneo S. Anselmo, 95, 403 p. (Studia Anselmiana, 116).

5702. REMOND (René). Le Catholicisme français et la société politique. Ecrits de circonstance (1947–1991). Paris, Editions de l'atelier/Editions ouvrieres, 95, 248 p.

5703. ROUVILLOIS (Samuel). Corps et sagesse: philosophie de la liturgie. Paris, Fayard, 95, 490 p. (Collection "Aletheia").

5704. TURBANTI (G.). Il contributo dei paesi di lingua tedesca e dell'Europa orientale al Concilio Vaticano II. *Cristianesimo nella storia*, 95, 16, 1, p. 141-160.

5705. Vaticano II fra attese e celebrazione (Il). A cura di Giuseppe ALBERIGO. Bologna, Il Mulino, 95, 250 p. (Testi e ricerche di scienze religiose, 13).

5706. WAGNER (Christine). Le dialogue sur la doctrine chrétienne de Juan de Valdès (1529). Paris, PUF, 95, 225 p. (Etudes d'histoire et de philosophie religieuses, 74).

Cf. nᵒ 1458

b. Geschichte des Papsttums.

5707. ANDRISANI (Gaetano). Bellarmino e Capecelatro cardinali di Capua. Caserta, s.i.e., 95, 110 p. (Saggi storici casertani, 4).

5708. BOCCHINI CAMAIANI (B.). The papacy and the new world. Concerning an edition of sources. *Cristianesimo nella storia*, 95, 16, 3, p. 521-552.

5709. CHAVASSE (Antoine). Les ancêtres du Missale Romanum (1570). Roma, Pontificio Ateneo S. Anselmo, 95, 94 p. (ill.). (Studia Anselmiana. Analecta liturgica, 20).

5710. GUASCO (Maurilio). Modernismo: i fatti, le idee, i personaggi. Cinisello Balsamo, Milano, San Paolo, 95, 214 p. (Universo teologia, 40).

5711. KUSS (Stephan). Römische Kurie, italienischer Staat, und faschistische Bewegung: der Vatikan und Italien in der Zeit nach dem Ersten Weltkrieg bis zur totalitaren "Wende" des Mussolini-Regimes (1919–1925). Frankfurt am Main, Lang, 95, 282 p. (ill.). (Europäische Hochschulschriften. Reihe III, Geschichte und ihre Hilfswissenschaften, 632).

5712. METZLER (Josef). America Pontificia: documenta pontificia ex registris et minutis praesertim ex Archivo secreto vaticano existentibus. Città del Vaticano, Libreria editrice vaticana, 95, 640 p. (Archivio Vaticano, Atti e documenti, Pontificio Comitato di scienze storiche, 3, 5).

5713. NASSI (Enrico), QUINZIO (Sergio), FAMILIARI (Rocco). Karol Wojtyla: la biografia. San Casciano Val di Pesa, Shakespeare and company, 95, 282 p.

5714. Paolo VI e la collegialità episcopale. Colloquio internazionale di studio. Brescia 25–27 settembre 1992. Brescia e Roma, Istituto Paolo VI, Edizioni Studium, 95, XIV-389 p. (Pubblicazioni dell'Istituto Paolo VI, 15).

5715. Papstgeschichte und Landesgeschichte. Festschrift für Hermann Jakobs zum 65. Geburtstag. Hrsg. v. Jürgen MIETHKE. Köln, Bohlau, 95, XIV-667 p. (ill.). (Beihefte zum Archiv für Kulturgeschichte, 39).

5716. PASSELECQ (Georges), SUCHECKY (Bernard). L'encyclique cachée de Pie XI. Une occasion manquée de l'Eglise face à l'antisémitisme. Paris, La Découverte, 95, 320 p. (Collection "L'Espace de l'histoire").

5717. SAVAGNONE (Giuseppe). La Chiesa di fronte alla mafia. Cinisello Balsamo, San Paolo, 95, 211 p. (Attualità e storia, 12).

5718. Toso (Mario). Welfare society. L'apporto dei pontefici da Leone XIII a Giovanni Paolo II. Roma, LAS, 95, 533 p. (Biblioteca di scienze religiose / Libreria Ateneo salesiano, 116).

5719. TYGIELSKI (Wojciech). Opinie nuncjuszy apostolskich na temat Polski XVI–XVII w. (Opinions des nonces apostoliques à propos de la Pologne aux XVIᵉ–XVIIᵉ s.). *Przegląd Historyczny*, 95, 85, 4, p. 351-362. [Eng. Summary].

5720. WIJNHOVEN (Joseph). Nuntius Pier Luigi Carafa (1627 September–1630 Dezember). Schöningh, Paderborn, 95, 4 vol., [s. p.]. (Catholic Church Apostolic Nunciature (Germany) / Görres-Gesellschaft: Nuntiaturberichte aus Deutschland, nebst ergänzenden Aktenstücken. Die Kölner Nuntiatur, 7).

5721. *Vacat*.

c. Spezialarbeiten.

* 5722. FUMASI (Eleonora). Mezzo secolo di ricerca storiografica sul movimento cattolico in Italia dal 1861 al 1945. Contributo a una bibliografia. Brescia, La Scuola, 95, 604 p. (Archivio per la storia del movimento sociale cattolico in Italia/Analisi e sintesi).

5723. BARANOWSKI (Andrzej). Oprawy uroczystości koronacyjnych wizerunków Marii [Matki Boskiej] na Rusi Koronnej w XVIII w. (Le cadre des cérémonies de couronnement des effigies de Notre-Dame en Ruthénie Royale au XVIIᵉ siècle). *Biuletyn Historii Sztuki*, 95, 57, 3-4, p. 299-322 (phot., dessins). [Eng. Summary].

5724. BELLONI (Cristina). Francesco della Croce: contributo alla storia della Chiesa ambrosiana nel Quattrocento. Milano, NED, 95, 350 p. (Archivio ambrosiano, 71).

5725. BERTOLI (Bruno), TRAMONTIN (Silvio). La chiesa di Venezia nel primo Novecento. Venezia, Studium Cattolico Veneziano, 95, 231 p. (ill.). (Contributi alla storia della Chiesa di Venezia, 9).

5726. BLET (Pierre). Le Clergé du grand siècle en ses assemblées (1615–1715). Paris, Editions du Cerf, 95, 529 p. (Histoire religieuse de la France).

5727. BOŃCZA-BYSTRZYCKI (Lech). Kościół katolicki na Pomorzu Zachodnim (1871–1945). (Eglise polonaise en Poméranie occidentale [1871–1945]). Koszalin et Poznań, nakł. autora, 95, 317 p. (phot., cartes 2). [Deutsche Zsfassung].

5728. BOGDANOWICZ (Stanisław). Karol Maria Antoni Splett – biskup gdański czasu wojny, więzień specjalny PRL [Polskiej Rzeczypospolitej Ludowej]. (Karol Maria Antoni Splett – évêque de Gdańsk en période de la guerre, prisonnier spécial de RPP [République Populaire de Pologne]). Gdańsk, Stella Maris, 95, XIX-356 p. (phot.).

5729. BUDNIAK (Józef). Jan Sarkander – patron jednoczącej się Europy. (Jan Sarkander – le patron de l'Europe en train de s'unifier). Cieszyn „4K", 95, 153 p. (phot., fig., dessins, cartes 2).

5730. BUONASORTE (Nicla). La politica religiosa italiana in Africa Orientale dopo la conquista (1936–1941). Studi Piacentini. Rivista dell'Istituto storico della Resistenza e dell'età contemporanea, 95, 17, p. 53-114.

5731. CAPRIOLI (Adriano), RIMOLDI (Antonio), VACCARO (Luciano), LANZANI (Vittorio). Storia religiosa della Lombardia. Vol. 11. Diocesi di Pavia. Brescia, La Scuola, 95, 524 p. (ill.).

5732. CÁRCEL ORTÍ (V.). Le cardinal Mercier et les études ecclésiastiques en Espagne. Revue d'Histoire Ecclésiastique, 95, 90, 1-2, p. 104-112.

5733. Catholiques entre monarchie et republique: Monseigneur Freppel en son temps, 1792–1892–1992. Actes du Colloque national de l'Université catholique de l'Ouest, Angers, 23–25 septembre 1992. Ed. par Bernard PLONGERON. Paris, Letouzey et Âne, 95, 238 p.

5734. CATTANEO (Massimo). Maria versus Marianne. I "miracoli" del 1796 ad Ancona. Cristianesimo nella storia, 95, 16, 1, p. 45-78.

5735. CESTARO (Antonio). Chiesa e società nel Mezzogiorno moderno e contemporaneo. Napoli, Edizioni scientifiche italiane, 95, 605 p. (Pubblicazioni dell'Universita degli studi di Salerno. Sezione Atti, convegni, miscellanee, 47).

5736. CIVIL (Pierre). Image et dévotion dans l'Espagne du XVIe siècle: le traité "Norte de Ydiotas" de Francisco de Monzon (1563). Paris, Presses de la Sorbonne Nouvelle, 95, 197 p. (ill.). (Textes et documents du Centre de recherche sur l'Espagne des XVIe et XVIIe sieclès, 5).

5737. DAROWSKI (Roman). Wojciech Sokołowski SJ (1586–1631) i jego filozofia. [Wojciech Sokołowski SJ (1586–1631) et sa philosophie]. Kraków, Wydawn. Apostolstwa Modlitwy, 95, 64 p. (Wydz. Filozof. Tow. Jezusowego w Krakowie. Teksty i Studia, 36). [Rés. français].

5738. DITCHFIELD (Simon Richard). Liturgy, sanctity and history in Tridentine Italy. Pietro Maria Campi and the preservation of the particular. Cambridge, Cambridge U. P., 95, XIV-397 p. (ill., maps). (Cambridge studies in Italian history and culture).

5739. DÓKA (Klára). A kalocsai érsékség birtokai a 18–19. században. (Les domaines de l'archevêché de Kalocsa aux XVIII–XIX siècles). Magyar egyhátört. vázlatok, 95, 7, 1-2, p. 89-152. – EADEM. Az esztergomi érsékség birtokai. (Les domaines de l'archevêché de Esztergom). Levéltári közl., 95, 66, 1-2, p. 93-119.

5740. DOMIN-JACOV (Maria). Opitius Pallavicini (1680–1688). Romae, Institutum Historicum Polonicum Romae, 95, 346 p. (Acta Nuntiaturae Polonae, 34).

5741. ESSERTEL (Y.). Réseaux et vocations missionaires dans le diocèse de Lyon de 1815 à 1962. Revue d'Histoire Ecclésiastique, 95, 90, 1-2, p. 49-70.

5742. FINCARDI (Marco). «Ici pas de Madone». Inondations et apparitions mariales dans les campagnes de la vallée du Po. Annales, 95, 50, 4, p. 829-854.

5743. FRANZINELLI (Mimmo). Stellette, croce e fascio littorio. L'assistenza religiosa a militari, balilla e camicie nere, 1919–1939. Milano, Franco Angeli, 95, 377 p.

5744. FURST (Carl Gerold). Il diritto canonico orientale nell'ordinamento ecclesiale. Città del Vaticano, Libreria Editrice Vaticana, 95, 274 p. (Bharanikulangara Kuriakose, Studi giuridici, 34).

5745. GĄSIOROWSKI (Antoni), SKIERSKA (Izabela). Średniowieczni oficiałowie gnieźnieńscy. (Les officiaux de Gniezno au Moyen Age). Roczniki Historyczne, 95, 61, p. 37-86. [Deutsche Zsfassung].

5746. GAUDIO (Angelo). Scuola, chiesa e fascismo: la scuola cattolica in Italia durante il fascismo (1922–1943). Brescia, La Scuola, 95, 223 p. (Paedagogica. Testi e studi storici).

5747. GEISSLER (Hermann). Gewissen und Wahrheit bei John Henry Kardinal Newman. Frankfurt am Main u. New York, Lang, 95, 224 p. (Theologie im Übergang, 12).

5748. GERGELY (Jenő). Concordatum hungaricum. A nyilas kormány konkordátum-tervezete 1945 elján. (Un projet de concordat du gouvernement des croix fléchées de l'année 1945). Századok, 95, 129, 3, p. 695-728.

5749. GŁÓWKA (Dariusz). Księgozbiory duchowieństwa płockiego w XVIII wieku. (Bibliothèques des ecclésiastiques de Płock au XVIIIe siècle). *Kwartalnik Historyczny*, 95, 102, 2, p. 15-26. [Eng. Summary].

5750. GRUSS (Heribert). Erzbischof Lorenz Jaeger als Kirchenführer im Dritten Reich. Tatsachen, Dokumente, Entwicklungen, Kontext, Probleme. Paderborn, Bonifatius, 95, 488 p. (ill.). (Zeitgeschichte im Erzbistum Paderborn, 3).

5751. HORGA (Ioan). L'Eglise gréco-catholique roumaine (Uniate) de Transylvanie à l'époque des Lumières. L'éveché d'Oradea (1780–1830). Lille, Université de Lille, 95, 605 p.

5752. JAMES (George Alfred). Interpreting religion: The phenomenological approaches of Pierre Daniel Chantepie de la Saussaye, W. Brede Kristensen, and Gerardus van der Leeuw. Washington, Catholic University of America Press, 95, XIV-304 p.

5753. Kirche, Recht und Wissenschaft. Festschrift für Albert Stein. Hrsg. v. Andrea BOLUMINSKI. Neuwied, Luchterhand, 95, VIII-259 p.

5754. Kirchenmusikalisches Erbe und Liturgie. Internationales wissenschaftliches Symposium an der Katholischen Universität Eichstätt am 18.–20. September 1989. Hrsg. v. Hubert UNVERRICHT. Tutzing, Schneider, 95, 212 p. (Eichstätter Abhandlungen zur Musikwissenschaft, 10).

5755. KLAUCK (Hans-Josef), RUPPERT (Lothar). Die Interpretation der Bibel in der Kirche: das Dokument der Päpstlichen Bibelkommission vom 23.4.1993. Stuttgart, Verlag Katholisches Bibelwerk, 95, 174 p. (Catholic Church Pontificia Commissio Biblica – Stuttgarter Bibelstudien, 161).

5756. KOSTERS (Christoph). Katholische Verbände und moderne Gesellschaft: Organisationsgeschichte und Vereinskultur im Bistum Münster 1918 bis 1945. Paderborn, Schoningh, 95, 684 p. (Veröffentlichungen der Kommission für Zeitgeschichte, 68).

5757. LOGAN (Oliver M.T.). The Venetian upper clergy in the sixteehth and early seventeenth centuries. A study in religious culture. Salzburg, Institut für Anglistik und Amerikanistik Universität Salzburg, 95, X-606 p.

5758. MATZ (Jean-Michel). Le développement tardif d'une religion civique dans une ville épiscopale. Les processions à Angers (v. 1450–1550). *In:* Religion civique à l'époque médiévale et moderne (La) [Cf. n° 4528], p. 351-366.

5759. MENGES (Evelyne Dominica). Die kirchliche Stiftung in der Bundesrepublik Deutschland: eine Untersuchung zur rechtlichen Identität der kirchlichen Stiftung staatlichen Rechts mit der kanonischen Stiftung. St. Ottilien, EOS, 95, LXXVIII-358 p. (Münchener theologische Studien, III, Kanonistische Abteilung 48).

5760. MIKRUT (Jan). Bischöfe aus Galizien berichten an Kaiser Franz I.: Ein Beitrag zur Geschichte der katholischen Kirche in der Habsburgermonarchie. Wien, Wiener Dom-Vlg, 95, 378 p. (ill.).

5761. MOLNÁR (Antal). Pietro Massarecchi antivari érsek és szendrődi apostoli adminisztrátor egyházlátogatási jelentése a hòdolt Dél-Magyarországròl, 1633. (Rapport de Pietro Massarecchi archevêque de Antivar et administrateur apostolique de Szendrő sur la visitation canonique de la Hongrie du Sud sous l'occupation turque). *Fons*, 95, 2, 2, p. 175-217.

5762. MORELLO (Giovanni), MADDALO (Silvia). Liturgia in figura: codici liturgici rinascimentali della Biblioteca apostolica vaticana. Città del Vaticano, Biblioteca apostolica vaticana, 95, 355 p. (ill.).

5763. NABYWANIEC (Stanisław). Uniccy biskupi przemyscy w latach 1610–1991. Szkice biograficzne. (Evêques uniates de Przemyśl dans les années 1610–1991. Esquisses biographiques). Rzeszów, Poligrafia Wyższego Sem. Duchownego, 95, 90 p. (phot., fig.).

5764. PAPINI (M.). The formation of a young catholic in the second half of the thirthies. Franco Rodano between the Marian congregation "La Scaletta" and the Liceo Visconti (1935–1940). *Cristianesimo nella storia*, 95, 16, 3, p. 553-586.

5765. PATEK (Artur). Z uwag nad położeniem Kościoła katolickiego w ZSRR w okresie międzywojennym. (Observations sur la position de l'Eglise catholique en URSS dans la période entre deux guerres). *Dzieje najnowsze*, 95, 27, 1, p. 1-12.

5766. PIECH (Stanisław). Dzieje Wydziału Teologicznego Uniwersytetu Jagiellońskiego w latach 1880–1939. (Histoire de la faculté théologique de l'Université Jagellonne dans les années 1880–1939). Kraków, Papieska Akad. Teolog. w Krakowie, 95, 258 p. (phot., fig.). (Studia do Dziejów Wydz. Teolog. Uniw. Jagiell., 6).

5767. PLEWKO (Jadwiga). Duszpasterstwo w Polonii w procesie jej integracji ze społeczeństwem kanadyjskim 1875–1988. (Prétrise de la Polonia [diaspora polonaise] dans les processus de son intégration à la société canadienne 1875–1988). Lublin, Red Wydawn. Kat. Uniw. Lub., 95, 464 p. (phot., fig.). (Bibl. Polonii, Ser. A: Studia, 7).

5768. POSSENTI (Vittorio). Cattolicesimo e modernità: Balbo, Del Noce, Rodano. Milano, Ares, 95, 229 p. (Collana Sagitta, 47).

5769. Przestrzeń i sacrum. Geografia kultury religijnej w Polsce i jej przemiany w okresie od XVII do XX w. na przykładzie ośrodków kultu i migracji pielgrzymkowych. (L'Espace et le sacré. La géographie de la culture religieuse en Pologne et ses changements du XVIIe au XXe s., sur l'exemple des centres de culte et de pèlerinage). Kraków, Inst. Geografii Uniw. Jagiell., 95, 328 p. (Eng. Summary, fig., dessins, cartes).

5770. RAABE (Thomas). SED-Staat und katholische Kirche: politische Beziehungen 1949–1961. Paderborn, Schöningh, 95, 294 p. (Veröffentlichungen der Kommission für Zeitgeschichte. B/70).

5771. REB (Sylvaine). L'Aufklärung catholique a Salzbourg. L'oeuvre réformatrice (1772–1803) de Hieronymus von Colloredo. Berne u. New York, Lang, 95, XVIII-1044 p. (Collection Contacts, III/33).

5772. RISKÓ (Mariann). A kárpátaljai görögkatolikus egyház kálváriája 1944-től a legalitás visszanyeréséig. (La calvaire de l'Eglise grécocatholique de la Ruthénie subcarpatique depuis 1944 à la reconquête de la légalité). *Magyar egyháztört. vázlatoká*, 95, 7, 1-2, p. 177-196.

5773. ROUX (Jacqueline). Sous l'etendard de Jeanne. Les fédérations diocesaines de jeunes filles, 1904-1945: une ACJF feminine? Paris, Ed. du Cerf, 95, 310 p. (ill.). (Histoire religieuse de la France, 5).

5774. SCHLOGL (Rudolf). Glaube und Religion in der Säkularisierung: die katholische Stadt Köln, Aachen, Münster 1700–1840. München, Oldenbourg, 95, 447 p.

5775. SCHRAUT (Barbara). Antonia Werr (1813–1868) und die Oberzeller Schwestern: geistliches Profil und sozialer Auftrag einer Frauenkongregation des 19. Jahrhunderts von der Grundung bis zur Gegenwart. Wurzburg, Schoningh, 95, XVI-369 p. (Quellen und Forschungen zur Geschichte des Bistums und Hochstifts Würzburg, 47).

5776. SCHUSTER (Raymund). Das kirchliche Amt bei John Henry Newman. Eine Historisch-systematische Untersuchung der Genese seines Priesterbildes im Kontext. Frankfurt am Main, Lang, 95, 322 p. (Europäische Hochschulschriften, XXIII/526).

5777. Semiotica del testo mistico. Atti del congresso internazionale per le celebrazioni centenarie di Sant'Ignazio di Loyola (1491/1556), San Giovanni della Croce (1542/1591), Fra Luigi di Leon (1527/1591). A cura di Giuseppe DE GENNARO. L'Aquila, Edizioni del gallo cedrone, 95, 1006 p. (ill.). (Pubblicazioni dell'Università della preghiera, 2).

5778. SEVEGRAND (Martine). Les enfants du bon Dieu: les catholiques français et la procréation au XXe siècle. Paris, Albin Michel, 95, 475 p. (Albin Michel histoire)

5779. *Vacat.*

5780. STEINER (Wolfgang). Die Lateinschule der St. Jakobs-Pfarrkirche in Innsbruck: ihr Aufstieg und Niedergang in der Zeit von 1420 bis 1634. *In*: Stadt und Kirche [Cf. n° 1309], p. 149-164.

5781. SZCZUDŁOWSKI (Piotr). Kościół katolicki wobec poewangelickich świątyń w Gdańsku [1945–1992]. (L'église catholique et les temples post-luthériens de Gdańsk [1945–1992]). *Nasza Przeszłość*, 95, 84, p. 257-301. [Deutsche Zsfassung].

5782. TOSI (Claudio). Repubblica e religione nella prima repubblica cisalpina (1796–1799). *Rivista di storia e letteratura religiosa*, 95, 31, p. 293-319.

5783. URBAŃSKI (Stanisław). Polska teologia życia mistycznego (1914–1939). [Théologie polonaise de la vie mystique (1914–1939)]. Warszawa, Akad. Teologii Kat., 95, 401 p. [Eng. Summary, Deutsche Zsfassung].

5784. WEISS (Otto). Der Modernismus in Deutschland: ein Beitrag zur Theologiegeschichte. Regensburg, Verlag Pustet, 95, XXII-632 p.

5785. Wunderbare Erscheinungen: Frauen und katholische Frömmigkeit im 19. und 20. Jahrhundert. Hrsg. v. Irmtraud Gotz von OLENHUSEN. Paderborn, Schöningh, 95, 251 p.

d. Ordensgeschichte.

* 5786. HAUSBERGER (Bernd). Jesuiten aus Mitteleuropa im kolonialen Mexiko: eine Bio-Bibliographie. Wien, Verlag für Geschichte und Politik, u. München, R. Oldenbourg, 95, 436 p. (map.). (Studien zur Geschichte und Kultur der Iberischen und Iberoamerikanischen Länder, 2 = Estudios sobre historia y cultura de los paises ibericos e iberoamericanos, 2).

* 5787. MORUJÃO (Isabel). Contributo para uma bibliografia cronológica da literatura monástica feminina portuguesa dos séculos XVII e XVIII: impressos. Lisboa, Univ. Católica Portuguesa, 95, 90 p. (História religiosa. Fontes e subsídios).

* 5788. POLGAR (László). Bibliographie sur l'histoire de la Compagnie de Jésus. *Archivum historicum Societatis Iesu*, 95, 64, 128, p. 287-459.

5789. BRUNELLI (Gianfranco). Monachesimo, laicità e vita religiosa. Bologna, EDB, 95, 198 p. (Problemi di vita religiosa).

5790. DE LA SELLE (Xavier). Le service des âmes à la cour: confesseurs et aumoniers des rois de France du XIIIe au XVe siècle. Paris, Ecole des chartes, 95, 364 p. (ill.). (Mémoires et documents de l'Ecole des chartes, 43).

5791. DELL'OMO (Mariano). Insediamenti monastici a Gaeta e nell'attuale diocesi. Montecassino, Pubblicazioni Cassinesi, 95, XXXII-225 p. (ill.). (Archivio storico di Montecassino, 8).

5792. EVANGELISTI (Silvia). L'uso e la trasmissione delle celle nel monastero di Santa Giulia di Brescia (1597–1688). *Quaderni storici*, 95, 30, 88 (1), p. 85-110.

5793. FERRARO (Domenico). Itinerari del volontarismo: teologia e politica al tempo di Luis de Léon. Milano, Franco Angeli, 95, 506 p. (Filosofia e scienza nel cinquecento e nel seicento, 42).

5794. GARMS (Jörg). Materialen zur Kunsttätigkeit der gegenreformatorischen Orden in Österreich und in anderen Ländern der Habsburgermonarchie bis 1800. 2: Das Archiv des Servitenordens. *Röm. Hist. Mitt.*, 95, 37, p. 145-161 (ill.).

5795. GARNOT (Benoit), DEREGNAUCOURT (Gilles). Le clergé delinquant XIIIe–XVIIIe siècle. Dijon, Editions universitaires de Dijon, 95, 191 p. (Publications de l'Université de Bourgogne, 80).

5796. GRABNER (Elfriede). Wunderglaube und Heilserwartung im barocken Klosterleben. Eine Prager Karmelitinnenchronik als Quelle zur Volksfrömmigkeit des 17. Jahrhunderts. *Österreichische Zeitschrift für Volkskunde*, 95, 49, 1, p. 1-40.

5797. HARASIMOWICZ (Jan). The role of Cistercian monasteries in the shaping of the cultural identity of Silesia in modern times. *Acta Poloniae historica*, 95, vol. 72, p. 49-63.

5798. IANNELLA (Cecilia). Malattia e salute nella predicazione di Giordano da Pisa. *Rivista di storia e letteratura religiosa*, 95, 31, p. 177-215.

5799. LAMBERT (Malcolm). Povertà francescana. La dottrina dell'assoluta povertà di Cristo e degli Apostoli nell'ordine francescano: 1210–1323. Milano, Edizioni biblioteca francescana, 95, 276 p. (Fonti e ricerche, 8).

5800. LEC (Zdzisław). Jezuici we Wrocławiu (1581–1776). (Les jésuites à Wrocław, 1581–1776). Wrocław, 95, 195 p. (Deutsche Zsfassung). (Papieski Fakultet Teolog. we Wrocławiu. Rozpr. Nauk., 8).

5801. MALATESTA (Edward), RAGUIN (Yves), DUDINK (Adrianus). Echanges culturels et religieux entre la Chine et l'Occident. San Francisco et Taipei, Ricci Institute for Chinese-Western Cultural History, Institut Ricci, 95, XLII-320 p. (ill.).

5802. MARIN (Richard). Dom Helder Camara, les puissants et les pauvres: pour une histoire de l'Eglise des pauvres dans le Nordeste bresilien, 1955–1985. Paris, Editions de l'atelier/Editions ouvrieres, 95, 366 p. (ill.).

5803. MARTINEZ QUESTA (Angel). Historia de los augustinos recoletos. I: Desde los origines hasta el siglo XIX. Madrid, Augustinus, 95, 750 p. (ill.).

5804. MERLO (Grado Giovanni). Gli inizi dell'ordine dei Frati Predicatori. Spunti per una riconsiderazione. *Rivista di storia e letteratura religiosa*, 95, 31, p. 415-441.

5805. MUNONO MUYEMBE (Bernard). Eglise, évangelisation et promotion humaine: le discours social des évêques africains. Fribourg et Paris, Editions Universitaires et Editions du Cerf, 95, 286 p. (Studien zur theologischen Ethik / Etudes d'éthique chrétienne. 63).

5806. Österreichs Stifte unter dem Hakenkreuz. Zeugnisse und Dokumente aus der Zeit des Nationalsozialismus 1938 bis 1945. Hrsg. von der Österreichischen Superiorkonferenz. Zusammengestellt und bearb. von Sebastian BOCK. Wien, Superiorkonferenz der Männl. Ordensgemeinschaften Österreichs, 95, 271 p. (Ordensnachrichten, 4A).

5807. PASCHE (Veronique), PARAVICINI BAGLIANI (Agostino). La parrocchia nel Medio Evo. Economia, scambi, solidarietà. Roma, Herder, 95, XXVII-325 p. (Italia sacra: studi e documenti di storia ecclesiastica, 53).

5808. PAVLÍK (Jan). Budou vás vydávat soudům. (They will send you to court). Tomo 1. Dějiny české provincie Tovaryšstva Ježíšova v době komunistického útlaku v letech 1950–1990. (The history of the Czech province of the Society of Jesus in the period of Communist oppression, 1950–1990). Praha, Societas, 95, 225 p.

5809. PIZZORUSSO (Giovanni). Roma nei Caraibi. L'organizzazione delle missioni cattoliche nelle Antille e in Guyana (1635–1675). Roma, Ecole française de Rome, 95, XVI-366 p. (ill.). (Collection de l'Ecole française de Rome, 207).

5810. ROBRES (Fernando Andres). La singularidad de la hermaña pequeña. Algunas consideraciones sobre el gobierno de la orden de Montesa y sus relaciones con la monarquía (siglos XVI–XVIII). *Hispania*, 95, 55, 190, p. 547-566.

5811. RUSCONI (Roberto). Through St. Francis. *Cristianesimo nella storia*, 95, 16, 3, p. 599-625.

5812. TAMBURINI (Filippo), AGNOLETTI (Attilio). Santi e peccatori. Confessioni e suppliche dai registri della Penitenzieria dell'Archivio Segreto Vaticano (1451–1586). Milano, Istituto di propaganda libraria, 95, 377 p. (ill.).

5813. TARDIEU (Jean-Pierre). L'inquisition de Lima et les hérétiques étrangers (XVIe–XVIIe siècles). Paris, L'Harmattan, 95, 175 p. (ill.). (Collection Recherches et documents. Amériques latines).

5814. TORRE (Angelo). Il consumo di devozioni: religione e comunità nelle campagne dell'ancien régime. Venezia, Marsilio, 95, XXIV-362 p. (Storia e scienze sociali).

5815. VASILIK (Vladimir). Franciscan manuscripts in Russia. *Archivum franciscanum historicum*, 95, 88, p. 533-58.

5816. VERDE (Armando F.). Movimenti savonaroliani e riformistici. Pistoia, Provincia romana dei Frati predicatori, 95, 533 p. (ill.). (Memorie domenicane, 25).

e. Missionsgeschichte.

5817. ILJA (Voldemar). Vennastekoguduse (Herrnhutluse) ajalugu Eestimaal (Pohja-Eest) 1730–1743. [Die Geschichte der Brüdergemeinde (Herrnhutertum) in Estland (Nord-Estland) 1730–1743. The history of the Fraternity of the Moravian Brethern (Herrnhuter) in Estonia (North-Estonia) 1730–1743]. Helsinki, Soc. Historiae Ecclesiasticae Fennica, 95, 296 p. (Eng. summary, Dt. Zfassung). (Suomen kirkkohist. seuran toim., 169).

5818. WŁOCZYK (Piotr). Adam Prosper Burzyński OFM, misjonarz w Egipcie na przełomie XVIII i XIX w. (Adam Prosper Burzyński OFM, missionnaire en Egypte à la fin du XVIIIe et au commencement du XIXe siècle). *Nasza Przeszłość*, 95, 84, p. 157-186 (phot., fig.). [Deutsche Zsfassung].

§ 3. Orthodoxie.

5819. AMIS (Robin). A different Christianity: early Christian esotericism and modern thought. New York, State University of New York Press, 95, XX-388 p. (SUNY series in Western esoteric traditions).

5820. COUNELIS (James Steve). Inheritance and change in Orthodox Christianity. Scranton a. London, University of Scranton Press a. Associated University Presses, 95, XVI-177 p.

5821. ENGLEZAKIS (Benedict), IOANNOU (Silouan), IOANNOU (Misael). Studies on the history of the church of Cyprus, IVth–XXth centuries. Aldershot, Variorum, 95, XIV-487 p. (ill.).

5822. FEDALTO (Giorgio). Le Chiese d'Oriente. Milano, Jaca Book, 95, VI-320 p.

5823. FENNELL (John Lister Illingworth). A history of the Russian church to 1448. London a. New York, Longman, 95, XII-266 p. (map).

5824. JOHNSON (Maxwell E.). The prayers of Sarapion of Thmuis: a literary, liturgical, and theological analysis. Roma, Pontificio Istituto orientale, 95, 298 p. (Orientalia Christiana analecta, 249).

5825. KRIČIENKO (O. V.). Pravoslavnyj khram v žizni russkikh dvorjan XVIII veka. (The Orthodox temple in the life of the Russian nobility in the XVIIIth century). Étnogr. obozrenie, 95, 5, p. 92-98.

5826. MAKRIDES, (Vasilios). Die religiöse Kritik am kopernikanischen Weltbild in Griechenland zwischen 1794 und 1821. Aspekte griechisch-orthodoxer Apologetik angesichts naturwissenschaftlicher Fortschritte. Frankfurt am Main, Lang, 95, 664 p. (Tübinger Beiträge zur Religionswissenschaft, 2).

5827. MARKIDES (Kyriacos C.). Riding with the lion: in search of mystical Christianity. London, Arkana, 95, 369 p.

5828. MOUSALIMAS (S. A.). The transition from Shamanism to Russian Orthodoxy in Alaska. Providence a. Oxford, Berghahn Books, 95, 254 p.

5829. NICHOLS (Aidan). Light from the East: authors and themes in orthodox theology. London, Sheen & Ward, 95, 234 p.

5830. OUSTERHOUT (Robert G.), BRUBAKER (Leslie). The sacred image East and West. Urbana, University of Illinois Press, 95, XIII-312 p. (ill.). (Illinois Byzantine studies, 4).

5831. PARKER-WAKEFIELD (Maurice). The facts about orthodox religions and spiritualism explained. London, Regency Press, 95, 519 p.

5832. PECHERSKAYA (Natalia A.), COATES (R.). The emancipation of Russian Christianity. Lewiston, Mellen Press, 95, XIV-119 p. (Toronto studies in theology, 33).

5833. PHILLIPS (Andrew). Orthodox Christianity and the English tradition. Hockwold-cum-Wilton, English Orthodox Trust in association with Anglo-Saxon Books, 95, 473 p. (ill.). (English Orthodox Trust).

5834. POPLAVSKAJA (Kh. V.). K voprosu o pravoslavnom missionerstve na Altae (30–60-e gody XIX veka). (The Orthodox missionary activity in the Altai in the 1830–1860's: some aspects of the problem). Étnogr. obozrenie, 95, 5, p. 99-109.

5835. RIMSKIJ (Sergej V.). Cerkovnaja reforma 60–70-kh godov XIX veka. (The church reform of 1860–1870's in Russia). Oteč. Ist., 95, 2, p. 166-175.

5836. Russkaja pravoslavnaja cerkov'i sovetskoe vremja (1917–1991): Materialy i dokumenty po istorii otnošenij meždu gosudarstvom i cerkov'ju. (The Russian Orthodox church in the Soviet period, 1917–1991. A history of the relations between the state and church. Documents and materials). Kn. 1. Kn. 2. Sost. G. ŠTRIKKER. Moskva: Propilei, 95, 2 vol., 399 p., 462 p.

5837. ŠKAROVSKIJ (Mikhail V.). Russkaja pravoslavnaja cerkov'v 1943–1957 godakh. (The Russian Orthodox church in 1943–1957). Vopr. Ist., 95, 8, p. 36-56.

5838. STANILOAE (Dumitru). Orthodoxe Dogmatik. Zürich u. Gutersloh, Benziger u. Mohn, 95, 3 vols., [s. p.]. (Ökumenische Theologie, 12, 15–16).

5839. STANTON (Leonard J.). The Optina Pustyn Monastery in the Russian literary imagination: iconic vision in works by Dostoevsky, Gogol, Tolstoy, and others. New York, Lang, 95, XVI-307 p. (Middlebury studies in Russian language and literature, 3).

5840. TAFT (Robert F.). Liturgy in Byzantium and beyond. Aldershot, Variorum, 95, XII-345 p. (Collected studies series, 493).

§ 4. Protestantismus.

* 5841. Archiv für Reformationsgeschichte. Beiheft Literaturbericht 1995. Archiv für Reformationsgeschichte, 95, 24, Literaturbericht, 1995, 188 p.

** 5842. CALVIN (Jean). Œuvres choisies. Edition présentée, établie et annotée par Olivier MILLET. Paris, Gallimard, 95, 336 p. (Folio classique, 2701).

** 5843. Correspondance de Théodore de Bèze. Vol. 18. 1577. Ed. par Alain DUFOUR, Béatrice NICOLLIER a. Reinhard BODENMANN. Genève, Droz, 95, XX-270 p. (Travaux d'Humanisme et Renaissance).

** 5844. Melanchthons Briefwechsel. T. 2. Texte. T. 8. Regeste 8072-9301 (1557–1567). Hrsg. v. Heinz SCHEIBLE u. Walter THÜRINGEN. Stuttgart, Frommann u. Bad Cannstatt, Holzboog, 95, 2 vol., 564 p., 470 p.

** 5845. Registres de la Compagnie des Pasteurs de Genève. T. 12. 1614–1616. Ed. par Gabriella CAHIER et Matteo CAMPAGNOLO. Genève, Droz, 95, XL-497 p. (Travaux d'Humanisme et Renaissance, 291).

5846. BLAUMEISER (Hubertus). Martin Luthers Kreuzestheologie: Schlüssel zu seiner Deutung von Mensch und Wirklichkeit; eine Untersuchung anhand der Operationes in Psalmos (1519–1521). Paderborn, Bonifatius, 95, 576 p. (Konfessionskundliche und kontroverstheologische Studien, 60).

5847. BOGÁRDI SZABÓ (István). Egyházvezetés és teològia a Magyarországi Református Egyházban 1948 és 1989 között. (Direction de l'Eglise et théologie dans l'Eglise réformée [calviniste] de Hongrie en 1948–1989). Debrecen, Ethnica, 95, 197 p.

5848. BRADY (Thomas A. jr). Protestant politics: Jacob Sturm (1489–1553). And the German reformation. Atlantic Highlands, Humanities Press, 95, XIX-449 p. (Studies in German histories).

5849. BUTIN (Philip Walker). Revelation, redemption, and response: Calvin's trinitarian understanding of the divine-human relationship. New York a. Oxford, Oxford U.P., 95, XII-232 p.

5850. CHRISTIN (Olivier). Les réformes: Luther, Calvin et les protestants. Paris, Gallimard, 95, 160 p. (ill.). (Découvertes Gallimard, 237).

5851. COTTRET (Bernard). Calvin. Biographie. Paris, Jean-Claude Lattès, 95, 456 p.

5852. D. Martin Luthers Werke. Hrsg. im Auftrag der Heidelberger Akademie der Wissenschaften von Ulrich Kopf. Weimar, Hermann Bohlaus Nachfolger, 95, VIII-635 p. (Lateinisches Sachregister zur Abteilung Schriften Band 1–60).

5853. DAVIS (Thomas J.). The clearest promises of God: the development of Calvin's eucharistic teaching. New York, AMS Press, 95, 398 p. (AMS studies in religious tradition, 1).

5854. Vacat.

5855. FANGMEIER (Jurgen), SCHOLL (Hans). Karl Barth und Johannes Calvin: Karl Barths Goettinger Calvin-Vorlesung von 1922. Neukirchen Vluyn, Neukirchener Verlag, 95, X-191 p.

5856. FIRPO (Massimo). Il "Beneficio di Cristo" e il concilio di Trento (1542–1546). *Rivista di storia e letteratura religiosa*, 95, 31, p. 45-72.

5857. FORNI (Guglielmo). The 'essence of Christianity': the hermeneutical question in the Protestant and modernist debate (1897–1904). Atlanta, Scholars Press, 95, 138 p. (University of South Florida international studies in formative Christianity and Judaism, 3).

5858. FOWLER (Robert Booth), HERTZKE (Allen D.). Religion and politics in America: faith, culture, and strategic choices. Boulder a. Oxford, Westview Press, 95, XIV-287 p.

5859. FRECH (Stephan Veit). Magnificat und Benedictus Deutsch: Martin Luthers bibelhumanistische Übersetzung in der Rezeption des Erasmus von Rotterdam. Bern, Lang, 95, 320 p. (Zürcher germanistische Studien, 44).

5860. GENEST (François). Les Protestants français dans les camps de concentration nazis. *In*: Nouvelles recherches sur l'univers concentrationnaire et d'extermination nazi [Cf. n° 4805], p. 231-247.

5861. GLEASON (Randall C.). John Calvin and John Owen on mortification: a comparative study in Reformed spirituality. New York, Lang, 95, X-183 p. (Studies in church history, 3).

5862. HENKEL (Annegret). Geistliche Erfahrung und Geistliche Übungen bei Ignatius von Loyola und Martin Luther. Die ignatianischen Exerzitien in ökumenischer Relevanz. Frankfurt am Main, Lang, 95, 402 p. (Europäische Hochschulschriften, 23/528).

5863. HOOLE (Charles R. A.). Modern Sannyasins: Protestant missionary contribution to Ceylon Tamil culture. Frankfurt am Main u. New York, Lang, 95, 366 p. (Studien zur interkulturellen Geschichte des Christentums, 94).

5864. HUTTON (Ronald). The English Reformation and the evidence of folklore. *Past and Present*, 95, 148, p. 89-116.

5865. JONES (Serene). Calvin and the rhetoric of piety. Louisville, Westminster John Knox Press, 95, X-238 p. (Columbia series in Reformed theology).

5866. KAEMPF (Bernard). La théologie pratique dans les facultés de théologie protestante francophones. *Revue des sciences religieuses*, 95, 69, p. 303-11.

5867. KINDER (A. Gordon). Spanish protestants and reformers in th sixteenth century. London, [s. n.], 95, 104 p.

5868. KUSUKAWA (Sachiko). The transformation of natural philosophy: the case of Philip Melanchthon. Cambridge a. New York, Cambridge U.P., 95, XV-246 p. (Ideas in context).

5869. LEEB (Rudolf). Beobachtungen zu Caspar Tauber: zur Rezeption reformatorischen Gedankengutes beim ersten Märtyrer der österreichischen Reformation. *Jb. f. Gesch. d. Protestantismus i. Österr.*, 94-95, 110-111, p. 21-45.

5870. LOHSE (Bernhard). Luthers Theologie in ihrer historischen Entwicklung und in ihrem systematischen Zusammenhang. Göttingen, Vandenhoeck & Ruprecht, 95, 378 p.

5871. Magyar (A) református egyház története. (Histoire de l'Eglise réformée [calvinienne] hongroise). Szerk. B/RÓ Sándor, SZILÁGYI István. Sárospatak, Ref. Koll., Theol. Akad., 95, 509 p.

5872. NEUMANN (Hans-Joachim). Luthers Leiden: die Krankheitsgeschichte des Reformators. Berlin, Wichern-Verlag, 95, 210 p. (ill.).

5873. NGIEN (Dennis). The suffering of God according to Martin Luther's 'Theologia Crucis'. New York, Lang, 95, XII-289 p. (American university studies. Series 7, Theology and religion, 181).

5874. NOWICKA (Ewa). Ewangelicyzm a polskość. Kryterium wyznaniowe i narodowe w świadomości społeczeństwa polskiego. (Evangélisme et polonité. Critères religieux et nationaux dans la conscience de la société polonaise). *Przegląd Polonijny*, 95, 21, 2, p. 47-64. [Eng. Summary].

5875. PACKULL (Werner O.). Hutterite beginnings: communitarian experiments during the Reformation. Baltimore a. London, Johns Hopkins U. P., 95, VIII-440 p. (ill.).

5876. PAUSZ (Josef). Christoph von Habermayer – Gründer der Evangelischen Gemeinde in Wiener Neustadt. *Jb. f. d. Gesch. d. Protestantismus i. Österr.*, 94-95, 110-111, p. 179-199 (ill.).

5877. PRANDI (Stefano). Influssi umanistici nella letteratura eterodossa del primo Cinquecento. *Rivista di storia e letteratura religiosa*, 95, 31, p. 217-33.

5878. PUCKETT (David Lee). John Calvin's exegesis of the Old Testament. Louisville, Westminster John Knox Press, 95, X-179 p. (Columbia series in Reformed theology).

5879. QUANTIN (Jean-Louis). Les jansénistes face à leurs adversaires. *Revue de l'histoire des religions*, 95, 212, p. 397-417.

5880. REINGRABNER (Gustav). Bemerkungen zur Geschichte des burgenländischen Luthertums seit 1974. *Jb. f. d. Gesch. d. Protestantismus i. Österr.*, 94-95, 110-111, p. 255-285. – IDEM. Ikonographische Beobachtungen zu den evangelischen Kirchen im Burgenland. *Burgenl. Heimatbl.*, 95, 57, 3, p. 97-116 (ill.).

5881. RUSSELL (William R.). Luther's theological testament: the Schmalkald articles. Minneapolis, Fortress Press, 95, XIV-192 p.

5882. RUSZKOWSKI (Janusz). Kościół ewangelicki w NRD. Geneza i rozwój aktywności opozycyjnej w latach 1971–1989. (Eglise évangélique en RDA. Genese et développement de l'activité d'opposition dans les années 1971–1989. Poznań, Inst. Zach., 95, 333 p. (Deutsche Zsfassung). (Studium Niemcoznawcze Inst. Zach., 69).

5883. SANDERS (Hanne). Bondevaekkelse og sekularisering. En protestantisk folkelig kultur i Danmark og Sverige 1820–1840. (Peasant revivalism and secularization. Protestant popular culture in Denmark and Sweden, 1820–1840). Stockholm, Historiska institutionen, Stockholm universitet a. København, Museum Tusculanums Forlag, 95, 392 p. (Studier i stads- och kommunhistoria, 12).

5884. SCHENKEL (Albert F.). The rich man and the kingdom: John D. Rockefeller Jr., and the Protestant establishment. Minneapolis, Fortress Press, 95, X-248 p. (ill.). (Harvard theological studies, 39).

5885. SCHWARZ (Karl). Von der Ersten zur Zweiten Republik: Die Evangelischen in Österreich und der Staat. *Jb. f. d. Gesch. d. Protestantismus i. Österr.*, 94-95, 110-111, p. 215-239.

5886. SPROXTON (Judy). Violence and religion: attitudes towards militancy in the French civil wars and the English Revolution. London a. New York, Routledge, 95, 103 p.

5887. STACKHOUSE (John G.). The historiography of Canadian Evangelianism. *Church History*, 95, 64, p. 27-34.

5888. STEIN (Stephen J.). America's Bible: canon, commentary and community. *Church History*, 95, 64, p. 169-84.

5889. STEINMETZ (David C.). Calvin in context. New York a. Oxford, Oxford U.P., 95, X-235 p.

5890. SZTURC (Jan). Protestantyzm na Śląsku (bez Śląska Cieszyńskiego. Bibliografia polskojęzyczna za lata 1945–1993. [Protestantisme en Silésie (sans la région de Cieszyn). Bibliographie en langue polonaise pour les années 1945–1993]. *Śląski Kwartalnik Historyczny. Sobótka*, 95, 50, 3-4, p. 283-292.

5891. TOLLEY (Bruce). Pastors and parishioners in Wurttemberg during the late Reformation, 1581–1621. Stanford, Stanford U. P., 95, XII-198 p. (tables).

5892. WALLACE (Ronald S.). Calvin's doctrine of the word and sacrament. Edinburgh, Scottish Academic Press, 95, XII-253 p.

5893. WAPPMANN (Volker). Durchbruch zur Toleranz. Die Religionspolitik des Pfalzgrafen Christian August von Sulzbach 1622–1708. Neustadt a.d. Aisch, Degener, 95, VII-314 p. (Einzelarbeiten aus der Kirchengeschichte Bayerns, 69).

5894. WOLGAST (Eike). Hochstift und Reformation. Studien zur Geschichte der Reichskirche zwischen 1517 und 1648. Stuttgart, Franz Steiner, 95, 375 p. (Beiträge zur Geschichte der Reichskirche in der Neuzeit, 16).

5895. ZIEGERHOFER (Anita). Die "Religionssache" auf den steirische Landtagen von 1527 bis 1564. *Jb. f. d. Gesch. des Protestantismus i. Österr.*, 94-95, 110-111, p. 47-68.

5896. ZIMMERMANN (Günther). Gottesbund und Gesetz in der Westminster Confessio. *Zeitschrift für Kirchengeschichte*, 95, 106, p. 179-99.

5897. ZUR MUHLEN (Karl-Heinz), BROSSEDER (Johannes). Reformatorisches Profil: Studien zum Weg Martin Luthers und der Reformation. Göttingen, Vandenhoeck & Ruprecht, 95, 408 p.

Cf. n°s 5371, 5699

§ 5. Nichtchristliche Religionen und Sekten.

5898. ABID (Mounir). Les débuts de la réglementation sanitaire du pélegrinage tunisien à la Mecque (1831–1866). *Revue d'Histoire Maghrébine*, 95, 79-80, p. 273-278.

5899. AGUWA (Jude C. U.). The Agwu deity in Igbo religion: a study of the patron spirit of divination and medicine in an African society. Enugu, Fourth Dimension, 95, X-162 p.

5900. ALEAZ (K. P.). Jesus in Neo-Vedanta: a meeting of Hinduism and Christianity. Delhi, Kant Publications, 95, XIV-242 p. (World religions relationship series, 2).

5901. AL-FARUQI (Ismail R.). Trialogue of the Abrahamic faiths. Papers presented to the Islamic. Beltsville, Amana Publications, 95, 103 p. (Issues of Islamic thought, 1).

5902. BABY (François). Enfer et paradis dans le catharisme du comté de Foix au XIVe siècle. In: Enfer et paradis [Cf. n° 1370], p. 275-299.

5903. BALZ (Heinrich). Where the faith has to live: studies in Bakossi society and religion. Berlin, Reimer Verlag, 95, XVI-404 p.

5904. BERNABE (Pons Luis F.). El evangelio de San Bernabe: un evangelio islamico español. Alicante, Universidad de Alicante, 95, 260 p.

5905. BONANATE (Ugo). Bibbia e Corano: i testi sacri confrontati. Torino, Bollati Boringhieri, 95, 265 p.

5906. BRAIBANTI (Ralph). The nature and structure of the Islamic world. Chicago, International Strategy and Policy Institute, 95, 108 p.

5907. BREGEL (Yuri). Bibliography of Islamic Central Asia. Bloomington, Indiana University, Research Institute for Inner Asian Studies, 95, 3 vol., [s. p.]. (Indiana University Uralic and Altaic series, 160).

5908. BROWN (Stuart E.). The nearest in affection: towards a Christian understanding of Islam. Valley Forge, Trinity Press International, 95, X-124 p. (Pathways books).

5909. CARDAILLAC (Yvette). Magie et répression, morisques et chrétiens: XVIe–XVIIe siècles. Revue d'Histoire Maghrébine, 95, 79-80, p. 421-462.

5910. CHAPMAN (Colin). Cross and crescent: responding to the challenge of Islam. Leicester, Inter-Varsity Press, 95, 346 p.

5911. DANFULANI (Umar Habila Dadem). Pebbles and deities: Pa divination among the Ngas, Mupun, and Mwaghavul in Nigeria. Frankfurt am Main, Lang, 95, 252 p. (European university studies, 23/551).

5912. DAY (John). Lectures on the religion of the Semites. Sheffield, Sheffield Academic Press, 95, 148 p. facsims (Journal for the study of the Old Testament supplement series, 183).

5913. DE GRUCHY (John W.), PROZESKY (Martin). Living faiths in South Africa. New York a. London, St. Martin's Press, 95, 241 p.

5914. DZIUBIŃSKI (Andrzej). Poturczeńcy polscy. Przyczynek do historii nawróceń na Islam w XVI–XVIII w. (Les Polonais chrétiens convertis à l'Islam. Contribution à l'histoire des conversions à l'Islam aux XVIe–XVIIIe siècles). Kwartalnik Historyczny, 95, 102, 1, p. 19-37. [Rés. Franç.].

5915. EL-SOLH (Camillia Fawzi), MABRO (Judy). Muslim women's choices: religious belief and social reality. Providence a. Oxford, Berg, 95, X-206 p. (Cross-cultural perspectives on women, 12).

5916. FISIY (Cyprian F.), GESCHIERE (Peter). Sorcellerie et politique en Afrique: la viande des autres. Paris, Karthala, 95, 300 p. (Collection Les Afriques).

5917. GODDARD (Hugh). Christians and Muslims: from double standards to mutual understanding. Richmond, Curzon Press, 95, XII-200 p.

5918. GREENBERG (Moshe). Studies in the Bible and Jewish thought. Philadelphia a. Jerusalem, Jewish Publication Society, 95, XVIII-462 p.

5919. GUARNEIRO (Antonio). Cosmology, rituals and society: preliminary observations on religious creeds in Iriomate-jiama. Cahiers d'Estrême-Asie, 95, 8, p. 1-40.

5920. GUERERE (A. Tabare). Las diosas negras: la santeria en femenino. Caracas, Venezuela, Alfadil Ediciones, 95, 138 p. (ill.). (Coleccion Vida alternativa, 7).

5921. HADDAD (Wadi` Zaydan), HADDAD (Yvonne Yazbeck). Christian-Muslim encounters. Gainesville, University Press of Florida, 95, XII-508 p. (Hartford Seminary Foundation).

5922. INOUE (Nobutaka), LAUBE (Johannes). Neureligionen: Stand ihrer Erforschung in Japan. Ein Handbuch. Wiesbaden, Harrassowitz, 95, XVIII-379 p. (Studies in oriental religions, 31).

5923. IRMSCHER (Johannes). Rapports entre juifs, chrétiens et musulmans. Eine Sammlung von Forschungsbeiträgen. Amsterdam, Hakkert, 95, 243 p.

5924. JEDREJ (M. C.). Ingessana: the religious institutions of a people of the Sudan-Ethiopia borderland, Leiden a. New York, Brill, 95, 180 p. (Studies on religion in Africa, 13).

5925. Vacat.

5926. Journal of Jewish Studies. Special Issue to commemorate the Twenty-Fifth year od Geza Vermes as editor. 95, 46, 367 p.

5927. KARUNARATNA (Charles W.). Sannyasi and saint: otherworldliness in some Hindu scriptures and in the New Testament. Ilford, Theos Logos, 95, VI-130 p.

5928. KASSAM (Tazim R.). Songs of wisdom and circles of dance: hymns of the Satpanth Isma'ili Muslim saint, Pir Shams. Albany, State University of New York Press, 95, XVI-424 p. (McGill studies in the history of religions).

5929. KELLY (Christopher). Civil and uncivil religions: Tocqueville on Hinduism and Islam. In: European integration and the European mind. Part 4 [Cf. n° 1334], p. 845-850.

5930. KOHLI (Narendra). Smarana-sakti ksharana. Nai Dilli, Vani Prakasana, 95, 76 p. (ill.).

5931. KRAEMER (David). Responses to suffering in classical rabbinic literature. New York a. Oxford, Oxford U.P., 95, XIII-261 p.

5932. KUSCHEL (Karl-Josef). Abraham: a symbol of hope for Jews, Christians and Muslims. New York, SCM Press, 95, XXIX-286 p.

5933. LANDA (Robert G.). Islam v istorii Rossii. (Islam in the Russian history). RAN. In-t vostokovedenija. Moskva, Izdatel'skaja firma "Vostočnaja literatura", RAN, 95, 312 p.

5934. MACHOBANE (L. B. B. J.). Basotho religion and Western thought. Edinburgh, Centre of African Studies, University of Edinburgh, 95, 57 p.

5935. MAINA (Kahumbi N.). Christian-Muslim relations in Kenya: an examination of issues of conflicts. Birmingham, Centre for the Study of Islam and Christian-Muslim Relations, Selly Oak Colleges, 95, 21 p. (CSIC papers. Africa, 17).

5936. MEISIG (Marion). Koenig Sibi und die Taube: Wandlung und Wanderung eines Erzählstoffes von Indien nach China. Wiesbaden, Harrassowitz, 95, VII-271p. (Studies in oriental religions, 35).

5937. MITRI (Tarek). Religion, law and society: a Christian-Muslim discussion. Geneva et Kampen, WCC Publications a. Kok Pharos Publishing, 95, XVI-137 p.

5938. MUSK (Bill A.). Touching the soul of Islam: sharing the gospel in Muslim cultures. Crowborough, Marc, 95, 256 p. (ill.).

5939. NWOSU (Ikechi Nwachukwu). Conversion in Luke-Acts and its pastoral implication for understanding the conversion of the Igbo of Nigeria. University of Nigeria, Nsukka Department of Religion, 95, 445 p.

5940. OGBAJIE (Chukwu). The impact of Christianity on the Igbo religion and culture. Umuahia (Abia State Nigeria), Ark Publishers, 95, XII-84 p. (ill.).

5941. PARRATT (John). Reinventing Christianity: African theology today. Grand Rapids a. Cambridge, Africa World Press, 95, X-217 p.

5942. SEIDEL (Anne). Taoïsm: religion non-officielle de la Chine. *Cahiers d'Estrême-Asie*, 95, 8, p. 1-40.

5943. SHARAN (Ishwar). The myth of Saint Thomas and the Mylapore Shiva Temple. New Delhi, Voice of India, 95, XVI-290 p.

5944. SHARF (Robert H.). Buddhist modernism and the rhetoric of meditative experience. *Numen*, 95, 42, 3, p. 228-283.

5945. SHARMA (Arvind). The philosophy of religion and Advaita Vedanta: a comparative study in religion and reason. University Park, Pennsylvania State U.P.,

95, VIII-232 p. (Hermeneutics, studies in the history of religions).

5946. SITZLER (Dorothea). "Vorwurf gegen Gott": ein religiöses Motiv im alten Orient (Ägypten und Mesopotamien). Wiesbaden, Harrassowitz, 95, XVI-249 p. (Studies in Oriental religions, 32).

5947. SMITH (Margaret). Studies in early mysticism in the Near and Middle East. Oxford a. Rockport, Oneworld, 95, VI-276 p.

5948. SOME (Malidoma Patrice). Of water and the spirit: ritual, magic and initiation in the life of an African shaman. New York a. London, Penguin, 95, 311 p. (Penguin Arkana).

5949. SOMMER (Deborah). Chinese religion: an anthology of sources. New York a. Oxford, Oxford U.P., 95, XXII-375 p.

5950. SPITZER (Schlomo J.). Die jüdische Gemeinde von Deutschkreutz. Wien, Köln u. Weimar, Böhlau, 95, 174 p. (ill.).

5951. STACEY (Vivienne). Women in Islam. London, Interserve, 95, 72 p.

5952. STOKES (Samuel). The India of my dreams: Samuel Stokes's challenge to Christian Mission. Delhi, ISPCK, 95, X-210 p.

5953. STOLLER (Paul). Embodying colonial memories: spirit possession, power, and the Hauka in West Africa. New York, a. London, Routledge, 95, XII-226 p. (ill.).

5954. STUBBE-DIARRA (Ira). Die Symbolik von Gift und Nektar in der klassischen indischen Literatur. Wiesbaden, Harrassowitz, 95, VII-154 p. (Studies in oriental religions, 33).

5955. Studia aramaica. New sources and new approaches: papers delivered at the London Conference of the Institute of Jewish Studies, University College London 26th–28th June 1991. Ed. by Markham J. GELLER a. Jonas C. GREENFIELD. Oxford a. New York, Oxford U. P. on behalf of the University of Manchester, 95, VIII-262 p. (ill.). (Journal of Semitic studies. Supplement 4).

5956. SWARUP (Ram). Hindu view of Christianity and Islam. New Delhi, Voice of India, 95, 136 p.

5957. SYED (Muhammad Aslam). Islam and democracy in Pakistan. Islamabad, National Institute of Historical and Cultural Research, 95, VI-309 p. (N.I.H.C.R. publication, 90).

5958. TALBOTT (Rick Franklin). Sacred sacrifice: ritual paradigms in Vedic religion and early Christianity. New York, Lang, 95, 356 p. (American university studies. Series IX19, History, 150).

5959. VELTRI (Giuseppe). Eine Tora für Koenig Talmai. Mohr, Tübingen, 95, XII-289 p.

5960. WAARDENBURG (Jacques). Scholarly approaches to religion, interreligious perceptions and

Islam. Bern, Lang, 95, XVI-464 p. (Studia religiosa helvetica Jahrbuch, 1).

5961. WILSON (H. S.). Islam in Africa: perspectives for Christian-Muslim relations. The WARC consultation, 6 to 10 June 1994, the Grace Bandawe Conference Centre, Blantyre, Malawi. Geneva, World Alliance of Reformed Churches, 95, 106 p. (World Alliance of Reformed Churches. Studies from the World Alliance of Reformed Churches, 29).

5962. WOLFFSOHN (Michael). Eternal guilt? New York, Columbia U.P., 95, XII-225 p.

5963. YOUNG (Richard Fox). The Bible trembled: the Hindu-Christian controversies of nineteenth-century Ceylon. Wien, Sammlung De Nobili, 95, 204 p. (Publications of the De Nobili Research Library, 22).

5964. Zirkel und Zionsstern. Bilder und Dokumente aus der versunkenen Welt des jüdisch-nationalen Korporationswesens. Ein Beitrag zur Geschichte des Zionismus auf akademischem Boden. Band 5. Hrsg. v. Harald SEEWANN. Graz, Selbstvlg, 95, 654 p. (Historia academica Judaica, 5)

M

BILDUNGSGESCHICHTE DER NEUZEIT

§ 1. Allgemeines. 5965-6056. – § 2. Akademien und wissenschaftliche Organisationen. 6057-6082. – § 3. Unterrichtsgeschichte. 6083-6153. – 4. Pressewesen. 6154-6215. – § 5. Philosophie und Weltanschauung. 6216-6375. – § 6. Exakte Wissenschaften. Technik, Naturwissenschaften und Medizin. 6376-6512. – § 7. Literatur (*a*. Allgemeines; *b*. Renaissance; *c*. Klassizismus; *d*. Romantik und Gegenwart). 6513-6713. – § 8. Bildende Kunst (*a*. Allgemeines; *b*. Architektur; *c*. Bildhauerei, Malerei, Graphik und Zeichenkunst; *d*. Kunstgewerbe und Volkskunst). 6714-6878.– § 9. Musik, Theater und Film. 6879-6986.

§ 1. Allgemeines.

* 5965. BALSAMO (Jean). La France et sa relation à l'Italie au XVIe siècle (bibliographie 1985–1994). *Nouvelle revue du XVIe siècle*, 95, 13, 2, p. 267-289.

* 5966. Bibliografia italiana di studi sull'Umanesimo e il Rinascimento. 1993. [1992. Cf. Bibl. 94, n° 5690.] Firenze, Olschki, 95, V-184 p. (Rinascimento, XXXIV. Supplemento.)

* 5967. Ilustración en America colonial: bibliografía crítica (La). Ed. por Diana SOTO ARANGO, Miguel Angel PUIG SAMPER y Luis Carlos ARBOLEDA. Madrid, Consejo Superior de Investigaciones Cientificas y Aranjuez, Madrid, Ediciones Doce Calles, 95, 233 p. (ill.). (Colección Actas).

5968. ADAMSON (Walter L.). The culture of Italian fascism and the fascist crisis of modernity: the case of Il Selvaggio. *Journal of Contemporary History*, 95, 30, 4, p. 555-576.

5969. ALTMAN (Janet Gurkin). La politique de l'art épistolaire au XVIIIe siècle. *In*: Art de la lettre, art de la conversation à l'époque classique en France [Cf. n° 5972], p. 131-144.

5970. ALVAREZ BARRIENTOS (Joaquin), LOPEZ (Francoio), URZAINQUI (Inmaculada). La república de las letras en la España del siglo XVIII. Madrid, Consejo Superior de Investigaciones Cientificas, 95, 226 p. (Monografias, 16).

5971. ANIKIN (Aleksej V.). Élementy sakral'nogo v russkikh revoljucionnykh teorijakh. (K istorii formirovanija sovetskoj ideologii). (Sacral elements in the Russian revolutionary theories. On the problem of Soviet ideology formation). *Oteč. Ist.*, 95, 1, p. 78-92.

5972. Art de la lettre, art de la conversation à l'époque classique en France. Actes du colloque de Wolfenbüttel, octobre 1991. Paris, Klincksieck, 95, 372 p. (ill.). [Cf. n^{os} <sélection> 5969, 5978, 5983, 5999, 6008, 6012, 6019, 6022, 6026.]

5973. ASCHER (Francois). Metapolis, ou, l'avenir des villes. Paris, Jacob, 95, 345 p.

5974. BACHMANN (Jörg J.). Zwischen Paris und Moskau. Deutsche bürgerliche Linksintellektuelle und die stalinistische Sowjetunion 1933–1939. Mannheim, Palatium im J. & J. Verlag, 95, 475 p. (Mannheimer historische Forschungen, 7).

5975. BADGER (Anthony J.). WARD (Brian). The making of Martin Luther King and the civil rights movement. Basingstoke, Macmillan, 95, XII-241 p. (Martin Luther King Jr Memorial Conference on Civil Rights and Race Relations).

5976. BAIRD (Catherine). Religious communism? Nicolai Berdyaev's contribution to Esprit's interpretation of communism. *Canadian Journal of History*, 95, 30, 1, p. 29-48.

5977. BALLA (Balint), STERBLING (Anton). Soziologie und Geschichte, Geschichte der Soziologie: Beiträge zur Osteuropaforschung. Hamburg, Kramer, 95, 262 p.

5978. BELLENGER (Yvonne). Le récit de voyage par lettres dans le Nouveau voyage d'Italie. *In*: Art de la lettre, art de la conversation à l'époque classique en France [Cf. n° 5972], p. 307-323.

5979. BERTHELOT (Jean-Michel). 1895, Durkheim: l'avènement de la sociologie scientifique. Toulouse, Presses universitaires du Mirail, 95, 186 p. (ill.). (Sociologiques).

5980. BJÖRNE (Lars). Patrioter och institutionalister. Den nordiske rättsvetenskapens historia. Part 1. Tiden före 1815. Stockholm, Institutet för rättshistorisk forskning, Nerenius & Santérus, 95, 443 p. (Skrifter utgivna av Institutet för rättshistorisk forskning. Serien I: Rättshistorikt Bibliotek, 52). [History of the Scandinavian science of law until 1815].

5981. BOLTE (Gerhard). Von Marx bis Horkheimer. Aspekte kritischer Theorie im 19. und 20. Jahrhundert. Darmstadt, Wissenschaftliche Buchgesellschaft, 95, XII-104 p.

5982. BOLZONI (Lina). La stanza della memoria. Modelli letterari e iconografici nell'età della stampa. Torino, Einaudi, 95, XXVIII-284 p. (ill.). (Saggi, 797).

5983. BONACCORSO (Giovanni). Une correspondance familiale: les lettres de Racine à sa sœur. In: Art de la lettre, art de la conversation à l'époque classique en France [Cf. n° 5972], p. 289-303.

5984. BOURGEOIS (Etienne), NIZET (Jean). Pression et legitimation: une approche constructive du pouvoir. Paris, Presses Universitaires de France, 95, 224 p.

5985. BRACCESI (L.). Poesia e memoria. Nuove proiezioni dell'antico. Roma, L'Erma di Bretschneider, 95, 197 p. (L'eredità dell'antico, 4).

5986. BURISCH (Wolfram). Das Elend des Exils: Theodor Geiger und die Soziologie. Hamburg, Europäische Verlagsanstalt, 95, 174 p.

5987. CARROLL (D.). French literary fascism. Nationalism, anti-semitism and the ideology of culture. Princeton, Princeton U. P., 95, IX-299 p.

5988. CECCARINI (E.). Olimpo laico: Francesco Compagna, Vittorio De Caprariis, Ugo La Malfa, Mario Pannunzio, Rosario Romeo, Altiero Spinelli. Firenze, Passigli, 95, 175 p.

5989. CHARLE (Christophe). Intellectuels, Bildungsbürgertum et professions au XIXe siècle. Essai de bilan historiographique comparé (France, Allemagne). Actes de la recherche en sciences sociales, 95, 106-107, p. 85-95.

5990. CHARTIER (Roger). Modèles de l'homme de lettres. In: Philosophes, écrivains et lecteurs en Europe au XVIIIe siècle [Cf. n° 6035], p. 14-25.

5991. Cultures et formations négociantes: dans l'Europe moderne. Sous la dir. de Franco ANGIOLINI et Daniel ROCHE. Paris, Editions de l'Ecole des hautes études en sciences sociales, 95, 593 p. (Civilisations et sociétés, 6).

5992. DAUPHIN (C.), LEBRUN-PEZERAT (P.), POUBLAN (D.). Ces bonnes lettres. Une correspondance familiale au XIXe siècle. Préf. de R. CHARTIER. Paris, Albin Michel, 95, 396 p. (ill.).

5993. DE NEGRONI (Barbara). Lectures interdites, le travail des censeurs au XVIIIe siècle, 1723–1774. Paris, A. Michel, 95, 385 p.

5994. DEMORIS (René). Le silence de Manon. PUF, Paris, 95, 126 p. (Le texte revé).

5995. DIONISOTTI (Carlo). Machiavelleria ultima. Rivista storica italiana, 95, 107, 1, p. 20-28.

5996. DODIER (Nicolas). Les hommes et les machines: la conscience collective dans les sociétés technicisées. Paris, Editions Metailie, 95, 384 p. (Collection "Leçons de choses.").

5997. DOOLEY (Brendan). La «Storia letteraria d'Italia» e la riabilitazione della scienza dei gesuiti. Rivista storica italiana, 95, 107, 2, p. 289-331.

5998. DORR-BACKES (Felicitas), NIEDER (Ludwig). Georg Simmel between modernity and postmodernity = Georg Simmel zwischen Moderne und Postmoderne. Würzburg, Koenigshausen und Neumann, 95, 204 p.

5999. DUCHENE (Roger). Lettre et conversation. In: Art de la lettre, art de la conversation à l'époque classique en France [Cf. n° 5972], p. 93-102.

6000. DURAND (Jean-Pierre). La Sociologie de Marx. Paris, Editions La Découverte, 95, 123 p. (Collection Repères, 173).

6001. DUVERNOY BOLENS (Jacqueline). L'homme zoologique. Race, et racisme chez les naturalistes de la première moité du XIXe siècle. L'Homme, 95, 35, p. 9-32.

6002. FAURE (Alain), POLLET (G.), WARIN (Pierre). La construction du sens dans les politiques publiques: débats autour de la notion de référéntiel. Paris, L'Harmattan, 95, 346 p. (Collection Logiques politiques, 29).

6003. FEHER (Katalin). Reformkori sajtóviták a nők művelődésének kezdeteiről. (Discussion dans la presse à l'époque des réformes sur les débuts des femmes). Magyar könyvszle., 95, 111, 3, p. 247-263.

6004. FELDHAY (Rivka). Galileo and the church. Political inquisition or critical dialogue? Cambridge, Cambridge U. P., 95, VIII-303 p.

6005. FIELD (Arthur). Un manoscritto di lettere del primo cancellierato di Leonardo Bruni. Archivio storico italiano, 95, 153, 565, p. 573-576.

6006. FREY (Lynda S.), FREY (Marsha L.). El tu: language and the French Revolution. In: European integration and the European mind. Part 3 [Cf. n° 1334], p. 505-510.

6007. GARRIDO PALAZON (Manuel). Historia literaria, enciclopedia y ciencia en el literato jesuita Juan Andrès: en torno a "Del origen, progresos y estado actual de toda literatura". Alicante, Instituto de Cultura "Juan Gil-Albert", 95, 215 p. (Colección "Ensayo e Investigación", 57).

6008. GIRAUD (Yves). De la lettre à l'entretien: Puget de La Serre et l'art de la conversation. In: Art de la lettre, art de la conversation à l'époque classique en France [Cf. n° 5972], p. 217-231.

6009. GISLAIN (Jean-Jacques), STEINER (Philippe). La sociologie économique, 1890–1920: Emile Durkheim, Vilfredo Pareto, Joseph Schumpeter, François Si-

1. ALLGEMEINES

miand, Thorstein Veblen et Max Weber. Paris, Presses universitaires de France 95, 235 p. (Sociologies).

6010. HABERMAS (Jürgen). Vorstudien und Ergänzungen zur Theorie des kommunikativen Handelns. Frankfurt am Main, Suhrkamp, 95, 606 p. (Suhrkamp Taschenbuch. Wissenschaft, 117).

6011. HALTTUNEN (Karen). Humanitarianism and the pornography of pain in Anglo-American culture. *American Historical Review*, 95, 100, 2, p. 303-334.

6012. HAROCHE-BOUZINAC (Geneviève). «Billets font conversation». De la théorie à la pratique: l'exemple de Voltaire. *In*: Art de la lettre, art de la conversation à l'époque classique en France [Cf. n° 5972], p. 341-354.

6013. HASKELL (Francis), TACHET (Alain), EVRARD (Louis). L'historien et les images. Paris, Gallimard, 95, 781 p. (ill.). (Bibliothèque illustrée des histoires).

6014. Incidenza dell'antico (L'). Studi in memoria di Ettore Lepore. Vol. 1. Atti del Convegno internazionale, Anacapri 24–28 marzo 1991; con la bibliografia ed un inedito di Ettore LEPORE. A cura di Alfredina STORCHI MARINO. Napoli, Luciano Editore, 95, [s. p.]. [Cf. n° <sélection> 1154.]

6015. Inventing human science: eighteenth-century domains. Ed. by Christopher FOX, Roy PORTER a. Robert WOKLER. Berkeley a. London, University of California Press, 95, XV-357 p.

6016. JESI (Furio). Germania segreta: miti nella cultura tedesca del '900. A cura di David BIDUSSA. Milano, Feltrinelli, 95, 234 p. (Mito e simbolo nella Germania moderna, 1).

6017. JOHNSON (Claudia). Equivocal beings: politics, gender, and sentimentality in the 1790s. Chicago, University of Chicago Press, 95, 239 p.

6018. JUAN (Salvador). Les formes élémentaires de la vie quotidienne. Paris, Presses universitaires de France, 95, 286 p.

6019. KAPP (Volker). L'art de la conversation dans les manuels oratoires de la fin du XVIIe siècle. *In*: Art de la lettre, art de la conversation à l'époque classique en France [Cf. n° 5972], p. 115-129.

6020. KEYNER (Tom). Smollett's Scotlands. *History Workshop*, 95, 40, p. 118-132.

6021. LACASSE (François D.). Mythes, savoirs et décisions politiques. Paris, Presses universitaires de France, 95, 277 p.

6022. LANDY-HOUILLON (Isabelle). Lettre et oralité. *In*: Art de la lettre, art de la conversation à l'époque classique en France [Cf. n° 5972], p. 81-91.

6023. Language and images of Renaissance Italy. Ed. by Alison BROWN. Oxford, Clarendon Press, 95, 335 p. [Cf. n° <choice> 753]

6024. LEROUX (Serge). La morale des élites et la morale des classes populaires: quelques considérations pour l'étude du processus d'acculturation au siècle des Lumières. *In*: European integration and the European mind. Part 3 [Cf. n° 1334], p. 225-233.

6025. MARTIN (Daniel). Cannibals and kings: Montaigne and the Valladolid hearings of 1550–1551. *In*: European integration and the European mind. Part 3 [Cf. n° 1334], p. 585-590.

6026. MELANÇON (Benoît). Diderot: l'autre de la lettre. Conversation et correspondance. *In*: Art de la lettre, art de la conversation à l'époque classique en France [Cf. n° 5972], p. 355-369.

6027. MENTGEN (Gerd). Der Würfelzoll und andere antijüdische Schikanen in Mittelalter und Früher Neuzeit. *Zeitschrift für Historisches Forschung*, 95, 22, p. 1-48.

6028. MONNIER (Raymonde). L'invention de la République et la dynamique culturelle démocratique. *In*: European integration and the European mind. Part 3 [Cf. n° 1334], p. 243-252.

6029. MUIR (Edward). The Italian renaissance in America. *American Historical Review*, 95, 100, 4, p. 1094-1118.

6030. Myten om det moderne. (The myth of the modernity). Ed. by Torstein ARISHOLM a. Henning LANGERUD. Oslo, Spartacus, 95, 276 p. (Seminarrekke for idéhistorie).

6031. NAUERT (Charles G. jr.). Humanism and the culture of Renaissance Europe. Cambridge, Cambridge U. P., 95, X-237 p. (New approaches to European history, 6).

6032. Nazisme (Le) et les savants. Ed. par Susanna MAGRI. *Genèses*, 95, 21, p. 2-95.

6033. Occidentalism: images of the West. Ed. by James G. CARRIER. Oxford, Clarendon Press, 95, X-268 p.

6034. PETER (Katalin). Papok és nemesek. Magyar művelődéstörténeti tanulmányok a reformácioval kezdődő másfél évszázadból. (Prêtes et nobles. Etudes d'histoire culturelle hongroise des XVI–XVII siècles). Budapest, Ráday Gyűjtemény, 95, 263 p. (A Ráday Gyűjtemény tanulmányai, 8).

6035. Philosophes, écrivains et lecteurs en Europe au XVIIIe siècle. Sous la dir. de D. MASSEAU. Valenciennes, Presses universitaires de Valenciennes, 95, 128 p. (Lez Valenciennes, 18). [Cf. n° <sélection> 5990.]

6036. PINCUS (Steve). "Coffee politicians does create": coffeehouses and restoration political culture. *Journal of modern history*, 95, 67, 4, p. 807-834.

6037. PIZER (John David). Toward a theory of radical origin, essays on modern German thought. Lincoln a. London, University of Nebraska Press, 95, XII-215 p. (Modern German culture and literature).

6038. POMEAU (René). Voltaire en son temps. Paris, Fayard et Oxford, Voltaire Foundation, 95, 2 vol., XVII-1036 p., 876 p. [avec la participation de Christiane MERVAUD et al.].

6039. POOVEY (Mary). The making of a social body: British cultural formation, 1830–1864. Chicago, University of Chicago Press, 95, 255 p.

6040. Prehistories of the future: the primitivist project and the culture of modernism. Ed. by Elazar BARKAN and Ronald BUSH. Stanford, Stanford U. P., 95, XII-449 p. (ill). (Cultural sitings).

6041. Race and Racism: American dilemmas revisited. Special numbers of *Salmagundi*, 104-105, 154 p.

6042. REMY (Jean). Georg Simmel. Ville et modernité. Paris, L'Harmattan, 95, 175 p. (ill.).

6043. Saperi della borghesia e storia dei concetti fra Otto e Novecento. Convegno storico 24–25 settembre 1993. A cura di Raffaella GHERARDI e Gustavo GOZZI. Bologna, Il Mulino, 95, 527 p. (Annali dell'Istituto storico italo-germanico. Quaderno, 42). [Cf. n° <scelta> 5039.]

6044. ŠČETININA (Galina I.). Idejnaja žizn'russkoj intelligencii, konec XIX–načalo XX veka. (The Russian intelligentsia's ideological life, the end of the XIXth–the beginning of the XXth centuries). Moskva, Nauka, RAN, In-t rossijskoj istorii, 95, 236 p.

6045. SOLAK (Zbigniew). Ausgewählte Bibliographie zu den deutsch-polnischen Beziehungen. Polnisches Schrifttum. *Inter finitimos*, 95, 8, p. 32-56.

6046. ŚRÓDKA (Andrzej). Uczeni polscy XIX–XX stulecia. (Les savants polonais des XIXe–XXe s.). T. 2. H – Ł. Warszawa, Aries, 582 p. (phot., fig.).

6047. Storia delle passioni. A cura di S. VEGETTI-FINZI. Roma e Bari, Laterza, 95, XXII-360 p. (Storia e società).

6048. SUEUR (L.). Rêver du paradis sur terre: la morale de la société protectrice des animaux de Paris au XIXe siècle. *Revue Historique*, 95, 119, 593, p. 135-155.

6049. SUGIMOTO (Yoshihiko). Bummei no Teikoku: Jūru Verunu to Furansu-teikoku-syugi-bunka. (Empire civilisateur: Jules Verne et impérialisme français). Tokyo, Yamakawa Shuppansha, 95, 446 p.

6050. SZÍJ (Rezső). Könyvkiadás, könyvművészet, társadalom. (Publication des livres, art bibliophile, société). Budapest, Szenci Molnár Társ., 95, 321 p.

6051. TÓTH (István György). Írás, olvasás, könyv a paraszti műveltségben a 17–18. században. (Écriture, lecture, livre dans la culture rurale aux XVII–XVIII siècles). *Századok*, 95, 129, 4, p. 817-856.

6052. VAN DÜLMEN (Richard). Historische Kulturforschung zur Frühen Neuzeit. Entwicklung, Probleme, Aufgaben. *Geschichte und Gesellschaft*, 95, 21, 3, p. 403-429.

6053. WANGERMANN (Ernst). Die Bilder der Französischen Revolution in der Habsburger Monarchie. *Österr. i. Gesch. u. Lit.*, 95, 39, 5b-6, p. 337-342.

6054. WIEDMANN (August). The German quest for primal origins in art, culture and politics, 1900–1933; die "Flucht in Urzustände". Lewiston, [s. n.], 95, IX-501 p. (Studies in German thought and history, 16).

6055. Witold Gombrowicz. Ed. par Malgorzata SMORAG. Numéro spécial de la *Revue des sciences humaines*, 95, 239, 170 p.

6056. ZEN'KOVSKIJ (Sergej A.). Russkoe staroobrjadčestvo: Duhovnye dviženija semnadcatogo veka. (Russia's old-believers. Spiritual movements of the seventeenth century). Moskva, Cerkov', 95, 528 p.

Cf. n[os] *1354, 1358, 4663*

§ 2. Akademien und wissenschaftliche Organisationen.

6057. ALVAZZI DEL FRATE (P.). Università napoleoniche negli «Studi romani»: il «Rapport» di Giovanni Ferri de Saint-Constant sull'istruzione pubblica (1812). Roma, Viella, 95, XLVII-265 p.

6058. AMOUROUX (Henri). Histoire des cinq academies. Paris, Perrin, 95, 464 p. (Institut de France).

6059. BARTOLINI (Roberto). Siena medicea: l'Accademia di Ippolito Agostini. *Annali della Scuola Normale Superiore di Pisa*, 95, 25, p. 1475-530.

6060. CORETH (Emerich). Die Theologische Fakultät Innsbruck. Ihre Geschichte und wissenschaftliche Arbeit von den Anfängen bis zur Gegenwart. Innsbruck, Leopold-Franzens-Univ., 95, 172 p. (Veröffentlichungen der Universität Innsbruck, 212).

6061. DAHRENDORF (Ralf). LSE. A history of the London School of Economics and Political Science, 1895–1995. Oxford, Oxford U. P., 95, XX-584 p.

6062. HARTWELL (Ronald Max). A history of the Mont Pelerin society. Indianapolis, Liberty Fund, 95, XIX-250 p.

6063. *Vacat.*

6064. HUSZÁR (Tibor). A hatalom rejtett dimenziói. Magyar Tudományos Tanács, 1948–1949. (Les dimensions occultes du pouvoir. Le Conseil Scientifique Hongrois, 1948–1949). Budapest, Akad. Kiadó, 95, 378 p.

6065. Italian academies of the sixteenth century. Ed. by D.S. CHAMBERS a. F. QUIVIGER. London, Warburg Institute, 95, 215 p. (Warburg Institute colloquia, 1).

6066. Jahre Institut für Slawistik an der Leopold-Franzens-Universität Innsbruck (XXV): 1970–1995. Hrsg. v. Ingeborg OHNHEISER. Innsbruck, Leopold-Franzens-Univ., 95, 96 p. (ill., Graph. Darstellungen). (Veröffentlichungen der Universität Innsbruck, 209).

6067. KALLINEN (Maija). Change and stability: natural philosophy at the Academy of Turku (1640–1713). Helsinki, Finnish Historical Society, 95, 439 p. (ill.). (Studia historica, 51).

6068. LaRUE (C. Steven). Händel and his singers: the creation of the Royal Academy operas, 1720–1728. Oxford a. New York, Clarendon Press a. Oxford U.P., 95, XIII-213 p. (Oxford monographs on music).

6069. MAAG (Karin). Seminary or university? The Genevan Academy and reformed higher education, 1560–1620. Aldershot a. Brookfield, Scolar Press, 95, 210 p. (St. Andrews studies in Reformation history).

6070. MADAJCZYK (Czesław). En rang serré, les intellectuels d'Europe? La fonction de congrès mondiaux d'intellectuels [1907–1950]. *Acta Poloniae historica*, 95, 72, p. 91-123.

6071. NEGRUZZO (Simona). Theologiam discere et docere: la facoltà teologica di Pavia nel XVI secolo. Milano, Cisalpino-Goliardica, 95, XIV-433 p. (ill.). (Fonti e studi per la storia dell'Universita di Pavia, 23).

6072. OBERKOFLER (Gerhard), GOLLER (Peter). Zur Geschichte der Universität Innsbruck (1669–1975). Innsbruck, Selbstvlg, 210 p. (ill.).

6073. OEXLE (Otto Gerhard). The British roots of the Max-Planck-Gesellschaft. London, German Historical Institute London, 95, 36 p.

6074. Oscar Montelius 150 years. Proceedings of a colloquium held in the Royal Academy of Letters, History and Antiquities, Stockholm, 13 May 1993. Ed. by Paul ASTROM. Stockholm, Kungl. Vitterhets Historie och Antikvitets Akademien, Almqvist & Wiksell International, 1995, 112 p. (Kungliga Vitterhets Historie och Antikvitets Akademien, 32).

6075. PETRACCHI (Giorgio). Un modello di diplomazia culturale: l'Istituto Italiano di Cultura per l'Ungheria, 1935–1943. *Storia contemporanea*, 95, 26, 3, p. 377-404.

6076. PISKUREWICZ (Jan). Ośrodki upowszechniania nauki polskiej we Włoszech 1918–1939. (Centres de diffusion de la science polonaise en Italie 1918–1939). *Kwartalnik Historii Nauki i Techniki*, 95, 40, 2, p. 57-70. [Eng. Summary]. – IDEM. Polska Akademia Umiejętności: próby organizowania nauki w pierwszych latach II Rzeczypospolitej (1919–1924). (L'Académie Polonaise des Facultés: tentatives d'organiser la recherche lors des premières années de la IIe République [Polonaise], 1919–1924). *Nauka Polska*, 95, 4, p. 47-74.

6077. PUŞCAŞ (Vasile). Universitate. Societate. Modernizare. Organizarea şi activitatea ştiinţifică a Universităţii din Cluj University, 1919–1940. (University. Modernization. The organization and scientific activity of the Cluj University, 1919–1940). Cluj-Napoca, Editura Presa Universitară Clujeană, 95, 310 p.

6078. *Vacat.*

6079. Rola towarzystw naukowych w rozwoju nauki polskiej w kontekście europejskim. Konferencja naukowa. (Rôle des associations scientifiques dans le développement de la science polonaise dans le contexte européen. Conférence scientifique). Ed. Waldemar PFEIFFER. Toruń, Wydawn. Uniw. M. Kopernika, 95, 112 p.

6080. STANTON (Domna C.), STEWART (Abigail J.). Feminisms in the academy. Ann Arbor, University of Michigan Press, 95, VI-361 p. (ill.). (Women and culture series).

6081. ÚJVÁRY (Gábor). "Iskola" a határom túl. A Római Magyar Intézet története, 1912–1945. ("École" au dehors de la frontière. Histoire de l'Institut Hongrois de Rome 1912–1945). *Levéltári szle.*, 95, 45, 4, p. 3-37.

6082. WEISZ (George). The medical mandarins. The French Academy of Medicine in the nineteenth and early twentieth centuries. New York a. Oxford, Oxford U.P., 95, XVIII-306 p. (ill.).

§ 3. Unterrichtsgeschichte.

* 6083. CASPARD (Pierre). Guide international de la recherche en histoire de l'education = International guide for research in the history of education. International Standing Conference for the History of Education/Institut national de recherche pedagogique Service d'histoire de l'education. Paris et Bern, Lang, 95, 275 p. (Institut national de recherche pedagogique).

6084. ADAMS (David Wallace). Education for extinction. American Indians and the boarding school experience, 1875–1928. Lawrence, University Press of Kansas, 95, XII-396 p. (ill.).

6085. ALDRICH (Richard). School and society in Victorian Britain: Joseph Payne and the new world of education. New York a. London, Garland, 95, XXVI-317 p. (ill.). (Garland reference library of social science, 935).

6086. ANDERSON (R. D.). Education and the Scottish people, 1750–1918. Oxford a. New York, Oxford U. P., 95, X-337 p. (ill.).

6087. ARTHUR (James). The ebbing tide. Policy and principles of Catholic education. Leominster, Gracewing, 95, X-300 p.

6088. BARATAS DIAZ (Luis Alfredo). La influencia francesa en el proyecto de reforma universitaria español de principios del siglo XX. Una analogia incompleta. *Hispania*, 95, 55, 190, p. 645-672.

6089. Bibliothekarisches Studium in Vergangenheit und Gegenwart. Festschrift aus Anlass des 80-jährigen Bestehens der bibliothekarischen Ausbildung in Leipzig im Oktober 1994. Hrsg. v. Engelbert PLASSMANN u. Dietmar KUMMER. Frankfurt am Main, Klostermann, 95, VI-292 p. (ill.) (Zeitschrift für Bibliothekswesen und Bibliographie, 62).

6090. BLOCH (Jean). Rousseauism and education in eighteenth-century France. Oxford, Voltaire Foundation, 95, XII-261 p. (Studies on Voltaire and the eighteenth century, 325).

6091. CASSANTA PEIXTO (Ana Maria). L'influence des idées étrangères sur l'éducation au Brésil. *Histoire de l'éducation*, 95, 65, p. 3-26.

6092. CHAŁUPCZAK (Henryk). Polsko-Katolickie Towarzystwo Szkolne na Warmię (1921–1939). [Association Scolaire Polonaise Catholique pour la région de Warmia (1921–1939)]. *Komunikaty Mazursko-Warmińskie*, 95, 39, 3, p. 249-268. [Deutsche Zsfassung].

6093. COBB (Christopher H.). Los milicianos de la cultura. Bilbao, Servicio Editorial, Universidad del Pais Vasco, 95, 214 p. (Historia contemporanea, Universidad del Pais Vasco, 6).

6094. DIEBOLT (C.). Le compte de l'éducation des universités en Prusse: 1868–1921. *Revue Historique*, 95, 119, 595, p. 85-108.

6095. DOROSZEWSKI (Jerzy). Praca oświatowa i kulturalna na Lubelszczyźnie w latach II Rzeczypospolitej [1918–1939]. (Oeuvre de l'instruction publique et culturelle dans la région de Lublin sous la IIe République de Pologne [1918–1939]). Lublin, Wydawn. Lub. Nowe, 95, 203 p. (Deutsche Zsfassung, phot., fig.). (Mater. i Studia z Dziej. Oświaty i Szkolnictwa w Latach II Rzeczypospolitej na Lubelszczyźnie, 2).

6096. Enseignement catholique en France aux XIXe et XXe siècles (L'). Actes du Colloque organisé par la Société d'histoire religieuse de la France (Toulouse, 18–20 mars 1994) et de la journée d'étude de l'Association française d'histoire religieuse contemporaine (Paris, 24 septembre 1994). *Revue d'histoire de l'Eglise de France*, 95, 81, 206, p. 7-294.

6097. ENYEDI (Sándor). Magyar nyelvű iskolahálózat Romániában, 1968–1972. (Le réseau des écoles de langue hongroise en Roumanie, 1968–1972). *Múltunk*, 95, 40, 1, p. 92-117.

6098. ERGETOWSKI (Ryszard). Studenckie organizacje Polaków w Lipsku w latach 1872–1919. (Organisations d'étudiants Polonais à Leipzig dans les années 1872–1919). *Przegląd Polonijny*, 95, 21, 2, p. 75-89. [Eng. Summary].

6099. FARREN (Sean). The politics of Irish education 1920–65. Belfast, Institute of Irish Studies, The Queen's University of Belfast, 95, XII-296 p.

6100. FRANK (Marie-Therese), ALLAIRE (Martine). Les politiques de l'education en France. De la maternelle au baccalauréat. Paris, La documentation française, 95, 925 p. (Collection retour aux textes).

6101. GEITZ (Henry). German influences on education in the United States to 1917. Washington, Cambridge a. New York, Cambridge U. P., 95, VI-301 p. (Publications of the German Historical Institute).

6102. GEMIE (Sharif). Women and schooling in France, 1815–1914: gender, authority, and identity in the female schooling sector. Keele, Keele U. P., 95, 240 p.

6103. GOLDMAN (Lawrence). Dons and workers: Oxford and adult education since 1850. Oxford a. New York, Oxford U. P., 95, X-363 p.

6104. GRAHAM (Gael). Gender, culture, and Christianity: American Protestant mission schools in China, 1880–1930. New York, Lang, 95, 231 p. (Asian thought and culture, 25).

6105. GRIMM (Gerald). Elitäre Bildungsinstitution oder "Bürgerschule"? Das österreichische Gymnasium zwischen Tradition und Innovation, 1773–1819. Frankfurt am Main, Berlin u. Bern, Lang, 95, X-607 p. (Aspekte pädagogischer Innovation, 20).

6106. GRÜTTNER (Michael). Studenten im Dritten Reich. Paderborn, München u. Wien, Schöningh, 95, 556 p.

6107. HAMMERSTEIN (Notker). Antisemitismus und deutsche Universitäten: 1871–1933. Frankfurt u. New York, Campus Verlag, 95, 123 p.

6108. HJORTSHØJ O'ROURKE (Kevin), WILLIAMSON (Jeffrey G.). Education, globalization and catch-up: Scandinavia in the Swedish mirror. *Scandinavian Economic History Review*, 95, 43, 3, p. 287-309.

6109. HOLMES (Brian), VOSKRESENSKAYA (Natalya). Russian education: tradition and transition. New York a. London, Garland, 95, XXX-364 p. (Garland reference library of social science, 906).

6110. IVANOV (Anatolij E.). Universitetskaja politika carskogo pravitel'stva nakanune revolucii 1905–1907 godov. (The university policy of the tsar's eve of 1905–1907 revolution). *Oteč. Ist.*, 95, 6, p. 93-105.

6111. JEISMANN (Karl E.). Die Hauptstadt als Bildungszentrum. *In*: Hauptstadt: Historische Perspektiven eines deutschen Themas [Cf. n° 1271], p. 213-229.

6112. KARANOVICH (Milenko). The development of education in Serbia and emergence of its intelligentsia (1838–1858). New York, Columbia U. P., 95, X-270 p. (East European monographs, 414).

6113. KERTZ (Walter). Technische Universität Braunschweig: vom Collegium Carolinum zur Technischen Universität, 1745–1995. Hildesheim, Olms, 95, XIV-491 p. (ill.).

6114. KRAGH (Jens). Mellem socialismens velsignelser og praktikable fremskridt : SF 1960–68. Odense, Odense universitetsforlag, 95, 329 p. (Odense University studies in history and social sciences, 182).

6115. KRAWCZYK (Jerzy). Galicyjskie szkolnictwo zawodowe w latach 1860–1918. (Education professionnelle en Galicie 1860–1918). Kraków, Universitas, 95, 295 p. (Deutsche Zsfassung).

3. UNTERRICHTSGESCHICHTE

6116. KULCZYKOWSKI (Mariusz). Żydzi-studenci Uniwersytetu Jagiellońskiego w dobie autonomii Galicji (1867-1918). (Les étudiants juifs de l'Université Jagellonne à l'époque de l'autonomie de la Galicie 1867-1918). Kraków, Księgarnia Akademicka, 95, 435 p. (Eng. summary). (Inst. Hist. Uniw. Jagiel., Studia nad Kształtowaniem się Inteligencji w Pol. w XIX i XX wieku, 3).

6117. LANGHOLM (Sivert). The new nationalism and the new universities: the case of Norway in the early nineteenth century. *Scandinavian Journal of History*, 95, 20, p. 51-60.

6118. LELORRAIN (Anne-Marie). Le rôle de l'école laïque et des instituteurs dans la formation agricole, 1870-1970. *Histoire de l'éducation*, 95, 66, p. 51-70.

6119. LEVINE (Susan). Degrees of equality: the American Association of University Women and the challenge of twentieth-century feminism. Philadelphia, Temple U. P., 95, XII-227 p. (ill.). (Critical perspectives on the past).

6120. LINCICOME (Mark Elwood). Principle, praxis, and the politics of educational reform in Meiji Japan. Honolulu, University of Hawaii Press, 95, X-298 p. (ill.).

6121. MAC LAUGHLIN (Martin L.). Humanist educators. *In*: Literary imitation in the italian Renaissance [Cf. n° 6569], p. 98-125.

6122. MARCHAND (Philippe). La formation professionnelle de l'adulte à Lille. *Histoire de l'éducation*, 95, 66, p. 137-58.

6123. MARRIOTT (Stuart). English-German relations in adult education, 1875-1955: a commentary and select bibliography. Leeds, University of Leeds Press, 95, XVI-269 p. (University of Leeds Study of Continuing Education Unit).

6124. MIASTKOWSKI (Leszko). Sylwetki łódzkich uczonych. Od Wolnej Wszechnicy Polskiej do Wydziału Ekonomiczno – Socjologicznego Uniwersytetu Łódzkiego. (Silhouettes des savants de Łódź. De l'Université polonais libre jusqu'à la faculté d'Economie et de Sociologie de l'Université de Łódź). Łódź, Wydawn. Uniw. Łódzkiego, 95, 313 p. (fig.).

6125. MOKRZECKI (Lech). Źródła do dziejów wychowania muzycznego w szkolnictwie staropolskim na przykładzie Prus Królewskich – próba charakterystyki. (Sources pour l'histoire de l'enseignement musical dans l'éducation ancien-polonaise sur l'exemple de la Prusse Royale. Essai de caractéristique). *Roczniki Gdański*, 95, 55, 1, p. 5-13. [Eng. Summary].

6126. MORGAN (Harry). Historical perspectives on the education of black children. Westport a. London, Praeger, 95, 237 p. (ill.).

6127. MURPHY (Michael). The Associated Catholic Charities of the Metropolis: for the educating, cloathing and apprenticing the children of poor Catholics and providing an asylum for destitute orphans, 1811-1861. North Harrow, Murphy, 95, VI- 316 p. (Studies in the education of Catholic poor children in nineteenth-century London).

6128. PEDERSEN (Henry). Skidthogen: beretningen om tre engelske flyvere, der meldte sig til R.A.F.'s stifindereskadriller. Odense, Odense universitetsforlag, 95, 225 p. (Odense University studies in history and social sciences, 185).

6129. PELCZAR (Roman). Szkolnictwo jezuickie w Jarosławiu 1575-1773 r. (L'enseignement des jésuites à Jarosław: 1575-1773). *Nasza Przeszłość*, 95, 84, p. 13-47. [Deutsche Zsfassung].

6130. PHILLIPS (David). Education in Germany. Tradition and reform in historical context. London a. New York, Routledge, 95, 292 p. (International developments in school reform).

6131. PIETSCH (Walter). Steirische Beiträge zur Schulgeschichte des 18. Jahrhunderts. *Z. d. Hist. Vereines f. Steiermark*, 95, 86, p. 237-275 (Dok., ill., Karten, Grundrisse).

6132. Pracownicy nauki i dydaktyki Uniwersytetu Mikołaja Kopernika 1945-1994. Materiały do bibliografii. (Chercheurs et professeurs de l'Université "Nicolas Copernic" 1945-1994). Matériaux biographiques. Aut.: Henryka DUCZKOWSKA-MORACZEWSKA, Maciej GOŁEMBIOWSKI, Renata KARPIESIUK. Réd. Sławomir KALEMBKA. Toruń, 95, 800 p. (phot., fig.). (Uniw. Mikołaja Kopernika w Toruniu).

6133. REESE (William J.). The origins of the American high school. New Haven a. London, Yale U. P., 95, XVIII-326 p. (ill).

6134. RESPONDEK (Peter). Besatzung, Entnazifizierung, Wiederaufbau. Die Universität Münster 1945-1952. Ein Beitrag zur Geschichte der deutsch-britischen Beziehungen nach dem zweiten Weltkrieg auf dem Bildungssektor. Münster, Agenda, 95, 295 p. (Agenda Geschichte 6).

6135. RÍOS ZÚÑIGA (Rosalina). La secularización de la enseñanza en Zacatecas. Del Colegio de San Luis Gonzaga al Instituto Literario (1784-1838). *Historia Mexicana*, 94-95, 44, p. 299-332.

6136. ROBIN (Ron). The barbed-wire college. Re-educating German POWs in the United States during World War II. Princeton a. Chichester, Princeton U. P., 95, X-217 p. (ill.).

6137. RUST (Val D.), RUST (Diane). The unification of German education. New York a. London, Garland Publishing, 95, XIV-369 p. (ill) (Garland reference library of social science, 960).

6138. SCHOTT (Walter). Das K.K. Taubstummen-Institut in Wien 1779-1918. Dargestellt nach historischen Überlieferungen und Dokumenten, mit einem Abriß der wichtigsten pädagogischen Strömungen aus der Geschichte der Gehörlosenbildung bis zum Ende der Habsburgermonarchie. Wien, Köln u. Weimar, Böhlau, 95, 344 p. (ill., Karten).

6139. SCUDERI (Graziella). Il pensiero educativo di Benedetto Croce. *Filosofia Oggi*, 95, 18, p. 81-94.

6140. SEBESTYÉN (Kálmán). Erdély református népoktatása, 1780–1848. (L'enseignement de premier degré réformé [calviniste] de Transylvanie, 1780–1848). Budapest, Püski, 95, 8, 136 p.

6141. SIVONEN (Seppo). White-collar or hoe handle? African education under British colonial policy 1920–1945. Helsinki, SHS, 95, 264 p. (Bibliotheca historica, 4.) (ill.).

6142. SUČKOV (Igor' V.). Socialnyj i duchovnyj oblik učitel'stva Rossii na rubeže XIX–XX vekov. (Social and spiritual aspects of the Russian teachers on the border of the XIXth and XXth centuries). *Oteč. Ist.*, 95, 1, p. 62-77.

6143. SZYMAŃSKI (Leonard). Kultura fizyczna w polityce II Rzeczypospolitej [1918–1939]. (Culture physique dans la politique de la seconde République Polonaise 1918–1939]. Wrocław, 95, 206 p. (phot., fig., dessins, cartes). (Akad. Wychowania Fiz. we Wrocławiu. Studia i Monografie, 47). [Eng. Summary].

6144. TEITELBAUM (Kenneth). Schooling for "good rebels". Socialism, american education, and the search for radical curriculum. New York a. London, Teachers College Press, 95, XII-258 p.

6145. TILKOVSZKY (Loránt). Nemzetiségi anyanyelvű oktatás Magyarországon a katolikus elemi népiskolákban, 1919–1944. (L'enseignement national en langue maternelle dans les écoles élémentaires catholiques de la Hongrie, 1919–1944). *Századok*, 95, 129, 6, p. 1251-1274.

6146. TITZE (Hartmut). Wachstum und Differenzierung der deutschen Universitäten 1830–1945. Göttingen, Vandenhoeck a. Ruprecht, 95, 357 p.

6147. TYACK (David), CUBAN (Larry). Tinkering toward utopia: a century of public school reform. Cambridge a. London, Harvard U. P., 95, 184 p. (ill.).

6148. Universitäten in Deutschland = Universities in Germany. Ed. by Christian BODE, Werner BECKER, Rainer KLOFAT in conjunction with Deutscher Akademischer Austauschdienst und Hochschulrektorenkonferenz. München a. New York, Prestel, 95, 632 p. (ill.).

6149. VINOVSKIS (Maris A.), RAVITCH (Diane). Learning from the past: what history teaches us about school reform. Baltimore a. London, Johns Hopkins U. P., 95, XIV-381 p.

6150. VINOVSKIS (Maris A.). Education, society, and economic opportunity: a historical perspective on persistent issues. New Haven a. London, Yale U. P., 95, XVI-235 p. (ill.).

6151. WALCZAK (Marian). Polskie środowisko szkolne na terenach wschodnich II Rzeczypospolitej (1939–1945). (Milieu scolaire polonais sur les territoires est de la IIe République [Polonaise]). *Przegląd Historyczno-Oświatowy*, 95, 38, 3-4, p. 177-200.

6152. YAZICI (Nesimi). Osmanlı Son Döneminde Libya'da Türk Dilinin Öğretimi Üzerine Bazı Gözlemler. (Quelques observations sur l'enseignement de la langue turque en Libye vers la fin de l'Empire Ottoman). *Belleten*, 95, 59, 224, p. 121-132.

6153. YOLALICI (M. Emin). Maarif Salnamelerine Göre Trabzon Vilayetinde Eğitim ve Öğretim Kurumları. (Les institutions d'enseignement et d'instruction dans le département de Trabzon d'après des Annales d'éducation). *Osmanlı Tarihi Araştırma ve Uygulama Merkezi Dergisi*, 95, 5, p. 435-473.

§ 4. Pressewesen.

** 6154. LAHARIE (Patrick). Contrôle de la presse, de la librairie et du colportage sous le Second Empire. 1852–1870. Inventaire des articles F^{18} 265 à 293, 552 à 555, 556 à 571 et 2345. Paris, Archives nationales, 95, LII-701 p.

6155. AHMAT (Adam). The vernacular press and the emergence of modern Indonesian consciousness (1855–1913). Ithaca, Cornell U. P., 95, XII-206 p. (Studies on Southeast Asia, 17).

6156. AYALON (Ami). The press in the Arab Middle East. A history. New York a. Oxford, Oxford U.P., 95, XIV-300 p. (Studies in Middle Eastern history).

6157. BARRERA (Carlos). Periodismo y franquismo. De la censura a la apertura. Barcelona, Ediciones Internacionales Universitarias, 95, 188 p. (Politica, cultura y sociedad). –IDEM. Sin mordaza. Veinte años de prensa en democracia. Madrid, Temas de Hoy, 95, 447 p. (Grandes temas, 40).

6158. BENJAMIN (Ionie). The black press in Britain. Staffordshire, Trentham Books, 95, VIII-134 p. (ill.).

6159. BERTAUD (Jean-Paul). La presse en l'an II: aperçu des recherches en cours. *In*: An II (L') [Cf. n° 4852], p. 161-172.

6160. BRODIE (Malcolm). The Tele. A history of the Belfast Telegraph. Belfast, Blackstaff Press, 95, XII-300 p. (ill.).

6161. BROWN (Walt). John Adams and the American press. Politics and journalism at the birth of the Republic. Jefferson a. London, McFarland, 95, X-213 p.

6162. CADIOLI (Renato). Letterati ed editori. Milano, Il saggiatore, 95, 224 p. (La cultura. Discussioni, 22).

6163. CARDUS (Salvador). Politica de paper. Premsa i poder a Catalunya (1981–1992). Barcelona, Edicions La Campana, 95, 351 p. (Edicions La Campana, 99).

4. PRESSEWESEN

6164. Catalogo storico delle Edizioni scientifiche italiane 1945–1995. Napoli, Edizioni scientifiche italiane, 95, 336 p. [contiene: CORSI (Ermanno), La ESI, Napoli e il Mezzogiorno, p. 9-10].

6165. DARNTON (Robert). The corpus of clandestine literature in France, 1769–1789. London a. New York, W. W. Norton, 95, 260 p.

6166. DE LLERA (L.). Prensa y censura en el Franquísmo (1936–1966). *Hispania sacra*, 95, 47, p. 5-36.

6167. Denních zpráv Hlavní správy tiskového dohledu (Z). 1957–1967. (From the daily reports of the Head Office of Press Supervision). Tomo 1–3. Praha, Ústav pro soudobé dějiny AV ČR, 95, 3 vol., 116 p., 125 p., 170 p. (Studijní materiály výzkumného projektu Československo 1945–1967, 5-7).

6168. DOUZOU (Laurent). La désobéissance. Histoire d'un mouvement et d'un journal clandestins, Liberation-Sud, 1940–1944. Paris, Jacob, 95, 480 p. (ill.).

6169. Edizioni elettriche. La rivoluzione editoriale e tipografica. Roma, De Luca, 95, 139 p. (ill.).

6170. Eighteenth century German book review (The). Ed. by Herbert ROWLAND a. Karl J. FINK. Heidelberg, Universitatsverlag C. Winter, 95, 214 p. (Beiträge zur neueren Literaturgeschichte, 3. Folge, 135).

6171. EMERY (Michael C.). On the front lines. Following America's foreign correspondents across the twentieth century. Washington, American U.P., 95, XVIII-346 p. (ill.). (American U.P. journalism history series).

6172. FONSECA (Wilton). A sombra do poder. A historia da Lusitania, 1944–1974. Lisboa, Edicoes Memoria do Tempo, 95, 163 p. (ill.). (Colecção Memoria do tempo).

6173. Fonti e studi di storia dell'editoria. A cura di Gianfranco TORTORELLI. Bologna, Baiesi, 95, 283 p.

6174. GERBER (Michael Rudiger). Die Schlesischen Provinzialblätter 1785–1849. Sigmaringen, Thorbecke, 95, 786 p. (Quellen und Darstellungen zur schlesischen Geschichte, 27).

6175. Giangiacomo Feltrinelli editore: catalogo storico 1955–1995. Milano, Feltrinelli, 95, 96 p. (tav.).

6176. GRANT (Alfred). Our American brethren. A history of letters in the British press during the American revolution, 1775–1781. Jefferson a. London, McFarland, 95, X-212 p.

6177. HALKIN (Ariela). The enemy reviewed: German popular literature through British eyes between the two world wars. Westport a. London, Praeger, 95, 211 p. (ill.).

6178. HARDT (Hanno), BRENNEN (Bonnie). Newsworkers. Toward a history of the rank and file. Minneapolis, University of Minnesota Press, 95, XIV-237 p.

6179. HARRIS (Bob). The London Evening Post and mid-eighteenth-century British politics. *English Historical Review*, 95, 110, 439, p. 1132-1156.

6180. HIBBS-LISSORGUES (Solange). Iglesia, prensa y sociedad en España (1868–1904). Alicante, Instituto de Cultura "Juan Gil-Albert", Diputación de Alicante, 95, 462 p. (Ensayo e investigación, 56).

6181. HUFFER (Jurgen Benedikt). Vom Lizenzpressesystem zur Wettbewerbspresse: Lizenzverleger und Altverleger im Rheinland und in Westfalen 1945–1953/54. München, Saur, 95, 376 p. (ill.). (Dortmunder Beiträge zur Zeitungsforschung, 54).

6182. HUTTNER (Markus). Britische Presse und nationalsozialistischer Kirchenkampf. Eine Untersuchung der 'Times' und des 'Manchester Guardian' von 1930 bis 1939. Paderborn, Schöningh, 95, 814 p. (ill.). (Veröffentlichungen der Kommission für Zeitgeschichte, 67).

6183. JOHANNES (G. J.). De barometer van de smaak: tijdschriften in Nederland 1770–1830. Den Haag, Sdu, 95, XIV-246 p. (Nederlandse cultuur in Europese context, 2).

6184. KHAN (Masood Ali). The history of Urdu press. A case study of Hyderabad. New Delhi, Classical Pub., 95, VI-140 p.

6185. KOHNEN (Richard). Pressepolitik des Deutschen Bundes. Methoden staatlicher Pressepolitik nach der Revolution von 1848. Tübingen, Niemeyer, 95, VIII-222 p. (Studien und Texte zur Sozialgeschichte der Literatur, 50).

6186. Kommunikationsrevolutionen. Die neuen Medien des 16. und 19. Jh. Hrsg. v. Michael NORTH. Wien, Köln u. Weimar, Böhlau, 95, 205 p. (Wirtschaft- und Sozialhistorische Studien, 3).

6187. LAZO (Alfonso). La Iglesia, la Falange y el fascismo. Un estudio sobre la prensa española de posguerra. Sevilla, Universidad de Sevilla, Secretariado de Publicaciones, 95, 359 p. (Colección de bolsillo. Universidad de Sevilla. Secretariado de Publicaciones, 144).

6188. MARABINI (Claudio). Letteratura bastarda. Giornalismo, narrativa e terza pagina. Milano, Camunia, 95, 371 p.

6189. MINOIS (Georges). Censure et culture sous l'Ancien Régime. Paris, Fayard, 95, 335 p.

6190. MIRA BENAVENT (Javier). Los limites penales a la libertad de expresión en los comienzos del regimen constitucional español. Valencia, Tirant Lo Blanch, 95, 341 p. (Tirant monografias, 29).

6191. MURIALDI (Paolo). La stampa italiana dalla liberazione alla crisi di fine secolo. Roma e Bari, Laterza, 95, 328 p. (Storia e società).

6192. MÜSSE (Wolfgang). Die Reichspresseschule: Journalisten für die Diktatur? Ein Beitrag zur Geschichte des Journalismus im dritten Reich. München, New Providence, London u. Paris, K. G. Saur, 95, 299 p. (Dortmunder Beiträge zur Zeitungsforschung, 53).

6193. NEVILLE (John F.). The press, the Rosenbergs, and the Cold War. Westport a. London, Praeger, 95, X-207 p.

6194. PAJKOSSY (Gábor). A reformkori Országgyűlési Tudósítások. (Les Országgyűlési Tudósítások [Renseignements de la diète] à l'époque des réformes). Levéltári közl.,95, 66, 1-2, p. 121-136.

6195. PASTA (Renato). Per una rilettura de «Il Caffè», 1764–1766. Rivista storica italiana, 95, 107, 3, p. 840-875.

6196. PIROŻYŃSKI (Jan). Z dziejów obiegu informacji w Europie XVI wieku. Nowiny z Polski w kolekcji Jana Jakuba Wicka w Zurychu z lat 1560–1587. (Histoire du circuit d'information en Europe au XVIe s. Nouvelles de Pologne d'entre 1560–1587 dans la collection de Jan Jakub Wick de Zürich). Kraków, 95, 361 p. (Deutsche Zsfassung). (Zesz. Nauk. Uniw. Jagiell. Prace Hist., 115).

6197. PISCHEDDA (Bruno). Due modernità. Le pagine culturali dell'Unità, 1945–1956. Milano, Angeli, 95, 271 p. (Quaderni Fondazione Feltrinelli, 48).

6198. POOLE (David N. J.). Stages of religious faith in the classical Reformation tradition: the covenant approach to the Ordo Salutis. Lewiston a. Lampeter, Edwin Mellen Press, 95, X-306 p.

6199. Public access to the Internet. Ed. by Brian KAHIN a. James KELLER. Cambridge, MIT Press, 95, 390 p.

6200. RĂDUICĂ (Georgeta), RĂDUICĂ (Nicolin). Dicționarul presei românești, 1731–1918. (The dictionary of Romanian press, 1731–118). București, Editura Științifică, 95, 560 p.

6201. RAGONE (Giovanni). Da Pierro ai Carabba. Avanguardie letterarie e nuova editoria del Sud fra Ottocento e Novecento. Archivio storico italiano, 95, 153, 565, p. 529-572.

6202. REQUATE (Jörg). Journalismus als Beruf. Entstehung und Entwicklung des Journalistenberufs im 19. Jahrhundert. Deutschland im internationalen Vergleich. Göttingen, Vandenhoeck & Ruprecht, 95, 500 p. (Kritische Studien zur Geschichtswissenschaft, 109).

6203. RINGDAL (Nils Johan). Kardinaler og kremmere: norske forleggere gjennom hundre år: Den norske forleggerforening 1895–1995. (Norwegian publishers through a houndred years. The Norwegian union of publishers 1895–1995). Oslo, Den norske forleggerforening, 95, 367 p. (ill.).

6204. ROBERTSON (Andrew W.). The language of democracy. Political rhetoric in the United States and Britain, 1790–1900. Ithaca a. London, Cornell U.P., 95, XVI-264 p. (ill.).

6205. SCHOEPP (Sebastian). Das Argentinische Tageblatt 1933–1945. Eine "bürgerliche Kampfzeitung" als Forum der Emigration. Vierteljahrshefte für Zeitgeschichte, 95, 95, 43, 1, p. 75-114.

6206. Scholarly editing. A guide to research. Ed. by D.C. GRELTHAM. New York, Modern Language Association of America, 95, VI-740 p.

6207. SCHUDSON (Michael). The power of news. Cambridge a. London, Harvard U.P., 95, 269 p.

6208. SIKLOS (Richard). Shades of Black: Conrad Black and the world's fastest growing press empire. London, Heinemann, 95, 466 p.

6209. SINOVA (Justino). El poder y la prensa. El control politico de la información en la España felipista. Barcelona, Ediciones Internacionales Universitarias, 95, 205 p. (Politica, cultura y sociedad).

6210. TESTI (Arnaldo). Giornalismo e potere negli Stati Uniti. Storica, 95, 2, 1, p. 103-118.

6211. TUCK (Jim). McCarthyism and New York's Hearst press. A study of roles in the witch hunt. Lanham a. London, U.P. of America, 95, 228 p.

6212. TUGAN- BARANOVSKIJ (Džuča M.). "Lošad' , kotoruiu ja pytalsja obuzdat'". Pečat'pri Napoleone. ("The horse I tried to curb". Mass media in Napoleon age). Nov. novejš. Ist., 95, 3, p. 158-179.

6213. "Wiadomości" [1945–1989] i okolice. Szkice i wspomnienia. "Informations" [1945–1989] et les environs. Esquisses et témoignages. Réd. Mirosław Adam SUPRUNIUK. Toruń, Uniw. M. Kopernika, 95, 275 p. (phot., fig.) (Archiwum "Wiadomości". Źródła i materiały do dziej. emigracji pol. po 1939 roku, 1). [Eng. Summary].

6214. YLÖNEN (Marja). Karin suomalainen: pilapiirrokset suomalaisuuden legitimointina. (Kari's Finn: political cartoons drawn by Kari Suomalainen published on the editorial pages of Helsingin Sanomat, 1951–1991). Tampere, Tampereen yliopisto, 95, 234 p. (Eng. Summary, ill.). (Acta Univ. Tamperensinsis, A 468).

6215. YODER (Edwin). Joe Alsop's cold war. A study of journalistic influence and intrigue. Chapel Hill a. London, University of North Carolina Press, 95, XII-220 p. (ill.).

Cf. n° 110

§ 5. Philosophie und Weltanschauung.

* 6216. Bibliografia degli scritti di Norberto Bobbio: 1934–1993. A cura di Carlo VIOLI. Roma e Bari, Laterza, 95, XLII-489 p.

* 6217. Bibliographie zu "Hegels Enzylopädie der philosophischen Wissenschaften im Grundrisse": Primär- und Sekundärliteratur 1817–1994. Hrsg. v. Karen GLOY u. Rainer LAMBRECHT. Stuttgart, Frommann u. Bad Cannstatt, Holzboog, 95, 123 p.

* 6218. BRODERSEN (Momme). Walter Benjamin: eine kommentierte Bibliographie. Morsum/Sylt, Cicero Presse, 95, 311p.

* 6219. SCHABERG (William H.). The Nietzsche canon: a publication history and bibliography. Chicago, University of Chicago Press, 95, XVI-281 p. (ill.).

** 6220. BENJAMIN (Walter). Gesammelte Briefe. Bd. 1. 1910–1918. Hrsg. v. Christoph GODDE u. Henri LONITZ. Frankfurt am Main, Suhrkamp, 95, 545 p. (Gesammelte Briefe. Walter Benjamin, 1).

** 6221. PICO DELLA MIRANDOLA (Giovanni). Conclusiones nongentae: le novecento Tesi dell'anno 1486. A cura di Albano BIONDI. Firenze, Olschki, 95, XXXVIII-157 p. (Centro internazionale di cultura "Giovanni Pico della Mirandola", Studi pichiani, 1).

6222. AHRENSDORF (Peter J.). The death of Socrates and the life of philosophy: an interpretation of Plato's Phaedo. New York, State University of New York Press, 95, X-238 p.

6223. ANDERSON (Kevin). Lenin, Hegel and Western Marxism. A critical study. Urbana, University of Illinois Press, 95, 311 p.

6224. APPELBAUM (David). The vision of Kant. Rockport a. Shaftesbury, Element, 95, 188 p. (The spirit of philosophy series).

6225. BALL (Terence). Reappraising political theory. Revisionist studies in the history of political thought. Oxford a. New York, Clarendon Press a. Oxford U.P., 95, XVI-310 p.

6226. BAMBACH (Charles). Heidegger, Dilthey, and the crisis of historicism. Ithaca, Cornell U. P., 95, XII-297 p.

6227. BARASH (Andrew Jeffrey). Heidegger et son siècle. Temps de l'Etre, temps de l'histoire. Paris, PUF, 95, 188 p.

6228. BARON (Marcia). Kantian ethics almost without apology. Ithaca a. London, Cornell U.P., 95, XIII-244 p.

6229. BAWDEN (Nina). The real Plato. London, Puffin, 95, 171 p.

6230. BEDNARCZYK (Andrzej). Z dziejów idei życia we wszechświecie. Epoka Oświecenia (Fontenelle, Huygens, Kant). [De l'histoire de l'idée de la vie dans l'univers. Epoque des Lumières (Fontenelle, Huygens, Kant)]. *Kwartalnik Historii Nauki i Techniki*, 95, 40, 3, p. 7-48. [Eng. Summary].

6231. BENCIVENGA (Ermanno). My Kantian ways. Berkeley a. London, University of California Press, 95, VIII-136 p.

6232. BENSAÏD (Daniel). Marx l'intempestif. Grandeurs et misères d'une aventure critique (XIXe–XXe siècles). Paris, Fayard, 95, 415 p.

6233. BERTHOLD-BOND (Daniel). Hegel's theory of madness. Albany, State University of New York Press, 95, XVIII-309 p. (SUNY series in Hegelian studies).

6234. BINDER (Dieter A.). Die diskrete Gesellschaft. Geschichte und Symbolik der Freimaurerei. Graz u. Wien, Vlg Styria, Ed. Kaleidoskop, 95, 239 p. (ill., Graph. Darstellungen).

6235. BIRN (Raymond). Rousseau senza frontiere. *Rivista storica italiana*, 95, 107, 3, p. 575-613.

6236. BLACKSON (Thomas A.). Inquiry, forms, and substances. A study in Plato's metaphysics and epistemology. Dordrecht a. London, Kluwer Academic, 95, VIII-226 p. (Philosophical studies series, 62).

6237. BLOSSER (Philip). Scheler's critique of Kant's ethics. Athens, Ohio U.P., 95, XVI-221 p. (Series in continental thought, 22).

6238. BODKAM (S.). La théorie ficinienne de la vacance de l'âme dans la Theologia Platonica: songe, prophétie et liberté. *Bibliothèque d'Humanisme et Renaissance*, 95, 57, 3, p. 537-550.

6239. BOLDT-IRONS (Leslie Anne). On Bataille. Critical essays. Albany, State University of New York Press, 95, VIII-338 p. (Intersections).

6240. BONDELI (Martin). Das Anfangsproblem bei Karl Leonhard Reinhold: eine systematische und entwicklungsgeschichtliche Untersuchung zur Philosophie Reinholds in der Zeit von 1789 bis 1803. Frankfurt am Main, Klostermann, 95, 445 p. (Philosophische Abhandlungen, 62).

6241. BOUCHER (David), CONNELLY (James), MODOOD (Tariq). Philosophy, history and civilization: interdisciplinary perspectives on R.G. Collingwood. Cardiff, University of Wales Press, 95, XVIII-388 p. (R. G. Collingwood Society).

6242. BRICKHOUSE (Thomas C.). Plato's Socrates. New York a. Oxford, Oxford U.P., 95, XIV-240 p.

6243. BRUDNER (Alan). The unity of the common law: studies in Hegelian jurisprudence. Berkeley a. London, University of California Press, 95, XII-354 p.

6244. BRUGERE (Fabienne). Esthétique et ressamblance chez Shaftesbury. *Revue de Métaphysique et de Morale*, 95, 100, p. 517-32.

6245. CALLORO (P.). A proposito di alcuni carteggi crociani. *Nuova rivista storica*, 95, 1, p. 162-170.

6246. CARABINE (Deirdre). The unknown God. Negative theology in the Platonic tradition: Plato to Eriugena. Louvain, Eerdmans, 95, XIV-358 p. (Louvain theological a. pastoral monographs, 19).

6247. CAYGILL (Howard). A Kant dictionary. Oxford a. Cambridge, Blackwell, 95, p. (The Blackwell philosopher dictionaries).

6248. CHARTIER (Roger). Généalogie et architecture de l'œuvre: Foucault lecteur de Foucault. *Les Cahiers de la Villa Gillet*, 95, 3, p. 188-203.

6249. COLLINS (Ardis B.). Hegel on the modern world. Albany, State University of New York Press, 95, xxi, 248 p. (Hegel Society of America Meeting).

6250. COROLEU (A.). Erasmus and Alfonso de Valdès: a note of the «Dialogo de Mercurio y Caron». *Bibliothèque d'Humanisme et Renaissance*, 95, 57, 2, p. 395-400.

6251. COUDERT (Allison). Leibniz and the Kabbalah. Dordrecht, London, Kluwer Academic, 95, XVIII-218 p. (Archives internationales d'histoire des idées = International archives of the history of ideas, 142).

6252. CREXELLS I VALLHONRAT (Joan). Obra completa.1: De Plato a Carles Riba. Barcelona, La Magrana, 95, 456 p.

6253. CRISTOFOLINI (Paolo). La Scienza nuova di Vico: introduzione alla lettura. Roma, NIS, 95, 165 p. (Seminario filosofico, 3). – IDEM. Vico et l'histoire. Paris, PUF, 95, 126 p. (Philosophies, 58).

6254. CROPSEY (Joseph). Plato's world: man's place in the cosmos. Chicago a. London, University of Chicago Press, 95, X-227 p.

6255. CUTROFELLO (Andrew). The owl at dawn. A sequel to Hegel's Phenomenology of spirit. Albany, State University of New York Press, 95, XII-196 p. (SUNY series in radical social and political theory).

6256. DAVIES (Martin L.). Identity or history? Marcus Herz and the end of the enlightenment. Detroit, Wayne State U.P., 95, XIV-344 p.

6257. DE PASCALE (Carla). Etica e diritto. La filosofia pratica di Fichte. Bologna, Il Mulino, 95, 368 p. (Annali dell'Istituto storico italo-germanico. Monografia, 26).

6258. DERRIDA (Jacques). Glas. Paris, Editions Galilée, 95, 291 p. (Collection la philosophie en effet).

6259. DI MAURO (A.). L'edizione Adelphi e l'edizione Bibliopolis delle opere di Croce. *Nuova rivista storica*, 95, 1, p. 156-161.

6260. DOLCINI (Carlo). Introduzione a Marsilio da Padova. Roma-Bari, Laterza, 95, 116 p. (I filosofi, 63).

6261. DROZ-VINCENT (Gabriel). L'atomisme dans le monisme épicurien. *Revue philosophique*, 95, 185, p. 3-17.

6262. EDEL (Susanne). Die individuelle Substanz bei Boehme und Leibniz. Die Kabbala als tertium comparationis für eine rezeptionsgeschichtliche Untersuchung. Stuttgart, Steiner, 95, 225 p. (Studia Leibnitiana, 23).

6263. FALKENSTEIN (Lorne). Kant's intuitionism. A commentary on the transcendental aesthetic. Toronto, London, University of Toronto Press, 95, 464 p.

6264. FEGER (Hans). Die Macht der Einbildungskraft in der Aesthetik Kants und Schillers. Heidelberg, Winter, 95, 351 p. (Probleme der Dichtung, 25).

6265. FELICE (Domenico). Immagini dell'Italia politica moderna nell'«Esprit des lois» di Montesquieu. *Pens. Pol.*, 95, 28, 2, p. 270-282.

6266. FEUER (Lewis S.). Varieties of scientific experience: emotive aims in scientific hypotheses. New Brunswick a. London, Transaction Publishers, 95, XX-445 p.

6267. FLAQUER (Jaume). Hegel y el romanticismo: la importancia de la rélación. Barcelona, Centre Borja, 95, 40 p. (Cuadernos Institut de Teologia Fondamental).

6268. FRAJESE (Vittorio). La politica di Ludovico Zuccolo e l'ambiente sarpiano. Contributo all'interpretazione di testi pubblici dissimulati. *Pens. Pol.*, 95, 28, 2, p. 151-177.

6269. GERAS (Norman). Solidarity in the conversation of humankind: the ungroundable liberalism of Richard Rorty. London a. New York, Verso, 95, 151 p.

6270. GIACOPINI (Vittorio). La figura del malvagio negli "Essays on the Law of Nature" di John Locke. *Cultura*, 95, 34, p. 433-84.

6271. GIBBONS (Sarah L.). Kant's theory of imagination. Bridging gaps in judgement and experience. Oxford, Clarendon Press, 95, VIII-205 p. (Oxford philosophical monographs).

6272. Ginguené (1748–1816), idéologue et médiateur. Colloque international, Bibliothèque municipale de Rennes, 2–4 avril 1992. Rennes, Presses Universitaires de Rennes, 292 p.

6273. GISEL (P.). Ernst Troeltsch: un dépassement des «Lumières». *Archives de sciences sociales des religions*, 95, 40, p. 83-94.

6274. GONZALEZ (Francisco J.). The third way: new directions in Platonic studies. London, Rowman a. Littlefield Publishers, 95, XII-269 p.

6275. GOODIN (Robert E.). Utilitarianism as a public philosophy. Cambridge a. New York, Cambridge U.P., 95, XII-352 p. (Cambridge studies in philosophy and public policy).

6276. GRAUPE (Heinz Mosche). The systematic nature of Jewish theology. Chicago, Academy Chicago Publishers, 95, 130 p.

6277. GRAY (John). Isaiah Berlin. London, Fontana Press, 95, VIII-189 p. (Modern masters series).

6278. GUILLAUME (Anne-Marie). Mal, mensonge et mauvaise foi: une lecture de Kant. Préface de Jean LADRIERE. Namur, Presses universitaires de Namur, 95, 549 p. (Collection "Philosophie", 3).

6279. HARRIS (H. S.). Hegel. Phenomenology and system. Indianapolis a. Cambridge, Hackett, 95, X-118 p.

6280. HAVAS (Katalin G.). Children, philosophy and logic from a dialectical point of view. *Logique et analyse*, 95, 38, p. 151-58.

5. PHILOSOPHIE UND WELTANSCHAUUNG

6281. Hérésie spinoziste (L'): la discussion sur le Tractatus theologico-politicus, 1670–1677, et la réception immediate du spinozisme: actes du Colloque international de Cortona, 10–14 Avril 1991 = The Spinozistic heresy: the debate on the Tractatus theologico-politicus, 1670–1677, and the immediate reception of spinozism: proceedings of the international Cortona Seminar, 10–14 April 1991. Publiés par Paolo CRISTOFOLINI. Amsterdam, APA-Holland U. P., 95, VIII-260 p.

6282. HOBSBAWM (Eric J.). Gramsci in Europa e in America. [Con scritti di Joseph BUTTIGIEG]. A cura di Antonio A. SANTUCCI. Roma e Bari, Laterza, 95, XIII-159 p. (Sagittari Laterza, 88).

6283. HOFFHEIMER (Michael H.). Eduard Gans and the Hegelian philosophy of law. Dordrecht a. London, Kluwer Academic Publishers, 95, XIII-134 p. (Archives internationales d'histoire des idées = International archives of the history of ideas, 143).

6284. HONNETH (Axel), ANDERSON (Joel). The struggle for recognition. The moral grammar of social conflicts. Cambridge, Polity Press, 95, XXII-215 p.

6285. HUANG (Jing-Xing). Philosophy, philology and politics in eighteenth-century China: Li Fu and the Lu-Wang school under the Ch'ing. Cambridge, Cambridge U.P., 95, XVI-204 p. (Cambridge studies in Chinese history, literature and institutions).

6286. HYLAND (Drew A.). Finitude and transcendence in the Platonic dialogues. Albany, State University of New York Press, 95, 208 p.

6287. JAMME (Christoph), WEISSER (Elisabeth). Politik und Geschichte: zu den Intentionen von G.W.F. Hegels Reformbill-Schrift. Bonn, Bouvier, 95, 320 p. (Hegel-Studien. Beiheft, 35).

6288. JOOS (Jean-Ernest). Kant et la question de l'autorité. Paris, L'Harmattan, 95, 223 p. (Collection La philosophie en commun).

6289. KAHANE (Howard). Contract ethics: evolutionary biology and the moral sentiments. Lanham, Rowman & Littlefield, 95, XIII-151 p. (Studies in social, political, and legal philosophy).

6290. KAUFMANN (Walter). Discovering the mind. New Brunswick a. London, Transaction Publishers, 95, XXXV-288 p.

6291. KEDOURIE (Elie), KEDOURIE (Sylvia), KEDOURIE (Helen). Hegel and Marx. Introductory lectures. Oxford a. Cambridge, Blackwell, 95, XII-216 p.

6292. KOLNAI (Aurel), DUNLOP (Francis). The utopian mind and other papers: a critical study in moral and political philosophy. London, Athlone Press, 95, XXXV-217 p.

6293. KONIG (Peter). Das Recht der Vernunft: Kant und Hegel über Denken, Erkennen und Handeln. Stuttgart-Bad Cannstatt, Frommann-Holzboog, 95, 438 p.

6294. KREISWIRTH (Martin), CARMICHAEL (Thomas). Constructive criticism: the human sciences in the age of theory. Toronto a. London, University of Toronto Press, 95, VIII-223 p. (ill.).

6295. KROIS (John Michael). Le carte inedite di Ernst Cassirer e l'edizione dei «Nachgelassene Manuskripte und Texte». *Rivista di storia della filosofia*, 95, 50, p. 871-888.

6296. LABBE (Yves). La question de Dieu dans les philosopheis contemporaines. *Revue des sciences religieuses*, 95, 69, p. 497-516.

6297. LEONHARD (Wolfgang). Die unbekannten Klassiker. Marx und Engels in der DDR. *Deut. Arch.*, 95, 28, 7, p. 709-720.

6298. LEVSTEIN (Ana). La invención de la locura en Michel Foucault. *Estudios*, 5, 95, p. 191-220.

6299. Liberalizm Zapada XVII–XX veka. (The Western liberalism, the XVIIth–XXth centuries). V. V. SOGRIN, A. I. PATRUŠEV, E. S. TOKAREVA, T. M. FADEEVA. Pod obščej redakciej V. V. SOGRINA. Moskva, RAN, In-t vseobščej istorii, 95, 227p.

6300. LÖWITH (Karl). Martin Heidegger and European nihilism. Ed. by Richard WOLIN. New York, Columbia U. P., 95, VIII-304 p.

6301. MADU (Ngozi). Public opinion in politics: Hegel's interpretation in his Philosophy of right 1821 in comparison with the Anglo-American political theory and history of ideas. Marburg, Tectum, 95, X-199 p.

6302. MAIA NETO (Jose R.). The Christianization of Pyrrhonism: scepticism and faith in Pascal, Kierkegaard, and Shestov. Dordrecht a. London, Kluwer Academic Publishers, 95, XVIII-151 p. (Archives internationales d'histoire des idées = International archives of the history of ideas, 144).

6303. MANCA (Sergio). Gli articoli di Nicolas-Antoine Boulanger per l'Encyclopédie. *Rivista storica italiana*, 95, 107, 3, p. 614-646.

6304. MANUEL (Frank Edward). A requiem for Karl Marx. Cambridge, Harvard U. P., 95, XI-255 p.

6305. MARCONI (Diego). Predicate logic in Wittgenstein's Tractatus. *Logique et analyse*, 95, 38, p. 179-90.

6306. MASTROIANNI (Giovanni). Rec. di A. Labriola, Il carteggio conservato nel Fondo del Pane. *Belfagor*, 95, 2, p. 243-249.

6307. Max Weber politique et histoire. *Rev. Eur. Sci. Soc.*, 95, 33, 101, p. 5-143 [Articles de G. DUPRAT, D. BEETHAM, C. COLLIOT-THELENE, S. BREUER, F. CHAZEL, W. KLER, P. ROSSI, J. M. VINCENT, H. BRUHNS, F. DRAUS]

6308. MENN (Stephen Philip). Plato on God as nous. Carbondale, Southern Illinois U.P., 95, XIII-86 p. (The Journal of the history of philosophy monograph series).

6309. MENNINGHAUS (Winfried). Walter Benjamins Theorie der Sprachmagie. Frankfurt am Main, Suhrkamp, 95, 282 p.

6310. Métaphysique (La) de Leibniz. Numéro spécial de la Revue de métaphysique et de morale. 95, 100, 1 [contiene: COUTURAT (Louis). Sur la métaphysique de Leibniz, p. 5-7. – LEIBNIZ (G.W.). Primae veritates, p. 7-30. – RAUZY (Jean-Baptiste). La conception leibnizienne de l'ordre, p. 31-48. – FICHANT (Michel). De la puissance à l'action, p. 49-82. – ZARKA (Yves-Charles). Leibniz et le droit subjectif, p. 83-94. – DE BOUZON (Frédéric). L'harmonie: métaphysique et phénomenalité, p. 95-120. DUCHESNAU (François). Leibniz et la méthode de la science, p. 121-24. – ROBINET (André). Leibniz: le meilleur des mondes par la balance de l'Europe, p. 125-27. SENTIS (Laurent). Saint Thomas d'Aquin et le mal, foi chrétienne et Théodicée, p. 127-30].

6311. MILLET (Olivier). La première réception des Essais de Montaigne (1580–1640). Paris, Champion, 95, 249 p.

6312. MITCHELL (Joshua). The fragility of freedom: Tocqueville on religion, democracy and the American future. Chicago a. London, University of Chicago Press, 95, XIII-273 p.

6313. MONTAGUE (Phillip). Punishment as societal-defense. London a. Lanham, Rowman & Littlefield, 95, XIV-175 p. (Studies in social, political and legal philosophy).

6314. MORGAN (Nicole). Le Sixième Continent: «L'Utopie» de Thomas More, nouvel espace épistémologique. Paris, Librairie Philosophique J. Vrin, 95, 172 p. (De Pétrarque à Descartes, 59).

6315. MORRISON (James C.), SCHULTZ (Johann). Exposition of Kant's critique of pure reason. Ottawa, University of Ottawa Press, 95, XXXII-216 p. (Collection Philosophica, 47).

6316. NAMOWICZ (Tadeusz). Johann Gottfried Herder. Z zagadnień przełomu oświecenia w Niemczech w drugiej połowie XVIII wieku. (Questions du tournant de l'époque des lumières en Allemagne dans la deuxième moitié du XVIIIe s.). Olsztyn, [s. n.], 95, 183 p. (Deutsche Zsfassung). (Ośrodek Badań Nauk. im. Wojciecha Kętrzyńskiego. Bibl. Olsztyńska, 29).

6317. NEGRETTO (Gabriel L.). ¿Qué es el decisionismo? Reflexiones en torno a la doctrina política de Carl Schmitt. Rev. Mexicana Cien. Pol., 95, 40, 161, p. 49-74.

6318. NEUJAHR (Philip J.). Kant's idealism. Macon, Mercer U.P., 95, VIII-134 p.

6319. OGONOWSKI (Zbigniew) La liberté de citoyen et la liberté religieuse dans la philosophie politique en Pologne au XVIIe siècle. Odrodzenie i Reformacja w Polsce, 95, 39, p. 155-162.

6320. PALMER (Bryan). La teoría crítica, el materialismo histórico y el supuesto fin del marxismo: retorno a la miseria de la teoría. Entrepasados, 95, 4, 9, p. 161-187.

6321. PATTEN (A.). Hegel's justification of private property. Hist. Polit. Thou., 95, 16, 4, p. 576-600.

6322. PATZOLD (Detlev). Spinoza, Aufklärung, Idealismus: die Substanz der Moderne. Frankfurt am Main a. New York, P. Lang, 95, 212 p. (Philosophie und Geschichte der Wissenschaften, 29).

6323. PIEROTTI (Piero). Prima di Machiavelli: Filarete e Francesco di Giorgio, consiglieri del principe. Pisa, Pacini, 95, 181 p. (Ecostoria, 6).

6324. PIWKO (Stanisław). La guerre juste selon André Frycz Modrzewski. Odrodzenie i Reformacja w Polsce, 95, 39, p. 51-54.

6325. PÖGGELER (Otto). Ein Ende der Geschichte? Von Hegel zu Fukuyama. Opladen, Westdeutscher Verlag, 95, 38 p. (Vorträge der Nordrhein-Westfälische Akademie der Wissenschaften. Geisteswissenschaften, 332).

6326. POULAKOS (John). Sophistical rhetoric in classical Greece. Columbia, University of South Carolina Press, 95, xiv-220 p. (Studies in rhetoric/communication).

6327. POZZO (Giovanni Maria). La vita e la storia come tensione etica nella VII lettera di Platone. Filosofia oggi, 95, 18, p. 9-30.

6328. RAIO (Giulio). Simbolismo tedesco: Kant, Cassirer, Szondi. Napoli, Bibliopolis, 95, 148 p. (Saggi bibliopolis, 51).

6329. Realismo antirealismo: aspetti del dibattito epistemologico contemporaneo. A cura di Alessandro PAGNINI. Scandicci, La nuova Italia, 95, 235 p. (Biblioteca di cultura, 201).

6330. REDHEAD (Brian). Plato to NATO. Studies in political thought. London, Penguin-BBC Books, 95, 222 p.

6331. REEVE (C. D. C.), COHEN (S. Marc), CURD (Patricia). Readings in ancient Greek philosophy: from Thales to Aristotle. Indianapolis a. Cambridge, Hackett, 95, XII-786 p.

6332. REINALTER (Helmut). Die österreichischen Jakobiner in mitteleuropäischem Zusammenhang. Österr. i. Gesch. u. Lit., 95, 39, 5b-6, p. 343-356.

6333. REINHARDT (Volker). Machiavellis helvetische Projektion. Neue Überlegungen zu einem alten Thema. Revue suisse d'histoire, 95, 45, 3, p. 301-329.

6334. REQUATE (Angela). Die Logik der Moralität in Hegels Philosophie des Rechts. Cuxhaven u. Dartford, Traude Junghans Verlag, 95, 126 p., (Hochschulschriften Philosophie, 19).

6335. Rise (The) of modern philosophy: the tension between the new and traditional philosophies from Machiavelli to Leibniz. Ed. by Tom SORELL. Oxford, Clarendon Press, 95, VIII-352 p.

6336. ROBERTS (David). Una nuova interpretazione del pensiero di Croce: lo storicismo crociano e il pensiero contemporaneo. Pisa, Istituti editoriali e poligrafici internazionali, 95, 125 p. (Idee e storia, 4).

6337. ROBINSON (T. M.). Plato's psychology. Phoenix, Toronto a. London, University of Toronto Press, 95, XXXII-202 p.

6338. ROCKER (Stephen). Hegel's rational religion: the validity of Hegel's argument for the identity in content of absolute religion and absolute philosophy. Madison a. London, Fairleigh Dickinson U.P. 95, 222 p.

6339. ROLLET (Jacques). Raymond Aron et la théorie du politique. *Pouvoirs*, 95, 73, p. 159-176.

6340. ROMANINI (Claudia). Antonio Labriola. Roma, Prospettiva, 95, 157 p.

6341. RUMMEL (Erika). The humanist-scholastic debate in the Renaissance and Reformation. Cambridge a. London, Harvard U. P., 95, IX-249 p. (Harvard historical studies, 120).

6342. SAATKAMP (Herman J.). Rorty and pragmatism: the philosopher responds to his critics. Nashville, Vanderbilt U.P., 95, XVI-258 p. (The Vanderbilt library of American philosophy).

6343. SASSO (Gennaro). Di Gentile, di Heidegger e della loro reciproca conoscenza. Documenti e aneddoti. *Cultura*, 95, 34, p. 35-46. – IDEM. Filosofia e idealismo. Vol. 2. Giovanni Gentile, Napoli, Bibliopolis, 95, 650 p. (Saggi Bibliopolis, 50). [contiene: L'atto, il tempo, la morte, p. 53-163; La questione dell'astratto e del concreto, p. 165-381; Gentile e Dante, p. 487-537; Glosse marginali di Giovanni Gentile a libri di Benedetto Croce, p. 539-611]. – IDEM. Gentile e il nazionalsocialismo. *Cultura*, 95, 34, p. 5-22.

6344. SAZBÓN (José). 'Crisis del marxismo': un antecedente fundador. *Estudios Sociales*, 95, 5, 8, p. 9-29.

6345. SCHARFF (Robert C.). Comte after positivism. Cambridge, New York, Cambridge U.P., 95, XVI-227 p. (Modern European philosophy).

6346. SCHERER (Irmgard). The crisis of judgment in Kant's three critiques: in search of a science of aesthetics. New York, Lang, 95, X-241 p. (New studies in aesthetics, 16).

6347. SEARS REYNOLDS (Jayne). Plato in Renaissance England. Dordrecht – London, Kluwer Academic Publishers, 95, XX-197 p. (Archives internationales d'histoire des idées = International archives of the history of ideas, 141).

6348. SERTL (Franz). Die Freidenkerbewegung in Österreich im zwanzigsten Jahrhundert. Wien, WUV-Univ.-Vlg, 95, VII-410 p. (ill., Karten, Graph. Darstellungen). (Dissertationen der Universität Wien, 5).

6349. SIMONS (Jon). Foucault and the political. London a New York, Routledge, 95, 152 p.

6350. SNYDER (Lee R.). The development of cognitive synthesis in Immanuel Kant and Edmund Husserl. Lewiston a. Lampeter, Mellen, 95, VI-322 p. (Studies in the history of philosophy, 36).

6351. SOTNAK (Eric). Primary and secondary divine decrees in the Leibniz-Arnaul correspondence. *Studia leibnitiana*, 95, 27, p. 85-134.

6352. STERBA (James P.). Social and political philosophy: classical western texts in feminist and multicultural perspectives. Belmont a. London, Wadswort, 95, XIV-539 p.

6353. STILLMAN (Robert E.). The new philosophy and universal languages in seventeenth-century England: Bacon, Hobbes, and Wilkins. Lewisburg, London a. Cranbury, Bucknell U.P., 95, 359 p.

6354. THOMAS MORE. Utopia. Latin text and English translation. Ed. by George M. LOGAN, Robert M. ADAMS a. Clarence H. MILLER. Cambridge, Cambridge U. P., 95, XLVI-290 p.

6355. TILLIETTE (Xavier). Recherches sur l'intuition intellectuelle de Kant à Hegel. Paris, Vrin, 95, 294 p. (Bibliothèque d'histoire de la philosophie. Nouvelle série).

6356. TIMMERMANS (Benoit). La résolution des problèmes de Descartes à Kant: l'analyse à l'age de la révolution scientifique. Paris, Presses Universitaires de France, 95, X-319 p. (Interrogation philosophique).

6357. TINGUELY (F.). Jean de Léry et les vestiges de la pensée analogique. *Bibliothèque d'Humanisme et Renaissance*, 95, 57, 1, p. 25-44.

6358. TORRANCE (John). Karl Marx's theory of ideas. Cambridge, Cambridge U. P., 95, 433 p.

6359. TRAPPE (Tobias). Zur Vorgeschichte der "transzendentalen Erfahrung". *Archiv für Begriffsgeschichte*, 95, 38, p. 178-200.

6360. TURI (Gabriele). Giovanni Gentile. Una biografia. Firenze, Giunti, 95, 544 p.

6361. TVARDOVSKAJA (Valentina A.), ITENBERG (Boris S.). Fridrikh Éngel's i Petr Tkačev: spor i soglasie. (Frederick Engels and Pytotr Tkačev: dispute and accord). *Nov. novejš. Ist.*, 95, 6, p. 103-120.

6362. UJMA (Christina). Ernst Blochs Konstruktion der Moderne aus Messianismus und Marxismus: Erörterungen mit Berücksichtigung von Lukàcs und Benjamin. Stuttgart, M & P, 95, 338 p.

6363. VERSTRAETEN (Pierre), FRANCO (Daniel). Hegel aujourd'hui. Paris, Vrin, 95, 232 p. (Annales de l'Institut de philosophie et de sciences morales, Université libre de Bruxelles)

6364. VISENTIN (Mauro). Ancora su Heidegger e il nazionalsocialismo. *Cultura*, 95, 34, p. 23-34.

6365. VITALE (Ermanno). La lettura diderotiana di Hobbes nell'Encyclopédie. *Pens. Pol.*, 95, 28, 3, p. 384-406.

6366. WALKER (John), SCHNEIDER (Helmut). History, spirit and experience: Hegel's conception of the historical task of philosophy in his age. Frankfurt am Main a. New York, Lang, 95, 179 p. (Hegeliana. Studien und Quellen zu Hegel und zum Hegelianismus, 2).

6367. WALTER (Stephan). Demokratisches Denken zwischen Hegel und Marx: die politische Philosophie Arnold Ruges: eine Studie zur Geschichte der Demokratie in Deutschland. Düsseldorf, Droste, 95, 421 p. (Beiträge zur Geschichte des Parlamentarismus und der politischen Parteien, 104).

6368. WARD (James F.). Heidegger's political thinking. Amherst, University of Massachusetts Press, 95, XXX-312 p.

6369. WEISSER-LOHMANN (Elisabeth), JAMME (Christoph). Politik und Geschichte: zu den Intentionen von G.W.F. Hegels Reformbill-Schrift. Bonn, Bouvier, 95, 320 p. (Hegel-Studien. Beiheft, 35).

6370. WICHT (Bernard). L'idée de milice et le modèle suisse dans la pensée de Machiavel. Lausanne, L'Age d'Homme, 95, 243 p.

6371. WLADIKA (Michael). Kant in Hegels 'Wissenschaft der Logik'. Frankfurt am Main, P. Lang, 95, XV-788 p. (Europäische Hochschulschriften. Reihe 20, Philosophie, 471).

6372. WOLFF-METTERNICH (Brigitta-Sophie von). Die Überwindung des mathematischen Erkenntnisideals: Kants Grenzbestimmung von Mathematik und Philosophie. Berlin, de Gruyter, 95, XII-225 p. (Quellen und Studien zur Philosophie, 39).

6373. WORTHINGTON (Glenn). Michael Oakeshott on life: waiting with Godot. *History of political thought*, 95, 16, p. 105-19.

6374. WRIGHT (Charles W.), HONNETH (Axel). The fragmented world of the social: essays in social and political philosophy. Albany, State University of New York Press, 95, XXV-343 p. (SUNY series in social and political thought).

6375. WYCZAŃSKI (Andrzej). Entre la moralisation et la vie politique [XVIe s.]. *Odrodzenie i Reformacja w Polsce*, 95, 39, p. 79-82.

Cf. n°s 1174-1231, 1512, 1513, 1519, 5647

§ 6. **Exakte Wissenschaften. Technik, Naturwissenschaften und Medizin.**

** 6376. Archivi (Gli) per la storia della scienza e della tecnica. Atti del convegno internazionale, Desenzano del Garda, 4–8 giugno 1991. Roma, Ministero per i Beni Culturali e Ambientali, Ufficio Centrale per i beni archivistici, 95, 2 vol., 732 p., 594 p. (Publicazioni degli archivi di Stato. Saggi, 36).

6377. ADAMSON (Donald). Blaise Pascal: mathematician, physicist and thinker about God. Basingstoke a. New York, Macmillan a. Martin's Press, 95, XII-297 p. (ill.).

6378. ANGLIN (W. S.), LAMBEK (Joachim). The heritage of Thales. New York, Springer-Verlag, 95, X-327 p. (Undergraduate texts in mathematics. Readings in mathematics).

6379. BALAKIER (Ann Stewart), BALAKIER (James J.). The spatial infinite at Greenwich in works by Christopher Wren, James Thornhill, and James Thomson: the Newton connection. Lewiston a. Lampeter, Mellen, 95, VIII-139 p. (ill.).

6380. BATES (Don). Knowledge and the scholarly medical traditions. Cambridge a. New York, Cambridge U.P., 95, XII-369 p.

6381. BERETTA (Marco). Bibliotheca lavoisieriana: the catalogue of the library of Antoine Laurent Lavoisier. Firenze, Olschki, 95, 363 p. (ill.). (Biblioteca di Nuncius. Studi e testi, 16. Uppsala studies in history of science, 20).

6382. BERTOLA (Francesco). Imago mundi: la rappresentazione del cosmo attraverso i secoli. Cittadella, Biblos, 95, 231 p. (ill.).

6383. BIAGIOLI (Mario). Le prince et les savants: la civilité scientifique au XVIIe siècle. *Annales*, 95, 50, 6, p. 1417-1454.

6384. BONNER (Thomas Neville). Becoming a physician: medical education in Britain, France, Germany and the United States, 1750–1945. New York a. Oxford, Oxford U.P., 95, XII-412 p.

6385. BOWLER (Peter J.), LESTER (Joseph). E. Ray Lankester and the making of modern British biology. London, British Society for the History of Science, 95, 220 p. (British Society for the History of Science, 9).

6386. BRIGAGLIA (Aldo), CILIBERTO (C.). Italian algebraic geometry between the two world wars. Kingston, Queen's University Press, 95, VIII-223 p. (ill.). (Queen's papers in pure and applied mathematics, 100).

6387. BROMAN (Thomas). Rethinking professionalization: theory, practice, and professional ideology in eighteenth-century German medicine. *Journal of modern history*, 95, 67, 4, p. 835-872.

6388. BUCCIANTINI (Massimo). Contro Galileo: alle origini dell'affaire. Firenze, Olschki, 95, 218 p. (Biblioteca di Nuncius. Studi e testi, 19).

6389. Çağini Yakalayan Osmanlı Devleti'nde Modern Haberleşme ve Ulaşim Teknikleri. (Les techniques d'information et de communication modernes dans l'Etat Ottoman). Ed. par Ekmeleddin İHSANOGLU. İstanbul, 95, IRCICA Yayınları, 710 p. (Ilim Tarihi Kaynakları ve Araştırmaları Serisi, 6).

6390. CALINGER (Ronald). Classics of mathematics. Englewood Cliffs, Prentice Hall, 95, XXII-793 p. (ill.).

6391. CAROL (Anne). Histoire de l'eugénisme en France: les medecins et la procréation, XIXe–XXe siècle. Paris, Editions du Seuil, 95, 381 p. (L'univers historique).

6392. CAVALLO (Sandra). Charity and power in early modern Italy: benefactors and their motives in Turin, 1541–1789. Cambridge a. New York, Cambridge U.P., 95, XVI-280 p. (ill.). (Cambridge history of medicine).

6393. CHAST (François). Histoire contemporaine des médicaments. Paris, La Découverte, 95, 388 p.

6394. CHATTOPADHYAYA (D. P.). Mathematics, astronomy and biology in Indian tradition: some conceptual preliminaries. New Delhi, Munshiram Manoharlal, 95, 128 p. (PHISPC monograph series on history of philosophy, science, and culture in India, 3).

6395. Ciencia Ilustrada (De la) a la Ciencia Romántica. Actas de las II Jornadas sobre "España y las expediciones cientificas en América y Filipinas". Ed. por Alejandro R. DÍEZ TORRE, Tomás MALLO y Daniel PACHECO FERNANDEZ. Madrid, Ateneo de Madrid, Editorial Doce Calles, 95, 642 p. (Colección Actas).

6396. CIFOLETTI (Giovanna). La 'question' de l'algèbre. Mathématiques et rhétorique des hommes de droit dans la France du XVIe siècle. *Annales*, 95, 50, 6, p. 1385-1417.

6397. CLARK (Stephen R. L.). How to live forever. Science fiction and philosophy. London a. New York, Routledge, 95, 223 p.

6398. Concepts, theories, and rationality in the biological sciences: the Second Pittsburgh-Konstanz Colloquium in the Philosophy of Science, University of Pittsburgh, October 1–4, 1993. Ed. by Gereon WOLTERS a. James G. LENNOX, in collaboration with Peter MAC LAUGHLIN. Konstanz, UVK, Universitätsverlag Konstanz a. Pittsburgh, University of Pittsburgh Press, 95, XI-417 p. (Pittsburgh-Konstanz series in the philosophy and history of science).

6399. COSMACINI (Giorgio). Storia della medicina e della sanità [Rassegna]. *Physis*, 95, 32, p. 137-42.

6400. COSTAGLIOLA (Jacques). Faut-il brûler Darwin? Ou l'imposture darwinienne. Paris, L'Harmattan, 95, 283 p. (Conversciences).

6401. DAHL (Per). Svensk ingenjörskonst under stormaktstiden. Olof Rudbecks tekniska undervisning och praktiska verksamhet. (Swedish art of engineering during the Age of Greatness: Olof Rusbeck`s teaching of technology and technical enterprises). Uppsala, Institutionen för idé- och lärdomshistoria, Uppsala universitet, 95, 338 p. (Skrifter av Institutionen för idé- och lärdomshistoria, 14).

6402. DARMON (Pierre). Louis Pasteur (1822–1895). Paris, Fayard, 95, 430 p.

6403. DASTON (Lorraine J.). Classical probability in the Enlightenment. Princeton a. Chichester, Princeton U.P., 95, XVIII-423 p. (ill.).

6404. DAVIES (Paul Charles William). About time: Einstein's unfinished revolution. London, Viking, 95, 316 p. (ill.).

6405. DAVIS (Philip J.), HERSH (Reuben), MARCHISOTTO (Elena). The companion guide to The mathematical experience, study edition. Boston, Birkhauser, 95, VI-120 p. (ill.).

6406. DAVIS (Philip W.). Alternative linguistics: descriptive and theoretical modes. Amsterdam, Philadelphia, John Benjamins Publishing Company, 95, VI-325 p. (Rice University Department of Linguistics Symposium/Amsterdam studies in the theory and history of linguistic science, 4/102).

6407. DEAR (Peter Robert). Discipline and experience. The mathematical way in the scientific revolution. Chicago a. London, University of Chicago Press, 95, XII-290 p. (ill.). (Science and its conceptual foundations).

6408. DEARBORN (David S. P.), BAUER (Brian S.). Astronomy and empire in the ancient Andes: the cultural origins of Inca sky watching. Austin, University of Texas Press, 95, XVI-220 p. (ill.).

6409. Dedekind to Godel (From): essays on the development of the foundations of mathematics. Ed. by Jaakko HINTIKKA. Dordrecht a. Boston, Kluwer Academic Publishers, 95, IX-459 p. (Synthese library, 251).

6410. DELPIANO (Patrizia). Per una storia della divulgazione scientifica nel Piemonte del Settecento: il «Giornale scientifico, letterario e delle arti» (1789–1790). *Rivista storica italiana*, 95, 107, 1, p. 29-67.

6411. DENNETT (Daniel Clement). Darwin's dangerous idea: evolution and the meanings of life. London, Allen Lane, 95, 586 p. (ill.). (Penguin science).

6412. DEPEW (David J.), WEBER (Bruce H.). Darwinism evolving: systems dynamics and the genealogy of natural selection. Cambridge, MIT Press, 95, XIII-588 p.

6413. DIKOTTER (Frank). Sex, culture and modernity in China: medical science and the construction of sexual identities in the early republican period. London, Hurst, 95, X-233 p. (ill.).

6414. DINGWALL (Helen M.). Physicians, surgeons and apothecaries: medical practice in seventeenth-century Edinburgh. East Linton, Tuckwell Press, 95, 262 p. (ill.). (Scottish historical review monographs, 1).

6415. DIXON (Laurinda S.). Perilous chastity: women and illness in pre-Enlightenment art and medicine. Ithaca a. London, Cornell U.P., 95, XVI-297 p.

6416. DREXLER (Alois). Die Aktion und der Kalkül des Unendlichkleinen. Zur Propädeutik der Wissenschaftstheorie bei Leibniz und Blondel. Frankfurt am Main, Lang, 95, 248 p. (Europäische Hochschulschriften, 20/466).

6417. EAGLE (M. R.). Exploring mathematics through history. Cambridge, Cambridge U.P., 95, IV-108 p. (ill.).

6418. *Vacat.*

6419. EPSTEIN (Julia). Altered conditions: disease, medicine, and storytelling. New York a. London, Routledge, 95, X-275 p. (ill.).

6420. ETAYO-PIÑOL (M. A.). Le livre médical espagnol à Lyon aux XVIe et XVIIe siècles: l'apport espagnol aux progrès de la médecine. *Revue Historique*, 95, 119, 595, p. 45-58.

6421. FERRARO (Giovanni), PALLADINO (Franco). Il calcolo sublime di Eulero e Lagrange esposto col Metodo sintetico nel progetto di Nicolò Fergola. Napoli, La citta del sole, 95, 241 p. (ill.). (Istituto italiano per gli studi filosofici, Seminari di scienze. Nuova serie, 6).

6422. FEYERABEND (Paul K.). Killing time: the autobiography of Paul Feyerabend. Chicago a. London, University of Chicago Press, 95, 192 p. (ill.).

6423. Galileo a Padova, 1592–1610. Atti delle celebrazioni galileiane, 1592–1992 (Università degli studi di Padova, Celebrazioni del 4. Centenario, 7 dicembre 1991–7 dicembre 1992). Vol. 1. L'anno galileiano: 7 dicembre 1991–7 dicembre 1992. Vol. 2. Galileo e la cultura padovana: convegno a cura dell'Accademia Patavina di scienze, lettere e arti, Padova, 13–15 febbraio 1992. A cura di G. SANTANIELLO. Vol. 4. Tribute to Galileo in Padua: international symposium a cura dell'Università di Padova, Padova, 2–6 dicembre 1992. Vol. 5. Occasioni galileiane: conferenze e convegni, Padova, maggio–novembre, 1992. Trieste, LINT, 95, 4 vol., X-257 p., XVI-484 p., X-398 p., X-390 p. (ill.).

6424. Galileo Galilei e la cultura veneziana. Atti del Convegno di studio promosso nell'ambito delle celebrazioni galileiane indette dall'Università degli studi di Padova (1592–1992). Venezia, Istituto veneto di scienze, lettere ed arti, 95, 421 p. (ill.).

6425. GARCÍA PINILLA (I. J.). On the identity of «Juan de Javara, medico y philosopho». *Bibliothèque d'Humanisme et Renaissance*, 95, 57, 1, p. 45-66.

6426. GENTILCORE (David). Contesting illness in Early Modern Naples: miracolati, physicians and the congregation of rites. *Past and Present*, 95, 148, p. 117-148.

6427. GILMAN (Sander L.). Picturing health and illness: images of identity and difference. Baltimore a. London, Johns Hopkins U.P., 95, 200 p. (ill.).

6428. GINDIKIN (S. G.). Horloges, pendules et mecanique céleste: mathematiciens et physiciens de la Renaissance à nos jours. Paris, Diderot Editeur, 95, VI-233 p. (ill.). (La règle et le compas).

6429. GOLDSTEIN (Thomas). Dawn of modern science: from the ancient Greeks to the Renaissance. New York, Da Capo Press, 95, 320 p.

6430. GUILLEN (Michael). Five equations that changed the world: the power and poetry of mathematics. New York, Brown, 95, VIII-277 p.

6431. GUSTAFSON (Robert K.). James Woodrow (1828–1907): scientist, theologian, intellectual leader. Lewiston a. Lampeter, Mellen, 95, XX-303 p. (Studies in American religion, 61).

6432. HAHN (Robert A.). Sickness and healing: an anthropological perspective. New Haven a. London, Yale U.P., 95, VIII-327 p.

6433. HALL (Lesley A.). 'Disinterested enthusiasm for sexual misconduct': the British society for the study of sex psychology, 1913–47. *Journal of Contemporary History*, 95, 30, 4, p. 665-686.

6434. HINTIKKA (Jaakko). From Dedekind to Gödel: essays on the development of the foundations of mathematics. Dordrecht, Kluwer Academic Publishers, 95, X-459 p. (Synthese library, 251).

6435. Hochgeehrter Herr Professor! Innig geliebter Louis! Ludwig Boltzmann – Henriette von Aigentler. Briefwechsel. Hrsg. v. Dieter FLAMM. Wien, Köln u. Weimar, Böhlau, 95, 329 p. (ill.). (Beiträge zur Wissenschaftsgeschichte und Wissenschaftsforschung, 2).

6436. HOLMES (Frederic L.). Les limites de la révolution chimique de Lavoisier. *Revue d'histoire des sciences*, 95, 48, p. 9-48.

6437. HØYRUP (Jens). On the mensuration of the "Liber mensurationum". Berlin, Max-Planck-Institut für Wissenschaftsgeschichte, 95, 36 p. (Preprint / Max-Planck-Institut fur Wissenschaftsgeschichte, 13).

6438. İHSANOGLU (Ekmeleddin), GÜNERGUN (Feza). Modernleşme Çağinda Osmanlı Bilimi. (La science ottomane à l'époque de la modernisation). İstanbul, [s. n.], 95, 622 p.

6439. JAMES (Jamie). The music of the spheres: music, science, and the natural order of the universe. New York, Copernicus Press, 95, XV-262 p. (ill.).

6440. JUDSON (Horace Freeland). The eighth day of creation: makers of the revolution in biology. London, Penguin, 95, 686 p.

6441. JUTTE (Robert), WOODWARD (John). Coping with sickness: historical aspects of health care in a European perspective. Sheffield, European Association for the History of Medicine and Health Publications, 95, 224 p. (European Association for the History of Medicine and Health).

6442. KAMMINGA (Harmke), CUNNINGHAM (Andrew). The science and culture of nutrition, 1840–1940. Amsterdam a. Atlanta, Rodopi, 95, VII-344 p. (The Wellcome Institute series in the history of medicine).

6443. KITCHER (Philip). The advancement of science. Science without legend, objectivity without illusions. New York a. Oxford, Oxford U.P., 95, VIII-421 p.

6444. Księga jubileuszowa 50 – lecia Politechniki Wrocławskiej 1945–1995. (Livre d'or pour les cinquante ans d'activité du Politechnique de Wrocław.

6. EXAKTE WISSENSCHAFTEN. TECHNIK, NATURWISSENSCHAFTEN UND MEDIZIN

Réd. Ryszard CZOCH. Wrocław, Oficyna Wydawn. Polit. Wrocł., 95, 498 p. (phot., fig.).

6445. LACHMUND (Jens), STOLLBERG (Gunnar). Patientenwelten: Krankheit und Medizin vom späten 18. bis zum frühen 20. Jahrhundert im Spiegel von Autobiographien. Opladen, Leske u. Budrich, 95, 242 p.

6446. LAMB (Ursula). Cosmographers and pilots of the Spanish maritime empire. Aldershot, Variorum, 95, XII-331 p. (ill.). (Collected studies series, 499).

6447. LANGLEY (Harold D.). A history of medicine in the early U.S. Navy. Baltimore a. London, Johns Hopkins U.P., 95, XX-435 p. (ill.).

6448. LAPLACE (Pierre Simon, marquis de). Philosophical essay on probabilities. Trans. a. ann. by Andrew I. DALE. New York a. London, Springer, 95, XVIII-270 p. (Sources in the history of mathematics and physical sciences, 13).

6449. LEDERER (Susan E.). Subjected to science: human experimentation in America before the Second World War. Baltimore a. London, Johns Hopkins U.P., 95, XVI-192 p. (ill.). (The Henry E. Sigerist series in the history of medicine).

6450. LEE (Stephen J.), BROOMAN (Josh). Medicine and public health: 1450 to the present day. Harlow, Longman, 95, 112 p. (ill.). (Longman history project. Study in development).

6451. LESTER (Joseph). E. Ray Lankester and the making of modern British biology. With additional material by Peter J. BOWLER. [S.l.], British Society for the History of Science, 95, 220 p. (BSHS monographs, 9 [i.e. 10]).

6452. LEVERINGTON (David). A history of astronomy from 1890 to the present. London a. New York, Springer-Verlag, 95, XII-387 p.

6453. LEVINA (Elena Solomonovna), VAVILOV (N. I.), LYSENKO (T. D.), TIMOFEEV-RESOVSKII (H. V.). Biologiia v SSSR: istoriia i istoriografiia. (History of biology in USSR). Moskva, AIRO-"XX", 95, 157 p.

6454. MAC GUIRE (J. E.), MELIA (Trevor), KRIPS (Henry). Science, reason, and rhetoric. Pittsburgh a. Konstanz, University of Pittsburgh Press a. Universitätsverlag Konstanz, 95, XX-322 p. (ill.). (Pittsburgh-Konstanz series in the philosophy and history of science).

6455. MANCOSU (Paolo). The philosophy of mathematics and mathematical practice in the seventeenth century. New York, Oxford U.P., 95, VIII-275 p.

6456. MARTZLOFF (Jean-Claude). A history of Chinese mathematics. Berlin, Springer, 95, XXIV-485 p. (ill.).

6457. MAXWELL (James Clerk). The scientific letters and papers of James Clerk Maxwell. Vol. 2. 1862–1873. Ed. by P. M. HARMAN. Cambridge, Cambridge U. P., 95, XXX-999 p.

6458. MICALE (Mark S.). Approaching Hysteria: disease and its interpretations. Princeton, Princeton U. P., 95, 327 p.

6459. Vacat.

6460. NAISH (Emily). Promoting the medical and allied sciences: a short history of science at the BMA. London, British Medical Association, 95, VIII-47 p. (ill.). (British Medical Association Board of Science and Education).

6461. Nature, histoire, société: essais en hommage à Jacques Roger. Rassemblés et présentés par Claude BLANCKAERT, Jean-Louis FISCHER et Roselyne REY. Paris, Klincksieck, 95, 454 p.

6462. NDAYE (Pap). Du nylon et des bombes. Du Pont de Nemours, l'Etat américain et le nucléaire, 1930–1960. *Annales*, 95, 50, 1, p. 53-74.

6463. NEWMAN (William R.). The philosophers' egg: the theory and practice in the alchemy of Roger Bacon. *In*: Crisi dell'alchimia (Le) [Cf. n° 4318], p. 75-101.

6464. NUTTON (Vivian), PORTER (Roy). The history of medical education in Britain. Amsterdam, Rodopi, 95, X-379 p. (The Wellcome Institute series in the history of medicine, 30).

6465. PAMMER (Michael). Vom Beichtzettel zum Impfzeugnis. Beamte, Ärzte, Priester und die Einführung der Vaccination. *Österr. i. Gesch. u. Lit.*, 95, 39, 1, p. 11-29.

6466. Pauli-Jung-Dialog (Der) und seine Bedeutung für die moderne Wissenschaft. Hrsg. v. H. ATMANSPACHER, H. PRIMAS u. E. WERTENSCHLAG-BIRKHAUSER. Berlin, Springer, 95, VIII-365 p. (ill.).

6467. PERLMAN (James S.). Science without limits: toward a theory of interaction between nature and knowledge. Amherst, Prometheus Books, 95, 358 p. (ill.).

6468. PETZ-GRABENBAUER (Maria). Zu Leben und Werk von Nikolaus Joseph Freiherr von Jacquin. *Wien. Gesch.-Bl.*, 95, 50, 3, p. 121-150 (ill.).

6469. PIASECKA (Janina Ewa). Książka francuska w geografii polskiej (XVII wiek–połowa XX wieku). (Le livre français dans la géographie polonaise, XVIIe s.–moitié du XX^{e}s.). *Kwartalnik Historii Nauki i Technik*, 95, 40, 3, p. 129-144. [Eng. Summary].

6470. Vacat.

6471. RAMIREZ (Santiago), COHEN (R. S.). Mexican studies in the history and philosophy of science. Dordrecht a. London, Kluwer Academic Publishers, 95, XII-280 p. (ill.). (Boston studies in the philosophy of science, 172).

6472. REY (Roselyne). The history of pain. Cambridge a. London, Harvard U.P., 95, 394 p.

6473. Rivoluzioni nelle scienze della vita (Le). A cura di Guido CIMINO e Bernardino FANTINI. Firenze, Olschki, 95, 261 p. (ill.). (Biblioteca di "Physis", 3).

6474. ROSEN (Edward), HILFSTEIN (Erna). Copernicus and his successors. London, Hambledon Press, 95, X-244 p. (ill.).

6475. ROSENBERG (Charles E.). The care of strangers: the rise of America's hospital system. Baltimore a. London, Johns Hopkins U.P., 95, X-437 p.

6476. ROSSITER (Margaret W.). Women scientists in America: before affirmative action, 1940–1972. Baltimore a. London, Johns Hopkins U.P., 95, XVIII-584 p. (ill.).

6477. ROTHMAN (David J.), KICELUK (Stephanie A.), MARCUS (Steven). Medicine and Western civilization. New Brunswick, Rutgers U.P., 95, XII-442 p. (ill.).

6478. RUDERMAN (David B.). Jewish thought and scientific discovery in early modern Europe. New Haven a. London, Yale U.P., 95, XII-392 p. (ill.).

6479. Santé et société au Quebec XIXe–XXe siècles. Sous la dir. de Peter KEATING et Othmar KEEL. Montréal, [s. n.], 95, 272 p.

6480. Savants et l'épistémologie vers la fin du XIXe siècle (Les). Dir. par Marco PANZA e J. C. PONT. Paris, Blanchard, 95, 282 p.

6481. SAWDAY (Jonathan). The body emblazoned: dissection and the human body in Renaissance culture. London a New York, Routledge, 95, XII-327 p.

6482. SCHLEINER (Winfried). Medical Ethics in the Renaissance. Washington, Georgetown U. P., 95, 230 p.

6483. SCHRÖDER (Eberhard). Ein mathematisches Manuskript aus dem 15. Jahrhundert (Staatsbibliothek Bamberg Handschrift aus Inc. Typ. Ic 1 44). München, Institut für Geschichte der Naturwissenschaften, 95, 362 p. (facsims.). (Algorismus, 16).

6484. SCHULZE (Winfried). Der Stifterverband für die deutsche Wissenschaft 1920–1995. Unter Mitarbeit von Sven BERGMANN und Gerd HELM. Berlin, Akademie, 95, 388 p.

6485. SIEGEL (Daniel M.). Text and context in Maxwell's electromagnetic theory. *Physis*, 95, 32, p. 125-40.

6486. SILVERS (Robert B.). Hidden histories of science. New York, New York Review of Books, 95, VIII-193 p. (ill.).

6487. SJOBERG (Boris). Fran Euklides till Hilbert. Historien om matematikens utveckling under tvatusen ar. Abo, Abo akademis forlag, 95, X-238 p.

6488. Słownik biograficzny techników polskich. (Dictionnaire biographique des techniciens polonais). Réd. en chef Tadeusz SKARŻYŃSKI et Zbigniew SKOCZYŃSKI. P. 6 Warszawa, Federacja Stow. Nauk. – Techn., 95, 189 p.

6489. SOLOWAY (Richard A.). The 'Perfect contraceptive': eugenics and birth control research in Britain and America in the interwar years. *Journal of Contemporary History*, 95, 30, 4, p. 637-664.

6490. STANEK (Aleksander). Historia chirurgii w Uniwersytecie Stefana Batorego w Wilnie w latach 1919–1939. (Histoire de la chirurgie à l'Université "Stefan Batory" de Vilnius dans les années 1919–1939.). Gdańsk, Akad. Medyczna, 95, 135 p. (phot., fig.).

6491. STOLZ (Joachim). Whitehead und Einstein: wissenschaftsgeschichtliche Studien in naturphilosophischer Absicht. Frankfurt am Main, Lang, 95, 244 p.

6492. SUEUR (L.). Les psychiatres français du XIXe siècle face à la folie. *Revue Historique*, 95, 119, 596, p. 243-258.

6493. SZAREJKO (Piotr). Słownik lekarzy polskich XIX wieku. Studia. (Dictionnaire des médecins polonais du XIXe s. Etudes). T. 3. Warszawa, Semper, 95, 432 p. (phot.).

6494. *Vacat.*

6495. TATON (René), WILSON (Curtis). The General history of astronomy. Planetary astronomy from the Renaissance to the rise of astrophysics. Cambridge, Cambridge U.P., 95, XIV-281 p. (ill.).

6496. TODD (Jan). Colonial technology. Science and the transfer of innovation to Australia. Cambridge a. New York, Cambridge U.P., 95, XII-300 p. ill. (Studies in Australian history).

6497. TÖRÖK (Enikő). Egy XVIII. századi polihisztor: Mikoviny Sámuel. (Un polyhistor du XVIII siècle: Sámuel Mikoviny [1700–1750]). *Fons*, 95, 2, 1, p. 73-90.

6498. TROUILLOT (Michel-Rolph). Silencing the past: power and the production of history. Boston, Beacon Press, 95, XX-191 p.

6499. WALKER (Mark). Nazi science: myth, truth, and the German atomic bomb. New York, Plenum Press, 95, VIII-325 p.

6500. WEAVER (Jefferson Hane), MOTZ (Lloyd). The story of astronomy. New York a. London, Plenum Press, 95, VIII-387 p.

6501. WEISSMANN (Gerald). Democracy and DNA: American dreams and medical progress. New York, Hill and Wang, 95, XX-263 p.

6502. WERTHEIM (Margaret). Pythagoras' trousers: God, physics, and the gender wars. New York, Times Books/Random House, 95, VIII-279 p.

6503. WHITFIELD (Peter). The mapping of the Heavens. London, British Library, 95, X-134 p. (ill.).

6504. WIESING (Urban). "Kunst oder Wissenschaft?": Konzeptionen der Medizin in der deutschen Romantik. Stuttgart-Bad Cannstatt, Frommann-Holzboog, 95, 365 p. (Medizin und Philosophie, 1).

6505. WILSON (Adrian). The making of man-midwifery: childbirth in England 1660–1770. Cambridge, Harvard U.P., 95, XII-239 p. (ill.).

6506. WILSON (Catherine). The invisible world: early modern philosophy and the invention of the microscope. Princeton, Princeton U. P., 95, X-280 p. (Studies in intellectual history and the history of philosophy).

6507. WOLFSCHMIDT (Gudrun). Milchstrasse, Nebel, Galaxien: Strukturen im Kosmos von Herschel bis Hubble. München, Deutsches Museum, 95, 186 p. (ill.). (Abhandlungen und Berichte / Deutsches Museum. Neue Folge, 11).

6508. YIP (Ka-che). Health and national reconstruction in Nationalist China: the development of modern health services, 1928–1937. Ann Arbor, Association for Asian Studies, 95, X-289 p. (Monograph and occasional paper series, 50).

6509. ZABUSKY (Stacia E.). Launching Europe. An ethnography of European cooperation in space science. Princeton, Princeton U. P., 95, 261 p.

6510. ZIMMERMANN (Völker). Paracelsus: das Werk, die Rezeption. Beiträge des Symposiums zum 500. Geburtstag von Theophrastus Bombastus von Hohenheim, genannt Paracelsus (1493–1541) an der Universität Basel am 3. und 4. Dezember 1993. Stuttgart, Steiner Verlag, 95, 227 p. (ill., facsim.).

6511. ZUIDERVAART (H. J.). Speculatie, wetenschap en vernunft: fysica en astronomie volgens Wytze Foppes Dongjuma (1707–1778), instrumentmaker te Leeuwarden. Ljouwert/Leeuwarden, Fryske Akademy, 95, 206 p. (ill., facsims, ports). (Fryske histoaryske rige, 12).

6512. ZWILLING (Robert). Natural sciences and human thought. Berlin a. New York, Springer-Verlag, 95, XII-228 p.

§ 7. Literatur.

a. Allgemeines

6513. BLOOM (Harold). The western canon. The books and schools of the ages. London, Macmillan, 1995, 578 p. (Papermac).

6514. BONN (Charles). Littératures des immigrations. Paris, L'Harmattan, 95, (Etudes littéraires maghrébines, 7-8).

6515. BOUNIN (Paule), CASALIS (Jacqueline). Les expressions littéraires françaises du Moyen âge, des origines à la fin du XIIe siècle. Paris, Ellipses-Marketing, 95, 125 p. (ill.).

6516. BULVER (Kathryn M.). La femme-demon, figurations de la femme dans la littérature fantastique. New York, Lang, 95, VIII-143 p. (Writing about women, 14).

6517. Comparare i comparatismi: la comparatistica letteraria oggi in Europa e nel mondo. A cura di Armando GNISCI e Franca SINOPOLI. Roma, Lithos, 95, 152 p. (Studi di letteratura comparata). [contiene: GNISCI (Armando). Introduzione, p. 9-13. – FRANCO CARVAHLAL (Tania). La letteratura comparata in America latina, p. 14-26. – IOSIHIKO (Kurtsukake). La letteratura comparata in Giappone, p. 27-36. – TIANZHEN (Xie), Le recenti tendenze della comparatistica letteraria cinese, p. 37-51. – DYSERINCK (Hugo), Il punto di vista sovranazionale dello studio letterario comparato e la sua applicazione all'imagologia, p. 52-66. – DURISIN (Dionyz), La comunità interletteraria: una categoria fondamentale del processo interletterario, p. 67-81. – PAL (Josef), L'Associazione Internazionale di letteratura comparata e i suoi lavori di storiografia letteraria, p. 82-88. – SUVIN (Darko), La letteratura comparata come prova di magia bianca, p. 89-98. – BADIN (Maria-Esther), Il pensiero letterario latino-americano, p. 99-122. – NERI (Francesca), La letteratura comparata e le teorie postcoloniali, p. 123-35. – SINOPOLI (Franca), La letteratura comparata nel dipartimento di italianistica de "La Sapienza" di Roma, p. 136-51].

6518. CONFIANT (Raphael), DAMOISON (David), LEBIELLE (Marcel). Les maîtres de la parole créole. Paris, Gallimard, 95, 201 p. (ill.).

6519. CSÓKÁS (László). A magyar írói foglalkozás kezdeteiről. (Des débuts de la profession d'écrivant en Hongrie). *Magyar könyvszle*, 95, 111, 3, p. 238-246.

6520. ENGEL (Vincent). La littérature des camps, la quête d'une parole juste, entre silence et bavardage. Louvain-la-Neuve, Les Lettres romanes, 95, 223 p. (Lettres romanes. Hors serie, 95).

6521. FELSENSTEIN (Frank). Anti-semitic stereotypes. A paradigm of otherness in English popular culture, 1660–1830. Baltimore a. London, Johns Hopkins U.P., 95, XVIII-350 p (ill.). (Johns Hopkins Jewish studies).

6522. GARMS-CORNIDES (Elisabeth). Tradizioni letterarie e attualità politica nella polemica antiaustriaca in Italia tra Sette- e Ottocento. *Röm. Hist. Mitt.*, 95, 37, p. 353-375.

6523. GUITTON (Edouard). La culpabilité dans la littérature française. Boulogne, L'ADIREL, 95, 248 p. (Travaux de litterature, 8).

6524. HUYSSEN (Andreas). Twilight memories, marking time in a culture of amnesia. New York a. London, Routledge, 95, X-292p. (ill.).

6525. JOUBERT (Jean-Louis), BAMBONEYEHO (Venant). Littératures francophones d'Afrique Centrale. Paris, Nathan, 95, 255 p. (ill.).

6526. Littérature maghrébine et littérature mondiale. Actes du colloque de Heidelberg, Octobre 1993. Ed. par Charles BONN et Arnold ROTHE. Würzburg, Königshausen u. Neumann, 95, 196 p.

6527. LIZ 2.0 Letteratura italiana Zanichelli. A cura di Eugenio PICCHI. CD-ROM dei testi della letteratura italiana. CD-ROM manuale di riferimento. Bologna, Zanichelli, 95.

6528. METZIDAKIS (Stamos). Difference unbound, the rise of pluralism in literature and criticism. Amsterdam, Rodopi, 95, 268 p. (Faux titre, 94).

6529. MITTERAND (Henri), PELLETIER (Alexis). Dictionnaire des oeuvres du XXe siecle, littérature française et francophone. Paris, Dictionnaires Le Robert, 95, XII-621 p. (Les usuels).

6530. ORLANDI (Giovanni). Perché non possiamo non dirci lachmanniani. *Filologia medioevale*, 95, 2, p. 1-42.

6531. Patrimoine littéraire européen. Anthologie en langue française. Dir. Par Jean-Claude POLET. T. 7. Etablissement des genres et retour du tragique (1515–1616). Bruxelles, De Boeck-Université, 95,XXXVIII-944 p.

6532. PIUS NGANDU (Nkashama). Le livre littéraire, bibliographie de la littérature du Congo. Paris, L'Harmattan, 95, 207 p. (Critiques littéraires).

6533. PUGLIESE (Silvia). Intorno alla retorica del testo elettronico. *Schede umanistiche*, 95, 1, p. 239-43.

6534. TRUNZ (Erich). Deutsche Literatur zwischen Späthumanismus und Barock, acht Studien. München, Beck, 95, 391 p. (ill.).

6535. Vier Literaturen der Schweiz (Die). Hrsg. v. Iso CAMARTIN. Zürich, Pro Helvetia Schweizer Kulturstiftung, 95, 161 p.

6536. WALL (Renate). Lexikon deutschsprachiger Schriftstellerinnen im Exil, 1933–1945. Freiburg i. Br, Kore, 95, 2 vol., [s. p.].

b. Renaissance.

* 6537. Bibliographie internationale de l'Humanisme et de la Renaissance. 1992 [1991. Cf. Bibl. 94, n° 6304] Ed. par Pierre DIDO et Claire MONNIER. Genève, Droz, 95, 504 p.

6538. ANDREWS (Lew). Story and space in Renaissance art. The rebirth of continuous narrative. Cambridge, Cambridge U. P., 95, XIV-188 p. (ill.).

6539. ARETINO (Pietro). I poemi cavallereschi. A cura di Danilo ROMEI. Roma, Salerno, 95, 456 p. (ill.). (Edizione nazionale delle opere di Pietro Aretino, 2).

6540. BALSAMO (J.). Les origines parisiennes du Tesoro politico (1589). *Bibliothèque d'Humanisme et Renaissance*, 95, 57, 1, p. 7-24.

6541. BANDERIER (C.). Le poème de la Création et le problème de son attribution à Agrippa D'Aubigné. *Bibliothèque d'Humanisme et Renaissance*, 95, 57, 3, p. 585-598.

6542. BELIN (Christian). L'œuvre de Pierre Charron (1541–1603). Littérature et théologie de Montaigne à Port-Royal. Paris, Champion, 95, 360 p. (Bibliothèque Littéraire de la Renaissance, 3, 31).

6543. BENASSI (Silvano). Gli antichi e le origini del moderno: motivi estetici tra letteratura e arti figurative. Bologna, CLUEB, 95, 222 p. (Relazioni e significati, 2).

6544. BENSON (Edward). Money and magic in Montaigne: the historicity of the Essais. Genève, Droz, 95, 197 p. (Travaux d'Humanisme et Renaissance, 295).

6545. BERNARDO TASSO. Rime. Vol. 1. A cura di Domenico CHIODO. Vol. 2. A cura di Vercingetorige MARTIGNONE. Torino, Edizioni Res, 95, 2 vol., 430 p., 430 p.

6546. BIANCARDI (Giovanni). L'ipotesi di un ordinamento calendariale del 'Canzoniere' petrarchesco. *Giornale storico della letteratura italiana*, 95, 172, p. 1-55.

6547. *Vacat.*

6548. BLANCHARD (Scott W.). Scholars' bedlam: Menippean satire in the Renaissance. Lewisburg, Bucknell U.P., 95, 205 p.

6549. BRAGANTINI (Renzo), FORNI (Pier Massimo). Lessico critico decameroniano. Torino, Bollati Boringhieri, 95, 498 p. (Studi e strumenti).

6550. BRAYBROOK (Jean). Space and time in Remy Belleau's 'Bergerie'. *Bibliothèque d'Humanisme et Renaissance*, 95, 67, p. 369-80.

6551. BURKE (Peter). The Fortunes of the «Courtier». The European reception of Castiglione's «Cortegiano». Cambridge, Polity Press, 95, 210 p. (ill.).

6552. CAPPELLO (Giovanni). Per un ordinamento delle 'Rime' di Dante. *Letture classensi*, 95, 24, p. 11-51.

6553. COLEMAN (Dorothy Gabe). Montaigne, quelques anciens et l'écriture des Essais. Paris, Champion, 95, 154 p. (Etudes montaignistes, 20).

6554. CRUZ (Anne J.). Los "Trionfi" en España: la poética petrarquista, la teoría de la traducción y la lengua vernácula en el siglo XVI. *Anuario de estudios medievales*, 95, 25, 1, p. 287-286.

6555. DANIELL (David). The language of Hamlet, the Hilda Hulme memorial lecture, 29 November 1994. London, University of London Press, 95, 26 p. (The Hilda Hulme memorial lecture).

6556. DI BENEDETTO (Arnaldo). Due note sulle rime del Tasso. *Giornale storico della letteratura italiana*, 95, 112, p. 261-70.

6557. DRUSI (Riccardo). La lingua 'cortigiana romana'. Note su un aspetto della questione cinquecentesca della lingua. Venezia, Il cardo, 95, 236 p. (Ricerche, Università degli studi di Venezia. Facoltà di lettere e filosofia).

6558. GAREFFI (Andrea). Ludovico Ariosto. Firenze, Lisciani e Giunti, 95, 128 p.

6559. GODMAN (Peter). Florentine humanism between Poliziano and Machiavelli. *Rinascimento*, 95, 25, p. 67-122.

6560. GURR (Andrew), CLEMENCE (Dominic). William Shakespeare, the extraordinary life of the most successful writer of all time. London, Harper Collins, 95, 192 p. (ill.).

6561. Jacques Lefèvre d'Etaples (1450?–1536). Actes du colloque d'Etaples, les 7 et 8 novembre 1992, organisé à l'initiative de la ville d'Etaples-sur-Mer avec la collaboration de l'Association des Professeurs d'Histoire et de Géographie. Dir. par Jean-François PERNOT. Paris, Champion, 95, 290 p.

6562. JAMES (Henry), WALKER (Greg). The politics of Gorboduc. *English Historical Review*, 95, 110, 435, p. 109-121.

6563. JARVIS (Simon). Scholars and gentlemen. Shakespearean textual criticism and representations of scholarly labour, 1725–1765. Oxford a. New York, Clarendon Press a. Oxford U.P., 95, X-234 p.

6564. JONES (John). Shakespeare at work. Oxford a. New York, Clarendon Press, 95, 292 p.

6565. KALLENDORF (Craig). From Virgil to Vida: the poeta theologus in Italian renaissance commentary. *Journal of the history of ideas*, 95, 56, 1, p. 41-62.

6566. LANIER (Douglas). 'Paradise regained' and the return of expressed. *Criticism*, 95, 37, p. 187-212.

6567. LIPPI BIGAZZI (V.). I commenti veneti all'«Ecerinis» del Musato e all'«Ars amandi» di Ovidio e i loro autori. *Italia medievale e umanistica*, 95, 38, p. 21-140.

6568. LOETSCHES (Andreas). Syntaktische Prestigesignale in der deutsche Prosa des 16. Jahrhundert. *Daphnis. Zeitschrift für Mittelere Deutsche Literatur*, 95, 24, p. 17-53.

6569. MAC LAUGHLIN (Martin L.). Literary imitation in the Italian renaissance. The theory and practice of literary imitation in Italy from Dante to Bembo. Oxford, Clarendon Press a. New York, Oxford U. P., 95, VIII-314 p. (Oxford modern languages and literature monographs). [Cf. n° <choice> 6121.]

6570. MARIOTTI (Scevola). Scritti medioevali e umanistici. A cura di Silvia RIZZO. Roma, Ed. di storia e letteratura, 95, XII-416 p.

6571. MARTELLI (Mario). Sul destinatario della canzone 'Spirito gentile' di Francesco Petrarca. *Medioevo e Rinascimento*, 95, 31, p. 91-120.

6572. MIRALLES MALDONADO (J. C.). Gabriele Faerno (1510–1561): la Métrica como disciplina auxiliar de la crítica textual. *Bibliothèque d'Humanisme et Renaissance*, 95, 57, 2, p. 407-418.

6573. MONFASANI (John). Byzantine scholars in Renaissance Italy: Cardinal Bessarion and other emigrés, selected essays. Aldershot, Variorum, 95, XII-351 p. (Collected studies series, cs485).

6574. NORLAND (Howard B.). Drama in early Tudor Britain, 1485–1558. Lincoln, University of Nebraska Press, 95, XXIX-394 p.

6575. O'BRIEN (John). Anacreon Redivivus. A study of Anacreontic translation in mid-sixteenth-century France. Ann Arbor, University of Michigan Press, 95, [s. p.].

6576. PANTIN (Isabelle). La Poésie du ciel en France dans la seconde moitié du seizième siècle. Genève, Droz, 95, 555 p. (Travaux d'Humanisme et Renaissance, 297).

6577. PASQUIER (Etienne). Pourparlers. Ed. par Béatrice SAYHI-PERIGOT. Paris, Champion, 95, 619 p. (Textes de la Renaissance, 7).

6578. PEACH (T.). Charles Estienne revu et augmenté: Le Paradoxe du plaider (1553) et le Deux Plaidoyers d'entre Monsieur Proces et Monsieur de Bon Accord (1570). *Bibliothèque d'Humanisme et Renaissance*, 95, 57, 1, p. 101-110.

6579. PETOLETTI (M.). «Ad utilitatem volentium studere in ipsa Comedia»: il commento dantesco di Alberico di Rosciate. *Italia medievale e umanistica*, 95, 38, p. 141-216.

6580. PHILIPPY (Patricia Berrahou). Love's remedies: recantation and Renaissance lyric poetry. Lewisburg, Bucknell U. P. a. London, Associated University Presses, 95, 261 p.

6581. PHILLIPS (Graham), KEATMAN (Martin). The Shakespeare conspiracy. London, Arrow, 95, VI-230 p (ill.).

6582. PICONE (Michelangelo). Il romanzo di Alatiel. *Studi sul Boccaccio*, 95, 23, p. 197-218.

6583. PREISIG (Florian). L'intertexte virgilien et ses enjeux dans 'L'infer' de Marot. *Bibliothèque d'Humanisme et Renaissance*, 95, 67, p. 569-84.

6584. REBHORN (Wayne A.). The emperor of men's mind: literature and the Renaissance discourse of rhetoric. Ithaca, Cornell U.P., 95, XVIII-276 p. (Rethoric and Society).

6585. Recueil de Farces (1450–1550). Tome 9. Textes établis, annotés et commentés par André TISSIER. Gènève, Droz, 95, 414 p. (Textes littéraires français, 456).

6586. SALWA (Piotr). Modelli letterali al servizio della politica – esempi novellistici. *Odrodzenie i Reformacja w Polsce*, 95, 39, p. 5-17.

6587. SMITH (Malcom C.). Ronsard and Du Bellay versus Bèze. Allusiveness in Renaissance literary texts. Genève, Droz, 95, 142 p. (Etudes de Philologie et d'Histoire, 48).

6588. Vacat.

6589. Théâtre français de la Renaissance. La Comédie à l'époque d'Henri II et de Charles IX. Première série. Vol. 7. 1561-1568. Firenze, Olschki et Paris, PUF, 95, 341 p.

6590. VELLI (Giuseppe). Petrarca e Boccaccio. Tradizione, memoria e scrittura. Padova, Antenore, 95, XII-276 p.

6591. VITI (Paolo), LELLI (Fabrizio). Pico e Poliziano. (Discussioni). *Archivio storico italiano*, 95, 153, 564, p. 369-386.

c. Klassizismus.

6592. BENREKASSA (Georges). Le langage des Lumières, concepts et savoir de la langue. Paris, Presses universitaires de France, 95, 353 p. (Ecriture).

6593. BRUNI (Arnaldo). Per la fortuna di Shakespeare. *Studi di filologia italiana*, 95, 53, p. 223-48.

6594. CERETTI (Marinella). Alessandro Verri fra illuminismo, preromanticismo e neoclassicismo. L'esempio delle tragedie storico-politiche. *Rivista storica italiana*, 95, 107, 1, p. 160-178.

6595. DENIS (Anne). Un testo inedito di Pietro Giannone. *Archivio storico italiano*, 95, 153, 566, p. 709-762.

6596. FLECK (Stephen H.). Music, dance, and laughter, comic creation in Molière's comedy-ballets. Paris a. Seattle, 95, 231 p. (Papers on French Seventeenth Century Literature, 88).

6597. GABRIELI (Vittorio). John Donne, Thomas More e Roma. *Rivista di letterature moderne e comparate*, 95, 48, p. 235-62.

6598. GAINES (James F.), KOPPISCH (Michael S.). Approaches to teaching Molière's Tartuffe and other plays. New York, Modern Language Association of America, 95, XII-166 p. (ill.). (Modern Language Association of America, Approaches to teaching world literature, 54).

6599. HANNEMANN (Beate). Im Zeichen der Sonne. Geschichte und Repertoire des Opernhauses "La Fenice" von seiner Gründung bis zum Wiener Kongress (1787–1814). Bern, Lang, 95, 332 p. (ill.).

6600. Italy in the Baroque. Selected readings. Ed. by Brendan DOOLEY. New York, Garland, 95, X-690 p.

6601. KRIEGLEDER (Wynfried). Die deutschsprachige Literatur des Josephinismus im europäischen Kontext. *Österreich in Geschichte und Literatur mit Geographie*, 95, 39, 5b-6, p. 374-384.

6602. KYLANDER (Britt-Marie). La vocabulaire de Molière, dans les comédies en alexandrins. Goteborg, Suede, Acta Universitatis Gothoburgensis, 95, 321 p. (ill.). (Romanica Gothoburgensia, 45).

6603. Memorie dei Georgofili (Le) rilette oggi (1753–1853). A cura di Franco SCARAMUZZI. Firenze, Accademia dei Georgofili, 95, 648 p.

6604. NUSSBAUM (Felicity). Torrid zones: maternity, sexuality, and empire in eighteenth-century English narratives. Baltimoer, Johns Hopkins U. P., 95, 264 p.

6605. PORTER (Dennis). Rousseau's legacy, emergence and eclipse of the writer in France. New York a. Oxford, Oxford U.P., 95, 306 p. (ill.).

6606. RAO (Anna Maria). Un «letterato faticatore» nell'Europa del Settecento: Michele Torcia (1736–1808). *Rivista storica italiana*, 95, 107, 3, p. 647-726.

6607. RIPOSIO (Donatella). Il labirinto della verità. aspetti del romanzo libertino del seicento. Alessandria, Edizioni dell'Orso, 95, 144 p. (Contributi e proposte).

6608. RUFI (Enrico). Le rêve laïque de Louis-Sebastien Mercier entre littérature et politique. Oxford, Voltaire Foundation, 95, VIII-234 p. (Studies on Voltaire and the eighteenth century, 326).

6609. SIMON (Alfred). Molière, ou la vie de Jean-Baptiste Poquelin, biographie. Paris, Seuil, 95, 555 p.

6610. SKRZYPEK (Marian). La fonction politique de la Réforme d'après les écrivains des Lumières polonaises. *Odrodzenie i Reformacja w Polsce*, 95, 39, p. 179-188.

d. Romantik und Gegenwart.

* 6611. ISELLA (Dante), REVERDINI (Niccolò). La vita di Alberto Pisani e i libri di Carlo Dossi. Milano, All'Insegna del Pesce d'Oro, 95, 122 p. (ill.). (Bibliografia del Novecento, 5).

6612. ADAMS (James Eli). Dandies and desert saints: styles of Victorian masculinity. Ithaca, Cornell U. P., 95, 249 p.

6613. AIRAKSINEN (Timo). The philosophy of the Marquis de Sade. London a. New York, Routledge, 95, VIII-200 p.

6614. ARNAUD (Jacqueline). La littérature belge de langue française, au-delà du réel. Paris, Editions L'Harmattan, 95, 187 p. (Université Paris-Nord Centre d'études littéraires francophones et comparées. Itineraires et contacts de cultures, 20).

6615. BAINBRIDGE (Simon). Napoleon and English Romanticism. Cambridge a. New York, Cambridge U. P., 95, XIV-259 p. (ill.). (Cambridge studies in Romanticism).

6616. Balzac, imprimeur et défenseur du livre. Paris, Paris-Musees, Des Cendres, 95, 236 p.

6617. BANCQUART (Marie Claire). Poesie de langue française, 1945–1960. Paris, PUF, 95, 327 p.

6618. BEN-GHIAT (Ruth). Fascism, writing, and memory: the realist aesthetics in Italy, 1930–1950. *Journal of modern history*, 95, 67, 3, p. 627-666.

6619. BERTRAND (Dominique). Dire le rire a l'âge classique, représenter pour mieux contrôler. Université de Provence, Aix-en-Provence, 95, 362 p.

6620. BYLES (Joan Montgomery). War, women, and poetry, 1914–1945, British and German writers and activists. Newark a. London, University of Delaware Press a. Associated U.P.es, 95, 198 p.

6621. CARETTI (Lanfranco). Manzoni e gli scrittori, da Goethe a Calvino. Roma e Bari, Laterza, 95, XII-154 p. (Biblioteca universale Laterza, 433).

6622. CHARLES (Michel). Introduction à l'étude des textes. Paris, Seuil, 95, 388 p. (Collection Poétique).

6623. CONNER (Tom). Dreams in French literature, the persistent voice. Amsterdam, Atlanta, GA, Rodopi, 95, 200 p. (University of Kentucky Foreign Language Conference [1991]; Faux titre, 92).

6624. Corps au XVIIe siècle (Le). Actes du premier colloque conjointement organisé par la North American Society for Seventeenth-Century French Literature et le Centre International de Rencontres sur le XVIIe Siècle, University of California, Santa Barbara, 17–19 mars 1994. Ed. by Ronald W. TOBIN. Paris, Papers on French Seventeenth Century French Literature, 95, 409 p. North American (Society for Seventeenth-Century French Literature/Centre international de Rencontres sur le XVIIe siècle).

6625. CRAIG (Gordon A.). The politics of the unpolitical, German writers and the problem of power, 1770–1871. New York a. Oxford, Oxford U.P., 95, XIV-190 p.

6626. CREMERIUS (Johannes). Freud und die Dichter. Freiburg i. Br., Kore, 95, 221 p.

6627. DARNTON (Robert). The forbidden best-sellers of pre-revolutionary France. New York a. London, W. W. Norton, 95, XXII-440 p.

6628. DE ROSA (Francesco). Le canzoni leopardiane, 1818–1822. *Annali della Scuola Normale Superiore di Pisa*, 95, 25, p. 619-74.

6629. DECLOEDT (Leopold R. G.). Imago Imperatoris. Franz Joseph I. in der österreichischen Belletristik der Zwischenkriegszeit. Wien, Köln u. Weimar, Böhlau, 95, 260 p. (ill.). (Literatur in der Geschichte, Geschichte in der Literatur, 31).

6630. DELBANCO (Nicholas). On Saul Bellow. *Salmagundi*, 95, 106, p. 81-85.

6631. Epreuve du lecteur (L'), livres et lectures dans le roman d'Ancien Régime. Actes du VIIIe colloque de la Société d'Analyse de la topique romanesque – Louvain – Anvers, 19–21 mai 1994. Ed. par Jan HERMAN et Paul PELCKMANS. Louvain, Paris, Peeters, 95, 502 p. (Société d'Analyse de la Topique Romanesque Colloque, Bibliothèque de l'information grammaticale, 31).

6632. FABRE (Giorgio). Sul «caso Moravia». *Quaderni di storia*, 95, 21, 42, p. 181-196.

6633. FETZER (John F.). Changing perceptions of Thomas Mann's Doctor Faustus, criticism, 1947–1992. Columbia, Camden House, 95, XVI-197 p. (Studies in German literature, linguistics, and culture. Literary criticism in perspective).

6634. FLITNER (Christine). Frauen in der Literaturkritik, Gisela Elsner und Elfriede Jelinek im Feuilleton der Bundesrepublik Deutschland. Pfaffenweiler, Centaurus-Verlagsgesellschaft, 95, 200 p. (Frauen in der Literaturgeschichte, 3).

6635. FOSCHI ALBERT (Marina). Friedrich Schlegels Theorie des Witzes und sein Roman Lucinde. New York, Lang, 95, 172 p. (Studies in modern German literature, 59).

6636. FREUNDLIEB (Dieter). Foucault and in study of literature. *Poetics today*, 95, 16, p. 301-44.

6637. FRIES (Helmut). Die grosse Katharsis, der Erste Weltkrieg in der Sicht deutscher Dichter und Gelehrter. Konstanz, Verlag am Hockgraben, 95, 2 vol., [s. p.].

6638. FRIES (Marilyn Sibley), BAHTI (Timothy). Jewish writers, German literature, the uneasy examples of Nelly Sachs and Walter Benjamin. Ann Arbor, University of Michigan Press, 95, X-221 p.

6639. FUSSO (Suzanne). Maidens in chilbirth: the Sistina Madonna in Dostojewsky's 'Devils'. *Slavic review*, 95, 54, p. 261-75.

6640. GARRIGUES (Emmanuel). Les jeux surréalistes, mars 1921–septembre 1962. Paris, Gallimard, 95, 311 p. (Archives du surréalisme, 5).

6641. GASSAMA (Makhily). La langue d'Ahmadou Kourouma, ou le français sous le soleil d'Afrique. Paris, Karthala, 95, 123 p.

6642. GERSON (Gal). Cultural subversion and the background of the Irish 'Easter Poets'. *Journal of Contemporary History*, 95, 30, 2, p. 333-347.

6643. GLENCROSS (Michael). Reconstructing Camelot, French Romantic medievalism and the Arthurian tradition. Cambridge, Brewer, 95, X-192 p. (Arthurian studies, 36).

6644. GOOD (Colin H.), DURRANI (Osman), HILLIARD (Kevin). The new Germany, literature and society after unification. Sheffield, Sheffield Academic Press, 95, XXIV-440 p. (ill.).

6645. GRAF (Johannes). 'Die notwendige Reise', Reisen und Reiseliteratur junger Autoren während des Nationalsozialismus. Stuttgart, M & P Verlag für Wissenschaft und Forschung, 95, 363 p.

6646. HANSEN (Thomas S.), POLLIN (Burton R.). The German face of Edgar Allan Poe, a study of literary references in his works. Columbia, Camden House, 95, 140 p.

6647. Italo Calvino: enciclopedia. Arte, scienza e letteratura. A cura di Marco BELPOLITI. Milano, Marcos y Marcos, 95, 322 p. (ill.). (Riga, 9).

6648. JASKUŁA (Roman). Literatura i historia Polski w wydawnictwach francuskich Karola Forstera w latach 1833–1879. (Littérature et histoire de la Pologne dans les éditions françaises de Karol Forster dans les années 1833–1879). *Kwartalnik Historii Nauki i Techniki*, 95, 40, 1, p. 59-81. [Eng. Summary].

6649. JUDGE (Anne), LAMOTHE (Solange). Stylistic developments in literary and non-literary French prose. Lewiston, Edwin Mellen Press, 95, VIII-292 p. (Studies in French literature, 19).

6650. KENNEDY (Kevin G.). Der junge Goethe in der Tradition des Petrarkismus. New York, P. Lang, 95, 129 p. (Studies in modern German literature, 48).

6651. KLUPPELHOLZ (Heinz). Die Innovation als Imitation, zu Fortsetzungen französischer Romane des 18. Jahrhunderts. Frankfurt am Main, Klostermann, 95, 303 p. (Analecta Romanica, 54).

6652. KNEIP (Heinz). Regulative Prinzipien und formulierte Poetik des sozialistischen Realismus, Untersuchungen zur Literaturkonzeption in der Sowjetunion und Polen (1945–1956). Frankfurt am Main, New York u. Lang, 95, 384 p.

6653. KONRAD (Susanne). Goethes "Wahlverwandschaften" und das Dilemma des Logozentrismus. Heidelberg, Winter, 95, XII-338 p (Beiträge zur neueren Literaturgeschichte, 3/144).

6654. LACKO (Miklós). Zsidòk a budapesti irodalomban, 1890–1930. (Les juifs dans la littérature de Budapest, 1890–1930). Budapesti negyed, 95, 3, 2, p. 107-126.

6655. LAGARDE (François). La persuasion et ses effets, essai sur la reception en France au dix-septième siecle. Paris a. Seattle, Papers on French seventeenth Century Literature, 95, 203 p.

6656. LANASRI (Ahmed). La littérature algerienne de l'entre-deux-guerres, Genèse et fonctionnement. Paris, Publisud, 95, 565 p. (Littératures arabes).

6657. LANDFESTER (Ulrike). Der Dichtung Schleier, zur poetischen Funktion von Kleidung in Goethes Frühwerk. Freiburg im Breisgau, Rombach, 95, 338 p. (Rombach Wissenschaft. Reihe Litterae, 30).

6658. LANGLAND (Elizabeth). Nobody's Angels: middle-class women and domestic ideology in Victorian culture. Ithaca, Cornell, U. P., 95, 268 p.

6659. LEMAIRE (Gérald-Georges). Futurisme. Paris, Editions du regard, 95, 214 p. (ill.).

6660. LOREY (Christoph). Die Ehe im klassischen Werk Goethes. Amsterdam a. Atlanta, Rodopi, 95, 308 p. (Amsterdamer Publikationen zur Sprache und Literatur, 118).

6661. MAC ILVANNEY (Liam). Robert Burns and the Calvinist radical tradition. History Workshop, 95, 40, p. 133-150.

6662. MAGGETTI (Daniel). L'invention de la littérature romande, 1830–1910. Lausanne, Payot, 95, 621 p.

6663. MAGRI (Veronique). Le discours sur l'autre, à travers quatre récits de voyage en Orient. Paris et Genève, Champion et Slatkine, 95, 426 p. (Travaux de linguistique quantitative, 55).

6664. MANZONI (Alessandro). I promessi sposi. Storia della colonna infame. A cura di Angelo STELLA e Cesare REPOSSI. Torino, Einaudi e Gallimard, 95, XCII-1327 p. (Biblioteca della Pléiade) [contiene: STELLA (Angelo). Introduzione, p. IX–XLIII].

6665. Manzoni tra due secoli. A cura di Francesco MATTESINI. Milano, Edizioni di vita e pensiero, 95, 212 p. (Scienze filologiche e letteratura, 32). [contiene <scelta>: SCARPATI (Claudio), Pietà e terrore nell'Adelchi, p. 77-99. – LANGELLA (Giuseppe), Il modello della conversione: Manzoni e Papini, p. 165-210].

6666. MARTINOIR (Francine de). La littérature occupée, les années de guerre, 1939–1945. Paris, Hatier, 95, XVI-303 p. (ill.). (Collection Brèves Littérature).

6667. MARX (Friedhelm). Erlesene Helden, Don Sylvio, Werther, Wilhelm Meister und die Literatur. Heidelberg, Winter, 95, 285 p. (Beiträge zur neueren Literaturgeschichte, 3/139).

6668. MATIJEVICH (Elke). The Zeitroman of the late Weimar Republic. New York, Lang, 95, VIII-197 p. (Studies in modern German literature, 77).

6669. MATUS (Jill L.). Unstable bodies: Victorian representations of sexuality and maternity. New York a. Manchester, Manchester U. P., 95, 280 p.

6670. MEHLMAN (Jeffrey). Genealogies of the text, essays on literature, psychoanalysis, and politics in modern France. Cambridge, New York, Cambridge U.P., 95, XII-262 p. (Cambridge studies in French, 54).

6671. Mélanges sur l'oeuvre de Paul Benichou. Ed. par Paul BENICHOU, Marc FUMAROLI et Tzvetan TODOROV. Paris, Gallimard, 95, 232 p.

6672. MILLER (Andrew H.). Novels behind glass: commodity, culture, and Victorian narrative. Cambridge, Cambridge U. P., 95, XI-242 p. (Literature, culture, theory, 17).

6673. MONTE (Lucia). Leopardi e il Werther. Napoli, Federico e Ardia, 95, 111 p. (Dal certo al vero, 12).

6674. MOUSSA (Sarga). La rélation orientale, enquête sur la communication dans les récits de voyage en Orient (1811–1861). Paris, Klincksieck, 95, 279 p. (Littérature des voyages, 9).

6675. NELSON (Claudia). Invisible men: fatherhood in Victorian periodicals, 1850–1910. Athens, University of Georgia Press, 95, 332 p.

6676. OJAIDE (Tanure). New trends in modern African poetry. Researches in african literatures, 95, 26, p. 4-20.

6677. Origins of Dracula (The): the background to Bram Stoker's Gothic masterpiece. Ed. by Clive LEATHERDALE. Westcliff-on-Sea, Desert Island Books, 95, 239 p.

6678. OZOUF (Mona). Les mots des femmes, essai sur la singularité française. Paris, Fayard, 95, 397 p.

6679. PANFILOWITSCH (Igor). Aleksandr Puskins 'Mednyj vsadnik', Deutungsgeschichte und Gehalt. München, Sagner, 95, 656 p. (Specimina philologiae Slavicae. Supplementband, 38).

6680. PELIKAN (Jaroslav Jan). Faust the theologian. New Haven a. London, Yale U.P., 95, XII-145 p.

6681. PERCHELLET (Jean-Pierre). L'ombre de Madame de Staël: la genèse de 'Wallenstein'. *Annales Benjamin Constant*, 95, 17, p. 37-49.

6682. PESSIN (Alain). La construction littéraire d'une vérité politique: Victor Hugo et la pénalité monstrueuse. *Tumultes*, 95, 6, p. 53-73.

6683. PLENZDORF (Ulrich), STADE (Martin), SCHLESINGER (Klaus). Berliner Geschichten, Operativer Schwerpunkt Selbstverlag', eine Autoren-Anthologie, wie sie entstand und von der Stasi verhindert wurde. Frankfurt am Main, Suhrkamp, 95, 316 p. (Suhrkamp Taschenbuch, 2256).

6684. PUTZ (Manfred). Nietzsche in American literature and thought. Columbia, Camden House, 95, 381 p. (Studies in German literature, linguistics, and culture).

6685. RADLER (Rudiger). Goethes 'Faust I' anders Gesehen, Neue und Visualisierte Interpretationen zu Grundfragen des Werkes. Paderborn, Schöningh, 95, 189 p (ill.) (Modellanalysen Literatur, 23).

6686. RHODES (Norman). Ibsen and the Greeks, the classical Greek dimension in selected works of Henrik Ibsen as mediated by German and Scandinavian culture. Lewisburg a. London, Bucknell U.P. a. Associated U.P., 95, 209 p.

6687. RICHTER (Matthias). Die Sprache jüdischer Figuren in der deutschen Literatur (1750–1933). Studien zu Form und Funktion. Göttingen, Wallstein, 95, 351 p.

6688. RONZEAUD (Pierre). L'Irrationnel au XVIIe siècle. Paris, Klincksieck, 95, 323 p. (Littératures classiques, 25).

6689. ROSENBLUM (Joseph). Thomas Holcroft. Literature and politics in England in the age of the French revolutions. Salzburg, Lewiston a. New York, Mellen, 95, IV-143 p. (Salzburg university studies. Salzburg Studies in English Literature: Poetic drama and poetic theory, 122).

6690. ROSS (Kristin). Fast cars, clean bodies, decolonization and the reordering of French culture. Cambridge a. London, MIT Press, 95, X-261 p. (ill.).

6691. RUPRECHT (Hans-George), LAURETTE (Pierre). Poétiques et imaginaires, francopolyphonie littéraire des Amériques. Paris, L'Harmattan, 95, 399 p. (Collection Critiques littéraires).

6692. SCHAFFRY (Andreas Michael). An der Schwelle zur Wissenschaft, ideologische Funktionen und gesellschaftliche Relevanz bei der Organisierung des Diskurses 'Altdeutsche Literatur' zwischen 1790 und 1815. München, Iudicium Verlag, 95, 273 p. (ill.).

6693. SCHMIDT (Claudia). Rückzüge und Aufbrüche, zur DDR-Literatur in der Gorbatschow-Aera. Frankfurt am Main u. New York, Lang, 95, 291 p. (Bochumer Schriften zur deutschen Literatur, 44).

6694. SCHNEIDER (Ulf-Michael). Propheten der Goethezeit, Sprache, Literatur und Wirkung der Inspirierten. Göttingen, Vandenhoeck u. Ruprecht, 95, 248 p. (Palaestra, 297).

6695. SCHNITZLER (Arthur). Tagebuch 1879–1931. 1923–1926. Unter Mitarbeit von Peter M. BRAUNWARTH [u. a.]. Hrsg. von der Kommission für Literarische Gebrauchsformen der Österr. Akad. der Wiss. Wien, Vlg der Österr. Akad. der Wiss., 95, 496 p.

6696. SCHOR (Naomi). Bad objects, essays popular and unpopular. Durham a. London, Duke U.P., 95, XVI-208 p. (ill.).

6697. SHELLEY (Percy Bysshe). Miscellaneous poetry, prose and translations from Bodleian MS. Shelley. Ed. by E. B. MURRAY. New York a. London, Garland, 95, L-534 p. (The Bodleian Shelley manuscripts, 21).

6698. SPIES (Bernhard). Ideologie und Utopie in der deutschen Literatur der Neuzeit. Würzburg, Königshausen u. Neumann, 95, 174 p. (ill.).

6699. STEEDMAN (Carolyn). Strange dislocations, childhood and the idea of human interiority, 1780–1930. London, Virago Press, 95, X-254 p.

6700. Sto lat baśni polskiej. (Cent ans de conte de fées polonais.). [Referaty sesji naukowej zorganizowanej w listopadzie 1994r. na Uniwersytecie Warszawskim]. (Cent ans du conte polonaise. Exposés de la session scientifique organisée en novembre 1994 à l'Université de Varsovie. Ouvrage collectif. Réd. par Grzegorz LESZCZYŃSKI. Warszawa, Fundacja „Książka dla Dziecka", 95, 113 p.

6701. SUDOLSKI (Zbigniew). Mickiewicz. Opowieść biograficzna. (Mickiewicz. Récit biographique). Warszawa, Ancher, 95, 918 p. (phot., fig.).

6702. SURDICH (Luigi). "In musica più idee": tra Montale e Caproni. *Rassegna della letteratura italiana*, 95, 3, p. 102-35.

6703. SUSSMAN (Herbert). Victorian masculinities. Cambridge, Cambridge U. P., 95, 227 p.

6704. Tempi del rinnovamento (I): gli spazi della diversità. Atti del convegno internazionale "Rinnovamento del codice narrativo in Italia dal 1945 al 1992". A cura di Serge VANVOLSEM, Franco MUSARRA e Bart VAN DER BOSCHE. Roma e Lovanio, Bulzoni, 95, 2 vol., 770 p., 702 p. (Leuven University, 5/6).

6705. THIELE (Eckhard). Literatur nach Stalins Tod, Sowjetliteratur und DDR-Literatur, Ilja Ehrenburg, Stephan Hermlin, Erwin Strittmatter, Christa Wolf, Juri Trifonow. Frankfurt am Main, Lang, 95, 237 p. (Europäische Hochschulschriften. I/1502).

6706. TIMMS (Edward). Karl Kraus: Satiriker der Apokalypse. Leben und Werk von 1874–1918. Wien, Deuticke, 95, 560 p. (ill., Werkverzeichnis K. Kraus).

6707. TOMASI DI LAMPEDUSA (Giuseppe). Opere. A cura di Nicoletta POLO. Introduzione di Gioacchino LANZA TOMASI. Milano, Mondadori, 1995, LX-1882 p. (Meridiani).

6708. VRETTOS (Athena). Somatic fictions: imagining illness in Victorian culture. Stanford, Stanford U. P., 95, 250 p.

6709. WAGNER (Irmgard). Critical approaches to Goethe's classical dramas, Iphigenie, Torquato Tasso, and Die natürliche Tochter. Columbia, Camden House, 95, 233 p. (Studies in German literature, linguistics, and culture. Literary criticism in perspective).

6710. WALKER (David H.). Outrage and insight, modern French writers and the 'fait divers'. Oxford a. Washington, Berg Publishers, 95, XII-269 p. (ill.). (Berg French studies).

6711. WALKER (Pierre A.). Reading Henry James in French cultural contexts. DeKalb, Northern Illinois U. P., 95, XXII-230 p.

6712. WENDE-HOHENBERGER (Waltraud). Goethe-Parodien, zur Wirkungsgeschichte eines Klassikers. Stuttgart, M & P Verlag fur Wissenschaft und Forschung, 95, 436 p.

6713. WOODCOCK (Bruce), COATES (John). Combative styles, romantic writing and ideology: two contrasting interpretations. Hull, University of Hull Press, 95, 151 p.

§ 8. Bildende Kunst.

a. Allgemeines.

6714. ABIODUN (Rowland). "What follows six is more than seven": understanding African art. London, British Museum, Department of Ethnography, 95, VI-321 p. (ill.). (British Museum Department of Ethnography – Occasional paper / British Museum, 105).

6715. AICHELBURG (Wladimir). Das Künstlerhaus, die Secession und der Hagenbund 1938–1945. Jb. d. Vereins f. Gesch. d. Stadt Wien, 95, 51, p. 5-34.

6716. Alchimie: art, histoire et mythes. Actes du 1er colloque international de la Societé d'étude de l'histoire de l'alchimie, Paris, Collège de France, 14–16 mars 199. Ed. par Didier KAHN et Sylvain MATTON. Paris et Milano, S.E.H.A. et Arche, 95, VI-847 p. (ill.). (Societé d'étude de l'histoire de l'alchimie, Textes et travaux de Chrysopoeia).

6717. ALTRICHTER (Helmut). Bilder erzählen Geschichte. Freiburg im Breisgau, Rombach, 95, 354 p. (ill.). (Rombach Wissenschaft. Reihe Historiae, 6).

6718. Arte, committenza ed economia a Roma e nelle corti del Rinascimento (1420–1530). Atti del Convegno internazionale, Roma, 24–27 ottobre 1990. A cura di Christoph Luitpold FROMMEL e Arnold ESCH. Torino, Einaudi, 95, XX-420 p. (80 p. di ill.). (Bibliotheca Hertziana/Deutsches Historisches Institut; Piccola biblioteca Einaudi, 630).

6719. BALBI DE CARO (Silvana). I Gonzaga: moneta, arte, storia. Milano, Electa, 95, 549 p. (ill.). (Centro Internazionale d'Arte e di Cultura di Palazzo Te).

6720. BARTLETT (Clive), EMBLETON (Gerry). English longbowman 1330–1515 AD. London, Reed Consumer, 95, 64 p. (ill.). (Warrior series, 11).

6721. BATORI (Armida). Marinetti e il futurismo a Milano: la grande Milano tradizione e futurista. Roma, De Luca, 95, 127 p. (ill.). (Biblioteca nazionale braidense, Accademia di belle arti).

6722. BATSCHMANN (Oskar). Nicolas Poussin [Poussin] 'Winter-Sintflucht': Jahreszeit oder Ende der Geschichte. In: Catastrophes [Cf. n° 6726], p. 38-48.

6723. BENJAMIN (Andrew E.). Abstraction. London a. New York, Academy Editions, 95, 96 p. (ill.).

6724. BERGMAN-CARTON (Janis). The woman of ideas in French art, 1830–1848. New Haven a. London, Yale U.P., 95, XVI-261 p. (ill.).

6725. BREDEKAMP (Horst), MEIER (Heinrich). Repräsentation und Bildmagie der Renaissance als Formproblem. München, Carl Friedrich von Siemens Stiftung, 95, 84 p. (ill.). (Carl Friedrich von Siemens Stiftung, 61.).

6726. Catastrophes. Communications faites au 19e Colloque de l'Association des historiens d'art, La Chaux-de-Fonds, 3–4 juin 1994. Zeitschrift für schweizerische Archäologie und Kunstgeschichte, 95, 52, 1, p. 1-86. [Cf. nos <sélection> 6722, 6777.]

6727. CAVALLARO (Anna). Temi profani e allegorie nell'Italia centrale del Quattrocento. Manziana (Roma), Vecchiarelli, 95, 119 p. (148 p. of plates).

6728. CHRIST (Carol T.), JORDAN (John O.). Victorian literature and the Victorian visual imagination. Berkeley a. London, University of California Press, 95, XXX-371 p. (ill.).

6729. ÇİFTÇİ (Fazil). Kastamonu Camileri-Türbeleri ve Diğer Tarihi Eserleri (Mosquées, tombeaux et les autres monuments historiques à Kastamonu). Ankara, Türk Diyanet Vakfı Kastamonu Şubesi, 95, 345 p.

6730. CORBO (Anna Maria), POMPONI (Massimo). Fonti per la storia artistica romana al tempo di Paolo V. Roma, Ministero per i beni culturali e ambientali, 95, 286 p. (Pubblicazioni degli Archivi di Stato. Strumenti, 121).

6731. CROW (Thomas E.). Emulation: making artists for revolutionary France. New Haven a. London, Yale U.P., 95, 364 p. (ill).

8. BILDENDE KUNST

6732. DAIBER (Hans). Schaufenster der Diktatur. Theater im Machtbereich Hitlers. Stuttgart, Neske, 95, 405 p. (ill.).

6733. DENKTAŞ (Mustafa). Karaman'daki Klasik Devir Osmanlı Yapıları. (Monuments ottomans de l'époque classique à Karaman). *Vakıflar Dergisi*, 95, 25, p. 125-147.

6734. Diderot on art. Ed. by John GOODMAN a. Thomas E. CROW New Haven a. London, Yale U.P., 95, 768 p. (ill.).

6735. DOWNTON (John), BESWICK (Francis). The death of art: incorporating Notes on philosophy and ethics. Sevenoaks, Kent, Hilda Downton, 95, X-115 p.

6736. DRECHSLER (Maximiliane). Zwischen Kunst und Kommerz: zur Geschichte des Ausstellungswesens zwischen 1775 und 1905. München, Deutscher Kunstverlag, 95, 215 p. (ill.).

6737. Estudos de arte e história: homenagem a Artur Nobre de Gusmao. Ed. Departamento de História da Arte da Faculdade de Ciências Sociais e Humanas da Universidade Nova de Lisboa. Lisboa, Vega, 95, 458 p. (ill.). (Artes. História).

6738. FARMAN (John). Art: a complete and utter history (without the boring bits). London, Macmillan, 95, VIII-200 p.

6739. FITTIPALDI (Teodoro), CASOLARO (Renato). Il Museo di San Martino di Napoli. Napoli, Electa, 95, 213 p. (ill.). (Soprintendenza ai beni artistici e storici di Napoli, Guide artistiche Electa Napoli).

6740. Florilegium: scritti di storia dell'arte in onore di Carlo Bertelli. Milano, Electa, 95, 216 p. (ill.).

6741. FORNARI SCHIANCHI (Lucia). I Farnese: arte e collezionismo. Milano, Electa, 95, 214 p. (ill.).

6742. GATES (Henry Louis), SCHOENER (Allon). Harlem on my mind: cultural capital of Black America, 1900–1968. New York, New Press, 95, 258 p. (ill.). (Metropolitan Museum of Art).

6743. GIESS (Frederique), DEBELFORT (Anne-Marie), FOUCART (Bruno). Le baron Taylor, l'Association des artistes et l'exposition du Bazar Bonne-Nouvelle en 1846. Paris, Fondation Taylor, 95, 300 p. (ill. et facsims.).

6744. GOLDSTEIN (Ann), RORIMER (Anne). Reconsidering the object of art, 1965–1975. Los Angeles a. Cambridge, MIT Press, 95, 335 p. (ill.).

6745. HARBINSON (Craig). La renaissance dans les pays du Nord. Paris, Flammarion, 95, 175 p. (ill.).

6746. História da arte portuguesa. Vol. 1. Da préhistória ao modo gótico. Vol. 2. Do modo gótico ao maneirismo. Vol. 3. Do Barroco à contemporaneidade. Dir. de Paulo PEREIRA. Lisboa, Temas e Debates, 95, 3 vol., 519 p., 537 p., 695 p.

6747. JOUIN (Pierre). Une liberté toute neuve: culture de masse et esthétique nouvelle dans la France des anneés 50. Paris, Klincksieck, 95, 308 p. (ill.).

6748. KAPLAN (Wendy). Designing modernity, The arts of reform and persuasion, 1885–1945. London, Thames and Hudson, 95, 352 p. (ill.). (Wolfsonian Foundation).

6749. KOWALCZYK (Jerzy). L'arte dell'antica Polonia nelle ricerche polacco-italiane [1955–1994]. *Biuletyn Historii Sztuki*, 95, 57, 1-2, p. 1-17. – IDEM. W setną rocznicę urodzin Profesora Mieczysława Gębarowicza [1893–1984]: M. Gębarowicz jako badacz sztuki ruskoukraińskiej. (La centième anniversaire de la naissance du Pr. Mieczysław Gębarowicz [1893–1984]: M. Gębarowicz en tant que chercheur dans le domaine de l'art ruthéno-ukrainien.). *Biuletyn Historii Sztuki*, 95, 57, 3-4, p. 217-225. [Eng. Summary].

6750. Kultura artystyczna Wielkiego Księstwa Litewskiego w epoce baroku. (Culture artistique du Grand Duché de Lituanie à l'époque baroque). Réd. Jerzy KOWALCZYK. Warszawa, Inst. Kultury, 95, 329 p. (English summary). Inst. Sztuki Pol. Akad. Nauk.

6751. LLORENTE (Angel). Arte e ideología en el franquismo, 1936–1951. Madrid, Visor, 95, 340 p. (ill.). (La balsa de la medusa, 73).

6752. MARGOLIS (Joseph). Interpretation radical but not unruly: the new puzzle of the arts and history. Berkeley a. London, University of California Press, 95, XIV-312 p.

6753. *Vacat.*

6754. MIRZOEFF (Nicholas). Silent poetry. Deafness, sign, and visual culture in modern France. Princeton a. Chichester, Princeton U.P., 95, XIV-317 p. (ill.).

6755. MONNIER (Gerard). L'art et ses institutions en France de la Révolution à nos jours. Paris, Gallimard, 95, 462 p. (Collection Folio/histoire, 66).

6756. NOCHLIN (Linda). Les Politiques de la vision: art, société et politique au XIXe siècle. Paris, Chambon, 95, 279 p. (ill.).

6757. NORMAN (Diana). Siena, Florence, and Padua: art, society and religion 1280–1400. New Haven, Yale University Press in association with the Open University, 95, X-260 p. (ill.).

6758. PADBERG (Gabriele). Georg Forster observateur d'oeuvres d'art: à l'époque des Vues sur le Rhin inférieur. Paris, Les Belles Lettres, 95, 341 p. (ill.). (Annales littéraires de l'Université de Besançon, 548).

6759. Paysage en Europe du XVIe au XVIIIe siècle (Le). Actes du Colloque organisé au musée du Louvre, Paris, 25–27 janvier 1990. Paris, Réunion des Musées nationaux, 95, 307 p. (ill.). [Cf. n[os] <sélection> 5624, 5629, 6811, 6812, 6817, 6834, 6841, 6845, 6847.]

6760. PERNIOLA (Mario). Enigmas. The Egyptian moment in society and art. London, Verso, 95, X-158 p.

6761. PERRY (Gillian). Women artists and the Parisian avant-garde: modernism and 'feminine' art, 1900 to the late 1920s. Manchester a. New York, New York a. Manchester U. P., 95, XIV-186 p. (ill.).

6762. PETERSEN (Swantje). Korrespondenzen zwischen Literatur und bildender Kunst im 20. Jahrhundert. Studien am Beispiel von S. Lenz – E. Nolde, A. Andersch – E. Barlach – P. Klee, H. Janssen – E. Jünger und G. Bekker. Frankfurt am Main, Lang, 95, XX-456 p. (Europäische Hochschulschriften XXVIII/ 277).

6763. PFOTENHAUER (Helmut), BERNAUER (Markus), MILLER (Norbert). Frühklassizismus. Position und Opposition: Winckelmann, Mengs, Heinse. Frankfurt am Main, Deutscher Klassiker Verlag, 95, 788 p. (ill.). (Bibliothek der Kunstliteratur, 2).

6764. REYNOLDS (Dee). Symbolist aesthetics and early abstract art: sites of imaginary space. Cambridge a. New York, Cambridge U. P. 95, XV-290 p. (ill). (Cambridge studies in French, 51).

6765. RILEY (Bridget), MAC GREGOR (Neil), KUDIELKA (Robert). Dialogues on art. London, Zwemmer, 95, 95 p. (ill.).

6766. ROBINSON (John Martin), BURTON (Peter), WALSHAW (Harland). Treasures of the English churches. London, Sinclair-Stevenson, 95, XVIII-426 p.

6767. RUBIN (Patricia). Giorgio Vasari: art and history. New Haven a. London, Yale U.P., 95, X-448 p. (ill.).

6768. RUSHING (W. Jackson). Native American art and the New York avant-garde. A history of cultural primitivism. Austin, University of Texas Press, 95, XII-250 p. (ill.). (American studies series).

6769. SCHEIFELE (Hans). Zur Geschichte der Plansammlung des Bundesdenkmalamtes. *Österr. Z. f. Kunst und Denkmalpflege*, 95, 49, 1-2, p. 80-87 (ill., Tab., Pläne).

6770. SMITH (Richard Candida). Utopia and dissent: art, poetry, and politics in California. Berkeley a. London, University of California Press, 95, XXVI-536 p. (ill.).

6771. SOLLERS (Philippe). Le cavalier du Louvre: Vivant Denon (1747–1825). Paris, Plon, 95, 287 p.

6772. SPIEGELMAN (Willard). Majestic indolence: English romantic poetry and the work of art. New York a. Oxford, Oxford U.P., 95, XII-221 p.

6773. STUPPERICH (Reinhard), SCHIERING (Wolfgang). Lebendige Antike: Rezeptionen der Antike in Politik, Kunst und Wissenschaft der Neuzeit. Mannheim, Palatium Verlag im J & J Verlag, 95, 223 p. (ill.). (Mannheimer historische Forschungen, 6).

6774. SUNDAR (Pushpa). Patrons and Philistines: arts and the state in British India, 1773–1947. Delhi a. Oxford, Oxford U.P., 95, VIII-294 p.

6775. TURNER (Frederick). The culture of hope. A new birth of the classical spirit. New York a. London, Free Press, 95, V-298 p.

6776. TURPIN (John). A school of art in Dublin since the eighteenth century. A history of the National College of Art and Design. Dublin, Gill a. Macmillan, 95, XX-710 p. (ill.).

6777. URSPRUNG (Philip). Katastrophen für das Salonpublikum. Die Sensationsbilder von Georges Rochegrosse [1859–1939] im ausgehenden XIX. Jahrhundert. *In*: Catastrophes [Cf. n° 6726], p. 63-71.

6778. VAREY (J. E.). Cartelera de los titeres y otras diversiones populares de Madrid: 1758–1840: estudio y documentos. Madrid, Tamesis y Woodbridge, Boydell & Brewer, 95, 491 p. (ill.). (Colección Tamesis. Serie C, Fuentes para la historia del teatro en Espana, 8).

6779. VASCO ROCCA (Sandra), BORGHINI (Gabriele). Giovanni V di Portogallo (1707–1750) e la cultura romana del suo tempo. Roma, Argos, 95, XVI-540 p. (ill.). (Ministero per i beni culturali e ambientali, Istituto centrale per il catalogo e la documentazione, Ospizio di San Michele).

6780. WELCH (Evelyn S.). Art and authority in Renaissance Milan. New Haven a. London, Yale U.P., 95, X-358 p. (ill.).

b. Architektur

* 6781. Paris XIXe–XXe siècles: urbanisme, architecture, espaces verts: bibliographie et sources imprimées à la Bibliothèque des archives de Paris. Ed. par Chantal AURE, avec la collaboration de Anne-Marie MORICE: guide des sources d'archives conservées aux archives de Paris, par Françoise BANAT et Marielle DUVERDIER; sous la direction de Jean-Marie JENN. Paris, Archives de Paris, 95, 542 p.

6782. BAILLIE SCOTT (M. H.). Houses and gardens: arts and crafts interiors. Woodbridge, Antique Collectors' Club, 95, 319 p. (ill.).

6783. BATEY (Mavis). Regency gardens. Princes Risborough, Shire, 95, 96 p. (ill.). (Shire garden history).

6784. BOEDER (Titus). Vergleich der Elemente und Konstruktionsprinzipien chinesischer und japanischer Wandelgärten des 17.–18. Jhs. Hamburg, [s. n.], 95, 212 p.

6785. CASSIANO (Antonio). Il Barocco a Lecce e nel Salento. Roma, De Luca, 95, XVI-431 p. (ill.). (Museo provinciale Sigismondo Castromediano – Centro di studi sul barocco).

6786. DESMOND (Ray). Kew: the history of the Royal Botanic Gardens. London, Harvill Press with the Royal Botanic Gardens, Kew, 95, XVI-466 p. (ill.).

6787. FAHR-BECKER (Gabriele). Wiener Werkstätte, 1903–1932. Köln a. London, Taschen, 95, 244 p. (ill.).

6788. HAMON-JUGNET (Marie), OUDIN-DOGLIONI (Catherine). Le Quai d'Orsay: l'hotel du ministre des Affaires étrangères. Paris, Editions du Felin, 95, 160 p.

6789. HARLANDER (Tilman). Zwischen Heimstätte und Wohnmaschine. Wohnungsbau und Wohnungspolitik in der Zeit des Nationalsozialismus. Basel, Berlin u. Boston, Birkhäuser, 95, 340 p. (Stadt – Planung – Geschichte, 18).

6790. KOMARIK (Dénes). Fezl Frigyes és megbízói. (Frigyes Feszl et ses mandants). *Budapesti negyed*, 95, 3, 3, p. 11-30.

6791. LE MOLLE (Roland). Giorgio Vasari: l'homme des Médicis. Paris, Grasset, 95, 475 p. (ill.).

6792. MEEKS (Carroll L. V.). The railroad station. An architectural history. New York a. London, Dover Publications, Constable, 95, XXVI-203 p. (ill.).

6793. MILETTE (Nicole). Parsons, Partridge, Tudway: an unsuspected garden design partnership, 1884–1914. York, Institute of Advanced Architectural Studies, University of York, 95, 24 p. (ill.).

6794. MURRELL (Kathleen Berton). St Petersburg: history, art and architecture. London, Flint River Press, 95, 144 p. (ill.).

6795. ÖZKARCI (Mehmet). Gaziantep Lala Mustafa Paşa Külliyesi. (Le Complexe de Lala Mustafa Paşa à Gaziantep). *Vakıflar Dergisi*, 95, 25, p. 39-67.

6796. PATAKFALVI (Endre). The plans and construction of the underground railway in Budapest, 1949–1956. *Acta hist. Art. Acad. Sci. Hungaricae*, 94-95, 37, 1-4, p. 295-332.

6797. PHILLIPS (Roger). A photographic garden history. London, Macmillan, 95, 319 p. (ill.).

6798. PICCOLO GIANNUZZI (Chiara). Fonti per il barocco leccese. Galatina, Congedo, 95, XVI-589 p. (ill.). (Lecce, Centro di studi sul Barocco, Archivio di Stato di Lecce, Studi di fonti archivistiche, storia e storia dell'arte, 1).

6799. THOENES (Christof). «La grande era bramantesca non è chiusa». L'architettura italiana del Rinascimento nella visione del fascismo. *Storia contemporanea*, 95, 26, 3, p. 441-450.

6800. WALLACE (William E.). Tomb of Julius II and other works in Rome. New York a. London, Garland, 95, XII-468 p. (ill.).

6801. WILLIAMSON (Tom). Polite landscapes: gardens and society in eighteenth-century England. Stroud a. Baltimore, Sutton a. Johns Hopkins U. P., 95, VIII-182 p. (ill. facsims, maps, plans).

c. Bildhauerei, Malerei, Graphik und Zeichenkunst.

** 6802. Carteggio indiretto di Michelangelo (Il). Vol. 2. A cura di Paola BAROCCHI, Kathleen LOACH BRAMANTI e Renzo RISTORI. Firenze, S. P. E. S. Editore, 95, XI-369 p.

6803. AMBROSE (Alison). Virtue and magnificence: art of the Italian Renaissance courts. New York, Harry N. Abrams, 95, 192 p. (ill.). (Perspectives).

6804. APOSTOLOS-CAPPADONA (Diane). The spirit and the vision: the influence of Christian romanticism on the development of 19th-century American art. Atlanta, Scholars Press, 95, XIV-234 p. (ill.).

6805. AYNUR (Hatice). İstanbul Çeşmeleri (1703–1730). (Les Fontaines d'Istanbul). İstanbul, İstanbul Büyükşehir Belediyesi, 95, 313 p. (Kültür İşleri Daire Bşk. Yay, 20).

6806. BAILEY (Martin). Dürer. London, Phaidon, 95, 126 p. (ill.).

6807. BARIŞTA (H. Orcun). İstanbul Çeşmeleri, Azapkapı Saliha Sultan Çeşmesi. (Les fontaines d'Istanbul: la fontaine de Saliha Sultane à Azapkabı). Ankara, [s. n.], 95, [s. p.].

6808. BERNARDINI (Maria Grazia). Tiziano: Amor sacro e amor profano. Milano, Electa, 95, 471 p. (ill.).

6809. BERNDT (Jaqueline). Phänomen Manga: Comic-Kulture in Japan. Berlin, Edition q, 95, 200 p. (ill.).

6810. BISCHOFF (Uwe). Die "Cassonebilder" des Piero di Cosimo. Fragen der Ikonographie. Frankfurt am Main a. New York, Lang, 95, 167 p. (ill.). (Europäische Hochschulschriften, XXVIII/229).

6811. BOSCHMA (Kees). Quelques considérations sur les vedute au XVIIIe siècle. *In*: Paysage en Europe du XVIe au XVIIIe siècle (Le) [Cf. n° 6759], p. 151-169.

6812. CHIARINI (Marco). Gaspard Dughet: ses liens avec ses contemporains et les paysagistes nordiques italianisants de la génération suivante. *In*: Paysage en Europe du XVIe au XVIIIe siècle (Le) [Cf. n° 6759], p. 105-118.

6813. CIARDI (Roberto Paolo). La tribuna del duomo di Pisa. Capolavori di due secoli. Milano, Electa, 95, 250 p. (ill.). (Opera della Primaziale pisana).

6814. COONIN (Victor). New documents concerning Desiderio da Settignano and Annalena Malatesta. *The Burlington Magazine*, 95, 137, p. 792-98.

6815. D'AMICO (Fabrizio). Roma 1950–59: il rinnovamento della pittura in Italia. Ferrara, Civiche gallerie d'arte moderna e contemporanea, 95, 153 p. (ill.).

6816. DANZER (Gudrun). Das steirische Eisenwesen in der Malerei und Graphik des 19. und 20. Jahrhunderts. Frankfurt am Main, Lang, 95, 290 p. (ill.). (Europäische Hochschulschriften, XXVIII/234).

6817. DEMORIS (René). Le paysage. Théorie et fantasme: Diderot et la tradition classique dans le Salon de 1767. *In*: Paysage en Europe du XVIe au XVIIIe siècle (Le) [Cf. n° 6759], p. 191-210.

6818. DEVISSCHER (Hans). Fiamminghi a Roma 1508–1608: kunstenaars uit de Nederlanden en het prinsbisdom Luik te Rome tijdens de Renaissance. Brussel, Snoeck-Ducaju & Zoon, 95, 475 p. (ill.).

6819. FRANCASTEL (Pierre). Bruegel. Paris, Hazan, 95, 237 p.

6820. FRASCINA (Francis). Meyer Shapiro's choice. My Lai, Guernica, MoMA and the Art Left, 1969–70. *Journal of Contemporary History*, 95, 30, 3-4, p. 481-512, p. 705-728.

6821. Fred Williams (1927–1982): [Exhibition] 1 November–2 December 1995. London, Marlborough Fine Art, 95, 44 p. (ill.).

6822. GREEN (Christopher). The European Avant-gardes: art in France and Western Europe 1904–1945: The Thyssen-Bornemisza Collection. London a. New York, Zwemmer, 95, 496 p. (ill.).

6823. HARDIE (Melissa). 100 years in Newlyn: diary of a gallery. Penzance, Patten Press in association with Newlyn Art Gallery, 95, 204 p. (ill.).

6824. HENNEN INSA (Christiane). "Karl zu Pferde": ikonologische Studien zu Anton van Dycks Reiterporträts Karls I. von England. Frankfurt am Main u. New York, Lang, 95, 276 p. (ill.). (Europäische Hochschulschriften. Reihe XXVIII, Kunstgeschichte, 225).

6825. HUMFREY (Peter). Painting in Renaissance Venice. New Haven a. London, Yale U. P., 95, VIII-320 p.

6826. KLEMM (David). Von Napoleon zu Bismarck. Geschichte in der deutschen Druckgraphik. Hamburg, Museum für Kunst und Gewerbe, 95, 159 p. (ill.).

6827. KUTSCHBACH (Doris). Albrecht Dürer: die Altare Dürer Albrecht. Stuttgart u. Zürich, Belser Verlag, 95, 168 p. (ill.).

6828. "Landschaft" und Landschaften im achtzehnten Jahrhundert: Tagung der deutschen Gesellschaft für die Erforschung des 18. Jahrhunderts, Herzog August Bibliothek Wolfenbüttel, 20. bis 23. November 1991. Hrsg. v. Heinke WUNDERLICH. Heidelberg, Winter, 95, 309 p. (ill.). (Beiträge zur Geschichte der Literatur und Kunst des 18. Jahrhunderts, 13).

6829. LAVIN MARILYN (Aronberg). Piero della Francesca and his legacy. Washington a. Hanover, National Gallery of Art, 95, 328 p. (National Gallery of Art – Center for Advanced Study in the Visual Arts: Symposium papers, 28).

6830. LEAVELL (Linda). Marianne Moore and the visual arts: prismatic color. Baton Rouge a. London, Louisiana State U.P., 95, XII-237 p. (ill).

6831. LIMOUZE (Dorothy A.), KURETSKY (Susan Donahue). The Felix M. Warburg print collection: a legacy of discernment. Vassar College Frances Lehman Loeb Art Center – Poughkeepsie, Frances Lehman Loeb Art Center, Vassar College, 95, 189 p. (ill.).

6832. LUCHS (Alison). Tullio Lombardo and ideal portrait sculpture in renaissance Venice, 1490–1530. Cambridge, Cambridge U. P., 95, XIV-306 p.

6833. MADERSBACHER (Lukas). Zu einer vergessenen Marientod-Tafel in der National Gallery in London. *Österreichische Zeitschrift für Kunst und Denkmalpflege*, 95, 49, 1-2, p. 21-28 (ill.).

6834. MANTION (Jean-Rémy). Desseins de paysages: du jardin au paysage à la fin du XVIIIe siècle. *In*: Paysage en Europe du XVIe au XVIIIe siècle (Le) [Cf. n° 6759], p. 277-290.

6835. MEYER (Franz). Marc Chagall. Paris, Flammarion, 95, 352 p. (1500 ill.).

6836. MILLER (Sanda). Constantin Brancusi. A survey of his work. Oxford a. New York, Clarendon Press a. Oxford U.P., 95, XXII-256 p. (ill.). (Clarendon studies in the history of art).

6837. MOISAN-JABŁOŃSKA (Krystyna). Obraz czyśćca w sztuce polskiego baroku. Studium ikonograficzno – ikonologiczne. (Image du purgatoire dans l'art baroque polonais. Etudes iconographique et iconologique). Warszawa, Semper, 95, 199 p. (Rés. franç.).

6838. MONSTADT (Brigitte). Judas beim Abendmahl: Figurenkonstellation und Bedeutung in Darstellungen von Giotto bis Andrea del Sarto. München, Scaneg, 95, XII-346 p. (ill.). (Beiträge zur Kunstwissenschaft, 57).

6839. MONTIAS (John Michael). Artists and artisans in Delft: a socio-economic study of the seventeenth century. Ann Arbor, U.M.I. Books on Demand, 95, XVI-424 p.

6840. MORRIS (Sarah P.). Daidalos and the origins of Greek art. Princeton, a. Chichester, Princeton U.P., 95, XXX-411 p. (ill.).

6841. MORTIER (Roland). Du «poétique local» au paysage pathétique ou l'évolution de la peinture de paysage, en France, après 1760. *In*: Paysage en Europe du XVIe au XVIIIe siècle (Le) [Cf. n° 6759], p. 291-307.

6842. Musées en Europe à la veille de l'ouverture du Louvre (Les). Actes du colloque organisé par le Service culturel du musée du Louvre à l'occasion de la commémoration du bicentenaire de l'ouverture du Louvre les 3, 4 et 5 juin 1993. Ed. par Edouard POMMIER. Paris, Musee du Louvre, Klincksieck, 95, 649 p. (ill.).

6843. NEUNER ANTJE (Maria). Das Triptychon in der frühen altniederländischen Malerei: Bildsprache und Aussagekraft einer Kompositionsform. Frankfurt am Main, Lang, 95, VIII-300 p. (ill.). (Europäische Hochschulschriften, 28/242).

6844. NOCHLIN (Linda), CHEIM (John). Andy Warhol nudes. Woodstock, Overlook Press, 95, 53 p. (ill.).

6845. OPPERMAN (Hal). François Desportes et le paysage: modernisme ou modernité. *In*: Paysage en Europe du XVIe au XVIIIe siècle (Le) [Cf. n° 6759], p. 171-189.

6846. READ (Peter). Picasso et Apollinaire: les métamorphoses de la mémoire, 1905–1973. Paris, Place, 95, 316 p. (ill.).

6847. ROLAND MICHEL (Marianne). Le paysage au XVIIIe siècle: théorie, einsegnement, sa place dans la doctrine académique. In: Paysage en Europe du XVIe au XVIIIe siècle (Le) [Cf. n° 6759], p. 211-229.

6848. ROOS (Jane Mayo). Landscapes of France: Impressionism and its rivals. London, The South Bank Centre, 95, 304 p. (ill.).

6849. RUSSO (Daniel). Religion civique et art monumental à Florence au XVIe siècle. La décoration peinte de la salle capitulaire à Sante-Marie-Nouvelle. In: Religion civique à l'époque médiévale et moderne (La) [Cf. n° 4528], p. 279-296.

6850. SANTOSUOSSO (A.). Giovanni Della Casa and his lost portrait by Titian. Bibliothèque d'Humanisme et Renaissance, 95, 57, 1, p. 111-118.

6851. SERRÃO (Vitor). A pintura maneirista em Portugal: a arte no tempo de Camoes. Ed. Comissão Nacional para as Comemoraçoes dos Descobrimentos Portugueses, Fundaçao das Descobertas Centro Cultural de Belém. Lisboa, C.N.C.D.P., 95, 511 p. (ill.).

6852. SEYMOUR (Charles). Michelangelo: the Sistine Chapel ceiling: illustrations, introductory essay, backgrounds and sources, critical essays. New York a. London, Norton, 95, XXI-243 p. (ill .). (Norton critical studies in art history).

6853. SILLEVIS (John). Rodin's first one-man show. The Burlington Magazine, 95, 137, p. 832-37.

6854. SIMONCELLI (Paolo). Pontormo e la cultura fiorentina. Archivio storico italiano, 95, 153, 565, p. 487-528.

6855. STUBBLEBINE (James H.). Giotto: the Arena Chapel frescoes: illustrations, introductory essay, backgrounds and sources, criticism. New York a. London, Norton, 95, XIII-218 p. (ill.). (A Norton critical study in art history).

6856. SZUBERT (Piotr). Rzeźba polska przełomu XIX i XX wieku. (Sculpture polonaise de la fin du XIXe / début XXe s.). Warszawa, Semper, 95, 114 p. (phot., fig., dessins).

6857. Taidevääremöksiä Suomessa. (Fakeries on paintings of known Finnish painters.) Publ. by The Criminal Police Association in Turku. Masku, Art Sherlock, 95, 240 p. (ill.).

6858. TARGOSZ (Karolina). Mikołaj Kopernik jednym z "Trzech filozofów" Giorgiona? (Nicolas Copernic fut-il l'un des "Trois philosophes" de Giorgione?). Kwartalnik Historii Nauki i Technik, 95, 40, 3, p. 49-85. [Eng. Summary].

6859. THEBERGE (Pierre), BISSONNETTE (Denise). Paradis perdus: l'Europe symboliste. Montréal, Musée des beaux-arts de Montréal, 95, 552 p. (ill.).

6860. THOMA (Petra). Philipp Jakob Rampl (1728–1809): ein bürgerlicher Bildhauer in Oberbayern zwischen Rokoko und Klassizismus. München, Kommissionsverlag Uni-Druck, 95, IV-290 p. (ill.). (Miscellanea Bavarica Monacensia, 166).

6861. VAISSE (Pierre). La Troisième République et les peintres. Art, histoire, societé. Paris, Flammarion, 95, 475 p.

6862. VENTURA (Leandro). Lorenzo Leonbruno. Un pittore a corte nella Mantova di primo Cinquecento. Roma, Bulzoni, 95, 354 p. (ill.). (Biblioteca del Cinquecento, 64).

6863. WENK (Silke). Versteinerte Weiblichkeit. Studien zur Allegorie in der Skulptur der Moderne. Wien, Köln u. Weimar, Böhlau, 95, 410 p.

6864. WILBERDING (E.). Cellini and the Salviati. Bibliothèque d'Humanisme et Renaissance, 95, 57, 3, p. 615-622.

d. Kunstgewerbe und Volkskunst.

6865. AKINSHA (Konstantin), KOZLOV (Grigorii). Stolen treasure: the hunt for the world's lost masterpieces, London, Weidenfeld & Nicolson, 95, XXIII-289 p. (ill.).

6866. CLARK (Garth). The potter's art. A complete history of pottery in Britain. London, Phaidon, 95, 239 p. (ill.).

6867. COOKE (Lynne), WOLLEN (Peter). Visual display: culture beyond appearances. Seattle, Bay Press, 95, 351 p. (ill.). (Dia Centre for the Arts – Discussions in contemporary culture, 10).

6868. COOREMAN (R.). Les Arts décoratifs aux Pays-Bas: à la période bourguignonne et sous les Habsbourg. Brussels, Musées royaux d'Art et d'Histoire, 95, 76 p. (ill.).

6869. Design history: an anthology. Ed. by Dennis P. DOORDAN. Cambridge, MIT Press, 95, XIV-274 p. (A Design issues reader).

6870. FAULKNER (Rupert). Japanese studio crafts: tradition and the avant-garde. London, Laurence King, 95, 192 p. (ill.).

6871. HASSELL (Geoff). Camberwell School of Arts and Crafts: its students and teachers, 1943–1960. Woodbridge, Antique Collectors' Club, 95, 239 p.

6872. HINE (Thomas). The total package: the evolution and secret meanings of boxes, bottles, cans, and tubes. Boston, a. London, Little a. Brown, 95, X-289 p. (ill.).

6873. MARTINIE (Henri). Art deco ornamental ironwork. New York a. London, Dover, Constable, 95, 106 p.

6874. SARPELLON (Giovanni). Miniature masterpieces: mosaic glass 1838–1924. München, Prestel, 95, 192 p.

6875. SPECTRE (Peter H.), LARKIN (David). Wooden ship: the art, history, and revival of wooden boat building. London, Cassell, 95, 427 p.

6876. TABURET-DELAHAYE (Elisabeth). L'orfèvrerie au poinçon d'Avignon. Revue de l'art, 95, 108, p. 5-23.

6877. THURRE (Daniel). Emaux celtes et continentaux du premier millénaire. Revue de l'art, 95, 108, p. 47-69.

6878. WOODS (Oona), HIPPSLEY (Paul). Seeing is believing? Murals in Derry. Derry, Guidhall Press, 95, 56 p.

§ 9. Musik, Theater und Film.

* 6879. Bibliographie der Filmseite und der Filmnachrichten des Pariser Tageblatts/Pariser Tageszeitung 1933–1940. Herausgegeben und mit einer Einleitung von Helmut G. ASPER; bibliographische Bearbeitung: Pariser Tageblatt 1933–1936, Cornelia FLEER; Pariser Tageszeitung 1933–1940, Christina GUMINSKI. Frankfurt am Main, Lang, 95, XVI-232 p. (Bibliographien zur Literatur- und Mediengeschichte, 5).

* 6880. HOFFMANN (Frank), COOPER (B. Lee). The literature of rock, III, 1984–1990: with additional material for the period 1954–1983. Metuchen a. London, Scarecrow Press, 95, XIX-1003 p.

6881. ALBERA (François). Cinéma sans frontières, 1896–1918. Images across borders. Aspects de l'internationalité dans le cinéma mondial. Représentations, marchés, influences. Lausanne-Québec, Payot-Nuit Blanche, 95, 383 p. (ill.).

6882. ALMANSI (Guido). Tra cinema e teatro. Venezia, Marsilio, 95, 126 p. (Gli specchi dello spettacolo).

6883. ALONGE (Roberto). Ibsen. L'opera e la fortuna scenica. Firenze, Le lettere, 95, 162 p. (Storia dello spettacolo. Manuali, 2). ·

6884. AMAR RODRÍGUEZ (Víctor Manuel). El negro en el cine de Argentina, Brasil y Cuba. Revista de História, 95, 132, p. 11-127.

6885. ARTIOLI (Umberto). Il combattimento invisibile. D'Annunzio tra romanzo e teatro. Roma e Bari, Laterza, 95, 254 p. (Biblioteca di cultura moderna, 1076).

6886. ASTON (Elaine). An introduction to feminism and theatre. London a. New York, Routledge, 95, IX, 166 p.

6887. Bach studies. Ed. by Daniel R. MELAMED. Cambridge, Cambridge U.P., 95, XIII-238 p.

6888. Bellezza (La) interiore. Il cinema di David Cronenberg. A cura di Michele CANOSA. Genova, Le Mani, 95, 166 p. (ill.).

6889. BERARDINELLI (Paula). Bill Evans. His contributions as a jazz pianist and an analysis of his musical style. Ann Arbor, UMI, 95, XVI, 334 p.

6890. BERNARDI (Sandro). Introduzione alla retorica del cinema. Firenze, Le Lettere, 95, 242 p. (Storia dello spettacolo. Manuali, 1).

6891. BERTELLI (Sergio). Corsari del tempo. Quando il cinema inventa la storia. (Guida pratica per registi distratti). Firenze, Ponte alle Grazie, 95, 357 p. (ill.).

6892. BICK (Ilsa J.). Boys in space: «Star trek», latency, and the neverending story. Cinema journal, 95, 35, 2, p. 43-60.

6893. Bielefelder Katalog Jazz. Schallplatten, Compact Discs, MusiCassetten, 1995. Stuttgart, Vereinigte Motor-Verlage, 95, 1472 p.

6894. BLACKADDER (Neil Martin). Offending the audience. Modern theatre as confrontation. Ann Arbor, UMI, 95, VII-300 p.

6895. Brewer's Cinema. A phrase and fable dictionary. London, Cassel, 95, 618 p.

6896. BRUNETTA (Giampiero). Il cinema di Hitchcock. Venezia, Marsilio, 95, 173 p. (Tascabili Marsilio, 23).

6897. BURNS (Lori). Bach's modal chorales. Stuyvesant, N.Y., Pendragon Press, 95, X-249 p. (Harmonologia series, 9).

6898. CAREW-REID (Micaela). Les fêtes florentines au temps de Laurent de Médicis. Firenze, Olschki, 95, 291 p.

6899. CARTER (Mia Elizabeth). Shades of jazz. Desire, difference and the politics of culture. Ann Arbor, UMI, 95, V-190 p.

6900. CASADIO (Gianfranco). Opera e cinema. La musica lirica nel cinema italiano dall'avvento del sonoro ad oggi. Ravenna, Longo, 95, 295 p. (ill.). (Musica, cinema, immagine e teatro, 15).

6901. Cinéma (Le) "direct". Dirigé par René PREDAL. Condé-sur-Noireau, Corlet-Télérama, 95, 216 p. (ill.). (CinémAction, 76).

6902. Cinéma (Le) des écrivains. Textes réunis par Antoine DE BAECQUE. Paris, Cahiers du cinéma, 95, 287 p.

6903. Cinéma (Le) fantastique. Réuni par Jean-Pierre PITON. Condé-sur-Noireau, Corlet, 95, 174 p. (ill.). (CinémAction, 74).

6904. «Con che soavità». Studies in Italian opera, song and dance, 1580–1740. Ed. by Iain FENLON a. Tim CARTER. Oxford, Clarendon Press, 95, X-336 p. (ill.).

6905. Concert des voix (Le) et des instruments à la Renaissance. Actes du XXXIVe Colloque international d'Etudes Humanistes. Ed. par Jean-Michel VACCARO. Paris, C. N. R. S., 95, 727 p.

6906. CRISE (Stefano). Come una veste al corpo. Interpreti mozartiani e prassi esecutiva all'epoca e nei luoghi di Mozart. Milano, Polyhymnia, 95, 261 p.

9. MUSIK, THEATER UND FILM

6907. Critica del testo musicale (La). Metodi e problemi della filologia musicale. A cura di Maria CARACI VELA. Lucca, Libreria Musicale Italiana, 95, XII-522 p. (Rinascimento, 35).

6908. DA VINCI NICHOLS (Nina), O'KEEFE BAZZONI (Jana). Pirandello and film. Lincoln, University of Nebraska Press, 95, XVI-244 p.

6909. DANIEL (Ute). Hoftheater. Zur Geschichte des Theaters und der Höfe im 18. und 19. Jahrhundert. Stuttgart, Klett-Cotta, 95, 537 p. (ill.).

6910. DEAN (Winton), KNAPP (John Merrill). Händel's operas, 1704–1726. Oxford, Clarendon Press, 95, XX-771 p.

6911. DENORA (Tia). Beethoven and the construction of genius. Musical politics in Vienna, 1792–1803. Berkeley, University of California Press, 95, XVII-232 p.

6912. Deutsche Theater in Pest und Ofen, 1770–1850. Hrsg. v. Hedvig BELITSKA-SCHOLZ u. Olga SOMORJA. Budapest, Argumentum, 95, 2 vol., 1276 p.

6913. DI BERNARDI (Vito). Introduzione allo studio del teatro indonesiano. Giava e Bali. Firenze, La casa Usher, 95, 255 p. (Guide teatro e spettacolo. Teatri orientali, 2).

6914. DUBOIS (Thomas A.). Finnish folk poetry and the Kalevala. New York-London, Garland, 95, XII, 328 p. (New perspectives in folklore, 1).

6915. Ecrire pour le théâtre. Les enjeux de l'écriture dramatique. Études réunies et présentées sous la direction de M.-Ch. AUTANT-MATHIEU. Paris, CNRS Éditions, 95, 199 p. (Spectacles, histoire, société).

6916. En travesti. Women, gender subversion, opera. Ed. by Corinne E. BLACKMER a. Patricia Juliana SMITH. New York, Columbia U.P., 95, 379 p. (ill.). (Between men – Between women).

6917. Est a ovest (Da). Cinema ungherese, 1987–1994. A cura di Vincenzo CAVANDOLI e Paolo VECCHI. Reggio Emilia, Ufficio Cinema del Comune, 95, 109 p. (ill.). (Quaderni di Ventiquattroalsecondo, 24).

6918. FULCI (Lucio). Miei mostri adorati. Racconti e scritti di cinema. Bologna, Pendragon, 95, 150 p. (L'inferno, 7).

6919. Gesuiti (I) e i primordi del teatro barocco in Europa. XVIII Convegno del Centro studi sul teatro medioevale e rinascimentale. A cura di Myriam CHIABÒ e Federico DOGLIO. Roma, Torre d'Orfeo, 95, 499 p.

6920. GOLDBERG (Lee). Science fiction filmmaking in the 1980s: interviews with actors, directors, producers, and writers. Jefferson a. London, McFarland, 95, XII-267 p. (ill.).

6921. GRECO (Franco Carmelo). La scena illustrata. Teatro, pittura e città a Napoli nell'Ottocento. Napoli, Pironti, 95, XXXIV-417 p.

6922. GRINDON (Lager). Body and soul: the structure of meaning in the boxing film genre. Cinema journal, 95, 35, 4, p. 54-69.

6923. HAMACHE (M.). Les Juifs dans les arts dramatiques au XIXe siècle. Regards croisés sur la tragédienne Rachel (1821–1858). Revue Historique, 95, 119, 593, p. 119-134.

6924. HEARTZ (Daniel). Haydn, Mozart and the Viennese School, 1740–1780. New York-London, Norton, 95, XXVIII-780 p.

6925. HOGDON (Pierre). Pleurnicher pour le cinéma français. Cahier du cinéma, 95, 489, p. 44-47.

6926. ISHAGHPOUR (Youssef). Opéra et théâtre dans le cinéma d'aujourd'hui. Paris, La Différence, 95, 99 p. (Mobile matière).

6927. ISOLA (Gianni). Dalla scatola della musica al radiocane. Radiofonia e tempo libero nell'Italia del Novecento. Storia in Lombardia, 95, 14, 1-2, p. 125-136.

6928. Jazz among the discourses. Ed. by Krin GABBARD. Durham-London, Duke U.P., 95, VIII-288 p.

6929. JONES (David Wyn). Beethoven: Pastoral symphony, Cambridge, Cambridge U.P., 95, X, 103 p. (Cambridge music handbooks).

6930. JONES (Stephen). Folk music of China. Living instrumental traditions. Oxford, Clarendon Press, 95, XXVII-422 p.

6931. JOUSSE (Thiérry). Cinq motifs pour Claude Chabrol. Cahier du cinéma, 95, 494, p. 34-35.

6932. JUST (Vladimír). Česká divadelní kultura 1945–1989 v datech a souvislostech. (Czech theatre culture, 1945–1989, in dates and in context). Tomo 1. Divadlo v totalitním systému (teze). Tomo 2. Kalendárium českého divadla 1945–1989. Praha, Divadelní ústav, 95, 469 p. (photogr., bibl.).

6933. KALLIONIEMI (Kari). Dadyfied image of Elvis Presley and the cultural polyphony of popular music. In: Monta tietä menneisyyteen [Cf. n° 1133], p. 39-48.

6934. KATER (Michael H.). Carl Orff im Dritten Reich. Vierteljahrshefte für Zeitgeschichte, 95, 95, 43, 1, p. 1-36.

6935. Keine Experimentierkunst. Musikleben an Städtischen Theatern in der Weimarer Republik. Hrsg. v. Dörte SCHMIDT u. Brigitta WEBER. Stuttgart u. Weimar, Metzler, 95, XII, 356 p.

6936. KERNEN (Alvin). Shakespeare, the king's playwright. Theater in the Stuart court, 1603–1613. New Haven-London, Yale U.P., 95, XXIII-230 p.

6937. KERR (David). African popular theatre. From pre-colonial times to the present day. London, Currey, 95, X-278 p. (Studies in African literature).

6938. KNEPLER (Georg). Wolfgang Amadé Mozart. Nuovi percorsi. Milano, Ricordi e Lucca, LIM, 95, 481 p.

6939. KORITZ (Amy). Gendering bodies/performing art. Dance and literature in early twentieth-century British culture. Ann Arbor, University of Michigan Press, 95, 218 p.

6940. KULIGOWSKA-KORZENIEWSKA (Anna). Scena obiecana. Teatr polski w Łodzi 1844–1918. (Scène de la grande promesse. Théâtre polonais de Łódź 1844–1918). Łódź, Wydawn. Łódzkie, 95, 318 p. (Deutsche Zsfassung, phot., fig.).

6941. LAURA (Ernesto G.). Parola d'autore. Gianni Puccini tra critica, letteratura e cinema. Roma, ANCCI, 95, 160 p.

6942. LEBEAU (Vicky). Lost angels. Psychoanalysis and cinema. London-New York, Routledge, 95, 172 p.

6943. LEGOY (C.). La figure du souverain médiéval sur les scènes parisiennes à la Restauration. *Revue Historique*, 95, 119, 594, p. 321-366.

6944. Leonardo Sciascia: cinema e letteratura. A cura di Sergio LANELLI. Pordenone, Cinemazero, 95, 158 p. [PIRRO (Ugo). Sceneggiare Sciascia, p. 59-65. CONNEZIO (Ermanno). Cinema e letteratura: due linguaggi diversi, p. 121-37].

6945. MANSURE (Victor Newell). The allemandes of Johann Sebastian Bach. A stylistic study. Ann Arbor, UMI, 95, XVI-268 p.

6946. MARSTON (Nicholas). Beethoven's Piano Sonata in E, Op. 109. Oxford, Clarendon Press, 95, XVIII-267 p. (Studies in musical genesis and structure).

6947. MARTIN CORRALES (Eloy). El cine español y las guerras de Marruecos (1896–1994). *Hispania*, 95, 55, 190, p. 693-708.

6948. MARTINELLI (Vittorio), BERNERDINI (Aldo). Il cinema muto italiano. I film degli anni d'oro. 1912. Torino e Roma, Nuova ERI, 95, 2 v.

6949. MEADOWS (Eddie S.). Jazz research and performance materials. A select annotated bibliography. New York a. London, Garland, 95, XLIII-806 p. (Garland library of music ethnology, 4).

6950. MELAMED (Daniel R.). J.S. Bach and the German motet. Cambridge, Cambridge U.P., 95, XV-229 p.

6951. MONALDINI (Sergio). Il teatro dei comici dell'arte a Bologna. *L'Archiginnasio*, 90, 95, p. 1-164 (ill.).

6952. Movies guide (The). Ed. by James PALLOT, New York, Perigee Book, 95, 1062 p.

6953. NEAL (Lucinda Jane). A search for primitive voice in post-modern theatre. Ann Arbor, UMI, 95, VI, 122 p.

6954. NELSON (Angela Marie S.). A theomusicological approach to rap. A model for the study of African American popular and folk musics. Ann Arbor, UMI, 95, X-343 p.

6955. Opera and the Enlightenment. Ed. by Thomas BAUMAN a. Marita PETZOLDT MAC CLYMONDS. Cambridge, Cambridge U.P., 95, XIII-317 p.

6956. PISCIOTTA (Eva Mae). The history of jazz choir in the United States. Ann Arbor, UMI, 95, IX-151 p.

6957. PITHON (Rémy). Cinéma et histoire, bilan historiographique. XXe siècle, 95, 48, p. 5-13.

6958. POGGI (Amedeo), VALLORA (Edgar). Beethoven. Signori, il catalogo è questo! Torino, Einaudi, 95, VI-733 p. (Gli struzzi, 473).

6959. PRICE (Curtis), MILHOUS (Judith), HUME (Robert D.). Italian opera in late eighteenth-century London. Vol. 1. The King's Theatre, Haymarket 1778–1791. Oxford, Clarendon, 95, XXV-698 p.

6960. Robert Desnos e il meraviglioso moderno. Una poetica surrealista del cinema (1923–1930). A cura di Riccardo MAZZONI e Federica GHISELLI. Pisa, ETS, 95, 127 p. (Le arti dello spettacolo, 9).

6961. ROMAGNOLI (Angela). Fra catene, fra stili, e fra veleni ... ossia Della scena di prigione nell'opera italiana (1690–1724). Lucca, Libreria musicale italiana, 95, 473 p. (ill.). (Studi e testi musicali. Nuova serie, 2).

6962. RONDOLINO (Gianni). Dizionario storico dei film. Torino, UTET, 95, 1378 p.

6963. RUSSO (Paolo). Come ascoltare le Passioni di Johann Sebastian Bach. Milano, Mursia, 95, 134 p.

6964. SABATIER (François). Miroirs de la musique. La musique et ses correspondances avec la littérature et les beaux-arts, 1800–1950. Paris, Fayard, 95, 728 p.

6965. SALA (Emilio). L'opera senza canto. Il mélo romantico e l'invenzione della colonna sonora. Venezia, Marsilio, 95, 266 p. (Musica critica).

6966. SARKAR (Bhaskar). Epic (Mis)takes: nation, religion and gender on television. *Quarterly Review of film and video*, 95, 16, 1, p. 59-75.

6967. SAUNDERS (Thomas J.). Art, ideology, and entertainment in Soviet cinema. *Canadian Journal of History*, 95, 30, 1, p. 85-92.

6968. Schermi di guerra. Cinema italiano 1939–1945. A cura di Mino ARGENTIERI. Roma, Bulzoni, 95, 382 p. (Cinema/studio, 7).

6969. SEIWERT (Elvira). Beethoven-Szenarien. Thomas Manns "Doktor Faustus" und Adornos Beethoven-Projekt. Stuttgart u. Weimar, Metzler, 95, 288 p.

6970. SINGER (Noel F.). Burmese dance and theatre. Kuala Lumpur, Oxford U.P., 95, XII-94 p. (ill.). (Images of Asia).

6971. SINISI (Silvana). Cambi di scena. Teatro e arti visive nelle poetiche del Novecento. Roma, Bulzoni, 95, 242 p. (tav.). (Biblioteca teatrale, 86).

6972. SNYDER (Lawrence D.). German poetry in song. An index of Lieder. Berkeley, Fallen Leaf Press, 95, XVIII-730 p. (Fallen Leaf reference books in music, 30).

6973. SOLOMON (Maynard). Mozart. A life. London, Pimlico, 95, XVI-640 p.

6974. SPINGER (Claudia). Eletronic eros. Bodies and desire in the postindustrial age. Austin, University of Texas Press, 95, XVI-340 p. (ill.).

6975. STAIGER (Janet). Bad women. Regulating sexuality in early American cinema. Minneapolis-London, University of Minnesota Press, 95, XVIII-226 p.

6976. Suomen musiikin historia. (The history of Finnish music). 1. Ruotsin vallan ajasta romantiikkaan: keskiaika – 1899. (From the Swedish era to Romantics: Middle ages – 1899). Ed by Fabian DAHLSTRÖM a. Erkki SALMENHAARA. 4. Aikamme musiikki: 1945–1993. (Modern music: 1945–1993). Ed. by Mikko HEINIÖ. Helsinki, WS, 95, 2 vol, 580 p., 568 p. (ill).

6977. SZYDŁOWSKA (Mariola). Cenzura teatralna w Galicji w dobie autonomicznej 1860–1918. (Censure théâtrale en Galicie à l'époque de l'autonomie 1860–1918). Kraków, Universitas, 95, 280 p. (phot., fig.). [Deutsche Zsfassung].

6978. Teatro (Il) musicale dalle origini al primo Settecento. Dir. da Alberto BASSO. Torino, UTET, 95, XV-462 p., (Musica in scena. Storia dello spettacolo musicale, 1).

6979. Théâtre (Le) et le temps qui passe. Mémoires singulières. Sous la diréction de Roger DELDIME. Carnières, Lansman, 95, 178 p. (Collection "Théatre événements", 7).

6980. THOMAS (Helen). Dance, modernity and culture. Explorations in the sociology of dance. London, Routledge, 95, X-206 p. ((ill.).

6981. TORDI (Rosita). Il manto di Lindoro. Rovani e il teatro d'opera. Roma, Bulzoni, 95, 305 p.

6982. VASEY (Ruth). Beyond sex and violence: the regulation of Hollywood movies 1922–1939. *Review of film and video,* 95, 16/4, p. 65-85.

6983. VERDONE (Mario). Storia del cinema italiano. Roma, Newton Compton, 95, 88 p. (Il sapere. Enciclopedia tascabile, 52).

6984. VOGEL (Martin). Musiktheater XI. Cagliostro, Goethes Gross-Cophta. Bonn, Orpheus, 95, 173 p. (Orpheus, 78).

6985. WINKLER (Martin M.). Cinema and the fall of Rome. *Transactions of the American philological Association,* 95, 125, p. 135-54.

6986. ŻÓRAWSKA-WITKOWSKA (Alina). Muzyka na dworze i w teatrze Stanisława Augusta. (La musique à la Cour et au Théâtre du [roi] Stanisław August [Poniatowski]). Warszawa, Arx Regia, 95, 370 p. (phot., fig., notes). [Eng. Summary].

Cf. n°s 434, 442, 1369

N

WIRTSCHAFTS- UND SOZIALGESCHICHTE DER NEUZEIT

§ 1. Volkswirtschaftslehre. 6987-7042. – § 2. Allgemeine Wirtschaftsgeschichte. 7043-7145. – § 3. Industrie, Bergbau und Verkehr. 7146-7199. – § 4. Handel. 7200-7232. – § 5. Landwirtschaft und Agrarprobleme. 7233-7268. – § 6. Geld- und Finanzwesen. 7269-7301. – § 7. Bevölkerungsbewegung und Städtebaukunst. 7302-7346. – § 8. Sozial- und Sittengeschichte. 7347-7489– § 9. Arbeiterbewegung und Sozialismus. 7490-7533.

§ 1. Volkswirtschaftslehre.

** 6987. BESOMI (Daniele). From the trade cycle to the essay in dynamic theory: the Harrod-Keynes correspondence, 1937–1938. *Hist. Polit. Ec.*, 95, 27, 2, p. 309-344.

** 6988. Catalogue (A) of the papers of John Maynard Keynes in King's College Library, Cambridge. Cambridge, Chadwyck-Healey, 95, XI-161p.

6989. ALMODOVAR (Antonio). A institucionalização da economia politica classica em Portugal. Porto, Edicoes Afrontamento, 95, 358 p. (Colecção Biblioteca das ciencias do homem. Historia, 7).

6990. ALTHUSSER (Louis). Sur la reproduction. Introduction de Jacques BIDET. Paris, PUF, 95, 314 p. (Actuel Marx confrontation).

6991. BALLARD (Bill). How Keynes became a post Keynesian. *J. Post. Keyn. Ec.*, 95, 17, 3, p. 325-336.

6992. BISHOP (John D.). Adam Smith's invisible hand argument. *J. Busin. Ethics*, 95, 14, 3, p. 165-180.

6993. BONNER (John). Economic efficiency and social justice: the development of utilitarian ideas in economics from Bentham to Edgeworth. Aldershot a. Brookfield, Edward Elgar, 95, 211 p.

6994. BREWER (Anthony), ELLIOT (John E.), FOLEY (Duncan K.), [et al.]. A minor post-Ricardian? Marx as an economist. *Hist. Polit. Ec.*, 95, 27, 1, p. 111-206.

6995. BREWER (Anthony). The concept of growth in eighteenth-century economics. *Hist. Polit. Ec.*, 95, 27, 4, p. 609-638.

6996. BRYAN (Dick). The internationalisation of capital and Marxian value theory. *Camb. J. Econ.*, 95, 19, 3, p. 421-440.

6997. CHALOUPEK (Günther). Long-term economic perspectives compared: Joseph Schumpeter and Werner Sombart. *Eur. J. Hist. Econ. Thou.*, 95, 2, 1, p. 127-150.

6998. CHAUVEL (Louis), FITOUSSI (Jean-Paul). Pareto and Pantaleoni: parallel lives and secant lives. *Riv. Pol. Ec.*, 95, 85, 3, p. 155-176.

6999. Classical tradition in economic thought (The). Ed. by Ingrid H. RIMA. Aldershot, For the History of Economics Society by Edward Elgar, 95, XII-121 p. (Perspectives on the history of economic thought, 11).

7000. DARD (Olivier). Voyage à l'intérieur d'X-Crise [le centre polytéchnicien d'études économiques, 1931–1939]. *XXe siècle*, 95, 47, p. 132-146.

7001. DAVIS (John Bryan). Keynes philosophical development. Cambridge, Cambridge U. P., 95, 196 p.

7002. DELMAS (Bernard), DELMAS (Thierry), STEINER (Philippe). La diffusion internationale de la physiocratie (XVIIIe–XIXe). Actes du Colloque international de Saint-Cloud. Grenoble, Presses universitaires de Grenoble, 95, 482 p. [Cf. n^{os} <sélection> 7002, 7038, 7041, 7160.] – IIDEM. Les physiocrates, la science de l'économie politique et l'Europe. *In*: La diffusion internationale de la physiocratie [Cf. n° 7002], p. 7-29.

7003. DONOGHUE (Mark). The wages-and-profits fund: classical remnants in Marshall's early theory of distribution. *Eur. J. Hist. Econ. Thou.*, 95, 2, 2, p. 355-374.

7004. DOW (Sheila C.). The appeal of neoclassical economics: some insights from Keynes's epistemology. *Camb. J. Econ.*, 95, 19, 6, p. 715-733.

7005. FAUCCI (Riccardo). L'economista scomodo. Vita e opere di Francesco Ferrara. Palermo, Sellerio Editore, 95, 316 p.

7006. FELIX (David). Biography of an idea: John Maynard Keynes and The general theory of employment, interest and money. New Brunswick, Transaction Publishers, 95, IX-285 p.

7007. FERGUSON (Niall). Keynes and the German inflation. *English Historical Review*, 95, 110, 436, p. 368-391.

7008. FLEETWOOD (Steve). Hayek's political economy: the socio-economics of order. London a New York, Routledge, 95, 178 p.

7009. FUKAZAWA (Katsumi). 18-seiki no furansurevanto bōeki to kokusai-kin'yū: Rū-shōkai-monjo no kawase-tegata (I) (II). (Franco-Levantine commerce and the international finance in the eighteenth century: bills of exchange in "fonds Roux"). *Shien*, 95, 132, p. 1-21.

7010. GEHRKE (Christian), KURZ (Heinz D.). Karl Marx on physiocracy. *Eur. J. Hist. Econ. Thou*, 95, 2, 1, p. 53-90.

7011. GERRARD (B.). Keynes, the Keynesians and the classics: a suggested interpretation. *Econ. J.*, 95, 105, 429, p. p. 445-458.

7012. HAGENLOCH (Thorsten). Religionssoziologie und Wissenschaftslehre bei Max Weber: kulturgeschichtliche Aspekte zur Entwicklung des modernen Kapitalismus. Weiden, Schuch, 95, 281 p.

7013. HAYEK (Friedrich August von). Contra Keynes and Cambridge: essays, correspondence. Ed. by Bruce CALDWELL. London, Routledge, 95, XI-269 p. (The collected works of F. A. Hayek, 9).

7014. Heterodox economic theories: true or false? Ed. by Fred MOSELEY. Aldershot, Edward Elgar, 95, XX-142 p.

7015. Historical evolution of the international political economy (The). Ed. by Christopher CHASE-DUNN. Aldershot, E. Elgar, 95, 2 vol., XIX-646 p., VIII-492 p. (Library of international political economy, 9).

7016. HOLLANDER (Samuel). Ricardo, the new view: collected essays. London, Routledge, 95, XIV-369 p.

7017. Idei N.D. Kondrat'eva i dinamika obshchestva na rubezhe tret'go tysiacheletiia. (The ideas of N. D. Kondrat'ev and dynamics of society abroad in third millennium). Ed. by Iurii Vladimirovich IAKOVETS. Moskva, Mezhdunar. fond N.D. Kondrat'eva, 95, 523 p.

7018. JOE (Hyeon-soo). Politische Ökonomie als Gesellschaftstheorie: Studien zur Marx-Rezeption von Isaak Iljitsch Rubin und Kozo Uno. Marburg, [s.n.], 95, 226 p.

7019. KAMIYAKA (Tsuneo). Meiji Keizai Seisakushi no Kenkyū. (The economic policy in the Meiji era). Tokyo, Hanawa Shobō, 95, 302 p.

7020. KURDAS (Chidem). Accumulation and technical change: Marx revisited. *Sci. Soc.*, 95, 59, 1, p. 52-68.

7021. LEVY (David M.). The partial spectator in The Wealth of Nations: a robust utilitarianism. *Eur. J. Hist. Econ. Thou.*, 95, 2, 2, p. 299-326. [On Adam Smith]

7022. LLOMBART (Vicent). Market for ideas and reception of physiocracy in Spain: some analytical and historical suggestions. *Eur. J. Hist. Econ. Thou.*, 95, 2, 1, p. 29-52.

7023. MATSUURA (Masataka). Nicchū Sensō-ki ni okeru Keizai to Seiji: Konoe Fumimaro to Ikeda. (Economic-political dynamics during the Sino-Japanese War, 1937–1945. Konoe Fumimaro and Ikeda). Tokyo, University of Tokyo Press, 95, 347 p.

7024. MESTMÄCKER (Ernst-Joachim). Wirtschaftsordnung und Geschichtsgesetz. *Ordo*, 95, 46, p. 9-25.

7025. MÉSZÁROS (István). Beyond capital: toward a theory of transition. London, Merlin Press a. New York, Monthly Review Press, 95, 994 p.

7026. MOSELEY (Fred). Capital in general and Marx's logical method: a response to Heinrich's critique. *Cap. Class*, 95, 56, p. 15-48.

7027. New perspectives on Keynes. Ed. by Allin F. COTTRELL a. Michael S. LAWLOR. Durham, Duke U. P., 95, VI-287 p. (History of Political Economy. Annual supplement, 1995).

7028. Nihon no Senji Keizai: Keikaku to Shijō. (Japan's wartime economy: planning and markets). Ed. by Akira HARA. Tokyo, University of Tokyo Press, 95, 313 p.

7029. NORTON (Bruce). The theory of monopoly capitalism and classical economics. *Hist. Polit. Ec.*, 95, p. 539-562.

7030. Origini (Alle) del pensiero economico in Italia. Vol. 1. Moneta e sviluppo negli economisti napoletani dei secoli XVII–XVIII. A cura di Alessandro RONCAGLIA. Bologna, Il Mulino, 95, 151 p. (Collana della Società italiana degli economisti).

7031. ORMAZABAL (Kepa M.). The law of diminishing marginal utility in Alfred Marshall's principles of economics. *Eur. J. Hist. Econ. Thou.*, 95, 2, 1, p. 91-126.

7032. OSWALD (Donald J.). Metaphysical beliefs and the foundations of Smithian political economy. *Hist. Polit. Ec.*, 95, 27, 3, p. 449-476.

7033. POMA (Lucio). Economia, giudizi e valori in Albert O. Hirschman. *Industria*, 95, 15, 1, p. 155-181.

7034. Post-Fordism: a reader. Ed. by Ash AMIN. Oxford a. Cambridge, Blackwell, 95, 435 p.

7035. SABOGAL TAMAYO (Julián). Historia del pensamiento económico colombiano (1850–1950). Bogota, Plaza & Janes, 95, 392 p.

7036. SMITH (Adam). Adam Smith's Wealth of nations: new interdisciplinary essays. Ed. by Stephen COPLEY a. Kathryn SUTHERLAND. Manchester, Manchester U. P., 95, XIII-205 p. (Texts in culture).

7037. SONG (Hyun-Ho). Adam Smith as an early pioneer of institutional individualism. *Hist. Polit. Ec.*, 95, 27, 3, p. 425-448.

7038. STEINER (Philippe). Quels principes pour l'économie politique? Charles Ganilh, German Garnier, Jean-Baptiste Say et la critique de la physiocratie. *In*: La diffusion internationale de la physiocratie [Cf. n° 7002], p. 209-230.

7039. Théorie de la régulation. L'état des savoirs. Sous la dir. de Robert BOYER et Yves SAILLARD. Paris, La Découverte, 95, 568 p.

7040. Theory of ethical economy in the historical school (The). Wilhelm Roscher, Lorenz von Stein, Gustav Schmoller, Wilhelm Dilthey and contemporary theory. Ed. by Peter KOSLOWSKI. Berlin, Heidelberg, New York a. Tokyo, Springer Verlag, 95, 343 p.

7041. VAGGI (Gianni). The limits of physiocracy and Smith's fortune. *In*: La diffusion internationale de la physiocratie [Cf. n° 7002], p. 59-77.

7042. Wilhelm Roscher and the "historical method". *J. Econ. Stud.*, 95, 22, 3-4-5, p. 4-220 [Articles by Jürgen G. BACKHAUS, Erich W. STREISSLER, Karl MILFORD, Peter R. SENN, Thanasis GIOURAS, Shigeki TOMO, Günter KRAUSE, H. R. C. WRIGHT, Jacob J. KRABBE, Harald HAGEMANN, Michael HUDSON, Yukihiro IKEDA]

§ 2. Allgemeine Wirtschaftsgeschichte.

* 7043. BELTRAN (Alain), RUFFAT (Michèle). L'histoire d'entreprise en France: essai bibliographique. *Cahiers de l'Institut d'histoire du temps présent*, 95, 30, p. 27-117.

* 7044. International bibliography of business history. Ed. by Francis GOODALL a. T. R. GOURVISH. London a New York, Routledge, 95, 300 p.

7045. ABE (Etsuo), FITZGERALD (Robert). Japanese economic success: timing, culture and organisational capability. *Bus. Hist.*, 95, 37, 2, p. p. 1-31.

7046. ALDCROFT (Derek Howard), MOREWOOD (Steven). Economic change in Eastern Europe since 1918. Aldershot a. Brookfield, Edward Elgar, 95, XIII-277 p.

7047. AMES (G.). Spice and sulphur: some evidence on the quest for economic stabilization in Portuguese Monsoon Asia, 1668-1682. *Journal of European Economic History*, 95, 24, 3, p. 465-488.

7048. ASSELAIN (Jean Charles). Histoire économique du XXe siècle. Vol. 1-2. Paris, Presses de Sciences PO, Dalloz, 95, 2 vol. [s. p.]. (Amphithéatre).

7049. BARDINI (Carlo), CARRERAS (Albert), LAINS (Pedro). The national accounts for Italy, Spain and Portugal. *Scandinavian Economic History Review*, 95, 43, 1, p. 115-146.

7050. BARNETT (Vincent). Soviet commodity markets during NEP. *Economic History Review*, 95, 48, 2, p. 329-352.

7051. BATOU (Jean). Les deux Europes aux vingt-deux visages, 1935-1970. *In*: Pour une histoire économique et sociale internationale [Cf. n° 1297], p. 229-246.

7052. BENABOUD (M'hammed). The economic situation of the Tetuan-Tanger region in 1857. *Revue d'Histoire Maghrébine*, 95, 79-80, p. 299-310.

7053. BEREND (Ivan T.). Industrialization on an obsolete technological basis. The international context of the economic performance of state socialist Central and Eastern Europe 1950-1989. *In*: Pour une histoire économique et sociale internationale [Cf. n° 1297], p. 247-266.

7054. BERGSTRÖM (Asta). Åstramning och expansion – den ekonomiska poilitiken i Sverige 1971-1982. Lund, Lund U. P., 1995, 313 p. (Lund studies in economic history, 2).

7055. BERNANKE (Ben S.). The macroeconomics of the Great Depression: a comparative approach. *J. Money C. B.*, 95, 27, 1, 1-28.

7056. BORRAS LLOP (Jose Maria). Actitudes patronales ante la regularización del trabajo infantil, en el transito del siglo XIX al XX. Salarios de subsistencia y economías domesticas. *Hispania*, 95, 55, 190, p. 629-644.

7057. BREZIS (E. S.), CROUZET (F. H.). The role of assignats during the French Revolution: an evil or a rescuer? *Journal of European Economic History*, 95, 24, 1, p. 7-40.

7058. BREZIS (Elise S.). Foreign capital flows in the century of Britain's Industrial Revolution: new estimates, controlled conjectures. *Economic History Review*, 95, 48, 1, p. 46-67.

7059. British economic development since 1945. Ed. by Alan BOOTH. Manchester, Manchester U. P., 95, XIV-166 p. (Documents in contemporary history).

7060. BUYST (Erik), SMITS (Jan Pieter), VAN ZANDEN (Jan Luiten). National accounts for the Low Countries, 1800-1900. *Scandinavian Economic History Review*, 95, 43, 1, p. 53-76.

7061. CASTRONOVO (Valerio). Storia economica d'Italia: dall'Ottocento ai giorni nostri. Torino, Einaudi, 95, VII-628 p.(Piccola biblioteca, 619).

7062. Choice, welfare, and development: a festschrift in honour of Amartya K. Sen. Ed. by K. BASU, P. PATTANAIK a. K. SUZUMURA. Oxford a. New York, Clarendon Press, 95, IX-343 p. (with a bibliography of Amartya K. Sen)

7063. CHRISTENSEN (Jørgen Peter), HJERPPE (Riitta), KRANTZ (Olle), NILSSON (Carl-Axel). Nordic historical national accounts since the 1880s. *Scandinavian Economic History Review*, 95, 43, 1, p. 30-52.

7064. CRAFTS (N. F. R.). Exogenus or endogenus growth? The Industrial Revolution reconsidered. *Journal of Economic History*, 95, 55, 4, p. 745-772. – IDEM. The golden age of economic growth in Western Europe, 1950–1973. *Economic History Review*, 95, 48, 3, p. 429-447.

7065. CRAFTS (Nick). Recent research on the national accounts of the UK, 1700–1939. *Scandinavian Economic History Review*, 95, 43, 1, p. 17-29.

7066. CROUZET (François). Les niveaux de vie en Europe à la fin du XVIIIe siècle: l'apport qualitatif. *In*: Pour une histoire économique et sociale internationale [Cf. n° 1297], p. 137-168.

7067. Cultures économiques et politiques économiques dans l'Empire tsariste et en URSS 1861–1950. Red. Jutta SCHERRER et Andrea GRAZIOSI. Paris, Ecole des hautes etudes en sciences sociales, 95, 213 p. (Cahiers du monde russe, 36/1–2).

7068. DAVID (Thomas). Un indice de la production industrielle de la Suisse durant l'entre-deux-guerres. *Revue suisse d'histoire*, 95, 45, 1, p. 109-130.

7069. DAVIET (Jean-Pierre). L'entreprise et ses fonctions: une géanalogie. *Cahiers de l'Institut d'histoire du temps présent*, 95, 30, p. 11-25.

7070. Dějiny hospodářství českých zemí od počátku industrializace do současnosti. Období první Československé republiky a německé okupace 1918–1945. (A history of the economy of the Bohemian Lands from the beginning of industrialization to the present. The first Czechoslovak Republic and the German occupation, 1918–1945). T. 3. Ed. by Vlastislav LACINA and Jaroslav PÁTEK. Praha, Karolinum, 95, 219 p. (bibl.).

7071. DINI (Bruno). L'economia fiorentina e l'Europa centro-orientale nelle fonti toscane. *Archivio storico italiano*, 95, 153, 566, p. 633-656.

7072. DUNBABIN (J. P. D.). The demographic causes of the Industrial Revolution. Some qualifications. *Journal of European Economic History*, 95, 24, 2, p. 405-410.

7073. DUNN (Cristopher Chase). The historical evolution of the international political economy. Aldershot, E. Edgar, 95, 2 vol., XIX-646 p., VIII-492 p.

7074. Economic development of Spain since 1870 (The). Ed. by Pablo MARTIN-ACENA a. James SIMPSON. (The economic development of modern Europe since 1870, 6). Aldershot a. Brookfield, Edward Elgar, 95, XVIII-564 p. (ill.).

7075. Economic history of modern Ethiopia (An). Vol. 1. The imperial era, 1941–1974. Ed. by Shiferaw BEKELE. Senegal, Codesria, VIII-334 p. (Codesria book series).

7076. Economic systems and state finance. Ed. by Richard BONNEY. Oxford, Clarendon Press, 95, XXI-652 p.

7077. Economie historique (L'). La longue période. Sériation, économétrie, interrogations. Actes du colloque d'économie historique, Paris, décembre 1994. *Economies et Société*, 95, 12, 295 p. [Cf. n^{os} <sélection> 7144, 7161, 7164, 7275.]

7078. EHRLICH (Eva), REVEZS (Gabor). Expectations and realities: trends in Hungary 1989–1994. *In*: Pour une histoire économique et sociale internationale [Cf. n° 1297], p. 267-282.

7079. ELTIS (David). The total product of Barbados, 1664–1701. *Journal of Economic History*, 95, 55, 2, p. 321-338.

7080. ENGERMAN (S. L.). The Atlantic economy of the eighteenth century: some speculation on economic development in Britain, America, Africa, and elsewhere. *Journal of European Economic History*, 95, 24, 1, p. 145-176.

7081. ESCOBAR (Arturo). Encountering development: the making and unmaking of the Third World. Princeton, Princeton U. P., 95, IX-290 p. (Princeton studies in culture/power/history).

7082. Europe's postwar recovery. Ed. by Barry EICHENGREEN. (Studies in monetary and financial history). Cambridge a. New York, Cambridge U. P., 95, IX-357 p.

7083. EVANS (E. W.), RICHARDSON (David). Hunting for rents: the economics of slaving in pre-colonial Africa. *Economic History Review*, 95, 48, 4, p. 665-686.

7084. FERGUSON (Niall). Paper and iron: Hamburg business and German politics in the era of inflation, 1897–1927. Cambridge, Cambridge U. P., 95, XIV-539 p.

7085. FEUERWERKER (Albert). Studies in the economic history of late imperial China: handicraft, modern industry, and the State. Ann Arbor, Center for Chinese Studies, University of Michigan, 95, 323 p. (Michigan monographs in Chinese studies, 70).

7086. Folk og erhverv – tilegnet Hans Christian Johansen. Ed. Anders Monrad MÖLLER. Odense, Odense Universitets forlag, 95, 359 p. [A collection of articles mainly on Danish economic history].

7087. FREMDLING (Rainer). German national accounts for the 19th and early 20th century. *Scandinavian Economic History Review*, 95, 43, 1, p. 77-100.

7088. GIBSON (A. J. S.), SMOUT (T. C.). Regional prices and market regions: the evolution of the early modern Scottish grain market. *Economic History Review*, 95, 48, 2, p. 258-282.

7089. HEDBERG (Lennart). Företagarfursten och framväxten av den starka staten. Hertig Karls resursexploatering i Närke 1581–1602. Örebro, Högskolan i Örebro, 95, IV, 382 p. (Örebro studies, 11). [The entrepreneur prince and the emergence of the strong state: Duke Charles' exploitation of resources in late 16th century Sweden].

7090. HEFEKER (C.). Interest groups, coalitions and monetary integration in the XIXth century. *Journal of European Economic History*, 95, 24, 3, p. 489-536.

7091. HJORTSHØJ O'ROURKE (Kevin), WILLIAMSON (Jeffrey G.). Open economy forces and late nineteenth century Swedish catch-up. A quantitative accounting. *Scandinavian Economic History Review*, 95, 43, 2, p. 171-203.

7092. HONNINGDAL GRYTTEN (Ola). The scale of Norwegian interwar unemployment in international perspectives. *Scandinavian Economic History Review*, 95, 43, 2, p. 226-250.

7093. HOWELL (David Luke). Capitalism from within: economy, society, and the state in a Japanese fishery. Berkeley a. London, University of California Press, 95, XIV-246 p.

7094. Innovations in the European economy between the wars. Ed. by François CARON. Berlin, de Gruyter, 95, X-330 p.

7095. JEQUIER (François). Une démographie des entreprises est-elle possible? *Revue suisse d'histoire*, 95, 45, 4, p. 490-501.

7096. Kapitalizm na Vostoke vo vtoroj polovine XX veka. (The Eastern capitalism in the second half of the XXth century). Avtorskij Kollektiv: V. G. RASTJANNIKOV, A. I. FURSOV, A. P. KOLONTAEV i drugie; Otv. red. V. G. RASTJANNIKOV (rukovditel'avtorskogo kollektiva), V. G. ŠIROKOV; Moskva, Vostočnaja literatura, RAN. In-t vostokovedenija, 95, 602 p.

7097. KAZGAN (Haydar). Osmanlıda Avrupa Finans Kapitali (Le Capital fiscal de l'Europe dans l'Empire Ottoman). İstanbul, Yapı Kredi Yayınları, 95, 225 p.

7098. KENNEDY (Kieran A.). The national accounts for Ireland in the nineteenth and twentieth centuries. *Scandinavian Economic History Review*, 95, 43, 1, p. 101-114.

7099. KESSLER (Christian). Le château et sa ville au Japon. Pouvoir et économie du XVIe au XVIIIe siècle. Avec la collaboration de Francis MOTHE et de Roland STEHLIN. Paris, Sudestasie, 95, 395 p.

7100. KHALIKOV (N. A.). Khozjajstvo tatar Povolž'ja i Urala: (Seredina XIX–načalo XX veka). (The economy of the Tatars of the Volga region and the Urals, the middle of the XIXth century–the beginning of the XXth centuries). AN Respubliki Tatarstan. In-t jazyka, literatury i istorii im. G. Ibragimova. – Kazan', 95, 235 p.

7101. KUDROV (Valentin). National accounts and international comparisons for the former Soviet Union. *Scandinavian Economic History Review*, 95, 43, 1, p. 147-166.

7102. KUMMEL (Gerhard). Transnationale Wirtschaftskooperation und der Nationalstaat: Deutsch-amerikanische Unternehmensbeziehungen in den dreissiger Jahren. Stuttgart, Franz Steiner, 95, 298 p. (Zeitschrift für Unternehmensgeschichte. Beiheft, 89).

7103. KÜTÜKOĞLU (Mübahat). Osmanlı Sosyal ve İktisadi Tarihi Kaynaklarından Temettü Defterleri (Registres d'impôt sur le revenu comme sources de l'histoire sociale et économique ottomane). *Belleten*, 95, 59, 225, p. 395-412.

7104. Labour's reward. Real wages and economic change in XIXth and XXth century Europe. Ed. by Peter SCHOLLIERS a. Vera ZAMAGNI. Aldershot a. Brookfield, Edward Elgar, 95, 300 p.

7105. LACINA (Vlastislav). Tempo růstu a etapy rozvoje hospodářství v meziválečném Československu. (Das Wachstumstempo und die Entwicklungsetappen der Wirtschaft in der Tschechoslowakei der Zwischenkriegszeit). *Český časopis historický*, 95, 93, 2, p. 223-243.

7106. LEVENSTEIN (Margaret). Mass production conquers the pool: firm organization and the nature of competition in the nineteenth century. *Journal of Economic History*, 95, 55, 3, p. 575-611.

7107. LEVI (Giovanni). La transformación de la tierra en mercancia: el caso Piamontes (1680–1717). *Hispania*, 95, 55, 191, p. 821-844.

7108. LICHT (Walter). Industrializing America: the nineteenth century. Baltimore a. London, Johns Hopkins U. P., 95, XVIII-219 p. (The American moment).

7109. LIN (Justin Yifu). The Needham puzzle: why the Industrial Revolution did not originate in China. *Econ. Dev. Cult. Change*, 95, 43, 2, p. 269-292.

7110. LOJÍN (Jaromír). Hospodářské důsledky sovětské okupace Československa 1968–1991. (The economic consequences of the Soviet occupation of Czechoslovakia, 1968–1991). Praha, Ústav pro soudobé dějiny AV ČR, 95, 58 p. (Materiály, studie, dokumenty, 8).

7111. LUNDGREN (Kurt). Why in Sweden? An analysis of the development of the large Swedish international firms from a learning perspective. *Scandinavian Economic History Review*, 95, 43, 2, p. 204-225.

7112. MAARBJERG (John P.). Scandinavia in the European world-economy, ca. 1570–1625. Some local evidence of economic integration. New York, Peter Lang, 95, 300 p.

7113. MADDISON (Angus). Monitoring the world economy, 1820–1992. Paris, Development Centre of the Organisation for Economic Co-operation and Development, 95, 255 p. (Development Centre studies).

7114. MANIAU (Joaquin). Compendio de la historia de la Real Hacienda de Nueva España. Con notas y comentarios de Alberto M. CARRENO; estudio preliminar de Marta MORINEAU. Mexico, Universidad Nacional Autonoma de Mexico, 95, XXVIII-149 p. (Serie C – Estudios historicos. Instituto de Investigaciones Juridicas, 49).

7115. MAYHEW (N. J.). Population, money supply, and the velocity of circulation in England, 1300–1700. *Economic History Review*, 95, 48, 2, p. 238-257.

7116. Mélanges offerts à Frédéric Mauro. Coordination et présentation par Guy MARTINIERE. Paris, Centro Cultural Calouste Gulbenkian, 95, XVII-1044 p. (ill.). (Arquivos do centro Cultural Calouste Gulbekian, 34). [Cf. n° <sélection> 7296.]

7117. MERCER (Helen). Constructing a competitive order: the hidden history of British antitrust policies. Cambridge a. New York, Cambridge U. P., 95, XI-274 p.

7118. Vacat.

7119. Naissance et mort des entreprises en Europe, XIXe–XXe siècles. Sous la dir. de Michael MOSS et Philippe JOBERT. Dijon, Publ. du Centre Georges Chevrier pour l'Histoire du Droit, 95, XVII-214 p. [Cf. n^{os} <sélection> 7307, 7322.]

7120. O'BRIEN (Patrick K.). The productivity of labour employed by European industries: the promise and dangers of a research programme in international economic history. In: Pour une histoire économique et sociale internationale [Cf. n° 1297], p. 283-300.

7121. O'GRADA (Cormac). Ireland: a new economic history, 1780–1939. Oxford, Clarendon Press, 95, XII-536 p.

7122. OKTAR (Tiğinçe Özkiper). Ereğli-Zonguldak Maden Kömürü Havzası'nin İktisadi Gelişimine İlişkin Bir İnceleme (Une étude sur le développement économique du bassin de l'houille à Ereğli-Zonguldak). *Marmara Üniversitesi İktisadi ve İdari Bilimler Fakültesi Dergisi*, 95, 11, 1-2, p. 133-139.

7123. OLSSON (Kent). Big business in Sweden. The golden age of the great Swedish shipyards, 1945–1974. *Scandinavian Economic History Review*, 95, 43, 3, p. 310-338.

7124. OWEN (Laura J.). Worker turnover in the 1920s: what labor-supply arguments don't tell us. *Journal of Economic History*, 95, 55, 4, p. 822-841.

7125. OWEN (Thomas C.). Russian corporate capitalism from Peter the Great to Perestroika. New York, Oxford U. P., 95, 259 p.

7126. På tröskeln till välfärden: välgörenhetsformer och arenor i Norden 1800–1930. Ed. by Marja T. SJÖBERG a. Tinne VAMMEN. Stockholm, Carlssons, 95, 261 p. [On the threshold of the welfare state: charity's former and speres in the Nordic countries before 1930].

7127. PÁTEK (Jaroslav). Možnosti a hranice rozvoje ekonomiky v meziválečném Československu a úloha hospodářského managementu. (The options and limits of economic development in interwar Czechoslovakia and the role of economic management). *Soudobé dějiny*, 95, 2, 2-3, p. 201-224.

7128. PEARSON (R.). The development of reinsurance markets in Europe during the nineteenth century. *Journal of European Economic History*, 95, 24, 3, p. 557-572.

7129. Predprinimatel'stvo na Urale: Istorija i sovremennost'. (Private business in the Urals: past and present. The XVIIIth–XXth centuries). V. N. ZADOROŽNYJ (rukovoditel'avtorskogo kollektiva), A. I. TATARKIN, L. A. ANTUF'EV i drugie. In-t ékonomiki Ural'skogo otdelenija RAN. – Ekaterinburg: Sredne- Ural'skoe knižnoe izdatel'stvo, 95, 252 p.

7130. PRUTSCH (Ursula). Das Geschäft mit der Hoffnung. Österreichische Auswanderung nach Brasilien 1918–1938. Wien, Köln u. Weimar, Böhlau, 95, 303 p. (ill.). (Böhlaus zeitgeschichtliche Bibliothek, 31).

7131. ROY (Tirthankar). Price movements in early twentieth-century India. *Economic History Review*, 95, 48, 1, p. 118-133.

7132. SANTUARI (A.). The Société Anonyme in France and the French Industrial Revolution, 1815–1848. *Journal of European Economic History*, 95, 24, 3, p. 587-618.

7133. SOLAR (Peter M.). Poor relief and English economic development before the Industrial Revolution. *Economic History Review*, 95, 48, 1, p. 1-22.

7134. SPOERER (Mark). "Wahre Bilanzen!" Die Steuerbilanz als unternehmenshistorische Quelle. *Zeitschrift für Unternehmensgeschichte*, 95, 40, 3, p. 158-179.

7135. SZOSTAK (Rick). Technological innovation and the great depression. Boulder a. Oxford, Westview, 95, XII-367 p.

7136. TAFT MORRIS (Cynthia). How fast and why did early capitalism benefit the majority? *Journal of Economic History*, 95, 55, 2, p. 211-226.

7137. TAKAMURA (Naosuke). Sai-Hakken Meiji no Keizai. (The Meiji economy pre-discovered). Tokyo, Hanawa Shobō, 95, 303 p.

7138. TEMIN (Peter). The 'Koreaboom' in West Germany: fact or fiction? *Economic History Review*, 95, 48, 4, p. 737-753.

7139. TOGNETTI (Sergio). Prezzi e salari nella Firenze tardomedievale: un profilo. *Archivio storico italiano*, 95, 153, 564, p. 263-334.

7140. TOMKA (Béla). Bankuralom, bankérdekeltség, bankellenőrzés. A magyarországi pénzintézetek ipari kapcsolatai a századfordulón, 1895–1913. (Domination des banques, intérêts des banques, contrôle des banques. Les relations des établissments financiers de Hongrie avec l'industrie au tournant du siècle, 1895–1913). *Tört. szle.*, 95, 37, 2, p. 171-207.

7141. TUREK (Otakar). Podíl ekonomiky na pádu komunismu v Československu. (The role of economics in the collapse of Communism in Czechoslovakia). Praha, Ústav pro soudobé dějiny AV ČR, 95, 106 p. (Sešity ÚSD, 23).

7142. VAN ZANDEN (J. L.). Tracing the beginning of the Kuznets curve: western Europe during the early modern period. *Economic History Review*, 95, 48, 4, p. 643-664.

7143. VEYRASSAT (Béatrice). Mais où est donc la différence? Modèles comparés de développement technologique (XIXe siècle). Historiographie internationale-historiographie suisse. In: Pour une histoire économique et sociale internationale [Cf. n° 1297], p. 205-228.

7144. VIDAL (Jean-François). L'histoire critique des catégories statistiques: un bref aperçu. In: Economie historique (L') [Cf. n° 7077], p. 253-269.

7145. YEAGER (Timothy J.). Encomienda or slavery? The Spanish crown's choice of labor organization in sixteenth-century Spanish America. Journal of Economic History, 95, 55, 4, p. 842-859.

Cf. n°s 1252, 1284, 1297, 7704

§ 3. Industrie, Bergbau und Verkehr.

7146. AHLSTROM (Goran). Technological development and industrial exhibitions, 1850–1914: Sweden in an international perspective. Lund, Lund U. P., 95, 251 p. (Lund studies in economic history, 5).

7147. ARASARATNAM (Sinnappah). Maritime trade, society and European influence in Southern Asia, 1600–1800. Aldershot, Variorum, 95, XII-299 p. (Collected studies series, CS471).

7148. ARIKAN (Muzaffer), TOLEDO (Paulino). "Turk Deniz Tarihi İle İlgili Belgeler" (Documents relatifs à l'histoire maritime des Turcs). Osmanlı Tarihi Araştırma Merkezi Dergisi, 95, 6, p. 387-408.

7149. Atlas zur Verkehrsgeschichte Schleswig-Holsteins im 19. Jahrhundert. Hrsg. u. bearb. v. Walter ASMUS, Andreas KUNZ u. Ingwer E. MOMSEN; unter Mitwirkung von Ulrike ALBRECHT [et al.]; Kartographie und graphische Datenverarbeitung Joachim Robert MOESCHL. Neumünster, Wachholtz, 95, 92 p. (ill.). (Studien zur Wirtschafts- und Sozialgeschichte Schleswig-Holsteins, 25).

7150. BEERBÜHL (Margrit Schulte). War England ein Sonderfall der Industrialisierung? Der ökonomische Einfluß der protestantischen Immigranten auf die Entwicklung der englischen Wirtschaft vor der Industrialisierung. Geschichte und Gesellschaft, 95, 21, 4, p. 479-505.

7151. BOOT (H. M.). How skilled were Lancashire cotton factory workers in 1833? Economic History Review, 95, 48, 2, p. 283-303.

7152. BOURNE (Russell). Americans on the move: a history of waterways, railways, and highways: with maps and illustrations from the Library of Congress. Golden, Fulcrum, 95, IX-133 p. (ill.).

7153. BURGHARDT (Uwe). Die Mechanisierung des Ruhrbergbaus, 1890–1930. München, Beck, 95, 437 p.

7154. BURT (Roger). The transformation of the non-ferrous metals industries in the seventeenth and eighteenth centuries. Economic History Review, 95, 48, 1, p. 23-45.

7155. CARRERAS (Albert). XIX and XX centuries transport history: current trend and new problems: a workshop. Organized by Albert CARRERAS, Andrea GIUNTINI a. Andreas KUNZ. Badia Fiesolana, European University Institute, Florence, Department of History and Civilization, 95, 77 p. (EUI working paper. HEC, 95/2).

7156. CUCARULL (J.). Le monde rural face aux mutations économiques: l'évolution de l'industrie textile en Ille-et-Vilaine dans la seconde moitié du XIXe siècle. Revue Historique, 95, 119, 595, p. 59-84.

7157. D'ANGIO (Agnes). Schneider & Cie et les travaux publics, 1895–1949. Préface de Dominique BARJOT. Paris, Ecole des chartes, 95, 396 p. (Mémoires et documents de l'Ecole des chartes, 45).

7158. DARRIEULAT (O.). De la mécanographie à l'informatique: retards et réussites de l'insertion de la compagnie des machines Bull (1931–1960). Revue Historique, 95, 119, 594, p. 367-388.

7159. DAVIDS (K.). Openness or secrecy? Industrial espionage in the Dutch Republic. Journal of European Economic History, 95, 24, 2, p. 333-348.

7160. DEMIER (Francis). «Néo-physiocratie» et première industrialisation française. In: La diffusion internationale de la physiocratie [Cf. n° 7002], p. 231-248.

7161. DORMOIS (Jean-Pierre), BARDINI (Carlo). La productivité du travail dans l'industrie de divers pays d'Europe avant 1914. In: Economie historique (L') [Cf. n° 7077], p. 77-103.

7162. Entwicklung der Motorisierung im Deutschen Reich und den Nachfolgestaaten (Die): Stuttgarter Tage zur Automobil- und Unternehmensgeschichte: eine Veranstaltung von Mercedes-Benz Classic – das Archiv. Hrsg. v. Harry NIEMANN u. Armin HERMANN. Stuttgart, F. Steiner, 95, 297 p. (GUG, 2).

7163. Fordism transformed: the development of production methods in the automobile industry. Ed. by Haruhito SHIOMI a. Kazuo WADA. Oxford a. New York, Oxford U. P., 95, VIII-320 p. (Fuji conference series, 1).

7164. GENESTE (Nathalie). Les spécialisations industrielles des régions françaises vers 1845. In: Economie historique (L') [Cf. n° 7077], p. 105-121.

7165. GILHAUS (Ulrike). "Schmerzenskinder der Industrie". Umweltverschmutzung, Umweltpolitik und sozialer Protest im Industriezeitalter in Westfalen 1845–1914. Paderborn, Schöningh, 95, XV-601 p. (Forschungen zur Regionalgeschichte, 12).

7166. GOTTWALDT (Alfred). Julius Dorpmüller, die Reichsbahn und die Autobahn. Verkehrspolitik und Leben des Verkehrsministers bis 1945. Berlin, Argon, 95, 136 p.

7167. HAMMACHE (Khalifa). A propos des deux navires algériens qu'étaient à Alexandrie avant la conquête d'Alger en 1830. Revue d'Histoire Maghrébine (Partie arabe), 95, 79-80, p. 423-437.

7168. HEIKKONEN (Esko). Reaping the bounty: McGormick Harvesting Machine Company turns abroad, 1870–1902. Helsinki, Finnish Historical Society, 95, 319 p. (Bibliotheca historica, 8). (ill., maps).

7169. Industrie Kultur. Mühlviertel, Waldviertel, Südböhmen. Reisen im Grenzland. Hrsg. v. Andrea KOMLOSY. Wien, Deuticke, 95, 256 p. (ill., Karten).

7170. Inland navigation and economic development in nineteenth-century Europe. Ed. by Andreas KUNZ a. John ARMSTRONG. Mainz, Verlag Philipp von Zabern, 95, X-330 p. (Veröffentlichungen des Instituts für Europäische Geschichte Mainz. Beiheft, 39).

7171. JOHNSON (Christopher H.). The life and death of industrial Languedoc, 1700–1920. New York a. Oxford, Oxford U. P., 95, 307 p.

7172. KARAOĞLU (Omer). XIX. Yüzyilda Osmanlı Sanayi ve Bir Devlet Teşebbüsü Örneği Olarak Zeytinburnu Demir Fabrikasi (L'industrie Ottomane au XIXe siècle et la fabrique de fer à Zeytinburnu comme exemple d'une entreprise d'Etat). *Türkiye Günlüğü*, 95, 37, p. 111-117.

7173. KATZ (Elaine N.). Outcrop and deep level mining in South Africa before the Anglo-Boer War: re-examining the Blainey thesis. *Economic History Review*, 95, 48, 2, p. 304-328. – EADEM. The underground route to mining: Afrikaners and the witwatersrand gold mining industry from 1902 to the 1907 miners' strike. *Journal of African History*, 95, 36, 3, p. 467-490.

7174. KIYOKAWA (Yukihiko). Nihon no Keizai Hatten to Gijutsu Fukyū. (Economic development and diffusion of technology in Japan). Tokyo, Tōyō Keizai Shimpōsha, 95, 358 p.

7175. KOKAZE (Hidemasa). Teikoku-Syugi-ka no Nihon-Kaiun: Kokusai Kyōsō to Taigai Jiritsu. (Japan's shipping under imperialism: international competition and independence). Tokyo, Yamakawa Shuppansha, 95, 341 p.

7176. KORALTÜRK (Murat). Kentleşme, Kentiçi Ulaşım, İstanbul ve Şirket-i Hayriye'nin Kuruluşu [Urbanisation, transport dans la ville, İstanbul et l'investissement de Şirket-i Hayriye (La Société concessionnaire du cabotage dans le Bosphore)]. *Marmara Üniversitesi İktisadi ve İdari Bilimler Fakültesi Dergisi*, 95, 10, 1-2, p. 53-113.

7177. LOUBET (Jean-Louis). Citroën, Peugeot, Renault et les autres. Soixante ans de stratégies. Paris, Le Monde Editions, 95, 637 p. (Mémoire d'entreprises).

7178. Magyar vasúttörténet. 1. Köt. A kezdetektől 1875–ig. (Histoire des chemins de fer de Hongrie. T.1. Des origines jusqu'à 1875). Főszerk. KOVÁCS László. Budapest, Közdok, 95, 415 p.

7179. MALONE (Michael Shawn). The microprocessor: a biography. Santa Clara, TELOS, 95, XIV-333 p.

7180. MEIKLE (Jeffrey L.). American plastic: a cultural history. New Brunswick a. London, Rutgers U. P., 95, 403 p.

7181. MEYER-LENZ (Johanna). Schiffbaukunst und Werftarbeit in Hamburg 1838–1896. Frankfurt am Main, Peter Lang, 95, 637 p.

7182. MONTERO (Manuel). La California del hierro: las minas y la modernización economica y social de Vizcaya. Bilbao, Beitia, 95, 285 p. (Beitia ensayo).

7183. MORRELL (J. B.). Bourgeois scientific societies and industrial innovation. *Journal of European Economic History*, 95, 24, 2, p. 311-332.

7184. MOUSSA (Bantenga). L'or des regions de Poura et de Gaoua: les vicissitudes de l'éxploitation coloniale, 1925–1960. *International Journal of African Historical Studies*, 95, 28, 3, p. 563-576.

7185. PASZKE (Andrzej), JERCZYŃSKI (Andrzej), KOZIARSKI (Stanisław Marian). 150 lat Drogi Żelaznej Warszawsko–Wiedeńskiej. (150 ans du Chemin de Fer varsovien et viennois). Warszawa, Centr. Dyr. Okręg. Kolei Państ., 95, 396 p. (phot., fig., dessins, cart).

7186. REMPORT (Zoltán). Magyarország vaskohászata az ipari forrdalom előestéjén, 1800–1850. (La sidèrurgie de la Hongrie à l'aube de la révolution industrielle, 1800–1850). Budapest, Montan-Press, 95, 362 p.

7187. RESCH (Andreas). Die alpenländische Senseindustrie um 1900. Industrialisierung am Beispiel des Redtenbacherwerks in Scharnstein, Oberösterreich. Wien, Köln u. Weimar, Böhlau, 95, 298 p. (ill., Karten, Graph. Darstellung). (Studien zur Wirtschaftsgeschichte und Wirtschaftspolitik, 3).

7188. Réseaux européens transnationaux XIXe–XXe siècles (Les): quels enjeux? Ed. par Michele MERGER, Albert CARRERAS et Andrea GIUNTINI. Nantes, Ouest editions, 95, 431 p.

7189. SAGAN (Iwona). Procesy uprzemysłowienia w powojennej Polsce [1944–1989]. (Processus d'industrialisation dans la Pologne de l'après-guerre [1944–1989]). Gdańsk, Gdańskie Tow. Nauk, 95, 142 p. (Eng. summary, Deutsche Zsfassung, carte). (Gdańskie Tow. Nauk, Wydz. 1 Nauk Społ. i Humanist., Ser. Monografii, 100).

7190. STOCKLY (Doris). Le système de l'Incanto des galées du marché à Venise (fin XIIIe–milieu XVe siècle). Leiden a. New York, E. J. Brill, 95, XVIII-434 p. (Medieval Mediterranean, 5).

7191. STUDENY (Christophe). L'invention de la vitesse: France, XVIIIe–XXe siècle. Paris, Gallimard, 95, 408 p. (Bibliothèque des histoires).

7192. SUÁREZ ARGÜELLO (Clara Elena). Sequía y crisis en el transporte novohispano en 1794–1795. *Historia Mexicana*, 94-95, 44, p. 385-402.

7193. TARNOVSKIJ (Konstantin N.). Melkaja promyšlennost' Rossii v konce XIX–načale XX veka. (The Russian small-scale industry at the end of the XIXth–the beginning of the XXth centuries). Otv. red. P. V. VOLOBUEV. Moskva, Nauka, RAN. In-t rossijskoj istorii, 95, 269 p.

7194. THERET (Bruno). A propos du rôle de l'Etat dans la mise en œuvre des infrastructures de transport et de communication, en France de 1815 à 1939. Les théories confrontées à l'histoire et à la mesure. *Histoire et mesure*, 95, 10, 1-2, p. 149-197.

7195. TIZLAK (Fahrettin). Osmanlı Devleti'nde Ham Bakır İşleme Merkezleri Olarak Tokat ve Diyarbakir. (Tokat et Diyarbakir comme des centres de l'exploitation de cuivre dans l'Empire Ottoman). *Belleten*, 95, 59, 226, p. 643-659.

7196. Transmanche et les liaisons maritimes (Le), XVIIIe–XXe siècles: actes du colloque de Boulogne-sur-Mer, 1–3 avril 1993. Sous la direction de Patrick VILLIERS et Christian PFISTER-LANGANAY. Lille, Université Charles-de-Gaulle, Lille III, 95, 248 p. (Revue du Nord. Collection Histoire, 9).

7197. WEIL (François). Capitalisme et industrialisation en Nouvelle-Angleterre, 1815–1845. *Annales*, 95, 50, 1, p. 29-52.

7198. ZACK-WILLIAMS (Alfred Babatunde). Tributors, supporters and merchant capital: mining and underdevelopment in Sierra Leone. Aldershot, Avebury, 95, VIII-239 p. (The making of modern Africa).

7199. ZETKA (James R.). Militancy, market dynamics, and workplace authority: the struggle over labor process outcomes in the U.S. automobile industry, 1946 to 1973. Albany, State University of New York Press, 95, XXVII-293 p. (SUNY series in American labor history).

Cf. n° 1137

§ 4. Handel.

7200. 19. Yüzyilda Osmanlı Dış Ticareti. (Le Commerce extérieure de l'Empire Ottoman au XIXe siècle). Ed. par Şevket PAMUK. Ankara, DİE, 95, [s. p.].

7201. AMINE (Mohamed). Les commerçants à Alger à la veille de 1830. *Revue d'Histoire Maghrébine*, 95, 77-78, p. 11-112.

7202. BONNETT (N. R.). Porto wine marchants: Sandeman in Porto, 1813–1831. *Journal of European Economic History*, 95, 24, 2, p. 239-270.

7203. BOROŃ (Iwona). Handel Górnego Śląska z Krakowem w dobie wojny trzydziestoletniej [1618–1648] na podstawie krakowskich ksiąg celnych. (Commerce de la Haute Silésie avec Cracovie à l'époque de la guerre de trente ans [1618–1648] sur la base des registres douaniers de Cracovie). Gliwice, [s. n.], 95, 99 p. (Muzeum w Gliwicach. Ser. Monograficzna, nr 5). [Deutsche Zsfassung].

7204. BOSTAN (İdris). Rusya'nın Karadeniz'de Ticarete Başlaması ve Osmanlı İmparatorluğu (1700–1787). [Le Commencement du commerce russe dans la Mer Noire et l'Empire Ottoman (1700–1787)]. *Belleten*, 95, 59, 225, p. 353-394.

7205. BOUBAKER (Sadok). La peste dans les pays du Maghreb: attitudes face au fléau et impacts sur l'activité commerciale (XVIe–XIXe siècles). *Revue d'Histoire Maghrébine*, 95, 79-80, p. 311-341.

7206. BROWN (John C.). Imperfect competition and Anglo-German trade rivalry: markets for cotton textiles before 1914. *Journal of Economic History*, 95, 55, 3, p. 494-527.

7207. CASALILLA (Bartolome Yun). Transacción mercantil y formas de transmisión de la propiedad territorial. *Hispania*, 95, 55, 191, p. 846-885.

7208. CIRONISOVÁ (Eva). Export plzeňského piva do Francie v 19. a 20. století. (Der Export von Pilsner Bier nach Frankreich im 19. und 20. Jahrhundert). *Minulostí Západočeského kraje*, 95, 30, p. 113-126.

7209. CSATÓ (Tamás). A belkereskedelem Magyarországon a 19–20. században. (Le commerce intérieur en Hongrie aux XIX–XX siècles). Budapest, Aula, 95, 248 p.

7210. DEMARCHI (Gustavo Ernesto). Los argentinos y la inflación. Buenos Aires, Nueva Generación, 95, VII-360 p. (Colección Scalabrini Ortiz).

7211. DOUMERC (Bernard), STOCKLY (Doris). L'évolution du capitalisme marchand à Venise: le financement des "galere da mercato" à la fin du XVe siècle. *Annales*, 95, 50, 1, p. 133-158.

7212. ERDEMIR (Ayşegül Demirhan). Anadolu Türklerinde Geleneksel Drogların (İlaçların) Ticareti. (Le Commerce de drogue traditionnel ches les Turcs anatoliens). *Türk Dünyası Araştırmaları*, 95, 96, p. 117-146.

7213. FUDGE (J.). Tudor-Habsburg trade wars and northern commercial networks 1486–1506. *Journal of European Economic History*, 95, 24, 3, p. 573-586.

7214. GECSÉNYI (Lajos). Bécs és a hódoltság kereskedelmi összeköttetései a 16. században. Thököly Sebestyén felemelkedésének hátteréhez. (Vienne et les relations commerciales du règime Ottoman dans le XVI siècle. Pour les dessous de l'ascension de Sebestyén Thököly). *Századok*, 95, 129, 4, p. 767-790.

7215. GULDON (Zanon), WIJACZKA (Jacek). Handel ekonomii litewskich z Królewcem w latach 1765–1768. (Le commerce des économies lithuaniennes avec Królewiec [Königsberg] dans les années 1765–1768). *Zapiski historyczne poświęcone historii Pomorza i Krajów Bałtyckich*, 95, 60, 2-3, p. 39-47. [Deutsche Zsfassung].

7216. HANCOCK (David). Citizens of the world: London merchants and the integration of the British Atlantic community, 1735–1785. Cambridge a. New York, Cambridge U. P., 95, XXIII-477 p.

7217. IMAŃSKA (Iwona). Rynek książki w Toruniu w pierwszej połowie XVIII wieku. (Le marché du livre à Toruń dans la première moitié du XVIIIe siècle). *Roczniki Biblioteczne*, 95, 39, 1-2, p. 39-47. [Eng. Summary].

7218. JDEY (Ahmed). Le commerce des habits de laine et ses produits dans les campagnes du Cap Bon en 1891: exemple d'un commerçant de Nabeul. *Revue d'Histoire Maghrébine* (Partie arabe), 95, 79-80, p. 393-412.

7219. JONES (Geoffrey). The evolution of international business: an introduction. London a. New York, Routledge, 95, XII-360 p.

7220. KUNTZ FICKER (Sandra). Empresa extranjera y mercado interno: el Ferrocarril Central Mexicano (1880–1907). Mexico, Colegio de Mexico, 95, 391 p.

7221. LANCASTER (William). The department store: a social history. London a. New York, Leicester U. P., 95, 212 p. (ill.).

7222. LAURILA (Juhani). Finnish-Soviet clearing trade and payment system: history and lessons. Helsinki, Bank of Finland, 95, 144 p. (Bank of Finland studies, A 94).

7223. LEMARCHAND (Yannick). Style mercantile ou mode des finances. Le choix d'un modèle comptable dans la France d'Ancien Régime. *Annales*, 95, 50, 1, p. 159-182.

7224. LOBATO FRANCO (Isabel). Compañias y negocios en la Cataluña preindustrial. Sevilla, Universidad de Sevilla, Secretariado de publicaciones, 95, 262 p.

7225. LOVEJOY (Paul E.), RICHARDSON (David). British abolition and its impact on slave prices along the Atlantic coast of Africa, 1783–1850. *Journal of Economic History*, 95, 55, 1, p. 98-119.

7226. MORTENSÖN (Ole). Renessansens fartöjer: sejlads og söfart i Danmark 1500–1650. Rudköbing, Langelands Museum, 95, 285 p. (Meddelelser fra Langelands museum). [The Danish navigation in the 16th century].

7227. PIUZ (Anne-Marie). Marchandises du commerce de Marseille à Genève et en Suisse au XVIIIe siècle. *In*: Pour une histoire économique et sociale internationale [Cf. n° 1297], p. 499-514.

7228. STEVENSON (Heon). Selling the dream: advertising the American automobile 1930–1980. London, Academy, 95, 287 p.

7229. STRAUBEL (Rolf). Kaufleute und Manufakturunternehmer. Stuttgart, Steiner, 95, 588 p.

7230. SUBTIL (José Manuel Louzada Lopes). O desembargo do Paco: 1750–1833. Lisboa, F.C.S.H. – U.N.L., 95, 856 p. (bibl.).

7231. SZLAJFER (Henryk). Garmisch-Partenkirchen. Trade among peripheral countries during the Great Depression: Polish-Argentinian trade in 1930s. *In*: Pour une histoire économique et sociale internationale [Cf. n° 1297], p. 541-546.

7232. WILSON (John Francis). British business history, 1720–1994. Manchester a. New York, Manchester U. P., 95, X-276 p.

§ 5. Landwirtschaft und Agrarprobleme.

* 7233. GIUDICI (Rita). Fonti per la storia dell'agricoltura italiana dalla fine del XV alla metà del XVIII secolo, saggio bibliografico. Milano, Vita e pensiero, 95, XXII-199 p. (Scienze storiche, 60. Contributi dell'Istituto di storia economica e sociale, 6).

———

7234. BEUTLER (Corinne). Vers une lecture scientifique de la littérature agricole du XVIe siècle. *In*: Histoire rurale en France (L') [Cf. n° 601], p. 224-230.

7235. BOULAINE (Jean). La fertilisation au XIXe siècle: routine et progrès. *In*: Histoire rurale en France (L') [Cf. n° 601], p. 242-244.

7236. Colonización agricola y gañadera en America: siglos XVI–XVIII: su impacto en la población aborigen. Ed. por Laura ESCOBARI DE QUEREJAZU. Quito, Ediciones Abya-Yala, 95, 434 p. (maps). (Coleccion "Biblioteca Abya-Yala", 25).

7237. Cotton, colonialism, and social history in Sub-Saharan Africa. Ed. by Allen ISAACMAN a. Richard ROBERTS. Portsmouth, Heinemann a. London, J. Currey, 95, XI-314 p. (Social history of Africa).

7238. DØRUM (Knut). Fikk overgangen til selveie betydning for fremveksten av husmannsvesenet ca. 1660–1850? (Was the Transition from tenancy to freehold peasant ownership important to the growth of the cotter system 1660–1850?). *Historisk Tidsskrift* (Norway), 95, 74, p. 145-170.

7239. FALCÓN (Romana). Descontento campesino e hispanofobia. La tierra caliente a mediados del siglo XIX. *Historia Mexicana*, 94-95, 44, p. 461-498.

7240. FERJANI (Khemaïs). Les salaires agricoles dans la région de Béja de 1956 (d'après les registres des notaires). *Revue d'Histoire Maghrébine* (Partie arabe), 95, 79-80, p. 539-566.

7241. GRAY (Peter). The Irish famine. London, Thames and Hudson, 95, 191 p. (New horizons).

7242. GUNST (Péter). Az Osztrák-Magyar Monarchie mezőgazdasága a századfordulón. (L'agriculture de la Monarchie Austro-Hongroise au tournant du siècle). *Századok*, 95, 129, 6, p. 1219-1250.

7243. HIGGS (Edward). Occupational censuses and the agricultural workforce in Victorian England and Wales. *Economic History Review*, 95, 48, 4, p. 700-716.

7244. KIRK (James). The books of assumption of the thirds of benefices: Scottish ecclesiastical rentals at the reformation. Oxford, Published for the British Academy by Oxford U. P., 95, LXXXVIII-896 p. (Records of social and economic history. New series, 21).

7245. KUBAČÁK (Antonín). Dějiny zemědělství v českých zemích. (A history of agriculture in the Bohemian Lands). Tomo 2. 1900–1989. Praha, Ministerstvo zemědělství ČR, 95, 254 p. (bibl.).

7246. KUEH (Y. Y.). Agricultural instability in China, 1931–1991: weather, technology, and institutions. Oxford, Clarendon Press, 95, XXV-387 p. (Studies on contemporary China).

7247. KUZNECOV (S. V.). Istočniki dija izučenija zemledel'českikh tradicij russkogo krest'janstva. (Konec XIX–načalo XX veka). (Sources for the study of agricultural traditions of the Russian peasants. Late XIXth–early XXth centuries). *Étnogr. obozrenie*, 95, 2, p. 104-112.

7248. LABROT (Gerard). Quand l'histoire murmure: villages et campagnes du Royaume de Naples (XVIe–XVIIIe siècle). Roma, Ecole française de Rome, 95, XII-686 p. (Collection de l'Ecole française de Rome, 202).

7249. LASERNA GAITÁN (Antonio I.). La visita de don José de Oraa a la gobernación de nueva Andalucia en 1788: la precariedad economica de la region y el desarollo de la agricultura indigena en la provincia de Cumana. *Boletin de la Academia Nacional de la Historia*, 95, 78, 2, [s. p.].

7250. Magyar (A) Tudományos Akadémia Agrártörténeti és Faluszociológiai Bizottsága tudományos ülésszaka az 1945. Évi földreform 50. évfordulója alkalmából. (Session scientifique de la Commission d'histoire agraire et sociologie rurale de l'Académie Hongroise des Sciences, consacrée au 50 anniversaire de la réforme agraire de 1945). *Agrártört. szle.*, 95, 37, 1-4, p. 3-77.

7251. MARTINEZ MARTIN (Manuel). Revolución liberal y cambio agrario en la Alta Andalucia. Granada, Universidad de Granada, 95, 358 p. (Biblioteca Chronica Nova de estudios historicos, 32).

7252. MAYAUD (Jean-Luc). Ruralité et politique dans la France du XIXe siècle. *In*: Histoire rurale en France (L') [Cf. n° 601], p. 133-136.

7253. MORINEAU (M.). Simples calculs relatifs à une prétendue révolution agricole survenue en France au XVIIIe siècle. *Revue Historique*, 95, 119, 593, p. 91-108.

7254. NIKONOV (Aleksandr A.). Spiral'mnogovekovoj dramy: agrarnaja nauka i politika Rossii (XVIII–XX veka). (The spiral of a centuries – long drama: agrarian science and politics in Russia from the XVIIIth through the XXth centuries). Moskva, Énciklopedija rossijskikh derevenʹ, 95, 571p.

7255. NISKANEN (Kirsti). Godsägare, småbrukare och jordbrukets modernisering. Södermanlands län 1875–1935. Stockholm, Almqvist & Wiksell International, 95, XIII, 275 p. (Stockholm studies in economic history, 21).

7256. OLSSON (Lars). På tröskeln till folkhemmet. Baltiska flyktingar och polska koncentrationslägerfångar som reservarbetskraft i skånskt jordbruk kring slutet av andra världskriget. Lund, Morgonrödnad, 95, 180 p. [The Baltic refugees and Polish concentration camp prisoners as a reserve manpower for the agriculture of Southern Swedish at the end of the World War Two].

7257. PALAIRET (M.). Rural Serbia in the light of the census of 1893. *Journal of European Economic History*, 95, 24, 1, p. 41-108.

7258. PAULMANN (Johannes). Ein Experiment der Sozialökonomie: Agrarische Siedlungspolitik in England und Wales vom Ende des 19. Jahrhunderts bis zum Beginn des Zweiten Weltkriegs. *Geschichte und Gesellschaft*, 95, 21, 4, p. 506-532.

7259. PERREN (Richard). Agriculture in depression, 1870–1940. Cambridge, Cambridge U. P., 95, VI-81 p. (New studies in economic and social history, 26).

7260. PIEL (Jean). Capitalismo agrario en el Peru. Lima, IFEA y Salta, Universidad Nacional de Salta, 95, 622 p. (Travaux de l'Institut français d'études andines, 78).

7261. Problemas agrarios y propiedad en Mexico, siglos XVIII y XIX. Introducción y selección de Margarita MENEGUS BORNEMANN. Mexico, El Colegio de Mexico, Centro de Estudios Historicos, 95, XXX-312 p. (Lecturas de "Historia mexicana", 11).

7262. RHODE (Paul W.). Learning, capital accumulation, and the transformation of California agriculture. *Journal of Economic History*, 95, 55, 4, p. 773-800.

7263. SALVATICI (Silvia). Un mondo in affanno: famiglie agricole nell'Italia fascista. *Passato e presente*, 95, 13, 36, p. 93-116.

7264. SIMPSON (James). Spanish agriculture: the long siesta, 1765–1965. Cambridge, Cambridge U. P., 95, XX-316 p. (Cambridge studies in modern economic history, 2).

7265. STINCHCOMBE (Arthur L.). Sugar island slavery in the age of enlightenment: the political economy of the Caribbean world. Princeton a. Chichester, Princeton U. P., 95, XVII-361 p.

7266. SURANYI (Béla). Földterület, művelési ág, földhasznosítás Magyarországon a XX. században. (Territoire, branche de la culture, emploie de la terre en Hongrie au XX siècle). *Agrártört. szle.*, 94, 36, 1-4, p. 363-416.

7267. SZAKÁCS (Sándor). A földreform és a kisüzemű mezőgazdaság, 1945–1948. (La réforme agraire et les petites propriétés, 1945–1948). *Agrártört. szle.*, 95, 37, 1-4, p. 79-183.

7268. Zemědělské družstevnictví. Kolektivizace zemědělství. Vznik JZD. 1948–1949. (Agricultural cooperatives. The collectivization of agriculture and the establishment of the Standard Farm Cooperative [JZD]. Ed. by Jiřina JUNĚCOVÁ a. Jana PŠENIČKOVÁ. Praha, Státní ústřední archiv, 95, 211 p.

§ 6. Geld- und Finanzwesen.

7269. AKYILDIZ (Ali). Osmanlı Finans Sisteminde Dönüm Noktası Kağıt Para ve Sosyo-Ekonomik Etkileri (Le Tournant dans le système fiscal ottoman: Le bank-note et ses influences socio-économiques). İstanbul, Eren Yayıncılık, 95, 408 p.

7270. ALATRI (Paolo). Riforme fiscali e crisi politiche nella Francia di Luigi XV. *Studi storici*, 95, 36, 2, p. 573-582.

7271. ALIMENTO (Antonella). Riforme fiscali e crisi politiche nella Francia di Luigi XV: dalla "taille tarifée" al catasto generale. Firenze, Olschki, 95, 396 p. (L'Officina dello storico, 1).

7272. Banking, currency, and finance in Europe between the wars. Ed. by Charles H. FEINSTEIN. Oxford, Clarendon Press, 95, XVIII-536 p.

7273. BARTH (Boris). Die deutsche Hochfinanz und die Imperialismen: Banken und Aussenpolitik vor 1914. Stuttgart, Franz Steiner, 95, 505 p. (Beiträge zur Kolonial- und Überseegeschichte, 61).

7274. BATUMLU (M. Ragib). Osmanlı Dönemi Borsa ve Mali Sistemi (La bourse et le sistème financière dans l'Empire Ottoman). İstanbul, İ.M.K.B. Yayınları, 95, 345 p

7275. BAYARD (Françoise). De la difficulté à élaborer des séries longues pour les finances de l'Ancien Régime en France. *In*: Economie historique (L') [Cf. n° 7077], p. 231-251.

7276. CARCELES DE GEA (Beatriz). Reforma y fraude fiscal en el reinado de Carlos II: la Sala de Millones (1658–1700). Madrid, Banco de España, Servicio de Estudios, 95, 154 p. (Estudios de historia economica, 31).

7277. CORREA BALLESTER (Jorge). La hacienda foral valenciana: el real patrimonio en el siglo XVII. Prologo de Mariano PESET. Valencia, Consell Valencia de Cultura, 95, [s. p.].

7278. DE IANNI (Nicola). Capitale e mercato azionario: la Fiat dal 1899 al 1961. Napoli, ESI, 95, 142 p. (Storia finanziaria, 2).

7279. Dette publique (La) en Amérique latine en perspective historique. Ed. par Reinhardt LIEHR. Frankfurt am Main, Vervuert Verlag et Madrid, Iberoamericana, 95, 527 p.

7280. Finanza e debito pubblico in Italia tra '800 e '900. Atti della seconda Giornata di studio Luigi Luzzatti per la storia dell'Italia contemporanea, Venezia, 25 novembre 1994. A cura di Paolo PECORARI. Venezia, Istituto veneto di scienze lettere ed arti, 95, 254 p. (Biblioteca luzzattiana, 4).

7281. FLANDREAU (Marc). Coin memories. Estimates of the French metallic currency 1840–1878. *Journal of European Economic History*, 95, 24, 2, p. 271-310. – IDEM. L'or du monde: la France et la stabilité du systeme monétaire international, 1848–1873. Paris, L'Harmattan, 95, 367 p. (Etudes d'économie politique. Sillery, Québec).

7282. GALL (Lothar), FELDMAN (Gerald D.), JAMES (Harold), [et. al.]. Die Deutsche Bank 1870–1995. München, Beck, 95, 1020 p.

7283. GARRETT (John R.). Monetary policy and expectations: market-control techniques and the Bank of England, 1925–1931. *Journal of Economic History*, 95, 55, 3, p. 612-636.

7284. HOFFMAN (Philip T.), POSTEL-VINAY (Gilles), ROSENTHAL (Jean-Laurent). Redistribution and long-term private debt in Paris, 1660–1726. *Journal of Economic History*, 95, 55, 2, p. 256-284.

7285. KOSTELENOS (George C.). Money and output in modern Greece: 1858–1938. Athens, Centre of Planning and Economic Research, 95, 481 p. (Studies. Kentro Programmatismou kai Oikonomikon Ereunon, 44).

7286. MARTINEZ LOPEZ-CANO (Maria del Pilar). El credito a largo plazo en el siglo XVI: Ciudad de Mexico, 1550–1620. Mexico, Universidad Nacional Autonoma de Mexico, 95, 208 p. (Serie de historia novohispana, 53).

7287. Měnové systémy na území Českých zemí 1892–1993. Sborník. (The currency system on the territory of the Bohemian Lands, 1892–1993). Opava, Ústav historie a muzeologie FPF Slezské univerzity, 95, 182 p.

7288. MOUSSAOUI-EL-KECHAI (Fella). Le système fiscal dans le rural du Beylik de Constantine durant la fin de la période ottomane (1771–1837). *Revue d'Histoire Maghrébine*, 95, 79-80, p. 463-474).

7289. MUELLER (R. C.). The Spufford thesis on foreign exchange: the evidence of exchange rates. *Journal of European Economic History*, 95, 24, 1, p. 121-130.

7290. NELSON WHITE (Eugene). The French Revolution and the politics of government finance, 1770–1815. *Journal of Economic History*, 95, 55, 2, p. 227-255.

7291. NISHIMURA (Shizuya). The French provincial banks, the Banque de France, and bill finance, 1890–1913. *Economic History Review*, 95, 48, 3, p. 536-554.

7292. PETROV (Jurij A.), KALMYKOV (Sergej V.). Sberegatel'noe delo v Rossii: Vekhi istorii. (The Russian savings bank). Moskva, K. I. T. , 95, 365p.

7293. PINAUD (P.-F.). Les ministres des Finances de 1790 à 1832: rupture ou continuité? *Revue Historique*, 95, 119, 594, p. 289-320.

7294. REDISH (Angela). The persistence of bimetallism in nineteenth-century France. *Economic History Review*, 95, 48, 4, p. 717-736.

7295. Ricerche per la storia della Banca d'Italia. Vol. 6. La bilancia dei pagamenti italiana, 1914–1931; i provvedimenti sui cambi in Italia, 1919–1936; istituzioni e società in Italia, 1936–1948; la Banca d'Inghilterra, 1694–1913. Scritti di Gian Carlo DE FALCO [et al.]. Roma e Bari, Laterza, 95, XI-438 p. (Collana storica della Banca d'Italia. Contributi, 6).

7296. ROMANO (Ruggiero). A propos des monnaies mexicaines au XVIIIe siècle. *In*: Pour une histoire économique et sociale internationale [Cf. n° 1297], p. 333-340. – IDEM. Quelques considérations sur monnaies et circulation monétaire dans le Méxique du XVIIIe siècle. In: Mélanges offerts à Frédéric Mauro [Cf. n° 7116], p. 763-770.

7297. SMILEY (Gene), KEEHN (Richard H.). Federal personal income tax policy in the 1920s. *Journal of Economic History*, 95, 55, 2, p. 285-303.

7298. SORIA (Víctor). La incorporación del apartado del oro y la plata a la Casa de Moneda y sus resultados de operación, 1778-1805. *Historia Mexicana*, 94-95, 44, p. 269-298.

7299. STEINDL (Frank George). Monetary interpretations of the great depression. Ann Arbor, University of Michigan Press, 95, XIV-197 p.

7300. TAMAKI (Norio). Japanese banking: a history, 1859-1959. Cambridge, Cambridge U. P., 95, XXI-289 p. (Studies in monetary and financial history).

7301. ZSCHALER (Frank). Öffentliche Finanzen und Finanzpolitik in Berlin, 1945-1961: eine vergleichende Untersuchung von Ost- und West-Berlin (mit Datenanhang 1945-1989). Berlin, De Gruyter, 95, XVIII-340 p. (Veröffentlichungen der Historischen Kommission zu Berlin, 88).

Cf. n° 5054

§ 7. Bevölkerungsbewegung und Städtebaukunst.

* 7302. GERHAN (David R.). Bibliography of American demographic history: the literature from 1984 to 1994. Westport a. London, Greenwood Press, 95, XX-339 p. (Bibliographies and indexes in American history, 30).

7303. BALSER (Frolinde). Aus Trümmern zu einem europäischen Zentrum. Geschichte der Stadt Frankfurt am Main 1945-1989. Sigmaringen, Thorbecke, 95. 511 p. (Veröffentl. der frankfurter historischen Kommission, 20).

7304. BALTA (Evangelia). Composition démographique et structure de l'habitat dans la ville de Serres aux XVe et XVIe siècles. *Osmanlı Araştırmaları*, 95, 15, p. 163-187.

7305. Be-és kitelepítések Közép-Európában a török uralom után, gazdasági szempontból. (Colonisation et éloignements en Europe Centrale après la domination turque, du point de vue économique). *Világtörténet*, 95, 3-4, p. 3-42.

7306. BODENSCHATZ (Harald), ENGSTFELD (Hans-Joachim), SEIFERT (Carsten). Berlin auf der Suche nach dem verlorenen Zentrum. Herausgegeben von der Architektenkammer Berlin. Hamburg, Junius, 95, 272 p.

7307. CHEVAILLER (Jean-Claude). La démographie des entreprises dans les départements français au XIXe siècle. In: Naissance et mort des entreprises en Europe, XIXe-XXe siècles [Cf. n° 7119], p. 125-139.

7308. Città e le sue storie (La). A cura di Carlo OLMO e Bernard LEPETIT. Torino, Einaudi, 95, VI-260 p. (Piccola biblioteca Einaudi, 617).

7309. CRAWFORD (Margaret). Building the workingman's paradise: the design of American company towns. London a. New York, Verso, 95, VIII-248 p. (Haymarket series).

7310. DAVID (Geza). 16-17. Yuzyıllarda Macaristan'in Demografik Durumu. (La situation démographique de la Hongrie aux XVIe-XVIIe siècles). *Belleten*, 95, 59, 225, p. 341-352.

7311. DERY (Attila). A Fővárosi Közmunkák Tanácsa, 1870-1948. Egy független városrendező hatóság. (Le Conseil des Travaux Publiques de la capitale. Un autorité indépendante des travaux d'urbanisme, 1870-1948). *Budapesti negyed*, 95, 3, 3, p. 77-96.

7312. ERDEI (Gyöngyi). A mintaadó polgármester. Bárczy István beruházási programja, 1906-1914. (Le maire-modèle. Le programme d'investitions de István Bárczy 1906-1914). *Budapesti negyed*, 95, 3, 3, p. 97-116.

7313. European urbanisation, social structure and problems between the eighteenth and twentieth century. Ed. by Desmond MAC CABE. Leicester, Centre for Urban History, University of Leicester, 95, II-159 p. (Eurocit).

7314. EVSEEV (Vladimir A.). Anglijskij gorod v tjudorovskuju epokhu: regiony i goroda. (The English towns during the Tudor age: regions and towns). Ivanovo, Ivanovskij gosudarstvennyj universitet, 95, 154 p.

7315. FEI (Silvano), GOBBI SICA (Grazia), SICA (Paolo). Firenze: profilo di storia urbana = Florence: an outline of urban history. Firenze, Alinea, 95, 216 p. (Saggi e documenti di storia dell'architettura, 22).

7316. Felvidék (A) települesienek nemzetiségi (anyanyelvi) megoszlása, 1880-1941. (La distribution des localités par nationalité [langue maternelle] en Haute-Hongrie [Slovaquie], 1880-1941). Összeáll. KEPECS József. Budapest, KSH, 95, 656 p.

7317. FERNADEZ (A.). La création en 1919 de la régie municipale du gaz et de l'életricité de Bordeaux. *Revue Historique*, 95, 119, 595, p. 109-122.

7318. FRIEDRICHS (Christopher R.). The early modern city 1450-1750. London a. New York, Longman, 95, X-381 p. (A history of urban society in Europe, 1).

7319. Fuentes para la historia urbana en el reino de Chile. Introducción y recopilación por Santiago Lorenzo SCHIAFFINO. Santiago, Academia Chilena de la Historia, 95, [s. p.]. (Serie de estudios y documentos para la historia de las ciudades del reino de Chile, 2).

7320. GALLEY (Chris). A model of early modern urban demography. *Economic History Review*, 95, 48, 3, p. 448-469.

7321. GJERDE (Jon), MAC CANTS (Anne). Fertility, marriage, and culture: demographic processes among Norwegian immigrants to the rural Middle West. *Journal of Economic History*, 95, 55, 4, p. 860-888.

7322. HIRSCH (Jean-Pierre). Naissance des sociétés, personnes et capitaux à Paris, Lille et Lyon en 1846 et 1866. In: Naissance et mort des entreprises en Europe, XIXe–XXe siècles [Cf. n° 7119], p. 141-156.

7323. HUCK (Paul). Infant mortality and living standards of English workers during the industrial revolution. *Journal of Economic History*, 95, 55, 3, p. 528-550.

7324. JAUHIAINEN (Jussi). Kaupunkisuunnittelu, kaupunkiuudistus ja kaupunkipolitiikka: kolme eurooppalaista esimerkkiä. (Urban planning, urban redevelopment and urban policy: three European examples). Turku, 95, 384 p. (Eng. summary, ill., maps). (Publ. Instituti Geographica Univ. Turkuensis, 146).

7325. JOHNSON (Eric A.). Urbanization and crime. Germany 1871–1914. Cambridge, Cambridge U. P., 95, 246 p.

7326. JORDAN (David Paul). Transforming Paris: the life and labors of Baron Haussmann. New York a. London, Free Press, 95, XXII-455 p.

7327. JORDE (Tine Susanne). Stockholms tjenestepiker under industrialiseringen: tjenestepikeyrkets funksjon i individets livsløp og i en ekspanderende storby. Stockholm, Stads- och kommunalhistoriska Institutet, 95, 187 p. (Studier i stads- och kommunalhistoria, 13).

7328. KEPSU (Saulo). Pietari ennen Pietaria – Nevansuun vaiheita ennen Pietarin kaupungin perustamista. (History of the Neva River delta before St. Petersburg was founded). Helsinki, SKS, 95, 128 p. (Eng. summary, ill., maps). (Suomal. Kirjall. Seuran toim., 608).

7329. LENGYEL (György). A gazdasági elit szegregációja és lakásviszonyai, 1920–1940. (La ségrégation et les conditions d'habitation de l'élite economique, 1920–1940). *Budapesti negyed*, 95, 3, 2, p. 127-136.

7330. LILJA (Sven). Stockholms befolkningsutveckling före 1800: problem, metoder och förklaringar. (The development of Stockholm's population before 1800: problems, methods and explanations). *Historisk Tidskrift* (Sweden), 95, 3, p. 304-338.

7331. Métropoles chinoises au XXe siècle (Les). Sous la direction de Christian HENRIOT; avec la collaboration de Alain DELISSEN. Paris, Arguments, 95, 265 p.

7332. MEYER (Jean), POUSSOU (Jean-Pierre). Etudes sur les villes françaises, milieu du XVIIe siècle à la veille de la Révolution française. Paris, SEDES, 95, 388 p. (Regards sur l'histoire. Histoire moderne, 48).

7333. MILLWARD (Robert), SHEARD (Sally). The urban fiscal problem, 1870–1914: government expenditure and finance in England and Wales. *Economic History Review*, 95, 48, 3, p. 501-535.

7334. Modern (A) város történeti dilemmai. (Les alternatifs historiques de la ville moderne). Szerk. GYÁNI Gábor. Debrecen, Csokonai, 95, 216 p.

7335. MÜDERRİSOĞLU (Fatih). Bani Çoban Mustafa Paşa ve Bir Osmanlı Şehri Gebze. (Gebze, une ville ottomane et son fondateur Çoban Mustafa Paşa). *Vakıflar Dergisi*, 95, 25, p 67-124.

7336. POLJAKOV (Jurij A.). Vozdejstvie gosudarstva na demografičeskie processy v SSSR (1920–1930-e-gody). (The influence of state on the demographic processes in the USSR. 1920's–1930's). *Vopr. Ist.*, 95, 3, p. 122-128.

7337. ROSŁANOWSKI (Tadeusz). La topographie sociale de l'urbanisme en Pologne et en Ukraine du XIVe aux XIXe/XXe siècles: question comparées. (VIIe colloque de la Commission des Sciences historiques près de l'Académie Polonaise des Sciences, Varsovie, les 14 et 15 décembre 1993). *Kwartalnik Historii Materialnej Polskiej Akademii Nauk*, 95, 43, 1, p. 9-14.

7338. SENJAVSKIJ (A. S.). Rossijskij gorod v 1960-e–80-e gody. (Russian town in the 1960's–1980's). Moskva, RAN. In-t rossijskoj istorii, 95, 264 p.

7339. Small towns in early modern Europe. Ed. by Peter CLARK. Cambridge, Cambridge U. P., 95, 310 p. (Themes in international urban history, 3).

7340. SMOUT (Christopher). The culture of migration: Scots as Europeans, 1500–1800. *History Workshop*, 95, 40, p. 108-117.

7341. SOLDO (Josip Ante). Sinjska krajina u 17. i 18. stoljeću, 1. (Sinjska Krajina in the seventeenth and eighteenth centuries). Sinj, Ogranak Matice hrvatske, 95, 259 p.

7342. VALLAT (Colette). Rome et ses borgate, 1960–1980: des marques urbaines à la ville diffuse. Préface de Anne-Marie SERONDE-BABONAUX. Roma, Ecole française de Rome, 95, 236 p. (Bibliothèque des écoles françaises d'Athènes et de Rome, 287).

7343. VERTLIEB (Vladimir). Osteuropäische Zuwanderung nach Österreich (1976–1991). Unter besonderer Berücksichtigung der Jüdischen Immigration aus der ehemaligen Sowjetunion. Quantitative und qualitative Aspekte. Wien, Inst. für Demographie der Österr. Akad. der Wiss., 95, 67 p. (Graph. Darstellungen). (Forschungsbericht des Instituts für Demographie der Österr. Akad. der Wiss., 15).

7344. WEIGL (Andreas). Eine Neuberechnung der Bevölkerungsentwicklung Wiens nach Bezirken 1777 bis 1869. *Wien. Gesch.-Bl.*, 95, 50, 4, p. 219-238 (Tab., Graph. Darstellungen).

7345. WEIR (David R.). Family income, mortality, and fertility on the eve of the demographic transition: a case study of Rosny-sous-Bois. *Journal of Economic History*, 95, 55, 1, p. 1-26.

7346. WIJACZKA (Jacek). Żydzi w Prusach Książęcych (1525–1701). (Les Juifs en Prusse Princière, 1525–

1701). *Komunikaty Mazursko-Warmińskie*, 95, 39, 1, p. 3-14. [Deutsche Zsfassung].

§ 8. Sozial- und Sittengeschichte.

7347. ABID (Mounir). Notes sur l'organisation médicale dans la Tunisie du XIXe siècle: une analyse préliminaire des documents de santé publique et de médecine d'après les registres des Archives Nationales de Tunisie. *Revue d'Histoire Maghrébine*, 95, 79-80, p. 475-479.

7348. AGUIRRE BELTRÁN (Gonzalo). Cuatro nobles titulados en contienda por la tierra. México, Centro de Investigaciones y Estudios Superiores en Antropología Social, 95, 256 p.

7349. ALBRICH (Thomas), MEIXNER (Wolfgang). Zwischen Legalität und Illegalität. Zur Mitgliederentwicklung, Alters- und Sozialstruktur der NSDAP in Tirol und Vorarlberg vor 1938. *Zeitgeschichte*, 95, 22, 5-6, p. 149-187 (Tab.).

7350. ALIBERTI (Giovanni). Élites e modello nobiliare nel secolo XIX. *Storia contemporanea*, 95, 26, 2, p. 211-226.

7351. ARRU (A.). Il servo. Storia di una carriera nel Settecento. Bologna, Il Mulino, 95, 241 p.

7352. BACSKAI (Vera). A pesti zsidóság a 19. század első felében. (Les Juifs de Pest dans la première moitié du XIX siecle). *Budapesti negyed*, 95, 3, 2, p. 5-21.

7353. Bakumatsu-Meiji-ki no Kokumin Kokka Keisei to Bunka Hen'yo. (Formation of the nation state and cultural change in the nineteenth-century Japan). Ed. by Nagao NISHIKAWA a. Syuji MATSUMIYA. Tokyo, Shin'yōsha, 95, 728 p.

7354. BELLAVITIS (Anna). «Per cittadini metterete ...». La stratificazione della società veneziana cinquecentesca tra norma giuridica e riconoscimento sociale. *Quaderni storici*, 95, 30, 89 (2), p. 359-384.

7355. BEN BELGHITH (Chibani). A propos du phénomène de la hausse de la dot au Sahel avant le protectorat selon des documents religieux. *Revue d'Histoire Maghrébine* (Partie arabe), 95, 79-80, p. 669-683.

7356. BERGMAN (Ulf). Från bondelots till yrkesmanlotsning i Östergötland 1537–1914. (From a peasant pilotage to the professional pilotage in eastern Sweden, 1537–1914). Lund, Lund U. P., 95, 408 p. (Bibliotheca Historica Lundensis, 85).

7357. BERTRAM (Martin). "Renaissance Mentality" in Italian testaments? *Journal of modern history*, 95, 67, 2, p. 358-369.

7358. BLASTENBREI (Peter). Kriminalität in Rom 1560–1585. Tübingen, Niemeyer, 95, IX-317 p. (Bibliothek des deutschen historischen Instituts in Rom, 82).

7359. BRUEGEL (M.). «Un sacrifice de plus à demander au soldat»: l'armée et l'introduction de la boîte de conserve dans l'alimentation française, 1872–1920. *Revue Historique*, 95, 119, 596, p. 259-284.

7360. BRUSINA (O. I). Kirgizija: social'nye posledstvija agrarnogo perenaselenija. (Kirgizia: social consequences of agrarian overcrowding). *Étnogr. obozrenie*, 95, 4, p. 96-106.

7361. BRUSTEIN (William), FALTER (Jürgen W.). Who joined the Nazi Party? Assessing theories of the social origins of nazism. *Zeitgeschichte*, 95, 22, 3-4, p. 83-108 (Diagr.).

7362. BURKE (Peter). Viewpoint: the invention of leisure in Early Modern Europe. *Past and Present*, 95, 146, p. 136-150.

7363. BUSCH (Margarete). Deutsche in St. Petersburg 1865–1914. Identität und Integration. Essen, Klartext, 95, 288 p. (Veröffentlichungen des Instituts für Kultur und Geschichte der Deutschen im östlichen Europa, 6).

7364. BUTEL (Paul). L'opium, histoire d'une fascination. Paris, Perrin, 95, 492 p.

7365. CAMMARANO (Fulvio). The professions in Parliament. *In*: Society and professions in Italy [Cf. n° 7458], p. 276-312.

7366. CAMPOS MARIN (Ricardo). La sociedad enferma: higiene y moral en España en la segunda mitad del siglo XIX y principios del XX. *Hispania*, 95, 55, 191, p. 1093-1112.

7367. CANOSA (Romano). Storia della criminalità in Italia dal 1946 a oggi. Milano, Feltrinelli, 95, 275 p. (Campi del sapere).

7368. CHINN (Carl). Poverty amidst prosperity. The urban poor in England, 1834–1914. Manchester a. New York, Manchester U. P. 95, X-182 p.

7369. Civilt samhälle kontra offentlig sektor. (The civil society against the public sector [in Sweden]). Ed. Lars TRÄGÅRDH. Stockholm, Studieförbundet Näringsliv och Samhälle (SNS), 95, 244 p.

7370. CLARK (Anna). The struggle for the breeches: gender and the making of the British working class. Berkeley a. Los Angeles, University of California Press, 95, XV-416 p.

7371. CLARK (Gregory), HUBERMAN (Michael), LINDERT (Peter H.). A British food puzzle, 1770–1850. *Economic History Review*, 95, 48, 2, p. 215-237.

7372. Consumption of culture (The), 1600–1800. Image, object, text. Ed.by Ann BERMINGHAM a. John BREWER. London a New York, Routledge, 95, XV-548 p.

7373. COSS (P. R.). The formation of the English gentry. *Past and Present*, 95, 147, p. 38-64.

7374. DE PLANHOL (Xavier). L'eau de neige. Le tiède et le frais. Histoire et géographie des boissons fraîches. Paris, Fayard, 95, 474 p.

7375. DESCIMON (Robert). Corpo cittadino, corpi di mestiere e borghesia a Parigi nel XVI e XVII secolo. Le libertà dei borghesi. *Quaderni storici*, 95, 30, 89 (2), p. 417-444.

7376. DONATI (Claudio). L'idea di nobiltà in Italia: secoli XIV–XVIII. Roma e Bari, Laterza, 95, VII-402 p. (Biblioteca universale Laterza, 438).

7377. DOWNS (Laura Lee). Manufacturing inequality: gender division in the French and British metalworking industries, 1914–1939. Ithaca, Cornell U. P., 95, 329 p.

7378. ECKSTEIN (Nicholas A.). The district of the green dragon. Neighbourhood life and social change in Renaissance Florence. Firenze, Olschki, 95, XXVI-274 p. (Rinascimento, 22).

7379. ENGMAN (Max). Peterburgska vägar. Helsingfors, Schildts, 95, 301 p. [Essays on the Finnish emigration to St Petersburg].

7380. Ethnicity, markets, and migration in the Andes: at the crossroads of history and anthropology. Ed. by Brooke LARSON a. Olivia HARRIS with Enrique TANDETER. Durham a. London, Duke U. P., 95, 428 p.

7381. FET (Jostein). Lesande bønder: litterær kultur i norske allmugesamfunn før 1840. (Reading peasants: literary culture in Norwegian peasant society before 1840). Oslo, Universitetsforlaget, 95, 442 p. (ill., bibl).

7382. FITZPATRICK (David). Famine, entitlements and seduction: captain Edmond Wynne in Ireland, 1846–1851. *English Historical Review*, 95, 110, 437, p. 596-619.

7383. FLYNN (Maureen). Blasphemy and the play of anger in sixteenth-century Spain. *Past and Present*, 95, 149, p. 29-56.

7384. FREVERT (Ute). "Man und Weib, und Weib und Mann". Geschlechterdifferenzen in der Moderne. München, Beck, 95, 254 p.

7385. FUGLUM (Per). Brennevinsforbudet i Norge. (Prohibition in Norway). Trondheim, Tapir, 95, 659 p.

7386. GALL (Lothar). Vom Stand zur Klasse? Zu Entstehung und Struktur der modernen Gesellschaft. *Historische Zeitschrift*, 95, 261, 1, p. 1-22.

7387. GARFINNKLE (Adam). Telltale hearts: the origins and impact of the Vietnam antiwar movement. London, Macmillan, 95, 370 p.

7388. Generations in conflict. Youth revolt and generations formation in Germany 1770–1968. Ed. by Mark ROSEMAN. Cambridge, Cambridge U. P., 95, 310 p. [Cf. n° <choice> 629.]

7389. GIARRIZZO (Giuseppe). Uomini e pesce. *Rivista storica italiana*, 95, 107, 1, p. 153-159.

7390. GLANTZ (Margo). Huérfanos y bandidos: los bandidos de Río Frío. *Historia Mexicana*, 94-95, 44, p. 141-165.

7391. GLAVE (Luis Miguel). Familia y poblamiento en el altiplano andino. *Andes*, 95-96, 7, p. 89-113.

7392. GRASSBY (Richard). The business community of seventeenth-century England. Cambridge, Cambridge U. P., 95, XXX-615 p.

7393. GYANI (Gabor). Hétköznapi Budapest. nagyvárosi élet a századfordulón. (Budapest de tous les jours. Vie de grande ville au tournant du siècle). Budapest, Városháza, 95, 104 p. (A város arcai).

7394. HÄKKINEN (Antti). Rahasta – vaan ei rakkaudesta. Prostituutio Helsingissä 1867–1939. (For money not for love. Prostitution in Helsinki, 1867–1949.) Helsinki, Otava, 95, 302, 16 p. (ill., maps.).

7395. HÄNNESTRAND (Bo). Människan, samhället och ledarhunden. Studier i ledarhundsarbetets historia. Uppsala, Uppsala Universitet, 95, 526 p. (Uppsala universitet. Studies in economic history, 36). [The man, the society and the dog. From the history of the guide dogs].

7396. HEAD-KÖNIG (Anne-Lise). La controverse sur les femmes mariées et l'emploi public dans l'entre-deux-guerres en Grande-Bretagne et en Suisse: jalons pour une étude comparative de l'évolution des emplois féminins dans l'administration publique en Europe. *In*: Pour une histoire économique et sociale internationale [Cf. n° 1297], p. 595-610.

7397. HERNÁNDEZ (Mauro). A la sombra de la Corona. Poder local y oligarquía urbana (Madrid, 1606–1808). Madrid, Siglo XXI Editores, 95, XIX-422 p. (Historia).

7398. HERR (Elizabeth). Women, marital status, and work opportunities in 1880 Colorado. *Journal of Economic History*, 95, 55, 2, p. 339-366.

7399. HORRELL (Sara), HUMPRIES (Jane). Women's labour force participation and the transition to the male-breadwinner family, 1790–1865. *Economic History Review*, 95, 48, 1, p. 89-117.

7400. HUNECKE (Volker). Der venezianische Adel am Ende der Republik 1646–1797: Demographie, Familie, Haushalt. Tubingen, Niemeyer, 95, X-466 p. (Bibliothek des Deutschen Historischen Instituts in Rom, 83).

7401. Ideale und Wirklichkeiten. Aspekte der Geschlechtergeschichte. Briefwechsel zwischen Hermine Cloeter, Emma Cloeter und Otto von Zwiedineck-Südenhorst 1893–1957. Hrsg v. Margret FRIEDRICH. Wien, Verlag der Österreichischen Akademie der Wissenschaften, 95, 575 p. (ill.). (Sitzungsberichte der Österreichische Akademie der Wissenschaften. Philosophisch-historische Klasse, 616).

7402. İPEK (Nedim). Anadolu'dan Amerika'ya Ermeni Göçü. (La migration des arméniens de l'Anatolie en Amérique). *Osmanlı Tarihi Araştırma Merkezi Dergisi*, 95, 6, p. 257-280.

7403. IRACE (Erminia). La nobiltà bifronte. Identità e coscienza aristocratica a Perugia tra XVI e XVII secolo. Milano, Unicopli, 95, 216 p.

7404. JOHNSON (Paul), NICHOLAS (Stephen). Male and female living standards in England and Wales, 1812–1857: evidence from criminal height records. *Economic History Review*, 95, 48, 3, p. 470-481.

7405. KAARNINEN (Mervi). Nykyajan tytöt: koulutus, luokka ja sukupuoli 1920- ja 1930-luvun Suomessa. (Modern girls: education, class and gender in Finland in the 1920s and 1930s). Helsinki, SHS, 95, 297 p. (Eng. summary, ill.). (Bibliotheca historica, 5).

7406. KARONEN (Petri). Brottsligheten i norden pa 1500- och 1600-talen. (Criminality in the north of Europe during the XVIth and XVIIth centuries). *Historisk Tidskrift* (Sweden), 95, 4, p. 67-74.

7407. KATES (Gary). The transgendered world of the Chevalier/Chevalière d'Eon. *Journal of modern history*, 95, 67, 3, p. 558-594.

7408. KAWAGOE (Osamu). Sei ni Yamu Shakai: Doitsu Aru Kindai no Kiseki. (The society corrupted by sexuality: traces of modern ages in German). Tokyo, Yamakawa Shuppansha, 95, 278 p.

7409. KAWAWAKE (Keiko). Jūhasseiki no Rondonsyōnin Bouzunkitto-ke no Jigyōtenkai. (The Bosanquet family enterprises in the eighteenth century). *Shirin*, 95, 78, 5, p. 1-41 (English summary).

7410. KNAPP (Éva). Vallásos társulatok, rekatolizáció és társadalmi átalakulás Kassán a 17–18. században. (Sociétés religieuses, actes des recatholiciser et transformation sociale á Cassovie dans les XVII–XVIII siècles). *Századok*, 95, 129, 4, p. 791-814.

7411. KOCKA (Jürgen). The middle classes in Europe. *Journal of modern history*, 95, 67, 4, p. 783-806.

7412. KOENKER (Diane P.). Men against women on the shop floor in early Soviet Russia: gender and class in the socialist workplace. *American Historical Review*, 95, 100, 5, p. 1438-1464.

7413. KRIEDTE (Peter). La dynastie des von der Leyen. Une famille de soyeux au XVIIIe siècle entre mennonisme et monde moderne. *Annales*, 95, 50, 4, p. 725-752.

7414. KUNZEL (Regina). Pulp fictions and problem girls: reading and rewriting single pregnancy in the Postwar United States. *American Historical Review*, 95, 100, 5, p. 1465-1487.

7415. LAHIRE (Bernard). Tableaux de familles. Heurs et malheurs scolaires en milieu populaire. Paris, Gallimard, 95, 297 p. (Hautes études).

7416. LÄHTEENMÄKI (Maria). Mahdollisuuksien aika. Työläisnaiset ja yhteiskunnan muutos 1910–30-luvun Suomessa. (The time of opportunities: working class women and social change in Finland from 1910 to 1930s.). Helsinki, SHS, 95, 348 p. (Biblioteca historica, 2.).

7417. LANGUE (Frédérique). El circulo las alianzas, estructuras familiares y estrategias economicas de la elite mantuana (siglo XVIII). *Boletin de la Academia Nacional de la Historia*, 95, 78, 1, [s. p.].

7418. LENGER (Friedrich). Großstädtische Eliten vor den Problemen der Urbanisierung. Skizze eines deutschamerikanischen Vergleichs 1870–1914. *Geschichte und Gesellschaft*, 95, 21, 3, p. 313-337.

7419. LILJEWALL (Britt). Bondevardag och samhällets förändring. Studier i och kring västsvenska dagböcker från 1800-talet. (Peasant everyday life and the changing society. Studies in and around the Western Swedish diaries from 19th century). Göteborg, Historiska institutionen, Universitetet, 95, 397 p. (Avhandlingar från Historiska institutionen i Göteborg, 10).

7420. LINCOLN (David). Settlement and servitude in Zululand, 1918–1948. *International Journal of African Historical Studies*, 95, 28, 1, p. 49-68.

7421. MAC CLINTOCK (Anne). Imperial leather: race, gender, and sexuality in the colonial context. London a New York, Routledge, 95, 449 p.

7422. MAC DOWELL (Laurel Sefton). Relief camp workers in Ontario during the great depression of the 1930s. *Canadian Historical Review*, 95, 76, 2, p. 205-228.

7423. MAKAROVIČ (Gorazd). Slovenci in čas: odnos do časa kot okvir in sestavina vsakdanjega življenja. (The Slovenes and the time: a relation to the time as a framework and a part of everyday life). Ljubljana, Krtina, 95, 446 p. (Knjižna zbirka Krt, 94).

7424. MÄNTYLÄ (Ilkka). Suomalaisen juoppouden kasvu. Kustavilaisen kauden alkoholipolitiikka. (The growth of Finnish drunkennes: the alcohol policy of the Gustavian era). Helsinki, SHS, 95, 253 p. (Eng. summary). (Hist. tutkim., 192).

7425. MEDICK (Hans). Una cultura delle apparenze. I vestiti e i loro colori a Laichingen (1750–1820). *Quaderni storici*, 95, 30, 89 (2), p. 515-538. – IDEM. Une culture de la considération. Les vêtements et leur couleurs à Laichingen entre 1750 et 1820. *Annales*, 95, 50, 4, p. 753-774.

7426. Migracje polityczne i ekonomiczne w krajach nadbałtyckich w XIX i XX w. (Migrations politiques et économiques dans les pays baltes aux XIXe et XXe s). Ouvrage collectif sous la réd. de Józef BORZYKOWSKI et Mieczysław WOJCIECHOWSKI. Gdańsk, Toruń, 95, 226 p. (Deutsche Zsfassung). (Inst. Hist. i Archiw. Uniw. M. Kopernika; Inst. Hist. Uniw. Gdańskiego).

7427. MITCHELL (Sally). The new girl: girls' culture in England, 1880–1915. New York, Columbia U. P., 95, IX-258 p.

7428. MONTEGUALDO ROBLEDO (María-Pilar). El espectáculo del poder. Fiestas reales en la Valencia Moderna. Preambulo de Rita BARBERÁ NOLLA. Presentación de Manuel TARANCÓN. València, Ajuntament de València, 95, 196 p. (ill.). (Colección Minor, 7).

7429. MOSELLE (Boaz). Allotments, enclosure, and proletarianization in early nineteenth-century southern England. *Economic History Review*, 95, 48, 3, p. 482-500.

7430. NAVARRETE (Maria Cristina). Historia social del negro en la colonia: Cartagena, siglo XVII. Cali, Universidad del Valle, 95, 128 p.

7431. Obemärkta. Det dagliga livets idéer. Ed. by Ronny AMBJÖRNSSON a. Sverker SÖRLIN. Stockholm, Carlssons, 95, 304 p. [Everyday life in the past on the grassroots level].

7432. Obščetvennaja žizn' v Central'noj Rossii v XVI–načale XX veka: Sbornik naučnykh trudov. (The social life in the Central Russia, the XVIth–the beginning of the XXth centuries. Collected studies). Voronežskij gosudarstvennyj universitet; Redkol.: M. D. KARPAČEV (otv. red.) i drugie. Voronež, Izdatel'stvo Voronežkogo universiteta, 95, 214p.

7433. OLLILA (Anne). Womens voluntary associations in Finland during the 1920s and 1930s. *Scandinavian Journal of History*, 95, 20, p. 97-108.

7434. ÖSTERBERG (Eva). Folk förr: historiska essäer. Stockholm, Atlantis, 95, 260 p. [The people in the past. Essays about the living conditions and mentalities of the Swedes].

7435. ÖZDEMİR (Rifat). Harput ve Çemişgezek'te Askeri Ailelerin Sosyo-Ekonomik Yapısı (1890–1919). (La structure socio-économique des familles militaires à Harput et Çemişkezek). *Belleten*, 95,59, 226, p. 739-835.

7436. PALSDOTTIR (Sigrun). Resistance to consumerism in Britain, 1920–1960. Oxford, [s. n.], 95, 67 p. (Thesis, University of Oxford, 1995)

7437. PANAYI (Panikos). German immigrants in Britain during the nineteenth century, 1815–1914. Oxford a. Washington, Berg, 95, 301 p.

7438. PAULSEN (Ivar Bjarne). Bibliografi over gårdsog ættesogne i Norge. (Books on family history in rural dictricts in Norway. A bibliography). Stavanger, Statsarkivet i Stavanger, 95, II-123 p.

7439. PLAINEMAISON (J.). La fête de la Quintaine à Saint-Léonard-de-Noblat (Haute-Vienne) et le cult du saint patron de la ville. *Revue Historique*, 95, 119, 596, p. 219-224.

7440. Politica della casa all'inizio del XX secolo (La). Atti della prima Giornata di studio Luigi Luzzatti per la storia dell'Italia contemporanea, Venezia, 3, dicembre 1993. A cura di Donatella CALABI. Venezia, Istituto veneto di scienze lettere e arti, 95, 295 p. (ill.). (Biblioteca luzzattiana, 3).

7441. POLJAKOV (Jurij A.). Problemy emigracii i adaptacii v svete istoričeskogo opyta. (Emigration and adaptation in the light of historical experience). *Nov. novejš. Ist.*, 95, 3, p. 8-15.

7442. POSADA (Marcelo), IULIANO (Rolando). Modernidad y rentabilidad. La "intelligentsia ganadera y los empresarios pecuarios. Godofredo Daireaux. *Revista de Historia de América*, 119, 95, p. 49-70.

7443. PRAK (Maarten). Cittadini, abitanti e forestieri. Una classificazione della popolazione di Amsterdam nella prima età moderna. *Quaderni storici*, 95, 30, 89 (2), p. 331-358.

7444. RABINOW (Paul). French modern. Norms and forms of the social environment. Chicago a. London, University of Chicago Press, 95, 454 p.

7445. REINDL-KIEL (Hedda). Wesirfinger und Frauenschenkel. Zur Sozialgeschichte der türkischen Küche. *Archiv für Kulturgeschichte*, 95, 77, p. 57-84.

7446. REYES (Juan Carlos). Delitos sexuales y penalización en la Venezuela del siglo XVIII, la criminalidad en Venezuela colonial: caso de bestialidad. *Boletin de la Academia Nacional de la Historia*, 95, 78, 4, [s. p.].

7447. Rok pruski. Życie codzienne wsi polskiej na przełomie XIX i XX w. w świetle korespondencji prasowych. (Anneé prussienne. La vie quotidienne de la campagne polonaise entre XIXe et XXe s. à la lumière des correspondances de presse. Ed. et avant propos Andrzej STANISZEWSKI. Olsztyn, [s. n.], 95, XVIII-339 p. (Studia i Mater. Wyższej Szkoły Pedagog. w Olsztynie, 75).

7448. ROMANELLI (Raffaele). Urban patricians and "bourgeois" society: a study of wealthy elites in Florence, 1862–1904. *Journal of Modern Italian Studies*, 95, 1, 1, p. 3-21.

7449. ROMANO (Ruggiero). Las Bulas Alejandrinas y el Tratado de Tordesillas en los orígenes del feudalismo americano. In: Tratado de Tordesillas (El) y su Epoca. T. 3 [Cf. n° 5631], p. 1541-1551.

7450. ROSANVALLON (Pierre), REBERIOUX (Madeleine), FRIDENSON (Patrick). Citoyenneté politique et citoyenneté sociale au XIXe siècle. Entretien. *Mouvement social*, 95, 171, p. 9-30.

7451. RUDERSDORF (Manfred). "Das Glück der Bettler". Justus Möser und die Welt der Armen. Mentalität und soziale Frage im Fürstbistum Osnabrück zwischen Aufklärung und Säkularisation. Münster, Aschendorff, 95, XX-415 p.

7452. SANDMO (Erling). Et virkeligt mandfolk. Teorier om kjoenn i det tidlig-moderne Europa. (Real men. Gender theories in early modern Europe). *Historisk Tidskrift* (Sweden), 95, 4, p. 477-508.

7453. SCARDOZZI (Mirella). Mestiere e famiglia a Firenze: un sondaggio sul censimento del 1841. *Passato e presente*, 95, 13, 34, p. 123-138.

7454. SCHILDT (Axel). Moderne Zeiten. Freizeit, Massenmedien und "Zeitgeist" in der Bundesrepublik der 50er Jahre. Hamburg, Christians, 95, 733 p. (Hamburger Beiträge zur Sozial- und Zeitgeschichte, 31).

7455. SCHLEGEL-MATTHIES (Kirsten). "Im Haus und am Herd": der Wandel des Hausfrauenbildes und der Hausarbeit 1880–1930. Stuttgart, Franz Steiner, 95, 292 p. (Studien zur Geschichte des Alltags, 14).

7456. SCHLUMBOHM (Jürgen). Quelques problèmes de micro-histoire d'une société locale. Construction de liens sociaux dans la paroisse de Belm (XVIIe–XIXe siècles). *Annales*, 95, 50, 4, p. 775-802.

7457. Shizoku no Rekishi-Shakaigakuteki Kenkyū: Bushi no Kindai. (A historical sociology of "Shizoku": Samurai and the modern ages). Ed. by Hidehiro SONODA. Nagoya, University of Nagoya Press, 95, 353 p.

7458. Society and professions in Italy 1860–1914. Ed. by M. MALATESTA. Cambridge, Cambridge U. P., 95, VIII-340 p. [Cf. n° <choice> 7365.]

7459. SOSA LLANOS (Pedro Vicente). Influencia del codigo negrero de 1789 en la insurrección de los negros de coro. *Boletin de la Academia Nacional de la Historia*, 95, 78, 2, [s. p.].

7460. SPREE (R.). Krankenhausentwicklung und Sozialpolitik in Deutschland während des 19. Jahrhunderts. *Historische Zeitschrift*, 95, 260, 1, p. 75-106.

7461. ŠTUHEC (Marko). Rdeča postelja, ščurki in solze vdove Prešeren: [plemiški zapuščinski inventarji 17. stoletja kot zgodovinski vir]. (Red bed, cockroaches and the tears of a widow Prešeren: 17th century inventories of aristocratic bequests as a historical source). Ljubljana, ŠKUC, Znanstveni inštitut Filozofske fakultete, 95, 201 p. (Studia humanitatis. Apes, 1).

7462. SVATEK (František). K dějinám sociálních elit první Československé republiky. (The Czechoslovak Republic's social élites). *Soudobé dějiny*, 95, 2, 2-3, p. 169-200.

7463. SVENSSON (Lars). Befattningssegregering efter kön. ett bidrag till förklaringen av lönegapet mellan kvinnliga och manliga kontorsandställda vid mitten av 1930-talet. (Professional segregation according to gender. A contribution to explanation of a wage gap between masculine and feminine white collar employees in the midst of 1930s). *Historisk Tidskrift* (Sweden), 95, 3, p. 277-304.

7464. Tempo libero e società di massa nell'Italia del Novecento. Postfazione di Stefano PIVATO. Scritti di M. ASSO [et al.]. Milano, Angeli, 95, 469 p. (ill.).

7465. Tempo libero, economia e società (II) (loisirs, tiempo libre, Freizeit), secc. XIII–XVIII: atti della 'Ventiseiesima Settimana di studi' 18–23 aprile 1994. A cura di Simona CAVACIOCCHI. Firenze, Le Monnier, 95, 888 p. (Pubblicazioni. Istituto internazionale di storia economica 'F. Datini' Prato. Serie II: Atti delle 'Settimane di studi' e altri convegni, 26).

7466. To in ono o meščanstvu v provinci. (This and that on the middle class in province). Ed. by Wolfgang ZITTA. Celje, Pokrajinski muzej, 95, 78 p.

7467. TOSH (John). Separation and intimacy in Victorian bourgeois marriage. *History Workshop*, 95, 40, p. 193-206.

7468. TRATNIK-VOLASKO (Marjeta), KOŠIR (Matevž). Čarovnice: predstave, procesi, pregoni v evropskih in slovenskih deželah. (The witches: notions, legal proceedings and witch-hunting in European countries and on Slovene territory). Ljubljana, Znanstveno in publicistično središče, 95, 270 p. (Zbirka Spekter, 1995, 2).

7469. TULVA (Taimi). Viron sosiaalityön muotoutuminen murroskaudella. (Social work in Estonia in a period of change). Rovaniemi, Lapin yliopisto, 95, 270 p. (Eng. Summary). (Acta Univ. Lappoensis, 8.).

7470. TÜRKDOĞAN (Orhan). Türk Ailesinin Yapısı ve Tarihi Gelişimi. (La structure de la famille turque et son développement historique). *Türk Dünyası Araştırmaları*, 95, 96, p. 1-47.

7471. VACULÍK (Jaroslav). Reemigrace zahraničních Čechů a Slováků v letech 1945–1948. (Reemigration of the Czechs and Slovaks living abroad, 1945–1948). *Slezský sborník*, 95, 93, 1/2, p. 53-58.

7472. VALLONE (Lynn). Disciplines of virtue: girls' culture in the eighteenth and nineteenth centuries. New Haven a. London, Yale U. P., 95, 230 p.

7473. Variationen der Liebe. Historische Psychologie der Geschlechterbeziehung. Hrsg. v. Thomas KORNBICHLER u. Wolfgang MAAZ. Tübingen, Diskord, 95, [s. p.] (Forum Psychohistorie, 4).

7474. VEBER (Václav). Ruská a ukrajinská emigrace v ČSR v letech 1918–1945. Sborník studií. (Russian and Ukrainian emigration in Czechoslovakia 1918–1945). T. 3. Praha, Ústav světových dějin FF UK, 95, 139 p.

7475. VENTURA (Piero). Le ambiguità di un privilegio: la cittadinanza napoletana tra Cinque e Seicento. *Quaderni storici*, 95, 30, 89 (2), p. 385-416.

7476. VIQUEIRA (Juan Pedro). Tributo y sociedad en Chiapas (1680–1721). *Historia Mexicana*, 94-95, 44, p. 237-267.

7477. WARIS (Elina). The extended family in Finnish Karelia. The family system in Ruokolahti 1750–1850. *Scandinavian Journal of History*, 95, 20, p. 109-128.

7478. WECKER (Regina). "... ein wunder Punkt für das Volkszählungswesen". Frauenarbeit und Statistik an der Wende vom 19. zum 20. Jahrhundert. *Revue suisse d'histoire*, 95, 45, 1, p. 80-93.

7479. WHITEMAN (Dorit Bader). Die Entwurzelten. Jüdische Lebensgeschichten nach der Flucht 1933 bis heute. Wien, Köln u. Weimar, Böhlau, 95, 393 p. (ill.). (Böhlaus zeitgeschichtliche Bibliothek, 29).

7480. WILDT (Michael). Consumer culture in 1950s West Germany. *History Workshop*, 95, 39, p. 23-41.

7481. WYROBISZ (Andrzej). Patterns of the family and woman in Old Poland. *Acta Poloniae historica*, 95, 71, p. 69-82.

7482. YAMAMOTO (Hideyuki). Nachizumu no Kioku: Nichijō Seikatsu kara Mita Daisan-Teikoku. (Memories of Nazism and everyday life in the Third Reich). Tokyo, Yamakawa Shuppansha, 95, 352 p.

7483. YEH (Wen-Hsin). Corporate space, communal time: everyday life in Shangai's Bank of China. *American Historical Review*, 95, 100, 1, p. 97-122.

7484. YORK (Deborah Valenze). The first industrial woman. Oxford, Oxford U. P.,95, IX-251 p.

7485. ŻARNOWSKA (Anna). Changes to the occupation and social status of women in Poland since the industrial revolution till 1939. *Acta Poloniae historica*, 95, 71, p. 123-131.

7486. ZILLIACUS (Ville). I samma båt: essäer om granskap och vänskap. Helsigfors, Schildts, 95, 165 p. [Essays on the neighbourly relations between the inhabitants of the both sides of the Gulf of Bothnia].

7487. ZILYNSKYJ (Bohdan). Ukrajinci v Čechách a na Moravě. (1894) 1917–1945 (1994). [Ukrains in Bohemia and Moravia. (1894) 1917–1945 (1994)]. Praha, X-Egem, 95, 128 p. (photogr.).

7488. ZSIDÓ (A) Budapest. Emlékek, szertartások, történelem. Szerk. KOMORÓCZY Géza. (Budapest juive. Mémoires, cérémonies, histoire). Budapest, Városháza-MTA Judaisztikai Csoport, 95, 2 vol., 793 p. (Hungaria Judaica 7).

7489. ZWETTLER (Otto). Češi a Němci v Čechách a na Moravě. (Czechs and Germans in Bohemia and Moravia). Tomo 1. 1848–1938. Tomo 2. 1938–1993. Brno, Akademické nakladatelství Cerm, 95, 2 vol., 16 p., 24 p.

§ 9. **Arbeiterbewegung und Sozialismus.**

7490. BEDANI (Gino). Politics and ideology in the Italian workers' movement: union development and the changing role of the Catholic and Communist subcultures in postwar Italy. Oxford, Berg Publishers, 95, XIII-365 p.

7491. BIANCHI (Roberto). Una rivolta popolare del «biennio rosso». I moti per i caroviveri a Firenze. *Passato e presente*, 95, 13, 35, p. 65-96.

7492. BLOMBERG (Eva). Män i mörker. Arbetsgivare, reformister och syndikalister. Politik och identitet i svensk gruvindustri 1910–1940. (Men in the dark. Employers, reformists and syndicalists. Politics and identity in the Swedish mining industry, 1910–1940). Stockholm, Almqvist & Wiksell international, 95, 432 p. (Stockholm studies in history, 53).

7493. BORSÁNYI (György). Gondolatok a Kommunisták Magyarországi Pártjának történetéről, 1918–1944. (Considérations concernant l'histoire du Parti des Communistes de Hongrie, 1918–1944). *Múltunk*, 95, 40, 1, p. 3-37.

7494. BOUYAHYA (Salem). Les relations syndicales tuniso-libyennes (1959–1966). *Revue d'Histoire Maghrébine* (Partie arabe), 95, 77-78, p. 57-95.

7495. CALLINICOS (Alex). Socialists in the trade unions. London, Bookmarks, 95, 79 p.

7496. DER (Aladár). Az osztrák szocialisták brünninemzetiségi programjáról. (Du programme de Brünn des socialistes Autrichiens concernant la question des nationalités). *Múltunk*, 95, 40, 4, p. 65-92.

7497. DI VITTORIO (Giuseppe). Il patto di Roma e la nascita della CGIL. A cura di Michele PISTILLO. Roma, Editori Riuniti, 95, XXX-139 p. (Studi, 79).

7498. DREYFUS (Michel). Histoire de la C.G.T: cent ans de syndicalisme en France. Bruxelles, Editions Complexe, 95, 407 p. (Questions au XXe siècle).

7499. EISNER (Freya). Kurt Eisners Ort in der sozialistischen Bewegung. *Vierteljahrshefte für Zeitgeschichte*, 95, 95, 43, 3, p. 407-436.

7500. ELLNER (Steve). El sindicalismo en Venezuela en el contexto democratico, 1958–1994. Caracas, Fondo Editorial Tropykos, Universidad de Oriente, 95, 351 p.

7501. FINNEY (Patrick B.). 'An evil for all concerned': Great Britain and minority protection after 1919. *Journal of Contemporary History*, 95, 30, 3, p. 533-551.

7502. FISCHER (Conan J.). Gab es am Ende der Weimarer Republik einen marxistischen Wählerblock? *Geschichte und Gesellschaft*, 95, 21, 1, p. 63-79.

7503. FURET (François). Le passé d'une illusion. Essai sur l'idée communiste au XXe siècle. Paris, Robert Laffont et Calmann-Lévy, 95, 580 p.

7504. GEORGI (Frank). L'invention de la CFDT 1957–1970: syndicalisme, catholicisme et politique dans la France de l'expansion. Préface de Antoine PROST. Paris, Les Editions de l'Atelier, CNRS Editions, 95, 651 p. (Patrimoine).

7505. Geschichte der Gewerkschaften in Bayern: eine Bibliographie. Zusammengestellt von Wolfgang KUCERA u. Lutz TIETMANN; herausgegeben vom Haus der Bayerischen Geschichte und dem Deutschen Gewerkschaftsbund, Landesbezirk Bayern. Augsburg, Haus der Bayerischen Geschichte, 95, 213 p. (Materialien zur Bayerischen Geschichte und Kultur, 2).

7506. GROSS (Jean-Pierre). Le projet de l'an II: promotion ouvrière et formation professionnelle. *In*: An II (L') [Cf. n° 4852], p. 209-221.

7507. HAMILTON (Gillian). Enforcement in apprenticeship contracts: were runaways a serious problem? Evidence from Montreal. *Journal of Economic History*, 95, 55, 3, p. 551-574.

9. ARBEITERBEWEGUNG UND SOZIALISMUS

7508. HÜBNER (Peter). Konsens, Konflikt und Kompromiß. Soziale Arbeiterinteressen und Sozialpolitik in der SBZ/DDR 1945–1970. Berlin, Akademie, 95, 247 p. (Zeithistorische Studien, 3).

7509. JUDINA (Ljudmila S.). Stačečnoe dviženie na Urale v 1905–1907 godakh: Khronika. (The strike movement in the Urals in the 1905–1907. Chronicle). Čeljabinsk, Čeljabinskij gosudarstvennyj universitet. Kafedra novejšej istorii Rossii, 95, 207 p.

7510. KAISER (Monika). Change and continuity in the development of the socialist unity party of Germany. *Journal of Contemporary History*, 95, 30, 4, p. 687-704.

7511. KOKO (Eugeniusz). W nadziei na zgodę. Polski ruch socjalistyczny wobec kwestii narodowościowej w Polsce (1918–1939). (En espérant la réconciliation. Mouvement socialiste polonais face à la question nationale en Pologne, 1918–1939). Gdańsk, Uniw. Gdański, 95, 247 p. (Eng. summary). (Rozpr. i Monogr., 207).

7512. KUJALA (Antti). Venäjän hallitus ja Suomen työväenliike 1899–1905. (The Russian Government and the Finnish workers' movement, 1899–1905). Helsinki, SHS, 95, 453, 8 p. (Eng. summary). (Hist. tutkim., 194).

7513. LIPP (Karlheinz). Religiöser Sozialismus und Pazifismus. Der Friedenskampf des Bundes der religiösen Sozialisten Deutschlands in der Weimarer Republik. Pfaffenweiler, Centaurus, 95, 222 p. (Reihe Geschichtswissenschaft, 35).

7514. MALLMANN (Klaus-Michael). Milieu, Radikalismus und lokale Gesellschaft. Zur Sozialgeschichte des Kommunismus in der Weimarer Republik. *Geschichte und Gesellschaft*, 95, 21, 1, p. 5-31.

7515. MALONEY (Thomas N.), WHATLEY (Warren C.). Making the effort: the contours of racial discrimination in Detroit's labor markets, 1920–1940. *Journal of Economic History*, 95, 55, 3, p. 465-493.

7516. MARTELLI (Roger). Le rouge et le bleu. Essai sur le communisme dans l'histoire française. Paris, Ed. de l'Atelier et Ed. ouvrières, 95, 286 .

7517. MASON (Timothy Wright). Nazism, fascism and the working class. Ed. by Jane CAPLAN. Cambridge a. New York, Cambridge U. P., 95, X-361 p.

7518. MATTHIESEN (Helge). Zwei Radikalisierungen: Bürgertum und Arbeiterschaft in Gotha 1918–1923. *Geschichte und Gesellschaft*, 95, 21, 1, p. 32-62.

7519. NAKANO (Tadashi). Igirisu-Kinsei-Toshi no Tenkai: Shakai Keizaishiteki Kenkyū. (Development of the modern English towns: socio-economic studies). Tokyo, Sōbunsha, 95, 532 p.

7520. NIELSEN (Michael Charles), MAILES (Gene). Hollywood's other blacklist: union struggles in the studio system. London, BFI Publishing, 95, XIII-178 p.

7521. OTÁHAL (Milan). Malý akční program Československého hnutí za demokratický socialismus (1971). (The little action programme of the Czechoslovak Movement for Democratic Socialism). *Soudobé dějiny*, 95, 2, 2-3, p. 374-398. (Suppl. Archiv soudobých dějin).

7522. PETER (Ulrich). Der "Bund der religiösen Sozialisten" in Berlin von 1919 bis 1933. Geschichte, Struktur, Theologie und Politik. Frankfurt am Main, Berlin u. Bern, Lang, 95, 696 p. (Europäische Hochschulschriften, 23. Theologie, 532).

7523. Raboĉee dviženie v Rosii 1895–fevral'1917 goda: Khronika. (Labour movement in Russia 1895–February of 1917: Chronicle). Redkol.: Ju. I. KIR'JANOV (ootv. red.) i drugie. Vup. 3. 1987 god. (1877). Sost. I. M. PUŠKAREVA (otv. sost.). Moskva, Sankt- Peterburg, Izdatel'stvo Russko-Baltijskij informacionnyj centr "Blic", Gosudarstvennaja služba Rossii i drugie, 95. 352 p.

7524. ROVERI (Alessandro). Il socialismo tradito: la sinistra italiana negli anni della Guerra fredda. Scandicci, La nuova Italia, 95, VIII-168 p. (Biblioteca di storia, 47).

7525. SALMINEN (Juhani). Kemi 1949. Suomen kohtaloratkaisu. Jyväskylä, Gummerus, 95, 393 p. [The decisive episode in the history of the Finnish workers movement].

7526. SERÇE (Erkan). 1923 İzmir-Aydın Demiryolu Grevi: Siyasal İktidar, Sermaye ve İşçi Sınıfı Üçgeni Üzerine Bir Deneme. (La Grève des ouvriers du chemin de fer d'Izmir-Aydin en 1923: un essai sur le triangle de l'autorité politique, le capital et la classe ouvrière). *Toplum ve Bilim*, 95, 66, p. 86-104.

7527. ŞIK (Yüksel). Osmanlı'dan Günümüze İşçi Hareketinin Evrimi (L'évolution du mouvement ouvrier de l'Empire Ottoman jusqu'à nos jours). İstanbul, Öteki Yayınları, 95, 320 p.

7528. Socialismes francais (Les), 1796–1866: formes du discours socialiste. Préface de Maurice AGULHON; textes recueillis par Jacques BIRNBERG, M. AGULHON [et al.]. Paris, SEDES, 95, 267 p. (Colloques de la "Societe des études romantiques").

7529. SOROKA (Józef Michał). Polska Partia Socjalistyczna wobec problemów kulturalno oświatowych 1918–1939. (Parti Socialiste Polonais face aux problèmes de culture et d'éducation 1918–1939). Wrocław, 95, 199 p. (Prace Nauk. Akad. Ekonom. im. Oskara Langego we Wrocławiu nr 700. Monogr. i Oprac., 110). [Eng. summary].

7530. STOLTZFUS (Nathan). Widerstand des Herzens. Der Protest in der Rosenstraße und die deutsch-jüdische Mischehe. *Geschichte und Gesellschaft*, 95, 21, 2, p. 218-247.

7531. STÖVER (Bernd). Loyalität statt Widerstand. Die sozialistischen Bewegung. *Vierteljahrshefte für Zeitgeschichte*, 95, 95, 43, 3, p. 437-472.

7532. TREMBICKA (Krystyna). Między apologią a negacją. Studium myśli politycznej Komunistycznej Partii Polskiej 1918–1932. (Entre apologie et négation. Etude sur la pensée politique du Parti Communiste Polonais dans les années 1918–1932.). Lublin, Wydawn. Uniw. M. Curie-Skłodowskiej, 95, 182 p.

7533. Wohlfahrt und Region. Beiträge zur historischen Rekonstruktion des Wohlfahrtsstaates in westfälischer und vergleichender Perspektive. Hrsg. v. Andreas WOLLASCH. Münster, Ardey, 95, 185 p. (Forum Regionalgeschichte, 5).

O

RECHTS- UND VERFASSUNGSGESCHICHTE DER NEUZEIT

§ 1. Allgemeine Rechtsgeschichte. 7534-7551. – § 2. Geschichte des Verfassungsrechts. 7552-7574. – § 3. Staatsrecht und öffentliche Einrichtungen. 7575-7616. – § 4. Zivil- und Strafrecht. 7616-7660. – § 5. Völkerrecht. 7661-7669.

§ 1. Allgemeine Rechtsgeschichte.

7534. CÍSAŘ (Jaromír). Vývoj československého zákonodárství v letech 1968–1970. (The evolution of Czechoslovak legislation, 1968–70). Praha, Ústav pro soudobé dějiny AV ČR, 95, 67 p. (Materiály, studie, dokumenty, 12).

7535. Deutsche (Die) Rechtsgeschichte in der NS-Zeit. Ihre Vorgeschichte und ihre Nachwirkungen. Hrsg. Joachim RÜCKERT u. Dietmar WILLOWEIT. Tübingen, Mohr, 95, 350 p.

7536. Deutsche (Die) und die italienische Rechtskultur im "Zeitalter der Vergleichung". Hrsg. v. Aldo MAZZACANE u. Reiner SCHULZE. Berlin, Duncker u. Humblot, 95, 245 p. (Schriften zur Europäischen Rechts- und Verfassungsgeschichte, 15).

7537. DIEDERICHSEN (Uwe). Innere Grenzen des Rechtsstaats. Der Staat, 95, 34, 1, p. 33-58.

7538. FAUTH (D.). Verfassungs- und Rechtsvorstellungen im Bauernkrieg, 1524/25. Zeitschrift der Savigny-Stiftung für Rechtsgeschichte. Kanonistische Abteilung, 95, 112, p. 225-248.

7539. GRODZISKI (Stanisław). O zadaniach i obowiązkach historii państwa i prawa polskiego wczoraj i dziś. (Les tâches et les devoirs de l'histoire de l'état et du droit polonais – hier et aujourd'hui). Czasopismo Prawno-Historyczne, 95, 46, 1-2, p. 19-29. [Rés. franç.].

7540. JARASS (Hans D.). Bausteine einer umfassenden Grundrechtsdogmatik. Archiv des öffentlichen Rechts, 95, 120, 3, p. 345-381.

7541. KOENEN (Andreas). Der Fall Carl Schmitt. Sein Aufstieg zum "Kronjuristen des Dritten Reiches". Darmstadt, Wissenschaftliche Buchgesellschaft, 95, X-979 p.

7542. LEWIS (A. D.). Montesquieu's Collectio Juris. Journal of Legal History, 95, 16, 3, p. 304-307.

7543. LUKOWSKI (Jerzy). Towards the ideal constitution: Rousseau, Montesquieu and 3 May 1791. Parliaments, Estates and Representation, 95, 15, p. 59-66.

7544. MOSCATI (Laura). L'interpretazione della Geschichte di Savigny nella scienza giuridica preunitaria. Rivista di storia del diritto italiano, 95, 68, p. 91-106.

7545. PETTERSSON (Ronny). Skifte och aganderätt. (Enclosures and property right). Historisk Tidskrift (Sweden), 95, 1, p. 1-33.

7546. PYLKKÄNEN (Anu). Substitute children and adoption in Finnish legal history. Scandinavian Journal of History, 95, 20, p. 129-140.

7547. QUARITSCH (H.). Giustizia politica: l'amnistia nella storia. A cura di P. P. PORTINARO. Milano, Giuffré, 95, VIII-187 p.

7548. SCHRECKENBERGER (Waldemar). Der moderne Verfassungsstaat und die Idee der Weltgemeinschaft. Der Staat, 95, 34, 4, p. 503-526.

7549. SCHWAB (Dieter). Geschichtliches Recht und moderne Zeiten. Heidelberg, Müller Juristischer Verlag, 95, 282 p.

7550. WALKER (David Maxwell). A legal history of Scotland. Vol. 3. The sixteenth century. Edinburgh, T & T Clark, 95, XVIII-871 p.

7551. YERUSHALMI (Yosef Hayim). "Diener von Königen und nicht Diener von Dienern": einige Aspekte der politischen Geschichte der Juden. Hrsg. v. Heinrich MEIER; aus dem Amerikanischen übersetzt von Wolfgang HEUSS. München, C.F. von Siemens Stiftung, 95, 61 p. (Themen, 58).

Cf. n°s 1232-1249, 5980

§ 2. Geschichte des Verfassungsrechts.

7552. ANGIOLINI (Vittorio). Costituente e costituito nell'Italia repubblicana. Padova, Casa edit. dott. A. Milani C.E.D.A.M., 95, XII-319 p.

7553. BACHNICK (Uwe). Die Verfassungsreformvorstellungen im nationalsozialistischen deutschen Reich und ihre Verwirklichung. Berlin, Duncker & Humblot, 95, 414 p. (Schriften zur Verfassungsgeschichte, 45).

7554. BOGDANOR (Vernon). The Monarchy and the Constitution. Oxford, Clarendon press, 95, XI-328 p.

7555. CALAMANDREI (Piero). Costruire la democrazia. Premesse alla Costituente. Con un saggio introduttivo di Paolo BARILE. Firenze, Vallecchi, 95, 170 p.

7556. CHIMENTI (Carlo). Addio prima Repubblica. Lineamenti della forma di governo italiana nell'esperienza di undici legislature. Torino, G. Giappichelli, 95, 352 p.

7557. Constitutional policy and change in Europe. Ed. by Joachim Jens HESSE a. Nevil JOHNSON. Oxford, Oxford U. P., 95, X-403 p.

7558. ERTAN (Temuçin F.). Osmanlı Devletin'de Anayasal Rejime Geçiş (1876 Kanun-i Esâsîsi). [Le passage au régime constitutionnel dans l'Empire Ottoman (La Constitution de 1876)]. *Hacettepe Üniversitesi Edebiyat Fakültesi Dergisi*, 95, 12, 1-2, p. 134-155.

7559. EUGSTER (Markus). Der brasilianische Verfassungsgebungsprocess von 1987–88. Bern, Stuttgart u. Wien, P. Haupt, 95, XV-403 p.

7560. FERREIRA DA CUNHA (Paulo). Para uma história constitucional do direito português. Coimbra, Almedina, 95, 455 p.

7561. FIORAVANTI (Maurizio). Le dottrine dello Stato e della costituzione. *In*: Storia dello stato italiano [Cf. n° 5048], p. 408-457.

7562. Gendai Nihon Sei-Kan Kankei no Keisei Katei. (Formation of relations between politics and bureaucrats in modern Japan). Ed. by Nihon Seiji Gakkai. Tokyo, Iwanami Shoten, 95, 272 p.

7563. GOTTSMANN (Andreas). Der Reichstag von Kremsier und die Regierung Schwarzenberg. Die Verfassungsdiskussion des Jahres 1848 im Spannungsfeld zwischen Reaktion und nationaler Frage. Wien, Verlag für Geschichte und Politik, Diss. Univ. Wien u. München, Oldenbourg, 95, 144 p. (Österreich-Archiv).

7564. HOĆEVAR (Rolf). Verfassungsreform zwischen Evolution und Revolution. *Zeitschrift für Parlamentsfragen*, 95, 26, 1, p. 24-40.

7565. KOCIAN (Jiří). Ústavněprávní poměr Čechů a Slováků v návrzích politických stran při přípravě Ústavy ČSR v letech 1946–1948. (Czecho-Slovak constitutional relations in the parties' proposals during the drafting of a new Czechoslovak Constitution, 1946–1948). *Soudobé dějiny*, 95, 2, 2-3, p. 399-471. (Suppl. Archiv soudobých dějin).

7566. Magyar alkotmánytörténet. (Histoire constitutionelle de Hongrie). Szerk. MEZEY Barna. Budapest, Osiris, 95, 406 p.

7567. Österreich. Kabinettsrat der Provisorischen Regierung Karl Renner 1945. Protokolle. 1: "... im eigenen Haus Ordnung schaffen". Protokolle des Kabinettsrates 29. April 1945 bis 10. Juli 1945. Im Auftrag der Österr. Gesellschaft für Historische Quellenstudien hrsg. v. Gertrude ENDERLE-BURCEL [u. a.]. Horn u. Wien, Berger, 95, XXXVI-457 p.

7568. PEÑA GONZALEZ (José). História politica del constitucionalismo español. Madrid, Prensa y ediciones iberoamericanas, 95, 415 p.

7569. PEUCHOT (Eric). L'influence des idées américaines sur les Constituants. *In*: France de la Révolution et les Etats-Unis d'Amérique (La) [Cf. n° 5593], p. 22-48.

7570. POMBENI (Paolo). La Costituente: un problema storico-politico. Bologna, Mulino, 95, 170 p. (Universale paperbacks Il Mulino, 301).

7571. Protokolle des Ministerrates der Ersten Republik, 1918–1938. Abteilung 9. Kabinett Dr. Kurt Schuschnigg. 29. Juli 1934 bis 11. März 1938. Band 3. 31. Mai 1935 bis 30. November 1935. Hrsg. v. Rudolf NECK [et al.]. Bearb. v. Gertrude ENDERLE-BURCEL. Wien, Verlag der Österreichischen Staatsdruckerei, 95, LXXIII-522 p. (Edition Juristische Literatur).

7572. PUTZER (Peter). Spuren der ersten Opfer des Rechtsbruchs 1731/1732 im deutschen Südwesten. *Jb. f. d. Gesch. d. Protestantismus i. Österr.*, 94-95, 110-111, p. 99-129.

7573. REDISH (Martin H.). The Constitution as political structure. New York a. Oxford, Oxford U. P., 95, IX-229 p.

7574. WOLFRUM (Carl Gert). Christian Sommer 1767–1835. Verfassungs- und Staatsverständnis eines deutschen Jakobiners. Berlin, Duncker & Humblot, 95, 255 p. (Schriften zur Verfassungsgeschichte, 46).

Cf. n°s 1174-1231, 4950

§ 3. Staatsrecht und öffentliche Einrichtungen.

* 7575. Bibliografia di storia delle istituzioni contemporanee. A cura di Sandro BULGARELLI, Rosanna DE LONGIS, Marco SCOLLO LAVIZZONI e Fernando VENTURINI. *Le carte e la storia*, 95, 1, 1, p. 36-49.

7576. ALADA (Adalet B.). Beledi Örgütlenmede İlk Basamak: Mahalle. Tarihsel Yaklaşım Çerçevesinde Bir Model Arayışı. [Le premier pas de l'organisation municipale: Mahalle (Quartier). Recherche d'un modèle dans le cadre d'une approche historique]. *Toplum ve Ekonomi*, 95, 8, p. 93-114. – IDEM. Tarihsel Gelişim Süreci İçinde İl İdaresi Düzenlemeleri ve Demokratikleşme Üzerine. (Sur les réformes de l'administration départementale et la démocratisation dans la processus historique). İstanbul Üniversitesi Siyasal Bilgiler Fakültesi Dergisi, 95, 10, p. 13-20.

3. STAATSRECHT UND ÖFFENTLICHE EINRICHTUNGEN

7577. AMELOTTI (Mario), COSTAMAGNA (Giorgio). Alle origini del notariato italiano. Milano, Giuffrè, 95, XIV-346 p. (Studi storici sul notariato italiano, 2).

7578. ANDREUCCI (Franco). La norma e la prassi. Le elezioni irregolari nell'Italia liberale (1861–1880). *Passato e presente*, 95, 13, 34, p. 39-78.

7579. Assemblées d'Etats dans la France méridionale à l'époque moderne (Les). Ed. par Anne BLANCHARD, Henri MICHEL et Elie PELAQUIER. Préf. de Jean BERENGER. Montpellier, Université Paul-Valery, 95, 299 p.

7580. BAYKARA (Tuncer). Osmanlı Reformunun İlk Zamanları: Yeniçeri Ocağının Kaldırılması ve İlk Tatbikat. (Les premiers pas de la Réforme Ottomane: la suppression du corps des Janissaires et les premières applications), *Tarih İncelemeleri Dergisi*, 95, 10, p. 1-11.

7581. BERSANI (Carlo). Lo Stato e il pluralismo nell'Italia contemporanea: corpi collettivi e diritto pubblico dall'età liberale alla Costituente. Torino, G. Giappichelli, 95, 173 p.

7582. BJÖRN (Claus). Lovene gives kraft: en biografi af Christian Colbjørnsen. (The laws should come into force. A biography of Christian Colbjörnsen). København, Landbohistoriske Selskab, 95, 295 p.

7583. BOWLES (Brett C.). La République régionale: stade occulté de la «synthèse républicaine». *French Review*, 95, 69, 1, p. 103-117.

7584. BURGER (Hannelore). Sprachenrecht und Sprachengerechtigkeit im österreichischen Unterrichtswesen 1867–1918. Wien, Vlg der Österr. Akad. der Wiss., 95, 284 p. (Graph. Darstellungen). (Studien zur Geschichte der Österreichisch-Ungarischen Monarchie, 26).

7585. CAPORAL (Stéphane). L' affirmation du principe d'égalité dans le droit public de la Révolution Française (1789–1799). Préface de Louis FAVOREU. Aix-en-Provence, Presses universitaires d'Aix-Marseille et Paris, Economica, 95, IV-339 p.

7586. CASSESE (Sabino). La ricezione di Dicey in Italia e in Francia. Contributo allo studio del mito dell'amministrazione senza diritto amministrativo. *Materiali per una storia della cultura giuridica*, 95, 25, 1, p. 107-131.

7587. CHURCH (S. D.). The rewards of royal service in the household of King John: a dissenting opinion. *English Historical Review*, 95, 110, 436, p. 277-302.

7588. DANWITZ (Thomas von). Vom Verwaltungsprivat- zum Verwaltungsgesellschaftsrecht. *Archiv des öffentlichen Rechts*, 95, 120, 4, p. 595-630.

7589. DE CECCO (Marcello), PEDONE (Antonio). Le istituzioni dell'economia. *In*: Storia dello stato italiano [Cf. n° 5048], p. 253-300.

7590. Gaetano Mosca, scienza politica e regime rappresentativo nell'età contemporanea. A cura di Carlo MONGARDINI. Roma, Bulzoni, 95, 528 p.

7591. GLETTLER (Monika). Vereine in zentralen Städten der Habsburgermonarchie im 19. und 20. Jahrhundert. Preßburg/Pozsony/Bratislava – Klagenfurt/Celovec. *Der Donauraum*, 95, 1, p. 29-38.

7592. GODINEAU (Dominique). Femmes et citoyenneté: pratiques et politique. *In*: An II (L') [Cf. n° 4852], p. 197-207.

7593. HÄUSLER (René). Der König – ideale Verschmelzung von Mythos und Funktionalität? Der Parlamentarismus als Katalysator für die Transformation der Monarchie zur "psychologischen" Staatsform. *Zeitschrift für Parlamentsfragen*, 95, 26, 3, p. 505-524.

7594. Justice royale (La) et le parlement de Paris (XIVe–XVIIe siècle). Ed. par Yves-Marie BERCE et Alfred SOMAN. Genève, Droz, 95, 186 p.

7595. KARPIK (Lucien). Les avocats: entre l'Etat, le public et le marché, XIIIe–XXe siècle. Paris, Gallimard, 95, 482 p.

7596. KENZ (David Et.). Le roi de justice et le martyr réformé. Etat sacré et désacralisé jusqu'à la veille de la première guerre de religion. *Bulletin de la Société de l'histoire du protestantisme français*, 95, 141, p. 27-67.

7597. MALANDAIN (Gilles). Les mouches de la police ou le vol des mots. Les gazetins de la police secrète et la surveillance de l'expression publique à Paris au deuxième quart du XVIIIe siècle. *Revue d'histoire moderne et contemporaine*, 95, 42, p. 376-404.

7598. MELIS (guido). L'amministrazione. *In*: Storia dello stato italiano [Cf. n° 5048], p. 187-252.

7599. MERLINI (Stefano). Il governo costituzionale. *In*: Storia dello stato italiano [Cf. n° 5048], p. 3-72.

7600. MONNIER (François). Doctrine et information générale. La naissance du contentieux administratif moderne. *Revue administrative*, 95, 48, 286, p. 348-354.

7601. NENNER (Howard). The right to be king: the succession to the crown of England, 1603–1714. Chapel Hill, University of North Carolina Press, 95, XIII-343 p. (Studies in legal history).

7602. NICCOLAI (Nadi). Contro il numero ignorante e proletario. Proporzionalismo e riforma elettorale in Italia (1870–1882). *Passato e presente*, 95, 13, 34, p. 79-100.

7603. Pays pyrénéens et pouvoirs centraux (XVIe–XXe). Dir. par Miche BRUNET, Serge BRUNET et Claudine PAILHES. [S. l.], Editions Milan, 95, 2 vol., 574 p., 320 p.

7604. PEREZ-BUSTAMANTE (Rogelio). História de las instituciones publicas de España. Madrid, Universidad Complutense, Facultad de Derecho, Servicio de Publicaciones, 95, 233 p.

7605. PIRETTI (Maria Serena). Le elezioni politiche in Italia dal 1848 a oggi. Roma e Bari, Laterza, 95, VIII-449 p.

7606. Politische Institutionen im Wandel. Hrsg. v. Birgitta NEDELMANN; unter Mitarbeit v. Thomas KOEPF. Opladen, Westdeutscher Verlag, 95, 411 p. (Kölner Zeitschrift für Soziologie und Sozialpsychologie. Sonderheft, 35).

7607. POMBENI (Paolo). La rappresentanza politica. In: Storia dello stato italiano [Cf. n° 5048], p. 73-125.

7608. RAGGIO (Osvaldo). Norme e pratiche. Gli statuti campestri come fonti per una storia locale. *Quaderni storici*, 95, 30, 88 (1), p. 155-194.

7609. ROMANELLI (Raffaele). Centralismo e autonomie. In: Storia dello stato italiano [Cf. n° 5048], p. 126-186.

7610. ROSSI-DORIA (Anna). Maternità e cittadinanza femminile. *Passato e presente*, 95, 13, 34, p. 171-178.

7611. SMEDLEY-WEILL (Anette). Les intendants de Louis XIV. Paris, Fayard, 95, 370 p.

7612. SOULE (Claude). Les assemblées provinciales au XVIIIe siècle: une tentative démocratique en France à la fin de l'Ancien Régime, origines et création. *Parliaments, Estates and Representation*, 95, 15, p. 93-100.

7613. THOMAS (Yves). Histoire de l'administration. Paris, la Découverte, 95, 122 p.

7614. WEISZ (Franz). Umstellung der personalen Organisation der ehemaligen Österreichischen Polizei auf jene des Deutschen Reiches. *Wien. Gesch.-Bl.*, 95, 50, 2, p. 79-95.

7615. WIEACKER (Franz). A history of private law in Europe, with particular reference to Germany. Foreword by Reinhard ZIMMERMANN. Oxford, Clarendon press, 95, XVII-509 p.

Cf. n°s 1174-1231, 3673

§ 4. Zivil- und Strafrecht.

* 7616. BUNGE (Jurgen). Zivilprozess und Zwangsvollstreckung in England: eine Gesamtdarstellung mit internationalem Zivilprozessrecht und einer Bibliographie. Berlin, Duncker und Humblot, 95, 297 p.

** 7617. DOLEMEYER (Barbara). Repertorium ungedruckter Quellen der Rechtsprechung: Deutschland, 1800–1945. Frankfurt am Main, V. Klostermann, 95, 2 vol., XXVI-1104 p. (Rechtsprechung. Materialien und Studien, 9.1, 9.2).

7618. AFFEK (Mariusz). Związki polsko-włoskie w naukach prawnych (1764–1795). Z dziejów humanitaryzacji prawa karnego w Polsce. [Rapports polono-italiens en sciences juridiques (1764–1795). De l'histoire de l'humanisation du droit pénal en Pologne]. Warszawa, 95, 204 p. (Pol. Akad. Nauk, Inst. Hist. Nauki. Monogr. z Dziej. Nauki i Techn., 152).

7619. AGO (Renata). Ruoli familiari e statuto giuridico. *Quaderni storici*, 95, 30, 88 (1), p. 111-134.

7620. ANDERSSON (Hans). Genus och rättskultur. Kvinnlig brottslighet i stormaktstidens Stockholm. (Gender and legal culture. Feminine criminality under the Swedish great power epoch). *Historisk Tidskrift* (Sweden), 95, 2, p. 129-160.

7621. APOSTOLIDES (Jean-Marie). Lycanthropie et rationalité juridique à l'aube du XVIIe siècle [l'affaire Jean Grenier devant le Parlement de Bordeaux, 1603]. *Littératures classiques*, 95, 25, p. 161-185.

7622. ARTIERES (Philippe). Crimes écrits: la collection d'autobiographies de criminels du professeur A. Lacassagne. *Genèses*, 95, 19, p. 48-67.

7623. BARRY (Jonathan). I significati della libertà: la libertà urbana nell'Inghilterra del XVII e XVIII secolo. *Quaderni storici*, 95, 30, 89 (2), p. 487-514.

7624. BART (Jean). Les anticipations de l'an II dans le droit de la famille, l'intégration des «enfants de la nature». In: An II (L') [Cf. n° 4852], p. 187-196.

7625. BAYOD LÓPEZ (María del Carmen). Suyetos de las capitulaciones matrimoniales aragonesas. Prólogo Jesús DELGADO ECHEVERRIA. Zaragoza, Institución "Fernando el Católico", 95, 353 p.

7626. Birth (The) of a criminal Code: the evolution of Canada's justice system. Ed. by Desmond H. BROWN. Toronto a. London, University of Toronto press, 95, XXXVIII-505 p.

7627. BOGUCKA (Maria). Law and crime in Poland in early modern times [XVIe–XVIIe s.]. *Acta Poloniae historica*, 95, 71, p. 175-195.

7628. BONFIELD (Lloyd). La distribuzione dei beni tra gli eredi negli atti di successione matrimoniale inglesi nell'età moderna. *Quaderni storici*, 95, 30, 88 (1), p. 63-84.

7629. BOUZID (Lamjed). Contribution à l'étude des prisons et des prisonniers au Caïdat de l'Aradh entre 1868 et 1881. *Revue d'Histoire Maghrébine* (Partie arabe), 95, 77-78, p. 11-35.

7630. BURDEAU (François). Histoire du droit administratif (de la Révolution au début des années 1970). Paris, PUF, 95, 494 p.

7631. CAVINA (Marco). Il potere del padre. Vol. 1. Configurazioni e 'ius corrigendi': lineamenti essenziali nella cultura giuridica italiana preunitaria (1804–1859). Vol. 2. La scuola giuridica estense e la promozione della patria potestà nel Ducato di Modena (1814–1859). Milano, A. Giuffrè, 95, 2 vol., 656 p.

7632. CERUTTI (Simona). Giustizia e località a Torino in età moderna: una ricerca in corso. *Quaderni storici*, 95, 30, 89 (2), p. 445-486.

7633. DESCIMON (Robert). L'union au domaine royal et le principe d'inaliénabilité: la construction d'une loi fondamentale aux XVIe et XVIIe siècles. *Droits*, 95, 22, p. 79-90.

7634. FARR (James F). Parlementaires and the paradox of power: sovereignty and jurisprudence in rapt cases in early modern Burgundy. *European history quarterly*, 95, 25, 3, p. 325-351.

7635. FONTAINE (Laurence). Devoluzione dei beni nelle valli alpine del Delfinato (XVII–XVIII secolo). *Quaderni storici*, 95, 30, 88 (1), p. 135-154.

7636. GARNOT (B.). La législation de la répression des crimes dans la France moderne (XVIe–XVIIIe siècle). *Revue Historique*, 95, 119, 593, p. 75-90.

7637. GUARNIERI (Carlo). L'ordine pubblico e la giustizia penale. *In*: Storia dello stato italiano [Cf. n° 5048], p. 365-407.

7638. GUHA (Sumit). An Indian penal régime: Maharashtra in the eighteenth century. *Past and Present*, 95, 147, p. 101-126.

7639. HERZOG (Tamar). La administración como fénomeno social: la justicia penal de la ciudad de Quito (1650–1750). Madrid, Centro de Estudios Constitucionales, 95, 352 p.

7640. KACZYŃSKA (Elżbieta). Town and countryside in penal judicature and criminality. Kingdom of Poland, 1815–1914. *Acta Poloniae historica*, 95, 71, p. 197-210.

7641. KALIFA (Dominique). L'encre et le sang. Récits de crimes et sociétés à la Belle Epoque. Paris, Fayard, 95, 352 p.

7642. KAMLER (Marcin). Penalties for common crimes in Polish towns 1550–1650. *Acta Poloniae historica*, 95, 71, p. 161-174.

7643. Karl Kraus contra ... Die Prozeßakten der Kanzlei Oskar Samek in der Wiener Stadt- und Landesbibliothek. 1. 1922–1927. Bearb. Und kommentiert v. Hermann BÖHM. Wien, Wiener Stadt- und Landesbibliothek, 95, XX-296 p. (Publikationen aus der Wiener Stadt- und Landesbibliothek, 2).

7644. KEPPLINGER (Maria). Schadenszauber- und Hexereivorwurf in dörflichen Konflikten. Dargestellt an zwei Zaubereiprozessen im Mülviertel an den Landgerichten Weinberg 1614–1618 und Oberwallsee 1663. *Jb.d. Oberösterr. Musealvereines I*, 95, 140, p. 145-180.

7645. KHAN (Zorina B.). Property rights and patent litigation in early nineteenth-century America. *Journal of Economic History*, 95, 55, 1, p. 58-97.

7646. KOLLROS (Ernst). Mühlviertler Hexen- und Zaubereiprozesse im Rahmen der europäischen Entwicklung. *Oberösterreichische Heimatblätter*, 95, 49, 1, p. 55-87.

7647. LAGUZZI (Marina). L'alienazione dei beni ecclesiastici in Toscana sotto Pietro Leopoldo: un sondaggio in Valdinievole. *Archivio storico italiano*, 95, 153, 564, p. 335-368.

7648. MAC CLENDON (Thomas V.). Tradition and domestic struggle in the courtroom: customary law and the control of women in segregation-era Natal. *International Journal of African Historical Studies*, 95, 28, 3, p. 527-562.

7649. MAZZACANE (Aldo). Una scienza per due regni. La penalistica napoletana della restaurazione. *Materiali per una storia della cultura giuridica*, 95, 25, p. 341-356.

7650. MELE (Franca). «Un nuovo cielo, una nuova terra». Le discussioni sulla deportazione nel Regno d'Italia dall'Unità al codice Zanardelli. *Materiali per una storia della cultura giuridica*, 95, 25, p. 357-404.

7651. PATIN (Maurice). [Témoignage]: l'exercice du droit de grâce par le général de Gaulle. *Espoir*, 95, 103, p. 74-79.

7652. RAHIKAINEN (Marjatta). The fading of compulsory labour: the displacement of work by hobbies in the reformatory schools of twentieth-century Finland. *Scandinavian Economic History Review*, 95, 43, 2, p. 251-262.

7653. RODOTÀ (Stefano). Le libertà e i diritti. *In*: Storia dello stato italiano [Cf. n° 5048], p. 301-364.

7654. ROGERS (James Steven). The early history of the law of bills and notes: a study of the origins of Anglo-American commercial law. Cambridge, Cambridge U. P., 95, XXV-267 p. (Cambridge studies in English legal history).

7655. SCHULTE-NOLKE (Hans). Das Reichsjustizamt und die Entstehung des Bürgerlichen Gesetzbuchs. Frankfurt am Main, Vittorio Klostermann, 95, XIX-378 p. (Ius Commune. Sonderhefte, Studien zur Europäischen Rechtsgeschichte, 71).

7656. Stein, 6. April 1945. Das Urteil des Volksgerichts Wien (August 1946) gegen die Verantwortlichen des Massakers im Zuchthaus Stein. Eine Veröffentlichung des Bundesministeriums für Justiz. Hrsg. v. Gerhard JAGSCHITZ [et al.]. Wien, Bundesministerium für Justiz, Dokumentationsarchiv des Österr. Widerstands, 95, 162 p.

7657. TÜRKMEN (Zekeriya). Osmanlı Devleti'nde Kapitülasyonların Uygulanışına Toplu Bir Bakış" (Une vue générale sur l'application des capitulations dans l'Etat Ottoman). *Osmanlı Tarihi Araştırma Merkezi Dergisi*, 95, 6, p. 325-342.

7658. Unjust enrichment: the comparative legal history of the law of restitution. Ed. by Eltjo J.H. SCHRAGE. Berlin, Duncker & Humblot, 95, 333 p. (Comparative studies in continental and Anglo-American legal history,15).

7659. WELLS (Charlotte C.). Law and citizenship in early modern France. Baltimore a. London, Johns Hopkins U. P., 95, 198 p.

7660. ZVJAGINCEV (A. G.), ORLOV (Ju. G.). Tajnye sovetniki imperii. Rossijskie prokurory, XIX vek. (The imperial Privy Councillors. The Russian prosecutors, the XIXth century). Moskva, Rossijskaja političeskaja énciklopedija, 95, 384 p.

§ 5. Völkerrecht.

7661. ABAŠIDZE (A. Kh.). Nacional'nye men'sinstva i pravo na samoopredelenie. (Meždunarodno-pravovye problemy). (Etnich minorities and the right to self-determination. International law issues). *Etnogr. obozrenie*, 95, 2, p. 149-158.

7662. CAGIANO DE AZEVEDO (Raimondo). Le migrazioni internazionali: il cammino di un dibattito. Torino, G. Giappichelli, 95, X-229 p.

7663. Deutsches internationales Privatrecht im 16. und 17. Jahrhundert: Materialien, Übersetzungen, Anmerkungen. Von Christian v. BAR und H. Peter DOPFFEL; unter Mitwirkung insbesondere von Dirk EFFERTZ, Franz NIEPER und Thomas STACKER. Tübingen, J.C.B. Mohr (Paul Siebeck), 95, [s. p.]. (Materialien zum ausländischen und internationalen Privatrecht, 39).

7664. Diritto della guerra e della pace di Alberico Gentili (II): atti del Convegno, quarta Giornata gentiliana: 21 settembre 1991. Milano, A. Giuffré, 95, 59 p.

7665. DRAKIDIS (Philippe). La Charte de l'Atlantique 1941. La déclaration des Nations Unies 1942. Sauvegardées par la Charte de l'O[rganisation des] N[ations] U[nies] arsenal prioritaire de paix et de Sécurité mondiales. Préface par Georges BOLARD et Daniel COLARD. Besançon, Centre de recherche et d'information politique et sociale, 95, 111 p. – IDEM. The Atlantic and United Nations Charters: common law prevailing for world peace and security. Besançon, Centre de recherche et d'information politique et sociale, 95, 158 p.

7666. GOYARD-FABRE (Simone). La guerre et le droit international dans la philosophie de Rousseau. *Etudes Jean-Jacques Rousseau*, 95, 7, p. 45-78.

7667. LIN (James C.). Humanitarianism and military force: humanitarian intervention and international society. [S. l.], [s. n.], 95, 265 p.

7668. Sanctions (Les) des Nations Unies dans le conflit de l'ex-Yougoslavie. Par Eugenios KALPYRIS, Richardt VORK et Antonio NAPOLITANO. Préface de Victor-Yves GHEBALI. Bruxelles, E. Bruylant et Paris, Libr. générale de droit et de jurisprudence, 95, XI-191 p.

7669. VOLF (Patrik-Paul). Der politische Flüchtling als Symbol der Zweiten Republik. Zur Asyl- und Flüchtlingspolitik in Österreich seit 1945. *Zeitgeschichte*, 95, 22, 11-12, p. 415-436.

Cf. n°s 1237, 7939

P

GESCHICHTE DER BEZIEHUNGEN ZWISCHEN DEN MODERNEN STAATEN

§ 1. Allgemeines. 7670-7795. – § 2. Kolonialgeschichte und Dekolonisation (*a.* Allgemeines; *b.* Asien; *c.* Afrika; *d.* Amerika; *e.* Ozeanien). 7796-7910. – § 3. Geschichte von 1500–1789 (*a.* Allgemeines; *b.* 1500–1648; *c.* 1648–1789). 7911-7973. – § 4. Geschichte von 1789–1815. 7974-8011. – § 5. Geschichte von 1815–1910. 8012-8071. – § 6. Geschichte von 1910–1935. Der Erste Weltkrieg. 8072-8199. – § 7. Geschichte von 1935–1945. Der Zweite Weltkrieg (*a.* Allgemeines; *b.* Diplomatie. Wirtschaft; *c.* Kriegshandlungen; *d.* Widerstand). 8200-8419. – § 8. Geschichte seit 1945. 8420-8802.

§ 1. Allgemeines.

** 7670. Corpus documental del Tratado de Tordesillas. Ed. por L. Adao da FONSECA, José Manuel RUIZ ASENCIO. Valladolid, Sociedad V Centenario del Tratado de Tordesillas, 95, 364 p.

** 7671. Fonti diplomatiche in età moderna e contemporanea. Atti del convegno internazionale di Lucca, 20–25 gennaio 1989. Roma, Ministero per i beni culturali e ambientali, Ufficio centrale per i beni archivistici, 95, 631 p. (Pubblicazioni degli Archivi di Stato, saggi, 33).

** 7672. Portugal et Bourgogne au XVe siècle (1384–1482): recueil de documents extraits des archives bourguignonnes. Ed. par J. PAVIOT. Paris, Centre Culturel Calouste Gulbenkian, 95, 595 p.

** 7673. Rossija-Švejcarija, 1813–1955: Dokumenty i materialy. (Russia-Switzerland, 1813–1955: Documents and materials). Moskva, Meždunarodyne otnošenija, Gosudarstvennaja služba Rossii i drugie, 623 p.

7674. ALLAIN (J.-C.). De la personalité au groupe de décision: leur pouvoir sur le cours de l'histoire internationale. *Relations Internationales*, 95, 83, p. 317-326.

7675. ANDREW (Christopher). For the president's eyes only: secret intelligence and the American presidency from Washington to Bush. London, Harper Collins, 95, 660 p.

7676. BAGNATO (Bruna). Storia di una illusione europea. Il progetto di unione doganale italo-francese. Londres, Lothian Foundation Press, 95, 336 p.

7677. BERCOVITCH (Jacob). Resolving international conflicts. Boulder, a. London, Lynne Riennert, 95, 279 p.

7678. BIELANSKI (Stefan). La Polonia nella geopolitica europea. *Relazioni Internazionali*, 95, 59, 36, p. 46-51.

7679. BJÖRGO (Narve), RIAN (Øystein), KAARTVEDT (Alf). Selvstendighet og union fra middelalderen til 1905. Oslo, Universitetsforlaget, 95, 416 p. (Norsk utenrikspolitikks historie, 1). [The history of the Norwegian foreign policy until 1905].

7680. BLACK (Jeremy). Empire and enlightenment in Edward Gibbon's treatment of international relations. *The International History Review*, 95, 17, p. 441-458.

7681. BOWER (Tom). The perfect English spy: Sir Dick White and the secret war 1935–90. London, Heinemann, 95, 426 p.

7682. BROWN (Chris). International theory and international society: the viability of the middle way? *Review of International Studies*, 95, 21, p. 183-196.

7683. BUTT (Gerald). The lion in the sand: the British in the Middle East. London, Bloomsbury, 95, V-215 p.

7684. CALANDRI (Elena). Islam, etnicità, nation building e politica estera nella Repubblica turca 1923–1991. *Storia delle Relazioni Internazionali*, 94-95/2, 10-11, p. 3-60.

7685. CHAN (Anson). Hong Kong: Europe's partner for the pacific century. *Studia Diplomatica*, 95, 48, 4, p. 65-72.

7686. CHARMELY (John). Churchill's grand alliance: the Anglo-American special relationship 1940–1957. London, Hodder & Stoughton, 95, XV-427 p.

7687. COLOMBO (Alessandro). Frammentazione e convivenza internazionale. *Relazioni Internazionali*, 95, 59, 31, p. 8-15.

7688. Contested territory: border disputes at the edge of the former Soviet empire. Ed. by Tuomas FORSBERG. Aldershot, Edward Elgar, 95, XI-267 p. (Studies of communism in transition).

7689. CREPEAU (François). Droit d'asile. De l'hospitalité aux contrôles migratoires. Bruxelles, Editions Bruylant, 95, 424 p.

7690. CURKINA (Iskra). Rusko-slovenski kulturni stiki: od konca 18. stoletja do leta 1914. Ljubljana, Slovenska matica, 95, 286 p.

7691. DADRIAN (Vahakn N.). The history of the Armenian genocide: ethnic conflict from the Balkans to Anatolia to the Caucasus. Providence, Berghahn Books, 95, XXVIII-452 p.

7692. DENMAN (R.). Missed chances: Britain and Europe in the twentieth century. *Political Quarterly*, 95, 66, 1, p. 36-45

7693. DI NOLFO (Ennio). Storia delle relazioni internazionali, 1918–1992. Bari, Laterza, 95, XX-1431 p.

7694. DOBSON (Alan P.). Anglo-American relations in the twentieth century: of friendship, conflict and the rise and decline of the superpowers. London, Routledge, 95, 199 p.

7695. DOGO (Marco). La guerra dei centosessant'anni, ovvero lo sfratto dei Musulmani dai Balcani. *Europa Europe*, 95, 4, 1, p. 39-58.

7696. DOWNS (George W.), ROCKE (David M.). Optimal imperfection? Domestic uncertainty and institutions in internationals relations. Princeton, Princeton U. P., 95, 159 p.

7697. DRAGUNOV (Georgij P.). Sovietskie voennoplennye, internirovannye v Švejcarii (1940–1948 gody). (The Russian prisoners-of-war, interned in Switzerland, 1940-1948). *Vopr. Ist.*, 95, 2, p. 123-132.

7698. DU REAU (Elisabeth). La France et l'Europe d'Aristide Briand à Robert Schuman. Naissance, déclin et redéploiement d'une politique étrangère (1929–1950). *Revue d'histoire moderne et contemporaine*, 95, 42, p. 556-567.

7699. DUROSELLE (J.-B.). L'histoire des relations internationales vue par un historien. *Relations Internationales*, 95, 83, p. 295-306.

7700. ECKES (Alfred E.). Opening America's market: US foreign trade policy since 1776. Chapel Hill a. London, University of North Carolina Press, 95, XXI-402 p.

7701. FAURIOL (Georges). Haitian frustrations: dilemmas for U. S. policy. Washington, Center for Strategic and International Studies, 95, [s. p.].

7702. FERRARI (Aldo). Costruzioni mitiche per una geopolitica della diversità russa. *Relazioni Internazionali*, 95, 59, 31, p. 36-43.

7703. FERRARIS (Luigi Vittorio). Le relazioni tra Italia e Germania: eredità e prospettive. *Europa Europe*, 95, 4, 2-3, p. 73-90.

7704. FOREMAN-PECK (James). History of the world economy: international economic relations since 1850. New York, Harvester- Wheatsheaf, 95, XVII-404 p. (ill.).

7705. FORSBERG (Tuomas). Contested territory: border disputes at the edge of the former Soviet empire. Aldershot a. Hants, Edward Elgar, 95, 267 p.

7706. FOUQUOIRE-BRILLET (E.). La Chine et ses voisins. *Relations Internationales*, 95, 81, p. 23-37.

7707. FREEDMAN (Lawrence). Alliance and the British way in warfare. *Review of International Studies*, 95, 21, p. 145-158.

7708. FUDGE (John D.). Cargoes, embargoes, and emissaries: the commercial and political interaction of England and the German Hanse, 1450–1510. Toronto, University of Toronto Press, 95, XX-265 p.

7709. GIRAULT (R.). Conjectures sur la conjoncture. *Relations Internationales*, 95, 82, p. 115-122.

7710. GLATZ (Ferenc). Hungarians and their neighbours in modern times, 1867–1950. Boulder, Social Science Monographs, 95, 347 p.

7711. Graensen i 75 år: 1920–1995. Ed. by Henrik BECKER-CHRISTENSEN. Aabenraa, Institut for graenseregions forskning. København, Told- og Skattehistorisk Selskab, 95, 304 p. P [The Danish-German frontier].

7712. GRANGE (D.). Le processus de décision en politique étrangère dans l'Italie libérale. *Relations Internationales*, 95, 84, p. 435-463.

7713. GRASSI (Fabio). Le battaglie diplomatiche relative alle occupazioni italiane in Turchia. *Annali dell'Istituto Ugo La Malfa*, 95, 10, p. 277-304.

7714. Großbritannien, das Empire und die Welt. Britische Außenpolitik zwischen "Größe" und "Selbstbehauptung" 1850–1990. Hrsg. v. Hans H. JANSEN u. Ursula LEHMKUHL. Bochum, Brockmeyer, 95, 474 p. (Veröff. des Arbeitskreises deutsche Englandforschung, 25).

7715. GUILLEN (P.). Écrire l'histoire de la politique extérieure de la France. *Relations Internationales*, 95, 83, p. 331-337.

7716. GUTJAHR (Lothar). Stability, integration and global responsability: Germany's changing perspectives on national interests. *Review of International Studies*, 95, 21, p. 301-318.

7717. HARASZTI (Éva). H. A Foreign Office és a magyar emigránsok, 1944–1954. (Le Foreign Office et les émigrés hongrois, 1944–1954). *Világtörténet*, 95, 3-4, p. 63-93

7718. HILDEBRAND (Klaus). Das vergangene Reich: deutsche Aussenpolitik von Bismarck bis Hitler, 1871–

1945. Stuttgart, Deutsche Verlags-Anstalt, 95, 1054 p.
– IDEM. Von Richelieu bis Kissinger. Die Herausforderungen der Macht und die Antworten der Staatskunst. *Vierteljahrshefte für Zeitgeschichte*, 95, 95, 43, 2, p. 195-220.

7719. HINDE (Robert A.), WATSON (Helen E.). War, a cruel necessity? The bases of institutionalized violence. London, Tauris, 95, 260 p.

7720. HOCKING (Brian), SMITH (Michael). World politics: an introduction to international relations. London, Hervester Wheatsheaf, 95, 353 p.

7721. HUPCHICK (Dennis P.). Conflict and chaos in eastern Europe. London, Macmillan, 95, 322 p.

7722. İLTER (Erdal). Ermeni Meselesinin Doğuşunda ve Gelişmesinde İngiltere'nin Rolü. (Le Role de l'Angleterre dans la naissance et le développement du problème arménien). *Osmanlı Tarihi Araştırma Merkezi Dergisi*, 95, 6, p. 155-172.

7723. INAYATULLAH (Naeem), BLANEY (David). Realizing sovereignty. *Review of International Studies*, 95, 21, p. 3-20.

7724. INCISA DI CAMERANA (Ludovico). Italia e America Latina: dallo strabismo all'attenzione. *Relazioni Internazionali*, 95, 59, 35, p. 55-63. – IDEM. La crisi delle medie potenze. *Relazioni Internazionali*, 95, 59, 34, p. 7-13.

7725. Insular dream: obsession and resistance (The). Ed. by K. VERSLUYS. Amsterdam, VU U. P., 95, 384 p. (European contributions to American studies)

7726. Istorija vnešnej politiki Rossii: Konec XV veka 1917 god. (The history of the Russian foreign policy: the end of the XVth century–1917.). RAN In-t rossijskoj istorii; Redkol. :A. N. SAKHAROV (otv. red.) i drugie. Pervaja polovina XIX veka. (Ot vojn Rossii protiv Napoleona do Parižskogo mira 1865 goda). (The first half of the XIXth century. From the Napoleonic Wars to the Paris peace 1856). Redkol: O. V. ORLIK (otv. red.) i drugie. Moskva, Meždunarodnye otnošenija, 95, 447 p.

7727. JOHNSON (Robert David). The peace progressives and American foreign relations. Cambridge, Harvard U. P., 95, 448 p. (bibl., ind.).

7728. KAHLER (Miles). International institution and the political economy of integration. Washington, The Brookings Institution, 95, 163 p.

7729. KASPI (A.). De Wilson à Roosevelt ou comment écrire l'histoire de la politique extérieure des États-Unis. *Relations Internationales*, 95, 83, p. 373-380.

7730. KENWORTHY (Eldon). America/Americas: myth in the making of US policy toward Latin America. University Park, Penn State Press, 95, 189 p.

7731. KEOGH (Dermot). Ireland and the Vatican: the politics and diplomacy of Church-State relations, 1922–1960. [s. l.], Cork U. P., 95, 410 p.

7732. KESKIN (Mustafa). Osmanlı Devleti Zamaninda Türk-Arap Münasebetlerine Bir Bakiş" (Un regard sur les relations turco-arabes au temps de l'Etat Ottoman). *Erciyes Üniversitesi Sosyal Bilimler Enstitüsü Dergisi*, 95, 6, p. 263-275.

7733. KIERNAN (Victor Gordon). Imperialism and its contradictions. London a. New York, Routledge, 95, XII-218 p.

7734. KIMURA (Mitsuhiko). The economics of Japanese imperialism in Korea, 1910–1939. *Economic History Review*, 95, 48, 3, p. 555-574.

7735. KISTANOV (Valerij O.). Japonija v ATR: Anatomija ékonomičeskikh i političeskikh otnošenij. (Japan in the Asia-Pacific region: the anatomy of economic and political relations). RAN. In-t vostokovedenija. Moskva, Vostočnaja literatura, 95, 335 p.

7736. KLEINSCHMIDT (Harald). Fatti e percezioni nella storia delle relazioni internazionali. *Relazioni Internazionali*, 95, 59, 31, p. 58-70.

7737. KLIMEK (Antonín), KUBŮ (Eduard). Československá zahraniční politika 1918–1938. Kapitoly z dějin mezinárodních vztahů. (Czechoslovak foreign policy, 1918–1938. Chapters from the history of international relations). Praha, Institut pro středoevropskou kulturu a politiku, 95, 115 p.

7738. KLOTZ (Audie). Norms in international relations: the struggle against apartheid. Ithaca, Cornell U. P., 95, 186 p.

7739. KOČETKOVA (Tat'jana Ju.). Voprosy sozdanija OON i sovetskaja diplomatija. (Some problems of the ONU foundation and the Soviet diplomacy). *Oteč. Ist.*, 95, 1, p. 28-48.

7740. KREIS (M.). La partecipation du peuple aux décisions de politique étrangère. Le cas de la Suisse. *Relations Internationales*, 95, 84, p. 425-434.

7741. Kriegsende im Norden. Vom heißen zum kalten Krieg. Hrsg. v. Robert BOHN u. Jürgen ELVERT. Stuttgart, Steiner, 95, 384 p. (Historische Mitteilungen, 14).

7742. KUPIECKI (Robert). Polityka zagraniczna Polski, 1918–1994. Warszawa, Scholar, 95, 295 p.

7743. LIEBICH (André). Mensheviks wage the Cold War. *Journal of Contemporary History*, 95, 30, 2, p. 247-264.

7744. LUMINARI (Laura). Armi all'Irak: obiettivi e mezzi della politica fascista in Medio Oriente (1931–1941). *Storia contemporanea*, 95, 26, 4, p. 537-574.

7745. LYONS (Gene M.), MASTANDUNO (Michael). Beyond Westphalia: state sovereignty and international intervention. Baltimore, Johns Hopkins U. P., 95, 324 p.

7746. MAC KENNA (Peter). Canada and the Inter-American system, 1890–1968. *Australian Journal of Politics and History*, 95, 41, 2, p. 253-270.

7747. Magyarország és a nagyhatalmak a 20. században. (La Hongrie et les grands pouvoirs au XXe siècle). Szerk., bevez. ROMICS Ignác. Budapest, Teleki Alapítvány, 95, 313 p.

7748. MARKWELL (Donald John). John Maynard Keynes and international relations: idealism, economic paths to war and peace, and post-war reconstruction. Oxford, University of Oxford, 95, X-319 p.

7749. MARQUINA (Antonio). Mediterraneo e sicurezza nell'ottica spagnola. *Relazioni Internazionali*, 95, 59, 34, p. 40-47.

7750. MELANDRI (P.). J.-B. Duroselle et les relations entre de Gaulle et les États-Unis. *Relations Internationales*, 95, 83, p. 389-395.

7751. MILZA (Pierre). J.-B. Duroselle et la théorie des relations internationales. *Relations Internationales*, 95, 83, p. 307-310.

7752. MINEAR (Larry), WEISS (Thomas G.). Mercy under fire: war and the global community. Boulder, Oxford, Westview, 95, 260 p.

7753. MORRELL (Gordon W.). Britain confronts the Stalin revolution: anglo-soviet relations and the Metro-Vickers crisis. Waterloo, Wilfrid Laurier U. P., 95, IX-204 p.

7754. MÜLLER (Klaus-Jürgen). The military in politics in France and Germany in the twentieth century. Oxford, Washington, Berg, 95, 176 p.

7755. NEILSON (Keith). Britain and the last tsar: British policy and Russia, 1894–1917. Oxford, Clarendon, 95, XV-408 p.

7756. Nemtsy o russkikh. [Deutsche über Russen]. Ed. by V. V. DROBYSHEV, I. D'IAKOV. Moskva, "Stolitsa", 95, 190 p.

7757. NEUMANN (Iver B.). Russia and the idea of Europe: a study in identity and international relations. London, Routledge, 95, 253 p.

7758. NIBLO (Stephen R.). War, diplomacy and development: the United States and Mexico, 1938–1954. Wilmington, SR Books, XX-320 p.

7759. Norge og Sovjetunionen 1917–1955: en utenrikspolitisk dokumentasjon. (Norway and the Soviet Union 1917–1955: Documentation relating to foreign politics). Ed. by Sven G. HOLTSMARK. Oslo, Cappelen, 95, 605 p.

7760. Norsk utenrikspolitikks historie. Vol. 1. BJØRGO (Narve), RIAN (Øystein), KAARTVEDT (Alf). Selvstendighet og union: fra middelalderen til 1905. Vol. 2. BERG (Roald). På egen hånd: 1905–1920. (The history of the Norwegian foreign policy. Vol. 1. Independence and union: from the Middle Ages to 1905. Vol 2. Norway independent: 1905–1920). Oslo, Universitetsforlaget, 95, 2 vol., 415 p., 400 p. (ill).

7761. OLMEDO BERNAL (Santiago). El dominio del Atlantico en la baja Edad Media: los títulos jurídicos de la expansión peninsular hasta el Tratado de Tordesillas. Valladolid, Sociedad V Centenario del Tratado de Tordesillas, 95, 485 p. (1 map). (Colección de história).

7762. OSIANDER (Andreas). Interdependenz der Staaten und Theorie der zwischenstaatlichen Beziehungen. Eine theoriegeschichtliche Untersuchung. *Politische Vierteljahresschrift*, 95, 36, 2, p. 243-266.

7763. ÖZCAN (Besim). 1877–1878 Harbine Kadar Osmanlı-Rus Münasebetleri. (Les relations entre l'Empire Ottoman et la Russie jusqu'à la guerre de 1877–1878). *Araştırma Dergisi*, 95, 22, p. 111-122.

7764. PAASI (Anssi). Territories, boundaries and consciousness: the changing geographies of the Finnish-Russian border. Chichester, John Wiley, 95, 353 p.

7765. PAPAGIANNAKES (Eleutherios). He exolothreusis tes Hellenikes homogeneias kai he Tourkike kata tes Hellados epivoule. Athena, Parousia, 95, 253 p.

7766. PETERI (Gyorgy). Revolutionary twenties: essays on international monetary and financial relations after World War I. Trondheim, Dept. Of History, University of Trondheim, 95, VII-204 p.

7767. PLATEN (Carl Henrik von). Stedingk. Curt von Stedingk (1746–1837): kosmopolit, krigare, diplomat hos Ludvig XVI, Gustav III ioch Katarina den stora. Stockholm, Atlantis, 95, 424 p.

7768. PORCILE (Gabriel). The challenge of cooperation: Argentina and Brazil, 1939–1955. *Journal of Latin American Studies*, 95, 27, p. 129-160.

7769. RENOUARD (F.). J.-B. Duroselle et les documents diplomatiques français. *Relations Internationales*, 95, 83, p. 339-342.

7770. RICHARDSON (Dick), STONE (Glyn). Decisions and diplomacy: essays in twentieth century international history: in memory of George Grun and Esmonde Robertson. London a. New York, Routledge, LSE, 95, XIV-230 p.

7771. ROBERTS (Adam). Communal conflict as a challenge to international organization: the case of former Yugoslavia. *Review of International Studies*, 95, 21, p. 389-410.

7772. ROBINSON (Thomas W.), SHAMBAUGH (David). Chinese foreign policy: theory and practice. Oxford, Clarendon, 95, 644 p.

7773. ROSSINI (Daniela). From Theodore Roosevelt to FDR: internationalism and isolationism in American foreign policy. Keele university, Ryburn, 95, 184 p.

7774. RUSSEL (Peter E.). Portugal, Spain, and the African Atlantic, 1343–1490: Chivalry and Crusade from John of Gaunt to Henry the Navigator. Brookfield, Ashgate, 95, 327 p. (map.).

7775. RYSTAD (Göran), BÖHME (Klaus-Richard), CARLGREN (Wilhelm M.). In quest of trade and security. The Baltic in power politics 1500–1900. Vol. 2. 1890–1990. Stockholm, PROBUS förlag, 95, 311 p.

7776. SANTORO (Carlo Maria). Le istituzioni della sicurezza e il concetto di occidente. *Relazioni Internazionali*, 95, 59, 36, p. 2-14.

7777. SCHIRMANN (Sylvain). Les relations économiques et financières franco-allemandes 1932-1939. Paris, Comité pour l'histoire économique et financière de la France, 95, 304 p.

7778. SCHULZE WESSEL (Martin). Russlands Blick auf Preussen: die polnische Frage in der Diplomatie und der politischen Öffentlichkeit des Zarenreiches und des Sowjetstaates 1697-1947. Stuttgart, Klett-Cotta, 95, 432 p.

7779. SCHUMAN (Maurice). Paradoxe sur deux victoires. *Revue des Deux Mondes*, 95, 11, p. 27-34.

7780. ŚLUSARCZYK (Jacek). Idea pokoju w europejskiej i polskiej myśli politycznej do 1939. Kompendium. (Idée de la paix dans la pensée politique européenne et polonaise jusqu'en 1939. Compendium). Warszawa, 95, 152 p. Inst. Studiów Polit. Pol. Akad. Nauk. [Eng. summary].

7781. SPIEZIO (Kim Edward). Beyond containment: reconstructing European security. Boulder, London, Lynne Rienner, 95, 156 p.

7782. STEINERT (M.). Renseignement et politique étrangère. *Relations Internationales*, 95, 84, p. 407-423.

7783. STUDDERT-KENNEDY (Gerald). Christianity, statecraft and Chatham House: Lionel Curtis and world order. *Diplomacy and Statecraft*, 95, 6, 2, p. 470-489.

7784. SUDOL (Adam). Polska na szachownicy weilkich mocarstw: sprawa polska w tajnej korespondencji dyplomatycznej, 1941-1945. Bydgoszcz, Wydawn. Uczelniane WSP w Bydgoszczy, 95, 249 p.

7785. TAYLOR (Alan John Percivale). From the Boer War to the Cold War: essays on twentieth-century Europe. Ed. by C. WRIGLEY. London, Hamish Hamilton, 95, XXV-454 p.

7786. TORKUNOV (A. V.), UFIMCEV (E. P.). Korejskaja problema novyj vzgljad. (The Korean problem: a new view, 1940-1950's). Moskva: Ankil, 95, 255 p.

7787. ULFSTEIN (Geir). The Svalbard Treaty. From terra nullius to Norwegian sovereignty. Oslo, Scandinavian U. P., 95, 572 p.

7788. UNGER (Brigitte), WAARDEN (Frans van). Convergence or diversity? Internationalization and economic policy reponse. Aldershot a. Hants, Avebury, 95, 376 p.

7789. UOLA (Mikko). Suomi ja Keskuksen Valtakunta. Suomen suhteet Kiinan tasavaltaan 1919-1949. (Finland and The Republic of China). Uusikaupunki, Author, 95, 360 p. (Eng. Summary).

7790. VAÏSSE (M.). De Plutarque à la Bombe: J.-B. Duroselle et l'étude de la stratégie. *Relations Internationales*, 95, 84, p. 327-330.

7791. VIGEZZI (Brunello). Le origini della prima guerra mondiale come problema di breve e di lungo periodo. *Storia contemporanea*, 95, 26, 2, p. 189-210.

7792. VITALE (Alessandro). Le concezioni imperiali grande-russa e serba. *Relazioni Internazionali*, 95, 59, 36, p. 15-26.

7793. WELCH (David A.). Justice and genesis of war. Cambridge, Cambridge U. P., 95, 335 p.

7794. ZARTMAN (I. William). Elusive peace: negotiating an end to civil wars. Washington, Brookings, 95, 393 p.

7795. ZILANOV (V. K.), KOSHKIN (A.A.), LATYSHEV (I.A.), PLOTNIKOV (A.IU.), SENCHENKO (I.A.). Russkie Kurily: istoriia i sovremennost': sbornik dokumentov po istorii formirovaniia russko-iaponskoi i sovetsko-iaponskoi granitsy. Moskva, Rossiiskaia akademiia estestvennykh nauk, 95, 181 p.

Cf. n°s 4580-4665, 5259

§ 2. Kolonialgeschichte und Dekolonisation.

a. Allgemeines.

7796. After colonialism: imperial histories and postcolonial displacements. Ed. by Gyan PRAKASH. Princeton, Princeton U. P., 95, VIII-352 p. (Princeton studies in culture/power/history).

7797. ALDEN (Dauril). The making of an enterprise: the Society of Jesus in Portugal, its empire, and beyond: 1540-1750. Stanford, Stanford U. P., 95, XXXVIII-707 p.

7798. BARATA (Manuel Themudo). Le Portugal et les conflits de la décolonisation: 1961-1974. *Guerres Mondiales et conflits contemporains*, 95, 45, 178, p. 63-90.

7799. BOSSENBROEK (Martin). The living tools of Empire: the recruetment of European soldiers for the Dutch Colonial Army, 1814-1909. *The Journal of Imperial and Commonwealth History*, 95, 23, p. 26-53.

7800. CARRUTHERS (Susan L.). Winning hearts and minds: British governments, the media and colonial counter-insurgency 1944-1960. London, Leicester U. P., 307-XI p.

7801. FEDOROWICH (Kent). Unfit for heroes: reconstruction and soldier settlement in the Empire between the Wars. Manchester, Manchester Univerity Press, 95, XI-243 p.

7802. GAUTHIER (Florence). Y a-t-il une politique des colonies en l'an II? *In*: An II (L') [Cf. n° 4852], p. 223-231.

7803. GOUDA (Frances). Dutch culture overseas: colonial practice in the Netherlands Indies, 1900-1942. Amsterdam, Amsterdam U. P., 95, IX-304 p. (ill.)

7804. HAVINDEN (Michael), MEREDITH (David). Colonialism and development: Britain and its tropical colonies, 1850–1960. London a. New York, Routledge, 95, XV-420 p.

7805. HAYTHORNTHWAITE (Philip John). The colonial wars source book. London, Arms and Armour Press, 95, 385 p.

7806. HINTJENS (Helen M.). Alternatives to independence: exploration in post-colonial relations. Aldershot a. Hampshire, Dartmouth, 95, 235 p.

7807. HUGGINS (Rita), JACOBS (Jane M.). Kooramindanjie: place and the postcolonial. *History Workshop*, 95, 39, p. 165-181.

7808. INGRAM (Edward). Empire-building and empire-builders. London, Frank Cass, 95, 231 p.

7809. KAGAN (Richard L.), PARKER (Geoffrey). Spain, Europe, and the Atlantic World: essay in honor of John H. Elliott. New York, Cambridge U. P., 95, 359 p. (graph.).

7810.LAVIN (Deborah). From empire to international Commonwealth: a biography of Lionel Curtis. Oxford, Clarendon Press, 95, [s. p.].

7811. Lines across the sea: colonial inheritance in the post colonial Pacific. Ed. by B. V. LAL and H. NELSON. Brisbane, Pacific History Society, 95, XVI-231 p.

7812. MARSHALL (P. J.). Imperial Britain. *The Journal of Imperial and Commonwealth History*, 95, 23, p. 379-394.

7813. MENNINGER (Annerose). Die Macht der Augenzeugen. Neue Welt und Kannibalen-Mythos 1492–1600. Stuttgart, Steiner, 95, 333 p. (Beiträge zur Kolonial- und Überseegeschichte, 64).

7814. MOCKAITIS (Thomas R.). British counterinsurgency in the post-Imperial Era. Manchester, Manchester U. P., 95, 165 p.

7815. MOORE (Bob). Anglo-American security policy and its threat to Dutch Colonial rule in the West Indies, 1940–42. *The Journal of Imperial and Commonwealth History*, 95, 23, p. 453-478.

7816. OSTERHAMMEL (Jürgen). Kolonialismus. Geschichte, Formen, Folgen. München, Beck, 95, 148 p.

7817. PAGDEN (Anthony). Lords of all the worlds: ideologies of Empire in Spain, Britain end France c.1500–c.1850. New Haven a. London, Yale U. P., 95, IX-244 p.

7818. SANGER (Clyde). Malcom MacDonald: bringing an end to empire. Liverpool, Liverpool U. P., 95, 498 p.

7819. VAN SPLUNTER (Jacob M.). Strategic minerals and decolonization: The United States and Great Britain versus the Netherlands, 1945–1951. *The International History Review*, 95, 17, p. 485-511.

b. Asien.

** 7820. STOCKWELL (A. J.). British documents on the end of Empire. Series B. Volume III. Malaya. Part I. The Malayan Union experiment 1942–1948. Part II. The communist insurrection 1948–1953. Part III. The alliance route to independence 1953–1957. London, HMSO, 95, 3 vol., 392 p., 486 p., 458 p.

7821. AKITA (Shigeru), TOWNSEND (Susan C.). Japanese perspectives on imperialism in Asia. Ed. by Janet HUNTER. London, Suntory-Toyota International Centre for Economics and Related Disciplines, London School of Economics, 95, 54 p.

7822. BROCHEUX (Pierre). Indochine: la colonisation ambigue (1858–1954). Paris, La Découverte, 95, 427 p.

7823. BURKE (S. M.), QURAISHI (Salim al Din). The British Raj in India: an historical review. Karachi, Oxford U. P., 95, XXV-699 p.

7824. CLYMER (Kenton J.). Quest of freedom: the United States and India's independence. New York, Columbia U. P., 95, XXI-393 p.

7825. FERREIRA (Ana Maria Pereira). Problemas marítimos entre Portugal e a Franca na primeira metade do seculo XVI. Redondo, Patrimonia, 95, 458 p. (ill.)

7826. FLORES (Maria da Conceição). Os portugueses e o Sião no seculo XVI. Lisboa, Comissão Nacional para as Comemorações dos Descobrimentos Portugueses, 95 179 p. (maps). (Mare liberum).

7827. GRAFTON (Bo). Sören Norby. Sjökrigare i Östersjön på 1500-talet. Visby, Odins Förlag, 95, 192 p. [The naval activities in the Baltic during the 16th century].

7828. HAGGARD (Stephan). Japanese colonialism and Korean development: a critique. La Jolla, Graduate School of International Relations and Pacific Studies, University of California, 95, 47 p.

7829. HEADLEY (John M.). Spain's Asian presence, 1565–1590: structures and aspirations. *Hispanic american historical review*, 95, 75, p. 623-646.

7830. India and the freedom struggle of Bangladesh (formerly eastern province of Pakistan). Ed. by M. S. DEORA. New Delhi, Discovery Pub. House, 95, XIX-356 p. (Afro-Asian liberation movement series).

7831. KA (Chih-ming). Japanese colonialism in Taiwan: land tenure, development, and dependency, 1895–1945. Boulder a. Oxford, Westview Press, 95, XXI-226 p.

7832. KERR (Ian J.). Building the railway of the Raj 1850–1900. Delhi, Oxford U. P., 95, XIX-254 p. (ill., maps).

7833. PANIKKAR (K. N.). Culture, ideology, hegemony: intellectuals and social consciousness in Colonial India. New Delhi, Tulika, 95, X-212 p.

2. KOLONIALGESCHICHTE UND DEKOLONISATION

7834. PEERS (Douglas M.). Between Mars and Mammon: colonial armies and the Garrison state in India 1819–1835. London, Tauris Academic Studies, 95, XI-289 p. (ill., maps)

7835. POPPLEWELL (Richard J.). Intelligence and imperial defence: British Intelligence and the defence of the Indian Empire, 1904–1924. London, Frank Cass, 95, 354 p.

7836. SMITH (Simon C.). British relations with the Malay Rulers from decentralization to Malayan independence 1930–1957. Kuala Lumpur, Oxford U. P., 95, X-234 p.

7837. SNYDER (Jed C.). After Empire: the emerging geopolitics of central Asia. Washington, Institute for National Strategic Studies, 95, 235 p.

7838. TERTRAIS (H.). Conjoncture française et guerre d'Indochine: le temps des périls (1945–1954). *Relations Internationales*, 95, 82, p. 197-211.

7839. Trade and finance in colonial India, 1750–1860. Ed. by ASIYA SIDDIQI. New Delhi a. New York, Oxford U. P., 95, VI-385 p.

7840. WEBSTER (Anthony). British expansions in South-East Asia and the role of Robert Farquhar, Lieutenant-Governor of Penang, 1804–1805. *The Journal of Imperial and Commonwealth History*, 95, 23, p. 1-25.

Cf. n°s 8803-9075

c. Afrika.

** 7841. BONO (Salvatore). Diario libico del tenente Mario Fiore (1911–1915). *Storia contemporanea*, 95, 26, 1, p. 47-56.

7842. ADEBAYO (A. G.). Jangali: fulani pastoralists and colonial taxation in Northern Nigeria. *International Journal of African Historical Studies*, 95, 28, 1, p. 113-150.

7843. ALEYA SGHAIER (Amira). Soixante jours de résistance populaire en Tunisie: du 14 janvier au 15 mars 1952. *Revue d'Histoire Maghrébine* (Partie arabe), 95, 77-78, p. 139-166.

7844. ALPERN (Stanley B.). What Africans got for their slaves: a master list of European trade goods. *History in Africa*, 95, 22, p. 5-43.

7845. ANGLIN (Douglas G.). Zambian crisis behaviour: confronting Rhodesia's unilateral declaration of independence 1965-1966. Montreal, McGill-Queen's U. P., 95, 389 p.

7846. AZZOU (El Mustafa). Les hommes d'affaires américains au Maroc avant 1956. *Guerres Mondiales et conflits contemporains*, 95, 45, 180, p. 129-142.

7847. BEHEBE (Ngwabi), RANGER (Terence). Soldiers in Zimbabwe's liberation war. London, James Currey, 95, XI-211 p.

7848. BEHRENDT (Stephen D.). The journal of an African slaver, 1789–1792, and the gold coast slave trade of William Collow. *History in Africa*, 95, 22, p. 61-71.

7849. BENJALLOUN (Abdelmajid). Maroc: la vérité sur le protectorat franco-espagnol: l'épopée d'Abd el Khalek Torres. *Revue d'Histoire Maghrébine*, 95, 77-78, p. 183-189.

7850. BENOIT (Bertrand). Le syndrome algérien: l'imaginaire de la politique algérienne de la France. Paris, L'Harmattan, 95, 191 p.

7851. BILLS (Scott L.). The Libyan arena: the United States, Britain, and the Council of Foreign Ministers, 1945-1948. Kent, Kent State U. P., 95, XV-209 p.

7852. BONO (Salvatore). Les Pays-Bas et la guerre de Libye (1911–1912). *Revue d'Histoire Maghrébine*, 95, 77-78, p. 127-134.

7853. CADIOLI (Beniamino). Poste e comunicazioni della Colonia Eritrea. Dall'insediamento di Assab all'occupazione di Massaua. Prato, Istituto di Studi Storici Postali, 95, 136 p.

7854. CAIOLI (Aldo). La terza repubblica francese e la svolta imperialista nell'Africa nera (1871–1900). Trieste, Università di Trieste, Dipartimento di scienze politiche, 95, 136 p. (Collana di studi storici. Storia ed istituzioni dell'Africa).

7855. CAMARA (Joao de Sousa da). Portugal na Commonwealth? Crise e ressurgimento em Mocambique. Braga, 95, 117 p.

7856. CAMEL (Florance). Une période troublée au Sahara: les révoltes touarègues et leur repression pendant la première guerre mondiale. *L'information historique*, 95, 57, 3, p. 100-108.

7857. CAPELA (José). O álcool na colonização do Sul do Save, 1860–1920. Maputo, [s.n.], 95, 90 p.

7858. COINTET (Michele). De Gaulle et l'Algérie française, 1958–1962. Paris, Perrin, 95, [s. p.].

7859. DEL FRA (Lino). Sciara Sciat: genocidio nell'oasi: l'esercito italiano a Tripoli. Roma, Datanews, 95, 103 p. (maps)

7860. DEORA (M. S.). India and the freedom struggle of Mozambique & Guinea-Bissau. New Delhi, Discovery Pub. House, 95, XVI-512 p.

7861. DHIFALLAH (Mohamed). Le territoire militaire de la soumission à la résistance: le cas des Nefzaouas (1881–1956). *Revue d'Histoire Maghrébine* (Partie arabe), 95, 79-80, p. 521-538.

7862. DUMBUYA (Peter A.). Tanganyika under international mandate, 1919–1946. Lanham, University Press of America, 95, [s. p.].

7863. DURANTON-CRABOL (Anne-Marie). Le temps de l'OAS. Bruxelles, Editions Complexe, 95, 319 p. (Questions au XXe siècle).

7864. FAIVRE (Maurice). Les combattants musulmans de la guerre d'Algérie. Des soldats sacrifiés. Paris, L'Harmattan, 95, 270 p. – IDEM. Les Français musulmans dans la guerre d'Algérie. 1. De l'engagement à la mobilitation. 2. Les représailles et l'oubli de la France. *Guerres Mondiales et Conflits Contemporains*, 95, 45, 177, 180, 139-166 p., 143-168 p.

7865. GIBBS (David N.). Political parties and international relations: the United States and the decolonization of Sub-Saharan Africa. *The International History Review*, 95, 17, p. 306-327.

7866. HARRIS (Robert L. Jr.). Le Nazioni Unite e la decolonizzazione dell'Africa. *Europa Europe*, 95, 4, 4, p. 59-74.

7867. HARRISON (Robert T.). Gladstone's imperialism in Egypt: techniques of domination. Westport, Greenwood Press, 95, 184 p.

7868. HASTINGS (Adrian). The Church in Africa, 1450-1950. New York, Oxford U. P., 95, XIV-706 p.

7869. HOISINGTON (William A. Jr.). Lyautey and the French conquest of Morocco. London a. Basingstoke, Macmillan, 95, VIII-276 p. (maps).

7870. IYOB (Ruth). The Eritrean stuggle for independence. Domination, resistance, nationalism 1941-1993. Cambridge, Cambridge U. P., 95, 198 p.

7871. JARRETT (Alfred Abosiah). The under-development of Africa: colonialism, neo-colonialism and socialism. Lanham, University Press of America, 95, XVIII-171 p.

7872. KUPARINEN (Eero). Valkoista Afrikkaa rakentamassa: Pohjolan miehet ja Kapmaa Hollannin Itä-Intian kauppakompanian hallintokaudella 1652-1795. (The making of White Africa – Northern Europeans in the Cape Settlement during the period of the Dutch East India Company's administration, 1652-1795). Turku, Turun yliopisto, 95, 285 p. (Eng. summary, ill., maps). (Turun yliopiston Historian laitos. Julk., 34).

7873. LABYADH (Salem). Tribu et colonisation: notes sur la révolte du Sud Tunisien (1915-1918). *Revue d'Histoire Maghrébine* (Partie arabe), 95, 77-78, p. 205-228.

7874. LOVEJOY (Paul E.), RICHARDSON (David). Competing markets for male and female slaves: prices in the interior of West Africa, 1780-1850. *International Journal of African Historical Studies*, 95, 28, 2, p. 261-294.

7875. LYNN (Martin). Law and Imperial expansion: the Niger delta courts of equity, c. 1850-85. *The Journal of Imperial and Commonwealth History*, 95, 23, p. 54-76.

7876. MALEK (Redha). L'Algérie à Evian: histoire des négociations secrètes, 1956-1962. Paris, Editions du Seuil, 95, 401 p. (ill.). (L'épreuve des faits).

7877. MARCUS (Harold Golden). The politics of empire: Ethiopia, Great Britain, and the United States, 1941-1974. Lawrenceville, Red Sea Press, 95, XII-205 p. (map).

7878. MUNENE (Macharia). The Truman administration and the decolonisation of sub-Saharan Africa. Nairobi, Nairobi U. P., 95, IX-242 p.

7879. MURPHY (Philip). Party, politics and decolonization: the conservative party and British colonial policy in Tropical Africa, 1951-1964. Oxford, Clarendon Press, 95, XII-259 p.

7880. OGOT (B. A.), OCHIENG (W. R.). Decolonization and indipendence in Kenya 1940-93. London, James Currey, 95, XVIII-270 p.

7881. Role of India in Angola's freedom struggle. Ed. by M. S. DEORA. New Delhi, Discovery Pub. House, 95, XVI-504 p. (Afro-Asian liberation movement series).

7882. Role of India in Namibia's freedom struggle. Ed. by M. S. DEORA. New Delhi, Discovery Pub. House, 95, 2 Vol., XVIII-991 p. (Afro-Asian liberation movement series).

7883. ROZANCEVA (Nina A.). OON v alžirskoj politike de Gollja. (1958-1962 gody). (Onu in the Algerian policy of de Gaulle, 1958-1962). *Nov. novejš. Ist.*, 95, 4, p. 64-75.

7884. RUGIIREHEH-RUNAKU (James B. M. N.). European interests in Uganda. Malunje, Spot, 95, 183 p. (map).

7885. SIKAINGA (Ahmad). Shari'a courts and the manumission of female slaves in the Sudan. *International Journal of African Historical Studies*, 95, 28, 1, p. 1-24.

7886. STOCKWELL (S. E.). Political strategies in British business during decolonization: the case of the Gold Coast/Ghana, 1945-57. *The Journal of Imperial and Commonwealth History*, 95, 23, p. 277-300.

7887. SVALESEN (Leif). The slave ship Fredensborg: history, shipwreck, and find. *History in Africa*, 95, 22, p. 455-458.

7888. THOMAS (Martin). The dilemmas of an ally of France: Britain's policy towards the Algerian Rebellion, 1954-62. *The Journal of Imperial and Commonwealth History*, 95, 23, p. 129-154.

7889. VILAR (Juan Bautista). Dos siglos de la presencia de España en Tabarka (1535-1741). *Revue d'Histoire Maghrébine*, 95, 77-78, p. 163-182.

7890. VOLTERRA (Alessandro). Verso la Colonia Eritrea: la legislazione e l'amministrazione (1887-1889). *Storia contemporanea*, 95, 26, 5, p. 817-852.

7891. WHITE (Shane), WHITE (Graham). Slave clothing and African culture in the eighteenth and nineteenth centuries. *Past and Present*, 95, 148, p. 149-186.

7892. WILLIS (Justin). "Men on the spot", and labor policy in British East Africa: the Mombasa water supply, 1911–1917. *International Journal of African Historical Studies*, 95, 28, 1, p. 25-48.

7893. ZOUBIR (Yahia H.). The United States, the Soviet Union and decolonisation of the Maghreb, 1945–1962. *Middle Eastern Studies*, 95, 31, 1, p. 58-84.

Cf. n°s 7237, 9076-9106

d. Amerika.

** 7894. BENTHAM (Jeremy). Colonies, commerce, and constitutional law: Rid yourselves of Ultramaria and other writings on Spain and Spanish America. Ed. by Philip SCHOFIELD. Oxford, Clarendon Press, 95, LXV-468 p. (The collected works of Jeremy Bentham)

7895. BERGAD (Laird W.), GARCÍA (Fe Iglesias), BARCIA (María del Carmen). The Cuban slave market, 1790–1880. Cambridge a. New York, Cambridge U. P., 95, XXI-245 p. (ill., tabs). (Cambridge Latin American Studies).

7896. BLANCO VALDES (Roberto Luis). El "problema americano" en las primeras Cortes liberales españolas, 1810–1814. Mexico, Universidad Nacional Autonoma de Mexico, 87 p.

7897. BURTON (Richard D. E.), RENO (Fred). French and West Indian: Martinique, Guadeloupe and French Guiana today. London, Macmillan Carribean, 95, 202 p.

7898. BUSTOS RODRIGUEZ (Manuel). Los comerciantes de la carrera de Indias en el Cadiz del siglo XVIII (1713–1775). Cadiz, Universidad de Cadiz, 343 p.

7899. COOK (Don). The long fuse: how England lost the American colonies, 1760–1785. New York, Atlantic Monthly, 95, 432 p.

7900. CORNBLIT (Oscar). Power and violence in the colonial city: Oruro from the mining renaissance to the rebellion of Tupac Amaru (1740–1782). Cambridge, Cambridge U. P., 95, X-230 p.

7901. Cultivating a landscape of peace: Iroquois-European encounters in seventeenth-century America. Ithaca a. London, Cornell U. P., 95, XII-280 p. (ill., maps).

7902. Envisioning America: English plans for the colonization of North America, 1580–1640. Ed. P. C. MANCALL. Boston, Bedford Books of St. Martin's Press, 95, X-182 p. (ill.).

7903. LEON-PORTILLA (Miguel). La flecha en el blanco: Francisco Tenamaztle y Bartolomé de las Casas en lucha por los derechos de los indigenas, 1541–1556. Mexico, Editorial Diana, 95, 193 p.

7904. MATHER (Ian Roderick). The role of the Royal Navy in the English Atlantic Empire, 1660–1720. [s. l.], 95, IX-425 p.

7905. OZ (Manuel Ferrer). La formación de un estado nacional en Mexico: el imperio y la república federal, 1821–1835. Mexico City, UNAM, 95, 379 p. (bibl.).

7906. Parliament and the Atlantic Empire. Ed. by Philip LAWSON. Edinburgh, Edinburgh U. P., 95, 130 p. (Parliamentary history)

7907. RODRIGUEZ BAQUERO (Luis). Encomienda y vida diaria entre los indios de Muzo (1550–1620). Bogotá, Instituto Colombiano de Cultura Hispánica, 95, 167 p.

7908. SALAS (Carmen Parrón). De las reformas borbónicas a la república: el consulado y el comercio marítimo de Lima, 1778–1821. San Javier, Imprenta de la Academia General del Aire, 95, 583 p. (ill.).

7909. TREXLER (Richard C.). Sex and conquest: gender violence, political order, and the european conquest of the Americas. Ithaca a. London, Cornell U. P., 95, XII-292 p.

Cf. n°s 4650, 7236, 9107-9118

e. Ozeanien.

7910. HIERY (Hermann Joseph). Das deutsche Reich in der Südsee (1900–1921). Eine Annäherung an die Erfahrungen verschiedener Kulturen. Göttingen, Vandenhoeck & Ruprecht, 95, 353 p. (Veröffentlichungen des deutschen historischen Instituts London, 37).

Cf. n°s 9119-9122

§ 3. Geschichte von 1500–1789.

a. Allgemeines.

7911. ARASARATNAM (S.). Maritime trade, society, and European influence in Southern Asia, 1600–1800. Aldershot, Variorum, 95, XII-299 p.

7912. ELLIS (Steven G.). Conquest and union: fashioning a British state, 1485–1725. London a. New York, Longman, 95, XII-336 p.

7913. Frankreich im europäischen Staatensystem der Frühen Neuzeit. Hrsg. v. Rainer BABEL. Sigmaringen, Thorbecke, 95, 240 p. (Francia, 35).

7914. KOLLER (Alexander). Die Vermittlung des Friedens von Vossem (1673) durch den jülich-bergischen Vizekanzler Stratmann: Pfalz-Neuburg, Frankreich und Brandenburg zwischen dem Frieden von Aachen und der Reichskriegserklärung an Ludwig XIV. (1668–1674). Münster, Aschendorff, 95, X-226 p.

7915. KRAFT (Ekkehard). Moskaus griechisches Jahrhundert. Russisch-griechische Beziehungen und metabyzantinischer Einfluß 1619–1694. Stuttgart, Steiner, 95, 223 p. (Quellen und Studien zur Geschichte des östlichen Europa, 43).

7916. MARCET-JUNCOSA (Alicia). Le rattachement du Roussillon à la France. Perpignan, Trabucaire, 95, 163 p.

7917. MEYER (Jean). La rivalité triangulaire franco-anglo-hollandaise du milieu du XVIIe siècle. *Histoire et stratégie maritimes. Histoire et Défense*, 95, 31, p. 7-27.

7918. NABER (Jaak). Motsättningarnas Narva: statlig svenskhetspolitik och tyskt lokalvälde i ett statsreglerat samhälle, 1581-1704. (Conflicting Narva: the Swedish state politics and the local German authorities, 1581-1704). Uppsala, Uppsala universitets Historiska institution, 95, III, 156 p. (Opuscula histoirica upsaliensia, 15).

b. 1500-1648.

** 7919. BERTHIER (Annie). Un document retrouvé: la première lettre de Soliman au roi François Ier (1526). *Turcica (Louvain)*, 95, 27, p. 263-266.

7920. ABULAFIA (David). The French descent into Renaissance Italy, 1494-1495. Aldershot, Variorum, 95, 496 p.

7921. ALONSO ACERO (Beatriz). España en Orano y Mazalquivir a fines del siglo XVI: el elemento turco en las relaciones entre cristianos y musulmanes. *Revue d'Histoire Maghrébine*, 95, 79-80, p. 279-288.

7922. ARBEL (Benjamin). Trading Nations: Jews and Venetians in the early modern Eastern Mediterranean. Leiden, E. J. Brill, 95, XI-237 p.

7923. ARIKAN (Muzaffer). XIV.-XVI. Yuzyillarda Turk-Ispanyol iliskileri ve denizcilik tarihimizle ilgili Ispanyol belgeleri. (Las relaciónes turco-españolas en los siglos XIV y XVI: documentos españoles relativos a la historia naval otomana). Ankara. Deniz Kuvvetleri Komutanligi Karargah basimevi, 95, 334 p.

7924. Austro-Turcica 1541-1552: diplomatische Akten des habsburgischen Gesandtschaftsverkehrs mit der Hohen Pforte im Zeitalter Suleymans des Prachtigen. Hrsg. v. Srecko M. DZAJA unter Mitarbeit von Günter WEISS. München , R. Oldenbourg, 95, XI-771 p.

7925. BAES (Christian). Un épisode de la querelle Habsbourg-Valois: la campagne de Henri II aux Pays Bas en 1554. *Revue belge de philologie et d'histoire*, 95, 73, 2, p. 319-341.

7926. BARTA (Gábor). Az elfelejtett hadszíntér. Megjegyzések a török-magyar szövetség előtörténetéhez. (Le champs de bataille oublié. Remarques concernant la préhistoire de l'alliance turco-hongroise). *Tört. szle.*, 95, 37, 1, p. 1-34.

7927. BUES (Almut). Stosunki Habsburgów z Polską i ich starania o polski tron w latach 1572-1573. (Les relations des Habsbourgs avec la Pologne et leurs démarches pour atteindre le trône polonais dans les années 1572-1573.). *Kwartalnik Historyczny*, 95, 102, 2, p. 3-14. [Deutsche Zsfassung].

7928. DENIZE (Eugen). Ţările Române şi Veneţia. Relaţii politice (1441-1541). De la Iancu de Hunedoara la Petru Rareş. [The Romanian countries and Venice. Political relations (1441-1541). From Iancu of Hunedoara to Petru Rareş]. Bucureşti, Editura Albatros, 95, 235 p.

7929. HAR-EL (Shai). Struggle for domination in the Middle East: the Ottoman-Mamluk War, 1485-91. Leiden, E. J. Brill, 95, XV-238 p. (ill., maps)

7930. HILLER (István). A firenzei diplomácia és Magyarország 1604-1648. (La diplomatie florentine et la Hongrie 1604-1648). *Tört. szle.*, 95, 37, 2, p. 151-169.

7931. HUGON (Alain). L'affaire l'Hoste ou la tentation espagnole (1604). *Revue d'histoire moderne et contemporaine*, 95, 42, p. 355-375.

7932. KROM (Mikhail M.). Mež Rus'ju i Litvoj: Zapadnorusskie zemli v sisteme russko-litovskikh otnošenij konca XV-pervoj treti XVI veka. (Between Rus' and Lithuania: the Western Russian land in the system of the Russian and Lithuanian relations, the end of the XVth-the first Rossijskoij of the XVIth centuries). Moskva, Arkheografičeskij centr, Arkheografičeskij centr, Rossijskij gosudarstvennyj arkhiv drevnikh aktov, 95, 294 p.

7933. LADEWIG PETERSEN (E.). Christian IV's skånske og norske fæstningsanlæg 1596-1622. (The fortress construction in Skåne [Danish possessions in the south of the Scandinavian peninsula] and Norway under Christian IV's early years 1596-1622). *Historisk Tidskrift* (Denmark), 95, 95, 2, p. 328-341.

7934. LOCKHART (Paul Douglas). Religion and princely liberties: Denmark's intervention in the Thirty Years War, 1618-1625. *The International History Review*, 95, 17, p. 1-22.

7935. NICOLLIER-DE WECK (Beatrice). Hubert Languet (1518-1581): un réseau politique international, de Melanchthon à Guillaume d'Orange. Genève, Droz, 95, XVIII, 678 p. (map, tabl.)

7936. NIEDERKORN (Jan P.). Gesandte, Vermittler, Schwindler. Von den Schwierigkeiten diplomatischer Kontakte mit orientalischen und osteuropäischen Mächten in der frühen Neuzeit. *Österr. Osthefte*, 95, 37, 4, p. 836-878.

7937. PEREIRA FERREIRA (Ana Maria). O Brasil e a Francia na primeira metade do século XVI: viagens e interesses. In memoriam Maria Olímpia Rocha Gil. *Archipélago. História* (Ponta Delgada), 95, 2, p. 123-130.

7938. PUDDU (Raffaele). L'assedio di Malta e la cavalleria mediterranea. *Dimensioni e problemi della ricerca storica*, 95, 2, p. 15-38.

7939. RINGMAR (Erik). The relevance of international law: a Hegelian interpretation of a peculiar seventeenth-century preoccupation. *Review of International Studies*, 95, 21, p. 87-104.

7940. SALLMANN (Jean-Michel). Le rêve italien de Charles VIII. *L'Histoire*, 95, 187, p. 58-63.

7941. SCHMIDT (Georg). Der dreißigjährige Krieg. München, Beck, 95, 116 p.

7942. SZAKÁLY (Ferenc). Ludovico Gritti in Hungary, 1529–1534. A historical insight into the beginnings of Turco-Habsburgian rivalry. Budapest, Akad. Kiadó, 95, 143 p. (Studia hist. Acad. Sci. hungaricae, 197).

7943. TEMIMI (Abdeljelil). La politique ottomane face à l'expulsion des Morisques et à leur passage en France et à Venise, 1609–1610. *Revue d'histoire maghrébine*, 95, 22, p. 397-420.

7944. TENENTI (Alberto). La Repubblica di Venezia e la Spagna di Filippo II e Filippo III. *Studi Veneziani*, 95, 30, p. 109-123.

7945. VIEJO YHARRASSARRY (Julian). El Baron de Lisola, la defensa de la monarquía católica y la Paz de Westfalia. *Annali di storia moderna e contemporanea*, 95, 1, p. 93-106.

7946. WHITING (John Roger Scott). The enterprise of England: the Spanish Armada. Stroud, Alan Stroud, 95, 248 p. (ill.).

7947. WOS (Jan Wladyslaw). La nonciature en Pologne de l'archevêque Hannibal de Capoue, 1586–1591. Trento, Dipartimento di scienze filologiche e storiche, 95, 100 p. (Labirinti).

c. 1648–1789.

7948. ABDERRAHIM (Abderrahim Abderrahman). The documents of Alexandria Court related to the Maghariba at the XVIIIth century. *Revue d'Histoire Maghrébine* (Partie arabe), 95, 77-78, p. 309-347.

7949. AKSAN (Virginia H.). An Ottoman statesman in war and peace: Ahmed Resmi Efendi, 1700–1783. Leiden, E.J. Brill, 95, XVIII-253 p. (ill., maps)

7950. ALTHOFF (Frank). Untersuchungen zum Gleichgewicht der Mächte in der Aussenpolitik Friedrichs des Grossen nach dem Siebenjährigen Krieg (1763–1786). Berlin, Duncker & Humblot, 95, 297 p.

7951. ANDERSON (Matthew Smith). The War of the Austrian Succession, 1740–1748. London, Longman, 95, XI-248 p.

7952. ANGUSIEWICZ (Sławomir). Najazdy tatarskie na Prusy książece (1656–1657). Legendy; fakty. [Invasions tartares sur la Prusse Princière (1656–1657). Légendes; faits]. *Komunikaty Mazursko-Warmińskie*, 95, 39, 3, p. 233-247. [Deutsche Zsfassung].

7953. BEACHEY (R. W.). A history of East Africa 1592–1902. London, Tauris, 95, 464 p.

7954. BECKMAN (Margareta). Under fransk fana! Royal suédois – ett svenskt regemente i fransk tjänst 1690–1791. Stockholm, Svenskt militärhistoriskt bibliotek, 95, 141 p. [The story of the Swedish regiment in the service of the kings of France].

7955. BELLINGERI (Giampiero). Un frammento di storia veneto-ottomana a Piacenza (sul ms turco "Landi 246" della Biblioteca Comunale: la Pace Perpetua del 1733). *Bullettino storico pistoiese*, 95, 90, p. 247-280 p.

7956. CAHNER (Max). Viatge d'un ambaixador català a la Franca de Lluis XIV. *Revista de Catalunya*, 95, 93, p. 23-44.

7957. ČERKASOV (Petr. P.). Dvuglavyj orel i korolevskie lilii: Stanovlenie russko-francuzskikh otnošenij v XVIII veke, 1700–1775. (L'aigle a deux têtes et le royal: les relations franco-russes au XVIIIe siècle 1700–1775). Moskva: Nauka, RAN. In-t vseobščej istorii, Centr francuzskikh istoričeskikh issledovanij, 95, 439 p.

7958. COX (B.). King William's European joint venture. Assen, The Netherlands, Van Gorcum, 95, IX-243 p. (ill., maps)

7959. FOHLEN (Claude). Jefferson à Paris, 1784–1789. Paris, Perrin, 95, 224 p.

7960. GRELL (Chantal). Les ambiguïtés du philhellénisme: l'ambassade du Comte de Choiseul-Gouffier auprès de la sublime Porte (1784–1792). *XVIIIe siècle*, 95, 27, p. 223-235.

7961. JACQ-HERGOUALC'H (Michel). La France et le Siam de 1680 à 1685: histoire d'un échec. *Revue française d'histoire d'Outre-Mer*, 95, 82, 308, p. 257-275.

7962. KAMIEŃSKI (Andrzej). Stany Prus książęcych wobec rządów brandenburskich w drugiej połowie XVII wieku. (Les Etats en Prusse Princière face au pouvoir brandenbourgeois dans la deuxième moitié du XVII s.). Olsztyn, [s. n.], 95, 181 p. (Deutsche Zsfassung). (Rozpr. i Mater. Ośrodka Badań Nauk. im.Wojciecha Kętrzyńskiego w Olsztynie, 148).

7963. KRUSZEWSKI (Eugeniusz). The Danish candidacy for the Polish throne in 1675. København, Polish-Scandinavian Research Institute, 95, 167 p.

7964. MARKIEWICZ (Mariusz). W cieniu kompanii Mórz Południowych. Rząd angielski wobec problemów gospodarczych w 1720 roku. (A l'ombre de la companie des Mers du Sud. Le gouvernement anglais face aux problèmes économiques en 1720.). *Studia Historyczne*, 95, 38, 1, p. 23-37. [Eng. Summary].

7965. PARVEV (Ivan). Habsburgs and Ottomans between Vienna and Belgrade (1683–1739). Boulder, East European Monographs, 95, XVIII 345 p.

7966. PERINI (Sergio). Venezia e la guerra di successione austriaca. *Archivio veneto*, 95, 144, p. 21-61.

7967. PRINCE (Munro). The Dutch affair and the fall of the Ancien Régime, 1784–1787. *The Historical journal*, 95, 38, 4, p. 875-905.

7968. PRITCHARD (James). Anatomy of a naval disaster: the 1746 French expedition to North America. Montréal a. Kingston, McGill-Queen's U. P., 95, XVI-318. (ill.).

7969. REESE (Armin). Europäische Hegemonie versus Weltreich. Außenpolitik in Europa 1648–1763. Idstein, Schulz-Kirchner, 95, 190 p. (Historisches Seminar, 7).

7970. SINKOLI (Anna). Frankreich, das Reich und die Reichsstände, 1697–1702. Frankfurt am Main, P. Lang, 95, 488 p.

7971. THEILER (Dominique). Projet Anglo-Helvétique d'établissement des réfugiés huguenots en Irlande, 1692–1694: Quel échec? Genève, Université de Genève, 95, 165 p. (ill., maps.)

7972. TRACY (Nicholas). Manila ransomed: the British assault on Manila in the Seven Years War. Exeter, University of Exeter Press, 95, X-158 p.

7973. VENNING (Timothy). Cromwellian foreign policy. London, Macmillan, 95, 270 p.

§ 4. Geschichte von 1789–1815.

7974. ALLISON (Robert J.). The crescent obscured: the United States and the Muslim world, 1776–1815. New York, Oxford U. P., 95, XVIII-266 p.

7975. AMINI (Iradj). Napoléon et la Perse: les relations franco-persanes sous le Prémier Empire, dans le contexte des rivalités entre la France, l'Angleterre et la Russie. Paris, Fondation Napoléon, 95, 254 p. (ill.)

7976. ARBOIT (Gérald). L'impossible rêve oriental de Napoléon. Souvenir napoléonien, 95, 58, 402, p. 27-37.

7977. ARNOLD (James R.). Napoleon conquers Austria: the 1809 campaign for Vienna. London, Arms and Armour, 95, VI-247 p.

7978. AUSTIN (Paul Britten). 1812: Napoleon in Moscow. London, Greenhill Books, 95, 264 p.

7979. BERTINI (Fabio). I rapporti tra la Francia del Direttorio, Bonaparte e San Marino. Studi romagnoli, 95, 46, p. 83-93.

7980. BIELECKI (Robert). Wielka Armia [Napoleona]. (La Grande Armée) [de Napoléon]. Warszawa, Bellona, 95, 563 p. (phot., fig., dessins).

7981. BLANC (Olivier). Les espions de la Révolution et de l'Empire. Paris, Perrin, 95, 371 p.

7982. BODINIER (Gilbert). Le rôle des officiers de la guerre d'Amérique dans la Revolution française. In: France de la Révolution et les Etats-Unis d'Amérique (La) [Cf. n° 5593], p. 80-111.

7983. BONNEL (Ulane). Les rapports maritimes France–Etats-Unis pendant la guerre d'Indépendance. In: France de la Révolution et les Etats-Unis d'Amérique (La) [Cf. n° 5593], p. 4-19.

7984. BOUDARD (René). Le débarquement anglais de Viareggio en décembre 1813 et les dernières semaines du gouvernement des Baciocchi en Toscane. Revue de l'Institut Napoléon, 95, 167, p. 7-30.

7985. CALDWELL (George). Rifles at Waterloo. Leicestershire, Bugle Horn, 95, 47 p. (ill., ports).

7986. CHARLIER (J.). Bataille de Waterloo. Revue belge d'histoire militaire, 95, 31, 3-4, p. 1-18.

7987. DE MATTEI (Roberto). Il proclama di Rimini e il problema italiano tra il 1813 e il 1815. Clio, 95, 31, p. 517-532.

7988. DUFRAISSE (Roger). Napoléon pour ou contre l'Europe. Souvenir napoléonien, 95, 58, 402, p. 4-25.

7989. FELDBÆK (Ole). De nordatlantiske øer og freden i Kiel 1814. (The North Atlantic islands and the peace treaty of Kiel 1814). Historisk Tidskrift (Denmark), 95, 95, 1, p. 24-34.

7990. FIOCCHI (Fabio). L'invasione austriaca dell'alto Vicentino nel 1809. Arte veneta, 95, 126, p. 61-83.

7991. GRAB (Alexander). Army, state and society: conscription and desertion in Napoleonic Italy (1802–1814). The Journal of modern history, 95, 67, 1, p. 25-54. – IDEM. State power, brigandage and rural resistance in Napoleonic Italy. European History Quarterly, 95, 25, p. 39-70.

7992. HARTLEY (J. M.). "It is the festival of the crown and sceptres": the diplomatic, commercial and domestic significance of the visite of Alexander I to England in 1814. Slavonic and East European Review, 95, 73, p. 246-268.

7993. INGRAM (Edward). The geopolitics of the first British expedition to Egypt: occupation and withdrawal, 1801–1803. Middle Eastern studies, 95, 31, p. 317-346.

7994. JONQUET (Michel). Le rôle de Napoléon dans le développement juridique du royaume de Bavière. Gnomon. Rev. int d'histoire du notariat, 95, 101, p. 16-20.

7995. Kriegsbereitschaft und Friedensordnung in Deutschland 1800–1814. Hrsg.v. Jost DÜLFFER. Münster, Lit, 95. 265 p. (Jahrbuch für historische Friedensforschung 3/1994).

7996. LEMAIRE (Jean-François). Thomas Jefferson, ambassadeur à Paris en 1789. In: France de la Révolution et les Etats-Unis d'Amérique (La) [Cf. n° 5593], p. 73-78.

7997. LENKEFI (Ferenc). Francia hadifoglyok Magyarországon 1793–1795. (Prisonniers de guerre français en Hongrie entre 1793–1795). Levéltari szle., 95, 45, 2, p. 35-48.

7998. LUXARDO DE FRANCHI (Nicolò). La caduta della Serenissima e la Dalmazia. La Rivista dalmatica, 95, 42, p. 161-168.

7999. MACKESY (Piers). British victory in Egypt, 1801: the end of Napoleon's conquest. London, Routledge, 95, XII-282 p. (maps)

8000. MANZARI (Giuliano). La difesa dell'arcipelago della Maddalena contro i Francesi (1793): Domenico e Agostino Millelire. *Bollettino d'archivio dell'Ufficio storico della Marina Militare*, 95, 9, 1, p. 83-103.

8001. MASSON (Philippe). Napoléon et l'Angleterre. *Souvenir napoléonien*, 95, 58, 400, p. 26-46; 401, p. 4-20.

8002. PASETZKY (Gilda). Das Erzbistum Salzburg und das revolutionäre Frankreich (1789–1803). Frankfurt am Main, Peter Lang, 95, IX-205 p.

8003. PILLORGET (René). La France et les Etats Unis en état de «quasi-guerre», 1793–1801. *In*: France de la Révolution et les Etats-Unis d'Amérique (La) [Cf. n° 5593], p. 50-68.

8004. Royaume anglo-corse (1794–1796) (Le). Actes du Colloque tenu à Bastia les 23 et 24 septembre 1994. *Bulletin de la Société des sciences historiques et naturelles de la Corse*, 95, 114, 670-671, 172 p.

8005. SCHNEID (Frederick C.). Soldiers of Napoleon's Kingdom of Italy: army, state, and society, 1800–1815. Boulder, Westview Press, 95, XIII-145 p. (maps)

8006. SIMMS (Brendan). "An odd question enough": Charles James Fox, the crown and the British policy during the Hanoverian crisis of 1806. *The Historical journal*, 95, 38, p. 567-596.

8007. TABLIT (Ali). Joel Barlow: U. S. Consul General at Algers: 1796–1797. *Revue d'Histoire Maghrébine*, 95, 79-80, p. 385-395.

8008. TEMIMI (Abdeljelil). La traité de paix entre la Régence de Tunis et Venise du mois de Mai 1792. *Revue d'Histoire Maghrébine*, 95, 77-78, p. 223-246.

8009. TULARD (Jean). Talleyrand et les Etats-Unis. *In*: France de la Révolution et les Etats-Unis d'Amérique (La) [Cf. n° 5593], p. 115-132.

8010. VILLANI (Pasquale). Agenti e diplomatici francesi in Italia durante la rivoluzione: Eymar e la sua missione a Genova (1793). *Studi storici*, 95, 36, p. 957-976.

8011. ZAJEWSKI (Władysław). Wielkie miasta Hanzy w polityce napoleońskiej. (Les grandes villes hanséatiques dans la politique napoléonienne). *Roczniki Gdański*, 95, 55, 2, p. 5-19. [Eng. Summary].

§ 5. Geschichte von 1815–1910.

8012. ARNOULET (François). Les papiers Destrées, Consul de France à Tripoli (1884–1896). *Revue d'Histoire Maghrébine*, 95, 79-80, p. 289-297.

8013. AVENEL (Jean). La défense de Montevideo par la marine française, 1845–1852. *Revue internationale d'histoire militaire*, 95, 75, p. 37-47.

8014. BINDER (Frederick Moore). James Buchanan and the Earl of Clarendon: an uncertain relationship. *Diplomacy and Statecraft*, 95, 6, 2, p. 323-341.

8015. BOLKHOVITINOV (Nikolaj N.). Rossja i načalo graždanskoj vojny v SŠA. Po arkhivnym materialam. (Russia and the origins of the Civil war in the USA. The archival materials). *Nov. novejš. Ist.*, 95, 3, p. 30-42.

8016. BOURGERIE (Raymond), LESOUEF (Pierre). L'expedition de Chine, 1860. *Revue internationale d'histoire militaire*, 95, 75, p. 63-75.

8017. BRAITHWAITE (Roderick). Palmerston and the Nunez: the affair within the affair, 1849–53. *The Journal of Imperial and Commonwealth History*, 95, 23, p. 395-426.

8018. BUZPINAR (S. T.). The Hijaz, Abdulhamid II and Amir Hussien's secret dealings with the British, 1877–80. *Middle Eastern Studies*, 95, 31, 1, p. 146-169.

8019. CARCEL ORTI (Vincente). La Congregación des Asuntos Eclesiásticos Extraordinarios y España (1814–1913). *Archivum historiae pontificiae*, 95, 33, p. 351-365.

8020. ÇAYCI (Abdurrahman). Büyük Sahra'da Türk-Fransiz Rekabeti (1858–1911). (La Concurrence turco-française dans le Sahara). Ankara, [s. n.], 95, 236 p.

8021. ČEPELKIN (M. A.). Rossijskaja diplomatija i ital'janskij vopros, 1856–1861. (The Russian diplomacy and the Italian issue, 1856–1861). Moskva, Akademija estestvennykh nauk RF. In-t special'nykh istoričeskikh disciplin rossijskoj, 95, 117 p.

8022. CSETRI (Elek). Az 1830–1831. évi lengyel felkelés menekültjei Erdélyben. (Les réfugiés de l'enlèvement polonais de 1830–31 en Transylvanie). *Tört. szle.*, 95, 37, 4, p. 385-410.

8023. DERREUMAUX (Edmond). L'occupation prussienne et saxonne à Roubaix de 1814 à 1818. *Bulletin de la Société d'émulation de Rubauix*, 95, 12, p. 1-6

8024. DIOSZEGI (István). Az Osztrák-Magyar Monarchia föderatív átalakításának kísérlete 1871-ben és a nemzetközi politika. (Essai de réorganisation fédérale de la Monarchie austro-hongroise en 1871 et la politique internationale). *Regio*, 95, 6, 3, p. 135-180. – IDEM. Magyarország helye a francia és a porosz külpolitikában, 1867–1868-ban. (La place de la Hongrie dans la politique éxterieure française et prussienne en 1867–1868). *Tört. szle.*, 95, 37, 4, p. 411-438.

8025. DUUS (Peter). The abacus and the sword: the japanese penetration of Korea, 1895–1910. Berkeley, University of California Press, 95, XIV-480 p.

8026. ENGİN (Vahdettin). Sultan II. Abdülhamid'e Düzenlenen Ermeni Suikasti ve Bu Sebeple Belçika İle Yaşanan Diplomatik Kriz" (L'Attentat arménien contre Abdülhamid II et la crise entre la Belgique et l'Empire Ottoman). *Belleten*, 95, 59, 225, p. 413-428.

8027. FORCADE (Olivier), GUELTON (Frédéric). L'éxpedition française en Syrie août 1860–juin 1861. *Revue internationale d'histoire militaire*, 95, 75, p. 49-62.

8028. FORNARO (Pasquale). Risorgimento italiano e questione ungherese (1849–1867): Marcello Cerruti e le intese politiche italo-magiare. Soveria Mannelli, Rubbettino, 95, 290 p.

8029. Francúzsko a stredná Európa. Vztahy medzi Francúzskom a strednou Európou v rokoch 1867–1914. Vzájomné vplyvy a predstavy. (La France et l'Europe Centrale. Les relations entre la France et l'Europe Centrale en 1867–1914. Impacts et images réciproques). Ed. par Bohumila FERENČUHOVÁ. Bratislava, Academic Electronic Press, 95, 169 p.

8030. GALLO (Klaus). De la invasión al reconocimiento: Gran Bretaña y El Rio de la Plata 1806–1826. Buenos Aires, A–Z Editora, 252 p.

8031. GEARY (Frank). The Act of Union, British-Irish, and pre-Famine deindustrialization. *Economic History Review*, 95, 48, 1, p. 68-88.

8032. GEORGES (Giorgos). Stis aparches tes Hellenikes exoterikes politikes. Athena, Kastaniote, 95, 236 p.

8033. GOUTTMAN (Alain). La guerre de Crimée. *Bulletin de la Société historique de Rueil-Malmaison*, 95, 20, p. 56-65.

8034. HAMPE (Karl-Alexander). Das auswärtige Amt in der Ära Bismarck. Bonn, Bouvier, 95, 256 p.

8035. HANSSEN (Jens-Peter). The effect of Ottoman rule on Beirut: the Wilaya of Beirut, 1888–1900. [s. l., s. e.], 95, 109 p.

8036. HEYDEMANN (Günther). Konstitution gegen Revolution: die britische Deutschland- und Italienpolitik 1815–1848. Göttingen, Vandenhoeck & Ruprecht, 95, 404 p.

8037. HUGHES (Michael). Diplomacy or drudgery? British consuls in Russia during the early twentieth century. *Diplomacy and Statecraft*, 95, 6, p. 176-195.

8038. JACKSON (William Godfrey Fothergill). The pomp of yesterday: the defence of India and the Suez Canal, 1798–1918. London, Brassey's, 95, X-262 p.

8039. JAŚKIEWICZ (Leszek). Carat i kwestia polska na początku XX wieku [1900–1904]. (Système tsariste et question polonaise au début du XXe siècle). *Przegląd Historyczny*, 95, 86, p. 29-46. [Eng. Summary].

8040. KIENIEWICZ (Jan). Rząd hiszpański wobec powstania styczniowego [1863]. (Le gouvernement espagnol face à l'insurrection du printemps 1863). *Przegląd Historyczny*, 95, 85, 4, p. 415-432. [Eng. Summary].

8041. KOLLANDER (Patricia A.). Politics for the defence? Bismark, Battenberg, and the origins of the Cartel of 1887. *The Journal of the German History Society*, 95, 13, p. 28-46.

8042. KUHLICH (Frank). Die deutschen Soldaten im Krieg von 1870–71: eine Darstellung der Situation und der Erfahrungen der deutschen Soldaten im deutsch-französischen Krieg. Frankfurt am Main, P. Lang, 95, 505 p. (1 folded map).

8043. LAMBERT-DANSENETTE (Jean). Histoire d'un "coup d'Etat" économique: le traité de commerce de janvier 1860 entre la France et l'Angleterre. *Souvenir napoléonien*, 95, 58, 403, p. 4-31.

8044. MAC LEAN (David). War, diplomacy, and informal Empire: Britain and the Republic of La Plata, 1836–1835. New York, St. Martin's Press, 95, 241 p.

8045. Makedoniia i Trakiia v borba za svoboda. [Macedonia and Thrace in a struggle for freedom]. Ed. by GEORGIEV (Velichko), TRIFONOV (Staiko). Sofiia, Makedonski nauchen in-t, 95, 815 p.

8046. MILLER (Carman). The unhappy warriors: conflict and nationality among Canadian Troops during the South Africa War. *The Journal of Imperial and Commonwealth History*, 95, 23, p. 77-104.

8047. MOLIS (Robert). Les francs-tireurs et les Garibaldi: soldats de la République: 1870–1871 en Bourgogne. Préface de Jean-Francois BAZIN. Paris, Editions Tiresias, 95, 362 p. (ill.).

8048. Montevideo, 1834–1859. A cura di D. RUOCCO. Napoli, Geocart edit, 95, XX-953 p. (Archivio di Stato di Torino, Consolati nazionali)

8049. MORENO FRAGINALS (Manuel). Cuba/España, España/Cuba: história comun. Presentación de Josep FONTANA. Barcelona, Critica, Grijalbo Mondadori, 95, 310 p. (ill.).

8050. O'CONNOR (Edward G.). The nature of British hegemony in the international economy, 1875–1914. [S. l.], [s. n.], 95, 45 p.

8051. OLENDER (Piotr). Wojna amerykańsko-hiszpańska na morzu 1898r. (La guerre maritime américano-espagnole en 1898). Warszawa, Lampart, 95, 213 p. (phot., fig., dessins, cartes).

8052. OTTE (T. G.). Great Britain, Germany, and the Far-Eastern crisis of 1897–98. *English historical review*, 95, 110, p. 1157-1179.

8053. PACAUT (Marcel). La guerre de 1870. *Société des amis des arts, sciences, archéologie et histoire locale de la Bresse louhannaise*, 95, 23, p. 29-37.

8054. PALOTÁS (Emil). Machtpolitik und Wirtschaftsinteressen: der Balkan und Russland in der österreichisch-ungarischen Aussenpolitik, 1878–1895. Budapest, Akademiai Kiadó, 95, 399 p.

8055. PAMUK (Sevket). 19. Yuzyilda Osmanli dis ticareti. (Ottoman foreign trade in the 19th century). Ankara, T.C. Basbakanlik Devlet Istatistik Enstitusu, 95, XXII-83 p. [Eng. Summary].

8056. PENNELL (Richard). State power in a chronically weak State: Spanish coastguards as pirates, 1814–50. *European History Quarterly*, 95, 25, p. 353-380.

8057. POLVINEN (Tuomo). Imperial Borderland: Bobrikov and the attempted russification of Finland, 1898–1904. London, Duke U. P., 95, 342 p.

8058. Powstaniec polski w Prusach wschodnich i na emigracji. Z dziejów wychodźstwa polskiego i myśli politycznej po 1831 roku. (Insurgé polonais en Prusse orientale et en émigration. De l'histoire de l'exil polonais et de la pensée politique après 1831). Réd. Sławomir KALEMBKA. Olsztyn, [s. n.], 95, 222 p. (cartes 3). (Studia i Mater. Wyższej Szkoły Pedagog. w Olsztynie, 69).

8059. POZZANI (Silvio). Verona 1822: i potentati della restaurazione respingono i delegati della Grecia insorta. *Studi storici Luigi Simeoni*, 95, 45, p. 249-264.

8060. RAYEN (Mohammed Rajei). Fezzan dans les stratégies politiques de la France (1830–1843). *Revue d'Histoire Maghrébine* (Partie arabe), 95, 79-80, p. 483-499.

8061. Regioni di frontiera nell'epoca dei nazionalismi. Alsazia e Lorena / Trento e Trieste 1870–1914. A cura di Angelo ARA e Eberhard KOLB. Bologna, Il Mulino, 95, 400 p. (Annali dell'Istituto storico italo-germanico in Trento. Quaderno, 41).

8062. RIVIERE (Peter). Absent-minded imperialism: Britain and the expansion of Empire in nineteenth-century Brazil. London, Tauris, 95, XII-194 p. (8 p. of plates, ill.).

8063. SAUNDERS (David). Russia and Ukraine under Alexander II: the Valuev edict of 1863. *The International History Review*, 95, 17, p. 23-50. – IDEM. Russia's Ukrainian policy (1847–1905): a demographic approach. *European History Quarterly*, 95, 25, p. 181-208.

8064. SIMS (Richard). Japan's rejection of alliance with France during the Franco-Chinese dispute of 1883–1885. *Journal of Asian history*, 95, 29, 2, p. 109-148.

8065. SMITH (Iain R.). The origins of the South African War, 1899–1902. London a. New York, Longman, 95, XIX-455 p.

8066. THOMPSON (Dennis W.). Prelude to the Sulphur War of 1840: the Neapolitan Perspective. *European History Quarterly*, 95, 25, p. 163-180.

8067. TILCHIN (William N.). Theodore Roosevelt, Anglo-American relations, and the Jamaica incident of 1907. *Diplomatic History*, 95, 19, p. 385-405.

8068. TUCK (Patrick J. N.). The French wolf and the Siamese lamb. The French threat to Siamese independence, 1858–1907. Bangkok a. Cheney, White Lotus, 95, XVIII-434 p.

8069. VEYRASSAT (B.). Chocs macro-économiques et négoce international. Le développement des relations de la Suisse avec l'outre-mer au XIXe siècle. *Relations Internationales*, 95, 82, p. 123-140.

8070. WAWRO (Geoffrey). The Habsburg Flucht nach Vorne in 1866: Domestic Political Origins of the Austro-Prussian War. *The International History Review*, 95, 17, p. 221-248.

8071. WHITE (John Albert). Transition to global rivalry: alliance diplomacy and the Quadruple Entente, 1895–1907. New York, Cambridge U. P., 95, XXIII-344 p.

§ 6. Geschichte von 1910–1935. Der Erste Weltkrieg.

8072. 1923 Metu Sausio Ivykiai Klaipedoje. Redaktore Roma NIKZENTAITIENE. Klaipeda, Klaipedos Universiteto Vakaru Lietuvos ir Prusijos istorijos centras, 95, 93 p. (Acta historica Universitatis Klaipedensis).

8073. Agents of empire: Anglo-Zionist intelligence operations, 1915–1919: Brigadier Walter Gribbon, Aaron Aaronsohn, and the nili ring. Ed. by A. VERRIER, London a. Washington, Brassey's, 95, XVI-342 p.

8074. ANDREWS (E. M.). "For Australia's wartime interests": W. M. Hughes and the push against Asquith, Britain, March–July 1916. *Australian Journal of Politics and History*, 95, 41, 2, p. 239-252.

8075. ATKINS (Martyn). Informal Empire in crisis: British diplomacy and the Chinese customs succession, 1927–1929. Ithaca, Cornell UP, 95, 142 p. (Cornell East Asia Series).

8076. BABIJ (Orest M.). The second labour government and British maritime security, 1929–31. *Diplomacy and Statecraft*, 95, 6, 3, p. 645-671.

8077. BADEL (L.). Trêve douanière, libéralisme et conjoncture (septembre 1929–mars 1930). *Relations Internationales*, 95, 82, p. 141-161.

8078. BALLARINI (Amleto). L'antidannunzio a Fiume: Riccardo Zanella. Trieste, Italo Svevo, 95, 372 p. (ill.). (Città di vita).

8079. BATOWSKI (Henryk). Zachód wobec granic Polski 1920–1940. Niektóre fakty mniej znane. (Occident face aux frontières polonaises 1920–1940. Certains faits moins connus). Łódź, Wydawn. Łódzkie, 95, 242 p. [Eng. summary].

8080. BAUDET (François). Alexis Léger et la Chine. Un apprentissage diplomatique (1922–1927). *Europe*, 95, 73, 799-800., p. 41-51.

8081. BEAUMONT (Joan). Australia's War, 1914–18. St. Leonards, Allen & Unwin, 95, XXII-195 p.

8082. BEKE (Gyorgy). Magyar afium Trianon fogsagaban. Budapest, Puski, 95, 128 p.

8083. BENNETT (G. H.). British foreign policy during the Curzon period, 1919–1924. New York, St Martin's Press, 95, XI-243 p.

8084. BENOIT (Fernand). Témoignage sur les attaques d'août et septembre 1917 devant Verdun. *Revue du Tarn*, 95, 158, p. 231-244.

8085. BERG (Roald). Norge på egen hånd 1905–1920. Oslo, Universitetsforlaget, 95, 401 p. (Norsk utenrikspolitikks historie, 2). [History of the Norwegian foreign policy].

8086. BERGER (F.). Les effets de la grande crise sur les relations franco-allemandes. L'exemple de la sidérurgie. *Relations Internationales*, 95, 82, p. 175-196.

8087. BERNEDE (Allain). Les troupes françaises en "mission d'interposition" en Hongrie, 1918–1919. *Revue internationale d'histoire militaire*, 95, 75, p. 111-131.

8088. BERSTEIN (Serge). "Gardons-nous de l'obsession du complot!". *L'Histoire*, 95, 189, p. 83-85.

8089. BERTOLASO (Marco). Die erste Runde im Kampf gegen Hitler? Frankreich, Großbritannien und die österreichische Frage 1933–34: eine Untersuchung der Außenpolitik der Westmächte in den ersten 18 Monaten des "Dritten Reiches" auf der Grundlage diplomatischer Akten. Hamburg, Kovac, 95, 299 p.

8090. BLAY (Jean-Pierre). La mission militaire française, son influence intellectuelle et technologique dans la formation des élites militaires brésiliennes (1919–1940). *Guerres Mondiales et Conflits Contemporains*, 95, 45, 177, p. 95-104.

8091. BOULANGER (Patrick). Des huiles en cuncurrence à Tetouan: un exemple des rivalités franco-espagnoles dans les années vingt. *Revue d'Histoire Maghrébine*, 95, 79-80, p. 343-346.

8092. BOURETTE-KNOWLES (Simon). The global micawber: Sir Robert Vansittart, the treasury and the global balance of power, 1933–35. *Diplomacy and Statecraft*, 95, 6, 1, p. 91-121.

8093. BRZEZIŃSKI (Andrzej Maciej). Dyplomacja polska wobec Międzynarodowego Instytutu Współpracy Intelektualnej w Paryżu (1925–1939). (Diplomatie polonaise face à l'Institut International de Coopération Intellectuelle [IICI] de Paris, 1925–1939). *Studia Historyczne*, 95, 38, 1, p. 73-88. [Eng. Summary].

8094. CANTERA CARLOMAGNO (Marcos). Ett folk av mänskligt granit: Sverige i den italienska utrikespolitiken 1932-1936. (The people of granit. Sweden in Italian foreign politics [and Fascist Italy in Swedish opinion], 1932–1936). Lund, Historiska media, 1995, 216 p.

8095. CASABIELHE (Olivier). Le Feu: roman de la Grande Guerre. *Guerres Mondiales et Conflits Contemporains*, 95, 45, 179, p. 135-146

8096. CHEVUTSCHI (Ludovic). L'intervention navale alliée en Lettonie, octobre–novembre 1919, l'exemple d'une collaboration franco-britannique. *Revue historique des Armeés*, 95, 1, p. 105-116.

8097. CONETTI (Giorgio). La composizione del Consiglio nella Società delle Nazioni. *Relazioni Internazionali*, 95, 59, 32, p. 29-32.

8098. CSÖPPUS (I.). The compensation question of Hungary after World War I. *Journal of European Economic History*, 95, 24, 2, p. 349-374.

8099. DARE (Robert). "Les cloches et les fanfares"; les réactions australiennes à la guerre de 1914. *Guerres Mondiales et conflits contemporains*, 95, 45, 179, p. 35-60.

8100. Decisions for war, 1914. Ed. by Keith WILSON. London, Ucl press, 95, IX-278 p.

8101. DIMITRIVA (Snezana). La politique extérieure française durant les anneés 1918–1920 et ses alternatives. *Bulgarian historical review*, 95, 23, 1, p. 103-122.

8102. Documents diplomatiques français sur l'histoire du Bassin des Carpates, 1918–1932. Vol. 2. Août 1919–Juin 1920. Réd. Par Magda ÁDAM, György LITVAN et Mária ORMOS. Budapest, Akad. Kiadó, 95, 676 p.

8103. DOUGLAS (Roy). The great war: 1914–1918. London, Routledge, 95, 157 p.

8104. DUTTON (David). La Grande-Bretagne, la France et la campagne de Salonique en 1917: l'alliance mise à l'épreuve. *Guerres Mondiales et conflits contemporains*, 95, 45, 180, p. 27-44.

8105. FARCY (Jean-Claude). Les camps de concentration français de la Première guerre mondiale (1914–1920). Paris, Anthropos-Economica, 95, 373 p.

8106. FERRIS (John R.). "Indulged in all too little"? Vansittart, intelligence and appeasement. *Diplomacy and Statecraft*, 95, 6, 1, p. 122-175.

8107. FOGLESONG (David S.). America's secret war against Bolshevism: US intervention in the Russian civil war, 1917–1920. Chapel Hill a. London, University of North Carolina Press, 95, X-386 p.

8108. FRANKS (Norman Leslie Robert). Bloody April – black September. London, Grub Steet, 95, 314 p.

8109. GEFFROY (Michel). Mission d'interposition en Turquie, 1921–1923: le corps d'occupation de Constantinople et la guerre gréco-turque. *Revue internationale d'histoire militaire*, 95, 75, p. 149-167.

8110. GILBERT (Martin). First World War. London, Harper Collins, 95, XXIV-616 p. (ill., maps.)

8111. GIORGI (Alessandro). Roncalli, von Papen e la pace. *Storia delle Relazioni Internazionali*, 94-95/2, 10-11, p. 211-228.

8112. GOTO-SHIBATA (Harumi). Japan and Britain in Shangai, 1925–1931. London a. Basingstoke, Macmillan, 95, XVI-196 p.

8113. HALL (Linda B.). Oil, banks, and politics: the United States and postrevolutionary Mexico, 1917–1924. Austin, University of Texas Press, 95, 224 p. (phot., bibl.)

8114. HAMARD (B.). Le transfert du Burgenland à l'Autriche 1918-1922, un arbitrage international de l'après-guerre. *Revue Historique*, 95, 119, 596, p. 285-306.

8115. HAUG (Karl Erik). Tyske krigsplaner og Norge under den første verdenskrig. (German war plans regarding Norway during the First World War). *Historisk Tidsskrift* (Norway), 95, 74, p. 423.

8116. HIERY (Hermann Joseph). The neglected war: the German South Pacific and the influence of World War I. Honolulu, University of Hawaii Press, 95, XVII-387 p. (ill., map).

8117. HOPKIRK (Peter). On secret service east of Costantinople: the plot to bring down the British Empire. Oxford, Oxford U. P., 95, XII-413 p.

8118. HORN (Martin). Alexandre Ribot et la coopération financière anglo-française 1914-1917. *Guerres Mondiales et conflits contemporains*, 95, 45, 180, p. 5-26. – IDEM. External finance in Anglo-French relations in the First World War, 1914-1917. *The International History Review*, 95, 17, p. 51-77.

8119. IANCU (Gheorghe). The ruling council. The integration of Transylvania into Romania 1918-1920. Cluj-Napoca, Center for Transylvanian Studies, The Roumanian Cultural Foundation, 95, 253 p. (Bibliotheca Rerum Transsilvaniae VIII).

8120. Intervencija na Severo-Zapade Rossii, 1917-1920 gody. (The intervention in the North-Western Russia, 1917-1920). RAN. In-t rossijskoj istorii. Sankt-Peterburgskij filial; Otv. red. V. A. ŠIŠKIN. Sankt-Peterburg: Nauka, 95, 394 p.

8121. JEANNESSON (Stanislas). Les objectifs rhénans de la politique française durant l'occupation de la Ruhr (1922-1924). *Revue d'Histoire Diplomatique*, 109, p. 369-389.

8122. KAPPEL (Hans). Les prisonniers de guerre danois dans le Cantal pendant la Première guerre mondiale. *Revue de la Haute-Auvergne*, 95, 57, 2, p. 137-143.

8123. KAZBUNDA (Karel). Otázka česko-německá v předvečer Velké války. Zrušení ústavnosti země České tzv. annenskými patenty z 26. července 1913. (The Czech-German question on the eve of the Great War. Annulment of the constitutionality of the Bohemian Lands by the so-called 'Patents of Annen', 26 July 1913). Praha, Karolinum, 95, 477 p.

8124. KENNEDY (Greg). Depression and security: aspects influencing the US Navy during the Hoover administration. *Diplomacy and Statecraft*, 95, 6, 2, p. 342-372.

8125. KENNEDY (Michael J.). Ireland and the League of Nations, 1919-1946: international relations, diplomacy and politics. Dublin, Irish Academic Press, 95, 285 p.

8126. KLEINE-AHLBRANDT (William Laird). The burden of victory: France, Britain, and the enforcement of the Versailles peace, 1919-1925. Lanham a. London, University Press of America, 95, XIII-342 p. (ill., maps)

8127. KNOCK (Thomas J.). To end all wars: Woodrow Wilson and the quest for a new world order. Princeton, Princeton U. P., 95, XVIII-381 p.

8128. KURTCEPHE (İsrafil). Türk-İtalyan İlişkileri (1911-1916). (Les Relations turco-italiennes). Ankara, [s. n.], 95, 279 p.

8129. LACAZE (Yvon). La genèse du traité d'alliance et d'amitié franco-tchécoslovaque de 1924. *Revue d'Histoire Diplomatique*, 95, 109, p. 115-134.

8130. LACHIVER (Alban). Le soutien humanitaire canadien-français à la France en 1914-1918. *Guerres Mondiales et Conflits Contemporains*, 95, 45, 179, p. 147-174.

8131. LENTIN (Antony). Several types of ambiguity: Lloyd George at the Paris Peace Conference. *Diplomacy and Statecraft*, 95, 6, 1, p. 223-251.

8132. LEPICK (Olivier). Et les Allemands inventèrent la guerre chimique. *L'Histoire*, 95, 187, p. 14-26.

8133. MACKERCHER (B. J. C.). The last old diplomat: Sir Robert Vansittart and the verities of British foreign policy, 1903-30. *Diplomacy and Statecraft*, 95, 6, 1, p. 1-38.

8134. MACLAREN (John). Intelligence, espionage, covert operations and cryptography, conducted before, during and after the Great War and the wars of intervention in Russia. Huddersfield, Macleren, 95, 8 Vol. [s. p.]

8135. MAGEE (Frank). "Limited liability"? Britain and the Treaty of Locarno. *20th Century British history*, 95, 6, p. 1-22.

8136. MAURER (John H.) The outbreak of the First World War: strategic planning, crisis decision making, and deterrence failure. Westport, Praeger, 95, XVII-149 p. (ill.). (Praeger studies in diplomacy and strategic thought).

8137. MECHOULAN (Eric). L'incomprénsion diplomatique franco-américaine, 1932-1933. *Revue d'histoire moderne et contemporaine*, 95, 42, p. 577-592.

8138. MEHNERT (Ute). Deutschland, Amerika und die "Gelbe Gefahr". Zur Karriere eines Schlagworts in der Großen Politik 1905-1917. Stuttgart, Franz Steiner Verlag, 95, 387 p.

8139. MICHÁLEK (Slavomír). Nádeje a vytriezvenia. Československo-americké hospodárske vzt'ahy v rokoch 1945-1951. (Hopes and disappointments Czechoslovak-American economic relations in the years 1945-1951). Bratislava, Veda, 95, 186 p.

8140. MICHEL (Bernard). L'Autriche et l'entrée dans la guerre en 1914. *Guerres Mondiales et conflits contemporains*, 95, 45, 179, p. 5-12.

8141. MICHELETTA (Luca). La dichiarazione dell'uguaglianza di diritti alla Germania dell'11 dicembre 1932. *Storia contemporanea*, 26, p. 695-730.

8142. MIKHUTINA (Irina V.). Tak skol'ko že sovietskikh voennoplennykh pogiblo v Pol'še v 1919–1921 godakh? (How many Soviet prisoners of war were killed in Poland in 1919–1921?). *Nov. novejš. Ist.*, 95, 3, p. 64-69.

8143. MORRISEY (Charles), [et al.]. "Giving a lead in the right direction": sir Robert Vansittart and the defence requirements sub-committ. *Diplomacy and Statecraft*, 95, 6, 1, p. 39-60.

8144. MOUTON (Marie-Renée). La Société des Nations et les intérêts de la France (1920–1924). Berne, Publications Universitaires Européennes, Peter Lang, 95, 597 p.

8145. MOYER (Lourence). Victory must be ours. Germany in the Great War, 1914–1918. London, Leo Cooper, 95, [s. p.].

8146. MÜHLE (Robert W.). Frankreich und Hitler: die französische Deutschland- und Aussenpolitik, 1933–1935. Paderborn, Schoningh, 95, 406 p.

8147. NAKANISHI (H.), SHIMAZU (N.). Japan and the First World War. London, Suntory-Toyota International Center for Economics and Related Discipline, London School of Economics, 95, 47 p.

8148. NASSON (Bill). Springboks ou autruches: les réactions sud-africaines au déclenchement de la guerre de 1914. *Guerres Mondiales et conflits contemporains*, 95, 45, 179, p. 61-82.

8149. Neutralidad de la España durante la Primera Guerra Mundial (La) (1914–1918). Ed. de N. AGUIRRE DE CARCER, Madrid, Ministerio de Asuntos Exteriores, 95, [s. p.].

8150. NIKOLAEVSKII (Boris Ivanovich). Tainye stranitsy istorii: Lenin i den'gi bol'shevistskoi organizatsii: biografiia Malenkova: Germaniia i russkie rivoliutsionery v gody pervoi mirovoi voiny: protokoly Politbiuro i dokumenty Osobogo otdela NKID SSSR, 1934. Moskva, Izd-vo Gumanitarnoi Literatury, 95, 507 p.

8151. NOUAILHAT (Y.-H.). Le rôle des États-Unis dans la Grande Guerre des Français, 1914–1918. *Relations Internationales*, 95, 83, p. 381-387.

8152. OPPELLAND (Torsten). Reichstag und Aussenpolitik im Ersten Weltkrieg: die deutschen Parteien und die Politik der USA 1914–1918. Dusseldorf, Droste, 95, 367 p.

8153. PACHECO-BORGES (V.). Des Français observant les Brésiliens: la correspondance diplomatique française (1930–1937). *Revue Historique*, 95, 119, 596, p. 307-326.

8154. PAŁUSZYŃSKI (Tomasz). Akcja polsko-łotewska w Łatgalii w styczniu 1920 roku. (L'action polono-lettonienne à Latgalie en janvier 1920). *Wojskowy Przegląd Historyczny*, 95, 40, 3-4, p. 22-36.

8155. PETROV (Metodi). Natsionalno-osvoboditelnoto dvizhenie v Zapadnite pokrainini, 1919–1934. Sofiia, Akademichno izd-vo "Marin Drinov", 95, 198 p. (ill.)

8156. PHILPOTT (William). Britain and France go to war: Anglo-French relations on the Western Front 1914–1918. *War in History*, 95, 2, p. 43-64.

8157. PISAREV (Jurij A.). Rossijsko-černogorskie otnošenija nakanune i vo vremja pervoj mirovoj vojny (1914–1916). (Relations between Russia and Montenegro on the eve and during World War I). *Oteč. Ist.*, 95, 2, p. 146-153.

8158. POLLMANN (Ferenc). A szövetségi együttműködés nehézségei. Osztrák-magyar-bolgár ellentétek Koszovó ügyében 1916 tavaszán. (Les difficultés de la coopération d'alliance. Dissentiments austro-hongrois-bulgares au sujet du Kosovo au printemps de 1916). *Hadtört. kozl.*, 95, 108, 4, p. 13-77.

8159. Powrót Polski na mapę Europy. Sesja naukowa poświęcona 70 rocznicy Traktatu Wersalskiego. (Retour de la Pologne sur la carte de l'Europe. Session scientifique consacrée au 70ᵉ anniversaire du Traité de Versailles). Lublin, les 22–24 mai 1989. Réd. par Czesław BLOCH et Zygmunt ZIELIŃSKI. Lublin, Redakcja Wydawnictw Katolickiego Uniwersytetu Lubelskiego, 95, 425 p. (Eng. summary, Deutsche Zsfassung, phot., fig., carte). (Kat. Uniw. Lub.).\P06

8160. PREDA (Dumitru). La Roumanie et sa guerre pour l'unité nationale: campagne de 1918–1919. Avant-propos de Liviu MANOR. București, Editions encyclopédiques, 95, 460 p., (plates, ill, maps).

8161. PRITZ (Pal). Magyar diplomácia a két háború között. Tanulmányok. (Diplomatie hongroise entre les deux guerres mondiales. Etudes). Budapest, Magyar Történelmi Társ., 95, 356 p.

8162. PROCACCI (Giovanna). La neutralité italienne et l'entrée en guerre. *Guerres Mondiales et conflits contemporains*, 95, 45, 179, p. 83-98.

8163. PUŠKAŠ (A. I.). Vnešnaja politika Vengrii, aprel'1927 goda–fevral'1934 goda. (The Hungarian foreign policy, April of 1927–February of 1934). Moskva, RAN. In-t slavjanovedenija i balkanistiki, 95, 316 p.

8164. RAUTKALLIO (Hannu). Suuri viha. Stalinin suomalaiset uhrit 1930-luvulla. (The major disaster. Stalins's Finnish victims in the 30s). Porvoo, WSOY, 95, 285 p.

8165. ROI (M. L.). From the Stresa front to the Triple Entente: sir Robert Vansittart, the Abyssinian crisis and the containment of Germany. *Diplomacy and Statecraft*, 95, 6, 1, p. 61-90.

8166. ROSTWOROWSKI (Wojciech). Polityka zagraniczna Polski 1918–1939). (La politique étrangère de la Pologne 1918–1939). *Dzieje najnowsze*, 95, 27, 1, p. 107-119.

8167. Sarajeva k Velké válce (Od). (Ab Sarajewo zum grossen Krieg). Tomo 1-2. Praha, Historický ústav Armády ČR, 95, 2 vol., 139 p., 130 p. (photogr.).

8168. SAREEN (Tilak Raj). Secret documents on Singapore mutiny, 1915. New Delhi, Mounto, 95, 866 p.

8169. SCHILD (Georg). Between ideology and Realpolitik: Woodrow Wilson and the Russian Revolution, 1917–1921. Westport, Conn, Greenwood Press, 95, 173 p.

8170. SCHIRMANN (S.). La dénonciation du traité de commerce franco-allemand d'août 1927: étapes et enjeux. *Relations Internationales*, 95, 82, p. 163-173.

8171. SELLERS (Leonard). The Hood battalion: royal naval division: Antwerp, Gallipoli, France 1914–1918. London, L. Cooper, 95, 334 p.

8172. SEVOST'JANOV (Grigorij N.). Sud'ba soglašenija Ruzvel't- Litvinov o dolgakh i kreditakh. 1934–1935 gody. Novye dokumenty. (The destiny of the Roosevelt-Litvinov agreement on debts and credits. 1934–1935. The new documents). *Nov. novejš. Ist.*, 95, 2, p. 115-134. – IDEM. Sud'ba soglašenija Ruzvel't-Litvinov o dolgakh i kreditakh. 1934–1935 gody. Novye dokumenty. Okončanie. (The fate of the Roosevelt-Litvinov agreement on debts and credits. 1934–1935. The new documents. The end). *Nov. novejš. Ist.*, 95, 3, p. 118-144.

8173. SHEREMET (Vitalii Ivanovich). Bosfor: Rossiia i Turtsiia v epokhu pervoi mirovoi voiny: po materialam russkoi voennoi razvedki. Moskva, Tekhnologicheskaia shkola biznesa, 95, 285 p.

8174. SHIMAZU (Naoko). The racial equality proposal at the 1919 Paris Peace Conference: Japanese motivations and Anglo-American responses. [S. l.], [s. n.], 95, 328 p.

8175. SONYEL (Salahi R.). Kurtuluş Savaşi Günlerinde İngiliz İstihbarat Servisi'nin Türkiye'deki Eylemleri (Les Actions du Service Secret de Grand-Bretagne dans la Turquie pendant la Guerre de l'Indépendance Turque). Ankara, Türk Tarih Kurumu Basimevi, 95, XVIII-373 p. (Türk Tarih Kurumu Yayınları. XVI. 70).

8176. SOUTOU (Georges-Henri), CASTELBAJAC (Ghislain de), GASQUET (Sébastien de). Recherches sur la France et le problème des nationalités pendant le Pemière Guerre mondiale, (Pologne, Ukraine, Lithuanie). Paris, Presses de l'Université de Paris-Sorbonne, 95, 239 p.

8177. SPECTOR (Sherman David). Romania at the Paris Peace Conference: a study of the diplomacy of Ioan I. C. Bratianu. Iaşi, Center for Romanian Studies, Romanian Cultural Foundation, 95, 355 p. (port., map.). (Romanian civilization studies).

8178. STAWECKI (Piotr). La fraternité d'armes polono-française (1914–1921). *Revue historique des Armées*, 95, 1, p. 105-116.

8179. STEEL (Nigel), HART (Peter). Defeat at Gallipoli. London, Papermac, 95, XVI-480 p.

8180. STENGERS (Jean). L'entrée en guerre de la Belgique. *Guerres Mondiales et conflits contemporains*, 95, 45, 179, p. 13-34.

8181. STĘPNIAK (Władysław). Potencjalna sojuszniczka czy drugorzędny partner? Grecja w polityce polskiej w latach 1920–1923. (Allié potentiel ou partenaire de second rang? La Grèce dans la politique polonaise des années 1920–1923). *Kwartalnik Historyczny*, 95, 102, 3-4, p. 151-167. [Eng. Summary].

8182. SUTTERLIN (Siegfried H.). Munich in the cobwebs of Berlin, Washington, and Moscow: foreign political tendencies in Bavaria, 1917–1919. New York, P. Lang, 95, XI-231 p.

8183. SZARKA (Laszlo). Szlovak nemzeti fejlodes, magyar nemzetisegi politika, 1867–1918. Pozsony, Kalligram Konyvkiado, 95, 340 p. (Mercurius konyvek).

8184. TARRANT (V. E.). Jutland: the German perspective: a new view of the great battle, 31 May 1916. London, Arms and Armour, 95, 318 p. (ill., plans).

8185. TELO (Antonio José). Le Portugal belligérant pendant la Grande Guerre 1914–1918. Entre l'Espagne et les Açores: le rôle de l'espace atlantique portugais dans la guerre. *Guerres Mondiales et conflits contemporains*, 95, 45, 178, p. 9-24.

8186. TORREY (Glenn E.). The revolutionary Russian Army and Romania, 1917. Pittsburgh, The Center for Russian & East European Studies, University of Pittsburgh, 95, II-94 p. (maps). (The Carl Beck papers in Russian and East European studies).

8187. Trianon and East Central Europe: antecedents and repercussions. Ed. By Bela K. KIRALY and Laszlo VESZPREMY. Boulder, Social Science Monographs, 95, VII-321 p. (maps). (War and society in East Central Europe).

8188. URMINSKÝ (Ivan). Letecké síly československých legií v Rusku 1918–1920. (The Air Force of the Czechoslovak Legions in Russia 1918–1920). *Historie a vojenství*, 95, 44, 4, p. 21-49 (ill.).

8189. VALENTA (Jaroslav). Nezdařený pokus o jednání mezi Čechy a Němci na přelomu let 1918–1919. (The failed attempt at Czecho-German Negotiations, 1918–1919). *Moderní dějiny*, 95, 3, p. 229-240.

8190. VINOGRADOV (Vladen N.). Ešče raz o novykh podkodakh k istorii pervoj mirovoj vojny. (About new approaches to the history of the First World War). *Nov. novejš. Ist.*, 95, 5, p. 62-74.

8191. WARSON (D. R.). Jean Pélissier and the Office Central des Nationalités, 1912–1919. *English Historical Review*, 95, 110, 439, p. 1191-1206.

8192. WIDACKI (Jan). Wywiad litewski w latach trzydziestych XX wieku jako przeciwnik wywiadu Korpusu Ochrony Pogranicza. (Le service des renseignements lithuanien pendant les années trente du XXe siècle en tant qu'adversaire des renseignements du

Corps de Défense des Frontières.). *Wojskowy Przegląd Historyczny*, 95, 40, 3-4, p. 85-94.

8193. WIECK (Jasper). Weg in die "Décadence". Frankreich und die mandschurische Krise, 1931–1933. Bonn, Bouvier, 95, 334 p.

8194. WILSON (Keith). Decision for war, 1914. London, UCL Press, 95, IX-278 p. (maps).

8195. WYSZCZELSKI (Lech). Warszawa 1920. (Varsovie en 1920). Warszawa, Bellona, 95, 293 p. (phot., fig., cartes).

8196. YLIKANGAS (Heikki). Vägen till Tammerfors: striden mellan röda och vita i finska inbördeskriget 1918. (The way to Tammerfors: the struggle between the Red and the White in the Finnish civil war). Stockholm, Atlantis, 95, 503 p.

8197. ZAMFIR (Zorin), BANCIU (Jean). Primul război mondial. (Première Guerre Mondiale). București, Editura Didactică și Pedagogică, 95, 419 p. (maps). (Pagini de istorie).

8198. ZNAMIEROWSKA-RAKK (Elżbieta). The policy of the Second Republic towards the Balkan states. *Acta Poloniae historica*, 95, 72, p. 77-90.

8199. ZURAWSKI VEL GRAJEWSKI (Przemyslaw Piotr). Sprawa ukrainska na konferencji pokojowej w Paryzu w roku 1919. Warszawa, Semper, 95, 128 p. (ill., maps).

Cf. nº 4642

§ 7. Geschichte von 1935–1945. Der Zweite Weltkrieg.

a. Allgemeines.

** 8200. Rzeczpospolita Polska czasu wojmy. Dziennik Ustaw RP i Monitor Polski 1939–1945. (République Polonaise en période de guerre. Journal Officiel de la RP et Moniteur Polonais 1939–1945). Avant propos de Ryszard KOCZOROWSKI et Lech WAŁĘSA. Préface de Adam STRZEMBOSZ. Réd. par Andrzej Krzysztof KUNERT. Warszawa, Kopia, 95, 858 p.

8201. 1938–1948. Les années de tourmente, de Munich à Prague. Dictionnaire critique. Sous la dir. De Jean-Pierre AZEMA et François BEDARIDA. Paris, Flammarion, 95, 1135 p.

8202. AJNENKIEL (Andrzej). Polska w koalicji antyhitlerowskiej. (La Pologne dans la coalition antihitlérienne). *Wojskowy Przegląd Historyczny*, 95, 40, 1-2, p. 1-10.

8203. ALLDRITT (Keith). The greatest of friends: Franklin D. Roosevelt and Winston Churchill, 1941–1945. London, Robert Hale, 95, 224 p.

8204. BALUK (Stefan Starba). Poles on the frontlines of World War II, 1939–1945. Warsaw, ARS Print Production, 95, 638 p. (ill.).

8205. BARROS (James), GREGOR (Richard). Double deception: Stalin, Hitler and the invasion of Russia. DeKalb, Northern Illinois U. P., 95, 307 p.

8206. BARTON (Brian). Northern Ireland in the Second World War. Belfast, Ulster Historical Foundation, 95, VI-164 p.

8207. BARTOŠ (Josef). Oběti nacistické okupace na severozápadní Moravě v letech 1938–1945. (Victims of the Nazi occupation in north-west Moravia, 1938–1945). *Severní Morava*, 95, 69, p. 21-30.

8208. BESSA (Carlos). Le Portugal neutre: la Seconde Guerre mondiale 1939–1945. Le Timor portugais dans la Deuxième Guerre mondiale. Martyres et luttes en territoire neutre. *Guerres Mondiales et conflits contemporains*, 95, 178, p. 43-62.

8209. BEST (Antony). Britain, Japan and Pearl Harbor: avoiding war in East Asia, 1936–41. London, Routledge a. LSE, 95, XII-260 p.

8210. BONA COSTA (Enrica). Dalla guerra alla pace. Italia e Francia 1940–1947. Milano, F. Angeli, 95, 312 p.

8211. BONALUME NETO (Ricardo). A nossa segunda guerra: os brasileiros em combate, 1942–1945. Rio de Janeiro, Expressão e Cultura, 95, 224 p. (ill., maps).

8212. BREUER (William B.). MacArthur's undercover war: spies, saboteurs, guerrillas, and secret missions. New York, J. Wiley and Sons, 95, XII-257 p. (plates, ill., maps).

8213. BURRIN (Philippe). La France à l'heure allemande 1940–1944. Paris, Seuil, 95, 560 p.

8214. BUZATU (Gh). Din istoria secretă a celui de-al doilea război mondial. București, Editura Stiintifică și Enciclopedică, 95, 2 vol., [s. p.]

8215. CAMOES (Filho). O canto do vento. Sao Paulo, Scritta, 95, 115 p. (plates, ill.).

8216. CATALA (Michel). La politique de la France face au problème de Tanger (1939–1940). *Guerres Mondiales et Conflits Contemporains*, 95, 45, 177, p. 67-78.

8217. COOPER (Artemis). Cairo in the war 1939–1945. London, Penguin, 95, XIII-370 p. (ill., maps)

8218. COUDRY (Georges). Le repatriement des ressortissant soviétiques de 1945 à 1947, avatars de la réciprocité. *Guerres Mondiales et Conflits Contemporains*, 95, 45, 178, p. 119-140

8219. CULL (Nicholas John). Selling war: the British propaganda campaign against American "neutrality" in World War II. Oxford a. New York, Oxfor UP, 95, XV-276 p.

8220. DANILOV (Valerij D.). Stalinskaja strategija načala vojny: plany i real'nost'. (Stalin's strategy of the beginning of the war: the plans and the realities, 1941–1945). *Oteč. Ist.*, 95, 3, p. 33-43.

8221. DAWS (Gavan). Prisoners of the Japanese: Pows of World War II in the Pacific – the powerful untold story. London, Robson, 95, 462 p. (ill.)

8222. DI NOLFO (Ennio). John Fowler e George Kennan: sei mesi troppo tardi. *Storia delle Relazioni Internazionali*, 94-95, 10-11, p. 3-24

8223. DOMBRÁDY (Lóránd). A magyar elszakadási törekvések és a hadsereg 1943-ban. (Les efforts du décrochage de la Hongrie et l'armée en 1943). *Századok*, 95, 129, 3, p. 493-534.

8224. Drogi śmierci. Ewakuacja więzień sowieckich z Kresów Wschodnich II Rzeczypospolitej w czerwcu i lipcu 1941. (Les voies de la mort. L'évacuation des prisons soviétiques des confins est de la IIe République de Pologne en juin et juillet 1941). Ed.: Krzysztof POPIŃSKI, Aleksander KOURIN, Aleksander GURJANOW. Warszawa, Karta, 95, 238 p. (Karta. Biała Seria, 1).

8225. DUBICKI (Tadeusz). Polscy uchodźcy w Rumunii 1939–1945. Studia i materiały. (Les refugiés polonais en Roumanie 1939–1945. Etudes et matériaux). Warszawa, Gryf, 95, 330 p. (phot., fig.). [Rés. franç., Deutsche Zsfassung].

8226. DUIGNAN (Peter). World War II in Europe: causes, course, and consequences. Stanford, Hoover Institution on War, Revolution and Peace, Stanford University, 95, 58 p.

8227. DYCZOK (Marta). Ukrainian refugees and displaced people at the end of World War II. Oxford, [s. n.], 95, XIV-336 p. (maps).

8228. False havens: the British Empire and the Holocaust. Ed. by Paul R. BARTROP. Lanham a. London, University Press of America, 95, XIV-293 p.

8229. FERTACZ (Sylwester). A contribution to the establishment and activity of the American Slavs Congress during World War II. *Acta Poloniae historica*, 95, vol. 72, p. 125-138.

8230. FREIRE (Antunes José). Roosevelt, Churchill, Salazar. A luta pelos Açores 1941–1945. Alfragide, Ediclube, 95, XI-163 p.

8231. GEBHART (Jan). Českoslovenští vojenští zpravodajci v Paříži (1939–1940). (The Czechoslovak Military Intelligence Officers in Paris. 1939–1940). *Moderní dějiny*, 95, 3, p. 129-138.

8232. GELLMAN (Irwin F.). Secret Affairs: Franklin Roosevelt, Cordell Hull, and Sumner Welles. Baltimore a. London, The Johns Hopkins U. P., 95, XVII-499 p.

8233. GENESE (Cecil). Nazi Germany and British guilt. Bournemouth, Purbeck, 95, III-260 p.

8234. GOBBI (Romolo). Chi ha provocato la seconda guerra mondiale? Una revisione nel segno della complessità. Padova, F. Muzzio, 95, V-124 p.

8235. GÓRSKI (Grzegorz). Ustrój Polskiego Państwa Podziemnego 1939–1944. Studium historyczno-prawne. (Système politique de l'Etat clandestin polonais 1939–1944. Etudes historique et juridique). Lublin, Kat. Uniw. Lub., 95, 345 p.

8236. GRABOWSKI (Waldemar). Delegatura Rządu Rzeczypospolitej Polskiej na Kraj. (Représentation/délégation en Pologne du Gouvernement en exil). Warszawa, Pax, 95, 293 p.

8237. GREŚ (Bolesław). Deportacja nauczycieli do ZSRR 1939–1941. (La déportation des enseignants en URSS entre 1939 et 1941). Warszawa, Zw. Naucz. Pol. Zarząd Gł., 95, 158 p.

8238. GUALTIERI (Roberto). Togliatti e la politica estera italiana: dalla Resistenza al Trattato di pace, 1943–1947. Prefazione di Giuliano PROCACCI. Roma, Editori riuniti, 95, XIII-281 p. (Gli studi)

8239. HALVORSEN (Terje). Kommunistpartiene og Stalin-Hitler-pakten. Et kritisk oppgjør med tradisjonelle oppfatninger. (The Communist Parties and the Stalin-Hitler pact. A critical view of traditional interpretation). *Historisk Tidsskrift* (Norway), 95, 74, p. 441.

8240. HARPER (John). Visioni dell'ordine internazionale durante la seconda guerra mondiale. *Europa Europe*, 95, 4, 4, p. 23-40.

8241. HARRISON (E. D. R.). Nazi Policies in Occupied Poland. *The Journal of the German History Society*, 95, 13, p. 233-244.

8242. HAUGE (Jens Christian). The liberation of Norway. Oslo, Gyldendal, 95, 201 p.

8243. HENSHALL (Philip). Vengeance: Hitler's nuclear weapon: fact or fiction? Stroud, A. Sutton, 95, 180 p.

8244. Vacat

8245. JENSEN (Tom B). Norsk lokalhistorisk krigshistorie om 2. verdenskrig 1940–1945: en bibliografi. (Norwegian local history concerning the Second World War 1940–1945. A bibliography). Oslo, Universitetsforlaget, 95, 249 p. (UBO skrifter, 26).

8246. JONES (Matthew). Britain, the United States and the Mediterranean war, 1942–1944. London, Macmillan, 95, 288 p.

8247. KARSAI (László). Jewish deportations in Carpatho-Ruthenia in 1944. *Acta univ. Szegediensis, Acta hist.*, 95, 101, p. 37-49.

8248. KEEGAN (John). The battle for history: refighting World War II. London, Pimlico, 95, 128 p.

8249. KITCHEN (Martin). Nazy Germany at War. London a. New York, Longman, 95, 329 p.

8250. KLINKHAMMER (Lutz). L'amministrazione tedesca di Bologna e il crollo della linea Gotica. *In*: Bologna in guerra [Cf. n° 8400], p. 133-155.

8251. KOŠKIN (Anatolij A.). Vstuplenie SSSR v vojnu s Japoniej v 195 godu. (The USSR's entry into the war against Japan in 1945). *Nov. novejš. Ist.*, 95, 4, p. 12-27.

8252. KRASUSKI (Wojciech). Tajna Organizacja Nauczycielska – współpraca organizacyjna, oświatowa i polityczna w ramacg Podziemnego Państwa Polskiego. (Organisation Secrète des Enseignants – coopération au niveau de l'organisation et de l'instruction dans le cadre de l'Etat Clandestin Polonais). *Przegląd Historyczno-Oświatowy*, 95, 38, 1-2, p. 61-74.

8253. KYNIN (Georgij P.). Germanskij vopros vo vzaimootnošenijakh SSSR, SŠA i Velikobritanii 1941–1943 godov. Obzor dokumentov. (The German issue in the relations between the USSR, the USA and Great Britain in 1941-1943. Review of the documents). *Nov. novejš. Ist.*, 95, 1, p. 91-113. – IDEM. Germanskij vopros vo vzaimootnošenijakh SSSR, SŠA i Velikobritanii 1944–1945 godov. (The German question in the relations between the USSR, the USA and Great Britain in 1944-1945). *Nov. novejš. Ist.*, 95, 4, p. 1045-132.

8254. LA GORCE (Paul-Marie de). 1939–45, une guerre inconnue. Paris, Flammarion, 95, 639 p. (ill.)

8255. LACAZE (Yvon). France and Munich: a study of decision making in international affairs. Boulder a. New York, East European Monographs, 95, 366 p. – EADEM. La France et le processus décisionnel de Munich. *Relations Internationales*, 95, 84, p. 465-484.

8256. LAGROU (Pieter). US politics of stabilization in liberated Europe. The view from the American Embassy in Brussels, 1944–46. *European History Quarterly*, 95, 25, p. 209-246.

8257. LAGZI (István). Number of Poles having escaped to the territory of Hungary during the Second World War. *Acta univ. Szegediensis, Acta hist.*, 95, 101, p. 11-25.

8258. LANEE (Ann), EMPERLEY (Howard). The rise and fall of the grand alliance 1941–45. London, Macmillan, 95, 264 p.

8259. LEGRO (Jeffrey W.). Cooperation under fire: Anglo-German restraint during World War II. Ithaca, London, Cornell U. P., 95, XII-255 p.

8260. LEITZ (Christian). Nazy Germany's struggle for Spanish wolfram during the Second World War. *European History Quarterly*, 95, 25, p. 71-92.

8261. LUCCHESI (Maria Luisa). "La politique des mains libres": il Belgio e la Francia tra il marzo 1936 e il 10 maggio 1940. *Storia delle Relazioni Internazionali*, 94-95, 10-11, p. 121-148.

8262. ŁUCZAK (Czesław). Od pierwszej do ostatniej godziny drugiej wojny światowej. Dzieje Polski i Polaków. (De la première jusqu'à la dernière heure de la deuxième guerre mondiale. Histoire de la Pologne et des Polonais). Poznań, Pracownia Serwisu Oprogramowania, 95, 532 p. (phot., fig., cartes).

8263. MACKSEY (Kenneth). The Hitler options: alternate decisions of World War II. London, Greenhill Books, 95, 224 p.

8264. MAGUIRE (Gloria Elizabeth). Anglo-american policy towards the free French. New York, St Martin's Press, 95, X-210 p. – EADEM. "Notre mal de tête commun": Churchill, Roosevelt, et de Gaulle, *Revue d'histoire moderne et contemporaine*, 95, 42, p. 593-608.

8265. MARSHALL (Jonathan). To have and have not: Southeast Asian raw materials and the origins of the Pacific War. Berkeley, University of California Press, 95, XVI-280 p.

8266. MEL'TJUKHOV (Mikhail I.). Ideologičeskie dokumenty maja–ijunja 1941 goda o sobytijakh vtoroj mirovoj vojny. (World War II in the ideological documents of May–June 1941). *Oteč. Ist.*, 95, 2, p. 70-85.

8267. MERCIER (Fabienne). Vichy face à Chiang Kai-shek. Paris, L'Harmattan, 95, 335 p. (Histoire Diplomatique).

8268. MINCHEV (Dimitur). Bulgarskite aktsionni komiteti v Makedoniia, 1941. Sofiia, Izd-vo na Ministerstvoto na otbranata 'Sv. Georgi Pobedonosets', 95, 174 p. (ill.).

8269. Národ se ubránil. 1939–1945. (The nation defended itself, 1939–1945). Praha, Sdružení MAC, 95, 109 p. (ill.). Suppl. Národní Osvobození.

8270. NĚMEČEK (Jan). Československý zahraniční odboj a sovětsko-finská válka 1939–1940. (The Czechoslovak resistance and the Soviet-Finnish War 1939–1940). *Moderní dějiny*, 95, 3, p. 139-158.

8271. NEVAKIVI (Jukko). Zdanov Suomessa: miksi meitä ei neuvostoliittolaisettu? (Zhdanov in Finland. Why we were not sovietisized?). Helsinki, Otava, 1995, 317 p.

8272. Nordmenn i fangenskap 1940–1945. Alfabetisk register. Ed. Kristian OTTOSEN. Oslo, Universitetsforlaget, 95, 692 p. [Norwegian prisoners in German as well as in French, Japanese and Soviet camps].

8273. Norsk krigsleksikon 1940–45. (The Norwegian war lexicon).Ed. Hans Fredrik DAHL. Oslo, Cappelen, 95, 468 p.

8274. ORSKI (Marek). Des Français au camp de concentration de Stuthof. Gdańsk, Marpress, 95, 90 p. (phot., fig.). (Grupy Państwowo-Narodościowe w Obozie koncentracyjnym Stuthof).

8275. OTTOSEN (Kristian). Historien om nordmenn i tysk fangenskap 1940–1945. (The history about Norwegians in German captivity 1940–1945). Oslo, Aschehoug, 95, 5 vol., [s. p.] (ill.).

8276. PANECKI (Tadeusz). Wysiłek zbrojny Polski w II wojnie światowej. (L'effort armé de la Pologne pendant la IIe guerre mondiale. *Wojskowy Przegląd Historyczny*, 95, 40, 1-2, p. 11-18.

8277. PARMAR (Inderjeet). Special interests, the state and the Anglo-American alliance 1939–1945. London, Frank Cass, 95, 200 p.

8278. PASÁK (Tomáš), DRÁPALA (Milan). Čeští vysokoškolští studenti v Sachsenhausenu a postoj protektorátní správy. (Czech University students in Sachsenhausen and the attitude of the protectorate administration). *Soudobé dějiny*, 95, 2, 4, p. 495-513.

8279. PASÁK (Tomáš). Problémy české kolaborace. (Problems of Czech collaboration). *In*: Dějiny a paměť - odboj a kolaborace za druhé světové války [Cf. n° 8401], p. 25-34.

8280. PASQUALINI (Maria Gabriella). Gli equilibri nel levante. La crisi di Alessandretta (1936–1939). Palermo, Edizioni Associate, 95, 340 p.

8281. PAVLOV (Anatolij G.). Sovetskaja voennaja razvedka nakanune Velikoi Otečestvennoj vojny. (The Soviet intelligence on the eve of the Great Patriotic War). *Nov. novejš. Ist.*, 95,1, p. 49-60. – IDEM. Voennaja razvedka SSSR v 19941–1945 godakh. (The Soviet intelligence in 1941–1945), *Nov. novejš. Ist.*, 95, 2, p. 28-38.

8282. Pearl Harbor revisited. Ed. by Robert W. LOVE. Basingstoke, Macmillan, 95, VIII-200 p.

8283. PECKA (Jindřich). Maďarští vojáci a české povstání 1945. (Hungarian troops and the Czech uprising of 1945). *Soudobé dějiny*, 95, 2, 4, p. 551-562. – IDEM. Váleční zajatci na území Protektorátu Čechy a Morava. (Prisoners of war in the Protectorate of Bohemia and Moravia, 1939–45). Praha, Ústav pro soudobé dějiny AV ČR, 95, 325 p., (bibl.). (Studie – materiály – dokumenty, 5).

8284. PETERSON (Edward Norman). An analytical history of World War II. New York, P. Lang, 95, 2 Vol., X-858 p. (American university studies).

8285. PIOTROWSKI (Tadeusz M.). Polish-Ukrainian relations during World War II: ethnic cleansing in Volhynia and Eastern Galicia. Toronto, Adam Mickiewicz Foundation, 95, 55 p. (map).

8286. PIPER (Franciszek). Arbeitseinsatz der Häftlinge aus dem KL Auschwitz. Oświęcim, Verlag Staatliches Museum, 95, 457 p. (phot., cartes).

8287. POLIT (Jakub). Japonia wobec paktu Ribbentrop-Mołotow. (Le Japon face au pacte Ribbentrop-Molotov). *Studia Historyczne*, 95, 38, 3, p. 397-411. [Eng. Summary].

8288. POLVINEN (Tuomo). J. K. Paasikivi: valtiomiehen elämäntyö. Vol. 3. 1939–1944. (J. K. Paasikivi: the life work of a statsman. Vol. 3. 1939–1944). Porvoo, WSOY, 95, VII-496 p.

8289. PONS (Silvio). Stalin e la guerra inevitabile, 1936–1941. Torino, Einaudi, 95, XII-342 p. (Biblioteca di cultura storica)

8290. Praca przymusowa Polaków w Trzeciej Rzeszy w latach 1939–1945. Polsko-niemieckie spotkania w Jankowicach koło Poznania w dniach 12–19 września 1993 roku. (Travaux forcés des polonais en IIIe Reich pendant les années 1939–1945. Entretiens polono-allemand à Jankowice près de Poznań, le 12–19 septembre 1993). Réd. par Stanisław NAWROCKI. Poznań, 95, 64 p. (Stow. Polaków Poszkodowanych przez Trzecią Rzeszę. Oddz. Wojew. w Poznaniu).

8291. RAACK (Richard C.). Stalin's drive to the West, 1938–1945: the origins of the Cold War. Stanford, Stanford U. P., 95, VIII-265 p.

8292. RAJSKIJ (Nikolaj S.). Vtoraja mirovaja vojna i sud'by pol'skikh voennoplennykh. (World War II and destinies of the Polish prisoners of war). *Oteč. Ist.*, 95, 4, p. 136-144.

8293. REAU (E. du). De la Décadence à l'Abîme: les Français devant la perspective d'un nouveau conflit mondial 1938–1939. *Relations Internationales*, 95, 83, p. 347-353.

8294. REYNOLDS (David). Rich relations: the American occupation of Britain, 1942-1945. London a. New York, HarperCollins a. Random House, 95, XXX-555 p.

8295. Rise and fall of the Grand Alliance (The), 1941–45. Ed. by Ann LANE and Howard TEMPERLEY. Basingstoke, Macmillan Press; New York, St. Martin's Press, 95, XVI-264 p. (ill.).

8296. ROBERTS (Geoffrey). Soviet policy and the Baltic States, 1939–40: a reappraisal. *Diplomacy and Statecraft*, 95, 6, 3, p. 672-700. – IDEM. The Soviet Union and the origins of the Second World War. Russo-German relations and the road to War, 1933–1941. London, Macmillan, 95, 192 p.

8297. ROSSI (Mario). La mission du colonel Passy aux Etas-Unis: inquiétudes et suspicions américaines (décembre 1944). *Guerres Mondiales et Conflits Contemporains*, 95, 45, 178, p. 115-118

8298. Ruch oporu wobec Trzeciej Rzeszy. (La Résistance face au IIIe Reich). Gdańsk, 95, 103 p. (Deutsche Zsfassung). (Uniw, Gdański, Rozpr. i Monografie).

8299. RŽEŠEVSKIJ (Oleg Aleksandrovich). Vtoraia mirovaia voina: aktual'nye problemy. Moskva, Nauka, 95, 367 p.

8300. SARIUSZ-SKĄPSKA (Izabela). Polscy świadkowie Gułagu. Literatura łagrowa 1939–1989. (Témoins polonais du Goulag. Littérature des camps soviétiques 1939–1989). Kraków, Universitas, 95, 358 p. (Rés. franç., Eng. Summary).

8301. SAWICKI (Tadeusz). Wpływ wojny z Japonią na politykę i strategię koalicji antyhitlerowskiej w Europie. (L'influence de la guerre avec le Japon sur la politique et la stratégie de la coalition antihitlérienne en Europe). *Wojskowy Przegląd Historyczny*, 95, 40, 3-4, p. 74-84.

8302. SCHREIBER (Gerhard), STEGMANN (Bernd), VOWEL (Detlef). Germany and the Second World War.

Volume III. The Mediterranean, South-East Europe, and North Africa 1939–1941. Oxford, Clarendon, 95, 822 p.

8303. SEMIRJAGA (Mikhaik I.). Sud'ba sovetskikh voennoplennykh. (The fates of the Soviet prisoners of war. 1941–1945). *Vopr. Ist.*, 95, 4, p. 19-33.

8304. SLÁDEK (Oldřich). Výsadky ze Sovětského svazu na Slovensko a do protektorátu v roce 1941. (Paratroops from the Soviet Union to Slovakia and the Protectorate, 1941). *Soudobé dějiny*, 95, 2, 4, p. 514-529.

8305. SLAVINSKIJ (Boris Nikolaevich). Pakt o nejatralitete meždu SSSR i Japoniej: diplomatičeskaja istoria, 1941–1945 gody. (The Soviet-Japanese neutrality treaty: diplomatic history, 1941–1945). Moskva, TOO "Novina", 95, 335 p.

8306. STEINBERG (Jonathan). The Third Reich reflected: German civil administration in the occupied Soviet Union, 1941–1944. *English Historical Review*, 95, 110, 437, p. 620-649.

8307. STONE (Glyn). Britain, France and Franco's Spain in the aftermath of the Spanish civil war. *Diplomacy and Statecraft*, 95, 6, 2, 373-407.

8308. STUDNICKI (Wladyslaw). Tragiczne manowce: proby przeciwdzialnia katastrofom narodowym, 1939–1945. Gdansk, Pomorska oficyna wydawniczo-reklamowa "MARIOL", 95, 216 p.

8309. SZAROTA (Tomasz). Życie codzienne w stolicach okupowanej Europy. Szkice historyczne, kronika wydarzeń. (Vie quotidienne dans les capitales européennes sous l'occupation. Esquisses historiques, chronique d'évenements). Warszawa, Państw. Inst. Wydawn., 95, 286 p. (phot.).

8310. THOMAS (Martin). The Anglo-French divorce over West Africa and the limitations of strategic planning, June–December 1940. *Diplomacy and Statecraft*, 95, 6, 1, p. 252-278.

8311. TORTZEN (Christian). Krigssejlerne: traek af dansk skibsfarts historie 1939–1945. (The story of Danish navigation during the war). Valby, Forlaget Pantheon, 95, 288 p.

8312. TSOKHAS (Kosmas). Anglo-Australian relations and the origins of the Pacific War. *History*, 95, 80, p. 400-420.

8313. TUSELL (Javier). Franco, España y la II Guerra Mundial: Entre el Eje y la neutralidad. Madrid, Temas de Hoy, 95, 709 p.

8314. Vårstormar: 1944 – krigsslutet skönjes. Ed. by Bo HULDT a. Klaus-Richard BÖHME. Stockholm, Probus, 95, 277 p. [Sweden and the World War in 1944].

8315. VERESS (Laura-Louise). Clear the line: Hungary's struggle to leave the Axis during the Second World War. Cleveland, Ohio, Prospero Publications, 95, XXII-404 p. (maps).

8316. Vtoraja mirovaja vojna: Aktual'nye problemy. (The Second World War: The actual problems). Otv. red. O. A. RŽEŠEVSKIJ. Moskva, Nauka, RAN, In-t vseobščej istorii, Associacija istorikov vtoroj mirovoj vojny, 95, 368 p.

8317. WECHSELMANN (Maj). De bruna förbindelserna. Ed. by Stefan LINDGREN. Stockholm, Ordfront, 95, 307 p. [The brown (i.e. nazist) connections of the Swedish military security service during the war years].

8318. WEINBERG (Gerhard Ludwig). Germany, Hitler, and World War II: essays in modern Germany and world history. Cambridge, New York a. Cambridge U. P., 95, VI-347 p.

8319. Wojsko Polskie w II wojnie Światowej. (Armée Polonaise dans la II Guerre Mondiale). Réd. Edward KOSPATH-PAWŁOWSKI. Warszawa, Bellona, 95, 325 p. (phot., fig., cartes).

8320. WORTH (Roland H.). No choice but war: the United States embargo against Japan and the eruption of war in the Pacific. Jefferson a. London, McFarland & Co, 95, XI-236 p.

8321. ŻERKO (Stanisław). Wymarzone przymierze Hitlera. Wielka Brytania w narodowosocjalistycznych koncepcjach i w polityce III Rzeszy do 1939 r. (L'alliance rêvée d'Hitler. La Grande Bretagne dans les conceptions national-socialistes et la politique du IIIe Reich jusqu'en 1939). Poznań, Inst. Zach., 95 440 p. (Studium Niemcoznawcze, 68). [Deutsche Zsfassung].

Cf. n° 1140

b. Diplomatie. Wirtschaft.

** 8322. Dokumenty vnešnej politiki, 1940–22 ijunja 1941. (Documents of the Soviet foreign policy, 1940–22 June 1941). T. 23. Kn. 1. 1 janvaria–31 oktjabrja 1940 goda. (Book one. January–October 1940). Redkol. G. É. MAMEDOV (predsedatel') i drugi. Ministerstvo inostrannykh del Rossijskoj Federacii. Moskva: Meždunarodyne otnošenija, 95, 746 p.

8323. AALDERS (Gerard), WIEBES (Cees). The art of cloaking ownership: the secret collaboration and protection of the German war industry by the neutrals: the case of Sweden. Amsterdam, Amsterdam U. P., Netherlands State Institute for War Documentation, 95, VII-210 p.

8324. Al Doilea Război Mondial. Transilvania şi aranjamentele europene (1940–1944). (World War II. Transylvania and European Agreements, 1940–1944). Ediţie, studiu introductiv, note: Dr. Vasile PUŞCAŞ. Cluj-Napoca, Centrul de Studii Transilvane, Fundaţia Culturală Română, 95, LXXV-163 p.

8325. ANDREINI (Ginevra). La "belle et bonne alliance": i rapporti franco-sovietici (1941–1945). *Storia delle Relazioni Internazionali*, 94-95, 10-11, p. 25-62

7. GESCHICHTE VON 1935–1945. DER ZWEITE WELTKRIEG

8326. ANTOHE (Ion). Răstigniri in România dupa Ialta. Bucureşti, Editura Albatros, 95, 503 p.

8327. BEZYMENSKIJ (Lev. A.). Vizit V. M. Molotova v Berlin v nojambre 1940 goda. V svete novykh dokumentov. (V. M. Molotov's visit to Berlin in November 1940. In the light of the new documents). *Nov. novejš. Ist.*, 95, 6, p. 121-143.

8328. BOYER DE SAINTE-SUZANNE (Raymond de). Dernière heures au Quai d'Orsay (16 mai–20 mai 1940). *Europe*, 95, 73, 799-800, p. 52-58.

8329. BREITMAN (Richard). A deal with the Nazi dictatorship? Himmler's alleged peace emissaries in Autumn 1943. *Journal of Contemporary History*, 95, 30, 3, p. 411-430.

8330. COUDRY (Georges). Le regroupement des ressortissantes soviétiques en France à la fin de la deuxième guerre mondiale: l'accord de Moscou du 29 juin 1945. *Guerres Mondiales et Conflits Contemporains*, 95, 45, 177, p. 105-130.

8331. CURAMI (Andrea). Otto settembre 1943. Documenti a margine dell'armistizio. *Italia Contemporanea*, 95, 201, p. 701-713.

8332. Czechoslovak Negotiations of the Establishment of Confederation and Aliance, 1939–1944. Czechoslovak diplomatic documents. Ed. by Ivan ŠŤOVÍČEK and Jaroslav VALENTA. Praha, Karolinum, 95, 449 p. (bibl.).

8333. DOCKRILL (Michael). The Foreign Office, dr. Eduard Benes and the Czechoslovak government-in-exile 1939–41. *Diplomacy and Statecraft*, 95, 6, 3, p. 701-718.

8334. ERIN (Mikhail E.), BARANOVA (Natalija V.). Nemcy v sovetskom plenu. (Po archivnym materialam Jaroslavskoj oblasti). (The Germans in the Soviet captivity. After archival materials of the Jaroslavl' oblast'). *Oteč. Ist.*, 95, 6, p. 133-142.

8335. ERIN (Mikhail E.). Sovetskie voennoplennye v Germanii v gody vtoroj mirovoj vojny. (The Soviet prisoners-of-war in Germany during the Second World War). *Vopr. Ist.*, 95, 11-12, p. 140-151.

8336. FORTMANN (Michael), [et al.]. Public diplomacy and dirty tricks: two faces of United States "informed penetration" of Latin American on the eve of World War II. *Diplomacy and Statecraft*, 95, 6, 2, p. 536-577.

8337. GUDERZO (Massimiliano). Madrid e l'arte della diplomazia. L'incognita spagnola nella seconda guerra mondiale. Firenze, Manent, 95, 538 p.

8338. IORDAN (Constantin). France and the guarantee to Romania, April 1939. *Intelligence and national Security*, 95, 10, 2, p. 242-272.

8339. KOCHAVI (Arieh J.). Britain, United States and Irish Neutrality, 1944–45. *European History Quarterly*, 95, 25, p. 93-116.

8340. LOMBARDI (Lapo). La Santa Sede e il nuovo confine sovietico-polacco nel 1945. *Storia delle Relazioni Internazionali*, 94-95, 10-11, p. 149-162.

8341. LUND (Joachim). Den danske østindsats 1941–43. Østrumudvalget i den politiske og økonomiske kollaboration. (The Danish contribution to the exploitation of the East 1941–43. Eastern Territory Committee and the collaboration [with Nazi Germany], political and economic). *Historisk Tidskrift* (Denmark), 95, 95, 1, p. 35-72.

8342. MACKENZIE (S. P.). The shackling crisis: a case-study in the dynamics of prisoner-of-war diplomacy in the Second World War. *The International History Review*, 95, 17, p. 78-98.

8343. MERGLEN (Général). Quelques réflexions historiques sur l'armistice franco-germano-italien de juin 1940. *Guerres Mondiales et Conflits Contemporains*, 95, 45, 177, p. 79-94.

8344. MOORE (Bob). British economic warfare and relations with the neutral Netherlands during the "Phoney War", September 1939 – May 1940. *War & Society*, 95, 13, p. 65-89.

8345. Nampō Kyōei-ken: Senji-Nihon no Tōnan-Ajia Keizai Shihai. (Greater east-Asia co-prosperitym sphere: Japan's Economic domination over south-east Asia in World War II) Ed. by Yasuyuki HIKITA. Tokyo, Taga Shuppan, 95, 857 p.

8346. NEAGOE (Sever). Teritoriul şi frontierele în istoria românilor. Bucureşti, Editura ministerului de interne, 95, 237 p. (maps, ill.). (Colecţia Valorile Patriei).

8347. PODLASEK (Maria). Wypedzenie Niemcow z terenow na wschod od Odry i Nysy Luzyckiej: relacje swiadkow. Warszawa, Wydawn. Polsko-Niemieckie, 95, 202 p. (4 leaves of plates).

8348. PRAZMOWSKA (Anita). Britain and Poland 1939–1943: the betrayed ally. Cambridge, Cambridge U. P., 95, 233 p.

8349. RÉTI (György). Magyar-olasz kapcsolatok az első Anschluss-kísérlettől az olasz német kiegyezés kezdetéig, 1934. április–1936. március. (Relations hungaro-italiennes de la première tentative d'Anschluss jusqu'aux débuts du compromis italo-allemand). *Múltunk*, 95, 40, 2, p. 67-96.

8350. SAJTI (Enikő). A. Hungarian-Croatian interstate relations, 1941–1944. *Acta univ. Szegediensis, Acta hist.*, 95, 101, p. 27-36.

8351. SAKHAROV (Andrej N.). Vojna i sovetskaja diplomatija: 1939–1945 gody. (The war and the Soviet diplomacy: 1939–1945). *Vopr. Ist.*, 95, 7, p. 26-45.

8352. SCHILD (Georg). Bretton Woods and Dumbarton Oaks: american economic and political postwar planning in the summer of 1944. New York, St Martin's Press, 95, XIII-254 p.

8353. ŞIŞCANU (Ion). Unionea Sovietică-România. 1940. Tratative în cadrul comisiilor mixte. (The Soviet Union-Romania. 1940. Negotiations within the Joint Commission). Chişinău, Editura Arc, 95, 270 p.

8354. STEINER (Herbert). Gestorben für Österreich: [Widerstand gegen Hitler: eine Dokumentation]. Wien, Locker, 95, 246 p.

8355. SZOKOLAY (Katalin). A lengyel-cseh tárgyalások és a magyarkérdés, 1939–1942. (Les entretiens polo-tchèques et la question hongroise). *Valóság*, 95, 38, 10, p. 42-57.

8356. TANAKA (Takashi). Les relations franco-japanaises de 1931 à 1941. *Guerres Mondiales et Conflits Contemporains*, 95, 45, 178, p. 91-102.

8357. URIARTE (Carmen). Las relaciónes hispano-turcas durante la guerra civil española, 1936–1939: el ocaso de la República Española desde la óptica de la República Turca. Madrid, Ministerio de Asuntos Exteriores, 95, XVII-207 p.

c. Kriegshandlungen.

8358. ASTOR (Gerald). Operation Iceberg: the invasion and conquest of Okinawa in World War II. New York, Donald I. Fine, 95, XII-480 p. (ill., maps).

8359. AXWORTHY (Mark). Third axis, fourth ally: Romanian armed forces in the European war, 1941–1945. London, Arms and Armour, 95, 368 p. (ill., maps).

8360. BAYROU (Maurice). Le B.M.2 sur le front de l'Atlantique. *Revue de la France libre*, 95, 289, p. 9-13.

8361. BOISSIEU (Alain de). La campagne de Normandie. *Espoir. Revue de l'Institut Charles de Gaulle*, 95, 100, p. 13-24.

8362. BOYD (Carl). The Japanese submarine force and World War II. Shrewsbury, Airlife, 95, XIV-272 p. (ill., plants, ports).

8363. CAÏTUCOLI (Georges). Hollande, 7 avril 1945, un stick S.A.S. en opérations. *Revue de la France libre*, 95, 289, p. 15-18. – IDEM. Les S.A.S et le débarquement. *Espoir. Revue de l'Institut Charles de Gaulle*, 95, 100, p. 48-58.

8364. CHESTERTON (Neville). Crete was my Waterloo: a true eyewitness account of the sinking of the Lancastria, the battle of Crete and P. O. W. Experiences 1940–45. London, Janus, 95, 11 p.

8365. CONNAUGHTON (R. M.), PIMLOTT (John), ANDERSON (Duncan). The battle for Manila. London, Bloomsbury, 95, 224 p. (ill., maps).

8366. FRIESER (Karl-Heinz). Blitzkrieglegende. Der Westfeldzug 1940. München, Oldenbourg, 95, XXII-473 p. (Operationen des zweiten Weltkrieges, 2).

8367. HARRIS (Sir Arthur). Despatch on war operations: 23rd February, 1942 to 8th May, 1945. London, Frank Cass, 95, 211 p.

8368. HUTTUNEN (Pertti). Linnoittaminen Suomussalmella ennen talvisotaa vuonna 1939 ja talvisodan aikana vuonna 1940. (Construction of defensive positions in Suomussalmi before and during the Winter War, in 1939–1940). *Studia historica Septentrionalia*, 95, 26, p. 45-65 (Eng. summary).

8369. JACKSON (Robert). Churchill's moat: the Channel war 1939–1945. Shrewsbury, Airlife, 95, 159 p. (ill.)

8370. KARLICKÝ (Vladimír). Byla chemická válka v září 1938 reálná?. Připravenost Československa na chemickou válku v roce 1938. (Was chemical warfare in September 1938 a real possibility? The preparedness of Czechoslovakia for chemical war in 1938). *Historie a vojenství*, 95, 44, 5, p. 38-78.

8371. KASPI (André). La libération de la France, juin 1944–janvier 1946. Paris, Perrin, 95, 562 p.

8372. KULOMAA (Jukka). Käpykaartiin? 1941–1944: sotilaskarkuruus Suomen armeijassa jatkosodan aikana. (Desertation in the Finnish army during the Continuation War of 1941–1944.) Helsinki, Painatuskeskus, 95, 510 p. (Eng. summary, ill.,maps).

8373. LEVINE (Alan J.). The Pacific War: Japan versus the allies. Westport a. London, Praeger, 95, IX-200 p.

8374. MARCHESI (Luigi), SOGNO (Edgardo), MILAN (Carlo). Per la libertà: il contributo militare italiano al servizio informazioni alleato, 8 settembre 1943–25 aprile 1945. Milano, Mursia, 95, 205 p. (Testimonianze fra cronaca e storia).

8375. MARION (Jacques). Neuf mois après "Overlord", le dernier débarquement de Normandie. *Etudes normandes*, 95, 44, 2, p. 87-96

8376. MARTIN (Jean-Pierre). Contraintes et enjeux politiques de l'offensive du détachement d'armée des Alpes au printemps 1945. *Revue historique des Armeés*, 95, 2, p. 3-15.

8377. MICHELET (Louis-Christian). La contribution militaire française à l'effort de guerre allié (1941–1945). *Guerres Mondiales et conflits contemporains*, 95, 45, 177, p. 7-20.

8378. MINNITI (Fortunato). Il nemico vero. Gli obiettivi dei piani di operazione contro la Gran Bretagna nel contesto etiopico (maggio 1935–maggio 1936). *Storia contemporanea*, 26, p. 575-602.

8379. NEILLANDS (Robin). The conquest of the Reich: from D-Day to VE day: a soldiers' history. London, Weidenfeld & Nicolson, 95, XVIII-301 p. (plates).

8380. OVERY (Richard). Why the allies won. London, Cape, 95, 396 p.

8381. PECKA (Jindřich). Na demarkační čáře. Americká armáda v Čechách v roce 1945. (On the demarcation line: the US Army in Bohemia, 1945). Praha, Ústav pro soudobé dějiny AV ČR, 95, 185 p. (Studie materiály – dokumenty, 6).

8382. PERRAS (Galen Roger). "Our position in the Far East would be stronger without the unsatisfactory commitment": Britain and the reinforcement of Hong Kong, 1941. *Canadian Journal of History*, 95, 30, 2, p. 231-259.

8383. ROCHAT (Giorgio). Una ricerca impossibile. Le perdite italiane nella seconda guerra mondiale. *Italia Contemporanea*, 95, 201, p. 687-700.

8384. Vacat.

8385. ROTARU (Jipa). Armata româna în al doilea război mondial. (Romanian army in the Second World War). Bucureşti, Editura Meridiane, 95, 213 p. (ill., maps).

8386. RŽEŠEVSKIJ (Oleg A.). Vzjat' Berlin! Novye dokumenty. (Capture Berlin! New documents). *Nov. novejš. Ist.*, 95, 4, p. 158-167.

8387. SAINT-HILLIER (Bernard). La I^e DFL durant la campagne d'Italie et le débarquement en Provence. *Espoir. Revue de l'Institut Charles de Gaulle*, 95, 100, p. 30-47

8388. SANDER (Rudolf). Válečná československá armáda v září roku 1938. (The Czechoslovak Army on a war footing in September 1938). *Historie a vojenství*, 95, 44, 6, p. 23-80.

8389. SENJAVSKAJA (Elena S.). Čelovek na vojne: opyt istoriko-psikhologičeskoj kharakteristiki rossijskogo kombatanta. (Man and the war: an historical and psychological study of the Russian combatant, 1941–1945). *Oteč. Ist.*, 95, 3, p. 7-15.

8390. SHIRREFF (David). Bare feet and bandoliers: Wingate, Sandford, the Patriots and the part they played in the liberation of Ethiopia. London, Radcliffe, 95, XXVVII-337 p. (ill., maps).

8391. SIMON (Jean). Le rôle des armées françaises dans la liberation du territoire national. *Espoir. Revue de l'Institut Charles de Gaulle*, 95, 100, p. 84-94.

8392. SMURTHWAITE (David). The Pacific War atlas, 1941–1945. London, HMSO, 95, 143 p.

8393. SZABO (Péter). Don-kanyar. A Magyar Királyi 2. Honvéd Hadsereg története, 1942–1943. (L'embouchure du Don. Histoire de la 2e Armée hongroise royale des Honvéd, 1942–1943). Budapest, Zrínyi, 95, 309 p.

8394. UNGVÁRY (Krisztián). A budapesti csata utolsó felvonása. A német-magyar védősereg kitörési kísérlete. (Le dernier acte de la bataille de Budapest. La tentative de sortie de l'armée défensive germano-hongroise). *Századok*, 95, 129, 6, p. 1275-1304.

8395. VERGINELLA (Marta), VOLK (Alessandro), COLJA (Katja). Ljudje v vojni: druga svetovna vojna v Trstu in na Primorskem. (People in war: the Second World War in Trieste and in the Primorska region). Koper, Zgodovinsko društvo za južno Primorsko, 95, 178 p. (ill.). (Knjižnica Annales, 9).

d. Widerstand.

* 8396. BØKER om Norges frihetskrig 1940–1945: en bibliografi. (Books concerning the Norwegian War of Independence during 1940–1945. A bibliography). Ed. by Hans LUIHN. Oslo, Grøndahl Dreyer: Frigjøringskomitéen, 95, 157 p. (ill.).

** 8397. Österreicher im Exil 1938–1945. Eine Dokumentation. USA 1938–1945. Bde 1–2. Einleitung, Auswahl und Bearb. von Peter EPPEL. Hrsg. Dokumentationsarchiv des Österreichischen Widerstands. Wien, Österr. Bundesvlg, Dokumentationsarchiv des Österr. Widerstands, 95, XII-547 p., 787 p. (ill.).

8398. ANDRAE (Friedrich). Auch gegen Frauen und Kinder: der Krieg der deutschen Wehrmacht gegen die Zivilbevölkerung in Italien 1943–1945. München, Piper, 95, 311 p.

8399. BERTRAM (Barbara). French resistance in Sussex. Pulborough, Barnworks, 95, XVI-76 p.

8400. Bologna in guerra. A cura di B. DALLA CASA e A. PRETI. Milano, Angeli, 95, 505 p. (Collana dell'Istituto nazionale per la storia del movimento di liberazione in Italia, 30). [Cf. n° <scelta> 8250.]

8401. Dějiny a paměť - odboj a kolaborace za druhé světové války. (History and memory. Resistance and collaboration during World War II). Ed. by Françoise MAYER [et al.]. Praha, Francouzský ústav pro výzkum ve společenských vědách, 95, 94 p. (Cahiers du CeFReS, 6/1995). [Cf. n^{os} <choice> 8279, 8407.]

8402. DOMORAD (Konstantin Il'ich). Razvedka i kontrrazvedka v partizanskom dvizhenii Belorussii 1941–1944 gg. Minsk, Navuka i tekhnika, 95, 254 p.

8403. GENTILE (Carlo). Settembre 1943. Documenti sull'attività della divisione «Leibstandarte-SS-Adolf Hitler» in Piemonte. *Il presente e la storia. Rivista dell'Istituto storico della resistenza in Cuneo e Provincia*, 95, 47, p. 75-130.

8404. GRGIČ (Silvo). Zločini okupatorjevih sodelavcev: monografija v treh knjigah. Knj. 1. Izven boja pobiti in na druge načine umorjeni, ranjeni in ujeti slovenski partizani. (The crimes of the occupier' collaborators: a monograph in three volumes. Vol. 1. The Slovene partisans killed outside battle or in other ways murdered, wounded and captured). Ljubljana, Društvo piscev zgodovine NOB Slovenije a. Novo mesto, Tiskarna Novo mesto, Dolenjska založba, 95, 554 p. (ill.).

8405. JANÁČEK (František). Odboj a jeho paměť. (Resistance and its memory). *In*: Dějiny a paměť – odboj a kolaborace za druhé světové války [Cf. n° 8401], 95, p. 35-49.

8406. KRAMER (Rita). Flames in the field: the story of four SOE agents in occupied France. London, Michael Joseph, 95, IX-338 p.

8407. *Vacat.*

8408. MOLETTE (Charles). Prêtres, religieux et religieuses dans la résistance au nazisme (1940–1945): essai de typologie. Paris, Fayard, 95, 225 p.

8409. NERI SERNERI (Simone). A past to be thrown away? History and politics in the Italian Resistance. *Contemporary European History Review*, 95, 4, 3, [s. p.]

8410. PAGE (Arthur L). Bella passeggiata: a walk in wartime Italy. Swindon, Newton, 95, X- 132 p. (ill., maps).

8411. RENDINA (Massimo). Dizionario della Resistenza italiana. Presentazione di Arrigo BOLDRINI. Roma, Editori Riuniti, 95, 218 p. (Uni ER).

8412. RICCIOLI (Jean-Louis). Les partisans italiens dans les Alpes. *Revue historique des Armeés*, 95, 2, p. 16-27.

8413. RUBY (Marcel). Résistance et contre-résistance à Lyon et en Rhône-Alpes. Lyon, Horvath, 95, 731 p. (ill.)

8414. SCHREIBER (Gerhard). L'eccidio di Caiazzo e le miserie della giustizia tedesca. *Italia Contemporanea*, 95, 201, p. 661-685.

8415. SIMPSON (William Cook). A Vatican lifeline: allied fugitives, aided by the Italian Resistance, foil the Gestapo in Nazi-occupied Rome, 1944. London, Leo Cooper, 95, X-230 p. (ill., maps)

8416. ŠOLC (Jiří). Smrt přála statečným. Osudy doc. Vladimíra Krajiny a jeho spolupracovníků v českém domácím odboji za druhé světové války. (Death granted to the brave. The fate of Docent Vladimír Krajina and his colleagues in the Czech home resistance during World War II). Praha, Vyšehrad, 95, 232 p. (photogr.).

8417. TRŠAN (Lojz). OF v Ljubljani: organiziranost v času italijanske okupacije 1941–1943. (Liberation Front in Ljubljana: organization in the period of Italian occupation 1941–1943). Ljubljana, Arhiv Republike Slovenije, 95, 197 p.

8418. VENNER (Dominique). Histoire critique de la Résistance. Paris, Pygmalion, 95, 502 p.

8419. WIEVIORKA (Olivier). Une certaine idée de la résistance: défense de la France, 1940–1949. Paris, Seuil, 95, 487 p. (L'Univers historique)

§ 8. Geschichte seit 1945.

** 8420. Arab league (The): British documentary sources. Ed. by Anita BURDETT. London, Archive Editions, 95, 10 Vol.

** 8421. Documents on British policy overseas Ed. by H. J. YASAMEE, K. A. HAMILTON, assisted by I. Warner, A. Lane. London, HMSO, 95, LIII- 377 p. (map).

8422. 1945: consequences and sequels of the Second World War. Montréal, September 2 1995. 18th international Congress of Historical Sciences. Paris, Institut d'Histoire du Temps Present, 95, 392 p. (*Bulletin du Comité international d'Histoire de la Deuxième guerre mondiale*, 27-28). [Cf. nos <choice> 4717, 4868, 4911.]

8423. ACHARYA (Amitav), STUUBS (Richard). New challenges for ASEAN: emerging policy issues. Vancouver, UBC Press, 95, 218 p.

8424. Adaptation and activism. The foreign policy of Denmark 1967–1993. Ed. Carsten DUE-NIELSEN, Nikolaj PETERSEN. København, Dansk Udenrigspolitisk Institute, Jurist- og Ökonomforbundets Forlag DJÖF Publishing, 95, 304 p.

8425. AGHA (Hussein J.), KHALIDI (Ahmad S.). Syria and Iran: rivalry and cooperation. London, Royal Institute of International Affairs, 95, 126 p.

8426. AKYOL (Nihat). Les relations euro-turques dans la perspective de l'Union douanière. *Rivista di Studi Politici Internazionali*, 95, 62, p. 381-391.

8427. ALAGAPPA (Muthiah). Regionalism and conflict menagement: a framework for analysis. *Review of International Studies*, 95, 21, p. 359-388.

8428. ALGER (Chadwick F.), LYONS (Gene M.), TRENT (John E.). The United Nations system: the policies of member state. Tokyo, United Nation U. P., 95, 510 p.

8429. ALLIN (Dana H.). Cold war illusions: America, Europe and Soviet power, 1969–1989. Basingstoke, Macmillan, 95, XV-267 p.

8430. American impact on postwar Germany (The). Ed. by Reiner POMMERIN. Providence a. Oxford, Berghahn, 95. XI-195 p.

8431. ANDERSON (James), BROOK (Chris), COCHRANE (Allan). A global world? Re-ordering political space. Buckingham, The Open University Press in assaciation with Oxford U. P., 95, 287 p.

8432. ANDREIS (Marco de), CALOGERO (Francesco). The soviet nuclear weapon legacy. Oxford, Oxford U. P. (with SIPRI, Stockolm), 95, 130 p.

8433. APPELIUS (S.). Die andere Besatzungsmacht: Britische Deutschland-Politik 1946–47. *Neue Gesellschaft /Frankfurter Hefte*, 95, 42, 3, p. 235-240.

8434. AYOOB (Mohammed). The Third World security predicament: state-making, regional conflict, and the international system. Boulder, Lynne Rienner, 95, 213 p.

8435. AYUBI (Nazih N.). Distant neighbours: the political economy of relations between Europe and the Middle East/North Africa. Reading. Ithaca, 95, [s. p.]

8436. BABIŃSKI (Grzegorz). W poszukiwaniu modelu wyjaśniania przemian etnicznych w Europie Środkowo-Wschodniej. O przydatności i nieprzydatności ogólnych teorii. (A la recherche du modèle expliquant les transitions éthniques en Europe Centrale et Orientale. Sur l'utilité et l'inutilité des théories générales). *Przegląd Polonijny*, 95, 21, 4, p. 69-80. [Eng. Summary].

8437. BAKER (James A.). The politics of diplomacy, revolution, war and peace, 1989–1992. New York, Putnam's Sons, 95, 687 p.

8438. BALDWIN (Richard), HAAPARANTA (Pertti), KIANDER (Jaako). Expanding membership of the European Union. Cambridge, Cambridge U. P., 95, 268 p.

8439. BALL (Simon J.). Military nuclear relations between the United States and Great Britain under the terms of the McMahon Act, 1946–1958. *The Historical Joural*, 95, 38, p. 439-454.

8440. BALOGH (Sándor). Erdély és a második világháború utáni békerendezés, 1945–1946. (La Transylvanie et les préparatifs de paix après la 2ᵉ guerre mondiale entre 1945 et 1946). *Századok*, 95, 129, 3, p. 535-571. – IDEM. Magyarország és szomszédai, 1945–1947. (La Hongrie et ses voisins). Budapest, História-MTA Történettud. Int., 95, 38 p. (História könyvtár, Előadások a történettud. műhelyeiből, 6).

8441. BANGURA (Abdul Karim). The effects of American foreign aid to Egypt, 1957–1987. Lewiston a. Lampeter, Mellen U. P., 95, XIV-240 p. (ill.)

8442. BARCLAY (Glen St J.). Problems in Australian foreign policy, January–June 1995. *Australian Journal of Politics and History*, 95, 41, 3, p. 339-355. – IDEM. Problems in Australian foreign policy, July–December 1994. *Australian Journal of Politics and History*, 95, 41, 2, p. 175-189.

8443. BARNETT (Michael). Partners in peace? The UN, regional organization, and peace-keeping. *Review of International Studies*, 95, 21, p. 411-434.

8444. BARNOUIN (B.), KAPUR (H.). La Chine face au système international. *Relations Internationales*, 95, 81, p. 13-21.

8445. BARRAVECCHIA (Giuseppe). Il peace-keeping e l'illusione dell'imparzialità. *Relazioni Internazionali*, 95, 59, 34, p. 58-62.

8446. *Vacat.*

8447. BAYLIS (John). Ambiguity and deterrence: British nuclear strategy 1945–1964. Oxford, Clarendon, 95, 495 p.

8448. BEAULIEU (Louis le Hardy de). Du déficit démocratique à l'Europe des citoyens. From democratic deficit to an Europe for citizens. Namur, Presses Universitaires de Namur, 95, 251 p.

8449. BÉKÉS (Csaba). The 1956 revolution and world politics. *Hungarian quarterly*, 95, 36, 138, p. 109-121.

8450. BELDA (Josef), BENČÍK (Antonín), PECKA (Jindřich). Podíl NDR na intervenci proti Československu v roce 1968. (The role of the DDR in the 1968 intervention in Czechoslovakia). Praha, Ústav pro soudobé dějiny AV ČR, 95, 45 p. (Materiály, studie, dokumenty, 10).

8451. BELMONTE (Laura). Anglo-American relations and the dismissal of Mac Arthur. *Diplomatic History*, 95, 19, p. 641-667.

8452. BENČÍK (Antonín). Sovětská vojska v Československu a «mírové úsilí» SSSR 1968-1973. (Soviet troops in Czechoslovakia and the 'peace efforts' of the USSR, 1968–1973). Praha, Ústav pro soudobé dějiny AV ČR, 95, 38 p. (Materiály, studie, dokumenty, 9).

8453. BENVENISTI (Meron). Intimate enemies: Jews and Arabs in a shared land. Berkeley, University of California Press, 95, 260 p.

8454. BERNASCONTI (Paolo). Nature et contenu juridique d'une convention internationale contre la corruption. *Rivista di Studi Politici Internazionali*, 95, 62, p. 279-287.

8455. BERNOV (Iurii Vladimirovich). Zapiski diplomata. Moskva, Parusa, 95, 191 p. (ill.).

8456. BIEBER (Roland), MONAR (Joerg). Justice and Home Affairs in the European Union, the development of the third pillar. Bruxelles, College of Europe a. European InterU. P., 95, [s. p.].

8457. BJERELD (Ulf), DEMKER (Marie). Utrikespolitiken som slagfält: de svenska partierna och utrikesfrågorna. (A study in the contemporary Swedish party struggle about foreign policy issues). Stockholm, Nerenius & Santérus, 95, 422 p. (Göteborg studies in politics, 33).

8458. BLASIUS (Rainer A.). Erwin Wickert und die Friedensnote des Bundesregierung vom 25. März 1966. *Vierteljahrshefte für Zeitgeschichte*, 95, 95, 43, 3, p. 539-554.

8459. BLUM (William). Killing hope: U. S. military and CIA interventions since World War II. Monroe M., Common Courage Press, 95, 457 p.

8460. BLUTH (Christoph). Britain, Germany and Western nuclear strategy. Opxford, Clarendon, 95, 322 p.

8461. BOCCIA (Corso Paolo). Le Nazioni Unite e la guerra fredda: occasioni mancate, impasses strutturali. *Europa Europe*, 95, 4, 4, p. 41-57.

8462. BONDE (Hans). Sport og international politik. Dansk gymnastik i stalinismens gennembrudsfase. (Sport and international politics. Danish gymnastics encounter Stalinism in its formative years). *Historisk Tidskrift* (Denmark), 95, 95, 2, p. 342-365.

8463. BORGERSRUD (Lars). Wollweber-organisationen i Norge. Nedgradert utg. Part 1–2. Oslo, Lars Borgersrud, 95, 2 vol., IX-665 p., 246 p. (University of Oslo Acta Humaniora). [The Soviet intelligence service in Norway in the Forties].

8464. BORHI (László). Az. Egyesült Államok Kelet-Európa-politikájának néhány kérdése, 1948–1956.

(Quelques questions de la politique des Etats-Unis concernant l'Europe Orientale, 1948–1956). *Tört. szle.*, 95, 37, 3, p. 277-300.

8465. BOSSUAT (G.). La choix de la petite Europe par la France (1957–1963). Une ambition pour la France et pour l'Europe. *Relations Internationales*, 95, 82, p. 213-235.

8466. BRANDS (H. W.). The wages of globalism: Lyndon Johnson and the limits of American power. New York a. Oxford, Oxford U. P., 95, VIII-294 p.

8467. BROEK (Hans Van Den). The common foreign and security policy in the context of the 1996 intergovernmental conference. *Studia Diplomatica*, 95, 4, p. 31-38.

8468. BROWN (Jeremy M.). Explaining the Reagan years in Central America: a world system perspective. Lanham, University Press of America, 95, 300 p. (bibl.).

8469. BRYANT (Ralph C.). International cooperation of national stabilization policies. Washington, The Brookings Institutiton, 95, 163 p.

8470. BUCKLEY (Roger). US-Japan alliance diplomacy 1945–1990. Cambridge, Cambridge U. P., 95, 225 p.

8471. BULLION (Alan J.). India, Sri Lanka and Tamil crisis 1976–1994. London, Pinter, 95, 226 p.

8472. BURGOGUE-LARSEN (Laurence). L'Espagne et la Communauté européenne. Bruxelles, Editions de l'Université de Bruxelles, 95, XVIII-469 p.

8473. BYSTROVA (N. E.). SSSR i problema sozdanija bez" - jadernykh zon v Rvrope (seredina 50-kh–konec 80-kh godov). (The USSR and the problem of the nuclear-free zones in Europe, the middle of the 1950's–the end of the 1980's). Moskva, RAN. In-t rossijskoj istorii, 95, 219 p.

8474. CABEZA DE MORANO (Marta Graciela). Sobre la ampliación hacia el Este de la Unión Europea. *Rivista di Studi Politici Internazionali*, 95, 62, p. 373-380.

8475. CACCAMO (Domenico). Panslavismo, eurasismo, guerra in Cecenia. *Rivista di Studi Politici Internazionali*, 95, 62, p. 337-351.

8476. CAGIATI (Andrea). Le prospettive di sviluppo dell'UEO. *Rivista di Studi Politici Internazionali*, 95, 62, p. 488-499.

8477. CAMPANA (Andrea). L'Italia e la questione cinese. Diplomazia, commercio e scelte politiche 1941–1962. *Storia delle Relazioni Internazionali*, 94-95/2, 10-11, p. 61-88.

8478. CARMAGNANI (Marcello). La cooperazione politica interamericana. *Relazioni Internazionali*, 95, 59, 35, p. 18-25.

8479. CHAITANYA (Rachana). The new world order. London, Sangam, 95, 191 p.

8480. CHERNOFF (Fred). After bipolarity: the vanishing threat, theories of cooperation, and the future of the Atlantic alliance. Ann Arbor, The University of Michigan Press, 95, 303 p.

8481. CHITRAKAR (Ramesh C.). Foreign investment and technology transfer in developing countries. Aldershot a. Hants, Avebury, 95, 241 p.

8482. CIAMPANI (Andrea). L'altra via per l'Europa. Forze sociali e organizzazione degli interessi nell'integrazione europea (1947–1957). Milano, F. Angeli, 95, 412 p.

8483. CIMBALA (Stephen J.). US military strategy and the Cold War endgame. London, Frank Cass, 95, VIII-271 p.

8484. CLARKE (Jonathan), CLAD (James). After the crusade: American foreign policy for the post-superpower age. Lanham, Madison Books, 95, 228 p.

8485. COHEN (Lenard J.). Broken bonds: Yugoslavia's disintegration and Balkan politics in transition. Boulder a. Oxford, Westview, 95, 386 p.

8486. COMBS (Arthur). The path not taken: the British alternative to U. S. policy in Vietnam, 1954–1956. *Diplomatic History*, 95, 19, p. 33-57.

8487. Conflict in Africa. Ed. by O. FURLEY. London, Tauris Academic Studies, 95, 324 p.

8488. CONFORTI (Benedetto). Il nuovo ruolo del Consiglio di sicurezza. *Relazioni Internazionali*, 95, 59, 32, p. 4-6.

8489. CONKLIN (Jeffrey Scott). Forging an East Asian foreign policy. Lanham, MD, University Press of America, 95, 789 p.

8490. CONNOLLY (Bernard). The rotten heart of Europe: the dirty war for Europe's money. London, Faber & Faber, 95, 427 p.

8491. CONZE (Eckart). Hegemonie durch Integration? Die amerikanische Europapolitik und ihre Herausforderung durch de Gaulle. *Vierteljahrshefte für Zeitgeschichte*, 95, 95, 43, 2, p. 297-340.

8492. CORDOVEZ (Diego), HARRISON (Selig S.). Out of Afghanistan: the inside story of the Soviet withdrawal. Oxford, Oxford U. P., 95, 450 p.

8493. CORNISH (Paul). The arms trade and Europe. London, Royal Institute of International Affairs and Pinter, 95, 117 p.

8494. COSTEL (Eric). La reconnaissance de l'alliance nucléaire anglo-américaine 1953–1958. *Revue d'Histoire Diplomatique*, 95, 109, p. 221-250.

8495. COTTEY (Andrew). East-Central Europe after the Cold War. London, Macmillan, 95, 208 p.

8496. COX (Michael). US foreign policy after the Cold War. London, RIIA, Pinter, 95, 160 p.

8. GESCHICHTE SEIT 1945

8497. CREMONI (Lucilla). Il conflitto arabo-israeliano nella "New York Review of Books": 1963–1993. *Storia delle Relazioni Internazionali*, 94-95, 10-11, p. 85-120.

8498. CROOME (John). Reshaping the world economy: a history of the Uruguay Round. Geneva, World Trade Organization, 95, 392 p.

8499. CSERESNYÉS (Ferenc). A magyarok hazatelepülése Ausztria brit övezetéből, 1945–1947. (La rentrée des Hongrois de la zone britannique de l'Autriche, 1945-1947). *Világtörténet*, 95, 1-2, p. 58-65.

8500. CUCCHI (Giuseppe). Costi ed efficacia dell'embargo nella crisi balcanica. *Relazioni Internazionali*, 95, 59, 31, p. 16-23.

8501. CURTIS (Mark). The ambiguities of power: British foreign policy since 1945. London a. New Jersey, Zed Books, 95, VI-250 p.

8502. CUTILEIRO (José). L'Union de L'Europe occidentale. Mythe et réalités. *Studia Diplomatica*, 95, 48, 3, p. 45-52.

8503. ČUVAKHIN (Dimitrij S.). S diplomatičeskoj missiej v Albanii. 1946–1952 gody. (Diplomatic mission in Albanija. 1946-1952). *Nov. novejš. Ist.*, 95, 1, p. 114-140.

8504. DAVIES (Philiph John). An American quarter century: US politics from Vietnam to Clinton. Manchester, Manchester U. P., 95, 279 p.

8505. DAVIS (M. Jane). Politics and international relations in the Middle East. Aldershot a. Hants, Edward Elgar, 95, 158 p.

8506. DAWISHA (Adeed), DAWISHA (Karen). The making of foreign policy in Russia and the new states of Eurasia. Armonk, NY, M. E. Sharpe, 95, 360 p.

8507. DAY (Richard B.). Cold War capitalism: the view from Moscow, 1945–1975. Armonk, M.E. Sharpe, 95, XVI-355 p.

8508. DE FRANCHIS (Amedeo). La politica estera di sicurezza dell'Unione europea. *Rivista di Studi Politici Internazionali*, 95, 62, p. 203-210.

8509. DE LUCA (Daniele). Gli Stati Uniti e i nuovi rapporti di forza in Medio Oriente: la dottrina Eisenhower, 1957–1958. *Storia delle Relazioni Internazionali*, 94-95/2, 10-11, p. 117-146. – IDEM. Il processo di polarizzazione e la politica difensiva mediorientale americana: il patto di Baghdad. *Clio*, 95, 31, p. 141-160.

8510. Vacat.

8511. DE SENARCLENS (Pierre). From Yalta to the Iron Courtain: the great powers and the origins of the Cold War. Oxford, Berg, 95 320 p.

8512. DEIGHTON (Anne). Building postwar Europe: national decision-makers and European institutions 1948-63. [S. l.], [s. n.], 95, 187 p.

8513. DELL (Edmund). The Schuman plan and the British abdication of leadership in Europe. Oxford a. New York, Oxford U. P., 95, XIV-323 p.

8514. DEUVE (Jean). La guerre secrète au Laos contre les communistes (1955–1964). Paris, L'Harmattan, 95, 311 p.

8515. DI GIUSTO (Stefano). L'avvio del riarmo tedesco-occidentale: tra la riproposizione di concezioni operative tradizionali e la nuclearizzazione dello scenario bellico europeo 1955–'56. *Storia delle Relazioni Internazionali*, 94-95, 10-11, p. 183-202.

8516. DOBBS-HIGGINSON (M. S.). Asia Pacific: its role in the new world order. Revised a. London, Mandarin, 95, 470 p.

8517. DOBRYNIN (Anatolii Fedorovich). In confidence: Moscow's ambassador to America's six Cold War presidents (1962–1986). New York, Times Books, Random House, 95, XIII-672 p. (ill.)

8518. DOKOS (Thanos). Negotiation for a CTBT 1958–1994. Lanham, University Press of America, 95, 298 p.

8519. DONNO (Antonio). Gli Stati Uniti, la Shoah e i primi anni di Israele (1938–1957). Firenze, La Giuntina, 95, 281 p.

8520. DORMAN (Andrew M.), TREACHER (Adrian). European security: an introduction to security issues in post Cold-War. Aldershot, Dartmouth, 95, 207 p.

8521. DOXEY (Margaret). "Something old, something new": the politics of recognition in post-Cold-War Europe. *Diplomacy and Statecraft*, 95, 6, 2, p. 303-322.

8522. DROUHAUD (Pascal). El Salvador: la longue marche vers la paix. *Guerres Mondiales et Conflits Contemporains*, 95, 45, 177, p. 185-194.

8523. Druhá světová válka a její důsledky. Teze referátů z vědeckého semináře Historického ústavu AV ČR. (The Second World War and its consequences. Theses of papers delivered at a seminar of the Historical Institute, the Czech Academy of Sciences). Praha, Historický ústav AV ČR, 95, 40 p.

8524. DUFFIELD (John S.). Power rules: the evolution of NATO's conventional force posture. Stanford, Stanford U. P., 95, 386 p.

8525. DUTTON (David). Statecraft and diplomacy in the twentieth century. Liverpool, Liverpool U. P., 95, 180 p.

8526. DUVAL (Marcel), MELANDRI (Pierre). Les Etats-Unis et la prolifération nucléaire: le cas français. *Revue d'Histoire Diplomatique*, 95, 109, p. 193-220.

8527. EDWARDS (Jill). The president, the archbishop and the envoy: religion and diplomacy in the Cold War. *Diplomacy and Statecraft*, 95, 6, 2, p. 490-511.

8528. EHRHART (Hans-Georg), KREIKEMEYER (Anna), ZAGORSKI (Andrei V.). Crisis menagement in the CIS: whither Russia? Baden-Baden, Nomos, 95, 256 p.

8529. EL-MUSTAFA (Azzou). Le nationalisme marocain et les Etas Unis d'Amérique (1945–1956). *Guerres Mondiales et Conflits Contemporains*, 95, 45, 177, p. 131-138.

8530. ESMAN (Milton J.), TELHAMI (Shibley). International organization and ethnic conflict. Ithaca, Cornell U. P., 95, 343 p.

8531. European security 2000. København, Copenhagen Political Studies Press (CORE publications) 95, 259 p.

8532. FARKAS (Richard P.). L'Est europeo alla riscoperta della ruota. *Relazioni Internazionali*, 95, 59, 31, p. 24-35.

8533. FARRAR-HOCKLEY (Anthony). The British part in the Korean war. Vol. II. An honourable discharge. London, HMSO Books, 95, 534 p.

8534. FAWCETT (Eric), NEWCOMBE (Hanna). United Nations reform: looking ahead after fifty years. Toronto, ON, Science for Peace, 95, 355 p.

8535. FELCMAN (Ondřej). Invaze a okupace. K úloze SSSR a sovětských vojsk ve vývoji Československa v letech 1968–1991. (Invasion and occupation. Concerning the role of the USSR and Soviet troops in Czechoslovak developments, 1968–1991). Praha, Ústav pro soudobé dějiny AV ČR, 95, 49 p.

8536. FERRETTI (Valdo). Fra neutralismo e alleanza occidentale. Il Commonwealth britannico e l'adesione del Giappone al Piano di Colombo. *Storia delle Relazioni Internazionali*, 94-95, 2, 10-11, p. 89-116.

8537. FERRIERE (Jacques de la). Israël, il y a vingt ans: souvenirs d'un "tremblement de terre". *Revue d'Histoire Diplomatique*, 95, 109, p. 89-114.

8538. FINKELSTEIN (Norman G.). Image and reality in the Israel-Palestine conflict. London, Verso, 95, 243 p.

8539. FISAS (Vicenc). Blue geopolitics: the United Nations reform and the future of the Blue Helmets. London, Pluto, 95, 184 p.

8540. FISZER (Józef). Stosunki kulturalne Polska-NRD w latach 1949–1990. (Relations culturelles Pologne-RDA dans les années 1949–1990). *Śląski Kwartalnik Historyczny*. Sobótka, 95, 50, 3-4, p. 195-209. [Deutsche Zsfassung].

8541. FLYNN (Gregory). Rethinking the hexagon: the new France in the new Europe. Boulder, Oxford, Westview, 95, 277 p.

8542. FOOT (Rosemary). The practice of power: US relations with China since 1949. Oxford, Oxford U. P., 95, 291 p.

8543. FRASER (Thomas G). The Arab-Israeli conflict. London, Macmillan, 95, XV-165 p. (map). (Studies in contemporary history).

8544. FREYMOND (J.). Présence de la Chine. *Relations Internationales*, 95, 81, p. 7-11.

8545. FRIEDMAN (Thomas L.). From Beirut to Jerusalem. New York a. London, Doubleday, 95, XV-588 p.

8546. GALA (Marilena). "Una logica e inevitabile necessità". La ricomposizione della special relationship anglo-americana dopo la crisi di Suez. *Storia delle Relazioni Internazionali*, 94-95, 10-11, p. 63-84.

8547. GALEAZZI (Marco). Roma-Belgrado. Gli anni della guerra fredda. Ravenna, Longo, 95, 214 p.

8548. GARDNER (Lloyd C.). Pay any price: Lyndon Johnson and the wars of Vietnam. Chicago, Ivan R. Dee, 95, XV-610 p.

8549. GAY (Bernard). La nouvelle frontière Lao-Vietnamienne: les accords de 1977–1990. Paris, L'Harmettan, 95, 345 p.

8550. GIBBONS (William Conrad). The US government and the Vietnam War: executive and legislative roles and relationship. Part IV. July 1965–January 1968. Princeton, NJ, Princeton U. P., 95, 969 p.

8551. GILLESPIE (R.), RODRIGO (F.), STORY (J.). Democratic Spain reshaping external relations in a changing world. London a. New York, Routledge, 95, 228 p.

8552. GINIEWSKI (Paul). La posture d'Israël dans le "processus de paix". *Rivista di Studi Politici Internazionali*, 95, 62, p. 352-364. – IDEM. Le "retour" de la Finlande, pont entre l'Ouest et l'Est. *Rivista di Studi Politici Internazionali*, 95, 62, p. 47-60.

8553. GINNATTASIO (Pietro). Difesa europea: passato e futuro. *Relazioni Internazionali*, 95, 59, 33, p. 44-49.

8554. GLEIJESES (Piero). Ships in the night: The CIA, the White House and the Bay of Pigs. *Journal of Latin American Studies*, 95, 27, p. 1-42.

8555. GLOVER (Audrey F.). National minorities in Europe. *Studia Diplomatica*, 95, 48, 3, p. 53-62.

8556. GODRON (Anne). Vers le réglement du contentieux frontalier sino-soviétique. *Revue d'Histoire Diplomatique*, 95, 109, p. 165-186.

8557. GOLDSWORTHY (David). British territories and Australian mini-imperialism in the 1950s. *Australian Journal of Politics and History*, 95, 41, 3, p. 356-372.

8558. GOODBY (James E.), IVANOV (Vladimir I.), SHIMOTAMAI (Nobuo). "Northen Territories" and beyond: Russian, Japanese, and American perspectives. Westport, Praeger, 95, 364 p.

8559. GOODBY (James E.). Regional conflicts: the challenge to US-Russian cooperation. Oxford, Oxford U. P., 95, 251 p.

8560. GORBAĆEV (Mikhail S.). Žizn' i reformy: V. 2. Knigakh. Moskva, Novosti, 95, 2 vol., 597 p., 653 p.

8561. GOUREVITCH (Peter), INOGUCHI (Takashi), PURRINGTON (Coutney). United States-Japan relations and international institutions after the Cold War. San Diego, Graduate school of International Relations and Pacific Studies, 95, 390 p.

8562. GOWLAND (D. A.), O'NEILL (B. C.), REID (A. L.). The European mosaic: contemporary politics, economics and culture. London, Longman, 95, 329 p.

8563. GREEN (Michael J.). Arming Japan: defense production, alliance politics, and the postwar search for autonomy. New York, Columbia U. P., 95, 206 p.

8564. GREGORY (Shaun). Le dispositif de commandment et de contrôle des forces nucléaires françaises pendant la guerre froid. *Revue d'Histoire Diplomatique*, 95, 109, p. 251-276.

8565. GRIECO (Joseph M.). The Maastricht treaty, economic and monetary union and the neo-realist research programme. *Review of International Studies*, 95, 21, p. 21-40.

8566. GRIMAUD (Nicole). La Tunisie à la recherche de sa sécurité. Paris, Presses Universitaires de France, 95, 222 p.

8567. GRUGEL (Jean). Politics and development in the Carribean Basin: Central America and the Carribean in the new world order. Basingstoke, Macmillan Press, 95, XII-270 p.

8568. GU (Weiqun). Conflicts of divided nations: the cases of China and Korea. New York a. Westport, Praeger, 95, X-263 p.

8569. GUASCONI (Maria Eleonora). La guerra psicologica quale strumento di lotta contro il comunismo in Italia: il piano Demagnetize. *Storia delle Relazioni Internazionali*, 94-95, 10-11, p. 163-182.

8570. HAGEMANN (Albrecht). Bonn und die Apartheid in Südafrika. Eine Denkschrift des Deutschen Botschafters Rudolf Holzhausen aus dem Jahr 1954. *Vierteljahrshefte für Zeitgeschichte*, 95, 95, 43, 4, p. 679-706.

8571. HALLIDAY (Fred). Islam and the myth of confrontation: religion and politics in the Middle East. London, I. B. Tauris, 95, 255 p.

8572. HALLIER (Hans-Joachim). La Santa Sede e la questione tedesca. Un capitolo della "Ostpolitik" vaticana dal 1945 al 1990. *Rivista di Studi Politici Internazionali*, 95, 62, p. 10-28.

8573. HALVERSON (Thomas E.). The last great nuclear debate: NATO and short-range nuclear weapons in the 1980s. London, Macmillan, 95, 219 p.

8574. HANABUSA (Masamichi). Is Japan changing? *Rivista di Studi Politici Internazionali*, 95, 62, p. 365-372.

8575. HANDERSON (Errol Anthony). Afrocentrism and world politics. London, Eurospan, 95, 222 p.

8576. HANHIMÄKI (Jussi). Self-restraint as containment: United States' economic policy, Finland, and the Soviet Union, 1945–1953. *The International History Review*, 95, 17, p. 287-305.

8577. HARE (William). The struggle for the Holy Land: Arabs, Jews and the emergence of Israel. Lanham a. London, Madison Books, 95, VIII-497 p.

8578. Harold Macmillan and Britain's world role. Ed. by Richard ALDOUS, Sabine LEE. London, Macmillan, 95, XV-161 p.

8579. HARRISON (D. M.). The organization of Europe. Developing a continental market order. London a. New York, Routledge, 95, 232 p.

8580. HARRISON (Selig S.), NISHIHARA (Masashi). UN Peacekeeping: Japanese and American perspectives. Washington, Brookings, 95, 178 p.

8581. HARVEY (Robert). The return of the strong: the drift to global disorder. London, MacMillan, 95, 350 p.

8582. HASSNER (Pierre). La violence et la paix. De la bombe atomique au nettoyage éthnique. Parigi, Esprit, 95, 398 p.

8583. HATZIVASSILIOU (Evanthis). Security and the European option: Greek foreign policy, 1952–1962. *Journal of Contemporary History*, 95, 30, 1, p. 187-202.

8584. HEIKAL (Mohamed). Secret channels: the inside story of Arab-Israeli peace negotiations. London, HarperCollins, 95, 572 p.

8585. HEITHAUS (Victoria). La Nato out-of-area. *Relazioni Internazionali*, 95, 59, 33, p. 18-22.

8586. HENGEVELD (R.), RODENBURG (J.). Embargo: apartheid's oil secrets revealed. Amsterdam, Amsterdam U. P., 95, 399 p.

8587. HENNINGHAM (Stephen). The Pacific Island states: security sovereignty in the post-Cold War world. London, Macmillan, 95, 174 p.

8588. HERMON (Elly). A propose du plan Félix Gaillard de pacte Méditerranéen. *Revue d'Histoire Diplomatique*, 95, 109, p. 3-28.

8589. HEURLIN (Bertel). Security problems in the new Europe. Copenhagen, Copenhagen Political Studies Press, 95, 123 p.

8590. HEY (Jeanne A. K.). Theories of dependent foreign policy and the case of Ecuador in 1980s. Athens, Ohio University Center for International Studies, 95, XIV-292 p.

8591. HOBDAY (Michael). Innovation in East Asia: the challenge of Japan. Aldershot a. Hants, Edward Elgar, 95, 224 p.

8592. HOLDSTOCK (Douglas), BARNABY (Frank). Hiroshima and Nagasaki: retrospect and prospect. London, Frank Cass, 95, 109 p.

8593. HOLM (Hans-Henrik), SØRENSEN (Georg). Whose world order? Uneven globalization and the end of the Cold War. Boulder a. Oxford, Westview, 95, 246 p.

8594. HOVORKA (Rostislav). Kronika dělení. Československo 1990–1992. (A chronicle of a division. Czechoslovakia, 1990–1992). Hodonín, Pedagogické středisko, 95, 93 p.

8595. HÜFNER (Klaus). Agenda for change: new tasks for the United Nations. Opladen a. Germany, Leske a. Budrich, 95, 312 p.

8596. Vacat.

8597. HURRELL (Andrew). Explaining the resurgence of regionalism in world politics. *Review of International Studies*, 95, 21, p. 331-328.

8598. INBAR (Efraim), SENDLER (Shmuel). The changing Israeli stategic equation: toward a security regime. *Review of International Studies*, 95, 21, p. 41-60.

8599. INBAR (Efraim). Regional security regimes: Israel and its neighbours. Albany, State University of New York Press, 95, 312 p.

8600. Interdependence versus integration: Denmark, Scandinavia and Western Europe, 1945–1960. Ed. by Thorsten B. OLESEN. Odense, Odense U. P., 95, 246 p. (Odense University Studies in History and Social Sciences, 193).

8601. ISHIDA (Takeshi). Shakai Kagaku Saikō: Haisen kara Hanseiki no Dōjidai Shi. (Rethinking social sciences in postwar Japan). Tokyo, University of Tokyo Press, 95, 308 p.

8602. ISRAELYAN (Victory). Inside the Kremlin during the Kippur war. University Park, Pennsylvania State Press, 95, XIX-238 p.

8603. JAGUARIBE (Helio). Potenzialità e opzioni future del Mercosud. *Relazioni Internazionali*, 95, 59, 35, p. 35-39.

8604. JAKÓ (Mariann). G. A magyar-szlovák lakosságcsere és előzményei, 1945–1948. (L'échange de la population hongroise et slovaque et ses antécédents, 1945–1948). Miskolc, Baz Megy. Levéltár, 95, 153 p.

8605. JANKOWIAK (Stanisław). Akcja "łączenia rodzin" między Polską a Niemiecką Republiką Demokratyczną w latach 1949–1954. (Action de "réintégration des familles" entre la Pologne et la République Démocratique d'Allemagne dans les années 1949–1954). *Przegląd Zachodni*, 95, 51, 3, p. 51-74.

8606. JANNUZZI (Giovanni). La Nato e la sicurezza europea. *Rivista di Studi Politici Internazionali*, 95, 62, p. 483-487.

8607. JENSEN (Richard). The culture of wars, 1965–1995: a historians' map. *Journal of Social History*, 95, 29, p. 17-37.

8608. JIAN (Chen). China's road to the Korean War: the making of the sino-american confrontation. New York, Columbia U. P., 95, XII-339 p.

8609. JONES (Barry), KEATING (Michael). The European Union and the regions. Oxford, Clarendon, 95, 306 p.

8610. JOYCE (M.). Preserving the sheikdom: London, Washington, Iraq, Kuwait, 1958–1961. *Middle Eastern Studies*, 95, 32, 2, p. 281-292

8611. KAISER (Wolfram). The bomb and Europe: Britain, France, and the EEC entry negotiations 1961–1963. *Journal of European Integration History*, 95, 1, 1, p. 65-85.

8612. KECHICHIAN (Joseph A.). Oman and the world: the emergence of an indipendent foreign policy. Santa Monica, RAND, 95, 409 p.

8613. KEDDIE (Nikki Ragozin). Iran and the Muslim world: resistance and revolution. Basingstoke, Macmillan, 95, X-303 p.

8614. KELLEHER (Catherine McArdle). The future of European security: an interim assessment. Washington, Brookings, 95, 216 p.

8615. KEMP (Goeffrey), GROSS STEIN (Janice). Powder keg in the Middle East: the struggle for Gulf security. Lanham, Rowman & Littlefield, 95, XI-417 p.

8616. KENEN (Peter B.). Economic and monetary union in Europe: moving beyond Maastricht. Cambridge, Cambridge U. P., 95, 219 p.

8617. KENNEDY-PIPE (Caroline). Stalin's cold war: Soviet strategies in Europe, 1943 to 1956. Manchester a. New York, Manchester U. P., 95, 218 p.

8618. KERTÉSZ (István) [1904–1986]. Magyar békeillúziók, 1945–1947. Oroszország és a Nyugat között. (Illusion hongroises de paix, 1945–1947. Entre la Russie et l'Orient). Jegyz., utószó GYARMATI György. Budapest, Európa, 95, 593 p. (Extra Hungariam).

8619. KHANNA (Jane). Southern China, Hong Kong and Taiwan: evolution of a subregional economy. Washington, Center for Strategic and International Studies, 95, 91 p.

8620. KINGSEED (Cole Christian). Eisenhower and the Suez Crisis of 1956. Baton Rouge, Louisiana State U. P., 95, XII-166 p. (Political traditions in foreign policy).

8621. KIWERSKA (Jadwiga). Między izolacjonizmem a zaangażowaniem. Europa w polityce Stanów Zjednoczonych od Wilsona do Roosevelta. (Entre isolationisme et engagement. L'Europe dans la politique des Etats Unis de Wilson à Roosevelt). Poznań, Inst. Zach., 95, 459 p. (English summary, phot., fig.). (Prace Inst. Zach., 61).

8622. KLARE (Michael). Rogue states and nuclear outlaws: America's search for a new foreign policy. New York, Hill and Wang, 95, 291 p.

8623. KNIPPING (Franz), MÜLLER (Klaus-Jürgen). Aus der Ohnmacht zur Bündnismacht. Das Machtproblem in der Bundesrepublik Deutschland 1945–1960. Paderborn, München, Wien u. Zürich, 95, 259 p.

8624. Vacat.

8625. KOLOBOV (Oleg. A.). Politika SŠA po otnošeniju k Izrailju i arabskim stranam na rubeze 80–90 godov XX veka: Monografija. (The United States of America policy towards the state of Izrael and the Arab countries on the edge of the 80–90 years of the XXth century: Monograph). Nižegorodskij gosudarstvennyj universitet im. N. I. Lobačevskogo. Nižnij Novgorod, Izdatel'sto nižegorodskogo universiteta, 95, 177 p.

8626. KOWALSKI (Wojciech). Liquidation of the effects of World War II in the area of culture. Warsaw, Inst. of Culture, 95, 115 p. (phot., fig.).

8627. KRASUSKI (Jerzy). Europa Zachodnia. Dzieje polityczne 1945–1993. (Europe occidentale. Histoire politique 1945–1993). Warszawa, Wydawn. Szkolne i Pedagog., 95, 350 p.

8628. KRAUSE (Keith), KNIGHT (W. Andy). State, society and the UN system: changing perspectives on multilateralism. Tokyo, United Nations U. P., 95, 267 p.

8629. KULIK (Boris T.). SŠA i Tajvan'protiv KNR. 1949–1952 gody. Novye arkhivnye materialy. (The USA and Taiwan against the CPR. New archival materials). *Nov. novejš. Ist.*, 95, 5, p. 19-40.

8630. LAGAZIO (Monica). Il piano Johnston e la politica americana nel Medio Oriente (1953–1955). *Clio*, 95, 31, p. 469-488.

8631. LAÏDI (Zaki). Power and purpose after the Cold War. Oxford, Berg, 95, 213 p.

8632. LAPPENKÜPER (Ulrich). Wilhelm Hausenstein, Adenauers erster Missions-chef in Paris. *Vierteljahrshefte für Zeitgeschichte*, 95, 95, 43, 4, p. 635-678.

8633. LARRES (Klaus). Eisenhower and the first forty days after Stalin's death: the incompatibility of detente and political warfare. *Diplomacy and Statecraft*, 95, 6, 2, p. 431-469. – IDEM. Politiken der Illusionen: Churchill, Eisenhower und die deutsche Frage 1945–1955. Göttingen, Vandenhoek & Ruprecht, 95, 334 p.

8634. LAURSEN (Finn). The political economy of European integration. The Hague, Kluwer Law International, 95, 314 p.

8635. LEBOW (Richard Ned), RISSE-KAPPEN (Thomas). International relations theory and the end of the Cold War. New York, Columbia U. P., 95, 292 p.

8636. LEE (David). Australia and Anglo-American disagreement over the Quemoy-Matsu Crisis, 1954–55. *The Journal of Imperial and Commonwealth History*, 95, 23, p. 105-128. – IDEM. Britain and Australia's defence policy, 1945–1949. *War & Society*, 95, 13, p. 61-80.

8637. LEE (Sabine). Anglo-German relations 1958–59: the postwar turning point? *Diplomacy and Statecraft*, 95, 6, 3, p. 787-808. – EADEM. Perception and reality: Anglo-German relations during the Berlin crisis 1958–1959. *The Journal of the German History Society*, 95, 13, p. 47-69.

8638. LEE (Steven Hugh). Outposts of Empire: Korea, Vietnam and the origins of the Cold War in Asia, 1949–1954. Kingston and Montreal, McGill-Queen's U. P., 95, XIV-295 p.

8639. LEIGH-PHIPPARD (Helen). US strategic export controls and aid to Britain, 1949-58. *Diplomacy and Statecraft*, 95, 6, 3, p. 719-752.

8640. LEITCH (Richard D.), KATO (Akira), WEINSTEIN (Martin E.). Japan's role in the post-cold war world. Westport a. London, Greenwood Press, 95, XVI-223 p. (Contributions in political science).

8641. LEVESQUE (Jacques). La fin d'un Empire. L'URSS et la libération de l'Europe de l'Est. Paris, Presses de la Fondation nationale des Sciences Politiques, 95, 331 p.

8642. LEVEY (Z.). Anglo-Israeli strategic relations, 1952–1956. *Middle Eastern Studies*, 95, 31, p. 772-802.

8643. LITTLE (Douglas). A puppet in search of a puppeteer? The United States, King Hussain, and Jordan, 1953–1970. *The International History Review*, 95, 17, p. 512-543.

8644. MA'OZ (Moshe). Syria and Israel: from war to peacemaking. Oxford, Clarendon , 95, 280 p.

8645. MAC CAULEY (Martin). The origins of the Cold War. London a. New York, Longman, 154 p.

8646. MAC INTYRE (David). Background to the ANZUS Pact: policy-making, strategy and diplomacy, 1945–55. London, Macmillan; Christchurch, Canterbury U. P., 95, VIII-464 p.

8647. MACMILLAN (John), LINKLATER (Andrew). Boundaries in question: new directions in international relations. London, Pinter, 95, 271 p.

8648. Magyar-osztrák kapcsolatok 1955–1956. (Relations hungaro-autrichennes, 1955–1956). Bevez. GECSENYI Lajos. *Társad. szle.*, 95, 50, 10, p. 78-90.

8649. MALONEY (Sean M.). Securing command of the sea. Nato naval planning 1948–1954. Annapolis, Naval Institute Press, 95, 276 p.

8650. MAN (Igor). Il risveglio islamico. *Rivista di Studi Politici Internazionali*, 95, 62, p. 35-46.

8651. MANDELBAUM (Michael). The strategic quadrangle: Russia, China, Japan and the United States. New York, Council on Foreign Relation Press, 95, 221 p.

8652. MARGIOTTA BROGLIO (Francesco). A sedici anni dall'inizio del pontificato di K. Wojtyla. Luci e ombre della recente politica estera del Vaticano. *Rivista di Studi Politici Internazionali*, 95, 62, p. 3-9.

8653. MARKIDES (Diana Weston). Britain's "New Look" policy for Cyprus and the Makarios-Harding talks, January 1955–March 1956. *The Journal of Imperial and Commonwealth History*, 95, 23, p. 479-502.

8654. *Vacat.*

8655. MARTÍN-MUÑZON (Gema). Islamismo e regimi nordafricani. *Relazioni Internazionali*, 95, 59, 36, p. 52-60.

8656. MARTSCHUKAT (Jürgen). Antiimperialismus, Öl und die Special Relationship: die Nationalisierung der Anglo-Iranian Oil Company im Iran 1951-54. Münster, Lit, 95, 355 p.

8657. MARTZ (John D.). United States policy in Latin America: a decade of crisis and challenge. Lincoln, University of Nebraska Press, 95, 407 p.

8658. MASKER (John Scott). Small states and security regimes: the international politics of nuclear non-proliferation in Nordic Europe and the South Pacific. Lanham, University Press of America, 95, 162 p.

8659. MAYERS (David). The ambassadors and America's soviet policy. New York, Oxford U. P., 95, VIII-335 p.

8660. MAZARR (Michael). North Korea and the bomb. London, Macmillan, 95, 290 p.

8661. MECHI (Lorenzo). Una vocazione sociale? Le azioni dell'Alta Autorità della CECA a favore dei lavoratori sotto le presidenze di Jean Monnet e di René Mayer. *Storia delle Relazioni Internazionali*, 94-95, 2, 10-11, p. 147-184.

8662. MELVERN (Linda). The ultimate crime: who betrayed the UN and why. London, Allison and Busby, 95, 442 p.

8663. MENDES DA COSTA MARTINS (Vitor Angelo). Le Portugal dans l'Union Europeénne. Realités et perspectives. *Studia Diplomatica*, 95, 48, 3, p. 33-44.

8664. MENDL (Wolf). Japan's Asia policy: regional security and global interests. London, Routledge, 95, 228 p.

8665. MENON (Anand). Explaining defence policy: the Mitterrand years. *Review of International Studies*, 95, 21, p. 279-300.

8666. MESSIA (José Luis). Por palabra de honor. La entrada de España en el Consejo de Europa (24–11–1977). Madrid, Colección Parteluz, 95, 215 p.

8667. MILLER (Benjamin). When opponents co-operate: great power conflict and collaboration in world politics. Ann Arbor, University of Michigan Press, 95, 354 p.

8668. MINGST (Karen A.). KARNS (Margaret P.). The United Nations in the post-Cold War era. Boulder a. Oxford, Westview, 95, 208 p.

8669. MLYN (Eric). The state, society and limited nuclear war. Albany, NY, State University of New York Press, 95, 241 p.

8670. MOORE (Alex). Un Américain au Laos aux débuts de l'aide américaine (1954–1957). Paris, L'Harmattan, 95, 288 p. (Mémoires asiatiques).

8671. MORPHET (Sally). The influence of states and groups of states on and in the Security Council and General Assembly, 1980–94. *Review of International Studies*, 95, 21, p. 435-[s. p.]

8672. MOTYL (Alexander J.). The post-Soviet nations: perspectives on the demise of the USSR. New York, Columbia U. P., 95, 322 p.

8673. MUNCK (Gerardo L.), KUMAR (Chetan). Civil conflicts and the conditions for successful international intervention: a comparative study of Cambodia and El Salvador. *Review of International Studies*, 95, 21, p. 159-182.

8674. MURFETT (Malcom M.). In Jeopardy: the Royal Navy and British far eastern defence policy 1945–1951. Oxford, Oxford U. P., 95, 178 p.

8675. MURILLO (Luis E.). The Noriega mess: the drugs, the canal, and why America invaded. Berkeley, Video-Books, 95, 1096 p. (ill., maps)

8676. NAIMARK (Norman M.). The Russians in the Germany: a history of the Soviet Zone of occupation, 1945–1949. Cambridge a. London, Harvard U. P., 95, XV-586 p.

8677. NARINSKIJ (Mikhail M.). Berlinskij krisis 1948–1949 godov. Novye dokumenty iz rossijskikh arkhivov. (The 1948–1949 Berlin crises. New documents from the Russian archives). *Nov. novejš. Ist.*, 95, 3, p. 16-29.

8678. NASH (Philip). Jumping jupiters: the US search for IRBM host countries in NATO, 1957–59. *Diplomacy and Statecraft*, 95, 6, 3, p. 753-786.

8679. NASTRI (Giuseppe G.). Testimonianza e riflessione sull'ex-Jugoslavia. Dei popoli soggetti a dure costrizioni. *Rivista di Studi Politici Internazionali*, 95, 62, p. 397-411.

8680. NELSON (Keith L.). The making of detente: Soviet-American relations in the shadow of Vietnam. Baltimore, Johns Hopkins U. P., 95, 217 p.

8681. NEVAER (Louis E. V.). Strategies for business in Mexico: free trade and the emergence of North America, Inc. Westport, Quorum Books, 95, 212 p.

8682. NEŽINSKIJ (Leonid N.), ČELYŠEV (Igor'A.). O doctrinal'nykh osnovakh sovetskoj vnešnej politiki v gody "kholodnoj vojny". (On a doctrinal base of the Soviet foreign policy in the years of the "cold war"). *Oteč. Ist.*, 95, 1, p. 3-27.

8683. NOBEL (Jaap W.). Morgenthau's struggle with power politics and the Cold War. *Review of International Studies*, 95, 21, p. 61-86.

8684. NOLAN (Peter). China's rise, Russia's fall. London, Macmillan, 95, 360 p.

8685. NORDLINGER (Eric A.). Isolationism reconfigured: American foreign policy for a new century. Princeton, Princeton U. P., 95, 335 p.

8686. NOVIK (Faina I.). Ustanovlenie diplomatičeskikh otnošenij meždu SSSR i FRG. (The establishment of diplomatic relations between the USSR and the FRG). *Oteč. Ist.*, 95, 6, p. 106-119.

8687. NOVOSSELOFF (Alexandre). Le processus de décision au sein du Conseil de Sécurité des Nations-Unis: une approche historique. *Revue d'Histoire Diplomatique*, 95, p. 275-304.

8688. NUTI (L.). L'administration Kennedy et sa politique italienne: un "test case" du processus de décision dans la politique étrangère des États-Unis. *Relations Internationales*, 95, 84, p. 485-500.

8689. *Vacat.*

8690. OLIVI (B.). L'Europa difficile. Storia politica della Comunità europea. Bologna, Il Mulino, 95, 548 p.

8691. Otwarta granica. Raport z badań na pograniczu polsko-niemieckim 1991–1993. (Frontière ouverte. Rapport d'études menées dans la zone frontalière polono-allemande 1991–1993). Réd. Stanisław LISIECKI. Poznań, Inst. Zach., 95, 387 p. (Deutsche Zsfassung, phot., cartes). (Ziemie Zach. Studia i Mater., 16).

8692. PAPACOSMA (Victor), HEISS (Mary Ann). NATO in the post-Cold War era: does it have a future? London, Macmillan, 95, 356 p.

8693. PARSONS (Sir Anthony). From cold war to hot peace: UN interventions 1947–1994. London, Michael Joseph, 95, X-278 p. (maps)

8694. PATERSON (Thomas G.). Contesting Castro: the United States and the triumph of the Cuban Revolution. New York a. Oxford, Oxford U. P., 95, XII-352 p.

8695. PAULÍK (Jan). Legalizace pobytu části sovětských intervenčních vojsk – uzavření smlouvy o podmínkách jejich tzv. dočasného pobytu v Československu. (Legalization of the basing of part of the Soviet troops of intervention. Signing the agreement on the terms and conditions of their so-called 'temporary basing' in Czechoslovakia. Praha, Ústav pro soudobé dějiny AV ČR, 95, 60 p.

8696. PAYNE (Richard J.). The clash with distant cultures: values, interests, and force in American foreign policy. Albany, SUNY, 95, 285 p.

8697. PECHATNOV (Vladimir Olegovich). The Big Three after World War II: new documents on Soviet thinking about post war relations with the United States and Great Britain. Washington, Woodrow Wilson International Center for Scholars, 95, 25 p.

8698. PEDRAZZI (Marco). Le relazioni del Consiglio all'Assemblea generale. *Relazioni Internazionali*, 95, 59, 32, p. 44-47.

8699. PERCIVAL (Mark). British political romance with Romania in the 1970s. *Contemporary European History*, 95, 4, p. 67-87.

8700. PERRONE (Nico). De Gasperi e l'America. Palermo, Sellerio, 95, 320 p. – IDEM. Obiettivo Mattei: petrolio, Stati Uniti e politica dell'ENI. Roma, Gamberetti, 95, 273 p. (ill.).

8701. PIKE (Fredrick B.). FDR's good neighbor policy: sixty years of generally gentle caos. Austin, TX, University of Texas Press, 95, XXVI-381 p.

8702. PINDER (John). European unity and world order. London, Federal Trust, 95, 60 p.

8703. POCAR (Fausto). Efficienza e trasparenza del Consiglio di sicurezza. *Relazioni Internazionali*, 95, 59, 32, p. 38-43.

8704. POGGIOLINI (Ilaria). Vietnam, 1968–73: l'alternativa diplomatica alla guerra. Firenze, Manent, 95, 145 p. (Il maestrale)

8705. Political economy of Korea-United States cooperation (The). Ed. by C. Fred BERGSTEN and Il SA KONG. Washington, Institute for International Economics, 95, IX-109 p.

8706. *Vacat.*

8707. Post-Soviet puzzles, mapping the political economy of the former Soviet Union. Ed. by Klaus SEGBERS a. Stephan DE SPIEGELEIRE. Baden-Baden, Nomos Verlagsgesellschaft, 95, 4 vol., 297 p., 511 p., 735 p., 179 p.

8708. POWER (Jonathan). A vision of hope: the fiftieth anniversary of the United Nations. London, Regency corporation, 95, 320 p. (col. ill.).

8709. PRADA (Pedro). Island under siege: the U.S. blockade of Cuba. Melbourne, Ocean Press, 95, 57 p.

8710. PRAWITZ (Jan). From nuclear option to non-nuclear promotion: the Swedish case. Stockholm, The Swedish Institute of international affairs, 95, VI,101 p. (Research report. The Swedish Institute of international affairs, 20).

8711. PREEG (Ernest H.). Traders in a brave new world: the Uruguay Round and the future of the international system. Chicago, University of Chicago Press, 95, 298 p.

8712. PROKŠ (Petr). Londýn a Praha na počátku míru. Příspěvek k historii československo-britských vztahů, květen 1945–květen 1946. (London und Prag am Beginn des Friedens. Beitrag zur Geschichte der tschechoslowakisch-britischen Beziehungen, Mai 1945–Mai 1946). *Český časopis historický*, 95, 93, 2, p. 263-277. – IDEM. Politická moc a sovětizace Československa (1945–1948). (Political Power and the Sovietization of Czechoslovakia. 1945–1948). *Moderní dějiny*, 95, 3, p. 173-212.

8713. RAMET (Sabrina Petra), ADAMOVICH (Ljubisa S.). Beyond Yugoslavia: politics, economics, and culture in a shattered community. Boulder, Oxford, Westview, 95, 502 p.

8714. RATHMELL (Andrew). Secret war in the Middle East: the covert struggle for Syria, 1949–1961. London, Tauris Academic Studies, 95, X-246 p. (Library of modern Middle East studies)

8715. RATNER (Steven). The new UN peacekeeping. London Macmillan, 95, 322 p.

8716. RAWNSLEY (Gary D.). How special is special? The Anglo-American alliance during the Cuban missile crisis. *Contemporary Record*, 95, 9, p. 586-601.

8717. RAY (James Lee). Democracy and international conflict: an evaluation of the democratic peace proposition. Columbia, University of South Carolina Press, 95, 243 p.

8718. REIN (Raanan). Israel's anti-Francoist policy (1948–53): motives and ideological justifications. *Diplomacy and Statecraft*, 95, 6, 2, p. 408-430.

8719. REY (M.-P.). L'URSS et l'Europe occidentale de 1956 à 1975: de l'ignorance méfiante à la coopération. *Relations Internationales*, 95, 82, p. 237-249.

8720. RICUPERO (Rubens). I processi d'integrazione in America Latina. *Relazioni Internazionali*, 95, 59, 35, p. 40-46.

8721. RIGHT (Hon). European security. *Studia Diplomatica*, 95, 48, 3, p. 17-32.

8722. RISSE-KAPPEN (Thomas). Cooperation among democracies: the European influence on US foreign policy. Princeton, Princeton U. P., 95, 250 p.

8723. RITTER (Archibald R. M.), KIRK (John M.). Cuba in the international system: normalization and integration. London, Macmillan, 95, 294 p.

8724. ROGERS (Daniel). Politics after Hitler. The western allies and the German Party System. London, Macmillan, 95, 206 p.

8725. ROSS (Robert S.). Negotiating cooperation: the United States and China 1969–1989. Stanford, Stanford U. P., 95, 349 p.

8726. RUANE (Kevin). Refusing to pay the price: British foreign policy and the pursuit of victory in Vietnam, 1952-4. *English Historical Review*, 95, 110, p. 70-92.

8727. RUFF (Mihály). Magyarország és az NDK kapcsolatairól, 1956. november–1958. március. (Des relations de la Hongrie et de la République Allemande Démocratique, novembre 1956–mars 1958). *Múltunk*, 95, 40, 2, p. 30-66.

8728. RYAN (David). U.S.-Sandinista diplomatic relations: voice of intolerance. London a. New York, Macmillan a. St. Martin's Press, 95, XII-274 p.

8729. RYRIE (William). First World, Third World. London, Macmillan, 95, XV-240 p. (ill.)

8730. SABA (Anna). Mémoires de Anna Saba Ministre plénipotentiaire d'Egypte. *Revue d'Histoire Diplomatique*, 95, 109, p. 29-66.

8731. SAHADEVAN (P.). India and overseas Indians: the case of Sri Lanka. Delhi, Kalinga, 95, 319 p.

8732. SALMINEN (Pertti). Puoluettomuuden nimeen. Sotilasjohto Kekkosen linjalla ja sen sivussa 1961–1966. (In the name of neutrality. Finnish military leadership in line and aside of president Kekkonen's policy in 1961–66). Helsinki, Kustannus OY Suomen Mies, 95, 389 p. (Suomen sotatieteellisen seuran julkaisua, 18).

8733. SANTORO (Carlo Maria). I nuovi poli geopolitici. *Relazioni Internazionali*, 95, 59, 33, p. 2-17. – IDEM. Il segreto delle Nazioni Unite. *Relazioni Internazionali*, 95, 59, 32, p. 7-9.

8734. SCHRÖDER (Hans-Jürgen). Deutsche Außenpolitik 1963–64. Die "Akten zur Auswärtigen Politik der Bundesrepublik Deutschland". *Vierteljahrshefte für Zeitgeschichte*, 95, 95, 43, 3, p. 521-538.

8735. SCHULZ (Brigitte). Development policy in the Cold War era: the two Germanies and Sub-Saharan Africa, 1960–1985. Münster, Lit, 95, 224 p. (Die DDR und die Dritte Welt)

8736. SELIVANOV (Igor' N.). Vnešnjaja politika Francii perioda Pjatoj respubliki: istoriografičeskie očerki. (The foreign policy of France in the Fifth Republic: essays in historiography, after 1958). Moskva, [s.n.], 95, 72 p.

8737. Sengo Nihon: Senryō to Sengo Kaikaku. (Postwar Japan: the occupation and post-war reformes). Ed. by Masanori NAKAMURA. Tokyo, Iwanami Shoten, 6 vol., 278 p., 305 p., 291 p., 301 p., 275 p., 295 p.

8738. SEVÓN (Cay). Visionen om Europa. Svensk neutralitet och europeisk återuppbyggnad 1945–1948. (The vision of Europe. Swedish neutrality and the European reconstruction). Helsingfors, Finsk Historisk Samfund, 95, 314 p.(Bibliotheca historica, 3).

8739. SHAMBAUGH (David). Greater China: the next superpower? Oxford, Clarendon, 95, 310 p.

8740. SHARP (Paul). The death of Soviet diplomacy (between the putsch of august 1991 and the dissolution of the USSR). *Diplomacy and Statecraft*, 95, 6, 3, p. 809-834.

8741. SHEARMAN (Peter). Russian foreign policy since 1990. Boulder a. Oxford, Westview, 95, 324 p.

8742. SILBER (Laura). The death of Yugoslavia. Harmondsworth, Penguin, 95, XXVII-400 p.

8743. SIMON (Françoise). Europe and Latin America in the world economy. Boulder a. London, Lynne Rienner, 95, 213 p.

8744. SINGH (Hari). Malaysia and the Cold War. *Diplomacy and Statecraft*, 95, 6, 2, p. 512-535.

8745. SMITH (David A.), BÖRÖCZ (József). A new world order? Global transformation in the late twentieth century. Westport, Greenwood Press, 95, 257 p.

8746. SMITH (Hazel). European Union, foreign policy and central America. London a. Basingstoke, Macmillan, 95, XXIII-234 p.

8747. So (Alvin Y.), CHIU (Stephen W. K.). East Asia and the world economy. London, Sage, 95, 307 p.

8748. Sovetskaja vnešnjaja politika v gody "kholodnoj vojny" (1945–1958): nove proctenie. (The Soviet foreign policy during the "Cold War", 1945–1958. A new outlook). Otv. red. L. N. NEŽINSKIJ. Moskva, Meždunarodnye otnošenija, In-t rossijskoj istorii RAN, 95, 509 p.

8749. Sovětské imperiální politice v Československu v letech 1945–1968 (O). Sborník příspěvků. (Concerning Soviet imperial policy in Czechoslovakia, 1945–1968. A volume of essays). Olomouc, Vyd. Univerzity Palackého, 95, 83 p. (Acta Universitatis Palackianae Olomucensis, Facultas Paedagogica. Civilia, 1).

8750. SPAINER (John W.). American foreign policy since World War II. Washington, CQ Press, 95, XIV-356 p. (ill., maps).

8751. SPANGER (Hans-Joachim), VALE (Peter). Bridges to the future: prospects for peace and security in southern Africa. Boulder a. Oxford, Westview, 95, 195 p.

8752. SPEAR (Joanna). Carter and arms sales: implementing the Carter administration's arms transfer policy. London, Macmillan, 95, 246 p.

8753. SRINIVAS CHARY (M.). The eagle end the peacock: US foreign policy toward India since independence. Westport, Greenwood Press, 95, XII-194 p.

8754. STATHAKIS (G.). U. S. economic policies in Post Civil War Greece, 1949–1953. Stabilization and monetary reform. *Journal of European Economic History*, 95, 24, 2, p. 375-404.

8755. STEHLE (Hansjakob). Zufälle auf dem Weg zur neuen Ostpolitik. Aufzeichnungen über ein geheimes Treffen Egon Bahrs mit einem polnischen Diplomaten 1968. *Vierteljahrshefte für Zeitgeschichte*, 95, 95, 43, 1, p. 159-172.

8756. STEVEN (Rob). Japan and the new world order. London, Macmillan, 95, 284 p.

8757. STEVENS (Willy). Mercosud: a Latin American regional integration of the second generation. *Studia Diplomatica*, 95, 48, 4, 49-64.

8758. STOCCHIERO (Andrea). Il partner europeo. *Relazioni Internazionali*, 95, 59, 35, p. 26-34.

8759. STORA (Benjamin). L'Algérie en 1995: la guerre, l'histoire, la politique: essai. Paris, Michalon, 95, 114 p. (Collection 'Idées et controverses')

8760. STRIKA (Vincenzo). Iraq e ONU, quattro anni dopo. *Nord e Sud*, 95, 42, 6, p. 123-134.

8761. STUECK (William Whitney). The Korean War: an international history. Princeton, Princeton U. P., 95, XII-484 p. (maps).

8762. SUMNY (Ralph), SALLA (Michael E.). Why the Cold War ended. Westport, Greenwood Press, 95, 278 p.

8763. Sverige inför en ny världsordning, 1945–50: formativa år för svensk utrikespolitik? (Sweden faced with a new world order, 1945–50: formative years for Swedish foreign policy?). Ed. by Charles SILVA a. Thomas JONTER. Stockholm, Utrikespolitiska Institutet, 95, 115 p. (Research report. Utrikespolitiska Institutet, 21).

8764. SWIETOCHOWSKI (Tadeusz). Russia and Azerbaijan: a borderland in transition. New York, Columbia U. P., 95, 290 p.

8765. TÄGIL (Sven). Ethnicity and nation building in the Nordic world. London, Hurst, 95, 333 p.

8766. TAL (L.). Britain and the Jordan crisis of 1958. *Middle Eastern Studies*, 95, 31, 1, p. 39-57.

8767. THOMPSON (Roger C.). Conflict or co-operation? Britain and Australia in the South Pacific, 1950–60. *The Journal of Imperial and Commonwealth History*, 95, 23, p. 301-324.

8768. TORCOLI (Francesco). Le relazioni italo-canadesi durante i primi anni del Patto Atlantico. Aspetti e problemi. *Storia contemporanea*, 95, 26, 4, p. 603-618.

8769. TOSCHI (Simona). Washington – London – Paris: an untenable triangle (1960–1963). *Journal of European Integration History*, 95, 1, 2, p. 81-109.

8770. TŮMA (Oldřich). «Žijeme ve velmi složité době». Záznam rozhovoru E. Honeckera a V. Biľaka 24.11.1988. ('We are living in a complicated time'. Minutes of a conversation between Erich Honecker and Vasil Biľak, 24 November 1988). *Soudobé dějiny*, 95, 2, 2-3, p. 361-373. (Suppl. Archiv soudobých dějin).

8771. *Vacat.*

8772. U istokov "socialističeskogo sodružestva": SSSR i vostočnoevropejskie strany v 1944–1949 godakh. (At the sources of the "socialist co-operation": the USSR and the countries of the Eastern Europe in the 1944–1949). Otv. red. L Ja. GIBIANSKIJ. Moskva, Nauka. RAN In-t slavjanovedenija i balkanistiki, 95, 208 p.

8773. UNDERHILL (Geoffrey R. D.). Keeping governments out of politics: transnational securities markets, regulatory cooperation and political legitimacy. *Review of International Studies*, 95, 21, p. 251-278.

8774. United Nations High Commission for Refugees. The state of the world's refugees: in search of solution. Oxford, Oxford U. P., 95, 264 p.

8775. United States and the use of force in the post-Cold War era (The). Ed. by Aspen Strategy Group. Washington, Brookings, 95, 289 p.

8776. United States-Japan relations and international institutions after the Cold War. Ed. by P. GOUREVITCH, T. INOGUCHI a. C. PURRINGTON. La Jolla, Graduate School of International Relations and Pacific Studies, University of California, 95, XIV-390 p.

8777. VARADI (Max). La separazione "dernier cri" della politica israeliana. *Rivista di Studi Politici Internazionali*, 95, 62, p. 163-169.

8778. VASQUEZ (John A.) [et al.]. Beyond confrontation: learning conflict resolution in the post-Cold War era. Ann Arbor, The University of Michigan Press. 95, 239 p.

8779. VECCHIONI (Domenico). Il Canale di Beagle. Storia di una controversia. *Rivista di Studi Politici Internazionali*, 95, 62, p. 537-543.

8780. VEDOVATO (Giuseppe). La cooperazione transfrontaliera dell'Europa di domani. *Rivista di Studi Politici Internazionali*, 95, 62, p. 211-249.

8781. VIBERT (Frank). Europe: a constitution for the millennium. Aldershot a. Hants, Dartmouth, 95, 239 p.

8782. VILLAUME (Poul). Allieret med forbehold. Danmerk, NATO og den kalde krig: en studie i dansk sikkerhetspolitik 1949-61. (An ally with reservation. Denmark, NATO and the cold war: a study in Danish defence policy). København, Forlaget Eirene, 95, 969 p.

8783. VITALE (Alessandro). La piovra russa. *Relazioni Internazionali*, 95, 59, 34, p. 14-23.

8784. VONDROVÁ (Jitka), NAVRÁTIL (Jaromír). Mezinárodní souvislosti československé krize 1967-1970. Prosinec 1967-červenec 1968. (Czechoslovak crisis in the international context, 1967-1970. Part One: December 1967 to July 1968). Brno, Doplněk, 95, 365 p. (Prameny k dějinám československé krize 1967-1970, 4/1).

8785. WAGNON-CHARPY (Sylvain). Les progressistes et le début de la guerre froide mars 1947 - mars 1948. *Revue d'Histoire Diplomatique*, 95, p. 135-164.

8786. WARNER (Daniel). New dimensions of peacekeeping. Dordrecht, Boston a. London, Martinus Nijhoff, 95, 210 p.

8787. WEBB (Michael C.). The political economy of policy coordination: international adjustment since 1945. Ithaca, Cornell U. P., 95, 269 p.

8788. WELCH (Claude E.). Protecting Human Rights in Africa. Roles and strategies of non-governmental organizations. Philadelphia, University of Pennsylvania Press, 95, 356 p.

8789. WHITTAKER (David J.). United Nations in action. London, University College London Press, 95, 304 p.

8790. WIENER (Jarrod). Making rules in the Uruguay Round of the GATT. Aldershot a. Hants, Dartmouth, 95, 248 p.

8791. WOODHOUSE (Roger). British policy towards France, 1945-51. London a. New York, Macmillan a. St. Martin's Press, 95, XIII-181 p.

8792. WOODWARD (Susan L.). Balkan tragedy. Chaos and dissolution after the Cold war. Washington, The Brookings Institution, 95, 536 p.

8793. WURM (Clemens). Western Europe and Germany. The beginnings of European integration 1945-1960. Oxford, Berg, 95, XIII-271 p.

8794. XIANG (Laxin). Recasting the imperial Far East: Britain and America in China, 1945-1950. Armonk a. London, M. E. Sharpe, 95, XI-259 p.

8795. YASUTOMO (Dennis T.). The new multilateralism in Japan's foreign policy. London, Macmillan, 95, 230 p.

8796. YETIV (Steve A.). America and the Persian Gulf: the third party dimension in world politics. New York, Praeger, 95, X-180 p.

8797. ZANARDI (Pierluigi Lamberti). Ampliamento del Consiglio e ruolo dei membri permanenti. *Relazioni Internazionali*, 95, 59, 32, p. 20-25.

8798. ZARTMAN (I. William), KREMENYUK (Victor A.). Cooperative security: reducing Third World wars. Syracuse, NY, Syracuse U. P., 95, 376 p.

8799. ZELIKOW (Philip), RICE (Condoleezaa). Germany unified and Europe transformed: a study in statecraft. Cambridge, MA, Harvard U. P., 95, 493 p.

8800. ZETTERBERG (Kent). I skuggan av Stalin: en säkerhetspolitisk balansgång: Sveriges bevakning av Finlands öde 1944-49. Stockhom, Probus, 95, 144 p. (Militärhögskolans Acta, B.2). [Keeping one`s balance: Swedish concern for the destiny of Finland in 1944-49].

8801. ZHANG (Shu Guang). Mao's military romanticism: China and the Korean War, 1950-1953. Lawrence, University Press of Kansas, 95, XIII-338.

8802. ZOUBIR (Yahia H.). U.S. and Soviet policies towards France's struggle with anticolonial nationalism in North Africa. *Canadian Journal of History*, 95, 30, 3, p. 439-466.

R

ASIEN

§ 1. Allgemeines. 8803-8809. – § 2. West- und Zentralasien. 8810-8814. – § 3. Südasien. 8815-8819. – § 4. Südostasien. 8820-8824. – § 5. China. 8825-9017. – § 6. Japan (vor 1868). 9018-9068. – § 7. Korea. 9069-9075.

§ 1. Allgemeines.

8803. CHALIAND (Gerard). Les empires nomades de la Mongolie au Danube: V^e–IVe siècles av. J.-C., XVe–XVIe siècles ap. J.-C. Paris, Perrin, 95, 220 p.

8804. CULAJA (Givi V.). Abkhazija i abkhazy v kontekste istorii Gruzii: (Domongol'skij period). Kratkie očerki. (Abkhazia and the Abkhazians in the context of the Georgian history. Before the Mongolian period. The brief essays). Moskva, RAN. In-t étnologii i antropologii im. N. N. Miklukho-Maklaja, 95, 171 p.

8805. DNEPROVSKIJ (K. A.), KORENEVSKIJ (S. N.), ÉRLIKH (V. P.). Novye pogrebenija "novoslobodnenskoj gruppy" u stanicy Kostromskoj v Zakuban'e. ("New burials" of Novoslobodnaya group from Kostromskaya village beyond the Kuban river). *Ros. arkheol.*, 95, 3, p. 119-130.

8806. Drevnie indoiranskie kul'tury Volgo-Ural'ja. (II tysiačeletie do novoj éry): Mežvuzovskij sbornik naučnykh trudov. (The ancient Indo-Iranian cultures of the Volgo-Urals region, the second millennium B. C. Collected studies). Samarskij gosudarstvenny pedagogičeskij universitet i drugie; Redkol.: I. B. VASIL'EV (otv. red.), O. V. KUZ'MINA. SAMARA, 95, 230 p.

8807. KATŌ (Hiroshi). Bunmei to Shite no Isuramu: Tagenteki Shakai Jojutsu no Kokoromi. (Islam as a civilization). Tokyo, University of Tokyo Press, 95, [s. p.].

8808. MURAI (Shōsuke). Higashi Ajia Ōkan: Kannshi to Gaiko. (The comunication in East Asia: Chinese poem and diplomacy). Tokyo, Asashi Shimbunsha, 95, 308 p.

8809. VERTOGRADOVA (Viktorija V.). Indijskaja épigrafika iz Kara-tepe v Starom Termeze: Problemy dešifrovki i interpretacii. (Indian epigraphical finds from Kara-tepe in Old Termez: The problems of deciphering and interpretation). Moskva: Nauka, RAN. In-t vostokovedenija, 95, 160 p.

Cf. n°s 7820-7840

§ 2. West- und Zentralasien.

8810. KOMAKI (Shōhei). Khorasen in the early 19th century. *Jōchi-ajia-gaku*, 95, 13, p. 79-108 (English summary).

8811. MIURA (Tōru). Damasukusu no madorasa to wakuhu. (The Madrasa and the Waqf in Damascus between the 5/11 and the 14/20 centuries: a historical survey). *Jōchi-ajia-gaku*, 95, 13, p. 21-62 (English summary).

8812. SAGUCHI (Tōru). Shinkyō Musurimu Kenkyū. (Study on Sinkiang Muslims). Tokyo, Yoshikawa Kobun kan, 95, 362 p.

8813. SCHOEBERLEIN-ENGEL (John Samuel). Guide to scholars of the history and culture of Central Asia. Cambridge, Harvard Central Asia Forum, 95, 313 p. (Research publications of the Harvard Central Asia Forum, 1).

8814. SUGIYAMA (Masaaki). Dai-Gen Urusu no Sandai Ōkoku: Kaishan-no Dakken to Sono Zengo. (The fundamental structure of Dai-on Ulus). *Kiyou*, 95, 34, p. 92-150.

§ 3. Südasien.

* 8815. LEE (Don Y.). An annotated bibliography on South Asia: historical research. Bloomington, Eastern Press, 95, 167 p.

8816. AWAYA (Toshie). Nanbūdiri-baromon no kāsuto kaikaku undō wo kangaeru. (Evaluating the Nambuditi caste reform movement). *Kiyō*, 95, 128, p. 141-178.

8817. MIZUSHIMA (Tsukasa). 18-seiki-matsu Chinguruputto-chiiki no Porigaru ni kansuru ichi-kosatsu. (A study on Poligars in Chingleput in the late 18th century). *Journal od Asian and African Studies*, 95, 48-49, p. 618-718.

8818. SCHMIDT (Karl J.). An atlas and survey of South Asian history. Armonk, M.E. Sharpe, 95, XV-168 p. (Sources and studies in world history).

8819. VANINA (Evgenija Ju.). Čelovek, vremja, religija (srednevekovaja Indija). (Man, time and religion. India in the Middle Ages). *Vopr. Ist.*, 95, 3, p. 136-144.

§ 4. Südostasien.

8820. BERZIN (Eduard O.). Jugi-Vostočnaja Azia s drevnejšikh vremen do XIII veka. (The Southeastern Asia from the earliest epochs till the XIIIth century). In-t vostokovedenija. Moskva: Vostočnaja literatura. 95, 347 p.

8821. FURUTA (Motoo). Betonamu no Sekaishi: Chūka Sekai kara Tōnan Ajia Sekai e. (Vietnam in the context of world history). Tokyo, University of Tokyo Press, 95, 274 p.

8822. Handbuch der Orientalistik. Abteilung 3. Südostasien. Band 8. PLUVIER (Jan M.). Historical atlas of South-East Asia. New York, E. J. Brill, 95, 64 p.

8823. MAC CLOUD (Donald G.). Southeast Asia: tradition and modernity in the contemporary world. Boulder a. Oxford, Westview Press, 95, XVII-360 p.

8824. SUENARI (Michio). Betonamu no "Kahu". (Genealogy in Vietnam). *Tokyo-daigaku tōyō-bunka kenkyū-jo Kiyo*, 95, 127, p 1-42.

§ 5. China.

* 8825. Handbuch der Orientalistik. Abteilung 4. China. Band 10. ZURNDORFER (Harriet). China bibliography: a research guide to reference works about China past and present. Leiden, New York a. Köln, E. J. Brill, 95, XIV-380 p.

8826. BAI (Hua). Mingdai zhouxian yashu de jianzhi yu zhouxian zhengzhi tizhi. (The construction of the county government and the county political system in Ming Dynasty). *Shixue jikan*, 95, 4, p. 16-23.

8827. BENEWICK (Robert), Wingrove (Paul). China in the 1990s. London, Macmillan, 95, 272 p.

8828. BENTON (Gregor), HUNTER (Alan). Wild lily, prairie fire: China's road to democracy, Yan'an to Tian'anmen 1942–1989. Princeton, Princeton U. P., 95, 361 p.

8829. CAO (Dawei). Zhongguo gudai de an guan nuzi jiaoyu. (Womens' education in ancient China Buddhist and Taoist temples and monasteries). *Zhongguo shi yanjiu*, 95, 3, p. 3-12.

8830. CAO (Liqiang). Zhongguo zhengfu dui zai Han Hua shang de baohu he guanli. (Chinese government's protection and management of Chinese businessmen in Korea). *Shixue jikan*, 95, 4, p. 31-34.

8831. CHEN (Keyun). Ming Qing Huizhou zongzu dui xiangcun tongzhi de jiaqiang. (The reinforcement of the control over the rural areas by Huizhou clans during the Ming and Qing periods). *Zhongguo shi yanjiu*, 95, 3, p. 47-55.

8832. CHEN (Lisong). Yijiusijiu qian Chaozhou zongzu cunluo shequ de yanjiu. (Pre-1949 Chaozhou clans's villages and communities). Shanghai, Shanghai Guji Chubanshe, 95, 135 p. (Chaoxian lishi wenhua congshu – Chaoxian History and Culture).

8833. CHEN (Shenyong). Qingdai shexue yu Zhongguo gudai guanban chudeng jiaoyu tizhi. (Community schools in the Qing dynasty and the system of officially sponsored primary education in Ancient China). *Lishi yanjiu*, 95, 6, p. 59-75.

8834. CHEN (Shiqi). Nanjing zhengfu de guanshui xingzheng gaige. (The Nanjing government's reform of custom administration). *Lishi yanjiu*, 95, 3, p. 133-144.

8835. CHEN (Siqi). Mai xiang guanshui zizhu de diyi bu. Guangdong guomin zhengfu kaizheng er-wu fujia shui. (The first step toward fiscal autonomy. The 2.5 additional tax of Guangdong republican government). *Jindai shi yanjiu*, 95, 1, p. 107-125.

8836. CHEN (Tiejian), HUANG (Lingjun). Beifa zhanzheng shiqi de Feng Zhang Ning Jiang yihe. (Peace talks among Chiang Kai-shek and Warlords during the North Expedition). *Jindai shi yanjiu*, 95, 6, p. 140-166.

8837. CHEN (Zhanyi). Ribenren yu Xianggang: Shijiu shiji jianwen lu. (The Japanese and Hong Kong: a chronicle of the XIX century). Hong Kong, Xianggang Jiaoyu Tushu, 95, V-259 p. (Yazhou Xueshu Wenku – Treasures of Asian Learning).

8838. CHENG (Minsheng). Lüe lun Songdai diyu wenhua. (An outline of regional cultures in the Song dynasty). *Lishi yanjiu*, 95, 1, p. 55-72.

8839. CHENG (Xiao), ZHANG (Ming). Wan Qing xiangcun shehui jiao guan. Dui jiaoan de yi zhong wenhua xinli jieshi. (Views on foreign religions in rural areas during the Late Qing. A cultural-psychological explanation of law suits involving religious disputes). *Lishi yanjiu*, 95, 5, p. 108-117.

8840. CHEVRIER (Y.). Un pays en voie de banalisation? Les paradoxes politiques de la réforme chinoise. *Relations Internationales*, 95, 81, p. 39-58.

8841. Chūgoku chūsei-shi kenkyū. (Studies of Medieval China). Kyōto, Kyōto U. P., 95, 531 p. [Cf. n° <choice> 8889.]

8842. Chūgoku kodai no kokka to minshū. (The state and the people in Ancient China). [S. l.], Kyūko shoin, 95, 859 p. [Cf. n° <choice> 8875.]

8843. DANIELS (Christian). 16–17 Seiki Fukke no Take-Gami Seizō Gijutsu. (Techniques for making bamboo paper in Fujian during XVIth and XVIIth centuries: Tiangong Kaifu paper making technology in its historical context). *Ajia Afurika Gengo Bunka Kenkyū*, 95, 48-49, p. 243-294.

8844. DENG (Ruiling). Yuandai Hangzhou xing xuanzhengyuan. (The bureau of religious affairs at Hangzhou in Yuan period). *Zhongguo shi yanjiu*, 95, 2, p. 85-94.

8845. DENG (Yibing). Qingdai qianqi de shiliang yunxiao he shichang. (Grain transportation and marketing during early Qing). *Lishi yanjiu*, 95, 4, p. 151-161.

8846. Difangzhi jichu zhishi xuanbian. (An anthology of basic knowledge on the Chinese local histories). A cura di Fengqi GUO, Zhaomin TIAN. Tianjin, Tianjin Shehui Kexueyuan Chubanshe, 95, 440 p. (Tianjin Difangzhi Congshu – Tianjin Collection of Local Histories, 1).

8847. DING (Sanqin). Jindai yilai Riben dui wo Guo Dongbei youzheng de qinduo. (The Seizing of postal administration in Northeastern China by Japan). *Lishi dang'an*, 95, 3, p. 105-110.

8848. DONG (Shili). Jindai huanwei xucheng zhidu shitan. (Investigation on the system of inheritance to the throne in Jin dynasty). *Shixue jikan*, 95, 3, p. 14-17.

8849. Dongbei Jun yu minchong kangri jiuwang yundong. (Northeast China Army and mass resistance and National Salvation Movement). Ed. by the Group for Party History Compilation in Northeastern Army. Beijing, Zhonggong Dangshi Chubanshe, 95, 226 p. (ill.). (Zhonggong Dongbeijun dangshi congshu – Collection of Party History in the Northeast Army).

8850. FAN (Jinmin). Qingdai Suzhou zongzu yitian de fazhan. (Development of the clan-owned land at Suzhou under the Qing). *Zhongguo shi yanjiu*, 95, 3, p. 56-68.

8851. FUJITA (Katsuhisa). "Shiki"-kou-honki to Shinso-no-saigetsuhyō: Shinmatsu ni-okeru So Kan no Rekishi-hyoka. (The Shih-Chi "Hsiang yu pen-chi" and "Monthly records during the Ch'in and Ch'u period: the historical assessment of Ch'u and Han during the late Ch'in dynasty). *Toyoshi-kenkyū*, 95, 54, 2, p. 29-61 (English summary).

8852. FUKUI (Shigemasa). Shin-kan Jidai ni Okeru Hakase Seido no Tenkai: Gogyō Hakase no Secchi wo Maguru Gigi Sairon. (The development of the Bosgi system during the Qin-han periods; doubts about the establishment of Wujiy-boshi by emperor Wu of the former Han). *Tōyōshi Kenkyū*, 95, 54, 1, p. 1-31 (Eng. summary).

8853. GAO (Rui). Zhongguo shanggu junshi shi. (Military history of Ancient China). Beijing, Junshi Kexue, 95, IX-604 p.

8854. GAO (Wangling). Shiba shiji Zhongguo de jingji fazhan he zhengfu zhengce. (Chinese economic development and government policy in eighteenth century). Beijing, Zhongguo Shehui Kexue Chubanshe, 95, 269 p. (Dongfang lishi xueshu wenku – Oriental History and Learning Series).

8855. Gaoxiong shi er erba xianguan renwu fangwen jilu. (Interviews of persons involved in the february 28 events in Gaoxiong municipality). Interviews by Xuechen Xu, Huifang Fang. Taibei, Zhongyang yanjiu jindaishi yanjiusuo, 95, 3 vol., 439 p., 470 p., 454 p. (Zhongyang yanjiuyuan jindai shi yanjiusuo koushu lishi congshu – Central Research Institute Modern History Department Oral History Collection, 54).

8856. GE (Jianxiong), CAO (Shuji). Dui Ming dai renkou zongshu de zin guji. (A new estimate of the vital statistics in Ming period). *Zhongguo shi yanjiu*, 95, 1, p. 33-44.

8857. GENG (Qingheng). Mingdai shu ji shi shu lüe. (An account of trainee officials in Ming period). *Zhongguo shi yanjiu*, 95, 1, p. 90-100.

8858. GILL (Bates), KIM (Taeho). China's arms acquisitions from abroad. Oxford, Oxford U. P., 95, 159 p.

8859. GONG (Liuzhu). Wuxue shengdian: "Sunzi bing fa" yu Zhongguo wenhua. (The great ceremony of military art. Sunzi's "Art of War" and Chinese culture). Kaifeng. Henan Daxue Chubanshe, 95, 315 p. (Yuandian Wenhua Congshu – Fundamental Canons).

8860. GOODMAN (Bryna). Native place, city and nation. Regional networks and identity in Shangai, 1853–1937. Berkeley a. Los Angeles, University of California Press, 95, 367 p.

8861. Guangdong lishi tidu ji. (Collection of historical maps of Guangdong province). Ed. by Guangdong Province Historical Maps Commission. Guangzhou, Guangdong Ditu Chubanshe, 95, 198 p. (bibl.).

8862. Guangzhou shi zhi. (History of Canton municipality). Ed. by Canton Municipality Local History Commission. Guangzhou, Guangzhou Chubanshe, 95, 21 vol., [s. p.].

8863. HAN (Daocheng). Dongbei lishi wenhua yanjiu. (Researches on the culture and history of the Northeast China). Taibei, Guoli bianyi guan, 95, 476 p. (ill.). (Rewen shehui kexue congshu – Collection of Human and Social Sciences).

8864. HIRASE (Takao). Chūgoku Kodai no koyomi ni Okeru "mizu" to "hi". (The "Aqua" and the "Fire" in the calendars of Ancient China). *In*: Bunmei-Gaku Gairon [Cf. n° 1326], p. 321-338.

8865. HOU (Baozhong). Zunyi huiyi. Jueding Zhongguo lishi mingyun de san tian. (The Zunyi conference.

the three days that determined China's destiny). Shanghai, Shanghai Renmin Chubanshe, 95, 258 p.

8866. HU (Cheng). Lüe lun wan Qing minzuzhuyi sichao dui bianjiang shiwu de gousi. (The conception of border affairs in nationalist thinking in late Qing). *Jindai shi yanjiu*, 95, 6, p. 14-32.

8867. HUANG (Meilan). Xueshu jiu guo. Zhishi fenzi lishi guan yu Zhongguo zhengce. (Learning for saving the country. Intellectuals' views on history and Chinese politics). Zhengzhou, Henan Renmin Chubanshe, 95, 290 p. (Zhongguo zhishi fenzi congshu – Chinese Intellectuals Collection).

8868. HUANG (Qichen). Aomen lishi. Zi yuangu – 1840 nian. (Macao's history. From antiquity to 1840). Macao, Aomen Lishi Xiehui, 95, 358 p.

8869. HUANG (Qiyi). Lishi de huangyuan. Gu wenhua de zhexue jiegou. (The wasteland of history. The philosophical structure of ancient culture). Chengdu, Bashu Shushe, 95, 800 p.

8870. JIANG (Boying). Zouchu kunjing de Mao Zedong. Ditu gaige zhanzheng de lishi baogao. (Mao Zedong overcomes difficulties. Historical report on the fight for the land reform). Fuzhou, Fujian Renmin Chubanshe, 95, 607 p. (bibl.).

8871. JIANG (Luming). Zhongguo guofang jingji lishi xingtai. (The historical pattern of Chinese national defense economy). Beijing, Guofang Daxue Chubanshe, 95, 480 p.

8872. JIANG (Min). Jiang Min xiansheng fangwen jilu. (Mr. Jiang Min speaks out). Interview by Xuechen XU. Transcripts by Jinglan Zeng. Taibei, Zhongyang yanjiu jindaishi yanjiusuo, 95, 206 p. (Zhongyang yanjiuyuan jindai shi yanjiusuo koushu lishi congshu – Central Research Institute Modern History Department Oral History Collection, 55).

8873. JIANG (Shoupeng), LIU (Huiwen). Ming Qing shiqi de guonei shichang. (The domestic market in Ming and Qing periods). *Shixue jikan*, 95, 2, p. 52-57.

8874. JU (Zhifen). Riben dui Huabei jingji de tongzhi he lüeduo. (Japanese control and plunder of North China economy). *Lishi yanjiu*, 95, 2, p. 96-106.

8875. KANEKO (Shūichi). Tō-chō teishitsu no etsubyo ni tsuite. (On the mausoleums of Tang dynasty). *In*: Chūgoku kodai no kokka to minshū [Cf. n° 8842], p. 499-516. – IDEM. Tō no Taisō, Shukusō tō no sokui ni tsuite: Jōi ni yoru sokui no tetsuzuki no kentō. (The procedure for the emperor's accession in Tang dynasty). *Yamanashi-Daigaku Kyōiku-gakubu Kenkyū-Hōkoku Jimbun-Shakai-Kagaku-Kei*, 95, 46, p. 22-33.

8876. KAWAMURA (Yasushi). Sō-dai Danrei kō. (A research about judicial precedents in Song China). *Kiyō*, 95, 126, p. 107-160.

8877. KIKUCHI (Hideaki). Min-Shin-ki no Ryōkō-nanbu-chiku ni-okeru Hakkaimin no Ido to Katsudo. (The influence of national policy on migration in southern Guangdong and Guangxi Provinces during the Ming and Qing dynasties). *Shigaku-Zasshi*, 95, 104, 11, p. 1-37 (English summary).

8878. KOSTJAEVA (Aleksandra S.). Tajnye obščestva Kitaja v pervoj četvrti XX veka. (The Chinese secret societies, the first quarter of the XXth century). Moskva, Vostočnaja literatura, 95, 240 p.

8879. LACKNER (M.). Quelques particularités linguistiques du discours politique en Chine. *Relations Internationales*, 95, 81, p. 77-88.

8880. LAI (Xinxia). Zhongguo difangzhi. (Chinese local histories). Taibei, Taiwan Commercial Press, 95, IV-VIII-250 p.

8881. LI (Enjun). Zhongguo lishi dilixue. (Historical geography of China). Beijing, Renmin Jiaotong Chubanshe, 95, 306 p. (bibl.).

8882. LI (Hongxi), ZHOU (Bing), LIU (Xihai). Xianggang miyue: Ri Jiang he tan bi dang. (Hong Kong secret pact: Japanese and Chiang Kai-shek peace talks). Hong Kong, Liwen, 95, VIII-330 p.

8883. LI (Longru). Hunan difangzhi kaoping. (An investigation on Hunan local histories). Changsha, Hunan Chubanshe, 95, II-VI-194 p.

8884. LI (Sheng). Zhong E Ili jiaoshe. (The Ili negotiations between China and Russia). Urumqi, Xinjiang Renmin Chubanshe, 95, 208 p. (Zhongguo bianjiang. Minzu lishi yanjiu zhinan congshu – Chinese Frontiers. Researches on National History).

8885. LI (Xiangjun). Qingdai jiumie de zhidu jianshe yu shehui xiaoguo. (The formation of institution for disaster relief in the Qing and their social effect). *Lishi yanjiu*, 95, 5, p. 71-88.

8886. LI (Yu), XIONG (Qiuliang). Lun Qingmo de gong si fa. (On late Qing company law). *Jindai shi yanjiu*, 95, 2, p. 95-108.

8887. LIANG (Binghua). Chengzhai yu Zhong Ying waijiao. (The walled city and Sino-British relations). Hong Kong, Qilin Shuyue, 95, XVII-331 p. (ill.). (Xianggang shi xilie – Hong Kong History Series, 3).

8888. LIANG (Shangxian). Shi shu 1922-1923nian Guangdong zhibi fengchao. (The agitation for Guangdong currency in 1922–1923). *Jindai shi yanjiu*, 95, 2, p. 190-215.

8889. LIGASAWA (Yasunori). Tōdai Fuhei-sei ni Okeru Fuhei no Ichi: Chūgoku Chūseiteki Heishi no Ichi Keitai to shite. (Soldiers' position in the military system of Tang China). *In*: Chūgoku chūsei-shi kenkyū [Cf. n° 8841], p. 61-106.

8890. LIN (Tianwai). Fangzhi xue yu difang shi yanjiu. (The study of local chronicles and local history research). Ed. by the National Bureau for Book Translation and Compilation. Taibei, Nantian Shuju, 95, XXVI-396 p.

8891. LIU (Aiwen). "Ai Guo Tu Zhi" haifang sixiang yanjiu. (Study on coastal defence thought in the "Hai Guo Tu Zhi). *Shixue jikan*, 95, 3, p. 60-69.

8892. LIU (Chaoming), ZHANG (Xian). Jianguo yilai shi da jingji guan. (The ten views on economy since the foundation of the People's Republic). Beijing, Zhongguo Jingji Chubanshe, 95, 269 p. (ill. 13 p.). (Zhongguo jingji de lishi yu weilai – The History and Future of Chinese Economy).

8893. LIU (Cunkuan). Zujie Xinjie. (Renting out the New Territories). Hong Kong, Sanlian Shudian, 95, IX-118 p., (ill.). (Xianggang lishi wenti ziliao xuanping – Selected Documents on Hong Kong History).

8894. LIU (Luya). Jiu Zhongguo de zhiyao gongye. (The medicine industry in old China). *Lishi dang'an*, 95, 2, p. 105-112.

8895. LIU (Pujiang). Jindai "tongjian tuipai" tanwei. (An investigation of the "General Survey and assessment of property" under the Jin 1115-1234). *Zhongguo shi yanjiu*, 95, 4, p. 27-35.

8896. LIU (Shuyong). Gezhan Jiulong. (Seizing Kowlon). Hong Kong, Sanlian Shudian, 95, II-VI-141 p. (ill.). (Xianggang lishi wenti ziliao xuanping – Selected Documents on Hong Kong History).

8897. LU (Huayu). Tangdai Changjiang xiayou dunsang cizhi ye zhi fazhan. (Development of sericulture and silk craftmanship in the Yangzi Delta in Tang). *Zhongguo shi yanjiu*, 95, 1, p. 12-20.

8898. LUO (Jiahuan), SHU (Jianmin). Zhongguo lishi shiqi de renkou bianqian yu huanjing baoyuan. (Population migrations and ecological protection in Chinese history). Beijing, Zhijin Gongye Chubanshe, 95, 289 p.

8899. LUO (Zhiji). Wanzu shehui lishi yu wenhua. (Wa minority's social history and culture). Beijing, Zhongyang Minzu Daxue Chubanshe, 95, 449 p. (ill. 8 p.).

8900. MA (Xiaoquan). Wan Qing zhengfu dui difang zizhi de caocong yu kongzhi. (The operation and control for the local self-government by the Qing). *Lishi dang'an*, 95, 4, p. 112-118.

8901. MA (Yi). Qin ren fu ji biaozhun shi tan. (On household registration adherent to stranger land under the Qin). *Zhongguo shi yanjiu*, 95, 4, p. 16-21.

8902. MA (Yong). Xinhai geming: xiandaihua de zhuguan yitu yu keguan xiaoguo. (The Republican Revolution: subjective intentions of modernization and objective results). *Jindai shi yanjiu*, 95, 1, p. 138-163.

8903. MAC KINLEY (Terry). The distribution of wealth in rural China. Armonk, M. E. Sharpe, 95, 215 p.

8904. MARCUS (Aage). Den blå drage: livskunst og billedkunst i det gamle Kina. (The art of life and the fine arts in ancient China). København, Spectrum, 95, 220 p.

8905. MATSUZAKI (Tsuneko). Bosō kara Mita Chūgoku Kodai Shakai: Shinsekki kara Zenkan Butei made. (Ancient Chinese society as seen from tombs: from the New Stone Age to the emperor Wu of the Former Han). *Sundai-shigaku*, 95, 93, p. 3-25.

8906. MI (Yizhi). Huanghe shangyou diqu lishi yu wenwu. (Local history and cultural relics along the Yellow River). Chongqing, Chongqing Chubanshe, 95, 763 p. (ill. 16 p.).

8907. MIN (Jie). Wuxu xuehui kao. (An evaluation of learning societies during the Hundred Days Reform). *Jindai shi yanjiu*, 95, 3, p. 39-76.

8908. MITANI (Takashi). Tenmon-Kai Saiko: shindai Chūgoku Minkan kessha no Ichikōsatsu. (Tianmen-hui reconsidered: a study of one secret society in XXth century north China). *Shakai-gaku Kenkyū*, 95, 34, p. 43-90 (English summary).

8909. MU (Qin). Zhonghua minzu lishi zhengti fazhan lun. (A organic developmental theory of the history of the Chinese nationalities). Beijing, Minzu Chubanshe, 95, 212 p.

8910. Nü qingnian dadui fangwen jilu. (The reminiscences of women's corps). Interviews by Sanjing CHEN. Taibei, Zhongyang yanjiu jindaishi yanjiusuo, 95, 541 p. (Zhongyang yanjiuyuan jindai shi yanjiusuo koushu lishi congshu – Central Research Institute Modern History Department Oral History Collection, 56).

8911. PI (Mingyong). Wan Qing junren de jingji zhuangkuang chutan. (On the economical conditions of military personnel in the Late Qing). *Jindai shi yanjiu*, 95, 1, p. 14-43.

8912. POO (Mu-Chou). The images of immortals and eminent monks. Religious mentality in early medieval China (4-6 c. A. D.). *Numen*, 95, 42, 2, p. 172-196.

8913. QI (Houjie), WANG (Xiaohua). Huang he hun: di yi, er, ba zhanqu kanzhan jishi. (Records of the war of resistance in the first, second and eighth war districts). Beijing, Zhongguo Dang'an Chubanshe, 95, VI-II-241 p. (Redian zhanzheng dang'an jiemi – Archival Secrets on the War, 1).

8914. QI (Shishen), GONG (Jianghong). Lun Ming Taizu, Chengzu shiqi dui Menggu de zhengce. (Ming dynasty emperors Taizu and Chengzu' policy toward Mongolia). *Shixue jikan*, 95, 3, p. 18-21.

8915. REN (Shiying). Tang dai liuwai guan de guanli zhidu. (Administrative system of "Out of the Run" officials in Tang period). *Zhongguo shi yanjiu*, 95, 1, p. 80-89.

8916. REN (Shuang). Wudai fenhe yu nan Tang de jingji wenhua. (The division and combination of the five dynasties and the economy and culture of South Tang dynasty). *Shixue jikan*, 95, 2, p. 29-35.

8917. Ri ju shiqi Taiwan ren fu dalu jingyan. (The experiences of the Taiwanese people seeking refuge in the mainland during the Japanese colonization). Ed. by the Oral History Commission of the Central Research Institute Modern History Department. Taibei, Zhongyang Yanjiuyuan Jindai Shi Yanjiusuo, 95, 244 p. (Zhongyang yanjiuyuan jindai shi yanjiusyo koushu lishi congshu – Central Research Institute Modern History Department Oral History Collection, 66).

8918. RUI (Kungai). Lun wan Qing de tielu jianshe yu zijin zhucuo. (On the railway construction and fund raising in the late Qing). *Lishi yanjiu*, 95, 4, p. 162-174.

8919. SAKAMOTO (Hiroko). Chūgoku Minzoku Shugi no Shinwa. (The legend of Chinese nationalism). *Shisō*, 95, 849, p. 61-84.

8920. SANG (Bing). Jiawu zhan hou Taiwan nei du guanshen yu gengzi jing wang yundong. (Members of the official – gentry class who returned from Taiwan after the Sino-Japanese War and the 1900 movement to serve the emperor with arms). *Lishi yanjiu*, 95, 6, p. 76-86.

8921. Shanxi Xinjun juesi di san zongdui. (The Third Column of the Shanxi New Army). Tomo 1. "Bufen fazhan shi". (A partial history). Tomo 2. "Huiyi lu" (Reminescences). Ed. by the Commission for the History of Shanxi New Army. Beijing, Zhonggong Dangshi Chubanshe, 95, 603, 477 p.

8922. SHAO (Yong). Yapian zhanzheng shiqi banghui. (The action of gangs during the Opium War). *Lishi dang'an*, 95, 3, p. 92-96.

8923. SHI (Zhongwen), HU (Xiaolin). Xinbian Zhongguo junshi shi. (New military history of China). Beijing, Renmin Chubanshe, 2 voll., [s. p.] (Baijuan ben Zhongguo quanshi – Chinese History in One Hundred Books).

8924. SONG (Dejin). Liao Jin funü de shehui diwei. (The women's social position under Liao and Jin dynasties). *Zhongguo shi yanjiu*, 95, 3, p. 21-31.

8925. SULLIVAN (Lawrence R.). China since Tiennanmen: political and social conflicts. Armonk a. New York, M. E. Sharpe, 95, 332 p.

8926. SUN (Yan). The Chinese reassessment of socialism, 1976–1992. Princeton, Princeton U. P., 95, 52 p.

8927. TAKAHASHI (Hidenao). Nisshin Sensō eno Michi. (The way to the Sino-Japanese War). Tokyo, Tōkyo Sōgensha, 95, 531 p.

8928. TAM (On Kit). Financial reform in China. London, Routledge, 95, 195 p.

8929. TANG (Ling). Kangzhan shiqi de tekuang zousi. (The special ores smuggling during the war of resistance). *Jindai shi yanjiu*, 95, 3, p. 148-159.

8930. TANG (Lixing). Huizhou Fang shi yu shehui bianqian. (Huizhou Fang Clan and social changes). *Lishi yanjiu*, 95, 1, p. 73-86.

8931. TANIGAWA (Michio). Zui-matsu no Nairan to Minshū: Hyōryō to Jiei. (Civil strife and the populase in the late Sui period: depredation and self-defense). *Tōyōshi kenkyū*, 95, 53-54, p. 55-81 (English summary).

8932. TANII (Yōko). Shin-dai Sokurei-shō Rei-kō. (Administrative regulations of the Qing dynasty). *Tōhō Gakuhō*, 95, 67, p. 137-239.

8933. TIAN (Maowu). Zhongguo lishi tixi xin lun. (A new systematic theory of Chinese history). Jinan, Shandong Daxue Chubanshe, 95, 352 p. (Shandong daxue wenshi shu xi – Shandong University Series on History and Culture).

8934. TIAN (Tao). Qingmo minchu zai Hua Jidujiao yiliao weisheng shiye ji qi zhuanyehua. (The medical activity of christian church in China and its specialization during late Qing and early republican Period). *Jindai shi yanjiu*, 95, 5, p. 169-185.

8935. TOMBA (Luigi). Città e anti-città nelle Comuni popolari cinesi (1958–1961). *Passato e presente*, 95, 13, 36, p. 55-84.

8936. TUO (Heti). Weiwuer lishi wenhua yanjiu. (History and culture of the Uigur). Beijing, Minzu Chubanshe, 95, 244 p. (ill. 6 p.).

8937. UMEHARA (Kaoru). Kei wa Taifu ni Noborazu: Sō-dai Kanin no Shobatsu. (The system of punishment for officials in Song China). *Tōhō Gakuhō*, 95, 67, p. 241-289.

8938. VASIL'EV (Leonid S.). Drevnij Kitaj. (Ancient China). Tom. 1. Predistorija, Šan'- In', Zapadnoe Čžou (do VIII veka do novoj éry). (Pre-history. Shang and the Western Chou civilizations. Before the VIIIth century B. C.). Moskva, Vostočnaja literatura, RAN. In-t vostokovedenija, 95, 378 p.

8939. WAN (Ming). Lun chuantong zhengzhi wenhua yu Ming chu zhengzhi. (On traditional political culture and the politics in early Ming dynasty). *Shixue jikan*, 95, 1, p. 58-66.

8940. WANG (Jingyu). Waiguo zai Hua jinrong huodong zhong de yinhang yu yinhang tuan. (Foreign banks and banking groups active in China 1895–1927). *Lishi yanjiu*, 95, 3, p. 111-132.

8941. WANG (Liangxing). 1929nian Zhongguo guoding shuize xingzhi zhi shuliang fenxi. (A quantitative analysis of the nature of China national tax regulations in 1929). *Jindai shi yanjiu*, 95, 4, p. 209-248.

8942. WANG (Qingcheng). Taiping Tianguo he Si shu Wu jing. (The Taiping heavenly kingdom and the four books and the five classics). *Lishi yanjiu*, 95, 3, p. 79-83.

8943. WANG (Saishi). Tangdai niangjiu ye chutan. (A survey of wine making industry in Tang period). *Zhongguo shi yanjiu*, 95, 1, p. 21-32.

8944. WANG (Shaohua). Chu tianyun. Diliu, jiu zhanqu kanzhan jishi. (Records of the war of resistance in the sixth and ninth war districts). Beijing, Zhongguo

Dang'an Chubanshe, 95, VI-231 p. (ill.). (Redian zhanzheng dang'an jiemi – Archival Secrets on the War, 4).

8945. WANG (Shunshen). Gandan xiangzhao. Rong ru yu Gong. Zhongguo Gongchandang lingdaode duodang hezuo zhidu de lishi kaocha. (Historical Investigation on PCC leaders in multiparty cooperation). Fuzhou, Fujian Renmin Chubanshe, 95, 438 p. (bibl.).

8946. WANG (Tianjiang). Jindai Henan nongcun de gao li dai. (High interest loans in modern Henan countryside). *Jindai shi yanjiu*, 95, 2, p. 34-53.

8947. WANG (Tingke). Mao Zedong duli zizhu sixiang de lishi fazhan. (The historical development of Mao Zedong's ideas of independency and autonomy). Chengdu, Sichuan Daxue Chubanshe, 95, 498 p.

8948. WANG (Tingyuan). Lun Huizhou shangbang de xingcheng yu fazhan. (The formation and development of the Huizhou trade group). *Zhongguo shi yanjiu*, 95, 3, p. 39-46.

8949. WANG (Xiaohua), WANG (Shaohua). Dongfang ji: di san, si, qi zhanqu kangzhan jishi. (Records of the war of resistance in the third, fourth, seventh war districts). Beijing, Zhongguo dang'an chubanshe, 95, II-VI-230 p. (ill.). (Redian zhanzheng dang'an jiemi – Archival Secrets on the War, 3).

8950. WANG (Xuezhen). Qing mo baolü de shishi. (The application of Press Law in late Qing). *Jindai shi yanjiu*, 95, 3, p. 77-91.

8951. WANG (Yongping). Lun Tang dai xuanhuishi. (On the comissioner of the court for proclaiming imperial majesty in Tang period). *Zhongguo shi yanjiu*, 95, 1, p. 73-79. – IDEM. Suidai Jiangnan shiren de fuchen. (The vicissitude of Jiangnan Literati during Sui dynasty). *Lishi yanjiu*, 95, 1, p. 42-54.

8952. WANG (Zijin). Qin Han shiqi qihou bianqian de lishixue kaocha. (A historiographical investigation on climate changes during Qin and Han era). *Lishi yanjiu*, 95, 2, p. 3-19.

8953. WARNER (Malcom). The management of human resources in Chinese industry. London, Macmillan, 95, 217 p.

8954. WEI (Qianzhi). Zhongguo gudai Youdairen de lishi gongxian. (Jews's historical contribution in ancient China). *Shixue yuekan* (Historical Science Monthly), 95, 3, p. 23-35.

8955. WEN (Qinming). 1944nian: Zhongguo shehui de lishixing zhuanlie. (1944: an historical turning point for Chinese society). *Jindai shi yanjiu*, 95, 4, p. 25-47.

8956. WEN (Rui). Lixiang, lishi yu shixian. Mao Zedong yu Zhongguo nongcun jingji biange. (Ideals, history and reality. Mao Zedong and the reform of Chinese peasant economy). Taiyuan, Shanxi Gaoxiao Lianhe Chubanshe, 95, 274 p. (ill.).

8957. WO-LAP LAM (Willy). China: after Deng Xiaoping. Chichester, John Wiley, 95, 497 p.

8958. WU (Lengxi). Yi Mao Zhuxi. Wo qinshen jingli de ruogan zhongda lishi shijian pianduan. (Remembering president Mao. Fragments on some important historical events as seen through my own experience). Beijing, Xinhua Chubanshe, 95, 167 p. (ill.).

8959. WU (Songdi). Songdai Fujian renkou yanjiu. (A Study of population in Fujian in Song period). *Zhongguo shi yanjiu*, 95, 2, pp. 50-58.

8960. WU (Tingqiu), ZHENG (Pengnian). Fojiao haishang chuanru Zhongguo zhi yanjiu. (Research of the entry of buddhism into China by the sea route). *Lishi yanjiu*, 95, 2, p. 20-39.

8961. WU (Tingyi). Liang Jin Nan Bei chao shizu menfa de tezheng. (Scholar clans and powerful families in the western and eastern Jin and southern and northern dynasties). *Shixue jikan*, 95, 1, p. 26-33.

8962. WU (Yining). Ren fu zheng lan de Songdai guanzhi. (The overstaffed official system during Song dynasty). *Shixue jikan*, 95, 2, p. 36-42.

8963. XI (Wuyi). 1895-1931nian Taiwan shilian maoyi yanjiu. Taiwan, Riben, dalu sanjiao maoyi kaocha. (Grain trade in Taiwan 1895–1931. An investigation on triangular trade among Taiwan, Japan and the mainland). *Jindai shi yanjiu*, 95, 5, p. 186-205.

8964. XIAO (Guojian). Xianggang gudai shi. (Ancient history of Hong Kong). Hongkong, Zhonghua, 95, II-150 p.

8965. XIAO (Hua). Jiang Jieshi "rangwai bi xian annei" zhengce yanjiu zongshu. (The formation of Chiang Kai-shek's anti-Japanese thought and its characteristics). *Mingguo dang'an* (Republican Archives), 95, 2, p. 71-78.

8966. XIE (Qing). Lun Qing mo lixue biyesheng kaoshi. (On the examination held for the students studying abroad at the end of the Qing dynasty). *Lishi dang'an*, 95, 2, p. 100-104.

8967. XIE (Yongguang). Xianggang kangri fengyun lu. (A record of the resistance against the Japanese in Hong Kong). Hong Kong, Tiandi, 95, VII-196 p. (ill.). – IDEM. Xianggang lunxian: Ri jun gong Gang shi ba ri zhanzheng jishi. (The occupation of Hong Kong: a chronicle of the eighteen days fight of the Japanese army to seize Hong Kong). Hong Kong, Commercial Press, 95, XIII-201 p. (ill.).

8968. XING (Tie). Ming Qing shiqi Kong fu xucheng zhidu. (The inheritance system of the house of Confucius during the Ming Qing period). *Lishi yanjiu*, 95, 6, p. 44-58.

8969. XIONG (Xianghui). Lishi de zhujiao. Huiyi Mao Zedong, Zhou Enlai ji si laoshuai. (Footnotes of history. Remembering Mao Zedong, Zhou Enlai and Four Old Commanders). Beijing, Zhonggong Zhongyang Dangxiao Chubanshe, 95, 204 p.

8970. XU (Xiuli). Jindai Huabei pingyuan de nongye gengzuo zhidu. (Agricultural systems in the North

China plains in modern Period). *Jindai shi yanjiu*, 95, 3, p. 112-131.

8971. YANG (Hongzhang). Li Dazheng yu jiu dang pai de guanxi. (Li Dazheng and the connection among old party factions). *Jindai shi yanjiu*, 95, 2, p. 159-175.

8972. YANG (Jiang). Jianguo yilai shi da jingji redian. (Ten important economic issues since the foundation of the People's Republic of China). Beijing, Zhongguo Jingji Chubanshe, 95, 161 p. (Zhongguo jingji de lishi yu weilai – History and Future of Chinese Economy).

8973. YANG (Tianshi). Jiang Jieshi yu qianqi Beifa zhanzheng de zhanlüe zhenglüe. (Jiang Kaishek's strategy and tactics during the early stage of the Northern Expedition). *Lishi yanjiu*, 95, 2, p. 69-81. – IDEM. Kong Xiangxi yu kanzhen shiqi de Zhong Ri mimi jiaoshe. (Kong Xiangxi and secret negotiations between China and Japan during the resistance war). *Jindai shi yanjiu*, 95, 5, p. 126-146.

8974. YANG (Zhaomin). Lu guo de lishi diwei yu Lu Guo shi yanjiu. (The historical position of the state of Lu and the study of its history). *Shixue jikan*, 95, 4, p. 16-23.

8975. YAO (Qi). Lun Min chu Zhongyang zhengfu zizhi xingshi zhi zheng. (The struggle about the organization shape of central government in early republic). *Lishi dang'an*, 95, 2, p. 113-118.

8976. YIN (Jiamin). Lishi xuanwo zhong de Jiang Jieshi yu Zhou Enlai. (Chiang Kai-shek and Zhou Enlai in the whirls of history). Beijing, Zhonggong Zhongyang Dangxiao Chubanshe, 95, 241 p.

8977. YU (Bailiu). Zhongyang Suqu jingji shi. (Economic history of the Central Soviet). Nanchang, Jiangxi Renmin Chubanshe, 95, 475 p. (Zhongyang Suqu shi yaniu congshu – Collection of Historical Researches on the Central Soviet).

8978. YU (Bingkuan). Wen Tonghe baguan yuanyou kaobian. (Investigation and analysis of Wen Tonghe dismissal from government post). *Lishi dang'an*, 95, 1, p. 113-121.

8979. YU (Shengwu), LIN (Shuyong). Ershi shiji de Xianggang. (XXth century Hong Kong). Hong Kong, Qilin Shuyue, 95, IV-331 p. (Xianggang shi xilie – Series on Hong Kong History, 2).

8980. YU (Shengwu). Gezhan Xianggang dao. (Seizing Hong Kong island). Hong Kong, Sanlian Shudian, 95, VI-107 p. (ill.). (Xianggang lishi wenti ziliao xuanping – Selected Documents on Hong Kong History).

8981. YU (Taishan). Qian Liang yu Xi yu guanxi shukao. (An investigation of the relations between the former Liang dynasty and the western regions). *Zhongguo shi yanjiu*, 95, 2, p. 139-144.

8982. YU (Tong). Riben tongzhi xia de Taiwan jinrong ye. (Taiwan banking and monetary business during the period of Japanese rule). *Minguo dang'an* (Republican Archives), 95, 1, p. 105-115.

8983. YU (Tongguan). Ming houqi Changcheng yanxian de minzu maoyi shichang. (The nationality trade markets along the great wall in late Ming). *Lishi yanjiu*, 95, 5, p. 55-70.

8984. YU (Wen). Minguo sanjun milu. (The Secrets of the republican three armed services). Beijing, Tuanjie, 95, VIII-313 p. (Minguo fengyun milu congshu – Secrets of the Republican Era).

8985. YU (Zhaopeng). Lun Song huizong yingzhi tonghuo pengzhang de shibai. (The failure of the inflation-halting policy under emperor Song Huizong). *Zhongguo shi yanjiu*, 95, 2, p. 59-67.

8986. ZANG (Jian). Nan Song nongcun "sheng zi bu ju" xianxiang zhi fenxi. (An analysis of practices of concealing birth of sons in the countryside under Southern Song). *Zhongguo shi yanjiu*, 95, 4, p. 75-83.

8987. ZENG (Yeying). Riben qinzhan Huabei haiguan ji qi houguo. (The Japanese seizing of North China customs and its consequences). *Jindai shi yanjiu*, 95, 4, p. 48-67.

8988. ZHAN (Qinghua). Zhongguo jindai haiguan zong shuiwu si. Muyong yangyuan tequan wenti xin lun. (The general tax bureau for customs in modern China. A new theory on the problem of the special power to enlist and use foreign experts). *Jindai shi yanjiu*, 95, 1, p. 89-106.

8989. ZHANG (Dongguang). Tang Song shiqi de shumi shuguan. (Gran Secretaries in the central government of the Tang and Song dynasties). *Lishi yanjiu*, 95, 4, p. 135-151.

8990. ZHANG (Fuqiang). Xi shi dong jian yu minchu Guangzhou chengshi de fazhan. (The urban development of Canton in early republic). *Jindai shi yanjiu*, 95, 5, p. 147-168.

8991. ZHANG (Hequan). Dong Han Guanzhong diqu wenhua fazhan de tezheng ji yixiang. (The characteristics and effect of cultural development in Guanzhong area of Eastern Han dynasty). *Shixue jikan*, 95, 2, p. 22-28.

8992. ZHANG (Jingru). Weiwu shiguan yu Zhonggong dang shixue. (Historical materialism and the historiography of PCC). Changsha, Hunan Chubanshe, 95, 225 p.

8993. ZHANG (Jinlong). Lingjun jiangjun yu bei Wei zhengzhi. (Imperial Guards Generals and Northern Wei politics). *Zhongguo shi yanjiu*, 95, 1, p. 54-62.

8994. ZHANG (Kaiyuan). Nanjing da tusha de lishi jianzheng. (An eyewitness's historical record of the Nanjing massacree). Wuhan, Hubei Renmin Chubanshe, 95, 320 p. (ill., bibl.).

8995. ZHANG (Quanming). Zhongguo lishi dili lungang. (Theoretical outlines of Chinese historical geography). Wuhan, Huazhong Shifang Daxue Chubanshe, 95, 358 p.

8996. ZHANG (Shiqu). Jindai Zhongguo wenhua minzuzhuyi. (Cultural nationalism in pre-modern China). *Lishi yanjiu*, 95, 5, p. 88-101.

8997. ZHANG (Weiran). Hunan lishi wenhua dili yanjiu. (Researches on Hunan history, culture and geography). Shanghai, Fudan Daxue Chubanshe, 95, 243 p. (Fudan Daxue poshi congshu – Collection from Fudan Daxue Doctoral Dissertations).

8998. ZHANG (Xuhua). Xiao Liang guanpin, guanban zhidu kaolüe. (A survey of the system of official levels and official setup of the Sourthern Liang of the Xiao Family). *Zhongguo shi yanjiu*, 95, 2, p. 78-84.

8999. ZHAO (Hongbao). Qingmo tongyuan weiji yu Tianjin shanghui de duice. (The late Qing copper crisis and the countermeasures of the Tianjin Chamber of Commerce). *Jindai shi yanjiu*, 95, 4, p. 172-187.

9000. ZHAO (Liren). Sun Zhongshan and Xu Xueqiu. (Sun Yatsen and Xu Xueqiu). *Jindai shi yanjiu*, 95, 1, p. 173-191.

9001. ZHAO (Shichao). Xunshou zhidu shitan. (The system of royal inspection). *Lishi yanjiu*, 95, 3, p. 3-15.

9002. ZHAO (Shiyu). Ming Qing shiqi Jiangnan miaohui yu Huabei miaohui de jidian bijiao. (Comparing temple fairs in Jiangnan and North China during Ming and Qing dynasties). *Shixue jikan*, 95, 1, p. 40-46.

9003. ZHAO (Yinglan). Lu Nanjing guomin zhengfu shiqi de xin zhengxue xi. (On the new political study group during the Nanjing decade). *Shixue jikan*, 95, 3, p. 32-38.

9004. ZHAO (Yuntian). Qingdai zhili bianchui de shuniu Lifan Yuan. (The office of border affairs: the axis of Qing border policy). Urumqi, Xinjiang Renmin Chubanshe, 95, 164 p. (Zhongguo bianjiang. Minzu lishi yanjiu zhinan congshu – Chinese Frontiers. Researches on National History).

9005. ZHENG (Qidong). Wan Qing sizhu ji qi shehui jingji yinxiang. (Private minting in late Qing and its socio-economic effects). *Jindai shi yanjiu*, 95, 4, p. 155-171.

9006. Zhonggong Dongbei Jun dang shi gaishu. (A general outline of party history in the northeast army). Ed. by the Group for compilation of Party History in the Northeastern Army. Beijing, Zhonggong Dangshi Chubanshe, 95, 261 p. (ill. 12 p.). (Zhonggong Dongbei Jun dangshi congshu – Collection of Party History in the Northeast Army, 1).

9007. Zhonggong Dongbei Jun dixia dang gongzuo huiyi. (Reminiscences of the underground party work in the northeast army). Ed. by the Group for compilation of Party History in the Northeastern Army. Beijing, Zhonggong Dangshi Chubanshe, 95, 724 p. (ill. 6 p.). (Zhonggong Dongbei Jun dangshi congshu – Collection of Party History in the Northeast Army).

9008. Zhonggong Dongbei jundang shi yigu renwu zhuan. (Biographies of deceased personalities of party history in the northeast army). Ed. by the Group for compilation of Party History in the Northeastern Army. Beijing, Zhonggong Dangshi Chubanshe, 95, 295 p. (Zhonggong Dongbei Jun dangshi congshu – Collection of Party History in the Northeast Army).

9009. Zhonggong Xizang dangshi da shi ji 1949–1994. (Main events of party history in Tibet 1949–1994). Ed. by the Tibet Autonomous Region Commission for Party History. Lhasa, Xizang Renmin Chubanshe, 95, 476 p. (ill. 16 p.).

9010. Zhongguo haijiang lishi yu xianzhuang yanjiu. (Researches on the history and contemporary situation of Chinese sea borders). Ed. by Yiran LU. Harbin, Heilongjiang Chubanshe, 95, 195 p. (Bianjiang shi di congshu – Collection on Border History and Territories).

9011. Zhongguo lishi diming da cidian. (Dictionary of locality names in Chinese history). Ed. by Songshan WEI. Guangzhou, Guangdong Jiaoyu Chubanshe, 95, XIV-1359 p. (ind.).

9012. Zhongguo lishi qiangzhen mulu. Gongyuan qian 23 shiji–gongyuan 1911 nian (Index to earthquakes in Chinese History. XXIII Century b.C.–1911 A.D.). Ed. by the National Bureau for Earthquakes Prevention. Beijing, Dizhen Chubanshe, 95, XV-514 p.

9013. ZHOU (Shaojing). Chaozhou huiguan shi hua. (History of Chaozhou guilds). Shanghai, Shanghai Guji Chubanshe, 95, 241 p. (ill.). (Chaoxian lishi wenhua congshu – Chaoxian History and Culture).

9014. ZHU (Baoqin). Cong Guomindang gaige dao Sun Zhongshan zheshi qianhou de Wang Jingwei. (Wang Jingwei from the KMT's reform to around Dr. Sun Yatsen's death). *Mingguo dang'an*, 95, 3, p. 84-90.

9015. ZHU (Ying). Qingmo xinzheng yu Qing chao tongzhi de miewang. (New politics and the end of Qing and the destruction of Qing power). *Jindai shi yanjiu*, 95, 2, p. 76-94.

9016. ZOU (Jingwen). Jindai Zhongguo gufen zhi. (The shareholding system in modern China). *Lishi dang'an*, 95, 3, p. 100-104.

9017. ZOU (Zhaozhen). Mao Zedong dui lishi de kaocha. (Mao Zedong's views on history). Beijing, Shoudu Shifan Daxue Chubanshe, 95, 288 p.

Cf. n° 7772

§ 6. Japan (vor 1868).

9018. AMINO (Yoshihiko). Akutō to Kaizoku; Nihon Chūsei no Shakai to Seiji. (Scoundrels and pirates; society and politics of Medieval Japan). Tokyo, Hōsei U. P., 95, 411 p.

9019. ARAKI (Moriaki). Nihon-Hōken-Shakai Seiritsu-shi-ron. (The establishment of feudal society in Japan). Vol. 2. Tokyo, Iwanami Shoten, 95, 307 p.

9020. ARIMOTO (Masao). Shinshū no Shūkyō-Shakai-shi. (A history of religious society of "Shinshu"). Tokyo, Yoshikawa Kōbunkan, 95, 406 p.

9021. ASAO (Naohiro). Toshi to Kinsei-Shakai wo Kangaeru: Nobunaga, Hideyoshi kara Tsunayoshi no Jidai made. (Towns and early modern society: from the age of Nobunaga and Hideyoshi to Tsunayoshi). Tokyo, Asahi Shimbunsha, 95, 337 p.

9022. Chūsei no Kukan wo Yomu. (Reading the medieval space). Ed. by Fumihiko GOMI. Tokyo, Yoshikawa Kōbunkan, 95, 448 p.

9023. Chūsei no Mura: Keikan wa katarikakeru. (Medieval villages of Japan: history through landscapes). Ed. by Susumu ISHII. Tokyo, University of Tokyo Press, 95, 253 p.

9024. Chūsei Shiryōron no Genzai to Kadai; Kōkogaku to Chūseishi Kenkyū. (The state and the problems of the Medieval sources; archaeology and the Medieval studies). Ed. by Yoshihiko AMINO, Susumu ISHII a. Kazuo TANIGUCHI. Tokyo, Meicho Shuppan, 95, 408 p.

9025. Chūsei tōgoku no butsuryū to toshi. (The trade distribution and towns i medieval eastern Japan). Ed. by Sumio MINEGISHI a. Shosuke MURAI. Tokyo, Yamawaka-Shuppan-Sha, 95, 300 p.

9026. Emaki ni Chūsei wo Yomu. (Reading the middle age in picture scrolls). Ed. by Yoshiaki FUJIWARA a. Fumihiko GOMI. Tokyo, Yoshikawa Kōbun Kan, 95, 344 p.

9027. FUJIKI (Hisashi). Le village et son seigneur (XIVe–XVIe siècles). Domination sur le territoire, autodéfense et justice. Annales, 95, 50, 2, p. 395-420. – IDEM. Sengoku-shi wo Miru Me. (Perspectives of the history of the Sengoku period). Tokyo, Azekura Shobo, 95, 337 p. – IDEM. Zōhyō-tachi no Senjō: Chūsei no Yōhei to Dorei-gari. (The battlefield of soldiers: the mercenary and slave-hunting). Tokyo, Asashi Shimbunsha, 95, 344 p.

9028. FUKAI (Jinzo). Kinsei no Chihō-Toshi to Chōnin. (Provincial towns and townspeople in early modern Japan). Tokyo, Yoshikawa-Kōbunkan, 95, 307 p.

9029. FUKUDA (Toyohiko). Muromachi Bakuhu to Kokujin Ikki. (Muromachi Bakufu and regional riots). Tokyo, Yoshikawa Kobunkan, 95, 329 p.

9030. HAGA (Norihiko). Chūsei Nihon no Seiji to Shiryō. (The politics and sources in Medieval Japan). Tokyo, Yoshikawa Kobunkan, 95, 390 p.

9031. HASHIMOTO (Yoshinori). Heian-kyō seiritsushi no kenkyū. (Syudy of the building of Heia-kyō). Tokyo, Hanawa-Shobō, 95, 462 p.

9032. HATTORI (Hideo). Keikan ni Saguru Chū-sei: Henbō suru Mura no Sugata to Shōen-shi-Kenkyū. (Seeking the landscape in the middle ages: changing villages and the study of the history of manors). Tokyo, Shin-Jinbutsu-Ōrai-Sha, 95, 611 p.

9033. HONGO (Kazuto). Chūsei Chōtei Soshō no Kenkyū. (Litigation in the imperial court in Medieval Japan). Tokyo, University of Tokyo Press, 95, 270 p.

9034. IECHIKA (Yoshiki). Bakumatsu-Seiji to Tōbaku Undō. (Politics at the end of the Edo period and the Anti-Shogunate movements. Tokyo, Yoshikawa Kōbunkan, 313 p.

9035. IENAGA (Junji). Muromachi Bakufu Shōgun Kenryoku no Kenkyū. (Studies in the power of Shogun in Muromachi Bakufu). Tokyo, University of Tokyo Press, 95, 423 p.

9036. IHARA (Kesao). Nihon Chusei no Kokusei to Kasei. (The national politics and household economy Medieval Japan). Tokyo, Azekura Shobō, 95, 598 p.

9037. ISHII (Osamu). Sekai Kyōkō to Nihon no "Keizai Gaikō", 1930–1936. (The depression and Japan's "Economic Diplomacy", 1930–1036). Tokyo, Keisō-Shobō, 95, 260 p.

9038. KATSUMATA (Shizou). 'Ikki', Ligues, conjurations et révoltes dans la société médiévale japonaise. Annales, 95, 50, 2, p. 373-394.

9039. KATSUYAMA (Seiji). Chūsei Nengu Seiritsu Shi no Kenkyū. (Studies in the formation of tribute system in the Middle Ages). Tokyo, Hanawa Shobō, 95, 480 p.

9040. Kindai Nihon to Igirisu Shiso. (Modern Japan and English thought). Ed. by Shirō SUGIHARA. Tokyo, Nihon Kaizai Hyoronsha, 95, 276 p.

9041. Kinsei Beisaku Tansaku-Chitai no Sonraku Shakai: Echigo-no-Kuni Iwate-mura Satō-ke Monjo no Kenkyū. (A village society in a rice-producing one-crop area in early modern Japan: research into the Sato family papers in the Iwate village of Echigo). Ed. by Takashi WATANABE. Tokyo, Iwata Shoten, 95, 444 p.

9042. Kinsei no Shakai-Shūdan: Yuisho to Gesetsu. (A history and statement of social groups in early modern times). Ed. by Hiroshi KURUSHIMA a. Nobuyuki YOSHIDA. Tokyo, Yamakawa Shuppansha, 95, 342 p.

9043. KITAHARA (Itoko). Toshi to Hinkon no Shakai-shi: Edo kara Tokyo e. (A social history of cities and poverty: from Edo to Tokyo). Tokyo, Yoshikawa Kōbunkan, 95, 375 p.

9044. KITAMURA (Masaki). Heian-kyō: Sono rekishi to kōzō. (The Heian capital: its history and structure). Tokyo, Yoshikawa-Kōbun-Kan, 95, 290 p.

9045. KUROITA (Nobuo). Heian Ōchō no Kyūtei Shakai. (Society of the Heianimperial court). Tokyo, Yoshikawa Kōbunkan, 95, 288 p.

9046. MAYUZUMI (Hiromichi). Mononobe, Sogashi to Kodai Ōken. (The clans of Mononobe and Soga and the ancient kingship). Tokyo, Yoshikawa Kōbunkan, 95, 254 p.

9047. MEZAKI (Tokue). Kizoku Shakai to Koten Bunka. (Aristocratic society and the classic culture). Tokyo, Yoshikawa Kōbunkan, 95, 307 p.

9048. MORISHITA (Toru). Nihon-Kinsei Koyō-Rōdōshi no Kenkyū. (A history of labor employment in early modern Japan). Tokyo, University of Tokyo Press, 95, 285 p.

9049. Nihon kodai-kokka no tenkai (jō)-(ge). (The development of the ancient Japanese state). Ed. by Teiji KADOWAKI. Kyoto, Shibunkaku-Shuppan, 95, 462 p. (jō)-468 p. (ge).

9050. Nihon-Kokka no Shiteki Tokushitsu. (Historical peculiarities of the Japanese state). Ed. by Asao Naohiro Kyōju Taikan-Kinen-Kai. Kyoto, Shibunkaku Shuppan, 95, 592 p.

9051. Nihon-Shakai no Shiteki Kōzō. (Historical structure of Japanese society). Ed. by Asao Naohiro Kyōju Taikan-Kinen-Kai. Kyoto, Shibunkaku Shuppan, 95, 570 p.

9052. NOMURA (Tadao). Narachō no seiji to fujiwarashi. (Politics in Nara period and the Fujiwara clan). Toky, Yoshikawa Kōbunkan, 95, 282 p.

9053. OGUCHI (Yujiro). Josei no iru Kinsei. (Women in early modern Japan). Tokyo, Keisō Shōbo, 95, 292 p.

9054. ŌHASHI (Nobuya). Nihon Kodai Ōken to Shizoku. (Kingship and clan in Ancient Japan). Tokyo, Yoshikawa Kōbunkan, 95, 398 p.

9055. OISHIO (Chihiro). Chūsei no Nanto Bukkyo. (The Buddhism at Nara in the Middle Age). Tokyo, Yoshikawa Kōbunkan, 95, 598 p.

9056. SASAKI (Ken'ichi). Kodai tōgoku shakai to kōtsū. (Society and transport in the ancient eastern Japan). Tokyo, Azekura-Shobō, 95, 398 p.

9057. SATŌ (Kazuhiko). «Des gens étranges à l'allure insolite». Contestation et valeurs nouvelles dans le Japon médiéval. Annales, 95, 50, 2, p. 307-340.

9058. SHIBATA (Shinichi). Shōwa-ki no Kōshitsu to Seiji Gaikō. (The imperial household and political diplomacy in the Showa period). Tokyo, Hara-Shobō, 95, 289 p.

9059. SMITH (Thomas C.). Nihon-Shakai-shi ni okeru Dentō to Sōzō: Kōgyō-ka Naizai-teki Syo-Yōin 1750–1920-nen. (Native conditions of Japanese industrialization, 1750–1920). Kyoto, Minerva Shobo, 95, 305 p.

9060. TANAKA (Yuko). Le monde comme représentation symbolique. Le Japon de l'époque d'Edo et l'univers du 'mitate'. Annales, 95, 50, 2, p. 259-282.

9061. TOLSTOGUZOV (Aleksandr A.). Očerki istorii Japonii VII–XIV vekov: Stanovlenie foedalizma. (Essays in the Japanese history in the VIIth–XIVth centuries. The emergence of feudalism). Moskva, Vostočnaja literatura, 95, 332 p.

9062. TORAO (Toshiya). Kodai Tōhoku to Ritsuryōhō. (Ritsuryo code in ancient Tohoku district). Tokyo, Yoshikawa Kōbunkan, 95, 260 p.

9063. WADA (Atsumu). Nihon Kodai no Girei to Saishi, Shinkō (jo), (chu), (ge). (Religious observance, ritual, and faith in Ancient Japan). Tokyo, Hanawa Shobo, 95, 3 vol., 488 p., 421 p., 496 p.

9064. WAKITA (Osamu). Hiranoya Takebee, Bakumatsu no Osaka wo Hashiru. (Takebee Hiranoya of Osaka in the last years of the Tokugawa Shogunate). Tokyo, Kadokawa Shoten, 95, 209 p.

9065. YAMADA (Kuniaki). Kamakura-fu to Kanto: Chūsei Seiji Chitsujo to Zaichi Shakai. (The Kamakura administration and eastern Japan: the political order and local society in the Middle Ages). Tokyo, Azekura Shobō, 95, 446 p.

9066. YAMAMOTO (Hirofumi). Sakoku to Kaikin no Jidai. (The age of isolation and "Prohibited Sea"). Tokyo, Azekura Shobō, 95, 263 p.

9067. YOSHIE (Akio). Eviter la souillure. Le processus de civilisation dans le Japon ancien. Annales, 95, 50, 2, p. 283-306.

9068. Zenkindai no Nippon to Higashi-Ajia. (Japan and East Asia in pre-modern times). Ed. by Takeo TANAKA. Tokyo, Yoshikawa Kobunkan, 95, 526 p.

§ 7. Korea.

9069. IDEO (Rosella). La Corea dall'annessione giapponese (1910) alla vigilia della guerra (1950): problemi ideologici e istituzionali. Trieste, Universita degli studi di Trieste, Dipartimento di scienze politiche, 95, 47 p. (Collana di studi storici).

9070. KIM (Song Whan). The rise of public sector banking: the Japanese banks in Korea, 1878–1938. [s. l.], University of Oxford, 95, XVIII-310 p. (ill.).

9071. LAN'KOV (A. N.). Političeskaja bor'ba v Koree XVI–XVIII vekov. (Political struggle in Korea of the XVIth–XVIIIth centuries). Sankt-Peterburg, Centr "Peterburgskoe vostokovedenie", 95, 197 p.

9072. LEE (Seong-si). Shiragi sou, Jizō no seiji gaikō jō no yakuwari. (The diplomatic role played by the monk Chajang of Silla). Chosen Bunka Kenkyū, 95, 2, p. 65-83 (English summary).

9073. South Korea's Minjung movement: the culture and politics of dissidence. Ed. by K. M. WELLS. Honolulu, University of Hawaii Press, 95, VIII-247 p. (ill.).

9074. TASHIRO (Kazuo), YONETANI (Hiroshi). So-ke Kyūzō "Tosho" to Mokuin. ("Tosho" or copper seals and wooden seals which used to be owned by the So family). Chosen Gakuho, 95, 156, p. 13-96 (English summary).

9075. TSUKIASHI (Tatsuhiko). Kōgo-kaikaku no Kindai Kokka Kōsō. (The concept of the modern state in the Kabo reform). Chosen-shi Kenkyukai Ronbunshu, 95, 33, p. 67-92 (English summary).

S

AFRIKA
(von der Urzeit bis zur Kolonisation)

* 9076. ALLEN (Christopher H.). Africa bibliography 1994. [1992-1993. Cf. Bibl. 94, n° 8473.] Edinbourg, Edinbourg U. P., 95, XXXVI-453 p.

** 9077. SHEN (John). New thoughts on the use of Chinese documents in the reconstruction of early Swahili history. *History in Africa*, 95, 22, p. 349-358.

9078. Afrique du Nord antique et médiévale (L'): monuments funéraires, institutions autochtones: actes du VIe Colloque international sur l'histoire et l'archéologie de l'Afrique du Nord, Pau, octobre 1993. Textes réunis par Pol TROUSSET. Paris, C.T.H.S, 95, 327 p.

9079. AKYEAMPONG (Emmanuel), OBENG (Pashington). Spirituality, gender, and power in Asante history. *International Journal of African Historical Studies*, 95, 28, 3, p. 481-508.

9080. ALAGOA (Ebiegberi Joe). People of the fish and eagle: a history of Okpoama in the Eastern Niger Delta. Lagos, Isengi Communications Ltd., 95, V-209 p. (ill.).

9081. ANDERSON (David M.), SETON (Rosemary). Archives and manuscripts collections relating to Africa held at the school of Oriental and African Studies, University of London. *History in Africa*, 95, 22, p. 45-60.

9082. BAY (Edna G.). Belief, legitimacy and the Kpojito: an institutional history of the 'Queen Mother' in precolonial Dahomey. *Journal of African History*, 95, 36, 1, p. 1-28.

9083. BENICHOU-SAFAR (Hélène). Les fouilles du tophet Salammbô à Carthage (1er partie). *Antiquités Africaines*, 95, 31, p. 81-199.

9084. BOUZID (Lamjed). Les Askia de Gao et les populations: contribution à l'étude des rapports entre le pouvoir et la société dans la boucle du Niger au XVIe siècle. *Revue d'Histoire Maghrébine*, 95, 79-80, p. 347-370.

9085. BUSSIERE (Jean). Lampes d'Algérie II. Lampes grecques, hellénistiques et tardo-républicaines. *Antiquités Africaines*, 95, 31, p. 231-276.

9086. CHELBI (Fethi), PASKOFF (Roland), TROUSSET (Pol). La baie d'Utique et son évolution depuis l'antiquité: une réévaluation géoarchéologique. *Antiquités Africaines*, 95, 31, p. 7-51.

9087. COPE (R. L.). Written in characters of blood? The reign of king Cetshwayo ka Mpande, 1872–79. *Journal of African History*, 95, 36, 2, p. 247-270.

9088. CORBIER (Paul), GASCOU (Jacques). Inscriptions de Tébessa d'après les archives de Paul-Albert Février. *Antiquités Africaines*, 95, 31, p. 277-323.

9089. DIAWARA (Mamadou). Oral sources and social differentiation in the Jarra Kingdom from the sixteenth century: a methodological approach. *History in Africa*, 95, 22, p. 123-139.

9090. EDDY (Michael R.). Politics and archaeology in the Canary Islands. *Antiquity*, 95, 69, 264, p. 44-445.

9091. EISENHOFER (Stefan). The origins of the Benin Kingship in the works of Jacob Egharevba. *History in Africa*, 95, 22, p. 141-163.

9092. FERCHIOU (Naïdé). Stucs puniques hellénistiques d'Utique. *Antiquités Africaines*, 95, 31, p. 53-79.

9093. Fotografia e storia dell'Africa. Atti del Convegno internazionale, Napoli-Roma 9–11 settembre 1992. A cura di Alessandro TRIULZI. Napoli, Istituto Universitario Orientale, 95, 266 p. (ill.).

9094. GAYIBOR (N. L.). Les Rois De Glidji: une chronologie revisée. *History in Africa*, 95, 22, p. 197-222.

9095. GUYER (Jane I.), BELINGA (S. M. Eno). Wealth in people as wealth in knowledge: accumulation and composition in Equatorial Africa. *Journal of African History*, 95, 36, 1, p. 91-120.

9096. HAIR (P. E. H.). Was Columbus' first very long voyage a voyage from Guinea? *History in Africa*, 95, 22, p. 223-237.

9097. HALLIER (Gilbert). Le monument circulaire du plateau de l'Odéon à Carthage: précisions sur la conception et la géométrie d'un parti original. *Antiquités Africaines*, 95, 31, p. 201-230.

9098. INSOLL (Timothy). A cache of hippopotamus ivory at Gao, Mali; and a hypothesis of its use. *Antiquity*, 95, 69, 263, p. 327-336.

9099. LAILY (P.A.), BRISSAUD (I.), FRONTIER (J.P.), JEHANNO (C.). Remploi de monnaies romaines à l'époque ziride. Analyse d'échantillons d'un trésor découvert à la Qal'a des Banu Hammâd (Algérie). *Antiquités Africaines*, 95, 31, p. 325-331.

9100. LAW (Robin). "Central and Eastern Wangara": an indigenous West African perception of the political and economic geography of the Slave Coast as recorded by Joseph Dupuis in Kumasi, 1820. *History in Africa*, 95, 22, p. 281-305. – IDEM. Historical source material from Togo and Benin. *History in Africa*, 95, 22, p. 445-446.

9101. MAC CALL (John). Rethinking ancestors in African culture. *Africa*, 95, 65, p. 256-70.

9102. MARK (Peter). Constructing identity: sixteenth- and seventeenth-century architecture in the Gambia-Geba region and the articulation of Luso-African ethnicity. *History in Africa*, 95, 22, p. 307-327.

9103. ŌTSUKA (Kazuo). Tekusuto no Mahudizumu: Sūdan no "Dochakushugi-undō" to sono Tenkai. (Mahdism described in texts: Sudanese "Nativistic Movement" from an anthropological perspective). Tokyo, University of Tokyo Press, 95, 255 p.

9104. PRESTON BLIER (Suzanne). The path of the leopard: motherhood and majesty in early Dahomè. *Journal of African History*, 95, 36, 3, p. 391-418.

9105. VANSINA (Jan). New linguistic evidence and 'The Bantu Expansion'. *Journal of African History*, 95, 36, 2, p. 173-196.

9106. WYLIE (Dan). "Proprietor of Natal": Henry Francis Fynn and the mythography of Shaka. *History in Africa*, 95, 22, p. 409-437.

Cf. n°s 1540, 7841-7893, 7953

T

AMERIKA
(von der Urzeit bis zur Kolonisation)

9107. ANGLES VARGAS (Victor). Pacarectambo y el origen de los Incas. Cusco, [s.n.], 95, 613 p.

9108. BROOKS (Francis J.). Motecuzoma xocoyotl, Hernan Cortes, and Bernal Diaz Del Castillo: the construction of an arrest. *Hispanic American Historical Review*, 95, 75, 2, 149-184.

9109. DAVIES (Nigel). The Incas. Niwot, University Press of Colorado, 95, X-259 p.

9110. EDMUNDS (R. David). Native Americans, new voices: American Indian history, 1895–1995. *American Historical Review*, 95, 100, 3, p. 717-740.

9111. GALLOWAY (Patricia). Choctaw genesis, 1500–1700. Lincoln a. London, University of Nebraska Press, 95, XV-411 p. (Indians of the Southeast).

9112. HAUPTMAN (Laurence M.). Tribes and tribulations: misconceptions about American Indians and their histories. Albuquerque, University of New Mexico Press, 95, XVI-164 p.

9113. HEMMING (John). Red gold: the conquest of the Brazilian indians. London, Papermac, 95, XVIII-685 p.

9114. LOVELL (William George) LUTZ (Christopher H.). Demography and empire: a guide to the population history of Spanish Central America, 1500–1821. Boulder a. Oxford, Westview Press, 95, XV-190 p. (Dellplain Latin American studies, 33).

9115. Mille ans de civilisations mésoaméricaines: des Mayas aux Azteques: mélanges en l'honneur de Jacques Soustelle. Réd. par Jacqueline DE DURAND-FOREST et Georges BAUDOT; préf. de Pierre CHAUNU. Paris, L'Harmattan, 95, 2 vol., [s. p.] (ill.).

9116. NERSESOV (Ja. N.). Rol'prirodnoj sredy v istorii drevnikh kul'tur Jugo-Zapada SŠA. (The environmental factor in the history of the ancient cultures in the South-West of the USA). *Ros. arkheol.*, 95, 4, p. 39-44.

9117. PEASE (G. Y, Franklin). Las cronicas y los Andes. Lima, Pontificia Universidad Catolica del Peru, Instituto Riva-Aguero y Mexico y Estados Unidos de America, Fondo de Cultura Economica, 95, 632 p. (Publicación. Pontificia Universidad Catolica del Peru, Instituto Riva-Aguero, 144; Sección de obras de história).

9118. RIESE (Berthold). Die Maya: Geschichte, Kultur, Religion. München, Beck, 95, 143 p. (Beck'sche Reihe. Wissen, 2026).

Cf. n°s 1083, 1475, 1476, 7894-7909

U

OZEANIEN
(von der Urzeit bis zur Kolonisation)

* 9119. SAUNDERS (Trish), TERRELL (Jennifer), PAYNE (Beverly Carron). Pacific history bibliography 1995. *Journal of Pacific history*, 95, 30, 3, p. 1-55.

9120. Cosmos and society in Oceania. Ed. by Daniel DE COPPET a. Andre ITEANU. Oxford, Berg, 95, VI-338 p. (ill.). (Explorations in anthropology. A University College London series).

9121. Politics of the secret (In Australian aborigines). Ed. by Christopher ANDERSON. Sydney, University of Sydney, 95, 142 p. (Oceania monograph, 45).

9122. South Pacific oral traditions. Ed. by Ruth FINNEGAN a. Margaret ORBELL. Bloomington, Indiana U. P., 95, 259 p. (Voices in performance and text).

Cf. nos 1041, 7910

AUTOREN- UND PERSONENREGISTER[1]

A

Aachen (Frieden von), 7914.
AALDERS (Gerard), 8323.
Aaronsohn (Aaron), 8073.
Abaelardus (Petrus), 4340, 4344, 4379.
ABAS (Syed Jan), 4175 a).
ABAŠIDZE (A.Kh.), 7661.
ABBE (Jean-Loup), 3178.
Abbenes (J. G. J.), 2273.
Abd el Khalek Torres, 7849.
ABDERRAHIM (Abderrahim Abderrahman), 7948.
Abdollahian (M. Andrew), 1290.
Abdulhamid II, sultano ottomano, 626, 8018, 8026.
ABE (Takeshi), 1137.
ABERTH (J.), 3690.
ABID (Mounir), 5898, 7347.
ABIODUN (Rowland), 6714.
ABITZ (Friedrich), 1759.
ABOU (Selim), 5214.
ABRAMENKO (Andrik), 1738.
ABRAMZON (Mikhail G.), 2606.
ABRET (Helga), 4661.
ABROMAIT (Heidran), 1178.
ABRUZZESE (S.), 1488.
ABUBAKRE (Razaq), 1540.
ABULAFIA (David), 3494, 7920.
ABU-LUGHOD (Janet), 848.
Acacius Melitensis, 3036.
ACCAME (Silvio), 764.
ACCAMPO (Elinor A.), 4851.
Acciaioli (Nicola), 3508.
ACCONCIA LONGO (Augusta), 3045.
ACHARYA (Amitav), 8423.
ACIEN (Manuel), 3550.
ACKERLY (Neal W.), 1569.
ADAM (Anne-Marie), 2488.
ÁDÁM (Magda), 8102.
Adamo de Citella, 3815.

ADAMOVICH (Ljubisa S.), 8713.
ADAMS (Barbara), 1760.
Adams (Brooks), 744.
ADAMS (David Wallace), 6084.
Adams (Henry), 734.
ADAMS (J. N.), 2510, 2749.
ADAMS (James Eli), 6612.
Adams (John), 6161.
ADAMSON (Donald), 6377.
ADAMSON (Walter L.), 5968.
ADDY MAXWELL (May Ann), 197.
ADEBAYO (A. G.), 7842.
Adémar de Chabannes, 739.
Adenauer (Konrad), 4818, 8632.
ADKIN (Neil), 2531.
ADNAN AL-BAKHIT (Muhammad), 368.
ADORNO (Francesco), 3922.
Adorno (Theodor Wiesengrund), 6969.
ADRADOS (F. R.), 2064.
AELBRECHT (V.), II.
ÆLFRIC, 3923.
AFFEK (Mariusz), 7618.
AFFICHARD (Joëlle), 1217.
AGAPETOS DIAKONOS, 3047.
AGHA (Hussein J.), 8425.
Agnellus Ravennas (Andreas), 683, 3302.
Agnes (Kaiserin), 3433.
AGNOLETTI (Attilio), 5812.
AGOSTI (Aldo), 842.
AGOSTINI (Filiberto), 5669.
Agostini (Ippolito), 6059.
AGOSTON (Gábor), 4585.
AGRAWAL (D.P.), 1626.
AGRIPPA D'AUBIGNÉ, 740, 6541.
Agrippina (Vipsania), 2642, 2912.
AGUET (Jean-Pierre), 1179.
AGUIRRE (Emiliano), 1596, 1608.
AGUIRRE BELTRÁN (Gonzalo), 7348.
AGUIRRE DE CARCER (N.), 8149.

AGULHON (Maurice), 7528.
AGUWA (Jude C. U.), 5899.
AHLSTRÖM (Christian), 991.
AHLSTROM (Goran), 7146.
AHMAD (Sayyid Maqbul), 368.
Ahmad Baba, 113.
AHMAT (Adam), 6155.
Ahmed Resmi Efendi, 7949.
AHMET (K.), 1734.
AHRENSDORF (Peter J.), 6222.
ÅHSBERG (Bengt), 5358.
AICHELBURG (Wladimir), 6715.
Aigentler (Henriette von), 6435.
AIGNER FORESTI (Luciana), 2439, 2502.
AILLOT (Michelle), 4541.
AIRAKSINEN (Timo), 6613.
AIRLIE (Stuart), 3692.
Aischylos, 2239, 2257, 2374.
AJNENKIEL (Andrzej), 8202.
AKEHURST (F. R. P.), 4007.
AKENSON (Donald Harman), 511.
AKIMOVA (O. A.), 1008.
AKINSHA (Konstantin), 6865.
AKITA (Shigeru), 7821.
AKKEMANS (Peter M. M. G.), 1627.
AKSAN (Virginia H.), 7949.
AKSENOV (Mikhail), 1605.
AKŚIN (Sina), 5510.
AKSJUTIN (Ju. V.), 5352.
AKTAN (Ali), 3.
AKYEAMPONG (Emmanuel), 9079.
AKYILDIZ (Ali), 45, 7269.
AKYOL (Nihat), 8426.
ALADA (Adalet B.), 7576.
ALAGAPPA (Muthiah), 8427.
ALAGOA (Ebiegberi Joe), 9080.
ALAMICHEL (Marie-Françoise), 4165.
ALARY (Luc), 474.
AL-ASSIOUTY (Sawat Anis), 1429.
ALATRI (Paolo), 5029, 7270.

---

1. Die slawischen und insbesondere die russische Eingennamen sind in ihrer einheimischen Form wiedergegeben, nach der gebräuchlichen Methode transkribiert und dementsprechend eingeordnet. Buchstaben mit diakritischen Zeichen sind bei den einfachen Buchstaben eingereiht (z. B. ć, ś, š, bei c, s). Die Umlaute der germanischen Sprachen (ä, ö, ø, ü) gelten als a, o, u. Die Abkürzungen M und Mc gelten ala Mac. Für die Namen der Christlichen Heiligen und der Päpste wurde die lateinische Form gewählt. Autorennamen wurden in Kapitälchen gesetzt..

ALBATS (Yevgenia), 5303.
ALBERA (François), 6881.
Alberico di Rosciate, 6579.
ALBERIGO (Giuseppe), 5705.
ALBERT (Jean-Pierre), 1430.
ALBERT (Rainer), 327.
ALBERT-SAMUEL (Colette), VI.
ALBERTAN-COPPOLA (Sylviane), 403.
ALBERTI (A.), 2233.
ALBERT-LLORCA (Marlène), 1430.
ALBERTSON (F. C.), 404.
Albertus Magnus, Sanctus, 4301, 4320, 4324.
ALBERZONI (Maria Pia), 4428.
ALBONICO (Aldo), 5029.
ALBONICO (P.), 25.
ALBRECHT (Dieter), 4607.
ALBRECHT (Ulrike), 7149.
ALBRECHT (Uwe), 4197.
ALBRICH (Thomas), 7349.
ALCALA (Angel), 3529.
ALCAMO (Jean-Claude), 3693.
ALCOCK (Leslie), 4542.
ALDCROFT (Derek Howard), 7046.
ALDEN (Dauril), 7797.
ALDOUS (Richard), 8578.
ALDRICH (Richard), 6085.
ALEAZ (K. P.), 5900.
Aleksandr I Romanov, imperatore di Russia, 7992.
Aleksandr II Romanov, imperatore di Russia, 8063.
ALEKSEEV (L. V.), 4543.
ALEKSIUN-MĄDRZAK (Natalia), 5234.
ALENIUS (Kari), 4836.
ALEXANDRE (Yardenna), 1885.
Alexandre le Jagellon, roi de Pologne, 5257.
ALEXANDRE-BIDON (Danièle), 3965.
Alexandros III hó Megas, re di Macedonia, 2113, 2116, 2368, 2390, 4192.
ALEXANDROV (Vladimir E.), 1539.
ALEXIOU (E.), 2234.
ALEXIOU (Stylianos), 4926.
ALEYA SGHAIER (Amira), 7843.
Al-Fārābī, 175.
AL-FARUQI (Ismail R.), 5901.
ALFIERI TONINI (Teresa), 2154.
ALFÖLDY (G.), 3203.
Alfonso III, rey de Léon, 735.
Alfonso I, rey de Aragona y de Navarra, 3480.
Alfonso V, rey de Aragona, Sicilia y Çardeña, 3598.
Alfonso VI, rey de Castilla y Léon, 3401.
Alfonso X, rey de Castilla y Léon, 553.

Alfred the Great, king of England, 3424.
ALGER (Chadwick F.), 8428.
ALIANI (Antonio), 3231.
ALIBERTI (Giovanni), 512, 7350.
ALIMENTO (Antonella), 7271.
ALISON (Nick), 2346.
Alkibiadēs, 2046, 2122, 2132.
ALLAIN (J.-C.), 7674.
ALLAIRE (Martine), 6100.
ALLAN (Pierre), 4666.
ALLDRITT (Keith), 8203.
ALLEGRÍA DE RIOJA (Jesús), 420.
ALLEN (Christopher H.), 9076.
ALLEN (Jim), 1570, 1616.
ALLEN (Pauline), 3048.
ALLIERES (Jacques), 4097.
ALLIN (Dana H.), 8429.
ALLISON (Robert J.), 7974.
ALLUE I BLANCH (Vicenc), 457.
ALMANSI (Guido), 6882.
ALMEIDA (M. M.), XVIII.
ALMODOVAR (Antonio), 6989.
ALONGE (Roberto), 6883.
ALONSO (Ana María), 5112.
ALONSO ACERO (Beatriz), 7921.
ALONSO JIMENEZ (Carmelo), 1590.
ALONSO-NUÑEZ (J. M.), 820, 2750.
ALPERN (Stanley B.), 7844.
ALPERÓVICH (M. S.), 513.
ALPERS (Michael), 2710.
ALPHANDÉRY (Paul), 3925.
AL-RAWI (Farouk N. H.), 1813.
Alsop (Joe), 6215.
ALSTON (Philip), 4702.
ALSTON (R.), 1761.
AL-TABARI (Abu Ja`far Muhammad b. Jarir), 3543.
ALTEKAMP (Stefan), 514.
ALTENMULLER (H.), 1979.
ALTÉS I AGUILÓ (Francesc Xavier), 3206.
ALTHOFF (Frank), 7950.
ALTHOFF (Gerd), 3926.
ALTHUSSER (Louis), 6990.
ALTMAN (Janet Gurkin), 5969.
ALTRICHTER (Helmut), 861, 6717.
ALVAR (Jaime), 1431.
ÁLVAREZ (Manue Lucas), 3243.
ALVAREZ BARRIENTOS (Joaquin), 5970.
ALVAREZ MARQUEZ (Carmen), 78.
ALVAREZ ROLDAN (Arturo), 1011.
ALVAZZI DEL FRATE (P.), 6057.
ALVIRA CABRER (Martin), 3927.
ALVIS (J.), 2347.
AMANO (Masatoshi), 1137.
AMAR RODRÍGUEZ (Víctor Manuel), 6884.
Amari (Michele), 741.
AMBJÖRNSSON (Ronny), 7431.

AMBROSE (Alison), 6803.
AMBROSIANI (Bjorn), 3577.
Ambrosius, Ep. Mediolanensis, Sanctus, 3003.
AMELANG (James S.), 515.
AMELOTTI (Mario), 7577.
AMES (G.), 7047.
Amiclas (Robert), 4146.
AMIET (Robert), 3261.
AMIN (Ash), 7034.
AMINE (Mohamed), 7201.
AMINI (Iradj), 7975.
AMINO (Yoshihiko), 1068, 9018, 9024.
AMIOTTI (Gabriella), 2607.
Amir Hussien, 8018.
AMIS (Robin), 5819.
AMITAI-PREISS (Reuven), 3544.
Ammianus Marcellinus, 805, 2548, 3044, 3056.
AMOUROUX (Henri), 6058.
Anacreōn, 6575.
ANATRA (Bruno), 517.
Anaxagoras, 2056.
ANAYA MERCHANT (Luis), 518.
Ancus Marcius, 2614.
ANDAH (Bassey W.), 685.
ANDERNACH (Norbert), 3180.
ANDERSEN (Henning), 344.
ANDERSEN (Per Sveas), 3341.
ANDERSON (Christopher), 9121.
ANDERSON (David M.), 9081.
ANDERSON (Duncan), 8365.
ANDERSON (James), 8431.
ANDERSON (Joel), 6284.
ANDERSON (Kevin), 6223.
ANDERSON (Matthew Smith), 7951.
ANDERSON (R. D.), 6086.
ANDERSON (R. G. W.), 475.
ANDERSON (Sean), 1069.
ANDERSSON (Hans), 7620.
ANDERSSON-SCHMITT (M.), 159.
Andokidēs, 2046, 2047.
ANDORLINI (I.), 1762.
ANDRAE (Friedrich), 8398.
András II, re d'Ungheria, 3469.
Andrea del Sarto, 6838.
Andrea di Samosata, 3036.
ANDREAE (Bernhard), 2859.
Andreas Agnellus, 683, 3302.
Andreas de Sancto Victore, 4385.
ANDREAU (Jean) , 775, 2441.
ANDREEV (Ju. V), 1995, 1996.
ANDREINI (Ginevra), 8325.
ANDREOLLI (Bruno), 3591.
ANDREOLLI (Cristina), 3283.
ANDREOZZI (Daniele), 4656.
ANDREUCCI (Franco), 7578.
ANDREW (Christopher), 5433, 7675.
Andrew the Fool, Sanctus, 3082.
ANDREWS (E. M.), 8074.

ANDREWS (Goeff), 4935.
ANDREWS (Lew), 6538.
ANDRISANI (Gaetano), 5707.
Anfilochio di Iconio, Sanctus, 3061.
ANFIMOV (A. M.), 5347.
Angelerio (Pietro), 3329.
ANGENENDT (A.), 4480.
ANGERHOFER (Paul J.), 197.
ANGIOLINI (Enrico), 3592, 5991.
ANGIOLINI (Vittorio), 7552.
ANGLES VARGAS (Victor), 9107.
ANGLET (Kurt), 850.
ANGLIN (Douglas G.), 7845.
ANGLIN (W. S.), 6378.
ANGOLD (Michael), 3093.
ANGULO RIVAS (Alfredo), 5581.
ANGUSIEWICZ (Sławomir), 7952.
ANIKIN (Aleksej V.), 5971.
ANIKOVICH (Michael), 1600.
ANIL (Yaşar Şahin), 1232.
ANKERSMIT (F. R.), 930, 934.
ANKO (Bostjan), 3287.
ANNAS (J.), 2100, 2182.
Annibale di Capua, 7974.
Anquetil-Duperron (Abraham Hyacinthe), 742.
ANRUP (Roland), 5085.
Antelami (Benedetto), 4177.
ANTER (Andreas), 1180.
ANTHONY (David W.), 1571.
ANTIN (Kirsti), V.
Antiphōn, 2171.
ANTOHE (Ion), 8326.
ANTOINE (Gerald), 343.
ANTONACCIO (Carla M.), 2348.
Antoni (Carlo), 743.
Antoninus (Titus Aurelius Fulvus), imperatore romano, 2059.
Antonius, Sanctus, 4475.
Antonius (C.), 2682.
ANTONOVA (E. V.), 1170, 1805.
ANTONOVA (I. A), 2608.
ANTUF'EV (L. A.), 7129.
ANYON (Roger), 1572.
ANZIDEI (Anna Paola), 1628.
APARICI (J.), 3787.
Apollinaire (Guillaume), 6846.
Apollonios Rhodios, 2291.
APOSKITE (Martha), 4926.
APOSTOLIDES (Jean-Marie), 7621.
APOSTOLOS-CAPPADONA (Diane), 6804.
APPELBAUM (David), 6224.
APPELIUS (S.), 8433.
APRILE (Renato), 984.
APULEIUS MADAURENSIS, 2532.
Apuleius (Lucius), 2802.
ARA (Angelo), 8061.
ARAKI (Moriaki), 9019.
ARALOVEC (N. A.), 5339.
ARALOVEC (Natal'ja A.), 5396.

ARASARATNAM (Sinnappah), 7147, 7911.
ARBEL (Benjamin), 7922.
ARBEZ (Fernand), 296.
ARBOIT (Gérald), 7976.
ARBOLEDA (Luis Carlos), 5967.
ARCHER (Rowena E.), 3491.
ARENA (Antonella), 2752.
Arendt (Hannah), 1201.
ARESTI (Cristina), 1.
ARETIN (Karl O. Frhr. Von), 4607.
ARETINO (Pietro), 6539.
ARGENTIERI (Mino), 6968.
ARIEW (Roger), 1509.
ARIKAN (Muzaffer), 7148, 7923.
ARIM (Meral), 5527.
ARIMOTO (Masao), 9020.
Ariosto (Ludovico), 6558.
ARIS (Rutherford), 802.
ARISAN (Kazim), 989.
ARISAN GÜNAY (Duygu), 989.
ARISHOLM (Torstein), 6030.
Aristeidēs, 2082.
Aristophanēs, 2048, 2087, 2276, 2305.
Aristotelēs, 175, 1511, 1518, 2049, 2050, 2051, 2053, 2074, 2267, 2273, 2280, 2303, 2331, 2315, 4267, 4303, 4321, 4334, 4388, 6331.
ARMBRUSTER (Barbara R.), 1653.
ARMISEN-MARCHETTI (Mireille), 2753.
ARMOGATHE (Jean-Robert), 1182.
ARMSTRONG (A.), 3928.
ARMSTRONG (John), 7170.
ARMSTRONG (Richard), 1591.
ARNALDI (Girolamo), 2961.
ARNAUD (Jacqueline), 6614.
Arnaud de Villeneuve, 4310, 6351.
Arnaut (Daniel), 4094.
ARNOLD (Clinton E.), 2962.
ARNOLD (James R.), 7977.
Arnold von Lübeck, 3926.
ARNOULET (François), 8012.
AROCA (Santiago), 4969.
Aron (Raymond), 6339.
ARRANZ (Miguel, S.J.), 3049.
Arrianus, 2052.
ARRIANZA (A.), 3593.
ARRIGHETTI (G.), 2237.
ARRIGHI (Vanna), 70.
ARRU (A.), 7351.
ARSLAN (Ermanno A.), 297.
ARSZYŃSKI (Marian), 4198, 4429.
Artaxerxes I, re di Persia, 2123.
ARTHUR (James), 6087.
ARTIERES (Philippe), 7622.
ARTIFONI (Enrico), 3428.
ARTIOLI (Umberto), 6885.
Arup (Erik), 744.

ASAJI (Keizō), 3388, 3429.
ASANTE (Emmanuel), 5634.
ASAO (Naohiro), 9021.
ASCHER (Abraham), 5305.
ASCHER (François), 5973.
ASCHERI (Mario), 1233.
ASHER (R. E.), 1080.
ASKWITH (Tom), 5082.
ASMUS (Walter), 7149.
ASOR ROSA (Alberto), 1550.
Aspasia of Miletus, 2133.
ASPER (Helmut G.), 6879.
ASPERTI (Stefano), 3929.
Asquith (lord Herbert Henry), 8074.
ASSELAIN (Jean Charles), 7048.
ASSMANN (Ian), 1764.
ASSO (M.), 7464.
ASTIGARRAGA (Juan Luis), 1421.
ASTON (Elaine), 6886.
ASTOR (Gerald), 8358.
ASTROM (Paul), 6074.
ATIYAH (Michael), 4175 a).
ATIYEH (George N.), 90.
ATKINS (Martyn), 8075.
ATKINSON (Charles), 4240.
ATMANSPACHER (H.), 6466.
AUBERGER (Janick), 2238.
Aubert (David), 4135.
AUBERT (R.), 1376.
AUBIN (Paul), 4849.
AUER (Alfred), 476.
Augustinus Aurelius, Sanctus, 330, 2941, 2943, 2975, 3019, 3076, 3028, 4130.
Augustus (Gaius Julius Caesar Octavianus), imperatore romano, 309, 2515, 2611, 2629, 2852, 2903.
AULIARD (C.), 2677.
AURE (Chantal), 6781.
Aurelius Symmachus (Quintus), 2598.
AURELL (Martin), 3694.
AURELL I CARDONA (Jaume), 3695.
AURISICCHIO (Carlo), 1629.
AUSENDA (G.), 990.
AUSTIN (N. J. E.), 2609.
AUSTIN (Paul Britten), 7978.
AUTANT-MATHIEU (M.-Ch.), 6915.
AUTENRIETH (Johane), 79.
AUZEPY (Marie-France), 3050, 3106.
AVALOS (Hector), 1720.
AVELLINI (Luisa), 80.
AVENEL (Jean), 8013.
Averlino (Antonio), 6323.
Avoseh (T. O.), 745.
AVRAM (Alexandre), 2026, 2349.
AVRIL (François), 151, 200, 4200.
AVRIL (J.), 3250.
AWAYA (Toshie), 8816.
AXWORTHY (Mark), 8359.

AYALON (Ami), 6156.
AYALON (Etan), 1677.
AYERBE IRIBAR (M. R.), 3181.
AYERS (Edward L.), 5588.
AYMARD (Maurice), 519, 600.
AYNUR (Hatice), 6805.
AYOOB (Mohammed), 8434.
AYRES (L.), 2313.
AYUBI (Nazih N.), 8435.
AZEMA (Jean-Pierre), 8201.
AZUAR (Rafael), 3545.
AZZARA (Claudio), 3594, 4418.
AZZOLINI (Luisa), 4599.
AZZOU (El Mustafa), 7846.

B

BAAKEN (Gerhard), 3595.
BAALBAKI (Ramzi), 1886.
BABA (Keiji), 2183.
BABEL (Rainer), 7913.
BABIĆ (Irina L.), 995.
BABIJ (Orest M.), 8076.
BABIŃSKI (Grzegorz), 8436.
BABY (François), 5902.
Bach (Johann Sebastian), 6945, 6887, 6897, 6950, 6963.
BACHMANN (Jörg J.), 5974.
BACHNICK (Uwe), 7553.
BACKHAUS (Fritz), 3541.
BACKHAUS (Jürgen G.), 7042.
BACKHOUSE (J.), 201.
BACKMAN (Clifford R.), 3489.
Bacon (Roger), 6463.
BÁCSKAI (Vera), 7352.
BADEL (L.), 8077.
BADER (A.), 1952.
BADER (Karl Siegfried), 3596.
BADER (Tibor), 1574.
BADGER (Anthony J.), 5975.
BADIN (Maria-Esther), 6517.
BAECHLER (Jean), 1252.
BAES (Christian), 7925.
BAGGE (Sverre), 3344.
BAGNALL (R. S.), 1968.
BAGNASCO (Gianni), 2442.
BAGNATO (Bruna), 7676.
BAHL (Vinay), 4976.
BAHN (Paul G.), 1597.
BAHTI (Timothy), 6638.
BAI (Hua), 8826.
BAILEY (Mark), 3696.
BAILEY (Martin), 6806.
BAILEY (Terence), 4241.
BAILLIE SCOTT (M. H.), 6782.
BAILLY (Antoine), 1253.
BAILO MODESTI (Gianni), 1630.
BAILYN (Bernard), 852.
BAINBRIDGE (Simon), 6615.
BAIRD (Catherine), 5976.

Bajazed II, 5521.
BAJONI (M. G.), 814.
BAKALOV (Georgi), 275.
BAKER (H.D.), 1739.
BAKER (James A.), 8437.
BAKER (Peter S.), 3952.
BAKHMATOVA (Marina), 5538.
Bakhtin (Mikhail Mikhailovich), 746, 1530, 2305.
BALADIER (Charles), 1380.
BALAKIER (Ann Stewart), 6379.
BALAKIER (James J.), 6379.
BALARD (Michel), 3925.
BALBI (G.), 3913.
BALBI DE CARO (Silvana), 6719.
BALCER (Jack Martin), 2114.
BALCOU (Jean), 832.
BALDINI (A. Enzo), 1181.
BALDWIN (Richard), 8438.
BALESTRACCI (Duccio), 3430.
BÁLINT (Csanád), 3345.
BALL (Simon J.), 8439.
BALL (Terence), 6225.
BALLA (Balint), 5977.
BALLARD (Bill), 6991.
BALLARINI (Amleto), 8078.
BALLETTO (Laura), 3597.
BALOGH (Sándor), 8440.
BALSAMO (Jean), 5965, 6540.
BALSER (Frolinde), 7303.
BALTA (Evangelia), 7304.
BALTY-GUESDON (M.-G.), 86.
BALUEV (Boris P.), 5307.
BALUK (Stefan Starba), 8204.
BALUŠKO (V. G.), 996.
BALZ (Heinrich), 5903.
Balzac (Honoré de), 6616.
BALZE (Felipe A. M. de la), 4679.
BAMBACH (Charles), 6226.
BAMBONEYEHO (Venant), 6525.
BANAC (Ivo), 5063.
BANAT (Francoise), 6781.
BANCIU (Jean), 8197.
BANCQUART (Marie Claire), 6617.
BANDERIER (C.), 6541.
BANDERIER (Gilles), 740.
BANGURA (Abdul Karim), 8441.
BANN (Stephen), 853.
BANNIARD (M.), 330.
BANNIARD (Michel), 3930.
BANNING (Lance), 5597.
BANTI (Alberto Mario), 4589, 4656.
BANTI (Ottavio), 5, 46.
BAR (Christian V.), 7663.
BARANOVA (Natalija V.), 8334.
BARANOWSKI (Andrzej), 5723.
BARANOWSKI (Shelley), 4758.
Barante (Prosper de), 830.
BARASH (Andrew Jeffrey), 6227.
BARATA (Manuel Themudo), 7798.

BARATAS DIAZ (Luis Alfredo), 6088.
BARATTOLO (Andrea), 1740.
BARBADILLO ALONSO (Javier), 425.
BARBANERA (Marcello), 2443.
BARBAS (Jean-Claude), 4853.
BARBER (Sarah), 4937.
BARBERÁ NOLLA (Rita), 7428.
BARBET (J.), 4282.
BARBIER (Frederic), 202.
BARBU (D.), 3107.
BARCIA (María del Carmen), 7895.
BARCLAY (Alistair), 1693.
BARCLAY (David E.), 4759.
BARCLAY (Glen St J.), 8442.
BARCLAY (Gordon J.), 1631.
BARDACH (Juliusz), 4590.
BÁRDI (Nándor), 5292.
BARDINI (Carlo), 7049, 7161.
BARDIS (Panos D.), 259.
BARDUCCI (Roberto), 3816.
BARELLO (Federico), 2444.
BARFOD (Jörgen H.), 4751.
BARIŚTA (H. Orcun), 6807.
BARILE (Paolo), 7555.
BARJOT (Dominique), 7157.
BARKAN (Elazar), 6040.
BARKER (E.), 1381, 2053.
BARKHUIZEN (J. H.), 3051.
BARKIN (Kenneth), 4760.
BARLOW (J.), 3931.
Barlow (Joel), 8007.
BARNABY (Frank), 8592.
BARNAY (Y.), 5209.
BARNES (Jonathan), 1511.
Barnes (Joshua), 2252.
BARNES (Philip), 4986.
BARNES (T. D.), 2610.
BARNETT (Correlli), 4936, 4965.
BARNETT (Michael), 8443.
BARNETT (Vincent), 7050.
BARNOUIN (B.), 8444.
BARNOVSKÝ (Michal), 5386.
BAROCCHI (Paola), 6802.
BAROFFIO (B. G.), 83.
BARON (Marcia), 6228.
BARRAL I ALTET (Xavier), 4181.
BARRANDON (J.-N.), 2034.
BARRAS (V.), 2071.
BARRATT (A.), 3898.
BARRAVECCHIA (Giuseppe), 8445.
BARRELL (Andrew D. M.), 4396.
BARRERA (Carlos), 6157.
BARRERA-GONZALEZ (Andres), 331.
BARRET (James), 2239.
BARRIE HALL (John), 2582.
BARRIERA (Darío), 520.
BARRIL VICENTE (Magdalena), 1654.
BARRINGER (J. M.), 2350.

AUTOREN- UND PERSONENREGISTER 367

BARRIO BARRIO (Juan Alfonso), 3598.
BARROS (James), 8205.
BARROS GUIMERANS (Carlos), 602.
BARROW (Geoffrey W. S.), 47.
BARRY (Jonathan), 7623.
BART (Jean), 7624.
BARTA (Gábor), 7926.
BARTA (János), 5541.
BARTELSON (Jens), 1183.
BARTH (Boris), 7273.
Barth (Karl), 5855.
BARTHELEMY (Dominique), 3697, 3932.
BARTL (Peter), 4673.
BARTLETT (Anne Clark), 3933.
BARTLETT (Clive), 6720.
BARTNICKI (Andrzej), 5597.
BARTOLINI (Roberto), 6059.
BARTOLO DA SASSOFERRATO, 3599.
BARTOLOME DE LAS CASAS, 5623, 7903.
BARTOLONI (F.), 6.
BARTON (Brian), 8206.
BARTON (Tamsyn), 2611.
BARTOŠ (Josef), 8207.
BARTOV (Omer), 854.
BARTROP (Paul R.), 8228.
BARTUSIS (Mark C.), 3108.
BAR-YOSEF (Ofer), 1617.
BARZMAN (John), 4854.
BASCH (Sophie), 4925.
BASCHET (J.), 4020.
BASHILOV (Vladimir A.), 1686.
BASSALYGO (Leonid A.), 4562.
BASSO (Alberto), 6978.
BASTERT (Katrin), 1806.
BASTIA (Patrizia), 3303.
BASTIAN (Jean-Pierre), 521.
BASU (K.), 7062.
BATCHELDER (A. G.), 2240.
BATES (David), 765.
BATES (Don), 6380.
BATESON (Donald), 3581.
BATEY (Mavis), 6783.
BATIĆ (Jerneja), 506.
BATKIN (Leonid M.), 5006.
BATKOV (A. M.), 5306.
BATORI (Armida), 6721.
BATOU (Jean), 1297, 7051.
BATOWSKI (Henryk), 8079.
BATSCHMANN (Oskar), 6722.
BAT-SHEVA (Albert), 3535.
BATTELLI (Giulio), 48.
BATTENBERG (Friedrich), 3518.
Battenberg (Louis Alexander), 8041.
Batthyány (Lajos), 5559.
BATTISTA (Gabriella), 3816.
BATTISTELLI (Pier Paolo), 5007.
BATTISTINI (Andrea), 855.
BATUMLU (M. Ragib), 7274.

BAUDET (François), 8080.
BAUDOT (Georges), 9115.
BAUDRY (G. H.), 1437.
Bauduin (F.), 379.
BAUER (Brian S.), 6408.
BAUMAN (Thomas), 6955.
BAUMANN (Martin), 1435.
BAUMGART (Susanne), 2963.
BAUMGÄRTNER (Ingrid), 3600, 3183, 3612.
BAUREPAIRE (P.-Y.), 4855.
BAUTZ (F.W.), 1422.
BAUTZ (T.), 1422.
BAWDEN (Nina), 6229.
BAXTER WOLF (Kenneth), 3934.
BAY (Edna G.), 9082.
BAYARD (Françoise), 7275.
BAYKARA (Tuncer), 7580.
BAYLIS (John), 8447.
BAYOD LÓPEZ (María del Carmen), 7625.
BAYRAKTAR (Nimet), 256.
BAYROU (Maurice), 8360.
BAZANT (Jan), 2860.
BAZIELICH (Barbara), 5264.
BAZIN (Jean-François), 8047.
BAZZANA (André), 1007.
BEACHEY (R. W.), 7953.
BEADLE (R.), 246.
BEAGON (Philip M.), 2964.
BEAL (Peter), 108.
Beard (Charles Ostin), 747.
BEARD (M.), 2711.
BEARMAN (P. J.), 1451.
BEARZOT (Cinzia), 2184.
BEATO DE LIÉBANA, 4458.
BEATON (J. M.), 1598.
Beatrice di Canossa, 3448.
BEATTIE (Blake), 4419, 4482.
Beatus Rhenanus, 837.
BEAULIEU (Louis le Hardy de), 8448.
BEAULIEU (Paul-Alain), 1807.
BEAUMONT (Joan), 8081.
BECCARIA (Gian Luigi), 332.
BECHTEL (G.), 203.
BECKA (Jan), 1071.
BECKER (A. S.), 2241.
BECKER (Jochen), 1366.
BECKER (Marjorie), 5113.
BECKER (Werner), 6148.
BECKER (Winfried), 4582.
BECKER-CHRISTENSEN (Henrik), 7711.
BECKERMAN (Paul), 4680.
BECKING (Bob), 1447.
BECKMAN (Margareta), 7954.
BEDANI (Gino), 7490.
BEDE, THE VENERABLE, 4268.
BEDARIDA (François), 600, 8201.
BEDNARCZYK (Andrzej), 6230.

BEDNARIK (Robert G.), 1599.
BEECH (George), 3935.
BEEKES (Robert S. P.), 2351.
BEER (Siegfried), 5169.
BEERBÜHL (Margrit Schulte), 7150.
BEETHAM (D.), 6307.
Beethoven (Ludwig van), 6911, 6929, 6946, 6958, 6969.
BÉGUIN (Daniel), 2242.
BEGUNOVA (Ju. K.), 5329.
BEHDAD (S.), 4990.
BEHEBE (Ngwabi), 7847.
BEHME (Thomas), 1184.
BEHREND (Hanna), 4761.
BEHRENDS (Okko), 2174, 3055.
BEHRENDT (Stephen D.), 7848.
BEHRMANN (Thomas), 62.
BEINART (W.), 5459.
BEINHART (William), 5447.
BEJAN (Adrian), 3346.
BEKE (Gyorgy), 8082.
BEKELE (Shiferaw), 7075.
BÉKÉS (Csaba), 8449.
BELARDI (Walter), 333.
BELCEV (Tasko D.), 997.
BELCHEM (John), 4591.
BELDA (Josef), 5491, 8450.
BÉLI (Gábor), 1234.
BELIEN (H. M.), 5144.
BELIN (Christian), 6542.
BELINGA (S. M. Eno), 9095.
BÉLIS (Annie), 2388.
BELISSA (Marc), 4918.
BELITSKA-SCHOLZ (Hedvig), 6912.
BELJAKOV (Aleksej A.), 5308.
BELKE (Klaus), 3054.
BELL (Brenda M.), 2754.
BELL (D. N.), 3936.
BELL (David), 4856.
BELL (Sandra M.), 5072.
Bellarmino (Roberto), Cardinale di Capua, 5707.
BELLAVITIS (Anna), 7354.
Belleau (Remy), 6550.
BELLENGER (Yvonne), 5978.
BELLI PASQUA (Ribaerta), 2445.
BELLINAZZI (Anna), 424.
BELLINGERI (Giampiero), 7955.
BELLONI (Cristina), 5724.
BELLOTTO (Nicoletta), 1808.
Bellow (Saul), 6630.
BELMONTE (Laura), 8451.
BELPOLITI (Marco), 6647.
BELTJENS (Alain), 4483.
BELTRAN (Alain), 7043.
BELTRAN (E.), 3937.
BELTRAN BERNAL (Trinidad), XIV.
BEM (Jeanne), 1537.
Bembo (Pietro), 6569.
BEN BELGHITH (Chibani), 7355.
BENĆÍK (Antonín), 8450, 8452.

BENABOUD (M'hammed), 7052.
BENACCHIO (Giannantonio), 1235.
BENASSI (Silvano), 6543.
BENCIVENGA (Ermanno), 6231.
BEN-DOV (Yoav), 1324.
Benedictus, Sanctus, 2940, 2995.
Benedictus XII, Papa, 4382.
Benedictus XIII, Papa, 4482.
Beneš (Eduard), 5470, 8333.
BENEŠ (Zdeněk), 523.
BENEVOLO (Leonardo), 1287.
BENEWICK (Robert), 8827.
BEN-GHIAT (Ruth), 6618.
BENHAMAMOUCHE (Fatima), 3938.
BENICHOU (Paul), 6671.
BENICHOU-SAFAR (Hélène), 9083.
BENIGNO (Francesco), 524, 1091.
BENJALLOUN (Abdelmajid), 7849.
BENJAMIN (Andrew E.), 6723.
BENJAMIN (Ionie), 6158.
Benjamin (Walter), 850, 6218, 6220, 6309, 6362, 6638.
BENKŐ (Loránd), 353.
BENKŐ (Péter), 5542.
Benn (Gottfried), 909.
BENNETT (Alvin LeRoy), 1072.
BENNETT (G. H.), 8083.
BENNETT (Tony), 477.
BENOÎT (Bertrand), 7850.
BENOIT (Fernand), 8084.
BENOIT (Paul), 3698.
BENOU (Lisa), 3065.
BENREKASSA (Georges), 6592.
BENSAÏD (Daniel), 6232.
BENSCH (Stephen P.), 3431.
BENSON (Edward), 6544.
BENTHAM (Jeremy), 6993, 7894.
BENTON (Gregor), 8828.
BENTON (Kenneth), 5434.
BENVENISTI (Meron), 8453.
BENVENUTI (A.), 4484.
BENZ (Lore), 2809.
BENZ (Wolfgang), 4762.
BERARDINELLI (Paula), 6889.
BERCE (Yves-Marie), 600, 1529, 7594.
BERCOVITCH (Jacob), 7677.
BERCOVITCH (Sacvan), 1532.
Berdyaev (Nicolai), 1207, 5976.
BEREND (Ivan T.), 7053.
BÉRENGER (Jean), 1073, 7579.
BERETTA (Marco), 6381.
BERG (Roald), 4592, 7760, 8085.
BERG (Warren G.), 1074.
BERGAD (Laird W.), 7895.
BERGAMELLI (Fernandino), 2932.
BERGE (Anders), 856.
BERGEMANN (Johannes), 2385.
BERGER (Albrecht), 3052, 3109.
BERGER (F.), 8086.
BERGER (Guy), 756.

BERGER (Helge), 4763.
BERGER (Stefan), 525.
BERGGREN (Henrik), 5359.
BERGHAUS (Peter), 228, 314.
BERGIER (Jean-François), 1254.
BERGMAN (Ulf), 7356.
BERGMAN-CARTON (Janis), 6724.
BERGMANN (Lothar), 1614.
BERGMANN (Sven), 6484.
BERGSTEN (Fred), 8705.
BERGSTRÖM (Asta), 7054.
BÉRI-LICHTNER (János), 5543.
BERKEY (Jonathan P.), 3546.
BERKHOUT (Carl T.), 3587.
BERLIN (Gail Ivy), 526.
Berlin (Isaiah), 6277.
BERLIOZ (Jacques), 3939.
BERMEJO BARRERA (José Carlos), 527, 857.
BERMINGHAM (Ann), 7372.
BERMON (Pascal), 3337.
Bernabe, Sanctus, 5904.
BERNABE (Pons Luis F.), 5904.
BERNANKE (Ben S.), 7055.
Bernanos (Georges), 4873.
BERNARD (Jean-Paul), 528.
Bernard de Montfaucon, 816.
BERNARD-GRIFFITHS (Simone), 831, 858.
BERNARDI (Philippe), 4178.
BERNARDI (Sandro), 6890.
BERNARDINI (Maria Grazia), 6808.
BERNARDINI (P. A.), 2097.
Bernardinus Senensis, Sanctus, 4517.
Bernardus, Abbas Claraevallensis, Sanctus, 597, 1415, 4269.
Bernart de Ventadorn, 4094.
BERNASCONTI (Paolo), 8454.
BERNAUER (Markus), 6763.
BERNDT (Jaqueline), 6809.
BERNECKER (Walther L.), 370.
BERNÈDE (Allain), 8087.
BERNERDINI (Aldo), 6948.
BERNHARD (Maria Ludwika), 1731.
BERNHARD (Michael), 4253, 5235.
BERNOV (Iurii Vladimirovich), 8455.
BERSANI (Carlo), 7581.
BERSTEIN (Serge), 4857, 8088.
BERTAUD (Jean-Paul), 6159.
BERTAUD (Madeleine), 587.
Bertelli (Carlo), 6740.
BERTELLI (Sergio), 1014, 6891.
BERTELLONI (Francisco), 4303.
BERTHE (Maurice), 3699.
Berthelier (Philibert), 5371.
BERTHELOT (Jean-Michel), 5979.
BERTHIER (Annie), 7919.
BERTHOLD-BOND (Daniel), 6233.
BERTHOUZOZ (Roger), 5688.
BERTI (Luca), 3700.

BERTINI (Fabio), 7979.
BERTINI (Ferruccio), 4054.
BERTOLA (Francesco), 6382.
BERTOLASO (Marco), 8089.
BERTOLI (Bruno), 5725.
BERTRAM (Barbara), 8399.
BERTRAM (Martin), 7357.
BERTRAND (Dominique), 6619.
BERTRAND (Georges), 373.
Bertrand du Mans, 3649.
BERZIN (Eduard O.), 8820.
BESOMI (Daniele), 6987.
BESSA (Carlos), 8208.
BESSMERTNY (Youri L.), 529, 530, 3701.
BEST (Antony), 8209.
BESWICK (Francis), 6735.
BETANCES (Emelio), 4830.
BETHELL (Leslie), 1060.
BETHENCOURT (Francisco), 1075.
BETTLES (Elizabeth), 1787.
BETTS (G.), 3088.
BEUTLER (Corinne), 7234.
BEVIR (Mark), 859, 4593.
BEWLEY (Robert), 1577.
BEYER (H.-V.), 3077.
BEYER-THOMA (Hermann), 5301.
Bèze (Théodore de), 6587.
BEZECZKY (Tamás), 2861.
BEZLER (Francis), 3347.
BEZYMENSKIJ (Lev. A.), 8327.
BHATT (Rakesh Kumar), 455.
Bil'ak (Vasil), 8770.
BIĆANIĆ (Rudolf), 5090.
BIAŁUŃSKI (Grzegorz), 3432.
Biały (Leszek), 3461.
BIAGIANTI (Ivo), 1255.
BIAGIOLI (Giuliana), 4647.
BIAGIOLI (Mario), 6383.
BIAGIONI (Mario), 5635.
BIANCARDI (Giovanni), 6546.
BIANCHI (Francesco), 1.
BIANCHI (Lorenzo), 815.
BIANCHI (Paola), 782.
BIANCHI (Roberto), 7491.
BIANCHI (S.), 4304.
Bianchi (Ugo), 748, 1477.
BIANCHINI (G.), 180.
BIANCIADI (Patrizia), 3661.
BIANCO (Maria Grazia), 2932.
BIANQUIS (T.), 1451.
BIARD (Michel), 4858.
BIARNE (J.), 2965.
BICK (Ilsa J.), 6892.
Bickerman (E.), 835.
BICKFORD-SMITH (Vivian), 5448.
BIDEAULT (Marise), 1367.
BIDERMAN (S.), 5636.
BIDET (Jacques), 6990.
BIDUSSA (David), 860, 6016.
BIEBER (Roland), 8456.

BIEDERMAN (S.), 1382.
BIEFANG (Andreas), 4764.
BIEG (Gebhard), 2489.
BIELANSKI (Stefan), 7678.
BIELECKI (Robert), 7980.
BIELIK (Miroslav), 5498.
BIEŃKOWSKI (Wiesław), XVII.
BIERING (Ralf), 2862.
BIGER (Gideon), 1911.
BIGET (Jean-Louis), 1293.
BIGGS (Bruce), 1041.
BIHL (Wolfdieter), XVI.
BIKAI (Patricia M.), 1887.
Bikerman (I. I.), 835.
Biko (Stephen), 5455.
BILE (Monique), 2155.
BÍLEK (Jiří), 5471.
BILLOWS (Richard A.), 1940, 2156.
BILLS (Scott L.), 7851.
BILLY (Pierre-Henri), 334.
BINAZZI (Gianfranco), 2931.
BINDER (Dieter A.), 6234.
BINDER (Frederick Moore), 998, 8014.
BINDER (G.), 2755.
BINDING (Günther), 4179.
BINNIE (Susan W. S.), 1239.
BINOCHE (Bertrand), 815.
BINSKI (Paul), 3397.
BIONDI (Albano), 6221.
Biondo (Flavio), 3940, 4013.
BIRCHLER (T.), 2071.
BIRLEY (A.), 2333.
BIRN (Raymond), 6235.
BIRNBERG (Jacques), 7528.
BÍRÓ (Sándor), 5871.
BIROLINI (Alain), 3702.
BISCHOFF (F. M.), 87.
BISCHOFF (Uwe), 6810.
BISCIONE (Michele), 743.
BISHOP (John D.), 6992.
Bismarck (Otto von), 4760, 6826, 7718, 8034, 8041.
BISSINGER (Manfred), 3110.
BISSON (Thomas N.), 3703, 3729.
BISSONNETTE (Denise), 6859.
BIVAR (A.D.H.), 1941.
BIZZOCCHI (Roberto), 531, 5681.
BJARNI (F. Einarsson), 3576.
BJERELD (Ulf), 8457.
BJØRGO (Narve), 7679, 7760.
BJÖRN (Claus), 7582.
BJÖRNE (Lars), 5980.
BLACK (Iris), 553.
BLACK (Jeremy), 7680.
BLACK (N. B.), 3909.
BLACKADDER (Neil Martin), 6894.
BLACKBURN (Mark), 3704.
BLACKMAN (S. A.), 88.
BLACKMER (Corinne E.), 6916.
BLACKSON (Thomas A.), 6236.

BLACK-VELDTRUP (Mechthild), 3433.
BLACKWELL (Christopher William), 2115.
BLAISE (Fabienne), 2054.
BLAIVE (Fréderic), 2827.
BLANC (Bernard), 2757.
BLANC (Odile), 405.
BLANC (Olivier), 7981.
BLANCHARD (Anne), 7579.
BLANCHARD (Joël), 3847.
BLANCHARD (Scott W.), 6548.
BLANCKAERT (Claude), 6461.
BLANCO VALDES (Roberto Luis), 7896.
BLANEY (David), 7723.
BLASCHKE (O. R.), 4765.
BLASIO (Maria Grazia), 3940.
BLASIUS (Rainer A.), 8458.
Blasius, Sanctus, 125, 126.
BLASTENBREI (Peter), 7358.
BLAUMEISER (Hubertus), 5846.
BLAY (Jean-Pierre), 8090.
BLÁZQUEZ (J.M.), 2863.
BLEANGY (C. H.), 1424.
BLECKMANN (Bruno), 2533.
BLEICKEN (Jochen), 1970, 2678.
BLET (Pierre), 5726.
BLOCH (Czesław), 8159.
BLOCH (Etienne), 749.
BLOCH (Howard), 462.
BLOCH (Jean), 6090.
Bloch (Marc), 731, 749.
BLOCH (Maurice), 532.
Bloch (Ernst), 6362.
BLODIG (Vojtěch), 5472.
BLOEDOX (Edmund F.), 2116.
BLOMBERG (Eva), 7492.
Blondel (Maurice), 6416.
BLOOM (Harold), 6513.
BLOOM (Ken), 1369.
BLOSSER (Philip), 6237.
Blum (Léon), 4912.
BLUM (William), 8459.
BLUMENAU (Semen F.), 533.
BLUNDELL (S.), 2185.
BLUTH (Christoph), 8460.
BOŃCZA-BYSTRZYCKI (Lech), 5727.
BOADA I VILALLONGA (Maria Teresa), 457.
Bobbio (Norberto), 1192, 6216.
Bobrikov (Nikolai Ivanovich), 8057.
Boccaccio (Giovanni), 4153, 6590.
BOCCHI (F.), 3281.
BOCCHI (Francesca), 4544.
BOCCHINI CAMAIANI (B.), 5708.
BOCCIA (Corso Paolo), 8461.
BÖCK (B.), 1809.
BOCK (Sebastian), 5806.
BODE (Christian), 6148.
BÖDEKER (H.-E.), 232.

BODEL (John), 2534.
BODENMANN (Reinhard), 5843.
BODENSCHATZ (Harald), 7306.
Bodin (Jean), 379, 1190.
BODINE (Walter R.), 1894.
BODINIER (Gilbert), 7982.
BODKAM (S.), 6238.
BODOR (András), 534.
BODSON (Liliane), 2712.
BOEDER (Titus), 6784.
BOERLIN-BRODBECK (Yvonne), 5624.
Boethius, 2535, 3339, 4273.
BOFFA (Giuseppe), 5397.
BOFFEY (J.), 89.
BOFFO (Laura), 2027.
BOGÁRDI SZABÓ (István), 5847.
BOGART (Leo), 5589.
BOGDANOR (Vernon), 7554.
BOGDANOV (Andrej P.), 535.
BOGDANOWICZ (Stanisław), 5728.
BOGUCKA (Maria), 1159, 7627.
BOGUCKI (Ambroży), 3434.
BÖHM (Hermann), 7643.
BÖHME (Klaus-Richard), 7775, 8314.
BOHN (Robert), 7741.
BOHN (Thomas), 812.
BOIS (Guy), 519.
BOISSIEU (Alain de), 8361.
BOISVERT (M.), 1409.
BOJKO (Krzysztof), 3435.
BOJOVIC (Bosko I.), 536.
BOLADO (AAlvarez Alfonso), 5435.
BOLAND (Margaret M.), 3941.
BOLARD (Georges), 7665.
BOLDRINI (Arrigo), 8411.
BOLDT-IRONS (Leslie Anne), 6239.
BOLENS (Lucie), 1256.
BOLGIANI (Franco), 770.
BOLKHOVITINOV (Nikolaj N.), 4594, 8015.
BOLOGNAN (Maria), 3303.
BOLTANSKI (Jean-Elie), 335.
BOLTE (Gerhard), 5981.
Boltzmann (Ludwig), 6435.
BOLUMINSKI (Andrea), 5753.
BOLZONI (Lina), 5982.
BÖMELBURG (Hans-Jürgen), 4766.
BÓNA (István), 3349.
BONACCORSO (Giovanni), 5983.
BONADONNA RUSSO (M. T.), 4459.
BONALUME NETO (Ricardo), 8211.
BONAMENTE (Giorgio), 2781.
BONANATE (Ugo), 5905.
BONAVENTURA de Balneoregio, Sanctus, 4271, 4324.
BOND (Gerald A.), 3942.
BONDE (Hans), 8462.
BONDELI (Martin), 6240.
BONELLI (Guido), 2055.

BONELLI (Renato), 4461.
BONFIELD (Lloyd), 7628.
BONGARD-LEVIN (G. M.), 835, 1732.
Bonghi (Onofrio), 484.
Bonifatius VIII, Papa, 3184.
BONIFAY (Michel), 2864.
BÖNINGER (Lorenz), 3943, 5008.
BONINO (Serge-Thomas), 4370.
BONK (Magdalena), 537.
BONN (Charles), 6514, 6526.
BONNASSIE (Pierre), 4493.
BONNEFOND-COUDRY (Marianne), 2612, 2865.
BONNEL (Ulane), 7983.
BONNER (Anthony), 4305.
BONNER (John), 6993.
BONNER (Thomas Neville), 6384.
BONNET (Corinne), 1888.
BONNET (Marie Rose), 3944.
BONNETT (N. R.), 7202.
BONNEY (Richard), 7076.
BONO (Salvatore), 7841, 7852.
BONOCORE (Marco), 3945.
BONOMI (Patricia U.), 5597.
BONVICINI (M.), 2737.
BOOCKMANN (Hartmut), 4187.
BOOKER (M. Keith), 746, 1530.
BOONE (Christopher), 4729.
BOONE (Graeme), 4244.
BOOT (H. M.), 7151.
BOOTH (Alan), 7059.
BORA (Siren), 4595.
BORDONE (Renato), 3844.
BORDREUIL (Pierre), 1918.
BORELLA (Vincent), 4859.
BORGERSRUD (Lars), 8463.
BORGES (María Elizia), 406.
BORGHETTI (M. N.), 584.
BORGHINI (Gabriele), 6779.
BORGIA (Luigi), 452.
BORGOLTE (M.), 3350.
BORGOLTE (Michael), 660, 1076.
BORHI (László), 8464.
BORISEVIĆ (G. V.), 4552.
BORK (B.), 4485.
BÖRKER-KLÄHN (Jutta), 1859.
BORKOPP (Brigitt), 3104.
BORNSTEIN (D.), 4486.
BORNSTEIN (Daniel E.), 4487.
BOROŃ (Iwona), 7203.
BÖRÖCZ (József), 8745.
BORRAS LLOP (Jose Maria), 7056.
BORREGUERO (Epifanio), 426.
BORRERO FERNANDEZ (Mercedes), 49.
Borromeo (Vitaliano), 3223.
BORSÁNYI (György), 7493.
BORSDORF (Axel), 371.
BORSI-KÁLMÁN (Béla), 5293.
BORST (A.), 3946.

BORTNEVSKIJ (Viktor G.), 5309.
BORZOMATI (Pietro), 5682.
BORZYKOWSKI (Józef), 7426.
BOS (Th. S. H.), XV.
BOSCÁ CODINA (José Vicente), 821.
BOSCHMA (Kees), 6811.
BOSCHOF (Egon), 3436.
BOSSENBROEK (Martin), 7799.
BOSSUAT (G.), 8465.
BOSTAN (İdris), 7204.
BOSWORTH (C. E.), 1451.
BOTALLA (Horacio), 906.
BOTHE (Michael), 1237.
BOTHWELL (Robert), 5073.
BOTOS (János), 5544.
BOTTALLA (Paola), 378.
BOUBAKER (Sadok), 7205.
BOUCHER (David), 943, 6241.
BOUCHERON (Patrick), 3705.
Bouchet (Jean), 3928.
BOUDARD (René), 7984.
BOUDON (J.-O.), 5683.
BOUDOURIS (K. J.), 1510.
BOUGARD (François), 3601.
BOUGEROL (J. G.), 4271.
BOUJU (Jacky), 538.
BOULAINE (Jean), 7235.
Boulanger (N.-A.), 842.
BOULANGER (Patrick), 8091.
BOULOGNE (Jacques), 2352.
BOUNIALES (Marinos Tzane), 4926.
BOUNIN (Paule), 6515.
BOUQUET (Jean), 2551.
BOURDIEU (Pierre), 862.
BOUREAU (Alain), 863, 3602, 4306.
BOURETTE-KNOWLES (Simon), 8092.
BOURGEOIS (Etienne), 5984.
BOURGEON (Jean-Louis), 4860.
BOURGERIE (Raymond), 8016.
BOURIN (Monique), 3706, 3765.
BOURKE (Cormac), 4184.
BOURKE (Stephen), 1735.
BOURNE (Russell), 7152.
BOURRIOT (F.), 2244.
BOUSQUET (Jacques), 4201.
BOUTIER (Jean), 940.
BOUTRY (Philippe), 539.
BOUYAHYA (Salem), 7494.
BOUZID (Lamjed), 7629, 9084.
BOVEN (Walter), 3264.
BOVESSE (Jean), II.
BOVYKIN (Dmitrij Ju.), 4861.
BOWDLER (Sandra), 1632.
BOWER (Tom), 7681.
BOWERSOCK (Glenn W.), 2966.
BOWLER (Peter J.), 6385, 6451.
BOWLES (Brett C.), 7583.
BOWLUS (Charles R.), 3407.
BOWMAN (William D.), 5170.
BOWYER (T. H.), 4977.

BOYD (Carl), 8362.
BOYD (Stephen), 5633.
BOYER (Paul), 5597.
BOYER (Régis), 769.
BOYER (Richard), 5114.
BOYER (Robert), 7039.
BOYLE (John F.), 4307.
Boysset (Bertrand), 3776.
BOZÓKY (Edina), 3947.
BOZZINI (Paola), 3197.
BRACCESI (L.), 5985.
Bracciolini (Poggio), 955, 4162.
BRACHMANN (Hansjürgen), 3710.
BRADLEY (Bruce A.), 1600.
Bradwardine (Thomas), 4394.
BRADY (Thomas A. jr), 5848.
BRADY (Thomas A.), 1100.
BRAET (Herman), 3811.
BRAGANTINI (Irene), 2866.
BRAGANTINI (Renzo), 6549.
BRAIBANTI (Ralph), 5906.
BRAIDA (Ludovica), 204.
BRAITHWAITE (Roderick), 8017.
BRAMBILLA AGENO (F.), 3900.
BRANCA (Vittore), 4488.
Brancusi (Constantin), 6836.
BRAND (Cordula), 1678.
BRAND (Paul), 3948.
BRANDS (H. W.), 8466.
BRANDT (Miroslav), 3351.
BRATCHELL (M. E.), 3437.
BRĂTIANU (Gheorghe I.), 5294.
Brătianu (Ioan I. C.), 8177.
BRATUKHIN (A. G.), 5306.
BRAUCKS (T.), 4480.
Braudel (Fernand), 750, 952.
BRAUER (Ralph W), 372.
BRAUN (Jean-Pierre), 2398.
BRAUNWARTH (Peter M.), 6695.
BRAYBROOK (Jean), 6550.
BREAUD-GAMBIER (Marie-Josèphe), 234.
BRECHON (Franck), 3603.
BRECKENRIDGE (Keith), 5449.
Brede Kristensen (W.), 5752.
BREDEKAMP (Horst), 479, 6725.
BREEN (Aidan), 3204.
BREGEL (Yuri), 5907.
BREITMAN (Richard), 8329.
BREMMER (Jan N.), 2960.
BRENNAN (Brian), 753.
BRENNAN (Tad), 2056.
BRENNEN (Bonnie), 6178.
BRENON (Anne), 4489.
BRENT (Allen), 2967.
BRENTJES (Burchard), 1860.
BRÉSARD (Luc), 2938.
BRETEL (Paul), 3949.
BRETT (Martin), 3604.
BRETTLER (Marc Zvi), 540.
BREUER (Christine), 2389.

BREUER (Claudia), 5398.
BREUER (Edward), 809.
BREUER (Stefan), 846, 6307.
BREUER (Tilmann), 541.
BREUER (William B.), 8212.
BREUGELMANS (R.), 248.
BREUILLY (John), 4944.
BREWER (Anthony), 6994, 6995.
BREWER (Charles), 4242.
BREWER (John), 7372.
BREZIS (Elise S.), 7057, 7058.
BRIAN (Eric), 864.
Briand (Aristide), 7698.
BRIANT (P.), 2117.
BRICKHOUSE (Thomas C.), 6242.
BRIGAGLIA (Aldo), 6386.
BRIGANTINI (Renzo), 4053.
BRIGHT (Charles), 4611.
Brill (E. J.), 1548.
BRINGMANN (K.), 2613.
BRINGMANN (Klaus), 2147.
BRINK (T.L.), 1383.
BRINKS (J. H.), 865.
BRIQUEL (Dominique), 2614, 2828.
BRISSAUD (I.), 9099.
BRITNEL (Richard H.), 3725.
BRITO (E.), 1377.
BRIXHE (Claude), 1980.
BRIZZI (G.), 2679.
BROCHEUX (Pierre), 7822.
BRODERSEN (Kai), 2615, 2659.
BRODERSEN (Momme), 6218.
BRODIE (Malcolm), 6160.
BROGI (Mario), 3179.
BROMAN (Thomas), 6387.
BROMM (G.), 50.
BROMSKI (Józef), 1568.
BRONKHORST (J.)., 1541.
BROOCK (Sebastian P.), 3053.
BROOK (Chris), 8431.
BROOKE (Christopher N. L.), 3187.
BROOKS (Francis J.), 9108.
BROOKS (Linda Marie), 1527.
BROOMAN (Josh), 6450.
BROSSE (Jacques), 4398.
BROSSEDER (Johannes), 5897.
BROWN (Alison), 6023.
BROWN (Andrew D.), 4490.
BROWN (B. R.), 2390.
BROWN (Chris), 7682.
BROWN (Cynthia J.), 205.
BROWN (Desmond H.), 7626.
BROWN (J. P.), 1889.
BROWN (Jeremy M.), 8468.
BROWN (John C.), 7206.
BROWN (Jonathan), 480.
BROWN (Peter), 1436, 2616, 2946, 3352.
BROWN (Richmond F.), 4966.
BROWN (Stuart E.), 5908.
BROWN (T. S.), 3111.

BROWN (Walt), 6161.
BROWNE (Gerald M.), 1765.
BROWNING (Robert), 3112.
BROWNRIGG (Linda L.), 147.
Brożek (Andrzej), 751.
BRUBAKER (L.), 3113.
BRUBAKER (Leslie), 4190, 5830.
BRUCE (Steve), 5637.
BRUCKNER (M. T.), 3917.
BRUDNER (Alan), 6243.
BRUEGEL (M.), 7359.
Bruegel (Pieter), 6819.
BRUFANI (Stefano), 4439.
BRUGÈRE (Fabienne), 6244.
BRUGNOLI (Giorgio), 206, 2536, 2758.
BRUGNONE (Antonietta), 2118.
BRUHNS (H.), 6307.
BRULE (P.), 2117.
BRUNDAGE (James A.), 3605.
BRUNE (Ghislain), 3707.
BRUNEAU (Philippe), 2391.
BRUNEL (Ghislain), 542, 601.
BRUNELLI (Gianfranco), 5789.
BRUNEL-LOBRICHON (Geneviève), 4477.
BRUNET (Miche), 7603.
BRUNET (Pierre), 373, 374.
BRUNET (Serge), 7603.
BRUNETTA (Giampiero), 6896.
BRUNI (Arnaldo), 6593.
Bruni (Leonardo), 752, 6005.
BRUNTERC'H (Jean-Pierre), 4545.
BRUSH (Kathryn L.), 553, 4176.
BRUSINA (O. I), 7360.
BRUSTEIN (William), 7361.
BRUUN (Christer), 2537.
BRYAN (Dick), 6996.
BRYANT (Ralph C.), 8469.
BRZEZIŃSKI (Andrzej Maciej), 8093.
BTANDTL (Markus), 51.
BUBENIK (Jaroslav), 5473.
BUBNOV (Nikolaj Ju.), 543.
BUC (P.), 3708.
BUCCI (Oddo), 3606.
BUCCIANTINI (Massimo), 1321, 6388.
Buchanan (James), 8014.
BUCHER (Bernadette), 4862.
BUCHER (Gregory S.), 2246.
BUCHHEIM (Hans), 1185.
BUCHREITER (N.), 2450.
BUCK (Robert J.), 2119.
BUCKL (Walter), 3340.
BUCKLEY (Roger), 8470.
BUCKLEY (Thomas), 1395.
BUDAK (Neven), 3709.
BUDINA (O. P.), 999.
BUDNIAK (Józef), 5729.
BUDNY (Mildred), 167.
BUES (Almut), 7927.

BUFFET (Jacky), 1257.
BUGNARD (Pierre-Philippe), 544.
BÜHLER (Pierre), 3950.
BUICAN (Denis), 1325.
BUITENHUIS (H.), 1719.
BUITRON-OLIVER (Diana), 2392.
Bukharin (Nikolaj Ivanovič), 5412.
BUKOV (K. I.), 5411.
BULGARELLI (Sandro), 7575.
BULLION (Alan J.), 8471.
BULVER (Kathryn M.), 6516.
BUNGE (Jurgen), 7616.
BUNSON (Matthew), 3353.
BUONASORTE (Nicla), 5730.
Burckhardt (Jacob), 753.
BURDEAU (François), 7630.
BURDETT (Anita), 8420.
BURDICK (Michael A.), 4681.
BURGARELLA (F.), 2617.
BURGER (Hannelore), 7584.
BURGERS (J. W. J.), 7.
BURGESS (Glyn S.), 3951.
BURGESS (Jonathan Seth), 2353.
BURGESS (R.W.), 2538.
BURGGRAAFF (W.), 1810.
BURGHARDT (Uwe), 7153.
BURGMAN (Verity), 4703.
BURGMANN (Ludwig), 3079.
BURGOGUE-LARSEN (Laurence), 8472.
BURGOS RINCON (Javier), 208.
BURGUIERE (André), 545.
BURIDANUS (Johannes), 4286.
BURISCH (Wolfram), 5986.
BURKE (Peter), 350, 6551, 7362.
BURKE (S. M.), 7823.
BURKE (Sean), 1528.
BURNETT (A.), 2713.
BURNETT (Charles Stuart F.), 4308.
Burns (Ken), 877.
BURNS (Lori), 6897.
Burns (Robert), 6661.
BURNS (Ross), 1890.
BURRIDGE (R. A.), 2247.
BURRIN (Philippe), 8213.
BURROWES (Robert D.), 1077.
BURT (Roger), 7154.
BURTON (J. B.), 2248.
BURTON (Peter), 6766.
BURTON (Richard D. E.), 7897.
Burzyński (Adam Prosper), 5818.
BUSCH (J. W.), 3711.
BUSCH (Margarete), 7363.
BUSCH (R.), 4480.
Bush (George Herbert Walker), 7675.
BUSH (Ronald), 6040.
BUSINO (Giovanni), 834, 1258.
BUŠKOV (V. I.), 5399.
BUSSE (Wilhelm G.), 97, 4546.
BUSSET (Thomas), 5367.

BUSSIÈRE (Jean), 9085.
BUSTOS RODRIGUEZ (Manuel), 7898.
BUSZKO (Józef), 5229.
BUTANAEV (Viktor Iakovlevich), 1000.
BUTEL (Paul), 7364.
BUTIN (Philip Walker), 5849.
BUTLER (John), 3712.
BUTLER (Marilyn), 839.
BUTOV (S. E.), 5310.
BUTT (Gerald), 7683.
BUTTERWECK (Christel), 2968.
BUTTIGIEG (Joseph), 6282.
BUTTLAR (Gertrud), 481.
BUTTRESS (Donald), 4204.
BUTURAC (Josip), 3265.
BUYST (Erik), 7060.
BUZATU (Gh), 8214.
BUZPINAR (S. T.), 8018.
BYLES (Joan Montgomery), 6620.
BYLINA (Stanisław), 4491.
BYLKOVA (V. P.), 2120.
BYNUM (Caroline W.), 2969.
BYNUM (Mary Rebecca), 2354.
BYRHTFERTH, 3952.
BYRN (Richard F. M.), 553.
BYRNES (Robert Francis), 798.
BYSTROVA (N. E.), 8473.

C

Caballinus de Cerronibus (Ioannes), 3896.
Cabanes (Emilio), 1696.
CABERO DOMÍNGUEZ (C.), 4547.
CABEZA DE MORANO (Marta Graciela), 8474.
CABEZUELO PLIEGO (José Vicente), 3607.
CABY (Cécile), 4431.
CACCAMO (Domenico), 8475.
CACCAMO Caltabiano (Maria), 2479.
CACHEY (Theodore J.), 3973.
CACIORGNA (Maria Teresa), 3608.
Cadden (Joan), 4309.
CADIOLI (Beniamino), 7853.
CADIOLI (Renato), 6162.
Caesar (Gaius Julius) 2602, 2604, 2754.
CAGIANO DE AZEVEDO (Raimondo), 7662.
CAGIATI (Andrea), 8476.
ÇAHA (Ömer), 5511.
CAHIER (Gabriella), 5845.
CAHILL (Thomas), 1327.
CAHN (Walter), 407.
CAHNER (Max), 7959.
CAIMARI (Lila M.), 4682.

CAIOLI (Aldo), 7854.
CAÏTUCOLI (Georges), 8363.
CALABI (Donatella), 7440.
CALAMANDREI (Piero), 7555.
CALANDRI (Elena), 7684.
CALDERARO (Michela), 378.
CALDWELL (Bruce), 7013.
CALDWELL (George), 7985.
Calibita (Giovanni), 3268.
CALIC (Marie-Janine), 4724.
Caligula (Caius Caesar Germanicus), imperatore romano, 2920.
CALINGER (Ronald), 6390.
CALLINICOS (Alex), 866, 7495.
CALLORO (P.), 6245.
Callu (Jean-Pierre), 2598.
CALO MARIANI (Maria Stella), 4182.
CALOGERO (Francesco), 8432.
Calvert (Frank), 1747.
CALVET (Antoine), 4310.
Calvet-Sébasti (Marie-Ange), 2928.
CALVIN (Jean), 5842, 5849, 5850, 5851, 5853, 5855, 5861, 5865, 5878, 5889, 5892.
Calvino (Italo), 6621, 6647.
Calvo Galvez (Matías), 2902.
Cam (Marie-Thérèse), 2601.
Camara (Helder), 5802.
CAMARA (Joao de Sousa da), 7855.
CÁMARA Serrano (Juan Antonio), 1656.
CAMARENA LAUCIRICA (Julio), 986.
CAMARTIN (Iso), 6535.
Cambiano (Giuseppe), 3103.
CAMEL (Florance), 7856.
Cameron (Alan), 2249, 2539.
Cameron (Averil), 3114.
CAMMARANO (Fulvio), 5009, 7365.
Camodeca (Giuseppe), 2511.
CAMOES (Filho), 8215.
Camoes (Luis Vaz de), 6851.
CAMPAGNOLO (Matteo), 5845.
CAMPANA (Andrea), 8477.
Campanile (Enrico), 2448.
CAMPBELL (Bruce M. S.), 3725.
Campbell (John Francis), 1694.
Campbell (Stuart), 1763.
Campi (Pietro Maria), 5738.
Camplani (Alberto), 2923.
Campos (A.), 209.
CAMPOS MARIN (Ricardo), 7366.
CANAL (Jordi), 546.
CANAL SANCHEZ-PAGIN (José M.), 3438.
CANAVAGGIO (Jean), 1545.
CANCIAN (P.), 547.
Cancik (H.), 2829.
Cancik-Kirschbaum (Eva), 1811.
Cancik-Lindemeier (H.), 2829.
Canfora (Luciano), 548, 2250, 3103, 3116.

Cangrande della Scala, 3901.
CANNARELLA (Carmelo), 4768.
CANNISTRARO (Philip V.), 4596.
CANNON (Joanna), 4460.
CAÑO SÁNCHEZ (Domingo), 441.
CANOSA (Michele), 6888.
CANOSA (Romano), 7367.
Canter (Dirk), 2252.
CANTERA CARLOMAGNO (Marcos), 8094.
Cantilena (Renata), 2393, 2449.
Cantu (Carla Maria), 3185.
Canzian (Dario), 3209.
CAO (Dawei), 8829.
CAO (Liqiang), 8830.
Cao (Shuji), 8856.
CAPANNELLI (E.), 3714.
CAPASSO (Mario), 92, 176.
Capdeville (Gérard), 2355, 2830.
Cape (Robert W., Jr.), 2540.
Capecelatro (Alfonso), Cardinale di Capua, 5707.
CAPELA (Jose), 7857.
Capella (Martianus), 4133.
Capgrave (John), 3266.
CAPITANI (Ovidio), 3281, 4423.
CAPLAN (Jane), 7517.
CAPORAL (Stéphane), 7585.
Capozza (M.), 2450.
CAPPELLO (Giovanni), 6552.
Capper (Brian J.), 2970.
CAPPI (D.), 757.
CAPPS (Walter H.), 5638.
CAPRIOLI (Adriano), 5731.
Caproni (Giorgio), 6702.
Carabba (Rocco), 6201.
CARABINE (Deirdre), 6246.
CARACI VELA (Maria), 6907.
Carafa (Pier Luigi), 5720.
CARAION (Marta), 408.
CARBONETTI VENDITTELLI (Cristina), 3233.
Carboni (Giovanni), 1628.
CÁRCEL ORTÍ (Vincente), 5732, 8019.
CARCELES DE GEA (Beatriz), 7276.
CARDAILLAC (Yvette), 5909.
Cardini (Franco), 3439.
Cardon (B.), 93.
CARDON (Bert), 4211.
CARDOZIER (Virgus Ray), 5590.
CARDUS (Salvador), 6163.
CARETTI (Lanfranco), 6621.
CAREW-REID (Micaela), 6898.
Carey (Christopher), 2157.
Cargill (J.), 2121.
CARILE (Antonio), 3425.
CARLETTI (Carlo), 8.
Carlevaris (A.), 4281.
CARLEVARO (Fabrizio), 1259.
CARLEY (Michael Jabara), 4597.

CARLGREN (Wilhelm M.), 7775.
Carlo I d'Angiò, re di Sicilia, 3929.
Carlos II, rey de España, 7276.
CARLSEN (Jesper), 2714.
Carlsson (Ingvar), 5362.
Carlucci (Claudia), 2451.
CARMACK (Robert M.), 4967.
CARMAGNANI (Marcello), 8478.
CARMI PARSONS (John), 3715.
CARMICHAEL (Thomas), 6294.
CARMILLY-WEINBERGER (Moshe), 4598.
CARMONA (Darío Acevedo), 5086.
CARMONA RUIZ (M. Antonia), 3609.
CAROL (Anne), 6391.
CARON (François), 7094.
CARONI (Pio), 3617.
CAROTI (Stefano), 4311.
CARR (A. D.), 3354.
Carr (Edward Hallett), 911.
Carradice (I.), 2186.
CARRASCO (Juan), 3716.
CARRASCO MANCHADO (Ana Isabel), 3490.
CARRE (M.-B.), 2220.
CARRENO (Alberto M.), 7114.
CARRERA DAMAS (German), 549.
CARRERAS (Albert), 7049, 7155, 7188.
CARRIER (James G.), 6033.
Carrillo Diaz-Pines (J.R.), 2916.
CARRION GUTIEZ (Manuel), 270.
CARROLL (D.), 5987.
CARROLL (Patrick J.), 5115.
Carruba (Onofrio), 1858, 1997.
CARRUTHERS (Susan L.), 7800.
Carter (J. B.), 1994.
Carter (James Earl), 8752.
CARTER (Mia Elizabeth), 6899.
CARTER (Tim), 6904.
CARUSI (Paola), 4312.
CASABIELHE (Olivier), 8095.
CASADIO (Gianfranco), 6900.
CASAGRANDE (Giovanna), 4492.
Casali (Sergio), 2581.
CASALILLA (Bartolome Yun), 7207.
CASALIS (Jacqueline), 6515.
CASELLA (Mario), 5010.
Casimir I, duc de Varsovie, 56.
CASOLARO (Renato), 6739.
CASPARD (Pierre), 6083.
CASPRINI (Flavio), 1260.
CASSAGNES (Sophie), 4202.
CASSANO (Raffaella), 4182.
CASSANTA PEIXTO (Ana Maria), 6091.
CASSESE (Sabino), 7586.
CASSIANO (Antonio), 6785.
Cassimatis (Hélène), 2453.
CASSINA (Cristina), 550.
Cassirer (Ernst), 6295, 6328.

Cassius Hemina (L.), 2592.
Casson (Lionel), 2251.
CASTAGNETTI (Andrea), 3515.
Castel (Corinne), 1812.
CASTELLANI (Cecilia), 867.
Castelli (Patrizia), 4021.
Castelli Montanari (Anna Luisa), 2564.
Castellvi (Georges), 2867.
Castiglione (Baldassarre), 6551.
Castorina (Alessandra), 2483.
CASTRILLO LLAMAS (M. Concepción), 4548.
Castriota (David), 2868.
Castro Ruz (Fidel), 8694.
CASTRONOVO (Valerio), 7061.
CATALA (Michel), 8216.
CATALAN (Jordi), 5436.
CATALAN MARTINEZ (Elena), 3610.
CATALDI PALAU (Annaclara), 94.
Cateni (Gabriele), 2495.
Caterina de' Ricci, Sancta, 4459.
CATEURA BENNASSER (Pau), 3717.
Catilina (Lucius Sergius), 2665.
CATTANEO (Massimo), 5684, 5734.
CATTARUZZA (Alejandro), 551.
CATULLUS (GAIUS VALERIUS), 2541, 2545, 2560, 2737.
CAUSSE (Louis), 4203.
CAVACIOCCHI (Simona), 7465.
CAVALLAR (Osvaldo), 3599.
CAVALLARO (Anna), 6727.
CAVALLERA (F.), 1448.
CAVALLO (Guglielmo), 9, 15, 255, 3117.
CAVALLO (Sandra), 6392.
CAVANDOLI (Vincenzo), 6917.
ÇAVDAR (Tevfik), 5512.
CAVIGLIA (Stefano), 5669.
CAVIGNEAUX (Antoine), 1813.
CAVINA (Marco), 7631.
CAWKWELL (George L.), 1971.
ÇAYCI (Abdurrahman), 8020.
CAYGILL (Howard), 6247.
Caylus (Anne-Claude-Philippe comte de), 755.
Ceauşescu (Nicolae), 5297.
CECCARINI (E.), 5988.
CECCHINI (E.), 3901.
CECCONI (Giovanni Alberto), 813.
CECCUTI (Cosimo), 5029.
Ceffi (Filippo), 4153.
CELANT (Alessandra), 1633.
Cellini (Benvenuto), 6864.
CELSUS (AULUS CORNELIUS), 2542.
ČELYŠEV (Igor'A.), 8682.
CENTANNI (Monica)1014.
CEPEDA (Isabel Vilares), 3954.
ČEPELKIN (M. A.), 8021.
CEPIC (Zdenko), 5390.
CERASUOLO (Salvatore), 2791.

CERCHIAI (Luca), 2454, 2490.
Cercidas de Mégalopolis, 2296.
CERDEÑO (Maria Luisa), 1696.
CERESA GASTALDO (Aldo), 2759.
CERETTI (Marinella), 6594.
ČERKASOV (Petr. P.), 7957.
ČERNJAK (Efim. B.), 868.
ČERNUKHA (V. G.), 5304.
ČERNYŠEVA (O. V.), 4651.
CERRETI (Claudio), 369.
CERRI (Giovanni), 2356.
Cerruti (Marcello), 8028.
CERUTTI (Simona), 7632.
CERVELLÓ AUTUORI (J.), 1766.
CESAREO (Vincenzo), 5639.
ČEŠKOV (Marat A.), 1078.
CESTARO (Antonio), 5735.
ÇETIN (Atilla), 427.
CETLIN (Ju. B.), 869.
Cetshwayo ka Mpande, king of Zululand, 9087.
CHABOD (Federico), 743, 4599.
Chabrol (Claude), 6931.
Chagall (Marc), 6835.
CHAITANYA (Rachana), 8479.
CHALIAND (Gerard), 8803.
CHALMETA (Pedro), 3547.
CHALOUPEK (Günther), 6997.
CHAŁUPCZAK (Henryk), 6092.
CHAMBERS (D. S.), 6065.
CHAMPION (Craige), 2028.
CHAN (Anson), 7685.
CHAN (Selina Ching), 1001.
CHANDHOKE (Neera), 1186.
CHANNON (John), 375.
CHANSON-JABEUR (Chantal), I.
Chantepie de la Saussaye (Pierre Daniel), 5752.
CHANTRE (Benoît), 826.
CHAPMAN (Colin), 5910.
CHAPPELL (Timothy D. J.), 1514.
CHAREILLE (Pascal), 3765.
CHARES (Mark), 1384.
Charitōn, 2057.
CHARLE (Christophe), 5989.
Charlemagne, röm.-deutscher Kaiser, König der Franken, 679, 3406, 4229.
CHARLES (Michel), 6622.
Charles IV, re d'Ungheria, 5562.
Charles VI, roi de France, 3199.
Charles VIII, roi de France, 118, 141, 7940.
Charles IX, roi de France, 4860, 6589.
CHARLESWORTH (H.), 1892.
CHARLET (Christian), 296.
CHARLIER (J.), 7986.
CHARMASSON (Thérèse), 428.
CHARMELY (John), 7686.
CHARON (Annie), 195.

CHARPIN (Dominique), 1814.
Charron (Pierre), 6542.
CHARTIER (Roger), 212, 255, 231, 456, 871, 1364, 5990, 5992, 6248.
CHARVÁT (Peter), 1815.
CHASE (Steven), 4313.
CHASE-DUNN (Christopher), 7015.
CHAST (François), 6393.
CHASTELAIN (G.), 3897.
Chateaubriand (François René de), 756.
CHATELAIN (Jean-Marc), 213.
CHÂTELLIER (Louis), 5685.
CHATTOPADHYAYA (D. P.), 6394.
CHATURVEDI (D. D.), IX.
CHAU (Wai-Shing), 2947.
CHAUCER (Geoffrey), 3956, 4092.
CHAUDHURI (Kirti N), 872.
CHAULEUR (Andrée), 429.
CHAUNU (Pierre), 4600, 4605, 9115.
CHAUVEL (Louis), 6998.
CHAUVIN (Yves), 3935.
CHAVASSE (Antoine), 5709.
CHAZEL (S.), 6307.
CHEDEVILLE (André), 3718.
CHEDOZEAU (B.), 791.
CHEIM (John), 6844.
CHELBI (Fethi), 9086.
CHEN (Keyun), 8831.
CHEN (Lisong), 8832.
CHEN (Sanjing), 8910.
CHEN (Shenyong), 8833.
CHEN (Shiqi), 8834.
CHEN (Siqi), 8835.
CHEN (Tiejian), 8836.
CHEN (Zhanyi), 8837.
CHÈNE (Catherine), 3719.
CHENEVAL (Francis), 1187.
CHENG (Minsheng), 8838.
CHENG (Xiao), 8839.
Chengzu, Ming emperor, 8914.
CHERICI (Armando), 2491.
CHERNOBAEV (A. A.), 615.
CHERNOFF (Fred), 8480.
CHERUBINI (Giovanni), 3720.
CHESTERTON (Neville), 8364.
CHEVAILLER (Jean-Claude), 7307.
CHEVALIER (Bernard), 3721.
CHEVALIER (Maxime), 986.
CHEVRIER (Y.), 8840.
CHEVUTSCHI (Ludovic), 8096.
CHIABÒ (Myriam), 6919.
CHIAM (Madelaine), 4702.
Chiang (Kai-shek), 8267, 8836, 8965, 8973, 8976.
CHIANOTIS (Angelos), 2345.
Chiara da Montefalco, Sancta, 4522.
CHIARINI (Marco), 6812.
CHICHOVA (I. A.), 2158.
CHIEFFO RAGUIN (Virginia), 4176.
CHIESA (Paolo), 3268, 3722, 3957.

CHIESI (G.), 3514.
CHIMENTI (Carlo), 7556.
CHINN (Carl), 7368.
CHIODO (Domenico), 6545.
CHITRAKAR (Ramesh C.), 8481.
CHITTOLINI (Giorgio), 3617.
CHIU (Stephen W. K.), 8747.
CHŁOPECKI (Jerzy), 5244.
Choiseul-Gouffier (Marie-Florent-Auguste Comte de), 7960.
CHRETIEN DE TROYES, 3899, 3958.
CHRIST (Carol T.), 6728.
CHRIST (Karl), 814, 2618.
CHRISTENSEN (Jørgen Peter), 7063.
Christian (William), 261.
Christian II, King of Denmark, 5656.
Christian IV, King of Denmark, 7933.
Christian VIII, King of Denmark, 4753.
CHRISTIANSEN (Erik), 1079.
CHRISTIN (Olivier), 5850.
Christine de Pizan, 3987.
Christopher (John), 262.
CHRZANOWSKI (Tadeusz), 5240.
CHUDZIAK (Wojciech), 4430.
CHURCH (S. D.), 7587.
Churchill (Winston Leonard Spencer), 4965, 5037, 7686, 8203, 8230, 8264, 8369, 8633.
CHWALBA (Andrzej), 5311.
Chydenius (Anders), 5366.
CIAMPANI (Andrea), 8482.
CIAMPI (Gabriella), 5029.
CIAMPOLTRINI (Giulio), 2394.
CANCIAN (Patrizia), 66.
CIAPPELLI (Giovanni), 3271, 3723.
CIARDI (Roberto Paolo), 6813.
CICALESE (Maria Luisa), 5029.
CICERO (M. TULLIUS), 2540, 2543, 2544, 2552, 2595, 2619, 2678, 2737, 2793, 2812.
CIFOLETTI (Giovanna), 6396.
Ç/FTÇ/ (Fazil), 6729.
CIGÁNEK (František), 5474.
CIGGAAR (Krijnie N.), 3118.
CILIBERTO (C.), 6386.
CIMBALA (Stephen J.), 8483.
CIMINO (Guido), 6473.
CINGANO (E.), 2097.
Cingio Severo (C.), 2520.
CINGOLANI (Stefano Maria), 3272.
CIOBANU (Mircea), 5295.
CIRONISOVÁ (Eva), 7208.
CÍSAŘ (Jaromír), 7534.
CÍSAŘOVSKÁ (Blanka), 214.
CITERNESI (Anna Corinna), 1321.
CITRONI (M.), 2760.
CIUFFOLETTI (Zeffiro), 5029.
CIVIL (Pierre), 5736.
CIZEK (E.), 805.

CLAD (James), 8484.
CLADIS (M. S.), 1440.
CLAGETT (Marshall), 1767.
CLANCY (Robert), 376.
Clara Assisiensis, Sancta, 4461, 4477.
Clarendon (George William Frederick Villiers Earl of), 8014.
CLARK (Anna), 7370.
CLARK (Christopher), 4769.
CLARK (Garth), 6866.
CLARK (Gregory), 7371.
CLARK (Katerina), 5312.
CLARK (Peter), 7339.
CLARK (Samuel), 1188.
CLARK (Stephen R. L.), 6397.
CLARK (Truman R.), 5271.
CLARKE (Helen), 3577.
CLARKE (Jonathan), 8484.
CLARYSSE (W.), 1768.
CLASSEN (A.), 3960.
Claudius (Tiberius), imperatore romano, 2515.
CLAUSI (B.), 784.
CLAUSS (James J.), 2545.
CLAUSS (M.), 3203.
CLAVAL (Paul), 377.
CLEMENCE (Dominic), 6560.
CLEMENS (Jacques), 3724.
CLEMENT (I. M.), 4274.
CLEMENTE (Guido), 4568.
CLEMENTI (Alessandro), 3611.
CLEMOES (Peter), 3962.
CLERC (Gisèle), 1785.
Clinton (William Jefferson), 5587, 5607, 8504.
Clodius Pulcher (Publius), 2669.
Cloeter (Emma), 7401.
Cloeter (Hermine), 7401.
CLOKE (Gillian), 2971.
CLOPPET (Christian), 2512.
CLOSE (David H), 4927.
CLUSE (Chr.), 4494.
CLYMER (Kenton J.), 7824.
COARELLI (Filippo), 2715.
COATES (John), 2395, 6713.
COATES (R.), 5832.
Çoban Mustafa Paşa, 7335.
COBB (Christopher H.), 6093.
COBBY (Anne Elizabeth), 3963.
COCCOLUTO (Giovanni), 2930.
COCHETTI (Maria), 179.
COCHRANE (Allan), 8431.
COCKE (Thomas), 4204.
COCKLE (W.E.H.), 2513.
COCKSHAW (Pierre), 2.
Coelestinus III, Papa, 4427.
COELHO (Maria Helena da Cruz), XVIII.
COELHO DIAS (Geraldo J. A.), 4432.

COFRANCESCO (Dino), 5011.
COHEN (B.), 2189.
COHEN (D.), 2159.
COHEN (Lenard J.), 8485.
COHEN (R. S.), 6471.
COHEN (Raymond), 1722.
COHEN (Robert S.), 1345, 1355.
COHEN (S. Marc), 6331.
COHEN (Yves), 873.
COHN (Samuel K.), 753.
COINTET (Michele), 7858.
COJOCARIU (Mihai), 5296.
COLAMARCO (Teresa), 3190.
COLARD (Daniel), 7665.
COLÁS (Santiago), 4683.
Colbjörnsen (Christian), 7582.
COLBOW (Gudrun), 1816.
COLE (Douglas), 482.
COLEMAN (Dorothy Gabe), 6553.
COLESANTI (Giulio), 2058.
COLETTE (Marie-Noël), 4243.
COLINET (A.), 3964.
COLISH (Marcia L.), 4314.
COLJA (Katja), 8395.
COLL I ROSELL (G.), 99.
COLLARD (C.), 2068.
COLLARD (Christopher), 2252.
COLLARD (F.), 781.
COLLARD (Franck), 781.
COLLART (Yves), 874.
COLLAS-HEDDELAND (Emmanuelle), 2059.
Collingwood (R. G.), 943, 6241.
COLLINS (Ardis B.), 6249.
COLLINS (James B.), 4863.
COLLINS (Randal), 552.
COLLINS (Roger), 3408.
COLLIOT-THÉLÈNE (C.), 6307.
COLLOMB (Pascal), 3196, 3273.
COLLON (Dominique), 1723, 1739.
Colloredo (Hieronymus von), 5771.
COLLOTTI (Enzo), 4770.
Collow (William), 7848.
COLOMBO (Alessandro), 7687.
COLOMBO (Arturo), 5029.
Colombo (Cristoforo), 9096.
COLONNA (Fanny), 4676.
COLONNA (Giovanni), 2492.
COLTON (Robert E.), 2761.
Combes (Emile), 4899.
COMBES (Robert), 2599.
COMBS (Arthur), 8486.
COMENDADOR REY (Beatriz), 1655.
COMET (Georges), 4315.
Compagna (Francesco), 5988.
Compagni (Dino), 757.
COMPAGNON (Antoine), 801.
COMPANYS I FARRERONS (Isabel), 3198.
Comte (Auguste Isidore Marie-François), 6345.

CONDELLO (E.), 11.
CONDELLO (Emma), 38.
CONETTI (Giorgio), 8097.
CONFIANT (Raphael), 6518.
CONFORTI (Benedetto), 8488.
CONFRARIA (Joao), 5273.
CONKLIN (Jeffrey Scott), 8489.
CONLON (Pierre M.), 4581.
CONNAUGHTON (R. M.), 8365.
CONNELLY (James), 943, 6241.
CONNER (Tom), 6623.
CONNEZIO (Ermanno), 6944.
CONNOLLY (Bernard), 8490.
CONRAD (C. F.), 2622.
CONSOLINO (Franca Ela), 2655, 2762, 2972.
CONSTABLE (Giles), 4316.
CONSTANTIN (Ion), 1081.
CONSTANTINE (S.), 4945.
Constantinus (Flavius Valerius), imperatore romano, 302, 679, 753, 2537, 2624, 2684, 2852.
CONTAMINE (Philippe), 3726, 3847.
CONTE (Emanuele), 3613.
CONTE (Patrice), 875.
CONTINI (Gianfranco), 1549, 4095.
CONTINISIO (Chiara), 1222.
CONTÒ (A.), 198.
CONTRENI (John J.), 3966.
CONTRERAS CORTES (Francisco), 1656.
Convenant (Gabriel de), 5369.
CONZE (Eckart), 8491.
COOGAN (Tim Pat), 4992.
COOK (Don), 7899.
COOK (James Wyatt), 4095.
COOKE (Lynne), 6867.
COONEY (Gabriel), 1634.
COONIN (Victor), 6814.
COOPE (Jessica), 4495.
COOPER (Artemis), 8217.
COOPER (B. Lee), 6880.
COOPER (Barbara M.), 5154.
COOPER (Frederick), 1082.
COOREMAN (R.), 6868.
COPE (R. L.), 9087.
Copernicus (Nicolaus), 6858.
COPLEY (Stephen), 7036.
COPPIETERS'T WALLANT (Bertrand), 2924, 4274.
COQUERY-VIDROVITCH (Catherine), I, 1261.
CORBIER (Mireille), 2508, 2681, 2869.
CORBIER (Paul), 9088.
CORBIN (Alain), 4887.
CORBO (Anna Maria), 6730.
CORBOZ (André), 5379.
CORDOVEZ (Diego), 8492.
CORETH (Emerich), 6060.

CORIA COLINO (Jesús I.), 3440.
CORISH (Patrick J.), 446.
CORMEAU (Christoph), 736.
CORNBLIT (Oscar), 7900.
Cornelius Gallus (Caius), 2573.
CORNELIUS (R.), 3894.
CORNELL (Saul), 876.
CORNELL (T. J.), 2456.
CORNISH (Paul), 8493.
COROLEU (A.), 6250.
CORON (S.), 242.
CORONA LORENZO (Mercedes), 441.
CORR (Helen), 4938.
CORRAO (Pietro), 3614.
CORRARATI (Patrizia), 3727.
CORREA BALLESTER (Jorge), 7277.
CORS I MEYA (Jordi), 1891.
CORSI (Ermanno), 6164.
Cortes (Hernàn), 9108.
CORTES PENA (Antonio Luis), 5640.
CORTESE (Ennio), 3615.
CORTESI (Mariarosa), 3233.
CORTONESI (Alfio), 3728.
COSGROVE (Denis), 4649.
COSI (Dario M.), 1386.
COSMA (Rita), 3233.
COSMACINI (Giorgio), 1330, 6399.
COSS (P. R.), 7373.
COSTA (Milton Carlos), 818.
COSTA (S.), 215.
COSTA BONA (Enrica), 8210.
COSTAGLIOLA (Jacques), 6400.
COSTAMAGNA (Giorgio), 7577.
COSTE (Jean), 3184.
COSTEL (Eric), 8494.
COTTEY (Anrew), 8495.
COTTIGNOLI (A.), 817.
COTTON (H.M.), 2513.
COTTRELL (Allin F.), 7027.
COTTRET (Bernard), 5851.
COUDERT (Allison), 6251.
COUDRY (Georges), 8218, 8330.
COULET (Noël), 4462.
COULIANO (Ioan P.), 1386.
COULSON (F. T.), 3968.
COUNELIS (James Steve), 5820.
COUPLAND (Simon), 3578.
COURTENAY (William J.), 4317.
COURTILLE (Anne), 4205.
COUTO (J.), 1083.
COUTURAT (Louis), 6310.
COUZINET (Marie-Dominique), 379, 1190.
COVELL (Maureen), 1084.
COWAN (Ian Borthwick), 4400.
COWDREY (H. E. J.), 4420.
COWEN (David), 1322.
COX (B.), 7958.
COX (Michael), 8496.

COZZI (G.), 5012.
CRACCO RUGGINI (Lellia), 2623, 2716, 2734.
CRAFTS (N. F. R.), 7064.
CRAFTS (Nick), 7065.
CRAGOE (Matthew), 4939.
CRAIG (Dick), 5140.
CRAIG (Gordon A.), 6625.
CRAVERI (Piero), 5013.
CRAWFORD (Barbara), 3588.
CRAWFORD (Margaret), 7309.
CREMASCOLI (Giuseppe), 4439.
CREMERIUS (Johannes), 6626.
CREMONI (Lucilla), 8497.
CREPEAU (François), 7689.
CREXELLS I VALLHONRAT (Joan), 6252.
CRIBB (J.), 1958.
CRIBB (Robert), 4987.
CRIELAARD (Jan Paul), 2002.
CRIPPS (Thomas), 877.
CRISCIANI (Chiara), 3970.
CRISE (Stefano), 6906.
CRISTIN (A.-M.), 12.
CRISTOFANI (Mauro), 2497.
CRISTOFOLINI (Paolo), 6253, 6281.
CRITCHLOW (Donald T.), 5597.
Croce (Benedetto) 743, 759, 6139, 6336, 6343.
CROCE (Paul Jerôme), 5641.
CROCE DA VILLA (Pierangela), 2621.
CROKE (Brian), 3056.
Cronenberg (David), 6888.
CRONIN (Mike), 4993.
CROOME (John), 8498.
CROPP (M. J.), 2068.
CROPSEY (Joseph), 6254.
CROSBY (Alfred W.), 554.
CROSS (F. M.), 101.
CROSSLEY (Ceri), 555.
CROTTI PASI (Renata), 3185.
CROUZEL (Henri), 2938.
CROUZET (F. H.), 7057.
CROUZET (François), 7066.
CROUZET-PAVAN (Elisabeth), 4551.
CROW (James), 1741.
CROW (Thomas E.), 6731, 6734.
CRUZ (Anne J.), 6554.
CRUZ (Manuel B.), 1191.
CSÁKY (Imre), 276.
CSAPODI (Csaba), 277, 3972.
CSAPODI (Zoltán), 4603.
CSATÓ (Tamás), 7209.
CSERESNYÉS (Ferenc), 8499.
CSETRI (Elek), 8022.
CSICSERY-RÓNAY (István), 5561.
CSIZMADIA (Ervin), 5545.
CSOHÁNI (János), 5546.
CSÓKÁS (László), 6519.
CSÖPPUS (I.), 8098.

CSUKA (János), 5064.
CUBAN (Larry), 6147.
ČUBAR'JAN (A. O.), 4651.
CUCARULL (J.), 7156.
CUCCHI (Giuseppe), 8500.
CUCCIOLI (R.), 2737.
CUCCIOLI MELLONI (Rita), 2586.
CUCHE (Francois-Xavier), 587.
CUETO (Marcos), 4722.
CUGUERO I CONCHELLO (Maria C.), 457.
CULAJA (Givi V.), 8804.
CULASSO GASTALDI (Enrica), 2457.
CULIANU (Ioan Petru), 1442.
CULL (Nicholas John), 8219.
CULLEN (Tracey), 1601.
CUMBERPATCH (C. G.), 1680.
Cumno (Irene), 34.
CUNIETTI-FERRANDO (Arnaldo J.), 298.
CUNILL GRAU (Pedro), 379.
CUNLIFFE (Barry), 1679, 1697.
CUNNINGHAM (Andrew), 6442.
CUNNINGHAM (M.B.), 3119.
CUNZ (Reiner), 327.
CUOMO (Glenn R.), 4804.
CUONO (Giovanni), 1641.
CUOZZO (Enrico), 3730, 3409, 3410.
CUPANE (Carolina), 3057, 3066, 3078, 3081.
CURAMI (Andrea), 8331.
CURCHIN (Leonard A.), 556, 2763.
CURD (Patricia), 6331.
CURKINA (Iskra), 7690.
CURRY (JaneLeftwich), 5236.
CURSENTE (Benoît), 3731.
Curtis (Lionel), 7783, 7810.
CURTIS (Mark), 8501.
Curtius (Ernst Robert), 1537.
CURTY (O.), 2030.
Curzon (George Nathaniel), 8083.
Cusanus (Nicolaus), 4339.
CUSCITO (Giuseppe), 2925.
CUSSINI (Eleonora), 1917.
CUST (Richard), 4940.
CUTILEIRO (José), 8502.
CUTINELLI-RÈNDINA (Emanuele), 759, 1176.
CUTROFELLO (Andrew), 6255.
CUTRONI (Aldina), 2458.
ČUVAKHIN (Dimitrij S.), 8503.
CYMBURSKIJ (V. L.), 1998.
CYRINO (M. S.), 2253.
CZAJA (Roman), 3732.
CZERSKA (Danuta), 5313.
CZICHON (Rainer Maria), 1817, 1861.
CZOCH (Ryszard), 6444.
CZOPEK-KOPCIUCH (Barbara), 336.
CZÖVEK (István), 5171.

D

D'Addario (Arnaldo), 452, 760.
D'AGOSTINO (Bruno), 2357.
D'AGOSTINO (F.), 1818.
D'AMBRA (Eve), 2870.
D'AMICO (Fabrizio), 6815.
D'ANGIO (Agnes), 7157.
D'Annunzio (Gabriele), 6885.
D'ARMS (J.H.), 2717.
D'HOOP (Alfred), 4713.
D'IAKOV (I.), 7756.
D'ONOFRIO, 4287.
DA CAMPAGNOLA (Stanislao), 4439.
DA FONSECA (L. Adao), 7670.
DA VINCI NICHOLS (Nina), 6908.
DĄBROWSKI (Jan), 3362.
DADRIAN (Vahakn N.), 7691.
DADSON (Trevor J.), 5437.
DAGRON (Gilbert), 3094.
DAHL (Hans Fredrik), 8273.
DAHL (Per), 6401.
DAHLSTRÖM (Fabian), 6976.
DAHM (Volker), 4771.
DAHRENDORF (Ralf), 6061.
DAIBER (Hans), 6732.
DAITO (Eisuke), 1137.
DAIX (Pierre), 750.
DAL CASON PATRIARCA (Francesca), 2514.
DAL COVOLO (Enrico), 1415, 2624, 2932.
DAL TOSO (Paola), 5686.
DALAI EMILIANI (M.), 3910.
DALARUN (Jacques), 4464.
DALBY (A.), 2187.
DALE (Andrew I.), 6448.
DALENA (Pietro), 3276.
DALES (R. C.), 4297.
DALEWSKI (Zbigniew), 5237.
DALLA (D.), 2737.
DALLA CASA (B.), 8400.
DALZELL (Ann), 4152.
Damianus, Sanctus, 4428.
DAMIEN (Robert), 458.
DAMOISON (David), 6518.
DAMON (Cynthia), 2682.
DAMOUSI (J.), 4705.
DANAHER (Kevin), 4730.
DANBOM (David B.), 5591.
DANDAMAEVA (M. M.), 2358.
DANDAMAYEV (Muhammad A.), 1943.
DANDOIS (Bernard), 897.
DANFULANI (Umar Habila Dadem), 5911.
DANGEL (Jacqueline), 337.
DANIEL (David Paul), 595.
DANIEL (Ute), 6909.
DANIEL (Yvonne), 5093.
DANIELL (David), 6555.

DANIELS (Christian), 8843.
DANILOV (A. A.), 5352.
DANILOV (Valerij D.), 8220.
DANN (Otto), 1211.
DANTE ALIGHIERI, 182, 3900, 3901, 3973, 3974, 5026, 6343, 6552, 6569.
DANWITZ (Thomas von), 7588.
DANYEL (Jürgen), 557, 588.
DANZER (Gudrun), 6816.
DARBO-PESCHANSKI (Catherine), 558.
DARBORD (Bernard), 1545.
DARD (Olivier), 7000.
DARDANO (Maurizio), 364.
DARE (Robert), 8099.
Darius I, re dei Persiani, 1950, 2116.
DARKEVIĆ (V. P.), 4552.
DARLINGTON (R. R.), 3289.
DARMON (Pierre), 6402.
DARNTON (Robert), 6165, 6627.
DAROWSKI (Roman), 5737.
DARRIEULAT (O.), 7158.
DARTMANN (Christoph), 4772.
DARTNELL (Michael Y.), 4864.
DARTON (Robert), 559.
Darwin (Charles Robert), 6400, 6411.
DASSMANN (Ernst), 2973.
DASTON (Lorraine J.), 6403.
DAUPHIN (C.), 5992.
DAVEAU (Suzanne), 395.
DAVID (Ephraim), 2061.
DAVID (Geza), 7310.
DAVID (Jean-Michel), 2683.
DAVID (Thomas), 1297, 7068.
DAVID-KIMBALL (Jeannine), 1686.
DAVIDS (Adelbert), 3124.
DAVIDS (Karel), 5152, 7159.
DAVIDSON (Alastair), 1192.
DAVIDSON (Donald A.), 1631.
DAVIDSON (John), 2359.
DAVIES (Benedict G.), 1771.
DAVIES (Jon), 5642.
DAVIES (M.), 216.
DAVIES (Malcom), 2254.
DAVIES (Martin L.), 6256.
DAVIES (Nigel), 9109.
DAVIES (Paul Charles William), 6404.
DAVIES (Philiph John), 8504.
DAVIES (Sue), 1787.
DAVIES (W. V.), 1726.
DAVIES (Wendy), 3400.
DAVIET (Jean-Pierre), 7069.
DAVILA (James R.), 1819.
DAVIS (H. W. C.), 3376.
DAVIS (John Bryan), 7001.
DAVIS (Judith M.), 4007.
DAVIS (M. Jane), 8505.
DAVIS (Philip J.), 6405.

DAVIS (Philip W.), 6406.
DAVIS (Thomas J.), 5853.
DAVRIL (Anselme), 192, 3904.
DAWISHA (Adeed), 8506.
DAWISHA (Karen), 8506.
DAWS (Gavan), 8221.
DAY (John), 1937, 5912.
DAY (Richard B.), 8507.
DE ANDREIS (Marco), 8432.
DE ANGELIS (Laura), 3492.
DE ANNA (Luigi G.), 3356.
DE ARMELLADA (B.), 4271.
DE AROZENA (B.P.), 2546.
DE AYALA MARTINEZ (Carlos), 3225.
De Aycinena (Juan Fermin), 4966.
DE BAECQUE (Antoine), 6902.
DE BOER (Dick E. H.), 3975.
De Bonald (Louis), 1220.
De Bono (Emilio), 5190.
DE BOO (J. A.), 285.
DE BORCHGRAVE (Christian), 3616.
DE BOUZON (Frédéric), 6310.
DE BOYER DE SAINTE-SUZANNE (Raymond), 8328.
DE BRUIJN (Erik), 1944.
DE BRUYN (O.), 2160.
DE BRY (Théodore), 5623.
DE CALLATAŸ (GoDefroid), 2547.
De Caprariis (Vittorio), 5988.
DE CASTELBAJAC (Ghislain), 8176.
DE CAZANOVE (Olivier), 2831.
DE CECCO (Marcello), 7589.
DE COCK (Jacques), 4865.
DE CONINCK-SMITH (Nina), 560.
DE COPPET (Daniel), 9120.
DE CRESCENTIIS (Petrus), 3277.
DE CUENCA (L. A.), 2064.
DE DONATO (Vittorio), 6.
DE DURAND-FOREST (Jacqueline), 9115.
DE FALCO (Gian Carlo), 7295.
DE FELICE (Alessandro), 5014.
DE FELICE (Franco), 5015.
DE FIGUEIREDO (Ivo), 5156.
DE FLEURQUIN (L.), 1377.
DE FOUCAULD (Jean-Baptiste), 1217.
DE FRANCHIS (AmeDeo), 8508.
De Francisci (Pietro), 761.
DE FRIAS CONDE (Fernando), 441.
De Gasperi (AlciDe), 8700.
DE GASQUET (Sébastien), 8176.
De Gaulle (Charles), 4892, 7651, 7750, 7858, 7883, 8264, 8491.
DE GENNARO (Giuseppe), 5777.
DE GIOVANNI BUZZONI (M.), 25.
DE GREGORIO (Giuseppe), 38.
DE GROSSI MAZZORIN (Jacopo), 1635.
DE GRUCHY (John W.), 5643, 5913.

DE GUIBERT (J.), 1448.
DE HALLEUX (A.), 1377.
DE HAMEL (C.), 102.
DE IANNI (Nicola), 7278.
De Javara (Juan), 6425.
DE JONG (Mayke) 4319, 4433.
DE KEGEL (Rolf), 3291.
DE LA FERRIERE (Jacques), 8537.
DE LA FUENTE (Alejandro), 5094.
DE LA GENIERE (Juliette), 2459.
DE LA IGLESIA (José Ignacio), 3568.
DE LA RONCIERE (Charles M.), 3733.
DE LA SELLE (Xavier), 5790.
DE LA VERONNE (Chantal), 5106.
DE LIBERA (Alain), 4301, 4320.
DE LLERA (L.), 6166.
DE LONGIS (Rosanna), 7575.
DE LUCA (Daniele), 8509.
DE LUCA (Don Giuseppe), 762, 1443.
DE LUCA (Francesco), 452.
DE LUNA (Giovanni), 842, 5016.
DE MADDALENA (Aldo), 1085.
DE MARCO (Vittorio), 5669.
DE MARTEL (G.), 4276.
De Martino (Ernesto), 1453, 1457.
DE MARTINO (Francesco), 2228.
DE MARTINO (Stefano), 1862.
DE MATTEI (Roberto), 7987.
DE MERINDOL (Christian), 3976, 4206.
DE MIGGRODE (Jacques), 5623.
De Moerbeke (Guillelmus), 4267, 4280.
DE MOGROBEJO (Endika), 271.
DE MOGROBEJO-ZABALA (Garikoitz), 271.
De Monzon (Francisco), 5736.
De Muris (Johannes), 260.
DE NEGRONI (Barbara), 5993.
DE NIE (Giselle), 790.
DE OLIVEIRA MARQUES (A. H.), 5274.
De Oraa (don José), 7249.
De Pals (Francesc), 3762.
DE PASCALE (Carla), 6257.
DE PLANHOL (Xavier), 7374.
DE RACHEWILTZ (Siegfried), 3796.
DE RIJK (L. M.).
DE RIJK (Lambert Marie), 4286, 4321.
DE ROMILLY (Jacqueline), 2122.
DE ROOS (Johan), 1879.
DE ROSA (Daniele), 3441.
DE ROSA (Francesco), 6628.
DE ROSA (Gabriele), 561, 758, 5644, 5669.
De' Rossi (Giovanni Battista), 763.
De Sade (Donatien Alphonse François Marquis), 6613.

De Sanctis (Gaetano), 764.
DE SANDRE GASPARINI (Giuseppina), 4496.
DE SENARCLENS (Pierre), 8511.
DE SENSI SESTITO (Giovanna), 2446.
DE SOUSA (Celeste Ribeiro), 1533.
DE SPIEGELEIRE (Stephan), 8707.
De Sürbeck (Pierre-Eugène), 304.
De Valdès (Alfonso), 6250.
De Valdès (Juan), 5706.
DE VEY MESTADGH (J.H.), 285.
De Vico Pisano (Roger), 4519.
De Villena (Juan Manuel), 3665.
DE VILLERS (Gauthier), 4714.
DE VIRGILIO (G.), 2974.
DE VIVO (A.), 837.
DE VRIES (Kelly R.), 3278.
Deák (Ferenc), 5559.
DEÁK (Ágnes), 5547.
DEAN (Winton), 6910.
DEAR (I.C.B.), 1140.
DEAR (Peter Robert), 6407.
DEARBORN (David S. P.), 6408.
DEBAE (Marguerite), 459.
DEBELFORT (Anne-Marie), 6743.
DEBORD (André), 3734.
DEBRU (Claude), 1333.
DECKER (Wolfgang), 2255.
DECLEVA (Enrico), 5024.
DECLICH (Francesca), 562.
DECLOEDT (Leopold R. G.), 6629.
DECRET (François), 2975.
Dedekind (Julius Wilhelm Richard), 6434.
DEFILIPPIS (Domenico), 3279.
DEGANI (Enzo), 3095.
DEGENRING (Susanne), 3599.
DEGL'INNOCENTI (Antonella), 4472.
DEGLER-SPENGLER (Brigitte), 5679.
DEGNBOL (Helle), 4088.
DEGREGORI (Carlos Ivàn), 5219.
DEGTJAREVA (A. Ja.), 5319.
Deguí (Pere), 4335.
DEHAY (Valérie), 4866.
DEHON (Pierre-Jacques), 2764.
Deichmann (Friedrich Wilhelm), 4180.
DEIGHTON (Anne), 8512.
DEJMEK (Jindřich), 5238.
DEKESEL (C. E.), 299.
DEKKER (J. C.), 5153.
DEL BOCA (Angelo), 4699.
DEL CAMPO (Alberto), 4458.
DEL FRA (Lino), 7859.
DEL ZOTTO (C.), 4271.
DELAIGUE (Marie-Christine), 1007.
DELAMONT (Sara), 1002.
DELAUNOIS (Jean-Marie), 4715.
DELBANCO (Nicholas), 6630.
DELCORNO (Carlo), 3977.
DELDIME (Roger), 6979.

DELGADO ECHEVERRÍA (Jesús), 7625.
Delisle (Léopold), 765.
DELISSEN (Alain), 7331.
DELL (Edmund), 8513.
DELL'OMO (Mariano), 5791.
Della Casa (Giovanni), 6850.
DELLA CASA (Philippe), 1657, 1691.
della Croce (Francesco), 5724.
DELLA CROCE (Giovanna Maria), 3283.
DELLA PERUTA (Franco), 5029.
DELLER (K.), 1724.
DELLSPERGER (Rudolf), 5673.
DELMAIRE (Bernard), 3735.
DELMAIRE (R.), 338.
DELMAIRE (Roland), 2684.
DELMAS (Bernard), 7002.
DELMAS (Thierry), 7002.
DELOGU (Paolo), 3411.
DELORT (Robert), 3736.
DELPIANO (Patrizia), 6410.
DELTERNE (M.), 3412.
DELUMEAU (Jean), 1444.
DEMANDT (Alexander), 814, 1347, 1725.
DEMARCHI (F.), 1488.
DEMARCHI (Gustavo Ernesto), 7210.
DEMARIS (Richard E.), 2832.
DEMBSKI (Günther), 300.
DEMENT'EV (Igor' P.), 747.
DEMERATH (N.J.), 1384.
Demetrius, 2051.
DÉMIER (Francis), 7160.
DEMIR (Fevzi), 5514.
DEMKER (Marie), 8457.
DEMONT (Paul), 1974.
DEMORIS (René), 5994, 6817.
DEMUELENAERE-DOUYERE (Christiane), 428.
DEN BOEFT (J.), 2548.
DEN BOER (Pim), 563.
DEN HENGST (D.), 2548.
DENG (Francis M.), 5462.
DENG (Ruiling), 8844.
DENG (Yibing), 8845.
Deng (Xiaoping), 8957.
Denikin (Anton Ivanovich), 5333.
DENING (Greg), 1003.
DENIS (Anne), 6595.
DENIZE (Eugen), 7928.
DENKTAŚ (Mustafa), 6733.
DENMAN (R.), 7692.
DENNERT (Martin), 3120.
DENNETT (Daniel Clement), 6411.
Dennis (George T.), 3157.
DENORA (Tia), 6911.
DENTIN (P.), 1445.
DEORA (M. S.), 7830, 7860, 7881, 7882.
DEPEW (David J.), 6412.

DEPREUX (Ph.), 3737.
DEPUYDT (Leo), 1769, 1945, 2123.
DER (Aladár), 7496.
DEREGNAUCOURT (Gilles), 5795.
DEREMETZ (Alain), 2765.
DERKS (H.), 2360.
DEROCHE (Vincent), 3058.
DEROUET (Bernard), 1262.
DERREUMAUX (Edmond), 8023.
DERRIDA (Jacques) , 1535, 6258.
DERVILLE (Alain), 1448, 3442, 3738.
DERWICH (Marek), 564, 4445.
DERY (Attila), 7311.
DESBROUSSES (Hélène), 1193.
Descartes (René), 1509, 6356.
DESCAT (R.), 2117.
DESCAT (Raymond), 775.
DESCHAMPS (L.), 2833.
DESCIMON (Robert), 7375, 7633.
DESCOEUDRES (Jean-Paul), 1735.
DESHMAN (R.), 104.
DESIDERI (Paolo), 2686.
Desiderio da Settignano, 6814.
DESMARAIS (Gaetan), 381.
DESMOND (Ray), 6786.
DESNIER (Jean-Luc), 2625.
Desnos (Robert), 6960.
Desportes (François), 6845.
DESPY (Georges), 3739.
DESTRO (Adriana), 2977.
DESTROOPER-GEORGIADES (Anne), 2188.
DESWARTE (Th.), 4421.
DEUBNER (Otfried), 1742.
DEUVE (Jean), 8514.
DEVAUCHELLE (R.), 217.
DEVILLERS (Olivier), 2549.
DEVINE (Andrew Mackay), 2256.
DEVISSCHER (Hans), 6818.
DEVOS (Paul), 3032.
DEVOTO (Guido), 2527.
DEZZA (Ettore), 3617.
DHÉNIN (Michel), 278.
DHIFALLAH (Mohamed), 7861.
DI BENEDETTO (Arnaldo), 6556.
DI BENEDETTO (Vincenzo), 2062, 2257, 2550.
DI BERNARDI (Vito), 6913.
DI CAMILLO (Ottavio), 566.
DI CARPEGNA FALCONIERI (Tommaso), 3740.
DI CAVE (Carlo), 3443.
DI DONATO (Riccardo), 1990.
DI FRAIA (Tomaso), 1658.
DI FRANCESCO (Amedeo), 3978.
di Giorgio (Francesco), 6323.
DI GIUSTO (Stefano), 8515.
DI LERNIA (Savino), 1636.
DI MAURO (A.), 6259.
DI NOLFO (Ennio), 7693, 8222.
DI RIENZO (Eugenio), 1177, 878.

DI VITTORIO (Giuseppe)., 7497.
DIACON (Todd), 4731.
Diacono (Paolo), 3272.
DIAKONOFF (Igor M.), 1446.
DIAWARA (Mamadou), 9089.
DÍAZ BODEGAS (P.), 3245.
Diaz Del Castillo (Bernal), 9108.
DIAZ Y DIAZ (Manuel C.), 105.
DIAZ-ANDREU (M), 1575.
DÍAZ-DEL-RÍO ESPAÑOL (Pedro), 1659.
Dicey (Albert Venn), 7586.
DICKERMAN (Edmund H.), 4919.
DICKINSON (Donald C.), 460.
DICKSON (P. G. M.), 5172.
Diderot (Denis), 6734, 6817.
DIDO (Pierre), 6537.
DIEBOLT (C.), 6094.
DIEDERICH (Toni), 274.
DIEDERICHSEN (Uwe), 7537.
DIEGO SANTOS (F.), 3205.
DIEM (Peter), 279.
DIERKENS (Alain), 1454.
DIESENER (Gerald), 779.
DIETL (Albert), 4177.
DIEZ DE VELASCO (Francisco), 1449.
DÍEZ TORRE (Alejandro R.), 6395.
DIHLE (A.), 2161.
DIJKSTRA (C. Th. J.), 3979.
DIJKSTRA (Klaas), 1893.
DIK (H.), 2258.
DIKOTTER (Frank), 6413.
DILCHER (R.), 2259.
DILKS (David N.), 4868.
DILLON (Matthew), 2260.
Dilthey (Wilhelm), 909, 6226, 7040.
DILWORTH (Mark), 4434.
DIMITRIVA (Snezana), 8101.
DIMOCK (G. E.), 2080.
DINET (Dominique), 4477.
DING (Sanqin), 8847.
DINGLEY (James), 4711.
DINGWALL (Helen M.), 6414.
DINI (Bruno), 3741, 7071.
Diodoros Sikelos, 766, 1954.
DIONISOTTI (Carlo), 218, 5995.
Dionysios Halikarnasseus, 1478.
DIOP (Samba), 1004.
DIÓSZEGI (István), 4584, 5173, 8024.
DIPPER (Christof), 1305.
Dirrheimer (Günter), 490.
DITCHFIELD (Simon Richard), 5738.
DITTMAN (Reinhard), 1806.
DIWO (Gérard), 4859.
DIXON (Laurinda S.), 6415.
DNEPROVSKIJ (K. A.), 8805.
DOBBS-HIGGINSON (M. S.), 8516.
DOBESCH (G.), 1975.
DOBLHOFER (Georg), 2245.
Doblin (Alfred), 909.
DOBOSZ (Józef), 4497.

DOBROV (G. W.), 2243.
DOBRYNIN (Anatolii Fedorovich), 8517.
DOBSON (Alan P.), 7694.
DOBSON (M.), 2195.
DOCAMPO CAPILLA (F. J.), 107.
DOCKES (Pierre), 1263.
DOCKRILL (Michael), 8333.
DODIER (Nicolas), 5996.
DODILLE (Norbert), 1331.
DODSON (Aidan), 1770.
DOGLIO (Federico), 6919.
DOGO (Marco), 7695.
DOHAR (William J.), 3742.
DOHERTY (L. E.), 2261.
DOIG (James A.), 3280.
DÓKA (Klára), 5739.
DOKOS (Thanos), 8518.
DOLATA (Jens), 2687.
DOLBEAU (François), 106, 3033.
DOLCI (Fabrizio), 5029.
DOLCINI (Carlo), 6260.
DOLEMEYER (Barbara), 7617.
DOLENZ (Heimo), 2898.
DOLHAR (Rafko), 5017.
DOMAŃSKI (Juliusz), 4498.
DOMBRÁDY (Loránd), 8223.
Domenica da paradiso, 4539.
Domenico di Perugia, Sanctus, 3274.
DOMINGOS (Manuela D.), 461.
DOMINGUEZ REBOIRAS (Fernando), 4302, 4322.
DOMINGUEZ RODRIGUEZ (A.), 107, 118, 141.
Dominici (Giovanni), 4486.
DOMIN-JACOV (Maria), 5740.
Domitia (Longina), 2917.
DOMNIN (Igor'V.), 5400.
DOMORAD (Konstantin Il'ich), 8402.
DONAGAN (Barbara), 4941.
DONALDSON (Gordon), 4942.
DONATI (P.), 2737.
DONATI (Claudio), 7376.
DONATI GIACOMINI (P.), 2737.
DONDARINI (Rolando), 3618, 3648.
DONDERER (Michael), 2871.
DONG (Shili), 8848.
Donne (John), 6597.
DONNINI (Francesco), 3816.
DONNINI (Mauro), 3034, 3619.
DONNO (Antonio), 8519.
DONOGHUE (Mark), 7003.
Donskoj (Dmitry), 767.
DOOLEY (Brendan), 5997, 6600.
DOORDAN (Dennis P.), 6869.
DOPFFEL (H. Peter), 7663.
DÖPP (S.), 2766.
DORATI (Marco), 2124.
DÖRFLINGER (Johannes), 382.
DORMAN (Andrew M.), 8520.

DORMOIS (Jean-Pierre), 7161.
DORONCHENKOV (Askol'd Ivanovich), 5314.
DOROSZEWSKI (Jerzy), 6095.
DORR-BACKES (Felicitas), 5998.
DORRIEN (Gary J.), 5645.
DØRUM (Knut), 7238.
DOSAL (Paul Jaime), 4968.
Dossi (Carlo), 6611.
DOSTALOVÁ (Růžena), 3121.
DOSTÁLOVÁ (R.), 568.
Dostoevsky (Fëdor Mikhailovič), 5839, 6639.
DOUGLAS (Roy), 8103.
DOUGLAS (William Alexander Binney), 5074.
DOUGNAC RODRÍGUEZ (Antonio), 5625.
DOUKELLIS (Panagiotis), 1743.
DOUMANI (Beshara), 5210.
DOUMERC (Bernard), 3743, 4553, 7211.
DOUZOU (Laurent), 6168.
DOVERE (Elio), 2978.
DOW (Sheila C.), 7004.
DOWNEY (Susan B.), 2872.
DOWNING (F. Gerald), 1895.
DOWNS (George W.), 7696.
DOWNS (Laura Lee), 7377.
DOWNTON (John), 6735.
DOXEY (Margaret), 8521.
Doyle (A. I.), 246.
DOYLE (William), 4869.
DRACK (Walter), 4435.
DRACONTIUS (Blossius Aemilius), 2551.
DRÄGER (P.), 2262.
DRAGOUMIS (Mark), 1169.
DRAGUNOV (Georgij P.), 7697.
DRAKIDIS (Philippe), 7665.
DRAPALA (Milan), 8278.
DRAPER (Peter), 4176.
DRAUS (F.), 6307.
DRAY (William H.), 879.
DRECHSLER (H.), 82.
DRECHSLER (Maximiliane), 6736.
DREHER (Martin), 2125.
DREW GRIFFITH (R.), 2263.
DREXLER (Alois), 6416.
DREYER (Mechthild), 4323.
Dreyfus (Alfred), 4873.
DREYFUS (Michel), 7498.
DRIJVERS (Jan Willem), 2548, 3953.
DRISCOLL (M. J.), 3575.
DROBYSHEV (V. V.), 7756.
DRÖGE (Kurt), 1251.
DROLET (Michael), 1175.
DRONFIELD (Jeremy), 1637.
DRONKE (P.), 3980.
DROUHAUD (Pascal), 8522.

Droysen (Johann Gustav), 768, 948.
DROZ-VINCENT (Gabriel), 6261.
DRUMMOND (Andrew), 2626.
DRUSI (Riccardo), 6557.
DRYGAS (Aleksander), 1332.
Du Bellay (Jean), 6587.
DU REAU (Elisabeth), 7698.
DUARA (Prasenjit), 880.
DUBICKI (Tadeusz), 8225.
DUBOIS (Henri), 3744.
DUBOIS (Jean-Daniel), 2979.
DUBOIS (Laurent), 2031.
DUBOIS (Thomas A.), 6914.
DUBOW (Saul), 5447, 5459.
DUBREUCQ (A.), 3290.
DUBROVSKIJ (A. M.), 4645.
DUBUIS (Olivier F.), 324.
DUBUIS (Pierre), 3745.
DUBY (Georges), 4181, 4449.
DUCAT (Jean), 2190, 2361.
DUCHEMIN (J.), 2362.
DUCHENE (Roger), 5999.
DUCHESNAU (François), 6310.
Duchesne (Louis), 763.
DUCHET (Michele), 569.
DUCLERT (Vincent), 4850, 4870.
DUCOS (M.), 2835.
DUCZKOWSKA-MORACZEWSKA (Henryka), 6132.
DUDINK (Adrianus), 5801.
DUDLEY (Dennine), 1944.
DUE-NIELSEN (Carsten), 8424.
DUFAURE (Jean-Jacques), 1743.
DUFFIELD (John S.), 8524.
DUFFY (John), 3122.
DUFOUR (Alain), 5843.
DUFOUR (Jean), 53, 3211.
DUFOURNET (J.), 3981.
DUFRAISSE (Roger), 7988.
DUGGAN (C.), 5025.
Dughet (Gaspard), 6812.
DUIGNAN (Peter), 8226.
DUJARDIN (Vincent), 4716.
DUKE (E. A.), 2098.
DULAC (L.), 3987.
DÜLFFER (Jost), 7995.
DUMBUYA (Peter A.), 7862.
DUMEZIL (Georges), 769, 1450.
DUMOULIN (Olivier), 570.
DUMVILLE (David N.), 3982.
DUMVILLE (David), 3262.
DUNBABIN (J. P. D.), 7072.
DUNBAR (N.), 2048.
DUNLOP (Francis), 6292.
DUNN (Cristopher Chase), 7073.
DUNN (Walter Scott), 5401.
DUNNAGE (Jonathan), 5018.
DUNNINGAN (John P.), 4994.
Duns Scotus (Johannes), 4389.
DUPRAT (G.), 6307.
DUPRONT (Alphonse), 770, 3925.

DUPUIS (J.), 1385.
Dupuis (Joseph), 9100.
DUPUY (Roger), 4871, 4904.
DURACK (Susan), 446.
DURAND (Aline), 3746.
DURAND (Jean-Pierre), 6000.
DURAND (Robert), 3747.
DURANTON-CRABOL (Anne-Marie), 7863.
Dürer (Albrecht), 6806, 6827.
DURIĆ (Rašid), 5065.
DURISIN (Dionyz), 6517.
Durkheim (Emile), 5979, 6009.
DURLIAT (Jean), 13, 3123.
Duroselle (Jean-Baptiste), 771, 7699, 7750, 7751, 7769, 7790.
DURRANI (Osman), 6644.
DURST (Margarete), 822.
DUSIŃSKA (Halina), 799.
DUTTON (David), 8104, 8525.
DUTTON (Y.), 98.
DUTU (Alexandru), 1331.
DUUS (Peter), 8025.
DUVAL (Marcel), 8526.
DUVERDIER (Marielle), 6781.
DUVERNOY BOLENS (Jacqueline), 6001.
DUVIOLS (Jean-Paul).
DUVOSQUEL (Jean-Marie), 3835.
DUZ' (Petr D.), 5315.
DYCZOK (Marta), 8227.
DYER (Christopher), 3748.
DYER (R. R.), 2552.
DYSERINCK (Hugo), 6517.
DYSKANT (Józef Wiesław), 1147.
DZAJA (Srecko M.), 7924.
DŽALL (E. Dz.), 1666.
DZIEDUSZYCKI (Wojciech), 3749.
DZIELSKA (M.), 2264.
DZIUBIŃSKI (Andrzej), 5914.

E

EAGLE (M. R.), 6417.
EASTWOOD (David), 839.
EAVERLY (Mary Ann), 2396.
EBBESEN (Sten), 4129.
EBERLEIN (Johann Konrad), 4207.
EBERSBACH (V.), 2767.
EBNÖTHER (Karl), 5368.
ECCLESHALL (Robert), 1175.
ECHEGARAY (Joaquín Gonzales), 4458.
ECK (Werner), 2515, 2718.
ECKES (Alfred E.), 7700.
Eckhart (Meister), 4337.
ECKSTEIN (Arthur M.), 828.
ECKSTEIN (Nicholas A.), 7378.
EDDEN (Valerie), 4499.
EDDY (Michael R.), 9090.

EDEL (Susanne), 6262.
ÉDEL'MAN (Ol'ga V.), 5317.
EDGERTON (Robert Breckenridge), 4922.
Edgeworth (Francis Ysidoro), 6993.
EDGREN (Lars), 970.
EDMUNDS (R. David), 9110.
EDMUNDSON (Mark), 1535.
ÉDOUARD-LAURENT (S.), 4872.
EDROIU (Nicolae), 14, 1090.
Edward III, king of England, 3278.
EDWARDS (A.), 89.
EDWARDS (Douglas A.), 1602.
EDWARDS (Jill), 8527.
EDWARDS (John), 3526.
EDWARDS (M. J.), 2047.
EDWARDS (Martha Lynn), 2191.
EDWARDS (P. C.), 1946.
EFFERTZ (Dirk), 7663.
EFIMOV (Nikolaj A.), 797.
EFTHYMIADIS (Stephanos), 3059.
EGAWA (Atsushi), 3388.
EGG (Markus), 1681.
EGGE (Åsmund), 5157.
EGGENBERGER (C.), 166.
EGGER (Christoph), 4422.
Egharevba (Jacob), 9091.
EHLERS (Joachim), 3444.
Ehrenburg (Ilja), 6705.
EHRENSVÄRD (Ulla), 1126.
EHRHART (Hans-Georg), 8528.
EHRLICH (Eva), 7078.
EICHENGREEN (Barry), 7082.
EIDE (T.), 1772.
Einstein (Albert), 6404, 6491.
EIRE (Carlos M. N.), 5687.
EISELE (J. A.), 1576.
EISENHOFER (Stefan), 9091.
Eisenhower (Dwight David), 8509, 8620, 8633.
EISNER (Freya), 7499.
Eisners (Kurt), 7499.
EITELJORG (Harrison), 2397.
Eiximenis (Francesc), 3517.
Ekaterina II, imperatrice di Russia, 5326, 7767.
EL MALKI (M'hamed), 4604.
ELAD (Amikam), 3549.
ELAYI (J.), 1896.
Eleanor of Castile, queen of England, 3715.
ELEUTERI (Paolo), 3096.
EL-FAÏZ (Mohammed), 1863.
Eliade (Mircea), 1489.
Elias (Norbert), 772.
Elisabetta, regina d'Ungheria, 4466.
ELLINGSEN (Mark), 5646.
ELLIOT (John E.), 6994.
ELLIOT SORUM (Christina), 2265.
ELLIOTT (John H.), 881, 7809.
Ellis (Peter Berresford), 1698.

ELLIS (Steven G.), 4937, 7912.
ELLISON (Christopher G.), 1384.
ELLNER (Steve), 7500.
EL-MARZOUKI (Fethi), 1092.
EL-MUSTAFA (Azzou), 8529.
Elsner (Gisela), 6634.
ELSNER (Jás), 2873.
EL-SOLH (Camillia Fawzi), 5915.
ELTIGANI (Eltigani E.), 5463.
ELTIS (David), 7079.
Elton (G. R.), 911.
ELVERT (Jürgen), 7741.
ELY (Richard), 1062.
ELY (Sidi Amar Ould), 113.
Emanuele Filiberto, duca di Savoia, 5028.
EMBLETON (Gerry), 6720.
EMECEN (Feridun), 430.
EMERY (Glles), 4324.
EMERY (Michael C.), 6171.
EMMONS (Terence), 571.
EMPERLEY (Howard), 8258.
ENDERLE-BURCEL (Gertrude), 7567, 7571.
ENDRESS (Gerhard), 3552.
ENGEHAUSEN (Frank), 4943.
ENGEL (Pál), 391.
ENGEL (Vincent), 6520.
ENGELBERT (Thomas), 5616.
ENGELMANN (Roger), 4774.
Engels (Friederich), 6297, 6361.
ENGERMAN (S. L.), 7080.
ENGİN (Vahdettin), 8026.
ENGLEZAKIS (Benedict), 5821.
ENGLISH (Barbara), VIII.
ENGLISH (Edward D.), 4366.
ENGLUND (Robert K.), 1820.
ENGMAN (Max), 4837, 7379.
ENGSTFELD (Hans-Joachim), 7306.
Enrique I, rey de Navarra, 3194.
Enrique III, rey de Castilla, 3503.
ENYEDI (Sándor), 6097.
Epifanio di Salamina, 2923.
EPPEL (Peter), 8397.
EPPRECHT (Marc), 5450.
EPSTEIN (Julia), 6419.
Erasmus Roterodamus (Desiderius), 3339, 5859, 6250.
ERASOV (Boris S.), 882.
Eratosthenes, 2063.
ERCILASUN (Ahmet B.), 1536.
ERDEI (Gyöngyi), 7312.
ERDEMIR (Ayşegül Demirhan), 7212.
ERDKAMP (Paul), 2719.
ERDÖ (Peter), 3621.
ERDOĞU (Burçin), 1744.
EREŚĆENKO (M. D.), 4635.
ERGENC (Ozer), 572.
ERGETOWSKI (Ryszard), 6098.
Erik av Pommern, 5160.

ERIKSON (K. O.), 1773.
ERIN (Mikhail E.), 8334, 8335.
Eriugena (Johannes Scotus), 6246.
ERLER (Mary C.), 4500.
ÉRLIKH (V. P.), 8805.
ERRERA (Andrea), 3622.
ERSKINE (Andrew), 1774.
ÉRSZEGI (Géza), 4437.
ERTAN (Temuçin F.), 7558.
ESCH (Arnold), 573, 6718.
ESCHER (Walter), 994.
ESCOBAR (Arturo), 7081.
ESCOBARI DE QUEREJAZU (Laura), 7236.
ESENWEIN (George), 5438.
ESMAN (Milton J.), 8530.
ESOLEN (A.), 2570.
ESPOSITO (Anna), 3520.
ESPOSITO (Enzo), 1524.
ESQUIVEL (José Antonio), 1587.
ESSERTEL (Y.), 5741.
ESTEBAN CASALDO (M. Eloísa), 431.
ESTELRICH (Jordi Gayà), 4295.
Esterházy (János), 5492.
ESTEVEZ (Jordi), 1613.
ESTEVEZ SOLA (Juan A.), 3296.
Estienne (Charles), 6578.
ESTIEZ (O.), 2688.
ESTOW (Clara), 3493.
ETAYO-PIÑOL (M. A.), 6420.
ETCHEPARE (Jaime Antonio), 4744.
ETEMAND (Bouda), 1264, 1297.
ETENYI (Nóra), 5548.
ÉTIENNE (J.), 1377.
ETIENNE (Gilbert), 1265.
ÉTIENNE (Roland), 2398.
ETZERDORFER (Irene), 5175.
EUGSTER (Markus), 7559.
Eukleidēs, 6487.
Euler (Leonhard), 6421.
EULER (Walter Andreas), 4325.
Euphebius, Sanctus, 3164.
Euripides, 2064, 2065, 2066, 2067, 2068, 2069, 2070, 2265, 2283, 2307, 2309.
Eusebius Caesariensis, 2536.
Eustathios, 3059.
EUTROPIUS, 2553.
EVANGELISTI (C.), 17.
EVANGELISTI (Silvia), 5792.
Evans (Bill), 6889.
EVANS (E. W.), 7083.
EVANS (Gillian Rosemary), 4326.
EVANS (M. J.), 109.
EVERS (Meindert), 5369.
EVIEUX (Pierre), 2980.
EVRARD (Louis), 6013.
EVSEEV (Vladimir A.), 7314.
EVZEROV (Robert Ja.), 1194.
Eymar (Ange Marie), 8010.

F

FABER (Riemer), 2554.
Faber Stapulensis (Jacobus), 4391, 6561.
FABIAN (B.), 199.
FABIETTI (Ugo), 1009.
FABRE (Giorgio), 813, 6632.
FABRE (Pierre-Antoine), 575.
FÁBREGA I GRAU (Angel), 3212.
FABRÉGUET (Michel), 4775.
FABRE-SERRIS (Jacqueline), 2769.
Fabro (Cornelio), 758.
FADEEVA (T. M.), 6299.
Faerno (Gabriele), 6572.
FAHR-BECKER (Gabriele), 6787.
FAIVRE (Antoine), 1455.
FAIVRE (Maurice), 7864.
FAIVRE (Xavier), 1821.
FAJFAR (Britta), 1456.
FAJFER (Luba), 5236.
FALCH (Sabine), 5176.
Falco (Giorgio), 773.
FALCÓN (Romana), 7239.
FALCÓN PÉREZ (M. P.), 4208.
FALKENSTEIN (Lorne), 6263.
FALKNER (Caroline), 2126.
FALLETTI (E.), 2516.
FALOLA (Toyin), 745.
FALTER (Jürgen W.), 7361.
FAMICIN (A. S.), 1010.
FAMILIARI (Rocco), 5713.
FAN (Jinmin), 8850.
Fang (Huifang), 8855.
FANGMEIER (Jurgen), 5855.
FANTINI (Bernardino), 6473.
Fantinus Taurianensis, Sanctus, 3045.
FARBER (Gertrud), 1822.
FARBMAN (Nikolaj V.), 4776.
FARCY (Jean-Claude), 8105.
FARENGA (Paola), 3985.
FARGE (Arlette), 883.
FARKAS (Richard P.), 8532.
FARMAN (John), 6738.
FAROQHI (Suraiya), 5515.
FAROUK (Ahmed), 5106.
Farquhar (Robert), 7840.
FARR (James F), 7634.
FARRAR-HOCKLEY (Anthony), 8533.
FARRELL (Thomas J.), 746.
FARREN (Sean), 6099.
FARRINGTON (Andrew), 2874.
FASOLI (Gina), 3281.
FATIO (Olivier), 5673.
FATTAL (Michel), 2267.
FAU (Jean-Claude), 4209.
FAUCCI (Riccardo), 7005.
FAULKNER (Rupert), 6870.
FAURE (Alain), 6002.
FAURIOL (Georges), 7701.

FAUTH (D.), 7538.
FAUTH (Wolfgang), 2364.
FAVA (Anna Serena), 301.
FAVI (Dolcino), 4873.
FAVINO (L.), 3623.
FAVOREU (Louis), 7585.
FAVREAU (Robert), 18, 188, 3202, 4210.
FAWCETT (Eric), 8534.
FAYER (Steve), 5595.
FEAR (A.T.), 2770.
FEATHERSTONE (Roger), 1577.
FEBRER ROMAGUERA (Manuel Vicent), 3624.
Febvre (Lucien), 749, 774.
FEDALTO (Giorgio), 5822.
Federico III, re di Sicilia, 3489.
FEDEROWICZ (Grażyna), 5227.
FEDERSPIEL (Michel), 2268.
FEDOROWICH (Kent), 7801.
FEDOSOVA (V. N.), 884.
FEE (Lian Kwen), 5385.
FEENSTRA (R.), 2680.
FEGER (Hans), 6264.
FEHÉR (Katalin), 6003.
FEHRENBACH (R. J.), 251.
FEI (Silvano), 7315.
FEINBERG (H. M.), 5451.
FEINER (Shmuel), 576.
FEINSTEIN (Charles H.), 7272.
FEISSEL (Denis), 2032.
FEISTNER (Edith), 3986.
FEITL (István), 5549.
FELBECKER (Sabine), 2981.
FELCMAN (Ondřej), 8535.
FELDBÆK (Ole), 5158, 7989.
FELDBAUER (Peter), 3551.
FELDHAY (Rivka), 6004.
FELDMAN (Gerald D.), 7282.
FELICE (Domenico), 6265.
FELICIANI (Angela), 449.
Feliciano (Felice), 198.
Felicita, sancta, 3033.
Felipe II, rey de España, 121, 4872, 7944.
Felipe III, rey de España, 7944.
FELIU (Francesc), 360.
FELIX (David), 7006.
FELLE (Antonio Enrico), 2926.
FELLER (Laurent), 3750.
FELLOWS JENSEN (Gillian), 3579.
FELSENSTEIN (Frank), 6521.
Feltrinelli (Giangiacomo), 6175.
FENLON (Iain), 6904.
FENNELL (John Lister Illingworth), 5823.
FERA (Vincenzo), 3988.
FERCHIOU (Naïdé), 9092.
Ferdinand I, röm.-deutscher Kaiser, 283.
FERENĆUHOVÁ (Bohumila), 8029.

Fergola (Nicolo), 6421.
FERGUSON (Niall), 4777, 7007, 7084.
FERGUSON (T. J.), 1572.
FERJANI (Khemaïs), 7240.
FERNADEZ (A.), 7317.
FERNÁNDEZ GÓMEZ (Marcos), 49.
FERNANDEZ QUINTERO (Norma), 1368.
FERNANDEZ TRABAL (Josep), 3751.
FERNANDEZ VIANA Y VIEITES (J. I.), 3216.
FERNANDEZ-MIRANDA (Manuel), 1660.
Fernando I, rey de Aragona y Sicilia, 827, 4114.
Fernando el Catolico, rey de Aragona, 288.
FERNILLOT (Y.), 211.
FEROTIN (M), 4277.
FERRANTE (Biagio), 3213.
FERRARA (A. J.), 1823.
Ferrara (Francesco), 7005.
FERRARI (Aldo), 7702.
FERRARI (Jean), 1195.
FERRARI (Michele C.), 4081.
FERRARIS (Luigi Vittorio), 7703.
FERRARO (Domenico), 5793.
FERRARO (Giovanni), 6421.
FERRARY (J.-L.), 2689.
FERREIRA (Ana Maria Pereira), 7825.
FERREIRA (Jaime Alberto do Couto), 5275.
FERREIRA DA CUNHA (Paulo), 7560.
FERRER (María Teresa), 3208.
FERRETTI (Maria), 577.
FERRETTI (Valdo), 8536.
Ferri de Saint-Constant (Giovanni), 6057.
FERRIS (John R.), 8106.
Ferris (Richard „Dick"), 5131.
FERRONE (Vincenzo), 5689.
FERTACZ (Sylwester), 8229.
FEST (Joachim), 4778.
Festetics (György), 394.
Feszl (Frigyes), 6790.
FET (Jostein), 7381.
FETZER (John F.), 6633.
FEUER (Lewis S.), 6266.
FEUERWERKER (Albert), 7085.
Février (Paul-Albert), 9088.
FEYERABEND (Paul K.), 6422.
FICHANT (Michel), 6310.
Fichte (Johann Gottlieb), 6257.
Ficker (Julius), 849.
FICKER (Sandra Kuntz), 5116.
FIELD (Arthur), 752, 6005.
Filangieri (Riccardo), 3242.
Filarete, 6323.
Filippo Neri, Sanctus, 4459.

FILIPPOV (Szergej), 885.
FILORAMO (Giovanni), 1380, 1416, 5669.
FIMIANI (Enzo), 4609.
FINCARDI (Marco), 5742.
FINK (Carole), 749.
FINK (Karl J.), 6170.
FINK (Paul), 5370.
FINKEL (Irving L.), 1824.
FINKELBERG (Margalit), 2193.
FINKELSTEIN (Israel), 1682, 1898.
FINKELSTEIN (Norman G.), 8538.
FINNEGAN (Rachel J.), 2194.
FINNEGAN (Ruth), 9122.
FINNEY (P. C.), 410.
FINNEY (Patrick B.), 7501.
FIOCCA (Giorgio), 5019.
FIOCCHI (Fabio), 7990.
FIORAVANTI (Maurizio), 7561.
Fiore (Mario), 7841.
FIORENTINO (Girolamo), 1636.
FIRPO (Massimo), 5690, 5856.
FIRSOV (Fridrikh Igorevich), 5601.
FISAS (Vicenc), 8539.
FISCHER (Albert), 4779.
FISCHER (Conan J.), 7502.
FISCHER (Jean-Louis), 6461.
FISHER-HANSEN (Tobias), 2440.
FISHMAN (Nina), 4935.
FISHMAN (Sarah), 4875.
FISIAK (Jacek), 355.
FISIY (Cyprian F.), 5916.
FISZER (Józef), 8540.
FITOUSSI (Jean-Paul), 6998.
FITTIPALDI (Teodoro), 6739.
FITZGERALD (William), 2771.
FITZPATRICK (David), 7382.
FITZPATRICK (Gerard), 1175.
FLACHENECKER (Helmut), 3752, 4438.
FLADBY (Rolf), 5166.
FLAIG (E.), 2690.
FLAMM (Dieter), 6435.
FLAMMARION (Edith), 578.
FLAMMARION (Hubert), 3191.
FLANDREAU (Marc), 7281.
FLAQUER (Jaume), 6267.
Flavio Biondo, 3940, 4013.
Flavius Josephus, 776, 2041, 2662.
Flavius Renatus Vegetius, 2600.
FLECK (Dieter), 1237.
FLECK (Stephen H.), 6596.
FLEER (Cornelia), 6879.
FLEETWOOD (Steve), 7008.
FLEMING (Andrew), 1661.
FLEMING (Robin), 579.
FLETCHER (H. G.), 250.
Flint (Robert), 777.
FLITNER (Christine), 6634.
FLOOD (J. L.), 226.
FLORES (Maria da Conceicao), 7826.

FLORI (Jean), 3753, 4501.
FLORIDI (Luciano), 1516.
FLORISTAN (José M.), 3060.
FLORKOWSKA-FRANĆIĆ (Halina), 751.
FLORUS (LUCIUS ANNEUS), 2750.
FLOTO (Inga), 744.
FLYNN (Gregory), 8541.
FLYNN (Maureen), 7383.
FLYNN (Sarah), 5595.
Focillon (Henri), 407.
FODOR (James), 5647.
FODOR (Pál), 5516.
FOFFANO (Tino), 4113.
FOGEL (Robert W.), 1266.
FÖGEN (Marie Theres), 3079, 3125, 3666.
FOGLESONG (David S.), 8107.
FOHLEN (Claude), 7959.
FOHLEN (Jeannine), 114.
FOLDA (Jaroslav), 4183.
FÖLDES (György), 5550.
FÖLDESI (Margit), 5551.
FOLDÖY (Oddveig), 3580.
FOLEY (Duncan K.), 6994.
FOLEY (John Miles), 3358.
FOLKERS (Karl H.), 886.
FOLLIET (Georges), 2927.
FONER (Eric), 5592.
FONSECA (Wilton), 6172.
FONT (Márta), 3445.
FONTAINE (Laurence), 7635.
FONTANA (Josep), 8049.
FONTANA (V.), 180.
FONTANELLA (Francesca), 2772.
Fontenelle (Fernarde Le Bovier de), 6230.
FOOT (M. R. D.), 1140.
FOOT (Rosemary), 8542.
Foppes Dongjuma (Wytze), 6511.
FORBES (Christopher), 2982.
FORCADE (Olivier), 8027.
FORDE (Simon), 553, 3338.
FOREMAN- PECK (James), 7704.
FORENBAHER (Stašo), 1676.
FOREVILLE (Raymonde), 3192.
FORMENTIN (M. R.), 96.
FORMIGARI (Lia), 345.
Formiggini (Angelo Fortunato), 773.
FORNARI SCHIANCHI (Lucia), 6741.
FORNARO (Pasquale), 8028.
FORNI (Guglielmo), 5857.
FORNI (Pier Massimo), 4053, 6549.
FORSBERG (Stig), 1683.
FORSBERG (Tuomas), 7688, 7705.
FÖRSTEL (Karl), 3074.
Forster (Georg), 6758.
FORSTER (Heinz), 1538.
Forster (Karol), 6648.
FORSTNER (Karl), 4502.
FORSYTH (William H.), 4212.

FORTASSIER (P.), 2269.
FORTMANN (Michael), 8336.
FORTUN PEREZ DE CIRIZA (Luis Javier), 3754.
FORZONI (Angiolo), 302.
FOSCHI ALBERT (Marina), 6635.
FOSS (J. E.), 2886.
FOSS (Michael), 3989.
FOSSE (Lars Martin), 1336.
Fossier (Robert), 3713, 4554.
FOSSUM (Jarl E.), 2983.
FOSTER (David William), 4684.
FOSTER (John L.), 1778.
FOTIADIS (Michael), 2399.
FOUACHE (Eric), 1743.
FOUCART (Bruno), 6743.
Foucault (Michel), 1203, 2200, 6248, 6298, 6349, 6636.
FOULON (Eric), 2196.
FOUQUOIRE-BRILLET (E.), 7706.
FOURACRE (Paul), 3400, 3413, 3625.
FOURNIER (Georges), 4876.
FOURNIOUX (B.), 280.
FOWLER (D. D.), 1576.
FOWLER (Elizabeth), 3626.
Fowler (John), 8222.
FOWLER (Robert Booth), 5858.
FOX (Anthony), 339.
Fox (Charles James), 8006.
FOX (Christopher), 6015.
FOXVOG (Daniel A.), 1825.
FRAJESE (Vittorio), 6268.
FRAME (Grant), 1826.
FRAME (Murray), 1061.
FRANCASTEL (Pierre), 6819.
FRANCE (J.), 2517.
FRANCE (Peter), 1553.
FRANCESCHINI BOLOGNESI RECCHI (Eugenia), 3126.
FRANCESCO DA BARBERINO, 3902.
FRANCHETTI PARDO (Vittorio), 2875.
Francis (Philip), 4977.
Franciscus Assisiensis, Sanctus, 4461, 4464, 4479, 4538.
FRANCO (Daniel), 6363.
Franco Bahamonde (Francisco), 8307, 8313.
FRANCO CARVAHLAL (Tania), 6517.
FRANÇOIS (Etienne), 4636.
François Iᵉʳ, roi de France, 7919.
FRANÇOIS (L.), II.
FRANGEUR (Renée), 887.
FRANK (Daniel), 3527.
FRANK (Erwin), 5203.
FRANK (Marie-Therese), 6100.
FRANKEL (David), 1603.
Franklin (Benjamin), 4782.
FRANKLIN (Michael J)., 4410, 4503.
FRANKS (Norman Leslie Robert), 8108.

Franz I, röm.-deutscher Kaiser, 5760.
Franz Joseph I, imperatore d'Austria e re d'Ungheria, 6629.
FRANZINA (Emilio), 5594.
FRANZINELLI (Mimmo), 5743.
FRASCARELLI (Alba), 2494.
FRASCHETTI (Augusto), 2555, 2837.
FRASCINA (Francis), 6820.
FRASER (Thomas G), 8543.
FRAZIK (Wojciech), XVII.
FRECH (Stephan Veit), 5859.
FREDELL (Joel), 3990.
Frederik VI, king of Denmark and Norway, 5158.
FREDOUILLE (Jean-Claude), 2984.
FREED (Joann), 2876.
FREEDMAN (Lawrence), 7707.
FREEMAN (Leslie G.), 4458.
FREIRE (Antunes José), 8230.
FREIRE (José Geraldes), 3991.
FREISE (Eckhard), 3992.
FREITAG (Ulrike), 580.
FREMDLING (Rainer), 7087.
FRENCH (Thomas), 4213.
FRENSCHKOWSKI (Marco), 2985.
FRENZ (Thomas), 54.
Freppel (Charles), 5733.
Fréret (Nicolas), 778, 815.
Freud (Sigmund), 6626.
FREUND (Stephan), 3993.
FREUNDLIEB (Dieter), 6636.
FREVERT (Ute), 7384.
FREY (Lynda S.), 1166, 6006.
FREY (Marsha L.), 1166, 6006.
Freyer (Hans), 779.
FREY-KUPPER (Suzanne), 324.
FREYMOND (J.), 8544.
Freyre (Gilberto), 780.
FRÉZOULS (E.), 1985.
FREZZA (Daria), 1196.
FRIDENSON (Patrick), 7450.
FRIED (Johannes), 3414.
FRIEDLÄNDER (Johann), 5197.
FRIEDMAN (J. B.), 221.
FRIEDMAN (Thomas L.), 8545.
FRIEDMAN (Yvonne), 3535.
Friedrich I (Barbarossa), röm.-deutscher Kaiser, 3449.
Friedrich II der Großen, König von Preußen, 1214, 7950.
Friedrich II von Hohenstaufen, röm.-deutscher Kaiser, 59, 60, 76, 112, 3478, 4182.
Friedrich III, röm.-deutscher Kaiser, 3502.
Friedrich Wilhelm IV, König von Preußen, 4759.
FRIEDRICH (Margret), 7401.
FRIEDRICH SILBER (Ilana), 4404.
FRIEDRICHS (Christopher R.), 7318.
FRIELINGHAUS (Heide), 2460.

FRIES (Helmut), 6637.
FRIES (Marilyn Sibley), 6638.
FRIESER (Karl-Heinz), 8366.
FRIOLI (D.), 19.
FROJANOV (Igor' Ja.), 5319.
FROLOV (S.), 1899.
FROLOVA (A. V.), 1012.
FROMMEL (Christoph Luitpold), 6718.
FRONTIER (J.P.), 9099.
FRONTISI-DUCROUX (F.), 2400.
FRUGONI (Chiara), 4177.
Frycz Modrzewski (André), 6324.
FRYDE (E. B.), 115.
FRYE (David), 3755.
FUÀ (O.), 2737.
FUBINI (Riccardo), 3201, 3994.
FUCHS (Rachel G.), 4851.
FUDGE (J.), 7213.
FUDGE (John D.), 7708.
FÜGEDI (Erik), 55.
FUGLUM (Per), 7385.
FUHRMANN (Rosi), 3756.
FUJIKI (Hisashi, 9027.
FUJISAVA (Fusatoshi), 5029.
FUJITA (Katsuhisa), 8851.
FUJIWARA (Yoshiaki), 9026.
FUKAI (Jinzo), 9028.
FUKAZAWA (Katsumi), 7009.
FUKUDA (Toyohiko), 9029.
FUKUI (Norihiko), 1095.
FUKUI (Shigemasa), 8852.
FUKUYAMA (Francis), 888, 6325.
FULBROOK (Mary), 4780.
FULCI (Lucio), 6918.
FUMAGALLI (F. M.), 3214.
FUMAGALLI (Vito), 3359, 3627, 3757.
FUMAROLI (Marc), 755, 6671.
FUMASI (Eleonora), 5722.
FURET (François), 7503.
FURIER (Andrzej), 5243.
FURIO (Antoni), 3758.
FURLEY (O.), 8487.
FURNO (Martine), 3995.
FURSOV (A. I.), 7096.
FURST (Carl Gerold), 5744.
FURUTA (Motoo), 8821.
FUSCO (Roberto), 3061.
FUSSO (Suzanne), 6639.
FYFE (W. H.), 2051.
Fynn (Henry Francis), 9106.

G

GABACCIA (Donna R.), 5597.
GABBA (Emilio), 581, 794, 2197.
GABBARD (Krin), 6928.
GABEL (Helmut), 4781.
GABELKO (O. L.), 2127.

GABRIELI (Vittorio), 6597.
GACK-SCHEIDING (Chr.), 260.
GADŽIEV (kamaludin S.), 1197.
GADDIS (John Lewis), 889.
GADILLE (Jacques), 1458.
GADKAR (R. D.), 4984.
GADOMSKI (Jerzy), 4214.
GAFFURI (Laura), 3996.
GAGNON (Claude), 4292.
GAGOS (T.), 2093.
Gaguin (R.), 781.
GAIBOV (V.), 1952.
GAIDE (François), 2556.
GAIER (Claude), 3759.
Gaillard (Félix), 8588.
GAILLARD (Jean-Michel), 4877.
GAILLARD (Michele), 582.
GAINES (James F.), 6598.
GAL (Zvi), 1900.
GALA (Marilena), 8546.
GALANDAUER (Jan), 5475.
Galante Garrone (Alessandro), 5011.
GALASSO (Giuseppe), 3415.
GALASSO (Luigi), 2580.
GALEAZZI (Marco), 8547.
Galēnos, 2071, 2242.
GALEOTTI (Mark), 4667.
GALEOTTI PAPI (Donatella), 2270.
Galesiotos (Jorge), 34.
Galilei (Galileo), 6388, 6423, 6424.
GALINIER (J.), 1438.
GALINIER (M.), 2877.
GALL (Lothar), 7282, 7386.
GALLAGHER (Tom), 5297.
GALLAVOTTI (Carlo), 1965.
GALLERANO (Nicola), 719, 5020.
GALLEY (Chris), 7320.
GALLIGAN (Brian), 4704.
GALLISTL (Bernhard), 2878.
GALLO (Italo), 2756, 3924.
GALLO (Klaus), 8030.
GALLOWAY (Andrew), 4327.
GALLOWAY (Patricia), 9111.
Gallus Cornelius (Caius), 2573.
GALNOOR (Itzhak), 5211.
GALOPPINI (Laura), 3446.
GALUZZI (Massimo), 890, 938.
GALVAGNO (Rosalba), 2773.
GALVAO-SOBRINHO (Carlos R.), 2986.
GAMBARARA (Daniele), 345.
GAMBERALE (Leopoldo), 2072.
GAMBLE (Harry Y.), 2987.
GAMESON (Richard), 116.
GAMKRELIDZE (T. V.), 329.
GANDINO (Germana), 4405.
GANGENI (Maria Luisa), 3760.
Ganilh (Charles), 7038.
Gans (Eduard), 6283.
GANZ (David), 20, 4328.
Gao (Rui), 8853.

GAO (Wangling), 8854.
GARAVAGLIA (Juan Carlos), 5117.
GARBRECHT (Günther), 2271.
GARCÍA (Fe Iglesias), 7895.
GARCIA-BELLIDO (PAZ), 313.
GARCIA BIOSCA (J. E.), 4554.
GARCÍA-CÁRCEL (Ricardo), 583.
GARCIA CUBERO (Luis), 270.
GARCIA DE CORTAZAR (José Angel), 3761.
GARCÍA MARSILLA (Juan Vicente), 3762.
GARCÍA MERCADAL (F.), 433.
GARCÍA-MERCADAL Y GARCÍA-LOYGORRI (Fernando), 281.
GARCÍA ORO (José), 222.
GARCÍA PINILLA (I. J.), 6425.
GARCIA-ROMERAL PEREZ (Carlos), 5621.
GARCIA TERUEL (G.), 3997.
GARDIES (Jean-Louis), 2162.
GARDIN (J. C.), 584.
GARDINER (Juliet), 1103.
GARDNER (Lloyd C.), 8548.
GAREEV (Makhmut A.), 5402.
GAREFFI (Andrea), 6558.
GARFAGNINI (Gian Carlo), 110.
GARFINNKLE (Adam), 7387.
GARGALLO DI CASTEL LENTINI (Gioacchino), 830.
Garibaldi (Giuseppe), 8047.
GARIN (E.), 759.
GARLAND (Lynda), 3127.
GARLAND (R.), 2198.
GARMS (Jörg), 5794.
GARMS-CORNIDES (Elisabeth), 6522.
Garnier (German), 7038.
GARNOT (Benoit), 5795, 7636.
GARRAFFO (Salvatore), 311, 2464.
GARRETT (John R.), 7283.
GARRIDO PALAZON (Manuel), 6007.
GARRIER (Gilbert), 1267.
GARRIGUES (Emmanuel), 6640.
GARRISSON (Janine), 4878.
GARROS (Veronique), 5405.
GARZELLA (Gabriella), 3763.
GASCOU (Jacques), 9088.
GĄSIOROWSKI (Antoni), 5745.
GĄSIOROWSKI (Stefan), XVII.
GASKELL (Philip), 223.
GASPARI (Gianmarco), 340.
GASSAMA (Makhily), 6641.
GATES (Henry Louis), 6742.
GATES (Marie-Henriette), 1745.
GAUCHET (M.), 1198.
GAUDEMET (Jean), 1236, 2988.
GAUDIO (Angelo), 5746.
GAUDRIAULT (R.), 224.
GAUNT (Simon), 3998.
GAUTHIER (Florence), 7802.
GAUTHIER (Philippe), 2033.

GAUTHIEZ (Bernard), 3628.
GAUTIER DALCHE (Patrick), 383, 3215.
GAVIGNAUD (Geneviève), 519, 585.
GAVROGLU (Kostas), 1335.
GAY (Bernard), 8549.
Gay (Peter), 782.
Gay Escoda (Joseph M.), 3620.
GAYÀ ESTELRICH (Jordi), 4289, 4329.
GAYIBOR (N. L.), 9094.
GAZICH (Roberto), 2774.
GAZIELLO (Catherine), 428.
GE (Jianxiong), 8856.
GE (Thierry), 1620.
GEARY (Frank), 8031.
GEARY (Patrick J.), 3629.
Gębarowicz (Mieczysław), 6749.
GEBHART (Jan), 8231.
GECSÉNYI (Lajos), 7214, 8648.
Geerlings (WILHELM), 2955.
GEFFROY (Michel), 8109.
GEHRKE (Christian), 7010.
GEHRKE (H.-J.), 2163.
GEIGER (Paul), 994.
GEISSLER (Hermann), 5747.
GEISTLINGER (Michael), 4834.
GEITZ (Henry), 6101.
GELLER (Markham), 2167, 5955.
GELLMAN (Irwin F.), 8232.
GELLRICH (Jesse M.), 586.
GEMIE (Sharif), 6102.
GEMMILL (Elizabeth), 303.
GENESE (Cecil), 8233.
GENEST (François), 5860.
GENESTE (Nathalie), 7164.
GENET (Jean-Philippe), 3447.
GENG (Qingheng), 8857.
GENICOT (L.), 3766.
GENTILCORE (David), 6426.
GENTILE (Carlo), 8403.
GENTILE (Emilio), 783, 4610, 5021.
Gentile (Giovanni), 6343, 6360.
Gentili (Alberico), 7664.
GENTILI (B.), 2097.
GENY (Évelyne), 2192, 2834.
GEORGES (Giorgos), 8032.
GEORGES (Robert A.), 1013.
GEORGI (Dieter), 2989.
GEORGI (Frank), 7504.
GEORGIANNA (Linda), 4000.
GEORGIEV (Velichko), 8045.
Georgius, Sanctus, 3174.
GERAS (Norman), 6269.
GERBER (Michael Rudiger), 6174.
GERBI (Sandro), 4782.
GERCMAN (E. V.), 1976.
GERGELY (Jenő), 5557, 5748.
GERGEN (Thomas), 1727.
GERHAN (David R.), 7302.
GERHARD (H.), 225.

GERICS (József), 3360.
GERLACH (Stefan), 1700.
GERMAIN (Marie-Odile), 483.
GERMAIN (René), 3767, 4557.
GERMAN RODRIGUEZ MARTIN (Francisco), 2879.
GERNER (Kristian), 1096.
GERÖ (András), 5552.
GERO (Stephen), 3128.
GERRARD (B.), 7011.
GERSON (Gal), 6642.
Gervasius von Tilbury, 3488.
Gervinus (Georg Gottfried), 785.
GESCHIERE (Peter), 5916.
GEYER (Michael), 4611.
GHALIB (Jama Mohamed), 5394.
GHEBALI (Victor-Yves), 7668.
GHERARDI (Raffaella), 6043.
Gherardus de Venetis, 4150.
GHIßAUF (Johannes), 3305.
GHIGGIA (P. C.), 2046.
GHILARDUCCI (Giuseppe), 3189.
GHINATO (Aurelio), 3197.
GHISALBERTI (Carlo), 5022, 5029.
GHISELLI (Federica), 6960.
GIACOPINI (Vittorio), 6270.
GIAMMARCO RAZZANO (Maria Carla), 2365.
GIANNINI (P.), 2097.
Giannone (Pietro), 439, 6595.
GIARDINA (G.), 2737.
GIARDINA (Giancarlo), 2586.
GIARRIZZO (Giuseppe), 589, 741, 768, 807, 813, 819, 845, 891, 1457, 7389.
Gibbon (Edward), 786, 7680.
GIBBONS (Sarah L.), 6271.
GIBBONS (William Conrad), 8550.
GIBBS (David N.), 7865.
GIBBS (Janis M.), 1250.
GIBIANSKIJ (L. Ja.), 8772.
GIBSON (A. J. S.), 7088.
GIBSON (Craig A.), 4330.
GIBSON (M. T.), 4273.
GIERSIEPEN (Helga), 24.
Gierszewski (Stanisław), 787.
GIESS (Frederique), 6743.
GIEYSZTOR (Aleksander), 1117.
GIFFORD (Prosser), 3969.
GIGANTE (Marcello), 2791.
GILBERT (Martin), 8110.
Gilbert of Sempringham, 4440.
GILCHER-HOLTEY (Ingrid), 4879.
GILES (F. J.), 1865.
GILHAUS (Ulrike), 7165.
GILIBERTI (F.), 227.
GILL (Bates), 8858.
GILL (C.), 1977.
GILL (Margaret A. V.), 2013.
GILLESPIE (R.), 8551.
GILLINGHAM (John), 553.

GILMAN (Sander L.), 6427.
GILULA (Dwora), 2073.
GIMENO BLAY (Francisco M.), 16, 21, 67.
GIMENO MENENDEZ (Francisco), 341.
GIMPEL'SON (Efim G.), 5403.
GINDIKIN (S. G.), 6428.
GINDIN (L. A.), 1998.
GINIEWSKI (Paul), 8552.
GINNATTASIO (Pietro), 8553.
GINSBORG (Paul), 892, 5029.
GINTER (Donald E.), 4962.
GINZBURG (Andrea), 1268.
GINZBURG (Carlo), 893.
GIOACCHINO DA FIORE, 4278.
Giordano da Pisa, 5798.
GIORGI (Alessandro), 8111.
GIORGIERI (Mauro), 1858.
GIORGIO (Arcangela Gabriela), 484.
GIOSUÈ (Daniela), 3266.
Giotto, 6838, 6855.
GIOURAS (Thanasis), 7042.
GIOVAGNOLI (Agostino), 5669.
Giovanna I d'Angiò, regina di Napoli, 4426.
Giovanni Crisostomo, 3029.
Giovanni Damasceno, 3064.
Giovanni di Capestrano, 3623.
GIOVANNI DI GARLANDIA, 3903.
Giovanni di Pian del Carpine, 3305.
Giovanni l'Elemosiniere, 3268.
Giovio (Paolo), 788.
Giraldi (Guglielmo), 153.
Girart de Roussillon, 4094.
GIRAUD (Yves), 6008.
GIRAULT (René), 1389, 7709.
GIRIA (Engenii), 1600.
GIRJA (E. Ju.), 1604.
GISEL (Pierre), 1452, 6273.
GISLAIN (Jean-Jacques), 6009.
GITIN (Seymour), 1923.
GIUA (Maria), 590.
Giuda Iscariota, 4062.
GIUDICI (Rita), 7233.
Giulio Ilariano (Q.), 2789.
GIUNTINI (Andrea), 7155, 7188.
GJERDE (Jon), 7321.
GJONGECAJ (Shpresa), 2199.
GJÖSTEIN RESI (Heid), 1687.
Gladstone (William Ewart), 7867.
GLANTZ (Margo), 7390.
GLASER-SCHMIDT (Elisabeth), 1201.
GLATZ (Ferenc), 391, 1124, 7710.
GLAVE (Luis Miguel), 7391.
GLEASON (Abbot), 1199.
GLEASON (Maud W.), 2775.
GLEASON (Randall C.), 5861.
GLEDHILL (John), 5118.
GLEI (Reinhold), 3062.
GLEIJESES (Piero), 8554.

GLEJSER (Herbert), 1269.
GŁEMBICKA (Halina), 5245.
GLENCROSS (Michael J.), 591, 6643.
GLENISSON (Jean), X.
GLESSGEN (Martin-Dietrich), 4097.
GLETTLER (Monika), 7591.
GLICK (Thomas F.), 5439.
GLOSÍKOVÁ (Viera), 1335.
GLOVER (Audrey F.), 8555.
GŁÓWKA (Dariusz), 5749.
GLOY (Karen), 6217.
GNISCI (Armando), 6517.
GNOCCHI (Claudia), 3416.
GOBBI (Romolo), 8234.
GOBBI SICA (Grazia), 7315.
GÖBEL (Robert), 22.
Goblet d'Alviella (Eugène), 1454.
GOBLOT (Jean-Jacques), 4880.
GODART (Louis), 1999, 2007.
GODDARD (Hugh), 5917.
GODDE (Christoph), 6220.
Godel (Kurt), 6434.
GODINEAU (Dominique), 7592.
GODMAN (Peter), 6559.
GODOY (Cristina), 906.
GODRON (Anne), 8556.
GODWIN (John), 2541.
Goebbels (Joseph), 4770, 4778.
GOEBEL (Ted), 1605.
GOERTZ (Hans-Jürgen), 894.
Goethe (Johann Wolfgang), 6621, 6650, 6653, 6657, 6660, 6685, 6709, 6712.
GOETZ (Hans-Werner), 1692, 3631.
GOEZ (Elke), 3448.
GOFF (B.), 2282.
Gogol (Nikolaj Vasilevič), 5839.
GOGRAFE (Rudiger), 1901.
GOGUEY (Dominique), 2720.
GOICHOT (Emile), 762.
GOŁĄB-JANKOWSKA (Ewa), 384.
GOLDBERG (Eric J.), 3398.
GOLDBERG (Lee), 6920.
GOLDBERG (P. J. P.), 3258.
GOLDBERG (S.M.), 2776.
GOLDHILL (S.), 2200.
GOLDING (Brian), 4440.
GOLDMAN (Lawrence), 6103.
GOLDSCHMIDT-LEHMANN (Ruth P.), 5208.
GOLDSTEIN (Ann), 6744.
GOLDSTEIN (Ivo), 3361.
GOLDSTEIN (Thomas), 6429.
GOLDSWORTHY (David), 8557.
GOLDTHWAITE (Richard A.), 3210.
GOŁEMBIOWSKI (Maciej), 6132.
GOLINELLI (Paolo), 3769, 4465.
GOLLER (Peter), 6072.
GOLOB (N.), 117.
GOLOVINA (V. A.), 1775.
GOLSON (Jack), 1607.

Gombrowicz (Witold), 6055.
GOMES (Rita Costa), 5276.
GOMEZ VOZMEDIANO (Miguel Fernando), 3770.
GOMI (Fumihiko), 9022, 9026.
GONÇALVES (Eduardo Candido Cordeiro), 5277.
GONCHAROVA (Victoria), 4245.
GONG (Jianghong), 8914.
GONG (Liuzhu), 8859.
GONG (Yushu), 1866.
GONTHIER (N.), 4331.
GONZALES I JIMENEZ (Manuel), 3771.
GONZALEZ (Francisco J.), 6274.
GONZALEZ ARCE (José Damián), 3772.
GONZALEZ BALASCH (M. T.), 3216.
GONZÁLEZ CASASNOVAS (Ignacio), 1066.
GONZÁLEZ ECHEGARAY (J.), 1902.
GONZALEZ PONCE (F.J.), 2557.
GONZÁLEZ-CASANOVAS (Roberto J.), 553.
GONZENBACH (Victorine von), 2880.
GOOD (Colin H.), 6644.
GOOD (Irene), 1662.
GOODALL (Francis), 7044.
GOODBY (James E.), 8558, 8559.
GOODICH (M.), 3971.
GOODICH (Michael E.), 3773.
GOODIN (Robert E.), 1189, 6275.
GOODMAN (Bryna), 8860.
GOODMAN (John), 6734.
GOODMAN (Jordan), 1329.
GOODMAN (Louis W.), 5582.
GOODNICK WESTENHOLZ (Joan), 1756.
GOOLD (G. P.), 2057.
GOPAL (Sarvepalli), 4980.
GÓRALSKI (Zbigniew), 5177.
GORBACHEV (Mikhail Sergeevič), 8560.
GORDESIANI (Rismag), 2810.
GORDON (R.), 2777.
GORDON (Robert P.), 1937.
GORE (Terry L.), 3774.
GORI PASTA (Orsola), 3495.
GÖRICH (Knut), 3449.
GORMAN (Vanessa B.), 2074.
GÖRNER (Karen), 1270.
GÓRSKI (Grzegorz), 8235.
GORSKIJ (Anton A.), 3496.
GORTER-VAN ROYEN (Laetitia V. G.), 5145.
GOSCHA (Christopher E.), 5616.
GOSDEN (Chris), 1638.
GOSEWINKEL (Dieter), 4612.
GOTO-SHIBATA (Harumi), 8112.
GOTTLOB (Michael), 592.
GOTTSMANN (Andreas), 7563.

Gottwald (Klement), 5475.
GOTTWALDT (Alfred), 7166.
GÖTZELT (Thomas), 1663.
GOU (L. DE), 5143.
GOUDA (Frances), 7803.
GOULEMOT (Jean), 844.
GOUMA-PETERSON (Th.), 3129.
GOURDIN (Pierre), 4558.
GOUREVITCH (Peter), 8561, 8776.
GOURVISH (T. R.), 7044.
GOUTTEBROZE (J. G.), 3450.
GOUTTMAN (Alain), 8033.
GOW (Andrew Colin), 3521.
GOWERS (Emily), 2628.
GOWLAND (D. A.), 8562.
GOYARD-FABRE (Simone), 7666.
GÖYÜNÇ (Nejat), 1015.
GOZZI (Gustavo), 6043.
GRAB (Alexander), 7991.
GRABNER (Elfriede), 5796.
Graboïs (Aryeth), 3971.
GRABOWSKI (Janusz), 56.
GRABOWSKI (Waldemar), 8236.
GRABOWSKY (V.), 5469.
GRACIOTTI (Sante), 4128, 4466.
GRAF (Christoph), 434.
GRAF (Johannes), 6645.
GRAFTON (Anthony), 813.
GRAFTON (Bo), 7827.
GRAHAM (Gael), 6104.
GRAHAM-CAMPBELL (James), 3581.
GRAIN-AYMERICH (Jean), 2498.
GRAINGER (John D.), 2128.
GRANDAZZI (A.), 531.
GRANGE (D.), 7712.
GRANT (Alexander), 717.
GRANT (Alfred), 6176.
GRANT (George Parkin), 261.
GRANT (Jacquelyn), 5648.
GRANT (Michael), 593, 2881.
GRANUCCI (Fiorenza), 356.
GRAPPE (Christian), 2990.
GRAS (Michel), 2461.
GRASSBY (Richard), 7392.
GRASSELLI (Gabriella), 4668.
GRASSI (Fabio), 7713.
GRATIEN (Brigitte), 1776.
GRAUPE (Heinz Mosche), 6276.
GRAY (John), 6277.
GRAY (Peter), 7241.
GRAY (Vivienne), 2272.
GRAYSON (C.), 3910.
GRAZIOSI (Andrea), 7067.
GREŚ (Bolesław), 8237.
GREAL (Jacqueline), 4477.
GREBEL'SKIJ (P. Kh.), 5316.
GRECO (Franco Carmelo), 6921.
GREEN (Anthony), 1763.
GREEN (Christopher), 6822.
GREEN (Louis), 3497.
GREEN (Michael J.), 8563.

GREEN (Miranda J.), 1701.
GREEN (S. J. D.), 895.
GREEN (William), 896.
GREENBERG (Moshe), 5918.
Greenblatt (Stephen), 789.
GREENE (Ellen), 2558, 2778.
GREENFIELD (Jonas C.), 5955.
GREENFIELD (Richard P.H.), 3130.
GREENHOUS (Brereton), 5074.
GREENHUT (Zvi), 1903.
GRÉGOIRE (Réginald), 4332.
GREGOR (Richard), 8205.
Gregorius (Vescovo di Agrigento), Sanctus, 3052.
GREGORIUS ACINDYNUS, 3063.
GREGORIUS CORINTHIUS, 3064.
Gregorius I Magnus, Papa, Sanctus, 2961.
Gregorius Nazianzenus, Sanctus, 2923, 2928.
Gregorius Palama, 3080.
Gregorius Turonensis, Sanctus, 790, 3931, 4362, 4518.
GREGORY (Andrew Pearce), 1947, 2518.
GREGORY (Justina), 2274.
GREGORY (Shaun), 8564.
GREGORY (T.), 4001.
GREILSAMMER (Myriam), 3299, 3775.
GRELL (Chantal), 594, 7960.
GRELTHAM (D. C.), 6206.
GRENDLER (P. F.), 229.
Grenier (Jean), 7621.
GRENIER (Jean-Yves), 529.
GRENVILLE (Anthony), 1526.
GRENZMANN (Ludger), 4187.
GRGIĆ (Silvo), 8404.
GRIBANOV (P. V.), 1016.
GRIBBIN (Joseph A.), 4505.
Gribbon (Walter), 8073.
GRICOLI IOKOI (Zilda Marcia), 4728.
GRIECO (Joseph M.), 8565.
GRIEP (Wolfgang), 5622.
GRIFFIN (J.), 2079, 2779.
GRIFFITH (Jeremy), 108.
GRIFFITH (Paddy), 3582.
GRIFFITHS (A.), 2330.
GRIFFO (Maurizio), 4978.
GRIGG (John), 4979.
GRIMALT (Joan O.), 1613.
GRIMAUD (Nicole), 8566.
GRIMM (Dieter), 1240.
GRIMM (Gerald), 6105.
GRINDON (Lager), 6922.
GRINEV (A. V.), 1017.
GRIŠINA (R. P.), 4635.
GRISWARD (Joël H.), 1450.
Gritti (Ludovico), 7942.
GRJAZNEVIĆ (P. A.), 3557.
GRODDEK (Detlev), 1867.

GRODECKI (Roman), 3362.
GRODZISKI (Stanisław), 7539.
GROENVELD (S.), 5146.
GROETHUYSEN (Bernhard), 897.
GROMADZIŃSKA (Krystyna), 5227.
GROMYKO (M. M.), 1018.
GROSS (Jean-Pierre), 7506.
GROSS STEIN (Janice), 8615.
GROSSE (Christian), 5371.
GROSSEL (Marie-Geneviève), 3955.
GROSSETESTE (ROBERT), 4297.
GROSSI (Paolo), 3632.
GROSSMAN (Janet Burnett), 2401.
GROTEN (Manfred), 57.
GROTH (Andrzej), 787.
GROTH (Siegfried), 5137.
GROTIUS (Hugo), 5142.
GROTTANELLI (Cristiano), 1391.
GRUBER (Ladislav), 5508.
GRUCA (Anna), XVII.
GRUEL-APERT (Lise), 1019.
GRUGEL (Jean), 8567.
Grun (George), 7770.
GRÜNBART (Michael), 5178.
GRUNEWALD (Michel), 4661.
GRUŠKO (Elena A.), 1020.
GRUSS (Heribert), 5750.
GRÜTTNER (Michael), 6106.
GU (Weiqun), 8568.
GUALTIERI (Roberto), 8238.
GUARDINO (Peter), 5119.
GUARNEIRO (Antonio), 5919.
GUARNIERI (Carlo), 7637.
GUASCO (Maurilio), 5710.
GUASCONI (Maria Eleonora), 8569.
GUBOGLO (Mikhail N.), 1200, 5320.
GUDERZO (Massimiliano), 8337.
GUELTON (Frédéric), 8027.
GUERBER (E.), 2164.
GUERERE (A. Tabare), 5920.
GUERET-LAFERTE (Michèle), 4215.
GUERIN (M. Victoria), 4002.
GUERRA (M. F.), 2034.
GUERREAU (Alain), 3776.
GUERREAU-JALABERT (Anita), 4003.
GUERRERO (Javier), 574.
GUEST (G.), 81.
Guglielmo di Recuperanza, 3213.
Guillaume de Saint Thierry, 4372.
GUGUEV (V. K.), 1097.
GUHA (Sumit), 7638.
GUICHARD (Pierre), 3965.
GUIDOT (B.), 3915.
GUILBERT (Sylvette), 3777.
GUILHAUMOU (Jacques), 4881.
GUILLAUME (Anne-Marie), 6278.
Guillaume d'Orange Nassau, 7935.
Guillaume de Breuil, 11.
GUILLAUME-COIRIER (Germaine), 2882.
GUILLAUMIN (Jean-Yves), 2535.

GUILLELMUS DE LA MARE, 4279.
GUILLELMUS DE MOERBEKE, 4267, 4280.
GUILLELMUS DURANTUS, 3904.
GUILLEMINOT (Geneviève), 195.
GUILLEN (Michael), 6430.
GUILLEN (P.), 7715.
GUILLON (Jean-Marie), 654.
GUILLOT (Ivan), 3698.
GUILLOT (Olivier), 3633.
GUILLOU (André), 3065.
GUIMIER-SORBETS (Anne-Marie), 2402.
GUINOT (Jean-Noë), 2991.
GUINOT RODRÍGUEZ (Enric), 3634, 4559.
GUIOMAR (Jean-Yves), 4613.
GUITTON (Edouard), 6523.
GULDON (Zanon), 7215.
GULJAEV (V. I.), 2000.
GULLICK (M.), 23.
GUMINSKI (Christina), 6879.
GÜNAY (Selçuk), 1021.
GÜNERGUN (Feza), 1352.
GÜNERGUN (Feza), 6438.
GUNNARSSON (Lars), 5360.
GUNNELL (Terry), 4004.
GUNST (Péter), 596, 7242.
GÜNTHER (H.-C.), 2070.
GÜNTHER (J.), 120.
GÜNTHER (Matthias), 2948.
GÜNZEL (B.), 77.
Guo (Fengqi), 8846.
GURJANOW (Aleksander), 8224.
GURNEY (O.R.), 1868.
GURR (Andrew), 6560.
GURŠTEJN (A. A.), 1337.
GURVAL (Robert Alan), 2629.
GUST (Wolfgang), 1098.
GUSTAFSON (Robert K.), 6431.
GUSTAFSSON (Harald), 5159.
Gustav III, re di Svezia, 7767.
GUTAS (Dimitri), 3552.
GUTIERREZ (Leandro H.), 4685.
GUTIERREZ (Ramon), 389.
GUTJAHR (Lothar), 7716.
GUY (Alain), 1517.
GUYADER (Josseline), 3635.
GUYAUX (Andre), 1537.
GUYER (Jane I.), 9095.
GUYOTJEANNIN (Olivier), 3778.
GYANI (Gabor), 7393.
GYARMATI (György), 5553.
GYARMATI (György), 8618.
GYEMANT (Ladislau), 5300.

H

HAAC' (A.), 811.
HAACKER (Klaus), 2992.

HAAPARANTA (Pertti), 8438.
HAASE (Richard), 1869.
HAASE (Wolfgang), 2826.
HABASH (Martha), 2276.
HABEKOST (Engelbert), 1551.
HABERMAS (Jürgen), 6010.
Habermayer (Christoph von), 5876.
HABERSTUMPF (Walter), 3451.
HABICHT (Christian), 2129.
HACKING (Ian), 898.
HACO (M.), 121.
HADDAD (Wadi' Zaydan), 5921.
HADDAD (Yvonne Yazbeck), 5921.
HADENIUS (Sven), 5361.
HADGRAFT (Nicholas), 167.
HADIDI (A.), 1904.
Hadrianus (Publius Aelius), imperatore romano, 1740.
Hadrianus IV, Papa, 58.
HADROVICS (László), 342.
HAFFNER (Alfred), 1702.
HAFID-MARTIN (Nicole), 5627.
HAFNER (Ralph), 899.
HAGA (Norihiko), 9030.
HAGEMANN (Albrecht), 8570.
HAGEMANN (Harald), 7042.
HAGENEDER (Othmar), 3239.
HAGENLOCH (Thorsten), 7012.
HÄGG (T.), 1772.
HAGGARD (Stephan), 7828.
HAGGH (Barbara), 4246, 4264.
HAGSPIEL (Hermann), 5179.
HAHM (D. E.), 2277.
HAHN (István), 1099.
HAHN (Robert A.), 6432.
HAIDACHER (Christoph), 52.
HAIG GAISSER (Julia), 2560.
HAIR (P.E. H.), 9096.
HAJNAL (Ivo), 2001.
HÄKKINEN (Antti), 7394.
HALE (Charles A.), 5120.
HALKIN (Ariela), 6177.
HALL (John Barrie), 2806.
HALL (Jonathan M.), 2201, 2403.
HALL (Lesley A.), 6433.
HALL (Linda B.), 8113.
HALLBERG (Göran), 3391.
HALLBERG (H.), 159.
HALLIDAY (Fred), 8571.
HALLIER (Gilbert), 9097.
HALLIER (Hans-Joachim), 8572.
HALLIWELL (S.), 2051.
HALLOF (Klaus), 2035.
HALLON (Ľudovít), 5387.
HALLS (W. D.), 4882.
HALSALL (Guy), 3780.
HALTTUNEN (Karen), 6011.
HAŁUBA (Stanisław), 1534.
HALVERSON (James), 4333.
HALVERSON (Thomas E.), 8573.
HALVORSEN (Terje), 8239.

HAMACHE (M.), 6923.
HAMAD (Bushra), 5464.
HAMARD (B.), 8114.
HAMEL (Debra), 2130.
HAMESSE (Jacqueline), 3348, 4006, 4334.
HAMILTON (Gillian), 7507.
HAMILTON (K. A.), 8421.
HAMLIN (William M.), 1022.
HAMMACHE (Khalifa), 7167.
HAMMAN (Adalbert G.), 2993.
HAMMAN (Adalbert-Gautier), 2937.
HAMMER (C. I.), 3781.
HAMMERSTEIN (Notker), 6107.
HAMON-JUGNET (Marie), 6788.
HAMPE (Karl-Alexander), 8034.
HAMPTON (Henry), 5595.
HAN (Daocheng), 8863.
HANABUSA (Masamichi), 8574.
HANCOCK (David), 7216.
Händel (Georg Friedrich), 6910.
HANDERSON (Errol Anthony), 8575.
Handley (E. W.), 2330.
HÄNDL-SAGAWE (Ursula), 2559.
HANDY (Lowell K.), 1920.
HANEGRAAFF (Wouter J.), 1387, 5649.
HANGARTNER (B.), 124.
HANHIMÄKI (Jussi), 8576.
HANKINSON (R. J.), 2278.
HANNA (N.), 4672.
HANNANT (Larry), 5075.
HANNEMANN (Beate), 6599.
HÄNNESTRAND (Bo), 7395.
Hannibal de Capoue, Archevêque, 7947.
HANSEN (G.C.), 2929.
HANSEN (Mogens Herman), 1986, 1988, 2279.
HANSEN (Thomas S.), 6646.
HANSSEN (Jens-Peter), 8035.
HANSSON (Pär), 1139.
HAQUIN (A.), 1377.
HARA (Akira), 7028.
HARA (Teruyuki), 1113.
HARASIMOWICZ (Jan), 5797.
HARASZTI (Éva), 7717.
HARBINSON (Craig), 6745.
HARBULOT (Jean-Pierre), 4859.
HARÐARSON (Gunnar), 4008.
HARDEN (David J.), 4614.
HARDIE (Melissa), 6823.
HARDING (Phillip), 2131.
HARDMAN (John), 4883.
Hardouin (Jean.), 791.
HARDT (Hanno), 6178.
HARE (William), 8577.
HAR-EL (Shai), 7929.
HARF (L.), 4216.
HARLANDER (Tilman), 6789.
HARMAN (P. M.), 6457.

HARMEL (Pierre).
HAROCHE-BOUZINAC (Geneviève), 6012.
Harpalos, 2115.
HARPER (John), 8240.
HARPER-BILL (Christopher), 4410, 4506.
HARRAK (Amir), 1905.
HARRILL (James Albert), 2994.
HARRINGTON (Joel), 4783.
HARRIS (Bob), 6179.
HARRIS (D.), 2202.
HARRIS (David), 1639.
HARRIS (H. S.), 6279.
HARRIS (J. William), 5596.
HARRIS (J.), 3131.
HARRIS (J.), 4217.
HARRIS (Olivia), 7380.
HARRIS (Robert L. jr.), 7866.
HARRIS (Sir Arthur), 8367.
HARRIS (W.V.), 2519.
HARRISON (D. M.), 8579.
HARRISON (E. D. R.), 8241.
HARRISON (Nicholas), 1542.
HARRISON (Robert T.), 7867.
HARRISON (S. J.).
HARRISON (Selig S.), 8492, 8580.
Harrod (sir Roy Forbes), 6987.
HARSÁNYI (Iván), 5539.
HART (Peter), 8179.
HÄRTEL (Helmar), 125.
HARTING-CORRÊA (A.), 4299.
HARTKAMP (A. S.), 2680.
HARTLEY (J. M.), 7992.
HARTMANN (Wilfried), 3636.
HARTMUT (Rüdiger Peter), 4789.
HARTOG (François), 900.
HARTWELL (Ronald Max), 6062.
HARVEY (D.), 2195.
HARVEY (Paul Dean Adshead), 282.
HARVEY (Robert), 8581.
HASHIMOTO (Yoshinori), 9031.
HASKELL (Francis), 6013.
HASLAM (M. H.), 2093.
HASSE (Klaus-Peter), 3637.
HASSELL (Geoff), 6871.
HASSIG (Debra), 4009.
HASSNER (Pierre), 8582.
HASTINGS (Adrian), 7868.
HATCHER (John), 3814.
HATTORI (Hideo), 9032.
HATTORI (Yoshihisa), 3388.
HATZIVASSILIOU (Evanthis), 8583.
HAUCAP-NAß (Anette), 126.
HAUG (Eldbjørg), 5160.
HAUG (Karl Erik), 8115.
HAUG (Walter), 4010.
HAUGE (Jens Christian), 8242.
HAUGERUD (Angelique), 5083.
HAUGHT (John F.), 5650.
Haupt (Georges), 792.

HAUPT (Herbert), 485.
HAUPTMAN (Laurence M.), 9112.
HAUPTNER (Rudolf), 5180.
HAUSBERGER (Bernd), 5786.
HAUSCHILD (Wolf-Dieter), 1392.
Hausenstein (Wilhelm), 8632.
HÄUSLER (René), 7593.
Haussmann (Georges Eugène), 7326.
HAUSTEIN (Jens), 4011.
HAVAS (Katalin G.), 6280.
HAVAS (Ladislaus), 2619.
HAVELKA (Miloš), 5502.
HAVELOCK (Christine Mitchell), 2404.
HAVERALS (M.), 1378.
HAVINDEN (Michael), 7804.
HAVRÁNEK (Jan), 5476.
HAWKINS (John David), 1739, 1870.
HAWLEY (Richard), 2748.
Haydn (Franz Joseph), 6924.
HAYE (Thomas), 4022.
HAYEK (Friedrich August von), 7008, 7013.
HAYNES (Deborah J.), 746.
HAYNES (G.), 1576.
HAYNES (John Earl), 5601.
HAYRAPETEAN (Srbuhi Poghosi), 1543.
HAYTHORNTHWAITE (Philip John), 7805.
HAYWARD (C. T. R.), 4298.
HAYWOOD (John), 3583.
HEAD (Randolph C.), 5372.
HEAD (Thomas), 4415.
HEAD-KÖNIG (Anne-Lise), 7396.
HEADLEY (John M.), 7829.
HEARTZ (Daniel), 6924.
HEATH (M.), 2076.
HEATHER (Peter), 2630.
Heckmann (Otto), 4784.
HEDBERG (Lennart), 7089.
HEDLUND (M.), 159.
HEDLUND (Stefan), 1096.
HEFEKER (C.), 7090.
HEFTNER (Herbert), 2132.
Hegel (Georg Wilhelm Friedrich), 793, 982, 6223, 6249, 6255, 6267, 6279, 6287, 6291, 6293, 6301, 6321, 6325, 6334, 6338, 6355, 6363, 6366, 6367, 6369, 6371.
HEGYI (Klára), 5554.
Heidegger (Martin), 6226, 6300, 6343, 6364, 6368.
HEIDEKING (Jürgen), 5587.
HEIKAL (Mohamed), 8584.
HEIKKONEN (Esko), 7168.
HEIL (Matthäus), 2631.
HEINAMAN (R.), 2236.
HEINIÖ (Mikko), 6976.
HEINRICH (Clark), 5651.

HEINRICHS (W. P.), 1451.
Heinrich IV, röm.-deutscher Kaiser, 57.
Heinrich VI, röm.-deutscher Kaiser, 3595.
HEINZER (Felix), 127.
HEINZL (Brigitte), 486.
HEISS (Mary Ann), 8692.
HEISZLER (Vilmos), 5181.
HEIT (Alfred), 293.
HEITHAUS (Victoria), 8585.
HELAS (Jean-Claude), 3782.
Helbig (Wolfgang), 794.
HELD (G. F.), 2280.
HELD (Winfried), 1746.
HELG (Aline), 5095.
HELLE (Egil), 5161.
HELLE (Knut), 3399, 3452, 3584, 5167.
HELLEMA (Duco), 5147.
HELLER (Leonid), 1202.
HELLINGA (L.), 235.
HELM (Gerd), 6484.
HELTZER (Michael), 1948.
Hemina (Lucius Cassius), 2592.
HEMMING (John), 9113.
HEN (Y.), 790.
HEN (Yitzhak), 4012.
HENDLEY (Matthew), 4946.
HENDRICKX (J.-P.), 1376.
HENDRICKX (Stan), 1777.
HENDRIX (G.), 597.
HENGEVELD (R.), 8586.
HENGSTL (Joachim), 1781.
HENKE (Klaus-Dietman), 4774.
HENKEL (Annegret), 5862.
HENNEN INSA (Christiane), 6824.
HENNESSY (Peter), 4615.
HENNING (Eckart), 274.
HENNINGHAM (Stephen), 8587.
HENRICHS (Laurent), 304.
HENRIOT (Christian), 7331.
HENRY (Madeleine Mary), 2133.
Henry II, king of England, 3484.
Henri II, roi de France, 6589, 7925.
Henri III, roi de France, 4903.
Henri IV, roi de France, 4919.
Henry of Huntingdon, 553.
Henry the Navigator, 7774.
HENSHALL (Philip), 8243.
HENTILÄ (Seppo), 4841.
HENTSCHEL (Klaus), 4784.
Hēracleitos, 2259.
HERBERT (Ulrich), 4884.
Herder (Johann Gottfried), 899, 6316.
HERLIHY (Kevin), 4995.
HERMAN (Arthur L. Jr.), 4885.
HERMAN (Jan), 6631.
HERMANN (Armin), 7162.
HERMANN (John P.), 4013.

Hermlin (Stephan), 6705.
Hermogenēs, 2076.
HERMON (Elly), 8588.
HERNÁNDEZ (Mauro), 7397.
HERNÁNDEZ GONZÁLES (Pablo J.), 5096.
HERNANDO (Joseph), 128.
HERNANDO GONZALO (Almudena), 1578.
Hērodotos, 2145, 2151, 2258, 2272.
HERR (Elizabeth), 7398.
HERRERA (Lorenzo), 4441.
HERRMANN (Georgina), 1960.
HERSCHER (Ellen), 2405.
HERSH (Reuben), 6405.
HERSHKOWITZ (Debra), 2281, 2780.
HERTZKE (Allen D.), 5858.
HERVE (Jean Claude), 1293.
Herz (Marcus), 6256.
HERZOG (Tamar), 7639.
HERZOG (Ze'ev), 1910.
Hēsiodos, 2356.
HESNARD (A.), 2517, 2884.
HESPANHA (António Manuel), 5278.
HESSE (Carla), 462.
HESSE (Joachim Jens), 4616, 7557.
Hettners (Alfred), 399.
HEUCK ALLEN (Susan), 1747.
HEUCLIN (Jean), 3638.
HEUMAN (Ella), 3309.
HEURLIN (Bertel), 8589.
HEUSS (Alfred), 795.
HEUSS (Wolfgang), 7551.
HEY (Jeanne A. K.), 8590.
HEYDEMANN (Günther), 8036.
HEYDENREUTER (Reinhard), 4928.
HIBBS-LISSORGUES (Solange), 6180.
HICKEN (W. F.), 2098.
HICKS (Michael), 3783.
HIDALGO NUCHERA (Patricio), 5223.
HIDOUCI (Ghazi), 4677.
Hieronymus, Sanctus, 784, 2531, 2536, 2538, 2578, 2759, 4298.
HIERY (Hermann Joseph), 7910, 8116.
HIESTAND (Augustus Rudolf), 3263.
HIESTAND (Rudolf), 58, 1305.
HIETANIEMI (Tuija), 4840.
HIGBY (Gregory J.), 1322.
HIGGS (Edward), 7243.
HIJMANS (B.L. Jr.), 2532.
HIKITA (Yasuyuki), 8345.
HILDEBRAND (Klaus), 7718.
HILDEBRANDT (R.), 3253.
HILDEGARDIS BINGENSIS, Sancta, 4281.
HILEY (David), 3284, 4252.
HILFSTEIN (Erna), 6474.
HILL (Jeremy David), 1680, 1703.
HILL (John M.), 4014.
HILL (Michael), 5385.

HILL (Stephen), 1741, 1748.
HILLARD (Kent), 1827.
HILLER (István), 7930.
HILLERS (Delbert R.), 1917.
HILLGARTH (Jocelyn Nigel), 3522, 4335.
HILLGRUBER (Michael), 2366.
HILLIARD (Kevin), 6644.
HILTON (R. H.), 4560.
HILTON (Rodney H.), 3498.
HILTON (Sylvia L.), 1066.
Himmler (Heinrich), 8329.
HINARD (François), 2728.
HINDE (Robert A.), 7719.
HINDESS (B.), 1203.
HINE (H. M.), 2266.
HINE (Thomas), 6872.
HINOJOSA MONTALVO (José), 3523.
HINSON (E. Glenn), 4407.
HINTERHUBER (Hartmann), 5182.
HINTIKKA (Jaakko), 6409, 6434.
HINTJENS (Helen M.), 7806.
HIPPEL (Wolfgang von), 4617.
Hippokratēs, 133, 2077.
Hippolytus Romanus, Sanctus, 2967.
HIPPSLEY (Paul), 6878.
HIRASE (Takao), 8864.
HIRSCH (Jean-Pierre), 7322.
Hirschman (Albert O.), 1285, 7033.
HIRSTEIN (James S.), 837.
Hitchcock (Alfred), 6896.
HITCHNER (R.B.), 2895.
Hitler (Adolf), 6732, 7718, 8089, 8146, 8205, 8239, 8243, 8263, 8318, 8321, 8354, 8403, 8724.
HJERPPE (Riitta), 7063.
HJORTSHØJ O'ROURKE (Kevin), 6108, 7091.
HOĆEVAR (Rolf), 7564.
HOARY (Paul), 446.
Hobbes (Thomas), 1203, 1208, 1226, 1519, 6365.
HOBBS (D. R.), 1644.
HOBDAY (Michael), 8591.
HOBSBAWM (Eric J.), 604, 4618, 6282.
HOCHHOLZER (E.), 3217.
HOCKING (Brian), 7720.
HOCQUET (Jean-Claude), 305, 3784.
HODGES (Donald C.), 5121.
HÖDL (Günther), XVI.
HÖDL (Uta), XVI.
HOENEN (Maarten J. F. M.), 4015, 4301, 4363.
HOENSCH (Jörg), 3499.
HOESLER (Joachim), 605.
HOFFER (Stanley E.), 2078.
HOFFHEIMER (Michael H.), 6283.
HOFFMAN (John P.), 1401.
HOFFMAN (P.), 1713.
HOFFMAN (Philip T.), 7284.

HOFFMANN (Frank), 6880.
HOFFMANN (Hartmut), 129, 3453.
HOFFMANN (Joachim), 5404.
HOFLACK (Kris), 4717.
HÖFLINGER (Klaus), 59.
HOFMANN (H.), 2275.
HOFMEISTER (Wilhelm), 4745.
HOFTIJZER (P. G.), 238.
HOGDON (Pierre), 6925.
HOHENBERG (Paul M.) 1272.
Hohenheim (Theophrastus Bombastus von), 6510.
HOISINGTON (William A.), 7869.
HOLCOT (Robert), 4336.
Holcroft (Thomas), 6689.
HOLDAWAY (Simon), 1606.
HOLDSTOCK (Douglas), 8592.
HOLDXAY (Simon), 1570.
HÖLKESKAMP (K.-J.), 2692.
HOLL (Béla), 4016.
HOLL (Imre), 4218.
HOLLAND (Luke), 4829.
HOLLANDER (Samuel), 7016.
HOLLARD (Dominique), 2203.
HOLLEN LEES (Lynn), 1272.
HOLLI (Melvin G.), 5598.
HOLLOWAY (Steven W.), 1920.
HOLLYWOOD (Amy), 4337.
HOLM (Hans-Henrik), 8593.
HOLMBERG (Ingrid E.), 2283.
HOLMES (Brian), 6109.
HOLMES (Frederic L.), 6436.
HOLT (Peter Malcolm), 3553.
HOLT (Thomas C.), 606.
HOLTON PIERCE (R.), 1772.
HOLTSMARK (Sven G.), 7759.
HOLTUS (G.), 4056.
HOLZ (Eva), XXI.
HOLZBACHOVÁ (Ivana), 607.
HOLZER (Georg), 346.
Holzhausen (Rudolf), 8570.
HOLZNAGEL (Franz-Joseph), 4017.
HOLZNER (Johann), 851.
HOMANN (Arne), 905.
Homēros, 2024, 2079, 2080, 2083, 2189, 2291, 2312, 2314, 2326, 2347, 2356.
HONDERICH (Ted), 1520.
Honecker (Erich), 8770.
HONGO (Kazuto), 9033.
HONNEFELDER (Ludger), 4338.
HONNETH (Axel), 6284, 6374.
HONNINGDAL GRYTTEN (Ola), 7092.
HOOD (John Y. B.), 3524.
HOOLE (Charles R. A.), 5863.
Hoover (Herbert Clark), 8124.
HOPE (Geoff), 1607.
Hope (James), 4964.
HOPKIRK (Peter), 8117.
HOPPE (Jiří), 5491.
HOPWOOD (Keith), 1966.

Horatius Flaccus (Quintus), 2561, 2562, 2597, 2737, 2782, 2792, 2795, 3332.
HORGA (Ioan), 5751.
Horkheimer (Marx), 5981.
HORN (Martin), 8118.
HORNE (Peter), 1577.
HOROWITZ (Joel), 4686.
HORRELL (Sara), 7399.
HORSFALL (Nicholas), 1548, 2783.
HORSTMANSHOFF (H. F. J.), 2235, 2751.
HORWITZ (Henry), 435.
HOSE (M.), 2204.
HOSHINO (Hidetoshi), 3785.
HÖSLE (Vittorio), 4339.
HOSSEINI (Hamid), 3554.
HOU (Baozhong), 8865.
HOUBEN (Hubert), 4442.
HOURCADE (Eduardo), 609, 906.
Houwink (H. J.), 1879.
HOVORKA (Rostislav), 8594.
HOWARD-JOHNSTON (James D.), 3132.
HOWELL (David Luke), 7093.
HOWELL (Peter), 2574.
HOYOS (Manuel), 1608.
HØYRUP (Jens), 1828, 6437.
HRBEK (Jaroslav), 5477.
HRIBAR (Tine), 5391.
HRUXKA (Blahoslav), 1829.
HU (Cheng), 8866.
HU (Xiaolin), 8923.
HUALDE (Jose Ignacio), 367.
HUANG (Jing-Xing). 6285.
HUANG (Lingjun), 8836.
HUANG (Meilan), 8867.
HUANG (Qichen), 8868.
HUANG (Qiyi), 8869.
HUBBARD (R.L.N.B.), 1579.
HUBBARD (William H.), 643.
Huber (Alfons), 849.
HUBERMAN (Michael), 7371.
HUBERT (Etienne), 3786.
HÜBINGER (Gangolf), 610.
HÜBNER (Peter), 7508.
HÜBNER (Wolfgang), 2563.
HUBSCHER (Ronald), 4886.
HUCK (Paul), 7323.
HUCKER (Bernd Ulrich), 4018.
HUDEMANN (Rainer), 4606.
HUDSON (Michael), 7042.
HUDSON (Robert), 375.
HUETE CABALLO (Ana Isabel), 441.
HUFF (Dietrich), 1949.
HUFFER (Jurgen Benedikt), 6181.
HÜFNER (Klaus), 8595.
HUGGINS (Rita), 7807.
Hughes (David G.), 4244.
HUGHES (Michael), 8037.

AUTOREN- UND PERSONENREGISTER 391

Hughes (W. M.), 8074.
HUGLO (Michel), 4247.
Hugo (Victor), 504, 6682.
HUGON (Alain), 7931.
HUGUES DE BALMA, 4282.
HUHN (Irmgard), 956.
HUIZINGA (Johan), 796, 937.
HULDT (Bo), 8314.
Hull (Cordell), 8232.
Hulme (Hilda), 6555.
HULTS (David S.), 987.
HUMBERT (Michel), 3000.
Humboldt (Alexander von), 1219.
HUME (Robert D.), 6959.
Hume (David), 1521.
HUMFREY (Peter), 6825.
HUMPRIES (Jane), 7399.
HUNECKE (Volker), 7400.
HUNGER (Herbert), 131, 3066, 3067, 3078, 3133.
HUNT (Lynn), 611, 903.
HUNTER (Alan), 8828.
HUNTER (Janet), 7821.
HUNTER (Rosemary), 1247.
Huntington (Henry E.), 460.
HUNWICK (J. O.), 1540.
HUPCHICK (Dennis P.), 7721.
HUPPERT (George), 907.
HURCOMBE (Linda), 1580.
HURINUI JONES (Pei Te), 1041.
HURRELL (Andrew), 8597.
HURWIT (Jeffrey M.), 2406.
Hussain ibn Talal, king of Jordan, 8643.
Husserl (Edmund), 1512, 6350.
HUSZAR (Lajos), 306.
HUSZÁR (Tibor), 6064.
HUTCHINGS (Kimberly), 1204.
HUTCHINSON (Ann M.), 4019.
HUTTER (Irmgard), 3134.
HUTTNER (Markus), 6182.
HUTTON (Ronald), 5864.
HUTTUNEN (Mika), 612.
HUTTUNEN (Pertti), 8368.
Huygens (Christiaan), 6230.
HUYS (M.), 2285.
HUYSE (Luc), 4717.
HUYSSEN (Andreas), 6524.
HYE (Franz-Heinz), 283, 1309.
HYLAND (Drew A.), 6286.
HYNDRÁKOVÁ (Anna), 5483.
Hypatia of Alexandria, 2264.
HYSLOP (Jonathan), 5452.

I

IAKOVETS (Iurii Vladimirovich), 7017.
IANCU (Gheorghe), 8119.
Iancu de Hunedoara, 7928.

IANNACCONE (Lawrence R.), 1384.
IANNELLA (Cecilia), 5798.
Ibsen (Henrik), 6686, 6883.
IDEO (Rosella), 9069.
IECHIKA (Yoshiki), 9034.
IENAGA (Junji), 9035.
IGGERS (Georg G.), 908, 930.
IGLESIA FERREIRÓS (Aquilino), 49, 3620.
Ignatius de Loyola, Sanctus, 5777, 5862.
IGUAL (D.), 3787.
IHARA (Kesao), 9036.
İHSANOGLU (Ekmeleddin), 256, 6389, 6438.
IKÄHEIMO (J.), 2017.
IKEDA (Yukihiro), 7042.
ILJA (Voldemar), 5817.
İLTER (Erdal), 7722.
IMAŃSKA (Iwona), 7217.
IMBACH (Ruedi), 4302.
IMBRUGLIA (G.), 759.
IMSEN (Steinar), 5162, 5166.
INALCIK (Halil), 5517.
INAYATULLAH (Naeem), 7723.
INBAR (Efraim), 8598, 8599.
INCISA DI CAMERANA (Ludovico), 7724.
INDELLI (G.), 2096.
INGLEBERT (Hervé), 2634.
INGLEBY (Richard), 1247.
INGLIS (Eric), 130.
INGRAM (Edward), 7808, 7993.
INGROSSO (Lorella), 760.
INNES (D. C.), 2051, 2266.
Innocentius III, Papa, 3071, 3239, 4422, 4423.
INOGUCHI (Takashi), 8561, 8776.
INOUE (Nobutaka), 5922.
INSABATO (E.), 3714.
INSOLL (Timothy), 9098.
INTIERI (Maria), 2447.
INVERNIZZI (Antonio), 1830.
IÔANNIDÈS (Phôtios S.), 2995.
IOANNOU (Misael), 5821.
IOANNOU (Silouan), 5821.
IOFFE (Genrikh Z.), 5322.
IOGNA-PRAT (Dominique), 4561.
IORDAN (Constantin), 8338.
IOSIHIKO (Kurtsukake), 6517.
IOVINO (Maria Rosa), 1641.
İPEK (Nedim), 7402.
IRACE (Erminia), 3286, 7403.
IRADIEL (P.), 3787.
IRANTZU (Aitziber), 271.
IRBLICH (Eva), 476.
Ireneus Lionensis, Sanctus, 3008.
IRMSCHER (Johannes), 3097, 5923.
ISAAC (B.), 2693.
ISAACMAN (Allen), 7237.
ISAKSSON (Christer), 5362.

ISELLA (Dante), 6611.
ISHAGHPOUR (Youssef), 6926.
ISHEMO (Shubi Lugemalila), 5134.
ISHIDA (Takeshi), 8601.
ISHII (Osamu), 9037.
ISHII (Susumu), 9023, 9024.
Isidorus Pelusiota, Sanctus, 2980.
IŠIN (Vjačeslav V.), 5323.
ISLAMOV (Tofik M.), 614.
Isockatēs, 2300, 2336.
ISOLA (Gianni), 6927.
ISRAEL (Jonathan), 5148.
ISRAELYAN (Victory), 8602.
ISSAWI (Charles), 1274.
ISTOMINA (Énessa G.), 5324.
ITEANU (Andre), 9120.
ITENBERG (Boris S.), 6361.
ITIER (Cesar), 363.
IULIANO (Rolando), 7442.
Iulianus (Flavius Claudius), imperatore romano, 2655, 2663, 2671, 2762, 3011, 3040.
Iulius Severianus, 2564.
IURCHENKO (T. G.), 746.
IUSTINUS (IUNIANUS MARCUS), 2750.
IVANĆIK (A. I.), 2003.
IVANOV (Anatolij E.), 6110.
IVANOV (Vjaceslav V.), 329.
IVANOV (Vladimir I.), 8558.
IVEREIGH (Austen), 4687.
IVERSEN (Gunilla), 4248.
Ivus, Sanctus, 4469.
IWAŃCZAK (Wojciech), 3788.
IWAMI (Toru), 5054.
IYOB (Ruth), 7870.
IZMOZIK (V. S.), 5406.
IZSÁK (Lajos), 5555.

J

JACKMAN (Donald C.), 3639.
JACKSON (Alvin), 4997.
JACKSON (Howard M.), 1779.
JACKSON (Robert), 8369.
JACKSON (S.), 2090.
JACKSON (William Godfrey Fothergill), 8038.
JACOBELLI (Luciana), 2885.
JACOBI (Klaus), 4340.
JACOBS (Jane M.), 7807.
JACOBS (Nicolas), 3789.
JACOBSEN (Gurli), 2721.
JACOBSEN (Roy), 5163.
JACOBSEN BUCKLEY (Jorunn), 1395.
JACOMY (Bruno), 488.
JACQ-HERGOUALC'H (Michel), 7961.
JACQUART (Danielle), 4341.
JACQUART (Jean), 617.

JACQUEMIN (A.), 1985.
Jacques d'Armagnac, 88.
Jacquin (Nikolaus Joseph Freiherr von), 6468.
Jaeger (Lorenz), 5750.
JAEGER (Michael), 909.
JÄGER (Wolfgang), 772.
JAGSCHITZ (Gerhard), 7656.
JAGUARIBE (Helio), 8603.
JAHN (Hubertus F.), 5325.
JAIN (Rekha), 307.
JAJLENKO (V. P.), 2608.
JAKIĆ (Ivan), 1275.
JAKO (Mariann), 8604.
JAKOBS (Hermann), 284.
Jakobs (Hermann), 5715.
JAKOBSON (Roman), 329.
JAKUŠEVSKIJ (Anatolij S.), 4785.
JAL (Paul), 2568.
JAMES (George Alfred), 5752.
JAMES (Harold), 7282.
JAMES (Henry), 6562, 6711.
JAMES (Jamie), 6439.
JAMES (Sharon L.), 2784.
James (William), 5641.
JAMME (Christoph), 6287, 6369.
JAMPOL'SKIJ (V. P.), 5415.
JAMZADEH (Parivash), 1950.
JANÁČEK (František), 8405.
JANIN (Valentin L.), 3365, 4562.
JANIŠOVÁ (Milena), 5478.
JANKOWIAK (Stanisław), 8605.
JANKOWSKI (Edmund), 1563.
JANNOT (Jean-René), 2499.
JANNUZZI (Giovanni), 8606.
JANŠA-ZORN (Olga), XXI.
JANSEN (Christian), 4587.
JANSEN (Hans H.), 7714.
JANSEN (K. L.), 3790.
JANSEN-WINKELN (Karl von), 1780.
JANTZ (Martina), 2785.
JANTZEN (Grace M.), 3791.
JARA (Álvaro), 4619.
JARASS (Hans D.), 7540.
JARAUSCH (Konrad H.), 618.
JAREB (Jere), 5091.
JARRETT (Alfred Abosiah), 7871.
JARVA (E.), 2407.
JARVIS (Simon), 6563.
JASHEMSKI (Wilhelmina F.), 2886.
JASINK (Anna Margherita), 1871.
JAŚKIEWICZ (Leszek), 8039.
JASKUŁA (Roman), 6648.
JAUHIAINEN (Jussi), 7324.
Jaume II el Justo, rey de Aragón, 3198.
JAURANT (Danielle), 3288.
JAZ'KOVA (A. A.), 4588.
JDEY (Ahmed), 1025, 7218.
Jean de Léry, 6357.
JEANEAU (Édouard A.), 4285.

JEANMOUGIN (Christian), 1324.
JEANNESSON (Stanislas), 8121.
JEANNOTAT (Claire-Marie), 5453.
JEAUNEAU (Edouard), 4379.
JEDREJ (M. C.), 5924.
Jefferson (Thomas), 5609, 7959, 7996.
JEHANNO (C.), 9099.
JEHNE (Martin), 2685, 2694.
JEISMANN (Karl E.), 6111.
JELAVICH (Peter), 910.
Jelinek (Elfriede), 6634.
JENAL (Georg), 2950.
JENKINS (Ian), 2408.
JENKINS (Keith), 911.
JENKS (Stuart), 3454.
JENN (Jean-Marie), 6781.
JENSEN (Bernard Eric), 1104.
JENSEN (Jorgen Steen), 308.
JENSEN (Richard), 8607.
JENSEN (Tom B.), 8245.
JEQUIER (François), 7095.
JERCZYŃSKI (Andrzej), 7185.
JESI (Furio), 860, 6016.
JESSEN (Ralph), 4786.
JESSENNE (Jean-Pierre), 4888.
Jesus Christus, 93, 388, 2956, 2977, 2979, 5698, 5799, 5856.
JETSON (Tim), 1062.
JIAN (Chen), 8608.
JIANG (Boying), 8870.
JIANG (Luming), 8871.
JIANG (Min), 8872.
JIANG (Shoupeng), 8873.
JIMENEZ (Pedro Angeles), 1368.
JOACHIM (Hans-Eckart), 1704.
JOANNÈS (Francis), 1831.
Joaõ V, rey do Portugal, 6779.
JOBERT (Philippe), 7119.
JOCHENS (Jenny), 3792.
JOCHUMS (Gabriele), 274.
JOE (Hyeon-soo), 7018.
JOHANNES (G. J.), 6183.
Johannes Antiochenus, 2565.
Johannes Chortasmenos, 3067.
Johannes Chrysostomus, Sanctus, 3029.
Johannes Damaskenos, 3062.
JOHANNES DE GARLANDIA, 4022.
Johannes Duns Scotus, 4389.
Johannes XXIII, Papa, 5669, 8111.
Johannes, Evangelista, Sanctus, 3017, 3225.
Johannes (Giovanni di Gerusalemme), Sanctus, 3050.
Johannes Paulus II, Papa, 5713, 5718, 8652.
Johannes Philoponos, 2942.
Johannes Scotus Eriugena, 6246.
Johansen (Hans Christian), 7086.
JOHANSEN (J.), 113.

JOHANSSON (Alf W.), 5363.
John, king of England, 7587.
John of Gaunt, 3855, 7774.
John of Oxford, 4506.
JOHN OF WORCESTER, 3289.
JOHNS (Sheridan), 5454.
JOHNSON (C.), 4277.
JOHNSON (Christopher H.), 7171.
JOHNSON (Claudia), 6017.
JOHNSON (Eric A.), 7325.
JOHNSON (Lesley), 553.
Johnson (Lyndon B.), 8466, 8548.
JOHNSON (Mark F.), 4342.
JOHNSON (Maxwell E.), 5824.
JOHNSON (Nevil), 4616, 7557.
JOHNSON (Paul), 7404.
JOHNSON (Robert David), 7727.
JOHNSTON (Wendy), 5076.
JOHNSTONE (Richard), 1247.
JOKIPII (Mauno), 1024.
JOLIVET (Jean), 4343.
JOLLEY (Nicholas), 1513.
JONAS D'ORLEANS, 3290.
JONES (Adrian), 4620.
JONES (Barry), 8609.
JONES (Charles), 347.
JONES (David Wyn), 6929.
JONES (E. D.), 3793.
JONES (Frederic J.), 4023.
JONES (Geoffrey), 7219.
JONES (H. G.), 487.
JONES (John), 6564.
JONES (Matthew), 8246.
JONES (Michael Owen).
JONES (Nicholas), 2165.
JONES (Peter M.), 4889.
JONES (Serene), 5865.
JONES (Stephen), 6930.
JONES ROCCOS (Linda), 2409.
JONES-DAVIES (M.T.), 598.
JONQUET (Michel), 7994.
JONSSON (Einar Már), 4024.
JONSSON (Ulf), 619, 1276.
JONTER (Thomas), 8763.
JOOS (Jean-Ernest), 6288.
JORDAN (David Paul), 7326.
JORDAN (John O.), 241, 6728.
JORDAN (Stefan), 793.
JORDE (Tine Susanne), 7327.
JØRGENSEN (Torstein), 1390.
JORIS (André), 3759.
JOSEPH (Gilbert M.), 5122.
Joseph d'Arimathie, 3914.
JOTISCHKY (Andrew), 4443.
JOUAN (François), 2367.
JOUANNA (Jacques), 133, 2286.
JOUANNO (Corinne), 2368.
JOUANNY (Robert), 4925.
JOUBERT (Jean-Louis), 6525.
JOUFFROY (Hélène), 2605.
Jouffroy (Jean), 3937.

Joufroi de Poitiers, 3981.
JOUIN (Pierre), 6747.
JOUSSE (Thiérry), 6931.
JOUTARD (Philippe), 654.
JOVER MAESTRE (Francisco Javier), 1664.
JOYCE (M.), 8610.
JOYCE (Patrick), 912.
Joyce (James), 1530.
JU (Zhifen), 8874.
JUAN (Salvador), 6018.
Juan de la Cruz, 5777.
JUCKES (Tim J.), 5455.
JUDGE (Anne), 6649.
JUDINA (Ljudmila S.), 7509.
JUDITH (George), 4025.
JUDSON (Horace Freeland), 6440.
JULIA (Dominique), 940.
Julia Domna, 2646.
Julianus (Flavius Claudius), imperatore romano, v. Iulianus.
Jumg (Carl), 1481.
JUNĚCOVÁ (Jiřina), 7268.
JUNGINGER (Horst), 1460.
JURAGA (Dubravka), 746.
Josephus Flavius, 776.
JUSSEN (B.), 3417.
JUSSILA (Osmo), 4841.
JUSSILA (Päivi Hannele), 4344.
JUST (Vladimír), 6932.
Justinianus I, imperatore di Bisanzio, 2684.
JUTTE (Robert), 6441.
Juvenalis (Decimus Junius), 2811.

K

KA (Chih-ming), 7831.
KAARNINEN (Mervi), 7405.
KAARTVEDT (Alf), 7679, 7760.
KABAYAMA (Kōichi), 1095, 3366, 3389.
KACZYŃSKA (Elżbieta), 7640.
KACZYŃSKA (Maria), 5227.
KADEL (Andrew), 2922.
Kadłubek (Wincenty), 3316.
KADOWAKI (Teiji), 9049.
KADROW (Sławomir), 1665.
KAELBLE (Hartmut), 4606.
KAEMPF (Bernard), 5866.
KAFADAR (Cemal), 5518.
KAGAN (Richard L.), 4655, 7809.
KAHANE (Howard), 6289.
KAHIN (Brian), 6199.
KAHLER (Miles), 7728.
KAHN (Didier), 4026, 6716.
KAISER (Monika), 7510.
KAISER (R.), 4444.
KAISER (Wolfram), 8611.
KAJAVA (Mika), 2722.

KAKAR (M. Hasan), 4669.
KALAMAKIS (D.), 3068.
KALATZI (Maria), 134.
KALEMBKA (Sławomir), 6132, 8058.
KALICZ (Nándor), 4219.
KALIFA (Dominique), 7641.
KALININA (I. V.), 411.
KALIŃSKI (Janusz), 5246.
KALITA–SKWIRZYŃSKA (Kazimiera), 4436.
KALLAS (Mariusz), 5231.
KALLENDORF (Craig), 6565.
KALLFELZ (Wolfgang), 3555.
Kallimachos, 2062, 2249.
KALLINEN (Maija), 6067.
KALLIONIEMI (Kari), 6933.
KALMYKOV (Sergej V.), 7292.
KALPYRIS (Eugenios), 7668.
KALUZA (Zénon), 4345.
KAMENSKIJ (Aleksandr B.), 5326.
KAMIEŃSKI (Andrzej), 7962.
KAMIYAKA (Tsuneo), 7019.
KAMLER (Marcin), 7642.
KAMM (Antony), 1107.
KAMMINGA (Harmke), 6442.
KANAO (T.), 3640.
KANDUS (Nataša), XXI.
KANEKO (Shūichi), 8875.
KANSU (Aykut), 5519.
Kant (Immanuel), 1204, 6224, 6230, 6237, 6247, 6263, 6264, 6271, 6278, 6288, 6315, 6318, 6328, 6293, 6346, 6350, 6355, 6356, 6371, 6372.
KANTOROVIĆ (A. R.), 2004.
KANYAMACHUMBI (P.), 5289.
KAPAŁA (Zbigniew), 5251.
KAPER (Olaf E.), 1782.
KAPLAN (Benjamin J.), 5149.
KAPLAN (Karel), 5478, 5479.
KAPLAN (Wendy), 6748.
KAPP (Volker), 6019.
KAPPEL (Hans), 8122.
KAPTEIJNS (Lidwien), 5395.
KAPUR (H.), 8444.
KARAGEORGHIS (V.), 2410.
KARAGÖZ (Mehmet), 5520.
KARANOVICH (Milenko), 6112.
KARAOĞLU (Omer), 7172.
KARKOWSKI (Bogumił), 463.
Karl, hertig, 7089.
Karl I der Große, röm-deutscher Kaiser, König der Franken, 679, 3406, 4229.
KARLBOM (Rolf), 233.
KARLICKÝ (Vladimír), 8370.
KARLSJÖ (Bertil), 3391.
KARLSSON (Michael), 5364.
KÁRNÍK (Zdeněk), 5480.
KARNS (Margaret P.), 8668.
KARONEN (Petri), 7406.

KARP (Theodore), 4249.
KARPAĆEV (M. D.), 7432.
KARPIESIUK (Renata), 6132.
KARPIK (Lucien), 7595.
KARPOZILOS (Apostolos), 3135.
KARSAI (László), 8247.
KARSTEN (Rudolph), 4787.
KARTAL (Metin), 1617.
KARUNARATNA (Charles W.), 5927.
KARWALE (W.R.), 5652.
KARWIESE (Stefan), 2369.
KASCHUBA (Wolfgang), 1032, 4621.
KASOZI (Abdu Basajabaka Kawalya), 5535.
KASPER (W.), 1398.
KASPI (André), 7729, 8371.
KASSAM (Tazim R.), 5928.
KAŠUBA (Margarita S.), 4622.
KATER (Michael H.), 6934.
KATES (Gary), 7407.
KATIĆIĆ (Radoslav), 1981.
KATO (Akira), 8640.
KATŌ (Hiroshi), 8807.
KATSOURIS (A. G.), 2288.
KATSUMATA (Shizou), 9038.
KATSUYAMA (Seiji), 9039.
KATZ (Dina), 1832.
KATZ (Elaine N.), 7173.
KATZ (Nathan), 1462.
KATZOFF (R.), 2166.
KAUFMANN (D.), 621.
KAUFMANN (Walter), 6290.
Kautskij (Karl), 4793.
Kautz (Jacob), 5633.
KAVYRCHINE (M.), 263.
KAWAGOE (Osamu), 7408.
KAWAMURA (Yasushi), 8876.
KAWANO (Kenji), 4890.
KAWAWAKE (Keiko), 7409.
KAY (Christian), 4144.
KAY (Sarah), 4027.
KAYA (Durmu), 2036.
KAZAKOV (M. M.), 2838.
KAZBUNDA (Karel), 8123.
KAZGAN (Haydar), 7097.
KAZHDAN (Alexander), 3098, 3136.
KAZIN (Michael), 5599.
KAŹMIERCZYK (Adam), 5228.
KEANEY (John J.), 2081.
KEARNS (Judy), 5527.
KEATING (Michael), 8609.
KEATING (Peter), 6479.
KEATMAN (Martin), 6581.
KEAVENEY (Arthur), 2635.
KECHICHIAN (Joseph A.), 8612.
KECSKEMÉTI (J.), 3984.
KEDDIE (Nikki Ragozin), 8613.
KEDOURIE (Elie), 6291.
KEDOURIE (Helen), 6291.
KEDOURIE (Sylvia), 6291.
KEDWARD (H. R.), 637, 4908.

KEE (Howard C.), 2997.
KEEGAN (John), 8248.
KEEHN (Richard H.), 7297.
KEEL (Othmar), 6479.
KEEN (Antony G.), 2134.
KEEP (John), 5407.
KEES (Thomas), 3499.
KEESLING (Catherine Marie), 2411.
KEHOE (Dennis P.), 1783.
Kekkonen (Urho Kaleva), 8732.
KELLEHER (Catherine McArdle), 8614.
KELLER (H.), 3455.
KELLER (Hagen), 62.
KELLER (James), 6199.
KELLEY (Donald), 777.
KELLNER (Hans), 934.
KELLY (Christopher), 5929.
KELLY (Douglas), 4028.
KELLY (Louis G.), 4290.
KELLY (Robert L.), 3641.
KELLY (Thomas Forrest), 4250.
KELLY (W. A.), 226.
Kemal (Mustafa Atatürk), 5528.
KEMP (Brian), 4507.
KEMP (Goeffrey), 8615.
KENAAN-KEDAR (Nurith), 4220.
KENDE (Tamás), 4623.
Kenderova (S.), 95.
KENDRICK PRITCHETT (W.), 2289.
KENEN (Peter B.), 8616.
KENIG (Evelyne), 3530.
Kennan (George), 8222.
KENNEDY (Greg), 8124.
KENNEDY (Hugh), 3556.
Kennedy (John Fitzgerald), 8688.
KENNEDY (Kevin G.), 6650.
KENNEDY (Kieran A.), 7098.
KENNEDY (Michael J.), 8125.
KENNEDY (Thomas C.), 4029.
KENNEDY-PIPE (Caroline), 8617.
KENNEL (Gunter), 2998.
KENNEL (N. M.), 2205.
KENNETH (Maxwell), 5279.
KENNY (Michael), 1175.
KENT (Bonnie), 4030.
KENWORTHY (Eldon), 7730.
KENZ (David Et.), 7596.
KEOGH (Dermot), 7731.
KEPECS (József), 7316.
KEPPLINGER (Maria), 7644.
KEPSU (Saulo), 7328.
KERBRAT (Pierre), 3456.
KERĆMAR (Vili), 1463.
Kerenskij (Aleksandr Fëdorovič), 5322.
Kerényi (Károly), 1461.
KERESZTÉNY (Balázs), 1339.
KERIVEN (Brigitte), VI.
KERKKONEN (Martti), 436.
KERMODE (Anita), 1556.

KERMODE (Frank), 1556, 1558.
KERN (Manfred), 4031.
KERNEN (Alvin), 6936.
KERR (David), 6937.
KERR (Ian J.), 7832.
KERSHAW (A. Peter), 1609.
KERSHAW (Ian), 4788.
KERSKEN (Norbert), 622.
KERTÉSZ (István), 8618.
KERTZ (Walter), 6113.
KESKIN (Mustafa), 7732.
KESSLER (Christian), 7099.
KESSLER (Ralf), 4789.
KESSLER (Ulrike), 3457.
KETTENHOFEN (Erich), 1951, 2636.
KEUL (Michael), X.
KEYNER (Tom), 6020.
Keynes (John Maynard), 6987, 6988, 6991, 7001, 7004, 7006, 7007, 7011, 7013, 7748.
KEYNES (Simon), 3219, 3262, 3418.
KHAĆTURJAN (Valerija M.), 623.
KHALIDI (Ahmad S.), 8425.
KHALIKOV (N. A.), 7100.
KHALIL (Elias L.), 624.
KHAN (Ansar Hussain), 4980.
KHAN (Masood Ali), 6184.
KHAN (Zorina B.), 7645.
KHANNA (Jane), 8619.
KHAPAEVA (Dina), 1108.
KHARAKWAL (Jeewan), 1626.
KHATIBI (A.), 25.
KHAZANOV (Anatolii Mikhailovich), 5327.
KHOMIĆ (L. V.), 1027.
KHOURY (Adel Theodor), 3062.
Khruschov (Nikita Sergeevitch), 5429.
KHRUSTALEV (Vladimir), 5351.
KIANDER (Jaako), 8438.
KICELUK (Stephanie A.), 6477.
Kidd (I. G.), 2313.
KIDD (Stephen W.), 5215.
KIDO (T.), 3367.
KIEFER (Thomas), 5694.
KIELMANSEGG (Peter Graf), 1201.
KIENAST (Hermann J.), 2386.
KIENIEWICZ (Jan), 8040.
KIENING (Christian), 4032.
KIERNAN (Victor Gordon), 7733.
KIESEWETTER (Hubert), 913.
KIKKAWA (Takeo), 1137.
KIKKERT (J. G), 4718.
KIKUCHI (Hideaki), 8877.
KILANI (Mondher), 5653.
KILCULLEN (J.), 4293.
KIM (K.), 3458.
KIM (Song Whan), 9070.
KIM (Taeho), 8858.
KIMURA (Mitsuhiko), 7734.
KIND (H.), 236, 237.

KINDER (A. Gordon), 5867.
KINDLEBERGER (Charles P.), 1277.
KING (Desmond S.), 5600.
King (Martin Luther), 5975.
KINGDON (Robert McCune), 5374.
KINGSEED (Cole Christian), 8620.
KINGSLEY (P.), 2290.
KINTZINGER (Marion), 625.
KINTZINGER (Martin), 4033.
KINZL (Konrad H.), 1973.
KIPPENBERG (Hans G.), 1464, 5670.
KIPPENBERG (Hans), 1465.
KIR'JANOV (Ju. I.), 7523.
KIRALY (Bela K.), 8187.
KIRBY (M. W.), 4945.
KIRCHHOFF (Hans), 4752.
KIRCHSCHLÄGER (Walter), 2951.
KIRIAKOPOULOS (G. C.), 4929.
KIRK (James), 7244.
KIRK (John M.), 8723.
KIRK (Robin), 5219.
KIRK (Tim), 1109.
Kirkby (John), 3240.
Kierkegaard (Söreen), 758.
Kirov (Sergej Mironovich), 797.
KIRPIĆNIKOVA (A. N.), 5329.
KIRSHNER (Julius), 3599.
KIS (Péter), 3459.
KISLINGER (Ewald), 3066, 3137.
KISLYJ (A. E.), 914.
KISS (Gábor), 4251.
KISS (Lajos), 348.
KISSANE (N.), 185.
Kissinger (Henry), 7718.
KISTANOV (Valerij O.), 7735.
KITAHARA (Itoko), 9043.
KITAMURA (Masaki), 9044.
KITCHEN (Martin), 8249.
KITCHER (Philip), 6443.
KIVIKÄS (Pekka), 1372.
KIWERSKA (Jadwiga), 8621.
KIYOKAWA (Yukihiko), 7174.
KIZWALTER (Tomasz), 1145.
KLANICZAY (Gábor), 4467.
KLANICZAY (Tibor), 4468.
KLARE (Michael), 8622.
KLASSEN (Thomas), 4034.
KLAUCK (Hans-Josef), 2952, 5755.
KLEHR (Harvey), 5601.
KLEIN (Emilio), 4749.
KLEIN (Erich), 5192.
KLEIN (Francesca), 3201.
KLEIN (S. R. E.), 5150.
KLEIN (T. A.-P.), 4035.
KLEINE-AHLBRANDT (William Laird), 8126.
KLEINERT (Claudia), 626.
KLEINPENNING (J. M. G.), 385.
KLEINSCHMIDT (H.), 3794.
KLEINSCHMIDT (Harald), 7736.
KLEMM (David), 6826.

KLENGEL (H.), 1724.
KLENKE (D.), 4790.
Kleopatra, 2297.
KLER (W.), 6307.
KLEVNJUK (O. V.), 5421.
KLIER (John Doyle), 5328.
KLIMEK (Antonín), 7737.
Kliment (Josef), 5489.
KLINGE (Matti), 1110.
KLINGER (J.), 1872.
KLINGHAMMER (István), 1340.
KLINKHAMMER (Lutz), 8250.
KLÍPA (Bohumír), 5481.
KLIPPEL (Diethelm), 1211.
Kliuchevskii (V. O.), 798.
KLÖCKENER (M.), 97.
KLOCZOWSKI (Jerzy), 627.
KLOFAT (Rainer), 6148.
KLOPPENBORG (Ria), 1387, 5649.
KLOS-BUZEK (Friederike), 4446.
KLOTZ (Audie), 7738.
KLUPPELHOLZ (Heinz), 6651.
KLUWE (E.), 2887.
KNAFLA (Louis A.), 1239.
KNAPP (Éva), 7410.
KNAPP (John Merrill), 6910.
KNEEPKENS (Corneille), 4346.
KNEIP (Heinz), 6652.
KNELL (Heiner), 2412.
KNEPLER (Georg), 6938.
KNIF (Henrik), 4947.
KNIGHT (V.), 2291.
KNIGHTINGALE (Pamela), 3795.
KNIGHTON (Henry), 3293.
KNIPPING (Franz), 8623.
KNOCK (Thomas J.), 8127.
KNOEPFLER (Denis), 2135.
KNORR (Ortwin), 2786.
KNOX (Peter E.), 2583.
KNÜTEL (Rolf), 3055.
KOĆETKOVA (Tat'jana Ju.), 7739.
KOCH (Guntram), 2859.
KOCH (Johannes), 1833.
KOCH (Petra), 136.
KOCH (Walter), 60.
KOCHANOWSKI (Jerzy), 5230.
KOCHAVI (Arieh J.), 8339.
KOCIAN (Jiří), 5470, 5482, 7565.
KOCKA (Jürgen), 772, 7411.
KOCSIS (Károly), 5388.
KOCZOROWSKI (Ryszard), 8200.
KOENEN (Andreas), 7541.
KOENKER (Diane P.), 7412.
KOEPF (Thomas), 7606.
KOERNER (E. F. K.), 1080.
KÖFLER (Werner), 52.
Kohl (Helmut), 4825.
KOHL (Philip L.), 1610.
KOHLI (Narendra), 5930.
KOHNEN (Richard), 6185.
KOIVISTO (Hanne), 1133.

KOKAZE (Hidemasa), 7175.
KOKO (Eugeniusz), 7511.
KOKOLAKIS (Minos), 2370.
KOLANOVIĆ (Josip), 3368.
KOLB (Eberhard), 8061.
KOLB (Frank), 1982.
KOLBABA (Tia M.), 3069.
KOLLANDER (Patricia A.), 8041.
KOLLER (Alexander), 7914.
KOLLER (Heinrich), 4036.
KOLLER (Manfred), 4221.
KOLLMANN (Wolgang), 4792.
KOLLROS (Ernst), 7646.
KOLNAI (Aurel), 6292.
KOLOBOV (Oleg. A.), 8625.
KOLONTAEV (A. P.), 7096.
KOLOVOU (Foteini), 3070.
KOLPAKOV (E. M.), 1028.
KÖLZER (Theo), 61.
KÖLZER (T.), 171.
KOMAKI (Shōhei), 8810.
KOMARIK (Dénes), 6790.
KOMLOSY (Andrea), 7169.
KOMMISRUD (Arne), 1111.
KOMONCHAK (J. A.), 1466.
KOMORÓCZY (Géza), 4598, 7488.
Kondrat'ev (N. D.), 7017.
KONEV (Aleksej Ju.), 5330.
Kong (Xiangxi), 8973.
KONIARIS (G. L.), 2085.
KONIAS (Andrzej), 386.
König (HILDEGARD), 2955.
KONIG (Peter), 6293.
KÖNIG (Roderich), 2588.
Konopka (Stanisław), 799.
KONRAD (B.), 97.
KONRAD (Susanne), 6653.
KONSTANT (D.), 2206.
Konstantinos Porfirogenitos, 3054.
KONTLER (László), 4644.
KONTORINI (Vassa), 2037.
KOOLE (R. A.), 5151.
KOOPER (Kate), 3035.
KOOPMANS (J.), 3912.
KOORING (Deborah), 1887.
KOORTBOJIAN (Michael), 2888.
KOPF (Ulrich), 5852.
KOPIEC (Jan), 628.
KOPOSSOV (Nikolaï), 915.
KOPPISCH (Michael S.), 6598.
KORALTÜRK (Murat), 7176.
KORELIN (A. P.), 5347.
KORENEVSKAYA (Natalya), 5405.
KORENEVSKIJ (S. N.), 8805.
KORHONEN (Teppo), 1006.
KORITZ (Amy), 6939.
KÖRMENDY (Adrienne), 3797.
KORNBICHLER (Thomas), 7473.
KORNBLUTH (Genevra), 4222.
KÖRNER (Hans M.), 1271.
Korniloff (Lavr Georgievič), 5322.

KOROLEVA (N. G.), 5331.
KORPELA (J.), 2723.
KORPELA (Jukka), 1029.
KORTÜM (Hans-Henning), 63.
KORŻIKHINA (T. P.), 5332.
KOS (Peter), 309.
KOSHELENKO (G.), 1952.
KOSHKIN (A. A.), 7795.
KOSI (Miha), 3369.
KOŠIR (Matevž), 7468.
KOSKI (Arto), 4847.
KOŠKIN (Anatolij A.), 8251.
KOSLOWSKI (Gerd), 4725.
KOSLOWSKI (Peter), 7040.
KOSPATH-PAWŁOWSKI (Edward), 8319.
KOSTADINOVA (Tatiana), 4742.
KOSTELENOS (George C.), 7285.
KOSTERS (Christoph), 5756.
KOSTIAL (Michaela), 2637.
KOSTJAEVA (Aleksandra S.), 8878.
KOTKIN (Stephen), 5408.
KOTTJE (Raymund), 24, 3642.
KOTTMAN (Paul), 916.
KOURIN (Aleksander), 8224.
Kourouma (Ahmadou), 6641.
KOUTRAKOU (Nike), 3138.
KOVACS (D.), 2066.
KOVACSICS (József), 3374.
KOVÁCZ (Péter), 3500.
KOVAL'ĆENKO (Ivan D.), 917.
KOVALEVSKAJA (V. B.), 918.
KOWALCZUK (Ilko-Sache), 4820.
KOWALCZYK (Jerzy), 6749, 6750.
KOWALESKI (Maryanne), 3798.
KOWALSKI (Wojciech), 489, 8626.
KOZIARSKI (Stanisław Marian), 7185.
KOZICKI (Richard J.), 1117.
KOZIEŁŁO-POKLEWSKI (Bohdan), 4791.
KOZLOV (Aleksandr I.), 5333.
KOZLOV (Grigorii), 6865.
KOZLOV (V. I.), 1030.
KOZLOWSKI (Janusz), 1617.
KRABBE (Jacob J.), 7042.
KRAEMER (David), 5931.
KRAFT (Ekkehard), 7915.
KRAG (Claus), 3584.
KRAGH (Jens), 6114.
KRAJEWSKA (Hanna), 437.
Krajina (Vladimír), 8416.
KRAMER (Rita), 8406.
KRAML (Hans), 4279.
KRANENBORG (R.), 1410.
KRANTZ (Olle), 7063.
KRASNOVSKAJA (N. A.), 1031.
KRASSER (Helmut), 2788.
KRASSOWSKI (Witold), 1373.
KRASUSKI (Jerzy), 349, 8627.
KRASUSKI (Wojciech), 8252.

KRAUS (Antje), 4792.
Kraus (Karl), 6706, 7643.
KRAUSE (Günter), 7042.
KRAUSE (Jens-Uwe), 2724, 2999.
KRAUSE (W.), 26.
KRAUSZ (Tamás), 5409.
KRAUTHEIMER (Richard), 4185.
KRAUTSCHICK (Stefan), 2565.
KRAVARI (Vassiliki), 3046.
KRAWCZYK (Jerzy), 6115.
KREIKEMEYER (Anna), 8528.
KREIS (M.), 7740.
KREISWIRTH (Martin), 6294.
KREJĆOVÁ (Helena), 5483.
KREMENYUK (Victor A.), 8798.
KRENKE (N. A.), 1684.
KRENTZ (P.), 2110.
KŘEŠTAN (Jiří), 5473.
KRESTEN (Otto), 3066, 3071, 3139.
KRETININ (Sergej V.), 4793.
KRETZENBACHER (Leopold), 4469.
KREUTER (S.), 2638.
KREWSON (Margrit Beran), 5585.
KRIĆIENKO (O. V.), 5825.
KRIEDTE (Peter), 7413.
KRIEGLEDER (Wynfried), 6601.
KRIEGSEISEN (Wojciech), 5247.
KRIERE (Karl R.), 2889.
KRINGS (Veronique), 1101.
KRIPS (Henry), 1359, 6454.
KRISCHER (Tilman), 2292.
KRISTENSSON (Gillis), 4038.
KRISTÓ (Gyula), 3370, 3460, 4039.
KRIŽEVSKAJA (L. Ja.), 1640.
KROEKER (P. Travis), 5654.
KROESCHELL (Karl), 3643.
KROGEL (Wolfgang), 5026.
KROIS (John Michael), 6295.
KRÓL (Joanna), 1563.
KROM (Mikhail M.), 7932.
KRONLUND (Jarl), 4842.
KROOS (Renate), 4040.
KRSANOV (Nikolaj A.), 5334.
KRUHEK (Milan), 1114.
KRUL (W. E.), 796.
KRUMBACHER (Karl), 3092.
KRUMME (Michael), 310.
KRUSZEWSKI (Eugeniusz S.), 5241, 7963.
KRZYŻANIAKOWA (Jadwiga), 4508.
Ktésias, 2124, 2238.
KUAN (Jeffrey K.), 1906.
KUBAĆAK (Antonín), 7245.
KUBINYI (András), 3531, 4408.
KUBŮ (Eduard), 5484, 7337.
KUĆERA (Martin), 5485.
KUCERA (Wolfgang), 7505.
KUĆKIN (Vladimir A.), 767.
KÜÇÜKDAG (Yusuf), 5521.
KUCZYNSKI (Michael P.), 4041.
KUDIELKA (Robert), 6765.

KUDRJAVCEVA (Elena P.), 5066.
KUDROV (Valentin), 7101.
KUEH (Y. Y.), 7246.
KUEHN (Thomas), 3644.
Kugler (Jacek), 1290.
KUHLICH (Frank), 8042.
KÜHNE (Hartmut), 1834.
KÜHNERT (Barbara), 2810.
KUHRT (Amelie), 1729.
KUJALA (Antti), 7512.
KUKSEWICZ (Zdzisław), 4347.
KULAVIG (Erik), 5336.
KULCSÁR (Péter), 4043, 4510.
KULCZYKOWSKI (Mariusz), 6116.
KULEMZIN (V. M.), 1023.
KULIGOWSKA-KORZENIEWSKA (Anna), 6940.
KULOMAA (Jukka), 8372.
KUMAR (Chetan), 8673.
KÜMIN (Beat), 804.
KUMMEL (Gerhard), 7102.
KUMMER (Dietmar), 6089.
KUNERT (Andrzej Krzysztof), 8200.
KÜNG (Hans), 5655.
KUNKEL (Wolfgang), 2695.
KUNT (M.), 5531.
KUNTZ FICKER (Sandra), 7220.
KUNZ (Andreas), 7149, 7155, 7170.
KUNZ (Hildegard), 5224.
KUNZEL (Regina), 7414.
KUPARINEN (Eero), 7872.
KUPIECKI (Robert), 5248, 7742.
KUPISCH (Berthold), 3055.
KURDAS (Chidem), 7020.
KURETSKY (Susan Donahue), 6831.
KURIEV (Murat M.), 4948.
KUROITA (Nobuo), 9045.
KURPERSHOEK (P. M.), 1033.
KURTCEPHE (İsrafil), 8128.
KURUCZ (Görgy), 1115.
KURUKIN (Igor'V.), 5354.
KURUSHIMA (Hiroshi), 9042.
KURZ (Gabriele), 1706.
KURZ (Heinz D.), 7010.
KUSCHEL (Karl-Josef), 5932.
KUSS (Stephan), 5711.
KÜSTER (Hansjörg), 1278.
KUSUKAWA (Sachiko), 5868.
KUSUMGAR (Sheela), 1626.
KUTLER (Stanley I.), 516.
KUTSCHBACH (Doris), 6827.
KUTSCHERA (F. von), 2293.
KUTTIANIMATTATHIL (J.), 1467.
KUTTIN (Bettina), XVI.
KUTTNER (Ann L.), 2890.
KÜTÜKOĞLU (Mübahat), 7103.
KUVŠINOV (Vladimir A.), 5337.
KUZ'MINA (O. V.), 8806.
KUZ'MIN (Ja. V.), 1666.
KUZNECOV (S. V.), 7247.
KVAŠONKIN (A. V.), 5421.

KYLANDER (Britt-Marie), 6602.
KYNIN (Georgij P.), 8253.

L

LA CAPRA (Dominick), 919.
LA FEBER (Walter), 4625.
LA GORCE (Paul-Marie de), 8254.
La Malfa (Ugo), 5988.
LA ROCCA (Cristina), 824.
LA TORRE (Gilka), 4723.
LA TORRE (Giuseppe), 5669.
LA VERGATA (Antonello), 1523.
LABARBE (Jules), 2082.
LABANDE (E. R.), 3202.
LABBE (Yves), 6296.
LABORIE (Pierre), 654.
Labriola (Antonio), 6306, 6340.
LABUDA (Gérard), 1102, 3461, 7248.
LABYADH (Salem), 7873.
LACAITA (Carlo G.), 5024.
Lacassagne (A.), 7622.
LACASSE (François D.), 6021.
LACAZE (Yvon), 8129, 8255.
LACHIVER (Alban), 8130.
LACHMUND (Jens), 6445.
LACINA (Vlastislav), 7070, 7105.
LACKENBACHER (Sylvie), 1784, 1907.
LACKNER (M.), 8879.
LACKÓ (Miklós), 6654.
LADERO QUESADA (Miguel Ángel), 3462.
LADEWIG PETERSEN (E.), 7933.
LADRIERE (Jean), 6278.
LAFFONT (Pierre-Yves), 3220.
LAFON (Xavier), 2891.
LAFONT (Bertrand), 1835.
LAFONTAINE-DOSOGNE (Jacqueline), 4186.
LAGARDE (Francois), 6655.
LAGARDERE (Vincent), 3558.
LAGARRIGA (I.), 1438.
LAGAZIO (Monica), 8630.
Lagrange (Giuseppe Luigi), 6421.
LAGREE (Michel), 1406.
LAGROU (Pieter), 8256.
LAGUNAS (Cecilia), 3799.
LAGUZZI (Marina), 7647.
LAGZI (István), 8257.
LAHARIE (Muriel), 412.
LAHARIE (Patrick), 6154.
LAHIRE (Bernard), 7415.
LÄHTEENMÄKI (Maria), 7416.
LAHUSEN (Thomas), 5405.
LAI (Cheng-Chung), 750.
LAI (Xinxia), 8880.
LAÏDI (Zaki), 8631.
LAILY (P.A.), 9099.
LAINS (Pedro), 5280, 7049.

LAIOU (Angeliki E.), 3140.
LAKARRA (Joseba A.), 367.
LAKE (M.), 4705.
LAKS (André), 2287.
LAL (B. V.), 7811.
LAM (Stanisław), 1568.
LAMARCA (M.), 210.
LAMARCHE (P.), 1448.
LAMB (Ursula), 5626, 6446.
LAMBEK (Joachim), 6378.
LAMBERT (Jean), 1468.
LAMBERT (Malcolm), 5799.
LAMBERT (Marie-Françoise), 2728.
LAMBERT (Nicholas A.), 4949.
LAMBERT (Peter), 629, 4794.
LAMBERT-DANSENETTE (Jean), 8043.
LAMBERTINI (Roberto), 4423.
LAMBINI (Gérard), 2207.
LAMBOT (Bernard), 1707.
LAMBRECHT (Rainer), 6217.
LAMBRECHTS (Roger), 2496.
LAMOINE (Georges), 4950.
LAMOREAUX (John C.), 2953.
LAMOTHE (Solange), 6649.
Lamprecht (Karl), 800.
LAN'KOV (A. N.), 9071.
LANA (Italo), 2789.
LANASRI (Ahmed), 6656.
LANCASTER (William), 7221.
LANCEL (Serge), 1908.
LANÇON (Pierre), 4223.
LANCONELLI (Angela), 3463.
LANDA (Robert G.), 1116, 5933.
LANDAU (Peter), 3645.
LANDERS (David S.), 1279.
LANDES (Richard), 739.
LANDFESTER (Ulrike), 6657.
Landino (Cristoforo), 3994.
LANDOLFI (Luciano), 2566.
LANDY-HOUILLON (Isabelle), 6022.
LANE (Ann), 8258, 8295, 8421.
LANELLI (Sergio), 6944.
LANG (H. W.), 230.
LANG (Helen S.), 1518.
LÁNG (Imre), 5602.
LANG (Timothy), 4951.
LANGELLA (Giuseppe), 6665.
LANGERUD (Henning), 6030.
LANGEWIESCHE (Dieter), 4626.
LANGHANS (Erika), 630.
LANGHOLM (Sivert), 6117.
LANGLAND (Elizabeth), 6658.
LANGLEY (Harold D.), 6447.
LANGLOIS (Claude), 5680.
LANGUE (Frédérique), 7417.
Languet (Hubert), 7935.
LANIADO (Avshalom), 2567.
LANIER (Douglas), 6566.
Lankester (E. Ray), 6385, 6451.
LANKHORST (Otto Stephanus), 238.

Lanson (Gustave), 801.
LANZA (Diego), 3103.
LANZA (Loredana), 4044.
LANZA TOMASI (Gioacchino), 6707.
LANZANI (Vittorio), 5731.
LAPIDGE (Michael), 3952, 4057, 4481.
LAPIED (Martine), 4881.
LAPLACE (Pierre Simon, marquis de), 6448.
Lapo da Castiglionchio, 4013.
LAPP (Benjamin), 4795.
LAPPENKÜPER (Ulrich), 8632.
ŁAPTOS (Józef), 4719.
LARKIN (David), 6875.
LAROCHE (Roland A.), 2294.
LARRAÑAGA ZULUETA (M.), 3221.
LARRÈRE (Catherine), 1205.
LARRES (Klaus), 8633.
LARRINGTON (Caroline), 3294.
LARSON (Brooke), 7380.
LARSON (J.), 2371.
LARSON (Pier M.), 631.
LARUE (C. Steven), 6068.
LASERNA GAITÁN (Antonio I.), 7249.
LASKAYA (Anne), 4045.
LATHAM (Anthony John Heaton), 1063.
LATTANZI (Vito), 993.
LATVAKANGAS (Arto), 632.
LATYSHEV (I.A.), 7795.
LAUBE (Johannes), 5922.
LAUDADIO (Valter), 3464.
LAUDE (P.), 1469.
LAUFENBERG (Heinrich), 97.
LAUKHIN (S. A.), 1611.
LAURA (Ernesto G.), 6941.
LAURENS (Jeannine), 1160.
LAURETTE (Pierre), 6691.
LAUREYS (Marc), 3896.
LAURIDSEN (John T.), 4754.
LAURILA (Juhani), 7222.
LAURIOUX (Bruno), 3800.
LAURSEN (Finn), 8634.
LAUSTEN (Martin Schwarz), 5656.
LAUTENSACH (Hermann), 395.
LAUTERBACH (Iris), 4767.
LAUTMAN (Françoise), 1388.
LAVENE (Béatrice), 4046.
LAVIN (Deborah), 7810.
LAVIN MARILYN (Aronberg), 6829.
Lavoisier (Antoine Laurent), 6381, 6436.
LAW (Robin), 9100.
LAW (Vivien), 4047.
LAWALL (Mark Lewis), 2208.
LAWLOR (Michael S.), 7027.
LAWSON (E. Thomas), 1396.
LAWSON (Philip), 7906.
LAWTON (C. L.), 2413.

LAZAROV (Ivan), 4743.
LAZEROW (Jama), 5657.
LAZO (Alfonso), 6187.
Lazzaroni (Pietro), 3314.
LE BLANC (Yvonne), 4048.
LE BOHEC (Yann), 2691.
LE BOULLUEC (Alain), 1441.
LE COZ (Raymond), 1397.
LE GLAY (Marcel), 2839.
LE GOFF (Jacques), 600, 633.
LE GUEN (B.), 2209.
LE GUILLOU (Louis), 811.
LE JAN (Régine), 3801.
LE MAY (Godfrey Hugh Lancelot), 5456.
LE MENE (Michel), 3802.
LE MOLLE (Roland), 6791.
Le Pen (Jean-Marie), 4897.
LE RIDER (Georges), 2210.
LE ROUX (Patrick), 2508.
LE ROY LADURIE (Emmanuel), 239, 749, 3969.
LE TURDU (Anna), 4796.
LE VOT (Gérard), 847.
LEARY (John), 5104.
LEATHERDALE (Clive), 6677.
LEAVELL (Linda), 6830.
LEB (Ioan-Vasile), 5695.
LEBEAU (Vicky), 6942.
LEBECQ (Stéphane), 4447.
LEBIELLE (Marcel), 6518.
LEBIODA (Tadeusz), 4797.
LEBOW (Richard Ned), 8635.
LEBRUN-PÉZERAT (P.), 5992.
LEC (Zdzisław), 5800.
LECKER (Michael), 1909.
LECLANT (Jean), 1785.
LECLERCQ (Jean), 4049.
LECOUTEUX (Claude), 4050.
LECZYK (Marian), 1102.
LEDERER (Susan E.), 6449.
LEE (David), 8636.
LEE (Don Y.), 8815.
LEE (Hoong Phun), 5105.
LEE (K. H.), 2068.
LEE (S. Y.), 2886.
LEE (Sabine), 8578, 8637.
LEE (Seong-si), 9072.
LEE (Stephen J.), 6450.
LEE (Steven Hugh), 8638.
LEEB (Rudolf), 5869.
LEEDHAM-GREEN (E. S.), 251.
LEERSSEN (josep), 1341.
LEFÈVRE (Eckard), 2790.
LEFÈVRE (F.), 2349.
LEFEVRE (François), 1983, 2042, 2136.
LEFEVRE (M.), 242.
Lefèvre d'Etaples (Jacques), 4391, 6561.
LEFF (Mark H.), 5603.

LEFORT (Jacques), 3046.
Léger (Alexis), 8080.
LEGGATT (S.), 2049.
LEGOY (C.), 6943.
LEGRAND (Catherine C.), 4831.
LEGRO (Jeffrey W.), 8259.
LEHMANN (Gustav Adolf), 810.
LEHMANN (Wilfred P.), 351.
LEHMKUHL (Ursula), 7714.
LEHTONEN (Tuomas M. S.), 4051.
Leibniz (Gottfried Wilhelm), 1513, 6251, 6262, 6310, 6335, 6351, 6416.
LEIGH-PHIPPARD (Helen), 8639.
LEITCH (Richard D.), 8640.
LEITZ (Christian), 8260.
LEJEUNE (Michel), 2007.
LELLI (Fabrizio), 6591.
LELORRAIN (Anne-Marie), 6118.
LEMA PUEYO (J. A.), 3221.
LEMAIRE (Gérald-Georges), 6659.
LEMAIRE (Jean-François), 7996.
LEMAITRE (Jean-Loup), 3222.
LEMANN (Nicholas), 634.
LEMARCHAND (Guy), 4891.
LEMARCHAND (Yannick), 7223.
LEMARIGNIER (Jean-François), 3646.
LEMON (Michael C.), 921.
LEMORINI (Cristina), 1641.
LENDLE (O.), 2111.
LENGER (Friedrich), 7418.
LENGYEL (György), 7329.
Lenin (Vladimir Ilič Uljanov), 5322, 6223, 8150.
LENKEFI (Ferenc), 7997.
LENNEIS (Eva), 1642.
LENNOX (James G.), 6398.
LENTES (T.), 4480.
LENTIN (Antony), 8131.
LENTINI (Maria Costanza), 311.
LENZ (Dirk), 2414.
LENZUNI (Anna), 137.
Leo ereticus, imperatore bizantino, 3045.
Leo IX, Papa, 4427.
Leo XIII, Papa, 5669, 5718.
LEONARDI (Claudio), 110, 3283, 3295, 3339, 3961, 4052.
Leonbruno (Lorenzo), 6862.
LEONHARD (Wolfgang).
LEONI (Diego), 3283.
LEON-PORTILLA (Miguel), 7903.
LEONTIADES (I. G.), 3077.
Léontios de Néapolis, 3058.
Leontios Presbyteros von Rom, 3052.
LEONTIS (A.), 2295.
Leopardi (Giacomo), 6673.
LEOTARD (Jean-Marc), 1617.
LEPETIT (Bernard), 529, 922, 1280, 7308.

LEPICK (Olivier), 8132.
LEPINE (David), 4511.
LEPLANT-MORA B., 3202.
LEPORE (Ettore), 6014.
LEPPIN (Volker), 1034.
LEPRE (Aurelio), 5027.
LEPROUX (Guy-Michel), 3199.
LERNER (Henri), 4892.
LERNER (Judith), 1953.
LERNER SIGAL (Victoria), 5123.
LEROUX (Serge), 6024.
LEROY (B.), 827.
LEROY (Géraldi), 4893.
LERSKI (Jerzy Jan), 1117.
LESKIEWICZOWA (Janina), 5233.
LESOUEF (Pierre), 8016.
LESOURD (Céline), 4894.
LESPAGNOL (André), 4895.
LESSER (Jeff), 4732.
LESTER (Joseph), 6385, 6451.
LESZCZYŃSKI (Grzegorz), 6700.
LETALDO DI MICY, 4054.
LETOUBLON (Françoise), 2211.
LETTA (Cesare), 2520.
LEVANONI (Amalia), 3559.
LEVEAU (Ph.), 2640.
LEVELEUX (Corinne), 3000.
LEVENSTEIN (Margaret), 7106.
LEVEQUE (Pierre), 1972, 2117.
LEVERINGTON (David), 6452.
LEVESQUE (Jacques), 8641.
LEVEY (Z.), 8642.
LEVI (Giovanni), 7107.
LEVI (Mario Attilio), 2696.
LEVICK (B.), 2521.
LEVICK (Barbara), 2748.
LEVIN (Saul), 3533.
LEVINA (Elena Solomonovna), 6453.
LEVINE (Alan J.), 8373.
LEVINE (Susan), 6119.
LEVSTEIN (Ana), 6298.
LEVY (David M.), 7021.
LEV-YADUN (Simcha), 1910.
LEWANDOWSKA (Małgorzata), 4436.
LEWIS (A. D.), 7542.
LEWIS (Andrew W.), 3267, 4512.
LEWIS (Bernard), 3534.
LEWIS (Earl), 635.
LEWIS (Jan), 636.
LEWIS (N.), 2093.
LEWIS (Peter S.), 3296.
LEWIS (R. J.), 2886.
LEWIS (S.), 4055.
LEWIS (R. A.), 1576.
LEYS (Colin), 5138.
LEYTE (Guillaume), 3647.
LHUILLIER (Virginie), 2168.
LI (Anshan), 4923.
Li (Dazheng), 8971.
LI (Enjun), 8881.
Li (Fu), 6285.

LI (Hongxi), 8882.
LI (Longru), 8883.
LI (Sheng), 8884.
LI (Xiangjun), 8885.
LI (Yu), 8886.
LIANG (Binghua), 8887.
LIANG (Shangxian), 8888.
LIBAEK (Ivar), 1119.
Libanios, 2083, 2671.
LIBRANDI (R.), 3906.
LICHT (Walter), 7108.
LICITRA (Vincenzo), 3329.
LIDÉN (Hans-Emil), 1480.
LIE (Einar), 5164.
LIEBICH (André), 7743.
LIEBL (Elsbeth), 994.
LIEHR (Reinhardt), 7279.
LIERTZ (Uta-Maria), 2509.
LIEVEN (Dominic), 4627.
LIEVENS (R.), 93.
LIFSCHITZ (Felice), 638, 3298.
LIGASAWA (Yasunori), 8889.
LIGHT (L.), 142.
LIIKANEN (Ilkka), 4843.
LILJA (Sven), 7330.
LILJEWALL (Britt), 7419.
LIM (Richard), 1730, 2641.
LIMA (Robert), 413.
LIMOUZE (Dorothy A.), 6831.
LIN (James C.), 7667.
LIN (Justin Yifu), 7109.
LIN (Shuyong), 8979.
LIN (Tianwai), 8890.
LINCICOME (Mark Elwood), 6120.
LINCOLN (David), 7420.
LIND (Michael), 5604.
LINDE (Samuel Bogumił), 352.
LINDE-LAURSEN (Anders), 1120.
LINDERSKI (J.), 2697.
LINDERT (Peter H.), 7371.
LINDGREN (Stefan), 8317.
LINDHOLM (Marcus), 4844.
LINDKVIST (Thomas), 3803.
LINDSAY (Hugh), 2642.
LINDSAY (W. M.), 4057.
LING (R.), 2892.
LINGER (Sandrine), 3649.
LINKE (Bernhard), 2643.
LINKLATER (Andrew), 8647.
LION (Brigitte), 1836.
LIOU (Bernard), 2601.
LIOU-GILLE (Bernadette), 2840.
LIPHSCHITZ (Nili), 1911.
LIPINSKAJA (V. A.), 1035.
LIPINSKI (Edouard), 1470.
LIPKA (Michael), 1750.
LIPP (Karlheinz), 7513.
LIPPI (E.), 84.
LIPPI BIGAZZI (V.), 6567.
LIPPOLIS (E.), 2464.
Lipszky (János), 394.

LIRIS (Elisabeth), 4896.
Lysias, 2086.
LISICYN (N. F.), 1612.
LISIECKI (Stanisław), 8691.
LISTOVA (T. A.), 1046.
LITAVRIN (G. G.), 1008.
LITTLE (Douglas), 8643.
LITTLEWOOD (A. R.), 3100.
LITVÁN (György), 8102.
LITVIN (Alter L.), 5338.
Litvinov (Maksim Maksimovič), 8172.
LITVINSKIJ (B. A.), 1170.
LITVINSKOGO (B. A.), 1170.
LITWIN (Jerzy), 1281.
LIU (Aiwen), 8891.
LIU (Chaoming), 8892.
LIU (Cunkuan), 8893.
LIU (Huiwen), 8873.
LIU (Luya), 8894.
LIU (Pujiang), 8895.
LIU (Shuyong), 8896.
LIU (Xihai), 8882.
Liutprando di Cremona, 4405.
LIUZZI (Dora), 2572.
LIVERANI (Mario), 392, 923.
Livius (Titus), 803, 2559, 2568.
LIVORSI (Franco), 1206.
LIZCANO PRESTEL (Rafael), 1656.
LIZISOWA (Maria Teresa), 3650.
LIZZI (Rita), 2644.
LLOMBART (Vicent), 7022.
LLORENTE (Angel), 6751.
LLOSA (Alvaro Vargas), 4969.
Lloyd George (David), 8131.
LOACH BRAMANTI (Kathleen), 6802.
LOBAĆEVA (N. P.), 1036.
LOBATO FRANCO (Isabel), 7224.
LOBEHE (Placido Alema), 5465.
LOCHNER (Michaela), 1667.
Locke (John), 6270.
LOCKHART (Paul Douglas), 7934.
LODGE (R. Anthony), 4097.
ŁODZIŃSKI (Sławomir), 5249.
LOETSCHES (Andreas), 6568.
LOEWENBERG (Peter), 924.
LOGAN (F. Donald), 3651.
LOGAN (George M.), 6354.
LOGAN (Oliver M.T.), 5757.
LOHR (C. H.), 4288.
Lohr (Charles H.), 4302.
LOHRER (Magnus), 5701.
LOHRMANN (Dietrich), 1282, 3652.
LOHSE (Bernhard), 5870.
LOJÍN (Jaromír), 7110.
LØKKE (Anne), 1283.
LOLLINI (F.), 139.
LOLLIO BARBERI (Olga), 492.
LOMBA (Joaquín), 3560.
LOMBARDI (Giuseppe), 3300.
LOMBARDI (Lapo), 8340.

Lombardo (Tullio), 6832.
LOMOSOVA (M. V.), 5421.
Longinos, 2051.
LONITZ (Henri), 6220.
LOPEZ (Francoio), 5970.
LOPEZ (Roberto J.), 5440.
LOPEZ BARJA DE QUIROGA (Pedro), 2725.
LÓPEZ BAYÓN (IGNACIO), 1617.
LOPEZ CASTRO (Jose Luis), 1912.
LOPEZ CRUCES (J. L.), 2296.
LOPEZ FEREZ (J. A.), 2083.
LOPEZ MORENO DE REDROJO (José Ramón), 1614.
LÓPEZ PADILLA (Juan Antonio), 1664.
LOPEZ PEREZ (María Dolores), 3501.
López Pumerejo (Alfonso), 5089.
LOPRENO (Dario), 1149.
LORANS (Elisabeth), 4563.
LORAUX (Nicole), 2169, 2212.
LORCH (Richard P.), 3561.
LORCIN (Marie-Thérèse), 3804, 3965.
LORCIN (Patricia M. E.), 1037.
LORD (Albert B.), 2328, 3371.
LORD (M. L.), 2328.
LORENTZ (John Henry), 1121.
LORENZ (Chris), 4798.
Lorenzo de' Medici, 6898.
LORENZO PINAR (Francisco Javier), 4470.
LORETO (Luigi), 2645.
LOREY (Christoph), 6660.
LORREN (Claude), 3779.
ŁOŚ (Andrzej), 2213.
ŁOSSOWSKI (Piotr), 1102.
LOTZE (Detlef), 1122.
LOUBET (Jean-Louis), 7177.
LOUIS (E.), 4564.
Louis VI, roi de France, 3211.
Louis VII, roi de France, 3267.
Louis XI, roi de France, 4345.
Louis XIV, roi de France, 4582, 4895, 7611, 7914.
Louis XV, roi de France, 4910, 4915, 7271, 7956.
Louis XVI, roi de France, 4883, 7767.
Louis XVIII, roi de France, 4861.
Loukianos Samosateus, 2084.
LOUNGHIS (Telemachos C.), 3141.
LOURENCO (Maria Paula Marcal), 5281.
LOVE (Robert W.), 8282.
LOVEJOY (Paul E.), 1329, 7225, 7874.
LOVELL (William George), 4970, 9114.
LOVIN (Robin W.), 5658.
LÖWENHARDT (John), 5340.

LÖWITH (Karl), 909, 6300.
LÖWY (Ilana), 925.
LOZA (Hugo).
LOZANO (Joan Miquel), 1613.
LU (Huayu), 8897.
LU (Yiran), 9010.
LUBO-LESNIĆENKO (E. I.), 1170.
Luca, Evangelista, Sanctus, 2939.
Lucanus (Marcus Annaeus), 2569.
LUCASSEN (Jan), 5152.
LUCCA (Rita), 2465.
LUCCHESI (Maria Luisa), 8261.
LUCCHI (P.), 139.
LUCHS (Alison), 6832.
LUCKETT (D. A.), 4952.
Lucretius Carus (Titus), 2570.
Lucullus, 2604.
ŁUCZAK (Czesław), 8262.
LUGAL (Mihin), 256.
Luigi di Leon, 5777.
LUIHN (Hans), 8396.
LUISELLI (Bruno), 3001.
LUKACS (Lajos), 5556.
Lukacs (György), 6362.
LUKINA (N. V.), 1023.
LUKINOJ (N. V.), 1023.
LUKOWSKI (Jerzy), 7543.
LULLUS (Raimundus), 3938, 4058, 4289, 4295, 4322, 4329, 4367, 4364, 4368, 4372, 4384, 4391.
LUMINARI (Laura), 7744.
LUNARI (Marco), 64.
LUND (Allan A.), 639.
LUND (Joachim), 8341.
LUND (John), 2893.
LUND (Niels), 3585.
LUNDEN (Kåre), 1342, 3372, 5159, 5165.
LUNDGREN (Kurt), 7111.
LUNDIN (A. G.), 438.
LUO (Jiahuan), 8898.
LUO (Zhiji), 8899.
LUONGO (Gennaro), 3036.
LUPO (S.), 759.
LUR'E (Jakov S.), 640.
LURAGHI (Nino), 641, 813, 841.
LUSNIA (Susann S.), 2646.
LUST (J.), 1377.
Luther (Martin), 865, 5656, 5846, 5850, 5852, 5859, 5862, 5870, 5872, 5873, 5881, 5897.
LÜTHI (Alfred), 4435.
LÜTKE WESTHUES (P.), 65.
LUTTERBACH (Hubertus), 4448, 4471, 4480, 4513.
LUTZ (Christopher H.), 9114.
Lu (Wang), 6285.
LUXARDO DE FRANCHI (Nicolò), 7998.
Luzzatti (Luigi), 7280.
LYDON (James F.), 553.

LYGDATE (John), 97.
LYNCH (Kathryn L.), 4059.
LYNE (R.O.A.M.), 2792.
LYNN (Martin), 7875.
LYON (B.), 701.
LYON (M.), 701.
LYONS (Gene M.), 7745, 8428.
LYSENKO (T. D.), 6453.

M

MA (Xiaoquan), 8900.
MA (Yi), 8901.
MA (Yong), 8902.
MA'OZ (Moshe), 8644.
MAAG (Karin), 6069.
MAARBJERG (John P.), 7112.
MAAS (Pauline Henriëtte Joanna Theresia), 4348.
MAAZ (Wolfgang), 7473.
Mabillon (Jean), 802.
Mably (Gabriel Bonnot de), 673.
MABRO (Judy), 5915.
Mac Arthur (Douglas), 8212, 8451.
MAC AULIFFE (Jane Dammen), 3543.
MAC CABE (Desmond), 7313.
MAC CALL (John), 9101.
MAC CANN (Gerard), 1175.
MAC CANTS (Anne), 7321.
MAC CAULEY (Martin), 8645.
MAC CAULEY (Robert N.), 1396.
MAC CHCHEON (R.T.), 1399.
MAC CLENDON (Thomas V.), 7648.
MAC CLINTOCK (Anne), 7421.
MAC CLOUD (Donald G.), 8823.
MAC CORMICK (Michael), 3142.
MAC COY (Jennifer), 5583.
MAC CREADY (William D.), 4409.
MAC CULLUM (Hugh), 5290.
MAC DONALD (Alasdair A.), 3953.
Mac Donald (Malcom), 7818.
MAC DONALD (R. A.), 286, 3465.
MAC DONOUGH (Christopher), 4167.
MAC DOWELL (Laurel Sefton), 7422.
MAC EVOY (J.), 4297.
MAC EWAN (G. J. P.), 1837.
MAC GING (B. C.), 119.
MAC GINNESS (Frederick J.), 5696.
MAC GINNIS (John), 1838.
MAC GLADE (James), 1581.
Mac Gormick (Cyrus Hall), 7168.
MAC GOVERN (Patrick E), 2415.
MAC GOWAN (Elizabeth P.), 2416.
MAC GRADE (A. S.), 4293.
MAC GREGOR (Neil), 6765.
MAC GUINNESS (Andrew), 282.
MAC GUIRE (Donald T., Jr.), 2571.

MAC GUIRE (J. E.), 1359, 6454.
MAC GURK (P.), 3289.
MAC HARDY (A. K.), 3653.
MAC ILVANNEY (Liam), 6661.
MAC INTYRE (Arnold Meredith), 4628.
MAC INTYRE (David), 8646.
MAC KEAN (Charles), 4953.
MAC KEE (Sally), 3805.
MAC KENNA (Peter), 7746.
MAC KINLEY (Terry), 8903.
MAC KINNON (James W.), 4254.
MAC KITTERICK (David), 464.
MAC KITTERICK (Rosamond), 146, 3373, 3378, 3419, 4060.
MAC LAUGHLIN (Martin L.), 6121, 6569.
MAC LAUGHLIN (Peter), 6398.
MAC LEAN (David), 8044.
MAC LEAN (Will), 3868.
MAC LEOD (W.), 1803.
MAC LEOLD (David), 1577.
MAC LOUGHLIN (Leslie J.), 5357.
Mac Mahon (Henry), 8439.
MAC MILLAN (Gordon), 4733.
MAC MILLIN (Arnold), 4711.
MAC NEILL (William H.), 926.
MAC QUEEN (E. I.), 1954.
MAC QUEEN (John), 3264.
MAC QUEEN (Winfred), 3264.
MAC ROBBIE (Angela), 4954.
Mac Sorley (Raonall), 286.
MACAN (Trpimir), 1123.
Macario de Heraclea-Pelagonia, 3060.
MACCAGNI (C.), 3910.
MACCARRONE (Michele), 4423.
MACCIONI RUJU (P. Alessandra), 493.
MACEDO (Jorge Borges), 927.
MACEDONIUS CONSUL, 3072.
MACGEER (Eric), 3143.
MACHAĆEK (Jiři), 4565.
Machiavelli (Niccolò), 803, 1176, 1218, 3922, 6323, 6333, 6335, 6370, 6559.
MACHOBANE (L. B. B. J.), 5934.
MACIAS (Santiago A. F.), 4566.
MACINTYRE (Stuart), 567.
MACKAY (Christopher S.), 2682.
MACKENDRICK (P.), 2793.
MACKENZIE (S. P.), 8342.
MACKERCHER (B. J. C.), 8133.
MACKESY (Piers), 7999.
MACKOWSKI (R. M.), 388.
MACKSEY (Kenneth), 8263.
MACLAREN (John), 8134.
Macmillan (Harold), 8578.
MACMILLAN (John), 8647.
MACTOUX (Marie-Madeleine), 2117, 2834, 2192.

MACUMBER (P. G.), 1946.
MADAJCZYK (Czesław), 6070.
MADAMS (Robert), 6354.
MADAS (Edit), 4061.
MADDALO (Silvia), 143, 5762.
MADDEN (J. A.), 3072.
MADDISON (Angus), 7113.
MADERSBACHER (Lukas), 6833.
Madison (James), 5609.
MADU (Ngozi), 6301.
MADUROWICZ-URBAŃSKA (Helena), 5244.
MAEDER (Ernesto J. A.), 389.
MAEHLER (Herwig), 2167.
MAEIR (Aren M.), 1913.
MAFFI (Alberto), 2170.
MAFRICI (Mirella), 4629.
MAGDELAIN (André), 2698.
MAGEE (Frank), 8135.
MAGGETTI (Daniel), 6662.
MAGGIONI (Giovanni Paolo), 4062.
MAGGIULLI (Gigliola), 2794.
MAGI SPINETTI (Antonio), 1.
MAGISTRALE (Francesco), 9.
MAGNAN (André), 844.
MAGNOU-NORTIER (Elisabeth), 3654, 4574.
MAGOCSI (Paul Robert.), 390.
MAGOON (Joseph), 509.
MAGRI (Susanna), 6032.
MAGRI (Veronique), 6663.
MAGUIRE (Gloria Elizabeth), 8264.
MAGUIRE (Henry), 3115, 3144.
Mahmud II, sultano ottomano, 5524.
MAHN-LOT (M.), 1038.
MAIA NETO (Jose R.), 6302.
MAIARELLI (A.), 3274.
MAIDEN (Martin), 354.
MAIER (C. T.), 4063.
MAIER (Charles S.), 4630.
MAIER (Charles), 4602.
MAIER (Hans), 4631.
MAIER (Harry O.), 2841.
MAILES (Gene), 7520.
MAILLARD (Brigitte), 5691.
MAILLARD (J. F.), 3984.
MAILLO (Felipe), 3562.
MAINA (Kahumbi N.), 5935.
MAIOCCHI (Roberto), 1343.
MAIRE VIGUEUR (Jean-Claude), 3226, 4567.
MAITLAND (Frederic William), 804.
MAITRE (Claire), 4255, 4449.
MAITRE (Jacques), 1388.
MAJER (Hans G.), 1168.
Maïeul, abbé de Cluny, 4561.
MAJEUR (Jean-Marie), 1458.
Makarios III (Michail Christodhulos Muskos), 8653.
MAKAROV (I. A.), 2137.
MAKAROVA (I. F.), 1008.

MAKAROVIĆ (Gorazd), 7423.
MAKDISI (George), 4349.
MAKK (Ferenc), 3301, 3460.
MAKKAI (Béla), 5183.
MAKKAY (János), 1685.
MAKRIDES, (Vasilios), 5826.
MAKRIS (Georgios), 3145.
MALACARNE (G.), 103.
MALAGUZZI (F.), 148.
MALAMUT (Elisabeth), 3146.
MALANDAIN (Gilles), 7597.
MALANIMA (Paolo), 1284.
Malatesta (Annalena), 6814.
MALATESTA (Edward), 5801.
MALATESTA (M.), 7458.
MALATO (Enrico), 1525.
MALECI (Stefano), 3073.
MALEK (Redha), 7876.
Malenkov (Georgij Maksimilianovič), 5429, 8150.
MALEUVRE (J.-Y.), 2795.
MALGERI (Francesco), 5669.
MALIA (Martin), 5410.
MALINA (Peter), 5184.
MALKIN (Irad), 2639.
MALLMANN (Klaus-Michael), 7514.
MALLO (Tomás), 6395.
MALLON (Florencia E.), 5124.
Malmberg (Lauri), 4846.
MALONE (Michael Shawn), 7179.
MALONEY (Sean M.), 8649.
MALONEY (Thomas N.), 7515.
MALPICA (Antonio), 3563.
MALTESE (Enrico V.), 3099, 3147.
MALTEZOU (Chryssa A.), 3148.
MALUKA (Zulfikar Khalid), 5204.
MALYŠEV (A. A.), 2647.
MAMBWINI KIVUILA-KIAKU (Joseph), 2796.
MAMEDOV (G. É.), 8322.
MAMMARELLA (Giuseppe), 5605.
MAMUROVSKI (Tasko), 5109.
MAN (Igor), 8650.
MAŇÁK (Jiří), 5486.
MANCA (Anna Gianna), 4799.
MANCA (Sergio), 842, 6303.
MANCALL (P. C.), 7902.
MANCHEL (Frank), 928.
MANCINI (Vincenzo), 494.
MANCOSU (Paolo), 6455.
MANDAL (Stephen), 1634.
Mandela (Nelson), 5455.
MANDELBAUM (Michael), 8651.
MANDIGORRA LLAVATA (María Luz), 67.
MANE (Perrine), 3806.
MANGO (Cyril), 15, 3094.
MANGO-TOMEI (Elsa), 5375.
Mani, 2979.
MANIACI (Marilena), 87, 149, 150.
MANIAU (Joaquin), 7114.

MANIKOWSKA (Halina), 4525.
Manilius (Marcus), 2572.
MANKIN (David), 2561.
MANKKI (Raija), V.
Mann (Thomas), 6633, 6969.
MANNELL (Joanne), 2894.
MANNINEN (Ohto), 4839.
MANNING (Eugène), 2, 4381.
MANNOVÁ (Elena), 595.
MANNS (Frédéric), 3002.
MANOR (Liviu), 8160.
MANSFIELD (Mary C.), 3655.
MANSINI (Guy), 4350.
MANSURE (Victor Newell), 6945.
MANTINI (Silvia), 1125, 4568.
MANTION (Jean-Rémy), 6834.
MÄNTYLÄ (Ilkka), 7424.
MANUEL (Frank Edward), 6304.
MANUEL II PALAIOLOGUS, imperatore bizantino, 3074I, 3089.
MANUWALD (Bernd), 2171.
Manutius (Aldus), 216, 218, 250.
MANZANO MORENO (Eduardo), 3564.
MANZARI (Giuliano), 8000.
MANZONI (Alessandro), 6621, 6664, 6665.
MANZONI (Gian Enrico), 2573.
Mao (Zedong), 8801, 8870, 8947, 8956, 8958, 8969, 9017.
MAR'INA (V. V.), 4659.
Mara (Maria Grazia), 1494.
MARABINI (Claudio), 6188.
MARASCO (Gabriele), 2297, 2797.
Marat (Jean-Paul), 4865.
MARAZZI (Federico), 3807.
MARBODO DI RENNES, 4472.
Marcabrun, 4094.
MARCACCINI (Carlo), 2372.
MARCATTO (Dario), 5690.
MARĆENKO (K. K.), 2008.
MARĆENKO (K. K.), 2023.
MARCET-JUNCOSA (Alicia), 7916.
MARCH (Duane A.), 1955.
MARCHAL (Guy P.), 4224.
MARCHAND (Philippe), 6122.
MARCHESI (Luigi), 8374.
MARCHESINI VELASCO (Simona), 2466.
MARCHETTI (Patrick), 2417.
MARCHISOTTO (Elena), 6405.
MARCON (S.), 140.
MARCONE (Arnaldo), 813, 2798.
MARCONI (Diego), 6305.
MARCOVICH (Miroslav), 2944.
MARCUS (Aage), 8904.
Marcus Aurelius (Antoninus), imperatore romano, 832.
MARCUS (Harold Golden), 7877.
MARCUS (Jonathan), 4897.
Marcus, Sanctus, 140.

MARCUS (Steven), 6477.
MARDEŠIĆ (Ivo), 1344.
Margarida de Cleves, 154.
MARGEL (Serge), 2298.
Margherita d'Ungheria, Sancta, 4468.
MARGIOTTA BROGLIO (Francesco), 8652.
MARGOLIS (A. D.), 5341.
MARGOLIS (Joseph), 6752.
Marguerite d'Autriche, reine d'Espagne, 459.
María de Valpuesta, Sancta, 3246.
Maria de Villabertran, Sancta, 3227.
Maria Teresa, imperatrice d'Austria, 5202, 5177.
Maria van Hongarije, reggente dei Paesi Bassi, 5145.
MARIANI CANOVA (G.), 153.
MARIN (Richard), 5802.
MARINI (Alfonso), 4461.
MARINO (Luigi), 645.
Marinus, Sanctus, 3034.
MARION (Jacques), 8375.
MARIOTTI (Scevola), 6570.
Marivaux (Pierre Carlet de Chamblain de), 673.
MARK (Peter), 9102.
MARKIDES (Diana Weston), 8653.
MARKIDES (Kyriacos C.), 5827.
MARKIEWICZ (Mariusz), 7964.
Markiōn, 3005.
MARKOFF (John), 4898.
MARKOV (G. E.), 1039.
MARKSCHIES (Christoph), 1400, 3003.
Marot (Jean), 6583.
MARÓTI (Egon), 2138.
Marpeck (Pilgram), 5633.
MARQUES PLANAGUMA (Josep M.), 3207, 3227.
MARQUINA (Antonio), 7749.
MARR (David George), 5617.
MARR (John), 2139, 2299.
MARRIOTT (Stuart), 6123.
MARROU (Henri-Irenée), 806.
MARROW (J. H.), 154.
MARRUS (Michael R.), 4632.
MARSDEN (Richard), 4225, 4514.
MARSH (Ian), 4706.
MARSHACK (Alexander), 1617.
Marshall (Alfred), 7003, 7031.
MARSHALL (Jonathan), 8265.
MARSHALL (P. J.), 7812.
Marsilio da Padova, 4355, 6260.
MARSTON (Nicholas), 6946.
MARTANI (M.), 465.
MARTELLI (Fabio), 5071.
MARTELLI (Mario), 4064, 6570.
MARTELLI (Roger), 7516.
MARTEM'JANOV (A. P.), 2726.

MARTHINSEN (Liv), 1093.
Marti (Jose), 5100.
MARTI (Sadurni), 360.
Martialis (Valerius Marcus), 2574, 2737.
MARTIGNONE (Vercingetorige), 6545.
MARTIN (C. J.), 2172.
MARTIN (Daniel), 6025.
MARTIN (G. H.), 3293.
MARTIN (Ged), 5077.
MARTIN (Henri-Jean), 202.
MARTIN (Jean-Marie), 3409, 3764, 3808, 4515.
MARTIN (Jean-Pierre), 8376.
MARTIN (Lutz), 1786.
MARTIN (Philippe), 5659.
MARTIN (Robert), 343.
MARTIN CORRALES (Eloy), 6947.
MARTÍN IGLESIAS (J.C.), 3037.
MARTIN-ACENA (Pablo), 7074.
MARTINELLI (Vittorio), 6948.
MARTÍNEZ (Samuel), 4972.
MARTINEZ LOPEZ-CANO (Maria del Pilar), 7286.
MARTINEZ MARTIN (Manuel), 7251.
MARTINEZ MARTINEZ (María), 3656.
MARTINEZ PIZARRO (Joaquin), 3302.
MARTINEZ QUESTA (Angel), 5803.
MARTINEZ QUIRCE (Francisco J.), 1654.
MARTINEZ-PINNA (Jorge), 2648.
MARTINICH (Aloysius P.), 1519.
MARTINIE (Henri), 6873.
MARTINIERE (Guy), 7116.
MARTIN-MUÑZON (Gema), 8655.
MARTINOIR (Francine de), 6666.
MARTOS ROMERO (Juan Antonio), 1614.
MARTSCHUKAT (Jürgen), 8656.
MARTYNOVA (Marina Ju.), 4622.
MARTZ (John D.), 8657.
MARTZLOFF (Jean-Claude), 6456.
MARVIN (Perry), 840.
MARWICK (Arthur), 929, 979.
MARX (C. W.), 4065.
MARX (Friedhelm), 6667.
Marx (Karl) , 6000, 6232, 6291, 6297, 6304, 6358, 6367, 7010, 7018, 7020, 7026.
MARY (André), 646.
MARZAHN (Joachim), 1839.
MARZIK (Thomas D.), 5498.
MAS CORNELLÀ (Martí), 1614.
MASARACCHIA (Agostino), 2300.
Masaryk (Tomaš Garrigue), 5485, 5497.
MASKER (John Scott), 8658.
MASLENNIKOV (A. A.), 2140.
MASLOWSKI (Tadeusz), 2543.

MASON (Hugh J.), 2649.
MASON (Timothy Wright), 7517.
MASON CLARK (Francelia), 4066.
MASONEN (Jaakko), 3586.
MASSA-PAIRAULT (Françoise-Hélène), 2727.
Massarecchi (Pietro), 5761.
MASSEAU (Didier), 844, 6035.
MASSENZIO (Marcello), 1472.
MASSEY (Doreen), 647.
MASSIE (Robert K.), 5342.
MASSING (J. M.), 155.
MASSON (Olivier), 2214.
MASSON (Philippe), 8001.
MASTANDREA (Paolo), 3038.
MASTANDUNO (Michael), 7745.
MASTROCINQUE (Attilio), 2141, 2621, 2650, 2842.
MASTROGREGORI (Massimo), 508, 648, 749.
MASTROIANNI (Giovanni), 6306.
MASTRULLO (G.), 227.
MASTRUZZO (A.), 28.
MATEI (Horia C.), 1127.
MATERNA (Ingo), 1128.
MATHER (Ian Roderick), 7904.
MATHEUS (Michael), 1105.
MATHIESON (Ian), 1787.
MATHON (G.), 1437.
MATIJEVICH (Elke), 6668.
MATJUKHIN (A. E.), 1582.
MATKOVIĆ (Hrvoje), 5092.
MATOS (Sérgio Carneiro de Campos), 649.
MATOSO (José), 1129.
MATSUMIYA (Syuji), 7353.
MATSUMOTO (Akira), 650.
MATSUURA (Masataka), 7023.
MATSUZAKI (Tsuneko), 8905.
Mattei (Enrico), 8700.
MATTESINI (Francesco), 6665.
MATTEUZZI (M.), 2084.
MATTHEWS (Caitlin), 1708.
MATTHEWS (Keith J.), 1583.
Matthews (Z. K.), 5455.
MATTHIESEN (Helge), 7518.
MATTINGLY (David J.), 2895.
MATTIOLI (Umberto), 2225, 2737.
MATTON (Sylvain), 4351, 6716.
MATTOS DE CASTRO (Hebe Maria), 4734.
MATTOSO (José), 3809, 4352.
MATUS (Jill L.), 6669.
MATVEEV (A. V.), 1573.
MATVEEV (N. P.), 1573.
MATZ (D.), 2215.
MATZ (Jean-Michel), 5758.
MAU (V. A.), 5343.
MAUDE (George), 1130.
MAUDUIT (Christine), 2301.
MAUGENEST (Denis), 5697.

MAUL (Stefan M.), 1840.
MAURER (John H.), 8136.
MAURER (K.), 2302.
MAURIN (Louis), 2522.
MAURITSCH (Peter), 2245.
MAURO (Frédéric), 1285, 7116.
Mauropous (John), 3136.
MAUSKOPF DELIYANNIS (D.), 3810.
Mauss (Marcell), 1440.
MAVCIC (Arne), 5392.
MAVROJANNIS (Theodoros), 2523.
MAVROMATIS (Lénos), 3065.
Maximus Planude, 3076.
Maximilian I von Habsburg, röm.-deutscher Kaiser, 3500.
Maximus Tyrius, 2085.
MAXWELL (Gordon S.), 1631.
MAXWELL (James Clerk), 6457, 6485.
MAXWELL (Robert L.), 197.
MAXWELL-HYSLOP (K. R.), 1788.
MAYAUD (Jean-Luc), 7252.
MAYER (Françoise), 8401.
MAYER (Jean), 1286.
Mayer (René), 8661.
MAYER (Wendy), 3048.
MAYER (Werner R.), 1841.
MAYER OLIVÉ (M.), 3203.
MAYERS (David), 8659.
MAYESKI (Marie Anne), 4353.
MAYHEW (N. J.), 7115.
MAYHEW (Nicholas), 303.
MAYO (Carlos A.), 4688.
MAYUZUMI (Hiromichi), 9046.
MAZARR (Michael), 8660.
MAŻEIKA (R.), 3375.
MAZHAR NOOR (Giovanni), 5660.
MAZZACANE (Aldo), 7536, 7649.
Mazzarino (Santo), 807.
MAZZEI (Marina), 2467.
MAZZINI (Innocenzo), 2575, 2737.
MAZZOCCA (Fernando), 5029.
MAZZOLENI (Danilo), 2933.
MAZZOLENI (Gilberto), 993, 1473.
Mazzoleni (Jole), 1087.
MAZZONI (Riccardo), 6960.
MAZZONIS (Filippo), 616.
MEADOWS (Eddie S.), 6949.
MEAGHER (R. M.), 2065.
MECHI (Lorenzo), 8661.
MECHOULAN (Eric), 8137.
Mechthild von Magdeburg, 4149, 4337.
MEDAGLIA (Mario), 1965.
MEDDA (E.), 2086.
MEDEROS MARTÍN (Alfredo), 1584.
MEDICK (Hans), 651, 7425.
MEDINA (Joao), 1131.
MEDING (Holger M.), 4691.
MEDNIKOVA (M. B.), 2647.
MEDVEDEV (Jurij M.), 1020.

MEEHAN (B.), 156.
MEEKS (Carroll L. V.), 6792.
MEGAW (Vincent), 1690.
MEHLMAN (Jeffrey), 6670.
MEHNERT (Ute), 8138.
MEIER (Heinrich), 6725, 7551.
MEIKLE (Jeffrey L.), 7180.
MEIKLE (S.), 2303.
MEILLET (Antoine), 356.
Meinecke (Friedrich), 808.
MEINEKE (Stefan), 808.
MEIRELES (Maria Adelaide), 243.
MEISIG (Marion), 5936.
MEISSNER (Andrzej), 5244.
MEIXNER (Wolfgang), 7349.
MEL'NIKOVA (Elena A.), 653.
MEL'TJUKHOV (Mikhail I.), 8266.
MELAMED (Daniel R.), 6887, 6950.
Melanchthon (Philip), 5868, 7935.
MELANÇON (Benoît), 6026.
MÉLANDRI (P.), 7750.
MELANDRI (Pierre), 8526.
MELBERG (Arne), 931.
MELE (Franca), 7650.
MÉLÈZE-MODRZEJEWSKI (J.), 1789.
MELIA (Trevor), 1359, 6454.
MELINZ (Gerhard), 5558.
MELIS (Guido), 7598.
MELJUKOVA (A. I.), 2009.
MELLOR (Ronald), 837.
MELVERN (Linda), 8662.
MELVILLE (Gert), 3466.
MELVILLE (Stephen), 726.
MELZER (Arthur M.), 904.
MENACHE (S.), 3971.
Menandros, 2288.
MENANT (François), 3764, 3812.
MENARD (P.), 3915.
MENCEL (Tadeusz), 5231.
Mendelssohn (Moses), 809.
MENDES DA COSTA MARTINS (Vitor Angelo), 8663.
MENDEZ SALCEDO (Ildefonso), 1132.
MENDL (Wolf), 8664.
MENDONCA (Manuela), 5282.
MENEGUS BORNEMANN (Margarita), 7261.
MENENDEZ PIDAL DE NAVASCUÉS (Faustino), 287.
MENESTÒ (Enrico), 4439.
MENGES (Evelyne Dominica), 5759.
MENICHETTI (Mauro), 2468.
MENJOT (D.), 4067.
MENN (Stephen Philip), 6308.
MENNELLA (Giovanni), 2930.
MENNINGER (Annerose), 7813.
MENNINGHAUS (Winfried), 6309.
MENON (Anand), 8665.
MENOZZI (Daniele), 5698.
MENTGEN (Gerd), 3536, 6027.

MENU (Michel), 1615.
MERCADO (Ruben Jose), 4689.
MERCER (Helen), 7117.
Mercier (Desiré), cardinal 5732.
MERCIER (Fabienne), 8267.
Mercier (Louis-Sébastien), 6608.
MEREDITH (David), 7804.
MERGER (Michele), 7188.
MERGLEN (Général), 8343.
MERIMSKIJ (Viktor A.), 4670.
MERKELBACH (R.), 1790.
MERLE (Gabriel), 4899.
MERLIN (Pierpaolo), 5028.
MERLINI (Stefano), 7599.
MERLO (Grado Giovanni), 5804.
MERLOTTI (Andrea), 439.
MERPERT (N. Ja.), 1668.
MERRAS (Merja), 1474.
MERRIAM (Louise Alice), 5586.
MERSCH (Andrea), 2418.
MEŚĆERJAKOV (A. N.), 1732.
MESKELL (Lynn), 1585.
MESSÍA (José Luis), 8666.
MESTERHÁZY (Károly), 3377.
MESTMÄCKER (Ernst-Joachim), 7024.
MESTRE GODES (Jesús), 4516.
MÉSZÁROS (István), 7025.
METZELTIN (M.), 4056.
METZIDAKIS (Stamos), 6528.
METZLER (Josef), 5712.
MEULDER (Marcel), 2799.
MEWES (Horst), 1201.
MEYER (Birgit), 4924.
MEYER (Christian), 157.
Meyer (Eduard), 810.
MEYER (Franz), 6835.
MEYER (Horst), 194.
MEYER (Jan-Waalke), 1873.
MEYER (Jean), 7332, 7917.
MEYER (K.), 3899.
MEYER (Kajsa), 3958.
MEYER-LENZ (Johanna), 7181.
MEYER-NOIREL (G.), 244.
MEYER-PETIT (Judith), 495.
MEYZA (Henryk), 2883.
MEZAKI (Tokue), 9047.
MEZEY (Barna), 7566.
MI (Yizhi), 8906.
MIASTKOWSKI (Leszko), 6124.
MICALE (Mark S.), 6458.
Michael Choniates, 3070.
Michael Italikos, 3122.
MICHAELIS DE MARBASIO, 4290.
MICHAILENKO (Valerij), 5344.
MICHAŁEK (Krzysztof), 5597.
MICHALEK (Slavomír), 8139.
MICHALIK (Jan), 1534.
MICHAŁOWSKA (Teresa), 4068.
MICHAUD (J.), 3202.
MICHAUD (Jean), 3228.

MICHAUD-FREJAVILLE (François), 3813.
MICHEL (Bernard), 8140.
MICHEL (Cécile), 1842.
MICHEL (Henri), 7579.
Michelangelo Buonarroti, 6852.
MICHELET (Jules), 811, 1212.
MICHELET (Louis-Christian), 8377.
MICHELETTA (Luca), 8141.
MICHELI (Gianni), 1346.
MICHON (P.), 4069.
MICHTA (Andrew A.), 5259.
Mickiewicz (Adam), 6701.
MICKWITZ (Joachim), 4845.
MIDDLEBROOK (Kevin J.), 5125.
MIDGETTE (Sally), 357.
MIEGGE (Mario), 656.
MIETHKE (Jürgen), 4411, 4354, 5715.
MIGEOTTE (Léopold), 2037.
MIGGIANO (Gabriella), 179.
MIGLIO (L.), 166.
MIGLIO (Massimo), 3304.
Mihai I, roi de Roumanie, 5295.
MIKASA (Takahito Prince), 1864.
MIKHUTINA (Irina V.), 8142.
MIKOCKI (Tomasz), 2896.
Mikoviny (Sámuel), 6497.
MIKRUT (Jan), 5760.
MIKUL'SKIJ (D. V.), 5399.
MILAN (Carlo), 8374.
MILANEZI (Silvia), 2373.
MILANO (E.), 103.
MILDE (Wolfgang), 4070.
MILES (Gary B.), 2800.
MILETTE (Nicole), 6793.
MILFORD (Karl), 7042.
MILHOU (Alain), 5623.
MILHOUS (Judith), 6959.
MILITAREV (A. Ju.), 1874.
Miljukov (Pavel N.), 812.
MILLA BATRES (Carlos), 1070.
MILLAR (F. G. B.), 2513.
MILLAR (Fergus), 2524.
Millelire (Agostino), 8000.
Millelire (Domenico), 8000.
MILLER (Alan S.), 1401.
MILLER (Andrew H.), 6672.
MILLER (Benjamin), 8667.
MILLER (Carman), 8046.
MILLER (Clarence H.), 6354.
MILLER (Edward), 3814.
MILLER (John), 4955.
MILLER (Joseph), 1250.
MILLER (Maureen C.), 3467.
MILLER (Norbert), 6763.
MILLER (Sanda), 6836.
MILLER (Simon), 5126.
MILLER (Timothy S.), 3157.
MILLER (Timothy), 1432.
MILLET (Olivier), 5842, 6311.

MILLIOT (Vincent), 414.
MILLWARD (Robert), 7333.
MILTON (Anthony), 5699.
MILTON (Sybil), 4800.
MILZA (Pierre), 4857, 7751.
MIMOUNI (Simon Claude), 3149.
MIN (Jie), 8907.
MINAMIKAWA (Takashi), 2651.
MINARINI (A.), 2737.
MINCHEV (Dimitur), 8268.
MINEAR (Larry), 7752.
MINEGISHI (Sumio), 9025.
MINEO (E. Igor), 3657.
MINERBI (Alessandra), 657.
MINGST (Karen A.), 8668.
Minicia Marcella, 2534.
MINNERATH (Roland), 2954.
MINNIS (A. J.), 4071.
MINNITI (Claudia), 1635.
MINNITI (Fortunato), 8378.
MINOIS (Georges), 6189.
MINUTI (Rolando), 658.
MINZONI-DÉROCHE (Angela), 1615.
MIRA BENAVENT (Javier), 6190.
MIRALLES MALDONADO (J. C.), 6572.
MIRAZITA (Iris), 3815.
MIRONOV (Konstantin Sergeevich), 510.
MIRZOEFF (Nicholas), 6754.
MISA (Thomas J), 5606.
Misch (Georg), 909.
MISTRETTA (Maria Beatrice), 4461.
MITANI (Takashi), 8908.
MITCHELL (Brian R.), 1288.
MITCHELL (Joshua), 6312.
MITCHELL (Maria), 4801.
MITCHELL (Sally), 7427.
Mithridatos VI Eupatoros, 2652.
MITRI (Tarek), 5937.
MITROVIC (Momcilo), 4727.
MITTAL (Satish Chandra), 659.
MITTELSTRASS (J.), 1515.
MITTERAND (Henri), 6529.
MITTERMAIER (Karl), 5030.
MITTERMAIR (Veronika), 5031.
Mitterrand (François), 8665.
MITTLER (E.), 199, 237.
MIURA (Tōru), 8811.
MIYAKE (Masaki), 932.
MIYAMOTO (Matao), 1137.
MIZUSHIMA (Tsukasa), 8817.
MLYN (Eric), 8669.
MŁYNARCZYK (Jolanta), 2883.
Mnesimachos, 2073.
MOCKAITIS (Thomas R.), 7814.
MODE (Markus), 1751.
MODIGLIANI (Anna), 3229.
MODONESI (Denise), 2525.
MODOOD (Tariq), 943, 943, 6241.
MOEGLIN (Jean-Marie), 3468.

MOELLER (Bernd), 4187.
MOELLER (E.), 4274.
MOESCHL (Joachim Robert), 7149.
MOGGI (Mauro), 2173.
MOGIL'NICKIJ (Boris G.), 1207.
MOGUS (Milan), 358.
MOHLER (Armin), 956.
MOHNHAUPT (Heinz), 1240.
MOHRS (Thomas), 1208.
MOISAN-JABŁOŃSKA (Krystyna), 6837.
MOKRZECKI (Lech), 6125.
MOLAS RIBALTA (Pere), XXII.
MOLENAT (Jea-Pierre), 3658.
MOLES (J. L.), 2304.
MOLETTE (Charles), 5700, 8408.
MOLEV (Evgenij A.), 2652.
MOLHO (Anthony), 3816.
Molière (Jean-Baptiste Poquelin), 6596, 6598, 6602, 6609.
MOLIS (Robert), 8047.
MOLLAY (Károly), 3817.
MÖLLENDORF (P. von), 2305.
MÖLLER (Anders Monrad), 4753.
MÖLLER (Astrid), 641.
MÖLLER (H.), 97.
MÖLLER (Hartmut), 4256.
MOLNÁR (András), 5559.
MOLNÁR (Antal), 5761.
MOLNÁR (Judit), 5560.
MOLODIN (V. I.), 1023, 1573.
Molotov (Viacheslav Mikhailovič Skryabin), 8327.
MOLTHAGEN (Joachim), 2653.
MOLYVIATI-TOPTSIS (Urania), 2576.
Momigliano (Arnaldo), 743, 813.
MOMMSEN (Hans), 4587, 4802.
Mommsen (Theodor), 814.
MOMMSEN (Wolfgang J.), 4803.
MOMSEN (Ingwer E.), 7149.
MONACI CASTAGNO (A.), 3004.
MONACO (Manuela), 1476.
MONALDINI (Sergio), 6951.
MONAR (Joerg), 8456.
MONCELON (Claire), 1502.
MONDRAIN (Brigitte), 245.
MONFASANI (John), 6573.
MONGARDINI (Carlo), 7590.
MONGILI (Alessandro), 1348.
Monnet (Jean), 8661.
MONNIER (Claire), 6537.
MONNIER (François), 7600.
MONNIER (Gerard), 6755.
MONNIER (Raymonde), 4900, 6028.
MONROE (C. R.), 1402.
MONSON (Don A.), 4072.
MONSTADT (Brigitte), 6838.
MONTACUTELLI (Maria), 4656.
MONTAGUE (Phillip), 6313.
Montaigne (Michel Eyquem de), 1022, 6025, 6311, 6542, 6544.

Montale (Eugenio), 6702.
MONTANA (Fausto), 2087.
MONTANA (Franco), 3064.
MONTANARI (Enrico), 1477.
MONTANARI (F.), 2306.
MONTANER FRUTOS (Alberto), 288.
MONTARDT I BOFARULL (Núria), 3198.
MONTE (Lucia), 6673.
MONTECCHI (G.), 220.
MONTEGUALDO ROBLEDO (María-Pilar), 7428.
Montelius (Oscar), 6074.
MONTERO (J. L.), 1669.
MONTERO (Manuel), 7182.
MONTERO (Santiago), 2843.
MONTERO RUIZ (Ignacio), 1660.
MONTES DE OCA NAVAS (Elvia), XIV.
MONTESANO (Marina), 4517.
Montesquieu (Charles Luis de), 815, 1213, 6265, 7542, 7543.
MONTGOMERY (Ingun), 1390.
MONTIAS (John Michael), 6839.
MOON (W. G.), 2426.
MOONEY (Linne R.), 3905, 4073.
MOORE (Alex), 8670.
MOORE (Bob), 7815, 8344.
MOORE (John C.), 3239.
MOORE (Keith), 440.
Moore (Marianne), 6830.
MOORE (Mary B.), 2419.
MOORHEAD (J.), 4518.
MORA (Clelia), 1858.
MORA (Fabio), 1478.
MORA (Gloria), 1575.
MORALES (Juan Antonio), 4723.
MORAND (A.-F.), 2071.
MORANDI (Alessandro), 2500.
MORANDI (Massimo), 2501.
MORANDI (Ubaldo), 3306.
Moravia (Alberto), 6632.
MORAWIECKI (Lesław), 2897.
MORDEK (Hubert), 3230, 4226.
More (Thomas), 6314, 6354, 6597.
MOREAU (Alain), 2374.
MOREIRA (Rafael), 5628.
MORELLE (Laurent), 3659.
MORELLET (André), 1177.
MORELLI (Marcello), 110.
MORELLO (G.), 143.
MORELLO (Giovanni), 5762.
MORENO (José Luis), 4690.
MORENO FRAGINALS (Manuel), 8049.
MORENZONI (Franco), 3818.
MOREROD (J.-D.), 4519.
MORESCHINI (Claudio), 2768, 2844.
MORETON (Jennifer), 264.
MORETTI (G.), 4133.
MOREWOOD (Steven), 7046.

MORGAN (Harry), 6126.
MORGAN (Kevin), 4935.
MORGAN (Llewelyn), 2577.
MORGAN (Nicole), 6314.
MORGAN (Peggy), 1403.
Morgenthau (Henry), 8683.
MORICE (Anne-Marie), 6781.
MORICEAU (Jean-Marc), 542, 601.
MORIKAWA (Hidemasa), 1137.
MORILLO (Stephen), 1134.
MORIMOTO (Yoshiki), 3819.
MORINEAU (Marta), 7114, 7253.
MORISHITA (Toru), 9048.
MORLET (Marie-Thérèse), 3820.
MORNATI (Lorenzo), 5032.
MORNET (Elisabeth), 3713.
MORO (Renato), 783.
Morone (Giovanni), 5690.
MORONI STAMPA (L.), 3514.
MOROZOV (Nikolaj N.), 5298.
MORPHET (Sally), 8671.
MORRELL (Gordon W.), 7753.
MORRELL (J. B.), 7183.
MORRIS (Christine), 2005.
MORRIS (Nancy), 5272.
MORRIS (Rosemary), 3150.
MORRIS (Sarah P.), 1994, 6840.
MORRISEY (Charles), 8143.
MORRISON (James C.), 6315.
MORSEY (R.), 661.
MORTENSÖN (Ole), 7226.
MORTIER (Roland), 6841.
MORUJÃO (Isabel), 5787.
MORWOOD (M. J.), 1644.
Mosca (Gaetano), 7590.
MOSCATI (Laura), 7544.
MOSELEY (Fred), 7014, 7026.
MOSELLE (Boaz), 7429.
Möser (Justus), 7451.
MOSETTIG (Ivan), 5067.
MOSHER STUARD (Susan), 3821.
MOSIICI (Luciana), 68.
MOSK (Carl), 5055.
MOSS (Michael), 7119.
MOSSAKOWSKI (Stanisław), 1479.
MOSSAY (Justin), 2935.
MOSSMAN (J.), 2307.
MOSTERT (Marco), 493.
MOTHE (Francis), 7099.
MOTIKA (Raoul), 1168.
MOTYL (Alexander J.), 8672.
MOTZ (Lloyd), 6500.
MOULAERT (Jan), 4720.
MOULINIER (Jean-Claude), 3307.
MOULINIER (Laurence), 4074.
MOUNTJOY (Penelope A.), 2010.
MOUREAUX (José-Michel), 1209.
MOURGUES (Jean-Louis), 2038.
MOUSALIMAS (S. A.), 5828.
MOUSSA (Bantenga), 7184.
MOUSSA (Sarga), 6674.

MOUSSAOUI-EL-KECHAI (Fella), 7288.
MOUSTAFA (Ahmed), 4175 a).
MOUTON (Marie-Renée), 8144.
MOYER (Lourence), 8145.
MOYSIDOU (Jasmine), 3151.
Mozart (Wolfgang Amadeus), 6906, 6924, 6938, 6973.
MOZZARELLI (Cesare), 1222.
MROCZKO (Teresa), 4198.
MROZEWICZ (Leszek), 1969.
MU (Qin), 8909.
MUCCHIELLI (Laurent), 662.
MÜDERR/SOĞLU (Fatih), 7335.
MUDRA (Miroslav), 5487.
MUELLER (R. C.), 7289.
MUGGLESTONE (Lynda), 359.
MUGIONE (Eliana), 2420.
Muhammad, 679.
MÜHLE (Robert W.), 8146.
MUIR (Edward), 6029.
MUIR (Lynette R.), 4075.
MUIR WRIGHT (Rosemary), 4227.
MUKOOZA SEJJENG (James), 5535.
MULDER-BAKKER (Anneke B.), 4076.
Müller (Adolf), 4808.
MÜLLER (Andreas E.), 3139.
MÜLLER (Christian), 1210.
MÜLLER (E. Maria), 3822.
MULLER (Franck), 5633.
MÜLLER (Friedhelm L.), 2553.
MÜLLER (G.), 1499.
MÜLLER (H.), 3255.
MÜLLER (Hans-Peter), 1914.
MÜLLER (Klaus-Jürgen), 7754, 8623.
MÜLLER (Konrad), 2587.
MÜLLER (Manfred), 1843.
MÜLLER (Rainer A.), 3823, 4633.
MÜLLER (Stefan), 2308.
MÜLLER (Ulrich), 1552.
MULLER (Walter), 2019.
MÜLLER (Wolfgang P.), 3308.
MULLETT (M.E.), 3152.
MULVEY ROBERTS (Marie), 1559.
MUNCK (Gerardo L.), 8673.
MUND-DOPCHIE (M.), 2088.
MUNDT (Robert J.), 1135.
MUNENE (Macharia), 7878.
MUNK OLSEN (Birger), 3961, 4077.
MUNONO MUYEMBE (Bernard), 5805.
MUÑOZ FERNÁNDEZ (Ángela), 4520.
MÜNSTERMANN (Hans), 2802.
Müntzer (Thomas), 656, 1214.
Murads III, sultano ottomano, 3510.
MURAI (Shōsuke), 8808, 9025.
Muratori (Ludovico Antonio), 817.
MURDOCH (B.), 4521.

MURDOCK (Carl J.), 4746.
MURFETT (Malcom M.), 8674.
MURIALDI (Paolo), 6191.
MURILLO (Luis E.), 8675.
MURIN (Jurij G.), 5412.
MURKEN (Jan), 4928.
Muromachi (Bakufu), 9029.
MURPH (Roxane C.), 3516.
MURPHY (David J.), 2089.
MURPHY (Michael), 6127.
MURPHY (Philip), 7879.
MURRAY (A. T.), 2080.
MURRAY (Alan V.), 553, 3338.
MURRAY (E. B.), 6697.
MURRAY (James), 69.
MURRAY (O.), 1273.
MURRELL (Kathleen Berton), 6794.
MUSACCHIO (Alberto), 1645.
MUSARRA (Franco), 6704.
MUSIL (Jiri), 5488.
MUSIL (Michal), 5489.
MUSILOVÁ (Dana), 4634.
MUSISI (Nakanyika), 5535.
MUSK (Bill A.), 5938.
MÜSSE (Wolfgang), 6192.
MUSSO (Olimpio), 3039.
Mussolini (Benito), 5027, 5030, 5711.
MUSSON (C. R.), 4542.
MUTAFCHIEVA (Vera P.), 4740.
MUYLLE (Marianne), 496.
MYERS (David N.), 663.
MYERS (Richard), 815.
MYHRE (Jon E.), 643.
MYLONAKI (Ioanna), 4930.
Myrsilus of Methymna, 2090.

N

NA'AMAN (Nadav), 1915.
NABER (Jaak), 7918.
Nabuco (Joaquim), 818.
NABYWANIEC (Stanisław), 5763.
NADAL CAÑELLAS (Juan), 3063.
NÄF (Beat), 2729, 2803.
NAFISSI (Massimo), 2375, 2464.
NAGATA (Yuzo), 5522.
NAGY (Ferenc), 5561.
Nagy (Imre), 5569.
NAGY (József), 5562.
NAIMARK (Norman M.), 8676.
NAISH (Emily), 6460.
NAKAMURA (Masanori), 8737.
NAKAMURA (Mitsuo), 1875.
NAKANISHI (H.), 8147.
NAKANO (Tadashi), 7519.
NALDINI (Mario), 2936, 4078, 4151.
NAMAZOVA (A. S.), 4648.
Namier (L. B.), 819.
NAMOWICZ (Tadeusz), 6316.

Napoléon Ier, empereur de France, 1919, 6615, 6826, 7975, 7976, 7977, 7978, 7979, 7980, 7988, 7994, 7999, 8001, 8005.
NAPOLITANO (Antonio), 7668.
NARDI (Carlo), 2934.
NARINSKIJ (Mikhail M.), 8677.
NARKISS (B.), 160.
NASH (Philip), 8678.
NAß (Klaus), 4079.
NASSI (Enrico), 5713.
NASSIET (Michel), 1349.
NASSON (Bill), 5457, 8148.
NASTRI (Giuseppe G.), 8679.
NATALI (C.), 2216.
NAUERT (Charles G. jr.), 6031.
NAUTA (L.), 796.
NAVA (Carmen), 4735.
NAVARRETE (Maria Cristina), 7430.
NAVARRO (G.), 3787.
NAVET (Georges), 1212.
NAVRÁTIL (Jaromír), 8784.
NAWROCKI (Stanisław), 8290.
NDAYE (Pap), 6462.
NEĆAS (Ctibor), 5490.
NEŽINSKIJ (L. N.), 8748.
NEŽINSKIJ (Leonid N.), 8682.
NEAGOE (Sever), 8346.
NEAL (Aubrey), 933.
NEAL (Lucinda Jane), 6953.
NEAUD (Pierrette M.), 1213.
NECIPOĞLU (Gürlu), 3565.
NECK (Rudolf), 7571.
NEDELMANN (Birgitta), 7606.
NEDERMAN (Cary J.), 4355.
NEDREBØ (Tore), 4637.
NEEDELL (Jeffrey D.), 780, 843.
NEEDLER (Martin C.), 5127.
NEES (Lawrence), 4188.
NEGRETTO (Gabriel L.), 6317.
NEGRI (Giovanni), 2699.
NEGRUZZO (Simona), 6071.
NEHAMAS (A.), 2091.
NEILLANDS (Robin), 8379.
NEILS (Jenifer), 2421.
NEILSON (Keith), 7755.
NEIRYNCK (F.), 1377.
NELSON (Angela Marie S.), 6954.
NELSON (Claudia), 6675.
NELSON (H.), 7811.
NELSON (Janet L.), 3420.
NELSON (Keith L.), 8680.
NELSON (Robert S.), 3153.
NELSON LIMERICK (Patricia), 665.
NELSON WHITE (Eugene), 7290.
NĚMEČEK (Jan), 8270.
NEMESKÜRTY (István), 5563.
NÉMETH (György), 1978.
NEMET-NEJAT (Karen R.), 1844.
NEMIROVSKIJ (E. L.), 161.
NENCI (Giuseppe), 2578.

NENNA (Marie-Dominique), 2402.
NENNER (Howard), 7601.
NEQUIRITO (Mauro), 3660.
NERI (Camillo), 1965.
NERI (Francesca), 6517.
Neri da Rimini, 162.
NERI SERNERI (Simone), 5033, 8409.
Nero (Claudius Caesar), imperatore romano, 2650.
NERSESOV (Ja. N.), 9116.
NESBITT (John), 3157.
NEUGEBAUER-MARESCH (Christine), 1642.
NEUJAHR (Philip J.), 6318.
NEUMANN (Hans), 1839.
NEUMANN (Hans-Joachim), 5872.
NEUMANN (Iver B.), 7757.
NEUMANN (U.), 2309.
NEUNER ANTJE (Maria), 6843.
NEUSNER (Jacob), 1979.
NEVAER (Louis E. V.), 8681.
NEVAKIVI (Jukko), 4841, 8271.
NEVILLE (John F.), 6193.
Nevsky (Alexander), 5329.
NEWCOMBE (Hanna), 8534.
NEWLANDS (Carole E.), 2804.
NEWMAN (Barbara), 4080.
Newman (John Henry), Kardinal, 5747, 5776.
NEWMAN (William R.).
NEWSINGER (John), 4998.
NEWTON (Francis), 4330.
Newton (Isaac), 656, 6379.
NGALAMULUME (Kalala), 666.
NGIEN (Dennis), 5873.
NÍ CHATÁIN (Próinséas), 3384.
NIBLO (Stephen R.), 7758.
NICASTRI (Luciano), 2756, 3924.
NICCOLAI (Nadi), 7602.
NICCOLI (Ottavia), 5034.
Niccolò de' Conti, 955.
Niccolò l'Arena, Sanctus, 3760.
NICGORSKI (Ann M.), 2422.
NICHOLAS (David), 3824.
NICHOLAS (Stephen), 7404.
NICHOLLS (David), 5661.
NICHOLLS (Mark), 4956.
NICHOLS (Aidan), 5829.
NICHOLS (Francis W.), 5662.
NICHOLS (Johanna), 329.
NICHOLSON (Oliver), 1956.
NICIEJA (Stanisław Sławomir), 5252.
NICO OTTAVIANI (Maria Grazia), 3661.
NICOLAI (Roberto), 2310.
NICOLAISEN (W. F. H.), 3381.
NICOLAU (Juan Carlos), 4692.
NICOLET-PIERRE (Hélène), 2199.
NICOLINI (S.), 215.
NICOLL (W. S. M.), 2098.
NICOLLIER (Béatrice), 5843.

NICOLLIER-DE WECK (Beatrice), 7935.
Nicomachus Flavianus, 2533.
NIDITCH (Susan), 1916.
Niebuhr (Reinhold), 5658.
NIEDER (Ludwig), 5998.
NIEDERER (Arnold), 994.
NIEDERHAUSER (Emil), 667, 1136.
NIEDERKORN (Jan P.), 7936.
NIEDERSTÄTTER (Alois), 3502.
NIEDHART (Gottfried), 4944.
NIEHAUS (Jeffrey Jay), 1916.
NIELSEN (Anne Marie), 2900.
NIELSEN (Michael Charles), 7520.
NIEMANN (Harry), 7162.
NIEPER (Franz), 7663.
NIEß (Ulrich), 3499.
NIETHAMMER (Lutz), 4587.
NIETO (F. J. Fernandez), 2142.
NIETO IBÁÑEZ (Jesús-María), 2836.
NIETO SORIA (José Manuel), 3503.
Nietzsche (Friedrich Wilhelm), 6684.
NIEWĘGŁOWSKI (Andrzej), 1586.
NIGDELIS (Pantelis M.), 2039.
NIGHTINGALE (A. W.), 2311.
Niketas Choniates, 3136.
NIKITINA (Tat'jana N.), 4931.
NIKLÍČEK (Ladislav), 4638.
NIKOLAEVSKII (Boris Ivanovich), 8150.
Nikolaos von Damaskos, 820.
Nikolaj I Romanov, imperatore di Russia 5346, 5356.
NIKONOV (Aleksandr A.), 7254.
NIKZENTAITIENE (Roma), 8072.
NILSSON (Ann-Marie), 4257.
NILSSON (Carl-Axel), 7063.
NINCI (Renzo), 3871.
NIPPEL (Wilfried), 2654.
Niqueux (Michel), 1202.
NIRENBERG (David), 1138.
NISHIHARA (Masashi), 8580.
NISHIKAWA (Nagao), 7353.
NISHIMURA (Shizuya), 7291.
NISKANEN (Kirsti), 7255.
NISTICÒ (R.), 1554.
NITOBURG (Éduard L.), 5663.
NITSCHKE (August), 3825.
NITSCHKE (Peter), 1214.
Nixon (Richard Milhous), 5607.
NIZET (Jean), 5984.
NOBEL (Jaap W.), 8683.
NOBLE (Thomas F. X.), 4415, 4424.
Nobre de Gusmao (Artur), 6737.
NOCHLIN (Linda), 6756, 6844.
NOE (Eralda), 2700.
NOEL (W.), 164.
NOGRADY (Árpád), 3469.
NOIRIEL (Gérard), 4639.
NOLAN (Peter), 8684.
NOLLA (Josep M.), 2867.

NOLTE (Hans-Heinrich), 1289.
NOMURA (Tadao), 9052.
Nonnos, 2092.
Norby (Sören), 7827.
NORBY (Trond), 643.
NORDBERG (Michael), 3379.
NORDLINGER (Eric A.), 8685.
NORELLI (Enrico), 3005.
Noriega Morena (Manuel Antonio), 8675.
NORLAND (Howard B.), 6574.
NORMAN (Diana), 4125, 6757.
NÖRR (Knut Wolfgang), 3662.
NORTH (John D.), 4356.
NORTH (Michael), 6186.
NORTH (Robert), 1427.
NORTON (Bruce), 7029.
NOSARTI (Lorenzo), 2579.
NOUAILHAT (Y.-H.), 8151.
NOUSCHI (André), 4678.
NOVIK (Faina I.), 8686.
NOVOPAŠIN (Jurij S.), 4640.
NOVOSSELOFF (Alexandre), 8687.
NOWAK (Tadeusz Marian), 1350.
NOWAK (Zenon Hubert), 3396, 4453.
NOWIŃSKI (Franciszek), 5253.
NOWICKA (Ewa), 5874.
NOY (David), 3218.
NOZAKI (Naoji), 3826.
NUGENT (Deniel), 5122.
NUOVO (Isabella), 3279.
NUSSBAUM (Felicity), 6604.
NUTI (L.)., 8688.
NUTTON (Vivian), 4357, 6464.
NWOSU (Ikechi Nwachukwu), 5939.
NYLANDER (Carl), 814.
NYSÆTER (Egil), 613.

O

Ó CORRÁIN (Donnchadh), 3421.
O'BALLANCE (Edgar), 4726.
O'BRIEN (John).
O'BRIEN (Patrick K.), 7120.
O'CARROLL (Maura), 4450.
O'CONNELL (James), 1602, 1616.
O'CONNOR (Edward G.), 8050.
O'CROININ (Daibhi), 3380.
O'DAY (Alan), 4999.
O'FAHEY (R. S.), 1540.
O'GORMAN (Richard), 3914.
O'GRADA (Cormac), 7121.
O'HAGAN (J. W.), 5000.
O'KANE (Rosemary H. T.), 4700.
O'KEEFE BAZZONI (Jana), 6908.
O'MEARA (John J.), 4285.
O'NEILL (B. C.), 8562.
O'REILLY (Kenneth), 5607.
O'SULLIVAN (Neil), 2143.

Oakeshott (Michael), 6373.
OBENG (Pashington), 9079.
ÖBERG (Jan), 3309.
OBERKOFLER (Gerhard), 849, 6072.
OBERLY (James W.), 5586.
OBERMAIER (Sabine), 4082.
OBRIST (Barbara), 4358.
OCCHIATO (Giuseppe), 3154.
OCHIENG (W. R.), 7880.
OCHMAN (Jerzy), 3537.
OCHOA DE OLZA EGUIRAN (Esperanza), 287.
OCHSENBEIN (P.), 10, 97.
OCKHAM (William of), 4293, 4321.
ODANAKA (Naoki), 4901.
ODED (Arye), 5536.
Òdena (José Trenchs), 821.
ODINCOV (Mikhail I.), 5413.
ÖDMAN (Per-Johan), 1351.
ÓDOR (Imre), 5564.
ODORICO (Paolo), 3065.
ODYNIEC (Wacław), 5254.
OELSNER (Joachim), 1845.
OEXLE (Otto Gerhard), 655, 668, 4083.
OGBAJIE (Chukwu), 5940.
OGILVIE (Denise), 428.
OGONOWSKI (Zbigniew), 6319.
OGOT (B. A.), 7880.
OGRIS (Alfred), 5185.
OGUCHI (Yujiro), 9053.
OHANA (David), 5005.
ŌHASHI (Nobuya), 9054.
OHLMEYER (Jane), 4996.
OHNHEISER (Ingeborg), 6066.
OIKONOMIDÈS (Nicolas), 3046, 3086.
OISHIO (Chihiro), 9055.
OJAIDE (Tanure), 6676.
OKTAR (Tiğinçe Özkiper), 7122.
OLÁBARRI (Ignacio), 935.
OLAI (Ericus), 3309.
OLÁVARRI (E.), 1670.
OLCZAK (Jerzy), 4430.
OLDEN (Anthony), 466.
OLDFIELD (John R.), 4957.
OLDRINI (Guido), 669.
OLEART (Oriol), 3664.
OLEF-KRAFFT (F.), 4084.
OLENDER (Piotr), 8051.
OLENHUSEN (Irmtraud Gotz von), 5785.
OLESEN (Thorsten B.), 8600.
Oliveira Martins (Joaquim Pedro de), 670.
OLIVER (Bobbie), 4707.
OLIVER (Judith), 165.
OLIVERA SERRANO (Cesar), 3665.
OLIVI (Bino), 8690.
OLLILA (Anne), 7433.
OLMEADOWS (Harry), 1481.

OLMEDO BERNAL (Santiago), 7761.
OLMO (Carlo), 7308.
OLNEY (Richard John), 1067.
OLSON (Paul A.), 4086.
OLSON (S. D.), 2312.
OLSSON (Kent), 7123.
OLSSON (Lars), 7256.
OMEL'ĆENKO (Nikolaj A.), 5414.
Omodeo (Adolfo), 822.
OMOSINI (Olufemi), 671.
ONIGA (Renato), 2805.
ÖNNERFORS (Alf), 2600.
OOSTERBOSCH (Michel), 69.
OPATRNÝ (Josef), 5097.
OPLL (Ferdinand), 936.
OPPELLAND (Torsten), 8152.
OPPERMAN (Hal), 6845.
ÓRAWSKA-WITKOWSKA (Alina), 6986.
ORBELL (Margaret), 9122.
ORCHARD (Andy), 4087.
Ordericus Vitalis, 3335.
ORESME (NICOLAUS), 4292, 4311.
Orff (Carl), 6934.
ORGANSKI (A. F. Kenneth), 1290.
ORIGENÉS, 2938.
ORIS (Michel), 1064.
ORLANDI (Giovanni), 6530.
ORLOV (Ju. G.), 7660.
ORLOVA (L. A.), 1666.
ORMAZABAL (Kepa M.), 7031.
ORME (Nicholas), 3827, 4089.
ORMOS (Mária), 8102.
ORMSBY-LENNON (Hugh), 1559.
ORNATO (Ezio), 149.
ORNATO (Monique), 173.
ORNEA (Zigu), 5299.
OROSIUS (PAULUS), 2750.
OROSZ (István), 5565.
ORSKI (Marek), 8274.
ORTALLI (Gherardo), 3828.
ORTAYLI (İlber), 1291, 5523.
ORTEGA CANADELL (Rosa), XXII.
ORTEGA PEREZ (Pascual), 3470.
ORTOLEVA (Vincenzo), 3075.
Orzechowski (Stanisław), 6588.
OSHIRO (Terumasa), 1876.
OSIANDER (Andreas), 7762.
OSOKINA (Elena A.), 5416.
OSTAPENKO (Galina S.), 4641.
ÖSTERBERG (Eva), 970, 7434.
OSTERHAMMEL (Jürgen), 7816.
OSTORERO (Martine), 3829.
OSTOS SALCEDO (Pilar), 49.
OSWALD (Donald J.), 7032.
OTÁHAL (Milan), 672, 7521.
OTOREPEC (Božo), 3310.
OTRANTO (Giorgio), 3006.
ŌTSUKA (Kazuo), 9103.
OTT (Joachim), 2730.
OTTE (Marcel), 1617.

OTTE (T. G.), 8052.
OTTEN (Heinrich), 1877.
OTTO (A. C.), 937.
Otto III, röm.-deutscher Kaiser, 3449.
OTTONE (Gabriella), 2376.
OTTOSEN (Kristian), 8272, 8275.
OUDIN-DOGLIONI (Catherine), 6788.
OULMONT (Philippe), 315.
OURSEL (Raymond), 4228.
OUSTERHOUT (R.), 3155.
OUSTERHOUT (Robert G.), 4190, 5830.
Ouy (Gilbert), 173.
OVERBECK (Franz), 1482.
OVERESCH (Manfred), 4806.
OVERGAAUW (Eef), 30.
OVERLAET (Bruno), 1957.
OVERY (Richard), 8380.
Ovidius Naso (Publius), 2580, 2581, 2582, 2583, 2752, 2757, 2769, 2773, 2804, 2806, 2822, 3924, 3968, 4141, 4153, 6567.
OVIEDO (Jose Miguel), 1555.
Owen (Dorothy M.), 4410.
Owen (John), 5861.
OWEN (Laura J.), 7124.
OWEN (Thomas C.), 7125.
OWEN HUGHES (Diane), 968.
OXHORN (Philiph D.), 4747.
ÖZ (Baki), 71.
OZ (Manuel Ferrer), 7905.
OZANNE (Henriette), 393.
ÖZCAN (Abdulkadir), 5513, 5524.
ÖZCAN (Besim), 7763.
ÖZDEM/R (Rifat), 5525, 7435.
ÖZKARCI (Mehmet), 6795.
ÖZKORUCUKLU (Hilmi), 1754.
OŻÓG (Krzysztof), 3504.
OZOUF (Mona), 6678.
OZTÜRK (Yücel), 1292.

P

PAASI (Anssi), 7764.
Paasikivi (J. K.), 8288.
PACAUT (Marcel), 8053.
PACE (Enzo), 5035.
PACH (Zsigmond Pál), 3830.
PACHECO FERNANDEZ (Daniel), 6395.
PACHECO-BORGES (V.), 8153.
PACI (G.), 31.
PACI (Gianfranco), 2781.
Pacifico di Verona, 824.
PACINI (Arturo), 4656.
PACIOCCO (R.), 4522.
PACKULL (Werner O.), 5875.
PAĆKO (Teresa), 384.
PACZKOWSKI (Andrzej), 5255.

PACZYŃSKA (Irena), 5229.
PADBERG (Gabriele), 6758.
PADBERG (Lutz E. von), 4523.
PADEL (Ruth), 1353.
PADOA SCHIOPPA (Antonio), 1241, 3617, 3667.
PADOVANI (Andrea), 3232.
PAGDEN (Anthony), 7817.
PAGE (Arthur L), 8410.
PAGE (R. I.), 167.
PAGE (Raymond Ian), 3587.
PAGEL (Jgen), 4642.
PAGNINI (Alessandro), 1523, 6329.
PAGNOTTA (L.), 3311.
PAIDAR (Parvin), 5205.
PAILHES (Claudine), 7603.
PAILLER (Jean-Marie), 2845.
Paisey (David L.), 226.
PAJĄKOWSKI (Włodzimierz), 1969.
PAJEWSKI (Janusz), 5256.
PAJKOSSY (Gábor),, 6194.
PAL (Josef), 6517.
PALACIOS MARTIN (Bonifacio), 3668, 4359.
PALAIRET (M.), 7257.
PALASIK (Mária), 5566.
PALENCIA HERREJON (Juan Ramón), 3831.
PÁLFFY (Géza), 5567.
PALLADINO (Franco), 6421.
Pallavicini (Opitius), 5740.
PALLECCHI (Pasquino), 1646.
PALLOT (James), 6952.
PALMER (Bryan), 6320.
PALMER (John Joseph N.), VIII.
Palmerston (Henry John Temple), 8017.
PALMIERI (Stefano), 3242.
PALOTÁS (Emil), 8054.
PALSDOTTIR (Sigrun), 7436.
PALUDAN (Helge), 4090.
PAŁUSZYŃSKI (Tomasz), 8154.
PAMMER (Michael), 6465.
PAMUK (Şevket), 7200, 8055.
PANAYI (Panikos), 7437.
PANAYOTAKIS (C.), 2807.
PANCIERA (Silvio), 2526.
PANECKI (Tadeusz), 8276.
PANELLA (Emilio), 3312.
PANELLA (Maria Antonietta), 484.
PANERO (Francesco), 3471.
PANFILOV (A. N.), 1573.
PANFILOWITSCH (Igor), 6679.
PANIAGUA PÉREZ (José Pablo), 1614.
PANIKKAR (K. N.), 7833.
PANIMOLLE (Salvatore A.), 2939.
Panissaro (Gregorio), 3234.
Pannunzio (Mario), 5988.
PANOURGIA (Eleni Neni K.), 1042.
PANOVSKA (Liljana), 5110.
Pantaleoni (Maffeo), 6998.

PANTELI (Stavros), 1141.
PANTELIC (Bratislav), 322.
PANTIN (Isabelle), 6576.
PANZA (Marco), 938, 6480.
PANZAC (D.), 5526.
PANZERA (Fabrizio), 5029.
PAOLI (Emore), 4439.
Paolino da Venezia, 3331.
Paolino di Nola, 2820.
PAPACHRYSSANTHIOU (Denise), 3046.
PAPACOSMA (Victor), 8692.
PAPADOPOULOS (Stratis), 2423.
PAPAGIANNAKES (Eleutherios), 7765.
PAPARIZOS (Antonios), 2218.
PAPATHOMOPOULOS (Manolis), 3076.
Papay (Gyula), 1340.
Papen (Franz von), 8111.
Papini (Giovanni), 6665.
PAPINI (M.), 5764.
PAPINI (Roberto), 5688.
PAPPAS (Nickolas), 1215.
Paracelsus, 6510.
PARADISO (Annalisa), 673.
PARAVICINI (Werner), 3186, 3832.
PARAVICINI BAGLIANI (Agostino), 4318, 4425, 4524, 5807.
PARCERO OUBIÑA (César), 1688.
PARDO RODRÍGUEZ (María Luisa), 49.
PARDOE (Colin), 1618.
PARENS (Joshua), 4360.
PARENTE (Anna Rita), 2469.
PARENTI (Adonella Barbara), 498.
Pareto (Vilfredo), 6009, 6998.
PARFITT (Keith), 1709.
PARISE (Nicola F.), 2424.
PARISSE (Michel), 3833.
PARKER (David S.), 5216.
PARKER (Dick), 5098.
PARKER (G.), 4655.
PARKER (Geoffrey), 7809.
PARKER (Peter), 1558.
PARKER (R. A. C.), 4965.
PARKER (Victor), 1752, 2144.
PARKER-WAKEFIELD (Maurice), 5831.
PARKINSON (R. B.), 1791.
PARLATO (Giuseppe), 5029.
PARMAR (Inderjeet), 8277.
Parmenides, 2356.
PAROLA (G.), 492.
PAROLI (Teresa), 1699, 4091.
PARPOLA (Simo), 1733.
PARR (Joy), 939.
PARRATT (John), 5941.
PARRY (Graham), 674.
PARSONS (David), 3587.
PARSONS (Sir Anthony), 8693.

PARVEV (Ivan), 7965.
PASAK (Tomáš), 8278, 8279.
Pascal (Blaise), 6377.
PASCHALIS (Michael), 2584.
PASCHE (Véronique), 4524, 5807.
PASCHOUD (François), 2808.
PASCUA ECHEGARAY (Esther), 3472.
PASETZKY (Gilda), 8002.
PASKOFF (Roland), 9086.
PASQUALINI (Maria Gabriella), 8280.
PASQUIER (Etienne), 825, 6577.
PASSELECQ (Georges), 5716.
Passy, (André Dewavrin, dit), colonel, 8297.
PASTA (Renato), 6195.
PASTENA (C.), 247.
Pasteur (Louis), 6402.
PASTEUR (Yvan), 1149.
PASTOR (Reyna), 3834.
PASTOR (Rodolfo F.), 675.
PASTOR BORGOÑÓN (H.), 1689.
PASTORE (Alessandro), 3617.
PASTOUREAU (Michel), 168.
PASZKE (Andrzej), 7185.
Paszkiewicz (Henryk), 957.
PATAKFALVI (Endre), 6796.
PATAR (Benoît), 4292.
PATEK (Artur), 5765.
PÁTEK (Jaroslav), 7070, 7127.
PATELL (Cyrus R. K.), 1532.
PATERSON (Thomas G.), 8694.
PATILLON (M.), 2104.
PATIN (Maurice), 7651.
PATRIARCA (Fátima), 5283.
PATRICH (Joseph), 3007, 3156.
PATRUŠEV (A. I.), 6299.
PATRUŠEV (Aleksandr I.), 800.
PATTANAIK (P.), 7062.
PATTEN (A.), 6321.
PATTEN (Robert L.), 241.
PATTERSON (Thomas C.), 644.
PATZOLD (Detlev), 6322.
PAUL (Gerhard), 4807.
PAULÍK (Jan), 8695.
PAULMANN (Johannes), 7258.
PAULSEN (Ivar Bjarne), 7438.
PAULSSON (Gunnar S.), 4755.
Paulus, Sanctus, 223, 2992, 3024.
Paulus Alexandrinus, 3083.
Paulus Diaconus, 3272.
Paulus V, Papa, 6730.
Paulus VI, Papa, 5714.
PAUSZ (Josef), 5876.
PAVIOT (J.), 7672.
PAVIOT (Jacques), 3505.
PAVLIK (Jan), 5808.
PAVLOV (Anatolij G.), 8281.
PAVLOV (Plamen), 4743.
PAVLOVSKAJA (A. I.), 2219.
PAYEN (Pascal), 1984.
PAYNE (Beverly Carron), 9119.

Payne (Joseph), 6085.
PAYNE (R. L.), 3908.
PAYNE (Richard J.), 8696.
PAZDERNIK (Charles F.), 2095.
PEACH (T.), 6578.
PEARCE (Mark), 794.
PEARCE (Susan Mary), 499.
PEARSON (R.), 7128.
PEASE (G. Y. Franklin), 9117.
PECERE (Oronzo), 3282, 3313.
PECHATNOV (Vladimir Olegovich), 8697.
PECHERSKAYA (Natalia A.), 5832.
PECKA (Jindřich), 5491, 8283, 8381, 8450.
PECORARI (Paolo), 7280.
PECORELLA (Corrado), 1242.
PEDERSEN (Henry), 6128.
PEDONE (Antonio), 7589.
PEDRAZZI (Marco), 8698.
Pedro I, rey de Castilla, 3493.
Pedro I, rey de Catalunya, 3517.
Pedro IV, rey de Aragón, 3668.
PEDRONI (Luigi), 2527, 2731.
PEERS (Douglas M.), 4981, 7834.
Péguy (Charles), 826.
Pekař (Josef), 5485.
PELAGATTI (Paola), 311.
PELAQUIER (Elie), 7579.
PELCKMANS (Paul), 6631.
PELCZAR (Roman), 6129.
PELIKAN (Jaroslav Jan), 6680.
Pélissier (Jean), 8191.
PELLEGRINI (Letizia), 169.
PELLEGRINI (Luigi), 4439.
PELLEGRINO (Carlo), 2585.
PELLETIER (Alexis), 6529.
PELLETIER (Monique),393.
PELLICCIA (H.), 2314.
PELLING (C. B. R.), 2266.
PELLIZZI (Camillo), 5049.
PELOILLE (Bernard), 1193.
PELON (Olivier), 2011.
PELOSI (Hebe Carmen), 774.
PELTERET (David A. E.), 3836.
PELTOLA (Pekka), 5139.
PELTONEN (Markku), 1216.
PELZ (Annegret), 5622.
PEÑA (José Antonio), 1587.
PEÑA (Milagros), 5217.
PEÑA BOCOS (Esther), 3837.
PEÑA GONZALEZ (José), 7568.
PENALVER CASTILLO (Manuel), 676.
PENE VIDARI (Gian Savino), 3617.
PENNELL (Richard), 8056.
PENNESTRI (S.), 316.
PENSOM (Roger), 4093.
PENVENNE (Jeanne Marie), 5135.
PERANI (Mauro), 170.
PERCHELLET (Jean-Pierre), 6681.
PERCIVAL (Mark), 8699.

PEREIRA (Michela), 4361.
PEREIRA (Paulo), 6746.
PEREIRA FERREIRA (Ana Maria), 7937.
PERETTO (Elio), 3008.
PEREZ (Christine), 2656.
PEREZ (Louis A.), 5099.
PEREZ BAREAS (Cristóbal), 1656.
Perez de Guzman (Fernan), 827.
PEREZ DE INESTROSA (José Luis), 1696.
PEREZ GONZALEZ (Maurilio), 3921.
PEREZ LOPEZ (Roberto), 441.
PEREZ MARTIN (Immaculada), 34.
PEREZ SARRION (G.), 5441.
PEREZ-BUSTAMANTE (Rogelio), 7604.
Periklēs, 2143.
PÉRIN (Patrick), 3779.
PERINI (Sergio), 7966.
PERLMAN (James S.), 6467.
PERNIOLA (Mario), 6760.
PERNOT (Jean-François), 6561.
Perón (Juan Domingo), 432, 4682, 4695.
Perotti (Niccolo), 3995.
Perpetua, sancta, 3033.
PERPILLOU-THOMAS (F.), 1792.
PERRAS (Galen Roger), 8382.
PERREN (Richard), 7259.
PERRENOND (Alfred), 1294.
Perrenot (Antonio), 3060.
PERRIE (Maureen), 5345.
PERRIN (M.), 1438.
PERRONE (Lorenzo), 3158.
PERRONE (Nico), 8700.
PERRONE-MOISÉS (Lyla), 5632.
PERROT (Jean-Claude), 941.
Perrot d'Ablancourt (Nicolas), 673.
PERRY (Gillian), 6761.
PERTHES (Volker), 5467.
PERTICI (Petra), 4569.
PERUGI (Maurizio), 4094.
PERUSSE (Roland I.), 4973.
PERUZZI (Emilio), 2470.
PERZ (Bertrand), 5186.
PESAVENTO (Luisa), 3314.
PESCE (Mauro), 2977.
PESCOSOLIDO (Guido), 834.
PESELY (George E.), 2315.
PESET (Mariano), 7277.
PESSIN (Alain), 6682.
PESTMAN (P. W.), 1793.
PESTRE (Dominique), 942.
Pétain (Philippe), 4853.
PETER (Jürgen), 677.
PÉTER (Katalin), 6034.
PETER (Ulrich), 7522.
PETERI (Gyorgy), 7766.
PETERS (Edward), 678.
PETERSEN (E. Ladewig), 72.

PETERSEN (Jens), 5029.
PETERSEN (Nikolaj), 8424.
PETERSEN (Swantje), 6762.
PETERSOHN (Jürgen), 73.
PETERSON (Edward Norman), 8284.
Peterson (Erik), 850.
PETIT (Carlos), 3669.
PETITFRERE (Claude), 4902.
PETITMENGIN (P.), 106.
PETITOT (Jean), 381.
PETKOV (Kiril), 1143.
PETKOVIC (Jelenka), 322.
PETOLETTI (M.), 6579.
Pëtr I Velikij [il Grande], imperatore di Russia, 5356, 7125.
PETRACCHI (Giorgio), 6075.
PETRALIA (Giuseppe), 679.
Petrarca (Francesco), 4023, 4049, 4092, 4095, 6571, 6590.
PETRI (Luce), 4362.
PETRO (Peter), 1557.
Petronius Arbiter, 2586, 2587, 2767, 2807.
PETROV (Jurij A.), 7292.
PETROV (Metodi), 8155.
PETRUCCI (Armando), 16, 35, 1354.
PETRUCCI NARDELLI (Franca), 467.
PETRUKHIN (Vladimir Ja.), 653, 1562, 4096.
PETRUS BERTIUS, 248.
Petrus Damiani, 3993.
PETRUS DE CRESCENTIIS, 4294.
PETRUS DE EBULO, 171.
PETRY (Klaus), 293.
PETTAS (William), 249.
PETTERSSON (Ronny), 7545.
PETTINATO (G.), 1919.
PETTIT (Philip), 1189.
PETZ-GRABENBAUER (Maria), 6468.
PETZNEK (Fridrich), 5187.
PETZOLDT MAC CLYMONDS (Marita), 6955.
PEUCHOT (Eric), 7569.
PEYLET (Gerard), 831.
PEZZAROSSA (Fulvio), 3303, 3315.
PEZZINO (Paolo), 680, 5036.
PFAFF (Richard W.), 144.
PFEIFFER (Waldemar), 6079.
PFIFFIG (Ambros J.), 2502.
PFISTER (Max), 4097.
PFISTER-LANGANAY (Christian), 7196.
PFOTENHAUER (Helmut), 6763.
Phaon (L. Domitius), 2518.
Philemon, 2790.
Philippos II, re di Macedonia, 1954.
Philip the Cleric, 3267.
PHILIPP (Jakob), 5178.
Philippe de Remy, 3981.
Philippe I, roi de France, 57.

Philippe II Auguste, roi de France, 53.
Philippe II le Bel, roi de France, 3263, 3412, 3672.
Philippe IV, 3683.
Philippe VI, roi de France, 3672.
Philippus (Marcus Julius), imperatore romano, 2658.
PHILIPPY (Patricia Berrahou), 6580.
PHILLIPS (Andrew), 5833.
PHILLIPS (David), 6130.
PHILLIPS (Graham), 6581.
PHILLIPS (John A.), 4958.
PHILLIPS (Roger), 6797.
PHILP (Mark), 839.
PHILPOTT (William), 8156.
PI (Mingyong), 8911.
Piłsudski (Józef), 5238.
PIANA TONIOLO (Paola), 3234.
PIASECKA (Janina Ewa), 6469.
PIATKOWSKI (A.), 2657.
PICARD (Jean-Michel), 3342.
Picasso (Pablo Ruiz), 6846.
PICCALUGA (Giulia), 3009.
PICCAT (Marco), 4229.
PICCHI (Eugenio), 6527.
PICCIRILLI (Luigi), 681.
PICCOLO GIANNUZZI (Chiara), 6798.
PICCOTTINI (Gernot), 2898, 2899.
PICHOT (Daniel), 3839.
PICHOTTE (Daniel), 3840.
PICO DELLA MIRANDOLA (Giovanni), 6221, 6591.
PICON (Antoine), 944.
PICONE (Michelangelo), 6582.
PIECH (Stanisław), 5766.
PIEL (Jean), 4971, 7260.
PIERARD (Richard), 1483.
PIERART (M.), 2145.
PIERART (Marcel), 2040.
PIÉRI (Dominique), 2864.
Piero dei Medici, 3495.
Piero della Francesca, 417, 3910, 6829.
Piero di Cosimo, 6810.
PIEROTTI (Piero), 6323.
Pierre de Saint-Flour, 4341.
Pierre l'Ermite, 4501.
Pierro (Luigi), 6201.
Petrus, Apostolus, Sanctus, 2954, 2990.
PIERROT (Roger), 500.
PIETA (Karol), 1705.
PIETKIEWICZ (Krzysztof), 5257.
PIETRI (Charles), 1458, 2949.
PIETRI (Luce), 2949.
Pietro da Barsegapè, 4521.
Pietro l'Athonita, 3080.
Pietro Leopoldo, Granduca di Toscana), 7647.
PIETSCH (Walter), 6131.

PIKE (Fredrick B.), 8701.
PIKHOJA (Rudol'f G.), 5417.
PIKOULAS (Y. A.), 2425.
PILÁT (Vladimír), 5471.
PILHOFER (Peter), 3010.
PILLORGET (René), 8003.
PIMLOTT (John), 8365.
PIMOUGUET (Isabelle), 2146.
PINA POLO (Francisco), 2701.
PINAUD (P.-F.), 7293.
PINAULT SORENSEN (Madeleine), 5629.
PINCUS (Steve), 6036.
Pindaros, 2097, 2109, 2257, 2314, 2367.
PINDER (Janice M.), 3297.
PINDER (John), 8702.
PINDL-BÜCHEL (Theodor), 4302, 4364.
PINELLI (Lucia), 3339.
Pinochet Ugarte (Augusto), 4748, 4750.
PINOTTI (P.), 2737.
PINTO (Antonio Costa), 5284.
PINTO (Giuliano), 3841.
PIOLANTI (Antonio), 4371.
PIOTROVSKIJ (B. B.), 3557.
PIOTROWSKI (Tadeusz M.), 8285.
PIPER (Franciszek), 8286.
PIPER (J.), 246.
PIPES (Richard), 5418.
Pirandello (Luigi), 6908.
PIRETTI (Maria Serena), 7605.
PIRILLO (Paolo), 3670.
PIRJEVEC (Jože), 5068.
PIROŻYŃSKI (Jan), 6196.
PIROUET (M. Louise), 1144.
PIRRO (Ugo), 6944.
PISAREV (Jurij A.), 8157.
PISCHEDDA (Bruno), 6197.
PISCIOTTA (Eva Mae), 6956.
PISKUREWICZ (Jan), 6076.
PISONI (Pier Giacomo), 3223.
PISTILLO (Michele), 7497.
PITHON (Rémy), 442, 6957.
PITON (Jean-Pierre), 6903.
PITUL'KO (V. V.), 1604.
Pius II, Papa, 4044.
Pius XI, Papa, 5716.
PIUS NGANDU (Nkashama), 6532.
PIUZ (Anne-Marie), 7227.
PIVATO (Stefano), 7464.
PIWKO (Stanisław), 6324.
PIXTON (Paul B.), 4526.
PIZARRO (Joaquin Martinez), 683.
PIZER (Donald), 1531.
PIZER (John David), 6037.
PIZZORUSSO (Giovanni), 5809.
PLACANICA (Augusto), 1295, 3382.
PLAINEMAISON (J.), 7439.
PLANAS BADENAS (Josefina), 172.

Planck (Max), 6073.
PLASS (P.), 2732.
PLASSMANN (Engelbert), 6089.
PLATEN (Carl Henrik von), 7767.
Plato, 175, 1215, 1224, 1521, 1522, 1528, 1535, 2089, 2091, 2098, 2099, 2100, 2293, 2311, 2318, 2322, 2325, 6222, 6229, 6236, 6242, 6246, 6252, 6308, 6327, 6330, 6337, 6347.
PLATOVA (A.), 1040.
PLATVOET (Jan), 1407, 5672.
Plautus (Titus Maccius), 2596, 2790, 2809.
PLAVA (Elmaz B.), 4674.
PLENZDORF (Ulrich), 6683.
PLETNEVA (S. A.), 1164.
PLEWKO (Jadwiga), 5767.
PLEZIA (Marian), 3316.
Plinius Secundus (Caecilius), minor, 3020.
Plinius Secundus, senior, 2588, 3946, 3994.
PLJUKHANOVA (Marija B.), 3383.
PLONGERON (Bernard), 5733.
PLOQUIN (Alain), 3698.
Plōtinos, 2101, 2102.
PLOTNIKOV (A.IU.), 7795.
PLOUG (Gunhild), 2900.
PLUMMER (John F.), 3956.
Ploutarchos, 175, 2072, 2103, 2250, 2323, 2334, 2344, 7790.
PLUVIER (Jan M), 8822.
POBOG-LENARTOWICZ (Anna), 4445.
POCAR (Fausto), 8703.
POCZIK (Szilveszter), 4643.
PODHRADSKY (Gerhard), 3235.
PODLASEK (Maria), 8347.
PODRAZA-KWIATKOWSKA (Maria), 5265.
Poe (Edgar Allan), 6646.
PÖGGELER (Otto), 6325.
POGGI (Amedeo), 6958.
POGGIOLINI (Ilaria), 8704.
POHL (Karl Heinrich), 4808.
PÖHLMANN (E.), 2429.
POKORNÝ (Jiři), 5188.
POKORNY (Rudolf), 3188.
POLET (Jean-Claude), 4092, 6531.
POLGÁR (László), 5788.
POLICHETTI (Antonio), 823.
POLINGER FOSTER (Karen), 2012.
POLIT (Jakub), 8287.
Poliziano (Angelo), 4064, 6559, 6591.
POLJAKOV (Jurij A.), 7336, 7441.
POLLAK (Detlef), 1408.
POLLARD (Sidney), 1296.
POLLARD (T.), 1739.
POLLET (G.), 6002.

POLLIN (Burton R.), 6646.
POLLMANN (Ferenc), 8158.
POLO (MARCO), 152.
POLO (Nicoletta), 6707.
POLO DE BEAULIEU (Marie-Anne), 3939.
PÖLÖSKEI (Ferenc), 5557.
POLVINEN (Tuomo), 8057, 8288.
Polybios, 828, 2256, 2277.
POMA (Lucio), 7033.
POMBENI (Paolo), 5037, 7570, 7607.
POMEAU (René), 6038.
POMIAN (Krzysztof), 945.
POMMERIN (Reiner), 8430.
POMMIER (Edouard), 501, 6842.
POMPER (Philip), 946.
POMPONI (Massimo), 6730.
PON (George), 3935.
PONIATOWSKA (Elena), 5128.
PONS (Frank Moya), 4832.
PONS (Nicole), 173.
PONS (Silvio), 8289.
PONS ALOS (Vicent), 3506.
PONT (J. C.), 6480.
PONTAL (Odette), 3236.
PONTANI (Anna), 3101.
Pontormo (Jacopo Carucci), 6854.
PONTRANDOLFO (Angela), 2427, 2471.
POO (Mu-Chou), 8912.
POOLE (David N. J.), 6198.
POOLE (Robert), 265.
POOVEY (Mary), 6039.
POPE (Rex), 4959.
POPELY (Gyula), 5492.
POPESCU (Emilian), 2846.
POPHAM (Mervyn R.), 2013.
POPIŃSKI (Krzysztof), 8224.
POPKO (Maciej), 1484.
POPLAVSKAJA (Kh. V.), 5834.
POPLIN (François), 2847.
POPOVA (V. A.), 1150.
POPPE (Andrzej), 3473.
POPPLEWELL (Richard J.), 7835.
POPRÁDY (Judit), 5568.
PORĘBSKI (Andrzej), 5189.
PORCH (Nick), 1619.
PORCIANI (Ilaria), 5029.
PORCILE (Gabriel), 7768.
Porete (Marguerite), 4337.
Porphyrius Tyrius, 2104.
PORTA (G.), 3333.
PORTALIER (M.), 3984.
PORTER (Dennis), 6605.
PORTER (Roy), 350, 786, 6015, 6464.
PORTINARO (P. P.), 7547.
PÒRTULAS (Jaume), 2377.
POSADA (Marcelo), 7442.
POSSENTI (Livia Dina), 2848.
POSSENTI (Vittorio), 5768.

POSTEL-LECOCQ (Sylvie), 234.
POSTEL-VINAY (Gilles), 7284.
POSTER (Mark), 947.
POSTGATE (J. N.), 1739.
POSTGATE (Nicholas), 1588.
POSTLES (D.), 3843.
POTEMKINA (T. M.), 1671.
POTESTÀ (Gian Luca), 4278.
PÓTÓ (János), XXIII.
POTTER (David), 4903.
POTTER (P.), 2077.
POTTS (D. T.), 1958.
POUBLAN (D.), 5992.
POULAKOS (John), 6326.
POULOUIN (Claude), 816.
Poussin (Nicolas), 6722.
POUSSOU (Jean-Pierre), 7332.
Powell (John Enoch), 829.
POWELL HARLEY (Marta), 4291.
POWER (Jonathan), 8708.
POZZANI (Silvio), 8059.
POZZI (Regina), 836.
POZZO (Giovanni Maria), 6327.
PRADA (Pedro), 8709.
PRAG (K.), 1921.
PRAK (Maarten), 7443.
PRAKASH (Gyan), 7796.
PRANDI (Stefano), 5877.
PRATESI (Alessandro), 6, 3233.
PRATT (Louise), 2316.
PRAWITZ (Jan), 8710.
PRAYON (Friedhelm), 2489.
PRAZMOWSKA (Anita), 8348.
PREĆAN (Vilém), 5494.
PREDA (Dumitru), 8160.
PREDAL (René), 6901.
PREEG (Ernest H.), 8711.
PREISIG (Florian), 6583.
PRESCENDI (F.), 2733.
PRESCOTT (Christopher), 1710.
Presley (Elvis), 6933.
PRESTON BLIER (Suzanne), 9104.
PRETI (A.), 8400.
PREVENIER (Walter), 69.
Prévost-d'Exiles (Antoine François), abbé, 403.
PRIAMI (E.), 4230.
PRICE (A. W.), 2317.
PRICE (Curtis), 6959.
PRICE (Munro), 4906.
PRICKARTZ (Cherles), 2658.
PRICOCO (Salvatore), 2940, 2976, 3011.
PRIMAS (H.), 6466.
PRINCE (Munro), 7967.
PRINZIVALLI (Emanuela), 2938.
Priselkov (Mikhail Dmitrievič), 640.
PRITCHARD (James), 7968.
PRITCHARD (P.), 2318.
PRITZ (Pal), 8161.
PRIZEL (Ilya), 5259.

PROCACCI (Giovanna), 8162.
PROCACCI (Giuliano), 1218, 8238.
PROCELLI (E.), 2472.
PROCHASSON (Christophe), 4907.
PROHASZKA (Marianne), 2473.
PROKHVATILOVA (A. S.), 5304.
PROKS (Petr), 8712.
Propertius Aurelius (Sextus), 2558, 2585, 2774, 2814, 3945.
Propp (Vladimir), 985.
Prosper d'Aquitaine, 2945.
Protagoras, 2143.
PROUD (Judith K.), 4908.
PROUDFOOT (Lindsay J.), 5001.
Proudhon (Pierre-Joseph), 1212.
PROVIDENTI (Elio), 443.
PROZESKY (Martin), 5913.
PRUENCA I BAYTONA (Esteve), 3207.
PRUNIER (Gerard), 5291.
PRUTSCH (Ursula), 7130.
PRYCE-JONES (David), 5419.
Psalter (Mary), 177.
Psellos (Michaēl Kōnstantinos), 3122.
PSENIĆKOVA (Jana), 7268.
Ptolemaios, 175.
Pucci (Francesco), 5635.
PUCCI (Silvio), 3200.
PUCCI BEN ZEEV (Miriam), 2041.
Puccini (Gianni), 6941.
PUCKETT (David Lee), 5878.
PUDDU (Raffaele), 7938.
Pufendorf (Samuel von), 1184, 1244.
PUGLIESE (Silvia), 6533.
PUIG I USTRELL (Pere), 3237.
PUIG SAMPER (Miguel Angel), 5967.
PUIGARNAU I TORELLÓ (Alfons), 3695.
PULIT (Marcin), 948.
PULZER (Peter), 4809.
PURCELL (Nicholas), 2849.
PURIN (Bernhard), 478.
PURRINGTON (Coutney), 8561, 8776.
PURSELL (Carroll W.), 5608.
PURVIS (Thomas L.), 1148.
PUŚCAŚ (Vasile), 1090, 6077, 8324.
PUŠKAREVA (I. M.), 7523.
PUŠKAREVA (N. L.), 1485.
PUŠKAŠ (A. I.), 8163.
Puskin (Aleksandr), 6679.
PUSTER (Rolf W.), 972.
PUTALLAZ (François-Xavier), 3671.
PUTNAM (Michael C.J.), 2589.
PUTTER (Ad), 4099.
PUTZ (Manfred), 6684.
PUTZER (Peter), 7572.
PYLKKÄNEN (Anu), 7546.
Pyrrhos, 2390.
Pythagora, 6502.

Q

QA'INI (Farzanah), 295.
QI (Houjie), 8913.
QI (Shishen), 8914.
QUANTIN (Jean-Louis), 5879.
QUAQUARELLI (L.), 198.
QUAQUARELLI (Leonardo), 3317.
QUARITSCH (H.), 7547.
QUATAERT (D.), 5534.
Quinet (Edgard), 831, 858.
QUINTO (Riccardo), 4365.
QUINZIO (Sergio), 5713.
QUIRINI-POPŁAWSKA (Danuta), 3482.
QUIVIGER (François), 6065.
QURAISHI (Salim al Din), 7823.

R

RAABE (Thomas), 5770.
RAACK (Richard C.), 8291.
RAAFLAUB (K.), 1988.
RAASTED (J.), 33.
RABAN (Sandra), 4412.
RABE (Susan A.), 4100.
RABEL (Claudia), 151.
RABIKAUSKAS (Paulius), 74.
RABINOW (Paul), 7444.
Racine (Jean), 5983.
RACINET (Philippe), 4570.
RACZ (Endre), 353.
RÁCZ (György), 289.
Radding (M. C.), 35.
Radegonda, sancta, 188.
RADI (Giovanna), 1672.
RADICE (Giles), 4810.
RADICKE (J.), 2105.
RADLER (Rudiger), 6685.
RĂDUICĂ (Georgeta), 6200.
RĂDUICĂ (Nicolin), 6200.
RĂDUȚIU (Aurel), 5300.
RADZIMIŃSKI (Andrzej), 4527.
RAEPSAET (Georges), 1298.
RAEPSAET-CHARLIER (Marie-Thérèse), 2528.
RAEVSKIJ (D. S.), 2014.
RAFAJ (Pavel), 5499.
RAFFAELLI (Renato), 2744, 2801.
RAFFESTIN (Claude), 1149.
RAFTERY (Barry), 1690.
RAFTI (P.), 4101.
RAGGIO (Osvaldo), 7608.
RAGONE (Franca), 3318.
RAGONE (Giovanni), 6201.
RAGUIN (Yves), 5801.
RAHIKAINEN (Marjatta), 7652.
RAHNEMA (S.), 4990.
Raimbaut d'Aurenga, 4094.
RAIMONDI (Ezio), 3303.

RAINER (Johann), 5190.
RAINER (M. János), 5569.
RAIO (Giulio), 6328.
RÄISÄNEN (Heikki), 3012.
RAITH (Jill), 4504.
RAJSKIJ (Nikolaj S.), 8292.
RAJTAR (Jan), 1705.
RAKHMATULLIN (Morgan A.), 5346.
Ralegh (Walter), 4956.
RAMAGE (Douglas E.), 4988.
RAMBOUSEK (Otakar), 5508.
RAMET (Sabrina Petra), 8713.
RAMIREZ (Santiago), 1345, 6471.
RAMIREZ FERNANDEZ (Cesar), 312.
RAMIREZ VAQUERO (Eloísa), 3507.
RAMOS AGUIRRE (Mikel), 287.
RAMOS DE CARVALHO (Joaqui), XVIII.
RAMOTOWSKA (Franciszka), 5233.
Rampl (Philipp Jakob), 6860.
RAMSEY (Frances M. R.), 4401.
RAMSEYER (J. Mark), 5056.
RANGER (Terence), 5383, 7847.
RANIANEN (Tuula), V.
RANIS (Peter), 4694.
Ranke (Leopold von), 753.
RANKOV (N.B.), 2609.
RANZATO (Gabriele), 4602.
RAO (Anna Maria), 1151, 6606.
RAO (Ida Giovanna), 3508.
RAO (Nandini), 1589.
RAPHAEL (L.), 1219.
RAPP (Claudia), 3159.
Rares (Petru), 7928.
RASSE (Paul), 502.
RASTJANNIKOV (V. G.), 7096.
RATAJ (Jan), 5500.
RATHJE (A.), 2474.
RATHMELL (Andrew), 8714.
RATNER (Steven), 8715.
RATTÉ (Christopher), 1757.
RAUF (Bulent), 5527.
RAUKAR (Tomoslav), 3845.
RAULFF (Ulrich), 749.
RAUNIO (Ari), 716.
RAUSCH (Andreas), 1673.
RAUTKALLIO (Hannu), 8164.
RAUTY (N.), 3249.
RAUTY (Natale), 266, 3238.
RAUZY (Jean-Baptiste), 6310.
RAVIOLA (Flavio), 2475.
RAVITCH (Diane), 6149.
Rawls (John), 1210.
RAWNSLEY (Gary D.), 8716.
RAY (James Lee), 8717.
RAYEN (Mohammed Rajei), 8060.
RAYNAUD (C.), 4102.
RAYNAUD (Christiane), 4189.
READ (Peter), 6846.
READINGS (Bill), 726.
Reagan (Ronald Wilson), 8468.

REAL (I.), 4473.
REAU (E. du), 8293.
REB (Sylvaine), 5771.
REBERIOUX (Madeleine), 7450.
REBHANN (Fritz M.), 5191.
REBHORN (Wayne A.), 6584.
REDEN (Sitta von), 2175, 2221.
REDHEAD (Brian), 6330.
REDISH (Angela), 7294.
REDISH (Martin H.), 7573.
REDMOUNT (Carol A.), 1794.
REDON (Odile), 3846.
REDONDO (A.), 5442.
REEDER (E. D.), 2217.
REEDY (W. Jay), 1220.
REESE (Armin), 7969.
REESE (William J.), 6133.
REEVE (C. D. C.), 6331.
REEVE (Michael D.), 3282.
REGELE (Ludwig W.), 5038.
REGLERO DE LA FUENTE (Carlos), 4571.
REGOLIOSI (Mariangela), 4103.
REHAK (P.), 2015.
REIBNITZ (Barbara von), 1482.
REID (A. L.), 8562.
REID (Jennifer), 5078.
REIDMANN (Josef), 3796.
REIFENBERG (Bernd), 468.
REIMERS (David M.), 998.
REIN (Raanan), 8718.
REINALTER (Helmut), 6332.
REINDL-KIEL (Hedda), 7445.
REINGRABNER (Gustav), 5880.
REINHARD (Wolfgang), 5693.
REINHARDT (Klaus), 4367.
REINHARDT (Volker), 6333.
Reinhold (Karl Leonhard), 6240.
REISCH (George), 870.
REISZ (T. Csaba), 394.
REITER (Eric H.), 4452.
REITER (Karin), 1959.
Rembrandt (Harmensz. van Rijn), 183.
REMENSNYDER (Amy Goodrich), 684.
REMOND (René), 5702.
REMPORT (Zoltán), 7186.
REMY (Jean), 6042.
REN (Shiying), 8915.
REN (Shuang), 8916.
RENAN (Ernest), 832.
RENARD (Etienne), 2850.
RENARD (Jean), 373.
RENDINA (Massimo), 8411.
RENGER (Johannes), 1846.
RENGGER (Nicholas J.), 1221.
RENNEBERG (Monika), 4784.
Renner (Karl), 7567.
RENNER (Rolf Günther), 1551.
RENNIE (Brian S.), 1486.

RENO (Fred), 7897.
RENOUARD (F.), 7769.
RENOUARD (Philippe), 234.
RENSHAW (Patrick), 1152.
REPOSSI (Cesare), 6664.
REPSTAD (Pål), 1487.
REQUATE (Angela), 6334.
REQUATE (Jörg), 6202.
REQUENA GALLERO (Manuel), 5443.
RÉQUES (Denis), 2106.
RESCH (Andreas), 7187.
RESLER (M.), 3918.
RESPONDEK (Peter), 6134.
RETAMERO (Felix), 317.
RETI (György), 5570, 8349.
REUSSE (F.), 686.
REVEL (Jacques), 903, 950.
REVELLI (Marco), 5016.
REVERDINI (Niccolò), 6611.
REVEZS (Gabor), 7078.
REY (M.-P.), 8719.
REY (Roselyne), 6461, 6472.
REYES (Juan Carlos), 7446.
REYNAUD (N.), 200.
REYNOLDS (David), 8294.
REYNOLDS (Dee), 6764.
REYNOLDS (Dwight Fletcher), 1045.
REYNOLDS (Roger E.), 4529.
REYNOLDS (Susan), 3848.
RHEIN (Reglinde), 4474.
RHOADS (David M.), 2956.
RHODE (Paul W.), 7262.
RHODES (Dennis Everard), 252.
RHODES (Norman), 6686.
RHODES (P. J.), 2176.
RHODES (R. F.), 2428.
RHYS ROBERTS (W.), 2051.
RIAN (Øystein), 4646, 5167, 7679, 7760.
Riba (Carles), 6252.
Ribbentrop (Joachim von), 8287.
RIBEIRO (Maria da Conceição), 5285.
RIBEIRO (Maria Manuela Tavares), XVIII.
RIBEIRO (Orlando), 395.
RIBÉMONT (B.), 3987.
RIBERA I LACOMBA (Albert), 2902.
RIBNIKAR (Slobodan), 322.
Ribot (Alexandre), 8118.
RIBOT GARCIA (Luis Antonio), 5631.
RICCA (Paolo), 5669.
RICCARDI (Andrea), 5029, 5669.
RICCIOLI (Jean-Louis), 8412.
RICE (Condoleezaa), 8799.
RICHARD (Jean), 3299.
Richard I, king of England, 3457.
Richard II, king of England, 3512.
RICHARDSON (David), 7083, 7225, 7874.

RICHARDSON (Dick), 7770.
RICHE (Pierre), 3342.
Richelieu (Armand-Jean du Plessis, cardinal de), 7718.
RICHEZ (Jean-Claude), 4859.
RICHLER (B.), 3214.
RICHTER (Matthias), 6687.
RICHTER (Melvin), 1223.
RICHTER (Michael), 3384.
RICHTER (Will), 3277, 4294.
RICHTER (William Lee), 1299.
RICHTER-BERGMEIER (Reinhilt), 4294.
RICO (Francisco), 1546.
Ricoeur (Paul), 5647.
RICUPERO (Rubens), 8720.
RIDDER (K.), 3253.
RIDINGS (Daniel), 3013.
RIECKHOFF-PAULI (Sabine), 1711.
RIEDEL (Volker), 2810, 2811.
RIEDERER (Josef), 2493.
RIEDINGER (Jeffrey), 5226.
RIEDINGER (Rudolf), 3047.
RIEDLINGER (Helmut), 4368.
RIEDMANN (Josef), 3509.
RIEGEL (Paul), 1538.
Riegl (Alois), 833.
RIEKS (Rudolf), 803.
RIES (Julien), 1420, 1488, 2941.
RIESE (Berthold), 9118.
RIGANTI (E.), 2737.
RIGAUD (Jean-Philippe), 1620.
RIGAUDIERE (Albert), 3672.
RIGBY (S. H.), 3849.
RIGBY (Val), 1690.
RIGGSBY (Andrew M.), 2812.
RIGHT (Hon), 8721.
RIGO (Antonio), 3080, 3160.
RIGON (Antonio), 4475.
RIGOTTI (Gianpaolo), 3076.
RILEY (Bridget), 6765.
RILL (Bernd), 3385.
RIMA (Ingrid H.), 6999.
RIMOLDI (Antonio), 5731.
RIMSKIJ (Sergej V.), 5835.
RINALDI (Rossella), 3850.
RINCÓN (J. M.), 1713.
RINDAL (Magnus), 3325.
RINEHART (Michael), 1367.
RINGDAL (Nils Johan), 6203.
RINGMAR (Erik), 7939.
Rinuccini (Alamanno), 3922.
RINUCCINI (C.), 3913.
RÍOS ZÚÑIGA (Rosalina), 6135.
RIOU (Yves-François), 175.
RIPOLL LÓPEZ (SERGIO), 1614.
RIPOSIO (Donatella), 6607.
RIPPE (Gérard), 3851.
RISKÓ (Mariann), 5772.
RISSE-KAPPEN (Thomas), 8635, 8722.

RISTORI (Renzo), 6802.
RITCHOT (Gilles), 381.
RITSCHL (Albrecht), 4763.
RITTER (Archibald R. M.), 8723.
RITTER (Gerhard Albert), 687.
RITTER (Stefan), 2903.
RIVES (J.), 2851.
RIVES (James R.), 2852.
RIVIERE (Peter), 8062.
RIX (Helmut), 2493.
RIZAKIS (Yvonne), 2417.
RIZZACASA (A.), 1489.
RIZZERIO (L.), 4297.
RIZZI (Alessandra), 3852.
RIZZO (Silvia), 3319, 4105, 6570.
ROBAYO (Juan Manuel), 5087.
ROBERT DE BORON, 3914.
ROBERT OF TORIGNI, 3335.
ROBERTS (Adam), 7771.
ROBERTS (David D.), 951.
ROBERTS (David), 6336.
ROBERTS (Geoffrey), 8296.
ROBERTS (Jane), 4144.
ROBERTS (Paul), 2463.
ROBERTS (R. H.), 1490.
ROBERTS (Richard), 7237.
ROBERTSON (Andrew W.), 6204.
ROBERTSON (Duncan), 4476.
Robertson (Esmonde), 7770.
Robespierre (Maximilien François Marie Isidore), 4879.
ROBIN (Ron), 6136.
ROBINET (André), 6310.
ROBINSON (D. B.), 2098.
ROBINSON (John Martin), 6766.
ROBINSON (O. F.), 2703, 3241.
ROBINSON (Philip), 4811.
ROBINSON (Thomas W.), 6337, 7772.
ROBLEDO SANZ (Beatriz), 1656.
ROBRES (Fernando Andres), 5810.
ROCCA (Giovanna), 2442.
ROCCARO (Cataldo), 4106.
Rocha Gil (Maria Olímpia), 7937.
ROCHAT (Giorgio), 8383.
ROCHE (Daniel), 5991.
Rochegrosse (Georges), 6777.
ROCHETTE (Bruno), 361, 2320.
ROCKE (David M.), 7696.
Rockefeller (John D. Jr), 5884.
ROCKER (Stephen), 6338.
ROCKWELL (Paul Vincent), 4107.
RODÀ (Isabel), 2867.
Rodano (Franco), 5764.
RODENBURG (J.), 8586.
RODER (Brigitte), 1712.
RODGER (N. A. M.), 3474.
Rodin (Auguste), 6853.
RODOTÀ (Stefano), 7653.
RODRIGO (F.), 8551.
RODRÍGUEZ (Jesús Antonio), 4909.

RODRIGUEZ ADRADOS (F.), 2222.
RODRIGUEZ ALCALDE (Angel), 1590.
RODRIGUEZ BAQUERO (Luis), 7907.
RODRIGUEZ CLAVEL (J. R.), 444.
RODRIGUEZ DIAZ (Elena E.), 3320.
RODRIGUEZ LIAÑEZ (L.), 36.
ROECK (Bernd),3919.
ROEMER (Thomas), 5666.
ROFFE (David), 688.
Roger (Jacques), 6461.
Roger of Hereford, 264.
ROGERS (Daniel), 8724.
ROGERS (James Steven), 7654.
ROGGEN (Héribert), 4454.
ROGISTER (John), 4910.
ROHLFING (H.), 236.
ROHMANN (Jens), 3161.
ROHR (Christoph), 4108.
ROI (M. L.), 8165.
ROISMAN (Joseph), 2113.
ROJAS (José), 4369.
ROJEK (Wojciech), 5232.
ROK (Bogdan), 5261.
ROLAND MICHEL (Marianne), 6847.
Roldán Hervás (JOSÉ MANUEL), 1153.
ROLIM CAPELATO (Maria Helena), III.
ROLLET (Jacques), 6339.
ROMAGNOLI (Angela), 6961.
ROMANELLI (Raffaele), 5039, 5048, 7448, 7609.
ROMANINI (Angiola Maria), 4572.
ROMANINI (Claudia), 6340.
ROMANO (Andrea), 689, 1362.
ROMANO (Ruggiero), 750, 952, 1154, 5040, 7296, 7449.
ROMANO (Sergio), 5029.
ROMEI (Danilo), 6539.
ROMEO (I.), 834.
Romeo (Rosario), 834, 5988.
RÖMER (Claudia), 3510.
ROMERO (Federico), 690.
ROMERO (Luis Alberto), 4685.
ROMERO TALLAFIGO (M.), 36.
ROMERO-POSE (Eugenio), 3014.
ROMICS (Ignác), 7747.
ROMLUND WITHERS (Bente), 328.
RÓNA-TAS (András), 22, 3386.
RONCAGLIA (Alessandro), 7030.
Roncalli (Angelo), 5669, 8111.
RONCONI (Lucia), 2476.
RONDOLINO (Gianni), 6962.
Ronsard (Pierre de), 6587.
RONZEAUD (Pierre), 6688.
ROOS (Jane Mayo), 6848.
Roosevelt (Franklin D.), 7729, 8172, 8203, 8230, 8232, 8621, 8264.
Roosevelt (Theodore), 5612, 7773, 8067.

ROPPER (G. J.), 1424.
ROQUES (D.), 2321.
RORDORF (Willy), 3015.
RORIMER (Anne), 6744.
Rorty (Richard), 911.
ROSŁANOWSKI (Tadeusz), 7337.
ROSA (Giovanna), 5029.
ROSA (Mario), 5681.
ROSANVALLON (Pierre), 7450.
ROSAS (Fernando), 1300.
RÖSCH (Gerhard), 3478.
ROSCHECK (Petra), 3499.
Roscher (Wilhelm), 7040.
ROSE (M. B.), 4945.
ROSENBERGER (Veit), 1967.
ROSEFELDT (Julian), 4767.
ROSELLI (Lucia), 445, 691.
ROSELLINI (Michela), 2590.
ROSEMAN (Mark), 4812, 7388.
ROSEMANN (P. W.), 4297.
ROSEN (Edward), 6474.
ROSEN (Haiim Baruch), 1924.
ROSEN (Kl.), 267.
ROSEN (Stanley), 1224.
ROSENBERG (Charles E.), 6475.
ROSENBERG (Samuel N.), 3955.
ROSENBLUM (Joseph), 196, 6689.
ROSENBLUTH (Frances M.), 5056.
ROSENSTEIN (Nathan), 2704.
ROSENTHAL (Anton), 5580.
ROSENTHAL (Jean-Laurent), 7284.
ROSIVACH (Vincent J.), 2591.
ROSLYNG-JENSEN (Palle), 4756.
ROSOKOKI (A.), 2063.
ROSONI (Isabella), 3673.
ROSS (Dorothy), 692.
Ross (John), 3240.
ROSS (Kristin), 6690.
ROSS (Robert S.), 8725.
ROSSETTI (Patrizia), 1641.
ROSSI (Leena), 1133.
ROSSI (Mario), 8297.
ROSSI (P.), 6307.
Rossi (Paolo), 1523.
ROSSIAUD (Jacques), 693.
ROSSI-DORIA (Anna), 7610.
ROSSINI (Daniela), 7773.
ROSSITER (Margaret W.), 6476.
Rostovtzeff (Michael Ivanovitch), 835.
ROSTWOROWSKI (Wojciech), 8166.
ROTARU (Jipa), 8385.
ROTH (Juliana), 988.
ROTH (Klaus), 988.
ROTH (Michael S.), 953.
ROTH (Norman), 3538.
ROTH (Paul), 870.
ROTHE (Arnold), 6526.
ROTHMAN (David J.), 6477.
ROTHSCHILD (Jean-Pierre), 3337.
ROTOLI (Vincenzo), 3102.

ROTT (Jean), 5633.
ROUCHE (Michel), 3674.
ROUILLARD (Jacques), 4849.
ROULAND (Norbert), 1243.
Rousseau (Jean-Jacques), 1195, 1205, 6235, 6605, 7543, 7666.
ROUSSEL (Claude), 3895.
ROUSSELLE (Aline), 2627.
ROUSSELLIER (Nicolas), 600.
ROUSSO (Henry), 4911.
ROUVILLOIS (Samuel), 5703.
ROUX (Jacqueline), 5773.
ROUX (Simone), 3853.
ROVAN (Joseph), 1155.
ROVERI (Alessandro), 7524.
ROVIRA LLORENS (Salvador), 1660.
ROWE (C. J.), 2099, 2319.
ROWLAND (Herbert), 6170.
ROWLANDS (Alison), 4813.
ROWSE (Alfred Leslie), 694.
ROY (Tirthankar), 7131.
ROZALIEV (Jurij N.), 5528.
ROZANCEVA (Nina A.), 7883.
RUANE (Kevin), 8726.
RUANO RUIZ (Encarnación), 1713.
RUBELLIN (Michel), 3244.
Rubin (Isaak Iljitsch), 7018.
RUBIN (Patricia), 6767.
RUBINSTEIN (Nicolai), 4231.
RUBINSTEIN (W. D.), 4708.
RUBIO GARCIA (Luis), 3528.
RUBIO VELA (Agustin), 75, 4573.
RUBLACK (Ulinka), 4814.
RUBY (Marcel), 8413.
RUBY (Pascal), 2477.
RUCK (Michael), 4757.
RÜCKERT (Joachim), 565, 7535.
RUDERMAN (David B.), 6478.
RUDERSDORF (Manfred), 7451.
RUDLOFF STANTON (Anne), 177.
RUDOLPH (Kurt), 748.
RUEDA MENDEZ (David), 5088.
RUELLO (F.), 4282.
RUFF (Mihály), 8727.
RUFFAT (Michèle), 7043.
RUFI (Enrico), 6608.
Ruges (Arnold), 6367.
RUGGERI (Paola), 2650.
RUGGIERI (Vincenzo, S.J.), 3162.
RUGGINI (Lellia), 2623, 2716, 2734.
RUGIIREHEH-RUNAKU (James B. M. N.), 5466, 7884.
RUGOLO (Carmela Maria), 3854.
RUHRBERG (Christine), 4109.
RUI (Kungai), 8918.
RUIZ ASENCIO (Jose Manuel), 7670.
RUIZ DE LOIZAGA (Saturnino), 3245, 3246.
RUIZ GOMEZ (Francisco), 695.
RUIZ IBAÑEZ (José Javier), 5444.

RULLI (Gabriella), 2814.
RUMI (Giorgio), 5029.
RUMMEL (Erika), 6341.
RUMSCHEID (Frank), 1753.
RUNBLOM (Harald), 1156.
RUNNELS (Curtis N.), 1593.
RUNNELS (Curtis), 2016.
RUOCCO (D.), 8048.
RÜPKE (Jörg), 268, 1500, 2815.
RUPPERT (Lothar), 5755.
RUPRECHT (Hans-George), 6691.
RUS (Martijn), 4110.
Rusbeck (Olof), 6401.
RUSCONI (Roberto), 4111, 5811.
RUSHING (W. Jackson), 6768.
RUSSEL (D.), 2051.
RUSSEL (Peter E.), 7774.
RUSSELL (James), 3163.
RUSSELL (P. E.), 3855.
RUSSELL (William R.), 5881.
RUSSMANN (Edna R.), 1795.
RUSSO (Daniel), 6849.
RUSSO (Paolo), 6963.
RUSSOCKI (Stanisław), 3675.
RUST (Diane), 6137.
RUST (Val D.), 6137.
RUSZKOWSKI (Janusz), 5882.
RUTGERS (L. V.), 1925.
RUTHERFORD (Ian), 1491.
RUTHERFORD (R. B.), 2322.
RUTTKAY (Elisabeth), 1642.
RUUSKANEN (J.-P.), 2017.
RYŚ (Jan), 4112.
RYAN (David), 8728.
RYBAKOV (B. A.), 4042.
RYBICKA (Małgorzata), 1647.
RYCHLÍK (Jan), 5498.
RYCKMAN (Thomas), 870.
RYCROFT (Simon), 4649.
RYDÉN (Lennart), 3082.
RYDSTRÖM (Jens), 1356.
RYRIE (William), 8729.
RYSTAD (Göran), 7775.
RYŻEWSKI (Wacław), 5251.
RŽEŠEVSKIJ (Oleg Aleksandrovich), 5335, 8299, 8316, 8386.

S

SAASTAMOINEN (Kari), 1244.
SAATKAMP (Herman J.), 6342.
SAAVEDRA GUERRERO (M.D.), 2705.
SABA (Anna), 8730.
SABATÉ (Flocel), 3511.
SABATIER (François), 6964.
SABBADINI (Remigio), 4113.
SABBATUCCI (Giovanni), 5029, 5047.
Sabinus, 2698.

SABOGAL TAMAYO (Julián), 7035.
SABROW (Martin), 603, 696.
SACCONI (Anna), 2018.
SACHS (Ignacy), 1301.
Sachs (Nelly), 6638.
SACKS (D.), 1357.
SADA (Luigi), 3321.
SAFTIEN (Volker), 1302.
SAFWAT (N. F.), 37.
SAGAN (Iwona), 7189.
SAGIV (David), 4671.
SAGONA (Antonio), 1754.
SAGONA (Claudia), 1754.
SAGUCHI (Tōru), 8812.
SAHADEVAN (P.), 8731.
SAHLINS (Marshall David), 697.
SAIANI (A.), 3903.
SAIBENE (Luigi), 1386.
SAILLARD (Yves), 7039.
SAINT-HILLIER (Bernard), 8387.
SAINT-ROCH (Patrick), 763.
SAINZ DE LA MAZA (Regina), 3208.
SÁINZ RIPA (E.), 3245.
Saitta (Armando), 836.
SAITTA (Biagio), 3539.
SAJTI (Enikő), 8350.
SAKAMOTO (Hiroko), 8919.
SAKHAROV (Andrej N.), 5348, 7726, 8351.
SAKONG (Il), 8705.
SALA (Emilio), 6965.
SALANOVA ALCALDE (Ramón), 447.
SALAS (Carmen Parrón), 7908.
Salazar (António de Oliveira), 5284, 8230.
SALEM (Elie A.), 5101.
SALERNO (Antonio), 1630, 1648.
SALIBA (George), 3083.
SALICRÚ I LLUCH (Roser), 3856, 4114.
SALISBURY (Chris), 1714.
SALLA (Michael E.), 8762.
SALLMANN (Jean-Michel), 7940.
SALLOIS (Jacques), 503.
Sallustius Crispus (Gaius), 2604, 2626, 2805.
SALMAN (Amer Shaker), 4175 a).
SALMANN (Elmar), 5701.
SALMENHAARA (Erkki), 6976.
SALMERI (Giovanni), 832.
SALMERÓN CASTRO (Alicia), 5129.
SALMINEN (Juhani), 7525.
SALMINEN (Pertti), 8732.
SALMON (P.), 2177.
SALMONOWICZ (Stanisław), 5263.
SALOMIES (Olli), 2509.
SALOMONI (Antonella), 448, 698.
SALRACH (Josep M.), 3857.
SALSON (Jean-Marie), 4232.
Saltman (Avrom), 3535.

SALVADÓ (Francisco J. Romero), 5445.
SALVATORI (Enrica), 3858.
SALVIAT (François), 2042.
Salviati (Giovanni), 94.
Salviati (Francesco), 6864.
SALVINI-PLAWEN (Luitfried), 4115.
SALWA (Piotr), 6586.
SAMAD (Yunas), 5206.
SAMARITANI (Antoinio), 3197.
Samek (Oskar), 7643.
SAMMER (Marianne), 753.
SAMPSON (Mary), 440.
SAMSOMOWICZ (Henryk), 3476.
SANCHEZ BELLA (Ismael), 1245.
SANCHEZ BENITO (J. M.), 3193.
SANCHEZ CERVELLO (Josep), 5286.
SANCHEZ GONZALEZ (A.), 36.
SANCHEZ JIMENEZ (Francisco), 2478.
SANCHEZ MARIANA (Manuel), 178, 3676, 3859.
SANCHEZ VIDAL (Agustin), 1546.
SANDER (Rudolf), 8388.
SANDERS (Hanne), 5883.
SANDERSON (Stephen K), 954.
SANDGRUBER (Roman), 1303.
SANDMO (Erling), 7452.
SANFILIPPO (Matteo), 5029.
SANG (Bing), 8920.
SANGER (Clyde), 7818.
Sanomat (Helsingin), 6214.
SANSONE (G. E.), 3902.
SANSTERRE (Jean-Marie), 415, 3164.
SANTANIELLO (G.), 6423.
SANTARELLI (Umberto), 3677.
SANTI (Francesco), 110, 3039, 4372.
SANTIEMMA (Adriano), 993.
SANTINI (Carlo), 206, 2592.
SANTOMASSIMO (Gianpasquale), 699, 5041.
SANTORO (Carlo Maria), 7776, 8733.
SANTORO (R.), 180.
SANTOS SANTOS (D.), 121.
SANTOSUOSSO (A.), 6850.
SANTUARI (A.), 7132.
SANTUCCI (Antonio A.), 6282.
SAPIEHA (Eustachy), 5239.
SAPRYKIN (S. Ju.), 835.
SARAĆ (M. S.), 1026.
SARADI (H.), 4478.
SARADI (Helen), 3165.
SARAIVA (António José), 3387, 5287.
SARDELLA (T.), 3016.
SARDET (Frédéric), 1304.
SAREEN (Tilak Raj), 8168.
SARIUSZ-SKĄPSKA (Izabella), 8300.
Sarkander (Jan), 5729.
SARKAR (Bhaskar), 6966.
SAROGNI (Emilia), 5042.

SARPELLON (Giovanni), 6874.
SARZI AMADE (Luca), 272.
SASAKI (Ken'ichi), 9056.
SASSE TATEO (Barbara), 3322.
SASSO (Gennaro), 6343.
SASSON (M.), 1721.
SATŌ (Kazuhiko), 9057.
SAUL (Nigel), 3512.
SAUNDERS (David), 8063.
SAUNDERS (John Joseph), 3567.
SAUNDERS (T. J.), 2050.
SAUNDERS (Thomas J.), 6967.
SAUNDERS (Trish), 9119.
SAUTEL (J.-H.), 174.
SAUVAGE (Martin), 1847.
SAUVAN (Y.), 86.
SAUZEAU (Pierre), 3017.
Sauzet (Robert), 5691.
SAVAGNONE (Giuseppe), 5717.
SAVĆENKO (E. I.), 2000.
SAVĆUV (Valerij V.), 1047.
Savigny (Friedrich Karl von), 7544.
Savonarola (Girolamo), 4539.
SAVY (Nicole), 504.
SAWDAY (Jonathan), 6481.
SAWICKI (Tadeusz), 8301.
Say (Jean-Baptiste), 7038.
SAYHI-PERIGOT (Béatrice), 6577.
SAZBÓN (José), 6344.
SBRIZIOLO (Itala Pia), 3323.
SCAGNO (Roberto), 1386.
SCALABRIN (Carlo), 1506.
SCALFATI (Silio P. P.), 46, 4416.
SCALIA (Giuseppe), 4116.
SCALLY (Robert James), 5002.
SCALON (Cesare), 469.
SCARAMUZZI (Franco), 6603.
SCARDIGLI (B.), 2103.
SCARDOZZI (Mirella), 7453.
SCARPATI (Claudio), 6665.
SCARROCCHIA (S.), 833.
SCARSELLA (A.), 253.
SCARZANELLA (Eugenia), 1048.
SCATENA (Giovanni), 3275.
SCATOZZA-HÖRICHT (Lucia A.), 2905.
SCATTERGOOD (V. J.), 4071.
Scaurus (Aemilius M.), 2246.
ŠĆETININA (Galina I.), 6044.
SCHABERG (William H.), 6219.
SCHADECK (Hans), 4555.
SCHAFFNER (Paul), 4117.
SCHAFFRY (Andreas Michael), 6692.
SCHALLER (Dieter), 4118.
SCHAMA (Simon), 1358.
SCHAMP (Jacques), 2323.
SCHARFF (Robert C.), 6345.
Scharling (Carl Henrik), 1422.
SCHAUDIG (Hanspeter), 1848.
SCHAUSBERGER (Franz), 5193.
SCHEIBLE (Heinz), 5844.

SCHEID (John), 2529, 2853.
SCHEIDEL (Walter), 2223, 2735.
SCHEIFELE (Hans), 6769.
SCHEIN (S.), 3971.
SCHELLER (Robert Walter Hans Peter), 4191.
SCHELLEWALD (Barbara), 3104.
SCHENK (Wolfgang), 2957.
SCHENKEL (Albert F.), 5884.
SCHENKER (Lukas), 5673.
Schenkeveld (D. M.), 2273.
SCHERER (Irmgard), 6346.
SCHERRER (Jutta), 7067.
SCHIAFFINO (Lorenzo), 7319.
SCHIAVETTO (Franco Lucio), 3329.
Schiemer (Leonhard), 5633.
SCHIERING (Wolfgang), 6773.
SCHIFFER (Elisabeth), 3057, 3078.
SCHILD (Georg), 8169, 8352.
SCHILDT (Axel), 7454.
Schiller (Johann Christoph Friedrich von), 6264.
SCHILLING (Heinz), 5693.
SCHINDEL (Ulrich), 4119.
Schindler (Oskar), 928.
SCHIOPPA (Simonetta), 449.
SCHIRMANN (Sylvain), 8170, 7777.
Schlaffer (Hans), 5633.
SCHLAG (W.), 132.
SCHLAGER (Karlheinz), 4258.
SCHLANGE-SCHÖNINGEN (Heinrich), 2660.
Schlegel (Friedrich), 6635.
SCHLEGEL-MATTHIES (Kirsten), 7455.
SCHLEINER (Winfried), 6482.
SCHLESINGER (Klaus), 6683.
SCHLICH (Thomas), 700.
SCHLOGL (Rudolf), 5774.
SCHLÖGEL (Karl), 4815.
SCHLUMBOHM (Jürgen), 7456.
SCHMÄDEKE (Jürgen), 4816.
SCHMIDL (Erwin A.), 490, 5194.
SCHMID-SIKIMIC (Biljana), 1691.
SCHMIDT (Claudia), 6693.
SCHMIDT (Dörte), 6935.
SCHMIDT (Georg), 7941.
SCHMIDT (Gérard), 1849.
SCHMIDT (Karl J.), 8818.
SCHMIDT (Paul Gerhard), 3292, 4120.
SCHMIDT (Peter R.), 644.
SCHMIDT (Thomas C.), 955.
SCHMIDT (V.), 2532.
SCHMIDT (Victor Michael), 4192.
SCHMIDT-DICK (Franziska), 318.
SCHMIDT-NOWARA (Christopher Ebert), 4650.
SCHMINCK (Andreas), 3079.
SCHMITT (Carl), 956, 6317, 7541.
SCHMITT (Ch.), 4056.

SCHMITT (J.-C.), 4020.
SCHMITT (Oliver J.), 3166.
Schmoller (Gustav), 7040.
SCHMUGGE (Ludwig), 4530.
SCHNEID (Frederick C.), 8005.
SCHNEIDER (Cathy Lisa), 4748.
SCHNEIDER (Helmut), 6366.
SCHNEIDER (Jakob Hans Josef), 4363.
SCHNEIDER (Katja), 2906.
SCHNEIDER (Robert J.), 3920.
SCHNEIDER (Ulf-Michael), 6694.
SCHNEIDMÜLLER (Bernd), 3477, 3486.
SCHNELL (B.), 97.
SCHNERB-LIÈVRE (Marion), 3326.
SCHNITZLER (Arthur), 6695.
SCHNURBEIN (Siegmar von), 2661.
SCHOBER (Richard), 5195.
SCHOCKENHOFF (E.), 3018.
SCHOEBERLEIN-ENGEL (John Samuel), 8813.
SCHOENER (Allon), 6742.
SCHOEPP (Sebastian), 6205.
SCHOFIELD (L.), 1726.
SCHOFIELD (Malcolm), 2287, 2324.
SCHOFIELD (Philip), 7894.
SCHOLL (Hans), 5855.
SCHOLL (R.), 1796.
SCHOLLIERS (Peter), 7104.
SCHOLTEN (Clemens), 2942.
SCHOLTEN (Helga), 2706.
SCHOORS (A.), 1728.
SCHOR (Naomi), 6696.
SCHÖRNER (Günther), 2907.
SCHOTT (Klausdieter), 3678.
SCHOTT (Walter), 6138.
SCHÖTTLER (Peter), 701, 749.
SCHOULER (B.), 3167.
SCHRAGE (Eltjo J.H.), 7658.
SCHRAUT (Barbara), 5775.
SCHRECKENBERGER (Waldemar), 7548.
SCHREIBER (Gerhard), 8302, 8414.
SCHREINER (Peter), 3092.
SCHRIJVERS (P. H.), 2235, 2751.
SCHRIRE (Carmel), 1591.
SCHRÖDER (Eberhard), 6483.
SCHRÖDER (Hans-Christoph), 4960.
SCHRÖDER (Hans-Jürgen), 8734.
SCHRÖDER (Iris), 4817.
Schubarth (Mateusz), 386.
SCHUBERT (C.), 2659.
SCHUCHARD (Christiane), 3247.
SCHUDSON (Michael), 6207.
SCHUHMACHER (Thomas X.), 1649.
SCHULER (S.), 4121.
SCHULTE-NOLKE (Hans), 7655.
SCHULTZ (Helga), 702.
SCHULTZ (J. P.), 1926.
SCHULTZ (James A.), 3860.

SCHULTZ (Johann), 6315.
SCHULZ (Brigitte), 8735.
SCHULZE (Reiner), 7536.
SCHULZE (Winfried), 4607, 6484.
SCHULZE WESSEL (Martin), 7778.
SCHUMACHER (Jan), 1390.
SCHUMAN (Maurice), 7779.
Schuman (Robert), 7698, 8513.
Schumpeter (Joseph), 6009, 6997.
SCHUNK-HELLER (Sabine), 4193.
Schuschnigg (Kurt), 7571.
SCHUSTER (Elisabeth), 362.
SCHUSTER (Raymund), 5776.
SCHÜTZ (Walter), 3248.
SCHWAB (Dieter), 7549.
SCHWABE (Klaus), 4606.
SCHWARCZ (Iskra I.), 957.
SCHWARTZ (Seth), 1755.
SCHWARZ (Hans-Peter), 4818.
SCHWARZ (Irene), 2736.
SCHWARZFUCHS (Simon), 3535.
SCHWEITZ (Arlette), 4887.
SCHWERHOFF (Gerd), 3861.
SCHWINGES (R. C.), 3182.
Sciascia (Leonardo), 6944.
SCOBBIE (Irene), 1157.
SCOLLO LAVIZZONI (Marco), 7575.
SCONOCCHIA (Sergio), 2593.
SCOPPOLA (Pietro), 5043.
SCORZA BARCELLONA (Francesco), 3040.
SCOTT (D.), 2325.
SCOTT (David), 1412.
SCOTT (Dominic), 1522.
SCOTT (H. M.), 4608.
SCOTT (T. Kermit), 3019.
SCOTTUS ERIUGENA (Iohannes), 4285, 6246.
SCRIBA (Friedemann), 5044.
SCUDERI (Graziella), 6139.
SCULLY (D. Eleanor), 3862.
SCULLY (Pamela), 5458.
SCULLY (S.), 2069.
SCULLY (Terence), 3862, 3863.
SEAFORD (Richard), 2326.
SEAGER (Richard Hughes), 5667.
SEALY (Judith), 1591.
SEARLE (Geoffrey R.), 4961.
SEARS REYNOLDS (Jayne), 6347.
SEBESTYÉN (Kálmán), 6140.
SEDLIAKOVÁ (Alžbeta), XX.
SEDOV (A. V.), 3557.
SEEBOHM (A.), 97.
SEEWANN (Harald), 5964.
SEGAL (Charles), 2107, 2327.
SEGARRA CRESPO (Diana), 2854.
SEGATTO (Jose Antonio), 4736.
SEGBERS (Klaus), 8707.
Ségolène, Sancta, 4473.
SEGONDS (A. P.), 2104.
SÉGUENNY (André), 5633.

SEGURA GRAÍÑO (Cristina), 3402.
SEGURET (Pierre), 4233.
SEIDEL (Anne), 5942.
SEIDEL (Carlos Collado), 5446.
SEIDENSTICKER (Mike), 958.
SEIFERT (Carsten), 7306.
SEIKALY (May), 5212.
SEIP (Anne-Lise), 5168.
SEIWERT (Elvira), 6969.
SEIWERT (Hubert), 1492.
SEKUNDA (N.), 2224.
SELGE (Kurt-Victor), 4278.
SELIGER (Maren), 5196.
SELINGMANN (Linda J.), 5218.
SELIVANOV (Igor' N.), 8736.
SELLERS (Leonard), 8171.
SELLERT (Wolfgang), 2174.
SELLIN (Volker), 959.
SELZ (Gebhard J.), 1850.
SEMENĆENKO (L. V.), 776.
SEMENOVKER (Boris A.), 3084.
SEMIRJAGA (Mihkaik I.), 8303.
SEMOTANOVA (Eva), 396.
SEMROV (Andrej), 309.
Sen (Amartya K.), 7062.
SENAC (Philippe), 3363.
SENATOR (Aleksej I.), 5057.
SENCHENKO (I. A.), 7795.
SENDLER (Shmuel), 8598.
Seneca (Annaeus Lucius), 2591, 2594, 2737, 2753, 3328.
SENEKOWITSCH (Martin), 5197.
SENELLART (Michel), 1225.
SENIN (A. S.), 5332.
SENJAVSKAJA (Elena S.), 8389.
SENJAVSKIJ (A. S.), 7338.
SENN (Peter R.), 7042.
SENTIS (Laurent), 6310.
ŞENTÜRK (Hüdai), 5529.
SERBAT (Guy), 2542.
SERBIN (Andrés), 5583.
SERCAMBI (G.), 3916.
SERÇE (Erkan), 7526.
SERGI (Giuseppe), 3844, 3881.
SERONDE-BABONAUX (Anne-Marie), 7342.
SERRA (Enrico), 771.
SERRAI (Alfredo), 179.
SERRANO (Monica), 5130.
SERRÃO (Vitor), 6851.
SERTL (Franz), 6348.
SESMA MUÑOZ (José Ángel), 3864.
SETH (Sanjay), 4982.
ŠETIĆ (Nevio), 5069.
SETON (Rosemary), 9081.
SETTESOLDI (Enzo), 3210.
SEVEGRAND (Martine), 5778.
SEVESTRE (Nicole), 4259.
SEVÓN (Cay), 8738.
SEVOST'JANOV (Grigorij N.), 5058, 8172.

Sextus Empiricus, 2108.
SEYMOUR (Charles), 6852.
SEYMOUR (M. C.), 4122.
Sforza (Francesco), 3514.
SHACKLETON BAILEY (D.R.), 2595.
Shaftesbury (Anthony Ashley Cooper, Earl of), 6244.
SHAHÎD (Irfan), 3168.
SHAKER (Sallama), 5530.
Shakespeare (William), 1022, 6560, 6564, 6581, 6593, 6936.
SHAMBAUGH (David), 7772, 8739.
SHAMMA (Samir), 319.
SHANK (Michael H.), 4123.
SHAO (Yong), 8922.
Shapiro (Meyer), 6820.
SHARAN (Ishwar), 5943.
SHARF (Robert H.), 5944.
SHARMA (Arvind), 5945.
SHARP (Paul), 8740.
SHAW (Brent D.), 2662.
SHAW (Carolyn Martin), 5084.
SHAW (Gregory), 4375.
SHAW (J. W.), 2006.
SHAW (M. C.), 2006.
SHAW (Prue), 3974.
SHEARD (Sally), 7333.
SHEARMAN (Peter), 8741.
SHEFTON (B. B.), 2503.
SHEHADI (Fadlou), 4260.
Sheldon (Charles Monroe), 1422.
SHELDON-WILLIAMS (I. P.), 4285.
SHELLENBERGER (Michael), 4730.
SHELLEY (Percy Bysshe), 6697.
SHELTON (J. C.), 2094.
SHEN (John), 9077.
SHEPARD (Jonathan), 3390.
SHEPARD S. WHITE (L.), 3917.
SHEPHERD (S. H. A.), 3907.
SHERBERG (Barbara), 2738.
SHEREMET (Vitalii Ivanovich), 8173.
SHERMAN (Claire Richter), 4124.
SHERMAN SEVERIN (Dorothy), 3865.
SHERMER (Michael), 870.
SHERRATT (Andrew), 1329.
SHERRY (Michael S.), 5610.
SHETLER (Jan), 5468.
SHI (Zhongwen), 8923.
SHIBATA (Michio), 1095.
SHIBATA (Shinichi), 9058.
SHIFFMAN (Gary Adam), 2226.
SHIHAB (Rafi`ullah), 5207.
SHIMAZU (Naoko), 8147, 8174.
SHIMOTAMAI (Nobuo), 8558.
SHIOMI (Haruhito), 7163.
SHIRREFF (David), 8390.
SHORE (Marlene), 703.
SCHOUTEN (M. T. A.), XV.
SHRIMPTON (Gordon), 841.
SHU (Jianmin), 8898.
SHUBERT (Adrian), 5438.

SIAT (Jeannine), 3020.
SIBYLLE (Eva), 3478.
SICA (Paolo), 7315.
SICARD (Patrice), 3337.
SIDDIQI (Asiya), 7839.
SIDOROV (V. V.), 1650.
SIEBERER (Wido), 960.
SIEDLER (Elfriede), XVI.
SIEGEL (Daniel M.), 6485.
SIEMS (Harald),3679.
SIERCK (Michael), 3403.
SIERRA (Sergio J.), 3532.
SIGAL (Pierre-André), 3324.
Sigismond, king of Hungary, 3875, 3972.
Sigismondo Tizio, 4154.
Sigismund von Luxemburg, röm.-deutscher Kaiser, 3499.
SIGNES (Juan), 3169.
SIGNORI (Gabriela), 416.
SIGNORINI (M.), 39.
SIGURDSSON (Jón Vidar), 5004.
SIHLER (A. L.), 1560.
SIJELMASSI (M.),25.
SIKAINGA (Ahmad), 7885.
ŞIK (Yüksel), 7527.
SIKLOS (Richard), 6208.
SILBER (Laura), 8742.
SILBERMAN (A.), 2052.
SILEO (L.), 4271.
SILEO (Leonardo), 4389.
Silio Italico, 206.
SILK (Mark), 5668.
SILLEVIS (John), 6853.
SILVA (Charles), 8763.
SILVERS (Robert B.), 6486.
SIMEK (Jan F.), 1620.
SIMEON (Dilip), 4983.
Simiand (François), 6009.
Simmel (Georg), 5998, 6042.
SIMMS (Brendan), 8006.
SIMÓ (Rafel), 1613.
SIMON (Alfred), 6609.
SIMON (Dieter), 3079.
SIMON (Françoise), 8743.
SIMON (Jean), 8391.
SIMON (Larry J.), 3866.
SIMON (Thomas), 3680.
SIMON (Zsuzsanna), 5571.
Simon de Montfort, 3883.
SIMONCELLI (Paolo), 754, 6854.
SIMONELLI (Antonietta), 2530.
SIMONETTA (S.), 3479.
SIMONETTI (Adele), 4531.
SIMONETTI (Giuseppina Abbolito), 4268.
SIMONETTI (Manlio), 1494, 3021.
SIMONITI (Vasko), 3867.
SIMONS (Jon), 6349.
SIMPSON (Ian A.), 1631.
SIMPSON (James), 7074, 7264.

SIMPSON (John), 1960.
SIMPSON (William Cook), 8415.
SIMS (Richard), 8064.
SIMS-WILLIAMS (P.), 4126.
ŞIMŞİRGİL (Ahmet), 1306.
SINERMA (Martti), 4846.
SINGER (Hans W.), 1307.
SINGER (Noel F.), 6970.
SINGH (Hari), 8744.
SINGH (R. G.), 4984.
SINGMAN (Jeffrey L.), 3868.
SINICROPI (G.), 3916.
SINISCALCO (Paolo), 1494, 3022.
SINISI (Silvana), 6971.
SINKEWICZ (Robert E.), 3085.
SINKOLI (Anna), 7970.
SINOPOLI (Franca), 6517.
SINOVA (Justino), 6209.
SIRERA (Josep Lluis), 1561.
SIRINELLI (J. F.), 600, 4867.
ŠIRINJA (Kirill K.), 4652.
SIRINJAN (Manja), 2929.
ŠIROKOV (V. G.), 7096.
SIRONEN (T.), 2480.
SLIŚCANU (Ion), 8353.
ŠIŠKIN (V. A.), 8120.
SITZLER (Dorothea), 5946.
SIVONEN (Seppo), 6141.
SJOBERG (Boris), 6487.
SJÖBERG (Marja T.), 7126.
SKAARE (Kolbjörn), 320.
SKAFTE JENSEN (Minna), 1547.
SKALNES (Tor), 5384.
ŠKAROVSKIJ (Mikhail V.), 5837.
SKARŻYŃSKI (Tadeusz), 6488.
SKIERSKA (Izabela), 5745.
SKINNER (Patricia), 3869.
SKŁADANKOWA (Maria), 1360.
SKOCZYŃSKI (Zbigniew), 6488.
SKOWRONEK (Jerzy), 450.
SKRYNNIKOV (Ruslan G.), 1158.
SKRZYPEK (Marian), 6610.
ŠKUNAEV (S. V.), 3392.
ŠKVORĆEVIĆ (Antun), 1493.
SLÁDEK (Oldřich), 8304.
SLAVINSKIJ (Boris Nikolaevich), 8305.
SLAVITT (D. R.), 2594.
SLINGS (A. H.), XV.
SLINGS (S. R.), 2273.
ŚLIWA (Michał), 727.
ŚLIWA (Monika), 4912.
SLOAN (Stephen), 1069.
SŁOCZYŃSKI (Henryk), 704.
SŁODKOWSKA (Inka), 5260.
SLUITER (I.), 2273.
ŚLUSARCZYK (Jacek), 7780.
SMADJA (Élisabeth), 2378, 2855.
SMAGA (Józef), 5311.
SMARR (J. L.), 3908.
SMEDLEY-WEILL (Anette), 7611.

SMEND (R.), 1961.
SMEYERS (M.), 93.
SMEYERS (Maurits), 4211.
SMILEY (Gene), 7297.
SMILEY (T. J.), 1521.
SMIRNOVA-SESLAVINSKAJA (M. V.), 1049.
Smith (Adam), 3554, 6992, 7036, 7037, 7041.
SMITH (Anthony D.), 553.
SMITH (Barry), 1512.
SMITH (Bonnie G.), 705.
SMITH (C. D.), 397.
SMITH (David A.), 8745.
SMITH (David M.), 3681.
SMITH (Dennis B.), 5059.
SMITH (H. S.), 1787, 2178.
SMITH (Harold E.), 1172.
SMITH (Hazel), 8746.
SMITH (Iain R.), 8065.
SMITH (J. J.), 4071.
SMITH (James Morton), 5609.
SMITH (Julia M. H.), 3423, 3870, 4414.
SMITH (L.), 4172.
SMITH (Lesley), 4173, 4273.
SMITH (M. L. R.), 5003.
SMITH (Malcom C.), 6587.
SMITH (Margaret), 5947.
SMITH (Michael), 7720.
SMITH (Patricia Juliana), 6916.
SMITH (R. R. R.), 1757.
SMITH (Richard Candida), 6770.
SMITH (Rowland), 2663.
SMITH (Simon C.), 7836.
SMITH (Susan L.), 4127.
SMITH (Thea Katharine), 2329.
SMITH (Thomas C.), 9059.
SMITH (Thurman L.), 294.
SMITH (William C.), 5583.
SMITS (Jan Pieter), 7060.
Smollett (Tobias George), 6020.
SMOŁUCHA (Janusz), 3513.
SMORAG (Malgorzata), 6055.
SMOUT (Christopher), 7340.
SMOUT (T. C.), 7088.
SMURTHWAITE (David), 8392.
SMYTH (Alfred P.), 3424.
SNAPE (Robert John), 470.
SNODGRASS (Mary Ellen), 1564.
SNYDER (Jed C.), 7837.
SNYDER (Lawrence D.), 6972.
SNYDER (Lee R.), 6350.
So (Alvin Y.), 8747.
SOAVE (Sergio), 5050.
SOBRAL CENTENO (Rui Manuel), 313.
SODEN (Wolfram von), 1927.
SOGNER (Sölvi), 643.
SOGNO (Edgardo), 8374.
SOGRIN (Vladimir V.), 5350, 6299.

ŠOKINA (Izabella E.), 4695.
Sokołowski (Wojciech SJ), 5737.
Sōkratēs, 2168, 2279, 2436, 6222, 6242.
SOLAK (Zbigniew), XVII, 6045.
SOLAR (Peter M.), 7133.
ŠOLC (Jiří), 8416.
SOLDO (Josip Ante), 7341.
SOLER I LLOPART (Albert), 4058.
SOLIGNAC (A.), 1448.
SOLIN (Heikki), 2509.
SOLLERS (Philippe), 6771.
SOLOMON (Maynard), 6973.
Solōn, 2054.
SOLOV'EVA (L. T.), 1050.
SOLOWAY (Richard A.), 6489.
SOMAKIAN (Manoug Joseph), 4698.
SOMAN (Alfred), 7594.
Sombart (Werner), 6997.
SOME (Malidoma Patrice), 5948.
SOMMELLA (Paolo), 2481.
SOMMER (D.), 1439.
SOMMER (Deborah), 5949.
SOMMERLECHNER (Andreas), 3239.
SOMMERSTEIN (Alan Herbert), 2228.
SOMMESTAD (Lena), 1276, 1308.
SOMOGYI (Éva), 5198.
SOMOGYI (Rosa Anna), 5045.
SOMOGYI (Stefano), 5045.
SOMORJA (Olga), 6912.
SONDHAUS (Lawrence), 4819.
SONG (Dejin), 8924.
SONG (Hyun-Ho), 7037.
Song (Huizong), 8985.
SONODA (Hidehiro), 7457.
SONYEL (Salahi R.), 8175.
Sophocles, 1993, 2240, 2286, 2327.
SORDI (Marta), 2504, 2620.
SORELL (Tom), 6335.
SØRENSEN (Georg), 8593.
SÖRENSEN (Öivind), 1119.
SORIA (Víctor), 7298.
SORICELLI (Gianluca), 2664.
SÖRLIN (Sverker), 7431.
SOROKA (Józef Michał), 7529.
SOSA LLANOS (Pedro Vicente), 5584, 7459.
SOSLAU (Eric), 292.
SOSLAU (Judy), 292.
SOSZYŃSKI (Jacek), 3327.
Sot (Michel), 582.
SOTNAK (Eric), 6351.
SOTNIKOVA (M. P.), 321.
SOTO (Lionel), 5100.
SOTO ARANGO (Diana), 5967.
SOUBIRAN (Jean), 2596.
SOUCY (Robert), 4913.
SOUFFRANT (Claude), 4974.
SOULE (Claude), 7612.
SOURIAC (René), 4914.
SOURVINOU-INWOOD (C.), 2227.

SOUSA (Bernardo Vasconcelos), 3872.
SOUSTAL (Peter), 3054.
Soustelle (Jacques), 9115.
SOUTHARD (Robert), 768.
SOUTHERN (R. W.), 4376.
SOUTO (Juan Antonio), 3569.
SOUTOU (Georges-Henri), 8176.
SOVERINI (P.), 2737.
SOWA (Zbigniew), 5244.
SOWINA (Urszula), 3873.
SPADOLINI (Giovanni), 5029.
SPAINER (John W.), 8750.
SPALINGER (Anthony), 1797.
SPALLANZANI (Marco), 3210.
SPALLONE (Maddalena), 3328.
SPANG (Paul), 5103.
SPANGER (Hans-Joachim), 8751.
SPARKS (Alister), 5460.
SPARR (Martin), 706.
SPATHARAKIS (I.), 181.
SPATHIS (Spyros), 1972.
SPATZ (L.), 1926.
SPAULDING (Jay), 3570.
Spaun (Anton von), 975.
SPEAKE (Graham), 1142.
SPEAR (Joanna), 8752.
SPECTOR (Sherman David), 8177.
SPECTRE (Peter H.), 6875.
SPEER (Andreas), 4270, 4377.
SPEIDEL (Michael P.), 2908.
SPENCER (N.), 2431.
Spengler (Oswald), 810.
Spenser (Edmund), 1022.
ŠPÉT (Jiří), 707.
SPEYER (Wolfgang), 1413.
SPICCIANI (A.), 3838.
SPIEGEL (Gabrielle M.), 961.
SPIEGEL (Joachim), 76.
SPIEGELMAN (Willard), 6772.
Spielberg (Steven), 928.
SPIES (Bernhard), 6698.
SPIESER (Jean-Michel), 3170.
SPIEZIO (Kim Edward), 7781.
SPINAZZOLA (Vittorio), 5029.
SPINDLER (Konrad), 1643.
Spinelli (Altiero), 5988.
SPINELLI (E.), 2108.
SPINGER (Claudia), 6974.
Spinoza (Baruch), 6322.
SPIRIDONOVIC (Srdan), 322.
SPITZER (Schlomo J.), 5950.
Splett (Karol Maria Antoni), 5728.
SPOERER (Mark), 7134.
SPOOR (Max), 5155.
ŠPOTOV (Boris M.), 5611.
SPOTTEL (Michael), 1051.
SPREE (R.), 7460.
SPRINGBORG (Patricia), 1226.
SPROXTON (Judy), 5886.
SPRUIT (J. E.), 2680.

SRAIEB (Noureddine), 5509.
SREJOVIC (Dragoslav), 322.
SRINIVAS CHARY (M.), 8753.
ŚRÓDKA (Andrzej), 1338, 6046.
STABRYŁA (S.), 2816.
STACEY (Vivienne), 5951.
STACHEL (John), 1335.
STACHNAL-TALANDA (Danuta), 384.
STACKER (Thomas), 7663.
STACKHOUSE (John G.), 5887.
STADE (Martin), 6683.
STADLER (Peter), 708.
STAEHELIN (Martin), 4187.
Staël de Launay (Marguerite-Jeanne Cordier, Madame de), 6681.
STÄHLI (M.), 158, 171.
STAIGER (Janet), 6975.
STAITI (C.), 4532.
Stalin (Iosif Visarionovič Džugašvili), 746, 5404, 5409, 5420, 6705, 7753, 8164, 8205, 8220, 8239, 8289, 8291, 8617, 8633, 8800.
STALLAERTS (Robert), 1160.
STALLEY (R. F.), 2053.
STALLS (Clay), 3480.
STAMBOULI (Andrés), 5583.
STANEK (Aleksander), 6490.
STANILOAE (Dumitru), 5838.
Stanislas di Scarbimiria, 4498.
STANISZEWSKI (Andrzej), 7447.
STANTON (Domna C.), 6080.
STANTON (Leonard J.), 5839.
STAPLETON (Timothy J.), 709.
STÄRK (Ekkehard), 2809.
STARK (Tamás), 5572.
STARKE (Frank), 1878.
STARN (Orin), 5219, 5220.
STAROBINSKI (Jean), 2071.
STARZYCZNÁ (Halina), 5503.
STASZEWSKI (Jacek), 5242.
STATHAKIS (G.), 8754.
STAUBACH (N.), 4130.
STAUFFACHER-SCHAUB (Marianne), 1482.
STAVIG (Ward), 1052.
STAVRIANOPOULOU (Efychia), 2345.
STAWECKI (Piotr), 8178.
STAZIO (Attilio), 2482.
STECHER (Gudrn Theresia), 4378.
Stedingk (Curt von), 7767.
STEEDMAN (Carolyn), 6699.
STEEL (Nigel), 8179.
STEEN (Jörgen), 325.
STEFANO DI LECCE, 3329.
Stegemann (EKKEHARD), 2958.
Stegemann (WOLFGANG), 2958.
STEGMANN (Bernd), 8302.
STEHLE (Hansjakob), 8755.
STEHLIN (Roland), 7099.

Stein (Albert), 5733.
Stein (Lorenz von), 7040.
STEIN (Stephen J.), 5888.
STEINBERG (Jonathan), 8306.
STEINBERG (Mark), 5351.
STEINBY (Eva Margareta), 387.
STEINDL (Frank George), 7299.
STEINER (Deborah Tarn), 2379.
STEINER (George), 1565.
STEINER (Herbert), 8354.
STEINER (Jan), 5503.
STEINER (Philippe), 6009, 7002, 7038.
STEINER (Ruth), 4261.
STEINER (Wolfgang), 5780.
STEINERT (M.), 7782.
STEINHÜBEL (Jan), 1161.
STEINKE (Klaus), 365.
STEINLE (Jürgen), 800.
STEINLE (Piero), 4767.
STEINMETZ (David C.)., 5889.
STEITKAMP (W.), 4624.
STELLA (Angelo), 6664.
STELLA (Francesco), 3911.
STELLA (Pietro), 5669.
STELZER (Winfried), 962.
STENGERS (Jean), 8180.
STEPAŠIN (S. V.), 5415.
Stephanus, Sanctus, protomartire, 2992.
STEPHENS (S. A.), 2045.
STEPHENSON (Gunther), 1414.
STĘPNIAK (Władysław), 8181.
STEPPAN (Markus), 1246.
STERBA (James P.), 6352.
STERBLING (Anton), 5977.
STERN (Fritz), 710.
STERNBERG (Th.), 2707.
STERN-GILLET (S.), 2331.
STERNINI (Mara), 2909.
STEVEN (Rob), 8756.
STEVENS (M.), 163.
STEVENS (Martin), 3983.
STEVENS (Susan T.), 2910.
STEVENS (W. M.), 4131.
STEVENS (Willy), 8757.
STEVENSON (Heon), 7228.
STEVENSON (J.), 4300.
STEVENSON (Jane), 4132.
STEVENSON (S. J.), 4542.
STEWART (Abigail J.), 6080.
STEWART (Hamish I.), 4744.
STEWART (Harry M.), 1798.
STEWART (Mary Lynn), 4851.
STEWART (Roberta), 2665.
Steyerers (Anton), 962.
STIEGMAN (Emero), 4269.
STIENNON (J.), 40.
STIETENCRON (Heinrich von), 1500.
STIH (Peter), 3481.
STILLE (Alexander), 5046.

STILLMAN (Robert E.), 6353.
STINCHCOMBE (Arthur L.), 7265.
STIPA (István), 5573.
STJERNØ (Steinar), 4657.
STOCCHIERO (Andrea), 8758.
STOCKLY (Doris), 7190, 7211.
STOCKWELL (A. J.), 7820.
STOCKWELL (S. E.), 7886.
STOK (F.), 2817.
Stoker (Bram), 6677.
STOKER (David), 3251.
STOKER (W.), 1410.
STOKES (Samuel), 5952.
STÖKLY (Doris), 3874.
STOLLBERG (Gunnar), 6445.
STOLLEIS (Michael), 1238.
STOLLER (Paul), 5953.
STOLLER (Richard), 5089.
STOLTE (A.), 182.
STOLTZFUS (Nathan), 7530.
Stolypin (P. A.), 5305.
STOLZ (Joachim), 6491.
STONE (Glyn), 7770, 8307.
STONE (Lawrence), 963.
STONE (Michael E.), 41.
STOOF (Magdalena), 1799.
STORA (Benjamin), 8759.
STORCHI MARINO (Alfredina), 6014.
STOREY (Robin Linsday), 3240, 4533.
STÖRK (L.), 187.
STORTI STORCHI (Claudia), 3617.
STORY (J.), 8551.
STOTZ (Peter), 4081.
STÖVER (Bernd), 7531.
ŠTOVÍČEK (Ivan), 8332.
STRABO (Walahfrid), 4299.
STRACHAN (J. C. G.), 2098.
STRASSNER (Erich), 366.
STRATMANN (Martina), 3188.
STRAUB (Christian), 4340.
STRAUB (Richard E. F.), 4135.
STRAUBEL (Rolf), 7229.
Strauss (Leo), 1201.
STRAUSS (Yael), 1913.
STRECK (Michael P.), 1851.
Streel (José), 4715.
STREISSLER (Erich W.), 7042.
Stresemann (Gustav), 4776.
STREVELER (Paul), 4336.
STRIKA (Vincenzo), 8760.
ŠTRIKKER (G.), 5836.
STRINGER (Keith J.), 717.
Strittmatter (Erwin), 6705.
STRONK (J. P.), 2112.
STROUD (Elaine C.), 1322.
STROUMSA (Gedaliahu A. G.), 5670.
STROUMSA (Guy G.), 1465.
STRUEVER (Nancy), 920.
STRZEMBOSZ (Adam), 8200.
STUBBE-DIARRA (Ira), 5954.

STUBBLEBINE (James H.), 6855.
STUDDERT-KENNEDY (Gerald), 7783.
STÜDELI (Bernhard), 4455.
STUDENY (Christophe), 7191.
STUDER (Basil), 2943, 5701.
STUDNICKI (Wladyslaw), 8308.
STUDT (Christoph), 4773.
STUECK (William Whitney), 8761.
ŠTUHEC (Marko), 7461.
STUIP (René Ernst Victor), 4373.
STUPPERICH (Reinhard), 6773.
STURGEON (Mary C.), 2911.
Sturm (Jacob), 5848.
STURM (Peter), 711.
STUUBS (Richard), 8423.
SUÁREZ (Margarite), 5221.
SUÁREZ ARGÜELLO (Clara Elena), 7192.
SUAREZ BILBAO (Fernando), 3540.
SUAU (Jean-Pierre), 4234.
SUBRENAT (J.), 3915.
SUBRENAT (Jean), 4136.
ŠUBRT (Jiří), 964.
SUBTIL (José Manuel Louzada Lopes), 7230.
SUCHCITZ (Andrzej), 5232.
SUCHECKY (Bernard), 5716.
SUCKALE (Robert), 4235.
SUCKALE-REDLEFSEN (Gude), 123.
SUĆKOV (Igor' V.), 6142.
SUDOL (Adam), 7784.
SUDOLSKI (Zbigniew), 6701.
SUENARI (Michio), 8824.
Suetonius (Tranquillus Gaius), 2817.
SUEUR (L.), 6048, 6492.
SUGIHARA (Shirō), 9040.
SUGIMOTO (Yoshihiko), 6049.
SUGIYAMA (Masaaki), 8814.
SUHL (Alfred), 3023.
SUK (Jiří), 5504.
SUKER (Dahir Mohamed), 5107.
SULERŻICKIJ (L. D.), 1666.
Suleiman I Kanuni, sultano ottomano, 5521, 7919, 7924.
SULLIVAN (Lawrence R.), 8925.
SULLIVAN (Richard E.), 3999.
SULLIVAN (S. D.), 2332.
SULLIVAN (Thomas), 4137.
Sulzbach (Christian August von), 5893.
SULZGRUBER (W.), 269.
SUMM (Harvey), 4737.
SUMMERS (G.D.), 1734.
SUMMERS (M. E. F.), 1734.
SUMNY (Ralph), 8762.
SUN (Yan), 8926.
Sun (Yatsen), 9000.
SUNDAR (Pushpa), 6774.
SUNDERMEYER (T.), 1495.
SUNDSTRÖM (Niclas), 1096.

SUPINO MARTINI (P.), 42.
SUPPLE (James J.), 825.
SUPRUNIUK (Mirosław Adam), 6213.
SURANYI (Béla), 7266.
SURCHAT (Pierre Louis), XIX.
SURDEZ (Muriel), 5376.
SURDICH (Luigi), 6702.
SURIKOV (I. E.), 2179.
SURTZ (Ronald E.), 4138.
SUSANETTI (D.), 2101.
SUSI (Eugenio), 3041.
SUSSMAN (Herbert), 6703.
SUTER (Andreas), 5377.
SUTHERLAND (Elizabeth H.), 2597.
SUTHERLAND (Kathryn), 7036.
SUTTERLIN (Siegfried H.), 8182.
SUVENIROV (Oleg F.), 5422.
SUVIN (Darko), 6517.
SUZUMURA (K.), 7062.
SUZZI VALLI (Roberta), 5049.
SVALESEN (Leif), 7887.
SVÁTEK (František), 7462.
SVENSON (Dominique), 2430.
SVENSSON (Lars), 7463.
SVENSTRUP (Thyge), 744.
SWADDLING (Judith), 2463.
SWANN (Julian), 4915.
SWANSON (R. N.), 4534.
SWARUP (Ram), 5956.
SWEARER (Donald K.), 1496.
SWEENEY (Del), 3691.
SWIETOCHOWSKI (Tadeusz), 8764.
SWITTE (Margaret L.), 4262.
SYED (Muhammad Aslam), 5957.
SYLOS LABINI (Paolo), 1227.
SYME (Ronald), 2333.
SYMINGTON (D.), 1739.
SYNAN (Edward A.), 4379.
SZABO (János), 1053.
SZABO (Péter), 8393.
SZAKÁCS (Sándor), 7267.
SZAKÁLY (Ferenc), 391, 7942.
SZAREJKO (Piotr), 6493.
SZARKA (Laszlo), 8183.
SZAROTA (Tomasz), 5266, 8309.
SZCZEPANIK (Krzysztof), 5248.
SZCZUDŁOWSKI (Piotr), 5781.
SZÉKELY (György), 4535.
SZELEST (H.), 2818.
SZENDEI (Janka), 4252.
SZENDREI (Janka), 4263.
SZIDAT (Joachim), 2739.
SZÍJ (Rezső), 6050.
SZILÁGYI (István), 5871.
SZKÁLY (Ferenc), 5574.
SZLAJFER (Henryk), 5235, 7231.
SZNYCER (Maurice), 1918.
SZOKOLAY (Katalin), 8355.
Szondi (Leopold), 6328.
SZÖRÉNYI (László), 4479.
SZOSTAK (Rick), 7135.

SZTURC (Jan), 5890.
SZUBERT (Piotr), 6856.
Szujski (Józef), 704.
SZYDŁOWSKA (Mariola), 6977.
SZYMAŃSKI (Józef), 4536.
SZYMAŃSKI (Leonard), 6143.

T

TABALUJAN (Carlo Hein), 4989.
TABLIT (Ali), 8007.
TABURET-DELAHAYE (Elisabeth), 6876.
TACHAU (Katherine H.), 4336.
TACHET (Alain), 6013.
Tacitus (Publius Cornelius), 837, 2549, 2796, 2799.
TAÇON (Paul S. C.), 1621.
TADINA (Nadežda A.), 1054.
TAFT (Robert F.), 5840.
TAFT MORRIS (Cynthia), 7136.
TÄGIL (Sven), 8765.
Taizu, Ming emperor, 8914.
TAKÁCS (Sarolta A.), 1800.
TAKAHASHI (Hidenao), 8927.
TAKAHASHI (Mutsuko), 5060.
TAKAHASHI (Yoshito), 1163.
TAKAMURA (Naosuke), 7137.
TAKAYAMA (H.), 3683.
TAKAYAMA (Hiroshi), 3394.
Takebee Hiranoya of Osaka, 9064.
TAL (L.), 8766.
TALBOTT (Rick Franklin), 5958.
TALIBI (Faramarz), 295.
Talleyrand-Périgord (Charles-Maurice prince de), 8009.
TAM (On Kit), 8928.
TAMAKI (Norio), 7300.
TAMBURINI (Filippo), 5812.
TANAKA (Mineo), 4139.
TANAKA (Takeshi), 8356.
TANAKA (Takeo), 9068.
TANAKA (Yuko), 9060.
TANDECKI (Janusz), 1310.
TANDETER (Enrique), 7380.
TANG (Ling), 8929.
TANG (Lixing), 8930.
TANGHERONI (Marco), 3446.
TANIGAWA (Michio), 8931.
TANIGUCHI (Kazuo), 9024.
TANII (Yōko), 8932.
Tannenbaum (Frank), 5120.
TANNER (Albert), 5378.
TANSINI (Raffaella), 2912.
TARAS (Raymond), 5267.
TARDIEU (Jean-Pierre), 5813.
TARGOSZ (Karolina), 4140, 6858.
TARNOVSKIJ (Konstantin N.), 7193.
Tarquinius Priscus, re di Roma, 2648.

TARRANT (Richard J.), 4141.
TARRANT (V. E.), 8184.
TARTAKOVSKIJ (A. G.), 5302.
TASCA (Angelo), 5050.
TASHIRO (Kazuo), 9074.
Tassilon III, 3737.
TASSO (BERNARDO), 6545.
Tasso (Torquato), 6556, 6709.
TATARINOV (Jurij B.), 4916.
TATARKIN (A. I.), 7129.
TATE (Georges), 519.
TATEO (Francesco), 4142.
TATIANUS (il Siro), 2944.
TATON (René), 6495.
Tauber (Caspar), 5869.
TAUBER (Eli'ezer), 4991.
TAUDEND (Klaus), 2148.
TAVIANI (Paolo), 1497.
TAYLOR (Alan John Percivale), 7785.
TAYLOR (Antony), 4944.
Taylor (Isidore-Justin-Severin), baron, 6743.
TAYLOR (Jack H.), 5174.
TAYLOR (Jane H. M.), 4172, 4173.
TAYLOR (Justin), 3024.
TAYLOR (Miriam S.), 3025.
TAYLOR (Pamela), 4575.
TAYLOR (Raymond M.), 5108.
TAYLOR HANSEN (Lawrence Douglas), 5131.
TAZBIR (Janusz), 1145.
TCHERNIA (André), 2229, 2740.
TECUSAN (M.), 1273.
TEDESCHI (C.), 43.
TEITELBAUM (Kenneth), 6144.
TEITLER (H. C.), 2548.
TEIXEIRA (Francisco Nuñes), 5136.
TEJRAL (Jaroslav), 1705.
TEKE (Zsuzsa), 3875.
TELEGIN (D. Ja.), 1651.
TELESKO (W.), 184.
TELESKO (Werner), 4537.
TELHAMI (Shibley), 8530.
Tell (William), 5372.
TELO (Antonio José), 8185.
TEMIMI (Abdeljelil), 712, 1065, 7943, 8008.
TEMIN (Peter), 7138.
TEMPERLEY (Howard), 8295.
Tenamaztle (Francisco), 7903.
TENENTI (Alberto).7944.
TENNANT (P.M.W.), 2856.
Teodorico, re dei Goti, 3425.
TERNI (Massimo), 1228.
TERPSTRA (Nicholas), 3876.
TERRELL (Jennifer), 9119.
TERTRAIS (H.), 7838.
TESHALE (Tibebu), 4701.
TESNIERE (Marie-Hélène), 3969.
TESSITORE (Fulvio), 965.

TESTI (Arnaldo), 5612, 6210.
THACKRAY (Arnold), 1328.
THAKUR (Ramesh), 4985.
Thalēs, 6331, 6378.
THAPAR (Romila), 713.
THEBERGE (Pierre), 6859.
THEBERT (Y.), 2666.
THEIBAULT (John C.), 4821.
THEILER (Dominique), 7971.
THEIS (Lioba), 3104.
Themistoklēs, 2139, 2299.
Theocritos, 2248, 2254, 2554.
Theodor Abu Qurra, 3062.
Théodore de Bèze, 5843.
Theodorus Studites, Sanctus, 3059.
THEODORE, Archbishop of Canterbury, Sanctus, 4300.
Théodoret de Cyr, 2991, 3090.
THEODORIDES (Jean), 1361.
Theodosius I, imperatore romano, 2672.
Theognis, 2316.
Theoleptos of Philadelpheia, 3085.
Theophanes Continuatus, 3169.
Theramenes, 2061, 2119.
Theresa de Avila, Sancta, 4138.
THERET (Bruno), 7194.
THIBODEAU (Thimothy M.), 3904.
THIELE (Eckhard), 6705.
THIERRY (André), 740.
THIERRY (Nicole), 3171.
Thiers (Augustin), 838.
THIESSEN (Werner), 2959.
THIJSSEN (Johannes M. M. H.), 4380.
THIREAU (Jean-Louis), 3687.
THIVEAUD (Jean-Marie), 1311.
THOEN (Erik), 3835.
THOENES (Christof), 6799.
THOMA (Petra), 6860.
THOMAS (Alfred), 1566.
Thomas Becket, Sanctus, 3712.
THOMAS (D.), 1739.
THOMAS (Helen), 6980.
THOMAS (Julian), 567.
THOMAS (M.), 132.
THOMAS (Martin), 7888, 8310.
THOMAS (Renate), 2913.
THOMAS (Rosalind), 2180.
THOMAS (Yves), 7613.
Thomas Aquinas, Sanctus, 758, 4307, 4324, 4342, 4369, 4370, 4371, 4388, 4392, 5943, 6310.
Thomas le Myésier, 4364.
THOME (J.), 2335.
THOMES (Paul), 1312.
THOMMEN (Lukas), 2741.
THOMPSON (Dennis W.), 8066.
THOMPSON (Michael), 3877.
THOMPSON (Roger C.), 8767.
Thompson (E. P.), 839.

Thomson (James), 6379.
THOMSON (Rodney M.), 4146, 4145.
Thornhill (James), 6379.
THOROCZKAY (Gábor), 714.
Thoukydidēs, 841, 2153, 2289, 2302, 2310.
THUILLIER (Jacques), 1567.
THUILLIER (Jean-Paul), 2505.
THUMSER (Matthias), 3878.
THUNMARK-NYLEN (Lena), 3589.
THÜRINGEN (Walter), 5844.
THURNER (Eugen), 966.
THURNER (Mark), 5222.
THURRE (Daniel), 6877.
TIAN (Maowu), 8933.
TIAN (Tao), 8934.
TIAN (Zhaomin), 8846.
Tiangong (Kaifu), 8843.
TIANZHEN (Xie), 6517.
Tiberius Julius Alexander, imperatore romano, 2038, 2603, 2657.
TIEDER (Irene), 811.
TIEKEN-BOON VAN OSTADE (Ingrid), 4147.
TIEMANN (Gabi), 988.
TIETMANN (Lutz), 7505.
Tiglath-Pileser III, king of Assyria, 1915.
TIGLER (Guido), 4194.
TILATTI (Andrea), 4148.
TILCHIN (William N.), 8067.
TILKOVSZKY (Loránt), 6145.
TILLARD (J.-M. R.), 1419.
TILLEY (Allen), 967.
TILLIETTE (Xavier), 6355.
TILLY (Ch.), 4601.
TIMMERMANS (Benoit), 6356.
TIMMS (Edward), 6706.
TIMOFEEV-RESOVSKII (H. V.), 6453.
TIMOŚĆUK (Boris A.), 1164.
TIMPSON (M. E.), 2886.
Tingsten (Herbert), 5363.
TINGUELY (F.), 6357.
TINNEFELD (Franz), 3089.
TISCHLER (Hans), 3955.
TISSIER (André), 6585.
TISSOT (Laurent), 1313.
Titus Aurelius Calpurnianus Apollonides, imperatore romano, 2608.
TITZE (Hartmut), 6146.
TIUTIUNDZHIEV (Ivan), 4743.
Tiziano Vecellio, 6808, 6850.
Tizio (Sigismondo), 4154.
TIZLAK (Fahrettin), 7195.
Tkačev (Pytotr), 6361.
TOBIA (Bruno), 5029.
TOBIN (Frank), 4149.
TOBIN (Ronald W.), 6624.
TOBLER (Hans Werner), 1314.

Tocqueville (Charles Alexis Henri Maurice Clérel de), 1179, 5929, 6312.
TODD (Jan), 6496.
TODD (Margo), 5671.
TODD (Robert B.), 829.
TODESCHINI (Giacomo), 3880.
TODOROV (Tzvetan), 969, 6671.
TODOROV (Vurban Nikolov), 4932.
Togliatti (Palmiro), 8238.
TOGNETTI (Sergio), 7139.
TOKAREVA (E. S.), 6299.
TOKAY (A. Gül), 5111.
TOKMAKOV (V. N.), 2667.
TOKMAN (Victor E.), 4749.
TOKODY (Gyula), 4822.
TOLDI (Ferenc), 5070.
TOLEDO (Paulino), 7148.
TOLLEY (Bruce), 5891.
TOLSTOGUZOV (Aleksandr A.), 9061.
Tolstoi (Nikita I.), 985.
Tolstoy (Lev Nikolaevič), 5839.
TOLU (Rosalia Manno), 424.
TOMASI DI LAMPEDUSA (Giuseppe), 6707.
TOMÁŠKOVÁ (Silvia), 1622.
TOMBA (Luigi), 8935.
TOMBS (Robert), 838.
TOMKA (Béla), 7140.
Tommaso di Giunta, 3311.
TOMMISSEN (Piet), 956.
TOMO (Shigeki), 7042.
TOMPKINS (Ian G.), 3090.
TONELOTTO (S.), 2450.
TONER (J.P.), 2742.
TONNERRE (Noël-Yves), 3684.
TOO (Y. L.), 2336.
TOPOLSKI (Jerzy), 1315.
TOPOROV (Vladimir N.), 3026.
TOPRAK (Zafer), 5532.
TORAO (Toshiya), 9062.
Torcia (Michele), 6606.
TORCOLI (Francesco), 8768.
TORDI (Rosita), 6981.
TORKE (Hans-Joachim), 5349.
TORKUNOV (A. V.), 7786.
TORO (María Celio), 5132.
TÖRÖK (Enikő), 6497.
TÖRÖK (József), 4150.
TÖRÖK (L.), 1772.
Török (Zsolt), 1340.
TORRA (J.), 210.
TORRACA (Luigi), 2380.
TORRANCE (John), 6358.
TORRE (Angelo), 4656, 5814.
TORRES (Joan Ramon), 1928.
TORRES PALOMO (M. Paz), 3550.
TORREY (Glenn E.), 8186.
TORRINI (Maurizio), 471.
TORRISI (Claudio), 1091.

TORTORELLI (Gianfranco), 6173, 773.
TORTORELLI GHIDINI (Marisa), 2043.
TORTZEN (Christian), 8311.
TOSCHI (Luca), 110.
TOSCHI (Simona), 8769.
TOSH (John), 7467.
TOSI (Claudio), 5782.
TOSI (R.), 2737.
TOSO (Mario), 5718.
TÓTH (Imre), 1405.
TÓTH (István György), 6051.
TÓTH (Sándor László), 3426.
TOTI (M. P.), 492.
Totting d'Oyta (Henryk), 4508.
TOUBERT (Pierre), 3881.
TOUCHETTE (Lori-Ann), 2914.
TOUMARKINE (Alexandre), 1055.
TOURNAVITOU (Iphigenia), 2020, 2021.
TOUZERY (Mireille), 4917.
TOWER HOLLIS (Susan), 1778.
TOWNSEND (R. F.), 2432.
TOWNSEND (Susan C.), 7821.
TOWNSON (Duncan), 1165.
Toynbee (Arnold), 840.
TRACY (Nicholas), 7972.
TRACY (S. V.), 1989.
TRÄGÅRDH (Lars), 7369.
Traianus (Marcus Ulpius), imperatore romano, 309, 3020.
TRAINA (Giusto), 766.
TRAMONTIN (Silvio), 5725.
TRAMPUS (Antonio), 715.
TRANCHO GALLO (Gonzalo), 1656.
TRANFAGLIA (Nicola), 5051.
TRANIELLO (Francesco), 5669.
TRAPP (E.), 3077.
TRAPPE (Tobias), 6359.
TRASK (R.L.), 367.
TRATNIK-VOLASKO (Marjeta), 7468.
TRAUTMANN (Thomas R.), 968.
TRAVAINI (Lucia), 323.
TREACHER (Adrian), 8520.
TREADGOLD (W.), 3105.
TREJSTER (M. Ju), 1097.
TREMBICKA (Krystyna), 7532.
TREMOLANTI (Ezio), 3254.
Trenchs i Òdena (Josep), 48, 67.
TRENT (John E.), 8428.
TREXLER (Richard C.), 4538, 7909.
TRIAUD (Jean-Louis), 1056.
TRIBE (Keith), 4823.
TRICARD (Jean), 3882.
TRIFONE (Pietro), 364.
TRIFONOV (Staiko), 8045.
Trifonow (Juri), 6705.
TRIGGER (Bruce G.), 1592.
TRIULZI (Alessandro), 9093.
TROCHET (Jean-René), 505.

TROELSGARD (C.), 33.
Troeltsch (Ernst), 6273.
TROJAN (Mieczysław), 5250.
TROMBETTA (Vincenzo), 471.
TRONCOSO (V. Alonso), 2181.
TROPPER (Josef), 1852, 1929.
TROTIGNON (Yves), 4824.
TROTTA (S.), 4153.
TROTTMANN (Christian), 4382.
TROUILLOT (Michel-Rolph), 6498.
TROUSSET (Pol), 9078, 9086.
TROY (Patrick), 4709.
TRŠAN (Lojz), 8417.
TRUDEL (Marcel), 5079.
TRUHART (Peter), 1167.
Truman (Harry S.), 7878.
TRUNZ (Erich), 6534.
TSAKMAKIS (Antonis), 2337.
TSAVARI (Isabella), 3076.
TSIPOPOULOU (Metaxia), 2022.
TSOKHAS (Kosmas), 8312.
TSOUNA-MAC KIRAHAN (V.), 2096.
TSUK (Tsvika), 1910.
TSUKIASHI (Tatsuhiko), 9075.
TSURUSHIMA (H.), 3483.
TUBACH (Jürgen), 1962.
TUCK (Jim), 6211.
TUCK (Patrick J. N.), 8068.
TÜDŐS (S. Kinga), 5575.
TUGAN-BARANOVSKIJ (Džuča M.), 6212.
TULARD (Jean), 8009.
TULVA (Taimi), 7469.
TŮMA (Oldřich), 8770.
TUMA (Renate), 5199.
TUNA-NÖRLING (Y.), 2433.
TUO (Heti), 8936.
Tupac Amaru, 7900.
TURBANTI (G.), 5704.
TURCHINI (Angelo), 5669.
TUREK (Otakar), 7141.
TURI (Gabriele), 6360.
TÜRKDOĞAN (Orhan), 7470.
TÜRKMEN (Zekeriya), 7657.
TURNER (Denys), 4383.
TURNER (Edith), 1497, 1501.
TURNER (Frederick), 6775.
TURNER (Ralph V.), 3484.
Turner (Victor), 1497, 1501.
TURPIN (John), 6776.
TURRINI (Patrizia), 4154.
TURTOLA (Martti), 716.
TURULL RUBINAT (Max), 3685.
TUŚ (Muhittin), 5533.
TUSA (Vincenzo), 2484, 2915.
TUSELL (Javier), 8313.
TVARDOVSKAJA (Valentina A.), 6361.
TWERASER (Kurt), 5200.
TYACK (David), 6147.
TYERMAN (C. J.), 3404.

TYGIELSKI (Wojciech), 5719.
TYSZKA (Przemysław), 398.
TZÉDAKIS (Yannis), 1999.
TZIFOPOULOS (Yannis Z.), 2338.

U

UDVARI (István), 5576.
UERPMANN (H.-P.), 1719.
UFIMCEV (E. P.), 7786.
Ugarte (Manuel), 5133.
UGOLINI (Gherardo), 2339.
UIBOPUU (Kaja), 2149.
UJMA (Christina), 6362.
ÚJVÁRY (Gábor), 6081.
ULFSTEIN (Geir), 7787.
ULLMANN (Manfred), 1930.
ULMANN (H.-P.), 4624.
ULPTS (Ingo), 4456.
ULRICH (Jens), 2668.
ULUNJAN (A. A.), 4933.
UMEHARA (Kaoru), 8937.
ÜNAL (Ahmet), 1880.
ÜNAL (Ingeborg), 4580.
UNDERHILL (Geoffrey R. D.), 8773.
UNFRIED (Berthold), 453.
UNGER (Brigitte), 7788.
UNGVÁRY (Krisztián), 8394.
Uno (Kozo), 7018.
UNVERRICHT (Hubert), 5754.
UOLA (Mikko), 7789.
URBAŃSKI (Stanisław), 5783.
Urbanus II, Papa, 4420.
URCIUOLI (G. M.), 1931.
URIARTE (Carmen), 8357.
URMINSKÝ (Ivan), 8188.
URSPRUNG (Philip), 6777.
URVOY (Dominique), 4384.
URZAINQUI (Inmaculada), 5970.
USSISHKIN (David), 1932.
USTINOVA (E. A.), 411.

V

VACCARO (Jean-Michel), 6905.
VACCARO (Luciano), 5731.
VÁCHOVÁ (Jana), 5470.
VACULÍK (Jaroslav), 7471.
VADKERTY (Katalin), 5505.
VAGGI (Gianni), 7041.
VAHL (W.), 290.
VAÏSSE (M.), 7790.
VAISSE (Pierre), 6861.
VALDÉS (C.), 1674.
VALDÉS (Fernando), 3571.
VALDÈS (Juan Gabriel), 4750.
VALE (Peter), 8751.
Valens, imperatore romano, 2670.
VALENSI (Lucette), 720, 742.

VALENTA (Jaroslav), 8189, 8332.
VALENTE (C.), 3883.
VALENTE (Vincenzo), 3321.
VALERIO (A.), 4539.
Valerius Maximus, 2599.
VALITSKAIA (A. P.), 746.
VALLAT (Colette), 7342.
VALLONE (Lynn), 7472.
VALLORA (Edgar), 6958.
VALSECCHI (B.), 44.
VAMMEN (Tinne), 7126.
VAN ANDEL (Tjeerd H.), 1593.
VAN ARK (Bart), 721.
VAN BREE (C.), 186.
VAN CAENEGEM (Raoul C.), 1248.
VAN DEN BROEK (Hans), 8467.
VAN DEN HOUT (Theo P. J.), 1879, 1881.
VAN DER BOSCHE (Bart), 6704.
VAN DER EIJK (Ph. J.), 2235, 2751.
VAN DER HORST (Pieter), 1434.
Van der Leeuw (Gerardus), 5752.
VAN DER MEER (L.B.), 2506.
VAN DER PARDT (R.T.), 2532.
VAN DER PIETER (W.), 1447.
VAN DER TOORN (Karel), 1407, 1447, 5672.
VAN DER WEE (Herman), 1316.
VAN DEURSEN (A. Th.), 5144.
VAN DEUSEN (Nancy), 4265.
VAN DONZEL (E.), 1451.
VAN DÜLMEN (Andrea), 1094.
VAN DÜLMEN (Richard), 6052.
VAN EENOO (Romain), II.
VAN EMDEN (Wolfgang), 4155.
VAN HEMELRYCK (T.), 3897.
VAN HOUTS (Elisabeth M. C.), 3330, 3335, 3395.
VAN KAN (F. J. W), 3405.
VAN KY (Nguyen), 5618.
VAN LERBERGHE (K.), 1728.
VAN LIERE (Franciscus A.), 4385.
VAN MAANEN (John), 1044.
VAN MINNEN (Peter), 2819, 3042.
VAN OORT (J.), 1471.
VAN SETTEN (G. J.), 5144.
VAN SLYCK (Abigail Ayres), 472.
VAN SPLUNTER (Jacob M.), 7819.
VAN TONGERLOO (A.), 1471.
VAN VLECK (Amelia), 3884.
VAN WAARDEN (Frans), 7788.
VAN WEERT-GAALMAN (M. E. J.), XV.
VAN ZANDEN (Jan Luiten), 7060, 7142.
VAN ZWIETEN (Jan W. M.), 4386.
VAN'T SPIJKER (Ienje), 4387.
VANDERJAGT (Ario J.), 4156.
VANDORPE (K.), 291.
VANĚK (Miroslav), 5506.
VANINA (Evgenija Ju.), 8819.

VANRIE (Andre), 4712.
VANSCHOENBEEK (Guy), 4721.
VANSÉVEREN (S.), 2340.
VANSINA (Jan), 971, 9105.
Vansittart (Robert sir), 8092, 8106, 8133, 8143, 8165.
VANVOLSEM (Serge), 6704.
VAQUERIZO GIL (D.), 2916.
VAQUINHAS (Irene Maria), 5288.
VAR'JAŠ (O. I.), 3393.
VARADI (Max), 8777.
VARANINI (Gian Maria), 3515, 3686.
VAREY (J. E.), 6778.
VARGA (János), 5577.
VARNER (Eric R.), 2917.
VARNI (Angelo), 5029.
VARPHES (Kostes A.), 4934.
Varro (Marcus Terentius), 2786.
VARVARO (A.), 4157.
Vasari (Giorgio), 6767, 6791.
VASCO ROCCA (Sandra), 6779.
VASEY (Ruth), 6982.
VASIL'EV (I. B.), 8806.
VASIL'EV (Leonid S.), 8938.
VASILIK (Vladimir), 5815.
VASOLI (Cesare), 1229, 4128, 4158.
VASQUES (Mario R.), IV.
VASQUEZ (John A.), 8778.
VAUCHEZ (André), 1458, 3184, 4528.
VAVILOV (N.), 6453.
VAYER (Lajos), 417.
VAZQUEZ VARELA (J. M.), 1594.
VEBER (Václav), 7474.
Veblen (Thorstein), 6009.
VECCHI (Paolo), 6917.
VECCHIO (Silvana), 4159.
VECCHIONI (Domenico), 8779.
VEDOVATO (Giuseppe), 8780.
VEENSTRA (Jan R.), 789.
VEGA (Bernardo), 4975.
VEGESACK (Thomas von), 5365.
Vegetius (Flavius Renatus), 2600.
VEGETTI-FINZI (S.), 6047.
VEKARIĆ (Nenad), 1317.
VELASCO DE ESPINOSA (Maria Teresa), 1368.
VELÁZQUEZ CANO (Julián), 1590.
VELIGIANNI (Chrissoula), 1963.
VELIMIROVI (M.), 3173.
VELLEKOOP (Kees), 4373.
VELLI (Giuseppe), 6590.
VELTRI (Giuseppe), 5959.
VENARD (Marc), 1458, 4236.
Venantius Fortunatus, 4025.
VENDEWALLE (Dirk), 5102.
VENDITTELLI (Marco), 3233, 3256.
VENEZIANI (Paolo), 473.
VENNER (Dominique), 8418.
VENNING (Timothy), 7973.
VENTURA (Angelo), 5024.

VENTURA (L.), 103.
VENTURA (Leandro), 6862.
VENTURA (Piero), 7475.
Venturi (Franco), 759, 842.
VENTURINI (Fernando), 7575.
VERA (Domenico) , 722, 2743.
VERBEKE (Gérard), 4388.
VERBEKE (Werner), 3811.
VERDE (Armando F.), 5816.
VERDONE (Mario), 6983.
VEREMES (Thanos M.), 1169.
VERESS (Laura-Louise), 8315.
VERGA (Marcello), 4660.
VERGER (Jacques), 3257, 4160.
Vergennes (Charles Gravier comte de), 4906.
Vergilius (Publius V. Maro), 2347, 2554, 2584, 2737, 2779, 2794, 6565.
VERGINELLA (Marta), 8395.
VERHELST (Stéphane), 3091.
VERHOEVEN (Marc), 1627.
VERHULST (Adriaan), 3835, 3885, 4576.
VERHUYCK (P.), 3912.
Vermes (Geza), 5926.
Vermeule (Emily Townsend), 1994.
VERMEULEN (Hans F.), 1011.
Vernanis (Guido), 1187.
VERNANT (Jean-Pierre) , 1990, 2381.
VERNETTE (Jean), 1502.
VERNUS (M.), 257.
VERRANDO (Giovanni Nino), 3043.
Verri (Alessandro), 6594.
VERRIER (A.), 8073.
VERSLUYS (K.), 7725.
VERSTRAETEN (Pierre), 6363.
VERTLIEB (Vladimir), 7343.
VERTOGRADOVA (Viktorija V.), 8809.
VERZÁR-BASS (M.), 2918.
VESPASIANO DA BISTICCI, 3919.
VESTER (Heinz-Günther), 973.
VESZPRÉMY (László), 3331, 8187.
VETH (Peter), 1623.
VETTER (Matthias), 5423.
VEYRASSAT (Béatrice), 7143, 8069.
VIALLANEIX (Paul), 811.
VIAN (F.), 2092.
VIAN (Giovanni Maria), 3027.
VIANSINO (Giovanni), 2569.
VIBERT (Frank), 8781.
VICENTE SERRADILLA (Ana Isabel), 441.
VICIANO (Pau), 723.
VICKERS (Miranda), 4675.
Vico (Giambattista), 855, 867, 6253.
Victor de Marseille, Sanctus, 3307.
VICTORIA (Jose Guadalupe), 1368.
Vida (Marco Girolamo), 6565.
VIDAL (Jean-François), 7144.

VIDAL (Nathalie), 454.
VIDAL CASTRO (Francisco), 3548.
VIDAL-NACQUET (Pierre), 974.
VIDOTTO (Vittorio), 5047.
VIEIRA (Manuel Joaquim), 3387.
VIERHAUS (Rudolf), 1364.
VIEJO YHARRASSARRY (Julian), 7945.
VIGANÒ (Lorenzo), 1933.
VIGEZZI (Brunello), 7791.
VIGUERA MOLINS (María Jesús), 3485, 3572.
VILANOVA (Mercedes), 724.
VILAR (Juan Bautista), 7889.
VILFAN (Sergij), XXI.
VILLA (Claudia), 189, 3332.
VILLANI (Filippo), 3333.
VILLANI (Matteo), 3333, 3886.
VILLANI (Pasquale), 8010.
VILLAR (Milagros), 4161.
VILLARD (Pierre), 1853.
VILLARI (P.), 5052.
VILLAUME (Poul), 8782.
VILLER (M.), 1448.
VILLIERS (Patrick), 7196.
VILLOCH VAZQUEZ (Victoria), 1595.
Villon (François), 3912.
VIÑA BRITO (Ana), 3887.
Vinay (Gustavo), 4052.
VINCENT (Catherine), 3888.
VINCENT (J. M.), 6307.
VINCENT (J.), 2341.
VINCENTE (Claudine-Adrienne), 1854.
VINCENTIUS BELVACENSIS, 3920.
VINCHESI (M.A.), 2820.
VINEL (Fr.), 2945.
VINOGRADOV (Ju. A.), 2023, 2150.
VINOGRADOV (Vladen N.), 8190.
VINOVSKIS (Maris A.), 6149, 6150.
VIOLANTE (Cinzio) , 3838, 3889, 4416.
VIOLI (Carlo), 6216.
VIQUEIRA (Juan Pedro), 7476.
VIRÁG (Zsuzsanna), 1675.
Virgilius Maro Grammaticus, 4047.
VIRLOUVET (Catherine), 2745.
VIROLI (Maurizio), 1363.
VIRRANKOSKI (Pentti), 5366.
VISCA (Danila), 1503.
VISCEGLIA (Maria Antonietta), 725.
VISCHER (Lukas), 5673.
VISENTIN (Mauro), 6364.
VISOTZKY (Burton L.), 1504.
VISSER (R.), 761.
VITALE (Alessandro), 7792, 8783.
VITALE (Ermanno), 6365.
VITALIS (Ordericus), 3335.
VITI (Goffredo), 4199.
VITI (Paolo), 4162, 452, 6591.
Vitruvius Pollio (Marcus), 2601.

VIVANTI (Corrado), 5053.
VIVARELLI (Roberto), 5029.
VIVEIROS DE CASTRO (Eduardo), 992.
VIVIERS (Didier), 1991, 2151.
VIZKELETY (András), 4163.
VJATKIN (Kirill S.), 4825.
Vladimir I Svyatoi, principe di Kiev, 3473.
Vladimiri (Paolo), 4498.
VOCI (Anna Maria), 4426.
VODE (Cvetka), XXI.
VOGEL (Martin), 6984.
VOGT-SPIRA (Gregor), 2809.
VOJNOV (A. F.), 5306.
VOLF (Patrik-Paul), 7669.
VOLK (Alessandro), 8395.
VOLK (Peter), 975.
VOLKOV (Mikhail Ja.), 5353.
VOLKOVA (Irina V.), 5354.
VOLLING (Thomas), 1715.
VOLOBUEV (O. V.), 5352.
VOLPILHAC-AUGER (Catherine), 578, 778.
Voltaire (François-Marie Arouet), 844, 1209, 6012, 6038.
VOLTERRA (Alessandro), 7890.
VON DER NAHMER (D.), 4485.
EUW (A. von), 97.
Stommeln (Christine von), 4109.
VONDROVÁ (Jitka), 8784.
VORK (Richardt), 7668.
VORLÄNDER (Hans), 1230.
VORONKOV (Vladimir I.), 4662.
VÖRÖS (Károly), 5578.
VORREUX (Damien), 4477.
VOSAHLIKOVA (Pavla), 1057.
VOSKRESENSKAYA (Natalya), 6109.
VOSS (K. C.), 1455.
VÖSSING (K.), 2821.
Vossler (Karl), 759.
VOTH (Hans-Joachim), 4826.
Vovelle (Michel), 845.
VOWEL (Detlef), 8302.
VRDOLJAK (Snježana), 1676.
VRETTOS (Athena), 6708.
VUILLEMIN-DIEM (Gudrum), 4267, 4280.
VYLCAN (Mikhail A.), 5424.

W

WAARDENBURG (Jacques), 5960.
WAARSENBURG (Demetrius J.), 2485.
WADA (Atsumu), 9063.
WADA (Kazuo), 7163.
WAELBROECK (Jean), 1318.
WAGNER (Armin), 5425.
WAGNER (Carlos G.), 1934.

WAGNER (Christine), 5706.
WAGNER (Irmgard), 6709.
WAGNER (Jonathan F.), 785.
WAGNER (Robert-Léon), 4143.
WAGNON-CHARPY (Sylvain), 8785.
WAGSTAFF (C.), 5025.
WAHL (Alfred), 4859.
WAHNICH (Sophie), 4918.
WAHRMAN (Dror), 4963.
WAIC (Marek), 5507.
WAITE (P. B.), 5080.
WAKITA (Osamu), 9064.
WALCZAK (Marian), 6151.
WALDENBERG (Marek), 727.
WAŁĘSA (Lech), 8200.
WALKER (Anita M.), 4919.
WALKER (Christopher B. F.), 1855.
WALKER (David H.), 6710.
WALKER (David Maxwell), 7550.
WALKER (Greg), 6562.
WALKER (John), 6366.
WALKER (Mark), 6499.
WALKER (Pierre A.), 6711.
WALKER (Susan), 2463.
WALKER BYNUM (Caroline), 4390.
WALL (Renate), 6536.
WALLACE (P. W.), 5620.
WALLACE (Ronald S.), 5892.
WALLACE (William E.), 6800.
WALLERSTRÖM (Thomas), 4577.
Walley (M. I.), 95.
WALLIS (Faith), 728.
WALSER (Gerold), 2602.
WALSHAW (Harland), 6766.
WALSHE (Peter), 5461.
WALTER (Christopher), 3174.
WALTER (François), 5379.
WALTER (Peter), 4302, 4391.
WALTER (Philippe), 1615.
WALTER (Stephan), 6367.
WALTERS ROBERTSON (Anne), 4166.
WALTHER (K. K.), 240.
WALTHER (Peter T.), 603.
WALZ (R.), 5674.
WAMERS (E.), 3890.
WAN (Ming), 8939.
WANATOWICZ (Maria), 5262.
WANDEL (Lee Palmer), 5380.
WANDRUSZKA (Nikolai), 3891.
WANG (Jingyu), 8940.
WANG (Liangxing), 8941.
WANG (Qingcheng), 8942.
WANG (Qinjia E.), 729.
WANG (Saishi), 8943.
WANG (Shaohua), 8944, 8949.
WANG (Shunshen), 8945.
WANG (Tao), 1588.
WANG (Tianjiang), 8946.
WANG (Tingke), 8947.
WANG (Tingyuan), 8948.

WANG (Xiaohua), 8913, 8949.
WANG (Xuezhen), 8950.
WANG (Yongping), 8951.
WANG (Zijin), 8952.
WANGERMANN (Ernst), 6053.
WANNAGAT (Detlev), 2434.
WAPPMANN (Volker), 5893.
WARD (A.), 4277.
WARD (Brian), 5975.
WARD (Harry Merrill), 5613.
WARD (James F.), 6368.
WARD (John O.), 3334.
WARDENGA (Ute), 399.
Warhol (Andy), 6844.
WARIN (Pierre), 6002.
WARIS (Elina), 7477.
WARKENTIN (Germaine), 4095.
WARNER (Daniel), 8786.
WARNER (I.), 8421.
WARNER (Malcom), 8953.
WARNER (Marina), 1058.
WARNER DE ROUEN, 4167.
WARREN (R.), 2069.
WARSON (D. R.), 8191.
WARTENBERG (U.), 2230.
WARTOFSKY (Marx W.), 1335.
Washington (George), 5587, 5607, 7675.
WASSERSTROM (Steven M), 3573.
WATANABE (Takashi), 9041.
WATERFIELD (R.), 2100.
WATSON (Helen E.), 7719.
WATSON (Nicholas), 4168.
WATSON (P. A.), 2231.
WATSON (P. M.), 1801.
WATSON (W. G. E.), 1935.
WATTEL-DE CROIZANT (Odile), 2919.
WAWRO (Geoffrey), 8070.
WAWRYKOW (Joseph P.), 4392.
WEATHERHEAD (Fran), 1802.
WEAVER (Jefferson Hane), 6500.
WEBB (Michael C.), 8787.
WEBER (Brigitta), 6935.
WEBER (Bruce H.), 6412.
WEBER (Ekkehard), 2502.
WEBER (Gregor), 2232.
WEBER (Martha), 1758.
Weber (Max), 846, 1180, 1464, 6009, 6307, 7012.
WEBER-JENISCH (Gabriele), 1716.
WEBSTER (Anthony), 7840.
WEBSTER (Margaret), 3827.
WECHSELMANN (Maj), 8317.
WECKER (Regina), 7478.
WEDDIGE (Hilkert), 4037.
WEEBER (Karl-Wilhelm), 1319.
WEEKS (Gregory), 4827.
WEGELER (Cornelia), 730.
WEGNER (Ilse), 1882.
WEGNER (Stefan), 1883.

WEHLER (Hans-Ulrich), 976, 4828.
WEI (Qianzhi), 8954.
WEI (Songshan), 9011.
Weibull (Lauritz), 744.
WEIGAND (Katharina), 1271.
WEIGL (Andreas), 7344.
WEIJERS (Olga), 4164, 4393.
WEIL (François), 7197.
WEILL (Claudie), 792.
WEINBERG (Gerhard Ludwig), 8318.
WEINBERGER (Jerry), 904.
WEINMANN-WALSER (Marlis), 2632.
WEINRICH (Lorenz), 4411.
WEINSTEIN (Martin E.), 8640.
WEIR (David R.), 7345.
WEISBROD (B.), 4587.
WEISL (Angela Jane), 4169.
WEISS (Gunter), 7924.
WEISS (Otto), 5784.
WEISS (Richard), 994.
WEIß (Stefan), 4427.
WEISS (Thomas G.), 7752.
WEISSER (Elisabeth), 6287.
WEISSER-LOHMANN (Elisabeth), 6369.
WEISSMANN (Gerald), 6501.
WEISZ (Franz), 5201, 7614.
WEISZ (George), 6082.
WEITHMANN (Michael W.), 1171.
WELCH (Claude E.), 8788.
WELCH (Cliff), 4738.
WELCH (David A.), 7793.
WELCH (Evelyn S.), 6780.
WELCH (Kathryn E.), 2669.
WELCHMAN (Jennifer), 1249.
WELKENHUYSEN (Andries), 3811.
Welles (Sumner), 8232.
Wellesly (Arthur), 4948.
WELLS (Charlotte C.), 7659.
WELLS (K. M.), 9073.
WELWEI (Karl-Wilhelm), 1692.
WEN (Qinming), 8955.
WEN (Rui), 8956.
Wen (Tonghe), 8978.
WENBORN (Neil), 1103.
WENDE-HOHENBERGER (Waltraud), 6712.
WENIGER (G.-C.), 1649.
WENK (Silke), 6863.
WENZEL (Horst), 190.
WENZEL (Siegfried), 4170.
WERNER (Ernst), 4416.
Werner (Jakob), 4081.
WERNER (Karl Ferdinand), 731, 3406.
WERNER (Michael), 977.
WERNER (R.), 2486.
WERNHER (Gretel), 2024.
Werr (Antonia), 5775.
WERTENSCHLAG-BIRKHAUSER (E.), 6466.

WERTHEIM (Margaret), 6502.
WESSEL (Marleen), 774.
WESSELING (H. L), 978.
WESSELS (Anton), 5675.
WEST (D.), 2562.
WEST (David R.), 2382.
WEST (Richard), 5619.
WESTERN (A. C.), 1803.
WETHERELL (Charles), 4958.
WETZEL (C.), 82.
WEYSS (Norbert), 5202.
WHALING (F.), 1418.
WHALING (Frank), 5676.
WHARTON (Annabel Jane), 4578.
WHATLEY (Warren C.), 7515.
WHEATLET (Pat), 2152.
WHEELER (Stephen M.), 2822.
WHELAN RICHARDSON (Regina), 446.
WHITBREAD (I. K.), 2435.
WHITCOMB (Donald), 1964.
White (Dick sir), 7681.
WHITE (Graham), 7891.
WHITE (Hayden), 911, 979.
WHITE (John Albert), 8071.
WHITE (Louise), 5537.
WHITE (Shane), 7891.
WHITEHEAD (D.), 2153.
Whitehead (Alfred North), 6491.
WHITEHORNE (J. E. G.), 2094.
WHITELAM (Keith W), 732.
WHITEMAN (Dorit Bader), 7479.
WHITFIELD (Peter), 6503.
WHITING (John Roger Scott), 7946.
WHITTAKER (David J.), 8789.
WICHT (Bernard), 6370.
Wick (Jan Jakub), 6196.
Wickert (Erwin), 8458.
WICKHAM (Chris), 3892.
WIDACKA (H.), 1371.
WIDACKA (Hanna), 1371.
WIDACKI (Jan), 8192.
WIEACKER (Franz), 7615.
WIEBE (D.), 1505.
WIEBE (Franz Josef), 2670.
WIEBE (Robert Huddleston), 5614.
WIEBES (Cees), 8323.
WIECK (Jasper), 8193.
WIEDMANN (Arnd), 5381.
WIEDMANN (August), 6054.
WIELAND (Georg), 3343, 4363.
WIELAND (Jan Wolfgang), 386.
WIELOCKX (R.), 1377.
WIEMER (Hans-Ulrich), 2671.
WIENER (Jarrod), 8790.
WIERDA (L.), 191.
WIERSCHOWSKI (Lothar), 2746.
WIERZCHOSŁAWSKI (Szczepan), 5268.
WIESEMANN (Jörg), 1320.
WIESING (Urban), 6504.

WIESMULLER (Wolfgang), 851.
WIESZ (Christoph), 4580.
WIEVIORKA (Olivier), 8419.
WIJACZKA (Jacek), 7215, 7346.
WIJNHOVEN (Joseph), 5720.
WILBERDING (E.), 6864.
WILCOX (Jonathan), 3923.
WILDT (Michael), 7480.
Wilhelm II, Dt. Kaiser u. König von Preussen, 4803.
WILKINS (J.), 2195.
WILKINSON (A. H.), 1804.
WILKINSON (Toby), 1588.
WILKINSON (Tony J.), 1936.
WILKS DOLNIKOWSKI (Edith), 4394.
WILLAERT (B.), 1377.
WILLCOCK (M. M.), 2109, 2544.
Willem I, Koning der Nederlanders en Belgen, 4718.
William of Conches, 4309.
WILLIAM OF JUMIÈGES, 3335.
William III, king of England, 7958.
WILLIAMS (Ann), 3487.
Williams (Fred), 6821.
WILLIAMS (J.), 4237.
WILLIAMS (Margaret H.), 2603.
WILLIAMS (Michael A.), 2383.
WILLIAMS (Robert John), 1717.
WILLIAMS (Stephen), 2672.
WILLIAMSON (Arthur H.), 4964.
WILLIAMSON (H. G. M.), 1937.
WILLIAMSON (Jeffrey G.), 6108, 7091.
WILLIAMSON (Tom), 6801.
WILLIS (Eliza J.), 4739.
WILLIS (Justin), 7892.
WILLOWEIT (Dietmar), 565, 7535.
WILMANNS (Juliane C.), 2747, 2823.
WILSON (A.), 3175.
WILSON (Adrian), 6505.
WILSON (Alistair Macintosh), 1365.
WILSON (Andrew), 980.
WILSON (Catherine), 6506.
WILSON (Curtis), 6495.
WILSON (David M.), 4195.
WILSON (H. S.), 5961.
WILSON (John Francis), 7232.
WILSON (Keith), 8100, 8194.
WILSON (Lynn B.), 1059.
Wilson (Thomas Woodrow), 7729, 8127, 8169, 8621.
WIN (May Kyi), 1172.
WINDEMUTH. (Marie-Luise), 3893.
WINGE (Harald), 5166.
WINGERATH (Halina), 2025.
Wingrove (Paul), 8827.
WINIUS (George D.), 5630.
WINKELMANN (Sylvia), 1736.
Winkler (Hans-Alexander), 1460.
WINKLER (J. J.), 2045.
WINKLER (Martin M.), 6985.

WINKLER (Ulrike), XVI.
WINOCK (Michel), 4920.
WINTER (Jay Murray), 4663.
WINTER (Werner), 329.
WIRTH (Gerhard), 2673.
Wisdom (Angelic), 4313.
WISEMAN (T. P.), 2857.
WISTRICH (Robert S.), 4658, 4829, 5005.
WITHERS (Charles W. J.), 400.
WITHERS (Paul), 328.
Witigowo, abbas, 415.
WITKAM (J. J.), 248.
WITKOWSKA-ZAREMBA (Elzbieta), 4266.
WITKOWSKI (Arianne), 5632.
WITSCHEL (Christian), 2708.
Wittgenstein (Ludwig Joseph), 1521, 6305.
WITTLIN (Curt), 3517.
WITTMANN (Roland), 2695.
WLADIKA (Michael), 6371.
WŁOCZYK (Piotr), 5818.
WŁODAREK (Andrzej), 4198.
WÖHRLE (Georg), 2342.
WOJCIECHOWSKI (Mieczysław), 7426.
WOJNA (Romuald), 5355.
WOJTASIK (Janusz), 5258.
Wojtyla (Karol), 5713, 8652.
WOKLER (Robert), 6015.
WO-LAP LAM (Willy), 8957.
WOLF (Aloise), 4171.
WOLF (Armin), 3488.
Wolf (Christa), 6705.
WOLF (K. B.), 733.
WOLF (Kirsten), 4005.
WOLFF (Etienne), 2551.
WOLFF-METTERNICH (Brigitta-Sophie von), 6372.
WOLFFSOHN (Michael), 5962.
WOLFRAM (Herwig), 1718, 3336, 3427.
WOLFRUM (Carl Gert), 7574.
WOLFSCHMIDT (Gudrun), 6507.
WOLGAST (Eike), 5894.
WOLIN (Richard), 6300.
WOLL (Ingrid), 4417.
WOLLASCH (Andreas), 7533.
WOLLEN (Peter), 6867.
WOLPERT (Andrew), 1992.
WOLTERS (Gereon), 6398.
WOOD (Eric Stuart), 401.
WOOD (Gordon S.), 734.
WOOD (Nancy), 637.
WOOD (Susan), 2920.
WOODCOCK (Bruce), 6713.
WOODHEAD (C.), 5531.
WOODHOUSE (Roger), 8791.
Woodrow (James), 6431.
WOODRUFF (P.), 2091.

WOODRUFF SMITH (David), 1512.
WOODS (David), 3044.
WOODS (Oona), 6878.
WOODWARD (D.), 163.
WOODWARD (Daniel), 3983.
WOODWARD (John), 6441.
WOODWARD (Susan L.), 8792.
WOOLF (Stuart), 4602.
WORMALD (Patrick), 3688.
WORP (K. A.), 2075.
WÖRRLE (M.), 1987.
WORTH (Roland H.), 8320.
WORTHINGTON (Glenn), 6373.
WORTMAN (Richard S.), 5356.
WOS (Jan Władysław), 7947.
WOS (K.), 2824.
WREGLESWORTH (John), 735.
Wren (Christopher), 6379.
WRIED (K.), 3182.
WRIGHT (Charles W.), 6374.
WRIGHT (Esmond), 5615.
WRIGHT (H. R. C.), 7042.
WRIGHT (M. R.), 2343.
WRIGHT (Neil), 4174.
WRIGLEY (C.), 7785.
WROBEL (Piotr), 1117.
WRONA (Janusz), 5269.
WRZESIŃSKI (Wojciech), 5264.
WU (Lengxi), 8958.
WU (Songdi), 8959.
WU (Tingqiu), 8960.
WU (Tingyi), 8961.
WU (Yining), 8962.
Wu, emperor of China, 8852, 8905.
WÜEST (Jakob), 4097.
WÜLFING (P.), 2825.
WUNDERLE (E.), 135.
WUNDERLICH (Heinke), 6828.
WUNSCHE (Raimund), 4928.
WURGAFT (Lewis), 981.
WÜRGLER (Andreas), 5382.
WURM (Clemens), 8793.
Wyclif (John), 3479.
WYCZAŃSKI (Andrzej), 6375.
WYLIE (Dan), 9106.
WYNN (Graeme), 5081.
Wynne (Edmond), 7382.
WYROBISZ (Andrzej), 7481.
WYROZUMSKA (Bożena), 3519.
WYROZUMSKI (Jerzy), 3362, 5244.
WYRWA (Andrzej Marek), 4457.
WYSZCZELSKI (Lech), 8195.

X

Xenophōn, 2110, 2111, 2112.
Xerses, re dei persiani, 2299.
XI (Wuyi), 8963.
XIANG (Laxin), 8794.
XIAO (Guojian), 8964.
XIAO (Hua), 8965.
XIE (Qing), 8966.
XIE (Yongguang), 8967.
XING (Tie), 8968.
XIONG (Qiuliang), 8886.
XIONG (Xianghui), 8969.
XU (Xiuli), 8970.
Xu (Xuechen), 8855, 8872.
Xu (Xueqiu), 9000.

Y

YABLONSKY (Leonid T.), 1686.
YADAVA (M.G.), 1626.
YALCINKAYA (Isin), 1617.
YAMADA (Kuniaki), 9065.
YAMADA (Masamichi), 1884.
YAMAMOTO (Hideyuki), 7482.
YAMAMOTO (Hirofumi), 9066.
YAMANOUCHI (Yasushi), 4653.
YAMAZAKI (Hiroaki), 1137.
YANG (Hongzhang), 8971.
YANG (Jiang), 8972.
YANG (Tianshi), 8973.
YANG (Zhaomin), 8974.
YANKELEVICH (Pablo), 5133.
YANNOPOULOS (Panayotis), 3176.
YAO (Qi), 8975.
YASAMEE (H. J.), 8421.
YASOUKA (Shigeaki), 1137.
YASUTOMO (Dennis T.), 8795.
Yavetz (Zvi), 2639.
YAZICI (Nesimi), 6152.
YEAGER (Timothy J.), 7145.
YEH (Wen-Hsin), 7483.
YELVINGTON (Kevin A.), 4664.
YEN (D. E.), 1624.
YERUSHALMI (Yosef Hayim), 7551.
YETIV (Steve A.), 8796.
YILDIRIM (Haci Osman), 421.
YIN (Jiamin), 8976.
YIOUNI (Paraskevi), 1652.
YIP (Ka-che), 6508.
YLI-JOKIPII (Pentti), 4847.
YLIKANGAS (Heikki), 8196.
YLÖNEN (Marja), 6214.
YODER (Edwin), 6215.
YOLALICI (M. Emin), 6153.
YON (Marguerite), 1918.
YONEKURA (Seiichirō), 1137.
YONETANI (Hiroshi), 9074.
YOO (Heon-Sik), 982.
YORK (Deborah Valenze), 7484.
YORK (Michael), 5677.
YOSHIDA (Nobuyuki), 9042.
YOSHIE (Akio), 9067.
YOSHIMI (Shun'ya), 5061.
YOUNG (Richard Fox), 5963.
YU (Bailiu), 8977.
YU (Bingkuan), 8978.
YU (Shengwu), 8979, 8980.
YU (Taishan), 8981.
YU (Tong), 8982.
YU (Tongguan), 8983.
YU (Wen), 8984.
YU (Zhaopeng), 8985.
YUI (Daizaburō), 5062.
YUI (Tsunehiko), 1137.

Z

ZABIB (Najib), 1173.
ZABUSKY (Stacia E.), 6509.
ZACCAGNINI (Carlo), 1856.
ZACCARIA (Raffaella Maria), 452.
ZACCHIGNA (Michele), 3689.
ZACHAR (József), 5579.
Zacharie, 3017.
ZACHOROWSKI (Stanisław), 3362.
ZACK-WILLIAMS (Alfred Babatunde), 7198.
ZADKA (Saul), 5213.
ZADORA-RIO (Elisabeth), 4579.
ZADOROŻNYJ (V. N.), 7129.
ZAGDOUN (Mary-Anne), 2344, 2387.
ZAGORSKI (Andrei V.), 8528.
ZAJEWSKI (Władysław), 8011.
ZAJKO (Vanda), 2384.
ZAK (W. F.), 1993.
ZAKERI (Mohsen), 3574.
ZAMAGNI (Vera), 7104.
ZAMBARBIERI (Annibale), 5669.
ZAMFIR (Zorin), 8197.
ZAMPONI (Stefano), 824.
Zanardelli (Giuseppe), 7650.
ZANARDI (Pierluigi Lamberti), 8797.
Zanella (Riccardo), 8078.
ZANG (Jian), 8986.
ZANKER (Paul), 1987, 2436, 2921.
ZANNI ROSIELLO (Isabella), 423.
ZAPPELLA (Giuseppina), 258.
ZAREMSKA (Hanna), 4525.
ZARKA (Yves Charles), 1231, 6310.
ŻARNOWSKA (Anna), 7485.
ZARTMAN (I. William), 7794, 8798.
ZASLAVSKY (Victor), 5426.
ZAWADZKI (Stefan), 1857.
ZAWADZKI (Tadeusz), 2674.
Ždanov (Andrei Aleksandrovič), 8271.
ZEBALZA ALDAVE (M. I.), 3259.
ZECCHINI (Giuseppe), 2604.
ZEILSTRA (Jurjen A.), 5678.
ZELIKOW (Philip), 8799.
ZEMAN (Georg), 4238.
ZEN'KOVSKIJ (Sergej A.), 6056.
ŻENDARA (Alicja), 1371.
Zeng (Jinglan), 8872.

ZENG (Yeying), 8987.
ŻERKO (Stanisław), 8321.
ZETKA (James R.), 7199.
ZETTERBERG (Kent), 8800.
ZETTERBERG (Seppo), 4835.
ZEVI (Fausto), 2437.
ZEZINA (Marija R.), 5427.
ZGÓRNIAK (Marian), 5232.
ZHAN (Qinghua), 8988.
ZHANG (Dongguang), 8989.
ZHANG (Fuqiang), 8990.
ZHANG (Hequan), 8991.
ZHANG (Jingru), 8992.
ZHANG (Jinlong), 8993.
ZHANG (Kaiyuan), 8994.
ZHANG (Ming), 8839.
ZHANG (Quanming), 8995.
ZHANG (Shiqu), 8996.
ZHANG (Shu Guang), 8801.
ZHANG (Weiran), 8997.
ZHANG (Xian), 8892.
ZHANG (Xuhua), 8998.
ZHANG (Yisbeng), 737.
ZHAO (Hongbao), 8999.
ZHAO (Liren), 9000.
ZHAO (Shichao), 9001.
ZHAO (Shiyu), 9002.
ZHAO (Yinglan), 9003.
ZHAO (Yuntian), 9004.
ZHENG (Pengnian), 8960.
ZHENG (Qidong), 9005.
ZHOU (Bing), 8882.
ZHOU (Shaojing), 9013.
Zhou (Enlai), 8969, 8976.
ZHU (Baoqin), 9014.
ZHU (Ying), 9015.

ZIADEH (Ghada), 1938.
ZIEGERHOFER (Anita), 5895.
ZIEGLER (E.), 10.
ZIEGLER (G.), 3028.
ZIEGLER (Joseph), 4273.
ZIEL (Wulfhild), 985.
ZIELIŃSKI (Tadeusz), 2675.
ZIELIŃSKI (Zygmunt), 8159.
ZIELINSKI (Bernd), 4921.
ZIER (Mark A.), 4285.
ZILANOV (V. K.), 7795.
ZILHÃO (João), 1625.
ZILLIACUS (Kim O.K.), 4848.
ZILLIACUS (Ville), 7486.
ZILYNSKYJ (Bohdan), 7487.
ZIMA (Veniamin F.), 5428.
ZIMMER (Gerhard), 2507.
ZIMMERMANN (Eduardo), 4696.
ZIMMERMANN (Günther), 5896.
ZIMMERMANN (Martin), 2676.
ZIMMERMANN (Reinhard), 7615.
ZIMMERMANN (Susan), 5558.
ZIMMERMANN (T. C. Price), 788.
ZIMMERMANN (Völker), 6510.
ZINCONE (Sergio), 3029.
ZINGEL (Michael), 738.
ZINMAN (M. Richard), 904.
ZIRLIN (Yael), 4239.
ZITTA (Wolfgang), 7466.
ZIWES (Franz-Josef), 3542.
ZMIJEWSKI (Josef), 3030.
ZNAMIEROWSKA-RAKK (Elżbieta), 8198.
ZOCCA (Elena), 2932, 3031.
ZOLOTAREV (M. I.), 2438.
ZOLOTAREV (V. A.), 5411.

ZOPPI (Mariella), 1375.
ZORAT (Marta), 2487.
ZORN (Jeffrey R.), 1939.
ZORZETTI (Nevio), 4098.
ZOTZ (Thomas), 4555.
ZOU (Jingwen), 9016.
ZOU (Zhaozhen), 9017.
ZOUBIR (Yahia H.), 7893, 8802.
ZSCHALER (Frank), 7301.
ZUBAR' (Vitalij M.), 2709, 2858.
ZUBAREV (V. G.), 402.
ZUBKOVA (Elena Ju.), 4665, 5429.
Zuccolo (Ludovico), 6268.
ZUCKERMAN (Constantine), 3177.
ZUIDERVAART (H. J.).
ZUINGHEDAU (Michel), 2601.
ZUKIER (Henri), 983.
ŽUKOV (Jurij N.), 5430.
ZUMBO (Antonio), 2447.
Zumthor (Paul), 847.
ZUPKO (Jack), 4395.
ZUR MUHLEN (Karl-Heinz), 5897.
ZURAWSKI VEL GRAJEWSKI (Przemyslaw Piotr), 8199.
ZURCHER (E. J.), 5534.
ŻUREK (Grzegorz), 2675.
ZURNDORFER (Harriet), 8825.
ZUTSHI (Patrick N. R.), 804, 3260.
ZVELEBIL (Kamil), 1541.
ZVJAGINCEV (A. G.), 7660.
ZWETTLER (Otto), 7489.
Zwiedineck-Südenhorst (Otto von), 7401.
ZWILLING (Robert), 6512.
ŻYCHLIŃSKI (Teodor), 273.
ŻYGULSKI (Zdzisław jun.), 5270.A

GEOGRAPHISCHES REGISTER

A

Abruzzo, 3611.
Acadia, 5078.
Açores, 8185.
Adrianople, 2609.
Adriatico (Mare), 2842.
Aegean Sea, 1726, 1996.
Afghanistan, 4666-4670, 8492.
Afrique, 466, 1063, 1082, 1288, 2520, 2640, 2855, 2895, 3123, 5916, 5961, 6641, 7080, 7866, 7868, 7871, 7872, 8487, 8788, 9076-9106. – A. centrale, 6525. – A. du Nord, 8320, 8435, 8802, 9078. – A. equatoriale, 9095. – A. méridionale, 5913, 8046, 8751. – A. noire, 1261, 7854. – A. occidentale, 5953, 7874, 8310, 9100. – A. orientale, 5730, 7892, 7953. – A. portugaise 1286. – A. subsaharienne, 7237, 7865, 7878, 8735. – A. tropicale, 7879.
Agrigento, 2443.
Aguillar de Anguita (Guadalajara), 1654.
Alaman Dağ, 3160.
Albanie, v. Shqiperi.
Alea, 2849.
Alessandretta, 8280.
Alexandria, 1774, 2402, 7948.
Alger, 7167, 7201, 8007.
Algérie, 1037, 4676-4678, 7858, 7864, 7876, 8759, 9085.
Alpes, 2503, 8376, 8412.
Alsace, 4859, 8061.
Amazon, 4733.
Amérique, 5657, 5668, 5712, 5858, 5967, 6029, 6282, 6395, 6449, 6475, 6476, 7080, 7236, 7402, 7901, 8138, 7982, 9107-9118. – British A., 6489. – A. centrale, 8468, 8567, 8746, 9114, 9115. – A. du Nord, 5654, 7902, 7968, 8681. – A. du Sud,1063, 4744. – A. espagn., 7145, 7894. – A. franç., 4849. – A. latine, 7724, 8720, 7279.

Ampurias, 2901.
Amsterdam, 7443.
Anatolia, 1021, 1864, 7402, 7691.
Ancona, 5734.
Andalucía, 3771, 7249.
Andes (Cordillera de los), 363, 5218, 5220, 9117.
Angers, 5758.
Angola, 7881.
Antilles (archipel et mer), 5809, 8567.
Antivar, 5761.
Aptera (Crète occidentale), 2355.
Arabian Sea, 872.
Arabie Saoudite, 5357.
Aragón, 288, 431, 3501, 3668.
Arcipelago della Maddalena, 8000.
Ardea, 2492.
Arezzo, 3700, 4419.
Argar, 1664.
Argentina, 620, 4679-4696, 6884, 7768.
Argive Plain, 2403.
Argos, 2425.
Arkadia, 2425.
Armenija, 4697-4698.
Arpi, 2467.
Arras, 3250.
Asie, 1063, 1288, 1738-1758, 7735, 7821, 7837, 8638, 8664. – A. centrale, 5907, 8813. – A. centrale-occidentale, 8810-8815. – A. de l'Est, 8209, 8345, 8591, 8747, 8808, 9068. – A. Mineure, 1484, 2003. – A. du Sud, 7147, 7911, 8815-8819. – A. du Sud-Est, 1496, 7840, 8265, 8820-8824.
Assab, 7853.
Assyria, 1733.
Astorga, 4547.
Atabey (Isparta), 2036.
Athēna, 1472, 1992, 2130, 2159, 2226, 2457, 2129, 2204, 2040, 2135, 2413.
Atlantique (Océan), 872, 3855, 4655, 7761, 7774, 7989, 8360.
Auschwitz, 8286.

Australia, 1570, 1598, 1602, 1609, 1616, 1618, 1623, 1624, 1644, 4702-4709, 6496, 8074, 8081, 8636, 8767.
Aversa, 3410.
Avignon, 3260, 4236, 6876.
Azerbajdžian, 8764.

B

Baghdad, 4349, 8509.
Bâlgarija, Bulgarie, 275, 4740-4743.
Balkaniques (pays, péninsule), 1136, 1274, 3586, 4588, 4622, 7691, 7695, 8054, 8485.
Baltique (mer, pays), 1126, 3356, 5254, 7775, 8296.
Bangladesh, 7830.
Banu Hammâd (Algérie), 9099.
Barbados, 7079.
Barcelona, 128, 210, 2901, 3212, 3431, 3856.
Bashkortostan, 1200.
Bay of Pigs, 8554.
Bayern, 3336, 7505, 7994, 8182.
Beagle (Canal), 8779.
Beitrawi, Jordan, 1921.
Béja, 7240.
Belgique, 4712-4721, 8026, 8180, 8261.
Belgrad, 7965, 8547.
Belm, 7456.
Belorussija, Russie Blanche, 4710-4711, 8402.
Benin, Dahomey, 9082, 9091, 9100, 9104.
Bergamo, 3233.
Bergara, 3195.
Berlin, 4768, 7301, 7306, 7522, 8181, 8327, 8386, 8637, 8677.
Beyrouth, 8035, 8545.
Bilbao, 3224.
Bithynia, 2127.
Black Sea, M. Noir, 1292, 2023, 7204.
Bohemia, v. Čechy.
Bolivia, 4722, 4723.

Bologna, 17, 423, 3315, 3456, 3850, 3876, 3891, 4349, 4544, 5018, 6951, 8250, 8400.
Bonn, 8570.
Bordeaux, 7317, 7621.
Bosnia-Hercegovina, 1136, 4724-4727.
Bosporus, 2150, 7176, 8173.
Bouches-du-Rhône, 4881.
Bourgogne, 7672, 8047.
Brünn, 7496.
Brabant, 4712, 4713.
Brandenburg, 7914.
Brasil, 1083, 1285, 4728-4739, 5277, 5632, 5802, 6091, 7768, 7937.
B.R.D., 5759, 8623, 8734.
Brescia, 5792.
British Isles, 3418, 3419, 3421, 3794.
Bronzo nel Fucino (L'Aquila), 1672.
Bruzio, 2450.
Bruxelles, 8256.
Budapest, 1675, 5181, 5558, 6654, 6796, 7393, 7488, 8394.
Bulgarie, v. Bâlgarija.
Buenos Aires, 4685, 4692.
Burgenland, 5880, 8114.
Burgundy, 7634.
Byzantion, Empire byzantin, 275, 2321, 2617, 2660, 2875, 3045-3177, 3345, 3722, 4180, 4398, 4418, 4478, 8109, 8117.

C

Cadiz, 7898.
Caiazzo, 8414.
Caieta, 2552.
Caire (Le), 8217.
Cajarc, 4550.
Calahorra, 3245.
Calais, 3280.
California, 5131, 6770, 7182, 7262.
Calzada-Logroño, 3245.
Cambodge, 5071, 8673.
Cambrai, 3250, 4246.
Cambrésis, 8079.
Cambridge, 167, 397, 3429, 3651, 7013.
Campania, 2449, 2483.
Campo de Gibraltar, 1614.
Canaan, 1898.
Canada, 511, 528, 5072-5081, 7626, 7746.
Canaries, Canary Islands, 9090.
Canary Islands, v. Canaries
Cantal, 8122.
Canton, 8990.
Cappadocia, 3171.
Capua, 5707.
Carlisle, 3240.
Caria, 1757.
Carniola, 3481.
Carpates (Bassin des), 8102.
Caribbean, v. Antilles.
Carthage, v. Carthago
Cartagena, 7430.
Carthago, Carthage, 1908, 2645, 2852, 2876, 2893, 2910, 9083, 9097.
Casale Monferrato, 3039.
Cassovie, 7410.
Castellò de la Plana, 3787.
Castilla, 675, 3438, 3462, 3593, 3761, 3837, 5443.
Cataluña, 99, 331, 3493, 3503, 3511, 3676, 3694, 3743, 3859, 4421, 6163, 7224.
Catania, 3760.
Caucasus, v. Kavkaz.
Caulonia, 2444.
Cecenia, 5243, 8475.
Čechy, Bohemia, 5506, 7070, 7245, 7487, 7489, 8123, 8283, 8381.
Československo, Czechoslovak Republic, 396, 1057, 5470-5508, 7070, 7462, 7110, 7127, 7141, 7474, 8370, 8450, 8452, 8594, 8695, 8712.
Ceylon, v. Sri Lanka.
Chalons-sur-Marne, 3777.
Chaozhou, 8832, 9013.
Chiapas, 7476.
Chicago, 1490.
Chile, 4744-4750, 7319.
China, 880, 1314, 5801, 5942, 5936, 6104, 6285, 6413, 6508, 6930, 7085, 7109, 7246, 7483, 7706, 7789, 8016, 8080, 8444, 8542, 8544, 8568, 8608, 8619, 8629, 8651, 8684, 8725, 8739, 8794, 8801, 8825-9017.
Chios, 2040, 3234.
Çiftlik (Sinop), 1748.
Ciudad de Mexico, 7286.
Clergy, 4533.
Cluny, 3228, 4561.
Coimbra, 5288.
Colombia, 574, 5085-5089.
Colorado, 7398.
Comacchio, 3197.
Conques (Anveyron), 4201, 4203, 4209, 4233.
Constantinople, v. Bysantion.
Córdoba, 4495.
Corée, v. Korea.
Corfinio, 2470.
Corinthia, 2354.
Corinthos, 2425, 2427.
Courcay, 4563.
Cracovia, v. Kracow.
Cremona, 3708.
Creta, v. Krētē.
Crimea, v. Krym.
Croatie, v. Hrvatska.
Cuba, 4650, 5093-5100, 8049, 8709, 8723.
Cuma, 2437, 2905.
Cyprus, v. Kypros.
Cyzicus, 1740.
Czechoslovak Republic, v. Československo.

D

Dahomey, v. Benin.
Dai-on Ulus, 8814.
Dakhleh Oasis, 1782.
Dalmacija, Dalmatie, 1657, 3845, 7998.
Damascus, v. Dimashq
Danmark, 4751-4756, 5883, 7226, 7934, 8424, 8600, 8782.
Danzig, v. Gdańsk.
D.D.R., 557, 603, 696, 4786, 4806, 4820, 5882, 6297, 6693, 6705, 7508, 8450, 8605, 8727.
Dead Sea, 1892.
Dēlos, 2021, 2398, 2402, 2523.
Delphoi, 1983, 2136, 2344, 2349, 2137, 2138.
Desna, 1650.
Detroit, 7515.
Deutschland, 187, 202, 525, 785, 862, 1105, 1109, 1574, 1711, 3826, 4438, 4613, 4637, 4589, 4636, 4642, 4725, 4757-4829, 5382, 5784, 6016, 6130, 6148, 6367, 6384, 6634, 6644, 7138, 7325, 7388, 7460, 7480, 7510, 7513, 7617, 7703, 7716, 7754, 7995, 8036, 8052, 8138, 8141, 8145, 8146, 8165, 8249, 8260, 8302, 8318, 8335, 8430, 8460, 8676, 8735, 8793, 8799.
Dimashq, Damascus, 8811.
Dominicana (República), 4830-4832.
Don, 2000.
Dublin, 6776.

E

Ebla, 1931, 1933.
Eboli, 1630.
Ebro, 3560.
Echigo, 9041.
Ecuador, 4719, 8590.
Edinburgh, 6414.
Egée (mer), 1996.

Egypte, 291, 1726, 1759-1804, 2479, 4671-46712, 5818, 5946, 7867, 7993, 7999, 8441, 8730.
El Cigarralejo (Murcia), 1713.
El Salvador, 8522, 8673.
England, 144, 251, 526, 1577, 3258, 3376, 3418, 3419, 3578, 3681, 3716, 3725, 3810, 3814, 3836, 3843, 3848, 3868, 3883, 4089, 4168, 4327, 4396, 4490, 4505, 4507, 4514, 4891, 4940, 4941, 4955, 4958, 4964, 5671, 6347, 6353, 6505, 6801, 7115, 7150, 7243, 7333, 7368, 7392, 7404, 7427, 7601, 7616, 7623, 7708, 7722, 7899, 7946, 7975, 7992, 8001, 8043.
Ephesos, 2164, 2959.
Eritrea, 2135, 7890.
España, 281, 331, 515, 546, 553, 1556, 2763, 2770, 2785, 2863, 3347, 3408, 3538, 3539, 3572, 3855, 4138, 4161, 4650, 4655, 5431-5446, 5640, 5261, 5732, 5970, 6180, 6209, 6395, 6554, 7022, 7049, 7074, 7366, 7383, 7604, 7774, 7809, 7817, 7829, 7889, 7894, 7921, 7944, 8019, 8049, 8149, 8185, 8307, 8313, 8472, 8551, 8666.
Ėstonija, 4833-4835, 5817, 7469.
Esztergom, 5739.
Ethiopia, 4699-4701, 5924, 7877.
Euboia, 2135.
Euphrate, 1731.
Europe, 235, 349, 501, 531, 690, 1241, 1134, 1272, 1327, 1370, 1593, 1660, 1680, 1681, 1995, 2351, 2441, 2463, 3294, 3348, 3352, 3357, 3367, 3375, 3379, 3556, 3716, 3729, 3741, 3835, 3892, 3930, 3953, 3984, 4126, 4130, 4227, 4242, 4315, 4376, 4414, 4493, 4525, 4585, 4597, 4599, 4602, 4606, 4607, 4609, 4616, 4637, 4648, 4655, 4763, 5028, 5664, 5729, 5991, 6031, 6035, 6070, 6196, 6282, 6478, 6517, 6606, 6759, 6842, 6859, 6919, 7002, 7066, 7071, 7097, 7104, 7119, 7128, 7161, 7170, 7272, 7339, 7362, 7396, 7406, 7411, 7452, 7557, 7615, 7685, 7692, 7698, 7757, 7785, 7969, 7809, 7988, 8159, 8226, 8256, 8301, 8429, 8435, 8448, 8465, 8473, 8482, 8490, 8493, 8512, 8513, 8521, 8541, 8555, 8579, 8589, 8611, 8616, 8617, 8621, 8627, 8690, 8738, 8743, 8780, 8781, 8799. – E. centrale, 450, 667, 1706, 3797, 4467, 4623, 4638, 5786, 7053, 7305, 8029, 8436. – E. centrale-occidentale, 3710. – E. centrale-orientale, 390, 627, 3875, 4590, 8187, 8495. – E. de l'Ouest, 1188, 2630, 3218, 3388, 3389, 3526, 3848, 4608, 4197, 6822, 7142, 8502, 8600, 8719, 8793. – E. du Nord, 4197, 4608, 4651, 8658. – E. du Sud-Est, 1097, 8302. – E. orientale, 450, 4608, 4620, 4623, 4635, 4640, 4644, 4654, 4659, 5704, 7046, 7053, 7721, 8436, 8641, 8464, 8772.
Evian, 7876.

F

Ferrara, 4021.
Fezzan, 8060.
Filipinas, Philippines, 5223-5226, 6395.
Finnland, v. Suomi.
Firenze, 424, 1125, 3201, 3312, 3723, 3733, 3741, 3785, 3816, 3875, 4568, 6757, 6849, 7378, 7448, 7315, 7453, 7491.
Fiume, 8078.
Fonte Tasca (Comune di Archi, Chieti), 1658.
France, 86, 173, 195, 200, 205, 211, 224, 393, 458, 503, 522, 563, 594, 600, 601, 637, 662, 684, 738, 738, 738, 862, 900, 1095, 1220, 1311, 3202, 3236, 3296, 3578, 3646, 3655, 3682, 3683, 3701, 3721, 3753, 3779, 3942, 3950, 3969, 3976, 4124, 4220, 4265, 4589, 4613, 4636, 4636, 4636, 4636, 4661, 4725, 4849-4921, 5624, 5685, 5697, 5790, 5965, 5972, 6090, 6096, 6100, 6102, 6165, 6384, 6391, 6575, 6576, 6627, 6655, 6670, 6731, 6747, 6754, 6755, 6822, 6841, 6848, 7043, 7191, 7194, 7208, 7223, 7252, 7253, 7270, 7271, 7275, 7294, 7498, 7504, 7579, 7586, 7636, 7659, 7698, 7715, 7754, 7817, 7850, 7864, 7913, 7914, 7916, 7937, 7943, 7961, 7970, 7975, 7983, 7979, 8002, 8003, 8012, 8029, 8043, 8060, 8064, 8089, 8104, 8126, 8130, 8144, 8156, 8176, 8193, 8210, 8213, 8216, 8255, 8261, 8264, 8307, 8330, 8338, 8371, 8406, 8419, 8465, 8541, 8611, 8736, 8791, 8802. – F. de l'Ouest, 3802. – F. du Nord, 3735.

Friuli, 469.
Fujian, 8959.

G

Gaeta, 2552, 3730, 5791.
Galicia, 5244, 5245, 6115, 6116, 6977, 5760, 8285.
Gallipoli, 8179.
Gambia-Geba region, 9102.
Gao (Mali), 9084, 9098.
Gaoua, 7184.
Gaoxiong, 8855.
Gdańsk, Danzig, 5728, 5781.
Gebze, 7335.
Genève, 5374, 7227.
Genova, 8010.
Gent, 4721.
Georgia, 1050.
Gerace, 3154.
Gerona, 2901.
Ghana, 4922-4924, 7886.
Glasgow, 4954.
Gold Coast, 4922, 7886.
Granada, 3485.
Grabfeldgau (Unterfranken), 1715.
Great Britain, 401, 475, 1344, 1526, 3588, 4126, 4184, 4273, 4868, 4935-4965, 5208, 5637, 6158, 6204, 6384, 6464, 6574, 6866, 7058, 7065, 7080, 7396, 7436, 7437, 7501, 7692, 7714, 7753, 7755, 7804, 7812, 7817, 7819, 7851, 7877, 8030, 8044, 8052, 8062, 8074, 8089, 8104, 8112, 8126, 8135, 8156, 8175, 8209, 8246, 8253, 8294, 8307, 8321, 8339, 8348, 8378, 8382, 8439, 8460, 8611, 8639, 8697, 8766, 8767, 8794.
Greece, v. Hellas.
Guadalupe, 7897.
Guangdong, 8835, 8861, 8888.
Guanzhong, 8991.
Guatemala, 4966-4971.
Guinea, 9096.
Guinée-Bissau, 7860.
Guyana, Guiana, 5809, 7897.

H

Haida, 1017.
Haifa, 5212.
Haïti, 1038, 4972-4975.
Hamburg, 7181.
Hampshire, 1697.
Hangzhou, 8844.
Hattusa, 1870, 1872.

Havre, 4854.
Hellas, Greece, 1169, 1449, 1579, 1601, 1889, 1965-2438, 2137, 2158, 2735, 2744, 2836, 3103, 3176, 4925-4934, 5826, 7285, 8059, 8181, 8754.
Helsinki, 7394.
Henan, 8946.
Hercegovina, 5529.
Hesse-Kassel, 4821.
Himalayas, 1626.
Hirakonpolis, 1760.
Hiroshima, 8592.
Hollywood, 1369, 6982.
Holy Land, v. Palestine.
Hong Kong, 7685, 8382, 8619, 8837, 8896, 8964, 8967, 8979.
Hongrie, v. Magyarorszàg.
Ḥorvat Teiman (Kuntillet 'Ajrud), 1677.
Howells, 1531.
Hrvatska, Croatie, 1160, 1344, 1676, 3361, 3709, 5059-5092.
Huizhou, 8831, 8930, 8948.
Hunan, 8883, 8997.
Hurvat Rosh Zayit, 1885.

I

Iberia, Ibérique (península), 1594, 1649, 1934, 3866.
Ili, 8884.
Illa d'Eivissa, 317.
Ille-et-Vilaine, 7156.
Iluro, 2901.
Imola, 3232.
India, 455, 659, 2229, 4976-4985, 5936, 5952, 6774, 7131, 7815, 7823, 7824, 7830, 7833, 7834, 7839, 7881, 7882, 8038, 8471, 8731, 8753, 8819.
Indochine, 7822, 7838.
Indonésie, 4986-4989.
Innsbruck, 5780, 6060, 6066, 6072.
Iran, 295, 1940-1964, 3017, 4990, 5205, 7975, 8425, 8613, 8656.
Iraq, 1021, 4991, 7744, 8760.
Ireland, 185, 553, 1327, 1341, 1526, 3342, 3380, 3384, 3421, 4184, 4273, 4992-5003, 7121, 7731, 7971, 8125, 8206.
Island, 5004.
Israel, 540, 732, 1889, 1915, 1923, 5005, 8519, 8537, 8538, 8552, 8577, 8599, 8625, 8644.
İstanbul, 1291, 6805, 6807.
Istria, 5069.
Italia, 35, 227, 323, 547, 616, 690, 1031, 1075, 1330, 1391, 1635, 2441, 2930, 2931, 3111, 3123, 3140, 3326, 3411, 3494, 3497, 3509, 3525, 3601, 3608, 3682, 3769, 3778, 3841, 3881, 3934, 4199, 4403, 4431, 4467, 4468, 4567, 5006-5053, 5639, 5669, 5681, 5711, 5722, 5738, 5746, 5965, 5978, 5997, 6023, 6076, 6265, 6522, 6573, 6600, 6727, 6815, 7030, 7061, 7049, 7263, 7280, 7367, 7440, 7464, 7490, 7552, 7578, 7586, 7605, 7650, 7703, 7712, 7724, 7920, 7991, 8005, 8010, 8210, 8094, 8398, 8410, 8477, 8569. – I. centro-meridionale, 3750. – I. centro-settentrionale, 66. – I. meridio-nale, 9, 1087, 3614, 3808, 3869, 4142, 5735. – I. settentrionale, 3467, 4465.
Izmir-Aydin, 7526.

J

Jabal Nablus, 5210.
Jalta, 8326, 8511.
Jamaica, 4749, 8067.
Jankowice, 8290.
Japan, 932, 1134, 3367, 5054-5070, 5922, 6120, 7028, 7174, 7175, 7353, 7562, 7735, 8064, 8112, 8147, 8209, 8287, 8301, 8320, 8345, 8373, 8470, 8536, 8561, 8563, 8574, 8591, 8601, 8651, 8664, 8737, 8756, 8776, 8795, 8847, 9018-9068.
Jazira, Iraq, 1936.
Jericho, 1924.
Jérusalem, 2954, 3549, 4483, 4578, 8545.
Jiangnam, 8951, 9002.
Jordan, 1801, 1887, 1944, 8643, 8766.
Jugoslavija, 5063-5070, 7668, 7771, 8485, 8679, 8713, 8742.

K

Kalocsa, 5739.
Karaman, 6733.
Kara-tepe, 8809.
Karelija, 7477.
Karst de Atapuerca (Burgos), 1608.
Kastamonu, 6729.
Kavkaz, Caucasus,1610, 7691.
Kellis, 2075.
Kent, 3483.
Kenya, 5082-5084, 5935, 7880.
Khersonesus, 2438, 2608.
Khorasen, 8810.

Kiel, 7989.
Kiev, 1651, 3473.
Kirgizia, 7360.
Klagenfurt, 5194.
Knōssos, 2013.
Kolbacz, 4436.
Königsberg, 7215.
Korea, 7734, 8025, 8568, 8638, 8660, 8705, 8830, 9069-9075.
Kos, 2033.
Kosovo, 8158.
Kostromskaya, 8805.
Kowlon, 8896.
Kracow, Cracovia, 4140, 5228, 7203.
Krētē, Creta 2022, 2006, 3110, 3148, 4929, 8364.
Krym, Crimea, 8033.
Kujawy, 647.
Kumasi, 9100.
Kurily, 7795.
Kypros, Cyprus,1141, 2405, 2410, 3518, 5620, 5821, 1773, 8653.

L

La Plata, 8044.
Laichingen, 7425.
Lancashire, 7151.
Lancastria, 8364.
Landtagen, 5895.
Langres, 3191.
Languedoc, 3220, 3706, 4876, 7171.
Laos, 8514, 8670.
Latgalie,1438, 4618, 4683, 8657, 8743, 8757, 8154.
Latvija, Lettonie, 8096.
Lauzerte, 3724.
Lazio, 3463, 3608.
Lebadea, 2375.
Lecce, 6785.
Legapzia, 3181.
Leipzig, 6098.
Leòn, 3401, 3438, 3799.
Lettonie, v. Latvija.
Liban, 5101.
Libye, 2764, 5012, 6152, 7852.
Lietuva, Lithuania, 7932, 8176.
Liguria, 2930.
Lille, 6122, 7322.
Lima, 5813, 7908.
Lithuania, v. Lietuva.
Liverpool, 1770.
Lleida, 4556.
Lleuda de Mediona, 3856.
Ljubljana, 3369, 8417.
Lombardia, 3449, 4428.
Locarno, 8135.
Łódź, 6940, 6124.
Lombardia, 5731.

London, 1531, 3948, 6061, 6833, 8712, 8769.
Lorraine, 3832, 4859, 5659, 8061.
Loroy, 3211.
Losanna, 3718, 4519, 5032.
Lucania, 2469.
Lucca, 3189, 3497.
Lusitania, 6172.
Luxembourg, 5103.
Lyon, 693, 3196, 5741, 6420, 7322, 8413.

M

Maastricht, 8565, 8616.
Macao, 8868.
Macédoine, 997, 5109-5111, 8045, 8268.
Madagascar, 631, 1084.
Madrasa, 8811.
Madrid, 178, 5687, 6778, 8337.
Maghreb, 7205, 7893.
Magna Grecia, 2292.
Magyarorszàg, Hongrie, 55, 223, 276, 391, 1115, 1405, 3360, 3374, 3500, 3531, 3621, 3875, 4016, 4437, 4510, 4535, 5292, 5539-5579, 5761, 5847, 6075, 6145, 6519, 7078, 7140, 7178, 7186, 7209, 7266, 7310, 7493, 7566, 7747, 7930, 7942, 7997, 8024, 8087, 8098, 8257, 8315, 8440, 8727.
Maine, 3839, 3840.
Makkah, Mekka, 5898.
Makri, 1652.
Malaya, Malaisie, 5104, 5104, 7820, 8744.
Mallorca, 3522, 3717.
Malopolska, 1665, 4112, 4214, 4536.
Malta, 1074, 7938.
Manila, 7972, 8365.
Mantova, 4572.
Maradi, 5154.
Marathonia, 2418.
Marathus, 2116.
Maroc, 1173, 5106, 5107, 6947, 7846, 7849, 7869.
Marseille, 2517, 2864, 2884, 3307, 4855, 4462, 7227.
Martinique, 7897.
Massalia, 2118.
Massaua, 7853.
Mauritania, 5108.
Mazalquivir, 7921.
Mediona I (Alt Penedès, Barcelona), 1613.
Méditerranée (mer), 1928, 3356, 3741, 3762, 3866, 8302, 2441, 2461, 7749. – M. orientale, 3451, 7922.
Mekka, v. Makkah.
Ménécée (Serrès), 3065.
Merida, 5581.
Meseta, 1659.
Mesia, 2726.
Mésopotamie, 1805-1857, 1863, 1893, 5946.
Metaponto, 2473.
Metz, 3256, 3780.
Mexico, 1314, 5112-5233, 5786, 7261, 7758, 7905, 8113, 8681.
Michoacán, 5118.
Milano, 64, 220, 3705, 3727, 6780.
Mill Hill, Deal, 1709.
Mödendorf, 5194.
Mombasa, 7892.
Momostenango, 4967.
Mongolia, 8803, 8914.
Montecassino, 180.
Monténégro, 5529, 8157.
Montesa, 5810.
Montevideo, 5580, 8013, 8048.
Montréal, 5076.
Montserrat, 3206.
Moravia, 1057, 5506, 7487, 7489, 8207, 8283.
Moskva, Moscou, 842, 3365, 3435, 3496, 4662, 5411, 5974, 7915, 7978, 8182, 8330, 8507, 8517.
Moyen Orient, 1274, 5947, 7683, 7929, 8435, 8505, 8571, 8615, 8509, 8630.
Mozambique, 5134-5136, 7855, 7860.
München, 4767, 4829, 8201, 8255.
Münster, 5756, 6134.
Murcia, 3440, 3528, 3656, 3773.
Muzo, 7907.
Mykēnē, 2020.

N

Nagasaki, 8592.
Namibia, 5137-5139, 7882.
Nanjing, 8834, 8994, 9003.
Napoli, 471, 2475, 4515, 6426, 6739, 6921.
Narbonne, 4421.
Narva, 7918.
Navarra, 287, 3194, 3259, 3507, 3754.
Nederland, Pays-Bas, 7, 238, 563, 4454, 5142-5153, 6183, 6818, 6868, 7159, 7819, 7852, 7925, 8344, 8363.
Negev, 1682.
New England, 7197.
New Guinea, 1607, 1638, 1639.
New Netherland, 5585.
New York, 998, 6768.
New Zealand, 1041, 5140, 5141.
Nicaragua, 5155.
Nicopolis, 1743.
Niger, 5154.
Niger (river), 9084. – Eastern N. Delta, 9080.
Nigeria, 5154, 5911, 5939, 7842, 7875.
Nil, 1731.
Norge, Norway, 320, 1119, 1390, 1480, 3341, 3344, 3575, 3584, 4637, 5156-5168, 6117, 7385, 7438, 7759, 7760, 7933, 8085, 8115, 8242, 8463.
Normandie, 3744, 5632, 8361, 8375.
Northampton, 4503.
Nottonville, 4570.
Nubia, 3570.

O

Océanie, 1288, 9119-9122.
Okinawa, 8358.
Öküzini cave (SW Anatolia), 1617.
Olbia, 2650.
Old Termez, 8809.
Olinto, 2427.
Ontario, 7422.
Orano, 7921.
Oruro, 7900.
Orvieto, 2491.
Österreich, 230, 437, 1642, 3336, 3509, 4221, 5169-5203, 5794, 5806, 6348, 7130, 7977, 8114, 8140, 8499, 8354.
Oxford, 6103.

P

Pacifique (Océan), 7735, 7811, 8221, 8320, 8587, 9119. – P. du Sud, 8587, 9122.
Paco, 7230.
Padova, 494, 4125, 6423, 6757.
Pagóry Radziejowskie, 1647.
Pakistan, 5204-5207, 5957, 7830.
Palermo, 247.
Palestine, 1755, 1903, 1904, 1906, 1911, 4183, 5208-5213, 8538, 8577.
Pampa, 4688.
Panfilia, 3162.
Paphlagonia, 1741.
Paraguay, 818, 5214-5215.
Paris, 381, 429, 474, 488, 495, 505, 4341, 4380, 4393, 4910, 4915,

4917, 5974, 6048, 6781, 7284, 7322, 7326, 7375, 7594, 7597, 7726, 7959, 7996, 8093, 8131, 8174, 8177, 8231, 8632, 8769.
Parma, 465, 3231, 4177.
Pas-de-Calais, 454.
Paternò, 3760.
Pavia, 297, 5731, 6071.
Pays-Bas, v. Nederland.
Pearl Harbor, 8209, 8282.
Peiraes, Pireus, 2175.
Pella, 2031.
Peloponnēsos, 2040, 2142.
Peltuinum, 2481.
Peñalosa (Baños de la Encina, Jaén,) 1656.
Penang, 7840.
Pergamon, 1742.
Perse, v. Iran.
Peru, 5124, 5216-5222, 7260.
Perugia, 3661, 7403.
Pest, 7352.
Petersburg, v. Sanktpeterburg.
Philippines, v. Filipinas.
Piacenza, 7955.
Picardie, 3652, 3784, 4447, 4541.
Piemonte, 148, 439, 3471, 5028, 6410, 7107, 8403.
Pireus, v. Peiraes.
Pisa, 3857, 6813.
Płock, 5749.
Poggibonsi, 3200.
Poitiers, 3888.
Poland, v. Polska.
Polska, Poland, 384, 437, 489,159, 1145, 1281, 1371, 1373, 1534, 3327, 3362, 3434, 3504, 4198, 4430, 4445, 4491, 4527, 4642, 4662, 5227-5270, 5311, 5719, 5728, 5769, 5767, 6095, 6196, 6319, 6648, 6749, 7189, 7481, 7485, 7511, 7618, 7627, 7640, 7678, 7784, 7927, 7947, 8142, 8159, 8166, 8176, 8200, 8202, 8224, 8236, 8241, 8262, 8276, 8348, 8540, 8605.
Poméranie, Pommern 4436, 5268, 5727.
Pompei, 758, 2885, 2921.
Pont-Euxin, 2052.
Pontus, 2652.
Porto, 243, 7202.
Portorico, 5271, 5272.
Portugal, 395, 670, 1075, 1131, 1300, 3387, 3855, 3991, 5273-5288, 5630, 6851, 6989, 7049, 7672, 7774, 7797, 7798, 7825, 7855, 8208, 8663, 8185.
Potosi, 298.
Poura, 7184.
Poznań, 8290.

Prague, v. Praha.
Praha, Prague, 4508, 8201, 8712.
Prato, 3580.
Prekmurie region, 3369.
Preußen, Prusse, 3432, 4429, 6094, 6125, 7346, 7778, 7952, 7962, 8058.
Primorska region, 8395.
Provence, 3944, 4178, 8387.
Prum, 3819.
Przemyśl, 5763.
Puerto Rico, 4650, 5271, 5272.
Puglia, 3322.

Q

Qara Qūzāq (Siria), 1670.
Quadrato di Torre Spaccata (Roma), v. Torre Spaccata.
Québec, 5073, 6479.
Quemoy-Matsu, 8636.
Quito, 7639.

R

Ravenna, 683, 3302, 4180, 4578.
R.D.A, v. D.D.R.
Reims, 175, 582, 3250.
Retz, 3707.
Rheinland, 6181.
Rhin, 1298.
Rhodesia, v. Zimbabwe.
Rimini, 7987.
Rio de Janeiro, 4729.
Rio de la Plata, 8030.
Rodhes, 2037, 2603.
Roma, 73, 492, 628, 722, 725, 794, 814, 1079, 1153, 1154, 1319, 1327, 1478, 1925, 1966, 1976, 1977, 1982, 2508-2921, 2915, 2954, 2966, 3011, 3035, 3229, 3260, 3266, 3517, 3520, 3608, 3740, 3786, 3878, 4421, 5044, 5696, 5809, 6081, 6597, 6718, 6800, 6818, 7342, 7358, 7497, 8415, 8547.
România, 1081, 1090, 5292-5300, 6097, 8119, 8160, 8177, 8186, 8225, 8326, 8338, 8353, 8699.
Rosny-sous-Bois, 7345.
Rossija, 375, 530, 543, 571, 577, 798, 885, 980, 1096, 1111, 1202, 3026, 3323, 4594, 4648, 5301-5356, 5414, 5815, 6056, 7254, 7412, 7523, 7673, 7755, 7757, 7763, 7778, 7975, 8015, 8037, 8054, 8063, 8134, 8157, 8173, 8188, 8205, 8506, 8528, 8651, 8618, 8684, 8764, 8884. – R. cen-

trale, 7432. – R. nord-occidentale, 8120. – R. occidentale, 7932.
Rothenburg, 4813.
Roubaix, 8023.
Rouen, 3628.
Roussillon, 7916.
Ruanda, 5289-5291.
Ruhr, 8121.
Ruokolahti, 7477.
Russia, v. Rossija.
Ruthenia, 1339, 5723, 5772, 8247.

S

Sabi Abyad, Syria, 1627.
Sachsenhausen, 8278.
Sahara, 7856, 8020.
Sanktpeterburg, Petersburg, 371, 5312, 6794, 7363, 7379.
Saint-Denis, 3178.
Saint-Léonard-de-Noblat (Haute-Vienne), 7439.
Salamanca, 446.
Salisbury, 4490.
Salento, 6785.
Salò, 5030.
Salonicco, 8104.
Salzburg, 3336, 4502, 5193, 5771, 8002.
Samos, 1746.
San Gimignano, 3179.
San Lazaro, 5225.
San Marino, 1255.
San Sebastian, 3221.
Santa Maria degli Angeli, 100.
Santiago, 3216.
São Paulo, 4728, 4738.
Saqqara, 1787.
Sarajevo, 4727, 8167.
Sardegna, 3446.
Scandinavia, 3325, 4004, 4008, 5241, 6108, 7112, 7933, 8600.
Schleswig-Holsteins, 7149.
Schweiz, Suisse, 5367-5382, 5624, 5673, 7068, 7227, 7396, 7673, 7697, 7740, 8069.
Sciara Sciat, 7859.
Scotland, 303, 658, 3421, 3465, 3581, 4938, 4400, 4942, 6020, 7550.
Scythia, 2764.
Seine, 1298.
Semide (Ardennes), 1707.
Senegal, 1004.
Serbie, v. Srbija.
Sevilla, 49, 78, 3609.
Shangai, 8112, 8860.
Shanxi, 8921.
Shqiperi, Albania, 4673-4675, 8503.

Siam, 7961.
Sibari, 2465.
Sibir', Siberia, 1035, 1605, 1612, 5330, 5253.
Sicilia, 741, 1091, 2440, 2458, 2472, 2479, 2915, 3281, 3385, 3478, 3489, 3525, 3614, 3657, 5629.
Side, 3162.
Siena, 4437, 4569, 6059, 6757.
Sierra Leone, 7198.
Silésie, Slesia, v. Śląsk.
Sinai, 1682, 1926.
Singapore, 5385, 8168.
Sintra (Lisbonne, Portugal) 1653.
Siracusa, 2457.
Skåne, 7933.
Śląsk, 386, 5262, 5264, 5797, 5890, 7203.
Slovensko, Slovaquie, 595, 1057, 4603, 5386-5389, 7105, 7316, 8304.
Slovenija, 451, 506, 1275, 1463, 3287, 3369, 5390-5393.
Sofia, 95.
Sogn, 1710.
Somalia, 5394, 5395.
Somme, 4866.
South Africa, 5447-5461, 8570.
Sparta, 2040, 2205.
Split, 2894, 5067.
Spoleto, 3661.
Srbija, Serbia, 6112, 7257.
Sri Lanka, Ceylon, 5863, 5963, 8471, 8731.
SSSR, 4627, 4642, 4667, 5396-5430, 5765, 6453, 6652, 7067, 7101, 7336, 7759, 7893, 8237, 8251, 8253, 8304, 8306, 8353, 8452, 8473, 8535, 8576, 8641, 8672, 8686, 8707, 8719, 8772.
St Kilda, 1661.
Stockholm, 7330.
Strasbourg, 737.
Stresa, 8165.
Stuthof, 8274.
Sudan, 1777, 1785, 5462-5466, 5924, 7885.
Suède, v. Sverige.
Südtirol, 5038, 5182.
Suez, 8038, 8620.
Suisse, v. Schweiz.
Sul do Save, 7857.
Suomi, Finnland, 436, 612, 1130, 4577, 4836-4848, 7405, 7433, 7652, 7789, 8057, 8271, 8552, 8576, 8800.
Sussex, 8399.
Suzhou, 8850.
Sverige, Suède, 632, 1157, 3803, 5358-5366, 5883, 7054, 7123,
7146, 7356, 7369, 8094, 8323, 8763.
Syme, 2126.
Syria, 1865, 1890, 1893, 1901, 1906, 2152, 2210, 4991, 5467, 8027, 8425, 8644, 8714.
Szendrő, 5761.

T

Tabarka, 7889.
Taiwan, 7831, 8619, 8629, 8963.
Tamil, 8471.
Tammerfors, 8196.
Tanganyika, v. Tanzania.
Tanger, 8216.
Tanzania, 5468, 7862.
Tarquinia, 2501.
Tartastan, 1200.
Tasmania, 1062, 1619.
Tayside Region (Scotland), 1631.
Tébessa, 9088.
Tell Kabri, 1689.
Tell en-Nasbeh, 1939.
Tell Qara Qūzāq (Siria), 1674.
Terragne (Manduria-Taranto), 1636.
Tetouan, 7052, 8091.
Thailand, 1172, 5469.
Thasos, 2423.
Thebes, 1770.
Thracia, 1744, 2112, 2372, 8045.
Tianjin, 8999.
Tibet, 9009.
Tierra del Fuego, 1048.
Ti'innik, 1938.
Tjumen, 1573.
Tlingit, 1017.
Togo, 9100.
Tokyo, 9043.
Toledo, 3658, 3669, 3770, 3831.
Tonkin, 5618.
Tordesillas, 5631, 7449, 7670, 7761.
Torino, 204, 7632.
Torre Águila (Barbaño-Montijo, Badajoz), 2879.
Torre Spaccata, 1628, 1629, 1633, 1635, 1645, 1646.
Toscana, 3430, 7647, 7984.
Touraine, 3697, 4563.
Tournai, 3278, 3250.
Trabzon, 6153.
Transilvania, 534, 1053, 4598, 5300, 5571, 5575, 5751, 6140, 8022, 8119, 8324, 8440.
Trento, 5856, 8061.
Trèves, 284.
Treviso, 84.
Trianon, 8082, 8187.

Trieste, 5017, 8061, 8395.
Tripoli, 7859, 8012.
Troja, 1747, 2360.
Tuna, 5529.
Tunis, 5509, 8008.
Tunisie, 1025, 1092, 2886, 5509, 7347, 7843, 8566.
Tunja, 5087.
Türkiye, Turkey, 1055, 1745, 5510-5534, 7713, 8109, 8173, 8175.
Turkmenistan, 1663.
Turku, 6067.
Turi, 2465.
Tuscia, 3252.
Tyre, 1915.

U

Üçagizli cave (Turkey), 1615.
Udine, 3310.
Uganda, 1144, 5535-5537, 7884.
Ugarit, 1907.
Uigur, 8936.
Ukraine, 980, 5538, 8063, 8176.
Umbria, 3661.
Ungheria, v. Magiarorszàg.
Urals, 1640, 1671, 7100, 7129, 7509.
Urbino, 3275.
U.R.S.S., v. S.S.S.R.
Uruguay, 385, 5580, 8498, 8711, 8790.
U.S.A., 4625, 4596, 4725, 5062, 5585-5615, 5663, 6101, 6136, 6204, 6210, 6384, 6956, 7414, 7729, 7750, 7758, 7819, 7824, 7851, 7865, 7877, 7893, 7974, 7983, 8003, 8009, 8015, 8107, 8113, 8151, 8152, 8246, 8253, 8256, 8297, 8320, 8429, 8336, 8339, 8439, 8464, 8470, 8509, 8517, 8519, 8526, 8561, 8529, 8621, 8622, 8625, 8629, 8643, 8651, 8657, 8688, 8694, 8697, 8700, 8705, 8725, 8728, 8794, 8796, 8776, 9116.
Utique, 9086, 9092.
Utrecht, 5149.

V

Valencia, 75, 2902, 3607, 4573, 7428.
Valdinievole, 3838.
Vallo di Diano, 5010.
Vallombrosa, 691.
Varsovie, v. Warszawa.
Vaticano, 7731.

Vendée, 4862, 4902.
Veneto, 3515, 3686.
Venezuela, 5581-5584.
Venosa, 4442.
Venezia, 216, 252, 494, 3874, 4194, 5725, 6832, 7190, 7211, 7928, 7943, 7944, 7966, 8008.
Venezuela, 5581-5585, 7446, 7500.
Verdun, 3256.
Verona, 65, 318, 3027, 8059.
Versailles, 8159, 8126.
Viareggio, 7984.
Vichy, 4875, 4882, 4892, 4908, 4921, 8267.
Vietnam, 5616-5619, 7387, 8486, 8504, 8548, 8550, 8638, 8680, 8704, 8726, 8821, 8824.
Vignale, 2451.
Viterbo, 3300.
Volhynia, 8285.

W

Wales, 3354, 3421, 7333, 7404.
Warmia, 6092.
Warszawa, Varsovie, 56, 8195.
Washington, 8182, 8769.
Waterloo, 7985, 7986, 8364.
Weimar, 4808, 6668, 6935, 7502, 7514.
Wessex, 1703.
Westfalen, 6181, 7165, 7745, 7945.
Westminster, 3397.
Wien, 478, 936, 4123, 5180, 5181, 5184, 5192, 5193, 5558, 5876, 6138, 6911, 7344, 7643, 7656, 7965.
Wisdom, 4086.
Wrocław, 5800, 6444.
Württemberg, 5891.

Y

Yalta, v. Jalta.
Yangzi, 8897.
Yellow River, 8906.
Yemen, 438, 1077.

Z

Zaire, 4714.
Zala, 5559.
Zambezi (Basin), 5134.
Zaragoza, 420.
Zeeland, 7.
Ziimshian, 1017.
Zimbabwe, 5383, 5384, 7845, 7847.
Zululand, 7420.
Zunyi, 8865.
Zypern, v. Kypros.